W9-AZP-077

THEODORE ROOSEVELT

Kathleen Dalton

★ ★ ★ ★ ★ ★ ★ ★ ★ ★ ★ ★ ★ ★ ★ ★ ★ ★ ★

THEODORE ROOSEVELT

☆ A STRENUOUS LIFE ☆

ALFRED A. KNOPF NEW YORK

2002

THIS IS A BORZOI BOOK
PUBLISHED BY ALFRED A. KNOPF

 Published in the United States by Alfred A. Knopf, a division of Random House, Inc., New York, and simultaneously in Canada by Random House of Canada Limited, Toronto.
Distributed by Random House, Inc., New York.
www.aaknopf.com

Owing to limitations of space, all acknowledgments for permission to reprint previously unpublished material may be found following the index.

Library of Congress Cataloging-in-Publication Data
Dalton, Kathleen (Kathleen M.)
Theodore Roosevelt : a strenuous life / Kathleen Dalton.—1st ed.
p. cm.
Includes bibliographical references and index.
ISBN 0-679-44663-X (alk. paper)
1. Roosevelt, Theodore, 1858–1919.
2. Presidents—United States—Biography. I. Title.
E757.D24 2002
973.91'1'092—dc21
[B] 2002022857

Manufactured in the United States of America
First Edition

For
Tony, Barbara, and Peter
with gratitude and love

Contents

Illustrations

Unless otherwise noted, all photographs and cartoons are from the Theodore Roosevelt Collection, Harvard College Library, by permission of the Houghton Library, Harvard University.

BETWEEN PAGES 150 AND 151

BETWEEN PAGES 406 AND 407

THEODORE ROOSEVELT

Introduction

THEODORE ROOSEVELT has become one of the enduring stock characters of American culture. He is so familiar to us in his aggressive exuberance that when his distinctive spectacles, mustache, and clenched teeth appear before us in a play or television commercial we need merely count the seconds until he utters the predictable "Bully!" He has so often been parodied that the *American Heritage Dictionary* uses a cartoon of TR to illustrate the word "caricature."[1]

Roosevelt draws our attention immediately, often leaving a quick impression. We see him personifying reliability in a newspaper ad for a bank or the spirit of boyish fun in a political cartoon. Even without words his image speaks to us.

His evocative power can carry a dollar value. Recognizing that he continues to strike an emotional chord with the public, advertisers have used Roosevelt's image to promote the Bible, computer diskettes, baking powder, investment firms, and malt liquor. More than eight decades after his death, the lasting persona of Theodore Roosevelt still can be found in millions of American homes: teddy bears are everywhere. Products sell better when endorsed by his catch phrases, such as "good to the last drop" Maxwell House coffee. TR theme restaurants serve up standard American cuisine using Rooseveltian sayings and Bull Moose–era decor. These restaurants embody the same insight that the owners of Moxie soda understood at the beginning of the twentieth century. When Moxie wanted a face to represent energy and intestinal fortitude they picked the president with the most "moxie."

America's affection for Theodore Roosevelt has a long history. He evoked a warm response from portions of the populace early in his political career. As a flamboyant New York state legislator and New York City police commissioner he won a devout local following. His national reputation grew further from his writing and his role as a U.S. Civil Service commissioner. As a doughty campaigner in the lively Bryan-McKinley presidential race in 1896, TR pulled in big audiences with a combination of colorful invective and lofty idealism.

Then, in 1898 he exploded into the national consciousness as one of the most touted heroes of the Spanish-American War. His presidency, of course, was the high watermark of his relationship with the American people, a time when the press hung on his every political word as well as his preachments on a great many other subjects. In his day he became the most revered president since Abraham Lincoln.

To many of his contemporaries Roosevelt was "the ideal man and statesman," both a president who grappled with modern problems and a charismatic leader who symbolized the people's highest ideals. As a third-party presidential candidate in 1912, running against the power and tradition of the two-party system, he achieved the impossible. Although he came in second to Democrat Woodrow Wilson, he beat the well-financed Republican incumbent, William Howard Taft, polling the largest percentage of the popular vote ever won by a third-party candidate in U.S. history.

His popularity extended beyond politics, for he was admired as a celebrity who stood for cherished beliefs and as an intellectual who reinterpreted the nation's past. From the 1880s he wrote for popular magazines from the *Ladies' Home Journal* to *Youth's Companion*, telling tales of his own adventures and giving advice on how people should conduct their lives. His readers were entertained and instructed by his articles about manly sports, proper family relations, who should go west, and good books to read on safari, all of which made him a highly paid and sought-after writer. When the Boy Scouts looked for the perfect role model to present to their young recruits, Theodore Roosevelt came to mind. Clearly, large segments of the public found him believable as a cultural authority. In 1913, when *American Magazine* took a poll to find out who was the "greatest man in the United States," TR won hands down.[2]

It is a testimony to his lasting popularity as an engaging national figure that in 1979 another popular magazine, *Newsweek*, featured him on its cover as a perennial American hero.[3] Among modern presidents it is TR who inspires the most active fan club, the Theodore Roosevelt Association. His life provides enough engaging material to inspire Broadway plays and movie scripts, and heavy traffic at historic sites.

But he left a more substantial legacy than mere popularity and entertainment value. Today he is heralded as the architect of the modern presidency, as a world leader who boldly reshaped the office to meet the needs of the new century and redefined America's place in the world. Theodore Roosevelt is alive and well in our memory, remembered as both an honored political leader and one of the most picturesque personalities who has ever enlivened the landscape.[4]

When the name of any historical personality slips into everyday usage—guaranteeing a knowing and amused response from the public—our vision of that personality is inevitably blurred. Whenever a figure in history has been canonized by generations of hero worshippers, as Roosevelt has been, it becomes harder for scholars to assess the real person beneath the image. His image blocks our view of him. Too often we see TR only as he is on Mount Rushmore, a larger-than-life monument carved in stone, unchanging, far from being flesh and blood, and quite imperturbable.

Yet we know that Theodore Roosevelt the person must be separable from TR the mythic creation of American culture. As a master politician and cultural leader he helped create his own legend, and therefore he provides any biographer with a special challenge. From the start of his political career his presentation of himself was shaped by his awareness of public scrutiny. He became a skilled politician who enjoyed playing to the crowd, shrewdly championing themes that evoked warm responses. His attunement to audience approval often carried over into his writing and private correspondence. His awareness of living his life for public consumption even crept into his relationship with his six children. He wrote them what they called "posterity letters," self-conscious missives intended for eventual public exposure. He expected, correctly, that the letters would be published, so he wrote them not only to stay close to his children, but to look good in the judgment of history.

As a result, he left a selective record of himself, much of which is well suited for use by admirers. He was most likely to censor himself during the years when his public role was largest. For example, he wrote his *Autobiography* not long after he ran for president on the Progressive, or Bull Moose, Party ticket in 1912. In it he purposely concealed the moments of pain, introspection, vacillation, regret, bumbling, self-doubt, and vulnerability which other, less public records show he had. Rather than explore his own torturous journey toward maturity and political understanding, he defended his record. Even his second wife, Edith Kermit Carow Roosevelt, admitted that her husband was often motivated to avoid facing grim realities about himself and others. She wrote his sister Anna Roosevelt Cowles: "He is not a nature who ever cares to talk over painful subjects."[5] Escape and flight from pain provided familiar devices to protect himself from his own strong emotions and from unpleasant facts he wanted to avoid.

Roosevelt preferred heroic themes to psychological reality in the stories he told about his life. A talented biographer and historian himself, he sought to keep his inner life and less attractive traits well hidden. He also encouraged his friends and authorized biographers to tell an upbeat, socially acceptable, stiff-upper-lipped version of his life. Many of his friends and biographers obliged him. He began, and they perpetuated, the myth that by force of will he cured himself of asthma. They perpetuated, too, the myth that from his minor post as assistant secretary of the navy he maneuvered the United States into war with Spain in 1898. Books about Roosevelt are often rich with dramatic adventure and colorful scenes, just as the Bull Moose would have wanted. His life story attracted many guardians. Family and friends edited or destroyed embarrassing letters and hid family secrets in order to keep the story of Roosevelt's life and times presentable.[6]

He cast himself as a hero in the many stories he told about himself. He shaped the plots and chose the virtues he would embody. As a young man well read in James Fenimore Cooper's and Francis Parkman's romanticization of the western pioneer, as well as the dime novel's simpler portrayal of western cowboys, TR styled himself as a new Leatherstocking, the lone hero who stood for innate morality in the midst of nature. As he headed west to lead "the wild, half adventurous life of a ranchman," Roosevelt entered the "hero land" of his favorite literature in order to become a hero himself.[7] He outfitted himself in buckskin cowboy garb and made sure he was photographed in it. Left unquenched by his western adventures, he looked elsewhere for testing grounds: his appetite for derring-do was insatiable.

He also suffered from what Mark Twain called "the Sir Walter disease," the eagerness to emulate the knights of yore chronicled by one of nineteenth-century American men's favorite authors, Sir Walter Scott.[8] Steeped since boyhood in stories of chivalric knights and military daring, TR saw his long-awaited "crowded hour" of battle in the Spanish-American War as a chance to transform himself into a Galahad. His self-aggrandizing book about the war made the conflict sound so much like a one-man crusade that humorist Finley Peter Dunne joked that it should be renamed "Alone in Cuba."

But *The Rough Riders* exalted more than one man's ride to glory; it celebrated the deep bonds between men forged in the melting pot of war. Roosevelt believed the War of 1898, like the Civil War, inspired a new spirit of brotherhood and nationalism. He saw his men as knights of the Roosevelt Round Table who, like King Arthur's loyal band, wagered their lives together in battle hoping that side by side they "might gain high military distinction" fighting for a high ideal.[9] When he advocated universal military training and the teaching of military drills in the public schools, he sought to unify his country by stamping a whole people with the mark of Galahad.

Most significantly for American history, Roosevelt fashioned himself as a heroic political leader, a fearless champion of the people. In reality, his days as a politician were filled with sedentary desk work and often tedious meetings, yet TR persisted in seeing himself in politics as a bold knight leading a life of action and daring. Office work would have palled on his spirits if he had not seen it in a heroic light, for he believed that any man who became a "time-server" in politics or any other job was better off dead.[10] But being a Galahad to him included fighting for increased corporate and government responsibility for workplace accidents and workers' well-being and a heightened national commitment to protect women and children workers. He wanted to bring Americans together, to replace a weak, divided government with a strong one, in order to do good at home and abroad. As he matured, the knight-errant he imagined himself fought more and more heated battles for social justice and democracy.

From the start of his political career in the New York Assembly his crusader's zeal for just battle and for reform marked him as a rare idealist mingling with self-interested party politicians. His hallmark motto which defined him as a heroic political crusader was "Aggressive fighting for the right is the noblest sport the world affords." In his writings, he portrayed the heroic "man in the arena" as a political version of Saint George slaying the dragon of "corruption which was eating away civic morality."[11]

Associating his own crusades with the heroics of Washington, Jackson, and Lincoln, Roosevelt argued that public service required a "healthy combativeness" because the people needed brave defenders. He accomplished more because he could draw clear battle lines to encourage greater public interest in politics. His drama showed voters it did, after all, matter who won. Responding to his dramatic style, cartoonists pictured TR as a knight-errant, Jack the Giant Killer, or Robin Hood crossing swords with new dastardly villains—the sinister bosses and the evil monopolies. As he cast himself in heroic roles again and again, his growing audience—large segments of the public—adored him for his entertaining gift of endowing politics with romance and for his colorful portrayal of resonant heroic archetypes.[12]

With eloquent writing and personal charm, TR persuaded many students of his life to replicate his heroic script. He worked directly with journalists and biographers to perpetuate his larger-than-life story. As a result, many writers produced legendary tales of Roosevelt's heroism. In their hands he became the ideal father, the greatest president, the American hero for all times.

Hermann Hagedorn, author of the best-selling *The Roosevelt Family of Sagamore Hill*, saw TR as an "enchanting Paul Bunyan-ish creature," an overmastering personality who "stands with the giants" of history.[13]

The trend toward accepting Roosevelt's heroic interpretation of his own life has not abated in our own time. If TR could have ghostwritten recent biographies he would have been "dee-lighted" to make the dubious claim, advanced by the publisher of one biography, that he "almost single-handedly brought about the Spanish-American War." He would have applauded the same biographer's naive insistence that "Teedie entered adolescence with no sexual or psychological doubts whatsoever." And he would have been pleased that his defenders still claim that TR never told a lie. Books that view him as towering "in a class by himself" above all other presidents tell the version Roosevelt wanted to be told.[14] Thrown off the trail by their hero's careful presentation of himself, too many writers have accepted at face value his explanation of his own behavior.

To see TR anew, then, we have to look beneath the heroics. Though genuinely courageous moments appear often in his life story, he was, in fact, not Sir Galahad twenty-four hours a day. Roosevelt's fondness for self-aggrandizing stories and heavily publicized adventures should not mislead us, but instead offer new insight into his personal needs. Bravery and manliness were crucial—sometimes excruciating—issues for him. He detested weakness and would have preferred a long, agonizing death to proving himself a coward. His need to live heroically, to keep on the move and live a strenuous life on occasion, drove him to dangerous extremes.

Our understanding of Theodore Roosevelt, blurred first by his own heroic constructs, is further clouded by the fact that America's memory of TR the man became confused with a cartoon. That cartoon character who waved the Big Stick and packed a pistol had become so familiar to the public that people accepted it as the real Roosevelt when Henry Pringle wrote his famous debunking biography in 1931. When Pringle portrayed Roosevelt as "the most adolescent of men" he hid within his use of modern psychology a systematic job of character assassination.[15] Although some of Pringle's criticisms were well founded, he unfairly made TR look foolish by trivializing his beliefs and his substantial accomplishments.

Following Pringle's lead, Richard Hofstadter—and the generations of historians he influenced—depicted Roosevelt as an emotionally overwrought, violent, unstable jingo and an insincere reformer to boot. Hofstadter's Roosevelt spoke the bombast of "a muscular and combative Polonius" and duped the gullible public by cynically serving as the "master therapist of the middle classes."[16] Generations of scholars adopted the cartoon caricature of TR wholesale. Since then Roosevelt has been repeatedly mauled by historians, ridiculed as a juvenile buffoon, a deeply flawed leader ruled primarily by personal ambition and militaristic bloodlust.

Because of the lasting influence of debunkers like Pringle, writers have repeated in one form or another Mark Twain's verdict that Roosevelt was "clearly insane . . . and insanest upon war and its supreme glories." Few stopped to ask why historians' portrayals of TR sounded so much like the epithets hurled at him by Democrats when he ran for office. Roosevelt's old foe William Jennings Bryan had been eager to impress upon the public's mind that TR was no more than "a man who loves war." TR's ambivalent friend and fellow historian Henry Adams added his own oft-quoted diagnosis "that Theodore is insane. . . . I see nothing for him but the asylum."[17]

Following Bryan and Adams, many historians have accepted the theory that Roosevelt was a bona fide neurotic, suffering from, as Thomas Bailey put it, "almost pathological bellicosity." Scientists, taking their cue from historians, have even listed him as a notable manic-depressive. Too often Theodore Roosevelt has been confused with a cartoon creation, remembered more for his frenetic visual kinship with Charlie Chaplin and the Keystone Cops than for his real personality.[18]

To assess Theodore Roosevelt's life and its meaning in the context of the fullness of American history—looking at cultural and social issues as well as political ones—requires us to question the debunkers as carefully as the writers who would canonize him. Neither the cartoon figure nor the standard heroic TR is real. Yet each has interfered with our understanding of him. To see him fairly requires a closer and more intimate look. His daily life and private relationships are recorded in stunning detail. Letters and diaries show Roosevelt the man, the husband, the father, the friend, the political leader, and he looks much less like a cartoon character and not at all like Paul Bunyan. Then, we must ask, who *was* Theodore Roosevelt—really?

He once wrote that if we want to understand the presidents, "the personal equation is always of vital consequence." "The personal equation" as I have applied it means seeing his life whole and in the larger context of his relationships, his evolving ideas, and his political acts. If there is a Horatio Alger story here it is not simply about a man who "made his own body." He made and remade his own remarkable character with the help of the people he loved, first and foremost his father. As a man TR matured slowly and learned important personal and political lessons within his developing union with his extraordinary second wife, Edith. Massachusetts political mastermind Henry Cabot Lodge mentored him early in his political career. He also became more of a person by reading omnivorously from an early age and using what he read to look into the future. Indeed, TR's self-making fell into three phases of learning—how to be a man, how to listen to and lead voters, and how to look into the future to give his country new direction. Often the courage he developed in his personal life came in handy when he faced a political challenge. From age fourteen, he insisted on living a strenuous life.[19]

Roosevelt is unique among presidents because he demanded so much of himself in office—solving national and international problems and making the presidency a modern and efficient voice of and for the people. His leadership transcended politics. He conceived of the presidency in broader terms than other presidents because he saw it as a "bully pulpit" for national uplift and inspiration. He preached as much as he politicked. He felt responsible for the well-being and morals of the whole country. He set an example of how a large, strenuous life could be led, and he invited others to renew their energies and apply them to public causes. He wanted to pull his country together to achieve a better life for all, and when he called for a Square Deal, he held out the promise to everyone that race, class, and ethnicity might no longer get in the way of full citizenship. Though he could not always deliver an America that judged a man on his merit, he reaffirmed in the new century that equality and inclusion would be prerequisites for true national unity.

After his presidency TR brought worldwide reform ideas into the conversation among America's progressive reformers, especially in his 1912 Bull Moose campaign for president. He was the first major national political leader to enlist the talents of the huge army of women volunteers and activists who had promoted reform during the early years of the Progressive Era, and late in life he turned himself into an effective suffrage campaigner in the long, hard fight to win the vote for women. He expected that he could remake himself in his sixties into the candidate for president in 1920 who would push for a modern welfare state with unemployment insurance, safe workplaces, and no child labor.

His legacy as a foreign policy leader had two sides, one imperial and one internationalist. He tried to make good on America's adventures in imperialism by concluding the Philippine-American War and by supervising affairs in Puerto Rico and Cuba. His intrusion in the Panamanian revolution against Colombia won the United States the Panama Canal, but showed the world, especially Latin Americans, that America's adventures in expansion were not over. As if to atone for past intrusions upon other nations' sovereignty, he embarked on a career of mediation and of building internationalist legal structures to ensure the peace. His diplomatic skill in making a workable peace to end the Russo-Japanese War made him the deserving recipient of the first Nobel Peace Prize won by an American. The United States gained respect around the world because of his efforts, but his successors too often recalled his legacy abroad as an aggressive one that justified later interventions.[20]

THE STORY THAT FOLLOWS is the result of a decades-long quest to find the real TR. My search began in the grogginess of a sleepless night in 1975. While I was studying for my doctoral exams as a history student at Johns Hopkins University, a doctor told me I had terminal cancer and only six months to live. Fortunately, his diagnosis was wrong and I was treated instead for a curable cancer and after a year given a new prognosis: "normal life expectancy." Suddenly I was free to begin my life over again in an act of creation—writing a dissertation. I picked up Richard Hofstadter's *American Political Tradition*, an influential chronicle of American leaders' feet of clay. As I reread his essay about Theodore Roosevelt, I found myself annoyed. I wondered why Hofstadter had ridiculed TR as a laughable cowboy and sham reformer, and I set out that night to find whether another side of Theodore Roosevelt existed.

Perhaps I decided to write about him because, as I recovered from my own medical trial, I was drawn to his struggle to hold on to life as an asthmatic child, or because I admired his warmth toward his children and his courage in running a quixotic race for president in 1912. Perhaps it was a generational grudge match against the fathers of my profession. I have almost nothing in common with TR except for his struggle with illness, his strong sense of familial attachments, and a few of his political ideas. We differ in gender, regional origins, social class, ethnicity, education, personality, and, most significantly, the times to which we belong. So I approach my subject across more than one wide abyss. Yet I have set as my scholarly task trying to understand how TR felt and how he looked at the world.

Just as I believe Hofstadter spoke for the tough guy revisionism of the Cold War, especially its sense of disappointment in American presidents, I am writing out of a fin-de-siècle revulsion against the refusal to look at ourselves, polarization, and anti-intellectualism too prominent in America at the start of the twenty-first century. Caricaturing the perceived opposition has been overdone. I hold the quaint belief that democracy will flourish only if citizens learn to understand each other across their differences, and this book stands as a gesture on behalf of scholarly as well as political and cultural willingness to listen.

I enjoyed immensely the detective work in my search to understand TR. In newly available manuscripts I found sides of him that had never been seen before—the operatic ham whose comic singing sent even his reserved wife,

Edith, into fits of laughter, the confiding father who taught his daughter Ethel to care for the needs of the poor, and even the bereaved college boy who drank too much and made a fool of himself. He did not always stand at Armageddon and battle for the Lord as he did in 1912. He danced, farmed, and told funny stories to his children. As he grew up he learned how to make people laugh and how to mix entertainment with high moral purpose.

Because character development and cultural and historical context are central to understanding TR, his story must begin in his early family world of horse-drawn omnibuses, gaslight, terrapin suppers, and cobblestone streets and end with his enlarged social world in a modern era filled with slick magazines, Buicks, gas warfare, apartment living, and streetcars. When he told a friend that he was "as well as a man with a bad disposition under good control can be," Roosevelt wrote part of my story of character development and change. The African-American scholar W.E.B. Du Bois posed one of the central questions of this biography when he asked the American Historical Association to judge people in history not merely by their faults, but to ask whether "they show[ed] any signs of a disposition to learn better things." Thus we judge Theodore Roosevelt. His wife Edith thought the best book ever written about him was the one that described him as having a character "far more complicated and intricate than is commonly supposed." Despite his admirable capacity for emotional and political growth, no one should mistake for the Mount Rushmore icon or the cartoon TR the story I tell about Roosevelt's strenuous life.[21]

He remains America's most fascinating president. His life was full of drama and challenge. He tried hard to push his country in a direction it did not want to go. He wanted to use the federal government as a moral force to serve the public good, to defend what he called social justice. Eager to expand the place of America on the world stage, TR promoted bold national assertion at a time when most of his countrymen cared little about foreign affairs. He worried about the increase of selfishness and materialism in the American character and argued that it must be tempered by family cohesion and duty to others. He also saw the unequal division of wealth in his own time as unfair and dangerous to true democracy. His ideas and concerns, even when they were wrong-headed, stand as challenges for our times. His strenuous life was passionate, entertaining, and constructive. May readers find some of what he lived inside this book.

☆ BOOK ONE ☆

Wherein a Young Duke Makes Himself a True Man

☆ CHAPTER ONE ☆

The Handicap of Riches

AMERICAN PRESIDENTS are not supposed to start out in life the way Theodore Roosevelt did. His was not a rags-to-riches story begun in a log cabin. He lacked humble origins. He could make no steady climb from modest economic beginnings toward the apex of fame or fortune because he was born near the top in wealth and social standing. Unlike Abraham Lincoln and Richard Nixon, he also did not have the type of sainted, self-sacrificing mother who could inspire his aspirations for a better life.

Instead, TR was born blessed with a millionaire grandfather and a distinguished family name. When he remembered his childhood, he had his sainted patrician father to thank for guiding his ascent. His privileged station, however, did not insulate him from facing serious trials in life. TR was born to wage a different kind of battle. Ahead of him lay a fateful struggle for life and identity—a fight grueling enough to allow him to see himself as a classic American self-made man.

Roosevelt's task of self-making began with the work of living up to past greatness. Often, when TR told the story of his childhood he began not with himself, but with his family's high standing. Proud to tell of his elite origins he wrote: "I was born in New York, October 27th 1858; my father of old dutch knickerbocker stock; my mother was a Georgian, descended from the revolutionary Governor Bulloch."[1]

TR's father, Theodore Roosevelt Senior (called Thee), gave his first son his name and admitted he loved him best of his four offspring. But with such favored love came the weight of familial expectations. The senior Roosevelt would look to young TR to prove he had enough "stern old Dutch blood" coursing in his veins to bring credit to the Roosevelt name.[2]

Roosevelts had been men of consequence, members of the Knickerbocker elite who had provided New York with leadership for generations. The family rose to economic prominence after the American Revolution when Isaac Roosevelt added Tory farmland to the family's already large holdings. The Roosevelts became one of the city's "governing families." TR's grandfather C.V.S. Roosevelt, a conservative merchant who thought of little besides trade, turned the family hardware business into a plate-glass importing firm, using his profits to buy up more Manhattan real estate. He later became a founder and director of the Chemical National Bank. C.V.S. Roosevelt's brother, Judge James I. Roosevelt, had been a congressman and prominent member of the New York Democratic Party before he was appointed to New York's highest court. Wealth, power, and social standing were part of the heritage Theodore was expected to preserve.[3]

Roosevelts, however, did not need to hold office to exercise power. The rise of popular voting rights in the Jacksonian age and the later arrival of vast numbers of immigrant voters, who were managed at the ballot box by Democratic Tammany Hall leaders and other competing bosses, challenged the old elite to fight harder than ever to shape their city's culture and politics. Businessmen eager for low labor costs initially welcomed rural and foreign newcomers, but they were thereafter unprepared to deal with competition in the political realm from bosses and their immigrant supporters and a large and often unemployed working class who hovered on the edge of starvation. In a chaotic city with a skyrocketing murder rate, twenty thousand prostitutes, an ineffective police force, gang rapes, highway robbery, and street fights, the old elite unfairly blamed the crisis on the wretched morals of the poor and the bosses who represented them in politics.

Men like the Roosevelts fought Democratic Boss Tweed when he insisted on fire protection by volunteer companies manned by his political cronies. The anti-Tweed forces won the right to hire a professional salaried fire company, and then further modernized Manhattan's government by creating a Metropolitan Board of Health that enforced new disinfectant codes and street-cleaning regulations. The anti-Tweed Citizens Association, so heavily funded and publicly led by Theodore's closest relatives that it was called a Rooseveltian oligarchy, finally ousted Tweed from power when Theodore was in his teens. Before he was old enough to shave, he had learned from his intensely political uncles and his father how to use newspaper exposés and scandals to arouse public outrage and bring about reform.[4]

Thee worked in his father's plate-glass importing firm, Roosevelt and Son, where he also managed the family's immense real estate, stock, banking, mining, and insurance holdings. When Theodore was a boy, C.V.S. Roosevelt and his five sons owned Manhattan's Piers Nine and Ten, a farm on Staten Island, land in upstate New York, stock in the New York Central Railroad, and property all over lower Manhattan. Thee and his brothers managed all their business concerns well enough to save time for civic reform and philanthropy, ministering with heartfelt noblesse oblige to the less fortunate members of society. The power of Roosevelt money and beneficence reverberated through Central Park, the Metropolitan Museum of Art, the American Museum of Natural History, Roosevelt Hospital, the Bellevue Training School for Nurses, the Children's Aid Society, and Thee's creation, the New York Orthopaedic Dispensary for the Deformed and Crippled.[5]

As a young man Theodore wrote with aristocratic pride: "The older races of the city made the mould into which the newer were poured." He did not doubt the value of leadership by those who presumed they were "the best men," but in his mature years he would take the position that the cultural authority and political power which accrued to his kind because they were upper class was built upon a system of unjust privilege. During Theodore's boyhood the old elite worked hard to remain keepers of the "mould" by incorporating newer industrial elites into their businesses, clubs, philanthropies, and social circles, where they taught them to invest in the cultural future of the city. Together they hoped to make New York a grand and dignified city worthy of pride around the world, rather than the stink hole of greedy commercialism and crime it was reputed to be. Not that nouveau riche stock traders and magnates like Jim Fisk and Jay Gould who used bribery and deception to corner markets after the Civil War were easily remade morally. The old elite remained suspicious of the suddenly rich who were "vikings in energy, unscrupulousness and violence, who swept through the land in railroad land grabs, in mining speculations, in purchase of legislatures, in stock dilutions, in great corners on stocks and grains"[6]

The striving industrial culture that emerged after the Civil War called upon elite women, presumed to be angelic repositories of morality, to elevate the moral tone of polite society by drawing clear social lines. When Caroline Astor stepped forward in the 1870s to form a bastion of gentility which became the socially select Four Hundred, Thee acted as one of her Patriarchs who extended invitations to grand balls to new and old worthies while excluding climbers with low morals. Edith Wharton in her *Age of Innocence* portrayed Knickerbockers like the Roosevelts as the van der Luydens, lofty patricians who expected to arbitrate a chaotic new society by speaking as the voice of cultural authority. Thee raised Theodore within the upper-class "mould" of old New York: he taught his son how to behave in receiving lines and when to wear patent leather shoes and a black tie. Most significantly, he provided him with a loving example of how one man can use his privilege to make society better.[7]

Thee had traveled enough as an importer and on Grand Tours to see that New York was inferior to the great European cities that he regarded as the vanguards of advancing world civilization. To bring home to Manhattan the benefits of the British Museum and the Louvre, he helped to found the American Museum of Natural History and planned the first building and the fledgling collections of the Metropolitan Museum of Art. His philanthropy applied science and art to the cause of making New York a more civilized city, and he favored the modernizing benefits of a cleaner water supply, less partisan police and firemen, and public health enforcement. Thee also hobnobbed with muscular Christians like Thomas Hughes in England, and became a convert to their belief that religion had become too feminized and ethereal and needed to be reformed by a spirit of aggressive manliness and athleticism. Rejecting the image of Jesus Christ as gentle, saintly, and long-suffering, muscular Christians reinterpreted him as a soldier of righteousness and vigor. They argued that training boys to see their bodies as one means of salvation, a "living sacrifice to God," was the best method to keep them away from sensuousness and self-indulgence. Not long after the Reverend Charles Kingsley began preaching muscular Christianity in England, his counterpart in the states, Bishop Phillips Brooks, spread his belief that "physical courage is a grand and precious thing" tied intimately with true Christian faith.[8] The Reverend Thomas Wentworth Higginson popularized the idea further that men could be made soldiers in service to Christ by toughening themselves with sports, and Brooks' hymn "Onward Christian Soldiers" spread the new muscular Christian cause across pews to schools and playing fields. Thee and his friends put the same spirit to use in reform and philanthropy to rejuvenate urban life in New York.[9]

To help the poor man climb and the wealthy man resist sin, Thee promoted muscular Christianity through the Young Men's Christian Association, the Children's Aid Society, and later through Dwight L. Moody's urban revivals. Thee worried that in an era when many youths moved to the city and stopped attending church, $4 million was being spent each year on the newly commercialized vice industry—from billiard saloons and brothels to "gambling hells" and pornographic bookstands. Vice and sin on an individual level were bad enough, but moral reformers like Thee believed that new businesses designed to commercialize sex (via dance halls, pornography, and brothels) sought to make huge profits out of pandering to human weakness—and, in doing so, pulled the whole society down. "Satan's empire" had to be stopped.

For Theodore, his father's muscular Christian cures defined the terms of his upbringing and his own later diagnosis of what ailed American culture.

Theodore learned at his father's knee that Christ himself was not a self-effacing saint but a "strong man physically, muscular, sinewy, enduring," a man who embodied moral purity and, in the Darwinian language of the day, "healthy animalism." Thee and his close friend William E. Dodge, Jr., saw to it that young clerks who moved to the city would have barbells and Bibles to help them withstand temptation in the new Y.M.C.A. building they erected in the Roosevelts' neighborhood. Thee often took Theodore with him when he preached manly fortitude and purity to the newsboys at his friend the Reverend Charles Loring Brace's Newsboys' Lodging House and his other missions. He made sure that Brace's houses provided boys with boxing gloves, horizontal bars, and exercise equipment because he believed they helped boys fight the "weakening of true masculine vigor, . . . [and] a hidden growth of secret and contagious vices" so rampant in their city. Thee's muscular Christianity argued not for dog-eat-dog social Darwinism or survival of the fittest, but for Christian obligation that man owed man across class divides. Like the rich benefactors in the popular stories written by Brace's other prominent patron, Horatio Alger, Jr., Thee felt obliged to be the deus ex machina who offered the poor a helping hand out of poverty—buying them a ticket to Albany to make a new start, sending them a winter's load of coal to heat their homes, or paying for their children's medical care. He even refused to acquire tenements because he did not want to profit from the meager earnings of the needy. Thee agreed with Brace's view that a boy could be made manlier and therefore purer if he could "gratify 'the savage in one's blood,' and lead a wild life in the woods," so the Children's Aid Society with Thee's help exported ninety thousand of New York's pauper children to the countryside of the Midwest and West.[10]

Theodore learned that muscular Christian exercise and the nature cure were democratic forms of salvation insofar as they promised to revive any type of man, but none of the Roosevelts understood fully that the power of noblesse oblige enabled them to impose their cures on less powerful men and boys, who were not always eager to be saved in this fashion. Thee disliked those who did not practice what they preached, so he took his children to the countryside in the summer, and promoted his own manliness and morality by riding, camping, and playing active sports including polo, fox hunting, and tennis.[11]

Theodore's atypical patrician boyhood, then, carried unusual lessons and examples. He was born into a clan who stood out among the New York elite as a strong, enduring, extended family self-assured in its outspokenness. His second cousin Nicholas wrote that "to be a Roosevelt was to be something distinctive—usually vital and energetic, often brilliant, generally intolerant, and always highly vocal. . . . they were openly and even zealously critical of each other." Their Hyde Park fifth cousin Franklin Delano Roosevelt later wrote that the longevity and "the virility of the Roosevelts" came from their "very democratic spirit," but Theodore's branch of the family allied themselves with the barely democratic remnants of the Federalist elite, the Jays, Livingstons, and Schuylers. Even though they accepted republicanism, civic virtue, and democratic participation as basic American ideals, the Manhattan Roosevelts were what TR's nephew Sheffield called "Dutch money-grubbers" who derived their clan identity from deep Hamiltonian, Federalist, and unequivocally aristocratic roots.[12]

TR grew up with a double legacy, carrying the weight of the Bulloch heritage of manly heroism as well. His southern mother, Martha "Mittie" Bulloch Roosevelt, made sure that her son heard about the military feats of her grandfather General Daniel Stewart in the American Revolution and her father, Major James Stephens Bulloch, a hero in Texas' War for Independence.[13]

Even the political leaders within the battling Bulloch clan were never content to let others do their fighting for them. Mittie's great-grandfather Archibald Bulloch, representative to the Continental Congress and commander in chief of Georgia at the outset of the American Revolution, personally led a war party against a Loyalist stronghold. Mittie's father, the "impetuous" Major James Bulloch, after his fighting days were over, married his stepmother-in-law, Martha Stewart Elliott, and in a flurry of scandal over the marriage left Savannah behind, packed up his wife, their children from previous marriages, and slaves, and moved to Roswell, Georgia. In Roswell the Bullochs settled on land which the Cherokees had recently held, before gold was discovered and President Andrew Jackson forced the native people to walk to Oklahoma on the infamous Trail of Tears. Though much less blessed with commercial success than the Roosevelts, TR's cavalier southern kin made their mark as a more daring and adventure-loving people.[14]

Just as Thee schooled him to lead society, Mittie's admiring stories of the Bullochs' courage, in a more subtle way, made Theodore see himself growing up to be the future vehicle for the Bulloch tradition. The Bulloch side of his upbringing gave him license to be more emotionally effusive than most of Old New York, but it also left him yearning for adventure. His only problem was that he was such a physical weakling as a child that the possibility of a brave, distinctive adulthood appeared ludicrous. His family feared he might not even live to be an adult.

* * *

THEODORE ROOSEVELT would always "speak of his childhood and early youth with a sense of detachment." When he looked back on himself as a child, he felt uneasy. Family pictures show him as a slender, pale-haired boy, costumed in infant dress, looking frail, but hardly deserving the self-contempt he later felt. His aversion to his past masked feelings of shame about the kind of boy he had been. He confessed: "For reasons which I am wholly unable to explain even to myself I somehow shrink from having a sketch of my younger days prepared." In fact, he found it unsettling to remember the long and painful years he spent as a captive of asthma. He detested the invalid he had been as a child.[15]

His life began on October 27, 1858, at 28 East Twentieth Street in New York City in a family who gave him a more intensely religious and moral upbringing than other children in the wealthy Gramercy Park neighborhood. Though Theodore grew up with a dual allegiance to his father's Dutch Reformed Church and his mother's Presbyterianism, it was Thee's evangelical fervor that permeated his childhood. When the Roosevelts prayed with their close friends the Dodges at regular Sunday prayer meetings, Theodore sang the evangelical hymn "Shall We Gather at the River?," knowing he belonged among the civilizers like his father who faced the daunting task of cleaning up a city and a nation.[16]

Theodore Senior did much more than teach his son Christian piety and social obligation. Each day he set an example of religious ethics in action. Thee was such a conscientious practicing Christian that when his neurasthenic wife turned away exhausted from the duties of motherhood to withdraw into invalidism, he frequently stepped into her place to nurture their children. Although many elite Victorian women suffered from similar bouts of neurasthenia, few husbands responded by mothering their children. Thee wrote to his ailing wife, Mittie: "I do not feel as if you can quite take care of yourself without my help," and she in turn told him that she loved being "dependent upon" him.[17]

Yet her extreme dependency on her husband had its price. Though Mittie was loving and playful with her children, her flamboyance affronted her stern husband. Before they were married, she wrote that she feared Thee with his "northern impressions of propriety" would "make quite a prude of poor 'little Mittie.' "[18]

Mittie and Thee met when he visited Bulloch Hall in 1850. Already their families were related: Thee's sister-in-law Mary West Roosevelt had a brother, Dr. Hilborne West, who wanted Thee to meet his wife Susan's stepsister Mittie. When Thee began courting Mittie, she struck him as a refreshingly pure and unaffected raven-haired beauty. Her soft and low southern accent beguiled him, as did her stories of graping and picnicking parties in the small Roswell community perched on the bluffs that overlook the Chattahoochee River. Her genteel background and her place in Savannah society, despite her family's precarious fortunes, made her an acceptable match for a Roosevelt. She was drawn to the earnest strength in his broad shoulders and steady gaze. She teased him about the other men who wanted to pursue her, but Thee knew he had won her heart unequivocally.

But theirs remained an attraction of unlikes. While the delicate but humorous Mittie had been called by her cousin "the wildest girl she had ever known," Thee was judged by his friends to be dogged, argumentative, and athletic. The contrast in Mittie's and Thee's temperaments inspired Thee's jocular elder brother Robert to reassure him that "between Mittie's liveliness and your solemnity you strike an even balance."[19]

Mittie and Thee's union started out happily after their Roswell wedding in December 1853. Bringing his bride north to live with him in New York, Thee found it a "great luxury to feel that there is one who really loves me, one center to which I can always turn." Passion and wit held this marriage in a precarious equilibrium. When Mittie returned to Roswell for a visit in 1855 she wrote flirtatiously home to her young husband:

> Oh how much I do love you. I am going to sit in your lap the moment you come. . . . How much I would have liked to have you carry me up in your arms . . . do you remember how I used to kiss you on the way up the stairs? . . . Anna says the first two or three nights I slept with her, I would throw my arms around her and call her darling, but that she knows I meant it for you, do you think so?[20]

Their earlier balance slowly tipped toward Thee's favor as their married life endured, in New York, in his world, living a short walk away from his parents' mansion on Union Square and next door to his brother Robert and his family in an attached double brownstone. Far from her mother and sister in Georgia, as an eighteen-year-old bride Mittie was "homesick for her own people" and for southern ways and country living. She was required to fit into the upright Roosevelt family and to follow the customs of what Edith Wharton called old New York's "hieroglyphic world, where the real thing was never said or done or even thought, but only represented by a set of arbitrary signs."[21] Mittie felt weighed down by her new duties in a world that strictly regulated the proper way to leave a calling card. She later pleaded with Thee: "I love you and wish to please you more than any one else in the whole world and will do everything I can to please you that is not unreasonable. . . . *don't be too hard upon me.*"[22]

Motherhood was not destined to be easy for Mittie. Their first child, Anna, born January 18, 1855, and called Bamie (for "bambino") by the family, became an invalid because of a spinal injury. An abscess formed over a hyperextended portion of her spine and caused her considerable pain all day (an injury which some of the family believed occurred when a maid dropped the child but others were sure had been polio). When the apparatus doctors put on the child had to be adjusted, she howled in agony. To keep her quiet, she was told stories or read to. The child's misery wore on her mother, who soon found that even when she reminded the maid to be gentle changing Bamie's dressings, she could not trust servants to give her ailing daughter the constant solicitude she needed. By the time she anticipated the birth of her second baby, Mittie pleaded with her sister Anna Bulloch and her mother, Martha Stewart Elliott Bulloch, to come to New York to help her on an emergency basis.

On the cold autumn day of Theodore's birth in 1858, Mittie took her regular midday carriage ride and went shopping before lunch. Then, after long hours of labor pains, her son Theodore Roosevelt Junior or Teedie arrived without forceps in the evening. As she recovered and nursed the small bundle in her arms, Mittie told her mother she thought the new baby "hideous . . . a cross between a terrapin and Dr. Young."[23]

When Theodore was two months old Grandmother Bulloch wanted to leave New York. She wrote Mittie's stepsister, Susan West, "I have been proposing to Mittie to go home but she cries at the mention of it . . . she thinks with a young baby, and Bamie such an invalid and sufferer that she ought not to be left alone."[24] So Mrs. Bulloch and her daughter Annie moved in with the Roosevelts. When Theodore's birth was followed by Elliott's on February 28, 1860, and Corinne's on September 27, 1861, Mittie often fell ill. Mittie had learned years earlier that it was, she wrote, a "good policy . . . to keep up the appearance of a cold" to solicit care from her mother, and she kept finding invalid ploys to keep her mother close. Mittie soon became a woman whose health declined with each year of marriage, as she suffered frequent digestive disorders, palpitations of the heart, nightmares which she called "horrors," obscure pains, and nerves. While Aunt Annie served as the children's tutor, Grandmother Bulloch cared for everyone's well-being, especially her "poor feeble child," Mittie.[25]

Mittie captured her children's fixed attention from her sickbed by telling them stories of the "stormy love affairs" and military exploits of her southern relatives and the amusing antics of her slaves back home in Georgia. Often wistful, she reminisced about her southern girlhood. She recalled her education at a girls' boarding school in Columbia, South Carolina, and a time when she was recognized by others as "intelligent" and possessing a "ready tongue."[26] A vivacious sprite who "does everything by impulse and with an air of perfect self-confidence," Theodore's mother provided him with an example of ebullience. She called him her "Butterfly" and encouraged him to become a ready talker whose clever verbal effusions in time equaled her own. Mittie amused her family by calling the much-visited Centennial Exposition in Philadelphia "thumbed over," just as Theodore would later entertain his public by coining clever original phrases such as the "lunatic fringe," "good to the last drop," or "my hat is in the ring."[27] Witty and starkly candid verbal outbursts always allowed Theodore to vent aggression and frustration, but, like his mother, he did not mean everything that came out of his mouth. While Elliott proved to be her "lovingest" son, Theodore, to Mittie's mind, became the family entertainer who returned her playful repartee in the most charming way imaginable.[28]

Mittie shared with her receptive eldest son her memories of southern duels and feuds and her fondness for novels of chivalry and romance, such as Charlotte Yonge's *Heir of Redclyffe* and the works of Sir Walter Scott. She told him romantic tales of the code duello and the men "who love the name of honor more than [they] fear death." Mittie peopled her son's imaginative world with noble-hearted aristocrats who fought courageously for high ideals.[29]

Schooling Theodore in southern definitions of manliness, Mittie was guilty of what one historian has termed "southern women's vicarious bloodthirstiness" in encouraging her son to dream of military crusades and duels to defend his honor. Through his mother's stories, Theodore said he learned about the "fine manly qualities" which "always appealed to" him in "the Southern Character." Later, as president, Roosevelt would eagerly remind southern voters of his connection with their region. He said he was genuinely proud that his "earliest training and principles were Southern," though he was careful to point out that his "manhood ha[d] largely been fought out in the North." And "fought out" were words chosen well.[30]

Mittie's invalidism served to keep her intermittently distant from her children and household cares, yet her lethargy was interrupted by expansive moods when her health improved for family outings, trips to resorts, and European Grand Tours. Edith Kermit Carow, a close childhood friend of the Roosevelt children and the woman who became Theodore's second wife, recalled Mittie as a woman who "was lovely to look at and had a great charm, and a knack with children," but no one remembered her for hard work or practicality. Mittie would kindly buy little Edith a china tea set that she would cherish for the rest of her life, but then find it tiresome to keep the house well provisioned. Thee took what normally would have been Mittie's tasks to his office: ordering a ton of coal to heat the house, ten pounds of block ice to be delivered daily, two quarts of terrapin for a dinner party, cod liver oil for their sick children, and case after case of Vichy water. As his bills from Tiffany's, A. T. Stewart's department store, and dressmakers proved, Mittie had sufficient vigor to consume according to her own fine taste, but from work her husband hired and fired servants, outfitted the house, and did other work usually reserved in their social strata for wives.[31]

Matching her maids' uniforms to the violets she kept in the parlor awoke Mrs. Roosevelt's enthusiasm, while keeping track of the money she spent did not. Mittie gloried in piling the Christmas table high with toys for her children, and she loved to watch their glee on Christmas morning. Reputed to be one of the great beauties of New York society, she could spend hours making sure that her pink silk-lined and ruffled muslin dress and matched pink parasol highlighted her looks.[32]

In fact, sometimes Mittie felt guilty—even calling herself a "deserter"—when she left her family to recover her health at stylish resorts or water cure establishments. Yet she continued to escape her home with regularity and with it the confining expectations placed on genteel Victorian women to be the angel of the house and moral beacon to her family, as well as the manager of practical domestic affairs and child-rearing. The epidemic of neurasthenia in the nineteenth century, a sloppily diagnosed nervous disease variously characterized by weariness, numbness, sleeplessness, palpitations, and a breakdown of "nervous" strength, gave medical permission for women like Mittie to take a break, to "move in neurasthenic circles" in New York and at water cure resorts, where homeopathic doctors urged women to control their own health, and women exchanged information about medical treatments as well as birth control advice. Illness may also have served as a tool to urge Thee to practice sexual restraint and to end their reproductive career early. After bearing four children in six years, Mittie abruptly stopped having children in her mid-twenties, probably due to abstinence or the birth control ideas she no doubt heard at water cure resorts.[33] Neurasthenia provided Mittie with a welcome ticket out of town, but her children regretted her elusiveness. A beautiful, but too often untouchable, objet d'art, Mittie was later judged by Theodore and Bamie as an extreme example of malingering and helpless femininity.[34]

THEE, THEN, held Theodore's childhood in his hands. Raised under his father's strict but loving guidance, Theodore was an exuberant child in his earliest years. He quickly learned to scramble ahead of his three siblings for the place of honor—the "cubby hole"—next to Thee on the sofa during the family's morning prayers. As the first son and the first healthy infant, he won adoration easily and gave love back freely. Thee meant the world to his son because he was the most reliable source of parental love, and he devoted immense energy to seeing that his namesake had a well-directed and happy childhood.

Yet Thee also stood, in Theodore's words, as a "big, powerful man, with a leonine face," an imposing and sometimes terrifying figure for his son. Because young Theodore identified with his father so much and wanted to please him so, Thee always remained for his son "the only man of whom I was ever really afraid." Each morning as Thee dressed for the office, his toddler Teedie would act as his father's adoring valet, as Thee told Mittie, "bringing me an indefinite supply of boots."[35]

Not everyone in the family was as delighted as his father by Theodore's inborn energy and brightness. Mittie warned Thee that "Teedie is the most affectionate and endearing little creature in his ways, but begins to require his father's discipline rather sadly. He is brimming full of mischief and has to be watched all the time." Grandmother Bulloch described the boy as "a mischievous little rogue" and compared him to her ancestors the Scottish "berserkers" who raged across the border to fight the English. Even though at the age of sixteen months Theodore had to share the family's attention with the new baby, Elliott, his "natural devilment" and tremendous enthusiasm for living seemed boundless.[36]

But Theodore's emotional development was soon disrupted by what his younger sister, Corinne, later called "much that was difficult and troublous." When the Civil War began, when Teedie was only two and a half, the family was divided in its sympathies. Mittie, her beloved sister Anna, and her mother, Grandmother Bulloch, were ardent Confederate supporters, and Thee, his brothers Jim, Rob, and Weir, as well as C.V.S. Roosevelt, sided with the Union.[37]

Bulloch men, proud of their ancestors' distinguished military records, quickly joined the Confederate forces. Being able-bodied, patriotic, and only twenty-nine years old, Thee believed he should enlist as a Union soldier. His long-stifled heroic feelings would finally have an outlet.

But Mittie used her delicate health to stop her husband from going to war. Bamie recalled: "Mother was very frail, and felt it would kill her for him to fight against her brothers." Out of regard for the zealous feelings of the woman he loved, Thee reluctantly paid $300 each for two substitutes. Next door in the adjoining Roosevelt house, Thee's brother Robert and his wife were also divided in opinion over the war, but Rob did not let her southern sympathies stop him from joining the New York State militia.[38]

Thee soon joined a Home Guard cavalry unit that drilled with swords in order to be prepared to defend New York City in case of Confederate attack. Yet he remained dissatisfied with himself for letting other men go to war for him. The public was full of disgust for those able-bodied men who bought a substitute. To obtain a substitute was judged an act of cowardice. According to Theodore Tilton, managing editor of the influential Congregational journal, the *Independent*, every "true man" should go to war. In Boston, historian Francis Parkman called for any man who still had "a lurking spark of manhood" to enlist. He declared that the "lingerers" who stayed at home should be shamed for their "miserable lethargy" in a time of national peril.[39]

Even Grandmother Bulloch thought it was unjust to allow some men to buy their way out of the war because the system "favors the rich at the expense of the poor." Thee's relentless conscience about his failure to fight in the war never rested. According to Bamie, he suffered for the remainder of his life from the shame that "he had done a very wrong thing in not having put every other feeling aside and joined the absolute fighting forces."[40]

Determined to serve at least in a noncombatant role, Thee left home in the fall of 1861 for almost two years on a mission of charity to aid soldiers' families, many of whom were left without food or money. Soldiers' pay was not systematically sent home to feed their families, nor were scattered private charities sufficient to help mothers and children with absent or dead breadwinners. One hungry woman who had come to the mayor's office in Manhattan to ask for help waited so long that her baby died there of starvation. Thee and his two close friends, Theodore Bronson and William E. Dodge, Jr., set up an Allotment Commission to allow soldiers to send portions of their pay home to support their families. They lobbied in Congress and with President Lincoln for the passage of an allotment law, and then personally traveled to war camps to sign up New York troops.[41]

Injured during his travels in a railroad accident and then suffering a nearly fatal case of typhoid fever, Thee threw himself into his war work with a dedication born of guilt. He wrote Mittie how he had ached from the cold as he stood for long hours on the damp encampment grounds, exhorting troop after troop to allot part of their pay to be sent home to their families. Because of his persuasion, at last, he said, "the scum of our city, seemed for the first time to recall their families."[42]

Though he failed to join the army, Thee proved to be a stalwart Union man. Witnessing the slaughter at Fredericksburg, he spontaneously took command of the evacuation of the wounded, shouting orders and getting bleeding men loaded onto hospital wagons. Back home for a visit, he and his brothers joined other elite New Yorkers to preach loyalty to the Union and service to the nation. As a member of the aristocratic Union League Club and its Loyal Publication Society, Thee joined his friend Francis Lieber in dispensing patriotic propaganda to enforce wartime loyalty. He gained an "education in nationality" volunteering to work with the Women's Central Association of Relief and the Sanitary Commission, which sent supplies and nurses to aid injured Union soldiers. Thee felt at home in organizations that promoted a stronger sense of American nationality and rejected the "state-ishness" and sectionalism that caused the war, and he approved of President Lincoln's "strengthening in every way Federal influence."[43]

His father's talk about stronger nationality shaped Theodore's later political views, and even during the war he was old enough to be pleased that his father had made friends with President and Mrs. Lincoln and that Thee was mistaken for Lincoln as he sat in the President's pew at church. Thee cherished the letters Lincoln had written him and wrote home to his family describing how the war-weary President brightened when his own small son ran into the room. In Theodore's mind his tall, bearded father and his father's friend President Lincoln were forever united, welded together in his memories of the Civil War as venerable giants. When TR became president he talked about Thee and Lincoln on his first night in the White House, for they always remained his two most important guiding spirits.

Thee's experiences in the Civil War provided his son's first lessons in history. Thee wrote home describing the personalities and conflicts he witnessed as he traveled in the highest political and social circles in Washington. Staying at Willard's Hotel, Thee and his new friend, Lincoln's young secretary, John Hay, listened to generals gossip about upcoming battles. Thee and Hay also heard drunken soldiers awaiting battle shooting wildly into the night air on Pennsylvania Avenue. Glad as he was to do valuable war-related work and meet Generals Sheridan, Sherman, and Grant, Thee never forgot that while he helped Mrs. Lincoln select bonnets, his brother-in-law James D. Bulloch was becoming a Confederate war hero for successfully navigating stores of ammunition through the Union naval blockade. Thee lectured the New York troops that allotting part of their army pay to be sent home to their families would enhance their "manliness," yet he remained haunted by shame because he had not gone to war.[44]

Back home in Manhattan, Theodore and his siblings were engulfed by the tense wartime atmosphere. Bamie always recalled "the terrible position my mother was in," being at odds with her husband and his family over the war. Mittie's disgruntled attitude toward her husband's absences filled her letters. Not long after Corinne's birth in the fall of 1861, Mittie told Thee that she had to write to him at night because it was "the only time unoccupied with the dear, troublesome little children deserted by their Papa." Calling her husband "my adventure loving Thee" and "my dear heartless Thee," she wrote him angrily a month later that she had been up six or seven times in the middle of the night with the sickly Teedie and that the still-ailing Bamie also awoke from her dreams calling out "Papa, Papa." Mittie even tried to get Thee to come home by pleading with him seductively that she missed him most after dark.[45]

Thee refused to let the pull of home diminish his sense of civic duty. He admitted to Mittie that when he came back for brief visits her morose good-byes bothered him. Yet he did not turn back in his hurry to catch a south-bound train. Roosevelt family legend maintains that in defiance Mittie hoisted a Confederate flag from her home on East Twentieth Street to celebrate a Southern victory, an act which, even in a city with considerable rebel sympathies, could have provoked mob retribution. Government agents arrested other people who displayed secessionist flags, and New Yorkers suspected of promoting Confederate interests were detained in Fort Lafayette, near Brooklyn. Federal employees, suspected spies, and voters in the border state of Maryland were forced to take loyalty oaths, and Thee's friend Francis Lieber even argued that aliens should be made to take oaths, too. In such an atmosphere Mittie's disloyal views would have been better kept quiet.[46]

Whether or not she expressed her political sympathies in public, everyone in the family's social circle knew Mittie and Thee were in conflict over the war. Mittie was proud of her brother's distinctive war record and the fact that Confederate soldiers were dressed in Roswell gray uniforms. Her father had been friends with Alexander H. Stephens, the fiery orator and vice president of the Confederacy, who argued that the subordination and inferior status of blacks were natural and just in both North and South. The Bullochs agreed with Stephens completely.

Mittie had once charmed dinner guests with her humorous dialect imitations of a Bulloch family slave, "Old Bess," in a fit of temper, but her mimicry now annoyed Thee, who could not convince her to stop. Finally, he silenced her by throwing her over his shoulder and carrying her bodily away from the company. Thee and his brothers, no doubt, found Mittie's slave tales even less amusing as they abandoned their former pro-slavery views and, swept along by wartime patriotism, supported Lincoln's emancipation policies. Robert Roosevelt would even be sent to Washington by the Union League Club to urge the adoption of the Thirteenth Amendment, which abolished slavery.[47]

It was a closely held family secret that Mittie's stepbrother James D. Bulloch, one of Jefferson Davis' secret agents, had been sent to Liverpool, England, to purchase cruisers and ironclad ships for the Confederacy from the Laird shipyards at Birkenhead. Mittie did not feel it necessary to hide her knowledge of her stepbrother's clandestine task from her in-laws. Her trust was misplaced, however.

Thee's brother and business partner James A. Roosevelt, fearing with good reason that English aid to the Confederacy might doom the Union cause, sent a message to Secretary of State William Seward to expose Bulloch's plan to build ships in England. James explained his action to Seward by saying he "would feel bound to denounce a brother . . . to save the Government."[48] And he did so even though he could have caused the death or capture of Mittie's adored stepbrother.

As it turned out, James Roosevelt's betrayal of Bulloch's plans did not succeed in blocking Confederate naval strategy. The famous *Alabama* raider, commissioned by Bulloch, escaped its berth in Liverpool in July 1862, some thought with English compliance, and headed across the Atlantic to shoot down armed and unarmed Northern ships. Along with other Confederate raiders, the *Alabama* wrought millions of dollars of destruction, sinking 257 ships and wounding the U.S. merchant marine. Northern newspapers denounced "these outrages upon our defenceless ships" when unprotected New Bedford whalers were sunk by the *Alabama.* Committees formed spontaneously to find ways to stop the Confederates from dominating the open seas and killing more Northern civilians on merchant ships. Across the North, the Bulloch name spelled infamy.[49]

Thee, Mittie, and their offspring usually joined Grandfather C.V.S. Roosevelt and Thee's brothers—Jim, Weir, and Rob and their wives—for cordial Saturday night dinners at the Roosevelt mansion around the corner on Fourteenth and Broadway on Union Square. But war changed the conversation. Mittie wrote to the absent Thee that at one family dinner she felt like an interloper, and when a political topic came up "I felt my blood boil." Before long Mittie told her husband that "something occurred there which has made me determine not to dine there again," and she refused to attend family dinners for the rest of the war.[50]

Thee demanded that Mittie keep up what he defined as the other social obligations of the family, including joining other women in the family working at the New York Sanitary Fair where they ran a "Knickerbocker kitchen" serving crullers, oly-koek cookies, and tea to fund war relief for the Union. He also required Mittie to entertain officials of the Union government "for political reasons," perhaps because Roosevelt and Son required a working relationship with government customs officers. Mittie gave in, but Grandmother Bulloch viewed such wartime parties as "absolutely sinful."[51]

To help the Confederacy, Mrs. Bulloch and her daughters had to resort to subterfuge. Even though she had little money left, Mrs. Bulloch sold some of her silver to finance hospital supplies for the Confederate soldiers being held in Union prison camps. Theodore's grandmother wondered whether she should return south to nurse her ailing son Daniel Stewart Elliott. In the end, though Mittie begged him not to, Thee got a pass to allow Mrs. Bulloch and Aunt Annie Bulloch to cross enemy lines to return to Georgia. But probably because of her advanced age and the danger involved in crossing into the Confederacy, Mrs. Bulloch finally decided that Mittie needed her to stay in New York.

INEVITABLY, Theodore, Bamie, Elliott, and Corinne were touched by the war and their family's conflict. When Thee left for Washington, Mittie conspired with her older children to wrap packages to send to the Confederacy, and they always recalled the "hushed and thrilling excitement" of packing a box "to run the blockade." Mittie proudly told her children of her stepbrother's skillful piloting through the naval blockade. His imagination piqued, Theodore invented a game called "running the blockade" which was based on their uncle James' adventures bringing his ship, the *Fingal*, through waters filled with Union patrollers. On a bridge in Central Park, he would play the Union boat and he would try to catch Bamie, the blockade runner desperately sailing to the safety of Confederate ports. Bamie recalled that it was "our favorite game for years afterward."[52]

Swept up in the war fever, Theodore was eager to imitate the Zouaves, the Union regiments dressed in red shirts, baggy pants, and colorful sashes and turbans. When Aunt Annie took him to be fitted for his own Zouave suit, he asked her: "Are me a soldier laddie too?" She told him: "Yes and I am the Captain," which motivated him to hold still long enough to be fitted for his uniform.[53]

Theodore's admiration for soldiers may have been heightened by seeing his uncle in state militia uniform or his father in Home Guard uniform, or hearing his uncle Rob's war letters read aloud. He could watch military parades from his grandfather's house on Union Square, where colorful scenes of waving flags and handkerchiefs added to the spectacle of loved ones saying farewell to departing men in uniform. War held more glory and less suffering for Theodore than for many children of war, who hid in fear underground as Vicksburg was shelled or who were caught in the path of armies.[54]

Yet war did bring physical danger to Theodore's Manhattan world. New York's Draft Riots broke out in July 1863 because poor men, many of them Irish immigrants, resented being drafted to fight in the Union army for a war that favored the rich. Poor men's anger boiled over at rich men like Thee who escaped the draft by paying for substitutes. Rioters believed that the battlefield's hospital wagons overflowed disproportionately with the poor, and they resented that the rich profited in safety from the war while their own kind lay slaughtered after the shooting stopped or died of scurvy at Andersonville prison. On the streets, mobs shouted "down with the rich men" and "there goes a $300 man."[55]

Around the corner from Theodore's house, among the many rich men expecting to be attacked, Elbridge Gerry tried to protect his uncle Peter Goelet's mansion by pushing furniture to blockade the windows and doors. Gerry even armed his servants to fight off the mob. Thee rushed away from his family's holiday at the stylish resort in Long Branch, New Jersey, to defend New York against the rioters. When he arrived in Manhattan, he found roving crowds had attacked abolitionists' homes, orphan asylums for black children, and draft enrollment offices. Rioters beat to death a colonel from the state troops. Then, street children set the victim afire, an appalling illustration that many at the bottom of society hated local authorities. Men who had once feared a surprise Confederate attack on New York saw how class warfare might overrun the city first.[56]

As armed bands of poor and working-class immigrants neared the rich cloisters of the Gramercy Park neighborhood, the scene proved dangerously reminiscent of the French Revolution and the European revolutions of 1848. Near Theodore's house, thirteen rioters were killed as they approached the home of Cyrus Field, the transatlantic cable promoter who served in the Union League Club with Thee. After rioters gained control of much of the city, Thee most likely joined the other wealthy members of the club who rescued riot victims and gathered their hunting weapons to stand guard to protect their clubhouse at 26 East Seventeenth Street, an edifice seen by many as the "Citadel of Privilege." Meanwhile, rioters' sniper fire rang out across the Roosevelts' neighborhood. After the editor of the *New York Times* fired a Gatling gun at the rioters from his rooftop and Union troops left the battlefield of Gettysburg to subdue the riot, peace returned to Manhattan, but more than a hundred people lay dead. The Draft Riots taught New York's elite that philanthropic work among the poor would not exempt them from being targeted by the fury of the "dangerous classes."

Several months later, when 250 members of the Union League Club donned top hats and formal Prince Albert coats and marched through rioters' neighborhoods from Union Square to Canal Street behind the black regiment they had recruited, Theodore's extended family was there to cheer. The deeper meaning of the day's pageantry was not emergent racial equality, but instead a reply to the rioters that law and order would prevail because of a temporary alliance of white and black to win the war and to keep bloody anarchy and class conflict at bay.[57]

While talk about the Draft Riots warned Theodore to fear the poor, the trumpeting of the feats of aristocratic war heroes like the martyred Robert Gould Shaw reaffirmed his family's pride of class. Shaw's sister Josephine Shaw Lowell became a regular visitor in their home, where she talked Sanitary Commission business and later State Charities Aid Association reform with Thee, and Theodore must have heard the inspiring story of her husband's death: In the midst of battle he was shot in the chest, his lung collapsed, and then his horse was shot out from under him. He remounted to fight again until "noble death" in relentless battle felled him as a fatal bullet severed his spine. War stories left indelible images of noble disfigurement in the mind of young TR.[58]

Civil War children like Theodore could not miss "the tremendous moral exaltation of those times nor the tremendous physical tension," as people close to them could think and talk of nothing else but the day's battle news and the chance that family and friends might be hurt. On the streets Theodore saw the wounded who returned in gruesome abundance. His contemporary Albert Beveridge would recall how his childhood was enlivened by the lively Civil War music of fife and drum, but he also remembered that he gained "a legacy of gloom . . . from that mute waiting for the ghastly news of loved ones' mangling or destruction."[59]

Though he lived in safety, the Civil War remained a traumatic event for Theodore, full of loss, grief, shock, insecurity, and conflict. Grandmother Bulloch and Uncle Daniel Elliott died during the war, his father was absent and in frequent danger for nearly half of it, and his family worried constantly about the outcome. When he visited his father at the Roosevelt and Son office on Pine Street, the veterans with missing limbs his father employed reminded him of the heroic scars worn by men of honor.

For the rest of his life Theodore expressed powerful emotion when he argued for the constructive effects of the Civil War. He saw it as an apocalyptic battle of the faithful against the forces of evil, which was the view promoted by Protestant clergymen who infused the war with biblical meaning. They taught that from the spilling of blood, sins would be remitted. He learned from them that "the extravagance and parade, the epicurism and effeminacy into which we were so fast running" would be cleansed by putting "our young men upon a training which will nourish their manly virtues."[60] War, preachers insisted, could save men's souls.

The war insinuated itself into every corner of his childhood. Before the war, Teedie had played at blocks or pretended to be a bear or a tame cat. But with Bamie he now played running the blockade. With Elliott he started acting out his most bellicose dreams through war games, taking the part of the "little rebellious soldier" and the "honored soldier." Encouraged to compete by Thee, they even fought battles, brother against brother, "with clubs." Steeped in the martial values of the Civil War and inspired by his mother's stories of Bulloch fighting valor, Theodore looked up to military heroes for the rest of his life, and he found repulsive, even disturbing, any notion of tragedy or waste in war.

On April 24, 1865, a photographer captured the sight of six-year-old Theodore and five-year-old Elliott watching from the second floor of Grandfather Roosevelt's mansion as President Lincoln's funeral procession passed through Union Square. Theodore looked with pride as the Invalid Corps haltingly trailed after the cortege. As Edith later recalled, she watched alongside the boys and burst out crying, overcome with grief at the sight of the Invalid Corps' wounds. Offended, Theodore locked her in a closet, so his reverie of hero worship for the honored veterans who brandished an "empty sleeve" could go uninterrupted.[61]

War had meant that Theodore was deprived of his most active parent for almost two years, and the fragile Mittie was too depressed about being left without her husband to give her children all the nurturance they needed. Though Aunt Annie, Grandmother Bulloch, and the devoted family nurse, Dora, managed the house and the four children well enough, Theodore felt the loss of his father deeply. When Thee returned for a brief visit, Teedie followed him closely, begging for attention, clasping the Testament that had belonged to Thee's recently deceased mother.[62]

Thee's family worshipped their reigning "benevolent Norse god" all the more in absentia, and, for Theodore, scarce contact with his father further enlarged Thee in his mind. A wonderful father who was so far elevated by his son's imagination would not be easy to live up to. Measuring his own progress against his extravagant idealization of his father encouraged him to set expansive, even boundless aspirations for himself. Theodore later admitted to a "hopeless sense of inferiority" to Thee.[63]

Theodore knew at an early age who his favorite parent was. He adored his father, but he had decidedly mixed feelings about his mother. Mittie had told her children stories about the Bullochs leaving their slaves trapped on a treadmill and her stepbrother Daniel Stewart Elliott even murdering his slave in a fit of rage, but in the wartime north the stories rang false. Bamie stopped sympathizing with the slave-owning Bullochs, and she later recalled that Mittie's stories made Theodore and her "intensely hate slavery."[64] One day he attempted a "partial vengeance" on his mother. As he said his evening prayers in front of her, young Theodore asked God to grant "the success of the Union arms." He prayed that the Union troops would "grind the Southern troops to powder." Mittie laughed at the child's earnest avowal, but she threatened Thee's wrath if the boy ever acted up that way again.[65]

During his father's absence, while family tension was at its height, Theodore's health had declined sharply. He begged his mother to "do tell Papa to come home," and the boy was soon overcome by very serious asthma. He suffered his first attack in June 1862, when he was three years old. Nothing seemed to relieve him from its strangling grip.[66]

Asthma and his consequent invalidism began to dominate Theodore's childhood. Wheezing and coughing, Theodore tried with all his might to pull air into his tight and congested lungs. His family knew that some children died of the affliction, and Theodore suffered the type of severe attacks that could prove fatal.

Although periods of relief often came, he never knew when a sudden and serious illness would strike him down. He was terrified by his inability to breathe, and frequently could not sleep: Attacks struck without warning, often at night. Acute asthma might pass quickly or take hold of him for days at a time. He recalled in his adulthood that during the Civil War "when the Union and Confederate troops were fighting . . . I was a little bit of a chap, and nobody seemed to think I would live."[67] Rarely free of asthma for long periods, he could count on ill health, including related respiratory ailments, intruding upon him a number of times each month.

When Theodore's attacks hit, a crisis atmosphere pervaded the household. The Roosevelts and Bullochs tried everything to help the boy and put the needs of the other children second because Theodore's life was at stake. The family sought the best medical advice, but to little avail.

Twenty-first-century physicians would have tried to identify and eliminate the possible sources of allergic reactions or infections which provoked his asthma. They would have provided inhalants or other medicines to cut down the inflammation and secretions of his lungs and open up his constricted bronchioles.

The duration of his asthma, especially the fact that it lasted into adulthood, suggests that TR had allergic asthma, probably caused in his childhood by ubiquitous coal dust, the black hair-cloth chairs that he recalled scratched his legs in the family's dining room, the heavy dust-laden Victorian draperies, animal hair from the Roosevelts' many pets and horses, and mold from a damp basement, all allergens which were further irritated by cigar smoke in his father's library. Asthma has biological rather than psychological roots, though family tensions probably exacerbated his ongoing condition. Today his severe asthma would be treatable and not destine a child to invalidism. In the 1860s it was life-threatening.[68]

Roosevelt's contemporaries who also suffered from chronic asthma often became nomads, if they could afford it, searching for a better place to breathe. Some relinquished their professions; others died young. No effective asthma medicine existed. No one could find what triggered his attacks, but the Roosevelts had their own suspicions: the weeds that grew outside their vacation house, his colds, and dust. Mittie wrote from Oyster Bay that "either from a cold or Ellie or Johnnie's tossing about the sofa cushions in the same room with him while we were at dinner, he had an attack of asthma and had to go in to the city . . . the dear little fellow is out here again looking much pulled down." The Roosevelts' doctors offered no more useful advice than to seek "change, plenty of fresh air, and exercise."[69]

Theodore's trials with asthma were multiplied by painful and unpleasant medical treatments. At first, when he suffered from related respiratory infections which produced swollen lymph glands on his neck, his parents merely massaged the lumps. His doctors soon proposed more drastic intervention: more than once they lanced his glands without anesthesia. Although "bleeding" and using leeches were declining as medical fashions in the nineteenth century, some respectable doctors still advocated bloodletting as a cure for children's respiratory ailments. Theodore was also forced to swallow medicines such as ipecac, quinine with iron, magnesia, rhubarb pills, and arrowroot.

When other treatments brought no improvement, Mittie and Thee applied heated mustard plasters to his chest. As a last resort, his father made him drink strong coffee and smoke cigars to stop the attacks. The Roosevelts also tried aggressive massage to stimulate his breathing, and Theodore complained in his diary: "I was rubbed so hard on the chest this morning that the blood came out."[70]

Eventually his parents became so desperate to improve their son's delicate health that they sent him, on their family doctor John Metcalfe's recommendation, to the office of the young neurologist George M. Beard, who specialized in the study of neurasthenia, or, as his famous book called it, *American Nervousness*. Sometime after 1868, Beard's partner, Alphonso D. Rockwell, who usually treated high-strung, excessively refined aristocrats who had inherited neurasthenia from a parent, began giving Theodore medical care using electrical charges.

Rockwell diagnosed Theodore as suffering from "the handicap of riches." The boy, he told Beard, was a typical case of excessive upper-class refinement, which others condemned as "the wretchedness of extreme civilization." Beard had warned that the roots of neurasthenia lay in the advances of modern American life. He blamed modern forces—steam power, the telegraph, scientific discoveries, the periodical press, and even women's increased intellectual activity—for wearing out the delicate nervous systems of brain workers and other cultured types who were multiplying in an affluent industrial world. Beard accepted the prevailing Victorian theories of cultural evolution: the belief that Africans, Indians, and aborigines—whom they saw as primitive or savage races—lived on the lowest rung of evolutionary development while higher evolutionary types progressed through stages of barbarism to reach "civilization," the advanced stage of cultural evolution which only the Anglo-Saxons had achieved. Neurasthenia, Beard wrote, was the price refined upper-class people paid for their evolution into self-controlled and advanced creatures.[71]

Rockwell recalled that he told Beard that Theodore "ought to make his mark in the world; but the difficulty is, he has a rich father." Thus he believed that the Roosevelts' affluence had generated the boy's pathology. To restore nervous energy, Beard and Rockwell attached electrical equipment to their patient's head and the abdomen or feet and sent a charge throughout the body to restore its energy and "vital force" in order to cure the patient of his "overcivilization."[72]

Years later, Theodore wrote Dr. Rockwell that he "had forgotten it entirely until your letter revived my memory . . . [of] the electrical instrument." He never recorded his impressions of what could have been an upsetting electrical treatment, although Dr. Rockwell, years after he had gone on to pioneer electrocution techniques, recalled that the boy had shown a great deal of curiosity about how the electricity worked. Electrotherapy and rest, however, did not cure Theodore's asthma or his alleged overcivilization.[73]

Mittie and Thee took Theodore to seek other treatments offered to victims of neurasthenia and overcivilization, including rest, water cures, and incessant travel. Thee even contemplated sending the boy to live in Denver to cure his asthma, but it proved impractical. Though Thee installed the same gymnasium equipment on his piazza that the Newsboys' Lodging House and the Y.M.C.A. used, his son's health was too precarious for a full dose of the exercise cure. So, for much of the boy's childhood his parents confined him to an invalid's life like his neurasthenic mother, searching for new medical cures and traveling with her to her favorite resorts. While the other children fared the best they could during his attacks, the family gathered around Theodore at its emotional center, watching him with anxious alarm because of his delicacy.

Although Theodore longed to be like his robust father, his asthma seemed to doom him to be like his mother. Edith Carow remembered him being "frail and ill" for much of his childhood, and he later told an interviewer he had been both "sickly and nervous" during his years as an invalid. Yet, around the time he was eight, the Roosevelts sent him, dressed in a velvet coat, to Thee's old tutor who now ran John McMullen's school for boys. Soon they saw that Theodore was too weak to withstand even the modest rigors of the nearby private school.[74]

Though Elliott remained with Mr. McMullen, Theodore had to be confined to private tutors and protected from contact with rougher children. When he and Elliott happened to encounter young "toughs" on the street, Teedie proved too weak and fearful to defend himself. So Elliott served as his bodyguard. Theodore had fitful bursts of energy and enjoyed many moments of play with Elliott and their heartier cousins Jimmy (James West), Frank, Johnny, and Emlen Roosevelt, but illness often prevented him from living a full life outside the sickroom.

Theodore later recalled that he "frequently had to be taken away on trips to find a place where I could breathe," often with Mittie. From the end of the Civil War until he was in his teens he and his mother traveled as nomadic health seekers. She was drawn to the relaxing world of resorts, sampling treatments at New Lebanon, Richfield Springs, Saratoga, Old Sweet Springs, Brattleboro, and White Sulphur Springs, and later she went to Carlsbad and Frangensbad during the family's European travels.[75]

Sometimes an atmosphere of desperation governed their trips. Not long before Theodore's twelfth birthday, Mittie rushed her son to the Richfield Springs water cure resort from Oyster Bay to avert an impending asthma attack with his "regular treatment" at the sulphur baths. There, Mittie took him to a doctor who told her that the air of sulphur baths was not good for asthmatics. Instead of listening to the doctor's advice, she telegraphed Thee, who telegraphed back ordering her to keep the boy there because the baths "would diminish wheeze."[76]

Bound to his mother by their common bond of weak health, Theodore in 1870 enumerated for Bamie his journeys in search of health, writing: "I have been several times sick since I came home and the result was that I visited Philadelphia, New York, Oyster Bay, Saratoga and Richfield."[77] In his diary and letters he recorded how often traveling in search of better health defined the middle years of his childhood: "Was sick so went to oyster bay by boat cars and coach"; "I was sick and so went in to the citty [*sic*]"; "I am here at Richfield now. Of course I came here because I was sick, and it is only ten hours in the cars and two in the boat from Oyster Bay, where I was."[78]

While Mittie found true happiness and a "supportive female environment" within the neurasthenic culture of spas, many of Thee's friends thought wealthy spa-visiting matrons like her and the neurasthenic men who sought health alongside them spelled national decline. Thee's friend Charles Loring Brace warned: "Those useless trips to crowded watering-places must be dropped for something—cheering, healthful, boyish—or we should be a nation of dyspeptics."[79] Critics of overcivilization targeted not just affluence itself; they also took potshots at well-worn American villains, especially antirepublican lovers of luxury. Women's invalid vacations at spas were disparaged as ominous portents by many of Thee's friends, including the editor of *Harper's Weekly*, George William Curtis, who wrote that "watering-place life is a full-dress parade of social weaknesses."[80]

In *Potiphar Papers*, Curtis satirized the "blighted circle" of rich families led by "scheming, or ambitious, or disappointed" wives who dragged their husbands and sons into "disgracing their manhood" by serving as a woman's "appendage" as she made the rounds of resort society. Theodore, who would soon read and admire *Potiphar Papers*, could easily wonder if he, by traveling to resorts as his mother's "appendage," had, in fact, demeaned his own manhood.[81]

In Theodore's youth, overcivilization became a shorthand expression for privileged men's many fears about how their class measured up. Scientific beliefs about cultural evolution and neurasthenia and social critics' understanding of overcivilization constituted iron cages of Victorian knowledge that bounded his childhood years. He was taught to blame growing urban licentiousness on the poorer "criminal classes," but his father also taught him to fear that the "better classes" had become too dainty to do battle against moral decay. Thomas Wentworth Higginson articulated for Americans at midcentury the male fear that higher standards of living were depleting men's bodies: "All civilization is a slow suicide of the race." After "refinement and culture" had wasted all of men's animal spirits, Higginson prophesied that American men would be left "in a condition like that of the little cherubs on old tombstones, all head and wings." Theodore later admitted that Higginson's early diagnosis of "race suicide" or "national emasculation" shaped his adult thinking about American men and the strenuous life, and his own early membership in the "nation of dyspeptics" would later make him all the more determined to fight the overcivilization in himself and in his country.[82]

Too sick to practice his father's muscular Christian beliefs, Theodore adapted to his childhood invalidism by becoming a scientist and a dreamer, studying natural history and collecting animals. As Mittie became more single-minded about keeping clean, Theodore responded by styling himself as a grubby "ornithological small boy" whose imagination flew far above the sickroom and the streets of New York with the birds he adored. Ironically, his way of loving birds was to shoot them and stuff them so that he could study them. He kept mice in his pockets just for shock value. He took pleasure in smelling of arsenic used to preserve specimens and keeping snakes in his room, proud to disobey his mother's codes of cleanliness. He wrote of himself: "The ornithological small boy, or indeed the boy with the taste for natural history of any kind, is generally the grubbiest of all" kinds of boys.[83]

Theodore made an invalid's life bearable by dreaming he could fight and explore side by side with the heroes of his favorite books. A "born hero-worshipper," he later recalled that his daydreams were often peopled by soldiers:

> From reading of the people I admired—ranging from the soldiers of Valley Forge, and Morgan's riflemen, to the heroes of my favorite stories—and from hearing of the feats performed by my Southern forefathers and kinsfolk, and from knowing my father, I felt a great admiration for men who were fearless and who could hold their own in the world, and I had a great desire to be like them. Until I was nearly fourteen I let this desire take no more definite shape than day-dreams.

On a day in 1868 when Theodore was suffering from an asthma attack, Mittie wrote Bamie that he "dressed up in rags to imitate a soldier."[84]

The Civil War haunted Theodore's mother, too, for Mittie was "never reconciled to the defeat of the Confederacy" or to her mother's death. Mittie gave up more time to invalidism (turning to ether and laudanum on occasion), and southern relatives visiting New York found that "Mittie felt it was too much for her and they should not have expected it of her" to attend extended Roosevelt family holiday dinners. In 1868, Thee had taken Mittie to visit Roswell, where she greeted her former slave Daddy Luke warmly, only to find he acknowledged her with eyes that looked dead. It saddened Mittie to find that the South and the girlhood she remembered had been lost forever.[85]

Theodore held only scant interest in his mother's state of mind during Reconstruction. Ignoring the fact that she still mourned friends who had died in the war, he asked her to go to battlefields to fetch him artifacts. From the quiet safety of Twentieth Street he collected and labeled specimens of war and nature, plants, wild animals, and other objects that fed his dreams and unlocked the mysteries of science. Like the cannibal who hoped to acquire the courage of his enemy by dining on him, the "ornithological small boy" captured exotic souvenirs of wild animal life, warfare, and Indians. He made them his own by writing about or drawing pictures of them, and sometimes displayed them in his own amateur Roosevelt Museum.

TR's love of stuffing animals soon became an obsession. But even here Theodore shared an underlying bond with his compulsive mother. Mittie could spend a whole week cleaning out one closet, and in the process lose all awareness of other people's demands on her. Theodore disconnected himself in the same way as he sorted and classified his burgeoning collection of different species.

A lover of books even as a toddler, Theodore had amused adults by bringing them the cumbersome David Livingstone's *Missionary Travels and Researches in Africa* and asking them to tell him about the heroic missionary who had been lost while exploring the Zambezi River. By the time he reached age seven he "crave[d] knowledge" of every kind, especially the scientific study of animal behavior.[86]

In fact, Mittie, an escape artist herself, understood her son's withdrawal into books, for she wrote: "Teedie has been engrossed with the 'Chaplet of Pearls,' having had Thee rudely tear from him his beloved geography over which he had pored. He told me last night that he thinks he would have died if it had not been for that geography."[87] As he gasped for breath, TR kept going by reading avidly, especially the adventures which featured struggle and triumph against danger by larger-than-life heroes. Already his imaginative life was peopled by the Ivanhoes, Robin Hoods, Natty Bumppos, and Civil War and American Revolutionary soldiers, all heroic male adventurers who transported him far from his sickbed.

Thee encouraged his dream life by reading him James Fenimore Cooper and supported his serious interest in science. Thee could afford to buy him almost any scientific book he wanted and arrange lessons for him with a professional taxidermist. Because Thee was one of the American Museum of Natural History's founders and financial backers, Theodore was the only child whom the ornithologist and director, Albert Bickmore, allowed to watch the unpacking of the famous Verreaux Collection, which featured 220,000 mounted mammals and almost 3,000 mounted birds.

His parents permitted him to house his own Roosevelt Museum of Natural History in his room, despite the inconvenience to his roommate, Elliott, and his collection grew to a thousand items by the time he was eleven. In addition to reading scholarly research papers to other members, Theodore proudly served as the museum's bird specialist, resident naturalist, and president of the Roosevelt library of natural history books. Years later, specimens he had captured would be valuable enough to find their way into the permanent collection of Bickmore's museum.[88]

Theodore was not alone in his quest to possess artifacts of alternative lives. In the latter half of the nineteenth century, many men and boys of the comfortable classes took up the popular hobby of collecting and classifying natural objects, and amateur natural history museums became the foundation for great public institutions. Nature was not the only territory to be conquered by Victorian acquisitiveness, for countless artistic and archaeological treasures from around the world found their way into Gilded Age collections. Isabella Stewart Gardner went after Italian paintings; Ned Warren bought Greek statues; William Sturgis Bigelow collected Asian art. The long imperial reach of Western travelers and collectors had deeper agendas than museum building and the pursuit of knowledge. When the Dodges acquired a Rembrandt they brought the authority of European high culture to bear on their ascendant economic status. American wealth could buy the best vacations the world had to offer, so at home the stuffed heads of big game announced that the master of the house, despite his management of stocks and bonds, had a touch of the caveman in him.[89]

Private collectors and museum builders also selected their displays didactically. In New York, art and natural history museum founders—Roosevelt, Dodge, Jesup, Blodgett, and Potter, among others—were men prominent in Protestant moral reform crusades, many of them muscular Christians who saw in wild animals and native people a shared category, a repository of valuable qualities lost in the march of advancing civilization. They gave money to museums for the same reasons they gave it to the Y.M.C.A.—to teach the virtues of struggle and simplicity, to counter the fancy-dress ball and sentimentality of the Victorian parlor with totems of essential maleness. The same men who "lamented the aboriginal strength the white man had lost" spent part of their fortunes to bring icons of "healthy animalism" and primitive masculinity to instruct New York in what it had forgotten about true manly living. If Theodore's asthma, indeed, came from overcivilization, then perhaps assembling souvenirs from the wilds, in his own museum and in the American Museum of Natural History, would bring to life the healthy natural man within him.[90]

During the years when his invalidism frustrated him most, Theodore warmed to museum founders' ideas about the sacred and curative force of nature and their embrace of primitive masculinity and "healthy animalism." He brought to his study of nature more than romantic notions about nature as a source of mystical rebirth. He wanted to learn scientific facts because science was the new truth of his age, and it shaped his view of the world as much as any other set of ideas. During Theodore's youth scientists and laymen debated the larger meanings of Charles Darwin's *Evolution of Species*, and the boy read Darwin eagerly. He did not share the fear expressed by many ministers about Darwin's theories that placing humans on a continuum of evolutionary development undermined their Christian belief that God created man in his image. Theodore chose to believe instead the teachings of "Darwin's bulldog," Thomas Huxley, who explained in *Man's Place in Nature* that the similar primate origins of apes and humans did not unseat God or reduce people to the status of beasts. Thus, Theodore could believe that God and evolution worked together.

He sought scientific knowledge voraciously, and saw in nature a miniature Civil War, predation and death everywhere. Despite the animal protection and conservation views he heard from his conservationist uncle Rob, as a youngster Theodore turned to nature as an outlet for his most aggressive impulses and liked wilderness stories best when man's aggression and wildlife's destruction went unchecked.[91] His favorite author, Mayne Reid, wrote stories of gruesome mortal combat and dismemberment, including one in which a mother helplessly watched an alligator kill her child, then used the remnants of her dead daughter's body as bait in order to take revenge on the murderous reptile. Theodore mentioned Reid's books five times in his *Autobiography*, remarking that he "so dearly loved" them as a child. Corinne remembered years later that young Theodore, sharing his view of nature as a battleground with his younger siblings, told them many tales, straight out of his fantasy life, "about jungles and bold, mighty and imaginary fights with strange beasts."[92]

Theodore's intellectual development was thriving. Blessed with an exceptional memory and abundant curiosity, the boy learned early to love literature, history, geography, and science. Corinne also recalled that her brother's "delicate health and his almost abnormal literary and scientific tastes had isolated him somewhat from the hurly-burly of ordinary school life, and even ordinary vacation life."[93]

He could not yet be the strong and healthy son his father wanted, but Theodore had already learned that the road to his father's favor was also paved with piety. Each Sunday when the family came home from church the children competed for their father's approval as they each hurried to write the best summary of the sermon and vied over who could do the best job memorizing two verses from the Bible. Thee encouraged their rivalry, especially when they fought over a chance to please him.

As a result, the children's rivalry intensified. Corinne, near the end of her life, still savored her glorious triumph over Theodore on the summer day during their stay in Loantaka, New Jersey, when Thee brought them "Pony Grant." She recalled that Thee offered to give the pony to the first child who dared to ride him. Hopping on Pony Grant before her brothers, Corinne always knew that, even though she was being raised to be a lady, she had her share of the Roosevelts' zest for living, perhaps more than her invalid brother did.[94]

Often, even when he lagged behind at similar physical competitions, Theodore outstripped the other children in contests of virtue. If a child had been extraordinarily good during the day, Thee would make him or her his assistant in preparing the salad dressing for dinner. For his father's sake, Theodore learned the stories in the Old Testament so well that they became "vivid pictures in his mind," which he could call up spontaneously in speeches for the rest of his life.[95]

As a child Theodore already stood out as the most aggressive and articulate young Roosevelt. Family members watched a "righteous ruthlessness" developing in him. Like his father he excelled at defining rights and wrongs not only for himself but for others. The family minister observed that Theodore "constantly reminded me of" his father in his impassioned attacks on evil.[96]

He guided his siblings, "leading, suggesting, explaining," taking center stage within the family as his due. Especially in his moral advocacy Theodore became his father's equal. Corinne saw Theodore as "truly the spirit of my father reincarnate." By the time he was an adolescent, TR was already a staunch Victorian moralist. Theodore's friends thought he was a "prig because of some strong positions he had taken toward certain usually condoned activities." He even let his Victorian moral decorum dictate his choice of companions. He wrote his father, hoping to elicit paternal approval: "Did you hear that Percy Cushion was a failure? He swore like a trooper and used disreputable language, so I gave him some pretty strong hints, which he at last took, and we do not see much more of him."[97]

While his intellectual achievements had reached nearly an adult level, his emotional development was delayed. He still played store and baby with the younger children. While his parents insisted upon his taking French, drawing, and dancing lessons to make sure he grew up as "cultured" as a boy of his class should be, TR preferred to practice Indian sign language and sketch violent scenes of Indian warfare.[98] Indeed, Theodore remained quite childish in his dealings with his peers. Having been "miserably jealous" of Elliott from an early age, Theodore at first banned his younger brother from museum membership, allowing instead his two serious-minded cousins Emlen and

Jimmy Roosevelt to join. He often roughhoused with Ellie, trying to put things down his back, and finally pushed him against a glass which cut his arm. Theodore proved himself an "inveterate tease" who exhibited a "superior attitude" toward younger children. His aloofness from others occasionally irritated his friends, who thought him socially inept because of his great fault, absentmindedness, which made him appear distracted and distant.[99] Fanny Smith Parsons, a childhood playmate and lifelong intimate friend, remembered Theodore's patronizing tone as he "came into the room one day in riding-clothes and tapped one of us younger ones on the top of our head with his riding-crop."[100]

For Theodore at age ten, the emotional patterns that emerged from his years as an invalid were already drawn: social awkwardness, withdrawal into books, self-centeredness rather than concern for others, intense dependency on a demanding but nurturing parent, a rivalrous disposition coupled with the habit of calling attention to his own inadequacies, the use of nature as an outlet for aggression, and a fierce moralism that imitated Thee. These childish patterns supported the development of his marked intellectual precocity, and they left room for him to give and receive love. But to become the kind of son his father wanted, he would have to confront his invalidism.[101]

Theodore grew up encased in iron cages of Victorian thought about cultural evolution, overcivilization, race suicide, class, mob violence, manliness and womanliness. As a child and a teen he was incapable of bending open those iron cages. Asthma and invalidism already imprisoned him so tightly that he had to worry about staying alive. But he did not have to worry alone.

When Theodore wheezed night after night with asthma, his father walked the floor carrying his son in his arms, comforting him until he could breathe again. Thee also took his son out for midnight rides in the family carriage in hopes that his lungs would open up in the night air. Years later, as an adult, Theodore told journalist Lincoln Steffens that his father remained a lifelong warming and curative presence in his life: "The thought of him now and always has been a sense of comfort. I could breathe, I could sleep, when he had me in his arms. My father—he got me breath, he got me lungs, strength—life."[102] In his mind, his dear father had saved his life. He worshipped Thee even more for being the force of comfort that kept him among the living. Yet, even in the protection of his father's arms, Theodore had to struggle to stay alive. The habit of struggle and the sense that death was nearby stayed with him forever.

Theodore wanted more than anything else in the world to be like his father and to live up to his lofty ideals. Thee had always been more comfortable pushing than praising his son. Theodore later recalled that his father sometimes "hesitated whether to tell me something favorable because he did not think a sugar diet was good for me."[103] Thee told his son that he wanted him to grow up to account for himself in the world. Thee hoped, too, that when he died his namesake would carry on his battles for reform and charity in New York. When the boy looked at himself against those high expectations, he saw mostly weakness and failure.

Once, after he suffered an especially bad attack of asthma, Theodore had a "nightmare dreaming that the devil was carrying me away." His asthma was like a devil that took away his chance to live up to his father's hopes for him. Yet, it was the fierce Thee, like the devil in Theodore's dream, who carried his son in his arms during his asthma attacks. It was Thee whose nearly demonic wrath terrified the boy. Though consciously Theodore viewed his father as a benignly powerful Norse god who held his life in his arms, subconsciously—in his dreams—the boy fearfully acknowledged that his deity had a darker side that might be brought to bear on him soon.[104]

On the brink of puberty, Theodore picked up Robert Browning's *Dramatic Romances*. He was taken aback by self-recognition as he read a poem about a young duke in "The Flight of the Duchess." He said he "felt discovered" when he read about the feckless young duke who had been shielded from other children and had never been called upon to test his worth in the outside world. He saw himself vividly in the story of the young duke, a delicate child who had traveled with his mother, "the sick tall yellow duchess."

The story of the young duke "pulled Theodore Roosevelt up sharp, like a lasso." It brought to the surface his own sense of captivity within a female invalid's domain. The poem also reminded him of his inadequacy compared to Thee and the Roosevelt and Bulloch traditions. A protected and sickly aristocrat, Theodore, as a child, had led a life like Browning's duke, devoid of either passion or purpose, secure in his high position, yet not sure he really deserved the honor. Try as he might, the young duke could not match his father's prowess in battle or in the hunt: "So all that the old Dukes had been without knowing it, / This Duke would fain know he was without being it." Nearly fifty years later, TR told a friend that he still remembered how this poem "strongly affected him," for he recognized that at the end of his childhood he was still suffering from the "handicap of riches."[105]

☆ CHAPTER TWO ☆

The Death of the Young Duke

THEE TOOK HIS FAMILY for a year-long Grand Tour of Europe in 1869, hoping travel would cure Theodore's asthma. When they left Theodore was especially sad to say good-bye to Edith and his cousins Jimmy and Emlen. As the Roosevelts traveled across Europe, Thee's domineering guidance felt punishing to his children. Theodore complained often to his diary about the pace, the dirt in the trains, his tiredness, and the demands made upon him to play with foreign children. He estimated that they had read fifty novels in the first five months of the trip. Just as Thee would insist that they speak only French at dinner on their summer vacations at home, he kept up Sunday school lessons for his children throughout their Grand Tour, making each one memorize and recite a parable and verse. Deprived of chances to play or nap, they sometimes spent as many as twelve hours at a time in railroad cars. It is no wonder that Theodore expressed relief when his mother told him the trip was already one-twelfth over. When Mittie showed Theodore a picture of Edith Carow, he wrote: "Her face stired [*sic*] up in me homesickness and longings for the past which will come again never, alack never." He held Edith and their days as childhood playmates closer to his heart because his departure from boyhood was proving so wrenching.[1]

Edith had been like a member of the Roosevelt family. When her father, Charles Carow, a wellborn Knickerbocker and Thee's old friend, failed in his shipping business, due in part to his alcoholism, his family moved from house to house. The Carows had settled in with Edith's Aunt Kermit, who lived behind the C.V.S. Roosevelt mansion. Corinne befriended Edith, who eagerly sought refuge at Theodore's house from her self-absorbed and critical mother and irritating sister Emily. So Mittie and Thee had welcomed her to take her first school lessons with Aunt Annie Bulloch, who for a few years after she married banker James K. Gracie remained the young Roosevelts' tutor.[2]

Everyone saw Edith as Corinne's best friend, yet she played house with Theodore and found in him a kindred booklover. Theodore recalled he "greatly liked the girls' stories" which he and Edith read together, such as *Little Women* and *An Old-Fashioned Girl*, though he later noted that he made this confession of his taste in books "at the cost of being deemed effeminate." Edith and Theodore looked with longing at the family lives which "girls' stories" portrayed—neither of them had mothers as unselfish and loving as Alcott's Marmee. While Theodore was on his Grand Tour, Gertrude Carow ushered Edith toward womanhood as it was practiced by Knickerbockers: She kept her out of school and ripped books out of her hands on the pretext of weak eyes. She preferred to have Edith dancing the court quadrille with Frank and Jimmy Roosevelt. As Theodore neared the time when he would be expected to become a man, he cared little for dancing and drawing room manners. He adored Edith, not for her grace in a ballroom, but for her literary bent and her companionship, and she liked him no less for being an invalid and dreamer who did not relinquish childhood easily. Edith kept a lock of Theodore's hair in her jewelry box and cherished every letter he sent her signed "Evere [sic] your loving friend."[3]

THE GRAND TOUR did not cure the boy's asthma. It was worse than ever, and after their return the Roosevelts spent the summer of 1870 rushing the boy from doctors to resorts. Theodore's troubled future as an asthmatic loomed even larger in Thee's worried mind because of other threats he faced in public life and within the family. Thee had left fifteen-year-old Bamie studying at Mlle. Souvestre's school for girls outside Paris, but he had to hurry to bring Bamie home after the Prussian armies had swept near her school on their way to conquer Paris in the Franco-Prussian War. Where Bamie had studied to become a cultured lady, the Paris Commune brought mob rule and destruction reminiscent of the Draft Riots. Back in New York, it confounded Thee further when his neurasthenic wife began to gain influence in society, as her "brilliant powers as a leader of a salon" drew the exclusive Faubourg St. Germain set to her "at homes," her days for receiving visitors. Thee discovered that the editor of the *New York Times*, John Bigelow, had sent her a book of poetry, and many nights he returned from his office to find a bevy of admirers gathered around his wife to hear her judgments about art and people. Mittie wielded her new social power by refusing to let Thee invite to dinner the lackluster Samuel J. Tilden, his ally in opposing Boss Tweed, and later a presidential candidate. Mittie also let Thee's witty friend John Hay, now a *New*

York Tribune reporter and frequent visitor to Twentieth Street, know that she thought his family connection—that is, class standing—negligible. Bamie cringed as she saw Mittie exercise her snobbish "little aristocratic, Southern feeling" on Hay. Yet, around the house Mittie remained her own inert and inept "little sweet dresden china self." Thee did not approve of the way his wife combined society leadership with escalating invalidism, so he took the responsibility for the household away from her and gave it to Bamie.[4]

Thee had hoped the Civil War would redeem his country, but instead in the early seventies his world seemed to be disintegrating, piece by piece, especially after the Orange Riot between warring Protestant and Catholic Irish immigrants killed sixty-two people not far from the Roosevelt home. He witnessed an era of scandal in the Grant administration and in the Tweed city government which made him and like-minded Protestant reformers believe sin and corruption had taken over their country. In postwar New York, rape, child molestation, and muggings went unpunished. Thee heard the stories about daughters drugged and kidnapped into prostitution and sons led astray by reading pornography or turning to drink in the working class "sporting male" brotherhood of the saloon. Sin seemed to multiply, and Thee was convinced that respectable people had lost control of the streets.[5]

Thee believed it was his duty as a citizen and a Christian to stand up against the immorality spreading around him. His brother Rob was so outraged in these years that he got himself elected to Congress, and together Thee and his brothers gave money to the Society for the Suppression of Vice's agent Anthony Comstock to wage a vigilante war against commercialized vice. Without a warrant, Comstock pulled a gun on dirty-book publishers and abortionists and used an ax to smash their wares. He allied himself with book banning in Boston and other cities at the same time that he and his supporters got a federal Comstock law passed to stop brothels and pornographers from using the federal mails. To thwart "conspiracies deep and black against the most sacred relations of home," Thee and his moral reform allies acted as a new conscience for Gilded Age America, using federal law to guard public morals from aggressive new businesses that sold sin.[6]

In Theodore's teens Thee organized prayer breakfasts for the successful Y.M.C.A. evangelist Dwight L. Moody, whose revival meetings drew audiences that totaled in the hundred thousands and set off nationwide mass conversions unequaled since the Second Great Awakening. Theodore most likely watched how the Reverend Moody used chopping arm gestures to preach against sin, because his adult style of public speaking copied both the gestures and the revivalist's plain-talking moral sincerity. At the urban revival meetings of the 1870s, Moody's partner, the singer Ira Sankey, often sang "How Firm a Foundation," which became Theodore's favorite hymn.[7]

Thee lost patience with his son's invalidism because he believed that weaklings were especially susceptible to the "moral typhoid" he feared was spreading across the nation. So, one day, probably in 1872, Thee demanded that the boy cast off his invalidism by force of will. He pointed out the inadequacies which troubled him most: The sickly Theodore paled in comparison with Elliott and cousins Emlen, Frank, and Jimmy, all of whom were on their way to hearty manhood. According to family members, Thee warned the boy: "Sickness is always a shame, and often a sin." Though she did not witness the event, Corinne reported that Thee said to his son: "Theodore, you have the mind but you have not the body, and without the help of the body the mind cannot go as far as it should." Theodore would turn fourteen that October, and his father believed that the boy had to become stronger physically to withstand the temptations of a corrupt society and to become a moral man who could influence his society for good.[8]

Thee told Theodore he must embrace manhood by adopting a rigorous body-building program, regardless of its effect on his asthma. The confrontation about Theodore's invalidism was charged with Thee's fears about his son's becoming strong enough to resist sexual temptation. He told him later: "If I had cause to doubt upon these important questions which come so much before all others" he would love his son less. According to Corinne, Thee told his son that he must make himself strong: "I am giving you the tools, but it is up to you to make your own body."[9]

Theodore was not a rebellious youngster, so, according to Corinne, he "looked up, throwing back his head in a characteristic fashion; then with a flash of those white teeth . . . he said, 'I'll make my body.' " A boy who later wrote "I owe everything I have or am to Father" could not bear to refuse. Edith later remembered that Theodore "saw his cousins and what they could do," and, realizing his inadequacy, "resolved to make himself strong."[10]

And so a new phase of Theodore's struggle for life and identity began, but he was faced with the daunting task of turning an asthmatic boy into a healthy man without the usual transitional social supports. Boys from the comfortable classes in his day pulled away gradually from the "civilizing" and feminine influences that sheltered their early childhoods by stepping into a larger world of boy culture where they played, unsupervised by adults, with boys their age, and practiced adult self-assertion and self-control which marked a halfway step toward the independent state that their culture defined as manhood. Theodore had been kept away from local boy culture because he was so helpless among ruffians that Elliott had to guard him. Finally, TR embarked upon his long search for the life of boisterous release and brotherhood he had missed.[11]

THEE SAW TO IT that his son's battle to "make his own body" began with daily trips to John Wood's gymnasium, where Theodore stood patiently at the chest-building machine, lifting weights slowly, pulling hard against the machine to increase his strength. Soon, changing his body became an all-consuming endeavor. With each hour spent body-building, Theodore hoped to become the kind of son his father wanted. Corinne later wrote that one of her "most vivid recollections" of her brother was "seeing him between horizontal bars, widening his chest by regular, monotonous motion."[12]

Success, unfortunately, did not come easily. Theodore was no more capable of curing asthma than the doctors had been. His body's transformation proceeded too slowly, as did the unmaking of his invalidism. Stronger upper-body muscles could not open up his tight bronchioles when an asthma attack engulfed him.[13] And the pressure from his father and from his own unforgiving conscience did not subside.

Then, for the first time ever, his father sent him away from the family during a flare-up of his asthma. Thee dispatched him north to Moosehead Lake in Maine to fight his asthma and timidity alone. Until that trip TR had rarely gone anywhere without escorts and defenders. For the rest of his life, he remembered his experience there.

He recorded his traumatic memory with rare candor in his *Autobiography*. He described himself as a "nervous and timid" child riding a stagecoach to Moosehead Lake, where he met two "mischievous" boys who discovered that he was a "foreordained and predestined victim." They "industriously proceeded to make life miserable" for him. Teasing him without mercy, the boys proved to Theodore how weak and timid he remained. Even after he tried to fight them, he found that in the blows that followed "either one singly could not only handle me with easy contempt, but handle me so as not to hurt me much and yet to prevent my doing any damage whatever in return."[14] Humiliated to the core, Theodore hated himself for being a sissy.

After his trip to Moosehead Lake, Theodore realized that remaining a weakling was intolerable, yet gradual body-building did not cure his asthma or bring him mastery over other boys. Although he would later claim that by building up his body he had effected a cure to his asthma, he had not. After Theodore's death, his sister Corinne told the truth to a sympathetic biographer:

> I wish I could tell you of something which really cured Theodore's asthma, but he never did recover in a definite way—and indeed suffered from it all his life, though in later years only at long separated intervals.[15]

Other family members, in interviews and private letters, confirmed that rather than curing himself of asthma, Roosevelt had well-documented but publicly concealed attacks later in life. While biographers have repeatedly accepted his self-created myth that by exercising he cured himself of asthma, the historical record says otherwise. He found ways to push asthma and invalidism out of the center of his life and to improve his stamina by exercise, but he never eradicated his disease.[16]

At first he met his father's demands to "make his own body" by regarding invalidism itself as his fiercest enemy. Theodore wanted to cut off all the ties he had with his mother's invalid world in order to smother the invalid within himself. He decided he hated the resorts that his mother enjoyed so much, calling them

> that quintessence of abomination, a large summer hotel at a watering place for underbred and overdressed girls, fat old female scandal mongers, and a select collection of assorted cripples and consumptives.[17]

His diatribe against "cripples and consumptives" expressed his fury over his mother's preference for a neurasthenic life and his own childhood captivity in her world. His hostility toward his mother came out "whenever his Mother would tell him to go and do something for her" and he replied, " 'Oh, yes, you pretty little thing!' but instead of doing it directly he would go and skin his birds."[18]

He tried harder than ever to live a life of heroic proportions. To practice heroic behavior he took boxing lessons from an ex-prizefighter, John Long. He surprised himself and his teacher with his ability to absorb hard punches and keep fighting. Boxing could knock the sissy out of him, and he said he also began "constantly forcing himself to do the difficult and even dangerous thing" in order to conquer his own fearfulness.[19]

As he went on a quest for vigor and a strenuous life, he practiced what one of his friends called "his policy of forcing the spirit to ignore the weakness of the flesh." He urged others to learn from his experience that "man does in fact become fearless by sheer dint of practicing fearlessness." He admitted he had been fearful in the beginning, of many things "ranging from grizzly bears to 'mean' horses and gun-fighters; but by acting as if I was not afraid I gradually ceased to be afraid."[20]

* * *

SINCE THEE BELIEVED that no cure equaled the sporting cure for invalids, he sent his fourteen-year-old son next door to see Uncle Rob for advice about a gun and then bought the boy a beginner's breechloader that Rob recommended. Elliott told Thee that Theodore had been within forty feet of a deer and had not seen it, so he also bought his nearsighted son glasses. Thee planned to strengthen his son further with a winter in the warm dry climate of Egypt, a boat trip down the Nile, and a visit to the Holy Lands. Then Thee would return to New York, and Mittie, accompanied by Bamie, would visit spas for her health and go to Paris for art and shopping. Thee planned to give Theodore the stern advantage of a German education in Dresden, where he, Elliott, and Corinne would study the German language intensively by living with local families for five months. Thee, who had inherited $3 million when C.V.S. died in 1871, planned to return early to New York to supervise the building of their ornate new home on West Fifty-seventh Street.[21]

Theodore little resembled the forlorn and homesick boy whose 1869–70 Grand Tour had been so miserable. Instead, on his 1872–73 trip he prowled for wild animals and explored out-of-the-way places. Mittie was struck by the sight of "miserably depressed looking women with veils" in Cairo, but Theodore wrote that when he got to Egypt, he had the "most exhilarating fun," for his family set sail on a native barge, or dahabeah, for two months of open-air life along the Nile. However, they were not completely roughing it. Included in the $5,000 rental price, numerous servants waited on them and another dahabeah followed loaded with supplies.[22]

While Mittie worried about being "dusty and dirty," Theodore loved their voyage down the river, for there he could script his own acts of courage and adventure. He relished vigorous donkey riding and exploring the pyramids. Allowed to roam the shores with his gun, shooting at will, along the Nile, Theodore played, sometimes overacted, the part of a brave hunter out of Mayne Reid's books, and he wrote home to Aunt Annie: "I think I have never enjoyed myself so much as in this month. There has always been something to do, for we could always fall back upon shooting when everything else fails us."[23]

Theodore boasted in letters to Edith Carow that he had killed "several hundred birds" with his new gun, but his more precise "Zoological Record" showed his catch for his two months in Egypt: 2 partridges, 3 quail, 37 doves, 81 pigeons, 18 large plover, 36 little shore birds, 8 Hoopoos, 8 cow heron, 1 gray heron, and 2 squirrels. Far from needing 81 pigeons for scientific study or practice in stuffing, he savored the aggressive act of shooting and the quantity of his catch.

Seeing almost every episode in his young life as a choice between passive invalidism and masculine vigor, Theodore frequently veered too far in the direction of recklessness. Corinne, who was rarely critical of her brother, wrote that, while they were in Egypt, TR took chances riding "mounted on an uncontrollable donkey" with "his gun slung across his shoulders in such a way as to render its proximity distinctly dangerous as he bumped absent-mindedly against them." He burned his pants with gunpowder, and took pride in having "tattoed [*sic*] myself with partially unburned grains of powder more than once." Bamie also remembered how he would put on his new glasses and "swing his gun over his shoulder," rushing away on his donkey to "ruthlessly lope after whatever object he had in view." She later said that Theodore was "always trying to break his neck."[24]

Proud of his injuries, he cultivated a breakneck style, describing himself in an inflated and devil-may-care way as a "hunter after large game." He gained such a reputation for carelessness with his gun that when he rode near a neighboring boat, the four college boys aboard expressed anxiety and fear about coming too close to the rash hunter. News of the wildness of the young Roosevelt did not deter the aging Ralph Waldo Emerson and his daughter Ellen from permitting the boy to row them from their dahabeah across the Nile to lunch on the Roosevelts' boat. The brief historic encounter between America's great romantic philosopher of nature and the future conservation president (whose love of nature would prompt him to change game protection and forest preservation policies) did not prove to be a time to muse over the salvation nature could offer. But the meeting was pleasant. Afterward, Ellen Emerson remarked that Theodore stood out as a likable boy with "red round cheeks, honest blue eyes, and perfectly brilliant teeth."[25]

DURING THE SUMMER of 1873, the Roosevelts placed their three younger children with the Minckwitz family in Dresden to further their studies. Theodore applied himself to studying German for long hours; he asked for more demanding lessons and got them. Elliott felt his brother's competitive spirit, and wrote home: "I could not be left behind so we are working harder than ever in our lives."[26]

Though he became more self-disciplined and independent of his parents in Dresden, Theodore just before his fifteenth birthday still had to struggle to avoid invalidism. He had to be sent out of the city because of asthma, and after his third attack he also contracted the mumps. In a moment of wishing to regress to earlier habits, TR confessed he would like to leave his regimen of studies to stay with his mother at a spa for the rest of the summer. Coming back to his senses and his father's agendas, Theodore reported stoically to his father that far from being held back by asthma, he left the resort and had wrestled, shot with an air rifle, played ball and tag, and gone walking. He wanted his father to know that, regardless of illness, he and Elliott would "have great fun with boxing, playing and everything else that we can 'cram in' to the time we have together."[27]

In Dresden, Theodore admired the German "capacity for hard work, and the sense of duty, the delight in studying literature and science, [and] the pride in the new Germany."[28] He discovered the *Nibelungenlied*, which he committed to memory, and he watched the "fascinating" Minckwitz boys, who were swordsmen and members of the dueling corps at the University of Leipzig. The Minckwitz boys were "much scarred," and one of them was called Sir Rhinoceros because the tip of his nose had been cut off and sewn on again after a duel.

Theodore looked up to them for wearing the results of their bravery on their faces, and he was eager to emulate them. Other American men also looked up to German youth as exemplars of honorable and well-defended manhood. Jurist Oliver Wendell Holmes, Jr., in his speech "The Soldier's Faith," praised the much-slashed Heidelberg students and reckless American polo players because "if once in a while in our rough riding a neck is broken, I regard it, not as a waste, but as a price well paid for the breeding of a race fit for headship and command."[29]

Theodore intended to be a part of the race fit for headship.

That summer boxing helped him prove his imperviousness to pain. To ensure regular practice, he and Elliott and their cousin Johnny Elliott formed a boxing club which they named the "mighty men of valor." Describing one hard-fought match with his brother Elliott, Theodore reported to his father:

> I was so weak however that I was driven accross [*sic*] the room, simply warding off blows, but then I almost disabled his left arm, and drove him back to the middle where some sharp boxing occurred. I got in one on his forehead which raised a bump, but my eye was made black and blue.[30]

Overjoyed to report he had seen "stars" after being pummeled, Theodore bragged to Aunt Annie that as a result of boxing, he was now a "bully boy with a black eye." He wrote his father: "If you offered rewards for bloody noses you would spend a fortune on me alone."[31]

By showing Elliott up, Theodore proved to himself that he was the better man. He relished beating Ellie as often as he could in boxing and in contests of strength and intellect. While they were studying German together,

Theodore let his father know that he was "equal to Ellie in the grammar," but that their teacher said "it is easier for me to study than for Elliott, and so I get longer lessons."[32]

That summer the Roosevelt children formed the Dresden Literary American Club, which prompted Elliott to write a violent story about a father who sharpened his knife and cut the throats of his three children. But their beloved mother was unjustly arrested for the heinous crime. Theodore ridiculed his brother's revealing story of a villainous father as an inadequate "coming down of a dime novel." Instead, he satirized family life ruined by the histrionics of a manipulative society matron mother. No matter that his villain was a mouse. His adventure in creative writing borrowed heavily from *Potiphar Papers* and scenes from his own family life.[33]

In November 1873, Mittie brought the children home to America. The day after they arrived Thee started Elliott and Theodore on lessons with a new tutor. In the winter of 1873–74 in their new home at West Fifty-seventh Street they entered a broader aristocratic social world which brought them into contact with nearby Fifth Avenue. The Panic of 1873 had thrown thousands out of work and ruined many businesses, but Thee's footmen still had claret uniforms and his landau kept its silver gilt trim. His letters were filled with irritation that the electric call system to his stables and the speaking tubes from his family's quarters to beckon the servants did not work, and that the gaslights were installed wrong. As they made new friends in a neighborhood peopled by the richest of the rich—the owners of the transportation systems that were reaching across the nation and the banks and insurance companies that financed them—Thee was determined to create a home with a level of convenience and civility which enabled his four teenage children to enjoy the benefits of living in a "well-known centre of social life and animation."[34]

Mittie and Thee agreed that the four young Roosevelts would need careful social sponsorship. Mittie chose suitable youths from similar elite backgrounds, including Edith Carow, to join her children in learning dancing at a regular class at Dodsworth's Ballroom, and Theodore, Elliott, and cousins Jimmy, Alfred, and Emlen scrambled to have Edith as a dancing partner. With Thee and Bamie's help and the applied industry of an enlarged household staff, Mittie was reported to have held a ball to which eleven hundred invitations were sent. While Uncle Robert entertained avant-gardists like Oscar Wilde, Thee and Mittie preferred the more staid society of Mrs. Astor, her lieutenant Ward McAllister, and their select Four Hundred. Thee drove a fast four-in-hand coach stylishly through Central Park, but he also worked on civic uplift in partnership with evangelical luminaries like William Dodge, Jr., Morris Jesup, and Henry Ward Beecher.[35]

Awkward among his peers, Theodore survived his entry into patrician society tolerably well because he wanted to please his sociable father. Within the family he could be hilariously funny and endearing, but his parents wanted him to learn to hold his own in society and in public life. Theodore, however, liked drawing lessons better than drawing rooms, and while he dutifully learned to dance, he preferred to go shooting. Though his future career might be in science, Theodore evidently told his drawing teacher he wanted to be a writer when he grew up.[36]

In Oyster Bay, the Roosevelts rented for several years a white-columned summer home which Mittie called Tranquility, where she could read quietly in the parlor near their large fireplace. But Theodore disliked too much tranquillity; his mother aggravated him no end when she refused to stop calling him her "precious Teddy" long after he had sprouted whiskers. Theodore sought relief from the propriety of their summer idylls by running races against his cousin Emlen and taking swims in Long Island Sound. He especially loved the long walks with his father as they explored the wooded countryside and shoreline around Oyster Bay.[37]

Their Oyster Bay summers also surrounded Theodore with adoring female attention from his sisters, who were equally fierce in their devotion to him. Corinne inherited Mittie's moodiness and the family called her "mercurial" because "she could cry and then she could laugh, like sunshine coming after rain," and she struggled mightily against elation mixed with "serious depression of spirits" all her life. Relatives observed that Corinne was "gifted & sentimental," as well as deeply "partisan" about her brother Theodore. Bamie, on the other hand, was "worldly, dispassionate," a true queenly cosmopolitan.[38]

Hardheaded and practical, Bamie disapproved of her younger sister's flightiness, but when Theodore also gave in to a "great flare-up of emotion" followed by "quiet embers," Bamie forgave his shifting emotions as signs of admirable sincerity. His sisters' lives revolved around their brother for the rest of their days but with a difference. Theodore called the demonstrative Corinne pet names—"naughty, purry, flirty mew-cat"—and cuddled her on his lap when he felt soulful or needed unambivalent praise or just playfulness. But he asked his "imperious" older sister, Bamie (who was also called Bye or Anna), for advice about etiquette and how to make his way in the larger world. He admired Bamie's brilliant conversation and her ability to work "with about fourteen business-man power." Theodore's devotion to his loved ones was "torrential," for he was passionately expressive toward them—and deeply loyal.[39]

When the Roosevelts spent their summers at Tranquility, Edith Carow and Fanny Smith (later Parsons) visited Corinne for weeks at a time, and they played charades, gave recitations, and laughed along with the rest of the Roosevelts' family and friends when Thee dressed up as a woman for amateur theatricals. Fanny thought Theodore was excitingly original and she hoped to curry favor with him by running down the steep sand banks of Cooper's Bluff at his side. Fanny's coquetry, however, was lost on the seventeen-year-old naturalist, who cared more for "ornithological enjoyment and reptilian rapture" than flirtation.[40]

Yet Theodore was happy to be enlisted to row out on the Sound with Edith, where they sat facing each other and cautiously renewed their old affection. He knew Edith would not line up easily among those who worshipped him. Later, when they exchanged letters and he denounced *The Arabian Nights* as immoral, Edith steadily asserted her judgment against his. She calmed down his categorical moralism by recalling how her beloved father's reading of *The Arabian Nights* tales to her had opened up a new world which she thought good for children. If such reading were done more often, Edith wrote, "there would positively be fewer commonplace grownup people,—certainly the bane of society." She stood up to "my dearest Mr. T.R." to defend imagination against his moralizing, reminding him of a truth they had learned together as children: that "while one can lose oneself in a book one can never be thoroughly unhappy."[41]

Theodore might have swallowed hard at being challenged by a young woman who was at least his equal in intelligence and better read in literature. He worked so hard as a young man to present a fierce and confident front to the world that people who challenged him often made him combative and defensive. Yet, he was not unnerved by Edith. She was all the more intriguing because she always granted him his dignity even when she stood him on his head intellectually. Moreover, she would never become one of the "commonplace grownup people."[42]

Thee hired Arthur Cutler, later the founder of Cutler School for boys, to tutor Theodore, Elliott, and their cousin Jimmy for college. After his rigorous studies in Dresden, Theodore was eager to immerse himself in books once more, hiding out from social demands as he read voraciously in natural history in the quiet of his own room. He studied English, mathematics, science, and history, as well as French, Latin, and Greek. Cutler regretted that the boy still lost week after week to illness, yet TR's self-discipline astounded his tutor. Each minute of his day was systematically arranged to make fast headway in his studies and physical self-improvement. Cutler often had to correct the boy's grammar and spelling, but he wrote that the "alert, vigorous character of young Roosevelt's mind" set him apart from his peers.[43]

The family saw that Theodore's new drive to make his body and his mind might destine him for great things, but his ascent occasioned Elliott's decline. Elliott's headaches and dizzy spells had increased in Dresden, where boxing may have caused a serious head injury. Like Mittie, he soon found that illness offered an evasion from family life. His ailments began to stand in the way of his riding with his father. Thee solicitously took him to England and to Florida to recover, but then in the fall of 1875, rather abruptly, despite the boy's dizzy spells and his need to take "antinervous medicine," Thee sent him off to the well-known Episcopalian boarding school St. Paul's. Many elite families placed their sons there so that its muscular Christian teachings would make men of them. Like his classmates, Elliott slept in a cold, damp alcove and had his weekly grade rankings read aloud at chapel. He made few friends and found that austerity governed playing field and classroom; soon he collapsed with "a bad rush of blood to my head" and faintness, which doctors labeled "hysteria." By early October the Reverend Henry Coit notified the Roosevelts that Elliott could not handle St. Paul's any longer. Thee sent Theodore to New Hampshire to pick up his younger brother, which he did, no doubt, with a mixture of empathy and triumph.[44]

Although they were fond of each other, Theodore judged Elliott harshly for failing to fight his illness. Thee pinned no more hopes on Elliott and sent him away to recuperate with a doctor and later on long hunting trips. In defeat Elliott headed toward a conventional elite path—riding to the hounds, cutting a dashing figure in polo matches, serving as a charming party guest, putting in an offhand performance at an undemanding job, and keeping up with the world of fashion. Yet Elliott's tender heart set him apart from the stern Roosevelt clan: when twenty-eight descendants of C.V.S. Roosevelt attended P. T. Barnum's Roman Hippodrome en masse, only Elliott recorded his worry about the showmen's cruelty toward the performing animals. Theodore understood he and his brother had different natures: he told Aunt Annie he recognized that "where he would naturally wish to surpass other men," his brother lacked a competitive spirit. When someone was ill in the family, Elliott would comfort, while Bamie managed, Corinne cried, and Theodore paced restlessly, impatient and fearful of inactivity.[45]

Seeing how close Theodore had become to their father, Elliott wrote to Thee as "Dear old Governor": "Oh. Father will you ever think *me* a 'noble boy', you are right about Tede he is one + no mistake a boy I would give a good deal to be like in many respects."[46] Perhaps Elliott's charm with women would give him his last chance to triumph over his older brother. He knew Theodore viewed Edith Carow as the most intelligent and attractive girl he had ever known. The year that Theodore prepared to go away to college, Elliott sent her flowers anonymously and began to pay calls on her. Though he never was aware of Elliott's secret pursuit of Edith, Theodore checkmated his brother unknowingly: While they had not yet spoken of it, Edith already loved Theodore "with all the passion of a girl who has never loved before." So she graciously discouraged Elliott's attentions.[47]

When Thee looked for a son to take his place in the great battle of life he saw Theodore. Thee brought his namesake to the Newsboys' Lodging House on Eighteenth Street where they could observe how he and his friend the Reverend Brace tried to convince poor boys to turn their backs on vice. He also took Theodore on inspection tours of his several charities and to Miss Sattery's Night School for Little Italians, where he required him to help, probably in the school's efforts to teach basic reading and writing skills to tenement children whom poverty had forced into factory jobs or work as flower sellers or organ grinders.[48]

Theodore learned important lessons when he saw his father speak in public using his own life as a moral example to instruct and inspire the newsboys, but he also learned that elite reformers' sense of social obligation to help others—their noblesse oblige—did not always evoke deference or gratitude from the men who defined themselves by their membership in the "sporting male culture" of saloons and brothels. Bowery boys saw more appeal in manly recreation—cockfighting, boxing, horse racing, drinking, and gambling—than in the prayer meeting and pious homilies offered by evangelical Protestants like Thee. When Theodore taught a mission class, he had to face an unruly bunch of boys who teased him about being "Teacher Four Eyes" and refused to accept him as a worthy instructor because of his upper-class dress and manners.[49]

Theodore was too sick, with asthma and respiratory infections, to study much in the winter of 1875–76, but that had not stopped him from skating so hard in Central Park that he knocked himself out for several hours. He got ready to leave for college in the fall, anticipating that he would enter the family business as his cousin Emlen did or that he would pursue a scientific career. Some members of the family still worried that he would not be healthy enough to endure a Cambridge winter. But he was determined to be equal to any challenge college offered him.[50]

When Theodore said good-bye to Edith and his family as he left for Harvard on September 27, 1876, he was still emotionally Thee's creature. He wished Arthur Cutler could go to college with him, but in truth it was his father's guiding hand he would miss the most. Yet, Theodore had made his first steps toward taking a more critical and independent stance. He knew his father felt guilty that men who could not afford to buy a substitute in the Civil War had fought in his place, so the boy reopened Thee's "deep wound" by telling him how much he disapproved. According to TR's son Archie, Thee's failure to serve "caused difficulty" between the two, but military service eventually provided one obvious means for TR to exceed the father he idolized.[51]

FRESHMAN THEODORE ROOSEVELT sat in his room at 16 Winthrop Street at Harvard College surrounded by the mementos of his New York home. Wearing slippers his parents had sent him, he "drew the rocking chair up to the fire, and spent the next half hour in toasting my feet and reading Lamb." His feeling of domestic comfort had been provided by Bamie, who took charge of decorating his room with wallpaper, furniture, a rug, and curtains. His asthma dictated that he take a second-story room off campus because the college's ground-floor rooms were considered unsafe for asthmatics. His father insisted that he seek medical care with Morrill Wyman, an expert on hayfever, but Theodore also went to the doctor for a wide variety of other ailments, including measles.[52]

The Harvard Theodore entered was an academically respectable regional men's college eager to imitate Oxford and English ways but more deeply flavored by Boston Brahminism. It was not the selective national research university it became in the next century. Two-thirds of his classmates lived within a hundred miles of Boston, and the social elite at Harvard duplicated the Brahmin pecking order. Admission standards were lax and scholarships few. For most students, college was a playful interlude before entering business or the professions, and much less serious academic work could be expected of Theodore's generation of Harvard men than their grandsons. Theodore later gave little credit to his education: "There was very little in my actual studies which helped me in after life."[53] Yet in his four years of college he did not stand still. He arrived far ahead of his peers in science, history, and languages—he spoke French, German, and Italian—and he left Harvard having broadened his knowledge in many ways. At the very least he made the acquaintance of a medieval history professor named Henry Adams and got to know Robert Bacon, Albert Bushnell Hart, and other classmates who would figure in his later literary and political careers. Most of all, he learned to make his way within his own privileged world.[54]

Many of Theodore's later complaints about his elite class grew out of his Harvard experience, for his classmates' "emulation of highbred cynicism and arrogant coolness" were anathema to the earnest and driven young Roosevelt. He editorialized in letters home that he found it "astonishing" "how few fellows have come here with any idea of getting an education." TR worried about the class antecedents of his peers, too, and preferred to mix only with other gentlemen. He was indignant that Harvard men of patrician families knew all too well the streetcars that led to brothels and saloons in Boston, but he led a more circumspect life.[55]

In college Theodore heard a great many of the new ideas and thinkers of his day. He heard Henry George, who taught that the extremes of wealth and poverty created by industrial capitalism could be alleviated by a land tax, and he heard Social Darwinist William Graham Sumner, who justified the increasing misery of the poor as their failure to win in the survival of the fittest. On his own TR devoured the works of Thomas Babington Macaulay, whose history taught that the brave English-speaking people were destined to rule "languid" Bengalis and other colonial types "fitted by habit for a foreign yoke."[56] But the youth found his intellectual home in science and morality.

Theodore stood out as different from his peers because he was energized by a rare intellectual intensity. He had already wondered about the implications of Darwinian theory for humans' obligation to lower animals and nature, and he was eager to hear what his Christian evolutionist natural history professor, Nathaniel Shaler, had to say about the interdependence of species, the dangers of deforestation, and the need for land reclamation. Shaler also tried to show his students how geography, including the open frontier, shaped history. He took his classes into the woods to see scars made by glaciers and taught Theodore, the youth said, how to walk in nature as an adventurous and observant scientist. The boy kept collecting specimens and reading on his own because he was passionate about science.[57]

Nor did Theodore have to leave muscular Christianity at home when he went to Harvard. His anatomy professor, philosopher William James, urged his students to strive "toward a high ideal of manliness." Though he attended required college chapel, Roosevelt greatly preferred Phillips Brooks' sermons at Trinity Church in Boston—often so crowded that Theodore had trouble hearing his every word.[58]

Though Brooks did not personally take the youth under his wing, as he did Theodore's college friend Endicott Peabody, his teachings reinforced what Thee had taught him about Christ's manly activism and the Social Gospel obligation of Christian men to walk among the poor. Theodore listened well when Brooks urged young men to push themselves to develop a strong spiritual and physical courage in order to wage the moral battles of their times. He took to heart Brooks' warning: "Self-consciousness is at the root of every cowardice. To think about one's self is death to real thought about any noble thing." If self-consciousness equaled cowardice, then Theodore would become a very brave man indeed.[59]

Late in Theodore's career at Harvard College, Dr. Dudley Sargent began his campaign to promote "manhood" by training college boys to build up their muscles and willpower with pulley-weight machines. But Theodore already knew how to design muscle-training regimens with what today is called aerobic exercise, and he regularly wrestled, boxed, ran, rowed, and walked, which lightened his asthma somewhat. He tried to box five times a week with a tutor, and wanted very badly to win the lightweight cup in boxing and wrestling. He failed, but his classmates admired his passion and honorable sportsmanship. Arthur Cutler had introduced Theodore to Bill Sewall, a rugged Maine wilderness guide, and during his college vacations TR went to Maine to hunt with Sewall. Getting along with "great, rough hospitable fellows" in the democracy of woodland survival showed him a larger social world where he might make a new place for himself. Returning to Harvard with "tales of exposure and hardship," Roosevelt was glad to have worldly experience to hold over his jaded classmates.[60]

Having grown up with deferential tutors, Theodore proved to be a student who demanded good service from his teachers. He soon earned a reputation for constantly asking questions and "always pinning the instructor down to hairbreadth points." Other students looked aghast when his geology professor finally exclaimed with irritation in his voice: "Now look here, Roosevelt, let me talk. I'm running this course."[61]

President Charles William Eliot, the father of Harvard's elective system, later claimed, even though he had no personal contact with the boy and would not have recognized him as an undergraduate, that Roosevelt was a loud intellectual lightweight. Eliot's memory was clouded by his later hatred of Roosevelt's foreign policy views. In George Palmer's philosophy class the young man spoke with explosive emphasis, almost spitting out his rapid-fire words, which one friend said was Roosevelt's way of overcoming an early speech impediment. Nevertheless, Palmer admired Roosevelt for organizing a group of street boys in East Cambridge into an informal mission class after he had been asked to resign as an Episcopal Sunday school teacher because he was a Presbyterian.[62]

Still troubled by asthma the first November he spent at Harvard and again in March of his freshman year, Theodore complained: "I have lost so much time in my studies through sickness." Thee also worried about the moral effects of college upon his son and advised him to "take care first of your soul, then of your health and lastly of your studies." To live up to his father's high moral standards made the task of gaining acceptance among other boys at college doubly difficult. Theodore did not mix easily with them at first, despite his social connections. He kept snakes in his room and was dismissed as eccentric by some classmates. William Hooper later recalled that he had thought Roosevelt was too puny and "a freak, a poseur, and half crazy." Even his friends recalled seeing the young man sitting in isolation in a great armchair near the roaring fire reading a book while raucous games went on around him. He concentrated so hard that he did not notice when his boots caught on fire. While the other Harvard boys drank together, Roosevelt prepared papers on the gills of crustaceans to be delivered at the Natural History Society.[63]

Theodore also failed to fit into the Harvard mold because he looked down on his classmates for their failure to live up to essential standards of decency. The *Boston Gazette* complained that Harvard students hurled insults from the galleries at the Globe Theater and indulged in behavior that was "coarse, brutal and indecent." Theodore reassured his family that he did not partake of the rowdy side of college life: "I do not find it nearly so hard as I expected not to drink and smoke, many of the fellows backing me up."[64]

Theodore explained that he tried to make up for his purity and religious ardor by impressing his classmates in other ways: "My ordinary companions in college would I think have a tendency to look down upon me for doing Sunday school work if I had not also been a corking boxer, a good runner, and a genial member of the Porcellian Club." In fact, he did not get into most clubs until late in his college career, and he gained a reputation as a prig who ran a man down at the Hasty Pudding Club because he sang a "smutty song." One classmate, Richard Welling, watched Theodore as he worked out in the gym, and judged him to be a "humble-minded chap . . . to be willing to give such a lady-like exhibition in a public place." Soon Welling revised his opinion. When they went skating through freezing wind on rough and treacherous ice at Fresh Pond, Welling thought that "any sane man would have voted to go home." But Theodore thrived on the chilling discomfort and danger of the skating, exclaiming, "Isn't this bully!" For three hours Welling marveled at TR's vitality and never again demeaned him.[65]

Early in his freshman year Theodore befriended Henry Davis Minot, a kindred spirit who loved science and cared more about moral purity than popularity. Both liked to identify birds in the wild and both disapproved of their classmates' forays into the urban "sporting male culture" with actresses and prostitutes. Both were socially marginal and scholarly boys who worried a great deal about being manly enough. Hal Minot suffered "terrors of the imagination" and feared that he had inherited a family mental illness; and he confessed: "I suffered from a dislike to the rougher boyish sports and to general society from a certain timidity, and from want of manliness; but now I am becoming manly."[66]

Together they went on a collecting trip to the Adirondacks in the summer of 1877 and published *The Summer Birds of the Adirondacks in Franklin County*, N.Y., which naturalist C. Hart Merriam praised as a scientific and meticulous bird list. Theodore brought Hal home to New York for a visit, and they planned to room together the following year because of their common scientific interests and deep personal sympathy. Hal recalled fondly one of the closest moments in their friendship when they sat by the firelight while Theodore talked to him about how strongly he condemned drinking and even worse sins.[67]

Theodore was neither popular nor self-confident in his first two years at Harvard. His vulnerability to the scorn of his peers showed how easily they could upset him. He grew mutton-chop sideburns to cover his callow face, then he shaved them off only to be teased by his classmates. He was touchy when Mittie had taunted him about his choice of friends: "Darling Motherling, How are you, you fussy little thing? . . . Seriously, darling, I wish you would avoid needlessly humiliating me, whenever I have a friend some few months older than I am."[68]

Before long, Harvard's social pressures and what Minot told Theodore was "the morally weakening, if not corrupting, influence of its social life" drove Hal into a "state of nervous excitability" and a breakdown. Although Hal said he had, like his friend Roosevelt, "a strong enough moral power to keep my troubles to myself, presenting a cheerful front to the world," he feared he might give in to "moral weakness" if he did not get help. TR urged him to see his own doctor, Morrill Wyman, but Hal left Harvard to seek treatment with another physician and finally wound up in an asylum. Though Theodore hated neurasthenics, invalids, and hypochondriacs with a passion born of his own experience, he showed remarkable sympathy for his friend's introspection and decline. Through all of Minot's troubles TR remained loyal to him and their friendship lasted long after his recovery.[69]

WHILE THEODORE struggled to find his place at Harvard, Thee became a nationally recognized civil service reformer. He had supported his fellow reformer Benjamin Bristow for president at the Cincinnati Republican convention of 1876 and had blocked the nomination of Senator Roscoe Conkling, opening the door instead to Rutherford B. Hayes. Conkling, a powerful and vain New York Republican boss known for his "turkey-gobbler strut" and habitual womanizing, took his defeat seriously and vowed revenge against the reformer who stole the presidency from him. Thee became a Hayes elector in the contested Tilden-Hayes election, and he was relieved when disputed Florida electors voted for his candidate. He saw no reason to fight for Reconstruction any longer even in its most moderate forms, and he sent his son his anti-boss political speeches to convert him to civil service reform. Theodore appreciated that his father held him as a trusted political confidant, and wrote him that there was no other fellow at Harvard who had "a Father who is also his best and most intimate friend, as you are mine."[70]

In 1877, Thee's new prominence in the civil service movement prompted President Hayes to appoint him the collector of the Port of New York, an act which Conkling's lieutenant Thomas C. Platt called "a straight-arm blow at the regular organization in our state." Hayes had already chosen Thee's friend John Jay to investigate the customs house, where he found ignorant, inefficient, and corrupt officials. Everyone knew Hayes was using Thee to make war on the entire New York Republican machine, so it came as no surprise when Conkling accused Thee of being his "bitter personal enemy" and set out to fight his appointment.[71]

The showdown between Hayes and Conkling came to a climax in the Senate's confirmation debates over Thee's appointment. Though civil service reformers saw the Roosevelt confirmation battle as a struggle between honest government and a corrupt patronage system, the controversy also reflected the tensions between factions within the Republican Party over race and Reconstruction. Chester A. Arthur and Conkling advocated vigorous enforcement of federal voting rights in the South while the Republican faction of William Maxwell Evarts and Roosevelt, like Liberal Republican presidential candidate Horace Greeley in 1872, urged abandonment of black voting rights, a speedy reconciliation between North and South, and an end to Reconstruction. Conkling made sure Thee's confirmation met defeat.[72]

Theodore saw his father's custom house fight as a tragic defeat of reformers by bosses. But he learned an even more ominous lesson. During the Rochester convention of New York Republicans, Conkling had lost his temper at elite reformers like Thee and George William Curtis and derided them as "man-milliners":

> There are about three hundred persons here who believe themselves to occupy the solar walk and the milky way, and even up there they lift their skirts very carefully for fear the heavens might stain them. Some of these people would vote against a man because he had been nominated. The mere fact of nomination and selection reduces him in their estima-

tion. They would have people fill the offices by nothing less than divine selection.[73]

Conkling's harsh words were echoed in the popular press, which caricatured civil service and other good government reformers as effeminate and precious creatures who were too fastidious and overprivileged to dirty their hands with politics. Conkling had drawn a crucial line in the sand between manly regular party politics and unmanly reformism. This told Theodore that regular party politics stood as the only "field upon which true manhood might be demonstrated and rewarded." Theodore did not doubt the correctness of his father's anti-boss independence, but the conflict did not make reform politics look like the career he sought.[74]

Unfazed by such assaults, Thee kept Theodore well informed of his progress in the Reform Club. The youth also read the day-to-day story of the fight over Thee's appointment in the *New York Tribune*. He wrote home to Bamie when it looked doubtful that their father would finally be confirmed that he was "glad on his account, but sorry for New York."[75]

In December 1877, Thee wrote his son that "a great weight was taken off my shoulders" when the Senate refused to confirm his appointment, and he warned him: "I fear for your future. We cannot stand so corrupt a government for any great length of time." Theodore understood his father wished him to carry on his work in politics, yet he still imagined himself becoming "a scientific man of the Audobon [*sic*], or Wilson, or Baird, or Coues type." Tragically, the coming weeks would magnify the customs house fight in Theodore's mind.[76]

Within days after Thee's defeat in the Senate his health declined. Theodore asked Bamie: "Does the doctor think it anything serious?" The youth was naturally absorbed with his own concerns, and the family did not want to tell him the doctors said it was cancer of the bowel. Theodore planned to come home for Christmas in a few days, and he told his sister: "My own health is excellent, and so, when I get home, I can with a clear conscience give him a rowing up for not taking better care of himself." Theodore thought the problem was that he "never does think of himself in anything." Even after he was called home suddenly when his father declined on December 21, he seemed unaware that his father's condition was terminal.[77]

At the end of his Christmas vacation, Theodore had his last conversation with Thee. Afterward, he wrote in his diary: "Today he told me I had never caused him a moment's pain; I should be less than human if I ever had, for he is the best, wisest and most loving of men, the type of all that is noble, brave, wise, and good." Thee had also told him that "after all I was the dearest of his children to him."[78]

As he returned to Harvard, Theodore still did not want to think hard about his father's illness. He said the vacation had come to a happy end, though he wished that Thee were feeling better. After Theodore's departure, Mittie, Elliott, Bamie, and Corinne took round-the-clock shifts by Thee's bedside as peritonitis set in. Elliott insisted upon being "with his father constantly." Though he promised "if there was danger" to inform Theodore, he made no effort to do so when Thee's death neared. When it was too late for Theodore to reach home in time to see his father before he died, Elliott finally telegraphed him.[79]

Theodore Roosevelt Senior's death on February 11, 1878, changed the family irrevocably. Thee had been its emotional mainstay, and no one could easily take his place. In his will he left his brothers Jim and Rob in charge of his money because Mittie was too impractical. The four Roosevelt children "felt we had to take care of Mother, and according to Father's will we were to allow her to live at 6 West 57th Street without paying rent." They recognized that Mittie's helplessness left them near orphans. Bamie said that without Thee "we all had to work out our own salvation." Thee had written Theodore that he hoped the responsibilities he had borne would prepare him "to take the father's place in the great battle of life," but at age nineteen Theodore was not ready to take charge of the family, its money and landholdings, or his father's political causes. He idealized Thee more than ever, saying: "Looking back on his life, it seems as if mine must be such a weak useless one in comparison."[80]

Theodore was so shocked by his father's death that he felt "as if part of my life had been taken away." He poured out his feelings of despair to his diary: "I feel that if it were not for the certainty that as he himself has so often said, 'he is not dead but gone before,' I should almost perish. With the help of my God I will try to lead such a life as Father would have wished me to." He avoided social contact for several weeks because he was afraid he would cry in public, and then confessed: "If I had very much time to think I believe I should almost go crazy." The boy fell into an episodic depression that lasted for months. He wrote in his diary to relieve his "very gloomy and desolate" moods, then he launched into intense activity ("must keep employed") to ward off feeling the depths of his loss. He saw no reason to get good grades with no father to please, and he wrote that "the aim and purpose of my life had been taken away." Back in his room at Harvard he sobbed alone, which he called "a good square breakdown." At night he suffered from feverish nightmares as he relived moments with his father.[81]

He marked the Bible Aunt Annie and Uncle Jimmie Gracie gave him with Thee's favorite passages, and when he came home for the summer after his sophomore year, the whole family tried to sing hymns they associated with Thee, but they found it too upsetting. Theodore wandered alone in the woods of Oyster Bay and wrote in despair:

> I often feel badly that such a wonderful man as Father should have had a son of so little worth as I. . . . I could not help reflecting sadly on how little use I am, or ever shall be in the world, not through lack of perseverance and good intentions, but through sheer inability. I realize more and more every day that I am as much inferior to Father morally and mentally as physically.[82]

In alternating lows of despair and highs of action he rowed, hunted, ran, and studied natural history, but he took less pleasure in his past recreations. Lost and alone without his father, Theodore searched for a new guide.

He sought counsel from his uncles—Jim and Robert Roosevelt and James Gracie—and from Bamie. His "intensely languid" "run-away mother" was no help. In grief he unburdened himself to a friend who had for a time lost control of his own emotions. To Hal Minot he wrote, "I have greatly felt the need of someone to talk to about my favourite pursuits and future prospects. I did some quite good work last summer, and this winter got my first Ipswich sparrow." In an age when many men believed that prolonged "sorrow . . . is proof of weakness of spirit," their shared religious beliefs inclined them to accept effusions of grief as something nobler than "weakness of spirit." Afterward, Theodore said Hal was "simply motherly in his care over me."[83]

Throughout the summer, Theodore searched desperately for moorings. He was still thinking about a career as a naturalist, though graduate study in Germany and a university post still seemed unreal to him. To become a reformer like his father required enough self-confidence to wage battle in the rough arena of politics—he was not ready yet. He had flirted with a number of young women he met in Brahmin and Knickerbocker social circles, but his deepest attachment was to a friend whose character stood out as more remarkable than her beauty. He sought comfort and understanding with the woman he associated with the safety of his childhood, Edith Carow, and at a party at Aunt Annie's house they paired off as a couple for a confidential talk. Before Thee died, Edith had been included in family visits to Cambridge, after which Theodore had written with proprietary pride that he had never seen "Edith looking prettier; everyone, and especially Harry Chapin and

Minot Weld admired her little Ladyship intensely, and she behaved as sweetly as she looked."[84]

Though family legend held that Thee discouraged his son from allying the Roosevelt name to the Carows as they sank in fortune and reputation, Theodore's friends and family expected he would marry her anyway. Friends described Edith as one of the best representatives of a Victorian generation which prized a "stern sense of duty" and self-control, and her reserve appealed to Theodore, who was less in command of himself.[85] Though he was rarely thoughtful about remembering birthdays, he sent Edith flowers on her seventeenth. Edith stayed at Tranquility visiting Corinne, and Theodore spent more and more time with her, hoping to move their fondness for each other into a commitment.[86]

But in August 1878, Theodore grew impetuous and needy in the throes of his grief. At Cold Spring Harbor on August 21, he and Edith had a "lovely morning" picking water lilies, but the next day their communion ended in conflict. No one knows what happened when he and Edith went alone in the late afternoon to the summerhouse near Tranquility. Whether or not he was too forward or proposed too precipitously, they argued and parted in anger. Edith recalled that he asked her to marry him more than once that year, but she refused. She may have been irritable because of the worsening of her father's alcoholism and the precarious state of her family's finances. Theodore afterward galloped his horse in the woods of Oyster Bay, riding it unusually hard. When a neighbor's dog barked at him as he rode by, he pulled out his revolver and shot it.[87]

Edith's pride seemed wounded by the encounter, too. It no doubt saddened her that by her next birthday Theodore inscribed his gift to her tepidly from "her sincere friend." Years later he finally described the incident to Bamie: "Eight years ago she and I had very intimate relations; one day there came a break for both of us had, and I suppose have, tempers that were far from being of the best. To no soul now living have either of us ever since spoken a word of this."[88]

On his return to college, Harvard's moral variety looked different to the young man. Now that his father was gone, he sought a new equation between maintaining moral purity and gaining social acceptance from the young men around him. The pressure from his father to remain morally pure had postponed his becoming one of the boys. He had lived so much of his life outside of normal boy culture and had idealized men's ways so long that becoming a part of a man's world posed a challenge. Hal Minot's mental collapse when he could not find a middle way between purity and Harvard's definition of manliness cautioned Roosevelt away from moral absolutism and harsh judgment of others. Theodore began drinking after his father's death, usually just to be sociable and accepted among other men and once or twice in genuine despair. He even got drunk a few times and confessed to his diary that wine "makes me awfully fighty."[89]

After TR became president and a national spokesman for moral reform, a few of his more malicious Harvard acquaintances insisted that he had been a "hard drinker" in college and had been asked to give up his Sunday school teaching post because he had dropped a bottle of claret on a sidewalk and been caught swearing about it. No corroborating evidence supports their charge. He had to give up his Sunday-school post because he was a member of another church. However, after his father's death, he certainly allied himself with a faster social set. His popularity increased and he was elected to the exclusive Porcellian Club. When he was voted one of the members of the Dickie, or DKE, his initiation task was to sit in a gallery of a Boston theater during a serious drama and applaud loudly, which he did so well he was kicked out.[90]

In October 1878 his classmate Dick Saltonstall invited Theodore to his home in Chestnut Hill where he met Dick's cousin Alice Hathaway Lee, a strikingly beautiful blond with vivid blue-gray eyes. TR told a friend: "See that girl? I am going to marry her, she won't have me, but I am going to have her!"[91]

Though Alice was only seventeen, her parents had already been driven to extreme measures to shoo away the legions of suitors who flocked to their house, which was next door to the Saltonstalls'. Alice looked no less desirable to Theodore for being a much-sought-after beauty. "Vivacious" and accustomed to praise and indulgence, Alice was as innocent as Edith Wharton's May Welland, who "with her long swinging gait her face wore the vacant serenity of a young marble athlete." She was the daughter of the circumspect banker George Cabot Lee of Lee, Higginson & Co., from a heavily intermarried and "exceedingly English" Boston Brahmin family proud of its ties to the Cabots, Lowells, Peabodys, Higginsons, Jacksons, and Saltonstalls. Alice had grown up closer to literary culture than Theodore: her uncle experimented in horticulture with Francis Parkman, and her cousin wrote books and consorted with Emerson. Yet, no matter how much they honored high culture and world travel, Henry Adams explained, Brahmins' preferred habitat was Boston, where "Harvard College and Unitarianism kept us all shallow." Brahmins admitted they had a "tendency to be arbitrary and intolerant and to look upon themselves as members of a higher and separate class," above even Knickerbockers, but class was not the real barrier that stood between Alice and Theodore.[92]

Theodore was a bumptious outsider who came on too strong. He professed his love for Alice too quickly and visited too often. He even admitted that the remainder of his college career was "passed in such incessant action, and such eager, restless, passionate pursuit of one all-absorbing object, that I have had but few moments to think in." His desperate pursuit of Alice followed so closely upon his grief over his father and his pursuit of Edith that they had to be related. In his eager courtship he sought another emotional center, a larger purpose to guide his life, and love to replace the bond he had lost. The challenge of winning Alice obsessed him, for both his honor among men and his need for affection seemed to be at stake, so he made "everything subordinate to winning her."[93]

Pursued so intensely by such an odd young man, Alice played coy and refused to show that she preferred him to other suitors. Thee had pushed his son to become a fighter, and rivals usually infused Theodore with combative and often creative energy. He brought more originality to his fight to win Alice than her other beaux. He campaigned by encirclement, winning his way into her family's heart by being himself. He made himself a boon companion to her uncle Leverett Saltonstall, who often stayed up late talking politics and ethics with the youth. When Theodore played lawn tennis with Alice and taught her new dances like the knickerbocker and five step, he made a point of including her plain-looking cousin Rose Saltonstall in the entertainment. He also roughhoused with Alice's nine-year-old brother, Georgie, and told the boy and his sister Bella tales of bears and wolves, and brought them into a dark room to scare them with ghost stories, which they adored. Georgie later recalled with affection the time he sledded with the exuberant Roosevelt and by accident they went headfirst through a barbed-wire fence. Theodore protected the boy and was unruffled by his own scratched face. By the end of his junior year Roosevelt had ingratiated himself enough to feel "like a very intimate relative" of the Lee and Saltonstall families. But Alice still would not consent to be his wife.[94]

When Theodore came back to New York he found Edith had won a literary competition and had proven herself a potential writer. They greeted each other at Aunt Annie's, but even though Edith made overtures of reconciliation, he dismissed her as "just the same sweet little flirt as ever" and wanted only to be her friend. Bamie had been playing "a rather superior sort of angel" and matchmaker for their cousin John Roosevelt, but she showed no interest in making a match between her beloved brother and Edith, whom Bamie viewed as too strong-willed to make a desirable sister-in-law. So Edith watched with dignified regret as Theodore drifted away from her.[95]

Theodore's behavior as a suitor followed the same emotional pattern of mood swings which he had recorded in detail in his diary in the months immediately after his father's death—elation alternated with despair. When he felt his spirits inflate, he rushed into restless activity but was plagued by anxiety and sleeplessness. Afterward, he fell into despondent states in which he expected the worst and poured out feelings of worthlessness.

One day he decided that Alice favored her neighbor Charlie Ware. He despaired and convinced himself that his campaign to win her had failed. Then, he suddenly veered erratically toward an aggressive, albeit chivalrous, solution to his feared loss. Friends found him wandering in the forest outside Cambridge distraught about Alice. He told them he wanted to challenge Ware to a duel. The threat of losing another loved one had disturbed his growing ability to moderate his moods. If Alice had known he had ordered dueling pistols, she might have laughed in wonderment, but his male peers understood why a duel over honor might appeal to a headstrong youth. Earlier that year a friend had asked Theodore to serve as a second in a duel, and he assented, though it never took place. Although talk of dueling was not considered extraordinary by his peers, it worried his family. Word reached the Roosevelts in New York of Theodore's delirious misery over Alice, and his cousin Jimmy left his classes at Columbia Medical School to bring the weary suitor home to rest.[96]

The dueling incident was only the most dramatic example of emotions carrying him away. On other occasions in 1879, Theodore spent money to excess and rode his horse so recklessly it was lamed. He even got into a fistfight at a DKE strawberry social. While quail hunting, he scratched his hands and arms in briars until his shirt was soaked with blood, but he did not stop to tend his injuries. If he kept moving, he thought, he could dampen and even out his rushes of energy: on a hunting trip to Maine cousin Emlen and Arthur Cutler "gave out" while Theodore climbed the 5,268 feet of Mount Katahdin. He dragged heavy canoes through rapids and came out soaked, pronouncing that he had had a "lovely time." Yet much of his life went on in even kilter. He attended classes that fall, studied, and took part at a measured gait in what he admitted was an excessive docket of club activities while he edited the *Harvard Advocate.* But he also sounded like a lost soul who drank in self-obliterating ways: he called it "drowning my sorrows." His mood swings became hardest to regulate when his fear of losing Alice overpowered him, and he had no one close enough to him to bring him back to his usual balance.[97]

His moods did not deter him from his "winter campaign" of winning Alice. He enlisted his mother and sisters to entertain the Lee family in New

York, but while the Lees were charmed, Alice still resisted. He was confounded by what he saw as the "changeableness of the female mind!" Theodore was tormented by worry that he would lose the precarious place he was gaining in her affections.[98]

Meanwhile, his close friendship with Hal Minot grew strained because of his mood swings and his embrace of mainstream Harvard habits. In the fall of 1879, Hal, who had recovered from his breakdown, visited his old friend at Harvard, but was appalled when Theodore got drunk and used foul language in public. As if Thee spoke from the grave to remind his son of his devout upbringing, Minot lambasted his friend:

> Now, remembering dearly these words, from the time when our friendship was the closest and warmest, do you suppose that I enjoyed the other night seeing you deliberately sacrifice your self-control, and yield to the silliest of all human indulgences, and hearing you talk shameful grossness before a woman whom I hope is respectable, and muddled nonsense about fighting sensible Charlie Ware with duelling pistols? . . . you were acting on the most casuistic and miserable argument, that, as you had been faithful and steady for a certain time, you were entitled to sacrifice independence, abandon your self-restraint, and have (as you call it) "a good time." . . . As regards the theory of compensation, could either of us bear to think of his father as saying to himself: "I have now been faithful to my wife for twenty years; and I feel entitled to abandon my principles, excite my passions, and seek criminal indulgence, just for once." . . . Surely, any indulgence that lowers us, is just as wrong for a mature, rational man of twenty, as for one of forty: the argument of "wild oats" is fit for only really thoughtless fools.—You have lowered yourself because you are capable of filling a high position and of exerting a high influence,—and I am not the only person who thinks this of you.[99]

Minot told Theodore that because "you have made up your mind to go back on yourself, I cannot feel as warmly toward you as I have felt."[100] In Minot's eyes, their bond of friendship had been sealed by a pledge of a shared moral standard, and Theodore had violated that bond.

TR meekly replied that he still looked to Hal as a friend and counselor, especially since his father was gone. He wanted their friendship to last, despite his lapse of judgment. He knew that during the time when he had been "pretty nearly crazy" over Alice, he had not behaved as his better self. Nevertheless, after months of "torture" when "I have hardly had one good night's rest," he kept hold of his sanity. He did not fight a duel, nor did he continue heavy drinking. He was close to winning his Holy Grail.[101]

His steady campaign and sincere avowals of love had begun to sway the young lady. In January 1880, Alice finally agreed to marry him. It took "heroic self-denial" for Theodore to tear himself away from her as he realized that now "I can hold her in my arms and kiss her and caress her and love her as much as I choose." He calmed down so much that on quiet evenings at Chestnut Hill, Alice could practice music while her intended read William Prescott's *Conquest of Mexico* with contentment. She loved him, but Alice grew apprehensive about losing all her freedom by marrying the intense and jealous man she called "Teddy" and "Teddykins." He reassured her that he would not be possessive or dictatorial: "The more good times you have—dancing, visiting or doing anything else you like—the happier I am." If she received a lot of attention from other men, he would not mind, and he reassured her: "You will always be your own mistress, and mine too."[102]

Evidently, women's lack of freedom and rights was on their minds in the spring of their engagement. Exactly two months after Alice agreed to marry him, Theodore began writing his senior thesis on "The Practicability of Equalizing Men and Women Before the Law," in which he asserted that "in an ideally perfect state of society strict justice would at once place both sexes on an equality," including equal rights of inheritance, the vote, and the right to go to law school. Anti-suffragist Francis Parkman had argued against "putting the ballot into hands unable to defend it," but TR, though he conceded that military service might be a legitimate criterion for voting, pointed out that women might even become "effective combatents [*sic*]" at some later date. He took the position, rare in a day when Harvard medical students demonstrated against the admission of a female student and very few private colleges or professional schools admitted women, that women should have equality before the law because, "though placed by education and surroundings at a disadvantage," women were "in no wise inferior as regards quickness or acuteness." Though Parkman and many others warned that "suffrage erodes civilization," TR did not see the dangers to men posed by the advancement of women. He was so willing to compromise with the fairer sex that he wrote that a woman should not be forced to assume her husband's name upon marriage.[103]

With their wedding set for his twenty-second birthday, he dismissed all thoughts of a career in science, which would most likely require study abroad. Instead, he enrolled in Columbia Law School. Having won Alice at long last, Theodore wrote: "It makes me so happy I am almost afraid." Indeed, he worried that he would not make her happy. Alice fretted, too, that she would prove "unworthy of such a noble man's love," but she assured him that she was not haunted by typical bridal apprehension about the marriage bed: "You must never think that I have the slightest fear at giving myself to you, I do love you so very much Teddy and trust you absolutely." He, in turn, told her: "I worship you so that it seems almost desecration to touch you; and yet when I am with you I can hardly let you out of my arms."[104]

Not long after Theodore and Alice became engaged, Dr. Dudley Sargent told Theodore that he had a dangerous heart condition which required abstention from exercise. Even climbing stairs might be dangerous. Theodore ignored his advice, and often ran three or four miles a day. He scoffed at the risk and often behaved as if activity dulled his anxiety. Before the wedding he was hounded by asthma and colic, so he went on a hunting trip with Elliott to Iowa, Minnesota, and the Dakota Territory, ending up in what Theodore called "the great, treeless, fenceless prairies" near the Red River. As he traveled TR noticed the dearth of class distinctions that separated a gentleman from a common farmer: "rural Americans" did not defer to aristocrats as readily as humble easterners and were "fiercely independent." He still viewed himself as their better, but he wrote home: "I don't wonder at their thinking us their equals, for we are dressed about as badly as mortals could be." He hoped the open-air life would "build me up" so he would not walk to the altar with any remnant of the frail "young duke" left in him.[105]

Asthma would not leave him alone, however. On his hunting trip it forced him to stay up all night, but he refused to let illness hold him back. In fact, he hunted with more determination because of it. His western trip made him feel like "twice the man" he had been, so as he headed east he picked up a fresh suitcase packed by Bamie, and arrived in Chestnut Hill as quickly as boats and trains allowed. He held Alice ever more tightly because he had missed her so much. A few days before the wedding Theodore could not hold still, so he visited his friend (and Alice's cousin) Endicott Peabody in Salem, where the two muscular Christians vigorously chopped down trees together. Alice evidently did not know of Dr. Sargent's warning or her letters would not have been so full of unambivalent praise for the fact that "Teddy" "takes a great deal of exercise." As their wedding approached Theodore's prevailing mood was exuberant—he was full of "wild spirits." He wrote in his diary: "I never can understand how I won her!"[106]

☆ CHAPTER THREE ☆

"My Heart Was Nearly Breaking"

ALICE HATHAWAY LEE and Theodore Roosevelt were married on his twenty-second birthday in 1880 at the Brookline First Parish Unitarian Church. Mingling with the predictable Brahmin and Knickerbocker guests was textile mill owner Amos A. Lawrence, who had paid for rifles used in John Brown's raid on Harpers Ferry but who preferred the more peaceful and profitable postwar era. Lawrence pronounced the ceremony and the reception afterward at the Lees' "a great wedding."[1] Theodore's favorite cousins, Emlen and James West Roosevelt, and his friend Endicott Peabody served among the ushers, and Elliott stood up for him as best man. Edith Carow was also present; Theodore had seen her alone and at family gatherings a number of times during his engagement, but no one knows what they said to each other. She "danced the soles off her shoes" at the reception and returned to New York still in love with the groom.[2]

After a night in Springfield, Alice and Theodore had the "loveliest honeymoon imaginable" at Tranquility, where Bamie had ordered all their meals ahead of time and arranged everything with the three servants who cared for them. Like many emotional issues in his life, Theodore found the early days of his marriage "too sacred to be written about."[3] The newlyweds enjoyed tennis and walked together along the shore of Oyster Bay. Alice played the piano for him and he read aloud to her. Then the young couple moved into 6 West Fifty-seventh Street with Mittie, Elliott, Corinne, and Bamie. Elliott chose the moment of Theodore's return to New York to take an extended hunting trip to India, and Theodore admitted he would not miss his younger brother. He signed his letters "Thee," and made it clear he wanted to assume his father's place in the family.

In the morning he walked more than fifty blocks downtown to attend classes at Columbia Law School, then located in lower Manhattan.

Sometime during that year he also began an informal apprenticeship at his uncle Robert Roosevelt's law office. His favorite class at Columbia was not law but political science with John Burgess, who would be remembered for teaching that superior Teutonic peoples would spread freedom around the world. TR had already been taught by the writing of Macaulay and others to see world history as a racial struggle which Anglo-Saxons or English-speaking peoples were destined to win because of their superior inheritance, and Burgess explained comparative legal history as a struggle for freedom which some nations won and others lost. Most afternoons Theodore turned his attention from law to the historical competition between nations as he settled into the Astor Library to write his naval history of the War of 1812, which he had started at Harvard. That fall in East Norwich, accompanied by one of Tranquility's black servants, he cast his first vote for president, for Republican James A. Garfield. It appeared that young Roosevelt had truly entered man's estate with a wife and the promise of a dual career in history and law, but he remained uncertain how he would make his mark in the world.[4]

Alice quickly fit into the Roosevelt family as an additional child to be reminded of her proper social duties by Bamie, whom Elliott called "the very model of a modern major-generaless!" Bamie turned down marriage proposals from men like James Roosevelt of Hyde Park because she preferred managing the family at West Fifty-seventh Street. She had explained to Alice that because Thee had expected so much of Theodore, his wife must "help him lead a true and noble life worthy of his Father's name," which included making room for his tight bonds with his sisters and helping him establish himself in society. Each afternoon when Theodore came home, Alice compliantly learned to call upstairs to Bamie and the others: "Teddy is here; come and share him." Alice did not mind that his family doted on Theodore so much, as long as he did the same for her.[5]

Theodore's marriage to Alice brought him as a full adult member into the Knickerbocker world of Patriarch Balls, dinner parties, and cotillions which required many evenings out. His close friends the Dodges and Leavitts gave parties to welcome Alice, and the Astors and Delanos eagerly swept the young couple into their social circles. At the height of the winter social season Alice and Theodore attended parties, balls, or dinners almost every night of the week. Though the groom enjoyed waltzing with Emily Post and took pride in having the most beautiful wife in town, he was not as satisfied as his nineteen-year-old bride with the narrow horizons of Knickerbocker society.

He would have preferred to stay at his desk to prove the American navy had better marksmen than Britain in 1812. He was less fascinated by society than by arcana such as when the British frigate *Java* left Spithead, England,

and how its bowsprit got caught in the *Constitution*'s mizzen rigging. Alice had trouble appreciating his priorities and was not ready to be a great man's helpmate. She resented her husband's intense writing jags, and would poke his arm and make marks on the paper to draw his attention away from his battle diagrams. His wife's playfulness charmed Roosevelt least when he felt most driven to make himself a man of consequence. Theodore found himself teasing his "baby wife" rather roughly and wishing they did not have so many social engagements.[6]

Alice was a loving but prim and conventional wife, and in practical matters she resembled Mittie, not Bamie. When they left for a five-month tour of Europe in May 1881, she expected him to arrange everything, and she leaned on him to care for her when she was violently seasick. Theodore found it tiresome to be his wife's nursemaid, and in his letters home he complained that as they entered new countries Alice "resents it as an impertinence if she is addressed in any language but english." As if to put distance between himself and the cushioned existence his wife preferred, he climbed the Matterhorn, though he later told Bill Sewall, his Maine guide, that he did it to show the English that a Yankee could climb as well as they did. Once more he defied doctor's orders in order to live a strenuous life. As they steamed down the Rhine, German table manners offended Alice, and she preferred to spend time reading her Baedeker's tourist guide and visiting familiar friends from Boston.[7]

Yet Theodore was no less "torrential" in his devotion to his child bride because of her love of comfort and familiar people and her unwillingness to help him amount to something in the world. When they were apart he wrote her passionately: "I could not live without you. . . . I care for nothing whatever else but you," and he signed his affectionate letters to her "Your lover and husband." But their relationship was changing. In courtship he had hungered for every moment he could be with her, but with each day of marriage Alice became the dependent seeker and he the sought. When they were apart, Alice wrote him beseechingly: "I am more homesick every moment—and at night miss your strong arm to lay my poor head on."[8]

Family members described TR as a restless law student and groom who missed his carefree Harvard days. When he went to the Harvard-Yale game he "nearly went wild & wished he was with the fellows." Mittie reported to Elliott, on his big-game hunt in India, that when Theodore heard the exciting details of his brother's adventure, he "longs to be with you and walks up and down the room like a Caged Lynx." Mittie added that when Alice asked for attention Theodore "smothered her with kisses and feels he is perfectly happy with her but sometime he must go off with his gun instead of pouring [*sic*] over Brown versus Jenkins, etc."[9]

From India, Elliott grew uneasy about what was happening within the Roosevelt family. After Corinne had her grand coming-out party in December 1880, the family, including Theodore, pressured her to marry her most eligible suitor, the loud and irascible but rich Scotsman Douglas Robinson, who managed the Astor properties. Robinson was a man's man who got on well with Theodore, but Corinne had misgivings about being "forced by her family to marry" a bully. She tried to break off the engagement, and Elliott wrote home urging the family to allow Corinne to do so because "it would be misery for both" to enter into a marriage in which the wife felt no love. But "after sobbing steadily" throughout her engagement, Corinne married Douglas and found his rages and jealousies so galling that she returned to Fifty-seventh Street as often as possible. Theodore made light of his younger sister's unhappiness because he had "four times too much to do," but Alice sympathized with her and wondered how candid she should be when extended family members asked her about Corinne's obvious gloom.[10]

Soon after he and Alice settled in New York, Theodore had become active in the local Republican organization in their "silk stocking" district that included West Fifty-seventh Street and nearby Fifth Avenue. His timing was opportune. President Hayes' brief foray into civil service reform had not accomplished much. When Hayes refused to run in 1880, bitter factional fights divided the Republican Party. James G. Blaine's machine men advocated Chinese exclusion and fought against a moral reform group that supported George F. Edmunds; a third faction was the Stalwarts, Grant loyalists who disliked the "old-woman policy of Granny Hayes." The convention deadlocked, but finally Republicans nominated, and, in November 1880, elected Civil War general James A. Garfield president.[11]

Though Theodore's party held the presidency, the Democratic Party dominated the South and was making enough inroads among northern laborers to recover the national political strength it had lost over the Civil War. So Republicans scrambled to find unifying issues: Roscoe Conkling preached against monopolies while Edmunds tried to build a Republican consensus around civil service reform and moral reform crusades like saving the institution of marriage by criminalizing Mormon polygamy. Blaine and John Sherman talked protective tariff. Then, in 1881, the heated squabbles among Republicans appeared to take a dangerous turn. A delusional Stalwart named Charles Guiteau killed President Garfield, thereby elevating Chester A. Arthur, also a Stalwart, to the presidency. As the public read every detail of Guiteau's long insanity trial, they put the blame for the murder on partisanship and office-seeking rather than seeing the shooting as the act of a madman. As a result, the civil service reform movement gained mass support for the first time, and by 1883 the Pendleton Civil Service Act became law. Former president Hayes warned that "bitter partisanship" was wicked, so New York Republicans looked for new men untainted by faction to run for office.[12]

In the fall of 1881, when Republicans were searching for responsible young men of good family to represent them in the legislature, they asked Theodore Roosevelt to run for state assemblyman against a machine politician, William Strew, the former head of the Lunatic Asylum at Blackwell's Island. The mantle of Thee's reputation as an independent reformer and philanthropist blessed Theodore with the benefit of "hereditary claims to the confidence" of the voters. He was endorsed by the *New York Evening Post*, the *New York Tribune*, and the *New York Times* and most of his father's friends, Joseph H. Choate, Morris K. Jesup, and even Boss Tweed's former lawyer, Elihu Root. Thee's friends and family could easily fund his son's campaign, and TR beat his opponent by 3,502 to 1,974 votes on November 8.[13]

Assemblyman Roosevelt promised at first to be nothing more than a flamboyant version of a typical patrician urban reformer of the Gilded Age—concerned about getting better administration of government by putting in office educated "best men" to oust working-class and ethnic professional party politicians from power. He took support from Anthony Comstock's backers and aligned himself with rich Protestant reformers who looked down upon Catholics, immigrants, and the poor, and who saw nothing wrong with Thomas Nast's cartoon portrayals of the Irish as ignorant apes in *Harper's Weekly*. He accepted the anti-Catholicism common among evangelical Protestants when he judged that "the average Catholic Irishman of the first generation, as represented in this Assembly is a low, venal, corrupt and unintelligent brute." Some civil service reformers in New York favored restricting the vote to men of property, and they made Theodore the vice president of their association. They were correct that political machines engaged in dishonest practices like voting fraud (hiring repeat voters, tampering with vote counts, and faking registration) and selling government favors and contracts, but civil service classification did not stop such practices altogether. Reformers took for granted the unproven proposition that the more educated a man, the more honest he was.[14]

Where Roosevelt differed from the typical patrician reformer of his day was in his growing admiration for and eagerness to make friends with less privileged men. As he had done at Harvard, he wanted to be accepted man to man. The other assemblymen were not so sure they wanted to accept him, however. At first he looked to them like a specimen of the "kid glove, scented, silk stocking, poodle-headed, degenerate aristocracy." He made a bad start when he appeared on the floor of the assembly dressed in his purple satin waistcoat. He was so "heedless" about his appearance that his family often teased him about his gaudy attire.[15]

Before long, his scrappiness on the floor of the assembly and his willingness to take unpopular stands won him allies and friends. He dropped many of his prejudices and befriended George Spinney and Isaac Hunt, who learned TR was fascinated by the "sporting male culture" of working-class entertainments. He never visited prostitutes and was incorruptible about money, but, according to his friends, he tried "anything and everything else," including drinking and gambling. Hunt and Spinney took him to an illegal cockfight in Troy, and when police raided it, they hustled him out just in time to avoid arrest.[16]

Already convinced that the Victorian parlor culture in which he was raised suffered from deep insufficiencies, Theodore found more authenticity in the characters he met in politics: he became fast friends with Jake Hess, a German Jew, and Joe Murray, an Irish Catholic immigrant. When Roosevelt faced election these friends learned to keep him away from saloonkeepers, whom he was likely to insult. Hess and Murray took care of the ethnic voters for him. At first TR played better to the Fifth Avenue and college athlete set, but after initial struggle and failure, he learned to speak in public and to use down-to-earth examples from his own life as Thee had done to find common ground with men from other classes. Moreover, he got on well with plain men like Billy O'Neill, the assemblyman who kept a country store in the Adirondacks. His adventures outside his own class shed a new light for him on the anti-immigrant and anti-party prejudices of the civil service reformers, who were blind to the fact that political parties were the best way to build a consensus to get things done. But many elite reformers were not interested in solving problems, and he was beginning to distrust the "silk stocking" reformer type who was "very refined" and who criticized practical politicians and was "wholly unable to grapple with real men in real life."[17]

Roosevelt broke out of the patrician reformer mold in other ways, too. When he could see how people's lives were affected, he veered toward genuine reform. From the start he was always more sympathetic to reforms that shielded women and children. Cigar-maker and labor leader Samuel Gompers had tried striking to win better wages for the men and women who made cigars, but employers fought hard to break the strike and it failed, even though cigar manufacturers admitted that lowered wages had left factory and tenement cigar workers to face near starvation.[18]

Finally, Gompers proposed a state law restricting the manufacturing of cigars in tenements, and he talked Roosevelt into visiting the homes where cigar-making went on. Theodore saw the face of poverty, especially the small children and their Bohemian immigrant mothers and fathers crowded alongside the stacks of tobacco. He recalled the tenement children he had met on his father's charitable rounds and remembered that Thee had abandoned popular laissez-faireism and advocated public rather than private solutions to social problems at the end of his life. The power of Thee's memory and the sight of tenement children pushed his son toward reform. TR not only supported but became one of the tenement house bill's loudest defenders. He argued on the floor of the assembly that stopping home cigar manufacturing was a public health measure and a first step toward seeing that immigrants led proper American family lives. The bill passed. But the young assemblyman was appalled when his reform was snuffed out by the branch of government that consistently supported employers in the Gilded Age: the courts.[19]

Theodore later said he went through "various oscillations of feeling before I 'found myself' politically." As a young politician, he often favored capital over labor: he opposed legislating eight-hour workdays and bills prohibiting prisons from selling for profit the forced labor of their inmates. But legislation for the good of the family appealed to him. He railed against organized liquor interests and showed a precocious interest in moral reform. He also fought to restrict the growing power of saloons with licensing fees and regulation. It startled a lot of people when Theodore called on the state legislature to pass a law punishing wife beaters by whipping them in public; he was shocked by what he read about husbands' cruelty toward their wives. When he was satirized in the press for his speech about public whippings he held his ground, and confessed: "I felt very angry and could not help saying what I did."[20]

His love of nature and his uncle Robert's commitment to conservation prompted him to offer to help the landscape designer Frederick Law Olmsted defend Central Park and the other parks of New York. Not much got done, and he found his work in politics harassing. But he learned to cross party lines for the sake of good legislation, and he formed a friendship with Democratic governor Grover Cleveland, who worked with him to make government in New York much more honest and accountable to the people. TR was already gaining attention for his courage in the political arena. After he got hold of correspondence showing the bribery of Judge T. R. Westbrook by financier Jay Gould, Roosevelt called for an investigation. When many assemblymen rose to the judge's defense and stopped TR from impeaching Westbrook, he was shocked. The battle for honest government was not going to be won easily.[21]

It was not enough to become one of the bright young stars of the New York Assembly at age twenty-three, he kept busy writing naval history with an eye to influencing national policy. America, he believed, needed to build a better navy. At first he did not feel equal to the task: his *Naval History of the War of 1812* had worried him when he could not get the story into the right words.[22] On the Liverpool leg of his honeymoon he talked over the need for naval preparedness with his uncle James Bulloch, who regretted that the Confederate navy had lacked a chance to build a fleet before the Civil War and who urged the U.S. Navy after the war to expand and prepare a force strong enough to protect a Panama Canal which Bulloch hoped the United States would control, rather than England or France.[23]

As Theodore wrote his naval history he aimed high: he wanted to make himself a historian like Francis Parkman or Macaulay. In December 1881, the completed manuscript of *The Naval War of 1812* sounded less like the Victorians' favorite historians and more like a young bulldog scholar barking out denunciations of the War Department's wartime strategy as a "triumph of imbecility." He also attacked Thomas Jefferson for his "criminal folly" in failing to prepare for war. He showed a talent for writing heroic battle scenes describing in vivid detail how men stood the test of battle and how well they died for their country, but he piled his numbers and tiny facts higher than most readers could bear. He indicted the most famous British historian of the war, William James, for "wilful [*sic*] misstatement," so his story read more like a prosecutor's case than true history.[24]

Nevertheless, he dug up so many new facts in the archives and compared conflicting accounts so well that his book added to scholarly knowledge of naval strategy. More significantly for his political career, Roosevelt became nationally recognized as a strong advocate of navalism. The navy thought his book important enough to put on every one of its ships. The book came out during congressional debates over America's weak coast defenses and at a time when Chile probably had a stronger navy than any other Western Hemisphere power. Though post–Civil War presidents had flirted with expansionism, none of them got very far without an adequate navy. Years before Alfred Thayer Mahan promoted the idea that a strong navy was vital to America's ability to assert itself in international markets and in power politics, Roosevelt declared himself for the navy as the key to America's expansion. Yet, even as he made a place for himself in the world of history and policy debates, TR wondered repeatedly "if I won't find everything in life too big for my abilities."[25]

Alice and Theodore moved to Albany for the winter of 1882, and they talked about buying a country house upstate. Though Theodore warmed immediately to politics, Alice was not making a promising start as a politician's wife. She missed Mittie, Corinne, and Bamie too much and found the cigar-smoking commoners who visited her husband in Albany distasteful. Theodore wanted to become a force in state politics but the task taken on by many political wives—offering hospitality and building friendships that would advance their husbands' careers—was not a job for Alice.

By the end of the year she urged Theodore to move back to New York City and to commute to Albany. He agreed. They bought their own brownstone at 55 West Forty-fifth Street where Alice received visitors on Tuesdays, but she did not feel competent to manage the household and had to call on Aunt Annie to help her order food and supervise the servants. In Albany, Theodore lost his bid to become speaker of the house, but he was appointed chairman of the Committee on Cities, which allowed him to throw himself into reforming New York City government.

Meanwhile, he and his family remained close friends with Edith Carow, though Edith never warmed to Alice. Charles Carow died an alcoholic death in March 1883, which was a blow to Edith, who was left to care for the selfish wing of the family—her mother, Gertrude, and sister Emily. A spinster's life burdened by debt awaited her. Once again, her Roosevelt ties offered a safe respite from the harsh climate of her own family life. Aunt Annie took Edith under her wing and spent many afternoons consoling her. Edith could have married any number of eligible men within her Knickerbocker social circle, but she showed "an utter lack of susceptibility" to them. If she could not marry the man she had always loved, she could content herself with the dignity of leading a solitary life. Eager to keep her friendship, Theodore took Edith for an occasional carriage ride in Riverside Park when Alice visited the Lees, but it was to Alice that he would "confide all of the little joys and pains of the day."[26]

Despite his success as a historian, Roosevelt's adult life was not becoming the substantial edifice he had hoped it would be. He disliked the practice of law and could not imagine himself spending the rest of his life in it. Later, he justified his decision to give up law on the basis of morality—that is, he was idealistic and legal education did not teach principles of justice. Family members said the law bored him because it was too slow. Though he might have made a fierce prosecuting attorney, his strong sense of justice would not rest until he found larger arenas where he could do honorable battle. His energies headed in several directions at once. He played ninety-one games of tennis that Fourth of July, and campaigned vigorously for reelection. He also delved into a career as a book publisher with a stationery business included in a partnership with Josephine Shaw Lowell's brother-in-law George Haven Putnam, who would publish his *Hunting Trips of a Ranchman*. And Theodore was managing his money recklessly. He lost track of how much he had in the bank and his check to Putnam for $20,000 bounced.[27]

In March 1882, Elliott returned to 6 West Fifty-seventh Street to find that Theodore was already well established as head of household. The triumphant hunter presented his mother with a tiger skin rug, and she resented it if he gave anyone else a similar gift. Unfortunately, Elliott also came home from India with habits of drink and a fondness for liaisons with "ladies not in his own rank," which he soon confided to Aunt Annie. His family excused his ill health and low spirits as Indian fever or epilepsy. Elliott conceded that "my idle character" and sin and "roughness and unworthiness . . . as a self-amusing dilettante" had relegated him justly to being inferior to his righteous and driven brother. He dabbled at writing about his hunt and talked about producing a novel, but he had no confidence that he had anything new to offer the world. A real estate job managing Astor properties with Douglas Robinson was a safe and forgiving harbor for his lax work habits.[28]

On ceremonial occasions like the christening of his godson Franklin Delano Roosevelt or Corinne's wedding that spring, Elliott won the hearts of guests easily, especially those who preferred to escape a political sermon from his brother. Mittie let her sons know that she, too, preferred Elliott's company. When Elliott fell in love with the stately beauty Anna Hall and married her in December 1883, Mittie feared she would lose his affections, but the rest of the family hoped it would settle him down. Knowing what a weak character he had, Aunt Annie warned Elliott: "You must be very pure and true now that you have secured the right to guard, love and cherish so sweet a girl as Anna."[29]

Theodore worried little about his inconsequential brother, but he had grown uneasy that after two years of marriage he and Alice were not yet parents. It made it harder that within three months after their wedding Corinne and Douglas were expecting and Theodore's cousins Alfred and John Roosevelt found wives and reproduced just as expeditiously. Theodore gushed to his cousin John that he could not get used to "your being a father" and promised to "get up my muscle just to give you a few thumps of admiration" for his accomplishment.[30]

Aggressive as he was in praising his cousin's good fortune in becoming a father, TR regretted that his own marriage remained barren, and that was not good news for a man who liked children and who was already on guard about his manliness. Alice suffered from a nervous disorder and gynecological troubles about which the family letters are silent except that Theodore wrote her from Albany: "I wish I could be with you while you have your nervous fits to cheer you and soothe you." Finally, they learned that Alice's gynecological problems could be cured. She had an operation, and then, at long last, she became pregnant in May 1883.[31]

Theodore's reaction to his impending fatherhood was jubilant but panicky. Asthma, cholera morbus, and rushes of manic energy plagued him for several months after Alice told him the news. As if he feared she would become even more dependent on him, when the legislative session ended in the spring, he found reasons to be away from her—in June he fled to Oyster Bay for his health and he planned to be gone for a long trip to the Dakotas in the fall. When they vacationed together at the resort of Richfield Springs, he admitted he was "bored out of my life by having nothing whatever to do," but it was also likely that he squirmed because he was reminded of his visits there as an asthmatic child. He and Alice planned to build a house on the hill in Oyster Bay near where Theodore had often walked with Thee, but the young husband shuddered at the thought of taking on too much adult responsibility at once. In August he installed Alice at Chestnut Hill for a separation of nearly two months and then "rushed in upon" his old friend Hal Minot to renew their friendship "now that the first excitement and absorption of his marriage has subsided."[32]

By the time Theodore reached Chicago in September he said he felt like a "fighting cock"; his health improved even before he got anywhere near a hunting ground. He reached the Little Missouri River in the Dakota Territory and hired Joe Ferris to guide him on a buffalo hunt. When a buffalo charged him, his pony reared and knocked his rifle against his head, gashing it until "blood poured over my face and into my eyes so that it blinded me for the moment." He lost the buffalo but recovered his sight. His enthusiastic letters about how robust and happy he felt away from New York and his hint that "there was a chance to make a great deal of money, very safely, in the cattle business" might have made Alice wonder if she would ever see him after their baby was born. In fact, without consulting her, he had already purchased two Dakota ranches and cattle and hired Sylvane Ferris and Will Merrifield to look after his new business.[33]

Later, he asked Bill Sewall, the Maine guide who had become his dear friend, to move west to supervise his Dakota cattle venture. Theodore intended to visit the ranches regularly to hunt and write stories about his adventures, but he would remain a New Yorker. He said he wanted to "try to keep in a position from which I may be able at some future time to again go into public life, or literary life." He might prove himself merely a rich dilettante who dabbled in ranching, writing, law, publishing, and politics, or he might succeed as a self-made superman who could excel in any number of fields at once.[34]

The role he seemed least interested in playing was husband. While Theodore hunted, Alice remained at Chestnut Hill, fragile but gaining some strength from short walks. With another session of the legislature opening that winter Theodore planned to spend more time in Albany to promote his reform charter bill to reduce Tammany's power over city government, so Alice moved back to 6 West Fifty-seventh Street to have Mittie and Bamie's company and no household to manage by herself.

As the winter of 1884 began, Theodore took it for granted that Alice's confinement would bring a normal birth, but he regretted being away from her in Albany and wrote her: "I wish I could be with you to rub you when you get 'crampy.' " The doctor predicted she would give birth around February 14, so Theodore let other worries preoccupy him—money, his own health, and the fate of his reform bill. He had hired a boxing instructor to spar with him during his weekdays, and on February 6 he wrote home proudly to Alice that he had bloodied the man's nose that day. Earlier that winter he had brought a few political friends home to be entertained by Alice and Mittie, and had started to regale them with the "shaved lion" story he liked to tell at Alice's expense: at the London Zoo she had asked him if the lions got their manes by being shaved like poodles. She begged him to stop and he complied, though he hated to miss a good story around his cronies.[35]

Back in Albany, his friends worried about his headlong rushes at issues and his explosive attacks on opponents and indiscretions which made them regard him "as a man would a ball of dynamite with a fuse in the process of burning." The political conflicts became so heated that Roosevelt knocked down one of his opponents with his fists. When his political enemies hired a woman to try to entice him into a compromising situation to ruin his career, TR recoiled and sent a detective to track the men down. He had just opened public hearings in which he intended to expose the corruption of New York City's Department of Public Works. His letters to his wife were full of his political problems—and they were no longer signed "Your lover and husband" but "With best love, Ever Your Fond."[36]

After a weekend with Alice in New York, Theodore left for Albany on the morning of February 12, confident that Bamie and Mrs. Lee (who had come down from Boston) would look after her. It excited him to hear that the reform bill was being called the Roosevelt bill. When he received a note from Alice which expressed her alarm about Mittie's latest illness, a high fever, he was preoccupied by so much serious business that he brushed aside news from home. Then news reached him that his baby daughter, named Alice by her mother, had been born later that day; it struck him as more good news, not a cause to rush back to the city. He stayed in Albany and did not make a move to return to the city even when a telegram told him that his wife was only "fairly well." Finally, an ominous second telegram alerted him to the direness of her condition: she was dying of Bright's disease.[37]

He took the next train home through a night of dense fog. He showed no signs of worry about Mittie's fever: in recent years she had always been working up one illness or another. When Theodore arrived home just before midnight on Wednesday, the thirteenth, he found Alice insensible and his mother near death from typhoid fever. He held Alice tightly in his arms as if to prevent her from slipping away from him, and had to be extracted to say good-bye to Mittie. By the end of Valentine's Day both women were dead.[38]

Theodore's grief over Alice was overwhelming and complicated. Her cousin Endicott Peabody hurried to New York and found his friend "wonderfully calm," yet his composure during the double funeral barely masked his deep suffering. TR had been taught by his father that "weakness is the greatest of crimes," so he could not show how distressed he was. Stunned by the magnitude of his loss, he was uneasy when he had to discuss Alice. Though the myth persists that he never spoke of her again after she died, it is simply not true. When he went west later that year he talked to Will Merrifield about her, and he mentioned her when he wrote a brief biographical sketch. To Hal Minot he talked freely about Alice and confessed that when she died "my heart was nearly breaking." Theodore wrote Hal: "The little baby is doing well; I shall call her Lee, for there can never be another Alice to me, nor could I have another, not even her own child, bear her name." For years afterward he could not stand to call his child Alice, but chose instead to call her Baby Lee or Sister.[39]

When Theodore wrote a memorial to his wife and mother he pointed out that Alice's death was much more tragic than that of Mittie, who, after all, had been languishing for years. His reaction to Mittie's death was not at all like his response to Thee's: no long diary entries about her, no conversations with friends and family documented his agony over losing his mother, no ruminations in his Bible's margins. His daughter Alice later confirmed that he "was not nearly so devoted to his mother as he was to his father." But the fact that both of his parents died young was troubling. In an era when doctors taught that degeneration or inherited weakness ran in families, Theodore could wonder whether he was from declining stock. Were Bamie's spinal deformity, Uncle Weir's paralysis, Corinne's asthma, and Elliott's dizzy fainting spells—and, more ominously, the cancer, neurasthenia, and early death that had struck down his parents—proof of a weak biological inheritance? As he gulped down the nitroglycerin pills that doctors had given him for his heart trouble, he faced the mortality of the people he had loved most and he restlessly feared his own time might be short.[40]

His deadened emotions made him write dramatically in his diary: "For joy or for sorrow my life has now been lived out." He comforted himself with action and grasped hastily to re-create the life he and Alice had imagined. He inherited $62,500 from his mother and signed a contract for $16,975 to build Leeholm in Oyster Bay, with a design reminiscent of Alice's house in Chestnut Hill, even though a ten-bedroom estate made no sense for a grieving widower who vowed never to remarry and who, as soon as his term in the state legislature ended, expected to divide his time between the Dakotas and New York.[41]

He left Bamie in charge of getting Baby Lee a wet nurse and raising her at the home she would buy at 689 Madison Avenue. Bamie supervised the closing up of 6 West Fifty-seventh Street, the division of family possessions, the sale of Theodore's house on West Forty-fifth Street, and the construction of Leeholm. She tried to comfort her brother as he alternated between a dull, stunned numbness and a fierce, manic insistence on work and never holding still long enough to think. He was candid about fearing that: "I should go mad if I were not employed" so his solution was to move fast, work hard, and escape introspection. He said: "Black care rarely sits behind a rider whose pace is fast enough," and he rode through life fast.[42]

If he felt guilt that he had not rushed home soon enough to his wife's bedside or that he had been bored by and had neglected his "pink baby wife," he showed it by pacing faster. Theodore returned to work at Albany just two days after Alice and Mittie's funeral, and he wrote Bill Sewall: "I have never believed it did any good to flinch or yield for any blow, nor does it lighten the pain to cease from working." He wrote to Bamie from his Albany hotel that he was glad "little Lee" was thriving, but he could not admit how badly he fared.[43]

While Bamie was picking up the pieces of Theodore's life, she also tried to aid Elliott's wife, Anna, in curbing her husband's wild night escapades. His first child, Eleanor, was born in the fall of 1884 but that did not settle him down; he still went "from one bad scrape" to another, drinking to excess and injuring himself with regularity. Though Bamie would never have much luck getting Elliott to accept adult responsibility, she filled in for Theodore knowing his grief would pass in time and he would return to being a reliable father. Aunt Annie took Baby Lee to visit her Boston grandparents and joined the Lees and Bamie in indulging the child's every whim.[44]

THE TRAGEDY of losing his wife bore down on TR's spirits. In the spring, summer, and fall of 1884, just when his grief held him in its tightest grip, he became embroiled in acrimonious Republican Party conflicts over the presidential race. He felt duty-bound to fight hard to win support for the nomination of reformer George Edmunds at the Republican state convention. Afterward he went to the national Republican nominating convention in Chicago as leader of New York's delegation. The problem for honest politicians like TR and his new friend from Massachusetts, Henry Cabot Lodge, was that the party was being steamrollered by the well-organized candidacy of James Blaine, a ruthless politician who operated by the rules of the spoilsmen they deplored—getting government jobs for political cronies and passing land grant bills in exchange for bribe money from railroads. A cartoonist in the political magazine *Puck* drew Blaine as a whore known for selling his political favors and giving the voters "Guano Statesmanship."[45]

At the convention Theodore tried everything to stop the party of Lincoln from giving its blessing to a rogue like Blaine. He made an impassioned speech to substitute John Lynch, a black delegate from Mississippi, for Blaine's corrupt choice for temporary chairman. His eloquence and invocation of the equal rights ideals once held dear by the party won Lynch's election but could not stop the nomination of Blaine. In the end, the convention was swept away by the "Blainiacs."

The nomination of a crook by the Republican Party posed a serious moral dilemma for Roosevelt. When the Edmunds men "pouted and sulked like whipped school boys," TR pouted with them. Like Lodge he "could only rage impotently." His mugwump friends decided they could not support the ticket, but it was not clear what stand TR would take in public.[46]

On the night that the convention nominated Blaine, about midnight Roosevelt met Horace White at the Grand Pacific Hotel, where White was writing a telegram to E. L. Godkin, the editor of the mugwump newspaper, the *New York Evening Post*, advising him what to do about Blaine. According to White, TR read the telegram and said: "If I were writing it I would say, 'Any proper Democratic nominee will have our hearty support.' " White interpreted this as Roosevelt's declaration of his own willingness to bolt and went to the newspapers with it. Roosevelt was infuriated that White twisted his private remark and made it public. He excused what he had said to White in another published letter to the editor: "I was savagely indignant at our defeat, and heated and excited with the sharpness of the struggle, I certainly felt bitterly angry at the result, and so expressed myself."[47]

After he spent a weekend with Henry Cabot Lodge at his summer house at Nahant, TR issued a statement declaring he was supporting Blaine. He flatly denied that he had ever promised to bolt. Then, Roosevelt, rather than Blaine, became the object of the mugwumps' fury. The mugwumps were convinced he had promised to oppose the Republican nominee with them, and, then, in a moment of calculation about his political future, he had gone over to the devil. In private, Theodore admitted that it was "impossible for me to say that I consider Blaine and Logan as fit nominees, or proper persons to fill the offices of President and Vice President," but in public he said he would support Blaine. The *Evening Post*, *Harper's Weekly*, the *Springfield Republican*, and the *Chicago Daily News* lined up against Blaine, and influential editors like Godkin declared that supporting Blaine put a man "knee-deep in perversion." After the Democrats nominated Grover Cleveland, the mugwumps threw their support to him, but TR and Lodge stayed loyal to the party of Lincoln.[48]

Mugwumps charged Roosevelt with selling out to machine politicians to further his own ambition. He was called a false reformer and a liar, and was pummeled by hostile mail. Under attack in the national press as he had never been before, TR was chagrined that his critics claimed that Lodge had duped him into supporting Blaine. He wrote Lodge: "The Boston Independents circulated through New York the idea that I was a misguided weakling, who would have liked to be honest, but who was held in moral thraldom by the unscrupulous machine-manipulator of Nahant."[49]

Lodge had, in fact, influenced Roosevelt to stick to his original decision to support Blaine. The start of a thirty-five-year "close and loving friendship" grew out of their controversial stand in 1884 when Lodge acted as his younger friend's father confessor, and their relationship combined mentoring for the younger man with a political alliance. Aside from Lodge's arguments for party regularity, Theodore judged on his own that supporting a Democrat was wrong. His father's party stood in his mind for noble causes: nationalism, national banking, the Homestead Act, and economic development. TR could not face leaving the "party of moral ideas" even when it nominated the likes of Blaine. He also disliked the idea of crossing party lines to support Cleveland with mugwumps who were routinely dismissed by Senator John J. Ingalls as "effeminate without being masculine or feminine." Roosevelt had been making a fine reputation for himself as a reform-minded Republican, but he did not want to waste his clout being trapped in the crossfire between independents and regular party men the way his father had been. Therefore, he stood up as a party regular, but certainly not an enthusiastic "Blainiac."[50]

Theodore urged Lodge not to take an active role in the 1884 campaign, but Lodge could not easily sit it out when he was running for a seat in Congress. Then, the news broke that Cleveland had fathered a child out of wedlock, which merely confirmed Theodore's view that he and Lodge had done the right thing by holding their noses and supporting Blaine.[51]

Roosevelt had gone back to his Dakota ranches in the summer, determined not to take part in the campaign, but as fall arrived he missed friends and home. He returned to the East to campaign for Lodge and for the party in New York. He warned voters that Cleveland as president would act beholden to the Democratic machine—the states' rights party that had brought disunion and that stood for the Dred Scott decision which held that blacks had no rights. Like other Republicans, TR "waved the bloody shirt" to remind voters that the Democrats were responsible for the infamy of secession, but voters had grown tired of hearing this old ploy. When the Reverend Samuel Burchard made even harsher attacks on the Democratic Party as the party of "rum, Romanism, and rebellion," the Republicans had gone too far. Cleveland won the presidency for the Democratic Party for the first time since the Civil War, not because of mugwump support or Burchard's anti-Catholic bigotry, but because the still-powerful boss Roscoe Conkling refused to mobilize his Republican voters for Blaine, whom he personally hated. Proud of Cleveland's victory, mugwumps were never going to forget that TR stood by Blaine.[52]

Roosevelt's aftertaste of 1884 was sour. When he met the "City's Saint," Josephine Shaw Lowell, on the train he told her he had to turn down a renomination to the assembly or else "everybody would have said" that "his political ambition" made him support Blaine. He promised to help her out with the State Charities Aid Association, but he felt so disgruntled that he said he was leaving politics forever. Mugwumps had hit him hard when he was downed by grief, and months later he admitted his "wrath still burns hot" at the "perverse lunatics" and "the white livered weakling" types among his former allies who lacked "the robuster virtues" and were too timid to engage in combat with "rough politicians." He urged Lodge to "hit the Mugwumps whenever you can."[53]

When Roosevelt looked back across the years, he judged the mugwumps to be insufferably elitist because they "distrusted the average citizen and shuddered over the 'coarseness' of the professional politicians." Their editors, like George William Curtis, he wrote, gave in to "backbiting, mean slander, and the snobbish worship of anything clothed in wealth and the outward appearance of conventional respectability." These "goody-goody," or Good Government, Goo-Goos lied freely, Roosevelt claimed, and ran newspapers "susceptible to influence by the privileged interests, and were almost or quite as hostile to manliness as they were to unrefined vice." His tirades echoed the fury of Conkling's man-milliner speech, and, though he liked to maintain his independence and his status as a reform-minded Republican, he had thrown in his lot with the regular politicians who demeaned the manhood of elite reformers like his father. From 1884 on he accepted Conkling's view that regular party loyalty was a sign of manliness.[54]

It was a comfort to him that he had acted in concert with Henry Cabot Lodge. The Lodge-Roosevelt friendship was built upon shared interests and complementary temperaments. A literary patrician, a fine horseman, and one of Thee's civil service reform allies, Lodge, like TR, planned to build a political career within the regular Republican Party, not with men of his own Brahmin class who were too fastidious to support imperfect candidates. Lodge knew who he was: a civil service reformer with some concern for the poor, and a hard-line, sound-money Brahmin immigration restrictionist, a fierce nationalist and navy man. The Civil War loomed large for both men: TR recalled exciting parades of soldiers and Lodge remembered cheering crowds surrounding his father's friend, abolitionist Senator Charles Sumner (who had been beaten senseless with a cane on the floor of the Senate by a defender of slavery). Theodore and Cabot admired military might and the same Olympians, especially Sumner, Lincoln, and Robert Gould Shaw.[55]

Some friends saw in Lodge a "slight feline quality." They said: "He purred with just the faintest suspicion of a snarl," and talked with an air of "detached intellectual superiority." But Theodore saw him as a cultivated scholar warmed up by "big boyishness." Lodge adored his young friend for overflowing with the spontaneity he lacked. Both were determined to prove that their generation was "just as patriotic, just as ready to sacrifice themselves for their country" as the brave Civil War soldiers they so honored. Both men had had their manhood challenged by working-class toughs in their youth, and both grew up with a fighting edge and a hatred of the effeminacy and "decrepit dilettantism" they saw in abundance in their own upper class. Both admired the English and American Puritans and the "men of action" in American history. Theodore, of course, carried his defensive pugnaciousness closer to the surface than Lodge did. Both punched opponents in the jaw before their careers were over.[56]

The New Yorker looked with some envy upon Lodge's life as a man of letters with a promising political career ahead of him. He also found Lodge's friends novelist William Dean Howells and jurist Oliver Wendell Holmes, Jr., charming. Lodge and TR became friendly competitors in sports, especially on horseback, and their parallel and sometimes overlapping writing careers egged them on to surpass the other and to scare up assignments for each other. They confessed their fears and weaknesses and often bragged in front of each other. TR, who believed he lagged behind his friend in writing and politics, said he regarded Lodge "with mild reverence" after Lodge told him that he could write an article of seven thousand words in three hours. Theodore told Lodge that in politics, "I am heartily glad you have taken command; it is an excellent thing in many ways, and will make you keep your grip. My own is now lost entirely, I regret to say."[57]

TR's somber mood deepened in the winter of 1885 when the anniversary of Alice's death reminded him of all he had lost. He envied Lodge's happy marriage to Nannie, Anna Cabot Mills Lodge, a beautiful Wellesley graduate and classical scholar who enjoyed quoting Dickens and Shakespeare to confound him. Lodge's frank spouse showed Theodore that he preferred women who were not the long-suffering and docile Patient Griselda type, and when Nannie teased him about an intellectual gaffe, he merely joked back: "My youth was an unlettered one."[58]

When the Lodges visited him at Leeholm, Theodore tried to get Nannie to run with him down Cooper's Bluff. She flatly refused. Afterward he said admiringly: "Nobody who heard her would ever again have accused her of possessing a timid or irresolute character." Nannie's forthrightness impressed him as well as her worldly concerns: she would join the Women's Educational and Industrial Union to help working women in Boston, and she sponsored the good works of the Visiting Nurses Association in Washington, D.C. He had animal skins he gathered from his western hunts turned into footmuffs for Nannie and confessed to her: "Indeed I would be almost ashamed to say how much I prize yours and Cabots good will and friendship. You see I never make friends at all easily; outside of my own family you two are really the only people for whom I genuinely care."[59]

Though the Lodges teased him a good deal, they also comforted him in his grief, and when he told bear stories to their small children, John, Bay, and Constance, he was reminded of his one-year-old daughter at home. Alice later felt peeved that her father let Bamie raise her at first, but she was not being entirely fair. He, in fact, had never abandoned the child. His western years were errands into the wilderness made by a grieving widower who lived more often in the East than the West. He would later swear under oath that he had lived in the West for three years and on other occasions said it was the "major part of seven years and off and on for nearly fifteen years" that he spent there. However, in 1884 he lived more than two-thirds of the year with Bamie and Baby Lee in New York and made only three trips to his ranches in the Dakotas. In 1885 the proportion was about the same, though in 1886 he visited the West for twenty-five weeks on two prolonged trips. After 1886 he became a full-time easterner again, except for hunting trips.[60]

From the time she could reason Baby Lee always knew her father was coming back to see her. He managed to make it home for her birthdays and Christmas, and, when Bamie traveled and left the child with servants or Aunt Annie, he sometimes returned to New York to make sure that Baby Lee was "in a condition of rampant and vocal good health." The family described Baby Lee to Bamie as "your baby," yet she remained Theodore's baby, too.

His relationship with "cunning little yellow headed baby Lee" was full of good-byes, but when he wrote affectionately to Bamie to "kiss the darling for me and tell her her father thinks of her and you very often," he testified both to his absence and his fond commitment to the child.[61]

For the three years that began in May 1884, Theodore and the "almost venerable" Bamie made a home together as a spinster-sister and widower-brother family at her house at 689 Madison Avenue, where she regularly entertained her brother's political and literary friends. She also served as the first mistress of Leeholm when it was being finished. She moved in furniture that had been at West Fifty-seventh Street and set the house into working order, and talked their cousin Frank Roosevelt into installing bells for the servants and their cousin John Elliott into putting in a road to the house. Bamie kept her brother's checkbook and watched over his business affairs and his clothes, and hosted his fox hunts at Leeholm. Most important of all, she helped him when he was so depressed or directionless that she feared he might give in to the "temptations to a life of sports and pleasure, to lettered ease, to an amateur's career in one of the fine arts."[62]

Bamie spoke up for Thee when she reminded her brother that he was the son chosen to do great things, and when he went west she kept him informed about local and national politics. She had long taken an interest in Thee's efforts to save New York from vice and in her brother's civil service reforms, and she kept up their network of social and political ties by serving on a variety of charitable boards. But Bamie was not willing to take steps like her friend Grace Dodge, an heiress who shocked her parents when she went off to work with the Reverend Brace and Mrs. Lowell and later founded working girls' societies and Columbia Teachers College. Bamie kept to a more traditional grande dame profile by working behind the scenes to promote her brother's dormant political career. She maintained her wealth by listening to the cautious financial counsel of Uncle Jim Roosevelt, Douglas Robinson, and George Cabot Lee, and invested her inheritance more wisely than Theodore, with whom she shared her funds. Her vast network of friends and her brother's career served as outlets for the public service career she might have had if she had lived a hundred years later. Friends noted: "It is seldom that two such personalities, so closely resembled, work together as one," and in grief Theodore leaned on his strong older sister. Bamie wrote: "It has been a real heart sorrow to me" for him to "lose these years without the possibility of doing his best & most telling work," but she would be ready to help him reenter the political arena when he finished his sojourn in the West.[63]

When guests spent a week with Theodore and Bamie at Leeholm they considered it "a signal piece of good fortune to have had the 'hunter politician' and his diplomatic sister so much to ourselves." Friends learned to correspond with TR through Bamie so that they were guaranteed a response. The siblings shared so many interests that Theodore talked of their having a literary-political salon. It was Bamie who suggested he read *Anna Karenina*, and she befriended the Lodges and with Cabot urged her brother to write less in the first person and to hold back articles that struck them as too egotistical. Most of Theodore's trophies from hunting came to Bamie to decorate what he called "our famous hall at Leeholm." But his reconstituted family still left a gaping hole in his life.[64]

In the Dakotas, Theodore's errand into the wilderness made him look long and hard at the desolate landscapes of the Bad Lands and the quiet of the spruce forests which, he told his diary, had "a weird, melancholy fascination for me." He came there to seek "enough excitement and fatigue to prevent over much thought," a cure for his troubling sleeplessness and sorrow. He wrote: "Nowhere, not even at sea, does a man feel more lonely than when riding over the far-reaching, seemingly never-ending plains," and in the Dakota plains he saw the land as a "death-like and measureless expanse." He said in despair that Baby Lee was better off without him, and his depressed spirits worried his family back home enough for them to make secret inquiries about him. They asked Bill Sewall to write each fortnight about Theodore's well-being because they knew he rode recklessly and dealt with unruly cowpunchers and neighbors without worrying about the consequences.[65]

At night Theodore listened to the wolves whose wails sounded as solitary as he felt. He had seen in Darwinian theory grounds for a new kinship between man and beast, and he believed that powerful, vigorous men of strong animal development must have some way in which their animal spirits can find vent." In the West he tried to live simply—as much like an animal as he could. He watched, chased, raised, herded, and killed animal life. His favorite companion was his horse, Manitou, whom he named with the Iroquois word for "animal spirit."[66]

Though in his sickly boyhood he had turned to nature as a balm and a comfort, he now welcomed, even invited, punishment from nature. He floundered in mudholes and quicksand and killed rattlesnakes. The "original condition of primeval wildness" around the Little Missouri River basin made him feel he had gone back in time to live a primitive life. He routinely spent thirteen hours in the saddle, and just before he came back to New York for Christmas in 1884 he hunted in fifty-degree-below-zero weather and froze his nose and cheek.[67]

Like the Puritans' journey to New England, Theodore's errand into the wilderness had two sides. He wanted to create a more perfect world for himself than the one he had escaped and to send a message back home to instruct the East in proper living. His more perfect world would be a utopia of male camaraderie where his eagerness for leadership was not belittled by critics, but that utopia took awhile to create. He arrived as a tenderfoot in spectacles, a suspicious sight for a town that did not always like what it got from strangers. He could not hide his "mole-like vision," his passion for birdsongs, or his Knickerbocker accent, clothes, and manners. One of TR's friends said: "In the beginning he was called a 'young squirt,' a 'weakling,' a 'punkin-lily,' a 'goo-goo,' a 'Jane Dandy,' a 'dude,' and was accused of the 'insufferable conceit' of 'banging his hair,' and uttering his r's in a manner regarded as effeminate in the West." No one in the money-starved Dakota Territory ever forgot that he was a rich New Yorker, a potential boss, benefactor, and customer, and his habit of handing out hundred-dollar bills to hunting guides reinforced the social distance between him and the plain folks of the West.[68]

But he was a rich man who stood up for his rights. He eagerly lived like the rest of the men—riding against the freezing wind, rounding up stray cattle, putting out brushfires, and crawling through cactus if he had to. Local men made a joke of his order, "Hasten forward quickly there!" Nevertheless, they saw "Mr. Roosevelt" was not much like the fragile, entitled specimens who vacationed at the dude ranch near his Maltese Cross spread or the arrogant French marquis whose cattle grazed on other men's land. Sewall spoke for the cowhands who worked for TR when he wrote: "We hitched well, somehow or other, from the start." The New Yorker proved he meant it when he quoted Anthony Trollope's bon mot: "It's dogged that does it," and the ranchmen admired him for making up in sheer persistence what he lacked in skill and experience. Roosevelt later said that he loved the West and the fresh start it gave him because of its "rugged and stalwart democracy" where "every man stands for what he actually is and can show himself to be."[69]

The message he sent back east was that America needed more western vigor. The didactic theme that ran through his many western magazine articles and his major western books—*Hunting Trips of a Ranchman* (1885), *Ranch Life and the Hunting Trail* (1888), *Thomas Hart Benton* (1887), *The Wilderness Hunter* (1893), and *The Winning of the West* (1889–96)—was that Americanness was a fierce frontier spirit more alive when plain folk fought their way west than when they settled into industrialized lives in the East. It was a frontier spirit he wanted to make national and to rekindle across class and regional lines. He used the West to teach the East that hunting and outdoor life "tend to bring out the best and manliest qualities in the men who follow them, and they should be encouraged in every way." Dime novels, which he devoured, and Buffalo Bill's Wild West shows taught the East what to expect of western fables, and he merely wrote himself into the pantheon of epic western frontier heroes. He lectured his readers that the great leaders of America—Lincoln, Washington, and Jackson—tested themselves first as hunters. His lesson for his readers was that manly feats in nature schooled men to lead and made them fit to be national heroes, so American politics would be led best by men who had been seasoned in the West.[70]

He had a Daniel Boone–Davy Crockett buckskin suit specially made so that he could pose in it for a photo at the beginning of his *Hunting Trips* book to reaffirm his frontier persona. He told a reporter for the *New York Tribune:*

> It would electrify some of my friends who have accused me of representing the kid-gloved element in politics if they could see me galloping over the plains, day in and day out, clad in a buckskin shirt and leather chaparajos, with a big sombrero on my head. For good healthy exercise I would strongly recommend some of our gilded youth to go West and try a short course of riding 'bucking' ponies and assist at the branding of a lot of Texas steers.[71]

He longed for even more glory than showing up his critics back home: near the end of his western adventure, he read sections of Napier's drum-beating descriptions of the Peninsular campaign to his cowhands, whom he prepared to fight a possible border war against Mexico. When the war did not materialize, TR wrote wistfully to Lodge: "I would surely have had behind me as utterly reckless a set of desperadoes, as ever sat in the saddle."[72]

As he built his career as a writer of books about the meaning of the West, he followed a famous line of genteel eastern writers, mostly Brahmins, who, like Richard Henry Dana, Jr., had left Harvard and had one great publishable adventure. Dana sailed around Cape Horn and described his life as a sailor among the colorful but "idle thriftless" californios in the coastal trade of California in the popular *Two Years Before the Mast.* Dime novels, Francis Parkman's western self-making, and the romantic vision of western landscapes painted by Thee's friend Albert Bierstadt informed TR's utopian vision of a West where the cowboy and hunter personified freedom. TR wrote that western life "is patriarchal in character: it is the life of men who live in the open, who tend their herds on horseback, who go armed and ready to guard their lives by their own prowess, whose wants are very simple and who call no man master."[73]

His political travails in 1884 encouraged him to idealize men of the West as impervious to domestication, completely independent of troublesome organizations and rules, and free of the "civilized" constraints on their angry and violent impulses against their rivals and critics. But in real life frontier and "civilization" overlapped. TR brushed aside complicating facts that sullied the image of absolute freedom on the frontier which he sought: the fact that his cattle grazed on land provided by the government, that most westerners were not masters of their own fate but impecunious employees, that the railroad regularly ran over and slaughtered his cattle, and that the local vigilante group caught and hanged horse thieves (and rejected TR for membership) by trampling on their freedom—that is, their right to a trial.[74]

Wildness as it was embodied in Roosevelt's West, then, was an imagined antidote for civilization at its most annoying. Like the stories of chivalry he and Lodge loved, TR dreamed that the West could offer him honor, freedom, and the essentials of life, rather than the overcivilized frills of bourgeois eastern society he knew too well. Ranching provided a chance to go back in time to tap his elemental skills, unlike doing industrialized work in the "humdrum, workaday business world." Yet he hoped not to abandon civilization but to use his western stories to reinvigorate it along more elemental and primitive masculine lines.[75]

He had his stationery embellished with a knight when he went west in the hope that he could bring to bear on modern life the lost world of chivalry. In his magazine stories he could be the knight who brought order to a lawless land by heroically tracking down thieves, and he could beat Indians at shooting contests without having to kill anyone. He could outsmart guides who saw him as an easy mark faster than he had foiled his opponents in the New York State Assembly. In fact, in the Dakotas it was easier to personify the knight on his stationery because the town government was not sewn up by Tammany Hall and competing Republican bosses. In the West he stood on safer ground than New York, where the only place he had found to stand had been in the crossfire between the machine men and the mugwumps.

He admitted that the "loneliness and freedom and the half adventurous nature of existence out here appeals to me very powerfully. . . . we are so very rarely able to actually and in real life dwell in our ideal hero land." Yet he always considered his western interlude a temporary phase when he was "playing at frontier hunter in good earnest." But his playacting looked real to his eastern audiences. With *The Hunting Trips of a Ranchman* he established himself as "the principal spokesman and historian of the cowboy, the chief interpreter of nature and the wild life of the West." His audiences accepted his romanticized lost Wild West and his praise for the belief that the only good Indian was a dead one.[76]

The West also gave him a chance to begin his long career as an author of advice literature for men. He wrote "Who Should Go West?" in *Harper's*

Weekly, urging weak-kneed young men not to go because it was a hard land requiring "the robuster and more virile virtues"—a place for men "made of fairly stern stuff" like himself.[77]

The more romance he offered, the more his audiences liked his western writing. When he wrote *Ranch Life and the Hunting Trail* he gave the photos of western scenes he had taken with his Kodak to his new friend, the artist Frederic Remington, who added yet another layer of romance as he turned them into illustrations for the book. TR's western books sold well at the same time that crowds hurried to see Buffalo Bill's Wild West show as it toured the country in the eighties. TR, Buffalo Bill, and Remington carried on the work of the dime novels in viewing the West as a land where civilization and its discontents could be evaded. In the nineteenth century many Europeans understood Americanness primarily via Buffalo Bill and western writers like TR. Most significantly, Roosevelt and other interpreters of the West served as the advance troops for a huge tourist industry and for a future mass migration.[78]

For Roosevelt personally, the West offered a welcome setting for his recovery from his loss of Alice and the political bludgeoning he took for supporting Blaine. He was a different person at the end of 1886 than when his wife died. Living among farm folk and foragers who worked as guides and hired hands, he took the irritating edge off his own upper-class accents; he put away his tails and pince-nez, wore a soft shirt, and ate at the kitchen table. He later said: "I never would have been President if it had not been for my experiences here in North Dakota. . . . And whatever of value there was in my work as President depended largely upon the fact that I knew and sympathized with our people as you can only know and sympathize with those with whom you have worked and with whom you have lived."[79]

He believed he had de-classed and re-manned himself in the West. The local people remembered how much he talked, how little he slept, and how curious he was about their irrigation schemes and the array of birds and animals in the Bad Lands. To them he had finessed, not erased, his class background. He remained "Mr. Roosevelt" "the boss," a likable but privileged outsider who took a turn at barn-cleaning duties. They liked him for sharing his extra gloves with a freezing boy, and for being more down-to-earth than the rest of his kind. He practiced leadership by talking his neighbors into joining the Little Missouri Stockmen's Association to band together against cattle thieves, and he was also noted for having stood up to barroom bullies, for capturing boat thieves, and for taking a young punk aside to lecture him not to become a drunk. He was a good neighbor who even organized funerals. If he dreamed his future held chances for national leadership, then having deep and affectionate roots in the West gave him an advantage in pulling a sprawling, divided nation together.[80]

His inheritance from Thee and Mittie financed his western adventure, but if he wanted to succeed as a capitalist he had come to the wrong place. Drought and blizzard killed his herds and the profit he had expected from selling cattle. By the end of 1886 half his inheritance was gone and he knew his ranching days were over. His wild Dakota Territory quickly became dominated by railroad men to whom the federal government gave hundreds of thousands of acres of land. Before long the Northern Pacific Railroad's James J. Hill explained to the residents: "You are now our children." Within thirty years farm folk would fight back against railroad domination of their politics and economy as Populists, progressives, and Non-Partisan Leaguers, but without great success. But at age twenty-eight Roosevelt was more interested in being Davy Crockett than being a capitalist like J. P. Morgan (or in fighting Morgan as the Populists did). He wisely left capitalism to his uncle Jim, Douglas Robinson, and later cousin Emlen, who managed his remaining inheritance, his railroad stock and landholdings, his Union Trust Company holdings, and his share of Roosevelt and Son. When he returned to politics, TR never presented himself as more qualified for public office because he had once been in business; he disliked men who lived for profit. Instead, he always boasted of the more romantic credential of having known the Wild West before it was lost and having experienced "toil and hardship and hunger and thirst" with the common cowboy and hired hand of the Dakotas.[81]

In truth, the West ultimately did not satisfy him. When he stayed in the cow camps, he often thought of home and read Swinburne "as a kind of antiseptic to alkali dust, tepid muddy water, frying-pan bread, sow-belly bacon, and the too-infrequent washing of sweat-drenched clothing." He recognized that he had not yet lived up to his father's—and now his own—expectation that he would make something of himself, but he did not know what to do next. When an offer to run the New York Board of Health as its president came up, he had trouble deciding and wrote to Corinne that he had become "really pretty philosophical about success or failure now."[82]

He turned down the job and tried to make more of a literary career for himself. He had promised to write a biography of Thomas Hart Benton for the prestigious American Statesman series. Without time to do much research, TR told Lodge he was "mainly evolving him from my inner consciousness." When he tried to gain the cooperation of Benton's daughter she did not respond but merely sent a clipping which said she was writing about her father herself. Annoyed, TR called her an "acursed [*sic*] old harridan" and pieced the "skeleton" of the book together sitting amidst drying strips of the elk and antelope that he had shot near his Elkhorn Ranch.[83]

Even judged next to biographies written by other Victorian gentleman-scholars, *Thomas Hart Benton* turned out to be a flimsy work because it shed so little light on Benton's character or experience. However, as a sustained nationalist interpretation of American history during Benton's Senate career, the book had merit. TR anticipated Frederick Jackson Turner's frontier thesis when he argued that the westward movement had shaped American character. He believed that the experience of "constant warfare" had turned the Kentucky, Tennessee, Arkansas, and Missouri settlers who pushed west at the end of the eighteenth century into belligerent expansionists inclined to see it as their manifest destiny to conquer other peoples.[84]

He judged Benton's street fights and brawls to be senseless, but he primarily used the book as a platform to rail against the "wealthy and timid bourgeoisie type" of the North who failed to understand America's potential greatness. Though he disliked the Jacksonians' anti-elite caste feeling, he announced himself sympathetic to Jacksonian and later forms of expansionism. Looking back at the period when U.S.-Canada and U.S.-Mexico national boundaries were unsettled, he insisted that the United States had as good a claim as Britain to western Canada—British Columbia, Saskatchewan, and Manitoba. Yet his expansionist appetite had its limits. He sharply criticized America's war with Mexico and the slaveholders' attempt to gain more slave territory by filibustering southward. Presidents Tyler and Polk, in TR's eyes, were worthless leaders because they were apologists for slavery, and the vain Mexican War leader General Winfield Scott he dismissed as "a wholly absurd and flatulent personage." In the end he praised Benton for his tenacious and unpopular defense of national interests against nullifiers and secessionists. He argued that Benton's "iron will and magnificent physique," made him better able to fight out the big political issues of his day. Lodge helped Roosevelt get a researcher to fill in the factual gaps in the book, but it remained less a biography than an eloquent declaration of TR's nationalism.[85]

When he returned to summer at Leeholm he lived like a country gentleman who promoted active and dangerous sports like fox hunting and polo to reinvigorate his own aristocratic class. London's *Pall Mall Gazette* credited him incorrectly with "having introduced fox-hunting" to America, a sport which Roosevelt liked because when you rode to the hounds the high jumps were more dangerous than polo, which he also played with abandon. In October 1885, Theodore was proud to have given, with Bamie's help, a successful breakfast to the Meadowbrook Hunt Club, which met at Leeholm.

He rode to the hounds across the hilly, uneven ground, leading the other horsemen, including the stylish banker August Belmont and the society figure Stanley Mortimer, in the first fever of the hunt. TR kept riding his horse fast even after it was lamed. As his animal jumped a high rail, it stumbled, dropping its rider on nearby rocks. Then the horse rolled over him heavily. When Theodore got up he was covered with blood, looking "like the walls of a slaughter house," his broken bone protruding, his arm "dangling." It might not have equaled a Civil War empty sleeve, but he was pleased to wear sporting wounds as a badge of courage.[86]

Though Bamie worried that both her brothers were turning into rich sporting fops, TR saw only virtue in risking his neck. He insisted that his friend Austin Wadsworth's fox hunt on his estate in Geneseo County was a "thoroughly democratic assemblage" because the dress of the hunters was not the formal garb worn on Long Island chases, but when he defended the sport in the pages of *The Century* he seemed to have lost track of the fact he knew when he toured tenements with Samuel Gompers: most Americans were too poor to own a horse, let alone ride to the hounds.[87]

IN THE URGENCY of his loneliness and his restless feeling that all his projects had met failure, he drifted briefly toward a playboy's life like the one his brother led, until a meeting intervened which helped him regain direction. After he was widowed, he told Bamie and Corinne that it would be easier for him to avoid contact with Edith Carow. She had visited Leeholm when she was staying with Aunt Annie at her nearby summer residence, Gracewood, but she had not seen Theodore there. In the fall of 1885, Theodore ran into Edith at Bamie's house on Madison Avenue, by chance or because Bamie let it happen. He was very glad to see her. In his loneliness he cut through his usual obtuseness about matters of the heart and realized that Edith still loved him. He began to see her as often as possible, though without telling his sisters.

Like other Victorians, Theodore believed that a first wife's death should not put an end to the love and loyalty a husband owed her. He had promised himself as a matter of honor never to remarry. But each time he saw Edith his old feelings for her came back. Her pride had been hurt by his marrying someone else, but her feelings for him had never changed. Almost unintentionally, he began to court her.

When on November 17, 1885, only six weeks after their first meeting, Theodore asked Edith to marry him, she consented. Their engagement, they decided, had to be marked by secrecy and a certain degree of self-denial. They postponed setting a wedding date for at least several months or until he could complete his ranching business in the West, and she could help her mother and sister Emily settle in Europe.

Theodore saw Edith almost daily in the early weeks of 1886. They hardly needed the months of courtship and engagement that custom required in order to get to know each other. Before long, their decision to wait for a year to be married proved to be trying. Theodore postponed his return to the Dakotas so that he could see Edith as much as possible, while his herds were watched by Bill Sewall.[88]

TR soon grew impatient with their long wait and struggled to hold himself back emotionally. Coming from a more gregarious and physically expressive family than Edith did, he was too forward in showing his love for her. She, however, did not hesitate to put him in his place. Years later he affectionately reminded her: "Do you remember when you were such a pretty engaged girl, and said to your lover 'no, Theodore, that I can not allo[w]'?"[89] She stood up to him with an authority and sureness that Alice had never had time to gain.

He left on March 15 for the Dakotas. She sailed for England in April not knowing when she would see him again. Headstrong as he was, Edith found Theodore a gentle suitor. When she reached London, Edith wrote him that she thought it amusing to watch his distant relative sing in *Carmen* because "his one idea of making love is to seize the prima donna's arm and shake her, violently." She added coyly: "I am so glad it is not your way." Gertrude urged her daughter to take more care of her looks now that she was engaged. Edith knew she was not the great beauty his first wife had been and conceded to Theodore: "I never used to think much about my looks if I knew my dress was all right; now I do care about being pretty for you, & every girl I see I think 'I wonder if I am as pretty as she is' or 'At any rate I am not quite as ugly as that girl.' "[90]

Edith was close to apologetic, however, about her emotional reticence. She knew she could not be as emotionally demonstrative as her future husband was:

> You know I love you very much & would do anything in the world to please you. I wish I could be sure my letters sound as much like myself as yours do like you. . . . You know all about me darling, I never could have loved anyone else. I love you with all the passion of a girl who has never loved before & please be patient with me when I cannot put my heart on paper.[91]

It was difficult to be thousands of miles away from each other for what turned out to be eight months until he could join her in England. While Edith and

Theodore were apart, she proved to be the more patient of the two. He asked for more letters than she had time to write, and he expressed more dissatisfaction with the long wait. Their letters recorded quite a different relationship than the one TR had with Alice—no baby talk or childlike dependency. And he deferred to Edith's better literary judgment.

Though he looked forward to marrying Edith, Theodore felt guilty about going back on his pledge to remain true to the memory of Alice. When he returned to Medora, Dakota, in March, according to his close friend Mrs. Tilden Selmes, he paced back and forth berating himself for loving Edith: "I have no constancy. I wish I could be constant." He felt uneasy, too, about facing what his remarriage would mean to Bamie and Baby Lee, who had been so happy to complete his household at Leeholm in the previous summer. Where would the new family-to-be leave them and how would he break the news? His solution was avoidance.[92]

He had not yet told anyone in his family that he and Edith were planning to meet in England to be married at the end of 1886. He wrote Corinne hinting that his western years were coming to an end: "It will fairly break my heart to have to give up this life, and especially my Rocky Mountain Hunting trip this fall. However if I continued to make long stays here I should very soon get to practically give up the east entirely."[93]

The news of his engagement leaked to the press before he had a chance to tell his sisters, and Bamie wrote him an injured letter doubting the truth of the report. Writhing with guilt over betraying Alice's memory and abandoning his older sister, he anticipated that Bamie would be hurt by his remarriage:

> I utterly disbelieve in and disapprove of second marraiges [*sic*]; I have always considered that they argued weakness in a man's character. You could not reproach me half as bitterly for my inconstancy and unfaithfulness, as I reproach myself. Were I sure there were a heaven my one prayer would be I might never go there, lest I should meet those I loved on earth who are dead. No matter what your judgement about myself I shall enter no plea against it. But I do very earnestly ask you not to visit my sins upon poor little Edith. It is certainly not her fault; the entire blame rests on my shoulders.[94]

Bamie had no choice but to welcome Edith graciously into the family.

Bamie and Corinne recognized more quickly than Theodore that Edith would not be a "baby wife." Corinne later said that she and Bamie were "horrified" about the engagement because Edith would not be as acquiescent as

Alice. They feared that Edith "would come between them" and the brother they adored. Bamie hoped Edith would encourage Theodore to return to politics, but none of the Roosevelts fully understood how much Edith would be like Thee, a goad to Theodore's conscience. Bamie was heartbroken that her brother's remarriage would tear apart yet another household she had run, and she wrote Nannie Lodge, who had become her special friend: "Theodore has against my will insisted on my keeping Baby, in fact for the present at least we will go on just as we are; all this sounds so crude in writing & it would have been a great thing to me could I but have talked over all these plans with you. . . . Edith we have known intimately always. She is very bright & attractive & I believe absolutely devoted to Theodore." Glad as she was that her brother would have a new start in life, their salon in the great hall at Leeholm, now renamed Sagamore Hill in deference to Edith's feelings, was over.[95]

To his surprise, the regular Republican Platt machine asked Roosevelt to run for mayor of New York against the popular and wealthy Democrat Abram S. Hewitt and the third-party labor advocate and well-known author of the single-tax treatise *Progress and Poverty*, Henry George. TR knew he had as much chance of being elected mayor "as I had of filling the throne of Bulgaria." He asked Lodge what he should do and Lodge advised against it. Theodore said he wished they could talk it over in person: "half an hour's talk with you would make me feel like a different man." But Lodge was running for Congress and had no time to see him, so Theodore ran anyway. He sought to earn "a better party standing" by competing as a sacrifice candidate, and he confided to his childhood friend Fanny Smith: "I took the nomination with extreme reluctance, and only because the prominent party men fairly implored me."[96]

In the 1886 mayor's race Hewitt had the support of Tammany Hall, wealthy Democrats, and Republicans who saw him as the best candidate to stop the popular and radical Henry George. Hewitt easily whipped up the anti-labor prejudices and fears of respectable rich and middle-class voters by reminding them of the violence associated with recent strikes. It did not matter to Hewitt that the labor movement had been blamed unfairly for killing policemen when a bomb exploded earlier that year during the Haymarket riot and for the violence that broke out when New York policemen attacked striking street railway workers. Because no right to strike existed in law or in the view of political leaders, strikes and other labor demonstrations—150 incidents were recorded—were routinely suppressed by state militia and National Guardsmen between 1877 and 1900. Though labor activism frightened many conservative citizens, George's Labor Party won the active support of large blocs of voters. George won support from labor, socialists, blacks, and many

Catholics; T. Thomas Fortune, editor of the black newspaper the *New York Age*; Frank J. Ferrell of the United Labor Party; Gompers; the Knights of Labor's Terence Powderly; Josephine Shaw Lowell, and the Social Gospel priest Edward McGlynn. Though George and his followers never endorsed violent tactics, Hewitt charged that the election of George would bring more Draft Riots. So Hewitt urged Republicans not to throw their votes away on Roosevelt but to stop George by voting Democratic.

George made his campaign issues economic inequality, starvation wages, crowded tenements, lack of playgrounds for the poor, and the high infant mortality rates in immigrant neighborhoods. He also argued for equal pay for equal work in public employment and heavier taxes on absentee landlords. TR allied himself with Hewitt in denouncing the Labor Party as a "class movement," and he denied that classes existed in America or that the existence of monopolies hurt wage earners.[97]

In a city with a strong Democratic machine Hewitt was almost certain to win, but TR fought as ferociously as if he had been a true contender. He dealt with George as unfairly as Hewitt did, lumping anarchists, socialists, and labor supporters together incorrectly as "people who have vague notions about the desirability of a general division of property in the interests of the many." He admitted that the misery of the working and poor classes was real, but he added that George and his supporters failed to realize that "these sufferings are irremediable in the first place by any law at all."[98]

Roosevelt warned that George and his kind would never stop at taxing land—they wanted to overturn private property altogether. He had the support of the Union League, the stand-pat *New York Times*, and his father's old friends, but the labor movement denounced him as "Whipping Post Roosevelt" for his moral reform proclivities and for representing the landlord class in its attempts to keep workers and tenants down. He replied with his first bald political lie: "I own no land at all except that on which I myself live." In the end Hewitt won, but George came in second with 68,110 votes, 8,000 more than TR received.[99]

In defeat Theodore felt optimistic and lighthearted. He had heard his campaign band play "Hail to the Chief" in recognition of his later potential, and he told Lodge he had had "first rate fun out of this canvass." He was annoyed that mugwumps supported Hewitt, proving to him that the "peculiarly large idiot vote among the so-called intelligent classes" was manipulated by his enemies who edited the *Evening Post*. At the end of a busy campaign he wrote Lodge that he did not mind losing and that as he assessed the way he had spent the last several weeks, most of all, he missed fox hunting.[100]

After the election, Bamie insisted on going with him to meet Edith. They left the almost three-year-old Baby Lee with Aunt Annie, and sailed to England, where Edith and Theodore were married at St. George's Church on Hanover Square in London on December 2. Bamie, Gertrude and Emily Carow, and Theodore's new British friend Cecil Spring Rice witnessed the wedding. TR had "not the slightest belief in my having any political future," but, allied with Edith, he looked forward to the years ahead in much better spirits than he had enjoyed for a long time.[101]

He had turned twenty-eight that fall, and he was still in the early stages of self-making. He would never amount to much politically if he merely lived a life of repeatedly making himself a man. He still needed to build on the lessons in democracy he had learned in the New York Assembly and in the West if he ever hoped to appeal to voters outside his own privileged world. As the *New York Herald* noted, he showed in the 1886 campaign he "understood the value of being kept before the public." He had more to learn about politics and people in his thirties.[102]

The West had helped him gain muscles and self-confidence in order to return home to battles he knew he must fight. His friends there liked him and accepted his leadership so eagerly that one crony said: "Most any sort of a man can be President of the United States. But that man could be elected marshal in any town in Texas!" The doctor who had treated Roosevelt's blistered feet when he captured boat thieves and walked them back to town across many miles of frozen countryside thought him "the most wonderful man I had ever met" because of his warmth and eagerness to "make the world a better place." His western writings in the years ahead would bring him fame as an interpreter of American nationality, and his personal ties to the West would help him transcend his eastern birth to become a national leader. He knew his Benton had been "a rather unequal book," but he was ready to learn to write better ones.[103]

The new life he began with Edith in 1887 had promise. The young lovers who misunderstood each other in the summerhouse eight and a half years earlier had known loneliness, loss, and hardship enough to temper their formerly hot heads. He brought more generosity and patience to his second marriage than he had to his first, and Edith did not need Bamie to assign her the task of working hard as a helpmate to an exceptional man who had not yet found the right outlet for his talents. Edith's Spartan courage equaled his own. She knew he still feared invalidism, cowardice, and inactivity, and that his temperamental highs and lows distracted him from keeping his sense of direction. Before their wedding Edith wrote to Theodore with affectionate humor, "Please try not to break your other arm until I can take care of you."[104]

☆ BOOK TWO ☆

Wherein a Gentleman Makes Himself a Man of the People

☆ CHAPTER FOUR ☆

The Sensitive Plant

THEODORE AND EDITH began their married life with a conventional Victorian wedding trip. The honeymoon cut them off from social obligations and family ties so their intimacy could develop and their commitment to each other be cemented. Edith's recollections of their "white hour" of first intimacy recalled a sacred "time which will never return." Theodore wrote home of Edith: "I don't think even I had known how wonderfully good and unselfish she was." Their travels through the south of France and to Italy's Bay of Spezia left her with warm memories of a place and a time that had brought her happiness. Theodore expressed exuberance coupled with contentment in the "absolutely idyllic weeks we passed," and later recalled that on a honeymoon "its [*sic*] a wonderful thing to have the 'first fine careless rapture,' and also the companionship of fun and humor, and the liking for the same things."[1]

The Roosevelts in their first months of marriage worried about money and the possibility they might have to close Sagamore Hill and move out to the Dakotas because Theodore's income dropped when his cattle investments went bad. With half his inheritance lost in his failing cattle business, Theodore had given instructions to Douglas Robinson to sell his favorite horse, Sagamore, but his brother-in-law found enough funds to help him pay his bills without doing it. Yet Edith was so worried about money that she told her husband she was willing to move west and "rough it" if their fortunes fell as precipitously as her father's had. Unlike his first wife, the second Mrs. Roosevelt did not expect that marriage would always be conducted under first-class conditions. She had fortitude to match his, and she had thrown in her lot with his, even if it meant a hard life of cattle ranching.[2]

Edith was not amenable to facing all the hard facts that came with her marriage. She did not forgive her husband easily on one sore point: After their falling-out, Theodore had preferred someone else. Family members recalled that she "always resented being the second choice and she never really forgave him his first marriage," and she later told her children Theodore had been bored by Alice. But she would not let the slight she had suffered stop her from loving him without hesitation.[3]

He must have reassured her in one way or another that she was a more satisfactory partner than Alice. She found it "cunning" that Theodore "used to say to me . . . that Eagles must mate with Eagles." Though Theodore may have seen her as a fitting mate, Edith proved to be as challenging as she was satisfactory. He found out slowly that she would not become a blind follower like his first wife or Corinne, Bamie, and Fanny Smith Parsons, who taught him to depend on "almost cloying adulation." These admiring women brought him practical help and, in his moments of self-doubt and insecurity, uncritical support. He also enjoyed the "hospitable inclinations" which made Bamie and Corinne endlessly accommodating to his needs and "able to entertain & make everyone love being" with them. If he telegraphed his sisters that he needed them to organize and host a political party at a moment's notice, they dropped everything to advance his career.[4]

Theodore would often try to pull Edith into his gregarious whirl on the same terms as his sisters. But Edith proved a less malleable, appreciative audience and playmate than he had hoped. She looked to him "so pretty and shy" at formal gatherings where he, by nature, pumped hands, slapped backs, and exuded warmth into every corner of the room, but he refused to let her hide on the sidelines. He persuaded her to dance with him. He felt sorry that "Poor, blessed Mother," as he called Edith after their family grew, remained so reticent.[5]

He had entered into an alliance with a woman who could make him laugh, however. She teased him about his bad French, bombast, and nasty habit of getting into accidents. She found his moralism as overblown as she had when they were engaged. On one speaking tour she "christened" her husband "the Prophet Jeremiah and laughed delightedly whenever she thought of it." In other words, he drew the benefit and occasionally felt the sting of having a mate who saw through him.[6]

She, in turn, adored his mimicry and accents and winning ways with children, horses, and dogs. Charmed as she was by the exuberance he brought to their shared life, Edith saw no reason to indulge his every whim. She told him bluntly that Corinne and Bamie spoiled him, and he reluctantly conceded that it was true. Unwittingly (or perhaps subconsciously), Theodore had brought an echo of Thee's stern conscience back into his life. He allied himself with a woman of judgment who chastened him when he failed to live up to the high ideals they shared. He took frequent refuge with his admirers after Edith developed the habit of making what her husband called "sudden and cunning raids on me, especially when I met with 'little adventures.' " Theodore later told friends that he had been lucky to marry "the sanest woman he has ever known," but at the start of their partnership many questions were waiting to be resolved. Their family life and his career were not yet defined. When he had left New York to meet her in London, he had no idea whether he would be a literary man or a politician or a cattleman.[7]

During their engagement Edith had called him her "sensitive plant" after a Shelley poem about a plant whose caretaker had died and left it to freeze in the hard winter, "a leafless wreck." Though TR would not like to be thought of as a tender plant by most of his acquaintances, he trusted his second wife to care for him and to know his sorrows and insecurities. There was so much about his life that he did not have to explain to her, so much they had shared from their days together on East Twentieth Street; he allowed himself to become her "sensitive plant" in private and to have her nurture his new growth.[8]

By February 1887, as the honeymooning couple marveled at the "vanished, old world splendour" of Venice in a snowstorm, Edith realized the discomfort she felt was probably morning sickness. In Rome her husband wrote six articles on ranch life and Edith edited them, and they found they liked to sightsee "in much the same way."[9]

Her pregnancy did not stop them from staying with Lord North at his English country house, where Theodore rode to hounds with the British aristocrats whom Knickerbockers saw as their social peers. Sensitive about condescension toward him as a specimen of a rough-hewn and backward new country, he was pleased to find himself welcomed as an equal in literary and aristocratic circles in London: "I, having begun by treating all the Englishmen I met with austere reserve, have, perhaps in consequence, become quite a lion." He met the writer John Morley, the reform-minded imperialist Joseph Chamberlain, and the historian George Trevelyan. The shrewd future student of American politics James Bryce took him to observe the House of Commons. Already Theodore had planned that, upon their return, he would take a three-week trip to the West to oversee his ranches. He and Edith talked over his hopes of making a literary career for himself and discussed their need for privacy at Sagamore Hill when they returned home.[10]

From abroad he informed Bamie, whom he called "the Manager of the Roosevelts," that the rules of the household she had set up were about to be changed. During the time he and Bamie shared Sagamore Hill he wrote in the sociable library on the ground floor where she and their many guests visited him often and jolly parties distracted him from his work. He told Bamie that he and Edith planned to create a "sanctum" in the third-floor Gun Room. There no one would be allowed to bother him while he wrote a biography of Gouverneur Morris, a New Yorker who helped make the American Revolution and frame the Constitution.[11]

During the couple's honeymoon, Bamie ruled Sagamore Hill and Baby Lee efficiently, hosting a party there in her brother's absence. She closed up the house for the winter, but the furnace she had put in proved inadequate and the pipes froze. Theodore had promised Bamie: "You shall keep Baby Lee, I of course paying the expense." Without consulting Edith, he had invited his sister to remain a part of his immediate family by continuing to spend her summers at Sagamore Hill. But he shifted his stance toward Bamie and Baby Lee because Edith believed she and Theodore should raise the child.[12]

By May 1887, when they came home, Bamie turned over the reins of Sagamore Hill, left three-year-old Baby Lee with them, and packed her bags for a trip to the South. Edith turned Bamie's sitting room on the second floor into a guest room for short-term visits. But Bamie parted on good terms with them and made her house at 689 Madison Avenue available whenever they wanted it. There Theodore sat on the floor and built block houses with Baby Lee and told her stories "about visionary beings" like himself "whose careers were varied and picturesque." Edith taught Baby Lee by the end of the summer to call her "Mama," but Bamie said "it almost broke my heart" to give the child up.[13]

After Theodore visited his Dakota ranches and saw starving cattle and corpses everywhere, he returned ready to embark on a new domestic life. The couple arranged to have Carow furniture sent to Sagamore Hill to add to the Roosevelt pieces Bamie had put there, and they moved Theodore's work up to the Gun Room and settled the Italian furniture they had bought in Florence into the dining room. They also hung up his latest mounted game trophies. Knowing how bereft Bamie felt, Edith wrote cordially to her that she would have a thousand questions about the house when she returned, and Theodore let his sister know that the trees she had planted were growing well.[14]

Together Edith and Theodore "fit up" the nursery in the long expectant summer days. After writing each morning, he played tennis and had canoe races and rifle contests with nearby Roosevelt relatives and neighbors. Most significantly, he stayed by his wife's side in her last months of pregnancy. He used old family connections to get the Jays to dig into their attic for John Jay–Gouverneur Morris letters. As he tried to define how important Morris had been in framing the Constitution, he talked over his subject's life with Edith and she edited his writing. He said his writing of the Morris book "goes drearily on by fits and starts; and in the intervals I chop vigorously and take

Edie rowing," but through his "fits and starts" he was learning to be a better writer. He showed historical acuity exceptional for his era when he observed that the American Revolution was "as much an uprising of democracy against aristocracy as it was a contest between America and England."[15]

In the 1880s and 1890s, TR was one among many historians who reassessed the meaning of the American Revolution. Because rapid railroad and factory expansion had sent industrial leaders seeking material gain and workers protesting for a living wage, Gilded Age America looked to many observers like a society that had lost its moral compass in the pursuit of wealth. If the country had temporarily abandoned its higher principles, TR and many others like him believed that history reinvoked could reunite the nation with its better self. Celebrations of the anniversaries of Lexington and Concord and the Declaration of Independence had marked the beginning in the 1870s of a broad Colonial Revival movement to recover America's colonial and Revolutionary heritage. The movement used historical lessons about simplicity, virtue, and patriotism to instruct wayward contemporaries.

TR appreciated the movement's tendency to lecture its own materialistic and corrupt era by invoking the imagined simplicity and honesty of the past. But he was less sympathetic with groups like the Daughters and Sons of the American Revolution, which tried to connect themselves to distinguished colonial and Revolutionary ancestors. Proud as he was that his ancestor Archibald Bulloch led the American Revolution in Georgia, he said that searching for one's noble inherited traits by tracing descent from accomplished ancestors was as stupid as trying to prove that a person's fondness for apples was due to his descent from Adam.[16]

Instead, Roosevelt preferred to use the past to unify the nation by recalling shared struggles and to assert America's worth among nations. He argued: "Our nation is that one among all the nations of the earth which holds in its hands the fate of the coming years." He also supported the rediscovery of the country's art and culture, which the opening of the American wing at the Metropolitan Museum heralded. Like his friends Lodge, Brander Matthews, and the genteel editor of the "intensely American" magazine *The Century*, Richard Watson Gilder, Roosevelt had become a literary nationalist hostile to Europeans who looked down on America as a "Paradise for Mediocrities" which lacked great ideas or minds. At the literary salon of Gilder and his wife, Helena, TR and Edith met American artists such as Cecilia Beaux and sculptor Augustus Saint-Gaudens, whom they admired as the creative lights of a new cultural Americanism. Roosevelt berated rank "Colonialism" whenever he saw it—among American aristocrats who aped British royalty and among men of letters who looked across the Atlantic and devalued their own literary roots in Cooper, Whitman, and Emerson. As a popular book reviewer TR praised authors like Owen Wister, who captured the "infinite picturesqueness" of American types and landscapes.[17]

In an era when English but not American literature was judged worth teaching in colleges, Roosevelt was invited to speak about the value of American writers to Brander Matthews' Columbia College class and got a cheering response from the students. He preached that western and southern men exhibited "the stern, manly qualities that are invaluable to a nation," and he refused to follow most Colonial Revivalists in their concentration on America's New England roots. TR loved "genuine Americana"—picturesque folk customs and American scenes and art and literature with a "daring Americanism of subject" and "democratic sympathies."[18]

But Roosevelt was not such a celebrant of America and its past accomplishments that he became an uncritical historian. Lodge wrote a biographical portrait of George Washington which found heroism and few faults, but TR relished the power of scientific fact too much to write filiopietistic biography. In *Gouverneur Morris* he praises Morris' vision of national unity but takes him to task for being less than a great democratic leader because he looked down on the common people. As he wrote about the elitism and antidemocratic tendencies of his Federalist forebears, Roosevelt began to confront the meaning for his own political career of the lesson he drew from Morris' life: no leader in a democracy could achieve greatness if he refused to listen to the common people and respect their needs.

But as a biographer, the twenty-eight-year-old Theodore still saw the world through the lens of the cultural evolutionary views he had learned as a boy: he asserted that rich, white Protestants were better suited to practice democracy than other people. In *Gouverneur Morris* he even praises property qualifications for voting and announces that the "half-savage negroid people in Hayti" were unfit for democracy and complains of the shortcomings of "priest-ridden peoples." He sounds like a young patrician who, despite all he had learned at cockfights in Troy and branding cattle alongside Dakota cowboys, was not ready for democratic leadership.[19]

His education for leadership was incomplete in other ways, too. He was developing an aggressive frankness in his writing that would later become the hallmark of his political success, but he still found himself insecure and nervous when he had to speak in public and when he faced political conflict. His defensiveness held him back, and Edith urged him to muster up a brave front. He nervously twisted his silver-rimmed glasses and anxiously clapped his hands before he spoke, which caused audiences to ask: "What's the matter with Roosevelt?"[20]

Edith could protect his work time and encourage him in his writing career, but she was ill prepared to teach him effective public speaking or to nurture his sympathy for the voting masses. As a Knickerbocker whose place among the elite had been more precarious than the Roosevelts', she held more tightly to Knickerbocker values and prejudices than her husband. She could be quick to dismiss as common outsiders like John Hay's rich midwestern wife who lacked her polish.[21]

It was striking, then, that Edith did not usually reinforce the aristocratic standards she and Theodore had learned as children. Instead, she encouraged in him the "applied Christianity" he had learned from Thee. As a devout Episcopalian, Edith often reminded her husband that his faith required "civic helpfulness," and she helped him realize that one of the problems he had to tackle in politics was Americans' lack of "social conscience." He told her his essay "Civic Helpfulness" would not have been written without her influence. She said it made her "proud" whenever he spoke up on behalf of her values in his writings on the Christian obligation to reach out "a helping hand" to the needier half of society. Though Bamie still busied herself advancing her brother's career by making friends with influential politicians—Thomas B. Reed, Lodge, and others—Edith aided her husband in a different direction. She encouraged him to hold on to Thee's Christian humanitarianism and live up to the teachings of his childhood, even as she urged him to develop a more self-controlled political voice.[22]

SIX WEEKS before Edith's due date in September 1887, they sent Baby Lee to stay with Corinne, while Theodore read Thackeray to his wife and tried to organize a polo club. While Baby Lee was away, they rowed out to West Harbor for a "divine" afternoon of reading and a picnic, returning to scenes of happy youthful days they had spent together. But they were no longer carefree teens. Family responsibilities would weigh heavily on them in the years ahead. Their day was blissful, but Theodore missed his daughter and having "no little girl to come in and sit on her small chair while Papa shaves, or to wait up in a long little white nightgown to kiss us good night."[23]

For the sake of her marriage Edith needed to find a way to make a place for herself within the extended Roosevelt family. Baby Lee preferred Bamie's company, and both of Theodore's sisters saw Edith as an interloper. Relatives agreed that neither of his sisters was "ever really in love with any man" because they both adored their brother absolutely. Bamie and Corinne enjoyed him so much that they "wanted to be with him every possible minute." So Edith could easily have found herself in the same position she had known in childhood, the Carow waif invited to visit the Roosevelt merriment.[24]

Edith, however, was much more grown-up than Alice Lee had been when she joined the tight Roosevelt family. She understood fully that marriage promised to be her first chance to define her own life, a life free from her former servitude to Gertrude and Emily. But with marriage to Theodore came the blessing and the curse of a menagerie. Bamie and Corinne were so absorbed in him and their lives "bound up" in his interests and success that they did not notice for a long time where that left Edith.[25]

For many years when Corinne's wild family of four children—Theodore, Corinny, Monroe, and Stewart Robinson—arrived at Sagamore Hill they disturbed Edith's repose. The little Robinsons followed Corinne's manic lead as they skated furiously, stayed up late to gaze at the stars, played a roughhouse version of musical chairs called "bumps," and walked far afield to spot birds and name wildflowers. Late nights and loud expressiveness reigned whenever the Robinsons barged in. Corinny later joked that she did not develop the power of speech until she was sixteen because her parents talked so much. The Robinsons' raucous charades and poetry recitations reminded Theodore of the old days at Tranquility, but too much wildness affronted Edith's dignity. Having a sister-in-law who turned cartwheels and recited her own sentimental poetry was a trial for her. Though Theodore characteristically told his sisters to visit often and stay as long as they wanted, Edith insisted that for the good of his writing they wait awhile to come back. His sisters learned that they had to mind "their p's and q's a little bit when they were with her."[26]

Edith and Theodore made a revised place in their family for Bamie, now demoted from commanding officer to the ladies' auxiliary. Bamie recognized that if she wanted frequent visits with Baby Lee she had to respect the prerogatives of the new mistress of Sagamore Hill. The child later said that Bamie "meant more to me than anyone," and when they were alone the generous aunt let the child have her own way. By contrast, Edith was a no-frills descendant of the Puritan theologian Jonathan Edwards, and she believed in rules and self-discipline for children. When conflicts arose, Theodore often did not know whose side to take.[27]

Despite her affection for Bamie, Edith found her sister-in-law controlling and imperious. She had nightmares that Bamie was peering down on her if she dressed the wrong way or committed breaches of good form. Bamie and Corinne adored Theodore's fondness for having whatever house he occupied "full of Tom, Dick, and Harry," but Edith tired easily of the Roosevelts' strenuous habit of socializing and declared: "I can't quite keep up with the pace but toil along panting." So Bamie and Corinne vied with each other to gather friends and plan lunches for their brother. They had much larger bank accounts than he did, so while he was "tramping the hills" in his early political career, his sisters were "paying the bills."[28]

When it was time for Edith to give birth in the fall, she needed to confront—and not for the last time—Bamie's problematic role. The expectant parents refused her offer to come and help, despite the fact that Theodore admitted he was "laid up by the worst attack of asthma I have had for a long while." Knowing childbirth would make her vulnerable, Edith did not want Sagamore Hill's first general to return to her command. In the meantime, Gertrude Carow cabled to say she was too ill to attend her daughter, which Theodore said did not bother his wife because "she has never reposed any trust" in her mother in times of "sickness or trouble." So she was attended by Theodore's cousin Dr. James West Roosevelt. Her husband stood by, more anxious than he cared to admit.[29]

On September 13, Theodore Roosevelt, Junior, was born to parents who were glad to have a boy. When Edith later mused over why people were so much more pleased to greet a boy baby she said it was "because they can do and we can only be." She had a few tearful moments as she adjusted to round-the-clock nursing and the demands of an infant without enough domestic help. But soon they established a new and loving family life: after Theodore was reassured that Edith had survived childbirth, he relaxed enough to start calling his daughter Alice. He also wrote Rector Endicott Peabody to save a place for Ted at Groton. Though Ted began his "hymn to the light" in the crib next to her bed at dawn, Edith took three-year-old Alice on walks and tried to pay attention to her needs. Theodore, who had been too upset about his first wife's death to enjoy Alice's infancy, savored Ted's babyhood. When Ted was old enough to be placed under the care of a maid in the nursery, he would beckon his indulgent father to pick him up from behind the nursery gate, with his little arms and legs waving so much that it made him "about as easy to carry as an electric starfish." Edith wrote that when Ted "sees his father he dances about clapping his hands calling 'Papa buppee tairs,' " for his father would take him downstairs to pat the "buppies," or animal heads, mounted on the wall.[30]

At Christmas, Elliott, his wife, Anna, and their three-year-old daughter, Eleanor, celebrated the holiday at Sagamore Hill. Elliott had long admired Edith, and her only fault in his eyes might be that as the daughter of an alcoholic her bar did not flow freely. She kept, instead, frugal decanters of iced tea in his room.[31]

Meanwhile, Alice and Eleanor proved to be congenial playmates. Though they were raised by Thee's sons, the women in their lives shaped them.

Largely because Edith's steady guidance made for a stable and loving childhood, Alice remained sunny and well loved through her father's frequent absences. Theodore discovered that Edith was the "most quietly conscientious and duty-performing person I ever met," which meant Alice got her full share of maternal attention. As she grew up, Alice often fought with her parsimonious stepmother, who disliked too much slavishness toward fashion but had to relent. She let the Lees or Bamie buy Alice whatever clothes and luxuries she wanted, and she allowed Bamie to sweep Alice away into the high society world of Adirondack camps and Newport mansions with her friends the very rich George Vanderbilts, the Bayard Cuttings, and the Whitelaw Reids—of whose ostentation Edith disapproved. Despite the fact she was raised almost by committee, Alice never suffered emotional and physical abandonment the way her cousin Eleanor did.[32]

Anna Hall Roosevelt, unlike Edith, had little interest in motherhood. Throughout Eleanor's childhood her mother flirted with young men while her husband slowly drank himself to death. Anna turned more parental tasks over to servants than Edith ever did. As a small child Eleanor was shocked when the steamer she and her parents were taking to Europe had a collision with another ship. In his rush to abandon the sinking ship, Elliott called on her to jump alone through gaping darkness into a lifeboat. "Terrified and shrieking," Eleanor jumped but afterward proved so disconsolate that her parents decided her presence would spoil their Grand Tour, so they dropped her off with Aunt Annie. Aunt Annie often took care of Eleanor, who, she said, was like "a storm tost bird," and from Aunt Annie's house in Oyster Bay or Bamie's home in Manhattan, Eleanor visited Sagamore Hill and grew up close to her cousins. Uncle Theodore read poetry to her in the Gun Room and took her to play chase in the Old Barn and to camp with her cousins. Aunt Edith also welcomed their neglected niece into the Sagamore Hill family circle. Elliott and Anna, in turn, never had enough of a home life to offer any surplus of love to Alice or her siblings.[33]

As they created a loving home together early in their marriage, Edith made two discoveries about her husband. Though he was much happier with her than he had been with his first wife, his pacing and restlessness did not disappear altogether. Kept indoors, he often found the temperature too warm, and he believed his health depended on frequent hunting trips. He remained eager to prove his manhood in the wild, which meant she often had to manage their growing family alone. When he began to disappear at regular intervals, she did not like it, but she did not want to tell him he should not go. Years later she advised her daughter Ethel never to let her husband get too "accustomed to being without you." Edith said her biggest mistake was in not trying to curb her husband's wanderlust early in their marriage.[34]

Edith frequently tried to call her husband home with affection. When Ted was about two months old and Theodore had been away hunting for five weeks, she wrote her peripatetic "Dearest love": "I dreampt last night you shot two bears & Sunday night dreams are supposed to come true I hope you may have some luck. . . . I do want you more & more I can't be happy without my own darling. Little Ted coos & laughs for his mamma & eats & grows like a little pig." She called her husband "my boy" and told him: "I am counting every day, only I do not want you to hurry back because I do not want you to leave me soon again." She worried all the time about his risk-taking and pleaded with him: "Do not do too many dangerous things." Her pleas were to no avail, but he sometimes found himself torn, eager to cut his trip short in order to return to her at the same time he wanted to stay west to harden himself.[35]

Her second discovery about the marriage was that her husband could not manage his own finances. She had to look after their money because Theodore was careless about what he spent and always assumed he had enough. He lost checks and forgot for years at a time to balance his checkbook. He berated himself for financial stunts he termed "unworthy of a middleclass chimpanzee," but he could not change. The only cure was to keep him on a budget. Edith gave him a set amount when he left in the morning (often $20). When he returned at night with empty pockets, he had no idea how he had spent it. Memories of her own family's financial struggles came back to amplify her real money worries, and as she hired and fired the staff and attempted to get her husband to limit himself to spending an amount closer to his income, they tried to turn Sagamore Hill into a working farm that would feed their family and cut their living expenses. Edith managed the farm and paid the farmer, gardener, coachman, and house servants, though Theodore liked to think he was in charge. He sometimes balked at the financial limitations she set on him, but he later told his friend Jacob Riis that Edith's competence had helped him get through life because men who were oblivious to finances "need such business partners."[36]

As 1888 BEGAN Bamie invited the financially strapped couple to live with her at 689 Madison Avenue during the winter months when Sagamore Hill was hard to keep warm, and they eagerly accepted, though it meant Edith became a guest rather than the mistress of the house. But Bamie found ways to make Edith feel at home, and she traveled often to give Edith her own dominion for brief spells. For Alice it was heaven to have all her adults under one roof, and she loved the smell of baking bread coming from Bamie's well-run kitchen. With Bamie's tall whiskered butler, Chamberlain, Alice happily gazed out the front window to see the snow fall day after day during the great Blizzard of 1888. Bamie had arranged to have Alice's short leg put in braces when she was two, and Edith was "terribly conscientious" about the child, stretching her Achilles tendon each night and insisting that the braces stay on her growing legs. Theodore proved to be an irritable and distracted husband while baby Ted teethed and gave them sleepless nights. When Edith had her picture taken with baby Ted, her tense husband said he did "not hate it as much as usual. He 'did not give a single dam' about it." Under the circumstances, Edith found Bamie was a much-needed sympathetic companion with similar intellectual interests, a helpful friend who provided extra servants and free advice about shopping and child care.[37]

That winter TR was worried that he could not support his family. By the end of the year he had committed himself to four sizable writing projects: submitting regular articles for *The Century* magazine; turning some of those articles into a book called *Ranch Life and the Hunting Trail*, researching and writing what turned out to be an ambitious four-volume *The Winning of the West*, and producing a history of New York City for Brander Matthews' American Historic Towns series. Before long, the history of New York was "weighing over" him "like a nightmare," as most of his ambitious literary projects did.[38]

But as he wrote he did not turn inward; he remained committed to public causes even when work bogged him down. At the same time he struggled to meet writing deadlines, Theodore and his friend George Bird Grinnell organized a club of big-game hunters, the Boone and Crockett Club, "to promote manly sport with the rifle." Most of Theodore's Boone and Crockett friends loved the West and wanted to preserve the natural world they had enjoyed on their hunts. But they lived in an age when no federal law protected America's national parks. In the early days when the Northern Pacific Railroad and concessionaires held sway, Yellowstone's land and animals were treated badly: geysers were rammed and closed up, vandals marred trees, hunters slaughtered animal populations, timber was cut and not replanted, and tourists littered the most visited spots. Then, private companies announced plans to bilk park visitors by charging high rates to pitch a tent or stay in a hotel.[39]

When the Boone and Crockett Club joined forces in Congress already fighting for the preservation of Yellowstone Park they succeeded in keeping public access reasonably priced. Later the club urged the establishment of Glacier National Park. As president of the Boone and Crockett Club, TR urged Congress to pass the Park Protection Act of 1894 and he lobbied further for the protection of the sequoias and Yosemite. The club's ideas about game protection were built on legal precedents set by early American village common land management practices and by state fish and game laws which Theodore's uncle Robert and other conservationists had urged. TR's pioneering work on behalf of game protection laws, the establishment of western forest reserves (which gave the President the power to turn federal forestland into forest reserves), and the expansion of the national park system made conservation history long before he held national office. Later, through the Boone and Crockett Club, TR, his friend Grant La Farge, and others founded the Bronx Zoo. At the same time Theodore kept up active membership in the Nineteenth Century Club, the Union League Club, the American Copyright League, the Civil Service Reform Association, and the Republican Party. Yet being an active citizen was not enough.[40]

He wanted to reshape American national government. So he found ways—writing articles and giving speeches—to keep his political career alive. Henry Cabot Lodge had gone to serve in Congress but he and Theodore still worked together to see that "the Republican party can steer clear of becoming a mere party of reaction." Gilded Age bosses expected to win elections in order to give their cronies jobs and to collect political assessment from officeholders in return. TR and Lodge, like other civil service reformers, wanted to attack the spoils system by awarding federal jobs instead to high scorers on civil service exams.[41]

Roosevelt applauded when Congressman Lodge proposed the Federal Elections Bill to guarantee blacks the right to vote in national elections. Lodge's bill was aimed at the South, where violence, intimidation, literacy tests, poll taxes, and other devices made for white-only primaries and general elections. Democrats had created a Solid South by prohibiting blacks from voting for the party of Lincoln. Critics of Lodge's bill did not want blacks to vote because they charged that the "tiger blood" of the dominant white race would not stand for usurpation by their inferiors. Blacks, on the other hand, heralded the Lodge bill as a much-needed reform of the election process. But its time had not yet come. A coalition of high-tariff Republicans, southern states' rights Democrats, and their free silver and Populist allies finally killed the Lodge bill, which was the last significant attempt in Congress to restore black voting rights in the South until the 1950s.[42]

But when they defended black voting rights in the early 1890s, Lodge and TR were hardly precursors of Martin Luther King, Jr. They were not fully committed to equality. Anthropologists taught their generation that "the black, the brown and the red races differ anatomically so much from the white" they could never be equal.[43]

Roosevelt, in fact, had a divided heart on matters of race. Sometimes he said blacks were inferior. He accepted the cultural evolutionary viewpoint that white races were more civilized and advanced than dark "savage" races. On occasion, he spoke up for the superiority of the English-speaking races and their need to dominate lesser people. "Civilization," as represented by the most technologically and culturally advanced nations, he argued, should be extended globally, by "order-loving races of the earth doing their duty" to get control of "the world's waste spaces." Though cultural evolutionary views were commonplace at the time, few Americans transformed them into foreign policy truths as boldly as TR. His assumption of the racial superiority of whites over Asian people fueled his wish to see America become dominant in the Pacific, and his belief that North Americans had superior ethnic stock justified his dismissing Colombians as "dagoes" and ignoring the opinions of Latin Americans and Africans because he saw them as "backward" racial types.

He said that because Americans were civilized they were justified in imposing their will on others: "No man is worth his salt who does not believe that the growth of his own country's influence is for the good of all those benighted people who have had the misfortune not to be born within its fold." He praised the British Empire on racial grounds for bringing "civilization" to "dark continents" and for putting down Islamic Mahdism in the Sudan. Roosevelt has to be classified as an imperialist and a condescending racialist at times during his public career, but such labels do not capture his full complexity.[44]

Even where racial theory was concerned, TR felt pulled in opposite directions. Race could be fixed or infinitely changeable to his way of thinking. He accepted cultural evolutionary racial hierarchies at the same time he was a scientist who believed in Lamarckian theory, which taught that any organism could exceed its biology by acquiring learned characteristics and skills from a good environment. Lamarckians, therefore, tended to accept the idea that all human capacity, including racial potential, was plastic and could be changed. Over time his scientific background made him ambivalent about permanent racial superiority, and he adopted the position that blacks had the same potential as whites because environment was more powerful than heredity.[45]

Furthermore, his contradictory racial views were often at odds with his basic egalitarian approach to people. On a personal level, he hated prejudice and wanted to see the diverse peoples of the earth as equals who deserved the same inherent rights. He often praised his Dutch ancestors in colonial Manhattan for insisting on racial tolerance and religious liberty even before there was an American nation.

In his important essay "True Americanism" he argued for "fair treatment" of all people on America's shores, and he also tried to promote a new spirit of brotherhood among immigrants and old stock people. He wrote that if the country could build a "community of interest among our people," ethnic and racial differences would matter less and a true national spirit would replace hatred between groups. He eventually defined his belief in fair play between all groups as the Square Deal and insisted: "To me the question of doing away with all race and religious bigotry in this country" was the most urgent question in public life. But in the years ahead he might show the racialist or the egalitarian side of his divided heart, depending on his mood and the audience he sought to please.[46]

While grappling with his own contradictory opinions, he usually found himself more optimistic than Lodge about immigrant potential. Restrictionists like Lodge viewed the new southern and eastern European influx with alarm because in some cities like New York the foreign-born and first-generation immigrant population would soon outnumber the native-born citizens. Lodge especially wanted to stop the growing number of poverty-stricken foreigners moving into American cities and birds of passage who came only to earn money and then returned to their native lands. After Roosevelt found out that three-quarters of New York City's population was foreign born or the children of immigrants, he understood better why Lodge feared the new immigration, and he even praised the Chinese Exclusion Act in a public speech.

But Roosevelt also criticized the anti-immigrant American Protective Association and other nativists who wanted to stop all immigration. He denounced the A.P.A. in an article in *Forum* magazine in 1894, and he declared that "it is an outrage to discriminate against" any loyal American "on account of creed or race." He disagreed with Lodge's extreme restrictionism because he believed foreigners could be assimilated: again he held the Lamarckian view that races could all reach the same level eventually. For Roosevelt an assimilated immigrant was a good immigrant, but poor Asians, European paupers, and foreign radicals looked to him like toxic stew meat for the melting pot. He gave qualified support to immigration restriction in the 1890s in hope of appealing to the segment of the labor movement that believed that cheap immigrant labor was a threat to their jobs and a stimulus to keep wages low. As Theodore spoke about nationalism and Americanism, he invited assimilated immigrants and native workingmen to avoid class conflict with privileged men like himself and to become instead one bold, American, heroic type—a manly fighter full of national pride.[47]

* * *

In the summer of 1888, Theodore, Edith, Alice, and Ted moved back to Sagamore Hill and Bamie went to England. That summer Theodore's Oyster Bay polo team played hard against Elliott's Meadowbrook team. Fiercely trying to beat his brother, TR fell to the ground when his horse threw him and he was "knocked senseless." Edith, who was again pregnant, saw her husband lying as still as a corpse and she was shaken by the experience. Without any good medical reason, Theodore was convinced that the miscarriage Edith had a week later was caused by the shock of witnessing his accident, and he blamed himself for the loss of the baby. He wrote Corinne: "The mischief of course came from my infernal tumble at the polo match. The tumble was nothing in itself; I have had twenty worse; but it looked bad, because I was knocked perfectly limp and senseless, and though I was all right in an hour, the mischief had been done to Edith." Corinne privately blamed Edith for letting the miscarriage happen. Not long after his wife's recovery, Theodore disappeared into the West to shoot bears.[48]

That October, when Theodore took to the stump to support Benjamin Harrison's campaign for president against Grover Cleveland, he took Edith with him on his twelve-day swing through Minnesota and Michigan. He defended immigration restriction as a means to keep wages up for the workingman, and he attacked the Democrats in Congress for blocking the admission of the Republican Dakotas to statehood at the same time they favored the admission of "polygamous Utah." On occasion TR used sarcasm to keen effect. He told an audience that he favored statehood for Washington and Montana even though they had elected Democrats as their territorial delegates in the last two elections. He added: "They won't do that in the future; they have since then adopted an excellent common school system." Laughter followed. His emerging campaign style was not built primarily upon humor, but his speeches often had funny moments. He knew how to get a laugh. For example, when a statue of General George B. McClellan was unveiled, TR quipped that it was unlike so many modern memorial statues that added "a new terror to death" for famous men. Voters recognized they were not seeing the usual Gilded Age politician.[49]

TR was jubilant when his party won the presidency. With a Republican administration forming, Cabot and Nannie Lodge were working to get their friend appointed to an important post, assistant secretary of state under the newly appointed secretary of state, James G. Blaine. Even though he was an expansionist himself, Blaine saw Roosevelt as a loudmouthed jingo and refused to work with him. So Lodge got his friend a place in the Civil Service Commission, a post which TR recalled "gave me my first opportunity to do big things."[50]

In May 1889, Theodore moved to Washington to fight the spoils system even though President Harrison was lukewarm about reform and used patronage to fill most federal positions. In private TR viewed Harrison's placement of a spoilsman as New York's postmaster as a black mark against the party and a political blunder. Theodore and his civil service reform friends, Lucius Swift and Charles Bonaparte, soon discovered that the civil service system was being corrupted. TR got three top officials removed from the tainted New York Customs House, a hotbed of corruption since the days when President Hayes tried to turn it over to Thee. Then, without asking Harrison's permission, Roosevelt impetuously went on an investigating tour of the President's home state of Indiana and looked into the behavior of Harrison's former law partner. TR's impolitic travels made headlines and produced a "galvanic shock" in the newspapers because he struck out so swiftly wherever he found corruption. But the headlines he won for investigating his own Republican administration did not make him popular at the White House. When they met, Harrison tapped the table with his fingers "nervously," acting as if he could not wait for each encounter with TR to end.[51]

The moral righteousness of being civil service commissioner and making reform "a living force" thrilled him. However, Theodore attracted enemies quickly and started his work in Washington under difficult conditions. He brought large quantities of unfinished writing with him, but Edith was not there to help him moderate his moods and encourage him to reconsider when he was tempted to expose a case of wrongdoing to his reporter friends. Edith worried that her husband's insecurity and nervousness, as well as his habit of verbal assault on opponents, would hinder him as he built the career in politics he wanted. Around the dinner table, he, like Mittie, entertained his family with mimicry, storytelling, and witty character assassination. But in public his bons mots sounded excessive. It had not been necessary for him to denounce the *New York World* for its "voluble scurrility, and versatile mendacity" and to announce in public that it was "edited by a rancorous kleptomaniac with a decided propensity for stealing trousers." Edith enlisted Cabot Lodge and both of them urged TR to hold back his verbal assaults. When cautioned that he had gone too far, too fast, Theodore reassured Cabot that he would cut down on his tendency to give frequent newspaper interviews.[52]

Away from his family, he bunked at the Lodges' house and worked long hours in the steamy Potomac summer. He and Edith decided in a moment of self-denial that the children were better off at Sagamore Hill with occasional visits from their father as his new job permitted. They followed their plan of removing the children from the capital every year until his civil service commissioner term ended in 1895. In the summer of 1889, Edith, again pregnant, saw him less than a total of two weeks, though he made time to vacation among the bears, hunting in the Rockies. His companion on the hunt was Bamie's young protégé, Robert Harry Munro Ferguson, an aristocrat from Scotland who had come to America to "make his way in the world," starting with long-term residence with Bamie or Theodore. Ferguson had a capacity for loyalty and helpfulness which Roosevelt appreciated in his years of ascent. TR was glad to hear from Lodge that President Harrison liked his work but hoped he would seek less dramatic publicity in the future.[53]

Roosevelt's outspoken advocacy of civil service reform brought him temporarily back into the good graces of the mugwumps, who looked to him to popularize the civil service cause. At one of their dinners the poet James Russell Lowell praised TR as "one so energetic, so full of zeal, and, still more, so full of fight." Roosevelt turned out to be the movement's best conduit to the people. But he did not think civil service was going to be a practical winning topic on the stump, and he still searched for the cause that would help him rise to higher office. He wrote Corinne: "I feel it is incumbent on me to try to amount to something, either in politics or literature, because I have deliberately given up the hope of going into a money-making business. Of course however my political life is but an interlude—it is quite impossible to continue long to do much, between two sets of kittle-cattle as the spoilsmen and the mugwumps."[54]

It made Theodore uncomfortable that when he attacked post offices that abused the law, the mugwump civil service reformers would praise him loudly and the regular Republicans would scowl at his excessive zeal. Harrison appointed one of his big campaign contributors, John Wanamaker of department store fame, to the crucial job of postmaster general. This enabled Wanamaker to distribute patronage positions to party supporters, and he had no intention of letting prime jobs be filled by civil service exam. TR pressed Harrison, and the President sided with Wanamaker, who fired thirty thousand fourth-class postmasters in order to distribute those jobs to loyal Republicans. Theodore could not walk away from such obvious spoilsmanship, so he went head-to-head against Wanamaker and exposed his violations of civil service laws. He launched a wholesale attack on the partisan donations Wanamaker required of his post office employees and asked Congress to investigate corruption in the post office. Not surprisingly, Congress found plenty.

Roosevelt wanted his literary efforts to equal the great, constructive work he was accomplishing in politics. But when he came home in the summer he paced restlessly whenever he closeted himself in the Gun Room with his unfinished manuscript of *The Winning of the West.* Having already mastered most of the printed sources, he went to Ottawa, Virginia, Tennessee, and

Kentucky to do research, but the press of deadlines forced him to cut short his manuscript work. TR told the story, in heroic terms, of the settlement in the late eighteenth century of Kentucky and Tennessee. The spread of the English-speaking peoples as a race into the West was a tale which he hoped would inspire a divided people to see itself as a united nation which represented advancing civilization—the spirit of freedom and democracy spreading ever westward.

In April 1889, after nine furious months of writing, he read his draft aloud to Edith. He had written the first two volumes of the book in less than a year and was so rushed to send them off to the publisher that he took scant care with style or substance. He thought them his best books.[55]

His earlier works had accustomed Roosevelt to critical reviews. Good and bad notices went into his scrapbook. Most reviews of *The Winning of the West* did not question his extreme admiration for the "grim, stern people, strong and simple, powerful for good and evil, swayed by gusts of stormy passion" who conquered the trans-Allegheny west "in the unending struggle with the wild ruggedness of nature . . . in the heroic age." Nor did they ponder why he chose the frontiersmen as the advance guard of Western civilization. His overlapping and dubious racial categories, which included "the English-speaking race," the "English race," "black barbarism," "the white, red, and black races," and the Irish Presbyterian "race," sound unscientific now, but were not exceptional then. At least he was more candid than other celebrants of white conquest when he noted that Americans, not just the British and their native allies during the American Revolution, often scalped their enemies.[56]

But two critical responses to his first two volumes of *The Winning of the West* bothered him. An expert reviewer in the *Atlantic Monthly* rebuked him for inaccurately identifying John Randolph of Roanoke as "a small western historian" and for several other minor errors. Though the review hurt, TR wrote the critic in a characteristically gracious spirit to thank him for the corrections, and afterward they entered into a cordial scholarly correspondence.[57]

Equally typical of TR was his combative reaction to a more threatening evaluation. That September, Theodore was accused of having borrowed parts of *The Winning of the West.* The western writer James R. Gilmore (pseudonym Edmund Kirke) charged in a letter to the *New York Sun:* "Roosevelt copies from Kirke whole pages, carefully avoiding actual plagiarism, but falling every now and then into some of his peculiar phrases, and continually committing what, in the case of Lawrence against Dana, was decided to be infringement of copyright." Gilmore, in fact, had tried to help Roosevelt gain access to documents in the Tennessee Historical Society, and he was angry now, not only because TR paraphrased his book so much, but because he charged Gilmore's book with "reckless misstatements." Now, in public letters, Roosevelt replied to Gilmore's attack by insisting that Gilmore's position was based on no evidence at all. By counterpunching hard and fast, TR won the dispute in the court of public opinion.[58]

Though he had not literally plagiarized Gilmore's book, Roosevelt had paraphrased its text rather sloppily. For example, Gilmore had described pioneer Kate Sherrill as "tall, straight as an arrow, and lithe as a hickory sapling," which in TR's close borrowing became: "a tall girl, brown-haired, comely, lithe and supple 'as a hickory sappling.' " However, heavy paraphrasing did not violate prevailing legal, scholarly, or popular standards. And although he identified himself with German "scientific" professional historians who relied on documentary evidence and he later joined the fledgling American Historical Association, Roosevelt wrote as a patrician amateur in an age before writing history in the United States had been professionalized and standards had been set for quotation and citation. TR had committed an amateur's crime of haste rather than of self-conscious theft.[59]

He had learned by now that aggressive counterattack would win the public's respect. After he wrote a scathing personal attack on Gilmore which was published in the *Sun*, Roosevelt told Lodge: "In my last letter I put the knife into him up to the hilt." He continued to paraphrase heavily from Gilmore in later volumes of *The Winning of the West*.[60]

While the debate over her husband's book played out in the fall, Edith gave birth prematurely to a second son, Kermit. Then, within a few months, she moved Alice, Ted, and baby Kermit to Washington, where they settled into a rented house at 1730 Jefferson Street, N.W. Once there, Edith continued to be pulled along in her husband's surging wake. He had promised her there would be no pregnancy in the summer of 1890 so that he could take her to see his western ranches and tour Yellowstone Park. And he kept his word. He was delighted to bring Edith to his ranches along with Bamie, Bob Ferguson, Cabot's son Bay Lodge, Corinne, and Douglas. Theodore showed them the stark ravines and the prairie dog towns. He introduced them to local characters like Hell Roaring Bill Jones, whose whiskey-soaked antics as a violence-prone law enforcement officer had enlivened so many of Theodore's fireside stories.

Edith was thrown by her horse at Yellowstone Park, but she withstood the rigors of the trip well and learned to love the scenes of many of her husband's fondest adventures. After the rest of the party left, Theodore hunted with Ferguson, but his horse bucked him so hard he "rather strained" his "loins" and was "cramped" into November. He wished he could keep the ranch open long enough to bring his sons there, but, even with Douglas Robinson and

Ferguson joining him in his investments, the future of his cattle venture in the West looked grim.[61]

In spite of their unsettled finances, the Roosevelts added two more children during the Civil Service Commission years: Ethel Carow Roosevelt was born in 1891 and Archibald Bulloch Roosevelt in 1894. TR liked a "household swarming with bunnies," as he called his children, and he loved to play with his large and boisterous family. He said to a friend that he wanted to be the father that Thee had been to him: "Unconsciously, I always find I am trying to model myself with my children on the way he was with us." Though less often at home than Thee had been, Theodore, like his father with him, spent a good deal of time with his children, roughhousing, reading to them, and teaching them new skills, swimming, riding, and football. TR later recalled that Sagamore Hill was a refuge where "we love a great many things—birds and trees and books, and all things beautiful, and horses and rifles and children and hard work and the joy of life." Around the time he finished his third volume of *The Winning of the West,* he was photographed outside the barn happily setting up handicap races between his brood and Corinne's and Emlen's children. The young Roosevelts remembered all their lives Father's ability to listen intently to them, and they recalled his wonderful ghost stories when he took them camping overnight. He did not fear to be demonstrative with his or his relatives' children, and he became their favorite playmate and friend.[62]

However, in the continuing adjustments that marriage requires, Edith and Theodore were not always in accord, especially about child-rearing. Both parents were "omnivorous readers" who loved to talk about books and to read aloud to their growing family, but they liked different books. She had read much more widely than he in literature and loved Milton, Shakespeare, Shelley, Trollope, and later writers like Conrad. Because he preferred the warlike Sienkiewicz, the *Nibelungenlied,* Sir Walter Scott, Longfellow, Cooper, Kipling, and Kingsley, she teased him about his literary judgment. She judged his fondness for the medievalism of Louise Imogen Guiney indefensibly sentimental. Theodore explained his lowbrow inclinations by insisting he was not as well educated as his wife. She admitted they had "different tastes," but added: "Perhaps that is one reason why I love him so much." She insisted the older children keep a classical dictionary next to them when she read certain books to them, which her husband did not. But they agreed about having the older children read the Bible daily, and both of them sought to bring poetry to the center of family life. They read and recited it together.[63]

His strenuous life also clashed with her sense of order. Sometimes he would be away from his family more than half the year, but the minute he returned home he promptly encouraged the children to be as expressive and active as possible. Edith had to deal with bedtime routines gone awry after he played bear and romped with them, and to him, but not her, the sight of a child mischievously climbing the icehouse roof looked like a risk worth taking.

When Edith tried to teach her children proper table manners, they had only to glance at their father's gobbling and finger-licking to drop all attempts at etiquette. He planned to ship each boy off to Groton as early as possible to make a man of him, but Edith disagreed. She finally convinced him to write Rector Peabody that Ted would not be enrolling until he was thirteen.

Both parents swam with the children, but Father dunked them and boisterously yelled to Alice, "Dive, Alicy, Dive." Cousin Eleanor cried when he pushed her to splash wildly with her cousins, and Alice recalled him as a sort of "sea monster who was flailing away in the water, peering nearsightedly at me without glasses and with his mustache glistening wet in the sunlight: the instigator of all those perfectly awful endurance tests masquerading as games!" Daring stood higher than decorum for Father. Even their adoring Auntie Bamie said of the Roosevelt children that she "never knew of such a badly brought up family." In his eagerness to instill "healthy animalism" in his brood, Theodore often pushed the children too hard, and he undermined his wife's authority whenever she gently tried to tame the "uproarious tribe pelting around."[64]

When Edith felt overwhelmed by the melee and took to her bed with a neuralgia headache, Theodore doubted she would be perfectly healthy until the children were old enough to go to school. Ill health made him squirm, so it was not with enthusiasm that he described Edith in the mid-1890s as "very much the worse for wear at the present time," and "all my children seem to be suffering under some of the divers ills to which infantile flesh is heir." The couple differed on how to handle the children's illnesses. Ted had asthma, which made Edith mildly protective and caused TR to push him even more, urging Ted to fight bullies, a paternal imperative which Ted said caused a "sinking" feeling in his "stomach."[65]

In raising his children Theodore followed the policy that "I would rather one of them should die than have them grow up weaklings," and he complained to the ever-sympathetic Bamie that Edith was "a little overconscientious in taking care of the ailments of the children." When he came home to Sagamore Hill, Theodore rekindled the spirit of adventure in his children and took them on "point-to-point" walks or scrambles where the rule was over, under, or through but never around—a rule which applied to sand dunes, barns, ponds with green scum on top, and rocky outcroppings.[66]

Edith eventually hardened herself to the injuries the children sustained on their adventures with Father, but his frequent misadventures wearied her.

In the summer of 1892, Theodore climbed up to repair the windmill which pumped water to the house, and its blade swung around and hit him in the head, gashing his forehead badly. He rushed into the house, blood pouring down his face. When Edith saw his latest injury, she told him not to bleed on the rug, but to go to the bathroom. He called it his "idiot spree with the windmill," but Sagamore Hill witnessed such mishaps often.[67]

Fortunately, Edith and Theodore's differences in the early years of marriage did not pull them apart. This was evident in the care with which they handled each other's visitors. When Theodore brought Bob Ferguson for long visits to Sagamore Hill, Edith found his odd schedule made more work for her. But she grew fond of the frail young man, too, and recognized he had become half-playmate and half–little brother to her husband after Elliott declined into alcoholism, so she found a way to draw him into her children's daily life. On the hot August day in 1891 when she gave birth to Ethel, Bob held the little bundle in his arms and agreed to be Ethel's godfather—in time he served as a beloved uncle for all six of the Roosevelt children. When the hypercritical duo of Emily and Gertrude Carow planted themselves by Edith's side for a five-month stay, Theodore made himself as gracious as possible to them because they were Edith's sister and mother.[68]

Archie later spoke for the others when he said their childhood left them with "all the memories of a large quarrelsome, fun-loving, & united family," and the Roosevelt children thrived in the security of knowing their parents loved each other. When Edith was away from her husband, she often put herself to sleep recalling their honeymoon, and she wrote him: I "think of our honeymoon days, & remember them all one by one, and hour by hour." For the rest of his life, he wrote her affectionate letters signed "Your own lover."[69]

In the winter when the family crowded together into its rented house in Washington, Edith would often walk her husband to work and have tea ready for him at five, after which he romped with the children. Their Ohio friends Bellamy and Maria Storer introduced them to a former superior court judge who came to town as solicitor general, William Howard Taft, and Will and Theodore often walked to work together. Theodore assumed that Taft had political ambitions like his own, but Taft longed for a spot on the Supreme Court. Edith and Theodore started "going out a great deal" to dinners with an assortment of political and literary people, including the Lodges, Henry Adams, John and Clara Hay, Speaker of the House Tom Reed, artist John La Farge (known for his stained-glass work), and Clarence King, former head of the U.S. Geological Survey.

The Roosevelts sometimes dined with the Hay-Adams-King circle of friends, called the "Five of Hearts," often at the matching houses architect

H. H. Richardson designed for Hay and Adams on Lafayette Square, where Adams had moved after his wife Clover's suicide in 1885. The Roosevelts learned about the exotic travels of La Farge and Adams, who had seen Japan with America's foremost Japanese art expert, Ernest Fenollosa. They became well acquainted, too, with Lodge's Buddhist friend, another Asian art specialist, Dr. William Sturgis Bigelow, who later became TR's tutor in Japanese exercise and history. Clarence King had the West in common with TR; he had mapped vast chunks of the region, and gained fame when he discovered the famed Golconda mine was a hoax.[70]

The Hay-Adams social circle amused the Roosevelts and enlarged their knowledge of the world. Adams, Hay, and King formed a tight circle of loyal friends, but compared to the vibrant young jingo and literary nationalist Theodore Roosevelt, they were decidedly squat in body, older in age and temperament, and more staid and patrician in their views. They published anonymously and were to one degree or another emotional and physical "paralytics"; Roosevelt looked at them as emblematic of a stifled class which made him want to trumpet his every adventure in print to inspire a more heroic America. His, not theirs, would be a strenuous life.[71]

But strenuosity needed restraints. Theodore joked that he needed Lodge and Edith around as foils at dinner parties because his own "tendency to orate" was "only held in check by the memory of the jeers of my wife and intimate friend." Edith found the Hay-Adams circle dinners "stiff" when her husband was absent because his ebullience played off so well against their wit and condescension. Edith found Mrs. Hay lacking in insight into what she read and Hay too full of his own wisdom, yet Adams intrigued her. She observed him walk away from a Shoreham Hotel dinner party given by the Hays because he was bored, and she wished she had the same nerve. His wide and comprehending reading in history, his "jim-jams" or dour moods, his widower's loneliness, and his (most often) unrequited love for the beautiful belle Elizabeth Cameron were no less endearing to Edith than the fact Adams respected her opinions more than those of the man he called "Theodore the Talkative."[72]

TR found John Hay, poet, diplomat, and journalist, "most amusing," and even more endearing because he had been close to his heroes, Thee and Lincoln. But Roosevelt chafed when Hay pontificated too much and treated him like a nephew forever in need of guidance. Theodore thought it unforgivably snobbish of the Hays to want to give their daughter Helen a debut abroad and to marry her off to an Astor connection, Payne Whitney. Theodore, in turn, struck the Hay-Adams circle as an entertaining but dangerous man to have in a drawing room: he had spilled coffee all over the dress of one governor's wife and bumptiously ripped another woman's hem with a clumsy step.[73]

Within the Hay-Adams orbit, TR looked with admiration upon Lizzie Cameron, unhappily wed to the hard-drinking Senator Don Cameron of Pennsylvania. Cameron was the legislative creature of railroad interests, and gossip columnists called the couple the "Beauty and the Beast." Theodore watched Lizzie flirt with Bob Ferguson and his brother Ronald, and agreed she was a singularly appealing beauty.[74] Edith observed that the violet-eyed Nannie Lodge always disliked other pretty women, especially Lizzie Cameron, but Edith found Lizzie the redeeming feature of many gatherings and they took French lessons together. Edith did not know that behind her back Lizzie criticized her for having too many children on a limited income or that Hay and Nannie Lodge had fallen in love and were seeing each other secretly. If she ever looked askance at her husband's admiration of Lizzie or his frequent flirtatious teasing of the woman he called "the Lodge Flower," Edith never let on. There was something so guilelessly demonstrable about her husband's feelings that Edith worried less about losing him to amours than to wars or the cunning of large game animals. And the time would come when the "other woman" who pulled her husband away from the marital hearth was the cheering crowd of voters.[75]

Edith kept up her reading and stayed well informed about public affairs, and she became a part of the women's club movement. Women's clubs sprang up across the country in the late nineteenth century. Women banded together to educate themselves, and often turned next to activism and the "social regeneration" of their country. Rather than line up with the half million middle-class crusaders against male drunkenness in the Woman's Christian Temperance Union, Edith joined a women's lunch club, and for a while she even taught a poetry class to other women. But she said that, "not being a 'new woman,'" she liked to read books about heroines "whose lives are absorbed in loving their husbands."[76]

TR depended upon his wife and counted on her willingness to let what Jane Addams called the "family claim" define her adult life, but he was enthusiastic about other women entering public life. When the Chicago philanthropist Bertha Palmer took charge of organizing the Woman's Building and American women's contribution to the Chicago World's Fair of 1893, Theodore encouraged Bamie to take a post on the Board of Lady Managers from New York. Though leaders in many states predictably celebrated the domestic and refining influence of women, Bamie praised their professional accomplishments in journalism and charity work. She also promoted the

Model Day Nursery at the fair which showed that working mothers could safely leave their children with expert child-care providers, and she chaired New York's Committee on Statistics, which brought new information to light about women workers. After the World's Fair, Bamie's assistant, Florence Lockwood, an advocate of workingwomen's clubs, and her future husband, the architect C. Grant La Farge, would become two of Theodore and Edith's closest friends. TR hunted with Grant and had him put an addition on Sagamore Hill, and he traded books and talked politics with Florence, who with Nannie Lodge, Fanny Parsons, and Martha Selmes became his only close female friends outside the family. He supported Bamie's endeavors enough to go in person to the Census Bureau and Carroll Wright's U.S. Department of Labor Statistics to track down information Bamie sought about women workers.[77]

When Bamie and her close friend Elizabeth Mills Reid, the wife of the owner of the *New York Tribune*, drew heavy press criticism for their day nursery work at the fair, TR got mad enough to talk about horsewhipping the editor. The Chicago World's Fair left a neoclassical architectural heritage in the city which TR and many others greatly admired at the same time it celebrated the nation's imperial potential, especially embodied by the Great White Way of lighted buildings. The fair's legacy for women and their budding political culture was to encourage them to unite to reform their home towns: Roosevelt's career would be altered when, in the wake of the fair, the Woman's Municipal League of New York fought the power of Tammany Hall. In coalition with male Good Government reformers, the Municipal League elected a reform slate led by William L. Strong in 1894. Women reform pioneers (and their male allies) built a model of reform in the 1890s which would shape change in the Progressive Era: expert investigators, often women social workers or male journalists, defined a social problem, won publicity to arouse the public's moral outrage, and then succeeded in getting reform legislation passed. Bamie met Jane Addams in Chicago and forged a link with Hull House women that would prove useful much later in her brother's career.[78]

SOME PUNDITS said TR's aggressive reforms ruined Harrison's chances of reelection. Roosevelt did not think much of the "little gray man in the White House," and when Grover Cleveland took the presidency back from Harrison in 1892, Theodore expected that his job would go to a Democrat. So he offered to resign. But Cleveland remembered their work together in New York and liked him enough to ask him to stay. Having a forthright Republican working for nonpartisan good government helped Cleveland keep his independent-mugwump supporters happy.[79]

Civil service reform, TR saw, was barely putting a dent in corruption. A U.S. Senate seat could still be bought from key state legislators for about $60,000; voting fraud was rampant; the government granted railroads about an eighth of the nation's land, and the president of New York Central Railroad paid over a million dollars to state officials to get a railroad rate bill passed. Graft from building the ornate neoclassical courthouses of the time ran into the millions. Stopping corruption in the Gilded Age proved to be a monumental job. Unintimidated by the magnitude of the problem, TR battled for justice wherever he could. He favored giving women, especially widows, a chance to take civil service tests, and he was furious when the new administration removed black women civil service employees in the Engraving Department without cause. When her husband got worked up too often over the *Evening Post's* criticism of his job performance, Edith worried that the reformer's life was wearing him out.[80]

His job was not his only source of frustration. His career in politics was stalled and he was restless to do bigger work. Corinne remembered seeing her brother with "that 'wistful' look" which turned into "a 'brooding' look" when the reality he faced stood at odds with "what he so strongly wanted it to be." When he imagined his own future, he declared that "a man ought to show he can go out into the world and hold his own with other men." He presented himself to his friends in New York politics as a man who knew logging camps and cow camps; he boasted, "I know the populists and the laboringmen well, and their faults." But he still had a lot to learn about street-corner politics.[81]

By the time he was thirty-three, Roosevelt had published eight books, but he was not satisfied to be a prolific writer. He had to keep writing to supplement his salary while he began to look around for what he would do next. Government work had not paid well. The Roosevelts went through what seemed to them like a "season of grinding poverty," which proved to be a nightmare to Edith. Keeping up two homes and traveling back and forth, not to mention supplying the wants of a large family, cost more than he was earning. By the end of 1893 he found their expenses had exceeded their income by $2,500, and he talked again about having to give up Sagamore Hill. He wrote Bamie: "My career has been a very pleasant, honorable and useful career for a man of means; but not the right career for a man without means." After he finished the next two volumes of *The Winning of the West*, he confessed he was "all at sea as to what I shall do afterwards." As if his career's stagnation, his relative financial distress, and the pain of long absences from his family were not enough, Theodore faced an agonizing dilemma because he did not know what to do about Elliott, who was slowly drinking himself to death.[82]

As early as 1890 he learned through friends that his brother had been drinking heavily and was traveling with a woman who was not his wife. Theodore reported it to Bamie with sarcastic disapproval: "Nice man, our brother." In 1891, after Elliott became so drunk and irrational that his pregnant wife, Anna, could not deal with him, Bamie hurried to see them in Europe, and tried to talk sense to him, but she wrote to Corinne that Elliott had become "utterly impossible." He insisted on his right to drink and spend as much as he wanted, and he refused to let Anna stop to rest during train trips as her doctor ordered. Then Katy Mann, a family servant, contacted Uncle Jim Roosevelt and asked for money because she was pregnant with Elliott's child. At first Theodore was inclined to believe his brother was innocent and offered to fight the suit she threatened in court. He would risk the "public scandal" if Elliott could promise him he had not been intimate with Katy Mann. But Elliott's history of using opiates and alcohol was well enough known in New York that he could not represent himself in court as a credible witness. When family members saw the baby, they recognized the truth. Theodore and Bamie agreed to pay what Katy Mann requested.[83]

Bamie reported that Anna was afraid of Elliott, and his drunken rages began again. Before long he became abusive toward his family. Edith understood the terrible experience Bamie was having trying to protect Anna and the children, and she wrote Bamie: "I have locked away the letters you wrote Theodore as to little Eleanor," which hints at abuse worse than violent rages that Eleanor may have endured from her father. Theodore refused to discuss the tragedy, because, as Edith remarked to Bamie, "He is not a nature who ever cares to talk over painful subjects." She urged Bamie to send Eleanor to spend the summer at Sagamore Hill, where she would be safe, but Bamie did not. Theodore cautioned Bamie to "keep a look out that he doesn't try to kidnap one of the children."[84]

In January 1892, TR went to France to extract promises from his brother that he would change his ways, but he returned convinced that Elliott was "out of his head." Edith and Theodore were shocked when the flighty Anna wrote that she and Elliott hoped to have more children. They agreed with Bamie that Elliott had to be put under the care of a responsible doctor. Finally, Theodore and Bamie, against the wishes of Aunt Annie and Corinne, petitioned for a writ of lunacy to have Elliott declared incompetent. After he had medical treatment, they put him into probationary exile in Virginia until he could prove he was sober and reliable enough to be reunited with his family.[85]

Theodore hated the fact the newspapers found out about the scandal, but he was more outraged that his brother had degenerated into a "dangerous maniac" who was "absolutely lacking in moral sense," a creature whose "moral depravity" was so great that it was not safe to allow Eleanor and the other children to see him unsupervised. "Anna has no moral right to condone his offences by again living with him," Theodore told Bamie, and he judged Anna's forgiving loyalty to her husband as "little short of criminal." Many Victorians believed that immorality could be transmitted to the next generation, and TR wrote Bamie that it was "dreadful to think of the inheritance" that lurked inside Anna's baby. For Theodore, Elliott's decline remained like a "brooding nightmare" throughout the early nineties.[86]

Theodore had once admired and envied his brother's heartiness, writing in *The Wilderness Hunter* that Elliott was a "well-grown, strong, and healthy . . . boy who deemed it unmanly to make any especial note of hardship or suffering." Now Elliott specialized in self-pity. He called the probation "wicked and foolish" and made irresponsible promises to little Eleanor about being together again someday. Elliott allowed his alienist (mental health practitioner) bills to be sent to his brother and claimed he had suffered more than Anna. Finally, he threatened suicide.[87]

When confronted by Theodore about becoming incompetent to work or care for his family or himself, Elliott broke down sobbing. In the fall he stayed with Aunt Annie at Gracewood, just down the road from Sagamore Hill, and he had a polite tea with Edith and Theodore. Eleanor visited her aunt and uncle in October, but they discouraged Elliott from seeing her or coming up from Virginia when Anna had an operation and then died of diphtheria in December.[88]

After her mother's death Eleanor and her brother lived with their grandmother Mary Ludlow Hall not far from Hyde Park, and Bamie warned Mrs. Hall not to let Elliott see his children at all. Edith held the opinion that nine-year-old Eleanor had been ruined by her family's tragedy: "I do not feel she has much of a chance poor little soul." Elliott moved back to New York, and became so delusional that he imagined armies coming after him and he tried to hit his mistress with a stick. One day he drove by Mrs. Hall's Manhattan townhouse in a hansom cab and Eleanor's governess let the child get into the cab with him. Afterward, even his staunch defender Corinne reprimanded Mrs. Hall never to let Eleanor be alone with Elliott again. Elliott died a lonely death on August 14, 1894, and when Theodore came to see his brother's body, Corinne said, "He was more overcome than I have ever seen him—cried like a little child for a long time." Eleanor said only, "I did want to see father once more," and she made the best of a dour and loveless existence living with her grandmother Hall. Mrs. Hall offered the girl a life among her own alcoholic sons, whose drunkenness required Eleanor to keep three locks on her bedroom door. Mrs. Hall was not cooperative when Bamie, Corinne,

Edith, Aunt Annie, and Theodore tried to influence Eleanor's upbringing, and Bamie briefly considered suing for custody of the child. But Aunt Annie saw Eleanor often, and the visits and long-distance affection she got from her father's siblings counted for something important in her upbringing, and the bond remained strong.[89]

In December 1893, Bamie heard that her old friend Helen Astor Roosevelt had died, leaving her husband (Franklin's half brother), James "Rosy" Roosevelt, a widower. Bamie saw in this tragedy a chance to help her distant cousin keep up his duties as first secretary of the American embassy in England and manage the care of his two children. When Bamie left to serve as Rosy's hostess and as surrogate mother for his daughter, Helen, and her brother, James, Theodore admitted he was "decidedly sad" and would miss his sister greatly. Bamie quickly made friends in diplomatic and aristocratic circles, and this enabled her to be Theodore and Cabot Lodge's informal diplomatic channel to Britain and the ambassador to the Court of St. James's, Thomas Bayard. She quietly worked to soften Bayard's opposition to the joint trusteeship of the Samoan Islands, which TR and Lodge supported, and she cultivated a bond with Sir Edward Grey, then under secretary of state for foreign affairs, who later became Theodore's valued friend and his behind-the-scenes connection with Britain's World War I cabinet. During the Cleveland administration's gold crisis, when TR and many others blamed England for blocking an international agreement which might have helped the United States restore silver to its earlier value, he wrote Bamie urging her to convey Lodge's ideas about bimetallism to America's friends in England.[90]

As she made friends for him, Bamie kept her brother in touch with the news from London. Edith's friend Teresa Richardson told her that Ambassador Bayard lacked respect in London diplomatic circles, and TR wrote Cabot that "she also gently implies that Rosy's position is chiefly due to what Bamie has done." Bamie's influence was all the more amazing because among the many physical disabilities she would have to bear before her life was over, the most socially debilitating one, deafness, had already taken hold.[91]

Bamie left her brother dumbfounded when she announced she was engaged to the embassy's divorced naval attaché William Sheffield Cowles, whom the family saw as "a dear, humdrum sort of person." TR hated to face the possible loss of his older sister's complete devotion to him, and the array of people for whom Bamie had also been a substitute mother—Alice, Eleanor, Bob Ferguson, Rosy Roosevelt, Helen Roosevelt, Corinne, and even Edith—shared some of the same sense of loss when she married Cowles in November 1895.[92]

Bamie reassured her brother that their relationship and her largesse toward him would not end: he and Edith could still use her house on Madison Avenue. Theodore found in his new brother-in-law, Will Cowles, a good if phlegmatic listener. Like TR, Will was a strong advocate of an enlarged navy, and he was completely loyal and devoted to Bamie and her family.[93]

WHILE ROOSEVELT stagnated at the Civil Service Commission, his country entered the worst depression so far in its history. Banks and businesses failed and unemployment lines grew longer. National leaders in Washington seemed not to care. On May Day in 1894, while the Senate debated TR's project, a bird and game preserve in Yellowstone Park, Jacob Coxey's ragtag "Army" of thousands of unemployed people marched to the Capitol. They asked Congress to hire men without jobs to build much needed roads until the depression ended. Marchers had come from as far away as Seattle. Some were captured as they headed east and put in makeshift prisoner-of-war camps by the U.S. Army; some stragglers like Jack London dropped out along the way. The peaceful but bedraggled crew who stayed with Coxey to the end assumed that in a democracy the government had to listen to the people. They were mistaken. Coxey's bill had been endorsed by the American Federation of Labor and introduced in both houses of Congress, but when Coxey began to speak at the Capitol he was arrested for walking on the grass. Little came from his long march.[94]

Like other patricians, TR assumed the worst of demonstrators and strikers, and he blamed the violence of the Haymarket Riot and the Great Railroad Strike of 1877 on strikers, not state troops or policemen. He agreed with his wealthy neighbors like the Vanderbilts who donated large sums to build the Seventh Avenue Armory in case class warfare broke out.

However, 1894 marked a major turning point in public perception of labor activism. The Pullman Company, a manufacturer of railroad passenger cars, cut its employees' wages but did not reduce the rents they paid in company housing. When George Pullman said he had "nothing to arbitrate," he was backed up by a formidable national organization of employers. In response, railroad unions stopped work and other unions organized sympathy strikes and boycotts. Soon transportation around the country was disrupted, and riots and fires charred the site of the Chicago World's Fair, leaving dark clouds over its grand vision of the nation's future. The Pullman strike had become a national crisis.

For much of that year Roosevelt played tennis regularly with railroad lawyer and attorney general Richard Olney, who convinced President Cleveland to use an omnibus injunction under the Sherman Anti-Trust Act to justify sending federal troops to quash the strike. Federal marshals invaded union offices, read union leader Eugene Debs' personal mail, and charged labor officials all over the country with obstructing federal mails. Illinois governor John Altgeld resisted federal intervention and blamed George Pullman for letting the families of his striking employees starve. The governor called for donations to keep workers alive, but newspapers shaped public opinion more than Altgeld. Much of the press routinely portrayed the strikers as violent mobs, but organized labor began to get a hearing. Americans did not agree about the ultimate meaning of the Pullman strike, but observers like Jane Addams called for renewed efforts to make both parties listen to each other and thereby rebuild the national community. The strike helped to make the moderate A.F.L. look respectable compared to the more assertive American Railway Union. Most significantly, George Pullman had been exposed as a cruel employer who would not talk to his workers.[95]

At first, TR saw the Pullman strike only in terms of urban disorder: he praised federal suppression of the strikers and denounced Governor Altgeld as a man who had harmed his country as much as Benedict Arnold. But then he reconsidered his view. He criticized "the mere money-getting American" in a magazine article and railed against types like Pullman, "the narrow, hard, selfish merchant or manufacturer who deliberately sets himself to work to keep the laborers he employs in a condition of dependence which will render them helpless to combine against him."[96]

TR did not come easily to his new position on labor and capital. During much of the depression of 1893–98 he had been in closer sympathy with boardrooms and landlords than workers. The suffering of laborers did not hit close to home. Hard times hurt people like the Roosevelts very little because they were the owners, not employees. Theodore's Uncle Jim and distant cousin James Roosevelt, Franklin D. Roosevelt's father, were fighting "shoulder to shoulder" to gain control of the Delaware and Hudson Railroad, a victory they won with the help of their allies in the Vanderbilt family. Edith inherited $30,000 from her uncle John during the depression and the interest helped her pay overdue bills. When Edith and Theodore were pressed for cash again, uncle Jim found a few thousand to give Theodore from his father's estate. In Roosevelt and Son and in Edith and Theodore's own private landholdings, the most direct effect of the depression was that there was a dearth of tenants to rent their property in lower Manhattan. Yet TR no longer saw the world only from the viewpoint of his own privileged economic class.[97]

While he wrestled with these issues, mourned over Elliott, and agonized over his own stalled career, Theodore's health grew more troublesome. He had a long bout of laryngitis in 1894 which prompted Edith to have a doctor spray his throat. His asthma attacks and other ailments were severe enough to confine him to the house. Each winter his bronchitis refused to go away, and that year it lasted so long and got so bad that he left work to take a pleasure trip. With his sportsman friend Austin Wadsworth, he went to Aiken, South Carolina, where he foxhunted, played polo, and raced. Back home, his cough came back within weeks, so Edith had him breathe pastilles and applied mustard plasters to his chest.[98]

When his illness would not subside, Theodore's cousin Dr. James West Roosevelt and Dr. Murray, a specialist, tried to unravel what was wrong. Edith wrote to Bamie:

> Dr. Murray holds to his opinion that all Theodore's difficulties originate with the heart and neurogastric nerve (I think this is right). He thinks owing to his very active life the heart is enlarged. He does not consider it at all serious, but evidently thinks all violent exercise a mistake which is diametrically opposed to West's opinion. He is giving Theodore digisaline. Theodore is really doing very well. Do not be anxious.[99]

More than a year later, Theodore complained that Edith "persists in regarding me as a frail invalid needing constant attention"; her "sensitive plant" took umbrage at her solicitous care and yet basked in her love. Lodge told him bluntly: "You need it."[100]

He had been her "sensitive plant" for eight years. Together they had made Sagamore Hill a home and produced four children to join Alice. TR's fruitful marriage had created a domestic world closer to the ideal of domesticity in the children's literature they had read together than what they had known as children. Edith proved his point that "the really able, intellectual, cultivated women have as a rule made the best wives and mothers; on the whole better mothers than the servile woman makes, and infinitely better than the vain, frivolous, shallow, tricky type which is not intellectual at all." Even before he had married Edith he had submerged his invalid self and built his body and his character to prove himself not just another upper-class wastrel. Edith had allied herself with Lodge, who guided Theodore into national politics. But most of all, she helped her husband grow up and regulate his nervousness and swings of emotion so that he could do effective work in the larger world. With her encouragement to live up to their ideals of "civic helpfulness" he had made himself much more than a patrician reformer. He had grown in compassion and understanding, even if she had not taught him to love Shakespeare or understand Chaucer. He had turned himself into a recognized historian and a good storyteller with a distinct moral viewpoint.[101]

Within the security and warmth of his second marriage, he made himself a substantial public servant with more potential for growth. As one of Theodore's college friends wrote to Edith: "You were indispensable to his full development. He would have been less, but for you. We old friends always knew this and we were silently grateful to you." He struggled against her severity at times, but he was grateful for what she had done for him, too. When friends of the Roosevelt children heard TR call her "Edith," they thought it "sounded particularly beautiful" because of the "tenderness" in his voice. Now she and Cabot prepared to help him find larger arenas where he could live up to all that they knew he could achieve. She was confident her husband would soon prove himself to be a "great man."[102]

☆ CHAPTER FIVE ☆

Soldier at the Moral Frontier and at War

THEODORE ROOSEVELT needed a larger arena to develop his talents, and he found it soon enough. The Good Government Clubs of New York and the Committee of Seventy, with the backing of prominent Republicans, urged him to run again for mayor of New York City in 1894. His prospects for winning were much better than in 1886. A large fusion movement had been energized by the crusading Reverend Charles Parkhurst and the Woman's Municipal League. The reform movement gained momentum from public outrage over the findings of the Lexow Committee. Clarence Lexow told the shocked public that prostitution in New York was conducted for the profit of the police via bribes from saloons and concert halls, and Parkhurst warned that the city under Tammany rule was governed by "a lying, perjuring, rum-soaked, libidinous lot of polluted harpies" who fed on New York's "quivering vitals." The time was ripe for a brave reformer. Corinne strongly urged her brother to run.[1]

But when he discussed it with Edith she was not encouraging. She did not want to leave Washington or face the prospect that he would be unemployed as soon as he was voted out of office. Based on his perception of her disapproval, TR suddenly withdrew his name and left on a western trip. As he ruminated over his decision, it rankled him and he blamed Edith. She wrote to Bamie:

> Theodore has been so sweet and good, but I cannot begin to describe how terribly I feel at having failed him at such an important time. It is just as I said to you he never should have married me, and then would have been free to take his own course. . . . I never realized for a minute how he felt over this, or that the mayoralty stood for so much to him, and I did not know either just in what way the nomination was offered; in fact I do not know now for I did not like to ask too much. I am too thankful that he is

> away now for I am utterly unnerved and a prey to the deepest despair, so that poor good Uncle Jimmie is the best companion I can have for he sees and knows nothing. I do not mean that I reproach myself with having made Theodore's decision for I never said anything until I thought it entirely formed, only if I knew what I do now I should have thrown all my influence in the scale with Corinne's and helped instead of hindering him. You say that I dislike to give my opinion. This is a lesson that will last my life, never to give it for it is utterly worthless when given,—worse than that in this case for it has helped to spoil some years of a life which I would have given my own for. I shall be myself again by Saturday when the darling gets back.[2]

On his hunting trip signs of his failing cattle venture caused Theodore to be "blue" and his run-down ranch and broken rocking chair made him "more melancholy than ever."[3]

Edith's "darling" returned to Sagamore Hill, where undercurrents of anger showed between them. After what she called "our worst evening," things got better and the tension "had not been quite as bad as I feared it might be." He wrote regretfully to Bamie that running for mayor was "the one golden chance which never returns." Hearing their distress, Bamie came back to America for a short visit and saw that the haggard Edith needed a change of scene, so she took her and the five young Roosevelts off to vacation in Vermont.[4]

Theodore told Lodge that the early fall had been "pretty bitter" for him, but he visited old friends in Boston. Even that was not all happy because Hal Minot had been killed in a train accident. Edith said her husband's travels had been "good tonics" to him as he returned to civil service work, which now seemed to him like "starting to go through Harvard again after graduating."[5]

His regret about the mayoralty race heightened when the reform candidate, William L. Strong, won election in November. Strong offered TR the street cleaning commissioner's job so that he could improve the system of sanitation in New York and make it nonpartisan. TR was tempted because he cared a lot about urban issues: he favored playgrounds for the poor, modern sanitation, rapid transit, and nonsectarian public schools. But street cleaning—with sixty thousand horses depositing tons of manure and urine each day on city streets—lacked romance, to say the least. TR said Lodge was keeping "a close eye on all my movements" and had advised him to wait for a better offer. As Lodge began aggressive management of his friend's political ascent, he urged Roosevelt to "go actively into the Presidential campaign" as a party speaker in 1896 and thereby build a national reputation.[6]

In December 1894, TR was confined to his room by his doctors when his bronchitis returned full force, and by Christmas he described Edith as ill and "thoroughly done out." Tensions between them over the mayor's race had faded, but neither brimmed over with marital bliss. After Theodore read an article by Bob Ferguson about visiting Eskimos and shooting reindeer, they began talking about making a trip to Alaska. The promise of shared adventure rewarmed their nest, even though their trip proved impossible.[7]

As 1895 began, Roosevelt became one of the first Americans to ski regularly (he called his skis Norwegian snowshoes). He started once more to enjoy the social life of Washington and "to deal with big interests, and big men." Mayor Strong, prompted by TR's friend Lemuel Quigg, indicated he would offer Roosevelt a position on the city's Police Commission, if he would accept. But TR was too dispirited about his career to jump at the chance.[8]

Edith enlisted Lodge's help. She fretted that in his current mood her husband was "much more interested in having Wister and Remington to dinner on Friday" than in taking the police job. She did not dare give Theodore direct advice this time. Instead, she urged Lodge to write him. Lodge did more than she asked. He went to New York and conferred with Mayor Strong, Quigg, Douglas Robinson, and TR's other political friends. Though Roosevelt insisted the job held no power, Lodge convinced him it was the next step forward and a place to do good work. So Theodore took the position.[9]

Whenever he started a new job TR threw himself into the work with his whole heart. On May 6, 1895, he bolted into police headquarters at 300 Mulberry Street determined to make the Police Commission an instrument of reform. The corrupt chief, Thomas F. Byrnes, told TR he had no chance to reform the system: "It will break you. You will yield. You are but human." TR countered with a threat of a public investigation into Byrnes' finances. Byrnes charged brothels and saloons "protection fees" of about $20 to $100 a month and amassed a fortune in real estate from bribes. After Roosevelt got enough proof, Chief Byrnes retired early.[10]

Next, TR got rid of Inspector "Clubber" Williams, famous for being too free with his nightstick. As the new president of the Police Commission, Roosevelt liked to tell himself he held "undisputed sway" over police affairs, but he was only one member of a four-man board which required a unanimous vote to act on many questions. He did not always get what he wanted. Roosevelt had an honest yes-man, Peter Conlin, appointed chief of police so that he could act as "the real chief." He took over many executive functions, such as supervising the cop on the beat. Knowing Mayor Strong had chosen him, above all, to confront the endemic vice and police corruption the Lexow

Report had exposed, TR applied his prodigious energies to watching what happened in every precinct and street corner in Manhattan.[11]

Each day, after taking the Long Island Railroad from Oyster Bay or leaving the care of Bamie's butler, Chamberlain, Roosevelt walked briskly or rode his bicycle to Mulberry Street. There he counted on the help of his new friend Jacob Riis, a Danish immigrant who had known poverty and homelessness firsthand before he became the police reporter for the *Evening Sun.* Roosevelt had sought out Riis after he wrote *How the Other Half Lives* in 1890 and offered to help him fight poor living conditions. As America's pioneer photojournalist, Riis showed interior scenes of crowded tenements to privileged readers, and his exposé helped fuel Parkhurst's crusade to reform city government. Riis encouraged TR to take a broad view of police reform as a city service for the poor as well as the rich. As a police reporter, Riis gathered facts to incite change. After watching tenement fires snuff out hundreds of lives, Riis discovered that bakeries on the ground floors of tenements often spread fire to residents on higher floors. So he convinced the city to zone bakeries out of tenements altogether. His resort to scientific fact when he found excess nitrites from sewage leaking into the city's water supply prevented a cholera epidemic. Riis became TR's most important ally in doing police work, and he changed forever the way Roosevelt saw his home town.[12]

Riis could show the new commissioner the city as no one else could, and he meant to show him more than crime. He recalled that TR wanted to learn everything about how the city lived at night, its sights and sounds as well as its human landscapes. The irony of a recent immigrant showing a native New Yorker the city where he was born reminded both of them that the Knickerbocker in evening clothes and pink shirts knew the club world of the Union League better than he knew the piers in the shadow of the Brooklyn Bridge or the shops of Delancey Street.[13]

Riis could guide Roosevelt to opium dens, abandoned children who lived under wharves, Mulberry Bend which "reeked with incest and murder," commercialized vice of all kinds in the Tenderloin, stripteases in concert halls and "mixed-race resorts," painted male prostitutes at American Mabille, and legions of ill-fed families whose dream of opportunity in a new land had proven to be a mirage. The reporter helped the commissioner see what cruel environments the poor inhabited and how the city's wealthy profited from high rents that overcrowded tenements brought. With Riis as his right-hand man Roosevelt learned the names and faces of the immigrant families who sewed shirts at home or peddled rags or fruit on the street.[14]

His friendship with Riis had a less competitive quality than his bond with Lodge, but it was another relationship that helped TR grow politically.

Theodore Roosevelt Senior,
Thee, TR's father

Martha Bulloch Roosevelt,
Mittie, TR's mother

Margaret Barnhill Roosevelt,
TR's grandmother

Cornelius Van Schaack (C.V.S.) Ro
TR's grandfather, one of the richest
New York

Robert Barnwell Roosevelt,
Uncle Rob

James Alfred Roosevelt,
Uncle Jim

Margaret Stewart Elliott Bulloch,
TR's grandmother

Anna Bulloch Gracie,
TR's aunt and earliest teacher

James Dunwody Bulloch, Confederate
agent and blockade runner

Theodore Roosevelt, around age two

Theodore at age seven

Irvine Bulloch, TR's uncle

TR sculling at Harvard

Hal, Henry Davis Minot, TR's close friend

Bamie and Baby Lee, February 1886

Alice Hathaway Lee Roosevelt

Edith Kermit Carow, TR's childhood friend, in 186

Clockwise: Theodore, Elliott, Corinne, and Edith, 1875, Oyster Bay

Anna (Nannie) Cabot Mills Lodge

Henry Cabot Lodge, Sr., senator, TR's mentor and foreign policy advisor

Jacob Riis, TR, and Bishop John Vincent, founder of Chautauqua. Riis taught TR about the problems new immigrants faced.

Roosevelt campaigning for McKinley with a Union veteran from the audience

Frederic Remington portrayed Roosevelt's charge up Kettle Hill.

An easterner turned western cowboy

Colonel Leonard Wood and Lieutenant Colonel Roosevelt and the Rough Riders

Mother taking Ethel, Kermit, Ted, and Alice to swim at Fleet's Pond, near Sagamore Hill

The Roosevelt family in 1895: TR, Archie, Ted, Alice, Kermit, Edith, and Ethel

Elliott and Eleanor at Old Saybrook

TR teaching Roosevelt cousins to play football, Ted and Alice in the foreground

Gifford Pinchot, chief forester, conservation advisor to TR

Cornelia Pinchot, Republican suffrage strategist

"Gentleman! The Senate will come to order." A cartoon from the New York World, *March 4, 1901*

'ice President Roosevelt tells reporters about President McKinley's condition outside the Milburn house

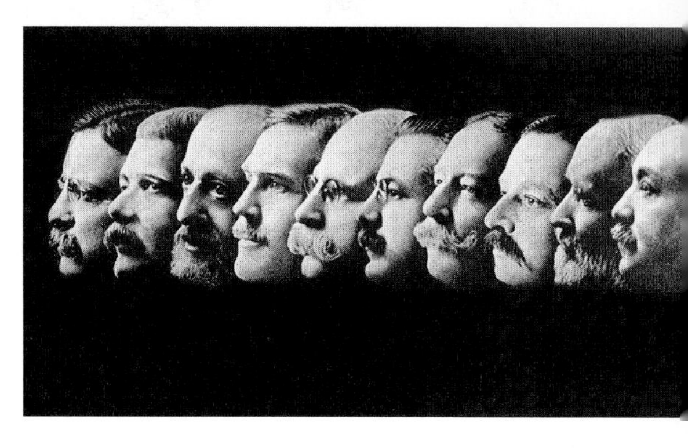

Above: Roosevelt and his cabinet—TR, Root, Straus, Garfield, Metcalf, Cortelyou, Taft, Meyer, Wilson, Bonaparte

Left: President Roosevelt in his office

The Tennis Cabinet (left to right): Captain Archibald Butt; William Phillips, assistant secretary of state; Herb Smith, commissioner of corporations; Beekman Winthrop, assistant secretary of the treasury; Gifford Pinchot, ch Forestry Service; Lawrence O. Murray, comptroller; Henry L. Stimson, district attorney; Herbert Satterlee, assis retary of the navy; John J. McIlhenny, civil service commissioner; Judge John C. Rose; Truman H. Newberry, sec the navy; Mr. George Woodruff, counsel to the Forestry Service; M. Jusserand, French ambassador; Mr. C. E finger; George von L. Meyer, postmaster general; Francis Leupp, commissioner of Indian affairs; Mr. Justice James R. Garfield, secretary of the interior; Marshall Seth Bullock; Solicitor General Hoyt; John C. Abernath Kelly, Indian agent; Robert Bacon, secretary of state; C. P. Neill, labor commissioner; William D. Sewall, collect toms; D. J. Keefe, commissioner of immigration; John C. O'Laughlin, assistant secretary of state; J. B. Reynold C. Pritchett; William Loeb, Jr., secretary to the President

Through Riis, the settlement house founder and visiting nurse organizer Lillian Wald enlisted TR to be an honorary member of the American Hero Club for ten- and eleven-year-old East Side boys. On one winter night Riis and Roosevelt went together to have dinner with Graham Wallas, the British Fabian socialist, at Wald's Henry Street Settlement. At the same dinner, Roosevelt greeted Felix Adler, housing reformer and founder of the Ethical Culture Society; William Dean Howells, the realist author; Seth Low, president of Columbia University and future mayor; and his old friends Brander Matthews and Richard Watson Gilder. On their way to Wald's dinner Roosevelt talked to a fruit peddler about how he made ends meet. At the dinner TR enjoyed imitating how the Italian "shrugged" and told him: "No good, no good. What I maka on de peanuta I lose on de dam' banan'." Wald recalled that TR learned more about politics from the individual people he met than from his vast reading.[15]

When Riis joined TR for midnight patrols to see if the police were covering their beats well, they had a larger agenda than checking up on the men in blue. They sought publicity. Riis and Roosevelt disguised themselves in black cloaks to see the sights of the city unheeded, but newspapermen tagged along and immortalized TR as a stealthy caliph Harun-al-Rashid from *The Arabian Nights*. On one early patrol Riis took TR along First, Second, and Third Avenues, where they found one policeman asleep on a butter barrel and quite a few absent from their beats. Commissioner Roosevelt, with reporter Richard Harding Davis and Riis in tow, discovered a patrolman evading his duty seated in an oyster bar. When TR asked him why he was not on his beat the patrolman got mad and told him off. The next day Roosevelt demoted the oyster bar dawdler, and word spread fast through the police force that the commissioner knew how to find loafers. He became such a local celebrity that whistles in the shape of "Roosey's teeth" were peddled on the streets of New York as novelties and the sight of the teeth alone could alarm cops. Davis, Riis, and reporter-novelist Stephen Crane dramatized TR's exploits for newspaper readers. He was even immortalized as a vaudeville character in a satire starring the famous actress Lillian Russell called *The Geezer* playing in Weber and Fields' Music Hall.[16]

Another time at two on a rainy night Riis took TR to the Church Street Police Lodging House, where he had stayed years before when he was a new homeless immigrant. Riis told Roosevelt about the epidemic of typhus that spread through lodging houses and how roughly he had been handled by a policeman. TR promptly closed all the police lodging facilities and set up a new system of municipal lodging houses, which was what Riis had wanted for years.[17]

Roosevelt's midnight patrols left him sleepy because he rarely stopped for a nap before he went to work the following morning. Edith disapproved of his grueling forty-hour patrol days, but she felt proud that when he took a cab home one night from an East Side meeting and he saw a policeman sitting down, smoking, rather than patrolling, he "sprang from the cab & administered a rebuke on the spot." Though they came from different worlds, Edith warmed up to Jacob and Elisabeth Riis when Theodore brought them home; it was clear to her that the little gray-haired immigrant with an accent worshipped her husband and expected the best of him. Her assessment proved correct: Riis once punched a man for speaking ill of TR.[18]

Edith had moved the children to Bamie's house on Madison Avenue and then to Sagamore Hill in May 1895, and she said that she could give up the pleasant life she had known in Washington more easily because it meant no long separations from her husband. Theodore rarely stayed in Manhattan more than a few nights a week and came home to Oyster Bay the rest of the time. She was especially glad not to have long separations from her husband because she was upset about her mother's death that April.

Commissioner Roosevelt was making a success of his police work, and his exuberant vitality made the public applaud him as a new crusading force in New York politics. Honest policemen liked him, too. He gave medals for gallantry—rewarding mounted horse policemen who stopped runaway carriages, patrolmen who stopped toughs who were beating up a peddler, or cops who saved people from burning buildings. He insisted on competitive sealed bids for contractors and stringent fiscal management. He replaced a hiring system of bribes and political cronyism with civil service exams. He also set standards for hiring taller, stronger, heavier, and smarter policemen. TR put on the police force a number of Jewish policemen because of their fluency in Yiddish and their understanding of life on the Lower East Side. When he was asked to stop an anti-Semitic preacher from giving a public speech to begin a crusade against Jews, he refused to interfere with the minister's right to free speech. Instead, he sent an entirely Jewish police contingent to keep order as "an object lesson" to teach people how foolish their prejudices were.[19]

TR did not confine himself to keeping the police clean. He served on the Health Board, too. In his assembly years he had explored tenements with Samuel Gompers to look for the hazards of turning them into places of work. Now with Riis he inspected tenements as a place to raise children. The worst rear apartments were so unhealthy that they produced a nearly one-third infant mortality rate. During hot summer nights children had nowhere to go because it was like an oven inside and there were few parks outside. In the middle of one heat wave so many horses died that the city could not remove them all, and children played among the carcasses. Riis told Roosevelt that children were coming out of saloons with mugs of beer, so they got a child to help them catch the saloonkeeper in lawbreaking. Based on Riis' information, Roosevelt also had the city seize sixteen of the unhealthiest tenements and tear them down.

The "vile crime and hideous vice" police had to confront disgusted Roosevelt. The "twilight phases of New York life" taught him the police needed to be "always on [their] guard." The moralist in him saw his police work as a fight to clean up vice to promote the advance of civilization and decency.[20]

His most controversial campaign began with his decision to enforce the state law requiring the Sunday closing of saloons. Roosevelt wanted to stop policemen from collecting bribes from bars. When a cop walked into a saloon it was often to receive a bribe for not enforcing the Sunday closing law or a small payment from the barkeep for not arresting the prostitutes or gamblers who worked upstairs. TR wanted to break the power of the liquor syndicates and the Tammany politicians in business with them. When he chose the saloon for his attack, he waged war on illicit ties between saloons and police as well as the bonds between the liquor business and Tammany Hall.

But his Sunday closing campaign was also a rich Protestant's war against the favorite recreation of poor immigrant men, many of them Catholics. Saloons functioned as civic centers for immigrant neighborhoods; they offered a polling place, the cheapest and safest drinks city dwellers could get, loans, advice, telephones, funerals for transients forgotten by everyone else, food, a lodging house, and recreation in the form of gambling, dancing, stripteases, and prostitution. Saloons were the workingmen's clubs, the heart of their sociability in a tough city.

Sunday drinking among immigrants had bothered moral reformers for years; Protestants also sought to create a more respectable and godly bourgeois society by winning Sunday restrictions on baseball games and rail service. Reformers attacked demon rum as "soul poison" and saloons as the hellish center of the "whore-making, criminal-making, madman-making business." The Prohibition Party and the Anti-Saloon League, with help from the Woman's Christian Temperance Union, won state and local dry laws and waged third-party challenges all over America. By the end of the nineties the issue of drink had polarized politics so much that in places where the Republican Party had defended restriction on drinking Democrats won new votes.[21]

TR wanted to use government to impose morals upon commerce but he had to walk a fine line because he saw prohibitionists as one-issue zealots who could threaten Republican victories. Instead of addressing the economic inequality which Populists and labor advocates saw as America's biggest problem, Roosevelt and Protestant reformers across the land pioneered on the "moral frontier," where they warred to improve the behavior of the wayward folk.[22]

At the same moment in 1895 that Frances Willard presented an uncomprehending President Grover Cleveland with a temperance petition signed by seven million people from around the world, TR listened to the tenor of his times and heeded the middle classes' concerns about moral reform. When he defended his Sunday closing policy in an article in the muckraking journal *McClure's Magazine* he agreed with temperance advocates that excessive drinking hurt the poor most and that the liquor industry spread "criminality" among the citizenry. To dramatize his Sunday closing campaign for the public, Roosevelt knew he needed a villain—the saloon where prostitution increased the profits earned by the liquor industry.[23]

He crusaded against "the violent tendencies of uncontrolled manhood" that saloons encouraged. He made surprise raids on houses of prostitution accompanied by Bob Ferguson, Stephen Crane, or Jacob Riis, and he boldly arrested customers, or johns, and prostitutes alike as well as brothel owners and operators. TR advocated the publication of the customers' names and harsh punishments for brothel owners. He also favored sending young girls new to the business to reformatories rather than prisons. He believed he had no choice but to hire plainclothesmen to pose as customers in brothels but he was criticized for entrapment. He confessed: "It is not a pleasant thing to deal with criminals and purveyors of vice." Newspapers attacked him but most of the city's ministers supported his war on vice. Cartoonists portrayed Roosevelt as a Puritan and even Mayor Strong joked about the Police Commission's puritanical tendencies. TR was called a nativist who favored "class legislation" and "hurting the poor man."[24]

At moments of high tension in the Sunday closing campaign, TR returned to the scenes of his youth, often with Riis, searching for inspiration in his father's memory. Though not superstitious, TR felt so strongly about his father's good influence on him that he had kept his father's letters near him "as Talismans against evil." He went out to his family's old summer place near Madison, New Jersey, where he had met John Hay, and he took Riis to Miss Sattery's Night School for Little Italians, where his father had made him help. Like Thee, he drove a "high phaeton" and wrote Bamie that it was like the one Thee drove at his age.

Riis had listened to his friend associate his own life and work with his father's, and collected stories about Thee for a magazine article. In it, he asserted: "It is not always an easy thing to keep the two Theodores apart." Riis wrote that Thee's worries about paupers and tenements and boys who had no safe place to grow up were the basis of his son's agendas. As Theodore struggled above all else to prove himself worthy to his dead father, he told Riis more than once, "How I wish father were here and could see it!"[25]

He was not the only crusader raiding brothels. Private preventative societies saw themselves as an "urban posse," and in that capacity already conducted busts on brothels and saloons. So the police commissioner's challenge was to develop a cooperative relationship with them and to assert the primacy of the government's authority to enforce the law. He made a point of befriending the Reverend Parkhurst, whose City Vigilance League made citizens' arrests when they found police corruption, and TR sent his officers to investigate Parkhurst's pet peeves. In turn, Parkhurst funded some of TR's anti-prostitution campaigns. Elbridge Gerry's Society for the Prevention of Cruelty to Children went after child seducers (New York had just raised the age of consent to eighteen), brothels that trafficked in children, and saloonkeepers who hired children to deliver "growlers" (buckets of beer). TR ordered his policemen to help Gerry and the S.P.C.C. At the same time, Anthony Comstock's Society for the Suppression of Vice raided pornography houses, saloons, homosexual gathering places, and brothels, but TR knew from Thee's friends who were still funding Comstock (Morris Jesup and William E. Dodge, Jr.) that the crusader was a law unto himself. Comstock wielded an ax and packed a rifle. He usurped police authority with federal permission because he had been given broad authority by the Comstock law of 1873 to stop birth control information and obscene materials from being sent through the federal mails. Roosevelt found it easier to send his bicycle squads to stop runaway horses than to curb the city's moral vigilantes.[26]

Nor was it easy to win unanimous support for his campaigns as police commissioner. One critic of his Sunday closing effort sent him a letter bomb which fizzled. In August 1895, TR wrote Lodge that the *New York World* and the *Journal* "nearly have epilepsy over me; there are few crimes which they do not accuse me of committing; and they are united in portraying me as spending my Sundays drinking heavily in the Union League Club." Even after he attended a parade held by the United Societies for Liberal Sunday Laws and saw banners protesting "Roosevelt's Russian Rule" and a coffin named "Teddyism," he insisted that "nothing could make me relax my grip on the liquor sellers."[27]

BUT HE WAS FAST LOSING the support of his own party. When he refused to hire incompetent veterans as police officers, the Grand Army of the Republic (G.A.R.) joined with the Republican Platt machine to get him indicted for violating an obscure law making it illegal to interfere with the rights of veterans. Though he won out against the veterans, his Sunday closing campaign drew increasing fire from Republicans. They feared he had lost working-class voters for the party, especially the traditionally Republican German beer-drinking vote. When the courts reinterpreted Sunday closing to prohibit the sale of all beverages, Roosevelt foolishly tried to shut down soda fountains, too. Many Republicans feared their party would lose the next election simply because a dynamo of political righteousness with a pince-nez and "snapping teeth" wanted to make a name for himself.[28]

Theodore felt lonely in his crusades and regretted that he had to conduct his Sunday closing campaign without the mentor he most needed. He wrote Senator Lodge that he wished "I could see you to talk over my difficulties!" Lodge advised him regularly via letters and urged him to think about building a long-term political base in New York by reaching out to new constituents. Edith and Cabot worked together, sometimes behind Theodore's back, to counsel restraint: "Talk as little as possible, except when you make a set speech which always helps."[29]

Lodge urged TR to use his police work as a stepping-stone to statewide office, probably a Senate seat, then to aim for the presidency. He advised him to keep his name before the voters: "Do not fail to go on the stump." He applauded TR's success in showing the public the corruption of Tammany Hall but urged him not to fight against the Platt machine, which controlled Republican politics in the state. TR balked because he saw Platt's influence was "simply poisonous. I cannot go in with him; no honest man of sincerity can," but he refused to join an anti-Platt bolt because he knew it was sure to hand victory to Tammany Hall.[30]

When a Platt-controlled Republican Party convention refused at first to back his Sunday closing campaign, TR was upset. He needed to unburden himself to Lodge about the strain of a job so tense with combat that he did not dare miss a day of work. After six months of ten-hour days, Theodore had dinner with Dr. William Sturgis Bigelow, who reported to Lodge: "He looks worn & tired, for him, and has lost much of his natural snap & buoyancy. At this rate it is only a question of time when he has a breakdown, and when he does it will be a bad one."[31]

When TR was too busy to return to Sagamore Hill for a week, Edith wrote him praising his recent speeches but admonishing him for a gratuitous attack he had made on the Goo-Goos, or Good Government reformers. She reminded her husband of Cabot's advice about avoiding unnecessary feuds. Despite what his mentor told him and his wife echoed, he could not stop himself from giving his critics "slashing blows."[32]

More trials awaited. TR discovered that one of the other commissioners, Andrew Parker, was "a scoundrelly intriguer" who worked secretly with corrupt members of the police force and Tammany Hall. Though TR tried hard to hire policemen in a nonpartisan manner under civil service rules, Parker charged him with using his position to get Democrats jobs. Parker even falsified numbers and political affiliations of the new hires to embarrass Roosevelt, and he spread rumors that instead of midnight patrols TR spent his evenings watching burlesque shows. Like the political bulldog he was, TR fought back and, with lawyer Elihu Root's assistance, had Parker tried for neglect of duty in the spring of 1896.[33]

When his childhood friend Fanny Smith Parsons watched him as he testified before the state senate in Albany, she expressed concern to Corinne about the way that TR's fervent beliefs "taxed his highly-strung nervous organization and made him appear less calm and assured than I would have liked to see him." Corinne passed along Fanny's comment to Theodore, who answered that Edith had already tried to get him to hide his "nervousness before the different crises that come up in the course of my very harassing work here, notably before the recent hearings by the Mayor." He promised Fanny he would try to hold himself together with a firmer hand in the future, but his fighting spirit often brought more emotions to the surface than he could suppress. He had trouble knowing how far to push his crusades. When he heard reports of nude actresses appearing in burlesque and vaudeville shows, he threatened to shut down the Olympia Garden Theater. But once he saw the show himself, he found only a tame tableau undeserving of censorship.[34]

At the height of his Sunday closing campaign and later in the Parker trial, Edith was so worried about her husband that she often left the children with the servants at Sagamore Hill and came into town to be with him. Afterward, she wrote Bamie that he had "such a worn and tired look." Parkhurst attacked him for not fighting vice hard enough, and Edith watched Theodore become "so worried and fussed that it [was] sometime before he calm[ed] down." His midnight "strolls told upon him dreadfully," and during the Parker trial she said he was "sleepless and nervous" much of the time.[35]

During the most dramatic episodes of his police work, Edith saw the anxiety and stress; Theodore saw the victories. He had professionalized the police force more effectively than any previous commissioner. His hiring systems would be adopted around the country, and he brought the Bertillon identification system, including photographs of the rogues' gallery and fingerprinting, into use. He added to the police detective's arsenal new photography labs, better patrol wagons, and steam launches.[36]

TR could also point to the fact that hospitals reported fewer alcohol-related injuries when he enforced Sunday closing; he had fired 200 policemen for dishonesty or incompetence; he got added funds so that he could appoint 1,700 new officers and give them updated professional training, including practice in marksmanship. He sent bicycle squads to patrol the streets and back alleys of the city and got them good press. Improving telephone communications was his most enduring technological gift to New York's law officers. And he was proud to claim that while he was commissioner no citizens were clubbed by police at political rallies or protest meetings. He gave credit to Riis for providing the vision that had guided his police work, but it was his own inimitable, strenuous style that had "shaken the Police Force to its very foundation." He had become a national symbol of clean government and municipal progress, known across the United States and in Europe. He told Lodge: "I have undoubtedly strengthened myself with the rank and file of our party," and Lodge assured him: "That Senatorship is getting well into sight, my dear boy."[37]

Though his reform could go no further, the most extraordinary outcome of TR's career as commissioner was that he established much warmer relations with the Lower East Side. Some of TR's friends like Frederic Remington looked down on immigrants as "a seething mass of smells, stale beer, and bad language," but Thee's son never saw the New Yorkers he met on the street as "vermin." His police work made him take a more engaged look at New York's ethnic neighborhoods and their people. As an assemblyman he had voted against minimum wage bills, but now he saw why they were needed.[38]

After his midnight patrols he became a regular visitor at Mike Lyon's Bowery restaurant, where he could learn about men and issues which the Good Government Clubs never considered. For example, he had thought little about the Irish land issue—poor farmers being evicted by rich landowners in a time of famine—and he slowly became an advocate of Irish home rule. He understood why, in 1891, Pope Leo XIII, in *Rerum novarum,* questioned the prevailing doctrine of liberty of contract which was so popular with courts that struck down laws protecting workers. Until he lived part of his days on the East Side, especially the Bowery and the Tenderloin, he did not comprehend that child labor and inhumane work were living issues to American Catholics. He learned, too, that newer immigrants were pushed to the bottom of the economic heap by prejudice and a harsh economic order. After he gave a speech at the Tee-To-Tum temperance club, he joined vigorously in waltzing with the East Side girls at the club, and the newspapers headlined it "Roosevelt Won the Girls' Hearts." Not surprisingly, he proved better doing an exuberant polka than a waltz, and the press heralded him as "the most popular man on the east side." His Sunday closing campaign had not irritated everyone in immigrant precincts, after all. When he campaigned for police reform by speaking to packed audiences in East Side meeting halls, he was pleased that he "never failed to carry the house" when critics challenged him.[39]

He preached temperance to the Catholic Total Abstinence Union's convention and received applause that usually belonged to "Big Tim" Sullivan. Sullivan was the compassionate Tammany ward boss and "King of the Bowery" who gave free Christmas dinners to hungry people out of his Bowery Democratic headquarters during the depression of the 1890s and later bought shoes for every child in his ward, but only if they came as members to the Democratic clubhouse. Roosevelt hoped he could win a few voters over to the Republican clubhouse without buying shoes or sending the children home with a growler of beer. Though a Tammany man like Big Tim should have been TR's sworn enemy, he found himself liking the Knickerbocker, especially after TR hired his cousin Jerry to be a policeman. In Roosevelt's continuing education about how politicians could win the hearts—or at least the votes—of the people, Sullivan provided a crash course in electioneering, ballot-box watching as a combat sport, and popular entertainment as a way to win votes. When TR ran for president in 1904 against Alton B. Parker, Congressman Sullivan "always kept a feeling of friendship" and remembered TR's days on the streets of New York. Big Tim sent word to Tammany ward heelers not "to commit any offense which would expose them to being put in the penitentiary in the interest of Parker's success."[40]

Few Protestant moral reformers ended their anti-saloon and anti-prostitution campaigns by making fast friends with the ethnic folk they had set out to uplift. But in Roosevelt's Police Commission years he may have been uplifted more than anyone else. His Knickerbocker superiority and entitlement had begun to fade. TR started to speak out for more democratic citizen participation to achieve "the higher life of cities," which he argued in widely read magazine articles could be achieved only by making life more livable for the average person. TR also wrote in praise of Riis' exposés of the hard living conditions for children in tenements and his work to establish parks and free libraries to make "the life of the day-laborer in our cities less onerous and more wholesome." Cities would never move forward, however, if the professional "know nothing" or nativist called the shots. Roosevelt boasted that in his police work "when one man attacked another because of his creed or his birthplace, I got rid of him in summary fashion." He disliked the prejudice against Catholics he saw at elite colleges, and he believed that "the question of doing away with all race and religious bigotry in this country, and of fusing us all into one people is the most important of all."[41]

Roosevelt was committed to a patriotic Americanization which taught a shared American culture, but he had started to redefine Americanness as a fluid amalgam enriched by the culture of the majority of voting New Yorkers who were foreign born. His nights on the Lower East Side had changed him. He had been hostile to professional sports and prizefighting. At first he warned against the dangers of passive spectatorship for the American "race" because "the existence of a caste of gladiators in the midst of a population which does not itself participate in manly sports is usually, as it was at Rome, a symptom of national decadence." He denounced prizefighting as "simply brutal and degrading" and fight fans as mostly "men who hover on the borderlines of criminality," but after working with the police force for a while, he became a fan of professional boxing and found that a love of the sport could be a bond that made his class status matter less to the men he encountered on the streets. TR counted among his new friends prizefighter John L. Sullivan, the son of an Irish hod carrier who fought his way to the heavyweight championship in 1882 and kept up "knocking out tours" long afterward. TR liked the boxer and urged him to get hold of his drinking habit.[42]

Though he took almost no time off in the summer of 1895, his opponents had stymied him so much that by mid-1896 he saw little chance to get much more done. Edith was overjoyed when he spent more time at home that summer, rowing across Long Island Sound with her and swimming with the children. TR did not let police work get in the way of his ongoing careers as an amateur field naturalist and mammalogist, as well as historian. He kept up his scientific reading and as a Harvard overseer urged the modernization of the teaching of zoology. He wrote a scientific essay for the journal *Science* in which he took issue with C. Hart Merriam's reclassification of coyotes into eleven different species. Merriam's new system emphasized small structural distinctions among the animals rather than broad commonalties. Roosevelt's argument so impressed professional scientists that they invited him to a debate with Merriam at the Biological Society's annual meeting. Later, when Merriam discovered a new species of elk he named it *Cervus Roosevelti* after his contentious friend.[43]

As he became less engaged by his police work, he finished volume 4 of *The Winning of the West* and was happy to find that *The Wilderness Hunter* and *Hero Tales from American History* were selling well. He kept up his work with the Boone and Crockett Club, editing three books with George Bird Grinnell on North American big game, and went to Medora to hunt during the summer of 1896. Nine-year-old Ted started public school at Cove School in Oyster Bay, and by winter he had learned to chop trees and ski alongside his father. Theodore made sure his namesake became "more like me as I am now than as I was when I was his age . . . more at home among other boys, and fonder of out-door sports."[44]

TR INTERRUPTED his police career to go on his own "knocking-out tours," campaigning for Republican nominee William McKinley in the presidential campaign of 1896. But he set aside his own reformist sympathies and went into the arena as a mainstream Republican, a loyal party minion. That year, the most class-conscious debate in American electoral history featured William Jennings Bryan as the defender of the working people against the forces of business and economic privilege. As one of McKinley's campaign surrogates, TR spoke out as a unifier who would teach the workingman to face economic hardship with manliness rather than envy the rich. But he also attacked Populists who ran on what he called the uncouth "no undershirt" platform and their leaders who would tear down the "decencies and elegancies of civilized life." When Bryan spoke out against economic privilege, TR warned the voters that Bryan would ignite dangerous class hatred. And he characterized the Bryan campaign as "fundamentally an attack on civilization; an appeal to the torch."[45]

Roosevelt's political invective was often misreported and it enraged him when newspapers like the *New York Journal* said he had talked of "meeting Altgeld sword in hand at the head of my regiment" and "standing up the silver leaders against a wall to be shot." He claimed he never made such violent statements, and though he conceded that Bryan was a "rather attractive man, a real orator," he thought the Great Commoner better fit to be a Baptist preacher than a president. In private, TR agreed with Bryan on many issues; for instance, he thought government ownership of telegraphs might be a good idea, but the Republican National Committee sent him to the stump as an advocate for a straight McKinley pro-business line.[46]

Bryan and TR campaigned as profoundly different personalities. Bryan proved to be less unlettered than astoundingly lacking in curiosity about the world of books and scientific discovery that animated TR's life. Bryan suspected experts, and believed that the spread of republican simplicity and virtue through individual salvation was the best way to promote the public good. Christ's concern for the poor and forgotten provided a model for Bryan, and he believed that the Republican Party favored business and that high tariffs hurt the small farmers who had to pay higher prices because of them. Bryan contended, too, that railroads and monopolies were the bullies of the new industrial economy. He sought a cure in expanding the money supply via silver coinage to help debtors, and he campaigned sincerely as "the representative of the under privileged."[47]

TR believed in public good, character, and republican virtue, too, but he was a more worldly thinker who had begun to see that modern industrial society was incapable of deep change without expert knowledge and without the intervention of the federal government in the economy. But in the 1896 campaign Roosevelt spoke out for the status quo. He praised the protective tariff, a growing international industrial economy that exploited labor and favored large corporations, and the gold standard. He built bridges between McKinley's mentor Mark Hanna and Lodge's big-donor friends in Boston, and spoke wherever the Republican National Committee sent him. TR preached well to solid burghers and even to the down-and-out in city missions, while Bryan sent his oratorical lightning through rural communities and mining towns and McKinley rested up in Canton, Ohio.[48]

Republicans amassed a $3 million campaign fund while Bryan raised only $300,000. The McKinley ticket got help from corporate campaign contributions and from employers who threatened to shut down their plants if workers elected Bryan. McKinley won by only 600,000 votes. It was a hotly fought election that produced an 80 percent turnout because real issues had been debated. Afterward, TR said that Mark Hanna had sold McKinley "as if he were a patent medicine," but he too had proven to be quite a salesman.[49]

Roosevelt read the election returns knowing he might get a job in the new administration. His police work had won him a national following and his writing had earned him added stature among reformers. In "The City in Modern Life" he had outlined a vision of better cities run by a "system of mixed individualism and collectivism." He believed that individuals should remain responsible for their own behavior yet city people as a group needed to make a collective commitment to planning their shared fate. City planning, professional fire and police forces, playgrounds, parks, housing regulation, policies to make housing affordable, and rapid transit were TR's prerequisites for modernizing city life. He had not campaigned on these progressive urban reform ideas, but anyone who followed his writing career understood that he stood for strong government and reform to make cities more humane places for average people.[50]

At the end of his Police Commission work, TR knew better how to manage intense political infighting and assaults on his character. It trained him for the presidency as no other job had. Years later Edith recalled the state her husband had been in when he was commissioner and she commented that she never saw him like that in the White House. While he was commissioner and when he campaigned for McKinley, he learned a lot about how to reach the average voter, and he trusted Lodge's assurance that he would someday need this knowledge.[51]

At Christmas time, as the Roosevelts waited anxiously to hear if TR would be called to join the McKinley administration, Theodore had "a violent attack of asthma" and smashed his head against the mantelpiece when putting a log into the fireplace. Bob Ferguson had come to Sagamore Hill for Thanksgiving and stayed until Christmas. Theodore and Bob took Ted on a ten-mile hike and together they cleared out a riding trail with axes. On Christmas morning the grown-ups happily watched as two-year-old Archie realized for the first time how much fun it was to open his stocking in his parents' bedroom before running up to the Gun Room for big presents.[52]

Meanwhile, Lodge tried to get TR made secretary of the navy, but McKinley worried that the impetuous young man would be too pushy and hard to control. McKinley knew that TR was a die-hard navalist who found it "sickening" that Congress refused to build a strong navy. Without adequate coastal defenses, TR had said, "We are actually at the mercy of a tenth rate country like Chile." These opinions gave McKinley pause, so Lodge urged TR to call on his friends Maria Longworth Nichols Storer and Bellamy Storer, close friends of the President-elect, to intercede on his behalf. McKinley thought TR "hotheaded and harum scarum," but Lodge and the Storers knew how to lobby him effectively. He owed money to the Storers and wanted to please Lodge, a leader of eastern Republicanism. TR stood out as a strong nationalist voice whose effective campaigning had to be rewarded, so McKinley reluctantly appointed him to the lesser post as assistant secretary of the navy.[53]

In April 1897, TR began his work in the Navy Department separated again from Edith, who was expecting their fifth baby in December. Edith stayed at Sagamore Hill and planned to move the children into their new rented Washington, D.C., house at 1810 N Street in early October. She was glad he got the job he wanted but Sagamore Hill—what he called their "child-infested house"—had been happier when she knew he was returning home most nights of the week and she could bundle the children into the farm wagon to meet him at the train station.[54]

That summer, Bamie and Will Cowles, with cousin Helen Roosevelt and her governess in tow, came back to reclaim 689 Madison Avenue and rented nearby Waldeck so that they could spend the summer close to Edith and the children. Reunited with her adoring Auntie Bye, thirteen-year-old Alice became fast friends with Helen, and when the two girls visited Bamie in New York they rode about town in a hansom cab and winked at all the men they met to make them "stare at us." Alice was already so beautiful that she did not have to misbehave to be noticed. From Bamie's house Alice conducted an extensive flirtation with her fifteen-year-old cousin Franklin Delano Roosevelt, to whom she coyly said: "I hope you have given me up, if not you had better." Franklin won an invitation to join in Sagamore Hill's annual Fourth of July celebrations, where he watched the fireworks with Alice, but Theodore did not notice whether the boy was smitten or not. As usual, he was more interested in teaching his children a hardy sport—that summer, it was football.[55]

In early August, Edith left the children at Sagamore Hill to spend time with her husband and get their new house settled. They had a romantic dinner at the Overlook Inn and watched a sunset without interruptions from the five children. Five months pregnant, Edith got exhausted "grappling" with the furniture "from the paloe-olithic, or Horse Hair cloth, stage of New York semi-civilization." TR fretted he would never get real exercise again, but planned to take Ted with him in the summer of 1898 to Medora to "pay one last visit to the ranch." Edith had intended only to stay a week, but after ten days she returned in response to the news that Ethel had contracted whooping cough.[56]

TR told Lodge that he wanted the Navy Department job "to be near you," but he also wanted very much to be in a position to build up the navy and to encourage the United States to follow a "large policy"—that is, one of expansion to gain American influence over the shape of the twentieth-century world. Roosevelt and Lodge judged it criminal for the United States to neglect its navy at a time when European powers and Japan were eyeing trading ports and spheres of influence all around the Pacific. After a planters' revolt turned Hawaii into an independent republic in 1893, talk of American annexation prompted Japan to send a warship, perhaps to protect its twenty-five thousand citizens who lived there, perhaps to block American annexation of the islands. TR had said in private that Cleveland should be impeached for refusing to annex Hawaii. Roosevelt and Lodge, along with naval advocate Alfred Thayer Mahan, saw it as a natural home for a strategic naval base to link a network of coaling stations which would make the United States a world naval power.[57]

Lodge and Roosevelt also watched Europe carefully for encroachments upon the New World. European powers' eagerness to acquire territory and military outposts to expand their influence had driven them to partition Africa and divide the treaty ports of China. When Cleveland was president, a crisis had erupted in Venezuela because of what Lodge called European "earth hunger." Britain and Germany threatened to occupy Venezuela, and Lodge and Roosevelt feared that South America would follow Africa as a scene of land-grabbing by European powers, and the region would be troubled by the constant danger of war. Critics said, "It is the trophies of Great Britain which will not allow Lodge and Roosevelt to sleep," but they believed war could be avoided if the United States took a strong stand reiterating the Monroe Doctrine to ward off European incursions.[58]

In the days when Cuba's war for independence against Spain began to dominate headlines, Lodge believed that Americans "must make up our minds whether we are to be dominant in the Western Hemisphere and keep it free from foreign invasion or whether we are to stand aside and let it be seized as Africa has been." By 1897, Lodge had become the recognized leader of the "large policy" advocates, and TR assisted him as a "quietly rampant 'Cuba Libre' man." Popular support for Cuban rebels was fueled by lurid reports in Joseph Pulitzer's *World* and William Randolph Hearst's *Journal* about concentration camps and the Spanish strip search of women suspected of being pro-Cuban spies. When Hearst stage-managed the dramatic rescue of the jailed daughter of an insurgent, public indignation over the mistreatment of Cuba soared. Few aside from the "large policy" advocates like Roosevelt and Lodge foresaw that Cuban unrest and the Filipino war for independence against Spain, which began in 1896, might provide the United States with a chance to fight Spain and take over its empire.[59]

TR spent his days getting the navy ready for war and lobbying with Congress for more defense spending. He was incensed over the poor planning that required American battleships to be docked for repairs abroad. He put together the statements of previous presidents in support of a strong navy, then distributed them to Congress. When his boss, Secretary John Long, was out of town Theodore proved deferential to varied requests from navy captains and took every opportunity to make his own decisions on issues of technology and construction. From his many scientific and literary acquaintances at the Cosmos Club, TR learned that the astronomer Samuel Langley had invented an airplane which could be used for military surveillance. Roosevelt got Langley a large grant from the War Department, thus playing a crucial role in the history of aviation. Fortunately for the energetic assistant secretary, Long proved to be "most kind, and at first acquiesced in what I did."[60]

The two months that TR acted as "the hot-weather secretary" while Long vacationed gave him an opening to promote his views with President McKinley. He dined with him and took carriage rides to explain the diplomatic value of making the American navy as strong as the Japanese. He also showed McKinley his strategic plans for a war with Spain. In order to protect undefended East Coast cities from the Spanish fleet, Roosevelt proposed to waylay its ships as early as possible in the war.[61]

TR obviously had more than an efficient navy in mind. He favored the annexation of Hawaii (he said, "in the interests of the White race" rather than let the Japanese take it) and the building of a canal connecting the Atlantic and Pacific so that the U.S. Navy could more readily exert its influence around the world. He believed Kaiser Wilhelm II of Germany had colonial designs on the New World which the United States must counter. Historians often argue that the depression of the mid-1890s sent policymakers looking for new overseas frontiers and markets to conquer, but U.S. imperialists were looking for more than a new economic frontier. Roosevelt and Lodge, both extravagant admirers of the idealism and nation-mindedness of the Civil War generation, sought to use empire and war to revive their nation's vigor and manhood.[62]

By the 1890s many men of Theodore's generation feared that the United States had lost its moral compass and its fighting spirit because of tame affluence. They envied the Civil War soldiers who had been "touched with fire," ennobled by a war that swept them up to serve high national purpose. A shared northern memory of the Civil War developed, erasing the bloodletting and horror and exalting the war as a "national regeneration." In the 1890s veterans like Oliver Wendell Holmes, Jr., evoked a sanitized and Homeric memory of the Civil War to remind youngsters of the need for selflessness, active citizenship, and fearlessness before the challenges of life. As muscular Christianity took firmer hold on American culture in the last decades of the century, more and more youths succumbed to this Civil War syndrome and dreamed of fighting like a "barbarian" for their nation in "a display of physical strength in battle." TR was not alone when he applauded Holmes and claimed that war itself, not just the Civil War, could make America a better, more Spartan and unified country.[63]

When he wrote Bob Ferguson with longing for "a general national buccaneering expedition to drive the Spaniards out of Cuba, the English out of Canada," TR's romanticized and nostalgic view of the Civil War inspired him to seek in war a strenuous life of self-sacrifice, service, and vigor. But that war spirit meant more to TR than willingness to fight and die. The Civil War spirit stood as the model for the kind of unselfish and active strenuous life he wanted people to live daily as an antidote to the aimless getting and spending of modern commercial life. Black leaders also remembered the Civil War as a providential battle for justice, and TR shared Frederick Douglass' view that the Civil War proved that the nation-state could be used as an instrument of justice and nationalism. When he wrote Bamie that America needed a war, he had in mind the strenuous Civil War cure.[64]

* * *

SECRETARY LONG told a friend that his assistant's pugnacity made him uncomfortable, but he appreciated the young man's attention to detail and his sophisticated understanding of strategy, technology, and diplomacy. But TR discovered that Long was not a true advocate of naval expansion, which made his own position awkward. Later, he told Jacob Riis he fought to get his friend George Dewey made commander of the Pacific fleet because Dewey had "a lion heart" and his courage might be needed in the days ahead.[65]

TR cultivated good press for the naval buildup by taking handpicked reporters and his friend Frederic Remington with him when he reviewed the fleet off Hampton Roads in September 1897. Before Edith brought the children to Washington that fall, her husband wrote her a letter full of wonder and admiration for America's fleet:

> I can not begin to describe the wonderful power and beauty of these giant warships, with their white hulls and towering superstructures. At night each was a blaze of light while the strings of shifting, many colored lanterns spoke and answered from ship to ship; and in the night practice with searchlights and rapid fire guns on a drifting target, the effect was as wildly beautiful as anything ever Turner dreamed. . . . the immense war-engines, throbbing with tremendous might. . . . I was aboard both the Iowa and the Puritan for their target practice, and really it was almost as exciting as if we had been going into action.[66]

Edith knew her husband was passionate about the navy and that his dreams of military glory had deep roots, but she hoped it would not mean that he would go into real action. With a sixth little Roosevelt on the way, Edith watched her country's slow procession toward war with deep apprehension.

Having his family join him in Washington made Roosevelt much happier, and he took them on scrambles up Rock Creek Park with Lodge's brother-in-law, another navalist, Harry Davis. He promised Davis and his sons that he could find "one or two places where they and my elder children can come sufficiently near breaking their necks to insure their enjoyment." Theodore then went up to Boston for a celebration of the *Constitution* and found the Navy Department under attack for selling alcohol to sailors in the Charlestown Navy Yard canteen. He promised that sports facilities and reading rooms would be provided and that men would be encouraged to drink cocoa and coffee instead of beer and wine.[67]

Edith went into labor unexpectedly in the middle of November and their son Quentin was born on the nineteenth. Complications from childbirth and the flu laid her low, though she rallied briefly in December; by January,

TR was "exceedingly put out" that he had to cancel a trip to the Boone and Crockett Club dinner in New York because she was too sick for him to leave. He described her uneasily as "an invalid."[68]

During the early days of 1898, Edith's illness worsened. TR tried to fill in for his wife as he took Kermit, Ethel, and Archie on their usual "Sunday Scrambles," sometimes including his friend Leonard Wood, who was an aggressive nationalist, the President's physician, and a veteran of the war against Geronimo. They crossed streams by tiptoeing on logs and picked their way through a cemetery by walking on top of a high brick wall. When Theodore led his men friends on scrambles, one-upsmanship was usually his agenda. He took pride in having outwalked a German military attaché, but he noted with frustration that his fierce gorilla-like friend Wood was unbeatable.[69]

TR often bemoaned the fact that desk work "does away with one's powers," but he might have added that being responsible for six children and an ailing wife, even with help from servants, also did away with his powers. While Edith was ill, he proved an indulgent parent: he bought the children flying squirrels as pets. As her long weeks of illness dragged on through January and February with no signs of ending, he felt confined by responsibility. More frustrated than ever when the Senate rejected McKinley's treaty to annex Hawaii, TR wrote his hunter friend Frederick C. Selous: "I long at times for the great rolling prairies of sun-dried yellow grass." He wondered if he would ever get to see the Alaskan wilderness Selous was exploring and yearned for romantic escape into the frontier.[70]

Edith's winter illness occurred at the worst time possible for Theodore: tensions with Spain over Cuba had heightened since the previous fall, and he expected that war might be imminent. But he had trouble convincing other people that he was right. For example, Long discovered that his assistant had authorized spending for repairs on ships that might be needed for war. The secretary thought the precautions unnecessary. TR was already making plans to be a part of the New York expeditionary force in case of war with Spain, but he found "the queer lack of imperial instinct that our people show" deeply disappointing.[71]

Roosevelt feared the President would invite national humiliation by refusing to stand up against Spain. After Cuban riots in Havana prompted the United States to send the *Maine* to safeguard Americans in January, the yellow press made public on February 9 the Spanish minister Enrique Depuy de Lôme's letter insulting McKinley as "weak" and "catering to the rabble, and, besides, a low politician." Roosevelt had been working for months to make sure America did not enter the war, as he put it, "butt end foremost." He wanted the United States to go to war headfirst, well prepared to fight and win and to use Cuba as a base to extend American naval power in the Caribbean. At this turning point in the nation's history, TR stood by, eager to play a crucial role in pulling America onto an international stage.[72]

When the *Maine* blew up on February 15, Roosevelt rushed to convince Congress that it had nothing to do with naval incompetence or a history of spontaneous explosion in the navy's battleships. Instead he insisted it "must be due to Spanish treachery." He was in the hot seat because he had to defend the soundness of the *Maine* at the same time he lobbied for war and heavier military expenditures in Congress. He urged McKinley's cabinet to warn Spain that if they sent their fleet to "our waters"—that is, the Caribbean—the United States would see it as an act of war.[73]

But family crises pulled him away from his work. Throughout early February, Edith had a fever of 101 and was not getting better. TR was slow to admit to himself how seriously ill she was. He called it grippe, sciatica, and neuralgia at first, and worried only that she would have to wean Quentin. He had Edith's childhood nurse, Mame, take Ethel, Kermit, and Archie to stay with family friends, and he tried to visit them as often as he could. He was also nonplused over Ted, who, he said, seemed to have "what I think is kind of a nervous breakdown." Ted suffered from headaches, melancholy, and a tendency to become "self-conscious," and he had been in bed depressed for several weeks. Doctors warned that Ted's nerves were "gone," and Father did not know what to do for his son or his wife. On February 26, when he could ignore Edith's illness no longer, TR called in the famous surgeon William Osler from Johns Hopkins University in Baltimore, who recommended immediate surgery because he found a large abscess in her psoas, or groin, muscle.[74]

While TR dragged his feet about Edith's operation because he could not bear to have her go under the knife, he was in a hurry to get ready for war. Hostilities could break out at any moment, yet McKinley and the army were neither prepared nor willing to fight. On the day before Osler saw Edith, TR went to the Old Executive Office Building and in Long's absence telegraphed Commander George Dewey to coal up and be ready to take Manila if war came. Historians have repeated the story that TR acted impetuously against orders when he ordered Dewey to Manila, but Long did not countermand the order when he returned to the office, and it was actually consistent with navy war plans. The clamor for war came from the yellow press, Congress, and large-policy advocates like Lodge while Roosevelt played a supporting role in the Navy Department.[75]

On March 5, Roosevelt got a second opinion from a gynecologist, who said Edith urgently needed surgery, and this time he heeded medical advice.

Corinne offered to take charge of domestic concerns, but he refused her help. He told her, "For two weeks we could not tell whether Edith would live or die" and he was so upset that "any sympathy would have made me nearly break down." After Edith's successful operation on March 6, Theodore reported to Bamie that his wife "behaved heroically; quiet, and even laughing, while I held her hand until the ghastly preparations had been made." Days later, after he heard that the Court of Inquiry confirmed that an outside mine had sunk the *Maine*, he wrote: "If there is a war I want to get away from here and get to the front if I possibly can."[76]

The Roosevelts' domestic troubles had not ended, however. Fourteen-year-old Alice refused to come home from her visit to Bamie in New York. Fortunately for TR, Bamie, despite her deafness, arthritis, and an unexpected but welcome pregnancy at age forty-three, took charge of the situation. She kept Alice calm and urged Theodore to send Ted to her so that he could be treated for his nervous problems by their mutual friend Dr. Alexander Lambert, a Cornell professor of medicine and expert on public health. Edith remained "terribly wasted" for three weeks after her operation, but not too wasted to tell her husband she did not want him to enlist if war came.[77]

Lambert wrote TR that Ted's problems were emotional ones caused by too much pressure from his father. TR promised Lambert, "I'll never push Ted again," and conceded with irritation that Edith was "well enough to feel the emotions of triumph. Hereafter I shall never press Ted in either body or mind." He confessed that he had been tough on Ted because the boy had the potential "to be all the things I would like to have been and wasn't, and it has been a great temptation to push him." He remembered often the invalid and weakling he had been as a child, and when Ted showed he also had his father's bookish and asthmatic tendencies, Theodore behaved as harshly as Thee had in pushing his son toward a combative manhood. He would never manage to keep his promise to ease up on Ted, but in the dramatic moments when European powers tried to prevent war between America and Spain, Roosevelt was willing to promise anything to keep the demands of family life at bay.[78]

Even after angry demonstrations in several cities followed the Court of Inquiry's report, peace was still possible if McKinley decided to hold his ground against advocates of war. For a while Spain's offers of compromise and cease-fire made peace look likely. Cuban rebels refused an armistice, but McKinley would not have to let them stop peace talks. The *Washington Post* warned the President to choose war or peace based on how manly he would appear: "a weak or vacillating policy would mean the overwhelming defeat of the Republican party and everlasting repudiation of the administration." McKinley almost certainly saw the cartoons which ridiculed him as a womanly figure in a bonnet and apron in the *New York Journal* and as a coward offering up the white feather of surrender in the *Chicago Tribune*. A crowd of ten thousand waited to hear McKinley's decision. The President opted for war.[79]

By April 11 the President sent his war message to Congress which explained that U.S. intervention could include "hostile constraint upon both the parties" in Cuba's war against Spain. In other words, suppression of the conflict between Cuba and Spain was the goal, not Cuba's freedom. Cuban rebels believed they were so close to ousting Spain by themselves that U.S. intervention would be harmful. McKinley and followers of the large policy refused to recognize or cooperate with the rebels and were annoyed when Congress passed the Teller Amendment which disclaimed American intent to annex Cuba. U.S. military leaders like General William Shafter declared that the multi-racial Cubans were "no more fit for self-government than gunpowder is for hell."[80]

Roosevelt, with his wife now on the mend, could devote himself with fewer distractions to preparing his nation for war. He felt so passionately about the war "that it is with very great difficulty I can restrain myself." The Navy Department had agreed upon his plan for operations, but the War Department and the army still boasted they could mobilize thousands of men overnight—yet they had no concrete transportation, recruitment, or supply plans. TR knew the army was dangerously disorganized, yet when McKinley called for volunteers, he enlisted as a volunteer cavalry officer in the army. On two occasions the President asked Roosevelt not to enlist but to stay in Washington to help manage the war, but he could not bear to sit out what might be the only war in his lifetime. He was infuriated that none of his friends or family wanted him to go. He and Edith talked over his passionate feelings on the subject, and she finally agreed that it was the only honorable thing for a man with his views to do.[81]

In retrospect, Alice and her cousin Corinney concurred that Thee's failure to fight in the Civil War had humiliated Theodore so much that it contributed to his desire to fight in the Spanish-American War. Corinney said: "He felt he had to explain it always, about the father he admired so hugely." Alice said she could always get a defensive reaction if she teased her father about Thee's failure to fight; taunts about manliness and cowardice were as telling with TR as they had been with McKinley. However, as the war began and Dewey defeated Spain's Pacific fleet in Manila Bay on May 1 and fifty thousand Cuban troops occupied much of the island, TR's greatest fear was that peace would break out before he got to fight.[82]

He refused initially the command of the First U.S. Volunteer Cavalry, or Rough Riders, which he had been organizing secretly for months, and asked instead that Leonard Wood be named colonel because of his superior military experience. TR did not accept command until in the heat of battle Wood was promoted and the Rough Riders needed Roosevelt to be their colonel. He and Edith "had a lovely last fortnight together," and then he gathered his Brooks Brothers uniform, the medicine chest Bamie sent, the field watch Corinne gave him, and multiple pairs of spectacles to take to the front. He said his good-byes to his family and left for San Antonio on May 12 to train his troops. Alice always remembered "the surge of apprehension and homesickness that came over me as he left." At his side would be Bob Ferguson, horseman-playboy Austin Wadsworth, socialites Woody Kane and Willy Tiffany, Douglas Robinson's cousin Kenneth, New Yorker Hamilton Fish, and several new friends—a fierce ex-sheriff from Arizona named Bucky O'Neill, a handsome Louisiana planter named John McIlhenny, and John Greenway, an Andover-Yale athlete from Arkansas. Many Indians joined up, but a part-Cherokee cowhand and bronco roper named Will Rogers was rejected by the Rough Riders because of his age—eighteen.[83]

After their brief training in San Antonio, TR hoped to take his men out of Galveston, but army orders doomed them and their horses to endure a badly coordinated four-day train ride to Tampa, where no food or orders awaited them. On June 2, Edith joined TR in Tampa. Wood allowed him to spend nights with Edith at the Tampa Bay Hotel as long as he arose at four and got to the camp ten miles away to drill with his men. Edith met the other officers and visited with Wintie and Margaret Chanler, Jack Astor, Ferguson, and Kenneth Robinson. When TR was ordered to report to sail to Cuba, Edith went home full of worry that she had seen her husband whole for the last time.[84]

TR was eager to get into battle, but the ordeal of waiting in the hot sun for the war to start grated on his nerves. Orders were given to load the men onto transports, but for several days the overcrowded ships were left to swelter in a sewerish canal. The men resorted to cooling themselves off by swimming in the bay until sharks appeared and forced them to climb back in the transports. TR did all he could for his men's comfort as Captain Allyn Capron drilled them to keep them in shape for what was ahead, but Roosevelt found the army's disorganization inhumane. He told Lodge that one manager "with autocratic authority" should force the railroads to cooperate, which was, in fact, the plan that Woodrow Wilson adopted in World War I.[85]

At home Edith wrote Lodge asking where her husband would be sent in case of serious injury and if she could go to take care of him. After she received TR's letter of June 15 chronicling the disorganization of the transport, she confessed to Cabot: "I feel so utterly helpless. If it had not seemed a clear duty to be with the children I should have stayed at Tampa."[86]

Finally, after some coordination between American forces and rebels took place, a Cuban pilot guided the Rough Riders' landing at Daiquirí on June 22. In the chaos of unloading the ships a few horses and men drowned. TR looked with condescension on the Cubans and called them "the grasshopper people," and Ferguson wrote home in disgust that the Cuban insurgents were "miserable hounds. . . . all of them niggers or half breed." Nevertheless, Cubans had kept Spanish troops away from the Americans' landing at Daiquirí. TR did not know why the landing had been so easy and pronounced the *insurrectos* ill dressed and "nearly useless."[87]

Ferguson wrote home, "Theodore has already a great hold" on the men under his command. When Spanish troops fired at the Rough Riders and the Tenth Cavalry in the jungle at Las Guásimas on June 24, it was hard to see the enemy, and in the skirmish Fish and Capron were killed. But TR advanced steadily through dense jungle terrain, with his troops subjecting the enemy to steady fire until they and the Tenth forced the Spanish fighters into retreat.[88]

TR's bravery at Las Guásimas hit the newspapers at home, thanks, in part, to a friend Bamie had cultivated for him, Richard Harding Davis, who fought alongside Lieutenant Colonel Roosevelt when he was not writing heroic stories about him. "All the children," Edith wrote Theodore, "crowd around me at mail time begging to hear what you have to say," and Ted asked for her help praying "to have Father brought home safe from the war." Eight-year-old Kermit was so upset about the danger his father faced that he asked to be cuddled in his mother's arms like the new baby, Quentin. When the report of Rough Rider casualties, including the death of Capron, appeared in the newspapers, Edith dropped her guard to Cabot: "I am proud of the Rough Riders and I realize that Theodore could not have staid [*sic*] in Washington, but oh how I wish it had been [possible] for him. He thought Capron his best captain,—such a fine, manly looking young fellow with all his life before him. . . . Do write me I cannot say how I turn to you and Nannie."[89]

On July 1 in the Battle of San Juan Heights, TR and his men crouched at the base of Kettle Hill, near San Juan Hill, where part of the battle also raged. Spanish artillery lobbed shells at them from the top of Kettle Hill, while he and his men waited in hundred-degree heat for orders to advance. Shrapnel whipped by him and a bullet grazed his wrist. TR's men were being shot down because indecisive commanders prevented them from advancing against the enemy or seeking enough shelter in the tall grass or in the San Juan River. In defiance, Bucky O'Neill stood smoking, exposing himself to

Spanish bullets and refusing calls to take cover. Before other soldiers could get him to crouch down, O'Neill was shot through the mouth and instantly killed. TR grew impatient to move his men forward.

When the order to advance finally came, other officers interpreted it as instruction to move up the hill slowly with heads down, because Kettle Hill was well fortified by entrenched Spanish troops shooting at them with Mausers. Spurred to attack boldly and disdainful of the caution of the other officers, TR mounted his horse and commanded his men to charge forward behind him up the hill. As he rushed to the crest of the hill leading his men and other regiments, heavy rifle fire and artillery shells exploded around him. One Rough Rider later described the moment: TR exposed himself to enemy fire without fear. As the American army and the Rough Rider volunteers took Kettle Hill his men were convinced he would be killed.[90]

Next, Roosevelt led his men to support General Hamilton S. Hawkins' conquest of nearby San Juan Hill, where they fought well but played a less decisive role than they had on Kettle Hill. Richard Harding Davis's story of TR's heroic charge merged in newspaper reports with his bravery at San Juan Hill and turned him into the hero of San Juan Hill. Roosevelt said that the black troops of the Tenth Cavalry saved his life by firing steadily to provide cover as they followed him in his charge, but he also wrote later that he had to pull a gun on black infantrymen to stop them from retreating. Later he also belittled the bravery of black soldiers he believed had avoided standing in the line of fire. He would be embroiled in controversies about who did what at the battle for the rest of his life.[91]

But even after the victory, American troops suffered heavy losses from Spanish counterattacks and were in great danger during the Battle of Santiago. TR was under fire on July 3, "the darkest day of the war," and his men were vulnerable both because Spanish bullets shot at them constantly and because they had little food or clean water. From the trenches outside Santiago, TR wrote to Lodge about the approach of a "terrible military disaster" in a tone of panic: "For God's [sake] have heavy reinforcements sent us instantly," in a pleading letter which Lodge deleted when he published their correspondence. Fortunately for Roosevelt and his troops, Spanish reinforcements were delayed by Cuban *insurrectos*. During the pause, the American navy defeated the Spanish fleet in Santiago harbor. Then, a truce, an invasion of Puerto Rico, and, finally, peace came.[92]

Though TR had not gone to war primarily to further his political ambitions, Lodge knew that war records had helped elect all the Gilded Age presidents but one. TR made the cover of *Harper's Weekly* and the headlines of newspapers everywhere. The politically ambitious William Randolph Hearst and William Jennings Bryan tried to fight in Cuba but were barred, and Hearst berated himself for "not raising the cowboy regiment I had in mind before Roosevelt raised his." Another would-be president, General Nelson A. Miles, was in Cuba but did not become a war hero, and he started saying in public that TR was never at San Juan Hill.[93]

But citizens, in general, honored Roosevelt as a worthy hero. Lodge wrote TR that he thought his friend's presidential prospects would be sterling after he made good in an intermediary office such as governor of New York. Even before TR was out of danger in Cuba, Lodge went to see his friends in New York. The senator was delighted that with the German navy already in position to capture a naval base in Manila, Dewey took the Philippines, and Congress, flushed with the excitement of the war, had annexed Hawaii and the Philippines while the U.S. Navy occupied Wake Island and Guam.[94]

While negotiations to end the war went on, TR's troops were stranded in Cuba under tropical heat, and he lamented, "Half of my men are dead, wounded or down with fever." He was made a colonel, but that did not give him the power to save his men from malaria or yellow fever. He bought food for them with his own money and made as much noise as he could with Lodge and the higher-ups in the army to get the men what they needed. Corinne mailed hampers of food, and Bamie, through her position on the executive committee of the Red Cross Auxiliary, sent nurses to care for the wounded, but not enough. TR declared in a letter (which Lodge never wanted published) that by their incompetence "the President & Secretary are causing dreadful loss of life."[95]

Mismanagement of the war shocked him. He wrote Lodge that some of his "half-starved" men were wounded but had no shelter in the rain or sun. Their paltry fare of hard tack made recovery harder. General Shafter, in TR's eyes, was an "unwieldy swine" who stayed away from the front lines and left his men to face a "hideous disaster." Roosevelt said he would "hang my head to think" how badly run the Cuban campaign had been. He signed a round robin letter with several generals requesting the removal of troops from the yellow fever area. He also wrote his own letter demanding the same thing. Both found their way into the newspapers, and army administrators were not pleased.[96]

The tragedy of the war was the army's botched supply and transportation systems, which caused inhumane treatment of the soldiers. The *Journal* and other newspapers ran exposés about the "embalmed" roast beef the army bought that was poisonous to the soldiers, and about the bad planning that left camps without food. The McKinley administration worried ineffectually about the disorganized medical care that left malaria and yellow fever cases to die.

Bob Ferguson had worried that the United States would become "the laughing stock of the world" and that the German military attaché sent to observe would tell the kaiser that Americans were too disorganized to fight. In France and Germany observers had expected Spain to raid Boston and New York and to defeat the upstart Americans. However, the victories at San Juan Heights and Manila redeemed America's military reputation. At long last the troops were ordered home, and Secretary of War Russell Alger eventually lost his job over the scandals.[97]

Theodore believed his wartime bravery warranted a medal of honor. His immediate superiors wrote letters urging the War Department to reward him. His men agreed, in part because of his courageous charge and in part because he had been so concerned about their well-being before and after the fighting. The soldiers said he treated them with "an almost fatherly, kindly attitude of forbearance and forgiveness." But the War Department found him a troubling "grandstander" who did not fall in well with military discipline. During the Battle of San Juan Heights, General Joseph Wheeler told Roosevelt he might be ordered by Shafter to retreat from his position on Kettle Hill. TR balked and said he might not obey such orders. Wood had to reprimand him for drinking beer with his men, and on another occasion he undermined a superior officer's authority by releasing a court-martialed soldier. He refused to be "a cog in a gigantic machine." Other army men resented the attention the Rough Rider received, for the public believed the press reports which made it seem like his war and his victory alone. TR's disobedience may not have been the deciding factor when his medal of honor was proposed, but after the round robin was published, the army refused him the honor it had given Wood and many other soldiers who had risked less.[98]

Later, Roosevelt confessed his dissatisfaction with his wartime heroism, declaring, according to one reporter, "I have always been unhappy, most unhappy, that I was not severely wounded in Cuba . . . in some . . . striking and disfiguring way." He told one of his combat buddies, "I rather envy you at least one of your wounds." Unsatisfied with himself because of the long shadow the Civil War cast over his life, TR admitted, "The only trouble was that there was not enough war to go around." Yet he knew he had written himself into history, and he told Lodge that the ten great days he spent fighting made his life complete: "I am quite content to go now . . . I am more than satisfied even though I die of yellow fever tomorrow, for at least I feel that I have done something which enables me to leave a name to the children of which they can rightly be proud."[99]

He had promised Kermit and Ted that if he were killed in battle they should have his sword and revolver, but for Edith, listening to her husband's plans to leave a proud name and a few mementos was heartbreaking. Alice comforted her sobbing stepmother when TR's letters written just before he went into battle arrived. Then, Uncle Jim Roosevelt died suddenly, and Edith wrote her husband: "I do not dare to let myself weep for poor Uncle Jim who was so kind and good to me for if I once break down all the longing for you and the terrible suspense & loneliness comes over me in a wave that I am helpless against."[100]

She held herself together to remain strong while Corinne fell into a "very nervous state" and Emily Carow had a "feverish attack" from the suspense. In August when TR was finally sent home to be quarantined at Camp Wyckoff at Long Island's Montauk Point, Edith and the children visited him in camp. And when he came home they did not expect the large crowds that greeted him in Oyster Bay or the delegations asking him to run for governor. Senator Lodge saw the snowballing effect of his friend's fame and even made sure New York political leaders heard how good a governor a war hero would make.[101]

The international aftermath of the war was tragic. American policymakers, in their ignorance of the Philippines and the varied people who inhabited its 1,200 islands, refused them independence and thus found themselves replacing Spain as the colonial authority over people who wanted self-government. When John Hay became McKinley's secretary of state in the fall of 1898, the President had already decided to "uplift" the Filipinos and Christianize them, despite the fact that anti-imperialists like Andrew Carnegie complained about the injustice of colonial rule. At first Roosevelt opposed outright annexation of all the islands and preferred the retention of one coaling station. After the Philippine revolution spread and independence leader Emilio Aguinaldo challenged America's right to be there, TR was one of those most eager to make war on the Filipinos. The Philippines became, TR later admitted, America's defensive "Achilles heel," and in the distant future they promised to be a troubling and expensive possession. But in 1898 the war looked like a glorious victory to the rising young nation and the proud young war hero–politician. America's reach into the Atlantic and Pacific to gain prominence as a world power changed the course of world history.[102]

☆ CHAPTER SIX ☆

A "Wild Gallup, at Breakneck Speed"

WHEN THEODORE ROOSEVELT disembarked from the troop transport that brought him back to Montauk Point, Long Island, on August 15, 1898, he was eager to go back to Cuba to fight some more. But Spain admitted defeat the next day. Only thirty-nine, he had to consider what came next, since he had resigned his post in the Navy Department. With his blossoming national fame and Lodge's management, he might look to move up in the political world. However, he had an unpromising electoral record in his home state of New York: he had been defeated for mayor of New York City in 1886 and had never been elected to any political position beyond the State Assembly. Since then his career had been built on appointed office. Nevertheless, as he helped to demobilize the Rough Riders at Camp Wyckoff and bid farewell to his friends from the Cuban campaign, he was besieged by political visitors asking him to run for governor. Soon he was running hard and testing his mettle on the campaign trail. He said America had "entered upon a new career" and so had he.[1]

TR was not quite prepared for the national "cult of Theodore Roosevelt." His lively book *The Rough Riders*, celebrating the many ethnic groups who fought side by side in brotherhood during the war, sold well in article and book form and helped make him a bigger celebrity. Flattering press reports had told the public he embodied the romantic ideals of their generation, and to a reading public schooled in Sir Walter Scott a new heroic Ivanhoe gave them hope in the aftermath of the grimy Gilded Age. Cheering crowds greeted him as he went in and out of Manhattan. Reporters asked him often if he would run for president.[2]

Entertainers capitalized on his story. Buffalo Bill signed up sixteen Rough Riders to reenact the Battle of San Juan Hill in his Wild West show, and another group of Rough Riders, including Tom Isbell, known as the invincible Cherokee, joined Buffalo Bill's competitor Zack Mulhall to perform steer roping with young Will Rogers in what was sometimes called "the famous Teddy Roosevelt cow boy band" or the Congress of Rough Riders and Ropers.[3]

The groundswell of popular enthusiasm for TR hit New York politics just as Republican Governor Frank Black was mired in a canal-dredging scandal. November promised to be a losing month for Republicans if they did not replace Black on the ticket. Boss Thomas Platt did not want to support Roosevelt because of his independent leanings and his Sunday closing crusades. But TR's friend Lemuel Quigg convinced Platt that TR was a crowd pleaser and a pliable party man. TR promised Platt to be moderate in exchange for a foreign policy plank and his machine's support. As he campaigned, Roosevelt was in the awkward position of having to defend or keep quiet about the Republican administration of the war, which he knew firsthand was negligent. Platt came of political age apprenticed to Roscoe Conkling and, like his mentor, "had the sincerest and the profoundest contempt," he said, for nonpartisan or independent reformers, whom he disparaged as "political hybrid[s]." But TR—after refusing the independents' nomination to please Platt—courted independent support and hoped to dampen reformers' third-party tendencies, which he knew would elect a Democrat.[4]

Candidate Roosevelt realized that tax policy and the merit system were not issues that worked on the stump. As he told Rudyard Kipling, he had learned to reach voters by "an appeal to their emotions." In 1898 love of country and pride in its victory over Spain stirred patriotic crowds well. America's rise to world power had taken less time than a schoolchild's summer vacation, and TR campaigned to enthusiastic throngs before the sobering reality of colonial responsibility had sunk in. He also praised unions, state factory inspection laws, and the closing down of sweatshops; he pledged a strong commitment to reform. As his campaign train traveled all over New York, one Rough Rider blew his bugle from the back of the caboose, bands played "There'll Be a Hot Time in the Old Town Tonight," and fans climbed aboard. By sheer force of personality, he drew crowds of twenty thousand and more along the sparsely populated Hudson River. Voters saw him as "sincerity 'six feet high.' " TR calmed down his raucous crowds by joking with them: "I want to ask you to let this be as much of a monologue as possible." They laughed and then listened.[5]

William Randolph Hearst, deeply jealous of the Rough Rider's fame, could not get the Democrats to nominate him to run against TR; they chose instead the more reliable Augustus Van Wyck, a staid New York Supreme Court judge from Brooklyn. Thereafter, Hearst unleashed the full force of his cartoonists and editorialists to ridicule Roosevelt as a spoiled child and political fake. Mugwump Carl Schurz refused to support TR because of his "fantastic notions as to the bodily exercise the American people need to keep them from Chinese degeneracy." In black neighborhoods Roosevelt praised the valor of black troops he had commanded in Cuba and said, "They can drink out of my canteen," but some black voters recalled his negative remarks about black troopers and refused to support him. Democratic boss Richard Croker lambasted TR for having used children as "stool pigeons" when he was police commissioner, and Roosevelt, in turn, denounced Croker's corrupt bossism at Tammany Hall and made Crokerism the real issue of the campaign. As Roosevelt whistle-stopped from the back of trains that toured the state, crowds ran after the cars to keep him in sight as long as possible. One supporter watched "as the train faded away and I saw him smiling waving his hat at the people and they in turn giving abundant evidence of their enthusiastic affection my eyes filled with tears."[6]

Edith was so glad to have him home from the war that for a while she could ignore the glare of publicity which followed the hero of San Juan Hill. She had stopped sharing her husband's war letters with the publicity-hungry Corinne, who ignored her sister-in-law's injunctions about keeping them private—she gave them to New Jersey newspapers. Edith rarely campaigned with her husband because his pace—forty speeches in two days—exhausted her. She did help him with his massive mail, and she wrote to thank friends like Seth Low when they helped her husband's campaign. Still, she confided in Lodge she was more preoccupied with Ted's continuing nervous collapse: "My poor little Ted is back where he was last winter."[7]

Theodore won election as governor that November, but only narrowly, by 17,794 votes, and though she was glad he achieved what he wanted Edith realized she did not like to have her family subjected to the rude public gaze. She paced up and down at the start of her husband's term and looked with disdain at the dismal old Governor's Mansion in Albany. She wondered how she could wrest a normal family life out of her husband's new circumstances.[8]

TR bustled into office, happy to have executive power for a change. He entertained a wide variety of people in the mansion—from his labor advisor George Gunton and the A.F.L.'s Samuel Gompers to every local assemblyman and boss whose vote he could attract. He got rid of the billiard tables in the Governor's Mansion and had a horizontal bar and wrestling mats installed. Before long, he and forester Gifford Pinchot wrestled out their competitive and affectionate bonds of friendship on the mats below. Between matches Pinchot wrote his conservation speeches and advised the governor on how to save the Adirondacks and the Palisades along the Hudson. Edith said she could "only peep from the stairs as they wear no shirts," and she was not surprised when the strenuous life of hard wrestling injured her husband's tendons and made his muscles sore.[9]

Being a hero felt exhilarating and affirming to the man they now called the Colonel, but fame also proved slightly dangerous. An armed crank was arrested before he broke into Sagamore Hill, so Jacob Riis took it upon himself to guard TR when he returned for visits to Oyster Bay and commuted to the city on the Long Island Railroad. He could no longer walk on the streets of New York without a crowd following him.

As their father busied himself with legislation and daily press conferences, the young Roosevelts discovered the cellar in the Governor's Mansion made a good home for the raccoon, possum, guinea pigs, rabbits, and squirrels they kept as pets, a fine arrangement until the stench wafted up to disturb Edith's guests in the parlor above. Eleanor wrote Bamie from Mlle. Souvestre's girls' school outside London that she was envious of Alice and Ted's family life in Albany and wished she were with them.[10]

Albany itself was, in Theodore's mind, "just like a little English cathedral town" with the very proper Bishop Doane shedding a quaint Anglican glow over the sleepy capital. That did not, in Edith's mind, make up for the lack of theater or art or intelligent company she had enjoyed in Washington and New York. She made the best of it by joining a ladies' discussion club where she could talk about English history and literature. Alice was bored by Albany's preoccupation with good works and athletics, which made her miss her friends in New York.

On the other hand, Edith was relieved to have no more Washington–New York commutes separating the family, and she enjoyed skating with her husband at the country club and sleighing with him that winter. Yet she felt "still frail" and took to her bed in the first few days of 1899. Sometimes the way her husband imposed the strenuous life on their sons upset her. A few days later TR wrote one Rough Rider not to come for a visit because "at the moment my family is having a breakdown," a reference to Ted's emotional problems which had prevented him from attending school for most of the previous year. Ignoring the promise he made to Lambert, Theodore pushed Ted toward mandatory vigor and wrote to a stranger what he expected from boys: "I am as intolerant of brutality and cruelty to the weak as I am intolerant of weakness or effeminacy. I want to see boys able to box, wrestle, play football and hold their own stoutly, not only in games, but when called upon to fight or resist oppression."[11]

Roosevelt stuck to his promise to consult Platt about whom he should appoint and the old man rather liked the "boy governor." Platt hoped that the heavy corporate financing of the campaign and the Republican organization would encourage the governor to run a "business government," but TR quickly disappointed him.[12]

Roosevelt surprised many people when on January 2 he gave his first annual message and called for the state to clean up its sweatshops and to do a better job inspecting its factories. He intended to pursue progressive reform of the kind that Robert M. La Follette would call for but rarely achieve. The New Yorker's willingness to compromise gave him a strategic advantage over the Wisconsin governor, who failed to get passed railroad rate regulation because in the give-and-take legislative process he disliked compromise.[13]

The kind of progressive reform TR advocated emerged from no coherent movement but from the work reformers did in the 1890s to address the new industrial and urban problems of hunger, crime, filthy streets, and economic exploitation. Progressivism began as a variety of local and state reform endeavors which gained momentum in the nineties. Social settlements, labor advocates, women's clubs, urban reformers, and business groups worked to upgrade the living standards of city dwellers and to increase the legal obligations of cities to protect those standards. Garbage collection, clean water, factory and tenement codes and inspection, and better schools were only a few of their goals. Public health professionals and social workers often worked with local merchants and landowners to ponder how far municipal ownership should go—should the city own its own water and garbage collection, its gas works, its public transportation system? In TR's home town, the development of the port and the subway system, and the reform of the city schools under a central administration were early progressive attempts at modernization through the expansion of public responsibility, and they were largely pushed by merchant Hamiltonianism typical of Thee's generation. But settlement house workers, urban working-class liberals, and other groups also worked for even more advanced reform at the turn of the century.[14]

Progressive reformers emboldened by the scientific authority they gained from new social science research discovered that TR was more receptive to their ideas than other politicians. In his first six months as governor he worked with the United Garment Workers to push through an eight-hour-day law which protected workers on public contracts—a law which he got extended to cover all state employees. He supported the Costello Anti-Sweatshop Act regulating tenements as workplaces, and signed a variety of weak consumer protection–pure food laws (laws requiring the labeling of dairy products, for example, provided no penalties for selling impure products). Jacob Riis watched the governor show extra pride whenever he "accomplished something for which his father had striven and paved the way."[15]

Roosevelt also built a record as a conservationist governor. He appointed men like the reform-minded businessman George W. Perkins to the Palisades Commission to protect that park along the Hudson, and he sought to make the Adirondacks and Catskills protected state parks. After a drought in the summer of 1899, fires broke out in the Adirondacks, and when local authorities refused to spend money on putting them out, Roosevelt sent emergency firefighters to save the forests. In addition, he got the Fish and Game Commission renamed the Forest, Fish, and Game Commission, and applied Pinchot's ideas about scientific management to New York forests. He also worked with the Audubon Society for bird protection. He wrote: "When I hear of the destruction of a species, I feel just as if all the works of some great writer had perished; as if we had lost all instead of only part of Polybius or Livy."[16]

Roosevelt's record as governor showed he was sympathetic toward reform, but he was not willing to take huge risks to win it. He supported proposals to extend woman suffrage incrementally, first for school board elections and gradually for other offices. But he did not then support a statewide suffrage or the national Anthony amendment. His record on race remained full of contradictions, yet it rated better for action than it did for privately racialist fulminations. In private he still wondered about "the natural limitations of the Negro." But he appointed blacks to state jobs and a visible spot on the Pan-American Exposition Board, and praised the abolitionist Frederick Douglass at the unveiling of a memorial. He consulted with the editor of the *New York Age*, T. Thomas Fortune, who spoke for the Afro-American League about how to advance the cause of blacks in New York. As a result, TR endorsed the Ellsberg anti-segregation bill which made it illegal to segregate public schools, a landmark integration bill that won passage in a Jim Crow era.[17]

Because reformers rightly saw Roosevelt as an ally, Florence Kelley volunteered to be the chief factory inspector for New York as she had been for Illinois when the reformer John Altgeld was governor. Her appointment had behind it the impressive backing of Jane Addams, Lillian Wald, Maud Nathan of New York's Consumers' League, and Jacob Riis. Despite Addams' personal visit and pleas, TR feared that if he appointed a radical woman, a socialist, from Chicago he would be charged with "Altgeldism" (Altgeld had defended the accused Haymarket bombers and Pullman strikers). Instead, he chose a male party loyalist who had been an elevator operator, and instructed him to listen to the expert advice of Kelley as he did his job.[18]

Factory inspectors had to patrol tenements where piecework and sweatshops commingled with crowded flats, and fires often spread from tattered cloth of the garment industry on the ground floor into the residential units above. As he had as police commissioner, Roosevelt followed Riis on tours through many five-story tenements. Afterward he proposed a new tenement house commission bill which imposed more penalties on landlords who refused to improve their lighting and sanitation. When he did not have time to tour, he asked Riis to investigate the possible human effects that bills before the legislature might have. He listened to Wald and the Consumers' League and supported their labeling campaign to let consumers know which goods were sewn in sweatshops. And he got a bill passed to require employers to provide seats for waitresses and women factory workers. The seventeen labor bills he signed as governor won him a loyal following among advocates of workingmen and -women like the Consumers' League. He pulled away from Republican Party dogmas and stood up for workers, conservation, and the regulation of monopolies, but Platt and his supporters in the state legislature fought him constantly.[19]

Roosevelt viewed his power from a strong moral perspective. He took the position that he would not approve a bill raising the salaries of New York City's public school teachers unless a system for evaluating teacher competence was included. He later wrote that his pardon power imposed "painful" duties on him. He grew "angry" when he was asked to pardon rapists, murderers, pornographers, and white slavers, and refused to do so. At the turn of the century, a life sentence meant an average of only fourteen years of imprisonment, so he came to favor the death penalty for murder and rape. He was called upon to pardon a woman, Martha Place, who was on death row for throwing sulfuric acid in her stepdaughter's face and smothering the girl, then taking an ax to her husband. After brief deliberation over the fact it would shock the public if he sent a woman to the electric chair, Roosevelt refused the pardon. However, he ordered that only reporters from the Associated Press and the Republican *New York Sun* be allowed to watch the electrocution, not any from the Hearst or Pulitzer papers because he expected they would sensationalize the details of Place's death to make him look like a woman killer.[20]

The thorniest problem he took on as governor was the previous administration's policy of granting generous franchises to corporations. The state had given traction corporations a near monopoly on the elevated subways of New York. Bridges and tunnels had been auctioned off to corporations to build and run for profit. TR disliked awarding monopolies to any company, and he believed that in certain cases, such as water, public ownership was the best way to provide cheap services to the people. The best he could do politically, however, was to limit the duration of the franchise and tax the corporation's profit, but when he supported a bill for that purpose, the Ford franchise tax bill, he angered Platt, who was funded by corporate donors hostile to such taxation. Thee's old friend Elihu Root represented the Whitney family's traction interests, and he was furious that Roosevelt wanted the public to benefit from the Whitney elevated train franchise. Platt pushed the governor to leave the Traction Trust alone.

The governor stood his ground, but the fight over the bill strained the Platt-Roosevelt relationship badly. When the bill was close to passage, Platt ordered his minion Speaker Fred Nixon to ignore the governor's special message urging legislators to vote for the bill. Nixon destroyed the message, and when TR heard what he had done threatened to come over to the assembly and read it himself. The bill passed, and TR told the celebrating assemblymen around him that he expected he had "ended" his "political career"—Platt would certainly not support him for reelection. The "boy governor" alienated Platt further when he fired Platt's ally Louis F. Payn, who had proven to be a corrupt superintendent of insurance. Payn warned: "He'll get you, too, soon." Platt had lost patience with Roosevelt and started to design ways to get him out of Albany.[21]

TR did not fully understand the growing popular agitation against monopolies, and he was inclined to dismiss it as "irrational," as he had Bryan's talk against privilege in 1896. But he knew that wealth was being concentrated by the merger movement that consolidated businesses. When U.S. Steel swallowed up 138 competitors someone got hurt—smaller businesses failed and workers were fired after mergers. A small group of monopolists was working to gain control of all the railroads and whole segments of the manufacturing sector. The 1890 census had shown that 9 percent of the population controlled 71 percent of the wealth, and in 1900 about three-quarters of the American people qualified as poor. As governor, TR found no more effective way to aid them than the stopgap of opening New York City armories to house the homeless during cold weather. He began gathering advice from experts and politicos about how government could use regulation and tax policy to stop the accumulation of too much power in private hands. He heard workingmen tell him as he spoke around the state that William Jennings Bryan was the only man who could control the trusts. He learned on his own that trusts were hard to control. When he won the passage of the Ford franchise tax bill, he underestimated his opposition. Afterward, corporations took him to court and blocked the tax on public franchises while he was governor.[22]

At the end of his first contentious several months in office he had left New York's corporations "howling like mad"; he said he wished he were fighting Filipinos rather than Boss Platt. At the same time, he remained critical of the growing popular anti-trust crusades, and though he favored putting corporations "fully at the service of the State and the people," he as yet had no good plan for how to do it.[23]

TR's political struggles did not deter him from speaking to the broad national audience that now looked to him as a hero and a leader for the new century. Not only was he regarded as presidential timber, but he was also recognized as a voice of a younger generation who would shape the new century. As a historian he had already spoken out on behalf of a vigorous new Americanism, and, perhaps most significantly, he was, after George Dewey, the most heralded hero in America's recent popular war. So when he was asked to give a speech in Chicago he was being offered a chance to define his country's future.

TR gave his famous "The Strenuous Life" speech at the Hamilton Club there on April 10, 1899. The talk touched a nerve and inspired a generation of young men to strive to lead more vigorous lives, to serve their country and to grasp world leadership. Roosevelt took as his task speaking to "all that is most American in the American character" and urging upon the American soul "not the doctrine of ignoble ease, but the doctrine of the strenuous life, the life of toil and effort, of labor and strife."

He warned his listeners not to go into the future "content to rot by inches in ignoble ease within our borders, taking no interest in what goes on beyond them, sunk in scrambling commercialism; heedless of the higher life, the life of aspiration, of toil and risk." The next task for the United States was governing its new territorial possessions, justly led by "stern men with empires in their brains," and if the country embraced "the life of strenuous endeavor" he promised "we shall ultimately win the goal of true national greatness." Kansas editor William Allen White said that the speech "excited controversy, fairly clamorous controversy," but it announced that "the Great Revival" of decency and renewed energy had begun.[24]

IN JUNE, TR went to Las Vegas and New Mexico Territory for Rough Rider reunions in a free private railroad car given him by the Atchison, Topeka, and Santa Fe Railroad. Crowds cheered him all along his route. He made a point of reporting to Platt how people in the West expressed their "wild enthusiasm"—as if he were a presidential candidate. On his return he endured a season of restlessness with the limited powers of the governorship, and he described himself as "just one cog in a complicated bit of machinery." Meanwhile, McKinley had made the Philippines part of an American empire, but his ignorance of the varied people he aimed to govern made colonial policy-making difficult and occupying American soldiers treated the Filipinos as childlike "gugus" who needed to be civilized. Roosevelt, who also looked at the Filipinos with racialist condescension, toyed with the idea of becoming secretary of war or governor general of the Philippines, but by midsummer Lodge already had a plan to get TR nominated as McKinley's running mate for the 1900 election. Edith felt the vice presidency was the wrong position for a man who liked power and activity, but TR saw that his precarious partnership with the Platt machine was disintegrating, so he was inclined at first to like the idea.[25]

Occasionally, though, he worried that politics might not be the right career for him. As he thought about what awaited him after he was governor, TR decided that his unfortunate habit of letting loose his opinions on many subjects "with some intemperance of expression" might doom him in politics and so hedged his bets by returning to his literary career. He signed a contract for $5,000 to write a life of Oliver Cromwell for Scribner's that summer, and despite days of malarial fever, which Edith dosed with quinine, he delved into a study of the Puritan leader who wanted to achieve what TR deemed the dangerous goal of creating a world "where civil government and social life alike should be based upon the Commandments set forth in the Bible." Though he judged that the Lord Protector's fearlessness and moralism had been virtues, he "lacked the power of self-repression possessed by Washington and Lincoln," notably when he lost his temper after a fruitless negotiation between Parliament and the army and childishly threw a pillow at the speaker before he stomped out of the room.[26]

After his first frustrating session trying to reform New York, TR reflected upon his own lapses in self-control and criticized Cromwell for being too impatient to build the legal systems that would guarantee lasting freedom for his people. He concluded that Cromwell's Parliament, which represented propertied voters and not a hereditary House of Lords, was more democratic than later Parliaments, but that the downfall of Puritan democracy had been Cromwell's fatal lust for power. His friend Arthur Lee wrote that Roosevelt "felt a certain affinity between Cromwell and himself," but Cromwell's religious dogmatism made TR want to reaffirm his own belief in religious toleration and a Social Gospel religion whereby believers of all faiths "best serve their God by serving their fellow men."[27]

By August he had finished a rough draft of his book, and Edith told him unexpectedly that she was going with him on his speaking tour around New York. Theodore joked slyly to Lodge, who knew how reticent about public contact Edith was: "I think I can see her now circulating among the wives" at the Pioneer picnic at Silver Lake. As Edith and Theodore made the rounds at county fairs and stopped at Niagara Falls and the Chautauqua lecture camp, she could enjoy watching her husband's obvious rapport with New York's people. Nevertheless, she still preferred the quiet days alone when he took an ax and she armed herself with a saw, and together they cleared brushwood for a new path along the edge of Cooper's Bluff.[28]

In September 1899, New York celebrated the return of George Dewey, now admiral, and honored him for his victory over the Spanish in Manila. Dewey Day brought huge crowds to see the North Atlantic Squadron as it sailed up the North River. "Welcome Dewey," strung in electric lights across the Brooklyn Bridge, Dewey flags, and Dewey Medals designed by Daniel Chester French grated on Roosevelt, though he went to McKinley's dinner for Dewey and prided himself on good relations with "the Navy game-cocks" like Dewey. He found Dewey's "thirst for notoriety" repulsive, and saw no signs of the same in his own blooming romance with the public. He was like a schoolboy going to his first dance over the question of how he should appear in the Dewey parade. Some wanted him to ride dressed like a "fake riding school master" at the head of the militia, but in the end he dressed as a governor in gray striped pants. Dewey's fame and the frustrations of being governor wore him down so much that when Austin Wadsworth asked him to go fox hunting that fall, he said he felt "about as sociable as a gut-shot bear."[29]

Edith did well managing the social side of being the governor's wife as well as keeping watch over the children. Her husband's larger salary, free house, and royalties from *The Rough Riders* allowed her to escape worry and duty as she never had before. In November 1899 her startled husband reported to Bamie, "Edith has just gone down in a fit of unwonted gayety to see Henry Irving and Ellen Terry in New York, leaving Miss Young and myself with the six children."[30]

The Roosevelts welcomed Emily Carow, German diplomat Hermann Speck von Sternberg, and the increasingly sickly Bob Ferguson to share their family Christmas that year, and Bamie sent Theodore such lavish gifts that Edith teased her about "pampering your butterfly brother." Speck and Bob took the children skating on the frozen meadow not far from the governor's mansion, and Bob more than ever was the uncle Elliott had never been to the six young Roosevelts. Edith and Theodore worried that Bob, as he agonized over the Boer War, would sign on with the Canadian Rough Riders and get himself killed. Before the next year was out, Theodore arranged a safe desk job for him—looking after the Astor family's vast real estate holdings with Douglas Robinson, a post not unlike the one Elliott had held before his decline.[31]

As the winter of 1900 began, TR went back to touring sweatshops with Jacob Riis, and he urged Riis to mobilize the civic reform groups to which he belonged to propose more legislation that he could champion in the legislature. Roosevelt preached in *The Century* magazine the importance of "fellow-feeling" or "willingness to treat a man as a man." He urged Americans to work together "on a plane of equality" "for a common object," a foreshadowing of a "square deal" for every man regardless of race, class, or creed. But dealing with men as equals was not in fashion in America then. In January, TR and Edith had entertained the well-known conservatory-trained black composer Harry Burleigh, who sang "The Absent Minded Beggar" for 350 of their guests, including some of the newsboys who had come up from New York. Edith praised Burleigh's interpretation of the song, based on "his own very spirited setting." She noted, however, that one of her guests' behavior was "very stupid" and no hotel in Albany would take in the singer, so the Roosevelts invited him to stay in the governor's mansion.[32]

Before Edith and Emily left on a vacation to Cuba, TR had what he called "a little too much strenuous life" while wrestling—he broke several ribs and dislocated a shoulder. As sole parent, he taught Ethel to ice-skate and kept the children occupied at the country club with great success. After Ted came home battered from a school yard fight with a boy he called a "Mick," Edith said her husband in her absence felt "the responsibility of the children in addition to his other cares while I am away, & I have had many pricks of conscience about leaving him." Nevertheless, her trip to Cuba was worth it to Edith because she followed "the trail the Rough Riders took to Guasimas" and she found it "almost too real."[33]

Most of the time, TR received plenty of personal help when he was governor; in fact, his sisters vied over who could be most useful to him politically. He often spent Friday and Saturday at 689 Madison Avenue, where Bamie hosted his breakfasts with Platt and his lieutenant Benjamin Odell. After Bamie moved to Washington in October 1899, Corinne turned her hospitality at 422 Madison Avenue over to her brother, who jokingly asked her: "Can I lunch at your house . . . with divers [*sic*] person of disreputable antecedents and no character?"[34]

EXPANSIONISM and its aftermath still occupied the governor's thoughts. He was not convinced the McKinley administration was forceful enough in dealing with the colonial dilemmas created by the war. He lobbied McKinley, the new secretary of war, Elihu Root, Senator Lodge, and Secretary of State John Hay, urging them to use force combined with diplomacy rather than diplomacy alone. He insisted that in the Philippines the army would have to fight harder because "we have the wolf by the ears and we cannot let him go safely," which was the same simile used by Thomas Jefferson about the holding of slaves. TR argued that "the reasoning which justifies our having made war against Sitting Bull also justifies our having checked the outbreaks of Aguinaldo and his followers." He also praised the rugged colonial administration of Leonard Wood in Cuba, where, along with improvements in sanitation, schools, and roads, Wood had Cubans publicly horsewhipped if they violated sanitary rules.[35]

Roosevelt then joined Lodge in the politically explosive act of speaking out against McKinley's canal plans. If the United States wanted to expand its protective role over the Western Hemisphere, it had to abandon its previous commitment in the Clayton-Bulwer Treaty that a canal be built jointly by the United States and Britain. After its difficult victory in the Boer War, Britain had little interest in such a project, so Hay, acting on McKinley's behalf, negotiated a treaty allowing the United States to pursue its own canal. Within a week after Hay submitted the treaty to the Senate on February 5, 1900, Roosevelt went to the estate of his supporter Frederick W. Holls near Yonkers to meet with Assistant Secretary of State David Jayne Hill, editor Albert Shaw, Nicholas Murray Butler, and Andrew Dickson White to plan an attack on the treaty because it did not guarantee for the United States the right to fortify and control the canal. The administration was "much disturbed" by the headlines made by the group's demand that any canal built between the two great oceans had to be fortified with American guns.[36]

Hay reprimanded the governor as if he were a wayward juvenile: "Cannot you leave a few things to the President and the Senate, who are charged with them by the Constitution?" TR replied like the brassy new generation he represented: he did not respect the "dead hand" of past treaty commitments. Finally, expansionists triumphed and amended the Hay-Pauncefote Treaty to say the canal would be fortified, thereby committing, in the eyes of TR's English friend Arthur Lee, a "gross disregard of international good manners." After Britain rejected the amended treaty, Lodge used diplomatic leverage in London to reach an understanding. Lodge and TR had been irritating, but nonetheless instrumental in clearing major obstacles for a U.S.-controlled and -fortified canal.[37]

By the end of his time in Albany, TR had made a stronger record than any other progressive governor as an advocate of conservation, especially in forest protection, the administration of the Adirondacks, and game and fish preservation. He had called for measures to achieve scientific water resource management and to prevent water pollution by the lumber industry, but he met legislative resistance. As governor TR said he had "always gone just as far forward as I could get people to go."[38]

But he knew his position as an independent Republican working with a corrupt boss would not last long: "If for some reason I should be weak," he said, "the Machine will throw me over." And Platt was already hard at work trying to convince McKinley and Mark Hanna they needed the Rough Rider on the 1900 ticket. Unfortunately, they were still smarting from TR's loud criticism of their foreign policy.[39]

Roosevelt had stifled talk of his challenging McKinley for the nomination in 1900 (Nelson A. Miles had tried to get him to run against the President with him), but it proved harder to dim Lodge's hope. Theodore told Cabot that the vice presidency with its modest salary and many expensive social obligations would make Edith worry too much about money. He made it clear to his supporters, however, that he wanted the presidential nomination in 1904, though he understood that by then "the kaleidoscope will have shaken and I shall be out of view." Lodge still hoped that at the very least his friend had a cabinet post or a Senate seat coming in McKinley's second term.[40]

The senator worked with Platt to convince Roosevelt's family and close friends to join them in pushing him toward the vice presidential nomination. Bamie was livid after Cabot came to her house in Washington and told her she was wrongheaded to advise her brother to stay in Albany. She, like Edith, feared what "comparatively inactive years" would do to him. TR lobbied against his own nomination with his many western allies, and when Edith arrived at the Republican convention in Philadelphia on June 18, 1900, she found him in his room at the Walton Hotel "being torn in every direction." She consulted several of his political friends, who gave her diametrically opposed advice. Edith urged her husband not to run but Lodge pushed him toward the vice presidency. Furthermore, the torchlight procession outside his balcony and the cries for "Teddy!" were seductive. Roosevelt listened to Lodge and let the convention cheer him at the top of their lungs and give him its nomination.[41]

After the Roosevelts' "melancholy little party" came home from the convention, the governor tried to save face by bragging that it was his immense popularity that made the vice presidency inevitable, not Platt's power within the party: "I stood Mr. Platt and his machine on their heads . . . but this simply solidified the entire remainder of the convention!" If he was elected vice president he hoped that "something will turn up to be done!"[42]

When TR went to Oklahoma City for a Rough Rider reunion and led a huge parade of Rough Riders, cowboys, Indians, marching bands, and Civil War veterans on Independence Day, it was hard to tell whether he was a potential national presidential hopeful or competition for Buffalo Bill's Wild

West Show. As he rode on his black charger and gave a speech to thirty thousand, TR belonged as much to the world of popular entertainment as he did to the world of politics. Later that day, he saw Zack Mulhall's cowboy band, including young Will Rogers, roping steers, and he praised Mulhall's sixteen-year-old daughter, Lucille, for her expert riding, which was no doubt more entertaining to him than watching yet another theatrical reenactment of the Battle of San Juan Hill. He later arranged for their Frisco Cowboy Band to play at McKinley's inauguration in March 1901. When Rogers made his way to Broadway as a vaudeville star, he became a Roosevelt family friend and named his horse Teddy. He always considered TR his favorite president.[43]

When Roosevelt returned to Oyster Bay, his doctors told him his throat was inflamed and that he had overdone it physically. Though they enjoyed quiet picnics with what they called "our own five" children, the Roosevelts were preoccupied with the scanty reports they received about the Boxer rebels, anti-foreign, spirit-possessed Chinese boys who had attacked foreign legations in Peking, with the secret blessing of the Dowager Empress. Theodore later applauded McKinley and Secretary of War Elihu Root's aggressive orders to send five thousand troops to lead the international Boxer Reprisal—an act of war without congressional consent.[44]

The nominee lived under "severe strain" in the summer and fall because he was pressed by the Republican National Committee to campaign everywhere even though he was exhausted and still trying to function as governor. As he campaigned out west, he was delighted to discover that men and boys had formed Rough Rider Clubs in town after town. At Green River, Wyoming, he won over the audience talking about the times when he and Edith had trouble paying the butcher bills. The crowd found him so sympathetic that a little girl came up to him and asked if he could get her father a civil service job, which newspaper reports said he tried to do when he returned to his campaign train.[45]

Roosevelt, the famous war hero, made a good vice-presidential running mate for McKinley because he campaigned fiercely against Democratic nominee William Jennings Bryan. The 1900 campaign inspired the comic writer and managing editor of the *Chicago Journal*, Finley Peter Dunne, to have his Irish barkeep Mr. Dooley point out that the two candidates for president looked alike—they both resembled the queen of patent medicines, Lydia Pinkham. McKinley stayed on his front porch, and, as Mr. Dooley said, " 'Tis Tiddy alone that's running, and he ain't running, he's galloping.' "[46]

Roosevelt had learned how to move crowds. In his 1898 governor's race when he made forty speeches in two days, he saw that great applause came from his remarks about everyday human traits—courage and honesty.

Human interest stories worked better on the stump than tariff policy. He disliked to "fester in the car and elbow to and from stagings where I address my audiences," and he was sorry to miss celebrating the Fourth of July with his children, but he understood that he had to make contact with more people than Bryan to win the election.[47]

An alert stump speaker could gain an education from his audience, and TR proved to be an attentive student of public opinion. When he spoke in states full of Union veterans like Indiana and Ohio, he planted a Grand Army of the Republic man in the front row and habitually "would interrupt himself, descend, shake hands with the veteran, and resume his speech." Observers said it was a "sure-fire" to win Roosevelt loud applause. When he said that the Republican Party of New York State had passed four-fifths of the laws "that now stand to benefit the wage-workers" he was greeted by "great applause." He also learned that campaigning side by side with a former W.C.T.U. officer, lawyer, and now nationally recognized Woman's National Republican Association leader, Judith Ellen Foster, helped him win votes in western states where women enjoyed suffrage.[48]

He developed a deft common touch that went far beyond baby kissing. He went down thousands of feet into mines and even crawled "belly-flat" into the jagged spaces of a gold vein; he tried drilling too. TR did not leave his character at home when he climbed up on the speaker's podium. In a small West Virginia town, Roosevelt was in the middle of giving a speech when a man tried to climb over the railing of the train to join him. Before guards could stop the interloper, TR ordered them to let him on the train; he suspended his speech, and threw his arms around the man and gave him a bear hug—he had recognized an old friend who had helped him when he was wounded in his Dakota ranch days and nothing would stop him from greeting him. But he also brought his bent for invective and slurred his opponents as cowards and liars and demagogues. According to Mr. Dooley, "Tiddy Rosenfelt opened th' battle mildly be insinuatin' that all dimmycrats was liars, horse thieves an' arnychists."[49]

And his campaign had its rough days. One stop away from Louisville, Kentucky, Roosevelt was about to speak at a public square despite a sore throat. But local Bryan supporters set out to sabotage his speech by blowing a steam whistle at a nearby mill so loudly that TR could not be heard. About fifty Bryanites interrupted Roosevelt with shouts of "Hurrah for Bryan!" Then, empty horse-drawn coal wagons drove through the crowd at top speed trying to disperse his audience. Though his sore throat made it difficult for him to shout down his opponents, he won the crowd back by yelling: "I call your attention to the attitude of Mr. Bryan's friends on the subject of law and order."[50]

Audiences in Populist territory often saw him as a representative of eastern moneyed interests. On September 26, Lodge and Roosevelt campaigned together in the town of Victor, Colorado. TR began attacking the Democratic Party for its suspected ties to the Ice Trust. To remind Roosevelt of the embalmed beef scandal which had reflected badly on the Republican conduct of the Spanish-American War, a man shouted: "What about the rotten beef?" TR replied angrily: "I ate it, and you'll never get near enough to be hit by a bullet or within five miles of it." His response, which defensively ridiculed a man for lack of war service, angered the crowd so much he had to be guarded as he left. Small boys threw rocks as his train sped out of town. Later, Democratic newspapers falsely accused Lodge and Roosevelt of appearing drunk there.[51]

On the stump Bryan and TR preached the same homely virtues of duty and God and patriotism. Though Bryan had criticized McKinley's imperial rule, he accepted the patriotic platitude that America had a God-given mission to civilize the rest of the world. Bryan also sounded xenophobic notes about how with its emphasis on imperialism and foreign trade the Republican Party was about to offer "their country into the hands of foreigners." The U.S.-Philippine War was still going on: when American sons were in battle political leaders were not likely to be allowed to criticize the war's wisdom. When Bryan raised legitimate questions about the country's adventure in imperialism, Roosevelt slammed him harshly saying: "The bullets that slay our men in Luzon are inspired by the denouncers of America here." It did not help Bryan that the Filipino independence leader Emilio Aguinaldo called his candidacy "a ray of hope." Anti-imperialist Charles Francis Adams said Bryan "can talk longer, and say less, than any man in Christendom" and those who looked for Bryan to expose the cruelties of the Philippine campaign or debate the dangers of defending such a far-flung empire were to be disappointed. Neither party wanted to debate segregation, and Bryan gave explicit support to white supremacist southern Democrats. No meaningful debate about foreign policy or race occurred during the 1900 campaign, and the triumphant Republicans liked it that way.[52]

As he had done in 1896, TR scared up the respectable vote by calling Bryan a demagogue and warning of his "populistic and communistic doctrines." But Roosevelt let his own views show more readily than in the last presidential campaign. He praised labor unions and the "great good" they conferred on working people. Based on his work as a progressive governor (but certainly not McKinley's as president), Roosevelt praised the eight-hour day, factory inspection, and tenement house regulation, and showed he was open-minded about the question of employers' liabilities and minimum hours. The

Democratic platform opposed using injunctions to stop strikes and had a more pro-worker philosophy, but Bryan did not reach out to urban laborers as effectively as TR. The Republican ticket had the support of most newspapers and big financial interests, but Hearst portrayed McKinley as the lapdog of the trusts. The publisher even set up the *Chicago American* to bolster the Great Commoner's campaign. TR hated Hearst with a passion and wanted "to get at him," but the best he could do was to prepare the New York National Guard to arrest Tammany and Hearst allies in case of voting fraud on election day. When November came, voters chose McKinley and prosperity.[53]

TR, some said, had beaten Bryan at his own game. He had the stamina to give nearly seven hundred speeches and to outtalk the "Boy Orator." After Roosevelt spoke, he sometimes greeted his audiences in person for as long as they lasted. Shaking hands with a war hero electrified crowds. Even the barely susceptible Mark Twain shook hands with TR and admitted afterward that he felt "a wave of welcome." Roosevelt's engagements for 1898 and 1900 alone added up to a thousand speeches. He covered a lot of territory—going 21,000 miles to visit twenty-four states. The *New York Times* estimated that TR had spoken to three million people before the 1900 campaign was over. Roosevelt said of his effective campaigning against Bryan: "Well, I drowned him out. I talked two words to his one. Maybe he was an oratorical cocktail, but I was his chaser."[54]

WHILE HIS FATHER was away campaigning, the unhappy Ted had started boarding school at Groton under the care of Rector Endicott Peabody, and Edith tried to comfort the homesick child long distance while she worried whether her husband took his sun cholera tablets for Cuban fever and throat problems. She dealt with Alice's sleepless nights, Kermit's illnesses, and Quentin's thumb-sucking, and tried to keep newspaper reports of the Victor riot from bringing back memories of the long weeks when her husband was in Cuba. Edith wrote him that the children missed him "dreadfully" and "Every minute I think of you, and hate to be comfortable at home while you are having such a horrid time." She tried to arrange to meet him secretly on the campaign trail without the press hearing about it, but it proved too difficult to manage. Hearing that he had invited guests to Sagamore Hill during the few days in October that they would have together, she resigned herself to having to share him with the rest of the world and she wrote him: "We can always have the night to hallow the day sweetheart. . . . I love you just as I did when we were married and I count the days until you are with me once more."[55]

On election night Edith and Theodore celebrated the Republican victory by drinking Miss Paulding's cherry bounce with the children. Supporters had sent them a dour small bear which romped beside the children before it had to be sent to the zoo. Edith confessed to Emily: "The V.P. is like the bridegroom at a wedding, no one even sees or thinks of him. . . . I hate having him in such a useless & empty position, & exposed to so many annoyances. . . . I don't care for this position." But her husband was in a self-congratulatory mood when he told a friend: "I was rather proud of myself that in all my speeches I did not say anything I had to take back." At the end of 1900, Edith saw the old century out staying up with Quentin, whose asthma kept him up all night, while her husband's inspirational speech calling on young men to face with bold spirits the moral challenges of the new century was read aloud to simultaneous Y.M.C.A. mass meetings all over the United States and Canada.[56]

After he said a morose farewell to Edith on January 7, Theodore left on a hunting trip in Colorado, healthy in body but low in spirits. He filled the time before his inauguration chasing cougar and lynx and killing a treed mountain lion with a knife. Edith was left to care for Quentin and Ted's asthma attacks, and she had Quentin's adenoids removed in the hope that it would diminish his inclination toward infections. When overdrawn bank notices arrived she wrote Theodore in amusement: "Ah ha! You are like the White Queen & can't do 'subtraction.' Your bank deficit is $80 now." But she missed her husband deeply.[57]

THE INAUGURATION on March 4, 1901, brought the Roosevelts temporarily back to Washington, accompanied by their six children, Uncle Jimmie Gracie, Corinne and Douglas and their four children, and, of course, Bob Ferguson. Edith said that at Union Station "Bamie met us at the train and hurried Theodore off before enough people recognized him to make a crush." It was not his first taste of celebrity, and it gave him less of a thrill than crowds cheering for his heroism in the war. Edith admiringly recorded in her diary that her husband "took the oath with great dignity & looked so young and handsome."[58]

She planned to spend most of the year at Sagamore Hill before moving to Washington to Bellamy and Maria Longworth Storer's house, which they had rented starting in October. After the rest of his family went back to Oyster Bay, the new vice president stayed with the Lodges in the capital and admitted he was "not doing any work and do not feel as though I [am] justifying my existence." Five days of presiding over the Senate and attending social functions showed him what a figurehead he had become, and he tactlessly wrote to Edith: "The whirl has been such that I have been too busy and too tired to miss you as I shall from now on." After Congress adjourned and no work turned up for him, he returned to Sagamore Hill, where he tutored Corinne in American history and arranged to study law with the Chief Justice when they moved back to Washington in the fall. When he advised Ted to "always try hard for the best, but don't grumble if you have to take something less," he was reminding himself that he ought not to grumble over his new job. But he did—often.[59]

His friends thought the vice presidency required the "suppression of the most characteristic traits of his nature." Since the crisis of his adolescence his greatest fear had been invalidism and inactivity, so the enforced idleness of the vice presidency palled on him. Alice later said that her father had a "melancholic streak which didn't come out very often but which was noticeable when it did. It ran in his family, I think." He could be "very fatalistic. . . . He thought for instance that the vice-presidency was the end of his career and he was very depressed about that." He feared that "my active work is over," and he confided to Fanny Parsons that Edith was unhappy about leaving their life in Albany: "But I mind it very much too; partly because I was so interested in the work."[60]

When he came back to revel in family life at Sagamore Hill, Edith knew her husband would bring the habits of the strenuous life to his relationship with the children. She issued an edict that he should only play bear with the younger children before supper because "tickle and 'grabble' . . . proved rather too exciting" at bedtime. He let their picnicking children wade in the water with their clothes on, and Edith could only react, he said, with "Roman-matron-like austerity" and regret that she could not give him her hot ginger tonic and punish him along with the children.[61]

When Edith had to go to Washington to see about the Storers' house, he taught Ethel how to ride. The mischievous but endearing toddler Quentin made his way into the Gun Room, where his father was writing, and managed to charm and harass him away from his work. Theodore chopped down trees that blocked their view of Long Island Sound, joined the Masons and got to know his neighbors better, and took time to watch the cherry trees bloom and the season of the bloodroot and violets come and go.[62]

Being vice president was not strenuous. He never drew close to McKinley and had little to do with formulating administration policy. Roosevelt looked upon the President as cold-blooded and unemotional, and he realized that neither McKinley nor his close advisor Mark Hanna "sympathize with my feelings or feel comfortable about me, because they cannot understand what it is that makes me act in certain ways at certain times, and therefore think me indiscreet and overimpulsive." William Allen White, the Kansas editor famous for his anti-Populist editorial "What's the Matter with Kansas?," tried to penetrate McKinley's circumspect persona and found Roosevelt's disdain was well founded: he was no more than "the statue in the park speaking." Hanna, TR believed, was determined to make sure he had no influence on McKinley or policy matters whatsoever.[63]

Though their social relationship with McKinley was warm, Edith as the Vice President's wife found it a tedious chore that she was expected to pay calls on Mrs. McKinley, who had succumbed to an epileptic fit on their last visit. Edith was glad, therefore, that Mrs. McKinley was not in the capital when she went to see about the Storers' house so she could avoid paying "a gruesome call at the White House."[64]

Roosevelt found time to organize a meeting of men who planned to support him when he ran for president in 1904; already Douglas Robinson was lining up donations. But TR also imagined himself unemployed after four years as vice president, and so planned to pick up the threads of his abandoned legal education. He felt discouraged about setting up a course of legal studies in Washington that would enable him to be admitted to the bar in New York, but finally Judge Alton B. Parker helped him.

Despite the uncertainty he faced about his future, he believed that public service had been a worthy path to take, and he wanted to encourage other men like him to follow it. With the help of Endicott Peabody and a Harvard student named Richard Derby he organized a conference on applied decency for select college men at Sagamore Hill in June 1901. He invited James B. Reynolds of the University Settlement to speak about his own experiences in social work. He also asked Woodrow Wilson, then only an obscure Princeton government professor, to join him and Rector Peabody in enlisting Harvard, Yale, and Princeton to encourage their students to go into politics. After his friendly visit with TR, Professor Wilson left Sagamore Hill "much heartened in many ideals." TR later spoke at Groton, where he urged Ted's classmates to embrace public service and the strenuous life or at the very least "not to take champagne or butlers with them on camping trips in the Adirondacks."[65]

He busied himself in the days of vice-presidential "unwarrantable idleness" by sending money to Rough Riders who landed in jail. He also contemplated the periodization of Greek history. In May he and Henry Cabot Lodge gave speeches in Buffalo at the opening of the Pan-American Exposition and on the way back Edith, Theodore, and Alice had an entertaining lunch on the train with Augustus Saint-Gaudens, whose memorial sculpture of Robert Gould Shaw and his Fifty-fourth Regiment on Boston Common TR admired extravagantly, and Finley Peter Dunne, whose Mr. Dooley had made ripe comedy out of TR's exploits. Roosevelt already knew the artist whose work he would later commission for American coins, but the memorable lunch would begin his friendship with Dunne.[66]

When TR went to Colorado in August to hunt, he was fighting off a bad case of bronchitis. Nevertheless, when he ran into Hamlin Garland, author of *Main-Travelled Roads*, at a Wild West rodeo in Colorado Springs, he took him to a breakfast with his local friends—Rough Rider cowboys and hunters. Garland heard TR tell stories of camping, hunting, and war, and was impressed by "Roosevelt's genius for friendship and his essential democracy." TR wrote home to Ethel that his wolf and coyote hunt had not been entirely successful but the "wild gallup, at breakneck speed, across plain & ravine, up & down hills, and in and out among prairie dog towns & badger holes is great sport."[67]

Though his bronchitis had turned into pleurisy and a chronic cold that summer, Roosevelt went on speaking tours in Minnesota and Vermont. He planned to break the pace with a family vacation in a four-room cottage next to the Tahawus Club, a hotel in a beautiful wild place in the Adirondacks from which they could hike and take camping and hunting trips. Before Edith could bundle the children up for the trip, Alice's jaw became infected and she required surgery at Roosevelt Hospital. Edith stood by her suffering stepdaughter and refused to let the doctors remove the child's front teeth.[68]

Then Quentin came down with an ear infection and wound up across the hall from Alice after doctors administered chloroform and lanced his ear. For five days doctors asked Edith to help them hold the child down for syringing treatments which made him "wake in an agony of apprehension at every footstep or voice" for days afterward. Theodore stayed over at the hospital to help his distressed wife. Before long, Archie came down with tonsillitis, and Edith struggled to get the children to the Tahawus Club before their "accumulating misfortunes" got worse.[69]

While the Roosevelts vacationed and waited for TR to join them, President McKinley visited the Pan-American Exposition in Buffalo. The nation was unprepared for the tragic event that was about to happen in the midst of America's turn-of-the-century calm. The Pan-American Exposition celebrated progress and international friendship. But not many months earlier Hearst's *New York Evening Journal* had attacked McKinley as a creature of big business unworthy of celebrating a progress that favored the few at the expense of the many: "If bad institutions and bad men can be got rid of only by killing, then the killing must be done." Outside the exposition's Temple of Music on September 6, 1901, McKinley refused to listen to the security agents who warned him against shaking hands with a large crowd.[70]

The President prepared to greet Leon Czolgosz, a man with his hand wrapped in a large handkerchief to conceal his gun. Czolgosz shot McKinley twice at almost point-blank range. James B. Parker, a black man, grabbed Czolgosz and saved the President from being shot a third time. He was taken to the Exposition Hospital for surgery (a bullet had pierced his stomach and pancreas), and then to the home on Delaware Avenue of the president of the exposition, John G. Milburn. That day TR had been visiting marble quarries near Rutland, Vermont, with his reform-minded friend Senator Redfield Procter. Then he had spoken at a Vermont Fish and Game League luncheon at Lake Champlain, where the news of the shooting reached him. Instead of joining Edith on vacation as he had planned, he hurried to Buffalo. Edith worried that her husband's four days of waiting in Buffalo for the President to recover created a strain on him.[71]

The doctors said the President's wounds were not fatal. One of them told Theodore that if McKinley "were a hospital case he would consider the President cured." Confident that medical authorities had guaranteed a full recovery, TR stopped in Oyster Bay first and then went back to the Adirondacks to be with his family.[72]

On September 12, Theodore, Edith, Ethel, and Kermit hiked in the rain to log houses, where they camped out for the night. The next day, Friday the thirteenth, Theodore climbed Mount Marcy and Edith went to Avalanche Lake. A messenger passed her party and carried urgent news up the mountain for TR: the President had relapsed. The doctors could not remove the bullet and it had caused an infection. As McKinley was struggling to stay alive, Theodore came back through the rain to have supper with Edith in the hotel. According to Edith, he "sent at once to the Lower works for further news, which came by 11 & 12 when we were in bed. He went at once to N[orth] Creek where a train was waiting." The news was that the President was slipping fast.[73]

McKinley died not long after 2 a.m. on September 14. Theodore took the train to Buffalo, where his friend Ansley Wilcox met him in a carriage, guarded by a cavalry detail. At the Milburn house he paid his respects to Mrs. McKinley and telegraphed the news to the "very tired & anxious" Edith to hurry their brood back to Oyster Bay. Corinne and Douglas had asked Bob Ferguson to go to Buffalo "in case the worst came," and Judge John R. Hazel administered the oath of office—evidently without a Bible—in Wilcox's parlor.[74]

Secretary of War Elihu Root and other cabinet members cried during the solemn swearing-in. TR behaved in a dignified manner throughout the proceedings, and he asked Wilcox for a copy of President Arthur's message after President Garfield was shot and used it as the basis for his first pronouncement. According to Ferguson, that night the youngest president in American history, knowing that the "world seemed pretty full of anarchy and darkness" for his companions, cheered them up with his wit at "the merriest of family dinners." For a moment he wanted to lift the gloom which had enveloped him and those closest to him through the long days since McKinley was shot. Despite his apparent command of the situation, Roosevelt was in a state of shock as he realized he was now President of the United States.[75]

He accompanied Mrs. McKinley and the casket that held her husband to Washington, where the dead president rested in the East Room of the White House. TR stayed with Bamie and tried to gather his strength for the challenge that faced him. From Oyster Bay, Edith wrote him that Archie had put black mourning bands on his dolls. Already she was getting letters from people all over the country offering advice about schooling her children in Washington. She had not yet figured out how to fit six children and two parents in four White House bedrooms. When she met her husband in New York on the sixteenth to go to McKinley's funeral, Edith observed: "Theodore came, looking very grave & older, but not at all nervous. All the country seems behind him."[76]

☆ CHAPTER SEVEN ☆

The Strong Man and a Weak State

IN THE AUTUMN morning sun on the twenty-second day of September, Theodore Roosevelt walked across Lafayette Park with a brisk step. The newspapermen who ran alongside as he went toward the White House had trouble keeping up. His friends described him as "an electric battery of inexhaustible energy." With high voltage came sparks, for, as his friends warned, "his combativeness is large." Having a fighter in charge of the government might break the inertia in the Capitol, but if this man lost his self-control he might be "completely dominated by a desire to destroy his adversary."[1] Self-control, then, would be the key to his presidency. If a strong man were to move a weak national government toward progress he would need to muster all the charm and political skill he possessed.

Before he took office TR had written that a president's strength depended largely on a "personal equation." In his case the "personal equation" for success was to keep himself steady and well rested enough to choose when to stand on principle and when to seek compromise in order to steer his country in a constructive direction.

He strode into his office with an air of self-confidence. Soon senators, representatives, cabinet officers and party leaders came to the room to see him, and he took command of the political discussions by nature, as if he had been entitled to power from birth.[2]

He understood why "the big men of my own party" were "sulky" and uneasy about his ascendancy. He knew that his "want of tact" posed a serious stumbling block to his success in the collaborative legislative partnership with Congress he hoped lay ahead of him. He could be as gregarious and charming as any man alive, and his humor and his "keen sense of the absurd" enabled him to step back and laugh at himself and others. One day Senator John Spooner of Wisconsin came to see TR in a state of advanced fury and after a little of the Roosevelt treatment said: "That man in the White House is stupendous. I went in as angry as a hornet, and before I was through in there I was liking him again in spite of myself." But, in the beginning, he was not as good as McKinley had been at "jollying" people up: Flattery, horse trading, and forgiveness were political skills that did not come easily to him. He never learned "small talk": too many important things needed to be said to waste time on chitchat. He put up his fists to fight too quickly in the political arena and too often defined differences of opinion in self-righteous terms. Yet he knew politics required competing interests and personalities to find common ground. Could he name that common ground?[3]

Among all the politicians who could have aided TR in winning support in Congress, the most influential was McKinley's advisor Senator Mark Hanna. But Hanna disliked Roosevelt, especially for his impetuousness and blunt talk. This powerful party leader had wanted civil service reform kept away from the party's platform and he disliked TR's reformist impulses. Hanna had advised McKinley, "It was a mistake to nominate that wild man." The new President feared Hanna wanted the 1904 presidential nomination for himself, but a more realistic danger was that Hanna had placed his loyalists so strategically in state and national positions that he could continue to dictate party policy. Even before Roosevelt could assess how many allies he had, Pulitzer's *World* pronounced that he had "no strong friends in the Senate" except Lodge.[4]

TR was determined to act as steward to the American people, more than a caretaker president, less than a king. But neither a steward nor a king could easily make all that was wrong in the land go right. The America Roosevelt was to govern at the turn of the century proved to be a violent and unjust country. In Kentucky, the state assembly overturned the election results in a heated contest for governor: armed men killed the assembly's pick for governor and a civil war almost broke out. Mark Twain called the almost uniquely American institution of lynching an "epidemic of bloody insanities," a crowd-abetted ritual violence perpetrated against southern blacks more often than ever before. Mississippi Democrat James K. Vardaman warned that every black in his state might be lynched if needed "to maintain white supremacy," and it was an era when Indians were burned at the stake and immigrants were rejected by officials at Ellis Island and Angel Island only to be sent home to face pogroms or poverty. It was also a time when college professor Andrew Sledd lost his job at Emory College for daring to criticize America's endemic racism.[5]

Most Americans feared the rest of the world and had never traveled abroad or even to large parts of their own country, so aliens—foreigners and new immigrants—looked dangerous. Almost half the nation lived close to the edge of poverty, and despite evidence that the new industrial economy offered many chances for upward mobility, those chances went more readily to old-stock white Protestants than newcomers. Economic opportunity was not open equally to all ethnic and racial groups, for Jews and Catholics faced job discrimination and restricted access to college and professional education. Some Italian immigrants at Ellis Island were enticed by labor agents into camps where they were held as captive workers, flogged, and sometimes starved to death. In 1900, 2.6 million southern blacks were illiterate and many were ensnared in debt peonage, which made it illegal for them to leave their jobs if they owed their employers money. Tuskegee president Booker T. Washington complained that any white man could use the debt peonage laws to send any black man to a chain gang or into virtual slavery to his employer.[6]

Newspapers were filled with accounts of pitched battles among competing economic interests. To combat ruinous competition which had plagued the business world throughout the last decades of the nineteenth century, companies hired spies and private armies, and fomented discontent in competitors' factories. Businessmen also embraced new technologies, new marketing devices, and finally new organizational innovations such as horizontal and vertical integration, mergers, holding companies, communities of interest among large stockholders, and cartels to increase market predictability. The merger movement which accelerated after the harsh depression of 1893 crushed many small firms. Monopolies packed even more political power than ever. No wonder that southern farmers and northern workers were up in arms about the robber barons and the "monster railroad trust." They feared an "invisible empire" of concentrated corporate economic power would "suck into its maw everything."[7]

The power of big business alarmed public opinion because its leaders behaved as if they were above the law—fixing prices, driving competitors out of business, neglecting workplace safety and product quality, and treating workers as if they had no rights. When his Florida East Coast Railway was being extended to reach the Florida Keys, Standard Oil magnate Henry M. Flagler assumed he was above the law when his men held workers at gunpoint so that they could not leave the construction site. The marketplace was being closed by monopolies out to destroy their competition. The big Ringling circus monopoly used its legal clout to stop shows like Pawnee Bill or Buffalo Bill's Rough Riders from playing at Madison Square Garden, and Standard Oil closed down competitors by any tactic, including intimidation and sabotage. Most businessmen assumed that all anti-competitive activity, called "restraint of trade" by the rarely used Sherman Anti-Trust Act, was beyond the reach of the law.[8]

In labor-capital conflicts, local police shot demonstrators, and employer-paid Pinkerton agents used clubs and guns to crush strikes. Businessmen regarded labor relations as none of the government's concern, except when Presidents Hayes and Cleveland called out federal troops to help employers put down strikes. When labor activist Mother Jones staged a march of child laborers from the mills she had no trouble finding for her front row little workers whose fingers and limbs had been taken off by machines: America had a higher rate of industrial accidents than any comparable country. No matter how valid workers' grievances were, courts favored employers, and TR's friend William Howard Taft as a circuit court judge ruled that workers had no right to strike if it interfered with interstate commerce. The Supreme Court had already blessed the growing use of militia to put down labor unrest. The government existed, the defenders of the status quo insisted, to keep big business on top.[9]

A quarter century of civil service reform had not eradicated political corruption and the use of patronage to keep party members loyal. Three-quarters of the Republican Party's national campaign funds came from corporations, especially manufacturers and financiers from Ohio, New York, and Pennsylvania. Republican donors expected their legislators to pass protective tariffs and other favors in return. Democrats played the same game, only with smaller coffers.[10]

The new President began his work knowing he would not have the power to put down all violence or eradicate all injustices. Most Gilded Age presidents had not even tried. Though recession-free economic growth had spread high hopes among reformers since 1897, Roosevelt, if he sided with reform, could expect to tangle with a stand-pat Senate elected by state legislators close to local economic interests. Congressmen expected to vote pork barrel boons to their local districts. Conservation of natural resources was not a major political issue for elected officials: forests sold to the highest bidder and lumber companies used dynamite to blow up age-old giant sequoias. Nature writer John Muir's protests on behalf of Yosemite's sequoias or the millions of acres of decimated forests did not register on Capitol Hill. The bloc of Confederate veterans in the Senate—Augustus O. Bacon of Georgia, Ben Tillman of South Carolina, among several others—stood for states' rights. Limited government was Congress' aim, not problem-solving. Salty old Uncle Joe Cannon, later Speaker of the House, had once joked to Gifford Pinchot that good legislation might get passed "if we didn't have a Senate of nits and lice."[11]

Roosevelt was also destined to work with one of the worst Supreme Courts in American history: it is remembered in legal history for vitiating state labor reform laws, sanctifying liberty of contract, and, in *Plessy* v. *Ferguson,* justifying racial segregation. The Court had ruled that unions must not commit "oppression" of their employers by asserting competing property rights, and it had undercut Congress' hope of putting true regulatory bite into the Interstate Commerce Commission.[12]

TR already had a keen understanding of the magnitude of the task before him: he had been a close observer of politics when the anti-trust suits of the Cleveland administration were negated by the Supreme Court; from his place on Harrison's Civil Service Commission he had fought against governmental inertia and corrupt party deals; he knew from his time as governor that business would resist most types of regulation. Yet he was not daunted. When Roosevelt finished his official business on September 22, he took a long horseback ride alone in Rock Creek Park to contemplate what "a dreadful thing to come into the Presidency this way" and what a monumental task revivifying the government would be. He later told a friend that he had "thought of Father all the time" in the first days as president as he slowly realized what had befallen him. He still missed his father and wished for his strength as he grappled with a daunting job. A few days earlier he had ventilated to his friend Nicholas Murray Butler "his lack of confidence in himself as President" and his fear he would fail at the job. Roosevelt had been "in a great state of emotional excitement about it," and Butler's optimistic attempts to buck him up failed.[13]

Edith could not be with him because she was closing Sagamore Hill and preparing the children for their move to Washington. So TR was "very anxious" that his sisters and their husbands and Bob Ferguson "should dine with him the first night that he slept in the old mansion." Only Bamie and Corinne knew how to comfort him with their unshaken faith in his aspirations. When TR was a homesick college boy, he had written of his sisters, "It does me positive good, morally and mentally, to be with them even for a short time."[14] Now he needed their support. Bamie and Will Cowles had already opened their house at 1733 N Street to her brother when he came to Washington after McKinley's death. While TR gave the sickly Ida McKinley time to move out of the White House, he had held cabinet meetings at the Cowles' house which the press dubbed "the Little White House."

As the dinner with his sisters began, Roosevelt did not speak of his anxieties. He asked them if they remembered that today was their father's birthday, and before they could reply he added warmly, "I have realized it as I signed various papers all day long, and I feel that it is a good omen that I begin my duties in this house on this day." In fact, Roosevelt added, "I feel as if my father's hand were on my shoulder, and as if there were a special blessing over the life I am to lead here."[15]

TR was not a superstitious man. He did not truck with palm readers, as Governor La Follette did, or with spiritualist mediums, like so many of his upper-class friends. But he believed in talismans and good omens connected to his father and his father's visits with Abraham Lincoln within these same walls. Corinne wrote that her brother's "romantic attachment" to the Executive Mansion derived from its association with his father and "the hero of his boyhood and manhood, Abraham Lincoln" and his wish to embody what they stood for.[16]

TR was sentimental enough about Lincoln to have boxwood cuttings from Lincoln's home planted at Sagamore Hill, and he later wore a ring holding a wisp of Lincoln's hair given him by John Hay. He admired Lincoln's egalitarian second inaugural address and what he called "Lincoln democracy; the democracy of the plain people, who are honest and possess common sense."[17] He echoed Lincoln in a 1903 speech at a New York State Fair when he declared: "We must treat each man on his worth and merits as a man. We must see that each is given a square deal, because he is entitled to no more and should receive no less." Roosevelt's Square Deal, the name he gave his domestic policies, came to symbolize a government that dealt fairly with every man, regardless of his wealth, creed, color, or religion. He told Hay that Lincoln also influenced him "to try to be good-natured and forebearing [*sic*] and to free myself from vindictiveness."[18]

Thee had taught his son his habit of struggle and self-defense, his moralism, his nationalism, his respect for the federal government as a defender of justice, his deep sense of public responsibility, and his Social Gospel commitment to the less fortunate. And he had accustomed his son to being the center of attention and the object of great adulation. Thee's spirit was reincarnated daily in the friends he had brought home in the 1860s and 1870s; now Secretary of State John Hay, Ambassador to England Joseph Hodges Choate, and Secretary of War Elihu Root would put up their restraining hands to hold back the young President.

Buoyed up, TR entered the presidential arena imbued with the fighting spirit his father taught him and he promised: "I am going to be full President." Observers noted that he showed "a firm determination to impose his will upon others." But there were formidable barriers to creating a progressive and unified country ruled by law and justice.[19]

When it came to challenging business interests and party patronage, Mark Hanna urged the new President to "go slow," but that was temperamentally impossible for him. TR's friend Edith Wharton believed that most people lived life as "a succession of pitiful compromises with fate, of concessions to old tradition, old beliefs, old charities and frailties," and such concessions would have to be a large part of the story of Roosevelt's first term.[20]

But TR was not most men. He had already denounced "men of wealth who sacrifice everything to getting wealth" and who "are equally careless of the working men, whom they oppress, and of the State, whose existence they imperil." In the 1900 campaign Roosevelt had asked his country: "Is America a weakling, to shrink from the world work of the great world-powers? No. The young giant of the West stands on a continent and clasps the crest of an ocean in either hand. Our nation, glorious in youth and strength, looks into the future with eager eyes and rejoices as a strong man to run a race." Roosevelt wanted to ready his country to do "world work" and to approach the future in the confident belief that good could be done at home and abroad. He refused to preside over a weakling state incapable of standing up for itself in the international arena, nor would he brook challenges to the authority of the federal government he led. He certainly would not be pleased if a pork barrel Congress or bullies in the form of monopolies or lynch mobs tried to push his nation-state around.[21]

When he appointed men to office he chose as few "pink-tea" weaklings as he could. He had to appoint certain regulars to build his own base within the party but he liked to work with hearty reformers like his "Tennis Cabinet," advisors who doubled as playmates. He attracted "incense swingers" who believed he could do no wrong, including muscular Christians like Gifford Pinchot, James R. Garfield, William Henry Moody, William Phillips, and Henry Stimson. At the end of the Roosevelt presidency, at an "incense swinger" luncheon, Stimson said that TR had "glorified each one by his friendship to that point when each man had been reborn in matters of principle, in character, and in mind." The "incense swingers" stood out as some of the ablest young men America had to offer—Pinchot, for example, had studied scientific forestry in France and Germany before helping to write early forest reserve legislation and protect New York's Adirondack Park. He was a devoted Roosevelt friend who had a talent for publicity and for making his foresters "feel like soldiers in a patriotic cause," and many scholars see him as the father of environmentalism in America. Garfield, Stimson, and Moody brought fine legal minds to the administration. Phillips got his start with TR, but went on to give long, vital State Department service for four decades; for F.D.R. he tried to prevent Mussolini's alliance with Hitler and under Truman he urged the creation of a Palestinian state to make peace last in the Middle East. Moody had gained fame for prosecuting alleged ax-murderer

Lizzie Borden, and Stimson had ahead of him a long career of distinguished service, among many other jobs, serving as secretary of war during World War II. TR remarked proudly that he had better men serving his administration than Lincoln; certainly they were more loyal to their boss.[22]

Under Roosevelt the incense swingers devoted themselves to public service: Garfield investigated violators of anti-trust laws, Moody tried to make the navy more efficient, and Stimson brought suit against the Sugar Trust. In the Roosevelt years more idealistic young men applied for government jobs than ever before; TR made public service a noble, manly calling and he sought loyal followers who respected expertise but believed character counted above all else. Even though he knew he would not move any legislative mountains in his first term, he aimed at nothing less than the bold goal of national rebirth.

He had asserted often that the rules of statecraft were the same as the rules of manhood: Thee had taught him that strength will be respected, but weakness invites bullying. He had complained when his son Kermit flinched before exploding roman candles on the Fourth of July: the boy had, he said, "not enough nerve," which was precisely what he thought was wrong with his country. TR held a strong nationalist and internationalist vision, and he hoped he could inspire America to action in the new century. He promised the nation that it should "know that the future is ours if we have in us the manhood to grasp it."[23]

Could the headstrong and dogged rules of his strenuous life make him a master of the collaborative art of governance and spark a national rebirth? This was an open question in his mind and in the minds of the people who knew him best. The art of governance in America at the turn of the century would require a near magician to graft modern systems, a world vision, and a renewed national spirit onto antiquated customs and parochial suspicions.

TR SAID he took office without detailed blueprints but with "certain strong convictions." Three days after McKinley's death he had started to shift appointment policy and within a year most of the cabinet had been replaced by younger and more progressive men. Though Roosevelt later said he did not begin his presidency with any plan of action, anyone who knew him well understood he had proven commitments—he was on record favoring conservation and a two-ocean navy joined by a fortified Isthmian canal; he supported the Monroe Doctrine and strong colonial management of America's new possessions; and as governor he had advocated factory, trust, and railroad regulation.[24]

When he visited the President, the English writer H. G. Wells judged Roosevelt to be a representative of the American spirit, especially its "creative purpose, the goodwill in men," but he saw TR less as a symbol of youthful, aggressive power in a bold new nation than as a symbol of "the seeking mind of America displayed," a restless but intensely curious intelligence looking for answers to questions posed by the new century. The "friendly peering snarl of his face" made him look "like a man with the sun in his eyes," perhaps a man with rare vision.[25]

Military aide Archie Butt observed that "the quickness of the man's physical movements" left "the impression of bounding in and out of the rooms." His mind, too, seemed to work double time, absorbing books, knowledge, facts with lightning-quick understanding. The French ambassador told Parisians that the new American President had read more widely in French literature than most Frenchmen, and word spread to European capitals that the United States finally had a cosmopolitan leader. In his own time he won election to the American Academy of Arts and Letters along with Mark Twain and William Dean Howells, and he would prove himself Thomas Jefferson's equal for fathoming broadly what constituted the best knowledge of his day, a rare presidential great mind.[26]

Roosevelt's scientific faith in experts led him to researchers and commissions to study national problems and seek solutions. He asked Carroll Wright, the statistician at the Department of Commerce and Labor, to study the Chicago meatpacking industry, the anthracite coal industry, and Colorado mining. When Congress blocked his conservation plans TR created the National Conservation Commission and later the Inland Waterways Commission to gain support for federal water projects. He used the Keep Commission to improve government efficiency and reduce paperwork and the Homes Commission to raise public health standards and to improve housing. Knowledge provided the prerequisite for problem-solving, and he hoped expert advice and grass-roots coalitions of progressives would help him in the formidable task of renovating the Republican Party—he called it "making an old party progressive."[27]

Though he respected experts and insisted upon an efficient flow of paper and visitors, TR was a hands-on politician. He slapped backs and gave out warm handshakes as he ushered politicos and advisors of all stripes to sit in the Mission-style rocking chair in his fireplaced office, where he welcomed them to join him in laughter and friendship. His thirty- by thirty-foot olive-walled office looked out on the tennis court, where he often ran strenuously after an elusive ball, but the jovial light of the art nouveau lamp and the informal manner of the talk convinced more than one visitor that the young President was growing "in suavity of manner."[28]

He knew who his allies were. He roared with laughter when Root teased him about what wreckage he was making of the economy or quipped that the President was really only about six years old, but he knew enough to keep the wry but corporate secretary out of his private meetings with Attorney General Philander Knox as they planned to prosecute trusts. Root was annoyed that the Northern Securities case took him by surprise despite his jocular relationship with TR. When Roosevelt met with George Cortelyou, Victor Metcalf, or Oscar Straus, his first, second, and third secretaries of commerce and labor, to talk about what the two million union members wanted, he did not invite Lodge or Hay, two close advisors who were effete enough to shrink from the handshake of a workingman. To his admirers, he looked like a modern Odysseus: "The guests streaming through the White House filed past a man who, in a level and docketed world, appeared to his generation as the reincarnation of forces primitive, overmastering, and heroic."[29]

When the Washington press corps held its satirical Gridiron Dinners they poked fun at the Roosevelt cabinet as a gathering of the secretary of football and some prizefighters and generals. These reflections of the President's interests made TR laugh loudly, perhaps more so than did his cabinet. He proved willing to be an intrusive supervisor, too, telling his secretary of war what size spur cavalry soldiers should wear and giving advice to the mint on how new coins should look. The secretaries grew used to his monopolizing the spotlight while they bent their needs to his. All news was his; all credit, his. He even took it for granted that they shared his enthusiasms. One day the cabinet waited to meet with him and he bounded in and alerted them that an extraordinary event had just happened. Expecting a diplomatic crisis, they were disappointed when they heard he had merely sighted a rare tropical bird outside the White House. He was the sun and they were distant planets.[30]

Kermit and Alice agreed that Father always liked to be "the bride at every wedding and the corpse at every funeral." After cabinet meetings it was the President who told the press what went on, not his cabinet. He stomped on leaks strenuously. His executive secretary, William Loeb, helped TR manage his press relations, and Loeb let the President use him to send up trial balloons. If a proposal to put chocolate brown uniforms on White House servants resulted in press attacks, Loeb took the blame and the idea was shelved. Gifford Pinchot worked so hard to promote conservation that his parents blamed Roosevelt for being "a vampire" who grew stronger by drinking the life's blood from the men who were devoted to him. Roosevelt's administrators did not complain when the President made himself, yet again, the centerpiece of their talks, especially when he read them Mr. Dooley's latest satire of him. But when the creator of Mr. Dooley's humor, Finley Peter Dunne, met the Roosevelts, Edith deflated her husband's ego for a moment: she made sure Theodore told Dunne that at a reception a young woman had gushed to him that she loved his book "Alone in Cuba."[31]

Roosevelt also turned the press into servants of his own purposes by giving them what they wanted—a good story. Thee taught him to perform recitations and theatricals with clarity and charm during Oyster Bay summers, and he had schooled himself for years on the campaign stump to build rapport with his audiences using simple themes. Indeed, TR had grown up to entertain—he became the great presidential master of self-dramatization. As one cartoonist who covered him wrote: his "genius" "for doing provocative, picturesque things" made good copy and "started discussion, stirred interest, aroused the bitterest antagonism and the most devoted loyalty."[32]

He gave reporters a permanent pressroom inside the White House with telephones, and he talked freely with his favorites, his "praise agents" or "fair-haired boys," at 1 p.m. on weekdays while he was being shaved. He befriended them and made them see events from his viewpoint, and they were so flattered they fell into line. As soon as he figured out that Joe Bishop would write a favorable account of anything he did, the President leaked news to Bishop on a regular basis. He would also charm magazine editor Walter Hines Page by talking with concern about how Page's sons were doing at Harvard, and when the press traveled with him he made sure they got fed whenever he did. He gave them off-the-record information and said: "If you even hint where you got it . . . I'll say you are a damned liar."[33]

He adapted his press relations to suit his personality—confiding, candid, warm, friendly, and, if crossed, vengeful. He expected confidential interviews to remain secret. Reporters who betrayed his trust were banished by the President to the Ananias Club, named after the biblical liar who was punished for his untruths by death. Once consigned to the Ananias Club a reporter could no longer obtain White House news in person.

TR let his critics' "savage attacks" and the betrayals of the press get under his skin. When journalist Henry Loomis Nelson professed warm sympathy for his views and then used the resulting interview to publish falsehood and slam the President by calling him socialistic, Roosevelt fumed privately against the "vicious, contemptible liar and blackguard." Edith and Lodge could usually restrain the President from making unseemly public attacks on his enemies, but they could not stop him from musing whether his attorney general "could get at" Nelson. He knew he was "personally of a slightly vindictive temperament," and when Jesse Carmichael of the *Boston Herald* printed a story about the Roosevelt children chasing a Thanksgiving turkey all over the White House lawn and grabbing its feathers, the President let his fury get the best of him. He banned the reporter and his newspaper from the White House. Then he tried to stop the U.S. Weather Bureau from sharing bulletins about storms with the entire city of Boston, but he could not get away with punishing a whole city. The *Herald* finally apologized and peace was restored.[34]

Like Pulitzer's discovery that pictures, human interest stories, and bold headlines sold newspapers, TR was the first president to realize that big deeds, human interest stories, and dramatic moments sold presidents and their policies to the voters. His well-planned hunts, his trip to Panama, his excursion in a submarine, even his plan to send the Great White Fleet on a cruise were dramatic presidential publicity stunts that worked. Humorists joked that when reporters followed him on his hunts they obligingly wrote that he killed five lions with one shot and that he merely had to hold out his knife to have a mountain lion impale itself on it. Though he had hoped to protect his family from the public gaze, he learned fast that they, too, made good copy. Roosevelt also claimed he "discovered Monday," the slow news day when he could capture the front page more easily. By the end of his presidency he had turned himself into a household word and an international celebrity. He also made government look a bit friendlier to the average American. Thanks to cooperative newspaper writers, a portion of the reading public embraced him as a personal friend.[35]

At the same time that mass circulation newspapers and magazines made him more popular, the rising power of publishing empires stood in his way. Pulitzer's *New York World* had over a million readers in New York alone and regularly took the populist (and often Democratic) position that aristocracy "ought to have no place in the republic." Pulitzer had lambasted the Republican Party for years for serving the millionaires who had deprived workingmen "of their fair share of the national wealth." Since the start of Roosevelt's career, Pulitzer had dismissed him as a conservative, "nice, dainty cultured," a "suckling reformer." William Randolph Hearst wanted to be president and organized three million voters into the National Association of Democratic Clubs to get himself elected. Hearst intended to use his newspapers, the *New York Journal*, the *Chicago American*, and the *San Francisco Examiner*, and his many magazines to tell a version of the news that would keep TR from being reelected in 1904. Roosevelt had to decide whether he should fight the media moguls head-on or cross over into their populist territory.[36]

Crowds had loved his effusive speaking style in 1900, but others labeled him a "demagogue" because of his appeal to the emotions of the mob. Newspapers called him "theatrical," and cartoonists portrayed him as a wild ruffian dressed in cowboy togs shooting opponents with lunatic abandon. His remark in *Gouverneur Morris* that Thomas Paine was a "filthy little atheist" came back to haunt him, and the press started to comb through his life and writings for unpresidential moments, of which there were plenty. Critics warned that he was "not fully trusted" to be president. The *New York World* labeled him "the strangest creature the White House ever held."[37]

Americans had never seen a president like TR: They would soon read in amazement about the chief executive scrambling up rock faces with panting ambassadors in tow. No other president practiced jiujitsu on his son on the living room rug or sparred with professional prizefighters or held a White House exhibition match between a Japanese jiujitsu expert and an American wrestler. Roosevelt proved to be so "full of animal spirits" that he went riding rain or shine, took twenty-nine-mile walks, and told stories as loudly and indiscreetly as any ward boss or country squire. So many people worried that "Prisidint Tiddy" was too young to be chief executive that Mr. Dooley joked that perhaps the boy President might play ball in the backyard instead of pondering weighty problems of foreign policy with his cabinet. But Dooley concluded that the office would "age" him. Indeed, the public was used to presidents who were Olympian and circumspect, and TR knew he had to act presidential or change the meaning of the word. He could not afford to let a bad public image hinder his policy aims—or his hopes of a second term.[38]

Politicians were then, as now, good at making promises. To offer in all boldness a Square Deal was to pretend that existing divides could be overcome and greater equality achieved. He did not seek to invite the Goliaths of the American status quo into full combat against him, but standing on principle and engaging in measured conflict over moderate reforms would be one of his prime strategies for change. He could use the "bully pulpit" to open new dialogues to push his agenda forward, inch by inch. With the press cultivated to broadcast his designs, Roosevelt also used illusion as one of his weapons: he liked to say "in our government 'if the red slayer think he slay,' it has about as much effect as if he actually does slay." In tariff disputes, antitrust prosecutions, and many other questions he made more noise than progress, but his rhetoric changed minds and renamed the common ground on which American politics stood.[39]

* * *

EARLY ON Theodore Roosevelt learned that as president he could inspire hidden emotions with the slightest gesture. Very soon he had offended a major section of the country: his mother's homeland, the South. When he invited Booker T. Washington to dinner at the White House on October 16, 1901, he had no idea that his dining with a black man would become a national crisis which would hurt his relations with the South. Expecting that Mark Hanna would challenge him for party leadership and possibly the Republican presidential nomination, TR had promised to meet with Washington, the most famous black leader of his day, to talk politics and to work together to thwart Hannaism in the party. Washington had gained fame for his 1895 "Atlanta Compromise" speech counseling caution and hard, but menial, work and industrial education for blacks. Nevertheless, he was fighting behind the scenes for racial justice. His "secret civil rights maneuverings"—raising money for legal challenges to grandfather clauses, white-only juries, and peonage—showed that there was more to him than racial accommodation and self-aggrandizement.[40]

In public Washington had argued that lynching "really indicates progress" because it established law and order among the criminal element. In private he worked with the historian and civil rights activist W.E.B. Du Bois to see if legal means could be found to stop Pullman car segregation. Washington wanted to convince TR to stop patronage for "lily-white" Republicans who favored taking the vote and Republican Party membership away from blacks in the South. Roosevelt opposed a lily-white Republican Party but did not know how best to loosen the Democratic stranglehold there. The President disliked what he saw in the South: Blacks paid taxes but could not walk into public libraries funded by their tax dollars. Nor could most of them vote or be sure their families were safe from white mob violence. In fact, both TR and Washington pandered to conservative white sensibilities in the South; both justified segregation as a way to protect blacks from hostile contact with whites. But both of them believed that it would help blacks if they strengthened the Republican Party in the South.[41]

After a reporter checked the White House guest book, the press reported the Booker T. Washington dinner. Southern newspapers loudly denounced the President for letting his wife and daughters sup with a black man. Washington's dinner with the Roosevelt family and TR's hunting friend, Colorado mine owner Philip B. Stewart, sent the southern press into a rage because presidents were supposed to be moral exemplars and the dinner violated widespread racial etiquette. The *Richmond Times* accused him of advocating by his invitation "that negroes shall mingle freely with whites in the social circle—that white women may receive attentions from negro men." Mississippi race-baiter James K. Vardaman denounced the dinner and called Roosevelt a "coon-flavored miscegenationist" who encouraged the violation of white women by black men. The one-eyed senator from South Carolina, "Pitchfork" Ben Tillman, warned: "The action of President Roosevelt in entertaining that nigger will necessitate our killing a thousand niggers in the South before they will learn their place again."[42]

Social equality was a charged issue at the turn of the century because racism was on the rise nationally. To stop black Republicans from voting, southern Democrats had spread the fear of black men raping white women. In fact, social equality also rubbed northern whites the wrong way. Even northern white civil rights activists refused to accept their black co-workers socially. Oswald Garrison Villard, editor of the *Evening Post* and later one of the founders of the National Association for the Advancement of Colored People (N.A.A.C.P.), would not invite his friend and ally W.E.B. Du Bois to his home.[43]

In an era when restaurants, schools, and most public places in the South and a great many in the North were segregated, the Roosevelts had entertained blacks in Albany and had William H. Lewis, the Massachusetts lawyer and ally of Washington, stay overnight at Sagamore Hill. Even after the controversy over the Washington dinner, the Roosevelts hosted many black social visitors—civil rights activist and president of the National Association of Colored Women, Mary Church Terrell, and delegations that included black Episcopal bishops. When the black composer Samuel Coleridge-Taylor conducted an African-American choral group singing his composition *Hiawatha* before an integrated audience, Edith made a point of being there.[44]

TR was shocked by the outrage newspapers registered over the Washington dinner, and he grew even more enraged when he read that Congressman Thomas Heflin of Alabama in a public speech declared that "if some Czolgosz had thrown a bomb under the table" where the presidential family sat Booker Washington, "no great harm would have been done the country." After Tillman started a fistfight with another senator during a debate, TR banned him from the White House. No matter how hard the President tried to win the affections of the "white whale" of the Solid South, many white southerners never forgave him for dining with a black man. Roosevelt later wrote that "the only wise and honorable and Christian thing to do is to treat each black man and each white man strictly on his merits as a man." However, in the uproar over the Washington dinner he saw vividly that the notion of equality was still a revolutionary idea.[45]

After the Washington dinner, Edith commented that all the southern cant about chivalry was hypocritical, and she held "but slight respect for our southern brother." Her husband admitted he had made a political blunder and regretted that he might have compromised Booker T. Washington's influence in the South: "I never thought much about it at the time. It seemed to me so natural & so proper." Even William Jennings Bryan denounced Roosevelt for promoting dangerous social equality, and TR said he felt "melancholy" about the depth of race hatred the incident uncovered.[46]

EDITH BEGAN her career as first lady in a state of shock. She barely had enough time to read all the advice she had received about where to send the children to school before she joined her husband for McKinley's funeral in Washington, which she later recalled "was one of the saddest things I had ever done," and was relieved that her husband was "not at all nervous." Then she sent fourteen-year-old Ted to Groton, and settled twelve-year-old Kermit at the Force School, a public school in the district, and ten-year-old Ethel as a weekday boarder at National Cathedral School, an Episcopal girls' academy. Later, seven-year-old Archie and almost four-year-old Quentin, along with servants and assorted dogs and guinea pigs, joined the family in the White House.[47]

Edith feared what being in the limelight would do to Alice, so she waited to bring the beautiful seventeen-year-old to the capital. Alice loved attention, and Edith knew that having the press corps fawning around might not be good for her. She sent Alice first into exile at Bamie's house in Farmington and then to Aunt Lizzie's at 4 West Fifty-seventh Street and the Lees at Chestnut Hill, arming all of the hostesses with "admonitions" for the child. Edith urged Emlen's wife, Christine, not to allow Alice to "accept any invitations"; instead, Alice should "absorb all the calm and repose that she can in Aunt Lizzie's house." Edith told the girl frankly: "In one way you will find this a hard position, but in others it will be delightful, & can do much for you that would have been financially impossible otherwise." Edith wanted to teach her stepdaughter to set an example of dignity and grace for the rest of the country, but Alice insulted her maid, disobeyed her hostesses, and threw a fit when she heard her parents planned only a modest White House debut for her in January.[48]

Alice later recalled: "My father was always taking me to task for gallivanting with 'society' and for not knowing more people like my cousin Eleanor." TR let Alice know that he admired Eleanor's serious nature and her way of taking an interest in other people and in social work. He held Eleanor up as a paragon to lambaste Alice's behavior—dancing the hootchie-kootchie, smoking, betting on horses, driving too fast, or cavorting in public with one of her many amours. Bamie, too, saw Eleanor as more typically Rooseveltian than Alice because of her intense interest in people and ideas, and the comparison hurt Alice. When newspapers detailed how Alice escaped the chaperonage of her maid between house visits, Edith postponed Alice's reunion with her family and threatened that she could "easily" be exiled for "the whole season at Newport."[49]

Edith found the Executive Mansion rat-infested and too small for her family, and the President joined his sons in rat-chasing during family dinners. Once the rodent problem subsided, Edith enjoyed having her husband working at home. TR told William Allen White: "You know, Will, Edie says it's like living over the store!" Edith loved walking "through the broad winding paths" of the White House flower gardens in the morning, "feeling very magnificent." She planted a colonial revival flower garden, after the style of Mount Vernon; her mint bed seasoned her husband's occasional juleps, and the rosebushes she planted lasted long past her husband's term of office. Though she missed the privacy of Sagamore Hill, she drew satisfaction from meeting interesting people and from helping her husband as much as she could. In addition to serving as her own White House housekeeper, Edith contributed to her husband's presidency by acting as an invisible advisor and by making the social side of his presidency go well. She learned how to set the tone for gatherings by inviting the right mixture of political people, close friends, New York Knickerbockers whom they'd known since childhood, and local social leaders, or "cave dwellers." She was offended by immorality and banned invitations to adulterers. She also held receptions for women reporters, had frequent meetings of cabinet wives, and advised her husband about cultural issues, art, music, architecture, and historic preservation.[50]

Theodore and Edith brought as much as they could of the arduous spirit of Sagamore Hill into the White House. "The true Roosevelt style," was, according to brother-in-law Douglas Robinson, "going it with a vengeance . . . not a minute unemployed eating, talking." TR put up a stuffed elk head in the State Dining Room, and Edith opened up the dark rooms that the invalid Mrs. McKinley had kept closed. But it soon became obvious that the White House was antiquated and in need of renovation, especially if it were to accommodate a rambunctious family of eight. So Edith added to her other duties the planning of a renovation with the renowned New York architects McKim, Mead, and White.[51]

No one stopped the children from making themselves at home in the old mansion. Before long Kermit was taking his pet kangaroo rat out of his pocket and letting it hop across the dining table to greet Jacob Riis, as he had done at Sagamore Hill. The President described how little their family life had changed since they moved to 1600 Pennsylvania Avenue: "I play bear with the children almost every night, and some child is invariably fearfully damaged in the play; but this does not seem to affect the ardor of their enjoyment. Poor Quentin still has a little asthma and cannot play, and I tell him stories and hum songs in a horse [*sic*] murmur until my brain fairly reels."[52]

The White House servants, most of them black, observed the Roosevelts' life at close range, and James Amos, in time, came to view TR as his personal friend and the most gregarious president the White House ever had. Amos saw that by nature Roosevelt liked people. No matter how hectic his presidential duties became he always said good-bye to his staff person by person, and he found time to get down on all fours for a pillow fight and tickle game with his children.[53]

The staff found Ethel, Archie, Kermit, and Quentin unruly, and gossips around the capital were appalled by their antics, especially after the young Roosevelts threw icicles which hit one policeman on the forehead and drew blood. They turned the White House into a playground and explored its farthest recesses, including the crawl spaces between floors. The nation's property suffered when the children heedlessly roller-skated over the new parquet floors in the East Room, and made spitballs and put them on the historic portraits. TR merely found it charming when Archie and Quentin built a brick fireplace and cooked bacon, thereby blocking a path outside of the White House portico, and he looked with amusement at his sons' habit of "making the lives of the policemen a burden to them." The children walked their stilts through the flower beds behind the White House and through the house itself without reproach, and TR rescued Quentin and his friends from being hit when their antics threatened to knock over the huge bust of Martin Van Buren from its pedestal. Even Edith admired "what a *fine* bad little boy" her son Quentin was.[54]

Having so many children present when sensitive political matters were being debated could have meant daily breaches of security. Relations between the United States and France had been hurt by France's sympathy with Spain in the War of 1898, and TR worked hard to repair matters. He befriended the erudite and charming French ambassador, Jules Jusserand, and often took him into the White House garden for private diplomatic negotiations. One day Quentin overheard everything they said because he and his friends were hiding up a tree nearby. Fortunately, TR and Edith kept the six young Roosevelts from talking about politics—most of the time. When outsiders asked the children who their father's favorite cabinet members were, they answered without thinking, "Mr. Root and Mr. Knox," which further shocked the capital.[55]

Because an anarchist had killed McKinley and an atmosphere of panic had sparked attacks on radicals and arrests of anarchists like Emma Goldman, Roosevelt had to pay attention first to calming the country down and second to addressing national security issues. He reassured the public that he would continue McKinley's policies, and the panic quickly subsided by the time he had moved into the White House. But security issues were more challenging. He found himself heading a government with no systematic intelligence plan, no contingency strategies in case of attack, and few qualified spies. If Czolgosz had acted as part of a conspiracy, the U.S. government would have little chance of finding who was in it. During the Civil War the War Department had hired private detectives to gather information about saboteurs and potential assassins, without great success. Later the Justice Department routinely borrowed Secret Service agents from the Treasury Department because it had no investigators of its own, and for the time being TR continued old precedents of intelligence-gathering. But he had in mind to make a weak state strong and modern as soon as he could.[56]

ON THE SECOND floor of the White House, Edith settled into her library next to her husband's private office and scanned numerous newspapers for him. He did not always need to read the articles because he had often planted the stories himself. He confided in her about even the most top secret subjects, so her private diaries sometimes reflected the latest news about the progress of a delicate diplomatic negotiation. Political associates noticed that Edith would knit on the sidelines while the President held political meetings and then after the guests left she would talk with him about his choices. Her closest ally in keeping her husband's bluster and impulse in check was Lodge. She also got along well with most of his other top advisors and their wives (though she did find Mrs. Root and Mrs. Taft trying). TR would describe William Loeb as "the man who socially and politically has been closest to me," but Edith ridiculed him as "Mr. Lo-eb."[57]

One day Gifford Pinchot overheard the presidential couple talking over the new Bureau of Corporations. Edith urged her husband to appoint the young, earnest son of President Garfield, James R. Garfield, who became one of TR's best administrators and friends. Edith could take pride in the fact that when her husband played tennis or threw medicine balls with Pinchot or Garfield and talked reform at the same time she had helped the threesome get started. One admirer of the working relationship between Edith and Theodore recalled: "As a team they produced a judgment that was not infallible, of course, but dangerously near it, humanly and politically."[58]

When the President asked Senator Lodge about his first message to Congress, Lodge advised him to ask Edith what she thought about his reference to Judas in his first draft, probably an inflammatory phrase about murderous anarchists. After listening to Edith, TR deleted that reference but still hit hard against anarchists. Czolgosz went to a speedy execution and anarchists with no connection to the assassination, including Emma Goldman, were rounded up by the police. Roosevelt called for anti-anarchist legislation in his annual message of December 1901 and asked for immigration restriction based on literacy which he hoped would "tend to decrease the sum of ignorance so potent in producing the envy, suspicion, malignant passion, and hatred of order out of which anarchistic sentiment inevitably springs." He urged a limitation on all poor immigrants, but Congress would only give him Chinese exclusion, which he accepted because he believed that the common "Chinaman" was "ruinous to the white race."[59]

NEWSPAPERS INSISTED that he had taken up his new duties "in depression of spirit," but the real story, the President said, was: "Now that I have gotten over the horror of the circumstances under which I came to the Presidency, I get real enjoyment out of the work." Pundits wondered how safe he would be, given his habit of riding and walking by himself. TR resisted Secret Service protection at first, preferring instead to carry his own gun. The McKinley assassination, however, still haunted Edith; she wrote that she could not put out of her mind the fear that the same thing would happen to her husband. Bamie quietly enlisted Bob Ferguson and other friends to guard her brother at large public gatherings, which, along with Theodore's eventual begrudging acceptance of Secret Service protection and their use of decoy railroad engines that traveled ahead of the President's train in order to detect anarchist bombs or sabotage of the tracks, eased some of Edith's anxieties. TR generally thought more about how to curb the trusts and whether or not to revise the tariffs; he worried not at all about his safety. Nevertheless, Edith worried about the new lines on his face and the effect that "the constraint and confinement of this new position" had on him. She and Bamie agreed, nonetheless, as they proudly watched the new President that he appeared like "a prophet who is charged with a message to deliver."[60]

While TR spent all too many of his work hours pondering who should get government jobs, Bamie's friends in the diplomatic service and the navy learned to count on her "dear help & suggestions & love" in greasing the wheels. Her friends the Whitelaw Reids and Mabel Boardman gained the President's ear and government posts through Bamie. Theodore had finally reached the place Bamie had dreamed of for him, and he joked significantly that "Auntie Bye is as dear as ever and oversees the entire nation." Her place in society as well as her knowledge and ease in diplomatic circles could be a boon to him. As she had in the nineties, she corresponded with many transcontinental luminaries, in part on his behalf. She urged Edith to hire her friend Belle Hagner as her social secretary and helped the first lady put together a staff to plan formal entertainments.[61]

Bamie brought her concern with protocol to the presidential couple's attention. She admitted to Corinne that when she visited the new President and witnessed the casual manners his visitors used around him, she wanted him instead to be "treated with a certain amount of formality." She thought it "rather absurd" when an acquaintance called him "by his first name when Cabot, unless entirely alone with him, would never dream of daring to!" After newspapers commented that the President was "undignified" when he ran across the field and jumped over the division fence at the Army-Navy football game, Will Cowles grumbled that TR had waved and pointed to friends at the game, too. Will and Bamie Cowles tried hard to encourage Theodore to behave more presidentially.[62]

Theodore and Edith sometimes sent Bamie their sick children, and often the younger Roosevelts found their way to the Cowles' for tea and sympathy when the bustle of White House life overwhelmed them. The President brought guests to Bamie's house when he wanted to escape press surveillance. She also provided a safe harbor for Eleanor when Franklin courted her against his mother's wishes, and she shepherded Alice to embassy parties and to the Chevy Chase Club to meet the right people and took the girl to baseball games. Auntie Bye tolerated Alice's frequent flirtations with handsome young military attachés, and kept open a sympathetic ear for both sides when Alice began to defy her parents more and more. Edith would pay Bamie a "long calm call" when she needed to talk to a friend or they would take "an enchanting walk" together to escape social duties.[63]

Gossips in Washington society held that "Mrs. Cowles tried to run Mrs. Theodore in the White House," because she was so used to managing people. Though Bamie ran neither the social nor political life of her brother's presidency, TR "counted a good deal" on his older sister's "reactions to things." Her political power was indirect: when a young Boston Brahmin was rude to her he almost lost his chance to build a diplomatic career. TR exploded in anger when a cabinet member went to Bamie first before seeing him about an administration problem, and she irritated Edith more than once with her tendency to say, "I would have nothing comfortably arranged if she had not attended to it!"[64]

Corinne had a different kind of influence over her brother's presidency. Human interest stories about the Roosevelts made their way into the press almost from the day that Ida McKinley left town. While Owen Wister was writing an article about the new President for *The Century* magazine, TR specifically asked him to leave out details about Edith and the children because his wife valued her privacy and they hoped to raise the children as normally as possible, to avoid making them feel "self-conscious." Nevertheless, details of his camping trips with his sons and nephews found their way into the newspapers, most likely fed them by Corinne. An unnamed Roosevelt nephew, probably Teddy Robinson, said that the great thing about roughing it with the President was that "Uncle Ted hasn't asked me once this week if I'd washed my face." Newspapers also reported that TR's "family absolutely idolize & worship him, from the oldest to the youngest member," which echoed the view of his staunchest idolater, Corinne.[65]

LIFE IN THE Roosevelt White House offered little insulation from public scrutiny. Family crises got into the news quickly. When Edith hurried on February 7, 1902, to Groton after Rector Peabody cabled that Ted was seriously ill with double pneumonia, press bulletins followed the boy's illness in detail—a fever of 102.4, pleurisy in the right lung, oxygen administered, boy fights for life. Edith stationed herself at her son's bedside and relied on Mame, White House servants, Theodore, and Bamie to look after the five children at home. She also had to ask Bamie to intercede on her behalf with the thick-witted Loeb, who bungled the forwarding of her letters.[66]

Reporters outside Ted's sickroom speculated about the Groton pneumonia epidemic which caused one student death and had closed the campus for two weeks. Rumors about meningitis did not deter the President from joining his wife at Groton when Ted remained critically ill and doctors said he might die. Edith watched Ted anxiously, while her husband met with reporters, exercised, and conducted the business of the country long distance. International tensions over Venezuela's failure to pay its debts to Germany and concerns over possible German expansion in the Caribbean were in the air, and the press had already begun to speculate about how Ted's death might affect foreign affairs.[67]

As their eldest son's life hung in the balance, Edith and Theodore had a lot to discuss, especially how their family was faring since he assumed the presidency. Ted had insisted on staying in a football game even after his collarbone had been broken and he also killed a tooth playing football. Though she knew her husband would praise injuries as badges of heartiness, she finally had prevailed on him to write Rector Peabody that he thought Ted was overdoing it at Groton. They often had serious talks about how hard the boy had been pushed—and had pushed himself. The rector, however, did not believe in letting up on the boys he educated.

Edith had wanted a private education for all her children, but TR had insisted upon sending Archie, Kermit, and, later, Quentin to nearby public schools because it would provide a more democratic experience. Archie recalled that his mother "felt that someone like my father, who had never attended either a public school or private school but had had a tutor until he went to Harvard to talk like an oracle on the subject did not make sense." Bamie had broached the possibility with Alice that they could attend the coronation of King Edward VII that spring, and Alice desperately wanted to go. Edith worried that it would be bad for Alice to be treated like visiting royalty, while TR disliked disagreeing with Bamie and denying his daughter what she wanted. As the crisis over Ted's health broke, the much relieved President went back to Washington to face the business community's reaction to his latest bombshell: the prosecution of the Northern Securities holding company for restraint of trade.[68]

ON FEBRUARY 19, 1902, the Roosevelt administration challenged the nation's railroad czars when it announced it was bringing an anti-trust suit against the Northern Securities Company. Populists, Bryan, and muckrakers had sounded the alarm over the sudden growth of trusts and monopolies long before TR picked up the issue; to a sizable bloc of public opinion railroads were the "octopus," "heejous monsthers [*sic*]," the villains in the human melodrama made by industrialization. Financial wars over control of railroad empires had reached a vicious stage. TR's handsome but vacuous college friend Robert Bacon, a partner of banker J. P. Morgan, had ruined his health trying to fight off a hostile takeover attempt of a portion of Morgan's railroad empire by E. H. Harriman acting in partnership with William Rockefeller, the Rockefeller-influenced National City Bank, and the bankers Kuhn, Loeb.[69]

Next, Harriman and Morgan sparked a Wall Street panic and ruined many investors over their fight for control of the Northern Pacific Railroad, and Morgan declared that he did not care about the larger economic consequences of his Wall Street dealings: "I owe the public nothing." After railroads all over the country had been consolidated by "Morganization," that is, mergers financed by private bankers like Morgan, they loomed as the largest and most powerful businesses in America. Morgan and Harriman finally made peace when they formed the huge Northern Securities holding company.[70]

Roosevelt saw that financiers could make or break the fragile new stock-dependent economy. The President would have liked to regulate the stock market but the best he could do was to try to stop a "financial Gorgon" like Morgan from exercising complete dominance over any segment of the economy. Not only did men like Morgan control large portions of the nation's transportation network, but newly merged railroads bought up mines and timber stands, thereby becoming the absentee employers of millions of workers. Morgan, his banks, and his railroads had gained unprecedented power and few believed they could be stopped. In Northern Securities the most powerful men in America—Morgan, Harriman, and James J. Hill—had built a railroad system that stretched from Seattle and San Francisco to Duluth and Chicago.[71]

TR's decision to prosecute Northern Securities was complicated. He told Corinne that as president "he never took any serious step or made any vital decision for his country without thinking first what position his father would have taken on the question," but in this case he would break loose from Thee. His father's eulogist and friend D. Willis James and other men once close to Thee were associated with Northern Securities Company, and Thee held Hamiltonian financial views rather than anti-monopoly sentiments like Andrew Jackson. TR grew up seeing banking and business consolidation as mildly uninteresting but not morally objectionable. After all, his uncle Jim and F.D.R.'s father bought up controlling interests in railroads and it helped the family's fortunes. Yet he had listened well to the popular outcry against monopolies. Experts advised him that if monopoly and other restrictions upon competition were allowed unrestricted growth, consumers would be hurt by higher rates, neglect of safety, and poor service. Roosevelt believed that a great president in the Lincoln mold would not hesitate to challenge anyone, even the richest and most powerful forces in the country, if the public good required it.[72]

Roosevelt knew he must act quickly and decisively to establish federal authority over the railroads early in his presidency while he was still popular. Rather than wait for Congress to pass a better law, he decided to use the Sherman Anti-Trust Act to stop railroad moguls from establishing a huge new western monopoly. He boldly announced that "trusts are the creatures of the State." Many financiers had believed the opposite. It took courage to challenge railroads, especially after President Grover Cleveland had been thwarted by the Supreme Court when he tried to apply the same laws. This bolt of news overshadowed in historic importance all other anti-trust prosecutions of the next three decades because it was the first time a president dared to stand up to the biggest corporations.[73]

Stocks fell and Wall Street accused TR of acting like a financial Rough Rider. A fistfight broke out on the floor of the Senate over Roosevelt's trust-busting, and visitor after visitor tried to convince him he must relent. But he would not. When Roosevelt launched investigations and prosecutions against Northern Securities, and later the Beef Trust and the Sugar Trust, he crossed over into the populist territory Pulitzer and Hearst had claimed as defenders of the little people's interests against the monopolists. He also took up the anti-monopoly rhetoric of Bryan and modified it for his own war against economic privilege—cartoonists pictured TR waving "the big stick" against corporate giants.

He knew the economic power of monopolies would not be crushed by a few anti-trust prosecutions, but he believed he had to stand up on behalf of the nation-state to defy men of great wealth. He later created the Antitrust Division of the Justice Department to make big business answer to the government on a regular basis. Even before the Supreme Court sustained him in using the Sherman Act to stop railroads from monopolizing regional transportation, railroads east and west dropped many of their pooling arrangements in order to avoid prosecution and bad publicity.[74]

However, Roosevelt feared that despite all he had gained in the realm of public support for his trust-busting, he might later suffer from the enemies he had made. Bamie knew Harriman socially and kept in close touch with financiers through her friendship with the Reids, and she did what she could to encourage a rapprochement with her brother. In time, however, she made her son Sheffield return Harriman's gift of a toy train set and she no longer invited the Harrimans to stay with her when they came to Washington. She told Sheffield one day as they rode in her carriage down Fifth Avenue and looked at the imitation Renaissance palaces which the robber barons had built that Uncle Theodore intended to discipline the newly wealthy.[75]

Edith brought Ted back to finish his recovery in the White House two days after the Northern Securities case broke. They arrived just in time for the first couple to bring Alice to New Jersey, where she christened Kaiser Wilhelm's racing yacht, *Meteor*, which his brother Prince Heinrich had come to claim during his state visit. The press published unfounded rumors that the elderly Prince Heinrich was smitten with the beautiful "Princess Alice," to whom he gave a diamond bracelet emblazoned with a menacing picture of the kaiser.

Magazines and the popular press heralded her as "Princess Alice," "sweet, naive," "the all-American girl," but her family knew otherwise. Alice pleaded with her parents to allow her to go to the coronation of Edward VII, but the press reported that Mark Hanna had told TR that the pungent "scent of monarchy" would be bad for the Republican Party. So TR finally told her she had to stay home and Bamie and Corinne went by themselves.[76]

Roosevelt found his patience tested daily by the human comedy of politics: he was called upon to take sides in a controversy over which admiral should get credit for the victory at Santiago in the Spanish-American War. Then he had to mediate an impossible personality conflict in the Immigration Service. To build his own power base among Republicans, he gave patronage positions to anti-Hanna factions in Alabama, Colorado, Kansas, Louisiana, Missouri, and South Carolina, which pulled him into state and local factional fighting. Last, but not least, he could not believe his ears when the ambitious and untrustworthy General Nelson A. Miles threatened he would reveal that the American army had committed atrocities in suppressing the Philippine revolt unless TR appointed him military commander there. Roosevelt knew blackmail when he saw it, and he thought even less of Miles because he had tried to cover up his own murderous responsibility in the Wounded Knee massacre. He wanted to fire Miles immediately and throw him down the White House steps. Self-control prevailed and TR held off on retiring Miles from the army until after his army bill passed. Even then, Miles' pension became a controversy because some southern Democrats in Congress did not want to vote to pension the officer who had held Jefferson Davis in chains at the end of the Civil War.[77]

Next, there was the messy aftermath from America's brief imperial adventure. The Filipino war for independence had sputtered along since February 1899 without resolution. McKinley had withdrawn many troops from the Philippines, and imperialists like Senator Albert Beveridge of Indiana thought America's "prestige suffered badly" as a result. When the war for Philippine independence resumed, 4,000 Americans died and, according to some estimates, 200,000 Filipinos were killed. Some American policymakers and soldiers looked down on Filipinos as childlike creatures, savages, or animals, and likened them to Native Americans and blacks: "They are not men. Honesty, truth, justice, pity—are either extinct among these people, or else still undeveloped." Many writers had argued that if modern American men had turned soft and shown signs of industrial age degeneracy, then exercising colonial rule and fighting wars would "manufacture manhood" in American soldiers. TR hoped, too, for the character-building effect the war might have on American men, but these hopes were dashed in 1902.[78]

Critics of American imperialism like Mark Twain had complained that "a universal reign of error" governed U.S. policy. By freeing the Philippines from Spain and then stealing the "once-captive's new freedom away from him," the United States had violated its own democratic principles: "We have debauched America's honor and blackened her face before the world." News about the war had been censored by the McKinley administration, but in the first half of 1902 embarrassing stories made their way into American newspapers. U.S. soldiers committed atrocities and reconcentration camps were set up in some areas to separate civilians from guerrillas. Camps in the Philippines looked to the Anti-Imperialist League like Butcher Weyler's camps in Cuba, but when they criticized the war, General Frederick Funston said he would rather see the anti-imperialists hanged for treason than lose another soldier fighting their war.[79]

American troops had tortured Filipino prisoners using the "water cure," and General "Howling Jake" Smith had ordered his men to "kill and burn" and shoot on sight any Filipino over age ten who ventured outside the reconcentration camps. Newspapers protested that instead of civilizing the Filipinos, the army had committed repeated acts of barbarism—rape, torture, and mutilation. Democratic newspapers were especially eager to tie Roosevelt and Root to the misdeeds and to brand them as "coparceners with the Jake Smith campaign of torture and murder."[80]

TR at first dismissed the atrocity stories as "utterly baseless slanders." Even after more reliable information came out, he refused to believe reports of water torture and massacres of civilians because he was sure they had not been based on official policy. He told Social Gospel minister Lyman Abbott: "I am very much afraid that the Democrats are deliberately following the policy of trying to keep alive the insurrection for political purposes." He implied that to criticize the administration was to give aid and comfort to the nation's enemies.[81]

When Senate hearings started, Lodge and Beveridge buried many disclosures of atrocities amidst lengthy army testimony about the problems they faced in the war. TR found it convenient to have Lodge defend the army's probity, and he wrote him that "with the Philippines I feel tolerably safe under your management." Like their mutual friend William Sturgis Bigelow, Lodge took the view that the atrocities were simply a response in kind to standard guerrilla practice in the Philippines, where "torture and castration of prisoners is as much a matter of course" to Filipinos "as taking prisoners."[82]

But anti-imperialism set in deeply enough outside of partisan circles to prompt the administration to go on the offensive to ward off further embarrassment over the atrocities. Root correctly denied that "kill and burn" had ever been official policy, and he ordered General Smith court-martialed to make the killing of civilians and the "howling wilderness" order look like the crime of one man rather than common army practice. After reports of sexual wrongdoing came to light, TR warned the soldiers about "moral uncleanliness and vicious living." Then he took great pains to shift public attention toward other villains on the public stage.[83]

TR made a point of dramatizing his own conflict with undemocratic elements in the South. He had been warned not to come to South Carolina by Senator Tillman's nephew because local feeling against him still ran high after his dinner with Booker T. Washington. Tillman's nephew packed a gun and was notorious for his violent tendencies. Of course, nothing could stop TR from speaking at the Charleston Exposition after such a threat. Edith said she was "frighten[ed]" by the possibility of violence, but she went with him for moral support, and he preached patriotism and reconciliation to a polite audience. Bamie felt "relief" that no "counter demonstration" or violence marred the President's visit. Several weeks later, on Memorial Day, Roosevelt launched a more aggressive counterattack against critics of American empire by pointing out that many of them complained about the lack of democracy in the Philippines but tolerated lynching in their own states. His remarks were widely reported and did not help his popularity with white supremacists, but it gave him the moral high ground once more.[84]

Lodge joined in the counterattack by delivering a stirring speech in the Senate: he promised that the administration would correct the mistakes made in the war but that loyal Americans should support their soldiers overseas. The diminutive senator from Wisconsin, John Spooner, denounced his Democratic opponents as a "syndicate of vituperation."[85]

The ongoing political donnybrook grew "very ugly" when TR fired a civil service employee for publicly criticizing his Philippine policy; Roosevelt insisted he could fire her on the grounds of "insolent insubordination" and because civil service rules prohibited classified employees from partisan utterances. He declared the insurrection over on the Fourth of July and signed the Cooper bill, which granted slightly more self-rule in the Philippines. He renamed Filipino insurgents "bandits," as the army shifted its fighting to subduing the Moros, Islamic islanders who resisted American rule. Roosevelt later claimed that no American had died in a war on foreign soil during his presidency, but, in fact, American deaths and the military conflict in the Philippines did not really end until 1914. The President had not come away from the atrocity scandal unscathed, but with Lodge's help he had won the public relations war.[86]

Under TR, the rest of American colonial rule took more peaceful shape than in the Philippines, but it was hardly a blessing to people under its sway. Puerto Ricans had welcomed U.S. occupation at first, but the United States soon restricted the right to universal manhood suffrage which the island had enjoyed under Spanish rule and limited democratic participation to the wealthy. The United States brought the right to get a divorce to Puerto Ricans and imposed a single standard of sexual morality by making adultery grounds for men or women to sue for divorce. The American program to "civilize" and modernize what it saw as "primitive" people brought severe restrictions on freedom of the press, and the U.S. presence increased racial attacks on Afro–Puerto Ricans. "Progressive colonialism" in Puerto Rico and Cuba encouraged United States investment, but corporate purchase of land for sugar production threw peasants off their small farms and they had little choice but to become low-paid wage workers. Colonial rule may have spread sewer systems and waterworks, but economic elites profited at the expense of workers throughout Cuba and Puerto Rico. McKinley and Roosevelt had ushered in an era in world politics when U.S. involvement abroad increased, often to the detriment of local people.[87]

FRUSTRATION GREETED any strong man who wanted to move a weak state forward. TR grappled with the problem that Walter Lippmann later defined in *Drift and Mastery:* the federal government was the only modern force capable of bringing an ordered and just nation out of the chaos of industrial upheaval by waging war on poverty and inequality and prohibiting greed and excess. But Congress had no interest in achieving mastery over a nation at drift. Roosevelt had to battle with Congress simply to bring better administration and some strengthening to the army and navy. He fought over the most modest conservation proposals because the two houses saw no need to conserve forests or water resources. He tried to prosecute the Beef Trust, to create a Bureau of Corporations and Labor, and to gain control of foreign policy. Finally, to win the Bureau of Corporations he floated in the press the explosive news that it was opposed by John D. Rockefeller, Jr., the much hated operator of the Standard Oil monopoly. He tried and failed at first to get Congress to aid Cuba by lightening the tariff placed on its products. Then, only a determined battle against the domestic sugar producers' lobby and the Democrats won Cuba the trade advantages Roosevelt wanted for them. Nor could he realize all the economic and social aid to the Philippines he thought necessary. He was finding his job was "one long experiment of checking one's own impulses with an iron hand and learning to subordinate one's own desires to what some hundreds of associates can be forced or cajoled or led into desiring."[88]

TR understood already that even though the United States had won a tentative place as a world power in 1898, men like Senator Eugene Hale and Joe

Cannon planned to block further naval development. To Roosevelt, this meant that the country's military would soon slip below its current low status. Hale even opposed the acquisition of the Danish Virgin Islands, which TR saw as a key to strategic protection of the Isthmian canal which he intended to build. Congress was prepared to thwart presidential diplomatic involvement in foreign affairs even when it cost nothing and promoted world peace. Roosevelt recognized that America could not stand as an equal of the major world powers until it gained further stature from taking a full and equal part in international diplomacy.

The navy needed more professional administration, target practice, and better ships, and the new President wanted the government to support research that would revolutionize warfare and perhaps travel, especially Samuel Langley's flying machine and the Wright Brothers' airplanes. Despite his qualms about what civilization and modernity did to sap man's vitality, TR was ready to be a state-builder and a modernizer who embraced the new technology of the twentieth century—the transpacific cable, more advanced documentary photography, Marconi's transatlantic wireless telegraph, and the medical research and public health campaigns that would save newborns, diminish the threat of malaria, and extend life expectancy. Though he realized that owning an automobile while he was in the White House would offend a public that saw it as the plaything of the rich, he was proud to be the first president to ride in a car, a submarine, and, after he left office, an airplane. He urged his country not to be afraid of the future, but he also wanted Americans to gain mastery over it, not to remain adrift.[89]

TR's definition of the new was evolutionary and scientific, and assumed a biological unity within mankind. And his Lamarckian and Darwinian scientific worldview taught him to see the human species as a changeable biological experiment capable of using its intelligence to create a better environment for itself. But progress could come, he believed, only if already "civilized" people led the way by harnessing science and rationality for humane purposes.

He believed nationalism and a strong central government could be the engines of progress. In Germany, Bismarck had used the coercive powers of the state to ban socialist opponents and achieve reform which created better schools and provided benefits to protect the average citizen from poverty and unemployment; in England, France, and parts of Scandinavia, stronger states had emerged to improve daily life for their citizens. Roosevelt held that a modern nation-state could achieve "national efficiency" only if its central government achieved enough power to establish minimal rules for the conduct of economic activity; thus, for the sake of efficiency he came to favor standardization of track, weights, measures, and currency, and to support enough economic regulation to ensure fairness in the marketplace. He believed problems could be solved; he did not always agree with all progressives about what solution to pick. "National efficiency" also made a nation strong enough to defend itself in case of war.

To keep his personal balance, he refreshed himself by taking his share of what he called "capital exercise." Bigelow came to the White House to show Roosevelt and Root the jiujitsu grips that Japanese soldiers studied to improve their self-control and strength. Roosevelt liked Japanese wrestling so much he hired a teacher to train him further. He wanted to learn the Japanese self-defense system, which he hoped would steel him physically and mentally for daily struggle. When the tensions of his job escalated, TR's malarial fever and sleeplessness returned, but he blamed his bad nights on the minor office-holders who clamored for appointment. When he could not sleep he stayed up and read books about paleontology, a tonic no other president has ever tried.[90]

He understood he could much better withstand the rigors of office, including attacks by the press and his critics in Congress, if he also fully immersed himself in the relief of family life. He sometimes feared that his tender feelings toward Edith and the children might "unman him" and make him less able to harden himself for the life of struggle he had chosen, but his intimate letters to them showed that, far from weakening him, they encouraged him and provided love and a fresh perspective. As the spring came in 1902, the Roosevelts listened on the south portico to the Marine Band playing cakewalks while local children crossed the White House lawn at the Easter Egg Roll. TR confided to Dr. Bigelow that "in the course of a walk up Rock Creek I turned a somersault on a pile of boulders and ruptured the muscles on one side of my back," but his injuries happened so often that they barely fazed him. According to Edith, "Theodore in spite of all his cares seems as well and in as good spirits as if he were in the midst of a holiday."[91]

But his family was not so restful that spring. One day in April, as Edith worked with Charles McKim to manage the White House renovation, the building of the West Wing and a tennis court, she read in the newspaper that two young men admitted to being in love with Alice. Edith confronted Alice about her dalliances, and the young woman fought back with "a foolish temper fit." The next day Edith, who had just learned she was pregnant, had a miscarriage which confined her to bed for eleven days. TR did not record how he felt about the pregnancy, the spat, or his wife's confinement. Edith left for Oyster Bay with the children on June 9 and stayed there most of the time until November, while TR settled into bachelor's quarters at Jackson Place.[92]

Sad that his wife was away, Roosevelt came to work in the White House where renovation "sounds like a boiler factory" as he found himself "up to my ears in fifteen different fights." He continued to work on building the Republican Party, going out of his way to welcome Mormon apostle Reed Smoot of Utah into the Senate while a controversy raged over seating a religious leader accused of polygamy. Smoot's critics were "cussing Roosevelt up hill and down dale," and the large and influential General Federation of Women's Clubs complained that seating a Mormon "shook the foundations of the American home." Once the President realized Smoot was anti-Hanna and not a polygamist, he helped him keep his Senate seat. And, best of all, Smoot turned out to be a rare ally on conservation; so if overcoming religious prejudice became part of the Square Deal creed of judging men by their merit and at the same time Utah became a Roosevelt state, TR got what he wanted.[93]

That summer when the President took up residence at Sagamore Hill, Oyster Bay became the Summer White House, with Loeb installed in an executive office over a store in the village and Secret Service men stationed outside the President's library. But politics did not take a vacation. A strike in the anthracite coal industry threatened to cut off the supply needed to heat the East in the coming winter. The coalfields were overdeveloped at the same time that the price was dropping, and the miners went on strike because their wages were not keeping up with the cost of living. After an 1897 massacre of striking workers at the Lattimer Mines in Pennsylvania, more miners had joined the United Mine Workers, the most powerful union within the A.F.L. The U.M.W.'s charismatic leader, John Mitchell, had joined Mark Hanna in making the National Civic Federation an agency for collective bargaining, but this time when 147,000 miners walked off their jobs in mid-1902, Hanna could not convince the owners to negotiate with Mitchell. J. P. Morgan's representative, George F. Baer, speaking for owners and the railroads that held many mines, said that unions were inherently violent and that "Christian men of property" like himself were the best protectors of labor's interests.[94]

After bread riots and the threat of coal famine frightened politicians, Socialist Victor Berger and many New York Democrats called on TR to take over the mines and retain them under government ownership for the good of the public. At the same time, many business leaders supported Baer in his refusal to talk with strikers. Lodge warned that if the strike went on too long Republicans might suffer in the off-year elections in November.[95]

On September 3, as TR was traveling from Pittsfield to Lenox, Massachusetts, on a speaking tour, the presidential carriage crossed a trolley track which was supposed to have been cleared. But a loaded trolley headed his way. The brakeman did not stop in time and the trolley slammed into the carriage and instantly killed Secret Service agent William Craig and one of the horses. TR and his secretary George Cortelyou were thrown thirty feet out of the carriage and injured. Roosevelt was hit hard in his left leg, his teeth were loosened, his cheek swollen and bruised, and his left eye blackened. When he returned home to Sagamore Hill, he found Kermit so upset that his father had been nearly killed and Craig was dead that he started carrying a gun and felt "he must be on hand to protect his Father" on his next trip.[96]

TR's supporters praised how in the midst of the trolley accident his "virility kept his nerves steady." But newspapers told the story that the President picked himself up and swore at the trolley driver with what Finley Peter Dunne's Mr. Dooley called "language like father used to make whin he hit his thumb with th' hammer." Mr. Dooley and many of his readers approved, however, because they said "Tiddy Rosenfelt" spoke from his heart and "he talks at th' man in front iv him."[97]

Despite his injuries the President held a secret meeting on September 16 at Sagamore Hill with three of the Senate's Big Four—Nelson Aldrich, John Spooner, William Boyd Allison (minus Orville Platt)—plus Lodge and Hanna, to talk over party prospects and the coal strike. Afterward, the President insisted on going on his next speaking tour, but by the time he reached Indianapolis an abscess on his leg was so serious he returned to Washington. What he called "this infernal leg trouble" left his limb numb and it had to be elevated all the time. Edith left Sagamore Hill to be with him at Jackson Place, and she found his leg had become "quite helpless." Then, after fever and infection set in, on September 28, as she stood by, doctors cut open his leg, giving him cocaine to ease the procedure.[98]

Because his illness excused them from social duties and the children remained in Oyster Bay, Edith and Theodore enjoyed the rare treat of quiet time alone reading during the coal crisis. He was amused by his wife's "air of triumph in attending me," but he found her "too pretty for anything" as he alternated between reading quietly and exploring with his advisors what actions he could legally take in settling the strike. He commanded Mitchell and the heads of the railroads that owned the mines to meet with him on October 3. At the conference the owners asked for troops to suppress the strike and Mitchell requested a commission to hear both sides. Baer and the other owners would not hear of a commission. TR found their arrogance "very exasperating" and wished he could have thrown Baer out the window.[99]

From the confines of his wheelchair the President "voyage[d] about with great ease," but could not get the owners to budge. He worked closely with Hanna, who had supported his Northern Securities prosecution and who agreed that presidential intervention might be needed in this strike. Roosevelt warned the owners that "the present system of ownership, or at least of management of the anthracite fields, is on trial." Root and Attorney General Philander Knox warned him to be cautious, but he decided he must act boldly and assemble ten thousand troops to take over the mines. To keep within the Constitution, he arranged for the governor of Pennsylvania to request the soldiers. He finally used a leak to scare the owners: he let newspapers print the rumor that he planned to take over the mines and run them through the army. Morgan quickly agreed to a commission. TR had managed a labor-management conflict more deftly than any president before him.[100]

At the end of the commission's hearings, the labor lawyer Clarence Darrow won a standing ovation as he described the miners' plight, and the workers won a 10 percent pay raise (without union recognition by the owners). TR's mediation had been a great victory for strong presidential leadership, and it improved his relationship with the labor movement for years to come. Despite his injuries he had shown remarkable stamina and diplomacy during the crisis; as usual, he had help. Before she returned to Oyster Bay on October 13 Edith made sure her husband had a masseur work on his stiff muscles, and she helped him get up and around on crutches.[101]

Congressmen who had fought Roosevelt's policies now tried to have their photos taken with him to help them win reelection. His successful resolution of the strike probably helped the Republican Party gain seats in the House. His actions represented a small step toward establishing the principle of collective bargaining which the Wagner Act would guarantee more than thirty years later. As John Hay put it, the strike let the President readjust labor-capital relations "at the psychologic moment" and win "enormous personal success," too.[102]

After he had recovered enough to take exercise again, Roosevelt tried a brief turkey shoot to regain his muscle tone and vigor, and then went on a bear hunt in Mississippi. Reporters and photographers who followed his excursion made it feel to him "like hunting with a 4th of July procession." When he made bad shots or had bad luck finding bears, newspapers reported it around the nation. Finally, his guides offered for him to shoot a bear they had tied to a tree. He refused, and Clifford Berryman published a cartoon immortalizing the incident as "Drawing the Line in Mississippi." Toy manufacturers made a bear based on the cartoon and the teddy bear was born.[103]

When he got home he found better sport, playing singlestick with his old playmate Brigadier General Leonard Wood, who had returned from his stint as colonial governor of Cuba. Helmeted and padded with breastplates and gauntlets, the two playmates used heavy sticks to smash each other on the head. Both came away with serious facial bruises. Over the next several months, Wood and Roosevelt delighted in many chances to "beat one another like carpets." At Christmas, Bob Ferguson rejoined the family in the newly renovated White House, which made for a better New Year's Day reception in the Blue Room because, as Edith noted, the President could greet people from a more protected position, and the addition of a West Wing made more room to separate office and living quarters.[104]

When his popularity grew, the "personal equation" changed for Roosevelt. He took more chances. He risked embroiling himself in conflicts over principle which hurt him politically in the long run. For example, in Indianola, Mississippi, the rising tide of prejudice caused whites to protest against black postmaster Minnie Cox because they wanted a white person to get her federal job. TR stood up for her because she had done good work and her appointment furthered his plan to use federal patronage to build an anti-lynching Republican Party in Mississippi. Indianola, regrettably, was within striking distance of race baiter James K. Vardaman's home town. There, his newspaper, *Commonwealth*, accused TR of trying to bring back Reconstruction and force black Republicanism on the state. When a local white citizens' group threatened Mrs. Cox and she resigned in fear, Roosevelt, on the advice of his postmaster general, decided to demonstrate "the majesty of the Federal Government" by closing the post office in her town.[105] Vardaman denounced the closure as "the work of a human coyote," a "political boll weevil pregnant with evil," and decided to run for governor in 1903. Vardaman's vitriolic anti-Roosevelt campaign got him elected, and by standing on principle over one federal postmaster TR had inspired the triumph of racial politics in Mississippi. The President denounced Vardaman as an "unspeakable creature," but would accept no blame for making him governor. He had not helped Mrs. Cox or the cause of racial justice much, either.[106]

But Vardaman's racism was not the only reason TR hated him. Vardaman was a Bryanite who saw robber barons taking over the national economy, ruining small farmers with high railroad rates while they gave rebates and passes to rich customers. He joined Bryan in advocating government ownership of railroads for the benefit of the people. The new governor sympathized deeply with poor white farmers and thought the Democratic Party should formally declare itself the party that defended all white men, rich or poor.[107]

TR, on the other hand, was friendlier than Vardaman with the railroads. He profited from railroad stock, took railroad passes for his family and campaign contributions from the companies, and gave a cabinet appointment to Paul Morton, the vice president of the Atchison, Topeka, and Santa Fe. Roosevelt had for many years worked within a party heavily funded and influenced by the biggest railroads. When he launched the Northern Securities prosecution, he was actually standing up against much more radical Bryanite railroad reform. He later endorsed the moderate Elkins Anti-Rebate Act and Hepburn Act, which regulated railroads but did not alter their status as monopolies. In fact, railroads commonly believed the Elkins ban on secret rebates would raise their revenues 15 percent. Economics as well as race made TR the enemy of populists like Vardaman, who used racism to unify poor whites into a radical political crusade.[108]

Like Vardaman, a new brand of unpredictable populists north and south were specters on Roosevelt's political horizon as they gained power in the Democratic Party and in the press. At Democratic mass meetings newly elected Congressman William Randolph Hearst attacked the Republican Party and trusts as evil Siamese twins. Hearst's wealth, his publishing empire, and his alliance with Tammany Hall gave him immense power, especially after he allied himself with Senator Edward Carmack and other congressional opponents of the President and set up his own political club. TR knew that the uncontrolled power of big business would become national issues if Hearst or Bryan ran against him for president in 1904—they would be likely to propose the public ownership of utilities and railroads.[109]

AFTER THE coal strike had been settled, TR felt "like throwing up my hands and going to the circus," but fraud and corruption were uncovered among his post office administrators so he had to divert energies in early 1903 to investigating the accusations. He found that corruption and profit-making from government contracts had been rife within McKinley's post office, and the mess proved "a worrying and disheartening business" because the scandal involved Republicans like the Roosevelts' friend Senator Don Cameron. Despite pleas from Lodge to ease up, Roosevelt faced the scandal squarely and with impressive tact, but nonetheless it proved embarrassing to the Republican Party. He had to prosecute fellow Republicans, which did not endear him to his own party regulars.[110]

Meanwhile foreign affairs were not going his way. A brawl over Venezuela seemed imminent when allies Great Britain, Germany, and Italy demanded the right to collect their debts in that country. The allies sank Venezuelan ships and landed troops to rescue their nationals. Then they shelled Castle Libertador and coastal cities and blockaded Venezuelan ports. Hay had used conciliatory terms when diplomats asked him whether the United States would take offense at European powers attacking a New World state, and he did not see such action as a violation of the Monroe Doctrine as long as the powers did not try to colonize South America.[111]

But Roosevelt disagreed because he believed Germany had designs on the Caribbean. He was distracted, however, by the usual flow of presidential life—worrying about the latest conflicts with Congress, inviting his ally, Princeton president Woodrow Wilson, to spend a few days, getting his exhausted attorney general to take a month's rest, socializing with his friends Henry Clay Frick, Edith Wharton, and Jane Addams, and trying without success to get William Howard Taft to take a place on the Supreme Court.[112]

Despite all that diverted him from solving the Venezuela crisis, the President saw vividly that he was "not out of the woods" because a state of war still existed less than a thousand miles from the tip of Florida as 1903 began. Hay recommended arbitration through the Hague Tribunal to resolve the debt collection problem without further violence; after briefly thinking about arbitrating himself, TR sent ships to observe the war zone and to discourage Germany from occupying cities. Shortly after Christmas he supported arbitration by the tribunal, which the allies agreed to in principle only.[113]

Germany extended its blockade and kept bombarding the coastal cities. TR feared that the kaiser would soon occupy the country. Press and public opinion in the United States moved from hostility to outrage over German aggression. Kaiser Wilhelm II wanted Germany to "work His will" upon the world as a great power to be "feared" by other countries. Despite the kaiser's overtures of friendship, TR knew Wilhelm II was a dangerous and untrustworthy "fuss-cat" whose pride was easily wounded if he were left out of great power talks. The kaiser was the only world leader who had ordered his troops in the Boxer Reprisal Expedition to act like Huns and take no prisoners. Roosevelt read the "incessant hysterical vacillations" of the kaiser's foreign policy as ominous signs that the new militarized German state might go to war at any time to gain land and power.[114]

Early in January 1903, TR wrote a fond and relaxed letter to Kermit about the way Tom Quartz, Alice's kitten, playfully grasped the pant legs of the Speaker of the House, Joe Cannon, as he walked downstairs after a meeting with the President. Within several weeks, however, Roosevelt's letters, despite his romps with his sons in their pajamas before formal dinners, revealed a shorter temper. He admitted to being in "a state of exasperation." Tension increased in early February when Germany refused to compromise or withdraw its ships. Arbitration was stalled; Germany made new demands and took what TR called "an impossible stand," while German newspapers boasted of their nation's naval strength. The President put Admiral Dewey's Caribbean fleet on alert and readied them for a fight.[115]

TR finally issued an ultimatum to Germany: let up on its blockade or prepare to face Dewey's fleet. When the new German ambassador Hermann

Speck von Sternberg, arrived in Washington, his old friend Roosevelt told him in no uncertain terms that the American public was incensed about the attacks on Venezuela: the United States would go to war if it had to. Speck telegraphed the kaiser about Roosevelt's demands: "I feel that the President does not place absolute trust in Germany's assurance that she will comply with the Monroe Doctrine." Rather than fight in the Caribbean, the kaiser backed down and lifted the blockade. Speck reassured the President that Germany had no territorial ambitions in the New World, but Roosevelt did not believe him. The crisis ended cordially enough by February 13, when the White House released the official story that negotiations had resolved the crisis. In fact, Roosevelt had used secret power politics and the threat of war. The kaiser praised the President for possessing "the strongest moral courage," but he did not intend to retire meekly from the international stage.[116]

Within the White House, tension had mounted among those who knew what was going on. TR admitted he had been "driven nearly mad" in early February, especially when Congress behaved, in Bamie's words, "like evil irresponsible beings." Tensions with Canada over which country owned the land near a recent gold discovery demanded his attention, too, as the Alaskan boundary dispute erupted. In the days when war with Germany could have broken out at any time, Edith felt faint and had to leave the table on the thirteenth, exhausted. Alice had overdrawn her allowance by about $1,000, and Edith snapped at her that she should have been an actress because she liked so much to be "conspicuous." After the crisis Edith regained her equanimity enough to give a dinner for Cousin Eleanor and to invite Ernest Fenollosa to lecture on Japanese art at the White House. She had time at last to visit her unhappy thirteen-year-old, Kermit, at Groton and to insist he come home for a rest. Though problems with Canada remained unsolved, the President's strenuous life had clearly returned to normal when he clambered up rocks and through streams with the Garfield and Roosevelt boys again.[117]

ROOSEVELT'S love of nature often provided a relief from politics. While he was busy dealing with an array of petitioners for jobs and political support, he looked out the window to see the spring migration of birds and then picked up the phone; he needed Hart Merriam, chief of the Biological Survey, to come over to make sure he had identified blackpoll warblers correctly as they perched in the tall elms behind the White House. Merriam confirmed that he was right. When Merriam had TR to dinner with a group of scientists, the President looked over his host's large collection of mammal skulls and impressed the other dinner guests when he identified many of them by genus.

The President took time to make lists of the birds he sighted on the grounds of the White House or on walks or rides in Rock Creek Park, and he remained proud that the snowy owl, Egyptian plovers, and spruce grouse he shot and mounted as a youngster were part of the permanent collection of the American Museum of Natural History. Ornithologists at the museum verified that during his presidential years TR sighted what may have been the last flock of the reportedly extinct *Ectopistes migratorius*—passenger pigeons. Merriam respected TR as a man who "would have been one of America's foremost naturalists" if politics had not distracted him.[118]

And distracted he was. Roosevelt proved effective as a peacemaker and as a domestic reformer by calculating how far he could go and who would go with him, but his heart trumped his head when it came to the political issue that mattered most to him, conservation. His love of the outdoors made the "personal equation" of his presidential leadership unique. He believed that America's shortsightedness about wasting its natural resources arose from a narrow commercial spirit, a greed which could only be tempered by more contact with the beautiful amplitude of the natural world. If he could make more people look with wonder at the timeless sequoias, perhaps he would persuade the architects of industrial progress to weigh more carefully the future costs of their exploitation of nature. His long-standing love of nature and commitment to science made him see a direct relationship between the waste of natural resources and America's failure to face its other problems in the new century; he declared: "The conservation of our natural resources and their proper use constitute the fundamental problem which underlies almost every other problem of our national life."[119]

He remembered vividly that when he was an invalid "ornithological small boy," his dearest companions were animals and the study of animal behavior his most compelling intellectual pursuit. He believed nature had saved him and facilitated his self-making. In conservation TR intended to replace his predecessors' "government by inaction" with his own brand of "government by intuition," doing what his heart told him must be done.[120]

Based on his observation of animal behavior TR even wondered about the "intellect and moral sense in animals," and he feared man's customary disregard of animal habitats would destroy whole species. He wrote ornithologist Frank Chapman that the destruction of species had to be stopped. And despite his official commitment to the policy of conservation of natural resources for use by humans, he held preservationist and romantic attachments to nature and animals far stronger than the average conservationist.[121]

His conservation program always had a moral agenda. He told the naturalist and nature writer John Burroughs that eastern men were turning into narrow-chested, pale, "degenerated" or overcivilized creatures who had forgotten how to breed and fight well, so he hoped America's wilderness would make them as hearty as Kentuckians or French Canadian woodsmen. He doubled the national parks for the same reason he endorsed fresh air farms for children and workers: the country had some of the most beautiful landscapes on earth, and its increasingly industrial and urban people, he believed, needed refreshment and restoration among the hills and trees.[122]

Often, because of political pressures, pragmatic ideas about "conservation for use" took precedence over the more comprehensive preservationist strategy which TR preferred. Nevertheless, he believed almost as deeply as John Muir in the salvation of the human spirit by the wilderness. Both Muir and Roosevelt thought they had discovered their truer selves in the woods, and they went there again and again to get the "parlor taste" out of their mouths. Both felt that mankind needed more "Wildness." Neither was sure that man was the center of God's creation; mountains, trees, and glaciers were sacred temples to Muir, while TR sensed a deeper kinship with birds and animals than he did with many men. Wilderness, Muir believed, offered new beginnings and taught mankind a "geography of hope," and Roosevelt agreed, though he explained his devotion to the natural world in the language of manhood and character building or in the language of scientific discovery.[123]

In the spring of 1903, TR needed to campaign in advance for the presidential election the following year and seek relief from White House life, so, following an old habit, he headed west. He took off on a two-month, fourteen-thousand-mile, western vote-getting tour, bringing his new friend Burroughs with him. As their train headed west, the President leaned out the window so that cowboys galloping past could shake his hand, and all along his route crowds gave him a much more enthusiastic greeting than when he had gone south. He made speeches in Pennsylvania, Illinois, Wisconsin, Minnesota, and South Dakota, and was reunited with neighbors from his Dakota days and some of his Rough Riders ("most of them," he noted, "with homicidal pasts"). Hell Roaring Bill Jones got so excited about the President's impending visit he drank himself into a stupor and could not make it to the train to say hello.[124]

If his western trip was meant to combine rest with the garnering of votes for 1904, it also provided more distance from reporters than his teddy bear hunt. After he laid the cornerstone at the gate to Yellowstone Park, he left the presidential party, including William Loeb, the Secret Service, and the press outside. He began his Yellowstone vacation with Burroughs, riding horseback into the woods, a naturalist eager to observe herds of elk at close range. When he heard an enticing birdsong he called to Burroughs, "Let's go run that bird down," urging the sixty-six-year-old to follow him at a fast trot. Burroughs surpassed most birders in his quick capacity to identify a bird by its song, and he found Roosevelt's tendency to turn a walk in the woods into a road race tiresome. Burroughs had nursed the Union wounded alongside his friend Walt Whitman, and he had known the "great father Emerson" and had dared to criticize his thinking. But TR impressed Burroughs as an American Sherlock Holmes with a scientific "detective eye" that could identify a wide range of birds quickly based on their identifying marks, and he taught the nature writer a lot about the behavior of large mammals they encountered in the park. Like the "ornithological small boy" he had once been, TR ran after a strange mouse which he thought might be a rare species, scooped it up in his hat, killed it, skinned it, and sent it back to Hart Merriam. Burroughs and a few guides watched Roosevelt spot his first pygmy owl with excitement. TR listened to the call of the night heron without interruption. For almost two weeks, he enjoyed outdoor life. He could laugh freely when he fell down skiing and he could hear the song of an ovenbird—all this a balm after a year and a half of constant conflict.[125]

After he left the park TR vowed he would write about the need to preserve the game he saw in Yellowstone. He and Burroughs became even closer friends, but the tactless Loeb sullied Burroughs' fond memories of the Yellowstone trip when he said that the President had hoped to quiet critics of his hunting by going into the woods with a famous nature writer and animal lover.[126]

Roosevelt also wanted three days alone camping with the president of the Sierra Club, John Muir, who was, he found, neither a scientist nor a bird lover. Muir had expressed disappointment that Emerson had visited Yosemite decades earlier without going camping with him, so TR made a point of carving time out of his schedule to do what Emerson had not done. Muir and Roosevelt took mules into Yosemite's woods, where Muir made a bed out of ferns and branches so that they could sleep out under "the solemn temple of the giant sequoias." The President judged the steaks he and Muir ate in the open air "Bully!" and the next night, when four inches of snow fell on their blankets, Roosevelt was "delighted." They looked up at the giant falls of El Capitan and stood together at Glacier Point, where the President discovered he had finally met a man who could outtalk him on the subject of the importance of nature. Muir hoped that their conversations would inspire new federal responsibility for saving the sequoias and Yosemite.[127]

Relieved to discover that at last America had a sincere conservationist in the White House, Muir wrote: "I fairly fell in love with him." After his trip with Muir, TR ordered the northern Sierras added to the national forest reserves and got Congress to fund protection of the giant sequoia trees which Muir had shown him in the Mariposa Big Tree Grove.[128]

The problem Roosevelt faced was that Congress did not think like John Muir. The administration had lost early legislative fights to bring scientific management to forest reserves because Speaker Cannon had attacked foresters and declared Congress would spend "not one cent for scenery." Cannon neatly scuttled preservation plans in the House. Many of Roosevelt's contemporaries viewed the conservation movement's warnings about the imminent forest depletion as "unadulterated humbug," and Congress refused to fund most of TR's conservation initiatives. The House would not agree to a bill providing game refuges in forest reserves and imposing penalties for trespassing and hunting.[129]

Roosevelt wanted to protect game animals and birds from indiscriminate killing. Though he continued to hunt and to urge others to build themselves up the same way, he deplored commercial hunters who killed countless animals capriciously. He believed in limited, regulated hunting and extensive animal protection. Angered when an Audubon Society game warden within the refuge system was murdered by illegal "bird-butchers," he attacked "short-sighted men who in their greed and selfishness will . . . rob our country of half its charm by their reckless extermination of all useful and beautiful wild things." He agreed with his opponents that "game belongs to the people," but he believed to future generations as well as current ones: "To lose the chance to see frigate-birds soaring in circles above the storm, or a file of pelicans winging their way homeward across the crimson afterglow of the sunset, or a myriad terns flashing in the bright light of midday as they hover in a shifting maze above the beach—why, the loss is like the loss of a gallery of the masterpieces of the artists of old time." Extinction would wipe out whole species, he feared, so he vowed to promote a more active federal program for game and bird protection, no matter what Congress said or did.[130]

He worked closely with game preserve advocates in the Boone and Crockett Club who wanted to extend the small number of federal wildlife reserves established under Benjamin Harrison. Roosevelt also found allies for his crusade among men like Muir and Burroughs and the General Federation of Women's Clubs, in which conservation had become a hot issue. He talked over his conservation goals with Sarah Platt Decker, president of the G.F.W.C., who threw her enthusiastic support behind him.[131]

And he refused to let Congress stop him from saving wildlife. When extinction threatened a rare breed of brook trout he simply ordered it to be revived in government hatcheries, and in gratitude scientists later renamed it the Roosevelt golden trout. When he found Congress would not authorize bird preserves he asked an advisor if any law prohibited him from creating a refuge on Pelican Island in Florida, and the aide said no. So he issued an order, and Pelican Island became a bird refuge. He started using executive orders to declare federal wildlife reservations, until there were fifty-two preserves which later became a national wildlife refuge system. The Audubon Society and other wildlife protection groups grew stronger because of the President's advocacy of their movement. Roosevelt became the best president wildlife ever had, but he did it by circumventing Congress.[132]

He sought other means to protect animals' habitats, especially some of his favorites: manatees, buffalo, and plovers. He cooperated with Pawnee Bill and the Bison Society to send buffalo from the Bronx Zoo to establish the National Bison Range at several western reserves under federal supervision. In doing so he helped save the buffalo, an almost extinct animal.[133]

Theodore and Edith supported the Audubon Society's bird protection activities, especially their campaign against using white heron plumes for ladies' hats. Even the Elks Clubs' habit of wearing real elks' horns made him concerned that elks might become extinct. He wanted to stop all spring shooting when animals tended their young, and he wished that public schools would teach children to protect and care for small birds. Though he could not issue orders to force schools to start environmental education, he took to the "bully pulpit" often during and after his presidency to build more public support for bird and game protection.

Roosevelt's concern about the depletion of the forests was tied to his love of animals because forests were their habitat. His long-standing hope was that what Frederick Jackson Turner called the closing of the frontier would not mean that the bond between man and wilderness would be broken forever. He asked Pinchot to write national policies on irrigation and forestry which provided the foundation for the reclamation of arid land by national government dam building and scientific management of forests to retain rainwater. After listening to the President's argument that forests had to be saved for posterity, one congressman quipped, "What has posterity ever done for me?"[134]

Because trees, water, mineral, and other resources were being depleted with dangerous rapidity, TR charged his administrators with the task of developing a coordinated resource policy which would include rivers and flood control. He believed experts should manage the use of forest and other resources wherever possible, but that often put him in conflict with local economic interests. When Pinchot worked as McKinley's confidential forest agent, he had seen how quickly the Homestake Mine, the Northern and Southern Pacific Railroads, and large cattle and sheep magnates encroached upon the forest reserves whenever the federal government failed to guard them. Pinchot wanted more federal control over land use. After the Oregon land fraud cases exposed the stealing of federal mineral and forest resources, Roosevelt could make a stronger plea to Congress to extend federal authority. Congress balked but finally agreed to transfer supervision of the national forests to the Department of Agriculture, where Roosevelt put Pinchot at the head of the new Forest Service. The Transfer Act gave Pinchot control of money from the lease of grazing land and waterpower within the forest reserves, which meant he did not have to beg Congress for a budget for forest protection each year. When Congress blocked Roosevelt from putting further western reserves under federal custody, TR and Pinchot set aside the "midnight reserves," sixteen million acres of land protected from sale, before the legislation prohibiting more reserves went into effect.[135]

Pinchot eventually gained control over much western land that did not contain forests. His policy of trying to make the Forest Service self-supporting meant that leasing resources for commercial purposes worked well while he was in charge, but his less conservation-minded successors exploited the leasing policy. Pinchot's federal fire prevention programs were popular enough, but the extensive protection of coal and forest lands made westerners so angry they called the chief forester "Czar Pinchot" and the Forest Service "Cossacks." When the government designated about a quarter of the state of Colorado as federal reserves, states' rights advocates held a "public lands convention" in Denver to protest against federal "outrages," which Senator Henry Teller predicted would reduce Coloradans to "servile peons." Despite charges of colonialism, by the end of his second term Roosevelt had done more than any other president to save trees and wilderness areas—he quadrupled federal forestland until 172 million acres were protected by law.[136]

TR spent much of his presidency "giving" assault to and "taking heavy blows" from Congress over conservation. Though they voted for "pork barrel" river and harbor bills all the time, Congress fought him on irrigation and water management legislation. In 1902, TR gave his support to a revised version of the Reclamation Act earlier proposed by the Nevada Democratic senator Francis Newlands to fund dams and channels that would provide water to arid farms and ranches in the West. Too many western farmers had claimed their land under the Lincoln-era Homestead Act only to find they had trouble competing with large landowners for scarce water resources. Roosevelt wanted to build dams to increase water available to farmers, but to win passage of the Reclamation Act he removed Newlands' radical rhetoric about nationalizing failed state reclamation projects. He also had to change his own party's mind about the irrigation issue. Reclamation meant federal redistribution of a scarce resource, so Cannon opposed it. But Roosevelt put pressure on the Speaker and lobbied the rest of his party's congressional delegation.[137]

Finally, he won the moderate Newlands Reclamation Act and claimed credit for it. The lax enforcement of the act, however, reduced the benefits for the average small farmer. Nevertheless, government-built dams generated electricity by waterpower and provided the public with cheaper electricity than profit-making private utility companies offered. Arizona's Roosevelt Dam stands as a monument to TR's water reforms. But his struggles with Congress did not stop after he won passage of the Reclamation Act. He wanted to stop the government's previous habit of giving waterpower rights to profit-making companies; instead, he would keep the rights in "stewardship" for the public. Waterpower companies hated his policy. When Congress passed a law to turn Muscle Shoals water resources over to a private firm in Tennessee, TR vetoed it, which made it possible many years later for Senator George Norris of Nebraska to fight for Muscle Shoals to become the publicly owned Tennessee Valley Authority.[138]

Roosevelt had gone to the mat so many times with Congress over conservation that he finally decided to turn to the public for support. At the Forest Service the publicity-minded Pinchot used a mailing-label machine to send hundreds of thousands of press releases to popularize conservation and praise Roosevelt's policies. To dramatize the work that he hoped his Inland Waterways Commission would do in 1907, TR went down the Mississippi in a steamboat with reporters, and he called the first conference of governors in American history to talk about conservation. He said the governors' conference "strengthened in the minds of our people the conviction that our natural resources are being consumed, wasted, and destroyed at a rate which threatens them with exhaustion." He asked Pinchot via the National Conservation Commission to draw up a national resource management plan, and in February 1909 he held a North American Conservation Conference which promised international cooperation.[139]

Congress did not appreciate the President bypassing it, however, and the newly elected senator from Mississippi, John Sharp Williams, called Roosevelt's commissions and public relations initiatives for conservation gross abuses of power. Congress accused the Forest Service press bureau of manipulating public opinion, and Congressman James Tawney's resolution to stop all presidential commissions became law after TR left office. Congress refused to fund the National Conservation Commission and many of Roosevelt's plans unraveled. He called for a World Conference on Conservation which never took place because Congress did not support it.[140]

Roosevelt took a broad view of what conservation meant beyond the preservation of animals, forests, and water resources. As a historian he understood how damaging deforestation had been to topsoil in other countries. In China and North Africa, he wrote, erosion seriously disrupted agriculture and the human environment. Yet Congress was not ready to heed his warnings that dust bowls would be the result of unregulated development in America. As an asthmatic his own sensitivity to smoke and dust may have made him more aware of the dangers of air pollution. Air pollution in coal-heated cities would not be regulated systematically by the federal government for six more decades, but TR ordered the District of Columbia to stop factories from spewing noxious smoke. He also told the branches of the federal government to make sure they did not pollute the air. He even saved a particularly beautiful elm on Lafayette Square from destruction, and when Fanny Smith Parsons wrote a best-selling book about wildflowers he applauded her and became militant about people not picking the favorites he shared with Edith—trilliums, arbutus, and bloodroot—on the grounds of Sagamore Hill.[141]

Roosevelt kept defending national parks, and he gave encouragement to the Sierra Club and Muir's efforts to save one of Yosemite's valleys from becoming the Hetch Hetchy Dam, against Pinchot's wishes. He created the huge Tongass National Forest in the territory of Alaska despite the opposition of Secretary of the Interior Ethan Hitchcock and even though no one in the government had studied the idea at length. He advocated the preservation of Niagara Falls, but federal-state jurisdictional conflicts prevented him from making it a national park. He expanded the national parks to include Oregon's Crater Lake Park, and he accepted Muir Woods as a gift to the federal government from William Kent, the eccentric millionaire and critic of John Muir, designating it a national monument.[142]

He finally discovered an ally in Congressman John F. Lacey, who pushed through the Antiquities Act to preserve "objects of historic or scientific interest." Preservation of the natural beauty of the American landscape struck Roosevelt as another duty owed to future generations, and it pleased preservationists when he interpreted the Antiquities Act broadly to include eighteen sites like Devils Tower in Wyoming, Inscription Rock in New Mexico, and Arizona's Petrified Forest. He heard of attempts to desecrate the rim of the Grand Canyon, which he had visited after seeing Muir in Yosemite, and asked Congress to make it a national park. It refused. So he defied Congress and applied the Antiquities Act, making 800,000 acres in the Grand Canyon a national monument. Finally, he added Washington's Mount Olympus to federally protected areas covered by the Lacey Act, though Woodrow Wilson later reduced the protected area to please local lumbermen.[143]

Roosevelt's conservation campaign had been a constant war between the executive branch and Congress. His edicts, vetoes, outbursts of frustration, and executive power grabs bespoke how difficult it had been to get anything done within the prevailing political climate. Without Pinchot, Newlands, Lacey, Muir, clubwomen lobbyists, and even the grudging votes of Cannon, however, he would have accomplished much less on behalf of conservation. TR recalled little collaboration and much lone combat, and claimed that all the important conservation landmarks of his administration "have been done by me without the assistance of Congress." Doubling the national parks and creating the first federal game preserves alone were great achievements. Historians agree that "TR was the right President at the right time" to conserve the natural environment.[144]

☆ CHAPTER EIGHT ☆

A Better Democrat

THEODORE ROOSEVELT once wrote a friend that in the presidency "a difficulty is also an opportunity." His difficulty in 1903 was leading a party committed to the status quo toward reform; his opportunity, to show the public he was their champion and that he could get America moving again. The Supreme Court approved his prosecution of Northern Securities, so he could extend his trust-busting and stop egregious "restraints of trade" by Standard Oil, which used intimidation and spies to run other refiners out of business. Roosevelt believed that action, even if controversial, was better than inactivity in the White House. With Bryan calling for more trust-busting, tariff reform, a federal income tax, woman suffrage, railroad regulation, the eight-hour workday, the Democrats could portray themselves as better defenders of the common man than the Republicans. TR was moving toward the Democrats on many issues, but he would not win the Republican nomination if he moved too fast on domestic reform. And if he took up the tariff question his party might be devoured by internal conflict. So, as other presidents discovered, it was easier to exert leadership in the realm of foreign policy than in the slow process of grappling with domestic issues or winning legislation from Congress.[1]

Roosevelt had declared that if the United States wanted to act as a world power to do justice around the world, as he believed it was doing in the Philippines, Cuba, and Puerto Rico, a bold spirit and perhaps some "rough surgery" might be needed at the onset. Where and when that "surgery" would come and how it would affect his chances of winning the Republican nomination and the presidency in 1904 were foremost in his mind. He was already annoyed that Russia had taken Manchuria and he told his secretary of state, John Hay, he believed Americans "would back me up" if the Russians had to be fought. Delegations of Jewish leaders asked him to protest czarist Russia's pogroms against Jews, especially the Kishinev massacre, so he conveyed their petition to American diplomats in Russia but did not risk war over that nation's anti-Semitism. Russia was too well allied with other powers to be the proper arena for the "rough surgery" the President had in mind.[2]

When he was on his western trip in 1903, TR sent Edith frequent letters and telegrams telling her how wonderful his time among his supporters had been. The large, enthusiastic crowds along the trail confirmed how popular he was at America's grass roots, which augured well for his chances in the election. Nevertheless, fears of failure at the polls haunted him. He questioned politicians throughout the West to assess Grover Cleveland's chances of beating him, and he worried that this Democrat would win Wall Street backing. TR garnered endorsements from the party faithful and maneuvered Hanna into endorsing his candidacy or looking like a fool. Hearst, too, was another rival who loomed larger in TR's mind than he did in reality, so when Roosevelt heard that federal postal workers had joined clubs on behalf of Hearst's candidacy he ordered them fired for violating civil service rules enforcing nonpartisanship. As he girded himself for more political combat, the President wrote John Burroughs that his western trip had "completely restored the tone of my body & mind, but of course I shall be utterly fagged out by the time I get home."[3]

While her husband was being photographed on a mule train in the Grand Canyon with a large band of politicians and journalists in tow, Edith confessed to Bamie that she was in "a low state of mind" over their long separation. She talked politics with Cabot as they rode up the Virginia bank of the Potomac River and urged him to alert her husband about impending trouble over corruption in the post office. Then, Archie and Quentin came down with the measles, and when Kermit's dog, Jack, died she cried and was so upset that she decided not to tell the boy until he got home from Groton. Her good humor was not completely restored when Quentin put Archie's pony, Algonquin, into the White House elevator and brought him to the family quarters on the second floor to cheer up his brother. Rides in Rock Creek Park with Gifford Pinchot buoyed her spirits, but she sorely missed her husband and worried about his safety the whole time he was gone. Theodore wrote Kermit, "I am now all eagerness to see mother," and he returned to her bearing a large collection of Navaho blankets and pottery and carrying Josiah the Badger for Archie.[4]

By the spring of 1903, Alice had started to collect a file of unfavorable clippings, and she finally admitted to herself that even though she was "just a woman" she longed to do something that mattered: "I should like to really count in all the big things that are going on." But she lived in an age that defined domesticity as woman's only natural place, so a fate unlike her brothers' awaited her. Her debut had introduced her to society, next marriage would be her fate, not college and a career. The press relished listing the young men who were in love with her or who claimed to have proposed to her. Her rebellion, smoking, and gambling were considered unladylike because she lived in a society that judged moral transgressions and bad habits "a thousand times more offensive when a woman is the offender." Later, the W.C.T.U., Christian Endeavor Societies, the Anti-Cigarette League, and even an Ohio Suffrage Club called on her as a prominent woman to set a good example by stopping smoking. TR forbade her to smoke under his roof, so she climbed on top of the roof to smoke. In the 1930s, Alice got even with the moral reformers by endorsing Lucky Strikes in a magazine ad.[5]

Alice continued to annoy her family by socializing with the exclusive Four Hundred, whose lives her father denounced for being "as stale as flat champagne." She irritated her parents further by losing her mother's engagement ring, and she enjoyed upsetting her father and stepmother with stories about the sexual exploits of her friends: "Why the poor dears were shocked when I happened to tell them that Jack Astor kept up a second establishment." She was also inconsiderate about her father's career. He asked her not to ride in automobiles because the public viewed them as aristocratic; she agreed, but within a week rode in wealthy socialite Robert Goelet's car because she found him attractive. Alice even begged her Lee grandparents to buy her a car, but they sided with TR and called her "extravagant."[6]

Edith admonished Alice that if she did not stop being so selfish, the family would "absolutely stop caring" for her. TR found it amusing when Alice then launched a brief campaign to behave like a proper young lady and live more in line with her family's values. She tried to read and exercise and discuss political affairs more often and "do a little for others . . . and pay some attention to the family." She read books about child labor, listened attentively to Lincoln Steffens over lunch, and scrubbed her closet under Edith's strict supervision. Alice was immensely pleased when Father took her to meet with Mark Hanna at his daughter Ruth's wedding to Medill McCormick in Cleveland. Crowds cheered for Alice as well as the President, and she was glad the meeting meant her father would be "on a nicer footing with Hanna than he has been before."[7]

The problem, however, was deeper than being a dutiful presidential daughter. Alice admitted that she was "fearfully jealous of cunning attractive bright and clever Ethel," who was a model daughter in her parents' eyes. Alice's campaign to look good again floundered when Cousin Eleanor began to visit them more often. Eleanor's uncles' drunkenness at Tivoli had forced her to leave Grandmother Hall's house and move in with Corinne, Bamie, and her cousin Susie Parish.[8]

It was exceptionally difficult for Alice to compete with the generous and well-informed Eleanor, whom cousin Franklin Roosevelt was already courting. Eleanor joined the Consumers' League, visited poor children at the Orthopaedic Hospital and volunteered at the Rivington Street Settlement House with other members of the Junior League; Alice went to parties and played the coquette. Even though the jealous Alice had not been interested in Franklin for years, she accepted his invitation to sail on his schooner, the *Half Moon*. When Alice found out that Bob Ferguson had become Eleanor's escort and that he had introduced her into artistic and bohemian social circles in New York, Alice made a play for him, which he quickly rebuffed. Eleanor, Bob, and Franklin were fond of Alice, but they found her "crazier than ever." One day Kermit and Quentin expressed their opinion of their older sister's antics when she and her friend actress Ethel Barrymore went upstairs to get their hats; the boys trapped them for an hour in the White House elevator.[9]

TR had never followed Thee's policy of giving each of his children undivided attention on his or her birthday. His style of fathering while he was president included telling bedtime stories, playing games of tickle, reading to them when they were sick, and giving them manly advice. He did not know how to handle Alice's defiance, and he did not yet understand why a woman might feel restless with her life chances. So he said he could either run the country or rein in Alice; in other words, he left to Edith the emotionally trying work of standing up to a rebellious child. Edith did not sympathize with Alice's longings for a larger life nor could she get Alice to meet her halfway on either intellectual or domestic grounds. By the end of 1903, Alice had given up on pleasing her parents: she returned to parties with the Four Hundred and public appearances with Broadway stars Ethel Barrymore and Maude Adams.[10]

The pressure of life in the White House caused new rifts between husband and wife. Edith was doing her part to make her husband's presidency a success, but he criticized her nonetheless. She became friendly with the wife of Secretary of the Interior Ethan Hitchcock and invited her to travel with the presidential party, which TR told her was a political blunder because he was planning to fire her husband. The first lady took to her bed with headaches after the demands of six children and the social season proved too hectic for her, but she rallied quickly because so many people depended on her.

Though the President appreciated all his wife did to make his life possible, he felt free to inspect her attire and to pronounce she looked too much like the cook in the simple white skirts and shirtwaist blouses so popular at the turn of the century. He urged her to dress in a manner more befitting her station. Theodore, Edith wrote her sister Emily, "much prefers me thin," so to please him she worked hard to stay slender.[11]

SEVERAL DIFFICULT political issues landed on TR's desk that year. He learned that a civil service employee, a bookbinder named W. A. Miller, had been fired from his job in the Government Printing Office because his union had disowned him. TR ordered Miller reinstated, which angered the union so much they threatened to strike. A crisis created by a job action in the federal government was worth avoiding, so the President called in advisors. When John Mitchell, the hero of the anthracite strike, and Samuel Gompers of the A.F.L. met with him, they agreed that Miller should remain in government service. The idea that a union could create a closed shop—a workplace which hired only union members in good standing—within the civil service system did not sit well with the public or the President. In the end, the Miller case won TR some popularity points with the "one-suspender men," the farmers and tradesmen who opposed the closed shop.[12]

That summer signs of a panic on Wall Street made Root nervous, and, in private, Roosevelt blamed it on J. P. Morgan and his kind for "the speculative watering of stocks on a giant scale." He regretted that if panic spread business leaders would blame it on his trust-busting and then "I shall have to pay for it" politically. He believed that if he had not prosecuted trusts, it would have "inevitably meant state ownership, or rather national ownership, of the railroads," and he fumed over the failure of people like Morgan and James J. Hill to see his viewpoint. Big-business leaders' recalcitrance in the anthracite strike coupled with attacks made on him by pro-business newspapers like the *Sun* inflamed the President. He complained to John Hay: "I can not stand more than a certain amount of uninterrupted association with men who are nothing but politicians, contractors, financiers, etc." He preferred to talk literature with Hay or birds with John Burroughs and even outdoor life with the plain folks he had met on his speaking tour. He invited muckrakers Lincoln Steffens and S. S. McClure to dine and tried to interest them in writing a sympathetic series of articles on his attempts to tame "malefactors of great wealth"; they agreed but then thought better of the idea. The best he could do to diminish the power of monopolists besides trust-busting, however, was to endorse further regulation and plant negative stories about the low ethical standards of businessmen with friends like Jacob Riis who wrote for popular magazines. His prosecution of Standard Oil for its many efforts to restrain trade and monopolize the oil-refining and marketing business, but elsewhere he trod with caution because he needed business votes and money in 1904.[13]

He could not let his critics or the volatility of the economy stop him from forging ahead on his plans to make American power felt abroad. Gold had been discovered in Alaska, prompting the Canadian government to lay claim to land that had been recognized on Canadian maps as belonging to the United States since the 1840s. He told Ferguson that "the Canadians have acted most foolishly" in making their claims, but not foolishly enough to provoke a fight. Ignoring Hay's advice to remember Britain's friendship above all else, Roosevelt sent eight hundred cavalrymen to British Columbia but wisely chose negotiation over war. He declared himself "delighted" when the Alaskan Boundary Commission (to which he had appointed Lodge) decided in America's favor. By the time the boundary dispute was settled his attention had shifted to a larger issue on the global stage—joining the Atlantic and Pacific Oceans.[14]

In the middle of an August downpour, the President asked Hay to come to Sagamore Hill. Throughout his presidency TR had been in the habit of trying ideas out on him. On Sundays after an exasperating week in the White House, Roosevelt would walk home from Reformed church services and stop for a visit at Hay's house on Lafayette Square, where he would talk out his bold plans in front of the avuncular secretary of state. Hay recalled that *if* "you can restrain him for the first fifteen minutes after he has conceived a new idea," the President would calm down and behave like a reasonable human being. During their three- or four-hour talk in Sagamore Hill's library that August, Hay did not put a damper on the President's foreign policy ambitions. "Rough surgery" was under consideration and the older man left, amused that the "Young Man Afraid of his waistband" was unhappy that the demanding workload of the presidency got in the way of his physical fitness regimen.[15]

Roosevelt had been eager to talk with Hay about the prospects for an American canal in Panama, which belonged to Colombia. Hay had proposed a deal to Colombia: in exchange for $15 million the United States would get the right to build a canal across Panama. Colombia had balked at the offer, for reasons unclear to TR. Some claimed that Germany had poisoned Colombia's relationship with the United States by spreading rumors that prejudiced Americans routinely called Colombians "dagoes," and that Germany was prepared to fund, behind the scenes, a Colombian canal. To plan American strategy in Panama, Hay and Roosevelt had to assess Germany's intentions in the region. After Germans had gained a foothold in southern Brazil, the President had tried cagey diplomacy: he told Ambassador Speck von

Sternberg that perhaps a German state in South America might stabilize the region. Speck, it turned out, heartily agreed, which told TR and the secretary of state they needed to keep a close watch on Germany's every move.[16]

Roosevelt's urgency about joining the Pacific and the Atlantic by building an American-run canal came from his reading of German intentions, as did his two-ocean naval strategy. The United States and France had wasted the last several decades negotiating fruitlessly for a route across Central America that had never materialized. From the beginning of his presidency Roosevelt assumed he would succeed where others had failed to acquire the right to build a canal. At first he imagined a Nicaraguan route would be the least expensive, but new information showed that Panama was a cheaper alternative. Colombia's legislature had stalled the agreement over the money the United States offered to pay them. Though Panamanians had tried to secede from Colombia many times in the nineteenth century, the United States had repeatedly supported Colombia in quashing the revolts. Perhaps, thought Roosevelt, the time had come to be less helpful to Colombia.[17]

He also consulted Mark Hanna about what he should do in Panama as diplomatic tensions increased with Colombia. The American consul in Bogotá warned Hay that the Colombians were so insulted by American treatment that even extra funds would not buy their cooperation, though other sources told the United States that more money would win Colombia's support for an American canal. Unconcerned that Colombia's decision-making was slowed down by a recent civil war and legislative logjams, TR impatiently complained to Hay that they should not allow the "lot of jackrabbits" in Colombia "to bar one of the future highways of civilization" forever.[18]

In October the President told Albert Shaw, the editor of the important magazine *The Review of Reviews*, that he had ruled out the possibility of fomenting a revolution in Panama but he would not mind if one happened without U.S. instigation. Coincidentally, on November 3, a revolt in Panama broke out. Later, canal organizer Philippe Bunau-Varilla claimed to have acted in "alliance" with the President in starting the Panamanian revolution. Though an alliance probably did not exist, Hay and Roosevelt had enough advance warning of a rebellion to send the *Nashville* and several other cruisers to the coast of Panama to make sure the insurrection succeeded. With American ships standing by, Panamanian nationalists revolted against Colombia and created an independent country willing to have an American-controlled canal built through it. The "rough surgery" Roosevelt was willing to conduct to extend American influence abroad was not needed. The Panamanian revolution triumphed with little bloodshed, and the United States recognized the Republic of Panama promptly, which was followed by a treaty for an American-built canal. When the President defended his support for the Panamanian revolution, Attorney General Knox advised him with tongue in cheek not to "let so great an achievement suffer from any taint of legality." Years later TR wrote that if the Panamanian revolution had not erupted he would have asked Congress to invade Panama "by force of arms" to get the right to build the canal.[19]

Roosevelt's actions, however, provoked outrage in several quarters. The Senate resisted his attempts to build a canal and accused him of usurping Congress' war-making powers. Missouri's Senator William Stone was disgusted that TR had promoted the Panamanian revolution. Senator Henry Teller of Colorado denounced the President for acting like a thief and for declaring to the world "we want" it and "therefore we take it." Pulitzer's *World* charged that behind the Panamanian revolution was a profit-making stock venture from which Douglas Robinson and other Roosevelt relatives profited, and Hearst's *Chicago American* denounced TR's actions as "a rough-riding assault upon another republic over the shattered wreckage of international law and diplomatic usage."[20]

When the Daughters of the Confederacy lauded Roosevelt's aid of Panamanian secessionism, he denied that his stance was meant as praise for the Confederate secession. Instead, he saw himself as Lincoln after Bull Run and Fredericksburg when critics lost sight of the larger historic questions at stake. Congressman Cannon laconically observed that with Panama to fight over he guessed no financial legislation would get passed this session. In the long weeks when the Panama treaty was being filibustered almost to death, TR conducted his own brand of social filibuster at dinner parties. Henry Adams moaned: "We were overwhelmed in a torrent of oratory, and at last I heard only the repetition of I-I-I- attached to indiscretions greater one than another." The President was "half-amused and half-angered" by the predictable opposition of presidential hopefuls, isolationists, and opposition newspapers, but he complained to Ted, "A goodly number of the Senators even of my own party have shown about as much backbone as so many angle worms." In private letters he berated some of his opponents as "a small body of shrill eunuchs" fearful of promoting national interests abroad. Despite strong opposition, by February 23, 1904, the Senate ratified the Hay–Bunau-Varilla Treaty and gave the canal its blessing, thanks largely to overwhelming public support.[21]

The Panama Canal became the cornerstone of Roosevelt's policies in the Western Hemisphere. His goal was to make the United States a major naval power capable of defending itself in worldwide conflicts in the Atlantic or the Pacific. He wanted the navy to be strong enough to defend itself at Pearl Harbor, the Philippines, in the Canal Zone and the Caribbean, and elsewhere in case of war. To achieve his goal, he believed, he had to make America's military presence felt in the New World. After he gained access to Panama he admitted that "it seems inevitable that the United States should assume an attitude of protection and regulation in regard to all these little states in the neighborhood of the Caribbean."[22]

When European powers prepared to use force in collecting unpaid debts from rebellion-torn Santo Domingo, the Dominican foreign minister requested his help and Roosevelt intervened. To ward off Germany and other powers looking to gain footholds in the New World, TR announced his Roosevelt Corollary to the Monroe Doctrine—that the United States would intervene in cases of "brutal wrongdoing or impotence." In fact, the United States had already acted as a regional police force for decades. Though TR intervened less often and with less violence than later presidents, the Roosevelt Corollary gave his blessing to a future history of interference in Latin America, which included support for military dictators and disregard for the legal rights and sensibilities of Latin Americans.

THE CONFLICTS and burdens of the presidency left Roosevelt in the fall of 1903 with "wild momentary longing" to hunt moose. He told Ted: "In politics, as in life generally, the strife is well nigh unceasing and breathing spots are few." On occasion, he made the strife worse. TR had talked too freely at a reception about the failings of Attorney General Knox, and the man to whom he spoke in confidence published the President's views as if their conversation had been an interview. Edith tried to stop all family members, including her husband, from letting such an event happen again.[23]

Politics was disappointing in the off-term. His friend Seth Low, the reform mayor of New York, had expanded civil service to replace patronage jobs in city government and pioneered the subway system, but the voters turned him out of office in 1903. TR said he was further disgusted to observe that Maryland voters had chosen as their senator Arthur Gorman, a scoundrel, who "won on a straight-out appeal to the basest race prejudice, and by successful misrepresentation of my position." Gorman also attacked Roosevelt for making too many black appointments, though the numbers show such federal selections declined under Roosevelt. But the President said lies and a shifting political tide would not affect him because "I have chosen my own line, and win or lose I shall fight it out on that line."[24]

As 1904 began he found it "awfully hard work keeping [his] temper in public life" because of the constant press scrutiny and personal attacks on him and his family.[25] He lost the shrewd, sarcastic conservative Elihu Root from his cabinet, Hay took ill, and he gained the huge yes-man William Howard Taft as secretary of war. TR said he missed Root dreadfully, and the daily work of keeping his combative ire in check proved harder with Hay and Root absent. Being under siege made him turn into a swashbuckler, lightning quick to reach for his rhetorical sword. When the *Brooklyn Eagle* ran an article charging that he had taken $80 million of personal patronage out of the Treasury, Roosevelt branded it "a malicious lie," which it was. He was annoyed that Hearst also attacked him for extravagance—an expensive naval review, a luxury yacht, grand presidential receptions in the White House, and renovations to the White House. TR refuted the charges by showing that the *Mayflower* was the yacht of the navy, the review was needed for the navy's morale, he personally paid for all the receptions, and Congress had recommended and financed the return of the Executive Mansion "to its old simple and stately dignity."[26]

After Congress refused to lower the age of eligibility for veterans' pensions to sixty-two, TR did it by executive order. He had for a long time sympathized with Civil War veterans, many of whom were too old to earn a living doing manual labor after that age. He also wanted to block a more extravagant pension bill that would have cost too much. The press and the Democrats criticized him for usurping congressional powers yet again. Of course, in an election year his pension ruling could win votes because veterans saw it as largesse. But the pension order also qualified as reform. TR reminded Riis that in New Zealand every civilian male at age sixty-five, regardless of his military record, received a much larger pension from the state. In that light his executive order could be seen as a small step toward a national old age pension reform that the United States would not institute until 1935.[27]

In the harsh winter of 1904, Roosevelt ventured into ice-covered Rock Creek Park, and fell down "full length" twice on a walk with Alex Lambert, Gifford Pinchot, and Jim Garfield. Afterward, he was quick to point out that his companions fell down much more than he had. His rheumatism, gout, and weight gain slowed him down, and he was finding it more difficult to get exercise. His work held him from nine in the morning until seven at night; then the social season required that he attend receptions and parties almost every night. On days when he had only a half hour to exercise he could trot his horse quickly around the Washington Monument or down to the Potomac, but it was not enough—he had to let off more steam.[28]

That winter TR and Edith had been faithfully visiting the ailing Mark Hanna, who had become a real friend. On the same day, February 15, that Hanna died and the Old Guard within the Republican Party lost its guiding spirit, Edith gave a reception for a future group of voters her husband would court, three hundred members of the National Woman's Suffrage Association. By 1904, women could vote for president in Colorado, Idaho, Utah, and Wyoming. Because the Republican Party had closer ties with the W.C.T.U. and other moral reform groups than the Democrats did, it had a better chance of winning women voters. Edith in private supported suffrage, though she would never say so in public, but TR did not give Susan B. Anthony his unconditional support for a national amendment when she came to the White House and asked for it (he said get another state first). It was slowly occurring to the President that the General Federation of Women's Clubs, the Daughters of the American Revolution (where Gifford Pinchot's mother held power), the woman-founded Pennsylvania Forestry Association, and women prominent in the Audubon Society and the Sierra Club were much more likely to lobby on behalf of his conservation bills than the mainstream of his own party. "A Million Women for Conservation," as one article counted it, wrote tens of thousands of letters to Congress about conservation while at least another million lobbied for some of the other causes TR favored, especially pure food and drug regulation and the abolition of child labor. As he struggled with his self-appointed task of "making an old party progressive," he looked for women allies. So he sent his old campaign companion Judith Ellen Foster west to win women voters for him in November.[29]

He wanted more than anything else to win the Republican nomination in 1904 and to be elected president, and he warily observed his likely rivals trying to make names for themselves. Congressman Hearst's advocacy of a bill to guarantee an eight-hour day for railroad workers won labor support, but his inability to make an effective public speech undermined his campaign. As the election year unfolded the *New York Evening Post* labeled a Hearst candidacy "unthinkable" because he was a "low voluptuary" whose liaisons with chorus girls would not stand up to public scrutiny.[30] As he looked ahead to the Republican nominating convention in June, Roosevelt had less control over his party than he wanted, and the uncertainty he faced made him dogmatic. He tried to assume command of the Republican National Committee, but the party's conservatives grumbled over his choice of George Cortelyou to head the committee. Then the Old Guard blocked his ideas about a platform and a running mate. He did not understand how anyone could disagree with what he had done: "Honestly I do not see that we have anything to defend." He told diplomat George Meyer he wanted the names of opponents of Cortelyou because "opposition to him" was "disloyalty to the republican party." When an employee of the Congressional Library (later Library of Congress) wrote to criticize his policy toward the South, TR told the librarian he thought the man should be fired because his remarks were "treasonable to the Government." Instead of letting Lincoln's magnanimous wisdom guide him through the election season, Roosevelt sounded more like John Adams confusing honest criticism of his administration's policy with disloyalty. Fortunately for his political future most of his intolerant moments were hidden from the public.[31]

When she moved the other children to Sagamore Hill for the summer, Edith left Alice under TR's supervision, and he proved to be a permissive parent. Oblivious to the prevailing social propriety, he allowed Alice to walk unchaperoned with a young man near Burnt Mills. TR even drew a map of good places to walk. Alice was determined to express herself whether or not her family approved—carrying a green snake, for example, named after Edith's sister Emily. Though the Lees gave her a generous allowance, Alice continued to overspend, and Edith wrote her angrily: "How would you like to have Archie give up college to pay your debts?" When newspapers published a letter written by a socially powerful congressman's wife criticizing White House social functions and Alice's "bumptious, awkward manners," TR personally confronted his daughter's critic. Nevertheless, his defense of his daughter did not stop her from being a political liability. The society scandal sheet *Town Topics* made snide remarks about her morals and reported that she had been "indulging freely in stimulants" at Newport.[32]

After many flirtations Alice focused more attention on a wealthy congressman from Ohio, Nicholas Longworth. Longworth was a relative of Maria Longworth Storer, proprietor of Rookwood Arts and Crafts pottery and the heiress who had talked McKinley into appointing TR assistant secretary of the navy. Mrs. Storer believed the President's debt to her could be paid by letting her meddle in Vatican diplomacy and Catholic politics; when she made public his letters about Catholic politics she proved to be "an awful trial" to the President. But Alice did not let her father's irritation with Nick's kin stop her. By the next summer Alice found ways to be alone with Longworth at Bar Harbor and before long in his study in Washington, and her diary told of his passionate caresses. After newspapers carried stories about her traveling unescorted with young men Alice got "a terrible lecture from Father & Mother on the family and my extravagance, lack of morals." The President confronted his daughter about her behavior, and he hoped something or someone would finally settle her down before she hurt his chances of winning in November.[33]

THE SOUTH remained the white whale of Roosevelt's political career. He still longed to be popular there, but he had little chance. He wrote a pleading letter to his southern critic John Sharp Williams complaining about violent attacks on him, but decided it was hopeless to send it. All Democrats had to do to win the Solid South in November 1904 was to keep black voters disenfranchised and distribute buttons with Roosevelt and Booker T. Washington labeled "Social Equality." Movies had never been used in political campaigning before 1904, and in May rumors began to spread around the Capitol that the Democrats had made a film dramatizing the friendship between Roosevelt and Washington. Feeling "great agitation" over the story, TR sent his Secret Service agents and the District of Columbia police to hunt down the moviemakers. They tracked the source of the film to New York, where the culprit turned out to be blackface minstrel-vaudevillian Lew Dockstadter, who had, in fact, portrayed Washington in a skit with actor Harry Ellis, who played the President. They had made a brief film with the Edison Kinetoscope Company, but no connection existed between Dockstadter and the Democratic Party.[34]

Nevertheless, the police demanded the print and when Dockstadter complied they burned it. Black newspapers charged TR with cowardice for trying so often to cover up his dinner with Booker T. Washington. Other papers charged him with dictatorial infringement upon citizens' rights—acting like a "Strenuous First Consul." Dockstadter made up a new vaudeville skit satirizing the strenuous President, which was not that hard to do.[35]

Ebullient before crowds, Roosevelt ignored Lodge's reassurances and in private agonized over what he feared might be his impending defeat at the polls. In his season of gathering tension, world events came to TR's rescue. On May 18, in Morocco, a bandit named Raisuli (Mulai Ahmed ben Mohammed) kidnapped Ion Perdicaris, a former resident of New Jersey. The President would not tolerate Americans being held hostage abroad, so he ordered warships to Tangier immediately. Diplomats exchanged urgent telegrams about Raisuli's extensive demands, which included a full pardon for the kidnapping and past crimes. Hay brought France into the crisis as the strongest European presence in Morocco and the only power capable of establishing order when bandits attacked foreigners or tribes revolted against the sultan. The sultan negotiated without success with Raisuli, and on June 15, Hay wrote with irritation in his diary that Raisuli had "a bad case of megalomania." TR ordered Hay not to cooperate with any blanket pardons: "Our position must now be to demand the death of those that harm" Perdicaris.[36]

Before negotiations reached a settlement or a joint expedition could be organized for an invasion of Morocco by France, England, and the United States, the Republican convention in Chicago had started. Party managers could see that with Roosevelt's nomination already sewn up, the convention would need some "artificial respiration." Hay wired the American consul in Morocco: "WE WANT PERDICARIS ALIVE OR RAISULI DEAD," largely so Joe Cannon could read the telegram in front of the full convention for the crowd effect, which was loud and enthusiastic. Aside from the incident's usefulness for playing to the grandstands, when the flag-waving passed, negotiation triumphed where threats of military action had failed. Perdicaris, whose U.S. citizenship was questionable anyway, went free. Spain and France worried that the United States wanted a naval base in Morocco more than Perdicaris' safety, and the kaiser, who had been excluded from negotiations, feared American favoritism toward France and the prospect that instability in Morocco would allow France to gather the country into its empire like Algeria.[37]

Roosevelt applauded the drama the telegram created, but he could only watch the convention from afar. Sitting presidents did not attend their own nominating conventions, but TR kept in touch by telegraph and telephone with Chicago. Despite the fact he was President and leader of his party, he had still not gained full control over the convention. He lost a crucial battle over his running mate, despite the fact that Root and Lodge actively worked the convention on his behalf. He had wanted Congressman Robert R. Hitt of Illinois to be his vice president, but E. H. Harriman and other powers in the party insisted upon the duller, more conservative Senator Charles Fairbanks of Indiana. Harriman may have won without much of a fight because Root and Lodge were so eager to placate the Wall Street wing of the party.[38]

Lodge also reported that, contrary to Roosevelt's wishes, the convention had added a platform plank that advocated the application of the clause of the Fourteenth Amendment which called for reducing a state's congressional delegation whenever racial disenfranchisement could be proved. William Monroe Trotter, editor of the *Boston Guardian*, and Congressman Edgar Crumpacker had long advocated such a plank, but TR and Booker T. Washington thought it too radical for the times. Roosevelt wanted to overturn the Solid South and white-only voting, but he did not want to revive the Civil War or stir up bitter memories of Reconstruction. Lodge said (and TR agreed) that the plank was "demanding something that in all probability we shall not have the nerve to do."[39] Though the convention did not go exactly as planned, Roosevelt got what he wanted, his party's enthusiastic endorsement. Lodge reported to TR that Root had quipped "that after the way in which he and I strained and racked our conscience in what we said of you in speech and platform it will be necessary for us to join some church which is able to give full absolution."[40]

Nevertheless, Hanna loyalists put a large picture of the dead senator in the center of the convention hall and kept TR's images to the side, which amused

Lodge. Roosevelt won the nomination handily and was the first vice president who, after ascending to the presidency upon the death of the President, won the nomination on his own—only Truman and Johnson would follow in his footsteps. But he did so with a deeply divided party.

As the fall campaign opened, Roosevelt, the Republican attack dog of 1896 and 1900, hungered to get into the fight, but his managers held him back. Sitting presidents did not slug it out on the campaign trail. Nevertheless, he could make speeches at strategic patriotic sites. He was the first president to speak where Lincoln gave his great Gettysburg Address; he traveled to the site of George Washington's suffering at Valley Forge and then went south to toast Stonewall Jackson's widow in Richmond. When he praised Jefferson Davis among southern voters he spoke for political effect and indulged in a bit of hypocrisy; in private TR still believed the president of the Confederacy was "an unhung traitor" on a moral par with betrayer Benedict Arnold. No matter how much he lauded Confederate heroes, his mother's homeland refused to warm up to him.[41]

Despite his worries, he lived the strenuous life as forcefully as ever that summer. TR watched with a mixture of regret and joy as his children became more independent. Ted and Kermit were allowed to go to the St. Louis World's Fair accompanied by friends, and later that year TR was proud that his eldest son killed his first bull moose, one with a fifty-six-inch spread of antlers. Ted refused to return to Groton in the fall of 1904, and he convinced his parents to let him stay home to study for his Harvard entrance exams on his own. Kermit hated Groton, too, and dreaded having to face Rector Peabody's strict regimen without his brother. Edith doubted that Ted could study amidst the social whirl of White House life, but she hired Matthew Hale to tutor him and Ted proved her worries unfounded.[42]

Even in jovial moments at Sagamore Hill, Roosevelt never forgot the coming election. His fate in 1904 depended upon whom the Democrats ran against him. He worried obsessively that a familiar figure like Grover Cleveland might be too hard to beat, but Lodge reassured him that Cleveland could not be nominated, nor could he ever be formidable again. Meanwhile, TR turned fundraising over to Cortelyou, who contacted Wall Street donors. At their nominating convention in St. Louis that July the Democrats sidestepped their best campaigner, Bryan, because of his losses in 1896 and 1900. Labor lawyer Clarence Darrow seconded the nomination of William Randolph Hearst, but Bryan did not trust Hearst and refused to endorse the publishing mogul who had paid him a generous salary for being one of his foreign correspondents. Tammany's aloofness toward Hearst threw the nomination to a stodgy appeals court judge, Alton B. Parker, and the Democrats' platform declared for immediate Philippine independence. Parker was a gold Democrat, more conservative than Roosevelt in that he disapproved of TR's antitrust prosecutions which were popular with voters. Nor was Parker good with crowds. He could not hold the Democratic ranks together, nor could he stop lifelong Democrats like young Franklin D. Roosevelt from voting for TR. Franklin said that he voted for Eleanor's uncle because "I felt he was a better Democrat than the Democratic candidates."[43]

Bryan stood lukewarm and disappointed on the sidelines watching as his party moved right to launch an attack on Roosevelt's radicalism. After Parker charged that 200,000 lives had been sacrificed in the Philippines, Lodge complained in private that the United States had never had more than 125,000 soldiers there, which showed that Lodge did not count the Filipino lives lost. Foreign policy questions did not arouse voters much, and on domestic issues Roosevelt knew how to appeal to crossover voters, Democrats who found him more sympathetic to unions and immigrants than Parker. That fall TR heard from Democratic campaigners that he had violated the Constitution, that he had never been at the Battle of San Juan Hill, that he toadied to labor unions, that he was the creature of the trusts, and that he had unpatriotically criticized Jefferson, Madison, and Jackson in his historical writings.

Ready to fight it out with his critics, he grew impatient against such accusations and the White House staff thought he was "looking for a scrap." He and Edith were so preoccupied by the campaign that they forgot Kermit's birthday, and Edith wrote the boy apologetically that, in truth, Father was worried he might lose. Friends and family tried to relieve some of the tension: "good angel" Bob Ferguson took Edith to dine at the St. Regis to get her away from constant talk of politics and members of the Tennis Cabinet kept the President walking fast and climbing steep hills.[44]

Lodge did not reduce Roosevelt's anxiety, however. He urged the President to make an appearance at the Grand Army of the Republic National Encampment, where Nelson A. Miles was capable of trying to undermine Roosevelt's strength among the veterans, but TR did not go because too many other groups would have called on him to make special visits. The President had to walk a fine line when fighting the Democrats. His strategy of courting the Democrats' populist and labor constituencies was working, and he wanted voters to see him as Franklin did, as "a better Democrat." But he could not afford to alienate his Republican base, which included a large eastern conservative faction. The usually Republican and pro-business *New York Sun* already invited defections when it charged that TR had "disarmed all his enemies" by adopting "every vestige" of Bryan's platform and that Roosevelt had become "the leader of the labor-unions" after the anthracite coal strike.

Fearing that the President had already alienated the pro-business wing of his party, Lodge calmed bankers and financiers in Boston and New York with promises that TR was going to be more moderate in his second term.[45]

Lodge worked quietly as TR's de facto campaign manager and found it "wiser to keep in the background." Meanwhile, Roosevelt sent his own bountiful advice to Cortelyou, and by October the intensity of the campaign pressed him to write three letters a day to his campaign manager at the Republican National Committee.

Parker proved to be a lackluster candidate, but he had staffers who knew how to do opposition research. As soon as they discovered how many corporations had donated big money to the Roosevelt campaign, Parker began pounding away at Cortelyouism: he charged that TR's campaign manager was using his previous knowledge as secretary of commerce and labor to hit up corporations for donations—asking them to donate or face prosecution. The *New York World* called Cortelyou "The President's Confidential Collector of Trust Tribute." Cortelyou was, indeed, in the process of collecting large and at that time legal corporate contributions, as were the Democrats on a smaller scale, but no evidence ever appeared which proved he had tied the donations to exemption from prosecution. But the fact that 73 percent of the President's campaign funds came from corporations made voters question the sincerity of his earlier trust-busting: whose side was he on?[46]

Desperate accusers claimed Roosevelt had advocated vigilantism in his biography of Oliver Cromwell and that he was a bought president. The incendiary Alabama congressman Thomas Heflin threatened to have Booker T. Washington lynched if he campaigned for the Republicans. Democrats called TR a dictator who was "unworthy to lace the shoestrings of President McKinley."[47]

The Square Deal had made significant inroads with ethnic voters, especially Jews and Catholics. Oscar Straus and Jacob Schiff left the Democrats to support TR because he had listened to B'nai B'rith and had forwarded their petition. Finley Peter Dunne's satirical Tiddy Rosenfelt had convinced other voters that the President was Jewish. TR told Dunne that he wished it were true, and he did nothing to correct the falsehood when he was the first president to make a visit to the Lower East Side. Roosevelt made sure immigrant voters knew he had cleaned up corruption at Ellis Island—sweeping out government officials, currency exchangers, and concessionaires who had cheated newcomers. Immigrants also liked seeing Catholics and Jews prominent in his administration. Jewish campaigners reminded voters: "All Jews, whatever their origin, glory in the President's sympathy for our people in Russia." The Irish vote, once reliably Democratic, crossed party lines because of the Square Deal's emphasis on tolerance and brotherhood across all social divisions. Roosevelt understood, too, that cartoonists would help him win votes by planting powerful images of him as Jack the Giant Killer fighting the trusts or as the brave wielder of the Big Stick at home and abroad.[48]

Lodge saw that the Parker candidacy was "going slowly but steadily to pieces" with voters, but the Roosevelts still feared the worst. The truth was closer to what William Jennings Bryan saw in Nebraska: that Parker stood for nothing compelling or appealing and the people's choice was clearly Roosevelt. Bryan, in fact, did not mind seeing the conservatives in his own party go down to defeat. But from Oyster Bay the clippings looked bad, and TR could no longer restrain himself from entering the arena for a knockout. His philosophy of campaigning, as he told Taft, was that on good days you paint circus posters to explain the issues to the voters and on bad days you engage in a rough contact sport: "Prize fights are won by knocking out the other man when he is groggy, and in hunting I always found it paid to make sure of sure things."[49]

TR personally appealed to old friends like Tim Sullivan, who agreed to have his Tammany buddies sit out Parker's campaign. After Parker attacked TR in the last week before the election, Roosevelt told his cabinet he could no longer contain himself. On Friday, November 4, Knox rushed over to the White House to stop the President, but Commissioner of Indian Affairs Francis Leupp and the Roosevelt family encouraged him to fight back. By that Saturday even Alice was caught up in listening to her father's drafts as the family talked over what he should say. He chose the words "monstrous" and "slanderous" and "falsehood" to belittle Parker's charge that Cortelyou had blackmailed corporations into making large contributions. No public opinion polling existed to gauge the effect his words had on the voters, but as his hard-hitting counterpunch went out to the press, he felt relieved that he had defended his good name. That night the President calmed himself down by reading poetry by Edwin Arlington Robinson. He admired the poet so much he later gave him a government job, though not out of political calculation: he already had the poet vote locked up.[50]

The tension had grown so much that TR admitted that "the last fortnight was nervous for both Edith and me." Early one morning before the election, Ted, Ethel, Edith, and Theodore were out riding, and as they crossed a rickety bridge, TR's horse, Rusty, stepped into a hole and "threw Father over his head." As he crashed to the ground the President got a bump on his head and a scratch on his nose. The family tried to conceal the accident from the press, but the *World* got wind of it anyway.[51]

TR had enjoyed the hoopla and theatrics of previous campaigns, but this year he had to act presidential and miss the playfulness of the canvassing. Booker T. Washington's most effective political organizer in New York, Charles W. Anderson, put together a Colored Republican Club there and supported TR's election with a song, "You're All Right, Teddy," penned by the author of the black national anthem, James Weldon Johnson, and his brother. Anderson agreed with TR's view that within Democratic ranks dwelled many enemies of "the black man's civil rights," and Anderson campaigned by spreading the word that the President consulted and respected black advisors. Later, Anderson ran a Republican Negro Bureau in the East to subsidize pro-Roosevelt black newspapers. TR's alliance with Booker T. Washington's Tuskegee machine, in fact, diminished the influence of more assertive black voices in the party such as Ferdinand Barnett and his wife, Ida B. Wells-Barnett. Soon after the election Roosevelt announced he wanted to appoint a well-known black man in New York to an important government job. So he chose Anderson as collector of Internal Revenue and Johnson got diplomatic posts in Venezuela and later Nicaragua.[52]

The day before the election he took a quiet walk in the White House garden with Edith and Alice before he boarded a train to Oyster Bay to vote. The train brought him back to the capital by 6:30 p.m. on election day, and Edith greeted him happily at the door. The first results told them it would be a landslide victory. Archie covered himself with campaign buttons and ran back and forth with the latest news from the telegraph room, while cabinet members, family, friends, and a worn-out Cortelyou joined the family for a party. Edith wrote that she felt "great surprise" that her husband had won an "overwhelming victory," and Alice noted that no previous president had received so many votes. The Solid South held as firm against him as it had against McKinley, except for Missouri. TR also felt jubilant that he would have Republican majorities in both houses of Congress, but he wrote Kermit: "It was a great comfort to feel, all during the last days when affairs looked doubtful, that no matter how things came out the really important thing was the lovely life I have with mother and with you children, and that compared to this home life everything else was of very small importance from the standpoint of happiness."[53]

The excitement of victory on election night moved TR to make a serious political blunder. He declared to a roomful of reporters that he would not run for a third term, though the Constitution would have allowed it and his landslide might be an argument for leaving open the option of a run in 1908. After his critics called him a Caesar and the South charged him with dictatorial tendencies worse than they suffered during Radical Reconstruction, he disavowed long-term ambition by promising not to seek reelection. When Roosevelt made his announcement it was obvious he had not deliberated over it with all of his advisors. Edith winced in surprise, but Lodge applauded it as a high-minded gesture. She proved to be correct because Congress soon started treating him as a lame duck president. His promise did not make him more popular with his critics, and it would come back to haunt him in his active post-presidential years. Too tense to eat in the final weeks of the campaign, Edith excused herself and went to bed to recover from overexcitement and electoral weariness.[54]

After Thanksgiving, TR and Edith took Corinne and Douglas and the children to the St. Louis Fair, where organizers put on a nationalist display of a hundred years of progress since the Louisiana Purchase. Visitors could see cultural evolutionary stages in the large anthropological Congress of Races meant to illustrate which races made progress. Zairean pygmies, Ainu aborigines from Japan, and costumed Native Americans were shown to illustrate the same theories as the nearby ethnological lab whose scientific measurements purported to show that savages and primitives had substandard brains.

TR had no large role in planning the fair, but he had endorsed government exhibits that showed Philippine products and people favorably enough to disprove southern Democrats' claim that Filipinos were unfit for eventual democracy. Philippine Igorot people appeared in G-strings, but their state of undress sparked an acrimonious debate. Moralists wanted the Igorots to cover up because they were against nudity at the fair, but anthropologist Frederick Starr warned that Western dress might kill them. Roosevelt at first ordered short pants to hide the Igorots' private parts and buttocks. Then, as the furor refused to die down, the exasperated President gave a "no pants" order. He wondered, however, "whether we were exploiting savagery to the detriment of civilization."[55]

The fair also celebrated the public excitement over inventions and products in the new century, incubators and airplanes, though many pundits warned that vast array of commercial ventures would "barnumize the fair." If the mélange of entertainments offended the President, he did not let on—the show encompassed reenactments of the Battle of Gettysburg and the Galveston flood, hootchie-kootchie dancers, aborigines from the ethnology exhibits competing in the fair's Olympic Games, and a large butter sculpture of Theodore Roosevelt. The President whose picture had already adorned Moxie soda pop ads unabashedly joined his own growing celebrity to other icons on display; he applauded the large crowds' enjoyment of the new sights and the new sounds of the popular chords of "Meet Me in St. Louis," and was undaunted by doctors' warnings that it might cause a breakdown to try to see the fair in one day as the Roosevelts did.[56]

Before he went to St. Louis, Theodore had strained his thigh badly and bruised it too, but he was careful not to limp in front of reporters as he hurried through the fair. He remembered: "I was taken through a lot of the buildings, streaking along pretty nearly as hard as I could walk from one place to another, while Mother, who was in beautiful walking trim, kept right up behind, and a mob of followers jostled after us." Alice had to do some "tall sprinting" and Corinne a "perpetual jog-trot" to keep up. Knowing that his family was also on display, he ordered Alice not to bet on horses when she took her cousin Corinny to the races, and Edith urged her not to be seen with a divorced socialite friend. TR had one criticism to make of the fair. When he got back from St. Louis he wrote to the organizer of the upcoming Jamestown Exposition to urge him to make sure African-Americans were allowed to plan their own exhibit "to show what they have done in three hundred years."[57]

Strenuous physical activity gave Theodore pleasure; adulation from the multitudes gave him honor and, when it came to him in the form of an avalanche of votes, power. He remained "very grateful to the American people," saying, "All that in me lies will be done during the next four years to show my appreciation," and he confessed to his new friend, French ambassador Jules Jusserand, that he adored popular acclaim: "I love it for the power it gives." Yet, acclaim would be hollow if he did not harness it to serve a purpose. Despite his popularity, he had won no major piece of legislation from Congress in his first term. Executive boldness had wrought anti-trust prosecutions, Panama, and the coal strike settlement. None of these changes would last beyond his presidency unless laws and public opinion were remade. He would try to win legislative victories in his second term, and he hoped for a national rebirth of conscience and vitality, too.[58]

With the coming of 1905, Lodge predicted in TR's second term significant agitation for tariff revision and the possible use of the labor vote by Gompers to "make trouble" for the Republican Party. Lodge saw every reason to slow down the President's impulse toward reform. The Russo-Japanese War, born of tensions over Russia's occupation of Manchuria and competition for influence over East Asia and the Pacific, had broken out and could upset the world balance of power at any moment. Roosevelt had no intention of listening to his friend's advice to be cautious. Instead, he secretly planned to use his landslide to change America: tackling workers' safety; employers' liability; the construction of new battleships, forts, and buildings; and the banning of railroad rebates. He hoped to spread progressive reform throughout the cities and states by using the District of Columbia as a model community with factory inspection laws, compulsory school attendance, a model juvenile court system, sanitary and housing regulation, new parks and playgrounds, child welfare laws, and a ban on child labor. His success at the polls encouraged him in his second term to propose new laws and to use his "bully pulpit" to define proper behavior for men and women. He told Congress he wanted to legislate married women out of factory jobs and bring in corporal punishment for husbands who beat their wives. After the election his opponents had more to oppose: they told stories about how TR behaved on election night, "crouching, and yelling as at a war dance and acting on the whole as an irresponsible boy." His bold plans looked like madness to critics, but like sanity to a host of new forces rising in American politics. Sane or not, he was ready to do a war dance with Congress. As always, he liked a good fight.[59]

☆ CHAPTER NINE ☆

"I So Thoroughly Believe in Reform"

THE NIGHT BEFORE his inauguration Roosevelt told John Hay how much he had appreciated his friendship as he began a new chapter of his life: "Tomorrow I shall come into my office in my own right. Then watch out for me!" He intended to lead his country into the twentieth century with the same vigor he had shown charging up Kettle Hill. Mark Twain thought TR was the Tom Sawyer of American politics, an awful, boyish show-off, but by 1905 Tom Sawyer would have figured out how to get Congress to do his bidding—at least he would get them to whitewash a fence for him. Roosevelt had not won great legislative victories yet but he was slowly learning how to use public opinion to make Congress cooperate with him. TR did not think of himself as a naughty but likable Tom Sawyer; he preferred to see himself as Sir Galahad.[1]

His second term began on March 4, 1905, a sunny but cold day. At the solemn swearing-in at the Capitol, as he promised to uphold the Constitution, TR wore the ring Hay had given him containing a lock of Lincoln's hair. Eleanor and Franklin Roosevelt, now engaged, arrived in Bamie's carriage and sat behind the President. An honor guard of Rough Riders surrounded him as he left the Capitol. After lunch with Jacob Riis, Uncle Robert Roosevelt, Corinne, Bamie, Grant and Florence La Farge, Bill Sewall, and other close friends and family members, the Roosevelts watched the pageantry of a flamboyant three-hour inaugural parade of thirty-five thousand walking down Pennsylvania Avenue. The Toledo Newsboys' Band celebrated Thee's charitable work and coal miners paraded along with Geronimo, Chief Joseph of the Nez Percé, cowboys, Filipino scouts, and 150 Harvard students in cap and gown. Theodore and Edith were reunited with innumerable friends of a lifetime at the huge inaugural ball that night. He said he would be "too much elated, if I did not have a very real and ever-present anxiety so to handle myself as to minimize the disappointment that many good people are sure to feel in what I am able to do."[2]

His supporters were excited to hear "There'll Be a Hot Time in the Old Town Tonight" played all over the city that week. There promised to be a hot time in the old capital, indeed, because Congress did not like his program of reform. His landslide and the Republican majorities in both houses did not mean the legislative branch would give up its constitutional right to govern as a partner of the presidency. If he alienated the legislators they could gather enough votes to obstruct his every wish. Roosevelt intended to "extend the sphere of Governmental action" in several directions—expanding railroad regulation to lower rates, holding employers responsible for workplace accidents, and exerting federal power over corporations.

Critics already denounced him as a would-be "czar" or "the Republican Bryan" and Senator Augustus O. Bacon called for an investigation of presidential usurpations of power. When the President's reform program stalled, his diplomatic successes gave him renewed prestige, which aided him in his sustained battles with Congress. Though he would be sidetracked in his second term by international crises and, on a few occasions, by his own blunders, he rarely lost sight of his boldest goal as president—using the federal government to solve the human problems created by the industrial age.[3]

During the campaign voters had told him their belief that tariffs—that is, import taxes to stifle competition from foreign goods—helped monopolies and hurt consumers. Government favoritism toward big manufacturers who benefited from the high tariffs had been a Democratic complaint for years. Even his cautious advisor Elihu Root, a corporation lawyer, saw the need for lowering the tariff. But when the President told Speaker of the House Joe Cannon and Senator Orville Platt he wanted tariff revision, they said no. Tariff was a sacred cow among stand-pat Republicans.[4]

TR backed down for the time being and instead took up railroad regulation. Speaker Cannon and the ascendant Big Four in the Senate—Aldrich, Spooner, Allison, and Platt—intended to block railroad reform, too. John D. Rockefeller, Jr.'s multi-millionaire father-in-law, Senator Nelson Aldrich, saw his own prosperity and the nation's economic well-being tied to its biggest business, the railroads, so he would not support any bill that might cut profits or reduce railroad power. "Railroad senators"—those who received campaign donations and free passes from the railroads—would not vote for a bill the industry opposed. They stalled regulation on Capitol Hill at the same time journalists exposed the special privileges—tax breaks, rebates, and land grants—railroads enjoyed.

Though he had not yet decided to support Senator Weldon Heyburn's pure food and drug bill, Roosevelt would not find it encouraging that the Senate found such a reform so preposterous that they played practical jokes on its sponsor. TR admitted to Kermit: "I am at times driven nearly wild both by the Senate and by the Speaker." He said he was "trying my best to get along somehow," but he feared his second term would end in "a hopeless snarl" with Congress. The stultifying routine of meetings, speeches, and the social season which filled his days and nights until Congress recessed could, he said, "drive me nearly melancholy mad."[5]

He sought relief by reading Tacitus and blackening his aide Roly Fortescue's eyes in a boxing match. He went riding in the middle of a blizzard and forded a freezing creek while chatting up his playmates who were also up to their waists in cold water. Chief White House usher Ike Hoover recalled TR working late, then walking to the Washington Monument at night, where he would take a run around the base while Secret Service men stood at a distance on guard.[6]

In the middle of his escalating hostilities with Congress, Roosevelt was being challenged to move to a new level of understanding in his long political education. Going into full dress combat did not work well when you had to work with your opponent again the next day. Name-calling, indiscreet ventilating against his rivals, and failure to compromise got him nowhere. Executive edicts might be righteous in his eyes, but they had alienated his partners in government. To promote reform he had to change the climate of opinion among politicians and their constituents alike, and he had to work in partnership with any allies he could find.

He later told Jane Addams: "I so thoroughly believe in reform," but he did not believe in just any reform. His growing progressivism had an urban social justice flavor to it. At a time when about a quarter of the workers in Alabama's cotton mills were children and every state had some kind of child labor problem, TR came out as a strong opponent. He allied himself with the Campaign Against Child Labor, which reformers like Felix Adler, Samuel McCune Lindsay, Jane Addams, James Cardinal Gibbons, and Florence Kelley advocated.[7]

However, when Senator Albert Beveridge proposed a federal law to prohibit the interstate transport of goods made by child laborers, TR refused to back him wholeheartedly. Because he had already asserted national authority over states' rights so many times, he feared an even greater coalition would build against him if he sought federal penetration into the workplace and the family to stop child labor.[8] Eventually, he would call for national legislation, but in the midst of his losing struggles with Congress in 1905 he urged states to restrain child labor. In the District of Columbia, where in practice he could act directly, he fought child labor more boldly. He asked Congress to give his new secretary of commerce and labor, Oscar Straus, money to investigate; Congress finally gave in, funding the investigation and then banning child labor there.[9]

To encourage progressive reformers in cities and states he sought to make the district a model city. He wanted to show what fine public education, parks, and playgrounds could do for the city's children, and he hoped to do away with alley tenements. The district lacked truancy laws, compulsory school attendance regulations, and a juvenile court. It was a poor, service workers' city, neglected by a Congress that was stingier with public funds than most municipal governments at the time. The district also suffered from a high death rate and a serious problem with tuberculosis. Black leaders from Howard University and Hampton and Tuskegee Institutes had already started an anti-tuberculosis campaign, but they benefited from new allies and money which the President could send their way. TR hoped that better building codes and condemnation of unsafe buildings would upgrade housing in the district, but when his Homes Commission recommended building public-funded low-cost housing, Congress refused. He brought Jacob Riis in to investigate and publicize the human suffering. Photojournalist Lewis Hine also documented in a historic series of photographs for the Homes Commission that within blocks of the Capitol houses stood without sewers or running water. But even here Roosevelt's reforms met resistance. In the end landlords sued and blocked his plans for tearing down dilapidated buildings, so reformers could do so only when they had funds for a playground or park to replace them. Democrat Albert Burleson of Texas opposed public playgrounds as "socialistic," and his party blocked funding.[10]

The President asked James B. Reynolds to investigate living conditions and the status of children in Washington and make recommendations, and in the end child labor laws, government regulation of insurance companies, employer liability laws, and pure food and drug laws were passed for the district. TR was proud that where he had authority he could prevent lynching altogether, and when Senator Heflin proposed to segregate the district's streetcar lines by law, Roosevelt and his party stopped him. The President also recommended the whipping post for wife beaters in the district, but did not win it. However, Congress did give in to his demands for a law forcing fathers to pay child support for their children.[11]

Congress responded to many of his ideas with disbelief. Unfriendly members of the press ridiculed Reynolds as TR's "Commissioner of Social Relations," and one society matron sniffed that the President was "devising" his reform agenda as one more way "to uplift and manage us." Senator Spooner, once a defender of the President's policies, accused him of trying to erase the power of the states and take all the power for himself.[12]

In his despairing moments when he saw the political "pendulum" swinging away from him, Roosevelt thought "of Lincoln, shambling, homely, with his strong, sad, and deeply furrowed face, all the time." As he pondered how far he could use the presidency in new and creative ways, he told friends he saw Lincoln in different rooms and halls. He hoped in his lifetime to see the Republican Party become "the real party of Lincoln again."[13]

Perhaps with Lincoln in mind, Roosevelt chose to make a quiet legal fight against the closest thing to slavery America had to offer: the peonage system in which employers held laborers captive because of debt. He was "appalled" by some of the revelations he heard about the system, so he empowered the Secret Service to investigate and his Justice Department to prosecute.[14]

His outrage was justified. Florida law allowed employers to imprison workers who owed them money, and no one bothered about legal due process in these cases. In Gainesville armed man hunters forced black workers back into peonage when they tried to escape from unfair labor contracts. Local sheriffs, rather than arresting the man hunters as kidnappers, aided them. Employers charged peons for transportation, water, food, and lodging, and held them prisoner until they paid up. To the President, this looked like slavery by another name, and state and local authorities were collaborating with employers. Peonage proved to be more common in areas where black disenfranchisement was complete, but even where blacks could vote they had little power to stop the collusion of employers, corporations, police, and courts which held the system in place. No National Association for the Advancement of Colored People existed to lobby against these practices when TR began his anti-peonage campaign. He believed, however, that no one could stop the practice if the federal government did not act.[15]

TR discovered labor agents were also transporting new European immigrants to the South to ensnare them in a system of debt peonage where they owed more than their wages to their bosses for transportation, food, or housing. Escaped workers from the turpentine industry were tracked down by hounds and beaten when caught. Employers forced Italian immigrants to work at gunpoint. Roosevelt knew he could not get federal legislation banning peonage through Congress, so he sent out government lawyers and investigators.

When Justice Department attorneys took employers to court for conspiracy to commit peonage, local Florida juries would not convict them. Roosevelt recognized the fervor and dedication of one legal crusader against immigrant peonage, Mary Grace Quackenbos, so he appointed her to investigate as his special assistant U.S. attorney in the South. She and the rest of the legal team prosecuted wherever they could find witnesses brave enough to testify. Though the campaign had only small success it served as an entering wedge of hope: later a black tenant farmers' union in Arkansas and the N.A.A.C.P. took up where the Roosevelt administration left off.[16]

TR had not decided to fight peonage to win votes, but he did have some vocal supporters. The Reverend Lyman Abbott, the Social Gospel minister, editor of *The Outlook* magazine, praised the peonage arrests in Alabama. Encouraged by presidential support, Booker T. Washington secretly raised money to launch legal challenges to the state contract-labor laws which made debtors liable to be sent into convict labor. TR urged his Justice Department to help Washington's lawyers, and their efforts paid off in *Bailey* v. *Alabama*, as the Supreme Court struck down the contract-labor laws. The *Bailey* case provided a rare early-twentieth-century moment when a black leader won presidential support for challenging one of the worst institutions of racism. But southern blacks were held down economically by so many legal and social devices that one legal victory was not enough to overturn a profitable system of racial oppression.[17]

Roosevelt also tried to influence southern courts to gain fairer treatment for blacks. Based in part on Grover Cleveland's and Booker T. Washington's recommendations, TR appointed a progressive lawyer, Thomas Goode Jones, to a federal judgeship. Jones ruled against employers who held workers in peonage, but most of the state and federal judiciary decided in favor of white bosses. Next the President tried to enlist muckrakers to expose peonage and the cruelties of convict labor in order to create broader public outrage against it, but anti-black sentiment was so pervasive in the North and South that he could not change public opinion about peonage laws, and few other judges followed Jones' lead. The President also turned to social scientist Frances Kellor to study what the federal government could do to stop the employment agencies that trapped immigrants into peonage and prostitution, and she worked with the Immigration Commission to put the agencies out of business. His critics often berated him for playing to the grandstand and courting votes at every opportunity, but in truth he was trying to turn the tide of public opinion and for the most part failed. Despite his own ambivalence about race, he wanted to hold "open the door of hope" to blacks in America.[18]

The backlash against the President's anti-peonage campaign reverberated throughout TR's second term. His most vitriolic enemies in the Senate—Bailey, Carmack, Bacon, and Tillman—had hated him for his dinner with Washington and now reviled him further because of his anti-peonage fight. Roosevelt considered them reactionaries who resisted "every measure to minimize the inequalities under which men lead their lives."[19] Even though he backed down on appointing blacks to federal jobs, he became for a while the most unpopular president in the South since the Civil War.[20] The logging and turpentine industries raised large defense funds to fight prosecution by the Justice Department. Southern business leaders and congressional representatives launched personal and political attacks on investigators in the Justice Department, including Attorney General Charles Bonaparte, Mary Grace Quackenbos, and Charles W. Russell. The Florida East Coast Railway tried to bribe witnesses to swear that no peonage existed in its construction crews, and even within the Roosevelt administration support for peonage prosecution flagged. Henry Stimson, TR's young U.S. attorney in New York, did not think the prosecution of such cases was as important as going after banks and trusts. When they accused him of seeking "negro domination," TR dismissed Tillman, Carmack, and others as Dickens characters out of *Martin Chuzzlewit*, but they continued to thwart many of his initiatives. He fought peonage while they worked for disenfranchisement, Jim Crow segregation, and the revocation of the Fifteenth Amendment.[21]

As he lost battle after battle, TR wished he had Lincoln's "invariable equanimity," but he kept moving forward guided by his own stormy disposition, morally purposeful but unforgiving. As his frustration with the limitation of his powers mounted, he unloaded his troubles on Edith, who suffered more than he did from the strain of daily battles and the harsh criticism leveled against him. After acrimonious sessions with Congress, he was the resilient one in the family. He bounced out of bed each day ready for battle, but Edith's neuralgic headaches came back when life seemed too hectic. She feared that she would never recover, and that she would languish as a "sofa person" for the rest of her days.[22]

To be sure, life at the start of the second term had its rewards for Edith. She enjoyed having Ignace Jan Paderewski play the new Steinway piano at a luncheon for retiring Commissioner Carroll Wright, and she relished the clever talk when they hosted Henry James, Augustus Saint-Gaudens, Henry Adams, and John La Farge at a "delightful" luncheon. Edith also liked to see old family friends from their early days in New York, like Louisa Lee Schuyler, Thee's old Sanitary Commission ally who now crusaded against preventable blindness.[23]

But good company could not make up for a disrupted family life. As usual, Alice was behaving badly, but she bothered Edith more than Theodore. Her "latest fad" was to talk on the telephone in her room with Nick Longworth, who was proving fonder of drink and the prostitutes on K Street than he was of Alice's temper tantrums. The elder Roosevelts did not know Alice and Nick kissed each other alone in the privacy of the congressman's study, but they were aware that Alice kept the family's servant with Edith's theater tickets out so late that Edith missed her engagement. Edith spoke sharply to her step-daughter about her thoughtlessness, but TR merely wrote Alice a brief reprimand.[24]

Alice fled often to Bamie's house, where Eleanor was planning part of her wedding to Franklin. Eleanor and her brother Hall had grown closer to Bamie and to their aunt and uncle in the White House. When Eleanor announced her engagement to Franklin, TR wrote the prospective groom: "I am as fond of Eleanor as if she were my daughter; and I like you, and trust you, and believe in you." He offered to have the wedding in the White House, but they scheduled it for New York. Uncle Theodore gave the bride away and slapped Franklin on the back, saying, "It's good to keep the name in the family." He then left the bride and groom standing alone as he held court in the next room, entertaining guests with stories. Nevertheless, he would play an increasingly important role in Eleanor and Franklin's life. "Uncle Theodore" guided and encouraged Franklin's budding political career and helped Eleanor learn to be a politician's wife. Franklin "really admired and respected and loved T.R." and took him as a mentor.[25]

The Roosevelts' matrimonial season had just begun. Bamie's other surrogate daughter, Rosy's daughter Helen Astor Roosevelt, was about to marry Corinne's eldest son, Theodore Douglas Robinson. Helen and Teddy Robinson's marriage united Astor and Roosevelt blood and money, and like Eleanor and Franklin's marriage it tied Oyster Bay and Hyde Park Roosevelts more tightly together. Meanwhile, the Roosevelts were quite shocked when Bob Ferguson announced that he would marry Isabella Selmes. She was the beautiful and free-spirited daughter of TR's close friends from his Dakota days and at eighteen she was a full twenty years younger than Bob. The news sent Bamie into emotional turmoil over losing the affections of the young man whose company she treasured, and, more surprisingly, Edith felt hurt that Bob had been so secretive about his romantic plans. Besides filling Elliott's place in the family, Bob had been the only one of her husband's close friends who had been concerned about Edith's well-being when her husband was distracted or off somewhere hunting bear or senators. Bob had also counseled her children and listened to her worries about them. Edith was so upset about Bob's marriage that she refused to invite him and his "child wife" for Christmas in 1905. Finally, TR, who rarely acted as the family mediator, saw how

Edith felt about Bob's marriage, and tried to stop Kermit from insisting that Bob and Isabella join Edith and the children on a family trip. Despite Theodore's continuing fondness for him, Ferguson never regained his position within the Roosevelt family after his marriage.[26]

WHEN TR left for his two-month tour of the West on April 2, 1905, and John Hay went to Europe to recover from heart disease, Secretary of War Taft remained "sitting on the lid" of foreign affairs. Roosevelt trusted Taft to act in his stead because he so often echoed the President's opinions and had proven himself a superb administrator in the Philippines and in the construction of the Panama Canal. Hoping travel and outdoor life would revive his energies for more struggle back in Washington, Roosevelt went to a Rough Rider reunion. He got a jubilant reception in Texas, and from there he and his close friend Dr. Alex Lambert went to Oklahoma to hunt wolves. He galloped ten miles behind greyhounds chasing the wolves, and the next day his muscles ached. After several more days of hard riding and speeches in Colorado, he came down with "Cuban fever," or malaria, and had to stay in camp. The worst part of having fever was his fear that the newspapers would make a big fuss over it, but they did not find out. Edith warned Kermit not to tell anyone about the fever because they would report it as typhoid, and she said she would "not have an easy moment until I get him safely home." News reached TR about developing crises in Europe and on the prospect for negotiations to settle the Russo-Japanese War, so he cut his trip short.[27]

The American press clamored to know who would replace Secretary of the Navy Paul Morton, and newsmen had been speculating about plausible candidates. TR gathered reporters together and told them: "Now, I have scooped you all!" His choice took them by surprise. TR named his old civil service ally, the peculiarly unnautical reformer Charles J. Bonaparte. Navy brass hated Bonaparte, but TR wanted him there because he was a Catholic, a clean government reformer, and a fierce enemy of Maryland's chief advocate of black disenfranchisement, Arthur Gorman. Most of all, Bonaparte was a loyal friend.[28]

By June, Roosevelt was embroiled in two simultaneous high-risk international episodes that would test his mediation skills—the Russo-Japanese War and the Moroccan crisis. The Russo-Japanese War had been raging in East Asia since the start of 1904, mostly over which country would control Manchuria. Japan and major Western powers were building large navies and planning for the possibility of a two-ocean war, and the new system of alliances could draw several nations into conflict at once. If the Russo-Japanese War did not stop soon, more loss of life and regional disorder would result.

In Europe, imperial competition also reached a dangerous juncture. That year France and Britain had become allies in the Entente Cordiale, which granted France free rein in Morocco—without consulting Germany. Kaiser Wilhelm took the Entente Cordiale's collusion as an insult and he became more sensitive to France's intrusions into Morocco. In March 1905 he went to Tangier and called for an international conference on the question of Moroccan independence. The kaiser hoped that his U.S. ambassador Speck von Sternberg's warm rapport with the President would enable him to enlist TR's help in guaranteeing an open door in Morocco. But as they rode horseback together one day, Roosevelt told Sternberg that the American people would never understand his meddling in Moroccan affairs. Speck had failed to listen carefully to the intent of TR's words and led the kaiser to believe that President Roosevelt harbored sympathy for the German presence in Morocco—that is, what TR called "the Kaiser's pipe dream."[29]

TR realized the danger of France and Germany competing for influence, and his friends Sternberg and French Ambassador Jusserand made sure he heard their countries' viewpoints on Morocco and the tensions in Europe. The President had a much more trusting relationship with Jusserand, who proved to be a more discreet and discerning listener than the German ambassador. Roosevelt shared diplomatic confidences with Jusserand, and believed in the accuracy of his statements of French intentions in North Africa.[30]

As tensions continued to escalate in Europe and war between France and Germany became a possibility, TR decided to intervene as a disinterested mediator in the Moroccan crisis. He asked Jusserand to urge France to hold talks with Germany in order to avoid war. Because Roosevelt and Lodge saw the kaiser as "unstable, crazy for notoriety," the gravest danger in Europe, they were eager to treat him with diplomatic finesse. Roosevelt flattered the kaiser, asking him to urge his cousin Czar Nicholas II of Russia to come to the negotiating table after his country had lost major battles in the Russo-Japanese War. The kaiser sought TR's praise eagerly: he did TR's bidding with the czar and agreed to work with the President to ease the Moroccan crisis, too. Edith wrote that if her husband's efforts succeeded "war may be averted over there." Finally, out of the efforts of European diplomats, ably assisted by Roosevelt's shrewd diplomacy, the Algeciras Conference convened and brought the Moroccan crisis to a peaceful end.[31]

Although he knew American diplomatic engagement with European affairs might be unpopular among isolationists at home, TR believed that modern weapons and technology made isolation impossible. If Americans had once claimed immunity from history and sailed "upon a summer sea" insulated from world politics, Roosevelt was convinced that the twentieth century would force a resistant people to abandon its innocence about the world. He envisioned his country gaining more credibility as a world power capable of bringing peace and advancing the cause of "civilization." Though he was suspicious of what would be known later as Wilsonian internationalism based on international law and organizations like the League of Nations, Roosevelt was becoming a cosmopolitan internationalist who wanted to promote cooperation and mediation wherever possible and who believed the United States could prevent war best by being actively engaged in world politics. He was careful to instruct diplomats not to obligate the U.S. in any way during the Algeciras Conference, where he attained his goal of increasing American diplomatic engagement. But after Algeciras, the kaiser's pride was wounded and his government was disrupted by what many German politicians saw as their country's failure to gain ground in Morocco. Despite plenty of flattery and careful diplomacy, TR had revealed that he favored France and Britain in the Moroccan negotiations, and the German leader brooded over it.[32]

TR had kept his extensive negotiations secret, but Democratic senators from the South got wind of them and demanded that all documents related to the Algeciras Conference be turned over to the Senate. Tillman and Bacon led the opposition to U.S. participation in the conference, but Lodge defended the administration's foreign policy. TR had no desire to court men like Tillman or Bacon, whom he held in contempt, nor did he hear their legitimate grievance that the Constitution had not given absolute power over foreign policy to the President for a good reason—the people's will could be represented by the Senate as well as the executive branch. Roosevelt dismissed them: "Creatures like Bacon, Morgan, et cetera, backed by the average yahoo among the Democratic Senators, are wholly indifferent to national honor or national welfare."[33]

When the Senate's opposition to the President's initiatives gained strength, TR accused them of trying to "reduce the Executive to impotency" and in private berated the legislators as "wholly incompetent" to manage foreign policy. The Senate turned down his arbitration treaties and refused for two years to approve the protocol which turned the collection of Santo Domingo's customs over to the United States. TR ignored the Senate and ran the Dominican customs anyway. He was also the first president who used executive agreements to avoid the process of fighting for Senate approval of his treaties, but in doing so he subverted the constitutional goal of Senate advice and consent. He believed that presidential control of foreign policy was faster, more efficient, and more discreet, and could offer other great powers continuity in contrast to the zigzagging and inconsistency of the legislative process.[34]

But an "imperial presidency" in foreign affairs was distinctly less open and democratic. In foreign policy, especially during the years when his secretary of state was John Hay, TR operated as a law unto himself. He did not consult or inform the Senate of the commitments he made to world leaders. In the Taft-Katsura Memorandum of 1905, the President agreed to Japanese control of Korea in exchange for Japan's recognition of U.S. interests in the Philippines, all without a word to the Senate. He failed to consult his cabinet, the State Department, or Congress about his mediation of the Russo-Japanese War.

Yet the impetuous imperialist who as a young man had wanted to invade Canada and as assistant secretary of the navy had urged the United States to acquire Hawaii, Cuba, Puerto Rico, the Philippines, and Guam was calming down. He discouraged Lodge's suggestion that America acquire Greenland, and merely coveted Denmark's possessions in the Virgin Islands. And though he still believed that imperial rule by English-speaking people or at least the French would be the only avenue toward economic development and "civilization" for Haitians, Islamic people he called "Mohammedans" in North Africa and the Middle East, and many Asian people, he finally recognized that Americans had no patience for doing the slow work of imposing colonial rule on unwilling subjects. He would have expanded American territory and influence further if given a free hand, but his congressional opponents, the press, and public opinion restrained him as a world leader. Nevertheless, he would push for as much world involvement as he could.[35]

Opportunity for more world leadership arrived in the middle of 1905. Japan had defeated Russia at the Battle of Port Arthur, but no terms of peace had been set. Roosevelt did not like the fact that a weakened Russia encouraged the kaiser to imagine himself unchallenged in central Europe. However, TR was no friend of the despotic Czar Nicholas, and he had thought it foolish of Russian Ambassador Count Arturo Cassini to tell him America should side with Russia because it was "fighting the battles of the white race." Faced with an internal revolt, Russia still refused to admit defeat. Next, the financially strapped Japan called upon TR to mediate terms of peace. He agreed, primarily to save lives and stabilize the military and diplomatic situation in the Pacific but also to demonstrate to voters the constructive possibilities of getting more involved with foreign affairs.[36]

As the Roosevelts moved to Sagamore Hill that summer, delicate negotiations were under way for the President to bring Japanese victors and the defeated Russians to the peace table and to avoid leaving either side in a position to make trouble in Asia. The summer was made much less private by the onrush of visitors to Oyster Bay preparing for the peace talks to be held in Portsmouth, New Hampshire. When the President greeted the aristocratic and touchy Count Sergius Witte and his associate ambassador, Baron Roman Rosen, negotiators for Russia, and Japan's foreign minister, Baron Jutarō Komura, and Ambassador Kogorō Takahira he saw that the Japanese hoped that their country could win an indemnity and territorial gains. Though defeated militarily, the Russians arrived without much inclination to make concessions.

As diplomats held preliminary talks with the President before formal meetings opened in August, Witte represented Russian interests clumsily, taking offense at the Roosevelts' lack of concern with protocol. The count found lunch at Sagamore Hill "almost indigestible" and rather uncouth—no wine, no tablecloth. When American Jews, including the investment banker Jacob Schiff, visited Count Witte, he dismissed their complaints about pogroms. The count was repelled by the "Jews swarming in New York," and he did not care for Schiff at all. The banker had floated wartime loans to the Japanese government, in part to register American disapproval of Russian anti-Semitism. The President judged the vain Witte worthless as a diplomat and his associate Rosen not much better, so he cabled Ambassador George Meyer in Moscow to talk directly with the czar. Roosevelt had already established a strong rapport with Ambassador Takahira and he got along well with Baron Komura, but he knew they had been instructed to win such a large indemnity from Russia that it might prevent a peace agreement.[37]

When the parties left Oyster Bay and boarded the presidential yacht, *Mayflower*, to sail to Portsmouth, Count Witte wanted to stop in Newport to see the grand castles, but TR worried that the Four Hundred would fawn all over the Russian aristocrat and treat Komura with rudeness, so he urged them northward. Witte looked down on Komura and told him: "There are no victors here, and therefore, no defeated." But Komura knew better. He began the talks by insisting that Japan receive a victor's indemnity. Witte refused to give him one. TR had urged Takahira to sue for peace earlier in the war, but the war party in Japan, including military leaders in the army and navy who had gained influence, pushed Japan's representatives to keep fighting and to hold out for an indemnity. By telegraph and telephone and emergency visits to Sagamore Hill by second-rung Portsmouth delegates and Roosevelt's college friend Kentaro Kanekō, Sagamore Hill kept in close touch with the peace talks. The President asked Takahira "to build a bridge of gold for the beaten enemy," because he knew Japan could spare no more young men and if war continued their nation might suffer famine or bankruptcy.[38]

By August 18 the Portsmouth delegations were deadlocked and it looked as if the war would go on. Roosevelt feared that a resumption would destabilize the region and interrupt trade. Edith worried that her husband would be embarrassed if the meetings "come to nothing in the end." He coaxed the Japanese not to leave the negotiations in disgust. Reportedly, he also warned the Japanese that the Russian government could fall if they did not make peace since the czar was already faced with mutinies, strikes, and a potential revolution. Schiff pointed out to Takahira that Russia still had abundant gold reserves to keep the war going whereas Japan's credit was precarious.[39]

The President finally decided it was time to go over the delegates' heads. He telegraphed Japan's emperor and Czar Nicholas II directly and instructed Ambassador Meyer to persuade the czar to compromise. TR reminded Nicholas that the Russian navy had been destroyed and that Japan was asking for no land on continental Russia, but he added in private: "I have led the horses to water, but Heaven only knows whether they will drink or start kicking one another beside the trough." Though both sides irritated him he wrote his British friend Arthur Lee, "There were moments when I earnestly wished I could get the entire Russian Government to the top of Cooper's Bluff and run them violently down a steep place into the sea."[40]

Before the peace negotiations had reached their denouement, more trouble broke out in Asia. On July 20, China's port cities, fired up by student nationalism and resentment of a long history of foreign intrusions, protested America's anti-Asian immigration policies by boycotting American-made goods. Not only had the United States restricted Chinese immigration, but the immigrants who made it to Angel Island were often treated roughly by immigration officials. The boycott spread from Shanghai to southern Chinese coastal cities and through Chinese overseas merchants to the Philippines and Japan, and sparked demonstrations and minor violence. Before the boycott the President had sent Will Taft on a congressional inspection visit to the Philippines, but the trip had soon become an Asian goodwill tour because he had allowed Alice (and Nick Longworth) to go along. Crowds were eager to see the famous President's daughter, and she and Taft made a cordial diplomatic stop in Japan, where Taft secretly gave the nod to Tokyo's control of Korea. Taft and Alice had visits with the Dowager Empress, whose empire was crumbling around her, but anti-American rioting forced them to cancel their trip to Canton. Despite gains Taft's group made in promoting goodwill, students still resented American power and prejudice, and before the end of the year the President sent ships to the Chinese coast and forced China into peaceful submission.[41]

While Alice received the attention she craved when she was treated as "temporary royalty" in Japan, the Philippines, China, and Korea, American newspapers were filled with stories of her meeting with the emperor of Japan and the empress of China. The boycotts even added an element of unexpected danger. While the President waited for news from Portsmouth and about his daughter's travels, he engaged in his own attention-getting behavior. He took a surprise dive under Long Island Sound in a submarine. He asked to hold the controls for a minute and managed to bring the vessel to the surface. Between his daring submarine ride, Alice's adventures in Asia, and the Portsmouth meetings, the headlines had been full of Roosevelt news all summer. But at any time the news could turn bad.[42]

Roosevelt tried to convince the Japanese that they could accept a peace without an official indemnity if Russia paid them for the care of their prisoners of war and gave them the southern half of Sakhalin Island. Both sides balked at his proposal. A crisis came at the end of August when the czar ordered his delegation home. Roosevelt convinced the Russian diplomats to disregard the order and keep on negotiating.

In a dramatic meeting, Witte confronted Komura with his last offer. Russia offered few compromises and no indemnity. It would grant Japan the southern portion of Sakhalin Island, which Japanese troops already occupied. After Tokyo sent word to compromise, Komura consented to avoid more war. At last the two sides agreed to the terms of the Portsmouth Treaty. But Komura had gained more than the terms of the treaty revealed. Japan's goals in the Russo-Japanese War had been to consolidate its dominion over Korea and to establish itself as a continental Asian power. It had also won American and Russian recognition of its growing spheres of influence in Korea and Manchuria, and Russia's promise to withdraw from southern Manchuria. The kaiser later claimed that the Peace of Portsmouth was "brought about by me in conjunction with President Roosevelt," but almost all other observers agreed with the French newspaper *Le Matin*, which called TR "the grand victor in this battle of giants."[43]

Roosevelt had demonstrated exceptional diplomatic skill and openness to new cultures and peoples in the negotiations. Although Tokyo's diplomats knew he supported Asian immigration restriction, they did not encounter in TR a bigot with a closed mind. It also helped that he had studied Japanese history and culture. Because of his long-standing admiration for medieval Europe and its legends of chivalry, it was not surprising that Roosevelt was drawn to the intertwined Japanese traditions of service, honor, and high principle, and admired the classic Japanese samurai story of the forty-seven ronins. He had shown, however, much less respect for the Chinese and their interest in Manchuria for they struck him as weak and submissive because their imperial government had been propped up by foreign armies since the Opium Wars.[44]

The Russian and Japanese delegations came separately to bid farewell to the President at Sagamore Hill. Kaneko brought a samurai sword as a gift of thanks from Japan; TR, in turn, sent the emperor a bearskin. Personal diplomacy could not institutionalize a new world order, but by mediating international disputes he threw the prestige of his office behind the internationalist claim that current diplomatic channels were insufficient and transnational organization was needed. The news of Portsmouth was widely heralded across Europe, especially at the Interparliamentary Union, where peace advocates met. In European capitals TR was seen as "more powerful than a King."[45]

The response was very different in Japan. The President had been extremely popular there before the war and many homes were decorated with his picture. When the terms of the treaty were announced, anti-treaty riots broke out in Tokyo over the lack of an indemnity, and seventeen people were killed and five hundred injured in the turmoil. Roosevelt was no longer viewed as Japan's friend by people on the street, but his rapport with Japanese diplomats carried the two nations peacefully until the next crisis broke in 1906. Kaiser Wilhelm II was eager to stir up even greater tensions between the United States and Japan in order to distract America from becoming a more active partner in European affairs; he even dreamed of an eventual German-Japanese alliance against the United States. Thanks to TR's careful diplomacy and his naval buildup, the kaiser's dream was postponed for thirty years. Around the world, rising leaders felt inspired by Japan's victory. To W. E. B. Du Bois it signaled the demise of "white supremacy" and to Jawaharlal Nehru the possibility of "Asian freedom from the thralldom of Europe."[46]

When William Loeb tracked the President down chopping trees in the far woods of Sagamore Hill he showed him the European press notices about the Portsmouth Treaty; TR told his aide he still felt apprehensive about its long-term effects. Despite his worries, the treaty added to his popularity in his own land. That fall when Edith and Theodore returned to Washington they were surprised to receive a jubilant welcome from well-wishers who lined Pennsylvania Avenue. He was even more surprised when he became the first American to win the Nobel Peace Prize, and widespread acclaim came to him for "sheath[ing] the swords of a million men."[47]

But TR wisely did not let praise go to his head. Serious problems remained. Japan had become a world power, and peace might turn to war overnight. As long as the United States restricted Japanese immigration and rioters insulted Asians on the West Coast, the President could find his country on the brink of war with Japan. When the San Francisco school board banned Chinese, Japanese, and Korean students from public schools in 1906, tensions erupted with Japan. Anti-Japanese agitation by white workers in the Asiatic Exclusion League and the Native Sons of the Golden West and mob assaults on Japanese-American workers insulted Tokyo further. Hearst had inflamed this campaign in his *San Francisco Examiner* and other papers, inveighing against what he called the "yellow flood" of Asian immigrants. He considered Asians incapable of assimilation and unworthy of citizenship. The publisher saw himself as "the attorney for the public," and on labor issues, public health, anti-trust agitation, and municipal ownership he may have been, but on Asians he was as much a race baiter and hate monger as James Vardaman. TR sent Californian Victor Metcalf west to negotiate with the school board so that Japanese-American children would not be insulted further.[48]

But the damage had been done. A Japanese newspaper, *Mainichi Shimbun*, protested: "Stand up, Japanese nation! Our countrymen have been HUMILIATED on the other side of the Pacific. Our poor boys and girls have been expelled from the public schools by the rascals of the United States, cruel and merciless like demons. . . . Why do we not insist on sending ships?" Japan's House of Peers even discussed the possibility of a Japanese-American war.[49]

As the war scare with Japan unfolded, TR worked diplomatically to show his respect toward Japan and to exert pressure on California. But his solution was to give Hearst and the anti-Japanese what they wanted most: curtailment of immigration. The President blocked the migration of Japanese workers from Hawaii and he asked Tokyo to restrict its own immigration to the United States if he could guarantee unsegregated schools in San Francisco. This "Gentleman's Agreement" brought a temporary resolution to the crisis, but Hearst nevertheless attacked Roosevelt for "truckling and turning pale" and bowing too low before an enemy race which he warned was already planning to defeat the United States in a Pacific war.[50]

During the war scare Congress still balked at Roosevelt's defense plans. Senator Eugene Hale of Maine opposed his call for speeding up battleship building in the aftermath of the Russo-Japanese War and the Moroccan crisis. TR complained privately that Hale was "an arrant physical coward" who also lacked patriotism. He understood Hale's opposition to defense spending only as an unmanliness that shrank from a fight, and he planned fleet reviews and patriotic speeches to win popular support. He was especially touchy about the fact that the *Army and Navy Journal* had compared America's battleships unfavorably with Japan's and had been critical of the investigation which exonerated Will Cowles in the 1904 collision of his ship, the *Missouri*, with another ship during naval maneuvers.[51]

With Hay's health declining, Roosevelt had acted as his own secretary of state for much of his first term. When Hay died in July 1905, the President convinced Elihu Root to reenter public life as Hay's successor. TR needed Root as a cautious counselor who could help him repair some of his misunderstandings with the Senate. Root relieved him of the burden of conducting daily foreign policy. Theodore and Edith found it comforting to have his humorous legal mind back in the cabinet. Hearst often berated Root as the "jackal" to the "hyenas" of Wall Street. In fact, Root did assume a Wall Street viewpoint on many of the President's domestic reforms, but in foreign policy he ran a somewhat less pro-business State Department than later secretaries.[52]

Root's greatest accomplishment was working out a more collaborative relationship with the Senate than TR ever had before. He listened to the Senate Foreign Relations Committee and did not bring them treaties he knew in advance they would not approve. Root found it tiresome to have to work with the President's fatuous college friend, Assistant Secretary of State Robert Bacon, but he admired Roosevelt's skill in seeking peace during the Morocco crisis and at Portsmouth. He inherited the challenging work of making the Algeciras Conference acceptable to the Senate and the American people, who were still skittish about diplomatic entanglements.[53]

Roosevelt, with Root's help, worked harder than ever before for peace. He realized that the nineteenth-century imperialist world order invited war and needed to be replaced by a better and more peaceful system, so he urged world leaders to use mediation and to build international institutions that would settle disputes before they caused war. He had proposed in his 1904 annual message that a Second Hague Conference would help resolve conflicts between nations, and he called for a "surer method than now exists of securing justice between nations."[54] After he let the czar take credit for calling a Second Hague Conference, TR asked that arms limitation be put on the agenda. He wished a tradition banning foreign travel did not stop American presidents from attending peace conferences, because he believed he could influence the kaiser and leaders from France and England to forestall an arms race—or at least to stop the building of ships bigger than Britain's huge *Dreadnought.* The late-nineteenth-century competition over arms made Krupp the biggest business in Europe; preparing for war had become so profitable and tied to nationalism that it was hard to stop. Germany announced before the Hague Conference that it would not allow discussion of arms limitations (and certainly not TR's proposal for a tonnage limitation on ships).[55]

Nevertheless, the Second Hague Conference took place in 1907, and Roosevelt helped to make a voluntary Court of International Justice "an operative force in history." Though he had threatened unilateral force to settle the Venezuelan debt crisis, he much preferred to rely on international law, which he increasingly saw as a vital tool to ensure peace, especially in minor conflicts that could be covered by arbitration treaties. When he proclaimed his policy of doing regional police duty in the Roosevelt Corollary, he outlined only one side of his foreign policy. He eventually modified the corollary by urging Latin American nations to establish their own institutions to resolve conflicts and to ward off European intrusion. He sent Root to the Pan-American Congress in Rio de Janeiro to improve relations within the hemisphere and to welcome increased trade. In Rio, Root told Latin Americans that the United States sought no territorial gains or "privileges of power" over them.[56]

Roosevelt learned to be a better hemispheric neighbor by the end of his presidency. He and Root worked to bolster the Central American justice system, to build a partnership with Mexico on regional peace initiatives, and to gain a place for Latin American representatives in international conferences. Roosevelt's diplomatic efforts behind the scenes to avert war between Brazil and Argentina over Uruguay may not have been the decisive factor in keeping the peace, but by the end of his second term many Latin American diplomats saw him more often as a peaceful partner than as a menacing imperialist.[57]

Despite his constructive diplomatic efforts, Roosevelt never became a good neighbor. He and Root privately viewed their neighbors to the south as "dagoes," and vowed to teach them and "the poor, little brown men" in the Philippines "what liberty means." Roosevelt favored active American economic penetration of the southland without giving thought to local political consequences; during his presidency the United Fruit Company and sugar companies gained a larger foothold in Cuba. Colombia, Cuba, Puerto Rico, and Santo Domingo had good reason not to revise their view of him as an aggressive presence in the region.[58]

The contradiction in Roosevelt's approach to foreign policy was that his aggressive posture—"We want" it, and so "we take it"—stood side by side with his internationalist commitment to negotiate, arbitrate, and build lasting structures to promote peace. His motto "Speak softly and carry a big stick" honored both sides of his foreign policy legacy, using diplomacy and force to promote national interests.[59]

* * *

LIVING IN the glare of public attention, the Roosevelts did not always see clearly what was happening to their children. In the fall of 1905, Ted started his freshman year at Harvard, followed around campus by "newspaper and kodak creatures." TR hoped that all the media attention would not give the boy a "big head." The slender but wiry youngster tried to please his father by making the football team, and opposing teams piled on top of him and purposely broke his nose. Father looked past Ted's suffering and announced that his namesake was upholding the family honor by excelling at sports. Kermit, nearly sixteen, returned to Groton reluctantly. He hated Rector Peabody and his Spartan regimen, which Kermit escaped by drinking, smoking, using opium, and sneaking out of his dormitory in the middle of the night. TR insisted that his sons adored Peabody and that their characters were being built by the Groton experience. Edith had a glimmering awareness of Kermit's surreptitious behavior, which she called his "besetting sin." She tried to reassure herself by telling the boy, "You are too much Father's son to find any attraction in immoral impurity," but he was an alcoholic in the making.[60]

Roosevelt decided to reform football, not because of Ted's experience, but in response to a threat made by the president of Harvard, Charles William Eliot. Eliot warned Harvard that he would abolish football there if its violence could not be curbed. An average of about three players a year were killed in college football, but the death of Harold Moore at the Union-N.Y.U. game in 1905, combined with spectacularly bad sportsmanship by players who gouged eyes or kicked tackled players in the stomach, brought football to a great crisis. *McClure's Magazine* had also published an exposé of the dangerous sport which pointed out how much it violated the amateur ideal and notions of fair play. Because he believed rough sports schooled boys in manly fortitude, TR could not let an anti-imperialist like Eliot "emasculate football." So he invited representatives from Harvard, Yale, and Princeton to meet at the White House on October 9. He hoped "to minimize the danger" without changing the rules to play "on too ladylike a basis."[61]

The President's football safety conference did not stop gratuitous violence at a Harvard-Yale game later that fall, where players inflicted intentional injuries on each other. Roosevelt kept defending the value of football, but Eliot asserted that the game was not only excessively violent but made "cheating and brutality" profitable. In response, Stanford, Berkeley, and Columbia abolished football, and Harvard also did so temporarily but only to force new rules of play—the addition of referees to stop brutality, a neutral zone at the line of scrimmage, and a ten-yard first-down rule, most of which were eventually adopted by other schools. At last, several groups of reformers put together an organization that later became the National College Athletic Association which, thanks to the President who loved football, made the game safer.[62]

TR HAD positioned himself somewhere between reform and party regularity for most of his career, and as he tried to push a conservative Congress toward reform, tensions developed in his close friendship with Senator Lodge. Root, Hay, and Lodge had maneuvered the President back to the center many times, but he had grown increasingly sympathetic with labor and progressive reform during his years in office. By 1906 his letters show that he was starting to balk at Lodge's advice.

TR could still be duped temporarily into following his friend's lead. Lodge talked the President into appointing to the Supreme Court the Massachusetts judge Oliver Wendell Holmes, Jr., who had made promising labor rulings. Edith dismissed the judge as "a vain old man," and once Roosevelt installed him on the Supreme Court he showed his true colors. Holmes voted against the interests of labor and against the President's anti-trust prosecutions, including Northern Securities. By advertising Holmes as a forward-thinking appointment, Lodge had pulled a fast one on his friend. TR said in disgust: "I could carve out of a banana a judge with more backbone than that." Henry Adams perceived early that Lodge could be the Rough Rider's undoing: "The most dangerous rock on Theodore's coast is Cabot. We all look for the inevitable shipwreck there."[63]

During TR's second term Lodge differed with him on labor, immigration, the inheritance tax, railroad rate-making, and pure food and drug legislation. Lodge even disliked the President's habit of ordering frequent cabinet shifts. For instance, during his presidency Roosevelt appointed Charles Bonaparte to investigate the post office scandals, then to the Board of Indian Commissioners, where he helped improve the quality of Indian agents, then to be secretary of the navy, and later attorney general. Lodge disliked Bonaparte and thought him "somewhat of a crank." Bonaparte enjoyed rotating jobs but quipped that "scratching names off [doors] so frequently may hurt the glass." Lodge also tried to talk the President into easing up on his investigations of corruption in the post office. Otherwise, the Democrats would use the scandal, as one Republican warned, to "beat the President's brains out." But Lodge's advice went unheeded.[64]

The senator also tried to talk him out of attacking malefactors of great wealth, but TR had begun to ignore his advice on domestic policy. Despite his efforts to pass the elections bill in the 1890s, Lodge had little interest in the racial questions raised by the Roosevelt administration's fight against peonage. He saw his job as keeping TR in touch with the business wing of the party, and he often took it upon himself to reassure party donors they had nothing to fear from the White House. Lodge was so eager to keep Roosevelt close to the mainstream Republican Party that he actively discouraged his fruitless efforts to pander to southern white Democratic voters. He talked him out of appointing Tennessee Democrat Horace Lurton to the Supreme Court; later, when President Taft appointed Lurton he turned out to be a poor judge. The Confederate veteran did not believe in the validity of the Fifteenth Amendment and he supported disenfranchisement.[65]

Lodge found his friend's growing ties with progressive reformers disturbing. When TR wanted to meet with settlement workers on a trip to Boston, Lodge refused to arrange it because he said they already supported him. Lodge warned TR that wages were going up too fast in cotton and woolen states, that agitation for tariff revision was growing, and that the labor vote under Gompers could "make trouble" for the Republicans in the fall congressional elections. He did not understand that TR favored improved wages and was trying to encourage labor to see his administration as its friend. Lodge heard echoes of the Paris Commune in calls from labor, farmers, and the Hearst press for the government to curb the trusts. His Brahmin nativism made him a pillar of the Immigration Restriction League, while TR had, in a qualified and expedient way, merely supported immigration restriction by literacy and in the Chinese Exclusion Act.[66]

Lodge was viscerally repelled by social contact with immigrants. As a scrappy urban politician who liked man-to-man banter, TR knew he had something to learn from the men of the Lower East Side; he bragged about his warm ties to ethnic and working-class men and his trace of Irish blood. Lodge never liked to mingle with the lower classes; when labor unionists insisted on meeting with him in his office he was startled to find "they were perfectly quiet & respectful & not for the most part bad looking."[67]

Perhaps the most acrimonious time in their second-term relationship came over railroad regulation. TR had shocked Lodge and other conservative Republicans when he called for an end to corporate campaign contributions and the regulation of interstate railroad rates. He also called for railroads to open their books to the government. When the President fought for passage of the Dolliver-Hepburn railroad regulation bill to give the Interstate Commerce Commission power to fix railroad rates, he intended to get the bill passed no matter who opposed him. Senate majority leader Nelson Aldrich believed he could sabotage the railroad bill by assigning TR's old nemesis

Ben Tillman to manage it. Aldrich assumed Tillman and Roosevelt could not work together.

Railroad senators warned that rate regulation was a step toward socialism and public ownership. Lodge agreed with them and opposed Roosevelt on the floor of the Senate with humor and dire warnings about the dangers such laws posed to business prosperity upon which, he pointed out, all employees depended. The President had no choice but to avoid his usual Republican allies and try to build a coalition with Senate Democrats and midwestern progressive Republicans like Jonathan Dolliver and Albert Cummins.

Because the President was not on speaking terms with Tillman, he leaned on a mutual acquaintance, former senator William E. Chandler, to act as a secret go-between. Finally, meeting face-to-face, Tillman and Roosevelt worked together to inch the bill along, but they still had trouble finding the necessary votes. To make matters worse, progressive Robert M. La Follette criticized TR for his attempts to compromise with what La Follette saw as the forces of evil. TR's temporary alliance with Democrats and his efforts to keep the progressive Republicans on his side might not work long enough to get the bill through.

In the middle of the legislative struggle, progressive journalism started to change the terms of debate over railroad regulation in Congress. David Graham Phillips accused the Senate of "treason" because of its corruption and dependency on corporate bribes. Lincoln Steffens blasted Senators Joseph Foraker and Nelson Aldrich as corrupt pawns of special interests in a piece called "What Aldrich Represents," and Ray Stannard Baker showed how railroads influenced politicians in a series of exposés that ran in *McClure's*. Railroads had given secret rebates to the Standard Oil Trust and the Sugar Trust, and their lobbyists had overplayed their hands in aggressive lobbying against the Dolliver-Hepburn bill. Though Roosevelt was locked in combat with the railroad senators and so might have been glad they were getting bad press, he instead lashed out against the muckrakers.[68]

The wear and tear of the political process was getting on the President's nerves, and in a well-publicized speech that gave the "muckrakers" their name, he blasted the investigative journalists who dug up scandals but had no interest in sustained analysis or reform. He likened them to the Man with the Muck-rake in John Bunyan's *Pilgrim's Progress* who concentrates on "filth on the floor" by reporting only what is "vile and debasing." His main complaint was their "indiscriminate assault," not the truthful reporting of evils. In private, he blamed Steffens' earlier attacks for Postmaster General Henry C. Payne's breakdown and death.[69]

Many newspaper writers were shocked by his speech because Roosevelt had many journalist friends and had worked closely with more responsible muckrakers throughout his career, especially Jacob Riis. TR had often tried to direct them toward writing about injustices he hoped to fight. He said he had the Hearst papers and the *New York Herald* in mind when he denounced muckrakers because they were "a potent enemy of those of us who are really striving in good faith to expose bad men and drive them from power."[70] In private letters he blasted Hearst as "the basest and most dangerous creature in American politics." He hated Hearst the most because he used the weapons of investigative journalism to advance his own political ambitions and he was one of the muckrakers who taught voters that Washington was all bad. One of Hearst's magazines, *Cosmopolitan,* accused Roosevelt in his speech of taking the side of the "muck." But the timing of TR's attack also suggests that, just as he was getting a few conservatives to vote his way on the railroad bill, the exposés hit and he lost the votes. He may have lashed out against muckrakers because they interrupted his deal-making.[71]

Roosevelt's long fight to win passage of the Dolliver-Hepburn Act came to a climax in May 1906. When Senator Albert Beveridge defected to Roosevelt's side, Aldrich snapped at him: "We'll get you for this." Finally, TR had to find a way to win a few Republican votes, so he proposed tariff reform, and then offered to take tariff off the bargaining table in exchange for votes. Suddenly, Aldrich and his followers surrendered.[72]

Then, on May 12, Tillman marched before the Senate and revealed his secret cooperation with the President and told the world that TR during their clandestine meetings had spoken ill of Senators Knox, Spooner, and Foraker. The embarrassment of having Roosevelt's indiscretions read into the *Congressional Record* so angered Lodge that he phoned the President for a denial. Of course, Roosevelt declared Tillman's statement "a deliberate and unqualified falsehood." In fact, TR was lying. His letters and conversation were filled with critical remarks about the three men whom he had disparaged in front of Tillman. After he made nasty comments about them in front of visiting Princeton students, his staff hastily telegraphed Princeton urging the boys not to repeat anything they had heard at the White House. In the end Tillman's revelations made no difference.[73]

Along with the President's legislative maneuvering, public opinion decided the fate of the bill. Roosevelt had gone to the people in speech after speech that spring until one railroad chieftain admitted that the President had so "roused the people that it was impossible for the Senate to stand against the popular demand." The Dolliver-Hepburn bill finally passed on May 18. The power of the conservative Republican leaders of the Senate never recovered because deep ideological and personal cleavages within the party exploded. TR had shattered his party's unity to pass the bill, and now he was heralded as the nation's greatest reformer.[74]

The Dolliver-Hepburn Act, however, did not win, in La Follette's eyes, "real justice" because it did not set rates but could only lower them after a complaint. TR agreed that further strengthening of the Interstate Commerce Commission and federal incorporation should be the next step toward making the economy serve the public good, but he knew the bill had been the best he could get passed that year.[75]

With each victory Roosevelt kept redefining himself as a reformer. In a speech before the Union League Club he declared that the people would not "tolerate the use of the vast power conferred by vast wealth, and especially by wealth in its corporate form, without lodging somewhere in the Government the still higher power" for defending the public interest. He tried to convince the people and Congress to give the federal government "the still higher power" to regulate economic relations, and even William Jennings Bryan admitted that Roosevelt stood for unequivocal reform.[76]

After the railroad bill, TR and Lodge found themselves more and more at odds. Lodge had been in the habit of asking the President for favors which would help Massachusetts—customs relief for picture frames for the Museum of Fine Arts, a letter of greeting for the city of Brookline, extra presidential appearances in vulnerable congressional districts, and battleships to defend Gloucester fishermen against Newfoundland's attempts to enforce international agreements about fishing rights. TR told Lodge that the Newfoundlanders were right and no warships were coming.

Yet their boyishly competitive bonds remained. As exhaustion, strained ankles, and rheumatism restricted TR's life from 1906, Lodge teased his friend that he was "sorry that you have reached the time of life when very violent physical exercise has ceased to be a rest." He pointed out, too, that unlike TR, he remained able to ride, chop wood, and swim without any problems.[77]

And presidential injuries had been multiplying. Roosevelt suffered from a cataract even before he received a sharp blow during a boxing match in 1904, and by the last year of his presidency he was completely blind in his left eye. Then his ax slipped one day while he was chopping wood and gashed his leg, and a riding injury reopened his trolley accident wound so his bone became inflamed again. For a while it looked as if he might need to have part of the bone removed. He complained that the sedentary political life of the presidency had "worked havoc with my physical ability," and finally his weak leg, gout, and rheumatism made it hard to recover his fitness. But he was determined not to show his vulnerability to the rivalrous Lodge.[78]

Lodge confided to another friend that he wished TR had not made quite so many progressive proposals in his message to Congress, yet he lobbied personally when he met with King Edward VII on the President's behalf to replace the inept Ambassador Mortimer Durand with TR's friend Cecil Spring Rice. The Lodges remained fixtures within the Roosevelt extended family. Theodore encouraged Cabot's son Bay in his career as a poet and appointed another son, John, to head the Freer Gallery at the Smithsonian. Cabot rendered behind-the-scenes help to Ted after one of the boy's drunken Harvard friends assaulted a policeman on the Boston Common and then ran away, leaving Ted to be hit in the face three times by angry officers. The Boston police issued a warrant for Ted's arrest because they said he would not give them his friend's name and had resisted arrest. Ted got off, thanks to Lodge.[79]

Beyond their political differences, TR appreciated Nannie and Cabot Lodge because most of his other social contacts looked at him solely as the President and would repeat what he said to the newspapers. The Lodges remained trusted and discreet companions. TR wrote Nannie fondly that when she and Cabot came to dinner at the White House they "could discuss the Hittite empire[,] the Pithecanthropus, and Magyar love songs, and the exact relations of the Volsungs saga to the Etzel of the Nibelungenlied, and of both to Attila—with interludes by Cabot about the rate bill, Beveridge, and other matters of more vivid contemporary interest." But the younger and more idealistic trio of William Henry Moody, James Garfield, and Gifford Pinchot played increasingly important roles in the President's life as allies and playmates in touch with the strenuous progressive spirit of the times. They crusaded at TR's side more boldly than Lodge could imagine. The President could send Garfield on his white charger to smash the Standard Oil trust while he and Pinchot were locked in combat with Congress over forest reserves. Moody toppled the Beef Trust and then TR sent him to the Supreme Court. Their shared adventures in Rock Creek Park and their common political causes strengthened the feeling of camaraderie between them. It was no accident that cartoonists often drew TR as a knight.[80]

Though still an indefatigable fighter, Roosevelt admitted that he was "driven well-nigh to death" by the pressure of politics that spring. Both houses of Congress had debated pursuing an investigation of the President because of a minor incident: the Secret Service had physically removed an irate woman, Laura Hull Morris, from the White House after she demanded that her husband be reinstated in his government job. As police took her to jail, she shrieked, clawed, and kicked them. Afterward, she charged the White House with rough handling and insults. Senator Tillman waved Mrs. Morris' torn taffeta dress on the floor of the Senate, where he denounced the President for being an unmanly brute and promoting an "imperial programme."[81]

TR had never laid eyes on Mrs. Morris, yet newspapers north and south editorialized against him and at first accepted her version of events. Democratic Congressman Morris Sheppard of Texas further orated on "the sacredness of motherhood" and how the ejection of Mrs. Morris was an insult to American womanhood. Finally, Mrs. Morris' neighbors testified that her frequent hysterical episodes occurred at home as well, and the whole affair faded except as a cautionary tale about press gullibility and congressional bombast.[82]

THROUGHOUT the spring the President found that strong calls for reform were coming from many fronts. He had assumed office aware of public health problems, and he knew that groups like the General Federation of Women's Clubs, Women's Health Protective Associations, and the W.C.T.U. had worked hard on the state and local levels to win the regulation of water, milk, and food. The W.C.T.U. had tried since the 1890s to ban laudanum-based baby soothers, poisonous "lost-manhood rebuilders," and Lydia Pinkham's opium-and-alcohol-laced compound cure-all for women's troubles.

Judith Ellen Foster, the Republican lawyer who had campaigned for TR in 1904, as well as respected women like Fannie Farmer, the cooking school and cookbook expert, advocated national pure food and drug regulation. Roosevelt learned that women who voted in the West were outraged about the use of opiates, locoweed, alcohol, and cocaine in over-the-counter drugs and medicines. He expected that Congress would see such a law as another unwise extension of federal authority, so he tried to do what the women wanted by using his executive powers. He ordered liquor taxes imposed on patent medicines that contained distilled spirits, and he told the post office to ban the mailing of false advertisements for medicines. His Homes Commission also warned the public that soft drinks like Coca-Cola, Dope, and Revive Ola contained cocaine, and he ordered his Department of Agriculture to start inspecting for tainted meat even before the Meat Inspection Act was passed.[83]

But women pure-food-and-drug reformers and their male allies believed the President had not done enough. Working with the Consumers' League and state public health officials, they insisted that permanent federal agencies with budgets for product testing were the only solution to the problem. *Ladies' Home Journal* and *Collier's* magazine began their own campaigns against patent medicines, which further aroused public opinion. Representatives of the Consumers' League, the American Medical Association, and the General Federation of Women's Clubs and the Agriculture Department's chemist Harvey Wiley met with TR and presented him with a petition showing they had broad popular support for pure food and drug legislation. He finally agreed to support the bill, and the women's groups and other allies such as the People's Lobby and Senator Weldon Heyburn pushed hard for its passage.[84]

Again, TR had to fight against Lodge, who was not sympathetic toward any regulation that business opposed. It looked as if the pure food and drug bill would never make it out of committee in the Senate. But grass-roots agitation pushed Congress to do what lobbyists told them not to do. Jane Addams urged women activists to write their representatives in Congress. The General Federation of Women's Clubs brought shocking displays of adulterated foods and drugs to show legislators on Capitol Hill. Inexplicably, Senator Nelson Aldrich dropped his opposition and brought the bill to the Senate floor (Loeb later claimed that TR had put heavy personal pressure on Aldrich). When the bill finally got to the Senate floor, it was Lodge himself who tried to amend it to please Massachusetts liquor and codfish industries.[85]

Though historians and journalists like to repeat the story that reading Upton Sinclair's *The Jungle* so sickened TR that he joined the pure food crusade, in fact, the book merely helped him publicize a cause he had supported in public for several months. Amidst journalistic revelations about tubercular beef and filthy slaughterhouses and the sensational publication of *The Jungle*, TR released the Neill-Reynolds Meat Inspection Report, which corroborated most of Sinclair's descriptions of unsanitary practices in meatpacking houses. The President had chosen the strategic moment for influencing Congress. At last, public outrage over the report got the meat inspection bill passed, and then Congress also broke the logjam on the Pure Food and Drug Act, which TR signed into law at the end of June. The President's opponents in the Senate called him "a humbug and a faker," but he had won legislation in 1906 that had seemed impossible a year before. Government chemist Harvey Wiley and members of Congress gave credit to organized women's groups, which had fought long and hard to get the bills passed, but TR and a mobilized public opinion also helped pass the landmark legislation.[86]

Roosevelt, as he moved left politically, found he was alienated from his own wealthy class. He did not know how to repair "the damage done to our country by the mere existence of these swollen and monstrous fortunes," but he decided that federal inheritance and income taxes were needed to take the excess wealth which ruined the characters of so many rich young men. America would be better off if large fortunes were put to public uses. Though he did not support giving excess wealth directly to the poor, he said he wanted "so far as it can be done by legislation, to favor the growth of intelligence and the diffusion of wealth in such a manner as will measurably avoid the extremes of swollen fortunes and grinding poverty." He told Kermit that "the very rich people seem to be in a mood to look at me as an anarchist" because of his anti-trust prosecutions and insistence on regulation.[87]

He had already refashioned the presidency and remodeled the government's relationship to the economy. He had developed new diplomatic finesse in order to make America effective in the cause of world peace. Yet he set even higher goals for himself in his final years in the White House. He worried about the moral decadence and materialism he saw spreading in the country. Since he could not convince Congress to aid him in attacking the excesses of millionaires and their monopolies or in doing anything to raise the moral standards of the country, in the last two years of his presidency he had decided to fight against the "malefactors of great wealth" using the weapon of rhetoric and to wage from his "bully pulpit" his own moral reform crusade to save "our own national soul."[88]

☆ CHAPTER TEN ☆

Saving "Our Own National Soul"

ONE DAY AFTER a heated game with men in his Tennis Cabinet, Theodore Roosevelt took tea in his office with Edith, Ambassador Jusserand, and diplomat William Phillips. An aide handed him a newspaper with headlines accusing him of serving alcoholic beverages to Welsh choirboys after they had sung for him in the East Room. The headlines played to the sensibilities of the W.C.T.U., which lamented that the dry White House of Lemonade Lucy Hayes was past.

TR put down the newspaper angrily and fulminated against the temperance forces and foolish newspapers as he paced the floor of his office and talked about demanding an apology. But Jusserand calmed him down and urged him to ignore the headlines. The President had served the choirboys sherry, and the temperance forces judged his moral lapse as even more upsetting because they saw him as America's foremost moral reformer.[1]

The essence of Roosevelt's distinctive presidential style came from something beyond his electric personality and clever gift for communication. When he saw an injustice he often spoke out against it, even when the wrong dwelled outside the usual purview of politics. He was perhaps the most intense moralist to serve in the White House, and he supported a wide variety of reforms aimed at how people lived their lives. In that sense TR was right at home with the Progressive Era's generation of reformers in their search for a new moral order in a world overrun by change. Progressives campaigned against demon rum, smoking, gambling, prostitution, and the white slave trade. Some of them also sought to regulate marriage and divorce, raise the age of consent for sexual relations, and censor newspapers and movies that might corrupt young minds. Roosevelt did not support every moral crusade of his era, but he spoke out often enough to be seen as standing among the leaders of their vast army.[2]

Public debate about the moral decadence of modern America had grown fairly heated as the twentieth century began. Commentators often warned that moral decline signaled a "national afternoon" which might be followed by weakness and downfall. If the Roman Empire could collapse so could America. TR's generation, like the characters in Booth Tarkington's *The Magnificent Ambersons*, had their daily lives turned upside down with a succession of newnesses—advancing industrialization, business concentrations, apartment house living, speculation on the stock market, women smoking in public, fast cars, media-made celebrities, and serial divorces. Panic was one of their responses to change and led them to seek legislative cures. For example, the president of the World Purity Federation blamed electricity, the telephone, and movies for bringing sin into the American home, and he and other crusaders argued that the nation could be made moral again by raising the age of consent and banning prostitution. Urging the government to protect the endangered family, the National Christian League for the Promotion of Social Purity called for adultery to be criminalized. Though they were not naive enough to believe they could stop all sin by passing laws against it, progressive reformers agreed that the time had come for government to set moral limits.[3]

Many progressives believed their generation was "stripped for a life-and-death wrestle" against the saloon and all the other forms of "commercialized vice," and that, after a struggle, the forces of progress and reason would triumph over evil. Senator George Frisbie Hoar of Massachusetts, a famous moralist, preached that the stakes were high—the future of the Republic depended on keeping its women pure. Moral reformers hoped they could stem the tide of modern laxness by legislating on the one hand and using persuasion and publicity on the other.[4]

Roosevelt had gone into politics in the first place because of his prime concern "for the spirit of public decency." As police commissioner he had pressed controversial Sunday closing enforcement, which pleased moral reformers and made many temperance advocates believe he was a prohibitionist, which he was not. He also had a gift for arguing in strong language for policies that would not normally inspire moral rhetoric—better docks for the navy and the need for game preserves. He had stated that he saw "no moral difference between gambling at cards or in lotteries or on the race track and gambling in the stock market," and he thought gambling ate away at a man's character. He said that the presidency gave him "a pulpit of an unusual character from which to preach" and that his popularity would be fleeting so he should use it to raise the moral tone of American society.[5]

He was especially disturbed by the turn-of-the-century "thirst for vapid excitement," which he saw spreading among the younger generations. So he began a campaign to preach to teachers and parents (and anyone else who would listen) the urgent need to convince "gilded youth" that "vapid idleness" was wrong and decency and hard work were right.[6]

When he advocated "the strenuous life" of bodily vigor, high moral activism, and public service he sounded like a preacher militant who had no doubts about his doctrine. Backstage, however, he talked over with Edith how he should carry out his responsibility to rebuild American character. The Roosevelts also discussed with their friends the sex scandals and easy divorces of the Four Hundred. They found it disturbing to hear young girls like Alice talk so freely about white slavery, infidelity, mistresses, and illicit affairs. Edith and Theodore disapproved of the rise of consumer culture, horse racing, gambling, nightclubs, and the high value that turn-of-the-century America placed on material comfort and commercial entertainment.

They disliked living in an age when scandal sheets told of socialites who committed adultery and got speedy divorces and then turned around and married again. Divorcées who flitted from marriage to marriage offended the Roosevelts' Victorian belief in the eternal binding commitment of marital vows. TR saw it as his public duty to draw a moral line to warn the American people against a permissiveness that he felt could lead only to national ruin. He argued that the preservation of the family was more important than "the question of the tariff, the currency, or even the regulation of railroad rates." Political reform was, he said, "subordinate to the great basic moral movements which mean the preservation of the individual in his or her relations to the home; because if the homes are all straight the state will take care of itself."[7]

The selfishness of his own upper class shocked him most. He was bothered by their self-indulgence and lack of interest in accepting a noblesse oblige responsibility for the rest of society. Millionaires got into the newspapers for extravagant foolishness—honoring a pet monkey at a formal dinner, passing out diamonds as party favors, seating guests at a black-tie dinner on horseback. The Four Hundred had taken the idea of lavish display, or conspicuous consumption, to new extremes at the turn of the century. They gained notoriety as they built castle-like homes in Newport and married their daughters to titled Europeans for the sake of gaining social status. The widely publicized antics of the spoiled aristocrats, TR feared, might teach the rest of society false values.

Roosevelt agreed with moral reformers that the American family was in a state of crisis. He worried that with the construction of great apartment houses in cities like New York where food could be delivered, "childless parents and unmarried people" could live a life of "luxury" but "with no proper thought for children." As people around the country debated the decline of the family and "the divorce crisis," Alice told her father and stepmother stories about young women marrying for money without the slightest intention of making a lifelong commitment to their husbands or having children.[8]

When the Interfaith Committee on Marriage and Divorce came to see the President in 1905 about the "loosening of marital ties," he told them that "if we have lost our own national soul," all other reforms could not save America. That year Mrs. Laura B. Corey made headlines when she got a quick Reno divorce after her husband dallied with a chorus girl; her case touched off a national debate about how easy the government should make getting a divorce. Divorces were increasing despite the fact that some states made remarriage illegal, and Episcopal and Catholic churches opposed remarriage after divorce. Many states would not grant divorces for grounds other than adultery or desertion. The National League for the Protection of the Family had been lobbying for stricter divorce laws in order to stop the "consecutive polygamy" which they believed increased when states permitted easy divorces. The Episcopal Church found allies in its anti-divorce campaign among Presbyterians and Baptists, and TR favored making divorce and marriage laws national, uniform, and strict in order to provide "all possible safeguards for the security of the family." He admitted to "bourgeois prejudices against domestic immorality," and his outrage grew "stronger directly in proportion as the social position of the offenders is higher."[9]

Theodore and Edith had been debating easy divorce with his college friend Robert Grant and his wife over dinner, and TR took a slightly more relaxed position than his wife on how easy it should be to get one. He did not want to ban all divorces, nor did he want to prohibit remarriage. He conceded that legislation could not stop impulsive marriages, adultery, or serial marriages, so he urged the church and the family to teach duty and purity to the young as prerequisites for making a permanent marriage bond which they would not violate. Though he did not believe in quick Reno divorces he thought moral suasion would prevent the decline of marriage as an institution far better than prohibitory legislation.[10]

Around the time the Interfaith Committee lobbied him about divorce laws, Roosevelt read Grant's novel *Unleavened Bread*. The President took a particular dislike to the character of Selma White Babcock Littleton Lyons, a self-centered member of the General Federation of Women's Clubs who divorced her unfaithful husband. Selma remarried twice but allowed her social, and later political, ambitions to stand in the way of having children. Grant used the character of Selma to skewer the numerous clubwomen who, he believed, meddled too much in public affairs, which he thought belonged rightfully to men. Grant also sought to warn his readers that the institution of marriage might come undone if women grew too independent. TR found Grant's warnings convincing. If ambition in women were the wave of the future and part of the problem with marriage and divorce, then it was time for Roosevelt to attack the Selmas from the "bully pulpit," which he did.[11]

TR first preached on the importance of keeping up family commitments and he chose to honor mothers who devoted themselves to their children, as Edith had done. When he made a widely publicized speech to the National Congress of Mothers (later the P.T.A.) in March 1905, he told his audience that a solid family life devoted to the well-being of children should remain the cornerstone of the Republic. He denounced Selma as "a thoroughly unlovely creature" whose selfishness in refusing to become a mother made her a creature who "merits contempt as hearty as any visited upon the soldier who runs away in battle." With the mother, he declared, "lies the foundation of all national happiness and greatness" and "her very name stands for loving unselfishness and self-abnegation, and in any society fit to exist, is fraught with associations which render it holy."[12]

It stood as no great act of political courage to defend sacred motherhood and pro-natalism before the Congress of Mothers in an era when every Fourth of July orator and aspiring politician praised mothers in flowery terms, but there is no doubt TR meant what he said. In effect, he evoked a well-worn cliché of republicanism, that private virtue was the underpinning of a healthy republic. He also implicitly defended Edith and her unselfish devotion to their six children as an example for future generations to follow. He was drawing a moral boundary between good and bad women at the same time he lectured men on the duties that fathers owed the family. He also drew a moral line between good and bad men when he advocated the severe punishment of wife beaters and fathers who failed to support their children.[13]

As governor and as president Roosevelt recommended public flogging for wife beaters. He was part of a faction that proposed flogging laws in twelve states to curb domestic violence. Maryland passed a forty lashes for wife beaters law in 1882 and Delaware followed suit in 1901, and in most flogging states the law was most rigorously enforced against black men. Roosevelt's public pronouncements evidently encouraged the passage of a similar law in Oregon in 1905. Opposition to flogging as a punishment for domestic violence came from Quakers, prison reformers, and others who viewed violent public shaming as too severe, but TR continued to support such laws for the rest of his life. In one sense he was not as extreme as the *World*, which proposed branding wife beaters with the letters W.B., but in another sense he took a position that did not help women much. By failing to support liberalized divorce laws he made it harder for abused women to leave violent marriages, and there was no evidence that flogging reduced wife beating or guaranteed women's safety. He differed from others who advocated flogging in one important way. In particular, he disagreed with former governor of Connecticut Simeon Baldwin, who argued for punishing rapists by castration. Instead, TR advocated capital punishment for the crime. He was unambivalent about drawing moral boundaries between bad men and good men, and he wanted the bad men severely punished.[14]

In his defense of motherhood as women's prime duty, the President conceded that exceptional women like Jane Addams might remain single and still be constructive members of society. Nevertheless, he did not want most women to go too far in seeking careers. Nor did he want them to forget why God put them on earth. He used Selma as a cautionary tale in order to reiterate that nonmaternal women and intentionally childless marriages were wrong, and that any "race that practiced suicide—would thereby conclusively show that it was unfit to exist." Just as he advocated anything but the life of ease and luxury for men he called for all women to embrace the strenuous life of unselfish motherhood.[15]

TR was eager to trumpet his views more widely, so when publisher Edward Bok offered him a chance to influence the opinions of women via his own column (half based on interview, half dictated) in the *Ladies' Home Journal*, the President agreed. The *Journal*'s nearly two million readers included western voters and legions of club activists. They read in his columns that the President had expanded his definition of the strenuous life to include "striving to better civic conditions," "writing a book or a poem," and "studying Indian songs in Pueblo villages." Most of all, the strenuous life included "patient mothers" who took special care of their children's "intellectual and moral education." When he celebrated mothers as heroines of the strenuous life he tried to win them over to become followers of his moral diagnosis.[16]

Early in the century, TR had already become the major American spokesman for the "race suicide panic"—that is, a panic over a declining national birthrate. Falling birthrate statistics alarmed him. The average number of children born to white Anglo-Saxon women had fallen from seven in 1800 to about four in 1880. Blacks and new immigrant groups did not suffer a similar decline. He bemoaned "race suicide" for two reasons: overall population decline weakened America and affluent white Protestants had lower birthrates than new immigrants and blacks. He had turned "race suicide" into a national controversy in 1902 when he wrote a public letter warning that the "right" people were not reproducing enough.[17]

Often he ignored the racial dimension of "race suicide" and called for more reproduction across the board. He urged motherhood on American women and used his December 1903 message to Congress to warn the country once more against the dangers of "willful sterility." He branded as sinful all intentionally childless men and women. "For the sake of the state," he said, all Americans should become "the fathers and mothers of many healthy children." Motherhood was a duty he believed each female citizen owed to the nation-state, just as military service was a duty owed by each male citizen. He especially criticized in women "a desire to be 'independent'—that is, to live one's life purely according to one's own desires." Furthermore, he warned that the ultimate result of childlessness would be "national death, race death."[18]

The birthrate did not change as a result of his admonitions, but large families became a sign of patriotism. Many agreed with him that motherhood was a patriotic duty, and they praised his pronouncements. When he spoke around the country, he often found large families waiting for him at railroad stations, led by mothers eager to win kudos for their bumper crop of children. Prominent magazines agreed with his diagnosis but blamed the declining birthrate on "sheer physiological failure, an actual loss of reproductive power" which modern life had wrought. Doctors did not know whether to blame declining birthrates on the higher education of women or on widespread untreatable venereal diseases which caused infertility.[19]

Roosevelt was the first—perhaps the only—president to admit that Americans were widely practicing birth control and to lecture them against the national consequences of their sexual practices—reducing the population. He attacked birth control because he associated it with prostitution. Moreover, he was upset by the women of his own social class, especially Alice's wealthy friends, rebelling against what he saw as their God-given duty to become mothers. Motherhood was clearly a nuisance to Alice's Newport friends. Further down the social scale, the graduates of women's colleges were less likely to marry and reproduce than their immigrant counterparts, and college women were entering the male-dominated professions in substantial numbers.

One of Roosevelt's greatest admirers, suffragist and author of the "Battle Hymn of the Republic" Julia Ward Howe, agreed that motherhood taught women "the sweetness of self-sacrifice" and should remain their highest goal in life, but other writers viewed children as "an expensive luxury" which most families could no longer afford in large numbers. Many women resented being told by the President that they should reproduce for the sake of the state, and popular magazines debated the issue heatedly. Social Gospel minister Walter Rauschenbusch agreed with many of TR's moral concerns but blamed the declining birthrate on grinding poverty and homelessness: the harsh industrial economy had made it harder to have large families. The anthropologist Elsie Clews Parsons also bemoaned the declining birthrate but said economic pressures made it difficult for working women to have children and pay the bills at the same time. Edith apparently agreed with her husband's views, but Alice was "humiliated, shamed and embarrassed" by her father's race suicide preaching. She quietly founded a Race Suicide Club among her friends based on their agreement not to reproduce or become self-sacrificing mothers.[20]

Most American feminists and suffrage advocates at the turn of the century did not yet view birth control as a goal of their movement. Quite unintentionally, however, Roosevelt forced factions of the movement to reconsider birth control as a woman's right worth defending; defenders of voluntary motherhood began to see TR's ideas as an outgrowth of Anthony Comstock's moral crusades against birth control, abortion, premarital sex, and free love. They believed the President's race suicide preachings were intended to keep women barefoot, pregnant, and away from political power. Groups within the women's movement took up the birth control crusade because of the extreme position he had taken.[21]

Progressive reformers like TR shared Anthony Comstock's concern for moral boundary-drawing. They also saw censorship as an important tool for uplifting American culture, bolstering the moral strength of young people, and preventing crime, especially in children. Censorship won broad public support through the National Congress of Mothers, the W.C.T.U.'s Department for the Suppression of Impure Literature, the General Federation of Women's Clubs, and church groups that worked to protect children from "dirty" books, shocking nude pictures, and tales of torture and perversion in the *Police Gazette*. Reformers like Jane Addams also worried that children would be hopelessly corrupted by movies. Many reformers, especially women in the W.C.T.U., believed that the main alternative to their protective moral vision was an amoral commercialized culture in which children read and saw anything that could be sold.[22]

TR agreed that in certain cases moral reform through censorship and social pressure was needed, and one such case was the sensational Thaw murder trial. On June 25, 1906, Harry Thaw shot famed architect Stanford White. When Thaw was brought to trial for murder, newspapers printed the sordid details that had led up to the murder: Thaw was an insane sadist who had competed with White for the attentions of actress Evelyn Nesbit, whom White had plied with champagne and raped when she was sixteen. Nesbit's ensuing affair with White and his many other sexual adventures made lurid reading when Thaw was on trial. Because Thaw had married Nesbit his lawyers tried to portray him as a wronged husband whose innocent wife had been ruined by White, an immoral home wrecker. Thaw's defense lawyer argued that his client had "struck for the purity of the home, for the purity of American womanhood, for the purity of American wives and daughters, and if he believed on that occasion that he was an instrument of Divine Providence, who shall say he was in error?" The President reacted with chagrin when the first Thaw trial was reported in the newspapers and wanted to keep the trial out of the news. White belonged to TR's social world and some commentators took the architect's turpitude as one more sign that morals within the elite were rotten to the core.[23]

Roosevelt knew White through his ties with the Four Hundred, the New York club world, their mutual friends, and the White House renovation. Perhaps he feared guilt by association. He had been accused of showing favoritism toward White's architectural firm in awarding government contracts, especially after McKim, Mead, and White renovated the White House. TR's primary motivation in seeking to suppress the Thaw trial news was not to avoid the taint of association with White. He sympathized with the opinions expressed in an avalanche of mail from concerned citizens who feared that the indecent disclosures about White and Nesbit in the newspapers would "excite prurient imaginations" and corrupt young minds.[24]

Roosevelt heard similar sentiments from mass meetings that called for the suppression of trial testimony. Roosevelt and other moral reformers believed the case might make premarital sex and sadomasochism fashionable and turn Thaw and Nesbit into celebrities. The President feared the public would also read of White's frequent sexual escapades and Thaw's cocaine addiction and approve of them. To save the "national soul" he urged his postmaster general to find out if the government had the power to stop mailing privileges for newspapers featuring the Thaw trial transcripts, but the postmaster said no such power existed. When the trial was turned into a play and later a movie called *The Unwritten Law*, the W.C.T.U. and other moral reform groups tried to ban it.[25]

TR took other strong moral stands to keep the youth of America innocent, and he fought immorality on many fronts. When a young man Alice met at Groton sent her a sexually explicit book about men's physiology, Roosevelt was outraged and notified Peabody. The President also refused to pardon a man who had passed obscene literature through the mails. Making a play for public support, he lamented that he did not have the "power to increase the sentence of the scoundrel."[26]

He also favored censoring movies if they had a "demoralizing" effect by promoting "race antagonism." He believed the movies of the black versus white Jack Johnson–James Jeffries fight should be banned, because whites had rioted in thirty cities after Johnson won. After protests by the W.C.T.U. chapters, which were eager to "mother the movies," prizefight films were prohibited altogether by several states and a federal law. As the leading spokesman for Victorian morality in American politics, TR used the power of the White House to exert moral leadership, but by urging censorship of movies he could not hold back the flood tide of racial conflict and more permissive and sensationalized attitudes toward sexuality.[27]

On occasion Roosevelt used the powers of the federal government to enforce private morality. When an alien took a woman who was not his wife to Canada, TR wanted to bar his reentry into the United States, and despite the fact the secretary of the interior advised him that it was not legal, the President ordered the man kept out. The *New York Herald* had published personal ads which advertised the services of prostitutes and TR ordered his Justice Department to fine the paper $3,000 for circulating obscene material.[28]

The white slave trade drew a great deal of public concern during the Progressive Era, and many evidently believed the exaggerated newspaper accounts of sixty thousand girls drugged and kidnapped into prostitution. Roosevelt stood on the same side of this explosive issue as James Mann, who later authored the Mann Act prohibiting the transport of women across state lines for immoral purposes. TR signed an international treaty to stifle the transport of captive women across national boundaries, and he recommended harsh punishment for the "flagrant man swine" who trapped girls into prostitution.[29]

Roosevelt also shared a prejudice against foreigners that was sometimes evident within the ranks of reformers. Despite contrary evidence presented by staff anthropologist Franz Boas, the President endorsed the findings of the Dillingham Commission, which blamed the prevalence of prostitution and the white slave trade on the "new immigration" from southern and eastern Europe.[30]

To the end of his public career Roosevelt remained on friendly grounds with many moral reformers. He praised his friend Father John J. Curran's work among the poor, including his support of the Total Abstinence Society, but he never gave his wholehearted support to the female-run temperance movement that blamed the decline of families on male drunkenness with its trail of irresponsibility, desertion, and violence. His police campaign for Sunday closings enhanced his credibility among male prohibitionists. Moreover, his friendship with Archbishop John Ireland, a leader of the Anti-Saloon League of America, helped to avert a showdown over how dry the President really was. The effect of his advocacy of moral reform was hard to gauge, but a college president wrote him that because of his crusades among students the "cynical disregard of any ethical standards in public life" had disappeared.[31]

However, in his endeavors to save "our own national soul," TR finally saw the inadequacy of his own moral boundary-drawing. He had recommended a strenuous life and a renewed moral stringency to cure the family's decline, race suicide, overcivilization, and immorality in an affluent age, but in the end this diagnosis no longer seemed broad enough.[32]

Women activists who shared his concerns with moral reform wanted to shift the "race suicide" conversation toward finding ways for the nation to help struggling mothers. They argued that if motherhood were a woman's duty, then the government should support its mothers. In a time of increased competition between nation-states for world supremacy, the American "race," Roosevelt argued, needed good breeders and fighters. Because he kept up with international trends via correspondence and his own voracious reading, he knew that in France, where the national birthrate had dropped far below America's, the depopulation crisis had also prompted national soul-searching. The French version of "race suicide panic" encouraged the government to spend more for infant and child health care and to consider social insurance—unemployment, health, and old age—to defuse socialist political competition and to make it easier for working women to become mothers. TR wished to remind women of their duties to the state, but his knowledge of the situation in France caused him to listen to what women activists were saying about how to save the family.[33]

He recognized the value of the women's crusade in motivating the government to help families in trouble. Many female reformers agreed with him that "the good old-fashioned home has absolutely broken down," but they urged him to bolster the family less by moral prescription and more by economic help. He finally decided to advocate pensions for widowed mothers so that they could stay home to care for their children. In 1909 he held the White House Conference on the Care of Dependent Children. There, he took a strong stand for mother's pensions. After his speech to the conference, women in the National Congress of Mothers and the General Federation of Women's Clubs campaigned for state-funded mother's pensions and the movement spread through the states like "wildfire." Because TR believed that motherhood was the female equivalent to men's military service, he felt that women who served the nation-state should, like veterans, be protected. If poor mothers had state support it would be easier to guard them and their children against moral evils like prostitution and child labor.[34]

Moral reform often pulled progressives like TR leftward. He believed that when no workers in a family brought home a living wage, high moral standards became a secondary concern. If industrial poverty sent children to work and mothers to brothels, to raise the moral level of the society reformers first had to alleviate poverty and inequality by creating a welfare state. He wrote that "the ruin of motherhood and childhood by the merciless exploitation of the labor of women and children is a crime of capital importance," and his solution was to denounce employers who mistreated women and child workers and to support labor's right to bargain collectively. He and his niece Eleanor supported the National Consumers' League's campaigns to use the power of consumers to boycott companies that refused to pay their workers a living wage or to comply with state factory laws. He admitted that in the crusade against prostitution male customers needed to be punished and women's lack of earning power outside of brothels had to be addressed. He said that a corporation that refused to pay women a living wage was "an enemy of morality, of religion, and of the state."[35]

He was glad when the Supreme Court upheld legislation limiting the hours of women workers in *Muller* v. *Oregon* in 1908. He was not quite ready to endorse all of Father John Ryan's radical "Programme of Social Reform By Legislation," which advocated public housing, public ownership of utilities, mines, and forests, and unemployment insurance. Yet by the end of his presidency he agreed with Ryan and many other reformers that America desperately needed protective labor legislation, the eight-hour workday, income and inheritance taxes, and the minimum wage. He also supported banning child labor, regulating women's work hours, and requiring children to attend school. TR saw these reforms as moral issues as closely tied to the preservation of the family as punishing wife beaters.[36]

During his second term, TR regularly paid court to women reformers and invoked the rhetoric of sacred motherhood to gain support for particular reform causes he favored. Because more women and children were working than ever before, Jane Addams and the Women's Trade Union League lobbied him successfully to get funding for a study of women and child workers. The women reformers used the resulting report as evidence that better factory inspection and safer workplaces were needed. He endorsed their plans for a federal Children's Bureau but Congress refused to create it while he was president. He agreed to serve on the advisory committee of the Mother's Congress, and to please its leaders and his friend juvenile court Judge Ben Lindsey, he also endorsed the juvenile court system, which offered counseling and rehabilitation for children convicted of crimes.[37]

Because TR believed that a president should also be a moral guardian protecting the people from corrupting influences, he talked with friends about "the lessons" he was trying to teach Americans. It bothered him that his listeners were not always attentive students. His injunctions to "breed freely" sounded like advocacy of sexual activity to some. When a toastmaster at a Texas banquet read a poem full of sexual innuendo about race suicide, Roosevelt took offense, and responded to the gauche remark with an eloquent and dismissive silence. An outspoken advocate for sex and reproduction only within marriage, he disapproved of jokes about sex.[38]

In the end, pounding his fist on the "bully pulpit" rarely resulted in successful proposals to Congress. He advocated a "very heavy tax on the celibate and the childless," which would produce public funds to be "given to the mothers of large families," but nothing came of it. Furthermore, he toyed with the eugenic idea that the government should prevent the unrestricted breeding of the feebleminded and chronic criminals to promote "race betterment," but was too ambivalent about eugenics to endorse any action. Most progressive eugenicists believed merely in exhorting the so-called "fit" to have more children. Drastic measures to improve the race came much later. America's eugenic experiments in sterilizing tens of thousands judged misfits by authorities and American eugenicists' intellectual guidance to the German Nazis occurred long after TR's lifetime.[39]

Over time Roosevelt backtracked on the question of "race suicide." He was criticized for encouraging large families, not just among the wealthy Yankee population but also among the very poor. Attacks on his pronouncements on "race suicide" prompted him to use the *Ladies' Home Journal* to modify his original position. Roosevelt heard his allies among settlement house workers and social scientists point out the grave threat to family life posed by high birthrates and high infant mortality rates among America's poorest classes. In response, he said he never intended to promote big families to the detriment of a mother's health, nor did he intend to promote families so big that they would be doomed to "a life of poverty and wretchedness."[40]

Years later, he went so far as to admit that China might be committing "race suicide" by reproducing too much. His son Ted, as governor general of the Philippines, many years later advocated birth control as a sound colonial policy and insisted that his father had intended his "race suicide" preaching to chastise the childless rich and not the struggling poor. No one in the family except Alice saw that TR's pronouncements on "race suicide" had stood as his attempt to keep modern women in their place.[41]

* * *

TR HOPED to save the national soul by moral reformation and cultural revival, so he appointed himself advocate and guardian of the people's culture. He argued in "Nationalism in Literature and Art" that when any culture was ready for a "blossoming" it needed active leadership to achieve real greatness. He believed his country was poised at such a moment because its ethnic and racial composition had jelled into an original American type ready to express creatively "the distinctive characteristics of our own national soul." His unequivocal cultural nationalism made him a passionate defender of "genuine Americana"; TR was the first president to make it patriotic to defend American artistic and literary creativity. He hoped for a revival of American culture similar to the Gaelic revival going on in Ireland at the same time.[42]

Walter Lippmann said that TR was "the first President who knew that the United States had come of age—that America was no longer a colony of Europe, and no longer an immature nation cringing on the outskirts of western civilization." He also praised Roosevelt for being the first president "to prepare the country spiritually and physically" to act as a key player on the world stage. Roosevelt expressed concern, however, that Americans had lived with so little world consciousness that they lacked "*savoir vivre*," and he aimed to teach them how to invent larger lives and to celebrate the depth and breadth of America's creativity. When he and Edith issued White House invitations and created a "salon" of writers, artists, musicians, reformers, and intellectuals, they wanted to show Americans and the rest of the world that there was greatness and largesse in American culture that deserved recognition.

They wished the nation to see that above money-getting the United States had produced many more profound national treasures, which the Roosevelts believed included writers Hamlin Garland, William Dean Howells, Henry James, Edwin Arlington Robinson, Mark Twain, Edith Wharton, and Owen Wister, as well as visual artists Cecilia Beaux, John La Farge, Frederic Remington, Augustus Saint-Gaudens, and Louis Tiffany, and native folklore, Negro spirituals, cowboy songs, and other forms of "genuine Americana." TR wished he could find donors for the starving but talented poets Corinne collected, but the best he could do was to get Robinson a job in the Treasury Department.[43]

The President worked with government agencies and the American Historical Association to preserve documents and to make sure professional history received its due as a major contributor to the interpretation of American life. He set up a preservation committee of historians, including Albert Bushnell Hart, J. Franklin Jameson, and Frederick Jackson Turner, to make sure that government documents were protected and published efficiently. And he advocated the preservation of historic sites, notably the protection of Edgar Allan Poe's cottage. He hobnobbed easily with scientists, academics, German-American intellectuals like Hugo Munsterberg, and scholars from many disciplines. Furthermore, he was America's best-read president: there were five thousand books in his library and many more scattered in bookcases around the house. He liked to talk literature with America's writers, and he often contemplated "what the literary future of my nation will be."[44]

Because he loved "genuine Americana" in all its forms TR wanted to celebrate it. He cared about the symbols that represented America and did not want his country only to imitate Europe. He thought the lions in front of the New York Public Library should be replaced by bisons, the buffalo being a unique American symbol. When Oklahoma—once largely a territory for displaced native people—became a state in 1907, TR asked Saint-Gaudens to use Indians as a symbol of Americanness on coins. He loved the folklore and folk songs of the West, and he encouraged John Lomax to collect cowboy songs. When Lomax published his collection, *Cowboy Songs*, TR wrote the introduction and praised the ballads' "sympathy for the outlaw." The endorsement increased the popularity of Lomax's work, and he and his son Alan went on to document the historic folk songs of field hands, slaves, cowboys, and railroad workers that would have been lost otherwise.[45]

TR's taste in music was warlike—Cheyenne victory songs, the outlaw ballad "Jesse James," the military "Danny Deever," and the Irish fight song Custer loved, "Garry Owen." But he was willing to learn from more expert minds. He listened to E. S. Curtis, Natalie Curtis, and Walter McClintock about the value of Indian music, and surprised White House guests by announcing at lunch one day that Natalie Curtis would sing an Indian song as grace. He praised "the depth and dignity of Indian thought" represented in her collection of Indian music. When Edith planned musicales her taste in music overruled his. She brought cellist Pablo Casals, pianist Ignace Jan Paderewski, and classically trained singers to perform for their guests, and she vetoed her husband's fondness for fight songs, which she thought undignified at the White House.[46]

When the erudite French ambassador, Jules Jusserand, told the President that Indian songs and black music were the potential sources of an original American contribution to world music, TR was impressed. In a condescending yet prophetic way he predicted to students at a local industrial school for blacks: "I feel that there is a very strong chance that gradually out of the capacity for melody that your race has we shall develop some school of American music." In addition to advocating that blacks represent their own history and accomplishments at the Jamestown Exposition, TR applauded the efforts of Arthur Schomburg and others to preserve black literary history and culture. Edith agreed that Negro spirituals had lasting value, so at White House entertainments she included them in her programs.[47]

TR's definition of "genuine Americana" was so elastic that it included gunfighters, sheriffs, and western desperadoes, whom the President praised as America's "Vikings." He believed such "Vikings" gave the American West its romance. So he gave a federal job to Pat Garrett, the lawman who captured outlaw Billy the Kid, and he made gambler-gunfighter Bat Masterson (and his lesser known friends Seth Bullock and Ben Daniels) a U.S. marshal. TR spent $50,000 in federal moneys to build the Cody Road in Yellowstone Park to please his friend Buffalo Bill, whose hunting lodge, dude ranch, and International Academy of Rough Riders needed a better highway to bring in tourists.[48]

Charles Fletcher Lummis, the father of the movement to preserve Spanish missions and a collector of Zuni folklore, came to Washington to ask his old college friend to help protect the land of southwest Indians. He heard in reply Roosevelt's famous "clicking" of his teeth when he slammed his fist on the table and vowed his support for a commission to investigate native land rights and back the pro-Indian reformers "to the last gun!" TR and Lummis wanted westernisms such as "horse wrangler" put in the dictionary, and Roosevelt endorsed Lummis' magazine, *Out West*, and later visited Lummis' South West Museum and his rock castle, El Alisal, to lend support to his efforts to make the history of the West better known. Winning national appreciation for the culture of his adopted region was especially dear to Roosevelt's heart.[49]

AUGUSTUS SAINT-GAUDENS praised TR as "probably the only President with any knowledge of art and artists." Roosevelt got the idea from Francis Millet to have a great artist design his inaugural medal, which made him feel "as if we had suddenly imported a little of Greece of the fifth or fourth centuries BC into America." He wanted America to appreciate its own art and to learn about the art of other cultures, especially Asia, and he arranged for Charles Freer to donate his great collection to the Smithsonian. It was not easy to convince the Smithsonian to accept this idiosyncratic collection because it included work by the controversial James McNeill Whistler and important pieces of Asian art, many of which had inspired Whistler. The Freer collection also brought the work of American artists Childe Hassam, Winslow Homer, John Singer Sargent, and Abbott Thayer to the Mall. Freer told the President that "without [his] good influence" no Freer Gallery would exist. TR served as regent of the Smithsonian Institution, and he became both a free source of advice on how to run the museum better and a major defender of its role as a promoter of the democratic dissemination of scientific and artistic knowledge.[50]

The Roosevelts were catholic in their artistic tastes, but they respected Saint-Gaudens' classicism and leaned toward the romanticism of P. Marcius Simonds, whose art they collected. They were proud to own original sculpture, including Frederic Remington's *The Bronco Buster* and Saint-Gaudens' *The Puritan* and Sargent sketches of Kermit and of the White House. Culturally, however, TR stood closely in sympathy with what one wing of the Arts and Crafts Movement advocated and for what Frank Lloyd Wright called an "innovative nostalgia," an attraction to a bare-bones aesthetic that honored plain living in the past.[51]

TR praised Charles Wagner's book *The Simple Life,* which called for a paring down of daily life to the essentials, and he invited the author to the White House. Roosevelt was pleased when Roycroft craftsman Elbert Hubbard heralded him as a kindred spirit and placed him on his Great Roster of the American Academy of Immortals. Arts and Crafts furniture maker and architect Gustav Stickley saw in Roosevelt's Square Deal a parallel movement to his own return to hardwood essentials and masculine remodeling of the female flourishes of the Victorian parlor. When he defended the "simple life" as an antidote to the excessive materialism of his age, TR also echoed Edward Bok's crusade in the *Ladies' Home Journal* to simplify domestic architecture and interior design. Bok endorsed the Arts and Crafts Movement's belief in replacing "repellently ornate" Victorian bric-a-brac with a "just" sense of beauty embodied in natural material, simple lines, and the revival of historic craftsmanship. The President who fought to reform politics and save America's soul was in Bok's and Stickley's minds "fired by the same vision" as the Arts and Crafts advocates who sought to democratize art and increase home ownership by building simple workers' bungalows.[52]

According to Lawrence Abbott, TR "felt that American history, scenery, flora, and fauna should minister to American art and literature and drama." He liked American writers to celebrate American scenes and to teach love of American landscapes. For Roosevelt tourism and conservation were allies; if he could encourage enough of his countrymen to ride a mule as he had in the heart of the Grand Canyon or sleep under the stars as he had in Yosemite, he had faith they would fight to preserve the natural wonders of America as vociferously as he did. He had proclaimed the Grand Canyon one of the "great sights every American should see." The irony was that he counseled patriotic tourism at the same time he ordered the preservation of the canyon. His order

"Leave it as it is" could not easily be reconciled with the growth of automobile tourism, which brought heavy use and occasional desecration to the country's natural wonders.[53]

TR also left his mark on Washington, where he insisted on the preservation of the open mall with its grand vista between the Capitol and the Washington Monument. He appreciated the grand design and beauty of European cities like Paris and knew of Frederick Law Olmsted's and Daniel Burnham's designs for urban landscapes, and his knowledge made him eager to make the capital a beautiful and progressive city. Though Edith deserved much of the credit for the simplicity and neoclassical detail of the White House renovation and expansion of 1902, TR had told Burnham to avoid gold ornamentation and to stick to eighteenth-century principles. The large greenhouses in back of the White House had many defenders, but when architects told him they interfered with their renovations the President issued the order: "Smash the glass-houses!" Later he had lions replaced by buffalo in the State Dining Room, a fitting legacy to remind later occupants of his aesthetics.[54]

Roosevelt also took firm hold of city planning and changed the capital forever. Before he became president, Congress had turned over a large part of the Mall to the Pennsylvania Railroad, but Roosevelt sent artistic experts McKim, Burnham, and Olmsted to come up with a plan to turn Washington into a City Beautiful by arranging buildings, streets, and parks more closely in accord with Pierre L'Enfant's original designs. Thanks to Burnham's intervention, the railroad agreed to move its operations off the Mall to government-funded Union Station, and Roosevelt thereafter defended the "open vista" of the Mall from all intruders. He also created a Fine Arts Council to promote public art and block new sculptures or buildings that would interfere with the plan. TR urged Congress in 1904 to create a National Gallery of Art, but Congress did not yet see the value in art—American or any other kind. Edith set up a gallery of first ladies' portraits in the White House and acquired for the Smithsonian the Harriet Lane Johnston Collection, which later became the nucleus of the Smithsonian American Art Museum.[55]

Not only did Roosevelt assume the role of steward of American culture, he also wanted to redefine America's cultural relationship with the rest of the world. Specifically, he wanted to save "our own national soul" by declaring America's cultural independence from Europe. His friends Thomas Lounsbury and Brander Matthews had been defending the reform of American spelling for years. They advocated giving up British spellings like "labour" for "labor" and making American English simpler and more phonetic than the King's English ("thorough" became "thoro"). Along with Andrew Carnegie, Matthews and Lounsbury had founded the Simplified Spelling Board, which

TR joined. Spelling reform touched a chord of cultural nationalism in TR. He wanted his countrymen to show their independence from the mother country; it was time to assert America's nationhood, certainly in art and literature, perhaps even on the high seas. So on August 27, 1906, without consulting Congress, he ordered the Government Printing Office to use the three hundred modified spellings advocated by the Simplified Spelling Board.[56]

As usual, he was unprepared for the magnitude of the outrage his order unleashed. His friend Lummis attacked it as "Deformed Spelling." In England he was called "despotic," and Congressman Champ Clark of Missouri, a Democrat, asked how long it would take to get a president "who will attend strictly to his constitutional functions and expend his energies only on subjects of great pith and moment." The *Baltimore Sun* asked if TR would now spell his name "Rusevelt" or "Butt-in-sky."[57]

Edith liked his defense of motherhood and attacks on divorce, but she was appalled when her husband suddenly came out in public for the spelling reform that many academics had proposed. He said she told him jokingly that he supported spelling reform only because he did not know "how to spell anything, and wish[ed] a wide latitude in consequence." His critics had complained so long about his kinglike behavior that for him to presume to appoint himself guardian of American English was to touch off another round of charges of dictatorship. He never understood fully why people got so upset about his attempt to institute simplified spelling, and by December 1906, Congress overruled his order. "Honor," "labor," and "check" (as opposed to "cheque") were already becoming the standard American spellings. So his short-lived edict merely publicized and hastened the trend toward Americanizing the spelling of English. TR continued to use the reforms in his own writing, however. Charles Bonaparte marveled at how little the flap had hurt the President with the public: "the average citizen laughed good-humoredly" and still loved TR as much as ever.[58]

During one of the President's campaigns to elevate American standards and defend real knowledge against fly-by-night popularizers, he got himself into more trouble than usual. When John Burroughs launched a literary offensive against inaccurate and sentimental nature writers like William J. Long and Ernest Thompson Seton, TR chimed in with his own attacks on "nature fakers." Authors who "endow animals with anthropomorphic powers" irritated TR. He told Burroughs: "I could not resist taking a smash at our friend Long," whom he considered "a pestiferous liar." Burroughs and Roosevelt objected to writers who told unscientific stories of birds running singing schools, a fox who calculated how to have the railroad run over his enemy, and a woodcock who set his own broken leg. Roosevelt admitted that a president should not get involved in literary controversies, especially when he was having "an awful time" with Congress. But he was disturbed to hear that public schools were assigning Long's animal stories and calling them natural history readers. He even attacked the implausible victory of the dog over the wolf in Jack London's popular boys' novel *White Fang.*[59]

Long counterattacked by charging TR was a "Gamekiller" who disliked nature writers because they had criticized his hunting. He questioned the President's credentials as a naturalist because "every time Mr. Roosevelt gets near the heart of a wild thing he invariably puts a bullet through it." After Long filled the newspapers with similar anti-Roosevelt remarks, the President's advisors urged him not to reply. Instead, scientists friendly to Roosevelt held a symposium which reaffirmed his position in order to lay the nature faker controversy to rest. TR still could not hold himself back: he published a second salvo at the "yellow journalists of the woods." Both London and Long fought back against "the big fakir" in the White House before the controversy finally died out. London, a novelist who did not present himself as a natural history writer, continued his career unharmed. But Long's books lost much of their public school audience. Seton went on unscathed to become the chief of the Boy Scouts.[60]

WHILE TR's reform program stalled and he entertained himself saving America's "own national soul," life in the White House took a heavy toll on the family. Though her own neuralgia put her in a wheelchair for a short time during the spring of 1906, Edith typically worried instead about her husband's health. She made sure he had his strong bowls of Puerto Rican coffee so that he could work steadily and remain "wonderfully calm during all this fussing over the rate bill." But she was worried that the stress of the presidency was hurting her husband and that he might start to feel, as Finley Peter Dunne warned humorously, that the White House was a "hateful prison." She told Kermit he could not have a tutor live with them at Sagamore Hill that summer because "I do not feel that Father is in a condition to have anything extra put upon him."[61]

TR refused to follow doctors' orders about his declining eyesight, so Edith had to "discipline" him "with deserved severity." He wrote Ethel, "I walk like an old man, rendered decrepit by rheumatism" when he and Edith toured the White House garden each morning. He wistfully remembered the early days of his presidency when he would watch Archie and Quentin playing happily in the sandbox outside his office, and he wrote Archie that such moments "would cheer me up a good deal now and then."[62]

Being unable to do all that needed to be done grated upon him. In April 1906 he heard news of the terrible earthquake in San Francisco, but no reliable cross-country telephone service existed. Telegraphic news did not give a complete picture at first of the devastating fire that followed the quake. TR sent as much aid as he could as quickly as possible, even ordering the Pacific fleet to transport medical supplies and aid in relief work. More than four hundred people perished, and it made his "blood boil" when he heard that the Red Cross refused to help the Chinese population of San Francisco.[63]

That summer TR got so tired that his effectiveness was compromised. At Sagamore Hill, Edith cared for him during "a suffering time" when he was confined to bed for several days, and Alex Lambert lanced the boils that had troubled him for three months. Edith also worried about Quentin's misbehavior and his lack of academic seriousness at school, and the "thin and nervous" Archie broke down with severe headaches for which his father recommended outdoor exercise. TR joked that his wife "feels more than ever that I am just the biggest of her children," and despite her protectiveness after his long battle for legislation in the spring, he was so weary that he made a series of blunders which marred his presidential record.[64]

His first that summer was invading Cuba. TR had supported the passage of the Platt Amendment, which called for Cuban independence but at the same time asserted many American privileges—control of a naval base, power over Cuban treaty-making, financial management of public debts, and the maintenance of order on the island. During Cuba's postwar prosperity it gained independence and a reciprocity treaty with the United States, which reduced the tariff on Cuban-grown sugar and gave rich profits to American investors in the Sugar Trust. American rule also pushed many Cubans out of landowning and into low-paid wage labor. By August 1906 rebels warred against the government because of its lack of democracy, and American investors got nervous.[65]

TR sent Bob Bacon, the serviceable Taft, and warships and troops on a "peace mission" to restore order. Before long, the peace mission became a "pacification" which lasted for more than two years. The President told diplomat Henry White: "Just at the moment I am so angry with that infernal little Cuban republic that I would like to wipe its people off the face of the earth." The floundering of his imperial dreams—first with a bloody war in the Philippines, then with civil war in Cuba—angered and frustrated him; he intervened in Cuba with great reluctance, but he intervened nonetheless. If TR had been a "Cuba Libre" man in 1895, he certainly was not one by 1906, and he told Kermit that he saw "no alternative" to running Cuba like the Philippines.[66]

Then he committed a second mistake by dismissing black soldiers who were accused of shooting up the town of Brownsville, Texas. In early August racial tensions in segregated Brownsville reached the boiling point after local citizens made it clear they did not welcome black soldiers from Fort Brown, a local army base. Rumors of an attempted rape provoked the mayor to worry about the safety of black troops. On the night of August 13, between ten and twenty unidentified assailants shot up the town, killing one man, but no one confessed to the raid. The mayor initially found no sign that black soldiers had been involved, but local people assumed the soldiers had been the raiders. Nor would soldiers in any of the companies at the nearby army base implicate another soldier. A Texas court found no soldier guilty of the crime. Yet TR accepted the townspeople's assumptions about who was guilty and blamed the black soldiers collectively for the raid.[67]

Roosevelt's mistake was discharging without honor black soldiers who had not been convicted of any crime. He had no evidence that any of them had done anything wrong. Although the President had considered Ted's refusal to tell on his friend to the Boston police an act of honor, when he asked the Brownsville soldiers to testify against their peers, they could not or would not. So he fired them. Among the discharged were six Medal of Honor winners, including Charles Frazier, a hero from the Spanish-American War.

Some of TR's northern critics judged his Brownsville decision to be "a play to the gallery" in the South so that he could keep control of the southern Republican Party. This is possible, though it also had the markings of a bad judgment call made in a hasty, tired moment. Ben Tillman said the Brownsville raid and all recent race riots were TR's fault because he had spread "the virus of social equality" among blacks and therefore invited violence. Tillman called for the Brownsville soldiers to get the death penalty.[68]

Texas Democratic Congressman James Slayden, normally one of Roosevelt's enemies, believed the black soldiers intentionally planned the assault on Brownsville, and he, like many other southern Democrats, approved of the discharge order. For political reasons, TR waited until November to announce his Brownsville decision, and weighed down by attacks and exhaustion he grew rigid and irascible about it. He would not listen to new information on the subject. Civil rights activist and writer Mary Church Terrell interceded with Secretary of War Taft while TR was in Panama and convinced him to delay the discharge order. The President overturned Taft's delay and dug in his heels even further.[69]

Brownsville proved to be such a miscarriage of justice that Senator Joseph Foraker called for a congressional investigation. TR lost control of himself at a Gridiron Club dinner because Foraker criticized him. The President shook his fist at Foraker and declared in a moment of rage: "Some of those men were bloody butchers; they ought to be hung. . . . It is my business and the business of nobody else. It is not the business of Congress. . . . If they pass a resolution to reinstate these men, I will veto it; if they pass it over my veto, I will pay no attention to it. I welcome impeachment." It was his most arrogant and imperious moment as president.[70]

Lodge urged TR to have Secret Service agents find out where Foraker was getting his facts in the case. Mrs. Foraker later claimed that the President had her husband's mail opened and offered to bribe him with an appointment if he would stop his investigation of Brownsville. TR hired detectives to prove that his discharge ruling on Brownsville had been right, and then he turned on Foraker and tried to drive him out of politics.

At the heart of his Brownsville decision was his long-standing ambivalence about race. His racial condescension and mistrust toward blacks and his concerns about "race suicide" came from his view that whites were superior. He had once believed in the "scientific race dogma" that taught that blacks and other groups had smaller cranial capacity, but the cultural evolutionary hierarchy of races had long been in conflict with his democratic belief in fair play and the Square Deal for all men. As a Lamarckian he had begun to question the prevailing scientific racial theory that had justified white racial dominance. By the 1890s, W.E.B. Du Bois and later anthropologist Franz Boas had begun to unravel scientific racism with evidence of blacks' cultural adaptation and achievement. But TR did not listen to them because he was not yet ready to shed his racialism. Nor was he ready to risk much for racial fairness. He appointed Robert H. Terrell the District of Columbia's first black judge, but after the South's hysterical reaction to his dinner with Booker T. Washington he backed off from making many black federal appointments.[71]

When a vicious riot broke out in Atlanta in 1906 he claimed he had no authority to send troops to bring order back, even though Booker T. Washington personally urged him to intervene and he had sent troops to quell labor disputes. Just as he did in the Philippines, he chose to defend the white man's burden and racial condescension in Brownsville.[72]

THEN THERE was the war that would not go away. After the main independence movement in the Philippines gave up, the Moros continued to resist. TR endorsed the "rough hand" approach Brigadier General Leonard Wood took. Controversy had flared when Roosevelt appointed his old singlestick opponent to a command in the islands. Congressmen charged that Wood, a military doctor, would never have been promoted or sent into combat if he had not been a playmate of the President. But Roosevelt ignored opponents like Mark Twain, who described Wood as "an ignorant and discredited mountebank . . . a target for the laughter of a thousand generations" because of his military airs.[73]

After trying to suppress the Islamic religion and customs like clan government and slavery in Mindanao and the Sulu archipelago, Wood set out to teach the Moros about civilization by giving them a good "spank." However, his policy went far beyond spanking. Taft inquired if "peaceful means rather than force" could be used to bring quiet among the Moros, but Wood was eager to prove his military prowess. TR did not try to stop Wood because he looked up to his friend and shared his view that the best way to manage races like the Moros was to show them who was boss. The hideous climax of Wood's two-year Moro campaign took place near Jolo in 1906. Hundreds of men, women, and children fleeing American rule hid in a 2,000-foot volcanic crater on Mount Dajo while Moro sniper fire strafed Wood's eight hundred men. In retaliation as much as self-defense, Wood's soldiers used machine guns to exterminate the six hundred Moros inside the crater.[74]

TR lauded Wood's Jolo massacre as a "brilliant feat of arms." The *New York Times* turned his praise into an unfriendly headline: "Women and Children Killed in Moro Battle: President Wires Congratulations to Troops." Though the Senate and the press called the administration down for killing civilians in a war that had been officially declared over for three years, the President promoted Wood to be commander of the Philippines Division of the army. Nevertheless, the controversy over the Jolo massacre and the Moro War faded quickly, save for an unpublished caustic comment by Mark Twain: "Roosevelt is far and away the worst President we have ever had." The press heralded TR as "the most popular man in the United States," but no longer did he look like Tom Sawyer to Twain. Nor was his own view of himself as an untarnished Sir Galahad as credible as it once had been.[75]

WITH THE CONTROVERSY over Brownsville swirling in his wake, Theodore and Edith left for an inspection tour of the future site of the Panama Canal in November 1906. On the *Louisiana*, one of his newest battleships, he read Milton and Tacitus, and walked up and down deck. He wanted to shovel coal with the coalmen, but when the ship pitched, his shovel sprayed coal on the white uniformed officer standing nearby. So his aides had to find other activities to occupy the President. When the ship stopped in Puerto Rico he thought "there is something pathetic and childlike about the people," and he found the Scottish-American commissioner of interior of Puerto Rico "such a handsome athletic fellow" with such high morals that TR hailed him as "a real Sir Galahad" whose rule would do the natives good, after they got over their horror of his kilts.[76]

In rainy Panama, Roosevelt tried to inspect everything—the locks, the workers' living quarters, the dams, the railroad, the mud. Frequent banquets and long speeches left him restless, and when he went to the site where the workers were digging deep into the earth he wanted to try to operate a steam shovel, so they let him. He wished he could collect specimens of the bright tropical birds he saw. He was immensely pleased at the progress in public health that American rule had brought in Panama. The Yellow Fever Commission had pointed to mosquitoes as the transmitters of the disease during the Spanish-American War, after which Roosevelt's strongman in Panama, General George Goethals, used mosquito abatement to improve public health for local people and the Caribbean workers who were building the canal. Killing disease-carrying mosquitoes and cleaning up microbes by constructing water and sewer systems made it safer to let the dirt fly on the canal. Roosevelt saw "the white men supervising matters and handling the machines" that cut deep into the earth at Culebra Cut, giving orders to "the tens of thousands of black men" hired from the West Indies to "do the rough manual labor," and he judged the arrangement as the proper relationship between the races in Panama.[77]

When Edith and Theodore returned to the States, he shifted his attention from canal inspection to literary achievement. He published a piece about the ancient Irish sagas in *The Century* magazine, celebrating the "huge splendid barbarians" like Conan and Cuchulain and the romantic heroines such as Maeve, Emer, and Deidre who sent their men on errands of bravery. He hoped "our great universities" would start to teach Celtic literature; perhaps young men would learn to live more heroically.[78]

IN 1907 new liberal movements in American political opinion were coming to the fore even as opposition to change became more entrenched in Congress. The Social Gospel minister Walter Rauschenbusch made a call to "social solidarity" and the equalization of wealth in *Christianity and the Social Crisis*. His fifty thousand readers, the growing numbers of Socialist Party voters, and the increasing left-progressive factions among Democrats and Republicans still did not make up a loud enough voice to guarantee change. American socialists had been promoting unemployment, sickness, and old-age insurance for years without any encouragement from Congress or the President. British Fabian socialists Beatrice and Sidney Webb, who had visited TR in the 1890s, were publicizing their "national minimums" program to use the government to prevent any citizen from falling beneath a minimum wage, or standard of health care and living. Labor in America, represented on a national level by the A.F.L., promoted the eight-hour workday and incremental gains through collective bargaining with employers, and their moderate proposals had won the support of major politicians. American labor was more likely to join regular political parties than to form workers' parties as British or German workers had done. But the United States lagged behind other Western industrial nations in building a welfare state: the Webbs called American political advancement "infantile."[79]

TR met with Rauschenbusch and listened to his social democratic ideas, and he expressed his humiliation "that at European international congresses on accidents the United States [is] singled out as the most belated among the nations in respect of employers' liability legislation."[80] His strong national pride was affronted by the fact the world community knew America lagged behind the rest of the "civilized" nations. Roosevelt criticized unsafe workplaces and spoke up for workmen's compensation so vehemently that public opinion shifted and workmen's compensation laws were enacted by twenty-one states.

TR brooded about other matters of social welfare when Jacob Riis told him about Denmark's effective system of old-age pensions. He also studied New Zealand's minimum wage legislation and its 1894 system of compulsory arbitration for intractable labor disputes. He argued that "the guiding intelligence of the man at the top" decided the success or failure of "any enterprise," and his intelligence told him that it was time for him to push harder for reform.[81]

Roosevelt saw his job as leading the nation toward reform through gradual, constitutional means—with an occasional jump-start of an executive order. Democratic means, however, required legislative consent. H. G. Wells thought TR sided with the forward-looking humanitarian movements of the day but could not harness reform energies while Congress was tied up in knots of its own making.[82]

The President's daily bursts of energy, however, were not sustained by the enduring patience and persistence he needed to keep working with Congress. Nor did his outburst against Foraker endear him to his colleagues on Capitol Hill. The long, slow process of governing required years of effort to get issues resolved. When he heard that the Dawes Severalty Act and the Indian agent system were not serving native people well and had provided graft for dishonest agents, TR called for an investigation. He had not started out as a friend to the Indian, but after attending a Lake Mohonk Conference of Friends of the

Indian in 1892 he had supported citizenship for natives and the abolition of the reservation system. Reformers like George Grinnell, Francis Leupp, Charles Fletcher Lummis, and Hart Merriam enlightened him further and convinced him native people were not getting a Square Deal.[83]

He stood up against attempts to steal tribal lands and force short haircuts on reluctant natives—"Civilizing by Scissors." And he threw his support to reformers' efforts to preserve native cultures and provide better administration on the reservations. He even tried to find places for homeless natives in the national forest reserve. Nevertheless, as president he remained committed to "civilizing" native people and he vetoed bills granting land claims or monetary grants to them. Legislation was too hard to achieve, so his Indian reform was won by executive orders and appointments.[84]

Meanwhile, TR's family life was threatened by a possible tragedy. Archie and Quentin had to be quarantined when Archie came down with diphtheria in March. The disease killed many of its victims because no effective cure existed at the time. Theodore wrote, "The little fellow had heart failure at noon today and his condition was very critical indeed for an hour." Despite Edith's vigilant care and an anti-toxin administered by Dr. Lambert, paralysis and permanent heart damage threatened the boy, but by the end of the month Archie had pulled through. The crisis over Archie had, Edith wrote, created "a terrible strain on Theodore," who was suffering with his own infected tooth.[85]

Because of the demands on his time, TR remained more oblivious to his children's real troubles than Edith. Although she did not know the extent of her favorite son Kermit's bad habits, she suspected something was wrong. When he went back to Groton full of burgundy after his March vacation, Peabody sternly lectured the boy on what a disappointment he was to his father, despite his high grades. Kermit got so mad at the rector that he lost his temper and "thought we were going to come to blows." Rector Peabody told Kermit he would not recommend him for college, but TR was more forgiving when Kermit came home in June. It was Bob Ferguson who finally talked Kermit out of quitting Groton altogether. But Kermit's habits did not change. He took time for "a few stiff drinks" before he boarded the train to Groton in the fall and he visited an opium den in Boston in his last year at the prep school.[86]

The strain of White House life had let up on the Roosevelts only where Alice was concerned. They were pleased when Nick Longworth and Alice were married; they were frankly relieved he was taking her off their hands. Edith noted wryly that Bamie liked to imagine that she had engineered the match, but Alice's diaries made it clear that mutual sexual attraction had brought them together. Edith arranged Alice's wedding for nine hundred people to be held in the East Room on February 17, 1906. She tried to plan the wedding to please not only Alice, but the Lees, Bamie, and the Longworths. When August Belmont, TR's polo playing friend, asked to be invited, the President complained that "the number of people at the wedding will be so great that we shall be fortunate if we escape a riot."[87]

The era of Alice's escapades had passed, and Kermit watched the human drama of the wedding reception with amusement, noting that Robert Goelet, Alice's old beau, looked "pretty glum." But the wedding went well, and the President was happy to have a meeting of forty Harvard men who had belonged to his Porcellian Club, including his new son-in-law. After the reception, Alice recalled, Edith was so exhausted that as her stepdaughter came to say good-bye and thank her, she snapped, "I want you to know that I'm glad to see you leave. You have never been anything but trouble." Though the remark seems uncharacteristic of Edith, Alice later insisted it was true. Alice remained close to her family after her marriage. No longer a political liability, she became a much more beloved member of the Roosevelt clan.[88]

Although Edith was no longer troubled by Alice's adolescent antics, she became increasingly concerned about her husband's short temper and outbursts. In the spring of 1905, the first lady had purchased with her own money a presidential retreat in the form of a primitive three-room cabin she called "my camp," Pine Knot, south of Charlottesville, Virginia, next to farms owned by their friends Joe and William Wilmer. Though no toilet, running water, or electricity graced the cabin, its occupants enjoyed a magnificent view of the Blue Ridge Mountains from the piazza. Edith took her husband there as often as she could for rest and a complete immersion in the simple life. At Pine Knot too she could keep him away from the White House's lavish meals. TR and Taft had gone on diets in 1905 because both had gained too much weight. Soon afterward Edith disapprovingly noticed Taft returning for repeated servings of venison sent her by Rough Rider John Greenway, and was determined to do a better job than Helen Taft in curbing her husband's eating. At Pine Knot Theodore ate simply and tramped through the woods all day sighting birds and hunting, undisturbed by Washington politics. Because she did not cook, he fried chicken for her over a kerosene stove. Unaccustomed as she was to emptying slop buckets and doing the dishes, Edith still enjoyed the rare opportunity to have her husband to herself.[89]

Despite trips to Pine Knot, by 1907 the strain of the presidency was taking a serious toll on her husband. It proved to be a year of growing labor unrest. Marxists led a racially integrated general strike in New Orleans. Socialists had gained power in several unions across the country, though conservative A.F.L. brotherhoods warred against their rising power. Bombings, open gunfire, and political assassinations marred the labor disputes in Idaho, where mine owners had embittered workers by refusing to eradicate dangerous conditions including fires.

Then, "Big Bill" Haywood and Charles Moyer of the Western Federation of Miners were arrested for the assassination of former governor Frank Steunenberg. Socialist Party leader Eugene Debs called the arrest of Haywood and Moyer "a hellish outrage" and reportedly threatened that if they went to the gallows, the governors of Idaho and Colorado and the capitalists from Wall Street who bought them "had better prepare to follow them." Clarence Darrow defended Haywood and Moyer, and daily reports of the trial filled the newspapers. TR saw danger in Debs' remarks and in the widespread support the accused assassins won in the labor movement. Fearing violent reprisals if they were convicted, TR allowed Secret Service head John E. Wilkie to place spies in the most radical wing of the labor movement.[90]

Idaho's Governor Frank Gooding wrote TR that he had sent a secret Pinkerton operative, Operative 21, to infiltrate Darrow's defense team, but it is not clear that Roosevelt ever saw Gooding's letter or that he approved of such tactics. The President warned Attorney General Moody that "tremendous pressure" was being brought to bear in Idaho to acquit Haywood, but he was also concerned about due process being violated in the way Haywood was extradited to Idaho to stand trial. However, when TR heard that mine owners were funding Idaho public authorities in charge of prosecuting Haywood and Moyer, he declared it a "bad mistake" and asked an editor he trusted to speak to the governor about it. In Idaho, TR had taken a hard law-and-order stand on many labor troubles and had sent federal troops, which had helped the owners more than the workers. He saw the Western Federation of Miners as another version of the Molly Maguires—criminal and violent leaders misleading "good, honest, stupid men in the ranks."[91]

Weeks before Haywood and Moyer went to trial, headlines announced another attack on TR's conduct of the presidency: "Roosevelt Begged Me, Wrote Harriman, to Raise Campaign Funds." This avowal brought back the old charges that George Cortelyou and TR had conducted a general shakedown of corporations and moneyed folk to bankroll the 1904 campaign. TR responded by inviting the press corps into William Loeb's office, where he offered them proof that Harriman's charge was "a deliberate and willful untruth." He was angry and before Edith or another advisor could stop him, he unwisely went on to blast Harriman for being an "undesirable citizen" like

Haywood and Moyer. After venting his rage at Harriman, TR felt relieved, and he confided to his cousin Emlen: "I was not altogether sorry that the opportunity came to smash him." But Haywood and Moyer were waiting trial, and TR did not stop to think about how his attack might influence the jury in Idaho. When he saw his mistake, he held friendly meetings with labor activists and insisted that his "undesirable citizen" comment did not mean he thought Haywood and Moyer were guilty.[92]

Nevertheless, socialists and labor unions, assisted by Abraham Cahan and the *Jewish Daily Forward*, as well as a variety of immigrant groups, held a gigantic protest against the President and a parade of support for Haywood and Moyer in New York City on May 4. More than forty thousand marched to the inspiring lilt of "La Marseillaise" and many wore buttons announcing "I Am an Undesirable Citizen." Reviled in his home town by the very constituents he had once called his own, TR was so irritable that Edith left him to eat his meals alone until he recovered his equanimity. His mood was not helped by the knowledge that similar parades were held in Boston, Rochester, Mobile, and Chicago. If he had known that A.F.L. affiliates managed to mute attacks on him in Chicago because they saw him as a possible ally after the anthracite coal strike, he would have seen it as a ray of hope in a political scene that was becoming increasingly polarized. In the end Haywood and Moyer were acquitted due to lack of evidence.[93]

With the crisis over, Edith insisted that her husband take some time off with her at Pine Knot. During that week he was excited about sighting passenger pigeons and walking far into the woods in search of birds. Then, he made a brief western trip that began with a stop at Mrs. McKinley's funeral. Afterward, he and Vice President Charles Fairbanks, who had no part in the administration except presiding over the Senate, walked through the countryside near Canton. They spotted bobolinks together and said hello to farmers whose houses they passed. Roosevelt still enjoyed speaking to small-town crowds from the backs of trains and having informal encounters with plain folks.[94]

But the specter of assassination came back to haunt the Roosevelts. With labor militancy and anti-capitalist rhetoric on the rise, TR found evidence that a radical named MacQueen had "preached my murder." He placed MacQueen under surveillance by the Secret Service. When TR and Edith were at Pine Knot, she "suffered terribly" because Loeb had not arranged adequate Secret Service protection. Although Archie kept a gun by his bed, Edith nevertheless "laid awake in terror stricken panic" because she felt so vulnerable to attack out in the country.[95]

When they came home to Oyster Bay that summer Edith saw some resilience returning as her husband happily joined in the haying with the farmers who ran the agricultural side of Sagamore Hill. Kermit worked with poor children at a summer camp run by Groton, and thirteen-year-old Archie spent many days sailing with his dog, Skip, in the dory his father bought him. But Theodore's flagging patience showed up again. Archie had recovered slowly from diphtheria and had been so troubled by headaches he could not study. In a rare scene of domestic squabbling, Edith watched her husband explode at the boy for neglecting his gun. Writing to Kermit she admitted that "we had a dreadful time." But TR, she said, had a personality capable of "a great flare-up of emotion" which soon calmed down into "quiet embers."[96]

Indeed, his anger at Archie, which was triggered by his disapproval of the boy's illness and mental slowness, quickly abated. He returned to the view that his fragile son was a good boy with "an extraordinary sense of honor and duty," sturdier in character than the chubby and undisciplined Quentin, whom TR warned "must not be a softy." But for the rest of his life Archie harbored resentment about being his father's inadequate son. Despite Archie's poor health and weak academic record, and the tragedy of Skip being run over by a car just as the summer ended, TR packed Archie off to start his career at Groton two days after the dog died.[97]

At the end of the summer Theodore and Edith felt sad to be leaving Sagamore Hill for the battlefront in Washington. He wrote Nannie Lodge: "I suppose I shall have an awful time with Congress this winter." He was right. That fall stocks fell and in the ensuing chaos depositors pulled their money out of banks. The Panic of 1907 was soon labeled the Roosevelt Panic by his opponents in the business community. TR complained that the Harriman–Standard Oil interests would do "literally anything they can to break me down," even blaming him for an economic downturn which he had not caused.[98]

In an era of no effective federal banking or securities regulation, trust companies were speculating recklessly with investors' estate money. In an effort to monopolize the copper market New York firms drove stocks higher and higher until the market crashed. Panic spread to other companies as ruined investors pulled their money out of banks. After there was a run on the Knickerbocker Trust Company, whose president had been a prominent copper speculator, the company failed and its president committed suicide, and several depositors followed his example. An atmosphere of panic engulfed New York and even Edith's close friend Teresa Richardson ran to the Knickerbocker Trust to withdraw her money. The President tried to calm the panic, but without federal deposit insurance or other means to guarantee banks or regulate the stock market, he was left with no choice but to cooperate with Wall Street and J. P. Morgan.[99]

When several big businesses went bankrupt Morgan asked TR for a meeting. Reluctantly, he met with Morgan and placed $25 million in government funds at Morgan's disposal so that he could salvage trust companies depleted by withdrawn deposits. TR worried that a "great depression" would follow the panic and laborers would lose their jobs. Lodge observed that "the investor class is very largely Republican," and he was concerned as stock prices fell lest they turn "angry and sore" against the President and his party. Consequently, Lodge set about reassuring Wall Street, and its equivalent State Street in Boston, that TR would only prosecute clear violators of the anti-trust laws.[100]

The panic was not caused by Roosevelt's anti-trust policies, though they may have hastened the downturn only because business investment slowed when the prospect for success became less predictable. But the underlying cause of the panic was the same as the Crash of 1929. In both cases, inadequate regulation left depositors unprotected, and as long as trust companies could speculate in stocks and make unreliable loans to customers who bought stocks on margin, no one could guarantee that any worldwide financial downturn might not provoke an American panic and depression. One segment of the press persisted in blaming Roosevelt's anti-trust prosecutions for causing the panic, and he received many letters of complaint about what Wall Street saw as his anti-business policies. Throughout the fall of 1907 the specter of the depression of 1893 hung over the country.[101]

In the middle of the economic crisis it became evident to the President that Morgan was a more crucial player than he in preventing a depression. TR did not like to stand at the sidelines, but when Morgan's agents asked him to promise not to launch an anti-trust prosecution if Morgan's U.S. Steel bought Tennessee Coal and Iron Company, he agreed. He knew the prosecution of anti-trust cases had not caused the panic or the recession, but as banks and businesses closed, and people were thrown out of work, he observed that "the anger of the people at large tends to become centered upon me." Therefore, he agreed to the merger because he did not want to make the economic situation worse.[102]

Nevertheless, TR became the scapegoat of the Panic of 1907. When federal district court judge Kenesaw Mountain Landis fined Standard Oil of Indiana $29 million for illegal rebates, the *New York Times* charged him with representing the current spirit of "vindictive savagery toward corporations," typical of the Roosevelt administration. Not only was the President charged with ruining the economy, but rumors spread through affluent social circles that he had a morphine habit on top of his insanity and drunkenness. Although TR found the rumors very amusing, Edith admitted that "the financial trouble [had] been hard upon" her husband.[103]

During the panic the President went hunting in the Louisiana canebrakes, where he camped next to a bayou surrounded by cypress trees and dense forest. He heard voodoo tales and hunted with Ben Lily, whom he thought a strange "religious fanatic," but an acceptable camping companion because he was "as hardy as a bear." Roosevelt's doctor, Surgeon General of the Navy Dr. Presley M. Rixey, also hunted with him and sent health reports to Edith reassuring her that the trip, though not dangerous, was "strenuous" enough to reduce her husband's ballooning weight. Roosevelt's arteriosclerosis had not been diagnosed yet, but his doctor knew the President's weight gain was a threat to his health. Writing to Edith that he was "very homesick" for her, TR promised to take only two meals a day when he got home. After he shot a 202-pound bear and drafted an article about his adventures, he came home and she was glad to see he was "in fine spirits & full of interesting tales of his travels."[104]

The Panic of 1907 was not the only challenge TR faced that year. The President also came under heavy attack for removing "In God We Trust" from American coins. He had asked Saint-Gaudens to design a series of artistic coins worthy of classical Greece or Rome. Saint-Gaudens told him that for aesthetic reasons he wanted to remove the motto that had been tacked on at the time of the Civil War. Many clergymen reacted as if Roosevelt had committed "an act of blasphemy" and had tried to censor the Bible or demean Christ. Denounced as a godless enemy of true Christian belief, TR was troubled about the campaign against his "godless coinage," which he called politically motivated "rot." The same lineup of enemies—Bacon, Carmack, and Tillman—denounced him as an enemy of the Christian faith. Roosevelt invited his secretary of commerce, Oscar Straus, to discuss the matter with him over dinner, and finally he agreed to give in as Congress postured over the need to bring America back to its "Christian, God-fearing, God-loving" system of coinage. Congress also refused TR's wish to have a Lincoln fifty-cent piece coined. The President knew when to back down in a losing battle, but he won the long-term war for "genuine Americana" in the form of more artistic coins. After Saint-Gaudens' death his students designed the buffalo nickel and his work inspired the Lincoln penny.[105]

Southern opposition to his "godless" coins reflected a distinctive brand of piety, but it also expressed persistent southern fear that TR was gathering more national power in his own hands in order to interfere further with their race relations. Indeed, southern Democrats, in backlash against his peonage campaign, looked for any means to block presidential programs and appointments. Senator James Taliaferro of Florida, for example, opposed one presidential appointee because, TR told Lodge, he had "done his duty up to the handle in these peonage cases."[106]

TR continued "taking heavy blows" from Congress throughout his last years in office. Congress would not agree to the four battleships he wanted, and he could not tell them about the intelligence he had received that the military party in Japan still threatened war, including an invasion of the West Coast. He warned his friend Baron Kanekō that the talk of war in Japan was an overreaction, but repeated American and Canadian insults to Japanese immigrants, especially mob attacks and legal restrictions, affected Tokyo's politics enough to encourage talk of Pan-Asianism, a future alliance of Asian people against the West. War planning in the United States needed to reach a more urgent stage. TR had pushed for the desegregation of San Francisco's schools, but he had little success putting a damper on anti-Asian outbreaks, even after he sent ships to quell riots. The war scare with Japan caused him to worry that a Pacific war might be imminent, so Roosevelt carried on a sustained campaign to get Congress to strengthen America's defensive capacity.[107]

Just as Japanese war hawks talked about fighting after the anti-Japanese riots, sensational press reports roused Americans' prejudice and spread the fear that Japan would soon invade the West Coast. When a Japanese citizen drew pictures of Fort Monroe, Virginians became alarmed that he was providing military intelligence to America's future enemy. Though they had no evidence of disloyalty among Japanese employees of the navy, officers ordered all Japanese nationals transferred away from battleships. TR sent a secret naval agent to East Asia to see if Japan was preparing for war and ordered the Naval War College to draw up War Plan Orange in case war came.[108]

TR had not been swept up in the hysteria of the war scare, but after Japan's victory in the Russo-Japanese War and the removal of Japan's ally Great Britain from active contention for naval supremacy there, he recognized the need to reassess America's battle readiness in the Pacific. He had long advocated contingency planning, increased military intelligence, and practice drills, so the navy would be prepared if attacked. He saw an important lesson in the fact that Russia's Baltic fleet had straggled in late, hampered by coaling and repair problems, to face defeat in the Battle of Tsushima. When naval strategists proposed that the Atlantic battleship fleet take a practice cruise around the Strait of Magellan to California, the President agreed.

Unfortunately, while Secretary of the Navy Victor Metcalf and other administration officials worked out the logistics of repairing damaged ships and providing 100,000 tons of coal to the fleet port-by-port as it sailed to the West Coast, news leaked to the press in June 1907 of the training cruise. TR denied reports and tried to keep the navy's planning secret, but he also wanted to reassure Americans along the Pacific coast that they would be defended if attacked. When Senator Eugene Hale threatened to cut off funds for coal for such a training cruise, he annoyed the President so much that TR, in defiance, gave orders to proceed with the sailing of the Great White Fleet. When senators complained about his plan, he declared he would never "permit anything so fraught with menace as the usurpation by any clique of Wall Street Senators of my function as Commander-in-Chief." The fleet idea proved to be much more than a display of American naval power; it was a costly but productive way to lobby Congress and the American people for more spending for the navy.[109]

Over three thousand men were pulled from other duties to staff the battleships and numerous destroyers and supply ships that followed them. Roosevelt did not bother to consult the Senate, his partner in making foreign policy. In his mind, the launching of the Great White Fleet on its cruise was the singular event in his presidency that brought him close to fulfilling the ideal of Sir Galahad.

The Roosevelts watched on December 16 as sixteen white-painted battleships steamed away from Hampton Roads. The President had the presidential yacht, *Mayflower*, follow the fleet out to sea. Rumors of Japanese submarine attacks and a secret ambush caused anxiety in the American press, and the navy received reports that Japan had bought mine layers to sabotage the fleet. TR warned the commander of the Great White Fleet, Rear Admiral Robley Evans, to make it a peaceful cruise but to be ready for any eventuality. At the same time he worked hard to calm public anxiety about Japan's intentions and to make sure Tokyo did not see the fleet as a threat or its voyage as a belligerent gesture.[110]

Secrecy was vital but security leaks plagued the trip. TR had told the ailing Evans that his tour would be extended to a round-the-world trip, and when Evans chose wireless telegraphy to share the news with the rest of the fleet, reporters overheard him onshore. Headlines trumpeting the world voyage elicited another presidential denial. The cruise advertised America's growing naval power, so the administration tried to suppress bad publicity about it. The administration tried to keep quiet the spinal meningitis, coaling problems, brawls between sailors and locals in ports, and a minor collision between two battleships, which marred the trip. Brazil, France, and Britain also used practice cruises to make sure they were prepared for war, but good press was especially crucial for America's venture because TR faced formidable opposition to naval preparedness for war. The voyage, however, was winning him more support for naval expansion—Americans were buying maps in unprecedented numbers to trace the fleet's progress. The Navy League and self-interested navalists such as munitions maker Irénée du Pont and steel man Henry Clay Frick applauded the undertaking.[111]

Success was not assured at the beginning of the fleet's journey. Fear of Japanese attack, though not based on realistic assessment of Japan's intentions, caught on in South American coastal cities. As the fleet made its way north in Pacific waters, Peruvian officials jailed a Japanese theater company to quell local worries about spying and sabotage. Critics feared the cruise signaled that Roosevelt was on the verge of assuming kinglike powers. When the State Department drafted TR's greetings to Peru "from me and my people" as the fleet docked in Lima, opponents of the voyage called it proof that the President thought of himself as a king who reigned supreme over "his" people. In fact, TR had not even seen the message, and like many flaps, it evaporated quickly. When Evans' flotilla joined the cruisers in the Pacific fleet in San Francisco Bay, Japanese-Americans showed their loyalty by donating large amounts of money to entertain the fleet's crew. A giant bonfire on Mount Tamalpais and an enthusiastic crowd of 300,000 welcomed the navy as it sailed into the bay.[112]

Japanese leaders, eager to quiet the war hawks in their own ranks, saw in the trip a diplomatic opportunity to build goodwill by inviting the fleet to visit Japan. TR agreed enthusiastically, though he made sure the American sailors would be on their best behavior while in Japanese ports so that they did not offend their hosts. By the second half of the cruise its goals were primarily diplomatic and after circumnavigating the globe and visiting twenty-six countries, the fleet's gains were mixed. Roosevelt had calmed relations with Japan and established the United States as a Pacific naval power, but he had to struggle further to make the military establishment and Congress cooperate with his preparedness plans.[113] The cruise had done little to dampen the growing international arms race. Kaiser Wilhelm later reassured Roosevelt that the voyage of the Great White Fleet had helped keep the peace in Europe; diplomats and naval planners who watched the display of American naval power were not so sure.[114]

The President convinced Congress to spend more to fortify Pearl Harbor and make it the center of Pacific defenses. He ordered the army and navy to work together on strategic planning, but it would take more than an executive order to heal the rivalry between the two branches of the service. He also ordered the army to get its officers in better shape physically in case of war and insisted that they be able to ride a horse or walk to prove their fitness. But his orders went unheeded.[115]

Roosevelt was proud that America's prestige had been enhanced by the cruise, but he had grown impatient with his critics and his constitutional partnership with Congress. One Democratic editor complained: "There isn't another government in the world which could afford to blow $20,000,000 for just one such spectacular but useless exhibition." The President's opponents warned that he had become a self-appointed dictator who had no more "respect for the Senate" than "a dog has for a marriage license."[116]

Even after the trip, no groundswell of popular support existed to make the military more efficient or to exercise U.S. power around the world. Roosevelt concluded that "public opinion should be properly educated" to face international power politics: "This people of ours simply does not understand how things are outside our own boundaries."[117]

ROOSEVELT'S relations with Congress reached an all-time low, so, with legislation stalled, he chose the end of his presidency to launch a rhetorical attack on the "purchased politician" and "law-defying wealth," and to call for a fairer distribution of wealth in America. His losing battles with Congress and the attacks making him the scapegoat for the Panic of 1907 embittered him. Though Root and Lodge tried hard to get him to tone down his rhetoric, in his first message to Congress in 1908 he insisted that "predatory wealth" be blamed for the Panic of 1907 because of its "speculative folly." For labor he promised workmen's compensation, the eight-hour day, and an end to automatic labor injunctions. He called for currency reform and new laws "to control law-defying wealth" such as stock market regulation and national incorporation and regulation of interstate businesses. This time Edith agreed with him that if he wanted to make Congress pass more reforms before he left office, he had to speak boldly. In doing so, however, he named names and personally attacked his opponents in the Standard Oil Company and other businesses. After he unleashed the tactless document he said: "I made up my mind that for once I would let myself go."[118]

Lodge tried in vain to get TR to stop talking about inheritance and income taxes and delicate political issues like Brownsville, and he teased his old friend about "the condition to which you have reduced" the American economy. Root sarcastically joked to Lodge that while the President had been busy making life miserable for flabby army officers who had to prove their fitness to fight a war by riding horses, "It has not yet been determined whether the attention of the Administration will be turned next towards the prevention of swollen bank accounts or the reduction of foreign commerce." Roosevelt's sense of humor still enabled him to laugh at himself, but he had good reason to wonder if his politics were any longer compatible with the beliefs held by Lodge, Root, and Taft. Congress resisted every one of the new ideas he proposed, and so did they.[119]

Outside the administration Roosevelt's message won mixed reviews. When Columbia University president Nicholas Murray Butler told TR that his moderate supporters reacted to his message to Congress "with grief and sorrow," the President replied angrily: "My real supporters—those whose deep convictions I most nearly represent—have hailed it as they have no other speech or action of mine for a long time." Later Roosevelt grumbled that Butler was "more royalist than the King himself," and they grew apart. Endicott Peabody was glad that his old friend had tried to convince the public that "thoroughgoing and radical control" of big business would be necessary, but in his elite social world Peabody also saw how much TR had alienated the wealthy. At receptions toward the end of his presidency, congressmen left the room to avoid having to shake hands with him.[120]

Nevertheless, Roosevelt's rhetorical war on political corruption and "law-defying wealth" won him grass-roots support. Ambassador James Bryce agreed that "nobody likes him now but the people." Many average Americans still appreciated the fact that the President guilelessly told a reporter his suit cost only $4. Observers noted that he had proven "wonderfully sensitive to the mood of the people," and it was the people he cared about most. Roosevelt had been successful at reaching the hearts and minds of the plain folk with his colorful speeches and his canny sense of using reporters as his press agents. For a while, when newspapers and political opponents heaped abuse on the White House in early 1908, men in eastern cities wore the white Roosevelt chrysanthemum on their lapels to show support for his campaign for "purity of motive, freedom from graft."[121]

When several railroads announced in 1908 they were cutting their employees' wages, TR stood up for workers in a public letter to the Interstate Commerce Commission. Business losses, he declared, should be "equitably distributed between capitalist and wageworker." His commissioner of labor thereafter mediated some of the wage disputes and the administration was able to prevent cuts, which Samuel Gompers applauded. Now, as Roosevelt felt the momentum building behind his advocacy of such issues, he started to "sincerely regret that this is not my first term."[122]

The most substantial accomplishment of his last year in office was his Governors' Conference on Conservation. For Gifford Pinchot the conference signaled the emergence of the conservation movement into national political prominence. Pinchot had enraged Congress by mailing millions of pieces of material promoting conservation to advertise the importance of his conference. The belief in publicity that he shared with the President was the basic premise behind the conference and established a historic precedent. It was the first national conference of governors, and it became the basis for coordination and conversation among state governments and for federal-state cooperation.[123]

For TR conservation remained "the great fundamental question of morality" in the nation. He warned the conference that half of the nation's timber was gone and a "timber famine" threatened the country. Mineral and gas deposits were diminished, and in some regions too much soil was exhausted. To make sure corporations did not take advantage of the ambiguous "Twilight land" between the powers of state and federal governments, Roosevelt called for one level of government or the other to exert "sovereign power" over natural resources such as water. He sought to make sure the public realized money from the use of its resources and to guarantee that corporate privileges were temporary. As a result of the conference, federal and state government began working harder on forest fire prevention and detection, and afterward Roosevelt added to the national forests the extensive Superior National Forest in Minnesota. But Congress was against TR's conservation program; they banned further press releases by the Forest Service and offered the President obstruction rather than help.[124]

As he anticipated the future the 1908 presidential election forced hard choices upon him and his supporters. He had promised to bow out, yet he still cared about the fight he was waging to change his country. The outpouring of support for another term made him reconsider. Newspapers ran headlines such as "The Whole Country Makes a Sweeping Demand for Another Term for President Roosevelt" and supporters urged him to take back his pledge not to run. Certainly, TR did not want the Democrats to win: Senator John Morgan of Alabama called for race to be the central issue with the Democrats taking a stand as a "white man's party." Nevertheless, TR listened to charges that he had become a king, a new Caesar, a "Bombastes Furioso," and the architect of financial ruin, and, faced with so many enemies, he stuck to his pledge. He decided to support William Howard Taft for the Republican nomination when his agreeable friend led him to believe he would keep his cabinet and extend the Square Deal. TR tried to cultivate livelier political skills in Taft, telling him to paint bright-colored posters, not detailed blueprints, for his audiences. And Roosevelt lavished advice on him about how to get his way around the Capitol.[125]

Yet he had reason to doubt the wisdom of his choice. He reprimanded Taft for sending a callous wage-cutting letter to War Department employees. He dressed down Taft crankily for his "frank avowal of the starvation wage theory." Most of the time, however, he preferred to look the other way and ignore the fact Taft was closer politically to Lodge and Root.[126]

In June, Roosevelt had to work hard to ward off a stampede at the Republican convention to nominate him for another term. Lodge had warned conservatives in the party that they should accept Taft or face another four years of Roosevelt's increasing radicalism. The "Taft or Roosevelt" threat worked, but on the convention floor, after Lodge as permanent chairman of the convention heralded TR as "the best abused and most popular man in the United States to-day," western delegates demonstrated so wildly that a stampede to renominate TR broke out. Lodge tried to restore civility to the convention, and failing in the attempt, he quelled the forty-nine-minute demonstration by ordering the band to drown it out with their rendition of "Garry Owen." At the White House, the President was in telegraphic communication with events on the convention floor and he put the brakes on the incipient revolt. Alice held court in the presidential box and enjoyed hearing the convention almost taken over by the delegates' cries of "Four-four-four years more!" As the cheering for TR died out, Taft got the nomination and won the election in November against William Jennings Bryan. Roosevelt now faced the end of his term of office.[127]

ROOSEVELT DESCRIBED his final year in the White House as a "war to the knife" against giant financial and political interests opposed to his reforms. In almost every case, he lost the battle for legislation but won the war for public opinion. He claimed not to mind the "terrific strain" because he knew in just a matter of months a long vacation awaited him. TR and Kermit planned an African hunting expedition to collect specimens for the Smithsonian and other museums. Edith worried that "when we leave the White House, I feel that we shall have to live off the garden which we will be forced to cultivate ourselves." Her husband was less concerned about money because on top of the inherited income each of them received he had saved over $41,000 in 1907 alone. Lucrative editorial and writing jobs were waiting for him; *Collier's* offered him $100,000 for reporting a round-the-world trip, and *McClure's*, *Scribner's*, and *Everybody's* magazines also tried to hire his pen. William Randolph Hearst sent one of his agents to invite Roosevelt to become a Hearst reporter, like Bryan. Instead, Roosevelt signed up to editorialize about political, social, and industrial issues for the Social Gospel journal, *The Outlook*, and he agreed to give his pieces about his African hunt to *Scribner's*. Although TR was leaving the White House, he was not planning to retire.[128]

On October 27, his fiftieth birthday, TR jumped his horse, Roswell, over a five-feet-eight-inch hurdle. That day he sat with his wife under the apple tree by the fountain behind the White House talking over the sad news that Bob Ferguson had been diagnosed with tuberculosis. Theodore judged the news tragic and Edith sadly picked the last rose of the season for her husband, who grew nostalgic about their White House years and the happiness they had known there. He wrote Archie after Quentin had a raucous sleepover with three friends that he had begun to feel "how old I had grown so that I was not needed in the play." He asked Archie: "Do you recollect how we all of us used to play hide-and-go-seek in the White House, and have obstacle races down the hall when you brought in your friends?"[129]

Edith looked forward to a quieter life alone with her husband at the conclusion of his presidency. After two miscarriages during their White House years, shehad finally resigned herself to the fact she could not have any more children. She also had difficulty reconciling herself to the pressure of public intrusions and the unremitting demands of life with Theodore. He noticed that she "brightened up and got over her headache" when at dinner she found she could score a few points off him in conversation, "every now and then making a sudden little assault upon me, just as I have seen a bird ruffle up its little feathers and give a sudden peck; then she would feel heart-smitten lest she had been too severe, and pet me to make up." After all their years together, Edith still enjoyed affectionate jabs at her mate, and he still liked to be "pet[ted]" up afterward.[130]

Their last Christmas in the White House, Edith had already begun to pare down their household in order to resume their more Spartan way of life at Sagamore Hill. She enjoyed hosting a Christmas luncheon for fifty and showed the first motion pictures in White House history—fittingly of a wolf hunt. Yet she looked forward to returning to Oyster Bay and rejoining her St. Hilda's sewing circle "not that they are interesting types, but that I really like them & feel a sympathy with their doings." On Christmas Day, Bamie entertained them for dinner and they were "all well and together" as TR galloped happily in the snow. As Edith watched her husband and heard his talk about going into serious work as a historian after Africa, she grew uneasy, observing that "it can't be easy to leave the helm even though one does it from choice."[131]

The White House overflowed with friends of the children at the time of Ethel's debut, but the younger generation's party disturbed the sleeping first couple. Humorously, TR wrote Ted about a tense domestic scene in which he was dressed only in pajamas:

> I was used by Mother as an instrument of summary vengeance. We were waked up at half past two by a most uncanny noise—apparently a thumping & shrill grunting in some remote part of the house. . . . Then I found that the squaw dance was proceeding with great vigor & hilarity in the inside room which opens off from the large room on the right of the stairs as you go up on the attic floor. I told them to stop at once & go to bed, but did not speak very severely, and in answer to a request from Ethel said they could go down & each get an apple in the pantry. By the time we reached the foot of that flight of stairs we encountered Mother in a most warlike mood, and the offenders were instantly smitten hip & thigh.[132]

The exuberant tribe of young adults reminded TR, as he wrote sadly to Bob Ferguson, "the days of the little family are past forever."[133]

TR's LAST DAYS as president ended with a bitter stalemate with Congress. His long struggle for self-control was floundering. His eagerness to triumph over his enemies overflowed into his quest for honest government. Like other presidents, TR relied on the Secret Service for investigations, so Attorney General Bonaparte sent agents to investigate land, postal, and timber fraud, and congressional misbehavior. Agents followed Senator Tillman because TR suspected him of making shady Oregon land deals.

Roosevelt also built a military intelligence group within the Naval War College to learn about other countries' military capacities. On occasion, he secretly hired private investigators to gather information for him and allowed agents to tap phones for the first time, all without congressional approval. Congress refused to fund spying despite the fact that almost every other major military power had large intelligence operations. Congress accused the president of sending out an unauthorized "army of spies." To improve national security and get the intelligence he needed, TR wanted to increase executive power no matter what the eventual cost might be to personal liberties. He defined himself as the steward of the public good, acting for the people in all areas not explicitly banned by the Constitution. He said: "I did not usurp power, but I did greatly broaden the use of Executive power." Congress thought he had gone too far and worried legitimately that a president could use spying for his own political purposes.[134]

At the same time, Roosevelt offended many legislators when he charged publicly that, based on information gathered by Secret Service agents, Tillman was trying to profit by revoking a railroad land grant. Congress responded by prohibiting the borrowing of intelligence agents, thereby confining the Secret Service to the tasks of physically protecting the President and hunting down counterfeiters. TR replied that members of Congress restricted him because they were afraid he would investigate their crooked dealings and put them in jail.[135]

As the House gathered to reply to his accusations, the overflowing galleries applauded each new speech attacking TR, who was on the ropes in his ongoing political boxing match with Congress. In the Senate, Tillman blasted the President so furiously that Lodge, acting as Theodore's loyal friend, tried to apply a gag rule. Lodge's bill forbade senators during a debate to make "offensive references" to other branches of government, but his colleagues would have none of it.[136]

TR refused to be stopped by Congress and its restrictions on investigators. Bonaparte urged Roosevelt to create a "special detective force" inside the Department of Justice to track down wrongdoing. It became the beginning of a federal detective force, later the Federal Bureau of Investigation. And Roosevelt made no secret of his feelings about the legislative branch: he told a congressman "he wished he had sixteen lions to turn loose in Congress." The congressman wondered if the lions might eat the wrong people. TR replied: "Not if they stayed long enough."[137]

AS PRESIDENT, Roosevelt had worked effectively and simultaneously for peace and a stronger navy, and though the stronger state he had built made its mistakes in ignoring the rights of other nations and neglecting equal rights at home it demonstrated a new strength that had the potential to do greater good at home and abroad in the future. By the end of his term he believed American imperialism was a doomed experiment because the populace did not support energetic ventures across the sea. Though he never conceded that his own country's brief and fitful adventures in acquiring an empire or gaining the Panama Canal were misguided, he did admit there had been problems with bringing order to the Philippines. He judged that public opinion in the United States was not ready to sustain the work of "civilizing" people from less advanced civilizations.[138]

His mediation of the Russo-Japanese War and his skillful diplomatic efforts to resolve dangerous differences between France and Germany at the Algeciras Conference argue for our seeing Theodore Roosevelt as a transitional internationalist figure between the diplomacy of imperialism and the generation ready to create a League of Nations to forestall war. He tried to halt the European naval race, though his own battleship building and sending the Great White Fleet around the world may not have promoted world peace. He made himself a symbol of international dialogue and America's active desire to prevent war. He should be remembered both as an imperialist and "as a major figure in the rise of American internationalism."[139]

Despite his legislative defeats, TR had been a forceful and effective president. He had brought expert advice into active public service to solve the social problems of his time. F.D.R. later called Gifford Pinchot one of the first "brain trusters," and Eleanor and Franklin agreed that their admiration for Uncle Theodore's problem-solving, expert presidential style, and warmth in reaching out to all the people shaped the New Deal.[140]

At times TR was optimistic about how far he had gone in taming the excesses of monopolies with his anti-trust prosecutions. Yet he knew he had not completely brought the "malefactors of great wealth" under control, or else he would not have called for new forms of supervision in his 1908 message. He had laid a legal and moral foundation for federal supervision of the economy upon which others would build. After Roosevelt's time in office, utility magnates like Samuel Insull and other shrewd business leaders learned to turn the regulatory tide to their own advantage. The coal operators muzzled George F. Baer and hired a press agent the next time they had a strike. In the long run the Rockefellers and other big-business leaders, after years of public outrage over their anti-labor policies, hired Ivy Lee, the father of public relations, to advise them how to do what Roosevelt had done, get publicity for the good things they did and keep the less popular things quiet. Defending the public good from inside the White House only became more difficult after TR's day.[141]

TR had built a stronger American nation-state. Manly nationalism and an appreciation of "genuine Americana" gained ground because of him. If his attempts to modernize his nation and protect the public interest met with partial victories, his fight was worth the effort. Perhaps his most important legacy as president was to be a vociferous advocate for the public good. He promoted conservation and encouraged the governors' conference to declare: "We agree that the sources of national wealth exist for the benefit of the People, and that monopoly thereof should not be tolerated."[142]

TR had shaken up the status quo. His disregard for constitutional niceties and dislike of legislative collaboration had a lot to do with the Congress of "nits and lice" who blocked his path, but he set a dangerous precedent for the "imperial presidency" that fed on war and bloated foreign policy powers.

Though their motives were often impure, the "nits and lice" in Congress deserved credit for trying to protect the Constitution and the people's rights. As a much-needed experiment in activism, compassion, and personalized governance, Roosevelt's strenuous presidency was without equal.

His presidency ended in national celebration when he greeted the Great White Fleet on its return to Hampton Roads on Washington's Birthday, February 22, 1909. When it was time to leave Washington, Edith and Theodore called on Cabot and Nannie Lodge and their children and grandchildren. Cabot remembered that there was an "abundance of emotion near the surface" during the visit. An exciting time in their lives was passing, never to return. Edith wrote Cabot: "I am so glad it is all over, and much as I love the White House and interesting as the life has been there are certain compensations in leaving it all behind me. Mr. Taft was so nice and big and beaming over his victory that it did one good to look at him."[143]

Roosevelt saw fewer compensations in leaving office, and he told William Jennings Bryan that he would miss the presidency when it was over:

> When you see me quoted in the press as welcoming the rest I will have after March the 3d take no stock in it, for I will confess to you confidentially that I like my job. The burdens of this great nation I have borne up under for the past seven years will not be laid aside with relief, as all presidents have heretofore said, but will be laid aside with a good deal of regret, for I have enjoyed every moment of this so-called arduous and exacting task.[144]

Though the other children viewed the end of the Roosevelt presidency with only a measure of regret, Quentin said: "There is a little hole in my heart when I think of leaving the White House!" Theodore talked of becoming a private citizen after his trip to Africa, but Edith recognized that "he has really forgotten how to be" anything but a public figure. Roosevelt and the people were still in love.[145]

☆ BOOK THREE ☆

Wherein a Politician Makes Himself a Prophet

☆ CHAPTER ELEVEN ☆

The World Citizen

BEFORE TR SAILED for Africa on March 23, he took his first drive through the new Hudson tunnel from Manhattan to New Jersey, where "a tremendous crowd" awaited him on the Hoboken pier. As he made his way toward his ship, public adoration exacted its price, for he was roughly "jostled" and nearly knocked down. Finally he stood on the deck of the liner *Hamburg* and waved good-bye to the thousands who had come to see him off. The demonstration lent credibility to reporters' claim that Roosevelt was "nearer to the people as a personal force than any President has ever been yet." John L. Sullivan gave him a lucky rabbit foot, which he carried in his pocket as a reminder that men like the aging pugilist wished him luck and would read his African hunting stories as their stories. As tugboats and ships of many sizes accompanied the steamer out to sea, a voice from the pier shouted to him: "Kill a lion for me, Teddy."[1]

Roosevelt set off on his post-presidential career basking in popularity, dressed in military uniform, enjoying the twenty-one-gun salute, yet unprepared to face the fact that a true retirement would be impossible because he still cared passionately about changing America. Large segments of the public still wanted his leadership. Edith observed her husband's popularity grow as he left office less with apprehension than with wry amusement at "how much people love Father and look upon him as Doctor cure-all." She shrewdly perceived that because "the country is crazy-mad about Father" the new man in the White House, Bill Taft, "must have a horrid time." As Henry Cabot Lodge watched from the pier, he was astounded that the throng watched "every movement" his friend "might make" as if he had become a "new Robinson Crusoe," and crowds in other countries watched, too, to see where this American scholar-cowboy-president would lead next.[2]

Theodore took it for granted that Taft would rise to the office he held. When he looked ahead to his Africa trip, he deceived himself further: "It will let me down to private life without that dull thud of which we hear so much. I will be away from it all, and by the time I come back it may be that I will have been sufficiently forgotten to be able to travel without being photographed." On one level he knew he was underestimating the tenacity of the public's attachment to him, but he did so to reconcile Edith to his long absence with the lame promise it would buy them the privacy and anonymity which she missed so much. He talked of being forgotten, but he had designed a dramatic hunting adventure and kept for himself the exclusive reporting rights on it in a mass circulation magazine. Was it quiet retirement or carefully managed fame that TR wanted?[3]

Having been pronounced the "most conspicuous and probably the most popular person in the world," Roosevelt was not yet ready to surrender public adulation. Nor could he in good conscience give up fighting for his favorite causes. Financially, he could have sought a quiet retirement, with a greater income than any previous former president. *The Outlook* paid him a $12,000 annual salary for writing editorials. Scribner's had given him $50,000 as an advance for his African articles and *African Game Trails*, which would be augmented by sizable royalties when the book became a best-seller. He still received a steady inheritance income, and Edith's own inheritance brought about $6,000 per year. The Roosevelts' income qualified them as unequivocally upper class, especially in an age when a factory worker in New York was lucky to get $45 a month.[4]

But money had never motivated TR. He was a man who had staked everything on a life of vigor and consequence. Fashioning a strenuous post-presidential one for himself would not be easy with so few appealing examples to follow. Of course, the president he admired most, Abraham Lincoln, never faced life after the presidency. Neither had McKinley nor Garfield. He could model himself after Rutherford B. Hayes and become a prison reformer and advocate of better education for blacks or remain in politics and run for president again like Grover Cleveland. When one Kentucky newspaper editor suggested that former presidents should simply be taken out and shot, he reflected a persistent national discomfort with leaders after their official powers are gone. Roosevelt found it so difficult to put his experience and fame to the right use that he exclaimed in frustration: "Oh Lord! I begin to think that the best use to which an ex-President could be put would be to have him knocked on the head."[5]

Newspapers reported that when TR took his leave from Edith and Quentin at Oyster Bay the morning he left for Africa, he had cried. Edith dreaded being away from her husband for a year, and she still feared that living separately could become "a fixed habit."[6] But she held her composure. His last family good-byes from Hoboken were to Corinne and Bamie, who acted as his hostesses at a shipboard farewell luncheon. Before Kermit joined his father on the liner he had been up late carousing with Harvard chums and had nearly been knifed in an opium den in Boston, and he was no doubt relieved that as they left port the acclaim for his father so filled the air that talk of his own shady adventures was, as usual, evaded.[7]

On board the *Hamburg* admirers were surprised by Roosevelt's "high-pitched rasping voice," haphazard manner of dress, and hurried gait. His good humor and gift for remembering names soon charmed all ages.[8] Despite suffering from his usual seasickness, the man they now called "the Colonel" plotted with the taxidermists on board how they would preserve and transport the scientifically valuable portion of his kill. He danced with the actress and reformer Ruth Draper, and worked out in the ship's gym, then circled the deck with his arm around Kermit's shoulder. When they landed in Italy, King Victor Emmanuel greeted TR and Kermit personally, and took them to tour the gruesome wreckage left by the recent earthquake at Messina, where reeking corpses still remained in the ruins. As president Roosevelt had sent more earthquake relief than any other nation, which cheering crowds in Italy remembered. He began to have an inkling that he had become not just a national but a worldwide celebrity. The New York Police Department's "Italian Sherlock Holmes," Joseph Petrosino, had prepared security for the former president's visit, but he was murdered by the criminal syndicate, the Black Hand, before TR got there.[9]

When he reached Africa the world press reported as if Roosevelt were the first great white hunter opening up "the dark continent."[10] Africa had been a center of world trade and culture for many centuries, and other safaris—Baron Rothschild, a Spanish duke, and the cartoonist John McCutcheon—hunted in the same area at the same time as TR. But the Roosevelt safari was world news, and it was being hotly debated back home. Professor Frederick Starr at the University of Chicago predicted that TR would die in Africa, killed by lions, sleeping sickness, or the strain of an extreme climate.[11] Roosevelt's old nemesis Nelson A. Miles declared that any man who shot elephants "must have a depraved mind," and humane societies and other anti-hunting forces agreed with him.[12]

Most of all, the press found itself missing Roosevelt's antics in Washington. Bored by Taft, by December the Washington press corps had formed a Back from Elba Club to force TR to run for a third term. Third-term talk had never stopped after the Roosevelt boom of 1908, but now Lodge reported widespread "constantly growing thought" that TR would "return to the Presidency." As a result the senator warned his friend not to repeat his blunder on election night 1904 by making any rash promises about his future. Opportunity followed him everywhere. Theodore insisted he had stopped thinking about politics and had "no destiny," but then lectured Lodge on the need for a federal inheritance tax.[13]

Now he was out to bag a lion. After his party landed in Alexandria and made its way to Mombasa, his hunt began officially on April 24, 1909, and by early May a rhinoceros had charged him at forty yards and a leopard had clawed a native porter before Kermit finally brought it down. When TR wrote Lodge about his adventures he followed his familiar pattern of magnifying the heroic and larger-than-life qualities of them—the mosquitoes, the roaring of lions and trumpeting of elephants just outside their camp each night, the death of a gun bearer of fever, the death of four porters of dysentery and two "mauled by beasts," and the eight deaths by sleeping sickness.[14]

His hunt was dangerous, but not because of privations in the field. His party of naturalists, guides, taxidermists, and 260 native porters, servants, and gun bearers traveled in relative comfort, never long deprived of adequate food. They made a waterless camp only once, and often broke their time on the plains or in the brush (rarely in rain forest or jungle) with visits to nearby ranches and farms.

The real danger came from living among wild predators. Under drought conditions prevailing in British East Africa at the time, lions seeking water and food attacked farms. The twelve men killed or mauled by lions that spring and summer and the men he met who were "maimed, or crippled for life" served as proof that his was a genuine adventure. So did trailside graves of hunters impaled by rhinos or trampled by charging herds. When Nandi spearmen surrounded a lion, Roosevelt watched with admiration when the lion fought back with claw and tooth as their spears pierced the lion's body. He was pleased that from their camp they could often hear "the yawning grunt of a questing lion."[15]

Roosevelt hunted for adventure and to challenge himself, but also to write. Each day's experiences became stories for *Scribner's Magazine.* He repeated the plot of danger faced bravely, so he deleted panic and fear from his narrative.

But in real life fear could not be edited out. After hunting in the limestone desert plain of the Sotik in July the Roosevelt expedition walked north to track hippopotami near Lake Naivasha. Though Theodore described hippo hunting as "not dangerous," one day he found himself surrounded all at once by several hippos, including one that butted his rowboat and another that approached him "open jawed." He panicked and shot wildly at them.[16] He wrote: "I object to anything like needless butchery," but, in this case, several animals died because he got scared.[17]

In August he was imperiled again. After he tracked a bull elephant for three days, TR shot it at thirty paces. Then, he caught sight of another bull, "so close that he could have touched me with his trunk." It looked as if the second bull would charge him. Stunned when he found his gun was empty, he did not know if he should run or stand still and risk being trampled. He jumped to the side to reload behind a tree while his guide stepped in and brought the elephant down with a timely shot.[18] Soon the excitement of a successful hunt was followed by a gory scene of men "all splashed with blood from head to foot" as they skinned and eviscerated the animal. Roosevelt roasted the elephant's heart over an open fire that night and ate it.[19]

Despite his pleasure in the hunt and his success collecting plentiful specimens for the Smithsonian and other museums, Theodore's worried letters home lingered over scenes of Kermit risking his life to get close to his prey. The boy chased cheetah "at breakneck speed." When his horse fell and then turned a somersault which threw him into bushes covered with thorns, he kept going. Theodore judged Kermit to be "as hardy as a young bull moose," but a reckless one nevertheless. Their safari company, Newland and Tarlton, hired a hunter to look out for the boy, but this did not stop Kermit from galloping his horse until it was exhausted. Then he ran after wild game on foot until he was lost, far from help. It disturbed Theodore that Kermit behaved very much like the boy who had hunted on the Nile in 1873, a boy who was "a little too reckless and keeps my heart in my throat, for I worry about him all the time."[20]

Theodore's letters were also filled with competitive feelings toward his son. Throughout his 1909 diary he berated himself for bad shooting, but consoled himself that he was still a better shot than his son. He was irked that Kermit could run faster and longer than he could. Aging, blindness in one eye, and illness haunted him as he "realized perfectly well, although I was only fifty, that I was no longer fit to do the things I had done." Theodore saw that Kermit needed "to supply the qualities that I once had had and now lacked."[21] As if to reassert that he was still the better man, he pointed out to his reading public twice in *African Game Trails* that the porters called him in Swahili Bwana Makuba, or "the Great Master," but they called Kermit only Bwana Merodadi, "the Dandy."[22] Near the end of the expedition, he resigned himself to the fact that "twenty is hardier and more active and endowed with better eyes than Fifty one."[23]

The Roosevelt expedition chronicled in *African Game Trails* brought wild animals into the lives of a staid industrial people to instruct them in "the hidden spirit of the wilderness."[24] TR reached out to a popular readership with his lurid dime novel style: "Hoofs thundered now and then, there were snortings and gruntings, occasional bellowings or roarings, or angry whinings, of fear or of cruel hunger or of savage lovemaking." Years earlier, he had written that the chase promoted manliness but now he also wanted to use his dramatic African adventures to remind his readers of the value of game preserves, zoos, and open wilderness in their own country. If his stories could inspire Americans to become a hardier people they might someday be more willing to accept a stronger state governed by more Spartan values, a nationalist government that would protect species, save its land and water, and take better care of all its children.[25]

He also stood up for the heroic vision of colonial conquest that Livingstone, Stanley, Matthew Arnold, and Kipling had promoted. Americans were late-arriving stragglers in the colonial game, but Roosevelt spoke for a world movement of technologically advanced civilized nations reaffirming their right to rule more primitive people. European domination of Africa was being threatened by native resistance, and fresh anti-colonial movements were organizing to repeat the African triumphs over Europeans: the Mahdist victory over Gordon in 1885 and the Abyssinian defeat of Italy at Adowa in 1896. Pleased that Germany named its crack southwestern African regiment after the Roosevelt Rough Riders, TR had written words of colonial moral support to Kaiser Wilhelm noting "how difficult it is for men in highly civilized countries to realize what grim work is needed in order to advance the outposts of civilization in the world's dark places."[26] He endorsed missionary work by Catholics and Protestants in Africa, because any form of Christianity was preferable, in TR's mind, to the African creeds with "bestial and revolting ritual and ceremony," which included self-mutilation.[27]

He was a critic of colonial cruelty, however, and *The Outlook* reproved Portugal and Belgium for exploiting blacks in the cocoa and rubber trade and for imposing harsh industrial slavery on their African subjects. He saw Uganda as a land that should be ruled by blacks, but he believed British jurisdiction in East Africa rested on a system of laws and rights superior to the customs of rival Mahdist and Sudanese sovereigns. He also opposed the colonial competition and national rivalry that was fueling the naval arms race, which he feared might lead to world war. *African Game Trails* sold about a million copies even after his adventures were serialized in newspapers around the world and *Scribner's Magazine*.[28]

One of the men Roosevelt befriended on his safari wrote: "I had never been with a man before who evidently considered every day what the world would think, say or write about his success or failure."[29] A mythic quest which he reported blow by blow required special rules. The great white hunter must get the first shot. When his guide R. J. Cuninghame shot a rare specimen, TR would not let him add it to the Smithsonian's collection because, as he told Cuninghame: "I don't want it possible to have it said with even a shadow of truth that I came out here and had things done for me."[30] Recalling how his Colorado hunting trip turned into a public relations disaster, he set up his African expedition so that he shot the most important game, and his party did nothing to insulate him from real conditions in the wild. His companions were told not to shoot any animals that attacked him "until Roosevelt was down."[31]

TR was careful about "not showing weakness" during his safari. He did not believe in whipping his porters as other "Great Masters" did, but neither was he lenient. He lost his temper when Gouvimali, his gun bearer, threatened to disobey orders. Kermit was trying to photograph a rhinoceros close-up, but Gouvimali raised his gun to shoot the rhino when it came dangerously nearby. TR ordered him to put down his weapon, but when Gouvimali resisted, Roosevelt slapped him across his face.[32]

As they read accounts of his safari Nannie Lodge and Edith thought newspaper reports of TR's hunting prowess must be exaggerated, and Elihu Root quipped: "Of course Theodore shot three lions with one bullet and Kermit shot one lion with three bullets."[33] Such reports did not bother the publicity-minded Roosevelt. In an age when nickelodeon theaters were trying to gain acceptance among respectable audiences, politicians often proved camera shy. Unlike most politicians of his day, Roosevelt liked to be filmed because movies reached a mass audience. He had originally agreed when Colonel Selig of Selig Polyscope asked if he could send a camera crew with him to Africa, but then changed his mind. Rebuffed, Selig made his picture anyway. He found tame lions and an actor to play the protagonists for a studio lot dramatization of *Hunting Big Game in Africa*, which many viewers accepted as real footage. One of Selig's tame lions, according to Hollywood legend, became the trademark lion roaring at the beginning of MGM movies. An animated cartoon of terrified animals hiding from Roosevelt and his gun also brought the safari to the attention of nickelodeon audiences.[34]

The publicity of his safari also made hunting big game more popular as a leisure-time activity for privileged men. They went to Africa as lion ropers, big-game balloonists, and long-bow hunters (leaving big game to suffer as living pincushions). Abercrombie and Fitch marketed the khaki waterproof "Roosevelt tent" he had used in Africa, and boys like Ernest Hemingway dressed up in khaki after reading *African Game Trails.* Hemingway later followed TR's path to East Africa, where he made friends with one of Roosevelt's guides and added Roosevelt references to his story "The Short Happy Life of Francis Macomber."[35]

WHILE HER husband bragged, "I am sunburnt and healthy, and look like a burly and rather unkempt ruffian," Edith waited testily at home.[36] Before she sent the "wild and mischievous" little Quentin back to Episcopal High School in Alexandria, Virginia, she cuddled him for a night in her bed, and she and Alice worried together that the boy's old "bustle" "had been paddled off him" by the school's strict masters.[37] After a night when a foghorn from Long Island Sound had intruded upon her gloomy sleep, Edith wrote: "I have been able to be as blue as I wished without good and busy little Auntie Bye to keep me up to the mark and I do believe that if it were not for the children *here* I would not have the nervous strength to live through these endless months of separation from Father. When I am alone and let myself think[,] I am done for, for self control is a moral muscle which exercise strengthens."[38]

As a former first lady the demands upon her time had not stopped. She became her husband's post-presidential staff, managing his mail with his secretary, Frank Harper, and running the family's finances. *Success* magazine asked her for a favorite recipe; she refused until she was reminded of all the political help the magazine had given her husband. To Kermit she joked about the relief she felt because she didn't have to make polite conversation at state functions any longer: "Ha! Ha! I don't have to talk with Takahira now." But she still watched politics and received visits from Gifford Pinchot and others who were becoming disenchanted with Taft.[39]

Edith expected that her husband would watch Taft with benign, removed avuncular interest. After Mrs. Taft found the responsibility of being first lady and the social whirl too much for her, Edith wrote her husband all she heard about Nellie Taft's "nervous collapse." But she spared him the worst Taft news.[40] When Taft destroyed the Roosevelt administration's Council on Fine Arts Edith confided in Kermit, not her husband, how upset she was.[41]

Theodore's robust and reassuring letters from Africa told her that frequent exercise and the open air helped his body recover from the desk work and worry of the presidency. He had walked off seventeen pounds on the hunt, but failed to mention several bouts of fever. Yet Edith worried that without her to take care of him he would not flourish, that his periods of frenetic activity, insomnia, and risk-taking would get the best of him. If an animal didn't kill him, his recurring leg infection might.[42]

In his father's absence, Ted wrote imperiously to Rector Peabody at Groton that he was now "in charge" of the Roosevelt family in case Archie happened to need a good paternal scolding.[43] In fact, Edith was as much in charge of the daily cares of the family as she had been when her husband was at home. Ted was trying to work his way up in business, and his mother had to comfort him when the girl he had been courting broke off their engagement. When news of the pompous letters Ted had been writing reached him in Africa, TR wrote Ethel: "Alas, alas, I fear it is just such a priggy, self-conscious, superior-creature kind of letter I doubtless often wrote at his age! I hope I am a nicer old grown-up than I was a young grown-up." Ted aired his romantic tribulations for Ethel and Edith, but not his father. Father wrote home manly bromides to Ted, patronizing advice to the dimmer bulb Archie, charming and affectionate animal stories to Quentin, and long confidential chats over family matters to Ethel, including suggestions for lightening up Edith's grim nature and relieving her habitual unnecessary worrying about money. Alice got only postcards.[44]

On November 5, Edith, while visiting her sister in Italy with Quentin, Ethel, and Archie, read newspaper reports that her husband had been killed. A neuralgia attack struck her down, and even after news arrived that he was alive, she refused to leave her sister's house. When she came back to Oyster Bay, Edith thought her husband's cheery letters from Africa sounded insufficiently homesick. She told him news of Orville Wright's latest flight, but to make him miss home she also sent him a picture of the apple trees in the Fairy Orchard, intended to bring back all the smells and memories of spring at Sagamore Hill.[45]

Theodore finally realized how difficult the separation was for Edith and how much he missed her. He responded:

> Oh, sweetest of all sweet girls, last night I dreamed that I was with you, and that our separation was but a dream; and when I waked up it was almost too hard to bear. Well, one must pay for everything; you have made the real happiness of my life; and so it is natural and right that I should [be] constantly more and more lonely without you. . . . Darling, I love you so. . . . How very happy we have been for these 23 years! Five days hence, on the 17th, is the anniversary of our engagement.[46]

It was just the kind of outpouring that always touched her and made her forgive his absences and lack of consideration. She had originally planned to meet him in late March 1910 for their European tour, but he asked her to leave earlier. He declared to Cecil Spring Rice: "Catch me ever leaving her for a year again, if I can help it!"[47]

There was another romance he could not give up. The American people and politics beckoned him. He was missed in Washington. In the White House the new President tripped over the tigerskin rug on the floor of the Blue Room, while Alice watched hoping for the fun of even greater gaffes. Taft wrote that when he heard someone call him "Mr. President," he still looked around for the real president. He hated crowds and press conferences, and quickly showed himself unready to practice the political lessons his mentor had taught him. Before long, cartoonists parodied Taft as a lost boy searching for his Teddy bear.[48]

Their contrasting styles made TR all the more popular, and the public sent buckets of fan mail to Sagamore Hill, not to 1600 Pennsylvania Avenue. When cartoonists drew Uncle Sam looking with longing across the Atlantic, they showed that Roosevelt's "grip on the people" had not ceased.[49]

Henry Cabot Lodge wrote him that Taft had replaced part of the Roosevelt cabinet, a move which the new President had led his friend to believe would never happen. Taft even tried to supplant Bamie's friend London ambassador Whitelaw Reid with former Harvard president Charles William Eliot, a man TR hated with a passion. Taft even credited his electoral victory equally to his brother Charles and to his predecessor, which made Roosevelt feel unappreciated.[50]

Furthermore, the Republican Party was crumbling under Taft's command. While TR had kept its progressive and conservative wings working together, Taft filled his cabinet with corporation lawyers and ignored progressive Republicans like La Follette. After promising tariff reduction in his campaign, he signed the Payne-Aldrich bill which set higher rates. He had tacitly approved of Roosevelt's calls for inheritance taxes, "a larger share of the wealth" for workers and farmers, and TR's criticisms of courts that blocked labor regulation. Then he backtracked on TR's policies and refused to support the Roosevelt ban on using injunctions to crush strikes.[51]

Fault lines within the Republican Party over tariff and social reform threatened a split, which Taft seemed helpless to prevent. Speaker Cannon ruled the House for the protection of business so blatantly that insurgents boycotted the Republican Party caucus there. Taft knew Cannon had to be removed, but still stood by him. Nor did the President stop the systematic punishment of insurgents by regular Republicans, who stripped them of their committee assignments and opposed their reelection. A *Chicago Tribune* poll showed that the Payne-Aldrich tariff and Cannon were unpopular. Taft could keep neither the public nor the press with him. He was, in short, not good at politics.[52]

While he was in Africa, Roosevelt's closest associates were operating on his behalf, with or without his blessing. Bamie spoke for him about his homecoming. Alice had buried a voodoo doll in the White House garden to jinx the Tafts and kept gathering information useful to her father, and Lodge played a two-faced game as he curried favor with Taft while seeking to undermine the President and unseat Cannon. Lodge also wrote his friend in Africa that he might be needed in 1912 to save the country from Taft.[53]

Gifford Pinchot made headlines feuding with the President. Pinchot accused Richard Ballinger, the new interior secretary, of dishonesty. Ballinger, suspect because he was a former lawyer for the Morgan-Guggenheim mining trust, had approved an illegal grant of Alaskan coal lands to those interests. Taft's administration had a good conservation record, but Pinchot saw Ballinger's mistake as proof that the President had betrayed Roosevelt's conservation policies and he went to the press. Then Taft fired Pinchot from his position as head of the Forestry Service for his anti-administration remarks, and the publicity-hungry Pinchot set out to stir up public opinion and align Roosevelt on his side. Congressional hearings on the Ballinger-Pinchot controversy filled the newspapers in the first half of 1910, and Edith thought that if Taft had simply "roared at" his warring employees "things might never have come to this pass." Alice, always more conservative than her stepmother, judged Taft correct in trying to rein in Pinchot's "practically rank socialism."[54]

When a runner brought the latest news to Lado Enclave in the Belgian Congo, TR was shocked to read that Taft had dumped Pinchot. But he turned quickly back to shooting white rhinoceros. He had abandoned his offspring—a revived federal government more capable of defending the public good—to be cared for by a politically inept "great pink porpoise of a man." Taft was his biggest mistake.

Even though he was out of the country, it did not take long before Roosevelt understood a political climate change was under way. At the same time that he began his Ugandan safari, new coalitions had formed back in America. In New York the strike of the shirtwaist makers was reported more sympathetically than previous labor conflicts because it involved women. Labor and wealth forged an unlikely alliance when suffragist Alva Belmont funded a lawyer for the Women's Trade Union League and won the support of the shirtwaist strike from the wealthy women of the Colony Club. The mink brigade of Colony Clubbers, led by Daisy Harriman, supported the strikers financially and acted as chauffeurs and picket watchers, which forced men in their social class and circle of friends, including Theodore Roosevelt, to take notice.[55]

Edith and Ethel sailed on February 16 to meet Theodore and Kermit in Africa, but not before Pinchot and James Garfield had come to Oyster Bay to give Mrs. Roosevelt their version of the Ballinger-Pinchot controversy. She encouraged them to stick by the administration as long as possible, but she saw that her husband would soon face pressure to submerge his own principles to suit Taft. She told Kermit quite bluntly: "I don't want him used to infuse popularity into the administration."[56]

On March 14, Edith and Ethel joined Kermit and Theodore in Khartoum. When Edith at last saw her husband waiting for her on the platform of the train station, she noted, with relief and pleasure, that he was "in splendid condition." It amused TR when Edith told him she had explained the politics of marriage to Ted's new fiancée, Eleanor Alexander, using her own peripatetic husband "as an awful example" of a mate who had needed a lot of reconstruction: "She was so charming and felt so much that she had both been wise and scored off me that I had to keep kissing her while she told me."[57]

Before they traveled up the Nile to Egypt, Roosevelt shipped his important scientific contribution to the Smithsonian: 8,463 vertebrates, 550 large mammals, 3,379 small mammals, and 2,784 birds. The expedition had come across the trail of ancient slave traders and sent home human skulls for physical anthropologists to study. Specimens also went to the San Francisco Museum, the Bronx Zoo, and the American Museum of Natural History, and several live animals to the National Zoo in Washington.[58]

Together the Roosevelts returned to scenes of his visit to the Nile on a dahabeah in 1873—Luxor, Karnak, and Cairo. They rode camels to the battlefield at Kerreri, where Kitchener fought the Khalifa and Gordon gave his life for the empire. Edith thought the pyramids "looming through a yellow sandstorm were wonderfully impressive. The sun hung in the sky a disk of pale gold." Theodore enjoyed racing horses against his son and showing his wife places he had described in letters to her in 1873, and for once he even permitted Ethel to direct their path using her tourist's Baedeker guide, which normally he hated. The Egyptians who tended their horses reportedly called Roosevelt the "man who never stops."[59]

When the Roosevelts reached Europe his hope that they would be able to enjoy private life again faded. TR's fame as a historian and scientific writer coupled with his presidency had brought him invitations to receive honorary degrees and give speeches at the University of Berlin, the Sorbonne, Cambridge, and Oxford, and to receive in person his Nobel Peace Prize in Christiania. Edith saw more clearly than her mate what lay ahead of them on tour.

She realized the grand drama would occur between the celebrity and his crowds, and she frankly disliked being one "who follows in his train." Instead of being a partner and helpmate she would enter his entourage. She preferred to get away with Theodore for a stay in Corfu "to have a chance to get acquainted with him again!" But the best they could arrange was a fleeting retracing of the Italian phase of their honeymoon. But before he and Edith had much of a chance to get reacquainted they were bombarded by official invitations and "rushed as if on a presidential tour."[60]

In Africa, TR had been hailed as "Mr. King of America!" and the same was true in Europe. He was delighted, however, that he and his wife could drive in an old-fashioned three-horse carriage and stay at the same hotel they had visited on their honeymoon, where they could listen to the "waves washing the wall beneath our balcony." Edith would recall fondly their "two delightful days on the Riviera," but crowds followed them everywhere, especially when they reached her sister Emily Carow's house in Porto Maurizio. After a visit from Pinchot, who had crossed the ocean under an assumed name, newspapers reported the falsehood that TR was willing to run for president again. Edith and Ethel soon escaped as private citizens to visit their literary friends in Paris, while TR and Kermit went to Venice, then Austria, after which the Orient Express brought them to meet Edith in Paris on April 20.[61]

In a speech at the Sorbonne, TR castigated the French for their declining birthrate while making common cause with them over the need for nations to seek peace and bring social justice to their own people. He had moved far beyond a Joseph Chamberlain–like concern with "national efficiency" and reached out to French Republicans like Georges Clemenceau as like-minded leaders who agreed with his social democracy, or what he called "the wise and democratic use of the powers of the State toward helping raise the individual standard of social and economic well-being" of all its people. Clemenceau adored TR, but by endorsing the nationalization of railroads and utilities, the Frenchman stood further left than did the American.[62]

French authorities liked Roosevelt's message about the birthrate so much they distributed it to fifty thousand schoolteachers, and the left praised his radical ideas. Theodore and Edith enjoyed visiting with intellectuals like Jusserand, and they met the sculptor Auguste Rodin and went to the Louvre. TR was inducted as an associate member of the Institut de France, which impressed Edith more than any other honor he had ever received. They watched airplane demonstrations, which were exciting in their newness, though also ominous evidence of France's war readiness. In a private moment, Theodore joined his wife for tea at 53, rue de Varenne with her distant cousin novelist Edith Wharton. The Roosevelts would not approve of

Wharton's having an affair (no matter how mentally ill or unfaithful her husband was), but her lover, Morton Fullerton, proved to be a perceptive new friend. He wrote in *Scribner's* that TR's sojourn to France equaled in historic importance the visit of Garibaldi because it symbolized the meeting of nations to herald new ideas—reform and internationalism—that could reshape the future. The philosopher William James, once a strong critic of Roosevelt's imperialism, praised the humane values articulated in his Sorbonne speech: "I myself regard Roosevelt, with all his faults, as a tremendously precious natural asset."[63]

The pace of Roosevelt's public performances across Europe caught up with him in the Netherlands, where Edith wrote:

> Father is so tired that whenever we go in a motor he falls asleep. The people are quite mad about him and stand in crowds around the hotel to see him go in and out and both nights I had to send him out on our balcony before they would disperse, though it was midnight.[64]

By the time he had toured Belgium, the Netherlands, Denmark, and reached Norway, he suffered from bronchitis and a high fever. Nevertheless, in Norway he and Edith became friends with King Haakon and Queen Maud, and Theodore played games with young Prince Olaf and "tossed him in the air, and rolled him on the floor" while the Dowager Empress of Russia watched. Roosevelt's appearances made such a hit throughout Norway that a brand of cigarettes was named after him—"Teddies." His Nobel Prize speech had worldwide importance because he warned against "unhealthy militarism in international relationships" at the moment major European powers were planning for war. He issued a challenge to leaders to work for arbitration, arms limitation, and a league of peace with international police power, which in the years ahead he hoped would make possible a world parliament and federation to protect the peace. The *London Morning Post* judged his league idea "too fantastic to be realized."[65]

War struck his European audiences as more realistic than a league of peace. On May 12, Kaiser Wilhelm watched as his brightly sashed and jack-booted student corpsmen stood with swords drawn at the former president's side for three hours as Roosevelt lectured twelve hundred people on familiar moral themes. Crowds were more subdued in their enthusiasm for him in Germany perhaps because he had become a "convenient symbol for Europe of American world power." He talked peace and international cooperation, but he represented a rising rival nation. He and Wilhelm spent several hours on horseback, both dressed in military outfits, reviewing a sham battle on the field of Döberitz. Roosevelt was disturbed by the preparations for war he had seen across the Continent: Count Zeppelin offered him a ride in a dirigible and he had seen impressive new French airplane squadrons.[66]

Andrew Carnegie had asked TR to speak to the kaiser about the possibility of arms reduction talks while he was in Germany. Roosevelt learned there that Germany and Austria expected a war with Britain. He heard too that German war plans included a flank march through Belgium. Nevertheless, he raised the question of disarmament with the kaiser, and told him he viewed the prospect of a war between England and Germany as an "unspeakable calamity." The kaiser had no sympathy for arms limitations and said he was not in complete control of his nation's foreign policy. Certainly Wilhelm would not be the man to take up the challenge of Roosevelt's Nobel Prize speech.[67]

In England, Roosevelt acted as special ambassador to the funeral of King Edward VII, where he marched in a procession with seven kings. At the Guildhall, he made a speech in which he tried to buck up England's faltering will to rule its empire. His talks with settlers in East Africa and administrators in Egypt had convinced him that Britain was not supporting its outposts, and he discussed his ideas ahead of time with King George and Foreign Secretary Sir Edward Grey. Yet his lecture shocked the British because he told them rather baldly that they had to keep their nerve as colonial rulers because they provided a major source of international stability. His speech—a rule or get out bromide—was, as Sherlock Holmes' creator, Sir Arthur Conan Doyle, put it, "a most unwarrantable intrusion into our affairs, but it was a calculated indiscretion, and very welcome, I believe, to those who were dealing with Egypt." As TR walked through the crowds to leave the Guildhall, he mischievously said to Doyle: "I say, I let them have it that time, didn't I!"[68]

Ambassador Whitelaw Reid spent most of Roosevelt's visit worrying that his guest would commit a horrible breach of etiquette. TR taunted Reid before King Edward's funeral services by joking in a stage whisper during a formal embassy reception: "I'm going to a wake tonight. I'm going to a wake tonight." Kermit and Ethel had grown tired of their father's effusive antics and had urged him not to take up so much space when he signed his name in guest books and not to speak with so many "I's." Before long the *New York World* put a running score on its front page—that year at 563,877,207—to record the number of times Roosevelt used "I" in his public addresses. In the face of such criticism Roosevelt complained: "I can't even say 'My Country 'tis of Thee' without being accused of egotism."[69]

His time abroad was not all show. As he contemplated his future, TR thought "there is nothing left for me to grasp at" politically. Yet, he was still a man intensely committed to ideas and causes. Freed from the compromises of office, he let his anger at the reactionaries in his own party simmer. His thoughts returned to the unfinished business of his presidency. While he was in Africa he scribbled in his pocket diary: "In the end a party of Haves produces a party of Have-nots by mere force of reflex action. Reaction at one end of the social scale invites revolution at the other end." This was only the first clue that in his unharnessed years he intended to grapple with the question of inequality.[70]

On his tour of Europe, Roosevelt praised true democracy and "equality of opportunity," and declared that "probably the best test of true love of liberty in any country is the way in which minorities are treated in that country." He declared himself in favor of social democracy everywhere. He had found the average European king intellectually dull and personally like a "sublimated vice-president," so he sought out the company of policymakers and "radical liberals." He evaded the "dress parade" side of his tour to meet with Europeans who were using an enlarged state to alleviate poverty. He, S. S. McClure, and Lawrence Abbott met with Germany's minister of state and public works, Paul Breitenbach, to discuss how to provide government assistance to the aged and the poor. In Denmark he inquired into old-age subsidies, and wherever he went he sought out discussions of industrial accidents, unemployment, and poverty with reform thinkers like Georges Clemenceau and John Morley. In England he asked to meet Lloyd George and confessed after their talks that he "took a real fancy" to the charismatic Welshman and his campaign for social insurance.[71]

Roosevelt understood he was returning to a nation where 2 percent of the people owned 60 percent of the wealth, and that workers at the bottom still had not gained a living wage. Though he did not want to face how little his own time in power had done to change those statistics, he believed he still had a future as a reformer or a reform propagandist. He came home ready to fight for social democracy.[72]

The biggest accomplishment of his tour was to impress Europe. His skill in French, Italian, and German, his wide literary and historical knowledge, and his high standing among scientists surprised many Europeans, who viewed Americans as rude, unlearned frontier people. English reporters were amazed that America's former president did not display "the natural slowness of the American mind."[73]

When the Roosevelts arrived in New York on June 18, they were greeted by one of the largest mass demonstrations in American history, a huge celebration with the harbor filled with destroyers, tugs, yachts, and boats of every size and a crowd of 100,000 waiting for TR's triumphal homecoming parade. Cornelius Vanderbilt had organized the event, though he rejected pleas from TR's friend Maud Nathan of the Consumers' League to allow women to join in the planning. Roosevelt's carriage was to be followed by six thousand Spanish-American War veterans and the Rough Riders on horseback, riding up Broadway and Fifth Avenue to Fifty-ninth Street.

When his liner set anchor, TR hugged Jacob Riis and warmly greeted Eleanor and Franklin and the other close relatives who had come to see him. In his brief public remarks he said he was "more glad than I can say that I am back in my own country, back among the people I love . . . I am eager to do my part in solving the problems which must be solved." It did not sound like retirement.[74]

Sagamore Hill was a welcome sight, though letters piled up and visitors and reporters flocked around the piazza and the front door. Edith and Theodore saw Ted married to Eleanor Butler Alexander, who would become their favorite daughter-in-law. The ex-president took only one day off after his homecoming before he started work at *The Outlook,* where people followed him to the United Charities Building at Fourth Avenue and Twenty-second Street. His office was situated in the building which had become the Social Gospel and social reform mecca of America. It was close enough to Florence Kelley of the Consumers' League and Paul Kellogg of *Survey* magazine for them to help him shape his developing program of reform. He had promised *The Outlook* twelve articles a year, and he and the other editors got along so well at first that the literary critic Hamilton Wright Mabie called him "great fun; a warm-hearted, affectionate, companionable giant, who makes everybody that knows him his friend."[75]

He had bought the family's first car as a consolation prize to Edith for their long separation, but it helped him more than it did Edith, since he could drive into the city and avoid crowds on the Long Island Railroad. Like Mr. Toad in *The Wind in the Willows,* he drove with more enthusiasm than precision, so Edith had to take the car keys away from him and give them to their chauffeur Charles Lee. At home, Mrs. Roosevelt was relieved not to have to be kissed by royalty anymore. Instead, she would put up with her husband's new interior decorating scheme: huge African animal heads attached to walls all over the first floor. When they finally had grandchildren, the young ones would crawl in the North Room on the skin of a Kenyan lion whose neck TR had broken. He usually forgot Edith's birthday, but from Africa he had brought her gifts of colobus monkey anklets and a beehive from his hunt which, judging from her reception, were "frightful failures."[76]

He barely had time to regale old friends with lion stories before the political situation erupted. Taft's quarrel with insurgents looked irreconcilable. TR was pressed daily to take sides, though it was the last thing he wanted to do. He said that Taft "had gone wrong on certain points; and then I also had to admit to myself that deep down underneath I had known all along he was wrong, on points as to which I had tried to deceive myself, by loudly proclaiming to myself that he was right." Roosevelt was determined to do what he could to heal the rift within the party and to avoid appearing as if he played any part in Taft's problems. While he was in Africa many of his supporters had started to describe themselves as part of a Progressive Movement in national politics.[77]

On June 27, after working in Sagamore's fields gathering hay for market, Roosevelt greeted Robert M. La Follette in his library, where the senator recited the sins of the Taft administration. TR was noncommittal about initiative and referendum proposals, but spoke in favor of the recall of judges. La Follette did not blame him for Taft's conservatism, and the senator left Oyster Bay pronouncing TR "the greatest living American."[78]

Soon men like the rich and "unbalanced" Rudolph Spreckels, whom Ted befriended after he and his wife, Eleanor, settled in San Francisco, were quick to climb on the La Follette presidential bandwagon, which TR considered an unstable vehicle. Roosevelt dismissed La Follette as a fame-hungry personality marred by "that touch of fanaticism" which made him incapable of running a national campaign with a broad coalition. But insurgency was in the air, and La Follette was its leader. His grass-roots organization in Wisconsin surpassed anything Roosevelt had achieved in faction-ridden New York. If a national Progressive Movement were launched by La Follette he would try to make the United States more democratic using the initiative, referendum, recall, direct election of senators, and presidential primaries. He believed that if the people ran politics, they could win tax justice and railroad regulation and finally America would become a progressive country.[79]

Roosevelt agreed with much of La Follette's program, but by 1912 he cared most passionately about the social justice issues—abolishing child labor and gaining recognition of workers' rights. He did not want progressives to fixate on electoral cure-alls, but to adopt "an elastic platform" which included transatlantic social programs like Lloyd George's old-age pensions. The British debate, spurred first by Fabian socialists, about using government to guarantee a "social minimum" standard of living impressed an urban Social Gospel reformer like TR. La Follette flattered himself that their cordial talks, agreement on many issues, and TR's stated lack of interest in running for president came close to an endorsement of his presidential ambitions. But they did not.[80]

TR's ex-presidency was about to reach a moment of truth. Edith let her own wishful thinking convince her that her husband would be appalled by the "serious demand for him to enter public life again" because she thought all he would want for the rest of his life would be to "stay at Sagamore with his family around him." He had promised he could be like the Greek general Timoleon who, after years in power, could forsake glory for retirement. But the quiet life was not strenuous enough.[81]

Gifford Pinchot, Gilson Gardner, and James Garfield came to Sagamore Hill to urge him to run for president in 1912, even though he had told them he did not want to play spoiler to the Taft administration. Reporters popped up when he and Edith went for walks in the woods around Oyster Bay to quiz him about politics. Besieged by requests for speeches and articles, urged on one side to run and on the other to support Taft or La Follette, he despaired: "I am almost worked to death. . . . I have all the work I had while President and no means of protecting myself." Edith wrote Bamie: "Poor [Theodore] is so harassed and worried that I could almost wish him back in Africa, and the worst is that he sees no way out of his present position."[82]

The lure of cheering crowds who grasped his hands over the rail of a departing campaign train and the urgency of a crusade tempted him. As he planned to give a series of speeches across the country in the summer of 1910, he found himself in a quandary. In spirit he was "with the insurgents" and wanted to use his speeches to float bold new ideas to see if they would catch on with the public, yet he needed to avoid making any public commitments because he had promised Lodge he would keep quiet.[83]

The political tension mounted until malarial fever and "opera singer's throat" brought Roosevelt down. He called the speeches he had promised to give that summer and fall "perfect nightmares," but Pinchot, William Allen White, Garfield, and Edith stepped in to help him prepare for his tour and work on drafts. His doctor told him not to talk at all so Edith wrote: "You can't think how funny it is to see Father entertaining them in silence [at political lunches] while I try to talk for him." In ill health Roosevelt chose what he told himself was a middle way—to remain unaligned but to exert leadership by pointing toward reforms that would revive democracy and provide more protection for the victims of laissez-faire industrial capitalism—workers, widows, children, the poor, and the aged. The result was not moderate at all.[84]

On August 31, Roosevelt made the most important speech of his political career on the "New Nationalism" at a memorial ceremony for John Brown at

Osawatomie, Kansas. After lunch at a mental hospital with local officials, TR climbed on top of a kitchen table before a crowd of thirty thousand to speak for over an hour, sounding familiar themes, but giving them a more radical tone. With insurgents arrayed on the stage behind him, he deviated from his prepared text and added impulsively: "No man is worth his salt in public life who makes on the stump a pledge which he does not keep after election; and, if he makes such a pledge and does not keep it, hunt him out of public life." The audience thought he was saying President Taft needed to be "hunted out of public life" and they cheered. Roosevelt went on to declare: "We must drive the special interests out of politics." He called for directors of companies to be held personally liable for corporate actions and for "swollen" fortunes to be put to public use by a graduated income tax and an inheritance tax. He said that currency reform, conservation, the direct primary, and the regulation of child labor were all required to achieve the larger good of "national efficiency," or "New Nationalism." And his audience responded enthusiastically.[85]

His New Nationalism address and later 1910 speeches showed that TR believed America was headed for a showdown. While he was in England he had predicted that a civil war between labor and capital would erupt in the United States, and his New Nationalism speech was his first post-presidential attempt to place himself at the head of the country's liberal trend and convince it to clean up its politics and provide a larger share of wealth to the worker. Roosevelt threw down the gauntlet to Taft when he invoked Lincoln's words "Labor is the superior of capital and deserves much the higher consideration." He defended workmen's compensation laws, and came out in support of the eight-hour day and labor's right to organize. In private he promised "to *eliminate* privilege, and to work for a more genuine equality of opportunity and for the betterment of the conditions of those who are not well off."[86]

Talk of a third party was already circulating, even an unlikely third party made up of Roosevelt, Bryan, and the insurgents. But TR hardly recognized what he had done. He still claimed to be the peacemaker of the Republican Party, and refused to face the fact that he had made the split in his party worse. Though he knew perfectly well the press watched each step he took for its national political meaning, he still maintained that he was free to say whatever he wanted, regardless of the effect. In Denver he made a public show of his closeness to direct democracy and municipal ownership reformers who had stopped a private company from making a profit from the municipal water supply. As he walked toward the speaker's platform he grabbed juvenile court judge Ben Lindsey, who had shocked local bosses with his muckraking attack on "the Beast" of corporate greed and crooked politics. TR endorsed

Lindsey and his work in front of the press and the assembled citizens. Spontaneity ruled most of Roosevelt's actions that fall as he bridled against the quiet, harnessed retirement Edith had in mind for him. She told herself she had "Father safely caged at Sagamore," but he was not a man to be caged, even by the wife he loved dearly. He told Kermit that his bold talk in Kansas and elsewhere was "merely another way of saying I am still alive."[87]

TR knew his post-Africa popularity would not last, but he was unprepared for the vitriolic personal attacks in the wake of his New Nationalism speech. Though he had consulted Oswald Garrison Villard of the *Evening Post* about the content of his talk ahead of time, the *Post* still judged it the speech of a "self-seeking, hypocritical braggart." He was also charged with insanity and rank socialism, and though he wrote James Bryce that he had merely said what Morley, Bryce, and many others at home and across the Atlantic had said already, it troubled him that the press and politicians in his own country "treat my remarks as if they indicated a determination to revive the Paris Commune." He believed that his New Nationalism speech had prompted Wall Street to launch "an organized crusade against me."[88]

Friends cajoled him into getting caught up in New York State politics to thwart a boss-dictated nomination. He acted as temporary chairman at the Republican State Convention in Saratoga in September and gained the nomination of his friend Henry Stimson for governor. In revenge, Republican boss William Barnes told his organization to sit out the election. TR could not get the Saratoga convention to budge on the tariff, for which he was criticized around the country, but he claimed: "I got from the convention the last ounce of radicalism it was possible to get."[89]

When TR met with Taft in New Haven that fall, the press reported inaccurately that Roosevelt had come as a supplicant "because I was in difficulties and needed Taft's support" to get Stimson elected. Being portrayed as a weak state reformer at the mercy of a president offended Roosevelt's pride and compounded the mistrust he felt about Taft and his press aides. He had known that getting involved in a state factional fight at Saratoga and a doomed governor's race were not dignified ways for a former president to use his prestige to further national causes, but he confessed: "I could not help myself."[90]

He could not help himself because he adored Stimson and his causes. A stiff, austere Wall Street lawyer and Good Government reformer who could not stand to be touched, Stimson had been one of the young men Roosevelt inspired to pursue public service. He had studied at Andover and Harvard Law School, gone west, and when he camped this young muscular Christian had "continually to be killing some poor damned animal or other." When he was President Roosevelt's favorite federal prosecutor, Stimson launched the salacious ads case against the *New York Herald* and the ill-advised Panama libel case against the *New York World* (TR went after the press for accusing his relatives of profiting from the canal), and he founded the National Conservation Association with Pinchot. TR twisted Stimson's arm to get him to run for governor and engineered his nomination, and together they framed a pro-labor platform. If Roosevelt had a political heir it was Stimson.[91]

In the fall of 1910, Roosevelt stumped all over the state for Stimson, telling crowds they stood together "for the rights of the laboring men." But TR campaigned as if he were the candidate. Workers lined up to hear "Teddy" in much larger numbers than "icicle" Stimson. He stole headlines again with stunts like going up in a bi-plane in St. Louis with flyer Arch Hoxsey, who was killed taking a similar flight a few weeks later. But in New York Roosevelt did not need stunts: he was the entertainment people wanted to see. TR urged them to vote for Stimson by reminding them when he was governor he fought for worker safety laws, the bakeshop law regulating hours, and the cigar factory law, and they greeted him with applause and cheers.[92]

Sometimes TR forgot to mention Stimson much at all and got so wound up in talking to responsive audiences that campaign staff had "to drag him off the stage backwards" to get him to stop talking. When he campaigned for himself, Stimson spoke on dry subjects with no zest in his delivery. Tammany's candidate, John Dix, attacked Roosevelt for his criticism of the Supreme Court ruling in the *Lochner* case, and warned that he was a "public menace." Dix even tried to scare voters into believing that their choice was between "Rooseveltism" or "business tranquillity."[93]

TR reveled in being back in front of a crowd. He loved hitting Tammany hard for its nasty habit of getting kickbacks on state contracts and reminded his audience that long before Tammany had attacked "the wild doctrines of Roosevelt" it had "denounced the imbecility of the administration of Abraham Lincoln." Using information provided by the Consumers' League, he blasted Dix and his financial backers for routinely violating labor laws and using child labor for eighteen hours a day in their businesses. He told voters that Stimson, not Dix, would fight to the death "against the dreadful system of exploiting the childhood of the nation."[94]

When Theodore returned from a ten-day speaking tour, Ethel helped her mother "hustle" Father upstairs for a rest. He had been careful as he campaigned not to hurt the chances of Democrat state senate candidate Franklin Roosevelt, who also sounded anti-boss themes in his campaign. TR wished FDR had views more like Corinne's charming son-in-law, Joe Alsop, but he heartily encouraged Franklin's political career and told Sara Roosevelt: "I'm so fond of that boy, I'd be shot for him."[95]

Roosevelt's close friendship with Gifford Pinchot suffered that fall because Pinchot thought TR had not been radical enough at Saratoga and so stayed away from the Stimson campaign. On the other side politically, TR was being pressed to say he supported Taft or that he would not run in 1912, but he refused because if he took himself out of consideration he would have no political clout left. One day he would confess to Ted that he would not accept the nomination no matter what, but then another day he and Stimson pondered his chances of returning to the White House. When Edith heard their speculations, she laughed and told her husband in no uncertain terms: "Put it out of your mind, Theodore, you will never be President of the United States again."[96]

☆ CHAPTER TWELVE ☆

A Progressive World Movement

ONE WARM EVENING, as the excitement grew at the end of the Stimson campaign, Theodore Roosevelt drove in an open car down Fifth Avenue with young lawyer and campaign aide Felix Frankfurter, who had worked for him prosecuting the Sugar Trust. When TR asked Frankfurter's campaign advice, the twenty-seven-year-old told him to talk more about Stimson and less about his own policies on the stump. Roosevelt had his share of yes-men as advisors, but he took this suggestion to heart and changed his strategy immediately. However, even timely issues and a revised campaign style could not elect Stimson, who lost to Dix by 67,000 votes. Republicans yielded control of the House of Representatives, and around the country Democrats and Republican insurgents beat stand-pat Republicans.

Smears against TR's reputation grew more hateful. He found he had to reassure his supporters that, contrary to the slander spread by his opponents, he had not drowned his sorrows with an alcoholic bender on election night. After the election season his spirits remained jovial at first as he played sports with Stimson, read William Cullen Bryant's version of the *Iliad*, and was as "gay as a lark" to be home at last.[1]

As always, his moods shifted. Friends who visited him in the winter of 1910–11 found him "in a most depressed state of mind" as he endured "six weeks of grey horror" watching Taft bumble, the Republican Party disintegrate, and progressive causes go unchampioned. For the many who criticized him for mucking around in state politics he answered: "The thing that would have hurt me most was to stay absolutely still, because I should have been attacked just as savagely as I am now attacked."[2]

He refused to move back to the center politically, but he was not sure what else to do with himself. He tried to make the best of his caged-wolf mood, when he confessed to his daughter-in-law Eleanor:

> What I now most want is just what is forced on me; to stay here in my own home with your mother-in-law, to walk and ride with her, and in the evening sit with her before the great wood fire in the north room and hear the wind shrieking outside; to chop trees and read books, and feel that I am justified in not working.[3]

Tammany was running New York City and state affairs, and much he cared about was not getting done. Voters had turned away from workplace safety regulation, and the thirty thousand factories in greater New York were not even required to provide fire escapes for their workers.

Though muckraking magazines habitually attacked "the special interests" and declared that "J.P. Morgan is the boss of the United States," no one had found a way to unite progressives, who headed in different directions. La Follette capitalized on the bad publicity that came out of TR's actions in the Saratoga convention and his New Nationalism speech to organize and raise funds for his own presidential ambitions. Roosevelt's followers flocked to La Follette, and Stimson would soon join the Taft administration as secretary of war. Pinchot was already talking about a third-party movement, which irritated his old chief. TR could not easily run for president, but he could not bear to keep out of politics, either. He had turned fifty-two that fall, still hardy except for occasional bouts of malaria and throat problems. He missed the strenuous life more than he could admit.[4]

Christmas 1910 found the Roosevelts unified but missing Ted, who was in San Francisco, and Archie, whom they had taken out of Groton temporarily and placed at the Evans School in Arizona because of his frail health. TR rode over the snow happy to have family gathered near him again. Back at the United Charities Building former shirtwaist factory worker and labor activist Leonora O'Reilly of the Women's Trade Union League talked over labor issues with him. He already knew her friend Mary Dreier, who briefly had been courted by the perennially eligible rich bachelor Gifford Pinchot. Together the women's reform network activists joined Frances Kellor in enlisting Roosevelt to work more actively beside them in their fight against child labor and for the improvement of conditions for working women. *The Outlook*, with TR's approval, had already praised the work of Louis Brandeis, the legal mastermind who had embarrassed the Taft forces in the Ballinger-Pinchot hearings. TR applauded when Brandeis mediated the cloakmakers' strike that fall, but more than mediation was needed.[5]

Over lunch with Pinchot and the *Collier's* editor, Norman Hapgood, early in 1911, TR said he would probably support Taft if he got the nomination in 1912. Pinchot bluntly called that "foolishness" and pressed him further: why not support La Follette? TR could not bring himself to endorse the senator, but made several overtures to meet with him so that they could discuss the best way to advance progressive ideas. He asked New Jersey reformer George Rublee to try to get Brandeis to prevent misunderstanding between progressive camps and to help him move the country ahead on labor and economic issues, but Brandeis declined because his close friend La Follette already feared that all his friends would desert him to urge TR to run for president. La Follette refused several offers to coordinate their efforts, because he gradually became suspicious of his supporters like Pinchot who loved TR best. For most of 1911, Roosevelt denied he had any interest in being 1912's sacrificial progressive lamb, but deep inside he did not know if he wanted to be drafted or left alone.[6]

In the same winter months Roosevelt found his way out of the doldrums by aligning himself squarely with the women's labor movement, the Consumers' League, and child labor reformers when he publicly endorsed the work of Frances Perkins of the New York Consumer's League in trying to get rid of child labor in canneries. After the Triangle Shirtwaist Company fire on March 25, 1911, killed over 140 women workers because the employers locked doors and failed to provide for fire safety, activists saw more vividly than ever the price average people paid for courts that blocked labor legislation. Eighty thousand workers stood in silent vigil in New York City on April 5, angered that the state had failed to pass the necessary safety legislation.[7]

In the wake of the Triangle Shirtwaist fire, Stimson chaired a committee of safety to prevent future workplace tragedies, and activists close to Roosevelt and his ideas became leaders in the "golden era in remedial factory legislation" which followed the creation of Robert Wagner's Factory Investigating Commission. His old friend Tim Sullivan mentored Perkins and helped her get passed an important bill limiting the hours women worked in New York's factories. Many of the programs Roosevelt had defended in the Stimson campaign, all basic goals of the Consumers' League, finally gained a hearing. Consumers' League representatives took TR to visit Pennsylvania coal country, where he talked with men covered in coal dust and visited homes without adequate sewer systems. Though he wrote magazine articles about what he had seen, he knew nothing would change for the miners and their families without government intervention. Climbing out of his own depression was harder when the state of his country made him so angry.[8]

His speeches told audiences stories intended to shock their consciences. He spoke about young girls who had lost arms in dangerous machinery and employers who would neither pay compensation nor provide safe working conditions. When he tried to build public support for the Consumers'

League's legislative program, Pauline Goldmark and Owen Lovejoy of the National Child Labor Committee drafted memos which he put directly into his speeches and articles. He took what he called his "ambulatory rareshow" to the South, where he described himself in Birmingham, Alabama, as a "radical" who believed that "unless the majority of our people share to a certain extent in the prosperity, then the success and the prosperity amount to very little." He was applauded when he called for "using the collective power of the people to build up the weak," but the South refused to listen to his calls for abolishing child labor in factories.[9]

Roosevelt's alliance with the women's reform network was forged out of a shared commitment to fight for social democracy, but the women activists irritated him when they tried to push him so far leftward that he lost credibility in the Republican Party. Consumers' League advocates Florence Kelley and Maud Nathan had started to convince him that protective laws for working women and the legislative crusade against white slavery would never be passed unless women got the vote. On his way to give a speech in Chicago he heard Jane Addams' arguments for suffrage and told her afterward: "If you're for it, I'm for it." The Consumers' League activist Molly Dewson urged him to support suffrage, and he could see that twenty-five million new women voters might be more inclined to support his causes than regular male Republican Party members. He moved from mild support of state-by-state suffrage to all-out backing for the national suffrage, or Anthony Amendment, but that put him out on a limb in party politics.[10]

Too restless to stay at home, he agreed to make a western speaking tour. He and Edith visited Hull House and their many social worker friends there, before he went to dedicate Roosevelt Dam. He enjoyed seeing the Grand Canyon again and hearing praise for his work to save it as a national monument. Then he, Ethel, and Edith visited Archie at the Evans School. Though Archie was happy to see his family, he later recalled that he knew he was the weakling son his father never accepted: "I suppose that subconsciously I realized I was a misfit." Theodore loved Archie, but did not hide the fact he thought him stupid. Before Archie's senior year at Groton his parents decided the boy would need extra tutoring if he ever hoped to pass Harvard's preliminary exams.[11]

Theodore and Edith stayed with Ted and his wife, Eleanor, in San Francisco, and TR gave a speech at the University of California at Berkeley announcing: "I took the Isthmus, started the canal, and left Congress—not to debate the canal, but to debate me," which reasserted his importance in history but also invited renewed criticisms of his foreign policy. When he was not bragging about his bold acts as president, he looked like a man who was trying to build a new political coalition. He met with leaders of women's clubs and breakfasted with organizations of women voters in Washington. He later told Maud Nathan that his contact with women voters in the West helped make him a supporter of the national suffrage amendment, but it is much likelier the conversion took place in his daily talks around the water cooler in the United Charities Building. He warned western voters against using the referendum to cut university budgets, but the Associated Press refused to cover his western speeches at all.[12]

When TR sat at his desk in the library at Sagamore Hill in the spring and summer of 1911 he could see the wisteria blooming outside his window, exactly as Edith intended when she planted it there to serve as a reminder of how peaceful home could be. He lamented that "an ex-president has only a small field of possible work open to him," and insisted he did "not care a rap" that he was being attacked as too radical or ambitious. But he was not being entirely honest with himself. He was sincerely distressed that Republican bosses stood between him and the people who wanted to follow him. He was not having much luck working up support for his new ideas among party regulars.[13]

Being adrift professionally gave him more time to devote to being a father and a husband, and he took the greatest pleasure in watching his family grow up. He accompanied Archie to the Bronx Zoo to watch the chimps and at night tutored him in civics and history while Edith helped the boy with French. While Edith supervised the paving of a new road to the house, Ethel helped her mother run Sagamore Hill, but she confided in her diary that she longed to hold down a real job.[14]

Near tragedy struck in the middle of Roosevelt's reacquaintance with family life. On September 30, Edith and Theodore were riding on the paved Cove Road near the blacksmith shop in Oyster Bay when an automobile frightened Edith's horse, Pine Knot. The horse reared, and she was thrown against the pavement "with great violence" and was almost killed. When the doctor arrived it was not clear she would wake up. For two days she remained unconscious, with the family waiting impatiently for news. By October 5 she was awake but had lost some of her memory and her sense of smell and taste. A distraught Theodore wrote Corinne:

> I think Edith is better, and I believe her to be out of danger; but her recovery is very slow, and the doctors' statement that the pain would vanish has not proved correct. She is still in real agony, and I do not know when she will be able to leave the bed. There was a slight concussion of the brain, and a slight dislocation of the three upper cervical vertebrae. She had a

> very narrow escape. We have a trained nurse, and have so far been able to get along with only one, as I take care of Edith during the night, though I generally have to call the nurse and Ethel at least once.[15]

She was dazed and semi-conscious for another ten days. The weeks of hovering by Edith's bedside and being her night nurse had, TR confessed, driven him "nearly mad."[16]

He rubbed her back and recited poetry to her, but his warlike poems were not a comfort for her splitting headache. Finally he had to hire a second trained nurse so that he could get some sleep. With the prospect of losing Edith ever present, he restlessly wrote long letters to friends and rode Pine Knot back to the scene of the accident, where the horse also tried to throw TR. He held firm to the saddle, though, and promised she would never ride Pine Knot again. At other times, he simply waited: "Sometimes I just sat quietly and held her hand."[17]

With mortality so present in his mind, Theodore watched his wife's recovery as she went from semi-consciousness to being "very frail and feeble" by November. He did not know if she would ever be herself again, which Ethel said was "so hard on Father." In San Francisco, Ted and Eleanor had produced the first Roosevelt grandchild, Gracie, and before her accident Edith had planted a grove of pine trees where little Gracie could play someday. When she became strong enough to talk, Edith said she was sorry that Gracie would be out of baby clothes before they could see her. Edith was too weak to travel, so Theodore spent Thanksgiving at Groton with Quentin, who had suddenly grown taller than his father.[18]

In the stressful several weeks after Edith's accident TR began to waver about 1912. Her always restraining hand no longer held him back from what she knew was a quixotic path. The terror of facing her near death was a reminder that time might be short for him, too. He began to behave as if the coming campaign might be his "last chance" to make government respond to the needs of its people. And in public addresses, his strongest emotions came out when he talked about protecting women.

TR had stayed close to home for most of the time since her accident, but he kept an engagement to speak on the "Conservation of Womanhood and Childhood" on October 20 in New York. In a strong speech that was his response to the tragedy of the Triangle fire, he praised the New York Factory Commission which had been set up in the wake of the fire and urged the passage of stringent laws to provide safe workplaces. He attacked the canners, the textile, candy, and collar manufacturers who had opposed the fifty-four-hour workweek bill that Frances Perkins had tried to shepherd through the legislature, and called it a disgrace that the South resisted efforts to prohibit child labor below the age of fourteen. He told the story of Alma Whaley, the Tennessee textile laborer who had been working ten hours a day, six days a week since she was ten. Rather than live a life of industrial slavery, TR pointed out with high drama, Whaley drank carbolic acid in a suicide pact with other child workers.

Conserving womanhood and childhood was the heart of his talk, but, on Pauline Goldmark's suggestion, he added that fatherhood, too, would be hurt if industries kept men working such long hours at such pay that they could not play a role in family life. Home manufacturing and chronic unemployment also diminished family life, and children were losing their childhoods because "our national government has proved so supine." A stronger state could save the family—all the families.[19]

Though TR spoke to an enthusiastic audience about substantial national issues, the Democratic *New York Times* described the speech only as an attack on the courts. The *Times* also reported that a suffragist ran up after he spoke and pinned a white suffrage ribbon on his chest reading "Woman want the Ballot." Roosevelt knew that getting the public aroused about issues like child labor would be difficult, but a small step was taken when Congress finally passed the Children's Bureau bill which he had supported as president.[20]

It felt like a political slap in the face when on the day before Roosevelt's fifty-third birthday, the Taft administration suddenly brought an anti-trust suit against the Steel Trust. Taft's lawyers attacked Roosevelt's 1907 approval of U.S. Steel's purchase of the Tennessee Coal and Iron Company. Stimson wrote: "It was certainly a most extraordinary charge for the lawyers of any administration to level without warning at an ex-President of their own party." Right away TR wrote an article for *The Outlook* about anti-trust policy in which he defended his decision in the U.S. Steel case and criticized Taft's anti-trust policy, which he said was aimed at re-creating the business conditions of the eighteenth century.[21]

He decided that the trust problem could be solved by a regulatory commission that would prevent unfair competitive practices among businesses and ensure fair labor conditions, including wage levels, hours, and safety at work. Furthermore, he argued that price regulation could protect the consumer. The edition of *The Outlook* describing his radical trust policy sold out quickly and stimulated more talk than ever about his candidacy for president. The small group of business leaders who were sympathetic to welfare capitalism, profit sharing, government regulation, and improved labor conditions, but not anti-trust suits, preferred TR's trust policy to Taft's. A few, like George

Perkins, launched a TR for President movement, raising funds with promises of more sympathetic regulation of business. Newspapers reported that Roosevelt did not know of Perkins' fundraising. But when Perkins sent potential supporters to Sagamore Hill, Roosevelt, cagey on the issues, asked them: "Could I carry your state?"[22]

Before Edith's accident and the Steel Trust suit, her husband had begged progressives not to urge him to run. Then, while she was still "very much shattered," he told his friend, governor of California Hiram Johnson, "Now I would not feel that I had the right to object to being sacrificed if it were necessary to sacrifice me, if we had to lead a forlorn hope." He thought his *Outlook* article on business regulation ignited "a strong undercurrent of feeling about me," and he knew by the large crowds who followed him that his popularity was still a potent national force but not one that would necessarily hit hard enough against the almost immovable object of boss-ridden party politics. TR had tried once more to work toward progressive unity by meeting, with La Follette's knowledge, with several of the Wisconsinite's closest lieutenants for a "very frank" talk. He said he would run only if the senator's campaign stalled. By December he told James Garfield that he could not say he would not run. Garfield knew the race was starting.[23]

In December, Theodore and Edith celebrated their silver anniversary alone. He toasted her recovery with her grandfather's Madeira. They were joined by a houseful of children for a subdued Christmas which Ethel summarized as "Horrid Christmas. Sister very depressed and ill. Ted Away. Mother weak. F[ather] preoccupied. Archie away. K[ermit] leaving early for a jaunt." Edith had a serious relapse in the form of a facial erysipelas infection after the holidays, so nurses had to be hired to minister hypodermics of morphine. Theodore kept quieter than usual about his political quandary, but he asked his friend Florence La Farge if he could hold a secret "political rendezvous" with Westchester boss William Ward at her house. In a few months Ward would turn up as one of TR's delegate managers.[24]

Roosevelt had reason to be preoccupied about America's need for better leadership as 1912 began. In January the Lawrence, Massachusetts, mill workers' strike drew headlines when the children whose parents were striking were sent away to ensure they would not starve or be caught up in strike violence. As the children boarded the train, the local police beat them. TR's friend Senator Miles Poindexter tried to bring the plight of the children to the attention of the Senate, where he found "a lot of self-satisfied old fossils . . . chuckling or jeering over the unfortunate condition of these mill workers." *The Outlook* published a tepid article on Lawrence because the Wobblies, or

Industrial Workers of the World (I.W.W.), had come to town to work with the local strike leadership, and TR was finding even the reform magazine too conservative.[25]

He disagreed strongly with the other *Outlook* editors on the subject of lynching, which he saw as a form of lawlessness as bad as letting rapists out on light bail. The burning alive of a black man by a mob in Coatesville, Pennsylvania, in the summer of 1911 shocked Roosevelt into action. He, Booker T. Washington, and the N.A.A.C.P. leadership lobbied *The Outlook* to fight lynching in its pages, and Roosevelt published an anti-lynching article and complained to other anti-lynching crusaders that public opinion was hard to arouse on the subject. Then he wrote, with Florence Kelley's help, an article speaking out in favor of suffrage where women wanted it, but one of the Abbotts edited out of his original draft his strongest praise for the positive effects of suffrage in helping women fight for better working conditions.[26]

Roosevelt had moved to a position which his supporters read as a shift: he said he was definitely not a candidate but if the nomination were presented to him as "a genuine popular demand" he would not "shirk a plain duty if it came unmistakably as a plain duty." If that public sentiment did not already exist, TR's friends knew how to stimulate it. La Follette's campaign was foundering because his appeal was limited to the Midwest, and he was judged by professional politicians to be incapable of mounting a serious challenge to Taft. Roosevelt men started putting his name on primary ballots across the country.[27]

In late January, Gifford Pinchot, Medill McCormick, and Gilson Gardner went to La Follette and asked him to withdraw from the race and support TR. Though the press and many of his supporters told him he could not win, the senator would not give up, even if his staying in the race meant factional infighting would undermine progressive causes. He could not admit that his campaign had not yet attracted strong support outside the Midwest or that lack of money made his winning the nomination unlikely. La Follette let himself get so tired his speeches were often incomprehensible. Then, he lost control of himself with a fist-shaking, cantankerous, and rambling tirade against newspaper publishers at the Periodical Publishers Dinner on February 2, where he berated publishers for thinking only of profit and rarely of careful reporting of the truth. Newspapers already hostile to the Wisconsinite's anti-capitalist rhetoric unfairly reported his performance as a nervous breakdown.[28]

La Follette believed that his candidacy had been undermined by his supporters who were Roosevelt's friends. As if to prove that the senator's suspicions had foundation, Pinchot let the press know that La Follette's erratic behavior had wrecked his candidacy. Next, his manager announced the campaign was over, which La Follette contradicted. Pundits declared that the senator's gaffe "puts the Rep[ublican] nomination . . . very definitely in the hands of Col Theodore Roosevelt."[29]

The suspense was building in February as rumors spread that TR would announce his candidacy any day. Evidence of widespread public support came from many quarters. Spontaneous Roosevelt meetings were being held across the country after local polls showed 60 percent of Republicans favored TR. Oklahoma was already reported to have three hundred Roosevelt Clubs. Then, by prearrangement with Sagamore Hill, the governors of seven states issued a public request for him to run.[30]

In private, on February 5, Roosevelt promised Pinchot, who already dreamed of founding a third party if TR did not get the Republican nomination, "he would 'stay through' if he did not get a single vote in the convention." He also asked Pinchot to write a platform for him. Pinchot may have misunderstood this as a commitment to bolt if the Republican nomination went to Taft, which was not TR's intent. Roosevelt reiterated his ideas about a New Nationalism in Columbus, where he spoke about the "Charter of Democracy," but then added controversial remarks on the recall of state judicial decisions. He argued that courts had blocked legislatures' attempts to address social and industrial injustice so the people needed some new device for overruling such decisions. His Columbus speech would come back to haunt him and some said would prevent him from being nominated, even though he had earlier spoken out for recall without starting an uproar.[31]

Early in February, Edith and Theodore moved into a cousin's house in Manhattan to escape the frigid winds of Sagamore Hill, but he evaded discussing what the months ahead might mean. Edith called the politics of 1912 "hateful" and said her husband's decision to run made her "gloomy." But she did not have the strength to try to stop him. He dismissed her sour mood, because, he said, "she has never regained her health." He evidently never considered the strain the campaign would bring upon his family, especially his fragile wife. She and Ethel planned a trip to the Caribbean to gain some stamina for what was coming.[32]

Alice called Edith on February 15 and learned that the announcement that TR would run was coming shortly. Nick Longworth declared that if Roosevelt challenged Taft for the Republican nomination, it would provoke a tragedy. He also told his wife he would not be able to run for Congress again because he owed allegiance to Taft and the Ohio Republicans, though he believed in most of the ideas of his father-in-law. Alice was certain Edith could bear the slander of a nasty campaign, but she was not sure how her own marriage would fare. When she came to Sagamore Hill to see Ted and Eleanor the next week, she got up early to talk politics alone with her father, who told her he thought Taft had a three-to-one chance of losing the nomination. Theodore at that moment believed he could win; the cheering crowds had lured him into political combat.[33]

On February 21, TR told a reporter: "My hat is in the ring, the fight is on and I am stripped to the buff." Alice and the rest of the family were "exploding with excitement." But his candidacy forced tough choices on his friends. Elihu Root's personal fondness for Roosevelt was not enough to make him a supporter, but he turned down Taft's pleas for help in the Ohio primary. A "miserably unhappy" Senator Lodge sought counsel with Alice, whom he considered "a good politician." Since his career was tied to the incumbent President and his views on recall and many direct democracy measures and labor issues were like Taft's he could not support his old friend. Former La Follette men like Amos and Gifford Pinchot, Gilson Gardner, Medill McCormick, and James Garfield eagerly joined the Roosevelt campaign along with Democrats like Ben Lindsey, who had been organizing Woodrow Wilson Clubs locally.[34]

Eleanor and Franklin Roosevelt adored Uncle Theodore and believed in many of his causes, though neither was as liberal as he on labor and suffrage issues in 1912. Franklin's budding career as a Democratic state senator stopped him from making any public gesture of support. Only Franklin's mother, Sara, sent money and turned up at Roosevelt headquarters, where she saw many relatives and friends. The 1912 conflict proved so painful to Archie Butt, the Roosevelts' military aide who had become like a brother to Taft, that he fled to Europe for a rest. Before he could come home to face his divided loyalty he died on the *Titanic.*[35]

With Roosevelt running, La Follette had little chance to be anything but a spoiler. But an adept spoiler he would be—attacking TR viciously in his serialized *Autobiography*, hinting that his rival was beholden to the railroads, and making the public charge that men like Gifford Pinchot had sabotaged the La Follette campaign. A year earlier when he had assumed TR would not run, he did all he could to praise the Colonel, but when his ambition was thwarted, La Follette lashed out at TR on the campaign trail as an "inconsequential playboy."[36]

March began "in mad haste" for TR because local authorities called him for jury duty just as he was setting up his campaign organization. Taft's forces were trying to stop states from choosing convention delegates by letting voters register their preference in presidential primaries, and the followers of Roosevelt and La Follette were backing primaries. The first primary, North Dakota, went to La Follette because of a local factional dispute, but TR blithely claimed it as a victory for anti-Taft forces. In a few nonprimary states where a caucus of party members voted unanimously for Roosevelt, it outraged him when the Taft organizers threw out the results and held new caucuses stacked with Taft men. Roosevelt had long known that any sitting president could manipulate the system to overrule what the voters wanted, especially in this era when caucuses chose more delegates than primaries. Nevertheless, he was shocked when Taft pulled strings to get the nomination.[37]

While Theodore struggled to run a campaign, Alice and Nick fought regularly. Alice was devoted to her father's cause, and Nick had finally decided to run for reelection and support Taft. She made repeated trips to Sagamore Hill to be closer to the action. Her father told her he could win the nomination if only the major newspapers would cover his views fairly. Hearst's *New York American*, Pulitzer's *New York World*, the *New York Times*, the conservative *Los Angeles Times*, and most other powerful papers were against him. But TR still had sympathetic coverage from the Scripps papers, *Munsey's*, the *Boston Transcript*, and the *New York Evening Mail*, the *New York Tribune*, the *Chicago Tribune*, the *Kansas City Star*, the *Philadelphia North American*, the *Washington Times*, the *American Review of Reviews*, *Collier's*, and, of course, *The Outlook*. He hoped that his popularity with the New York Press Club would help him get more positive coverage.[38]

Alice saw 1912 as her chance—at long last—to win her father's love. As he left work at *The Outlook*, she met him on the Long Island Railroad and went with him to Sagamore Hill. While Ethel and Edith were on vacation in the Caribbean, Alice talked nonstop politics with him over a rare dinner when they had no visitors. It was her first chance to be her father's advisor and a respected political mind, and, if she alienated her husband in the process, it was worth it to her. Alice hated to return to Washington, where she soon got into an argument when her friends accused TR of mad ambition, and Nick told her unequivocally to "shut up" about her father's candidacy. Alice thought Edith had been "stony and unsympathetic about F[ather]" and his campaign, so she sought to replace her stepmother as the loyal family member who was "with [him] mind heart and soul."[39]

Edith cabled her husband that she was extending her trip southward, and he wrote in exasperation to Kermit: "I don't know how it was settled as to which one's health demanded the Costa Rica trip!" He predicted that when he asked her why she stayed away so long his wife would "be very pretty and alert and defiant, and explain that it is because she has grown so independent on account of my going to Africa and leaving her all alone." He admitted to being lonely without Edith, but Alice's visit had been a comfort. He explained to Kermit that Alice "felt she just had to see me because of course all respectable society is now apoplectic with rage over me."[40]

His campaign for the nomination, however, was even more daunting because he had inadequate staff support. Before long, Roosevelt was "driven nearly to death." Newspapers were accusing him of being on the take from Andrew Carnegie because the steel magnate had funded part of the Smithsonian collection from TR's Africa trip. Alice chose the heat of the campaign to consort with the enemy, attending Washington parties for the Tafts where she flirted with William Randolph Hearst, with whom she made a date to meet at the Democratic convention. Hearst, she knew, agreed with her father on many issues, but nothing she could say or do could stop him from following a vicious anti-Roosevelt editorial policy. The publisher resurrected stale charges of Standard Oil influence over the Republican Party, just as Pulitzer's *World* would claim that TR was a pawn of big corporate interests. Though her father considered Hearst an "unspeakable blackguard," Alice saw him again to find out as much as possible about his plans to sabotage her father's campaign and elect a Democratic candidate.[41]

With a race for the nomination to be run, Theodore's spirits, even under attack, brightened considerably. Edith observed wryly: "He always answers to the spur," and the stimulation of being in the running again made him feel more alive.[42] After Ben Lindsey visited TR at Sagamore Hill he wrote home to friends in Colorado:

> I had a *great* visit with T.R. He is *just* great, great! Never saw him in better, fitter shape for the fight, and *radical*—just as radical as we want him. Had a private conference with him and his manager, Mr. [Medill] McCormick last night at Sagamore Hill. *Just a few friends*, Anne Morgan among them.[43]

Anne Morgan had been a prominent Mink Brigade supporter of the Triangle strike, and her left-of-center views were distinctly at odds with her father, J. P. Morgan, who bankrolled Taft. But her presence signaled a new constituency working for Roosevelt that spring, the women's reform network. He had followed their advice on social justice, and they saw his campaign as a logical extension of their presence in municipal reform, settlement work, and the labor movement. Woman's Roosevelt Leagues cropped up across the country long before any campaign organization existed in most states. Ethel's friend Dorothy Whitney Straight joined Anne Morgan, the Pinchots, Lucius Littauer, and others in financing Roosevelt's spring campaign for the Republican nomination.[44]

The season opened when Roosevelt's manager Medill McCormick challenged Taft to meet his opponent in direct primaries. The presidential race in 1912 would not be like the one in 1904 because for the first time primaries were a major factor in choosing nominees, and no one was sure how it would work. Fourteen states were holding primaries to select delegates. Before presidential primaries were invented by progressive reformers, party regulars and officials voted in caucus or held closed meetings to choose delegates to the nominating convention. In 1912 far more states held caucuses than primaries, so incumbents, from the President down to the county chairman, could push caucuses toward the candidate they preferred, in this case, Taft. Though primaries drew the greatest press coverage and seemed to gauge best the will of the people, what mattered most was the final delegate count when the nominating convention began, as Roosevelt would soon discover.

TR became an advocate of primaries because they let more voters choose the party's nominee, and they loosened officials' control over the nomination process. He welcomed the new era of successive primaries, which the press reported as a series of horse races because when it came to vote-getting he had become quite a thoroughbred. Media interpreters had never spoken with one voice, but during his presidency they had spread his viewpoint and news of his greatest political feats across the land. He had no reason to expect different treatment now, and he urged more states to adopt primaries as quickly as possible.

When progressives like TR introduced presidential primaries, they prolonged the decision-making process and brought it into fuller public view. Voters in primary states received more attention from candidates than voters in caucus states. In the long run, primaries also enlarged the role of the media, and donors gained influence because multi-state primary campaigns in the public view were more expensive to run than secretive caucuses.

The Republican nominating process was not supposed to be like 1908, when TR dictated from Washington the selection of Taft. Primaries were invented to make the search for delegates more challenging. But not all primary states were holding free elections. In New York the Democratic Murphy machine and the Republican Barnes machine specialized in voting fraud and voter confusion with fourteen-foot-long ballots in some districts. So Roosevelt had to run against corruption first and Taft second. New York's Roosevelt

Committee offered $500 to anyone who could prove polling place impropriety. It was no accident that poll inspectors were being politically pressured and fired as the primary approached.[45]

Caucus states were even worse. Roosevelt men were excluded from caucuses in the South where blacks were largely disenfranchised and a white Republican was hard to find, and Taft sent organizers to make sure southern delegates would go his way. In hotly contested caucus states talk about federal officeholders being pressured to support Taft started as early as March, and no one dared run a front porch campaign in 1912.[46]

AT THE STAR Casino in New York City on March 25, while Roosevelt was in the middle of a deeply felt speech about voting fraud and how hard it was to guarantee impartial poll watchers, he was interrupted by a woman who shouted from the audience: "Should not the women be allowed to vote, Mr. Roosevelt?" He responded politely that he thought women should vote to decide whether they should get suffrage. She persisted with other questions until the angry crowd cried: "Order! order!" and "Woman, you go home and take care of your children." TR called on the crowd not to throw her out, but the woman would not stop asking questions. She shouted: "You are no square deal, Mr. Roosevelt." Confusion reigned as the crowd hissed and booed. The band started to play, and it was impossible for TR to go on with his speech. He tried to regain control of the meeting, saying, as she was removed by special police: "Friends, wait a minute; wait a minute. Now, I am particularly anxious to treat any woman with the utmost respect. . . . Anything that the women of the country want, I want to give them."[47]

The crowd was his again. He was a seasoned stump campaigner who had had many speeches disrupted by critics, hecklers, and opponents over the years. Yet, even when he managed a heckler graciously, he had not anticipated how disruptive it would be when his speeches were interrupted by suffragists. He wanted them on his side, so he moved closer to declaring himself on their issue.

On April 2, TR left Sagamore for a five-state, nine-day campaign trip "naturally very fussed" over the support Taft would get from the Lorimer machine in Illinois. He campaigned to large audiences and canvassed voters with the help of Hull House and a wide range of Illinois progressives and labor people. He beat Taft handily in the Illinois primary and campaigned in Pennsylvania, where he told Gifford Pinchot he had "his fighting clothes on." He held up before the crowd a pay envelope of a mill worker whose wage was $25 but who had debts to his employer for rent and purchases at the company store totaling $23.23. Roosevelt charged this practice was an "outrage," and his audience cheered. He won another stunning victory in Pennsylvania, which would soon be followed by triumphs in Nebraska, Oregon, California, and Maryland.[48]

Taft finally decided to fight back. Angered by his benefactor's criticisms of the courts and egged on by his advisors, Taft took on the Osawatomie speech, declaring: "When the demagogue mounts the platform and announces that he prefers the man above the dollar he ought to be interrogated as to what he means thereby." TR countered that he had merely been quoting Abraham Lincoln about putting the man above the dollar.[49] Taft had also claimed that the Colonel belonged among the "political emotionalists and neurotics," that he was promoting class hatred, and that he was a dangerous man.[50] Roosevelt replied that Taft was the bosses' candidate, that he had "been disloyal to our past friendship" in the vicious way he had conducted his campaign, and charged him with a "scandalous abuse of patronage" in pressuring federal officeholders to support him at the convention.[51]

And it soon got even nastier. Lodge's ambitious son-in-law, August Gardner, accused Roosevelt of having protected the International Harvester Company from anti-trust prosecution as president. Worse yet, Taft produced documents to add suspicion about the suit, and the contest threatened to degenerate into name-calling and debates about who said what at cabinet meetings in 1907.

When Roosevelt warned voters that "if on this continent we merely build another country of great but unjustly divided material prosperity, we shall have done nothing," he made wealthy voters nervous. As they gathered in their mansions and private clubs, many of his Harvard classmates "now felt sure he was crazy." California newspapers were spreading reports that TR had been drunk on the campaign trail. Taft warned that Roosevelt "would hurry us into a condition which would find no parallel except in the French Revolution." Irwin Cobb of Pulitzer's *World* wrote that Roosevelt was "the most cunning and adroit demagogue that modern civilization has produced since Napoleon III."[52]

Taft announced that the primary vote in his home state of Ohio would decide the nomination. He tried to win the black vote by criticizing TR for discharging innocent soldiers in the Brownsville case, but the Roosevelt campaign pointed out that Taft as secretary of war had recommended the dismissal. When he was criticized for breaking the third-term tradition, TR dredged up the fact that Taft's father had been active in the third term for Grant movement in 1880, and that, as long as the terms were not consecutive, charges of dictatorship were ridiculous.[53]

Their Ohio showdown proved to be a strain on Roosevelt because he had "no right hand man" in the state and had to act as his own advance man and take care of travel plans. He won the black vote there by stating he stood for "equality of opportunity"; he also had a better record than Taft on appointing blacks to office, preaching against lynching, and building long-term relationships with black leaders. He told Ohio audiences that Taft "has forgotten the plain people," and on primary day Roosevelt beat Taft in his home state by 47,000 votes.[54]

In private, the feud made for ugly feelings. Roosevelt seethed that Taft was a "puzzlewit" who was "behaving like a blackguard," and Taft grieved over "the hold which Roosevelt still has over the plain people" and broke down sobbing after he had attacked his old friend. A mutual friend visited TR to express Taft's private hope that after the campaign they could return to their former warm friendship. But the President also bitterly awaited the day when "almost the insanity of megalomania that possess[es] Theodore Roosevelt will make [itself] known to the American people." Taft found the campaign he was waging distasteful and seriously considered withdrawing from the race. But he stayed in because he believed his rival's judicial recall plan was dangerous. Both men got so caught up in the personal emotions of their feud that they lost track of the issues.[55]

TR came home to Sagamore Hill believing that his Ohio victory "should settle the question of the nomination." He told friends that if the newspapers reported more accurately what he said, people would support him in droves. Furthermore, he convinced himself that he had enough delegates to win the nomination even though he knew the Republican National Committee had the power to disqualify contested delegates. He had, in fact, won 278 delegates in the primaries, far more than Taft's 48 and La Follette's 36. But he ignored the fact that the struggle was not over. The contest over delegates had already threatened to break out into violence more than once: In Missouri men armed with baseball bats fought each other at the "ball bat convention" to see whether their state would go for Taft or Roosevelt. In Michigan state troops had to stop fights between Taft and Roosevelt men. The convention would not be cut and dried for Roosevelt.[56]

The excitement of the campaign had spread into his family. Kermit stayed up all night in Roosevelt headquarters in Boston to hear the disappointing news that his father had split the Massachusetts delegation with Taft. Ethel and the Roosevelt cousins were jubilant over each victory as they worked in Roosevelt campaign headquarters in Manhattan. Ethel wrote that the "campaign is all that means anything to us now." Edith stayed at Sagamore Hill for most of the time comforting Alice over the phone when her Longworth in-laws were nasty to her, and Nick forbade her to visit him in Ohio because she was so outspoken in support of her father. Before her accident Edith had been involved in a movement to provide villagers with more recreation, including a park, bandstand, and tennis court, but now she had limited energy, which she saved for her children, especially Alice, who wrote in her diary that her stepmother had been "so dear & kind & sympathetic."[57]

All spring Alice was obsessed with her father's campaign. She read ten newspapers a day and kept on the phone to the campaign and the family. When Lodge asked Nick to write TR to stop him from attacking Governor Murray Crane of Massachusetts, Alice judged Lodge's request "a piece of unparalleled cheek" which proved that Lodge had lost all "sense of proportion." Since most of her social world in Washington accepted the "power mad" view of her father's campaign, she found herself defending TR again and again at embassy receptions. As her marriage became strained, she alternated between being "nearly wild with excitement and anticipation" and taking to her bed with odd pains. She timed her trips to Sagamore Hill to coincide with her father's homecomings, and she appreciated Edith's calm as they walked to Cooper's Bluff and sat on the beach looking at the far-off mist on Long Island Sound.[58]

In the middle of his father's political struggle, Archie wrote what TR called "vulgar and profane" remarks about Rector Endicott Peabody on the outside of a letter he sent to a friend at Groton and was promptly expelled for it. Always oblivious to how much his four sons disliked Peabody and Groton, Theodore wrote his old friend that he was sure Archie "loves" you, but he was "passing through a phase of thinking it manly to be tough and swear." Edith was furious that the rector had bothered her husband instead of taking the matter up with her first, and Archie's standing in the family sank to its lowest depths ever.[59]

Edith was proud that her husband was "making an uphill fight for what he believes in," but she did find amusement in the fact that his hair had been straight before but "is now curling vigorously,—due to psychical electricity doubtless!" She was used to having him criticized in public and she confided to friends: "When I am angry or sad I remember that the mountain tops are always lonely." She worried about Quentin, who was being ostracized at Groton for his father's politics. Cruelty from his peers, she said, ate away at his "big tender heart," which always reminded her of Thee's. After the "spiteful folly" of Lodge's son-in-law attacking TR's action in the International Harvester case, Edith wrote Bamie that Theodore "bears all these worries and hurts marvelously," though his voice was hoarse and his chest was "tired."[60]

If presidential primaries and popular votes had been the deciding factors in 1912, TR unequivocally would have won the Republican nomination. But primaries were new and in most states party caucuses could be manipulated by the incumbent. After the primary season TR had won 411 convention votes, Taft 201, La Follette 36, Albert Cummins 10, and 420 were either uninstructed or disputed. The Taft-controlled Republican National Committee would decide on the contested delegates, which did not bode well for TR.[61]

When Roosevelt finally had a chance to relax by early June, he suspected what lay ahead at the Republican convention. Taft forces would not give up easily, though gossips reported to Alice that the President was sleeping a lot and Mrs. Taft was so upset she was "incoherent." TR's humor had not disappeared in the duress of the campaign, and he joked that "Mr. Taft only discovered that I was dangerous to the people after I discovered that he was useless to the people." Reporters told him they had heard he would break with tradition and make a personal appearance at the Republican convention. Newspapers recorded that he made a "comical grimace" and replied: "By George! that's the first time I'd heard it. But with my Machiavellian disposition, I may have concealed it from myself, don't you know."[62]

He was forced to go to Chicago, however, when his convention managers complained that a Taft steamroller was stealing delegates. Roosevelt bundled together a horde of relatives and took the train there on June 14. They were greeted by fifty thousand supporters who had broken through police lines, "cheering at the top of their lungs." Out on Michigan Avenue ten thousand handbills announced that TR would soon walk on the waters of Lake Michigan. To make the primaries count as the voice of the people, Kermit met with delegates at party headquarters and Roosevelt spoke with small groups at the Congress Hotel to hold their votes. William Jennings Bryan, present as a Hearst newspaper reporter, found his old rival "as buoyant as I have ever seen him." Bryan thought the attendance of the "leading candidate" at a party convention—a first—added a touch of novelty to an already contentious show.[63]

Bands played "There'll Be a Hot Time in the Old Town Tonight" when TR waved to crowds from his hotel balcony, and no one slept much. When he addressed a huge mass meeting Roosevelt spoke with great emotion to remind his followers that the progressive cause was much larger than a contest over the presidential nomination:

> What happens to me is not of the slightest consequence; I am to be used, as in doubtful battle any man is used, to his hurt or not, so long as he is useful, and is then cast aside or left to die. I wish you to feel this. I mean it; and I shall need no sympathy when you are through with me, for this

> fight is far too great to permit us to concern ourselves about any man's welfare. . . . We fight in honorable fashion for the good of mankind; fearless of the future; unheeding of our individual fate; with unflinching hearts and undimmed eyes; we stand at Armageddon, and we battle for the Lord.[64]

Reporter Bryan wrote that when TR got around to talking issues he sounded a whole lot like a Democrat, even a Bryan Democrat. When he heard Roosevelt denounce the evil influence of special privilege and corporate greed, Bryan could only remark dryly: "He probably feels more strongly stirred to action to-day because he was so long unconscious of the forces at work thwarting the popular will." For TR's die-hard followers every word was truth, every word was original, every word was an invitation to act. That night Alice wrote: "You could feel the tension in the air."[65]

Roosevelt fed on the sociability and excitement of the convention. When William Allen White brought the young short-story writer Edna Ferber to the Congress Hotel to meet the former president, he dropped politics to tell her that in her next story she should have her popular businesswoman heroine Emma McChesney combine marriage and a career. Ferber was "disarmed" and charmed. Edith would hardly recommend combining marriage with the arduous career of politician's wife because she was "dead tired" as she gave a tea for newspaperwomen and received friends and supporters from around the country. Because of her weak health she felt the "strain of these days" more than anyone else. She and Alice had suggested cuts in her husband's Armageddon speech, and Edith helped mobilize the family to work toward the nomination of the man the conventioneers called the "Big Noise."[66]

The Taft-dominated credentials committee would decide which of the 252 contested seats rightfully belonged to Taft, Roosevelt, or La Follette. Early reports looked bad for Roosevelt. The irony was that Taft did not want the nomination anymore. He told a supporter that he was staying in the race to save the country from Roosevelt's radicalism. Ethel, who now felt "that politics is all that's worth while," overheard meetings in her parents' rooms about plans for the Roosevelt forces to "bolt" if the credentials committee refused to seat legally elected Roosevelt delegates. Some recalled that TR argued against a third party even after the outcome of the fight over delegates became clear, yet others believed he had been moving toward the third-party idea for a long time.[67]

Roosevelt's advisors, Learned Hand, George Rublee, and Joseph Cotton, found him uncomprehending about the tariff and open-minded about most reform issues, but convinced unequivocally that the Republican Party was "a class party" under Taft. Even before the convention, TR had written: "I have absolutely no affiliations with any party," and as the convention proceeded he came to the realization that he was not a Republican anymore.[68]

The Taft-dominated platform committee turned down the most revered woman in America, Jane Addams, when she asked it to endorse woman suffrage, and rejected prominent social workers who presented a platform for national minimums modeled after the British program of the same name. Paul Kellogg of *Survey* magazine then brought the national minimums platform to TR, who had already supported most of its planks, and got a more sympathetic hearing. Roosevelt had already been talking about a national health service and a social welfare bureau in the federal government, and Florence Kelley had given him an abundance of facts and figures about the need for a minimum wage.[69]

When the convention finally opened at the Coliseum, hope lingered that Roosevelt would be nominated because he had won so many delegates in the primaries. One tipsy Rough Rider threatened to shoot up the convention if the nomination was stolen from his old colonel, so TR turned the man over to his valet, James Amos, who got the man so drunk he could not pick up his gun.[70]

Taft had chosen as his convention manager the Albany Republican boss, William Barnes, who was later charged with taking kickbacks on the state's printing contract. Barnes told the delegates that they must "preserve the Republic and the Constitution against monarchy" by voting against TR, which disgusted young Nicholas Roosevelt, who was running errands for his cousin Theodore. In the eyes of the cynical Pennsylvania boss Boies Penrose, who took money from mill owners to block child labor legislation, all progressive reformers like the teetotaler Gifford Pinchot really needed was a good stiff drink. With bosses like Barnes, Lorimer, and Penrose lined up against them, Roosevelt supporters were going to lose no matter how much they shouted about reform at the convention.[71]

TR proved "wonderfully cheerful" until he saw the forces arrayed against him. La Follette delegates threw their support to Taft to elect Elihu Root as temporary chairman, a serious defeat for Roosevelt. To have his old friends Lodge and Root in control of the convention made his impending defeat even more painful. Root let contested delegates vote, which meant that the fraudulent had as much influence as the elected. La Follette then instructed his delegates to do all they could to prevent Roosevelt's nomination. Then, Governor Herbert Hadley of Missouri and Senator Cummins were proposed as compromise candidates. Though Edith was lying down with a headache, TR called her into a meeting with his advisors, and she apparently urged him to step aside so that Hadley could get the nomination. But he did not take her advice because he could not let go of a nomination which he believed the voters had given him. Roosevelt would not release his delegates until the fraudulent ones were expelled.[72]

Grass-roots supporters on the floor loved Roosevelt. When on the second day of the convention a woman dressed in white—the color of the suffragists—stood up in the balcony and waved a picture of TR, she set off a forty-minute demonstration and parade around the perimeter of the Coliseum. She was joined by a swaying golden California bear sent by Hiram Johnson's stalwarts. Though the demonstration turned the convention floor into pandemonium, it did not change the roll call. News came that TR's men had walked out of the credentials committee after the Taft men disqualified 90 elected Roosevelt delegates. Of the 252 contested seats the committee awarded 238 to Taft. California's Roosevelt delegation wanted to walk out of the convention altogether, but the caucus decided it was "best to keep silent but not leave."[73]

The credentials fight had determined the outcome of the convention, and on June 20, TR wrote that "successful fraud and deliberate theft" had ruined the Republican Party. Even Taft's most sympathetic biographer later admitted that "a proportion of the Taft delegates had been illegally chosen." When Senator Warren G. Harding of Ohio put Taft's name in nomination, the convention was disrupted by gallery cries of "steamroller" and chants of "Choo-choo" as Roosevelt delegates, now numbering 343, sat refusing to participate.[74]

Alice's feverish desire to be everywhere, to know everything, and to will the right outcome into being pushed her to forget that her husband, who sat next to her in the Roosevelt family seats, watched Harding's nominating speech for Taft without seeing him as she did. When Harding told Nick he would gladly support him for governor, Alice chimed in to say that they would not accept any such crumbs from his vile hands. Stunned that she would presume to speak for him, and so peremptorily, Nick was "furious" with her.[75]

Taft won the Republican nomination that night without high drama or a conviction that he could win in November. Instead of paying attention to that awful fact, Alice was completely caught up in the "spirit buoyancy & enthusiasm" of the Roosevelt delegates who met at Orchestra Hall to begin a third party. A young social worker had organized a parade of supporters wearing red bandannas, and TR wore one around his neck as he spoke to his new party. Because Alice saw that meeting as "one of the greatest nights of my life—A new party has come into being," she was angry that Nick did not share her enthusiasm. What Ethel called "Crusaders in their Holy War" listened as TR prepared them for what promised to be a "hard fight."[76]

Back home after Chicago, ready to plan for the third party, TR waited to see whom the Democrats would nominate. He knew he could win if the Democrats chose the conservative Champ Clark. They might pick Woodrow Wilson, who had an outstanding record as a reform governor of New Jersey. He supported the regulation of utilities and advocated a corrupt practices law, a workmen's compensation law, and the direct election of senators. Roosevelt thought he would probably lose to Wilson, who would get the Solid Democratic South and many progressive votes. Even William Jennings Bryan had been disgusted when Taft claimed his party had been saved by his nomination. Bryan wrote that Taft showed "an astounding indifference to the intelligence of the public" because "both he and Senator Root know that he was not the choice of a majority of the Republican voters." Furthermore, Bryan understood that TR could win in November if Clark got the nomination, so when the Democratic convention met in Baltimore in July, Bryan threw his support to Wilson and to a platform that called for a single-term presidency.[77]

With Wilson running, TR could have positioned himself as a centrist and calmed the fears of those who saw him as a threat to the Republic. At times in the 1912 presidential campaign, he did try reassurance as a campaign strategy. But his major reason for running what he knew in his more reasonable moods would be a losing race was to move the American polity left, to introduce new ideas that others, perhaps Wilson, would carry into legislation. As letters from supporters around the country poured in, it was clear that TR's talk against special privilege had touched a deep nerve. The magnitude of his mail alone was a testament to public concern about a "crisis unparalleled since the decade prior to the Civil War." In response, he kept running hard. Though bosses like Barnes would demonize Roosevelt as a new Jacobin, his followers believed that he "incarnate[d] social justice."[78]

Taft dismissed TR as "a freak, almost, in the zoological garden" and "the most dangerous man that we have had in this country since its origin," a demagogue who wanted to turn his adherents into "Holy Rollers." But he also dismissed Wilson as an opportunist who gave "purring and ladylike" speeches. The National Progressive Party, which was now being called the Bull Moose Party because of TR's remark about feeling "as fit as a Bull Moose," sought to become a permanent alternative to the two old parties which TR called mere "husks." It became America's closest flirtation with creating a multi-partied system.[79]

Roosevelt asked Gifford Pinchot, George Rublee, and Learned Hand to work on the Bull Moose platform, which sent donor George Perkins into "a perpetual state of jitters" as he waited to see how radical it would be. TR listened as well to his Female Brain Trust, especially Jane Addams, Frances Kellor, and Florence Kelley, and to his social worker allies, Henry Moskowitz, John Kingsbury, and Paul Kellogg, who helped write the historic social welfare planks—minimum wage, old-age insurance, health insurance. At a time when most mainstream party leaders, including Taft and Wilson, considered the minimum wage a dangerous quack remedy, Kelley credited the Bull Moose campaign for its passage in eight states.[80]

TR finally took the full suffrage plunge and endorsed the Anthony Amendment at a time when coming out for woman suffrage invited attacks on a man's masculinity. For example, the reporter Will Irwin, who marched for woman suffrage in Manhattan parades, was jeered at as a "Sissy," and one aristocratic hostess spat in his face.[81]

Roosevelt's old concerns about manliness and his desire to appear as forceful as possible in a year when he had come out for suffrage made him careful about what kind of figure he cut in the newsreels. When Pathé News came to make a newsreel of his life at Sagamore Hill for use in the fall campaign he refused to be filmed playing tennis because, he said, "some people think tennis is effeminate." Instead, he asked to be shown jumping with his horse, playing with his dogs, and chopping down a tree.[82]

Reform groups had high expectations for the platform, especially on race. The most advanced leaders of the N.A.A.C.P., including Jane Addams, W.E.B. Du Bois, Henry Moskowitz, Joel Spingarn, and Lillian Wald, hoped that the Roosevelt campaign would help them fight disenfranchisement, lynching, and segregation. What they had not expected was Roosevelt's anger at southern black Republicans. TR was especially bitter about the charges that Taft paid black delegates in the South to vote against the Roosevelt ticket. Before TR came to the Bull Moose convention in August, Du Bois, working through his N.A.A.C.P. allies Spingarn and Addams, presented a racial equality plank to the platform committee. Du Bois recommended two ideas that TR privately favored: ending lynching and cutting southern congressional delegations where blacks were not allowed to vote. Most significantly, Du Bois included the prohibition of segregation in housing laws, the military, education, and public transportation. He had, in effect, asked the Bull Moose to kill Jim Crow. Newspapers said Roosevelt accepted Du Bois' racial equality plank.[83]

But he did not. Roosevelt said he feared it would ignite racial conflict. He recalled the sting of the attacks on him for socializing with Booker T. Washington, and he knew men like Josephus Daniels, Walter Hines Page, and Thomas Dixon, Jr., had recently risen to power across the South by inciting race hatred and posing as defenders of endangered white womanhood when they disenfranchised blacks. If he supported Du Bois he would lose the South and create an uproar in the North. He still dreamed of winning the Solid South away from the Democrats, and he told his friend John Parker of Louisiana: "Really if I could carry one of the eleven ex-Confederate states, I should feel as though I could die happy."[84]

His divided heart on race made him at once ready both to abandon all pretenses of seeking racial justice if he could win back the presidency and fight for what he knew was right. On one level he agreed with Du Bois' goals, but he viewed them as unattainable in 1912. Roosevelt had denounced the southern Democrats for grasping power "by encouraging the hatred of the white man for the black," and he had been one of the few white national voices to call the southern rape scare false and pernicious. But he was also feeling spiteful about the criticism he had drawn from Niagara Conference activists like Du Bois for his dismissal of the Brownsville soldiers. He decided not to risk further controversy by advocating racial equality in his platform.[85]

He also faced a moral dilemma about seating contested delegates from the South. Roosevelt never accepted a blanket policy of seating only "lily-white" delegates, but after years of trying to build a Republican Party in the South in partnership with Washington, TR now turned against the black men from the rotten-borough districts in the South for electing fraudulent Taft delegates in Chicago. In a public letter to delegate Julian Harris of Georgia he wrote that though he supported equal rights for blacks, he also believed an integrated Republican Party had failed in the South. He ordered the credentials committee to give each disputed delegation a fair hearing, but after his Harris letter they decided in favor of few southern black delegates. Delegates like William Flinn protested "lily-whitism" in the Bull Moose Party, but the credentials committee also refused to seat delegates representing Asian-Americans from Hawaii. The committee asserted that Progressives wanted "a white man's party."[86]

Roosevelt rationalized the emerging racial policies of the Bull Moose Party by claiming that enlightened white Progressive leaders would "set their faces sternly against lynch law and mob violence" and make war on peonage and "fight to keep the school funds equitably divided between white and colored schools." TR promised that the Bull Moose Party would act "with fuller recognition of the rights of the colored man than ever the Republican Party did." Newspapers reported that on the grass-roots level in the North and the South the Progressive Party was open to blacks, and in New York the Bull Moose state committee recommended that wherever blacks were a substantial part of the population they should be guaranteed 10 percent representation among the state's delegation.[87]

With his racial equality platform rejected, Du Bois understandably left the Bull Moose Party and embraced Wilson. Roosevelt's failure to stand up for racial equality seriously marred his record as a reformer, even though he later served on an N.A.A.C.P. committee and tried to get the Republican Party to accept some of Du Bois' proposals in its 1916 platform.[88]

Despite his unwillingness to tie the goal of racial justice to his Bull Moose campaign, TR kept the support of many black leaders. Black progressives formed local organizations and held a national "Roosevelt Progressive Colored Republican" convention. In states like Indiana leading black politicians supported the Bull Moose Party. The radical editor of the *African Methodist Episcopal Church Review*, Reverdy Ransom, left the party with Du Bois, but the conservative minister Francis Grimke stayed with TR. Many founders of the Niagara movement, the N.A.A.C.P., and the National Urban League stood by Roosevelt because of his commitment to social reform. Booker T. Washington could not afford to leave the Republican Party and give up his influence over federal appointments, but because of his past working relationship with Roosevelt he could not bear to campaign actively for Taft.[89]

Most black voters believed they had nowhere better to go and expected even less of Wilson and Taft on race. The Socialist Party nominated Eugene Debs for president, and he stood up against segregation no matter how many votes it cost him, but his party included plenty of bigots like Victor Berger. Northern grass-roots black voters still saw TR as their major white champion, and S. Willie Layton, president of the influential though disenfranchised Black Baptist Women's Convention, threw her support to the Progressive Party. Roosevelt, however, looked like a tarnished hero to many black voters. As one black newspaper said about Brownsville: "President Roosevelt may like Colored folks, but he has a 'devilish mean way' of showing it."[90]

Though Roosevelt was not yet ready to accept the challenge of reforming race in America, the Bull Moose platform took on a great many other issues. Like social democrats in Europe, the Progressives advocated government guarantees of a minimum level of economic welfare via unemployment insurance, a minimum wage, health insurance, and pensions. Roosevelt's aides sent word to Lloyd George that the Bull Moosers were "fighting on the Lloyd George programme." Gas and water socialism was welcome in the party, and so were redistributive taxes on inheritance, income, and corporations.[91]

When TR arrived in Chicago for the Bull Moose convention in August, the National Progressive Party had already, with his blessing, placed itself squarely to the left of the Republicans and Democrats and on many issues quite close to the Socialist Party. After a stirring keynote speech by Albert Beveridge calling for "social brotherhood" TR's nomination was seconded by Ben Lindsey and Jane Addams, who became the first woman to give a nominating speech at a major party convention. As a representative of American women and the conscience of the social justice side of progressivism, Addams spoke explicitly about the Bull Moose Party being the harbinger which would bring America up to the reform standards already achieved by other countries:

> The new party has become the American exponent of a world-wide movement toward juster social conditions, a movement which the United States, lagging behind other great nations, has been unaccountably slow to embody in political action.
>
> I second the nomination of Theodore Roosevelt because he is one of the few men in our public life who has been responsive to the social appeal and who has caught the significance of the modern movement. Because of that, because the programme will require a leader of invincible courage, of open mind, of democratic sympathies, one endowed with power to interpret the common man and to identify himself with the common lot, I heartily second the nomination.[92]

The Bull Moose platform, or "Contract with the People," advocated the right of labor to organize in unions, conservation, the limitation of campaign spending, woman suffrage, the eight-hour day, the six-day week, legislation for safer workplaces, and, most significantly, social insurance for unemployment, old age, and sickness. It no doubt gave Addams a sense of satisfaction that the platform called for immigrants to be given "a larger share of American opportunity."[93]

The scene at the Chicago Coliseum was one of hope and excitement over Roosevelt's willingness to harness his popularity to a united front of reform groups, and Addams and others relished the "curious moment of release from inhibitions" afforded by the "barn raising of a new party." Though the convention was often described by historians as having the flavor of a Protestant revival meeting, among the fourteen thousand rich and poor, elected and self-appointed delegates who came from all over the country, a significant force of the newly politically arrived walked the convention floor: more women than any party convention had ever had; more immigrants, Jews, and Catholics than a Republican convention had ever seen; and black delegates from Arkansas, Delaware, Illinois, Indiana, Kentucky, Maryland, Massachusetts, New Jersey, Ohio, Pennsylvania, Rhode Island, Tennessee, and West Virginia. Newspaper reporters claimed they saw as many as a quarter of the convention seats filled by women, and they were surprised when the Massachusetts state delegation proposed that it was time to choose a woman as the party's vice-presidential nominee. But calmer estimates showed fewer than forty women delegates.[94]

Though the press, especially the *New York Times*, complained how "feminized" the campaign had become, many voters recalled that the candidate stood for revived and strenuous manliness in the minds of many Americans. Partisanship, like gun owning, belonged mainly to men in 1912, but thanks to women advisors and activists in the Bull Moose Party, the women's reform network now claimed the right to leave the ladies' auxiliary behind and make party politics coeducational.[95]

Senator Albert J. Beveridge, the man who Mr. Dooley said gave speeches you could waltz to, chaired the convention, but the mood in the Coliseum was not a waltz. "Battle Hymn of the Republic" and "Onward Christian Soldiers" fit the mood of high moral purpose, but the delegates sang in the coming days a more original and expansive set of tunes: "Oh, You Beautiful Moose," "Roosevelt, My Roosevelt," and "The Red Bandanna." Oscar Straus, the Women's Trade Union League's Mary Dreier, southern black delegate Dr. W. H. Suggs, and Catholic John J. Leary sang along on behalf of a party that advertised itself as knowing "no North, no South, no East, no West, no Race, no Creed, no Sex."[96]

A friend of the Socialist candidate Eugene Debs attended the Bull Moose convention and wrote back to him in astonishment:

> There is something strikingly significant in the gathering together of 14,000 men and women from all parts of the nation to declare that they no longer were republicans, thus severing the political ties of a life time. I sat within twenty feet of Roosevelt and there were times when I could have shut my eyes and readily believed that I was listening to a Socialist soap boxer! In the decorations, red predominated and the red bandana was very much in evidence. My prediction that Roosevelt would steal our platform bodily has been fulfilled. I am also firmly convinced that he is to be the central figure around which the campaign will be waged this year.[97]

The *New York Times* dismissed the gathering as "a convention of fanatics" and "a convention managed by women and has-beens," and it denounced Roosevelt for preaching "socialism and Revolution." Indeed, TR had never advocated reform by violence, revolution, or state ownership of the means of production; he was, in fact, an anti-socialist social democrat. But former Populists Mary Elizabeth Lease and Tom Watson jumped on the Bull Moose bandwagon because they, too, saw something radical at its core. In Europe the press saw Bull Moose proposals with no alarm because they were familiar "advanced doctrines that have been floating around in American and European politics for years."[98]

Edith, who was never swept up in hero worship for her husband, admired what he stood for and found the Progressive Party convention "far more serious and constructive" than the Republican convention. For her it was the climax of her husband's long commitment to a Social Gospel. Though John Parker and Ben Lindsey were considered for the vice-presidential nomination, TR picked California's Hiram Johnson. Edith was touched by the many volunteers and strong family support the campaign drew, and she was glad that her husband started the campaign season in "fine and dandy" shape.[99]

Formidable enemies waited, however, ready to attack when Roosevelt's fall campaign began. He had anticipated from the start that he had "to step in and take the hammering" for the "whole movement" of progressive reform. But the hammering he received exceeded his worst fears. Newspapers, almost entirely owned by conservative Democrats or Republicans, denounced the former president as ambition-mad and radical. In the *Houston Post* he was arraigned as "the first president whose chief personal characteristic was mendacity, the first to glory in duplicity, the first braggart, the first bully." The press heaped the same abuse on him that he and Hewitt had given Henry George in 1886. Believing what they read in the papers, socialites lectured Alice on TR's overweening lust for power, and ambitious politicians like Warren G. Harding called him a "communist."[100]

Rather than credit TR with his crucial support of food regulation, pure food and drug advocate Harvey Wiley accused him of regulating in the interests of industry rather than consumers, and Wiley went on the stump to call the Bull Moose "essentially dangerous to free institutions." Southern editors rehashed their old complaints about TR's advocacy of "social equality" when he ate dinner with two black Progressives in Providence. Harvard's ex-president Charles Eliot charged Roosevelt with disregarding the Constitution in seeking another term, though no provision against third terms existed at the time. Following Roosevelt as he gave campaign speeches in Charleston, Atlanta, Birmingham, Chattanooga, Louisville, and Chicago was a young reader of Pulitzer's *New York World* who carried a Colt revolver.[101]

Edith wanted to help her husband fight for what he believed in the fall campaign, so she ministered to his everyday needs. Though she was not fully recovered from her accident, she made sure her husband had clean shirts to wear and went to the public library to get books for him to read on his long train trips across the country. She advised Corinne that she could help by mailing him books along the way: "He likes a new book on history or science or a novel which is *not* a problem novel, but one in which he can consistently act the hero's part, or a good novel of trash." Because he knew she worried about his safety too much, he typically did not tell her about the assassination threats he received or about the attacker whom reporters said the Bull Moose repelled with a jiujitsu move.[102]

As always, Roosevelt left the unpleasantness about money to someone else. A Women's National Committee was set up "mainly for raising money," and friends of the family were generous, especially Olivia Cutting and Dorothy Whitney Straight. Ethel worked on the finance committee in New York, where large donations were also collected from Elon Hooker, Frank Munsey, Douglas Robinson, and Emlen Roosevelt. Pinchot cultivated a prospective donor named Cornelia Bryce, but fell in love with her rather than winning a big donation. But the campaign had limited appeal to the very wealthy because of its advocacy of inheritance and graduated income taxes. After all, receipts for donations to the party carried the redistributive slogan "Pass Prosperity Around."[103]

Inventor Thomas Edison made the loudest and most important celebrity endorsement of Roosevelt, and the campaign handed out pamphlets in which Edison said a vote for TR was a vote for the "equalization of wealth." And the inventor of the incandescent light bulb and the motion picture made a small campaign contribution. In New York, nephew Teddy Robinson rented an old house on Washington Square West for headquarters, and from that home base Gifford Pinchot, social workers like Mary Simkhovitch, and the actor William Gillette, who had brought Sherlock Holmes to American theaters, spoke to enthusiastic crowds of Italian-American Bull Moosers.[104]

To reach the goal of $300,000 needed to run the fall campaign, Ethel and the women's committees around the country sold Bull Moose stamps in drugstores and started a People's Dollar Campaign. Women's colleges organized Moosette Leagues, and Simkhovitch and Ruth Hanna McCormick put together a Founder's Day celebration featuring women supporters. The Bull Moose stores in Chicago and New York marketed TR badges, stuffed moose, bronze lapel pins, and red silk bandannas with the Colonel's face imprinted on them. The National Women's Trade Union League's Margaret Dreier Robins, her sister Mary Dreier, and several other women labor leaders gladly took leadership positions in the new party.[105]

Women played a more prominent role in presidential politics during the Progressive Party's brief life than they ever had before or ever would again until Molly Dewson and Eleanor Roosevelt made the women's division a vital force in the Democratic Party. Future members of Congress Ruth

McCormick and Isabella Ferguson (later Greenway) gained experience as Bull Moose organizers, which encouraged them to launch their own political careers later on. Though the Bull Moose usually waffled on the question of banning demon rum, dressmakers from the W.C.T.U. joined the party enthusiastically. The campaign adopted advertising techniques popular in the suffrage movement, such as displays in store windows, posters, and celebrity appearances by Lillian Russell. Russell spoke on TR's behalf at rallies all over the East Coast, and Progressive Party pamphlets also reflected women's influence when they argued that a true democracy should not deny rights based on sex. One cartoonist showed a party wife and mother telling her husband at the breakfast table: "In the future, Henry, please do not refer to me as the 'Missus': Call me the moosus."[106]

The Progressive Party was innovative, not only in its acceptance of women's contributions as advisors and fundraisers, but in its embrace of technology. TR made at least three sound recordings with the Victor Talking Machine Company, including "Why the Trusts and Bosses Oppose the Progressive Party." But this did not diminish his followers' understanding that Roosevelt stood for a strenuous life in which modernity could be mastered by strong hands that lived in close touch with nature and the romance of the past. Followers came to him from odd places and for odd reasons. Some supporters saw in a Bull Moose aesthetic the promise of a reformed culture more sympathetic to plain people and plain living. Hull House advocates of the Arts and Crafts Movement called for a "just" sense of beauty, and organized for the Bull Moose all over the state of Illinois. Conservation-minded designer Gustav Stickley and his ideological kinsman Charles Fletcher Lummis became Bull Moosers, too.[107]

As the fall began back home at Sagamore Hill, however, Edith said she felt "actually black and blue with successive blows!" from the many departures—Kermit after graduation from Harvard had taken a job with the British Railway in Brazil, Archie had been sent to finish high school at Phillips Academy, Andover, Quentin returned to Groton, Alice was back in the capital. Twenty-one-year-old Ethel lived as strenuous a life as she could—dining with Maxfield Parrish, seeing Ty Cobb play baseball and Harry Houdini perform his escape stunts, learning to do the turkey trot, and, all the while, working as a campaign volunteer for her father. Before Theodore's departure for the campaign trail he had taken his wife rowing, and he wrote that he found her "as charming and pretty . . . as when she was the slender girl I made love to—and I can't help making love to her now." She worried that his throat would give out again or that he would exhaust himself, so Emlen's son George, another volunteer, sent her regular state-of-the-candidate telegrams.[108]

Roosevelt campaigned as he never had before. He remained angry at what had happened in Chicago and the untruths that newspapers and people like Barnes told about him. He explained on the stump that principle drove him: "As this movement has developed, instead of my growing less radical, I have grown more radical." Motion pictures of TR speaking from the back of trains showed him smiling at crowds and having a good time, because men, women, and children wearing red bandannas listened to him when he said: "This country will not be a good place for any of us to live in if it is not a reasonably good place for all of us to live in."[109]

He cheerfully embraced "the deluge of travel and dust and howling and fatigue" that went with full days of speaking as he traveled to thirty-eight states. He laughed heartily when local Progressives tried to greet him with moose calls, and he spoke affectionately to the "little Bull Mooses" who flocked around the train on his whistle-stops. He even kept his equanimity when roman candles were thrown his way and when the wooden platform on which he spoke collapsed. Whistle-stop campaign techniques were already being supplemented by door-to-door and telephone canvassers, electric signs, and mass mailing of printed matter, but TR still loved the nostalgic human drama of the torchlight parades which greeted him in small towns.[110]

For all the amusements and trials of being on the stump again, he and Edith never forgot that their close friends Elihu Root and Henry Cabot Lodge helped Taft make sure Roosevelt did not get the nomination. Years later, Edith still had angry dreams about Root. She took some satisfaction when Lodge was to speak in Boston that a thousand Republicans went instead to a Roosevelt meeting featuring young cousin George Roosevelt. When Roosevelt campaigned in Massachusetts everyone knew he alluded to Lodge when he talked about the "shame and indignation" he felt when certain New England senators supported the theft of delegates in Chicago. In private he also amused guests with the riddle, how was Lodge like a New England farm? The answer, TR replied, was that both were "highly cultivated but entirely sterile!" But Lodge continued to write warm personal notes to his old friend all through the campaign year, and the replies, though at times guarded, told him their friendship would survive. The New Yorker wrote him: "My dear fellow, you could not do anything that would make me lose my warm personal affection for you." Root and Taft, on the other hand, would not be forgiven as easily.[111]

The campaign grew more complicated when a "real war with no weapons barred" broke out between Roosevelt and Wilson in October. TR had to go over Wilson's daily statements and rewrite speeches on the train before "pillorying the Professor." He criticized Wilson's inactivity against trusts in New

Jersey and the fact that Wilson said he did not understand the Progressive platform. Wilson's defense of limited government, Roosevelt stated, sounded to him like a defense of laissez-faire and liberty of contract. He accused Wilson of knowing "nothing of actual living conditions of our wageworkers" and proposing economic policies that would cause a bigger crash than that of 1893. Wilson, in turn, said monopolies would have free run of the economy if TR were elected and he charged his opponent (falsely) with taking Standard Oil contributions in 1904 and U.S. Steel money in 1912. TR replied that Wilson accepted Wall Street donations, too, and represented Wall Street's financial views.[112]

Because Taft was so unpopular and ineffective as a candidate the campaign had become a two-way race between Roosevelt and Wilson. The remarkable fight hinged on issues, momentum, eloquence, and intangibles like trust. When Elihu Root heard of Wilson's extramarital affair with Mary Allen Peck Hulbert, he could have advanced the Taft campaign by using the information to undermine public trust in the candidate. If TR learned of Wilson's secret, he judged it foul play to let a sex scandal determine an election's outcome. Fearful that his sins would be exposed, Wilson fought even more feverishly against Roosevelt, calling him a defender of the special interests and a friend to monopolies.[113]

New constituencies and new state parties with Progressive slates were developing as Roosevelt's train headed west. Though women did not yet have the full franchise in New York, the Bull Moose state convention welcomed about 10 percent women delegates, organized by Alice Carpenter's Woman's Roosevelt League. In September the Colonel found he had such strong support from women voters that extra women-only meetings had to be added to his tour in Spokane, and in Los Angeles a Jane Addams chorus of a thousand women greeted him. After talking with women activists in the West, TR started speaking out for one of their pet issues—moving elections away from saloons and into the public schools.[114]

TR called for an equal partnership of the sexes within the Bull Moose Party, so for the first time in U.S. history women served alongside men on the national committee and on the party's state committees, though without full equality. Women like Margaret Dreier Robins became favorite Progressive stump speakers and she traveled around the country on the Woman's Roosevelt Special Train.[115]

The Bull Moose himself spoke up for even more than suffrage and "equality of right." Harvard's Eliot hated TR for welcoming women to participate in his party's leadership and so attacked Jane Addams because she was what he called "an old maid," and, therefore, a bad choice to be "held up in the limelight as an example for other women to follow." Roosevelt defended Addams and other unmarried women, and argued in a searing speech that women "have precisely the same right to speak in politics" as men. When the *New York Times* joined Eliot in denouncing Addams' seconding speech, TR retorted that "one of the memories of the Convention which I shall always cherish is the fact that Jane Addams seconded my nomination." TR said that it had been Jane Addams, Frances Kellor, and Florence Kelley who had convinced him, based on their expert knowledge and experience, "that working girls would be helped by the suffrage."[116]

The Progressive Party's discovery of the unrecognized electoral potential of women voters and organizers was not altogether new. Even where they could not vote, women had counted in politics. TR's sisters had been lining up allies, building networks, and even making phone calls for their brother for years. The Woman's Municipal League had been a factor in the fight against boss rule in New York, while women's organizations had worked hard to reform cities and towns across the country. Women's auxiliaries to the Republican and Democratic Parties had been around for a long time. But 1912 marked the height of the women's reform network's influence before national suffrage became a fact.

The first woman in U.S. history to cast an electoral vote for president was the Moosette Helen B. Scott, who voted for TR. Politicians could see how well women's organizations could get out the vote, but the regular parties still resisted women's participation. Nevertheless, minister Raymond Robins, whose moral reformism aimed at uplifting men's behavior in the Men and Religion Forward Movement, believed the Progressive Party's example was spreading: "The fellowship and service of women in politics has advanced wonderfully in all parties, and all parties vie with each other to be thought Progressive."[117]

As the fall wore on, Roosevelt delved happily into combat with his rivals and warm contact with cheering crowds. He was quick to lash out at opponents who sent a squad of "Truth Tellers" to "dog" his tour. In Marquette, Michigan, TR was heckled by a man who challenged his praise of Hiram Johnson's accomplishments and the minimum wage for women; as young cousin Philip Roosevelt reported, as soon as TR found out that the man was a local Republican "scalliwag [*sic*]," "he tore the hide off the man's words holding up to scorn his past record, his partner's record, and his assault on Johnson. It certainly was spectacular."[118]

By mid-October, Roosevelt's campaign reached its zenith. The Bull Moose was as happy as he had ever been, though he said he could not possibly keep up the pace of twenty speeches a day until November. Raymond

Robins wrote his sister-in-law Mary Dreier: "Saturday was a great day for the big Bull Moose in this little old Chicago. He spoke to over 25,000 people and over ten thousand tried to hear him without success." TR had also given a rousing speech to eight thousand immigrants on the West Side of Chicago, then he returned to the Coliseum where the thirteen thousand seats were filled within eleven minutes after the doors opened. Men hung from the iron girders under the balcony so they could "hear Teddy."[119]

But a Colt revolver waited in one of the crowds. On October 14 outside the Gilpatrick Hotel in Milwaukee, Roosevelt entered the car that was to drive him to his next speaking engagement. He turned and lifted his hat to wave toward the people who lined the sidewalk, when a man standing nearby shot TR in the chest. Stunned and wounded he fell backward. When his aide Henry Cochems put his arm around him, the wounded candidate said only: "They have pinked me." His stenographer wrestled with John Schrank, a paranoid-schizophrenic former bartender obsessed by the third-term issue, and knocked him to the ground to prevent him from shooting again. Roosevelt called out not to hurt the gunman. He made sure he was not bleeding from the mouth and then, despite the pain, announced that he would go on to his speaking engagement as planned. Doctors in the crowd were horrified that a bleeding man would endanger his life for an insignificant speech, but no one dared stop him.

Despite pain, the loss of blood, and the bullet lodged near his lung, Roosevelt went to the hall and spoke for an hour and a half to a mortified audience. Seeing this as a chance to talk "without having his sincerity questioned," he said, "this is my big chance, and I am going to make that speech if I die doing it." TR showed his blood-stained shirt to his audience and explained that he had been shot but added: "It takes more than that to kill a Bull Moose." He called his would-be assassin a "coward" and said: "It is a very natural thing that weak and vicious minds should be inflamed to acts of violence by the kind of foul mendacity and abuse that have been heaped upon me for the last three months in the interests not only of Mr. Debs, but of Mr. Wilson and Mr. Taft." Reiterating that he "would not speak to you insincerely within five minutes of being shot" he tried to lay to rest charges that "insane ambition" drove him to run. Instead, he said he was running "to stand for the sacred rights of childhood and womanhood . . . to see that manhood is not crushed out of the men who toil by excessive hours of labor, by underpayment, by injustice and oppression."[120]

Roosevelt's glasses case, overcoat, suspenders, and thick folded speech kept the bullet from penetrating farther into his chest, but it nevertheless broke a rib and caused bleeding. He was taken to Mercy Hospital in Chicago, but before he left Milwaukee he telegraphed Edith that the wound was "purely superficial. . . . I very earnestly beg you not to come out. I am not nearly as bad hurt as I have been again and again with a fall from my horse. Everything possible is being done for me by everybody."[121]

Of course, she was already determined to go to him because no one else could make him listen to doctor's orders. Doctors recalled that TR was "very much wrought up after the accident," and when he reached Mercy Hospital he eagerly awaited his wife. When Edith arrived she found his breathing labored due to his broken rib, which also caused a severe pain in his side. Doctors watched him for signs of lockjaw or blood poisoning, but his life was not in danger.[122]

Edith, Ethel, and Alice allowed almost no one to see him in the hospital, but TR insisted on talking to a few reporters. The Roosevelt women, however, welcomed Jane Addams to speak with him about granting suffrage to the District of Columbia as soon as he took office. The "impatient patient" shook hands with the nuns who had been his nurses and left the hospital on the twenty-first in a wheelchair. Edith brought him back to Sagamore Hill and cared for him without help. As TR recuperated he played with little Gracie untiringly, and Groton let Quentin come home to see his father. Edith was encouraged by his recovery: "It will be some time before he is free from discomfort and I know he ought not to use his right arm as much as he does," but by the end of October he could sleep on his right side again. Doctors warned her that her own serious bout of eczema and weakened health were reactions to the shooting. Her husband's appetite came back and soon the chicken bones were "stacked like cordwood" around his plate, which disgusted Edith. A servant who observed TR eating declared that "the bullet was never made could kill a man that can eat as much fried chicken as that and live." By Halloween supporters in New Mexico led by Isabella Ferguson were holding a Bull Moose Masquerade Ball to celebrate the recovery of their hero, some dressed in Teddy costumes.[123]

The campaign hoped that the nearly "lavish post-mortem praises" their candidate received after he was shot might turn into a win on election day. The would-be assassin, Schrank, had dreamed that President McKinley told him TR had been his murderer and asked him to "avenge" his death. Schrank provoked a nationwide debate about crime, "moral insanity," and the evil influence of saloons. Bull Moose campaign manager Senator Joseph Dixon blamed the shooting on inflammatory reporting by the reactionary press, which had trumpeted Taft's charge that TR was a threat to free institutions. Roosevelt had been attacked for a multitude of sins, including being endorsed by too many writers.[124]

Schrank was finally confined to a prison ward for the criminally insane, where Bull Moose inmates taunted him. Wilson announced that he would stop campaigning out of deference to his wounded opponent, but TR thought the campaign should go on while he recuperated. His surrogates, especially Hiram Johnson and Oscar Straus, hit Wilson hard for his anti-immigrant writings and lack of concrete proposals for reform.[125]

Roosevelt finally agreed to hire the Burns detective agency for protection, and a thousand policemen guarded him when he gave his last major speech of the campaign at Madison Square Garden on October 30. As he spoke, he could not lift his right arm for his customary fist-pounding gesture, but otherwise did a "tremendously impressive" job in his adoring daughter Ethel's eyes. Thee's old friend Louisa Lee Schuyler sat in the audience and was proud to call herself a Bull Mooser, which pleased Edith and Theodore as a blessing from the Civil War generation they so revered.[126]

Public sympathy shifted after Roosevelt was shot. Oddsmakers, who had rated the Bull Moose's chances of winning at four to one before the shooting, now saw his chances improved to almost two to one. Edith was amused when Quentin wrote to say even Rector Peabody would vote the Progressive ticket. In his last campaign interview, TR said that the participation of women, especially his loyal Female Brain Trust, had been the greatest inspiration of the campaign and that if elected he would call a special session of Congress to pass the social justice planks which the *New York Times* said were "practically dictated to him" by Addams, Kellor, and Margaret Dreier Robins. Roosevelt told one of his supporters that Jane Addams probably would have a cabinet post.[127]

After a quiet walk on November 5, Edith and Theodore awaited evening phone calls telling them the state-by-state election returns. By dinner time they knew Wilson was winning. TR earned 4,119,538 votes against Wilson's 6,293,454 and Taft's 3,484,980. With an even smaller campaign budget and weaker organization than the Bull Moose Party, Socialist Eugene Debs received 900,672 votes. Later Ethel wrote: "Of course its [*sic*] a great disappointment but we expected it. The worst blow is that Taft makes a much better showing than we expected. . . . F[ather] seems wonderfully brave and smiling." The next morning Ethel and Edith broke into sobs over breakfast, but Theodore remained "undaunted." He told the press: "The battle is just begun." Booker T. Washington visited to explain why he had sat out the election, and Roosevelt said he "honored" the choice, which left Washington thinking his old ally was "a bigger man than I thought he was before."[128]

Already the Bull Moose Party's accomplishments were impressive. They had made a better showing in 1912 than the Republicans had in 1856, when they were a fledgling third party. Thirteen new Progressive congressmen and

Left: Alice in 1902

ed, Archie, TR, Quentin, and Kermit, 1904

TR at the Army-Navy football game. Behind him in the stands are Ethel and Ted; seated to his right are Loeb and Edith, and behind him Bamie. Princeton, December 1905

Jane Addams, founder of Hull Hous
crusader against child labor, and th
most admired woman in America

Florence Kelley, National Consumers' League advocate and defender of the minimum wage

The President and Booker T. Washington at Tuskegee Institute

Below: Frances Kellor and Mary Dreier, members of TR's 1912 Female Brain Trust, leaders in the National Women's Trade Union League

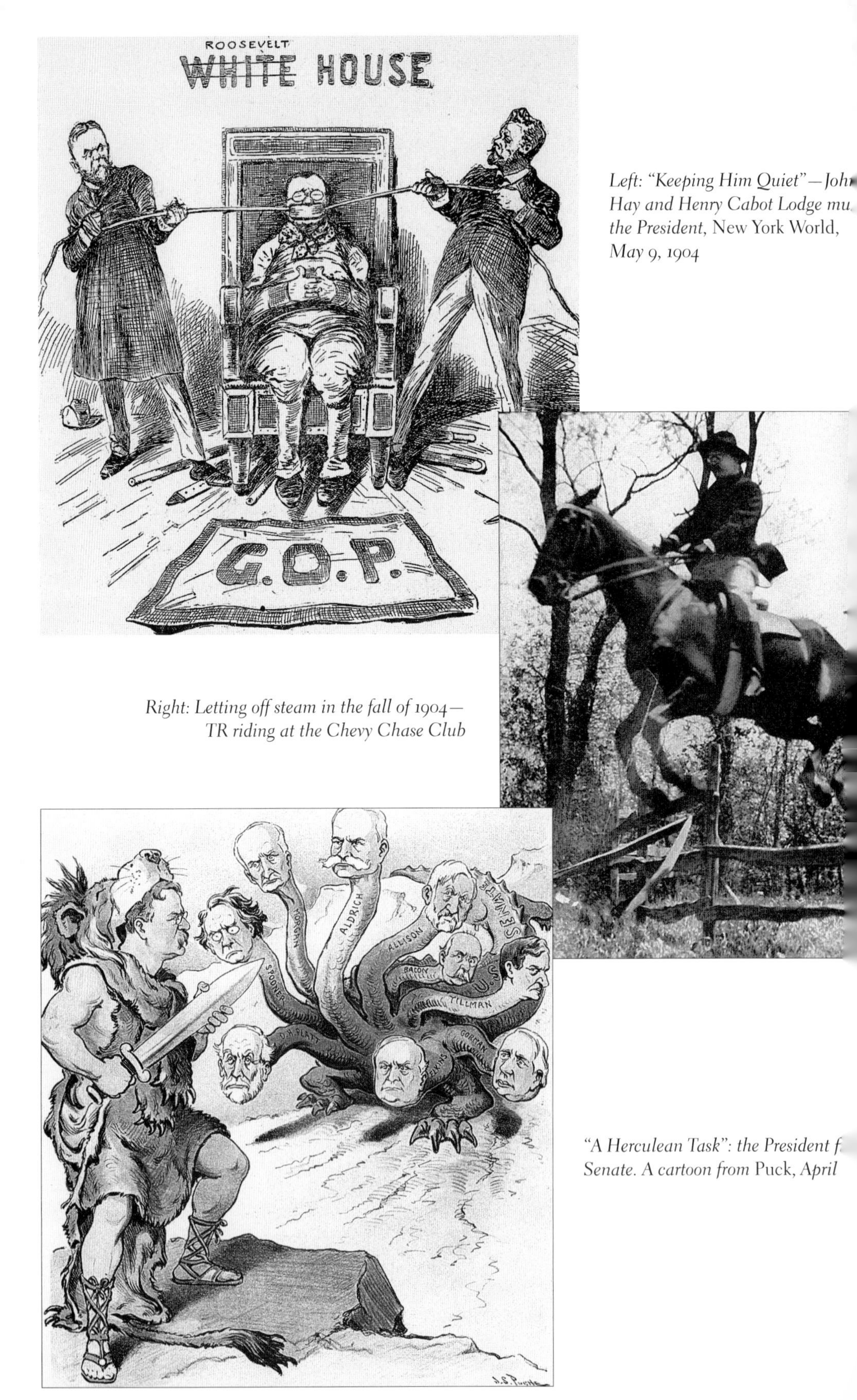

Left: "Keeping Him Quiet"—John Hay and Henry Cabot Lodge mu the President, New York World, *May 9, 1904*

Right: Letting off steam in the fall of 1904— TR riding at the Chevy Chase Club

"A Herculean Task": the President f Senate. A cartoon from Puck, *April*

Sergei Witte, Baron Rosen, TR, Baron Komura, Minister Takahira

Augustus Saint-Gaudens' ten-dollar Indian-head coin

Lodge and Taft drift politically away from TR during his second term.

The President and the backbone of the navy

Roosevelt in Africa

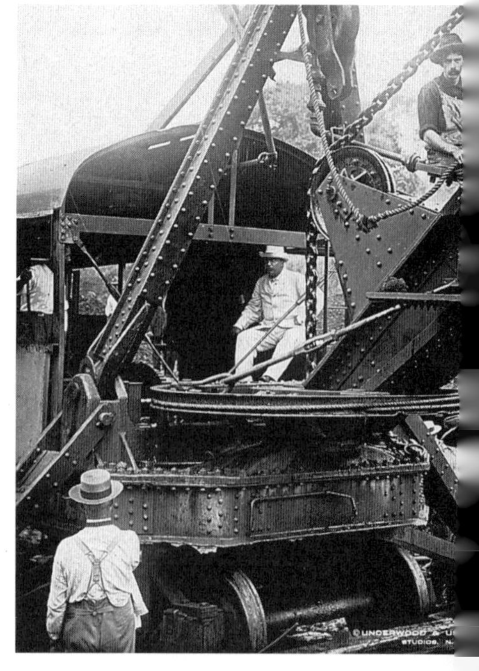

TR in Panama, operating the steam shov
at Culebra Cut, November 1906

Nicholas Longworth, Alice Roosevelt Longworth, and the President, 1906

Right: Quentin on Algonquin

Pine Knot, presidential retreat

He devotes a few moments to San Domingo

He hands Mr. Castro a few

He jumps on the U. S. Senate

He dashes off an essay about the race question

He lands on the Standard Oil Co.

He attends a banquet in New Yor

He superintends the preparations for Inauguration Day

He passes a hot message to the Senate

He pauses for a moment to mak plans for a hunting trip

"One of Roosevelt's Quiet Days," a cartoon by John McCutcheon

The Great White Fleet's return from its round-the-world cruise

TR gives the New Nationalism speech while standing on a kitchen table

Above: TR watches troop maneuvers with Kaiser Wilhelm II

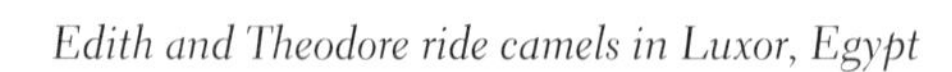

Edith and Theodore ride camels in Luxor, Egypt

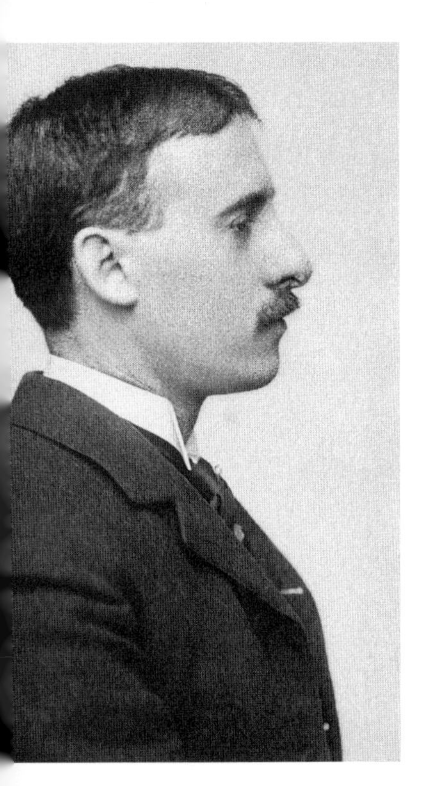

Henry Stimson, Roosevelt protégé, U.S. attorney, and TR's chosen candidate for governor of New York in 1910

Above: TR waving his hat as he greets crowds in 1912

Left: Colored Bull Moose picnic

Left: TR, lawyer W. H. van Benschoten, and F.D.R testified for Uncle Theodore in the Barnes trial, Syr May 1915

Right: TR and Alice often talked politics.

Below: Ethel and TR entering the church before her wedding, April 1913

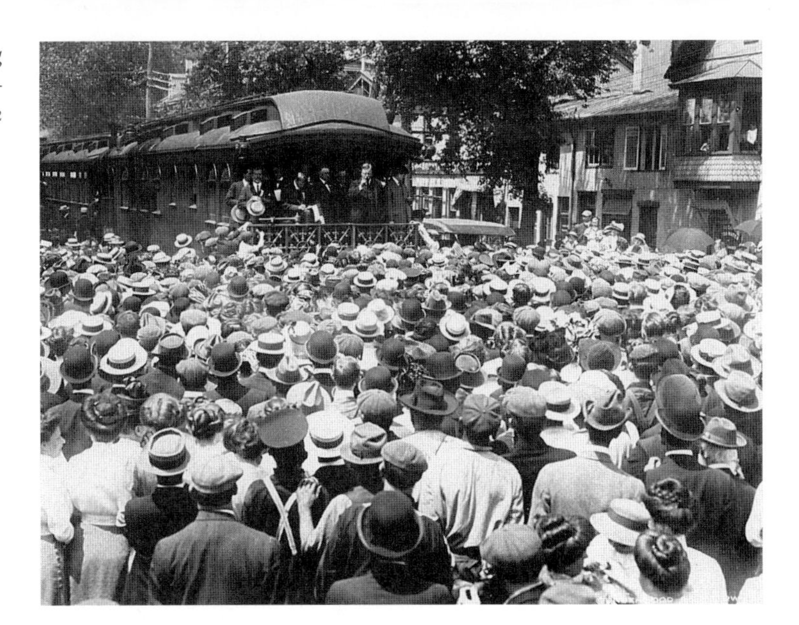

TR campaigning during a whistle-stop tour in 1912

Left: The Progressive Party Convention, Chicago, August 1912

Roosevelt and Colonel Rondon before entering the River of Doubt

Left to right: William Jennings Bryan, Secretary of the Navy Josephus Daniels, President Woodrow Wilson, Assistant Secretary of State William Phillips, and Assistant Secretary of the Navy Franklin Delano Roosevelt, 1915

Clifford Berryman's cartoo TR's World War I editorial

"Pass Prosperity Around" was the slogan for the Bull Moose Party in 1912.

Helen Mills Reid, Vira Whitehouse, TR, and Harriet Laidlaw:
New York suffrage leaders hold a meeting and reception at Sagamore Hill, 1917.

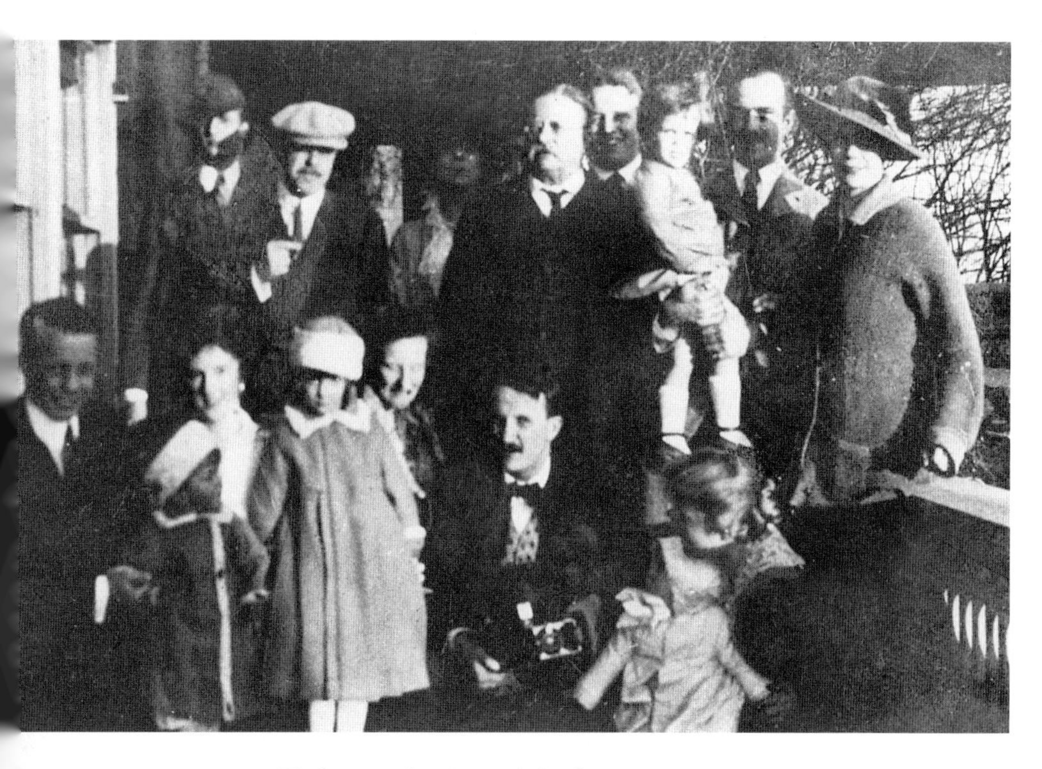

The last complete Roosevelt family picture

The President and first lady

TR holds his place in a book while a photographer snaps his picture with Edith.

260 state legislators had been elected. The minimum wage had been popularized; labor had gained new defenders of their right to collective bargaining; TR had wagered his popularity to fight for the idea that Americans should not suffer because of old age, unemployment, and illness. Later historians would assert that the Bull Moose Party foreshadowed Franklin Roosevelt's Democratic coalition of the thirties, but others argued that Progressive Party voters lured urban immigrants away from Republican rather than Democratic ranks.[129]

TR saw the deeper meaning of the campaign in his attempt to change people's minds about what Americans owed to each other. He said he had pleaded "the cause of the crippled brakeman on a railroad, of the overworked girl in a factory, of the stunted child toiling at inhuman labor." For a political party to step so far away from politics as usual to talk about the obligation that the whole society owed to those who struggled was enough to "fill" Mary Simkhovitch and other social workers "with thanksgiving."[130]

He wrote his "dear friends" Mary Dreier and Frances Kellor that the party must look to the future and the work they still needed to do together to shift the mainstream of American politics. Few outside the campaign saw 1912 as the epic drama of a heroic warrior fighting to the death against what used to be his own armies; few saw it as a battle waged by a strong man who saw the harm done by a weak state. But Edith Wharton wrote: "Our Theodore is a good deal more saga-like than anything in Wuthering Heights."[131]

LOYAL FAMILY member Douglas Robinson felt as if "somebody had given me a blow in the solar plexus" when the election results came in. Big crowds had led them to hope that TR would win an upset victory. Instead, the Bull Moose Party had guaranteed Woodrow Wilson's triumph. For Roosevelt, his disappointing showing at the polls hurt much more than the bullet that still pained him if he moved too suddenly. In its brief existence, the Progressive Party had come "into this world making a noise like 10,000 babies," but had not had time to grow up enough to overcome the established two-party system. It did not console Roosevelt to know that, after all the racial controversies swirling around the platform and the convention, he had won 60 percent of the African-American vote nationally.[132]

He had proven once again that he was the ultimate "slugger" in American politics, but when the cheering stopped so did his high spirits. The "dull thud" he had avoided by going to Africa in 1909 would hit him hard after the 1912 election. At first he looked upon Wilson with a kindly eye, hoping he would prove himself a true progressive.[133]

But his own fall from grace hurt. The editor of the *Louisville Courier-Journal*, Henry Watterson, denounced the large Bull Moose vote as the product of hero worship and the American preference for Caesarism over constitutional processes. Watterson found it ominous that the women voters of the western "suffragettes" states voted Progressive and that TR won the new suffrage state, California. He called Bull Moosers dangerous "nationalists" who "have 'nigger' on the brain." He portrayed Roosevelt as "an opportunist without convictions, one who had never been a man of the people, bred an aristocrat—a patrician, unstable in all his mental processes and moral conclusions; a child of fortune, selfish, self-willed and dangerously ambitious." Since July, Roosevelt had suspected he would lose, but the defeat and accusations still hurt. So many had turned their back on him in battle. Henry Adams dismissed his old friend as nothing more than a "chewed-up cud."[134]

As 1912 came to a close, Edith watched her husband's sorrow, and she wrote Kermit: "The disappointment went deeper than he admits to himself at the result of the election." *The Outlook* subscribers were leaving in large numbers so the Abbotts warned Roosevelt they might not be able to give him a salary much longer. TR blamed himself for the magazine's decline, and Edith wrote: "He was hurt and grim because so many of those he cared for did not stand with him, and in the excitement of the fight he did not have time to think of it as he has now." After being so harshly vilified in the campaign, Roosevelt felt so low that he began contemplating how the end of his life would turn out.[135]

Dr. Alex Lambert was called on "short notice" to Sagamore Hill in December. Theodore told Lambert he had been "shunned by old friends and neighbors, treated like an outcast," and described himself as "unspeakably lonesome." Although the family tried to hide the fact from biographers, Lambert later said he found Roosevelt mired in a mood of "desolation." The family would later concede that TR suffered that winter from a "bruised spirit," but they would not allow anyone to describe him as clinically depressed.[136]

After such a recent escape from a righteous end in Milwaukee, Roosevelt, despite Lambert's sympathy, contemplated the subject of heroic death. He wrote about the nobility in Antarctic explorer Robert Scott's dying words, composed after another man beat him to the pole: "We took risks . . . but bow to the will of Providence, determined to do our best to the last." Finding his own place on "the long honor roll of those men who 'do and dare and die at need' " captured Roosevelt's thoughts in 1913.[137]

But it was the wrong moment for Theodore, like the *Titanic*, to slip with his lost cause into the icy sea. He had to find a more heroic ending to his final chapter of life. In the weeks after the election he felt the loss almost as intensely as the death of someone he loved. Even the former pleasures of daily life with Edith at Sagamore Hill rang hollow. His old bustle to get tasks done so that he could reward himself with an afternoon sunlight walk with her had lost its magic. Death had been with him since his childhood days of gasping for breath. Dying itself struck much less terror in Roosevelt than coming to a bland or ignominious end.

When Sir Edward Grey wondered whether he would have been as brave in speaking so long if he had bled from a bullet wound, TR reassured his friend that he too would "have shown the absolute coolness and courage and lack of thought of self that your brother showed when mauled by the lion." Roosevelt confessed that he had made the Milwaukee speech "in the very unlikely event of the wound being mortal I wished to die with my boots on, so to speak. It has always seemed to me that the best way to die would be in doing something that ought to be done, whether leading a regiment or doing something else." But the gunshot had not killed him. With a reprieve at hand, how could he keep doing something worthwhile until he could meet a worthy death?[138]

He disliked Shakespeare's story of a man angry when his time passed before he was ready, perhaps because he did not like to see the raging King Lear emerging in himself. An indomitable will would prove to be inflexible armor for this stage of living. Aging well required something more subtle than the headlong drive to win. Willfulness and his long-standing combativeness toward rivals might interfere with his ability to fight selflessly for high purposes. The roar of crowds, the seduction of political flatterers, the temptation to heroics, in short, his desire for glory, competed with his urge to keep fighting a steady and uphill fight for social justice. His path to political usefulness was blocked by his many foes in old parties, but most of all by President-elect Wilson.[139]

In the first weeks and months after the election, TR still wrote about Wilson in tempered language. He had hopes that journalists like Joe Bishop would be treated better now that Wilson was president "because Taft showed himself to be a plain fool, and Wilson is not a fool." TR even praised Wilson in private for his "adroitness" in the campaign and for talking an "ardent but diffuse progressiveness."[140]

Roosevelt doubted, however, that Wilson would get much done as a progressive president because of his commitment to the Democrats' states' rights philosophy and his failure to understand social justice. Deep reform, in his opinion, could be forged only by an activist federal government led by a strong executive. Wilson's Industrial Relations Commission produced little, and the new President refused at first to support child labor reform. He supported the Aldrich version of currency reform and did nothing for women. The Bull Moose conceded, however, that Wilson had the potential to "make a great record and rivet the attention of the country upon him." And a great record for Wilson meant no more record for TR. While he waited to see how Wilson would do, Roosevelt said: "I am absolutely helpless—probably more helpless than any other man in America."[141]

If Wilson snuffed out TR's last hopes as a progressive leader, would the last years of the great Bull Moose drag out, devoid of purpose? With Schrank's bullet lodged in his chest for the rest of his life, Roosevelt felt in his shortened wind and enlarged girth the cumulative effects of unhealthy campaign living. He might console himself and his supporters by remembering how he had influenced the "choir invisible" of minds changed forever by the "educational value of the campaign." Yet he felt the costs more sharply than the legacy. He knew that the 1912 campaign had hurt his standing with the American people. Perhaps the romance he had with the public was over.[142]

Rumors of TR's drunkenness had been spread during the campaign by Democratic and Republican newspapers alike. When he heard the same lies about his drunkenness repeated too many times, he finally lost patience. The editor of a small-town paper, the *Iron Age*, a staunch Republican named George Newett, had written:

> Roosevelt lies and curses in a most disgusting way; he gets drunk, too, and that not infrequently, and all his intimates know about it. All who oppose him are wreckers of the country, liars, knaves and undesirables. He alone is pure and entitled to a halo. Rats. For so great a fighter, self-styled, he is the poorest loser we ever knew![143]

TR decided to sue Newett for libel, and in December, as he prepared for the trial, he warned his Michigan-based lawyer, James H. Pound, that Newett was "hunting everywhere to find testimony against me." Ready to fight, Roosevelt lined up his closest friends and associates to prove that he was not much of a drinker at all. Then Newett found a journalist, J. Martin Miller, who said he was willing to testify about specific occasions when he saw Roosevelt drunk.[144]

Roosevelt's integrity was also being questioned by his fellow naturalists. In *Auk* magazine Francis Allen accused TR of as many as fifty misrepresentations in his published criticisms of Abbott H. Thayer's views on protective coloration in animals. Allen said he had proof of Roosevelt's "inaccurate habit of mind." But scientists rallied around the accuracy of Roosevelt's statements, and the editor of *Auk* wrote TR an apology for publishing Allen's partisan attack.[145]

Though the family would try to be upbeat, it had been a difficult chapter in their lives. Fifteen-year-old Quentin was still being hazed at Groton for his father's politics. The boy admitted to Auntie Bye, but not his father, that he had had "a pretty hard time up here." When he went into the shower in his dormitory a classmate stole his towel. As soon as Quentin chased the boy outside to reclaim it, other boys blockaded the door so the only way he could get back inside was to walk naked in front of several ladies. Quentin expected Peabody to suspend him for public nudity, but the mishap eluded the rector.[146]

The year 1912 also had more permanent victims. Alice discovered Nick had been unfaithful to her, but she knew that Theodore and Edith disapproved of a member of their family getting a divorce. They believed that duty and commitment should come before personal happiness. After building his career standing up for the sanctity of marriage and old-fashioned moral codes, TR feared that a scandal in his family would undermine the very institutions and ideals he stood for. Alice understood that a divorce in the Roosevelt family would constitute what Ethel would later call a "betrayal of the trust of the American people."[147]

So Alice chose marital repair and tried to play the part of a good politician's wife by doing flood relief work. Her "annoying red female" of an antisuffragist mother-in-law never stopped harping on the sins of the Bull Moose, so as late as 1914, Alice wrote Auntie Bye in exasperation that she contemplated becoming "an active suffragist just to spite her." Quiet sexual transgression and an acerbic wit provided easier rebellions against a loutish husband and insufferable in-laws. At Sagamore Hill everyone knew that Alice was going through a horrible time.[148]

The 1912 campaign had opened up new worlds for the ardently progressive Ethel, and seeing her father's Female Brain Trust in action made her want to help people through the Progressive Social Service which TR and Frances Kellor set up in 1913 or perhaps she could organize social services in a hospital. No wonder that as 1912 ended, Ethel agonized over Dr. Richard Derby's long-standing marriage proposal. She wanted to postpone married life so that she could at least have the adventure of going to Brazil to visit Kermit, who had announced to the family that he might be away for a decade. She even asked her parents if she could work with Jane Addams at Hull House, but they said no because she was too young. Ethel's situation resembled Grace Dodge's dilemma in the 1880s: after growing up with parents who exposed her to the important work of reform and charity, Dodge had wanted to lead a public life of "good works," a fate her parents considered unthinkable. Edith and Theodore thought Dick Derby a perfect match for Ethel: He was a moneyed young doctor with a social conscience. Groton and Harvard had trained Dick, and he had been one of the outstanding college men TR had brought to Sagamore Hill to launch into public service careers.[149]

BEING BUSY might dissipate TR's grief for a while; having work piled high on his desk might approximate true purposefulness. After answering twenty-five thousand letters in 1912 alone, he was used to managing a tidal wave of correspondence each day. In the winter of 1912–13 he also spent long hours at his desk making sure his voice would not be lost on the American scene. He contemplated going into motion pictures, possibly as a lecturer, but he chose not to for fear of "commercializing what I did as President." He traveled many miles and spent some of his own money to keep the Progressive Party alive. His admirers predicted that the White House would be his in 1916, so why should he reconcile himself to a quiet life?[150]

After the election he had written Fanny Parsons, who was to have a private lunch with him in New York: "I shall not try to put on paper the multitude of things I have to say to you." Especially in this period when Edith and Theodore went through a mild estrangement, Edith jealously found their childhood friend Fanny still "very pretty and affected." TR held Fanny dear for being what Edith was not, an adoring audience when he was licking his campaign wounds.[151]

Still weakened by her near-fatal accident in 1911, Edith was having her neuralgia, lethargy, migraines, eczema, and other ailments treated with prescribed rest and thyroid supplements. While everyone else around Roosevelt had been giddy with the excitement of the campaign, she had waited, tense and apprehensive, knowing that the shooting in Milwaukee could happen at any time, hoping he would survive to embrace their quiet life at Sagamore in November. Theodore described his wife as still not well, and he felt responsible.

When her wounded and "rather blue" warrior returned to her at Sagamore Hill, he could not bear to seek respite for long. He brought home to Edith telegrams, phone calls, daily bags of mail, and plentiful guests. He brought, too, abundant tension and excitement as reporters called upon him almost daily to flash his famous smile and react to world events.[152]

Christmas 1912 found the Roosevelts of Sagamore Hill united again for well-loved family traditions. Together, Theodore and Edith sang Christmas carols in a snowstorm as they gathered on Christmas Eve in the North Room with Quentin, Archie, Ted, his wife Eleanor, and Ethel. Because of the snow,

Ted and Eleanor had left Gracie home to spend Christmas with the servants, which disappointed her eager grandparents.

On Christmas morning Theodore arose early as usual and woke Edith up with a kiss. Then the family opened their stockings in Theodore and Edith's bedroom, as they had done when the children were small. After the holiday Edith took ill again, probably with the same gynecological troubles that would linger until 1915, but Ethel, Quentin, and Archie managed on their own when on December 27 TR rode the train to Boston to spend three days with William Sturgis Bigelow and deliver an address as president of the American Historical Association.

Roosevelt reaffirmed a romantic's view of history, of heroic tales, of lofty dreams, of "the glory of triumphant violence" and banners flying above great hosts of warriors. He hoped that when the history of his own time was written "it will show that the forces working for good in our national life outweigh the forces working for evil." Historians who had wanted him to serve as president of the A.H.A. considered him worthy especially for his advocacy of preserving historical records when he was president. TR's defense of the life of the mind and of the value of teaching history as an essential part of all education earned him respect across the profession.[153]

When he planned his trip to Boston he sought to insulate himself from unpleasant confrontations with his critics. He told Bigelow he wanted to see a few Massachusetts Progressives or scholars at breakfast or dinner. To avoid contact with the Republicans who often visited his sister Bamie in Farmington, he told her that when he stopped at her house en route from Boston he wanted to see "no one who is not in the Progressive Party." To further reduce contact with his political foes and with the clubmen who hated him for being a traitor to his class, he resigned from the Century Association.

As 1912 finally ended, TR's spirits remained low. Helplessness did not set well with the Bull Moose. Yet the editor of the *New York Evening Mail* would later write that Roosevelt "seemed to me never so great, never so inspiring, as during this after-the-White-House period." In the years when Roosevelt spoke out most boldly as a prophet for causes he held dear and became a pariah for it, he "reminded" the editor "of an imprisoned soul struggling vainly for freedom."[154]

☆ CHAPTER THIRTEEN ☆

The Bull Moose Unheard

THEODORE AND EDITH took their familiar walk over to Cooper's Bluff on January 2, 1913, in the frigid air which would shortly freeze the pipes in their bedroom at Sagamore Hill. He claimed that his wife kept him "under rigid discipline," but in the years after his 1912 defeat no discipline worked. She could not count on him to control his eating, talking, or risk-taking. Edith watched apprehensively as her husband struggled to redeem his reputation as a worthy national hero in the Newett libel trial and in a dangerous Brazilian adventure. Losing the goodwill of the American people hurt him, yet he courageously wagered what public favor he had left by standing up for liberal reform. He lost credibility, too, when he attacked Woodrow Wilson in vicious and personal terms. When in the years after 1912 her husband alternately cultivated and damaged his reputation, Edith found "taking care of Father" harder than ever.[1]

When they returned from Cooper's Bluff, *The Outlook*'s editor, Lawrence Abbott, dined with them and spent the night so that he could work with TR on his autobiography.[2] Abbott hoped to revive *The Outlook* by publishing the autobiography serially. Roosevelt took on the project to argue for the cause of reform and reingratiate himself with his public. Dispirited about what he saw as his loss of credibility, he fought on with pen and tongue because he believed that the "only safety" for the future of America lay with "a sane and temperate radicalism."[3]

Roosevelt chose to bare his soul as a reformer in his autobiography to win back an electorate that had not voted for him. By describing the slow, but sincere, development of his progressive views he hoped to prove to his public that he was not a power-hungry fake. Edith talked the book over with her husband and counseled him, as she had many times, to preserve whatever shreds of privacy were left to them. Despite her warnings, he lowered the veil on his private life whenever it served the larger purposes of his *Autobiography*. He knew human interest stories about his personal growth and his family life could convince people he was sincere and that his politics were, after all, safe. His own life had always been his secret weapon in politics. Because he had struggled against illness, corruption, and privilege, he was more qualified to preach from the bully pulpit. In his *Autobiography* he perpetuated the myth that he had overcome asthma by exercising, which placed his life story squarely in the self-made man myth and made it a self-help guide to inspire others in their own struggles against the trials of life. Corinne said he never conquered asthma completely, but he justified stretching the truth because people needed to look up to heroes.[4]

Because Edith had known him since childhood, as he wrote, they could reminisce about dancing together in Mr. Dodsworth's classes. They had memories of Tranquility summers with Mittie and Thee and rows on Long Island Sound when he courted her during his vacations from Harvard. The bond of shared nostalgia extended far, but still left taboo subjects between them which proved also unfit for his memoirs, especially Alice Lee. Wherever he could, Theodore sidestepped his own emotional land mines. It was safe to talk about coming from a Knickerbocker family or his grandmother's slave-owning life at Bulloch Hall, but not his failed cattle investment, Elliott's profligacy, his daughter Alice's wildness, or Brownsville. TR, unlike La Follette in his *Autobiography*, commanded enough artistry to portray himself as a brave adventurer and crusader in scenes of stock romance. Unwilling to take a hard look inward, he wanted most of all to give the reader a good time and win back his public. Over lunch he talked more honestly with his family and regaled Ethel with hilarious Mittie stories. But the book he created offered up a sincere and historic defense of using the government to protect the public from predatory capitalism. He defended the way he had lived his life in one of America's most endearing political autobiographies.[5]

Writing the book was bound to be a political process because his words still carried so much weight. With California about to pass a law forbidding Japanese-Americans to own land, there was talk of war between Japan and the United States. Rumors circulated that TR intended to release information that would further irritate the Japanese government, so he had to issue a careful denial that his *Autobiography* would contain any inflammatory material about Japan. Though he circulated his early drafts widely, there remained a steady stream of complaints about what he had written. African-Americans took offense at his use of the word "darky," and Mrs. Pinchot did not think the ex-president had given her boy Gifford enough credit for the Roosevelt administration's conservation policies.[6]

TR held back his true feelings as he wrote because he knew bitterness was poor entertainment. He tried not to expose how he really felt about his enemies, but in private he raged against Nicholas Murray Butler, who had become the "little brother of the rich" and "the people who, by their ceaseless and intemperate abuse," had "excited" Schrank to want to kill him.[7]

His fury over 1912 did not fade. Progressives around the country were being punished for their support of him. In Idaho, the editor and the publisher of a local Progressive newspaper were thrown into jail for daring to criticize the local court that had kept the Bull Moose off the ballot. Shocked by this blatant violation of the First Amendment, TR sent telegrams to a long list of people that he was "outraged and indignant beyond measure" at such a violation of citizens' rights. The Progressives stayed in jail.

In the winter of 1913 he was disheartened to find that the Republican Party sought revenge on the Bull Moosers but had not listened to their ideas. Republicans in Maine adopted a few of the more innocuous Progressive planks to bring straying Progressive voters back into Republican ranks. More often they chose retribution. TR answered letter after letter from minor political appointees who had been fired by Taft loyalists for being Bull Moosers. Taft later punished Bull Mooser Learned Hand by blocking his appointment to the Supreme Court. By the spring of 1913 wealthy Progressive Party donors Frank Munsey and Dan Hanna had broken with the reformers, heading back, with money and followers, to the G.O.P. George Perkins saved the day by funding Progressive newspapers and national party offices in Washington and New York, but TR knew the regular parties would fight hard to keep a third party off the ballot.[8]

While Roosevelt's defeated troops were being battered, more powerful attacks were aimed at the Bull Moose himself. In February 1913, Congress debated whether to alter the Constitution to stop what TR had done in 1912. The Roosevelt Amendment to create a one-term six-year presidency was proposed to prevent him from running again in 1916. Roosevelt judged that a six-year presidency would be bad for the country in cases like the Civil War, when Lincoln had been desperately needed for two terms to hold the country together. He was prepared, nevertheless, to face public rebuke graciously, but the amendment failed.[9]

Bull Moosers also fought among themselves. Amos and Gifford Pinchot started a vendetta against Perkins which the ex-president tried to quash. Perkins' ties to J. P. Morgan and the corporate world bothered anti-capitalist Bull Moosers but not the Bull Moose himself. Without the money and organizational acumen of Perkins there would have been no party, so Roosevelt asked him to publicize his profit-sharing plan for workers in order to convince the dissenters that the Progressive from U.S. Steel really was pro-labor.[10]

Without the focus of a presidential election, Progressives headed in so many directions that TR could not always keep track of them. Perkins talked up compulsory voting at the Honest Ballot Association, while George L. Record still harped on the single tax as a cure-all. Western Progressives favored nationwide prohibition to cut down on family violence, while eastern Progressives saw the crusade to ban drink as a lame cause. After meeting with feuding camps of Bull Moosers, the great mimic entertained Edith and Ethel with an opéra bouffe version of the war. But he put humor aside the next day and applied his energy to holding the party together.[11]

Freed from the hindrance of office and party regularity, Roosevelt and his closest advisors continued to move leftward. In January 1913, on behalf of the Progressive Party, he invited his old friend Lillian Wald of the Henry Street Settlement to have lunch with him at *The Outlook* offices so that she could talk with the staff about the latest garment workers' strike on the East Side. She recalled the lunch as a "jolly occasion, with joking and much laughter and exchange of stories." But TR insisted on knowing everything about the job action—the issues, the reason the sides were at odds, and the conditions of the workers. He asked Wald for the names of the strikers, presumably so that he could talk with them when he visited the picket line. Wald had tried to interest President-elect Wilson in labor issues that week and had found him formal and uninterested. When she went back to Henry Street, she told the residents it was Roosevelt, not Wilson, who cared about workers: "He knew how to draw one out, how to get at all the human interest in the dispute."[12]

TR visited the garment workers, who were striking for union recognition and better wages. The workers were girls in their teens, many Turkish Jews and recent immigrants from Spain, who worked twelve-hour days for low wages—from $2.50 to $8 a week—out of which their employer charged them for sewing machine rentals, electricity, and drinking water. The lawyer for the white goods manufacturers, Harry A. Gordon, believed in the "Vicegerent of God"—that employers should answer only to God for their treatment of their workers. Roosevelt wrote in a public letter that they should have the right to join a union and it was an outrage that workers were being fired simply because they had unionized.[13]

He told the newspapers that he felt a "deep sympathy" for the strikers, and promised Mary Dreier to do whatever he could for women industrial workers. After his visit the strikers won most of their demands. The long-term solution he and his allies sought was investigation and the passage of laws creating minimum wage boards set up by employees and employers, an idea very much like the National Recovery Act of the New Deal.[14]

Roosevelt's response to the strike stood in sharp contrast with that of the A.F.L.'s Samuel Gompers, who had little interest in marginal women workers. The Female Brain Trust who had aided TR in the 1912 campaign now kept him informed and fired up about social and economic justice. When martial law was declared in a violent West Virginia bituminous coal labor dispute, Roosevelt denounced mine owners for exploiting workers and courts for issuing injunctions against labor unions. In the past he had been inclined to blame breaches of law and order on striking workers, but after 1912, thanks to his advisors, he saw owners' mistreatment of employees as being at the heart of the ensuing riots.[15]

The Female Brain Trust also urged Roosevelt to become more vocal about suffrage because women voters were more likely to support Progressive causes, and he did. Maud Nathan and others talked Roosevelt into being the keynote speaker at the Suffrage Pageant at the Metropolitan Opera House on May 2. Newspapers reported that Moosettes were "nervous" about what the "race suicide" president would say, but the audience warmed up to Roosevelt quickly and applauded his praise for Nathan, Jane Addams, and Florence Kelley and their work on child labor, immigration, and the minimum wage. He pointedly hailed the importance of suffrage as "our cause." For a former president to praise women's capacity for "statesmanship" and acknowledge in public how much he counted on the advice of women advisors was a breakthrough for all women.[16]

But with the Newett libel case over his drinking habits pending, he moved on to controversial ground when he talked of his 1912 campaign in Michigan: "I saw placards, 'Vote Against Woman Suffrage,' in the saloons out there." When he heard audible "gasps of surprise" from the audience, Roosevelt corrected himself: "I mean, I saw them on the outside of the saloons, of course." The women in the audience broke into relieved laughter. He won them over completely when he made fun of those who claimed women were not physically capable of voting, and he told them he believed that the underworld, the red light district, and the bosses would be defeated if women got the vote. TR said that at the time of the Seneca Falls Declaration most people believed that "the family would be ruined if it was not based on the theory of masterful headship" by the husband, but "a far nobler and higher ideal . . . the ideal of an equal partnership of duty and right between the man and the woman" had supplanted the older form of marriage. He concluded: "The measure of the growth of civilization is the increased respect for the woman who is neither a doll nor a drudge."[17]

He discovered that outside of suffrage, social work, and reform circles, his ideas fell on deaf audiences. Undeterred, he still argued for women to be put on county committees so that they could influence the party nominating process. In the years 1912–18, when he became deeply committed to women's equality, public opinion still headed the other way, especially after instances of sabotage in Britain were blamed on the Pankhursts, and an English suffragist committed suicide by throwing herself in front of a horse on Derby Day. Hostility toward feminism became more overt and the press branded it as "subversive of the very foundations of social stability" and said the militants had "killed all womanliness in thousands of young girls."[18]

Roosevelt's advanced feminism was confined by its deep Victorian commitment to the determining power of gender difference. He had built his cultural leadership on calling on men and women to hew to gender duties. How comfortable would he be with the violation of gender boundaries in dress, sexuality, work, and behavior that feminists used to define larger lives for themselves? Getting the vote seemed a just women's demand; eroding the power of Victorian respectability to enlarge the sexual freedom of women struck him as immoral. To the end of his life he insisted that a woman's "primal and most essential duty" was motherhood and large families were a racial necessity. In classically Victorian terms he saw woman as "the high priestess of the race," capable of statesmanship based on her identity as a mother. Despite his indulgence toward Alice, he never understood her rebellion against proper Victorian womanhood. Nevertheless, he could accept the Women's Trade Union League's insistence upon safeguarding women as future mothers by protective legislation. His closest women friends remembered him as a compulsive talker who nevertheless listened to women's opinions better than most political men of his generation.[19]

When TR told Fanny Parsons that he imagined women in politics would be good at campaigning for pure milk legislation because they understood babies, she laughed in his face. She told him she "had no intention of limiting my activities to milk for babies." Ridicule from one of his most devoted friends "really annoyed" him, but Fanny's laughter taught him to expect women to be interested in much more than municipal housekeeping.[20]

The Progressive Party proved to be a dynamic force in American politics. Despite the opposition it faced, the party enjoyed success for a while, winning minimum hours and wage laws, workmen's compensation, widows' pensions, and other legislation on the state level. Bull Mooser George Rublee joined the Wilson administration and pushed a child labor law through Congress, and the party won forty-two state offices. As its national membership grew, Bull Moosers had two senators and gained twenty seats in the House. Five thousand Moose Clubs were founded around the country to spread Roosevelt's ideas. Massachusetts had a Federation of Progressive Women and many states had Boys' Progressive Clubs.[21]

The Bull Moose Party fostered more innovation than the Republicans and Democrats because it combined electoral politics with a quest for solutions to social problems using a "party laboratory, manned by experts." Roosevelt created the Progressive National Service (P.N.S.), headed by Frances Kellor, to study social problems and develop plans for broad educational and legislative initiatives which the party would promote. Because courts had struck down labor legislation protecting the health and safety of workers, the P.N.S. advocated protective legislation for women and allied itself closely with the Consumers' League.[22]

Roosevelt planned a nationwide Progressive network which would spread its message through modern advertising techniques, movies, Chautauqua speakers, and a vast number of volunteers, all funded by small contributions from "the people" and not the wealthy. He asked Jane Addams to create "A Plan of Work" for the establishment of six service bureaus, researching and recommending reforms for labor, children, social insurance, immigration, and social and industrial justice. Gifford Pinchot worked on conservation and George L. Record on democracy, but most of the P.N.S. effort was tied to women, children, and labor issues.[23]

TR acted as the mouthpiece of the Female Brain Trust, taking to the stump speeches filled with their statistics and proposals at the same time they acted as his ambassadors to the Lower East Side. Roosevelt's Female Brain Trust served as a much smarter legislative research bureau than La Follette had ever had from the University of Wisconsin. Corinne, Ethel, Mary Dreier, and Frances Kellor worked with him daily to keep the issues of 1912 alive. Twenty-one states had Progressive Service organizations by 1914 and its members lobbied successfully for an Industrial Relations Commission and less successfully for its Progressive Congressional Program.[24]

On his post-1912 speaking tours, Roosevelt dramatized the human cost of laissez-faire industrialism as no other politician had ever done. He told the story of Sarah Knisley, a young woman whose arm had been crushed in an industrial accident, and promised Mary Dreier he would do "whatever I can do for those whom you rightly call the most helpless group of the great industrial army of America."[25]

Though critics still insisted that TR used the Progressive Party only as a vehicle for the promotion of his own ambitions, his behavior showed they were wrong. He channeled his earnings as a writer into Progressive coffers after his chances of being a candidate had grown dim. When he told Kermit that using "an aggressive educational fight" "to advance the principles" of true progressivism meant more to him than regaining the White House, he spoke the truth. Frances Kellor's book about prison conditions shocked Roosevelt so much that he gave a speech defending the rehabilitation of prisoners and attacking the convict lease system which profited states more than prisoners. He knew he won no votes by attacking convict labor, but he felt righteous anger about what Kellor had shown him. He understood he had lost in 1912 because small businessmen and prosperous farmers who might have voted for him considered him "too radical," yet he went on supporting much "too radical" ideas for the rest of his life.[26]

He wanted to repair his relationship with the American people, but he insisted on doing it on his own terms. While he and his women allies lobbied for the abolition of child labor and the passage of protective legislation for women, most national politicians were as oblivious of women as political partners as William Jennings Bryan who, according to William Allen White, "seemed not to know that there was another sex than his."[27]

ROOSEVELT'S romance with America proved to be as tumultuous as ever. His devotees voted him into electoral history: no other third-party candidate had ever beaten an incumbent vote for vote. Yet many more loved him than voted for him. After he lost the election and was reviled by critics, an *American Magazine* poll anointed him the "greatest man in the United States." An *Independent* magazine poll rated Roosevelt "America's most useful citizen. . . . He has a hold on the public that he can sway it more powerfully than any man now living." But he decided to spend what credibility he had left to advance ideas that were not always popular.[28]

Though more committed to social justice ideals than winning elections, TR tried to build up the Progressive Party, speaking at dinners and receptions regularly in the first half of 1913. The Progressive National Service enlisted John Dewey and Thomas Edison to promote reforms in education while another group including the actor William Gillette and writers Franklin P. Adams, Will Irwin, and Samuel Merwin planned to use movies to dramatize Progressive causes. Even a simple reception of the Nassau County Progressives "rather knocked" Edith out in her state of weakened health, but she worried more about Theodore than about herself: "Theodore works like a dog. He is not having an easy time poor dear."[29]

He wanted anything but an easy time. While he wrote his autobiography, he put his American Historical Association talk together with the speeches he had given on his 1910 post-Africa trip so that Scribner's could publish them as *History as Literature, and Other Essays.* His co-author, Edmund Heller, came to Sagamore Hill off and on to work with him on the *Life-Histories of African Game Animals,* which Scribner's also published. Roosevelt made speeches urging the party faithful to keep fighting politically until they had achieved their goal: "to compel the rich to divide with the poor."[30]

While TR struggled to move the country toward reform, Dick Derby pressed his courtship of Ethel as he worked as an attending surgeon at St. Luke's Hospital and at the Ruptured and Crippled Hospital in New York. Like Ethel, Dick was an ardent Progressive who thought Ted and Eleanor were becoming shallow society people. In February, Ethel finally agreed to marry Dick. Having listened carefully to TR's prison reform speech, they planned when they were married to hire only ex-prisoners as servants.[31]

Distracted by having to plan Ethel's wedding, Edith regretted that she could not help TR with all of his political and literary work. But she had gained enough strength to see that his mail got answered and made sure meals were on the table for his many unannounced guests. In one week at Sagamore Hill, even in the relative quiet of his eclipse in 1913, as many as 175 meals were served to the family and legions of guests. Edith listened as he read her drafts of speeches and chapters. When his hours at his desk expanded too much, she would simply come into the library and announce that his workday was over.[32]

On April 4 in Oyster Bay's Christ Church, Ethel and Dick were married. Endicott Peabody assisted in the ceremony, and among the three hundred guests TR welcomed a reunion of his cronies, including the Abbotts, Robert Bacon, George Cortelyou, Henry Cabot Lodge, William Loeb, George L. Meyer, Frank Munsey, Fanny Parsons, Gifford Pinchot, Jacob Riis, Franklin Roosevelt, and Henry White. (Niece Eleanor missed the wedding because she was expecting.) The press jostled the guests, however, and crowds of onlookers tore Ethel's veil and picked over the interior of the church for mementos. Newspapers reported that Roosevelt also disrupted the dignity of the event by asking a local band to play ragtime as the bride and groom left the church. As Ethel boarded the steamer with Dick to honeymoon in Europe, she realized that she was no longer her mother's child, no longer Edith's assistant in keeping a great man's life "going smoothly." For Edith, however, the wedding held more compensations than sorrows. It pleased her that Ethel would follow her example and become an "old-fashioned wife" who would not be too independent.[33]

TR longed to be buoyed by a political crusade or a raucous audience, and he wrote his honeymooning daughter: "I am working with heated unintelligence at my 'biography' and I fairly loathe it, now." He restlessly began planning a trip to South America: at first he imagined he would spread the word of progressivism on a speaking tour. Then the drama of crossing the Mato Grosso, the Brazilian equivalent of the Wild West, took hold. However, Edith and his doctors strongly opposed the idea of foreign adventure.[34]

He finished his *Autobiography* in time to leave on May 24 for the Newett trial in Marquette, Michigan, where he hoped to put to rest some of the ugly lies told about him in 1912. A *New York Times* reporter who traveled on the train with him wrote that he showed signs of "weary impatience" with the ordeal he faced and had "less of his old buoyancy" about him. Roosevelt knew ahead of time that Newett's witnesses might charge that he had been so drunk at Union Station in St. Louis on October 11, 1910, before a memorable airplane ride with Arch Hoxsey, that he could barely walk out of the depot. Rumors of surprise witnesses circulated as well as the rumor that the journalist J. Martin Miller said that he had drunk whiskey at a dinner for Uncle Joe Cannon, which TR knew was a "pure lie."[35]

He brightened quickly when enthusiastic supporters in this Bull Moose town greeted his arrival. When TR opened his testimony grimly on Tuesday morning, the ailing Newett, a small-town editor known for his acid tongue and temperance views, did not appear. Reporters saw "nothing mirthful" in Roosevelt's "curiously protruding jaw" as he spoke in his own defense. Careful to avoid his college years when he did drink to excess a few times, he testified that since his maturity he had never been under the influence of alcohol and that he took whiskey or brandy only under doctor's orders for his chronically weak throat. He said he drank white wine with Poland water at home and Madeira or champagne on rare occasions. He recalled having five or six mint juleps when he lived in the White House. He did not say he was an abstainer, but merely "very abstemious," which was true.[36]

His witnesses were formidable. His friends Robert Bacon, O. K. Davis, James Garfield, Alex Lambert, Gifford Pinchot, Jacob Riis, and cousin Emlen Roosevelt testified he was no drunk. He was merely a gesticulating, exuberant character. Admiral Dewey, who had known him since 1891, said that TR was never drunk but merely "full of spirits, full of life and animation. All who knew him knew his peculiarities in that respect."[37]

Newett's case dissolved when Miller, his star witness, fled to Canada because he had been indicted for grand larceny. Without eyewitness testimony, Newett's lawyers tried to insinuate that politicians, an occupational group held in low esteem by the general public, were often fond of drink, but Roosevelt pointed out that his frequent associates were also naturalists and historians, less alcoholically suspect groups. Reporters watched as Roosevelt "wriggled and gesticulated as he listened. He made faces, he muttered, he nodded in approval, or he said 'No!' with violent shakings of his head."[38]

Finally, Newett read in court a statement of retraction. Though he could have asked for $10,000, TR waived damages because his goal had always been to repair his reputation. It was no surprise when the jury found for Roosevelt and awarded him six cents damages. The courtroom erupted in cheers and he was barely able to prevent the spectators from carrying him out of the room on their shoulders. Humorists joked afterward, "In other words, the Colonel would have us believe that a man isn't necessarily drunk every time he acts that way."[39]

TR returned to Edith "in good spirits" and allowed himself a three-day holiday. The whole family felt "an immense relief," though Edith worried about lawyers' fees and travel expenses for so many witnesses. He relished the "heaps & heaps" of congratulatory telegrams that poured in from around the country, proof that he was making his way back into the nation's good graces.[40]

But a revealing incident showed TR was ambivalent about always having to live his life to win public approval. On May 2, just days before he left for the Newett trial, he had behaved recklessly. That afternoon, Edith wrote that during a convivial visit on the first floor Theodore and several friends "had emptied the whiskey decanters." She left the house and turned their further alcoholic entertainment over to James Amos, their butler. TR consoled himself and his friends with whiskey at a time when reporters could have walked up to a window and his Newett defense would have been blown sky high.[41]

Roosevelt had exhausted his patience with the slow political process and the frustration of trying to educate public opinion until he struck out, quite literally, against what he hated most in modern America. The sexual immorality detailed by the Evelyn Nesbit stories mounted up like an invading army that would bring in its aftermath the destruction of the family, and, before long, total moral decline. When he looked immorality in the face, he lashed out against it. He was in friendly contact with young men who worked in other offices in *The Outlook*'s building. On one memorable occasion they were celebrating a special triumph, and they invited TR to join their party. He was not offended by the inebriated good fellowship that surrounded him at the affair, and they toasted him and drank to his health.

But another less endearing toast followed. One drunk said: "Let us drink to our *sweethearts,*—our *friends' wives.*" Before the young man knew what hit him, TR lunged forward and "struck a blow right on his chin, which sent him twenty feet." Having repulsed the voice of boasting adultery, he left the room, followed by the sound of applause.[42]

SOON AFTER her husband won the Newett case, Edith hurried to Italy to be with her sister Emily during surgery. Before she departed TR and Edith spent the night together at Ted and Eleanor's in New York, and he wrote his wife afterward that she should extend her trip to Russia and Spain, two places she had always wanted to see. During Edith's long absence, from June until early August, he found himself in an entirely altered mood. He was "dreadfully homesick" for his wife and he "did hate to have the pretty thing go!"[43]

But his loneliness did not deter him from working magic with worshipful audiences. When he walked into a Rochester, New York, auditorium in June 1913 a capacity crowd filled the room and many had to stand in the aisles. A small boy dressed in a white suit was lifted onto the stage to sing while a big band played "Roosevelt, My Roosevelt." Loud cheering from the Bull Moose crowd turned into a roar of excitement when they first caught sight of their leader coming into the hall. His adoring audience greeted him with prolonged moose calls. He smiled at them and then let loose with his own moose calls, and declared with wry humor: "It takes a trained zoologist to distinguish between a tiger and a moose." His joke sunk in and the audience "went wild."[44]

Roosevelt told his audience that the time had come for a "new collective morality" and shift of more of the tax burden to the "unearned increment" on income from stocks and bonds, like a capital gains tax. He also defended raising men's morality by establishing the same moral law for the two sexes. Such ideas won him little recognition in the newspapers.[45]

The year 1913 marked the height of the "age of socialist inquiry" in which reformers asked how government could be taken from economic interests and put into the hands of the average citizen. Reformers borrowed practical socialist ideals like the ones Beatrice and Sidney Webb promoted in England. Their eclectic search for solutions did not imply an embrace of Karl Marx, nor was it simply ameliorative welfare capitalism. TR and his allies aimed to enlarge definitions of the public good, to elucidate a vision of America as a great humane commonwealth, to revive democracy by preventing extremes of wealth and poverty "by collective action through the agencies of government."[46]

He recommended Vladimir Simkhovitch's book on socialism to several friends because it repudiated state socialism while defending the incorporation of socialist ideas into a democratic framework. Roosevelt and

Simkhovitch saw promise in Eduard Bernstein's proposals for expanding definitions of the common welfare by gradual and democratic adoption of socialist methods of ending poverty. When H. J. Whigham of *Metropolitan Magazine* asked Roosevelt to write about socialism, he declined because of the press of other work, but added: "I am friendly to the kind of Socialism of which you speak. I am utterly against the kind of Socialism of Debs, and that kind of applied Socialism . . . which means the break-up of the family. But as you say, I am not to be frightened in the least by the word Socialism, or of ideas because they are called Socialistic."[47]

As a popular magazine writer he still defended the strenuous life, and urged "the cultivation of those primitive virile qualities which are lost in any decadent and luxurious over-civilization." He also recommended "getting back to nature." He became the patron saint of G. Stanley Hall's remasculinization movement to cleanse public education of its feminization and to reclaim boys from their mothers' influence. The interest he had taken in education and teaching boys to lead the strenuous life through athletics led him to be invited to review ten thousand boys from New York City's Public Schools' Athletic League as they drilled and ran races in Central Park. Thousands cheered when he preached that athletics would serve as a "leveling force which makes for democracy." Baron Pierre de Coubertin read Roosevelt's defense of athletics and the outdoor life to the Olympic Council. Yet, as athleticism swept the public schools in America, and TR was hailed as the guiding spirit of a new more strenuous and masculine culture, he still longed for a more unequivocal reconciliation with his public and for more heroic roles for himself.[48]

With Edith away in Europe, TR felt freer to expand his proposed speaking trip to South America to include a project he knew she strongly opposed. He had become cronies with Father Zahm, an independent-thinking Darwinian Catholic priest and explorer, and together they planned to traverse South America from Uruguay to Venezuela. Zahm convinced Roosevelt that travel to the interior of Brazil's Amazon jungle was as safe as "a promenade down . . . Fifth Avenue."[49]

Theodore's letters to Edith were secretive about the extensive plans he was making. She told Kermit that TR wanted to go to South America in October "partly in order to be away from home at election time," and that he "needs more scope, and since he can't be President must go away from home to have it." During their long separation in 1913, Edith felt "like the homesick school boy." If her husband went far away from her again, it would be even more worrisome because she knew he longed for dangerous adventure more than ever, yet he had less stamina and will to survive it.[50]

Roosevelt had already won the backing for his South American trip from Henry Fairfield Osborn of the American Museum of Natural History, who recommended that he collect rare specimens for the museum with the help of ornithologist George K. Cherrie, a specialist in South American birds, and Leo Miller, a mammalogist. The South American crew would be funded in part, as his African trip had been, by his childhood playmate and Woodrow Wilson's college roommate Cleveland Dodge. Though he took genuine care with the scientific plans for the trip, he trusted Father Zahm to plan their travel and seemed unfazed when his friend cavalierly proposed a journey of several weeks mostly overland and then upriver with steel-hulled boats.[51]

After seeing the Hopi Snake Dance in Arizona with Quentin and Archie, TR returned home on August 25 to marital tensions. Edith felt irritated that "in his letters to me he preserves a Sphinx-like silence & except for the fact that he sails on Oct. 4—I know nothing of his plans." Clearly miffed, she heard from Ted's mother-in-law that her husband confided more freely to his in-laws about his plans than to her. When she finally heard the whole story of her husband's intended trek through the Brazilian wilderness, Edith announced that she was joining him on his speaking tour. She wrote to Kermit to plead with him to accompany his father to stop him from taking too many risks. Kermit replied that he did not want to follow in the wake of his father's folly. At age twenty-four he had his own slow-starting career and his proposal of marriage to Belle Willard on his mind, and in September he was recovering from broken ribs and missing teeth suffered when he fell forty feet from atop a steel beam while he was bridge-building near São Paulo.[52]

But Edith would not let it rest. In case recklessness and impulsive heroics set in, she cajoled Kermit to be ready to be his father's protector. Reluctantly, Kermit agreed to take on his mother's role of the great man's guardian, but his father's pride had to be spared. In front of TR, Kermit was to insist that he could "make much of this trip with Father" to advance his own career. Theodore never knew that Kermit came along on his trip because Edith pleaded with him to act as her surrogate.[53]

The day before he departed for South America, more than two thousand Bull Moose supporters met to hear Roosevelt's farewell speech under a glass roof at the Garden of the Dance at the New York Theater. The crowd may have been one-third female but they nevertheless stomped their feet, waved their napkins, and shouted, "We want Teddy!" TR was especially touched that his niece Eleanor had left her busy Washington duties, caring for small children and entertaining to advance her husband's career as assistant secretary of the navy, to join in the cheering tribute. He was much happier to see her than the many "wild asses of the desert" among his squabbling followers.

Extracting himself from his supporters' devotion was not easy, but he bid them good-bye at last by promising them: "All my life I have been engaged in work which culminated during the last eighteen months; and of all my political life it is these eighteen months to which I look back with most unalloyed satisfaction. . . . I know that in the end, whatever may befall us personally, the cause will win." In TR's allusion to "whatever may befall us personally" was a clue that he already contemplated not returning to "the almost intolerable burden of my political work."[54]

The next day, October 4, the Roosevelt expedition, including Father Zahm, valet Jacob Sigg, Arctic explorer Anthony Fiala, and Cherrie, accompanied by Edith and her niece Margaret Roosevelt, prepared to set sail on the S.S. *Van Dyck*. Roosevelt, dressed in a gray business suit punctuated by a red carnation, bounded up the gangplank, fresh from an early-morning haircut and a cheerful breakfast with Fanny Parsons, Corinne, and Alex Lambert. He reassured photographers and newspaper reporters that he would come back in "fighting trim" for the 1914 elections, when Progressives would again challenge the two established parties.[55]

Edith said her husband's sense of release, as he bid farewell to the demands of the Progressive Party on the dock that day, reminded her of "Christian in *Pilgrim's Progress* when the burden fell from his back." TR laughed more wholeheartedly than he had in years as he watched the antics of passengers at their deck games, and his jubilant mood prompted him to dance a sailor's hornpipe for the assembled guests at dinner.[56]

Once their southward journey was under way, he put out of his mind the irritating charges made by a Republican newspaper in Brooklyn that he had promoted the Progressive Party out of a secret hope of electing Democrats. Unfettered by her usual cares, too, Edith had not left a forwarding address for her sister Emily, and could rest easy knowing that Ethel would keep track of Quentin at Groton and Archie at Harvard. Refreshed by ocean air, TR wrote Henry Cabot Lodge that the cruise would be a good thing for Edith because at Sagamore Hill she wore herself out with work, while on ship she stayed in her stateroom reading until lunch. Lodge envied his friend's upcoming adventure while he recovered at home in Massachusetts from a duodenal ulcer with a perforation which he insisted had been just as big as TR's gunshot wound. Yet, Lodge, like Edith, worried about TR because he knew of explorers who had gone into the same "particularly unhealthy region" of Brazil only to die there of fever spread by mosquitoes or to be killed by natives.[57]

Overflowing and exuberant, TR at 220 pounds could no more discipline his appetite than his flow of work and visitors at Sagamore Hill. While on shipboard he walked an hour, skipped lunch—and then still overate. His weight was a hazard except when he threw it into the ship's tug-of-war between married and single men. As he had on many public occasions, he weighed in heavily on the side of marriage and won.[58]

When the ship reached Bahia, Kermit greeted them, and together they traveled to Rio, where they were swept up in the official round of activities—dinners, speeches, tours, receptions. Housed luxuriously in Princess Isabella's palace, Edith and Theodore felt welcome but besieged by official events and people. Foreign Minister Lauro Müller told the ex-president that the Brazilian government wanted him to consider altering his travel plans. Noted Brazilian explorer Colonel Candido Rondon had located the headwaters of an uncharted River of Doubt, which Müller hoped TR would explore. If Roosevelt agreed to chart the river from its source to its mouth, he could stand in history alongside Champlain or risk everything like Scott in an attempt to advance the reach of civilization around the globe. Both possibilities thrilled TR, and he snatched this new adventure without a second thought, as if it were a lifeline.

Müller wanted to take advantage of Roosevelt's publicity value. A worldwide celebrity who doubled as a prolific travel writer could enhance Brazil's prospects with international investors and tourists. Unlike earlier Brazilian diplomats who had feared U.S. encroachments into the Amazon, Müller welcomed an enlarged American trade presence, which he hoped TR's trip would bring. No one knew where the River of Doubt led, how long it was, or whether it flowed into the Madeira, Tapajós, Gy-Paraná, or Amazon River.[59]

Roosevelt's eagerness for exploration did not waver when he learned that Zahm had minimized the real danger they might face and that their steel-hulled motorboats would be worthless. He did not care if Brazil used him to bring international attention and trade to compensate economically for the collapse of the Amazon rubber trade. One Brazilian businessman put a cash value on TR's éclat: each day he traveled in their land was worth a million dollars to Brazil.[60]

When Henry Fairfield Osborn heard the news that the original museum expedition had been co-opted by the Brazilian government, he was angry. He called the plan reckless and warned that the museum might refuse to support the venture at all because the region was so unsafe. Osborn cautioned that Roosevelt might "not return alive." Unfazed, TR replied: "If it is necessary for me to leave my bones in South America, I am quite ready to do so." Edith had not been entirely surprised that his trip had been expanded. She had never had much luck standing in the way of her husband's ardor for danger.[61]

As the Brazil Railway took the Roosevelts through the new and rugged towns of the southernmost states, TR spoke to crowd after crowd and dictated almost an article a day to his secretary, Frank Harper, who mailed them off to *The Outlook*. Theodore found the adulation of his tour refreshing. Edith observed that her husband "scarcely sleeps" yet felt "perfectly well."[62]

Throughout his month and a half of speaking tours, TR tried to spread progressive ideals while also giving conciliatory foreign policy speeches markedly free from earlier imperial condescension. No longer sounding like the man who in 1901 had urged European powers to "spank" any South American state that "misbehaves," he sought more cooperative relations with the continent and sounded a respectful tone. In his October 24 speech, "American Internationalism" in Rio, he called for a unified Western Hemisphere with Argentina, Brazil, and Chile working for peace on equal footing with the United States.[63]

In Buenos Aires, TR met crowds estimated upwards of 250,000. A young girl threw roses toward his party, making a direct hit at him, knocking his glasses off his face. He responded with good humor, a smile, and a bow.[64]

In South America he and his political ideas were very much alive. As he preached Progressive Party doctrines, he befriended Argentina's Jacob Riis, Francisco P. Moreno, and the pro-labor socialist president of Uruguay, José Batlle y Ordóñez, who was trying to convince his legislature to pass laws establishing an eight-hour day, old-age pensions, and workmen's compensation.[65]

Finally, it was almost time for Edith and Margaret Roosevelt to sail home from Valparaíso. Edith had longed to return to Sagamore Hill "a thousand times" and had admitted to Ethel: "I feel a trifle down for I have not been able to help Fa[ther]." But she had made him laugh by imitating his clumsy French after a state dinner at Tucumán. They rode to the heights of the Andes and enjoyed the dramatic peaks together, and, most of all, they rejoiced in their reunion with their favorite son, Kermit. Kermit wrote to Belle Willard, who had just accepted his proposal, that his mother was "dreadfully worried" about their exploration and that she had been actively preparing him for his role as his father's protector.[66]

The night Edith left Theodore, November 26, Kermit described his father as feeling "quiet and sad." Theodore knew Edith feared he would never return to Sagamore Hill. But he would not give up what he called "his last chance to be a boy" for anything, not even his wife.[67]

Theodore and Kermit crossed the Andes on horses, traveling through southern Argentina. TR enjoyed singing cowboy songs to himself, reminiscing about his western days. Without Edith to guard his health, he gorged himself at a sheep ranch, eating ribs and flank and asking to carry the haunches home for a later snack. Exuberant again, he woke up his traveling companions at 3:30 a.m. with a Sioux war cry: "Whoo-oo-oop-ee!"[68]

A river steamer took Theodore and Kermit to meet Colonel Rondon. Even before the reorganized Roosevelt-Rondon expedition stopped at Corumbá, TR decided that he liked the half-Indian and half-Portuguese Rondon, a fearless spit-and-polish military man and explorer who had charted rivers, built roads and telegraph lines, and peaceably brought native people into the Brazilian nation. But tensions soon emerged within the expedition. George Cherrie complained in his diary that the trip was badly organized, and Kermit already resented Zahm for being "a foolish well meaning little fellow, who mislead [*sic*] father greatly."[69]

On Christmas Eve a homesick TR was "covered with prickly heat," as he wrote home to Edith from a putrid "hot little sidewheel steamer jammed with men, dogs, bags and belongings, partially cured and rather bad smelling skins, and the like." "Drenched with sweat most of the waking hours," he found most nights too hot for sleeping, but he reassured his wife: "I enjoy it; but my dainty little sweetheart most certainly would not."[70]

After Roosevelt injured his knee jumping off one of the boats that had taken them north he felt more like an "old man." He turned his pen to adventure and travel articles for *Scribner's*, determined to associate himself in the hunt and on the page with vitality and heroism. He carried with him two classic texts of chivalric romance, the *Chanson de Roland* and Sir Walter Scott's *Quentin Durward*. TR's hero, Roland, chose heroic death over asking for help, and Quentin, an emissary for a foreign king, saved the monarch's life by killing a wild boar with a spear. TR wrote that he had always dreamed of repeating Quentin Durward's feat, and when he stopped at the fazenda (estate) São João to hunt he saw his chance. He borrowed a spear from Dom João and used it to kill a "valiant and truculent" boar.[71]

On the four-hundred-mile muleback trip northward from Tapirapuan, TR withstood 104-degree days and rode long hours in the sun across the sandy plains of the Planalto, the Brazilian highlands, and then into the Amazon valley. Fascinated by the blood-sucking bats that preyed on cattle and men in the region, he watched with interest as the Brazilian packmen disciplined their bucking and overloaded oxen. Though he grew homesick for Edith, he found peace of mind reciting Longfellow's "Saga of King Olaf" and selections from Kipling and Keats to himself.[72]

At night, around the campfire, in anticipation of danger ahead, the men traded stories of adventure gone awry—Rondon had nearly starved living only on jungle fruit while laying down a trail for telegraph lines and Fiala had been stalked by polar bears while stranded in the Arctic.[73] The campfire circle regaled TR with stories about piranha that inhabited the rivers they were soon to cross. Rondon said he had lost a toe and had been attacked by the killer fish. Cherrie also had scars to prove that piranha were dangerous. Knowing his audience back home, TR wrote up the piranha tales for his *Scribner's* series and became the first popular natural history writer to publicize the man-eating cannibal fish of the Amazon.[74] He reported luridly: "They mutilate swimmers—in every river town in Paraguay there are men who have been thus mutilated; they will rend and devour alive any wounded man or beast; for blood excites them to madness."[75] Danger and the chance to write a harrowing story enticed him to bathe in piranha-infested waters, which Kermit promptly photographed. Fortunately, no fish accepted TR's invitation.

Newsreel photographers and reporters had recorded his speaking tour, but TR banned them from his River of Doubt trip because he wanted to report its drama as he saw it. Men back home needed to hear about the "wild, naked savages" and the still-open frontiers which stood as a summons to their courage. He encouraged settlers to come to the Brazilian lands, plains and rain forest alike, which were "as well fitted for stock-raising as Oklahoma."[76] Through his Brazilian articles TR introduced readers to "dark-skinned, lean, hard-faced men, in slouch-hats, worn shirts and trousers, and fringed leather aprons, with heavy spurs on their bare feet" because he wanted to awaken a manly spirit of adventure in their overtamed souls.[77]

Even before they reached the River of Doubt the expedition of two hundred saddle and pack animals nearly foundered over heat prostration and disorganization. Father Zahm complained so much and offered so little help that Cherrie's and Kermit's patience wore thin. Trailside remnants of ill-fated expeditions, bleached skeletons of oxen and mules, were joined ominously by the cast-off excess boxes of the Roosevelt-Rondon expedition. At the magnificent Utiarity Falls they faced a crisis.[78]

On previous South American adventures, Zahm had been carried in a sedan chair across the Andes by local natives, but Roosevelt would not countenance this. The priest had so irritated TR that on February 1, Roosevelt composed a letter, which he asked other members of the party to sign, saying that for the good of the expedition Zahm must make his way to "settled country at once." TR sent Zahm and several others away because if the expedition was to survive the journey the party had to be reduced to a small core of hardy men. He also had to intervene with Rondon to convince him that luxurious tents and crates of candy were impractical to pack into densely vegetated terrain where they would have to be carried over steep hills by *camaradas*, or native porters.[79]

Then Roosevelt discovered that Rondon had forgotten to pack several crates of food. The river might prove to be several hundred miles long and the rainy season would make hunting and foraging difficult, so their twenty-two men—TR, Rondon, his navigator friend Lyra, the naturalist Cherrie, Kermit, Dr. Cajazeira, and sixteen *camaradas*—needed three or four months' worth of rations. Sending for more food would delay them until the river might be too low for safe travel, so TR chose to go ahead and gamble that they could reach the end of the River of Doubt before their food ran out. Wagering his own life for a heroic mission was a proper choice, but risking the lives of his son and the rest of the expedition was different.[80]

The Rondon-Roosevelt expedition prepared to embark on the River of Doubt February 27. The local natives, the Nhambiquaras, had murdered two Brazilian employees of Rondon's Telegraph Commission and left them buried standing up where the expedition found them. When they sent their last cables to Edith from Utiarity Falls, they began their river exploration with foreboding.[81]

When Edith received news from Kermit telling her that her husband had been suffering from his usual sleeplessness, a minor leg injury, and missing her terribly she responded that because her husband "went of his own volition" she could not be too sympathetic. She added: "I never felt it was a wise trip but probably I was wrong." But she faithfully tended his political garden in his absence, attending Progressive functions and answering his mail.[82]

On his journey Theodore had stomped to death a poisonous coral snake as it approached him in camp and had his underwear eaten by termites. Unfazed, he handed out chocolate to the *camaradas* and kept up everyone's good cheer. Yet when they surveyed the rushing water as it twisted and veered farther away from the last Brazilian settlement, Cherrie estimated that at the rate they were going they would be about thirty-five days' short of food. Kermit grew impatient with the long delays they endured when rapids blocked their progress on the river. The *camaradas* labored long hours doing back-wrenching portages of canoes and baggage along the shore. Meanwhile TR wrote a book about their adventures and fortified himself by reading the Stoic Epictetus.[83]

On March 15 the River of Doubt provided serious trouble at Broken Canoe Rapids. Kermit took the lead dugout, which ventured ahead of the others. What happened next became a matter of dispute. TR wrote that while listening for the sound of rapids ahead of him, Kermit commanded his canoemen, Simplicio and João, to stay close enough to shore to avoid being pulled into the vortex of a dangerous waterfall ahead. Then, a whirlpool pulled them into the falls. Rondon claimed that Kermit had been rash and had intentionally forced the canoemen to head straight into the rapids.[84]

The rushing water enveloped Kermit's canoe as it crashed down into the falls ahead. In the descent, his helmet jammed over his face holding the water in and the air out. At the bottom of the falls another whirlpool overturned his canoe. Ten days' worth of food supplies and the canoe disappeared, and, worst of all, Simplicio was never seen again. Theodore ran ahead onshore to see if his son had survived and found Kermit still breathing. TR admitted that "the fear of some fatal accident befalling him was always a nightmare to me."[85]

From that moment, the excitement of the journey turned to apprehension. More rapids awaited them, smashing their canoes and blocking their passage to the river ahead. They were forced to build dugouts and then lower them with ropes down steep passages or to carve out a path for them along the dense vegetation along the shore. While the *camaradas* did most of the grueling labor of the eight-hour portages to reach navigable stretches of the river, Rondon explored the shore with his dog, Lobo. Howls reminiscent of calls issued by spider monkeys rang out as two arrows pierced and killed Lobo. If native hunters living along the River of Doubt were close enough to shoot the dog, the whole expedition was in danger. Rondon hurried back to camp to put the expedition on armed guard to prepare for an attack.

The next days of the journey tested everyone's fortitude. The arrows that had killed Rondon's dog kept the men from venturing too far from the shore in search of food; Rondon put everyone on shortened rations, but he soon found that someone was stealing food from their scarce supplies. The calls of armed natives nearby in the forest reminded them that they could be attacked at any time.

To keep up the spirits of the group Rondon decided that it was time to hold a ceremony changing the name of the river to the Rio Roosevelt, but as they posted a marker TR and Kermit realized their chances of getting out alive grew poorer with each delay. Tension mounted among the men. Rondon wanted to chart with care every turn of the river, but Kermit and TR, when faced with privation and the prospect of Indian attack, saw the need for haste. Even so, each time dugouts were lost, the whole expedition was forced to stop long enough to hew more vessels out of trees. Cherrie wrote in his diary that he doubted whether all of them would ever make it to Manáos alive.[86]

On March 27 they reached a particularly treacherous bend in the river and two dugouts overturned and were caught against boulders. To stop them from being pulled into the rapids and destroyed, TR rushed chest-deep into the water where he, Kermit, and several *camaradas* worked for three hours to pull out the tangled dugouts. In the struggle Roosevelt bruised and scraped his leg severely. Abscesses soon formed at the site of his old carriage accident injury. Within a day, malaria and a high fever struck him down.

After following the river for six weeks the men were exhausted. Traversing rapid after rapid and portaging through dense jungle had worn them down. Fever made some delirious, yet the *camaradas* still had to pitch camp in the dark and in the rain. Under way again, they discovered on March 28 that the river before them ran through miles of rapids tucked into an almost impassable gorge bordered by steep, "nearly vertical" hills. Turning around to head back to their starting point while fighting against the current was impossible, but moving forward through rapids encased by canyons which blocked their path would require more than heroic energy. And they were running out of food. They had no choice but to cut their baggage further, and even that did not guarantee they could cross the steep hills.[87]

Rondon wanted to abandon the dugouts, but Kermit convinced him to use ropes to lower the crafts down the falls. They set up camp at one of the heights which approached the site where the series of rapids rushed downward. On March 30, Kermit and the *camaradas* worked to lower the dugouts with ropes only to have one smashed on the rocks. His bedridden father sweated with high fever as the "very disheartened" men hurried to move the dugouts. According to Cherrie, they believed that "Indians were on all sides" of their camp.[88]

When camp was finally set up at the bottom of a waterfall, TR could walk only with assistance from Cherrie. He moved from his sickbed slowly across the precarious rock face to a new resting place. Kermit wrote that he was "worried a lot about Father's heart," most likely because of the palpitations and shortness of breath he had been suffering. On April 2, when it seemed unlikely they could make it out together, an even greater sense of crisis took hold. Rondon called for "every man to fight for himself" to escape the jungle on his own. But Kermit convinced the group to stick together and keep trying to move the dugouts down the rapids.[89]

TR's high fever made him ramble. Stranded in mossy hills reminiscent of Chinese prints he had seen at William Sturgis Bigelow's house, he recited over and over Samuel Taylor Coleridge's "Kubla Khan," which tells of a "deep romantic chasm," "a savage place" "with ceaseless turmoil seething, / As if this earth in fast thick pants were breathing. . . . And 'mid this tumult Kubla heard from far / Ancestral voices prophesying war!" If he did not return from his delirium, he was at least being defeated by a formidable foe he saw in poetic terms, "the devil of evil wild nature in the tropics."[90]

He became too sick to walk and worried that Kermit might not survive if an invalid held the expedition back. Kermit understood well why his father would rather die than know "he was a burden." Cherrie recalled that TR said: "Cherrie, I want you and Kermit to go ahead. We have reached the point where some of us must stop. I feel I am only a burden to the party." They had packed morphine in the medical supplies, and Kermit, Dr. Cajazeira, Rondon, and Cherrie took turns keeping watch over Roosevelt to make sure he did not "make the great sacrifice" and end his life to save theirs. But before TR could sacrifice himself to save others, he came close to dying of natural causes. Cherrie later said: "There were a good many days, a good many mornings, when I looked at Colonel Roosevelt and said to myself, he won't be with us tonight; and I would say the same thing in the evening, he can't possibly live until morning."[91]

Cut to half-rations and subsisting mostly on palm hearts, the company was nearly starving. The *camarada* Julio, whom Kermit called a "shirker," had been stealing food for days. His supervisor, Sergeant Paixão, had hit him and reprimanded him severely because his selfishness might cost other men their lives. On April 3 the strain of living under danger and deprivation for so long caused Julio to crack. After a dispute he shot Paixão and fled into the forest. The same day, as the rain pounded on them, Theodore "had a very bad go of fever, was delirious." Kermit stayed up until midnight with his father until Dr. Cajazeira and then Rondon took over. Kermit admitted that he was "in a blue funk, as I have been for some time to get Father out of the country."[92]

The next day Kermit had fever, too, and found his father faint. TR's fever and chills were compounded by his painfully swollen leg. When it was time to move onto the open river again, the *camaradas* had to carry him to place him in a dugout, where he was exposed to a bruising hailstorm. That night in another fever TR begged Rondon to leave him, but, like Kermit, the explorer refused.[93]

Edith knew nothing of her husband's abject state. She wrote Bamie: "I felt that Theodore was tired and jaded and that the jungle became a desired haven of refuge in his mind." She regretted that the beloved haven she and Sagamore Hill offered had not satisfied him. In the first days of April, as her apprehension grew, Edith took Kermit's intended, Belle Willard, to the opera, where she lost her worries in beautiful arias "until I felt that S. America did not exist, and I was only 'a little bit of string' after all, and nothing mattered much."[94]

Edith's insistence on sending Kermit to protect TR saved his life. Despite Theodore's characteristic unselfishness and courage under duress, the hero of the expedition was not the aging man who had risked other lives to satisfy his wanderlust. Kermit stayed up with his father and made sure that the morphine was out of reach. He pushed Rondon to keep moving, and he did all he could to get the canoes down the rapids safely. He put his life on the line using ropes and his physical strength to move the dugouts past the steepest mountains. No one rose to the test with more foresight and concern for others.

As they paddled along once more, Julio called to them from the bank. They argued about whether or not to let him rejoin the party. Kermit wrote that Rondon "vacillated about Julio with 100 lies," but in the end, "after a fight," TR prevailed, and Julio was left behind, to starve or die at the hands of the natives. Rondon's entirely different version of the conflict claimed that Roosevelt acquiesced in an attempted but failed capture of Julio.[95]

Rondon and the Roosevelts continued to differ sharply about how fast the expedition should move. Kermit reported that Rondon wanted to stop and chart the river but TR stopped him. Rondon did not seem to realize how urgent it was to get TR to food and medical care. Rondon, in turn, resented the delay caused when Kermit sent men to find his lost dog, Trigueiro. On April 9, Kermit's fever was such that he could not walk and the next day he suffered from head- and backaches. TR's leg remained "very inflamed" and by the sixteenth had to be lanced without anesthesia. Brave as he was under the knife, he remained seriously ill and his son was apprehensive. With dwindling food and "no knowledge of what's ahead of us," Kermit and his father thought the end was near for all of them. Dysentery, fever, and hunger left everyone weak. According to Rondon, TR's abscessed leg "showed signs of erysipelas," which could mean that a strep infection would spread beyond his wound and into his bloodstream.[96]

But finally their luck turned. They found a deserted rubberman's hut and an old man nearby who told them they were in the Castanho. TR was too sick to get out of the dugout. As they came farther downriver, the expedition frightened settlers, who ran away or picked up guns expecting an Indian attack. With food at last, they could only hope that they would find a settlement before it was too late for TR, who "was scarcely able to stand up on his sick leg."[97]

By the time they reached the Rio Branco, Kermit thought his father "still very far from well," and he hooked up a canoe cover to shelter him from the sun. Kermit tried to rush the party along because TR's dysentery had opened a fistula in his buttocks which became infected and made sitting painful. He had also lost more than fifty pounds and suffered gastrointestinal upset that made it nearly impossible to eat.[98]

Within a few days they had contracted for a boat to take them to Manáos. After his ordeal of forty-eight days Roosevelt was still among the living when an ambulance carried him away. Of the *camaradas* who started the journey Simplicio, Paixão, and Julio did not make it to Manáos. Roosevelt had shown compassion for the *camaradas:* he shared his food with them, but until the end they ate out of different food supplies.

On Roosevelt's earlier Mato Grosso trip the white hunters had sent out a young "swarthy" native to scout dangerous ground ahead, and TR reported in *Through the Brazilian Wilderness* that they named him Nips after the monkey in *Swiss Family Robinson* who was used as a taster to protect the family from poisonous food. Though he admired their courage, TR saw the *camaradas* and other natives he met in Brazil with racial condescension.[99]

While he barely survived the ordeal, Roosevelt claimed it as a heroic triumph. He wrote: "Genuine wilderness exploration is as dangerous as warfare. The conquest of wild nature demands the utmost vigor, hardihood, and daring, and takes from the conquerors a heavy toll of life and health." Still too weak to get out of bed, he wrote his friend Arthur Lee from the Amazon, saying that after he attended Kermit's wedding in Madrid on June 11 he planned to come to London. He asked Lee to let the Royal Geographical Society know he was willing to give a talk on his South American exploration. He was proud of having charted "an absolutely unknown river," "the biggest affluent of the biggest affluent of the mightiest river in the world." He later likened the Rio Roosevelt to the Rhine.[100]

When TR wrote *Through the Brazilian Wilderness,* his version of the events of March 27 through April 17 differed markedly from what other members of the party recorded:

> While in the water trying to help with an upset canoe I had by my own clumsiness bruised my leg against a bowlder [*sic*]; and the resulting inflammation was somewhat bothersome. I now had a sharp attack of fever, but thanks to the excellent care of the doctor, was over it in about forty-eight hours; but Kermit's fever grew worse and he was unable to work for a day or two. We could walk over the portages, however.[101]

Though TR tried to dismiss his situation as somehow equivalent to Kermit's, he added in an offhand way that while his son had been bruised, he "was in worse shape" due to his abscess. He did not mention his despair, his heart trouble, the threat of erysipelas, the fistula, the possibility of suicide, his inability to walk, being carried by the *camaradas,* his delirium, or his nearness to death.[102]

Significantly, he pronounced: "No man has any business to go on such a trip as ours unless he will refuse to jeopardize the welfare of his associates by any delay caused by a weakness or ailment of his. It is his duty to go forward, if necessary on all fours, until he drops. Fortunately, I was put to no such test."

Yet, if the truth had been told, he *had* been put to the test, quite starkly. He belittled his ill health on the trip by recalling only: "I remained in good shape until we had passed the last rapids of the chasms," which was simply not accurate. TR told heroic stories of River of Doubt days without further mention of his own near death on the trip, as if to excise his vulnerability as easily as a surgeon cuts out a wart.[103]

ON APRIL 30 the cable Edith had been waiting for arrived: her husband had survived. Homecoming for Theodore on May 19 meant a happy reunion with his wife, but it also meant that before he was out of quarantine reporters asked him if he would be the Progressives' candidate for New York governor. The newspapers had reported only that he suffered from boils, so Edith had no idea that he had barely survived or that he walked with a cane.[104]

She was astonished to see how much weight he had lost. TR made light of the fever and chills he still suffered and his open abscesses, but admitted his ills more freely to male friends to whom wounds would be heroic emblems of suffering in extremity. He had already told her to expect him to go into New York by the end of the week, where Fanny Parsons found him "so full of enthusiasm and sympathy and so simple and boyish with it all."[105]

In the White House, President Wilson issued an apology to Colombia for Roosevelt's support of the Panamanian revolution and asked Congress to pay an indemnity to that country. Rising above the political fray would be difficult for Roosevelt now. It could provide little solace to see the new President thwarted by the same enemies who had made his own presidency so frustrating: after Wilson pleased organized labor by appointing William B. Wilson, the former head of the United Mine Workers, secretary of labor, Senator Tillman and a coalition of southern conservatives blocked his labor program, except for the toothless Clayton Anti-Trust Act. Cartoons portrayed TR as feeling jealousy toward Wilson because the President drew applause for personally addressing Congress and winning progressive reforms like lowering the tariff, passing a graduated income tax, and creating the Federal Reserve Board. But Roosevelt was stung less by being upstaged than by direct affronts. Most irksome, his claims to have charted an undiscovered river nearly a thousand miles long were being challenged by explorers and geographers, and he wrote Arthur Lee: "Of course, anything more preposterous than to question what I have done cannot be imagined."[106]

While TR had been indulging his romantic impulse to escape to another hero land, many of the causes he cared for had foundered. The Progressive Party fell into crisis when Frances Kellor and George Perkins could no longer work together. Bosses were putting "faux moose" candidates on the ballot to confuse voters, and striking miners had been gunned down by state militia in Colorado's Ludlow Massacre. No national politician stood up to stop Rockefeller mining interests from crushing the local United Mine Workers.[107]

While TR was in Brazil, Wilson had done something aggravating to the Bull Moose: he had inaugurated a policy of segregation in the federal government, causing the loss of black patronage jobs for the first time since the Civil War and the spread of Jim Crow customs into agencies. Lynching increased under Wilson, and Jim Crow window service became the official policy of the post office.[108]

Sagamore Hill was once more overrun by reporters. Telegrams overwhelmed Ethel, who despite her new baby, Richard Derby, Jr., was helping her mother manage mail and visitors while TR conferred with Perkins. Edith was pleased by her husband's weight loss and said: "I am doing my best to keep his wonderful figure and in consequence I fear starving my guests." Amidst the glare of attention his arrival caused, Theodore was more relieved to be reunited with Edith than he had ever been. His fever returned, yet he left her again to take a steamer for Europe a mere eleven days after his return from Brazil. Edith was still too frail to go to Spain for Kermit's wedding to Belle Willard, the daughter of Wilson's ambassador to Madrid. TR and Alice, however, danced through a flurry of events—wedding parties and seeing the Escorial, the Prado, El Greco's house, cathedrals, and palaces. Their trip struck Alice as being "like a movie run at several times life speed."[109]

Theodore wrote Edith that he got along very well with the king and queen of Spain and that "Belle and Kermit were so dear!—I believe she will be his sweetheart almost, but not entirely, as you are mine." He saw no signs of hard feelings over 1898. After visits to France and England, he met Harry Houdini on the return steamer but socialized little because he was plagued by a resurgence of fever. Nevertheless, he left within a week after his return to Edith on June 23 to speak for Gifford Pinchot's Bull Moose Senate campaign in Pennsylvania.[110]

With so many causes asking for Roosevelt's help, he returned to the frustrating way of life that had sent him to Brazil. He remained a celebrity of whom great things were expected, yet he lacked political power or sufficient staff to answer his mail. Still devoted to the cause of game preservation and conservation of natural resources, he called his own country "perhaps the chief offender among civilized nations in permitting the destruction and pollution of nature." It troubled him that "in the United States we turn our rivers and streams into sewers and dumping-grounds, we pollute the air, we destroy forests, and exterminate fishes, birds, and mammals—not to speak of vulgarizing charming landscapes with hideous advertisements." Although he preferred a uniform federal game protection law rather than forty-eight separate ones, he agreed to do whatever he could for the campaign to stop California from destroying its game birds through the "excessive hunting which free marketing brings." He warned readers of *The Outlook* about the extinction of game and birds which Audubon Societies and refuges sought to prevent, and he called for all national forests to be turned into game preserves.[111]

Roosevelt saw electoral politics as the key to all reforms, but he remained a dangerous pariah in the minds of party leaders. William Barnes, Republican boss of Albany, was suing him for libel—for calling Barnes a boss. If the New York Progressive Party had not posed a looming threat to Barnes' power base, he would not have sued its leader. So TR wearily hired lawyers and began another time-consuming and expensive legal battle.[112]

He admitted that he might have to run for president as a Progressive in 1916 because the Republican Party was still too conservative and closed to new ideas. He said the Wilson administration was "a menace to our national honor, and an obstacle to our social and economic well being at home." Pundits were calling for TR and FDR to run against each other for New York governor, but "Uncle" Theodore loved Eleanor and Franklin too much to enter such a contest. The press speculated that TR might even throw his support to FDR because he held such a high opinion of him. FDR ran instead for the Senate, but a Tammany man won the Democratic nomination. Conservatives, especially bosses he had attacked, portrayed TR "as broken in body and permanently impaired in mind" after his River of Doubt trip, so that he could be dismissed as a "force in public life." Knowing that her husband turned to Lincoln in times of great stress, Edith gave him an inspirational Lincoln dinner speech to read. In a life of many resurrections, she helped him ready himself emotionally for another encore.[113]

But was recovery possible? Though his leg was healing, he regretted that his fever "hangs on in rather irritating fashion and is a debilitating thing." Edith, ill herself with gynecological problems, called Dr. Lambert in mid-July to examine her husband's infected larynx and evaluate his overall condition. She said the doctor had to get a medical history from her husband's traveling companions because "it is hard for Father to tell about himself." TR's fistula had not healed, and he was generally run-down. Lambert recommended total rest "or he will never be really well again," and he advised that Roosevelt "not go into any strenuous campaign *this* year."[114]

In the summer of 1914, TR promised to get "six weeks real rest so as to be in trim for a reasonable number of speeches in the Fall," but he doubted that he would ever be able to return to "all my former good condition." He broke off his affiliation with *The Outlook* to expand his fight for domestic reform and to pursue more lucrative arrangements with the socialist magazine *Metropolitan* ($25,000 a year) and with the Wheeler Syndicate's newspaper, the *Philadelphia North American*. Before he hit the trail to campaign for Progressives across the country, he corrected the draft of *Through the Brazilian Wilderness* and tried to set limits on whom he would see. But "real rest" made him uneasy because of its resemblance to the invalid world he had inhabited as a child. Between family picnics, he played tennis for two hours with Archie.[115]

In September, Ted wrote disapprovingly: "Father is on a loathly trip through New York State, speaking for the present candidates, who have absolutely no chance. . . . His sence [*sic*] of loyalty is so strong that I think at times it carries him to a quixotic extent." Against doctor's orders, he returned from a trip to New Orleans only to board a train days later for Chicago to speak on behalf of Raymond Robins, who was running for the Senate on the Progressive ticket. Hostile newspapers trivialized Robins' message of reform, but TR, Medill and Ruth McCormick, the Dreier family, and most of Hull House, the Women's City Club, and the Women's Trade Union League joined the campaign. Roosevelt described Robins as the "man with whom I have been in closest sympathy" on the issues, which included suffrage and the right to collective bargaining. Robins lost, but Bull Moosers still held twenty seats in the House of Representatives and were running promising candidates around the country, so TR considered it worth the strain to give over 110 speeches for the party that fall.[116]

Roosevelt still attracted so much "slander and mendacity" from his political enemies that he anticipated he might need to step out of the limelight to allow Hiram Johnson or Albert Beveridge to come forward as Progressive "presidential timber" in 1916. They would be better candidates, he said, because "they are not as radical as I am." He campaigned without making conciliatory gestures toward the Republican Party that might win him their nomination in 1916. He stumped with James Garfield in Ohio, but he found his audiences were losing patience with talk of domestic reform because their attention had turned elsewhere—to the Great War, to the dance steps of Irene and Vernon Castle, to baseball.[117]

When the 1914 election returns came in, Republicans swept the East. Where Bull Moosers aligned themselves with prohibition forces, workers voted Democratic, which TR had predicted. Though the Progressive Party had established itself in Congress and in many states, the old Bull Moose was saddened to see how people voted in November. Voters during a serious recession "with a whoop of joy" had gone back to the bosses. He said in disgust that "the dog returned to his vomit." Women voting in nine states had not turned the tide. Not long after his fifty-sixth birthday and the election, Theodore described himself as "no longer fit, physically or in any other way, to continue to lead an active life, and am really glad that it has become my duty to stay quietly at Sagamore Hill and loaf and invite my soul."[118]

He was not the only quixotic spirit in the family. After the Great War had broken out in August, his son-in-law Dick Derby was asked to work as a surgeon caring for Allied soldiers in the American Hospital at Neuilly. Ethel went to Paris with him and left their baby, Richard, with her parents. TR was proud that they wanted to "do their part in this great world tragedy," but he confessed to Ethel: "Our anxiety about you is great." While Ethel and Dick were abroad, Grandfather Roosevelt found six-month-old Richard Derby an irresistible distraction from the frustrations of politics. Each morning he would rise early and carry Richard to see and touch the gaslights in the nursery.[119]

In August, Theodore Roosevelt had seen a "great black tornado [that] trembles on the edge of Europe." Earlier, he had predicted that the war in the Balkans and the collapse of the Ottoman Empire could unsettle affairs in Europe, while "our own special prize idiot, Bryan, and his ridiculous and insincere chief, Mr. Wilson, are prattling pleasantly about the steps they are taking to procure universal peace by little arbitration treaties which promise impossibilities, and which would not be worth the paper on which they are written in any serious crisis." He added: "It is not a good thing for a country to have a professional yodeler, a human trombone like Mr. Bryan as Secretary of State" or a "college president with . . . a hypocritical ability to deceive plain people" yet with "no real knowledge or wisdom" about foreign policy heading the country.[120]

The Great War looked at first to Roosevelt as a "frightful tragedy" which did not require American intervention. The writer Herbert Croly was visiting Sagamore Hill at the time, and they agreed that if Britain defeated Germany and Russian despotism was left to reign on the Continent it would be a disaster. Even after Germany invaded Belgium and declared that the Treaty of London guaranteeing its neutrality was no more than "a scrap of paper," TR supported Wilson's neutrality policy.[121]

The Allies and the Central Powers saw Roosevelt as a key influence upon American public opinion, and both sides had designs on him. After TR heard from German leaders specific details of their plans to invade New York in case the United States went to war, he viewed the conflict as one of German aggression, not self-defense. The passion with which TR would denounce pro-Germans had a great deal to do with his desire to distance himself from his former closeness to German-American intellectuals and from his earlier praise for the German welfare state. And he believed Germany ruthlessly violated human rights in its conduct of the war.[122]

British friends also campaigned to win TR over to their side by trying to prove that Germany was motivated by an "ideal of world conquest." The British were investigating the stories that German troops had committed atrocities against the Belgians, including rape and mutilation. Roosevelt had not seen the war as one of German aggression until he met with the Belgian commissioners in the fall of 1914. The avalanche of British propaganda about German sexual abuse and torture of women and their use of civilians as screens to protect their own soldiers from enemy attack also changed his mind.[123]

Atrocity stories about German soldiers cutting off the right hands of Belgian boys to prevent them from shooting back were confirmed for TR by a trusted eyewitness. Ethel said she saw Belgian refugees arriving in France, among them "a lot of little boys with their right hands cut off." Roosevelt grew livid and abandoned his support of Wilson's neutrality. He defined the war, thereafter, not as an imperial competition or the result of the reckless arms race. Instead, he saw it as caused primarily by the kaiser's megalomania and German soldiers' violation of the codes of civilized conduct. The atrocity stories troubled Kermit, who wrote his father that the Germans were "a loathsome abscess on the face of the world; if you have to cut off an arm because of an infection, cut it off." Later the record would show that some atrocity stories about German treatment of civilians in Belgium were based on verifiable fact. About 5,500 civilians were killed by German soldiers in reprisals for mostly imagined resistance.[124]

Roosevelt's essays about the war in the *Philadelphia North American* warned that what happened to Belgium could happen to the United States because of Germany's already well-developed plans for an invasion. He attacked the Taft and Wilson administrations' faith in arbitration treaties to keep the peace and called instead for "an international posse comitatus" of law-abiding countries to suppress outlaw nations.[125]

He also charged that the Wilson administration was unprepared for war with Mexico or Germany. Wilson found it disconcerting when his assistant secretary of the navy, Franklin Delano Roosevelt, confirmed that what TR said about military readiness was correct. While both Roosevelts were internationalists who saw the Great War as an imminent danger to the United States, Wilson and most of his advisors believed, with Jefferson, that America was "kindly separated by nature and a wide ocean" from the ugly rivalries of Europe. So Secretary of the Navy Josephus Daniels repudiated FDR's statement and tried to silence the young man. From 1914 to 1918, Daniels would have trouble keeping FDR quiet about the administration's failure to prepare for war, despite Wilson's gag order which required silence from federal officials. But Wilson had no power to silence TR.[126]

By Christmas the Bull Moose had recovered a small fraction of his stamina by taking long autumn rows on Long Island Sound with Edith. As the family circle gathered for the holiday, the reality of the war hit home. Ethel came back from France in need of an operation, yet strong enough to tell stories about what she had seen and heard in the hospital—patients with both eyes gone, amputations, tales of drunken German troops and German artillery purposely firing on the Red Cross. With the Allies and Central Powers locked in a "death grip," only the British army prevented the conquest of France.[127]

As 1915 began, TR could see little to praise in Wilson's foreign policy. By refusing to recognize the government of strongman Victoriano Huerta in Mexico, Wilson had, Roosevelt claimed, favored the revolutionaries who fought to unseat him. When the Mexican Revolution spilled over to U.S. border towns and Wilson invaded the country, TR said the President had bungled the crisis. If he had been president, he said, he would have recognized Huerta or established an American protectorate over Mexico to restore order.[128]

Wilson kept American troops in Vera Cruz to stop arms sales to Huerta until the Constitutionalist revolutionary leader Venustiano Carranza gained power near the end of the summer of 1914. After revolutionaries Pancho Villa and Emiliano Zapata called for "bread and justice" and factionalism triumphed, a civil war broke out among revolutionary armies and the power of the Roman Catholic Church was challenged by rebels.[129]

In his *Metropolitan* articles Roosevelt attacked Wilson's policy as too tame and pointed out to Catholic readers that the failed Mexico policy had not prevented the rape and murder of nuns. Border raids that caused the deaths of Americans, talk of Mexican land reform, and state ownership of oil and mining rights struck TR as affronts to American honor, and when Wilson asked him to mediate the conflict, he refused. Roosevelt was too much at odds with administration policy to act as a peacemaker.[130]

Ted saw that his father was edgy and so invited Colonel Gordon Johnston to visit Sagamore Hill, where talk soon shifted to raising a volunteer force in case the United States entered the European war or one started with Mexico. TR made a list of his friends and acquaintances with whom he would like to face battle. He added his sons' names without asking them. His romantic fantasies about riding in France with "my division of mounted riflemen" reflected how in 1915 most Americans had not yet understood how war would be transformed by the new technology—poison gas, aerial bombardment, new automatic rifles, and long-range artillery. Oliver Wendell Holmes, Jr., insisted in 1914: "Except in exceptional circumstances I think the improved weapons mean smaller losses." The romantic view of war spread by the Civil War syndrome and chivalric literature also made men like Jack London repeat the old myth that war could provide a "Pentecostal cleansing." When Frank Knox joined Theodore in his military planning, Edith dismissed it as "two small boys playing at soldiers."[131]

By the end of January, Roosevelt's health again collapsed. After being miserable with fever and infection, he recovered, but unfolding events left him irate. Being clearly pro-Allied in a country divided and officially neutral about the war was not easy for him. Germany declared its submarines would attack neutral ships in the war zone around Britain, and the British also interfered with U.S. shipping enough to disrupt its neutral trade. Roosevelt feared that Wilson was inclined to reprimand and even fight Britain.[132]

Thereafter, TR tried to fashion himself as a behind-the-scenes mediator to improve U.S. relations with the Allies, especially Britain. Through Bamie's friend Foreign Secretary Sir Edward Grey, he urged the British War Cabinet to try harder not to interfere with American trade. He also advised the British to cooperate with American war correspondents so that they could tell the Allied side of the war. He thought war news in America suffered from an anti-Allied bias because William Randolph Hearst hated the English. Germany had welcomed many American journalists behind its lines, and John Reed and Robert Dunn had fired shots toward French lines from German trenches in February. TR declared they should be "courtmartialed and shot." After the rape of Belgium, Roosevelt wondered, how could anyone fail to support the Allies?[133]

Yet he also opened 1915 with a proposal, published in the January 4 issue of *The Independent*, for a League of Nations, which was to be a tribunal of "efficient civilized nations—those that are efficient in war as well as in peace" that would join "by solemn covenant" to guarantee that their rights were respected and to use their "combined military strength . . . against any recalcitrant nation." While his league sounded more like the big-power alliance system that provoked the Great War or a collective security pact such as NATO, it provided legal means for arbitrating conflicts between countries. Unlike Taft and Wilson's style of arbitration, in which treaties were easily broken, Roosevelt proposed to "put force back of righteousness."[134]

Again, he preached a diplomacy of deterrence based on his personal experience that weakness invited bullying, and he insisted that "what is thus true in private life is similarly true in international life." He added that before a league could be planned, America needed to face its own lack of preparation to defend itself. He pointed out that national defense was still judged a low priority because Wilson insisted to Congress that the country was in "no danger," and Taft dismissed the rising concern about preparedness as "mild hysteria."[135]

Bryan and Daniels were confirmed pacifists, but within the administration the President relied more and more on the informal advice of Texas millionaire Colonel Edward House. House tried to negotiate a peaceful settlement to the war, yet he quietly sympathized with the Allies and met with preparedness advocates within the administration, especially FDR, and two former members of the Roosevelt administration, Secretary of the Interior Franklin K. Lane and the State Department's William Phillips. Franklin Roosevelt provided Theodore with inside information during the war, and like his "affectionate Uncle," the future president worked against the peace advocates within the administration, who, he believed, were so ignorant about preparedness that they, like Henry Ford, "thought a submarine was something to eat."[136]

In TR's mind, preparedness stood for the strenuous life, courage, physical vigor, and high idealism and public service based on love of country. He advocated universal military training to help immigrants and other youths learn middle-class ways just as Hull House and the Henry Street Settlement had done for many children—to give them medical care and teach them hygiene, brotherhood, and patriotism. Training camps would have a leveling effect, imbuing young men with the same muscular Christian ethics that TR's father had advocated. But military democratization, he argued, would work better than athletic leveling had in the schools because "the son of the capitalist and the son of the day laborer, the son of the Railway President and the son of the brakeman, the sons of farmer, lawyer, doctor, carpenter and clerk would all go in together, would sleep in the same dog tents, eat the same food, go on the same hikes, profit by the same discipline, and learn to honor and take pride in the same flag." Officers would be chosen by merit, not class standing or wealth, which would provide an avenue of social mobility for poor but able men. Training would make some young men better industrial workers and others better industrial bosses afterward.[137]

Roosevelt's arguments for universal military training echoed the reasoning that had brought compulsory athletics for boys in public schools: both promised to increase fitness and self-discipline, inspire youths to a heartier manhood, build character, teach team cooperation, and diminish class distinctions by having all young men mingle on a level playing field. TR believed that universal suffrage should depend on universal service and that training camps could serve as "great factories of Americanism" and "huge Universities of American citizenship."[138]

The patron saint of the preparedness movement was Leonard Wood, who longed to teach young trainees the values of "regularity, thoroughness, promptness, respect for authority." Because they were disgusted by unmanly aristocratic drunks and undisciplined plebeians, Wood and TR expected that the "physical culture features of military training [would] develop a new and better [form of] American manhood."[139]

Preparedness did not always equal militarism or reactionary politics. Walter Lippmann and FDR endorsed universal military training because they agreed with TR that it "means cooperation and the establishment of a collective national spirit. This means laying the foundation for further steps in social reform." If reform could not win the day because bosses still ruled the ballot box, perhaps reform and a strengthened democratic state would emerge from the national emergency. In TR's mind, universal military training was a logical successor to the now-defunct Progressive National Service. However, many of his Bull Moose supporters did not agree.[140]

Wood, with Roosevelt's support, put together a voluntary officers' training program in Plattsburg, New York, for men who could afford to pay their own expenses, but the Wilson administration balked at it. Half the men there were from Harvard, where muscular Christianity still reigned among the aristocratic student body. Places like Yale, "the great middle class college," sent fewer men, Ted said, because "the middle classes are not naturally gallant."[141]

Though many preparedness leaders like the hidebound conservative Democrat Henry Watterson hated Roosevelt, TR served as honorary president of the National Security League, which boasted fifty thousand members and local branches in forty-two states by October 1915. The N.S.L.'s Henry Wise Wood declared that in case of war only Theodore Roosevelt was "fit to remasculinize what has become an almost demasculinized America," but many preparedness leaders did not want to associate their cause too closely with a radical like Roosevelt, whose name they would not allow their families to utter at the dinner table. Corinne furthered her own career in the N.S.L. by acting as her brother's surrogate at its conventions. When the N.S.L. seemed too nonpartisan, TR also endorsed the more openly anti-Wilson American Defense Society.[142]

Despite his commitment to preparedness, Roosevelt still fought domestic conservatism with vigor. The sharp recession of 1913–14 had shown him how much the country needed Bull Moose social insurance plans. He called for a federal unemployment bureau and the federal hiring of the jobless for needed public works projects, both Progressive Party ideas being promoted by its congressional members. Some 45.5 percent of union workers in New York City in 1913 were unemployed as a result of the recession, so with TR's approval Progressives in Congress proposed a bill to create a national bureau of employment. If legislation failed, he hoped private funds could provide unemployment relief or jobs. Frances Kellor, Grace Vanderbilt, and Corinne asked him to help them raise funds for the Interchurch Committee on Unemployment, which he did when he spoke at the Metropolitan Opera House on January 26, 1915, where he raised twenty or thirty thousand dollars.[143]

After his unemployment speech was over TR had a convivial dinner with the three organizers. He did not mind that his devoted admirers hung on his every word at dinner, and he reported to Kermit that

> Mother would not go to the meeting or to the supper. There was no reason why she should have gone to the former; but I think if she could have made up her mind to it she would have really enjoyed being at the supper, for she is just as pretty and attractive as ever; and there were plenty of people in whom she might have been interested. However, she not only would not come but persists in thinking that I was bored but didn't know it! As a matter of fact, I had an extremely good time.[144]

Edith disliked the "aroma of plutocracy" around Grace Vanderbilt, and so preferred to stay home at Sagamore Hill.[145]

As Edith's ill health made her cling more reclusively to their home, her husband admitted in a letter to Kermit that, as much as he loved his home base and its guardian angel, "every fortnight or so I like to get in town for a day or a night to see a few people in whom I am interested." In fact, he went to town quite often in the first half of 1915. That winter he had dinner at Corinne's house in Manhattan with the Lodges and on other occasions saw the Richard Harding Davises, Cecil Spring Rice, and Grant and Florence La Farge. Ted described his father that winter as having "a beautiful time dining in town with various friends of his."[146]

TR rarely criticized Edith's lack of "hospitable inclinations" directly, but he did complain to Archie that she saw herself as "martyr" weighed down by burdens not easily cast aside in order to have fun. After Edith discovered that her husband had never bothered to read her description of her travels in the letters she wrote him while he was in Africa, she came to the painful realization that she, like his first wife, sometimes bored him. Ethel, in retrospect, said of her mother, "I don't think she liked clever people or good talk" as much as TR did, and his sisters thought she had become "deeply possessive" and eager to keep her husband "to herself as much as possible." At the very least, Edith wanted the "privilege of growing old peacefully together," but her mate was still a live wire.[147]

On his many excursions to Manhattan, ostensibly to see his grandchildren or to work at his *Metropolitan* office, TR had another agenda, which he evidently did not always mention to Edith. He visited the widowed Fanny Parsons at her apartment for occasional lunches and dinners with and without Corinne. Edith, in fact, had always been jealous of the "very pretty and affected" Fanny, who "had a way with the gentlemen." Ethel recalled that TR's "southern blood fairly overflowed talking" to Fanny, which explained why Edith "always used to say darkly that when she died we would see Mrs P. installed in her place!"[148]

In her memoirs Fanny recalled their visits as moments when he brought to her house "that extraordinary sense of radiance and vitality—of something that could hardly be kept bottled up but must explode, suffusing the room with a kind of ebullient atmosphere." She, in turn, appealed to him because she was an effusive, pretty, lifelong friend who laughed more freely and judged him less insightfully than his wife. Like TR, Fanny was a follower of nature writer John Burroughs, and she had the gumption to march into Charles Scribner's office in 1892 and talk herself into a book contract and a career as a successful nature writer. She joined her friend Roosevelt in New York suffrage and reform politics. His relatives observed that she "understood TR better than almost anyone else did." Yet, for all his warm friendship and intimate laughter with Fanny, Theodore never wavered in his devotion and fidelity to his wife.[149]

Seeing Fanny kept him from feeling as if he were a defunct, old man, a political pariah. For the same reason he sought out creative and lively people. Just as he had made the White House a welcoming place for artists and writers, he was drawn to Manhattan to steep himself in its intellectual vitality. The city and its people kept pulling him back because of the street life and contention, the noise and the new ideas, the crowds and the broad spectacle of human life in a time of ferment.

The creative atmosphere that Roosevelt enjoyed took place in a moment when new politics coalesced with a season of cultural awakening. In the same days when Van Wyck Brooks heralded America's Coming of Age and modernist sensibilities incubated in Greenwich Village, Theodore usually steered clear of the followers of Nietzsche, free lovers, Wobblies, and the anarchists who mingled with Eugene O'Neill and Edna St. Vincent Millay around Washington Square. Once in a while the more radical, avant-garde Greenwich Village world spilled over into his magazine and social work circles because of common editors and overlapping causes. TR knew William Hard, Freda Kirchwey, Walter Lippmann, John Reed, Lincoln Steffens, and Gertrude Vanderbilt Whitney, all of whom were among the "movers and shakers" who frequented Village intellectual havens like Mabel Dodge's salon. Roosevelt's favorite intellectual, Lippmann was fresh from visiting Fabian socialists and an array of "intellectual samurai" in England, and he found in TR one of his best sounding boards for new ideas. They agreed that the United States needed a stronger government to guarantee a national minimum standard of life for all citizens, and together they mused over the question Lippmann posed in *Drift and Mastery*: "The real problem of collectivism is the difficulty of combining popular control with administrative power."[150]

Ethel's best friend, Dorothy Straight, had offered Herbert Croly, Walter Weyl, and Walter Lippmann money to publish a progressive magazine, *The New Republic*, which became a voice of cultural nationalism and reform with TR, Learned Hand, and Felix Frankfurter advising them informally. If Dorothy had been their angel, in its early years TR served as the *New Republic*'s God. Though he and Lippmann fell out over Wilson's Mexico policy, Lippmann always saw Roosevelt as the ideal president.[151]

TR found plenty of bright people to ruminate with him over how America should leave its cultural immaturity behind. He welcomed newness and innovation up to a point, lauding Henri Bergson, W. H. Hudson, and Robert Frost, but he thought William Dean Howells' novels more uplifting than Stephen Crane's. In fact, it upset him that Crane's hero in *The Red Badge of Courage* experiences so many doubts about soldiering. His friendship with modernist art collector and literary promoter John Quinn encouraged TR to see useful parallels between Irish and American cultural revivals. As president he had publicized the Gaelic revival promoted by Quinn and Lady Gregory, and he applauded their introduction of Yeats, Joyce, and Synge to American audiences. After he left office he wrote again that Americans would do well to emulate the Gaelic revival to appreciate and stimulate the flowering of their own national culture.[152]

In 1911 Roosevelt dined in Manhattan with Quinn, Lady Gregory, Finley Peter Dunne, and Colonel Robert Temple Emmet before they went to see Synge's controversial *Playboy of the Western World*. Audiences elsewhere had thrown stink bombs and vegetables onto the stage, but TR loved the play and clapped loudly. As *Playboy* toured America the actors were harassed and threats were made on Lady Gregory's life. Philadelphia tried to ban the play for immorality because two unmarried characters spend the night together.

Yet TR saw no need for censorship. The play stood in his mind as living proof of the creative power of nationality.[153]

At the 1913 Armory Show, Quinn ushered TR around rooms filled with paintings by European modernists including Paul Cézanne and Paul Gauguin and Americans Arthur B. Davies, Walt Kuhn, and John Sloan, and sculpture by Gutzon Borglum. Roosevelt thought much of the show was "Bully!," especially the American art which depicted scenes of American subjects. He was not yet ready to endorse wholesale a modernist revolt against stilted traditions. Quinn urged TR to write about the show which he did, with surprising sympathy.[154]

The Colonel warmed up to the realism and city scenes of the Ashcan School at a time when most art critics hated them. He wrote of the Armory Show that "the seeing eye was there" in Sloan's tenement scenes and in the painting *The Terminal Yards*. He also praised Davies and George Bellows. But he did not entirely comprehend modern art, except for its celebration of primitivism. Cubism, he wrote, paralleled extremists in the political "lunatic fringe." Never drawn to Edith's favorite painter, Cecilia Beaux, who depicted feminine and domestic scenes and painted lovely portraits of Mrs. Roosevelt and Ethel, TR remained loyal to his favorites: Turner, Remington, Rembrandt, and P. Marcius Simonds. Yet he appreciated Maxfield Parrish, whose nudes and nymphs shocked the Comstocks of his generation. He could see in the Armory Show a piece of what the cultural nationalists and city lovers of the American Renaissance had to say. Artistic authenticity for Roosevelt could be had in the scenes of plain people leading plain lives in Manhattan. Above all, he believed, America had to come up with its own, preferably masculine, native art.[155]

His cultural nationalist aesthetic had been schooled by his many years of walking the neighborhoods of Manhattan, which prompted him to write about the Bowery as he imagined Dante would have seen it, as "one of the great highways of humanity, a highway of seething life, of varied interest, of fun, of work, of sordid and terrible tragedy." He wished the Bowery had its own Dante who could write out "the eternal mysteries" of the everyday. Dante looked at "people of no permanent importance" in the larger schemes of history and saw "those tremendous qualities of the human soul which dwarf all differences in outward and visible form and station." Those common people, he wrote, became apt literary subjects because of their "passions" and "great souls" "whom no torture, no disaster, no failure of the most absolute kind could force to yield or to bow before the dread powers that had mastered them."[156]

A Dante for the Bowery could weave city stories into an epic American landscape alongside the "trust magnates and politicians and editors and magazine writers" who, TR jested, might belong in "the fifth chasm of the eighth circle of the Inferno." No matter how sympathetically he wrote about the city that had made him or how well he used social documentary stories in his stump speeches to dramatize the plight of workers, he knew he would never be America's Dante. His love of Americana could not make up for the artistry needed to "express the soul of a nation" in story form. The best he could do was to encourage better American writers to follow Walt Whitman in remembering the souls of the common folk when they wrote. He held the opinion, too, that American writers should "write as Americans" of the places that defined them.[157]

Years before, he had joked with Bamie about their creating a literary salon where cultivated people interested in ideas and politics could meet. But now it was Corinne who organized such a salon for him in New York. At her house at 422 Madison Avenue, he met Robert Frost and told him how much he admired his poem "A Servant to Servants," about the farmer's wife who struggles to hold on to her sanity. Knowing of TR's friendliness toward writers, Ezra Pound asked Quinn to enlist his help to get the "prohibitive" tariff on books lightened and to establish international copyright law.[158]

Quinn's success in broadening TR's taste in art did not overhaul his literary sensibilities, which remained more Victorian realist than modernist, anti-Conrad, pro-Howells. Unlike Edith, Theodore remained oblivious of most of Quinn's modernist friends. Yet intellectuals of many bents considered him a companionable and open-minded bibliophile with whom they could find a true meeting of minds. The bacteriologist and poet Hans Zinsser, like jurist Learned Hand, moved from being a Bull Mooser to becoming a close intellectual peer and Roosevelt family friend. TR's visits with the art critic Royal Cortissoz, Edna Ferber, Hamlin Garland, Mary Roberts Rinehart, Booth Tarkington, and many others made him feel as if he were still in the middle of creative progress, even if politics left him stalled. Van Wyck Brooks spoke for many in the prewar generation of writers when he declared Roosevelt was a "genius."[159]

Roosevelt's intellectual curiosity ranged broadly. In 1915 alone he wrote articles about John Muir, conservation, and spoke out against book censorship. He made himself a lively part of New York's vibrant magazine world by holding court at the Harvard Club with the editors and writers of *The Outlook, Metropolitan, Collier's, McClure's, Ladies' Home Journal,* and *The New Republic.* He oversaw a short-story contest for *Collier's,* and he began a secret collaboration with Edward Bok, editor of the *Ladies' Home Journal.* TR acted informally as Bok's literary editor and wrote anonymous articles and finally a regular column called "Men" in which he gave advice about fatherhood, family relationships, work, and the public schools.[160]

He did not, however, find all of the intellectuals he met in Manhattan congenial. Fellow *Metropolitan* writer John Reed wrote about the preparedness movement as a cabal of munitions makers, a charge which infuriated Roosevelt. Around the office Reed liked to get a rise out of the ex-president by defending Pancho Villa, and it worked every time. When TR denounced Villa as "a murderer and a bigamist," Reed replied, "Well, I believe in bigamy." TR shot back, "I am glad, John Reed, to find that you believe in something." When Roosevelt and Reed fell into a shouting match, the *Metropolitan*'s editors stopped them before two of the magazine world's most popular writers did damage to each other.[161]

TR's literary life and his advocacy of nationalism in literature took tangible form in the Vigilantes, a group of writers and artists whom he and the young German-American Hermann Hagedorn pulled together. The Vigilantes pledged through their writings to cultivate in the reading public a spirit of public service and nationalism. They hoped to muster "the spiritual forces of the country" through writing and art. In fact, their literary nationalism was closely linked to their support for preparedness and the Allies in the Great War. Samuel Hopkins Adams, Edna Ferber, Hamlin Garland, Will Irwin, E. A. Robinson, Booth Tarkington, Hendrik Van Loon, and William Allen White joined TR and Corinne in pledging to write often to stir up patriotism. By the end of the Great War the Vigilantes' articles appeared in fifteen thousand newspapers.[162]

Lines of visitors often awaited the ex-president at his *Metropolitan* office. One day a Chinese general asked him to come to China to help modernize its institutions. TR declared he was too busy and that the Chinese needed to learn to defend themselves before they could do anything else. He had just published a collection of his political essays, with a title provided by Edith, *Fear God and Take Your Own Part,* and was about to publish travel writings and other essays in *Booklover's Holidays in the Open.*[163]

Throughout the spring of 1915, he worried about Edith's health. She finally went into the hospital for gynecological surgery, probably a hysterectomy, required by symptoms that had troubled her for over a year and which for part of that time appear to have necessitated separate bedrooms. He and Ted waited through "the severe and trying operation" on April 15. As she recovered, TR read aloud to her "The Man from Snowy River." He found her depression after her surgery understandable and temporary. Edith was, in his words, "frail and weak still," "propped up in bed in a pretty pink kimono" when he left for almost a month in Syracuse, where boss William Barnes was suing him for libel. He considered it a "silver lining" that she could not attend the proceedings because she took such conflicts so to heart and would find several weeks of legal machinations disagreeable.[164]

Barnes accused Roosevelt of libel for calling him a corrupt boss, yet Ethel said she was "horribly depressed" about her father's trial because Barnes "must know he is lying." When the judge ruled that Roosevelt had "to give proof such as would be necessary in order to convict Barnes of a crime instead of proof such as ought to convince a majority of the voters that he is an improper public servant," TR believed the judge had thrust the burden of proof on the wrong party. After long days of defending himself in court, he expected defeat, which wore on his nerves.[165]

World events overshadowed the trial. On May 7, a German submarine torpedoed and sank the passenger liner *Lusitania* off the Irish coast, killing 1,198, including 128 American men, women, and children. Germany had published warnings to civilians not to travel into the war zone on passenger ships, and German agents personally cautioned Americans on the dock not to board the *Lusitania*, which secretly carried 6 million rounds of ammunition and explosive shrapnel shells to the British war effort.[166]

With the Barnes trial going badly for him, with his personal and political fate in the hands of a jury which included a German-American presumed to be sympathetic to the kaiser, TR might have been prudent to remain silent about the *Lusitania*. But he stepped out of the courtroom and gave a statement to a *New York Times* reporter calling the sinking "an act of piracy." He wrote a searing article, "Murder on the High Seas," for the *Metropolitan* which called for the United States to "act promptly" to cut off trade with Germany and impound German ships in U.S. harbors. His editor, H. J. Whigham, telegraphed that he hesitated to print it because he feared it would antagonize the jury, but TR replied: "By all means publish immediately." President Wilson declared on May 10: "There is such a thing as a man being too proud to fight. There is such a thing as a nation being so right that it does not need to convince others by force that it is right." Roosevelt judged Wilson's statement as the most irritating example of cowardice he had ever heard in his life.[167]

While the public debated the *Lusitania* crisis, the judge in the Barnes trial seemed set against Roosevelt and struck out of the record much of his evidence. Discouraged, TR wrote Ethel: "This practically ends the case, so far as any hope of my winning is concerned."[168]

As they had in the Newett case, Roosevelt's closest friends and family members stood up for him in public. FDR made the trip to Syracuse to support "Uncle Theodore," who wrote home to Edith: "Franklin Roosevelt was up here yesterday and made the best witness we had yet had, bar Davenport." FDR could speak from personal experience fighting against the collusion between Republican and Democratic bosses and their power over the state legislature and the nominating process.[169]

On the witness stand, TR played so well to the jury that he had to be asked to restrain his remarks. Despite the judge's bias, the jury, in the end, found TR's "unguarded candor" more impressive than Barnes' "furtive" demeanor. The jury denied that Roosevelt had committed libel, and he wrote Kermit how relieved he was to have won the galling case. As he left town, he cordially invited the entire jury to visit him at Sagamore Hill. He had promised that the Barnes trial would bring the "death knell of bossism," yet even in defeat bossism still ruled Albany and the trial cost the Roosevelts $50,000.[170]

The sinking of the *Lusitania* shifted American public opinion away from Germany, but not toward war. Wilson decided to respond with a series of diplomatic notes, which prompted his pacifist secretary of state, Bryan, to resign on June 8. Theodore wrote to Kermit that he was "heartily disgusted" with the administration's conduct of foreign policy. Yet he knew that Wilson's diplomatic protests to Germany suited the national mood of isolation better than his own call for an armed defense of America's rights.[171]

In the middle of debates over preparedness and Germany's assault upon America's neutral rights, the press uncovered a small German propaganda and sabotage spy ring in the United States. The Berlin government secretly planned to use propaganda to stifle support for the Allies in America, and to use sabotage and bombs to blow up munitions plants that made arms to sell to the Allies. A propaganda network financed by Germany acquired the *New York Evening Mail* and provided funds to influence a few other papers and the National German-American Alliance. Germany failed to gain a controlling interest in the *Washington Post* and *New York Sun*. Allied propagandists exaggerated the size and competence of German infiltration when they claimed that America was "spy-ridden," but the threat was nonetheless real.[172]

Wilson tried to keep revelations about internal subversion quiet because it would help interventionists like TR stir up support for the Allies. British intelligence officers gave Wilson evidence that America was widely infiltrated by German spies. Wilson had proof that a number of German agents had been sent to America to foment strikes, disrupt war production for the Allies, and fund pro-German and anti-intervention propaganda.[173]

In August 1915, Secret Service agents impounded a German diplomat's briefcase after he fell asleep on a New York elevated train. His papers offered substantial documentary proof of a secret propaganda network which tried to undermine support for the Allies while it encouraged backing for Germany or at least U.S. neutrality in the Great War. Neutrality groups sang "Deutschland über Alles" at their conventions and sold German war bonds and souvenirs of the kaiser in the United States, yet the $25 million Germany spent here for propaganda in the first years of the war bought less support for Germany than parallel British efforts. Wilson had the German embassy's phones tapped, but he kept quiet about the full extent of German covert operations until newspapers broke the briefcase story.[174]

Pro-German propaganda and sabotage inside the United States struck TR, his English friends, and the preparedness movement as downright dangerous. They viewed Wilson's response as worse than inadequate. Meanwhile, the Roosevelts were so sure that the country would be pulled into the war that Ted and others began organizing the American Legion, a reserve of men ready to fight in case of war. The Roosevelts and their preparedness allies planned the legion from the start as "the G.A.R. of the Great War," a less pension-hungry but no less politically powerful successor to the Union veterans' Grand Army of the Republic. Ted saw in the organization the seeds of his own political career and was not bothered by its whites-only policies.[175]

For most of 1915 and 1916 Wilson retained public support for being "too proud to fight." Theodore could not understand why stories of sabotage and spies, the rape of Belgium, and atrocities did not stir a huge public uproar. In this period when his views were offensive to a large segment of the public, he thought long and hard about how to change opinion. New media like movies and advertising reached people who missed stump speeches and preparedness parades. TR learned from Hearst that invasion movies had a novel power to evoke racial prejudice in the service of playing on the emotions of the audience. Hearst's *Patria*, a racist movie about a Mexican-Japanese plan to conquer the United States, stirred up so much hatred that Wilson asked Hearst to tone it down.[176]

When TR's flashy new Oyster Bay neighbor, J. Stuart Blackton, asked him for help in making a movie about a German invasion of America to show their countrymen they were unprepared for war, the Colonel refused to appear in it himself. But he recruited Elihu Root (with whom he had reconciled), Cornelius Vanderbilt, Leonard Wood, New York's reform mayor John P. Mitchel, Lyman Abbott, and Admiral George Dewey to help produce and then publicize the film. The result was the influential invasion film *The Battle Cry of Peace*. Millions flocked to theaters to see the Capitol in ruins, but peace sentiment still ran strong outside of eastern cities.[177]

In his latest book, *America and the World War*, Roosevelt opened fire against Wilson for his failure to stand up to the Germans. He accused the

President of representing a "cult of cowardice." TR's invective was so personal and out of tune with public opinion in 1915 that even his most loyal supporters pressed him to moderate his diatribes. Fanny Parsons had urged self-editing on him, but he always broke his promises to moderate his tongue. William Allen White wrote the Bull Moose to stop insulting Wilson personally: "Your cistern is dry on politics. If I were you I would discuss anything in the world except politics. . . . I might take a side swipe at the national moving picture censorship but I would not have anything to do with friend Bryan or friend Wilson. . . . You will be a lot stronger if you do not have their blood on your hands." White could have prodded Roosevelt to criticize Wilson's new policy of censoring the news about Mexico and the Great War, but that would wait for another year. When White suggested he write a history of the Progressive Party, TR demurred, saying: "I am more like a corpse than like the cistern of which you spoke" about whom obituaries could be written later. He described himself merely as "a very crippled old man," but Democrats opposed to preparedness saw him as an "old cannon loose on the deck in a storm."[178]

The "old cannon" viewed preparedness as a reform that would produce a more active and democratic citizenry resistant to manipulation by bosses. His political opponents criticized his sentiments as militarist, socialist, and tending toward dictatorship. Controversy would not allow him to rest at Sagamore Hill to "lick his wounds." Instead, he was "more likely to lick his wounders!" When propaganda agent George Sylvester Viereck criticized him for being "unfair to Germany," TR lashed back that Viereck ought to give up being an American citizen and go back to fight in the German army where he belonged. Viereck became for Roosevelt the archetype of the disloyal hyphenate, while his friend Hermann Hagedorn, whom TR considered a good German-American because he opposed Germany in the war, stood by TR in trying to prepare America for intervention to help the Allies.[179]

Wilson had previously dismissed agitation for preparedness as a sign that "some amongst us are nervous and excited," but after the *Lusitania* sinking and the exposure of the German propaganda and sabotage networks he was forced to face the fact that the United States might be swept into a war it was unprepared to fight. But unpreparedness had its own advocates. German Ambassador Johann von Bernstorff met secretly with peace advocate and editor of *The Nation* Oswald Garrison Villard, to talk about how in this delicate diplomatic climate German views of the war could be publicized more effectively in America.[180]

TR told Kermit that even though "I very earnestly hope for peace," the United States seemed destined to fight Germany sooner or later. He contacted Washington "about raising a Division of mounted riflemen," but his proposal was considered laughable.[181] Stymied by bosses, conservatives in both parties, and a hostile press when he talked domestic reform, Roosevelt lived under "a continual nervous strain" as he devoted more and more time to promoting preparedness and intervention, knowing he would alienate many of his reform allies who, like Jane Addams and Lillian Wald, believed there was no such thing as a "just war." He wrote Kermit:

> In politics I have now become like an engine in a snow storm; I have plowed my way through until I have accumulated so much snow on the cow catcher that it has brought me to a halt. . . . The consistent and vicious attacks made upon me for many years ha[ve] had a cumulative effect; and the majority of our people are bound now that I shall not come back into public life.[182]

He wished he could run foreign policy toward Mexico and Europe, but was confined to being an irritated spectator. He felt age bearing down on his spirits, and he suffered from new aches and pains "as I move slowly and clumsily."[183]

In the spring and summer of 1915, TR stepped up his criticism of the peace movement, especially the women in it who had been his reform allies. Wald never agreed with Charlotte Perkins Gilman's indictment of war as "maleness in its absurdest extremes," but she nevertheless served in the American Union Against Militarism and the Woman's Peace Party, where the war was often blamed on masculinity, and the "motherhood instinct" was cited as proof that women should not by nature support war. Jane Addams came home from the Hague International Congress of Women and visits to European leaders eager to promote peace. On July 9, Addams said at Carnegie Hall that soldiers in the Great War called it "the old men's war" and were sent into bayonet charges drunk or dosed with ether because they couldn't face the carnage any other way.[184]

Many preparedness advocates charged Addams with disloyalty, and Roosevelt judged the participants in the Hague Conference "both base and silly." TR called the women's peace movement a "shrieking sisterhood" and their leader "poor bleeding Jane." He wrote to Lord Bryce: "As for Jane Addams and the other well-meaning women who plead for peace without daring even to protest against the infamous wrongs, the infamies worse than death which their sisters in France and Belgium have suffered, I lack patience to speak of them."[185]

The competition between preparedness and peace movements to win over public opinion had evolved into a debate about gender. TR had been willing to agree that "the mother half of humanity" had something to teach men about morality and reform, but he did not accept the women pacifists' claim that the instinct of motherhood with its desire to protect life made women opponents by nature of arms races and war. Instead, he judged women who wanted peace as unnatural because they were not selfless and brave enough to have their sons go to battle. Later, Addams squared off against her old friend when she tried to stop public school physical education classes from being used to give boys military training. Roosevelt's side won control over the public schools: for many years after the Great War, New York State required sixteen- to nineteen-year-old boys to attend three hours of military drill a week.[186]

Hoping to be a part of the preparedness movement, Ted took the summer off from Wall Street to join forty-five other members of Harvard's Porcellian Club training to be officers at Plattsburg. Archie did so well in training that he was slated for a captaincy if a volunteer army were called up, and Archie and Ted began their campaign to encourage Kermit and Quentin to come to Plattsburg to prove they had the right military stuff in them. Quentin attended the Students' Camp, but he never took to military life the way Ted and Archie did. Kermit flatly refused to go into training.[187]

When Edith recovered from her operation, she and her husband took a trip in June 1915 to visit ardent Progressive John Parker in Louisiana. Theodore had recently broken his ribs, but he would not let his discomfort be public. To reduce the demands on them as they traveled south, such as crowds that called for him to make impromptu speeches at two in the morning from the back of the train, TR let out that Edith had been ill. At Pass Christian on the edge of the Gulf of Mexico, he spent five days on an Audubon Society boat visiting bird refuges with photographer Herbert Job. When Roosevelt wrote up the trip for *Scribner's*, he denounced the "reckless extermination of all useful and beautiful wild things," especially by those who violated game protection laws to hunt indiscriminately. He walked along the shore barefoot watching birds and became once more the "ornithological small boy" whose spirit flew with the birds far away from his usual world. He and Edith were happy to get away from the cold winds that leaked through the North Room windows, and together they listened to the mockingbirds at dawn, as he wrote, "when the crescent of the dying moon had risen above the growing light in the east."[188]

FDR rode part of the way home with them to talk politics, and Edith returned to Sagamore looking to her husband "infinitely better and more like her old self." Later, TR spoke at the Plattsburg camp, where he berated the hyphenated American, the pacifist, the "college sissy," and the man with "a mean soul" who opposed preparedness. He denounced professional German-Americans for having "preached and practiced what comes perilously near to treason against the United States," and he accused the Wilson administration of following a pro-German foreign policy. He even compared selling arms to Germany with the immorality of giving a gun to a white slaver. When his remarks were reported widely in the newspapers, Secretary of War Lindley Garrison sent a telegram reprimanding Major General Leonard Wood for permitting such harsh criticism of the President on federal property.[189]

WHAT BOTHERED Roosevelt most, he admitted, was that Wilson was correct in reading public sentiment and "I am completely out of accord with public feeling. . . . Meanwhile I can do no good." When the Turks massacred countless Armenians that year, TR was appalled. But his writing about it failed to stir up public outrage. Wilson, TR declared, "has made up his mind that the bulk of our people care for nothing but money getting, and motors, and the movies, and dread nothing so much as risk to their soft bodies, or interference with their easy lives."[190]

Feeling helpless, he went to the Tourilli Club, a private game preserve northwest of Quebec City, to hunt with Alex Lambert in September. An advocate of progressive public health reforms, Lambert was in the middle of a campaign to win the support of his colleagues in the American Medical Association for compulsory national health insurance, and he and the ex-president opposed profit-making health insurance schemes.[191]

No matter how much he contemplated progressive reforms, the shadow of the Great War descended over Roosevelt's trip and his nature writing about it. His descriptions of his hunt became reveries on human, not animal, extinction and the role of manliness in the dreadful struggle for survival. TR saw his French-Canadian guides as embodiments of "strapping" manhood, fathers of large families, and they turned his thoughts to the loss of "race supremacy" of the English-speaking people because of "sheer dwindling in the birthrate." The calls of wild loons and eagle owls reminded him that among his overcivilized countrymen "the atrophy of the healthy sex instinct" doomed them to be overrun by other groups. Under such a cloud of preoccupation, beavers looked fecund to him, hares prolific, and he noted with disapproval the slow breeding of porcupines, surely an apt reminder of his belief that only the creatures that fight and breed well can rise in the world.[192]

His ability to hold his head up in the company of strapping young men was called into doubt on this trip as it had not been since he went to Moosehead Lake as a boy. Roosevelt was convinced that racial competition would be won by sturdy men who lived a strenuous life, the Germans and the Japanese, but perhaps not the tame Americans; and he said he did not feel fit for the strenuous life anymore.

As he and his guides made their way through the forest, he shot one bull moose, but then an even larger animal chased him in his canoe back and forth on the lake. The moose, aggressive during the rut of mating season, shook his antlers at TR, "bent on man-killing." The moose "swaggered along grunting, it kept its mouth open, and lolled out its tongue over its muzzle" threatening TR for an hour. When he scrambled onto land the moose charged after him "like a locomotive" and it frightened Roosevelt. As the moose charged nearer and nearer, TR's guides shouted for him to defend himself. Finally he shot the animal four times before it died. He confessed afterward that he had not done well, and he wrote Kermit: "I shall never again make an exhibition of my self by going on a hunting trip. I'm past it!"[193]

More humiliation awaited him on his return to America, this time from a "faux bull moose." After Wilson heard from his advisors that the preparedness movement had "a sinister political purpose to embarrass and, if possible, to force" his hand, the President decided to beat his rivals at their own game by talking nationalism and asking Congress for more defense funds. Wilson had also decided "to out-Teddy T.R." by co-opting the language of preparedness in his own speeches.[194]

Not to be outdone by a rival, TR, in a searing speech at Carnegie Hall in October, blasted "hyphenated Americans" who served the kaiser in the United States. When he spoke to Congress on December 8, Wilson copied Roosevelt's attacks on ethnics, calling for those who "poured the poison of disloyalty into the very arteries of our national life" to be "crushed out." He and TR together unleashed an anti-hyphen movement. Wilson also invented a new category of disloyalty, Americans who refused to be neutral: "Some men among us have so far forgotten themselves and their honor as citizens as to put their passionate sympathy with one or the other side in the Great European conflict above their regard for the peace and dignity of the United States." The remark infuriated TR, who understood that the "adroit demagogue" in the White House was calling him a disloyal American.[195]

Affecting the course of world events was still within King Lear's grasp. TR bragged to Kermit: "I have doubtless been the main factor in forcing Wilson to eat his own words and come out for preparedness."[196] Though Edith was taking an interest in war relief and preparedness in her quiet, private way, she primarily concerned herself with distracting her husband from politics. He took fewer trips to Manhattan, and when they celebrated the thirtieth anniversary of their engagement, TR wrote that "it is a great blessing for lovers to grow old together." Edith looked to him "as charming and bewitching as ever; & all her ways are so attractive, & she is so interesting. Rather absurd for a fat, rheumatic, blind old man to speak this way, isn't it?" He admitted that his wife "looks so pretty and charming that now and then I have to get up and make love to her—which is rather absurd on the part of a gouty old man."[197]

Christmas 1915 brought all the Roosevelt children home except Kermit, and for three days the house overflowed with talk and festivities. Theodore called his Christmas poems "cave-man efforts," but his family received them "with rapture." Before breakfast he took his grandchildren Richard, Ted, and Gracie (but not Ted and Eleanor's tiny infant Cornelius) downstairs one at a time "piggy-back" to pet the "buppies." While he was out riding over Christmas holidays TR's horse slipped on an icy section of asphalt road, fell, and rolled over him. But he walked away from the accident unhurt. TR, who now kept his seven sharp axes in the elephant foot receptacle by the hall door, organized a chopping expedition or a walk most days, and he found Alice "as amusing as ever, and a real help to me politically." Ted was pleased that after the sinking of the *Lusitania* "Father seems to have had a very considerable recrudescence of popularity and influence," but the family doubted that he could do anything more in 1916 than to push the GOP to choose a candidate acceptable to Bull Moose sensibilities.[198]

Roosevelt found himself in an uncomfortable position in 1916 because the Progressive Party had floundered and the Republicans had fallen "completely under the control of the reactionaries." He judged his chances of winning the presidency slim even if he did "hold my nose and swallow the nauseous dose" of rejoining the Republicans. Lodge was already preparing TR to step aside and accept Supreme Court Justice Charles Evans Hughes as a candidate who could reconcile the Bull Moose with the Republican Old Guard in order to beat Wilson. Roosevelt considered Hughes a "cold, selfish man" who knew little of foreign affairs, but he thought Hughes might do a better job than Wilson.[199]

America remained divided between a vociferous preparedness movement and those who favored neutrality. Americans of Irish and German descent usually wanted the United States to stay out of the Great War, while interventionists were a vocal and growing minority. Large preparedness parades in May demonstrated the size and power of those who wanted the government to increase spending on defense and ready the armed forces in case of war. On May 13, 100,000 would march in the Preparedness Day parade in New York City, including most of the Roosevelts. Ted's wife, Eleanor, organized women into preparedness battalions, Ethel addressed envelopes, and even Edith marched alongside Eleanor in the parade. Across from the reviewing stand a peace advocate held up a lonely banner asking: "Are you sure you are right?"[200]

Because TR and other preparedness advocates kept hammering the President for being weak on preparedness, Wilson's personal secretary, Joseph Tumulty, advised him to lead a preparedness parade with newsreel cameras running. When the President marched in New York City on June 14, he intentionally draped a flag over his shoulder and had TR's relative FDR march in his wake. Tumulty believed that Wilson "cleverly outwitted his enemies and took command of the forces in the country demanding preparedness." For TR it was a late and insincere conversion: Wilson was only "going through the motions of being for national preparedness."[201]

Heightened election-year partisanship prompted the youthful Franklin to claim in a public speech that during TR's presidency the navy was so ill run that the Great White Fleet had had to borrow officers and equipment to make its round-the-world trip. The Colonel, restrained by personal affection and family loyalty, gently and in private reprimanded FDR for his error. Any other member of the Wilson administration would have received a verbal blast that made headlines.[202]

Edith did not want her husband to run for president in 1916. He had suffered two relapses in March and April, with fever, croup, and general debility which lasted through the summer. The family feared he had whooping cough. He was still "talking social reform," but Edith knew his low spirits and irascibility would only get worse in the heat of a campaign. He was torn between his desire to run domestic and foreign policy and his realistic assessment that Bull Moose views were too radical for voters and the two parties were too strong to defeat. Republicans, after all, still saw him as Benedict Arnold. When Progressive Party groups organized to put TR's name on the Michigan and Massachusetts primary ballots, he said he did not want the nomination and would not allow a faction to fight on his behalf. But he left an opening when he said, from his February vacation in the Caribbean: "It would be a mistake to nominate me unless the country has in its mood something of the heroic."[203]

His followers campaigned for him in several primary contests with support from preparedness forces, munitions makers, Catholics angry about Wilson's Mexico policy, farmers, and other progressives in the new Roosevelt Non-Partisan League, social workers who had not joined the peace movement, and, of course, the Bull Moose faithful. For a while peace talks went on between TR and Pennsylvania's Republican boss Boies Penrose. Roosevelt let his followers pursue his candidacy as a Progressive because it would give the Bull Moosers more bargaining power in June to push the Republicans to accept domestic reform. At the end of May, supporters converged on Sagamore Hill to demonstrate how many people were behind his candidacy.[204]

If TR ran in 1916, he knew he would face the animosities and character assassination of 1912 all over again. If his own nomination as a Republican looked impossible, he hoped a Progressive or liberal candidate could be nominated because he saw Wilson as a foreign policy failure and a lukewarm reformer. While TR campaigned for woman suffrage actively and described himself as "an ardent suffragist," Wilson still opposed the Anthony Amendment. Roosevelt had long advocated the abolition of child labor, but Wilson had doubted that the federal government had the power to regulate it. Wilson had won important reforms like the Federal Reserve System and the Federal Trade Commission, but he opposed rural credits (via federally funded farm loan banks), collective bargaining, and social insurance. But an election year pushed Wilson to try to win over progressive voters by praising Bull Moose ideas. He changed his position on rural credits, child labor, appointed labor lawyer Louis Brandeis to the Supreme Court, and actively cultivated TR's 1912 constituency.[205]

When both Bull Moose and Republican conventions opened in Chicago on June 7, the Roosevelt family was "all strung high with excitement over the convention" and the distant chance that the Republicans might turn to TR. Ethel believed that "the people surely want him," but, as Alice noted about 1912, "any one who has been in politics knows that crowds and enthusiasm do not have much relation to majorities." Roosevelt and George Perkins had made the mistake of scheduling the Bull Moose assembly at the same time as the Republican convention, because they hoped to use the Progressive Party to exert pressure on the Republicans.[206]

During the conventions, Theodore spent long hours in Oyster Bay on the phone to Perkins, who was more interested in engineering a reconciliation between the Progressives and the GOP than in moving the Republicans leftward. Meanwhile, Ted politicked with black delegates at Roosevelt Republican headquarters in Chicago, where statuettes of the ex-president and the flag held the inscription "I am for peace with honor." With the telephone receiver pressed to his ear, TR wearily listened to promises of support for his candidacy. Then he heard the news that the Old Guard had pulled strings against him. Midwest German-Americans opposed him because he favored the Allies and intervention, and party regulars like Penrose refused to forget 1912.[207]

Alice, like Perkins, mingled with the Republican delegates. William Randolph Hearst urged her to convince her father to come to the convention to make sure the Old Guard did not keep its stranglehold on the party. In print

Hearst asked Roosevelt "to come to Chicago to use your splendid ability and mighty influence . . . to establish a permanent, patriotic, radical party." But TR knew from past experience Hearst wanted the presidency for himself so badly that his views and alliances would shift capriciously to achieve that goal.[208]

On June 10 the Republican convention, which TR thought "a peculiarly sordid body," nominated Charles Evans Hughes for president. The old Bull Moose had predicted the result, yet it felt like one more rejection, one more disappointment. Three days after Hughes was nominated, the ailing Theodore coughed so violently he tore a ligament in his side and spent the next several days in pain.[209]

The Progressive Party chose him for president, but he refused to accept the nomination because it would guarantee once again the election of Wilson. After he called on the party to nominate someone who favored preparedness, TR impulsively suggested Henry Cabot Lodge, which felt like "a slap in the face to every Progressive" because Lodge remained a hidebound conservative, an opponent of labor unions, immigrants, and woman suffrage. Walter Lippmann described "this tragic farce" as a disagreement between two beloveds, leader and followers, over how to break up: "Should the Progressive party kill itself, or should Roosevelt be made to bear the onus of killing it?" The convention of Bull Moosers nominated him in defiance, and he refused them. Murder, not suicide, was their choice.[210]

But Hughes' nomination signaled an odd triumph for the Bull Moose, too. Roosevelt insisted that a reformer like Hughes would never have been nominated if it had not been for the influence of Progressive ideas on the voters and the party, and he was probably correct. Perkins wrangled himself and TR's allies Harold Ickes, Chester H. Rowell, Oscar Straus, and James R. Garfield onto the Republican Campaign Committee. Frances Kellor ran the Women's Committee of the National Hughes Alliance, which sent the Women's Campaign Train filled with former Bull Moose women on an 11,000-mile campaign tour. Hughes was no stand-pat Republican but a proven civic reformer who as Supreme Court Justice had upheld labor laws and the rights of women. He supported rural credits for farmers, federal workmen's compensation laws, and the eight-hour day in certain industries, and stood left of Wilson on many issues. Hughes' *Republican Campaign Text-Book* charged that the Democratic Party under Wilson had committed a grave error in seeking to "eliminate and humiliate the negro" in the federal government. Though Roosevelt found Hughes too stiff, when he dined with the candidate late in June, he told Ethel afterward that the man "really was trying to, well,—be human."[211]

He endorsed Hughes and urged his followers to do so but they did not listen to him. As Bull Moose defections to Wilson's camp grew more numerous each day, Wilson's popularity galled TR. It exasperated Roosevelt when Wilson barely responded to sabotage and referred to all the parties in the European war, including the invaded Belgians, as "madmen." War, in fact, struck very close to home that summer. On July 30, German spies sabotaged the munitions depot on Black Tom promontory in New York harbor, causing twenty minutes of huge explosions that could be heard as far away as Maryland. Shrapnel flew into the Statue of Liberty and Ellis Island and skyscraper windows were shattered in Manhattan, yet conclusive proof that Germany was responsible for the incident did not emerge until later. Berlin believed that if it sabotaged munitions and stalled shipments to the Allies, bombed the Capitol, and used germ warfare against Americans and their stock animals it could undermine the Allied war effort. Though it succeeded in blowing up a few munitions plants, most of Germany's plans failed.[212]

WHILE ETHEL was away from Sagamore Hill to recover from a lingering illness and Dick Derby trained at Plattsburg, Roosevelt was happy to entertain his grandson, who, though he was not yet three, had just been read *Treasure Island.* TR bid him goodnight saying, "Goodnight, Jim Hawkins," to which Richard would reply, "Good night, John Silver." On quiet days together in the North Room, Richard asked his grandfather to "perform for him the 'Dance of Old Man Kangaroo.' " The old man obliged him, doing the dance repeatedly, to Richard's great delight.[213]

When the fall vote-getting season started, Hughes fell flat as a campaigner. On the stump he spoke lifelessly as he tried to go after Wilson on Mexico and labor issues. FDR and other Wilsonites declared that Hughes had fallen under the influence of untrustworthy politicians. The Republican National Committee called on TR to "perform a personal rescue act" on Hughes' bland campaign. Flattered to have the GOP court him as a campaign asset, he would help, but, rather than follow Hughes' campaign tunes, he would sing his own.[214]

Campaigning wholeheartedly for Hughes was hard because Roosevelt had never really liked the man he called "the bearded iceberg." He did not forget that Hughes had refused to testify for him in the Barnes trial. The National German-American Alliance had flocked to Hughes the previous spring in order to block TR's nomination, and that fall Hughes talked preparedness while actively courting German-American groups who opposed intervention. Nor was Hughes in accord with Roosevelt on all domestic issues, especially progressive taxation and a living wage. Nevertheless, Wilson's failure to help the Allies when they were in desperate need made electing Hughes a lofty enough goal to justify suppressing his rivalrous feelings.[215]

The challenge was greater than mustering the energy for a life of constant speaking and missed sleep in a Pullman car. The old question of self-control followed TR on tour. He started out by charging that Wilson's weakness had "invited the murder of our men, women and children by Mexican bandits on land and by German submarines on the sea." He was already in print reminding voters that Wilson's failure to prevent German submarines from killing Americans had caused a Mexican newspaper to call Americans a "degraded people." Whether Hughes or the Republican National Committee desired it or not, TR said he would continue "fighting the battle of the Allies" for American public opinion throughout the 1916 campaign.[216]

As long as Hughes failed to talk about questions of social justice, Roosevelt could not draw many Bull Moosers into the Hughes camp. The leader of the militant National Woman's Party, Alice Paul, who "always regarded" Roosevelt "as an ally," visited Sagamore Hill to plan strategies for moving Hughes into the woman suffrage fight. TR shared Paul's disappointment that the Republican platform failed to endorse the federal suffrage amendment and he agreed to lean on Hughes personally. Prodded by TR, Hughes agreed to speak before the Woman's Roosevelt League, where, in a surprise move, he broke with the R.N.C. and declared his support for the Anthony Amendment. The press said Hughes' bold announcement had caught Wilson "napping."[217]

With women voting for president in twelve western states Hughes gained an early advantage in the contest for their votes. The National Woman's Party declared that it would fight Wilson's reelection because, as TR's friend Abby Scott Baker said: "Mr. Wilson thoroughly despises women, and all his beautiful dreams of democracy and self-government are for men." Wilson controlled the damage by meeting with the National American Woman Suffrage Association's Anna Howard Shaw to convince her that he would be more sympathetic to suffrage, which she took as as "clean a promise as ever a man made."[218]

Yet Wilson was a tiger whose stripes would never change on some issues. Having shown little concern about gross inequities that left poorer people carrying more than their share of the tax burden, Wilson opposed Senator George Norris, Robert M. La Follette, and others' efforts to ask the wealthy to shoulder more of the burden of increased defense spending through excess profits taxes, taxes on corporate capital surplus, munitions taxes, and increased inheritance and estate taxes. TR, in contrast, supported tax justice and later advocated a higher excess profits tax than La Follette did.[219]

And then there was race. After federal jobs had been lost and Jim Crow made policy in the federal government in Wilson's first term, black leaders finally saw the President for the racial reactionary that he was. While TR had required his cabinet to climb rock faces like sturdy men, Wilson, after all, had made his cabinet listen to his "darky" stories. Claiming that segregation was a benefit for blacks and a humane way to protect them from white hostility, Wilson had insulted *Boston Guardian* editor William Trotter and shown he was deaf to protests against his policies. The N.A.A.C.P.'s *The Crisis* saw Wilson as a "representative of the southern Negro-hating oligarchy" and called on black voters not to support the Democrats.[220]

TR's long-standing ties with black voters clearly helped Hughes win 78 percent of the Harlem vote in November. Disenfranchised in the South and politically neglected by most Republicans in the North, black voters had trouble making themselves heard, but where they spoke, they spoke for TR and Hughes over Wilson.[221]

While Hughes still searched for a campaign issue, Ida Tarbell told Wilson: "With a moving picture political hero like T.R. performing free for the whole country, it is up to the Democrats to do a little decent performing themselves." So Wilson hired anti-vice crusader and muckraking journalist George Creel and Robert Woolley's publicity bureau to use modern public relations techniques to get Wilson reelected, which TR later called "the most brilliant achievement in the history of American politics." Though Creel's plans for negative campaigning made donor Henry Ford balk at the "rough stuff" of character assassination and innuendo, he got out his checkbook anyway. Hearst and Cleveland Dodge anted up, too.[222]

Taking Creel's advice, Wilson began making speeches saying that Hughes meant war. The campaign promised American mothers that a vote for Wilson meant their sons would not become "cannon-fodder," and that "if you want WAR, vote for HUGHES!" Wilson warned the voters that "the only articulate voice, a very articulate voice," on the Republican side—that is, TR—"professes opinions and purposes at which the rest in private shiver and demur," but which would bring war if Hughes were elected. The Democratic Party spread rumors that Hughes would appoint TR his secretary of state and that TR would run Hughes' foreign policy.[223]

On October 8 the German submarine U-53, after a visit to Newport, sank six European ships off the coast of Nantucket. The stock market dropped as more Americans realized their vulnerability to attack. Wilson warned German Ambassador von Bernstorff that such submarine strikes could throw the election to the pro-war Republicans. Desperate because the Allied naval blockade of their ports was starving their populace, German military leaders secretly pushed for total submarine warfare, which would certainly force any American president, even the pacific Wilson, into the war. In his last book Harvard psychologist Hugo Münsterberg denounced the wave of popular suspicion of German-Americans which TR and Wilson had fueled as "the pogrom of the hyphen," yet he spread suspicion of German-Americans further by predicting that the "war will end with the spiritual triumph of the German nation."[224]

By late October, Wilson had been warned by Berlin that if he did not intervene to bring the warring parties to the peace table then unrestricted submarine warfare was on its way. Knowing that he might be unable to keep America out of war much longer, Wilson still ran an antiwar campaign by playing on the emotions of a public eager for peace.[225]

The President tried once more in vain to bring the war to an end. Wilson's peace initiatives looked to Britain's war minister, Lloyd George, like "pro-German" attempts to "butt in" by a neutral power "too proud to fight," but not too proud to lecture other countries how to conduct their affairs. Lloyd George reasoned that a premature truce would leave Germany powerful enough to regather its strength for an even bloodier conflict, so he called on the Allies to fight "to the finish—to a knockout." TR agreed with Lloyd George. He hated to see Wilson exploiting the peace issue while the threat of war hung so palpably over America. In private, TR despised "the lily-livered skunk in the White House" more than ever.[226]

Roosevelt took off on his tour for Hughes on October 17, acting as "a jovial master of ceremonies" and storyteller on the journey for the aides and reporters who traveled with him. TR insisted that everyone eat together in his private railroad car. The wire service and *New York Tribune* reporter Ned Lewis, who had never been given the time of day when he traveled with the Hughes train, within hours of meeting Roosevelt felt as if "I've known him for a long while." Lewis described to his mother the journalists' "cordial and democratic" friendship with the ex-president: "The Colonel has caught us in his arms, figuratively speaking, and are all struggling against his bosom."[227]

As their train headed south, Louisville "went wild" for Roosevelt despite mud and rain. He came to town elated as he was heralded by factory whistles and exploding rockets. But Lewis saw TR's exhilarated mood plummet as "an expression of fatigue flash[ed]" over his formerly animated face where "a touch of sadness" started to show. Roosevelt played veteran campaigner as naturally as he chopped wood for the fire in the North Room. He deftly and "invariably picked out a little baby hoisted on some father's shoulder and reminded his hearers that 102 like that child went down on the Lusitania." He offered listeners his gift for bringing abstract political issues down to the personal level, and as journalists watched him whistle-stopping in Kentucky they wrote that "to see the Colonel standing bareheaded in the cold mountain rain telling pinch-faced, unnourished mountaineers that their ancestors were 'not too proud to fight' was enough to make you run for a typewriter." The engine of Roosevelt's train broke down twice so he extended his remarks spontaneously until the train once more chugged away. As the crowds ran after the steaming train, the Bull Moose shook their hands out his compartment window. As an afterthought, the newspapermen tossed out Hughes buttons as darkness closed upon the departing train in the Kentucky night.

By the time they reached Arizona, Lewis wrote, they had become Roosevelt's confidants and he had made friends with their friends who had joined the train along the way. TR told funny stories and put on a playful Irish brogue ("FOINE" for fine), thereby convincing the journalists that he was "the greatest American humorist." In Phoenix, Pueblo Indians and cowboys in flivvers met the Roosevelt special, which had come three thousand miles in ninety-six hours. In 100-degree weather in a baseball park set in cactus country, TR's face dripped with sweat while he unleashed his "almost savage Roosevelt snarl" denouncing Wilson's foreign policy.[228]

When Roosevelt motored to the outskirts of Denver to visit J. C. Shaffer, owner of a newspaper chain, he got covered by mud splashed from the passing autos, but it did not deter him from speaking that night before eight thousand women about his support for suffrage. As he went to another speaking engagement, "Wilson hecklers stirred Roosevelt to a terrible rage and he called them several kinds of scoundrels in his own, patented smashing style."[229]

TR's arrival in Chicago was greeted by a raucous street demonstration, with him standing in his open car waving his old black hat at the cheering multitudes. Republican leaders had taken him aside at the train station to urge him to moderate his words, but he refused. What the Republican National Committee hoped would be a rescue act for the faltering Hughes campaign had become a truth squad for intervention and progressivism. The German-American press denounced TR as "the wild man of Oyster Bay" because of his emotional pro-Allied rhetoric. That rhetoric caused the GOP to discreetly cancel his speeches in St. Louis and Cincinnati, and former Progressives kept him out of California because of his foreign policy diatribes.[230]

In Chicago, the day before his fifty-ninth birthday, Roosevelt joined the speakers from the Hughes Women's Special Train, featuring a veritable Bull Moose reunion of Mary Antin, Katharine Bement Davis, Rheta Child Dorr, and Margaret Dreier Robins. Every other speaker was shouted down with cries of "We want Teddy!" Four thousand women "created a shrill, hysterical bedlam" when Roosevelt crossed the stage. Wilson hecklers tried to disrupt his speech, but the *New York Tribune* reporter wrote: "Even the Wilson supporters love Roosevelt but think he's on the wrong side this year."[231]

When the trip was over, and they had traveled 6,300 miles in twelve days together, TR bid farewell to his new journalist friends, telling them that he had "had a bully good time on this tour." All fall he had chafed at having to work with the Republican Old Guard. He had found it "very galling to have to take any action which helps these scoundrels." He added as he bid the newspapermen good-bye, "Gentlemen, remember this, if Mr. Hughes is elected Nov. 7 I shall never be seen in politics again. I'm through."[232]

Finally, election day arrived. Through much of the fall, TR and Hughes had coordinated their two-headed campaign over the phone, with Hughes urging him to soften his attacks on "hyphenated" Americans so that he could not be misunderstood to be denouncing immigrants. TR had pushed Hughes without much success to speak out more forcefully on preparedness and social justice. Roosevelt had found working with such a prim anti-gambling reformer a bit hard to bear, and at the end of the campaign he teased him: "Now, at the risk of causing a shock to your principles, I desire to say that I would like to make a bet that you will carry New York by over a hundred thousand."[233]

Hughes' lack of verve and TR's rage still added up to sizable inroads into Wilson's popularity. On November 7 newspapers reported that Hughes had swept the East. The outcome of the election was unclear for weeks. Day by day, however, votes from the West and the Solid South trickled in and Hughes' victory faded. Wilson's promises of peace coupled with his suffrage pledge paid off when he won ten of the twelve states where women voted. Roosevelt wrote William Allen White that voters who chose Wilson because of the "he kept us out of war" slogan represented no more than cowardice, and he thought that Hughes' infernal "pussy-footing and lack of vision" as well as his conservatism on social issues had lost the crucial state, California.[234]

Wilson lost the black vote altogether. Though he won narrowly by 591,385 votes nationwide, his harsh racial policies paid off in electoral votes: the South swept him to victory once more. TR's final effect on the 1916 campaign cut both ways because he mobilized the intervention vote more effectively than Hughes while also proving more adept at scaring away peace and German-American voters.

His reelection secured, Wilson backed down on his support for suffrage. The National Woman's Party felt so betrayed that at the start of 1917 they began picketing the White House. Before the year was out their group would irritate the President so much that they would be arrested for their peaceful protest, confined to a workhouse, vilified for going on a hunger strike to protest their rough treatment, and then force-fed. While TR had welcomed tutelage by activists like Frances Kellor, Wilson had never recovered from his early "chilled, scandalized feeling that always overcomes me when I see and hear women speak in public."[235]

Despite Wilson's many campaign promises, domestic reform was noticeably absent from his inaugural address. TR found it painful that so many of his Bull Moose faithful supported a president who had done little for their causes. Though he had been glad to return to campaigning and work that mattered, Roosevelt remained the Bull Moose unheard.[236]

☆ CHAPTER FOURTEEN ☆

Why Is Roosevelt Unjailed?

IN THE AFTERMATH OF 1916, political cartoonists pictured Roosevelt as an exuberant Falstaff who laughed at Hughes' defeat because it made more likely his own triumph in 1920. Back home at Sagamore Hill, no one was jubilant. Roosevelt sadly wished he could have been the Lincoln of the Great War, for he believed he could have saved many lives by entering and ending the conflict promptly. He mused that if he had been elected in 1916, "I would also have fought for the industrial regeneration of this country along the lines of the 1912 platform, and fought hard and, I think, effectively."[1]

His critics (and most later historians) would ignore his call for progressive programs and tell only stories of warmongering and hatred of Wilson in the last years of Roosevelt's life. He joked that they simplified his motivation as "ambition o'erleaped itself." But they were missing a story of a determined reformer who despite illness and loss stayed committed to Bull Moose ideas to the end of his life. He also remained a major political voice during the Great War and almost got himself put in jail for criticizing Wilson. Roosevelt lived out his final years as a tragic hero who readied himself to be the Sir Galahad of World War I or in the presidential race in 1920, yet he was doomed to die before he found his grail.[2]

Still hoping to avoid war, Wilson, in a stirring speech to the Senate on January 22, 1917, called for "peace without victory," including a world League of Nations, freedom of the seas, "a peace between equals," arms limitations, self-determination of large and small nations around the globe, and an end to entangling alliances. Because Wilson's speech undercut nationalism, the Allies were furious to have "that ass President Wilson" reinterpret the meaning of their war. Germany was poised to gamble that all-out submarine warfare could knock out Britain long before an antiwar Wilson could mobilize his peace-loving people for a real fight. It was a gamble Germany almost won.

On January 31 the German government announced it was resuming unrestricted submarine warfare, but Wilson still hoped to avoid the struggle.[3]

Roosevelt decided he could do the most good for America by "dying in a reasonably honorable fashion" leading a division of volunteers in the European war. Roosevelt wanted to lead an inclusive division of fighting Americans. He believed that a strong, well-defended nation united for war and reform should set aside prejudice to defend and extend democracy, but the Wilson administration generally disagreed—black volunteers were excluded from fighting in the navy, the marines, and the Army Air Corps. TR urged Hamilton Fish, Jr., and William Schieffelin to organize a regiment or more of black volunteers. From all over the country black lawyers, ministers, waiters, tailors, college graduates, and day laborers wrote him volunteering to serve because, as one New York bookkeeper wrote, "I know that my race will make no difference with you."[4]

While Roosevelt prepared for war, Wilson found he could not hold out for peace any longer. On February 25 two Americans were killed off the coast of Ireland when German submarines sank the armed liner *Laconia*. Wilson's intelligence sources also intercepted the Zimmermann telegram, a diplomatic bombshell. German Foreign Secretary Arthur Zimmermann did not fear American military strength, but to make sure the United States was unable to fight in Europe alongside the Allies, he invited Mexico to ally with Germany and offered it a sizable reward: Texas, Arizona, and New Mexico. Germany also suggested that Mexico initiate an alliance with Japan against America.

Public reaction to the Zimmermann telegram moved the United States toward war. Wilson asked Congress to authorize the arming of merchant ships so that they could defend themselves against submarines. When opponents of war, including Robert La Follette, filibustered his armed ship bill, Wilson let loose with an angry tirade against the "little group of willful men, representing no opinion but their own, [who] have rendered the great Government of the United States helpless and contemptible." White House usher Ike Hoover said he "never knew" the President "to be more peevish." Wilson had so successfully called La Follette's patriotism into question that the senator was hung in effigy and denounced as pro-German. The intolerance of wartime had arrived.[5]

America's help was urgently needed because the Great War was going badly for the Allies. Massive slaughter at Verdun and the Somme in 1916 had driven British and French soldiers to question the wisdom of generals like Douglas Haig and Robert Nivelle, who sent hundreds of thousands of soldiers to their deaths without achieving victory. Then, nearly half the French army mutinied and Czar Nicholas was forced to abdicate in favor of the democratic socialist government of Alexander Kerensky. Wilson was pleased that the "naive majesty" of the Russian people had defeated czarist autocracy, making Russia, at long last, worthy to have America fight at its side.[6]

On April 2, Wilson, in his message to Congress, declared that a state of war already existed. The Great War was now an American fight, but Wilson urged his country to fight for higher purposes than nationalism and territorial gain: "The world must be made safe for democracy." The next day marked a poignant moment in TR's life. He stopped in Washington on his way back from a devil fishing expedition in Florida and revisited the scenes of his lost power. But Wilson and Lodge were too busy to see him.

On April 10, Roosevelt went back to the White House to ask Wilson to let him take a division of volunteers to France. During their surprisingly cordial forty-five-minute meeting, Roosevelt suggested they put their past differences behind them, and, according to Alice, he said: "Mr. President, all that has gone before is as dust on a windy street." Wilson later said that TR had joked that he would "promise not to come back" if the President let him fight in France.[7]

The President, in turn, asked Roosevelt's support for his army bill authorizing conscription. TR told Wilson he had gathered an organization which newspapers estimated at between 54,000 and 200,000 men, including 25,000 African-American volunteers and officers eager to win full citizenship by fighting in the war. He promised to support Wilson's army bill although he regretted that it lacked universal military training. He left the White House smiling, and Wilson admitted he had found him charming, "a great big boy," with "a sweetness about him that is very compelling."[8]

The Roosevelt division's romantic appeal drew popular acclaim and strong editorial support across the country. Men like Henry Stimson and Leonard Wood wanted to go to war alongside TR, his sons, his son-in-law Dick Derby, the highest-ranking black army officer, Charles Young, and a large assortment of Rough Riders and political buddies. John L. Sullivan said that anyone who could not see the appeal of the Roosevelt Division "hadn't any soul."[9]

The old Bull Moose had been looking for a heroic ending to his life since 1913. He wrote that he was "entirely willing, and indeed a little more than willing, to finish in a decent manner by dying at the front" if he could only have this last chance to serve his country.[10]

Wilson pondered Roosevelt's division knowing that the last time that TR was in uniform the regular army viewed him as a troublemaker. The Roosevelt Division confronted powerful adversaries. Senator James Vardaman objected to the draft because "millions of Negroes who will come under the measure will be armed, [and] I know of no greater menace to the South than this." With help from TR and FDR, the N.A.A.C.P.'s Joel Spingarn and Leonard Wood established a camp to train black officers, another affront to white supremacists.

As he thought about the Roosevelt Division, Wilson had every reason to fear TR politically and therefore to prevent another San Juan Hill from electing TR president in 1920. So he turned TR down. The head of the Army League declared publicly that "he believed Roosevelt incompetent to lead a large military force," and senators attacked his "impetuosity" and "lack of judgment," claiming that in the San Juan Hill fight his troops had been rescued by black soldiers. The rejection hurt TR deeply.[11]

In June he offered his services to both France and England. Though they wanted Roosevelt's help both governments did not wish to alienate Wilson whom they hoped they could convince to send extensive aid. TR considered serving with Canada, then dismissed the idea. He finally understood the awful fact that during the Great War he was consigned to stay at home with the women and children, and he told Ted: "I need not grumble about fate; I had my day, and it was a good day." His habit of stifling despair with activity moved him just four days later to dance "pigeon-wings in time" with Ethel, Dick, and young Richard as the Victrola in the North Room played Custer's "Garry Owen."[12]

TR kept on the move, stirring up patriotism as his father and uncles had done through the Union League in the Civil War. He wrote searing editorials in the *Kansas City Star*, which newspapers reprinted across the country. On June 7, after Lieutenant John Philip Sousa led his band in "Rule Britannia," "La Marsellaise," and the "Star-Spangled Banner" at a meeting of the American Medical Association in New York, Roosevelt called on doctors to enlist to care for the wounded at the front. A crowd of six thousand shouted, "Three cheers for Teddy," who told them that war slackers were "miserable creatures who should be hunted out of society by self-respecting men and women."[13]

Though Wilson kept him out of war, Roosevelt could send surrogates into battle. He promised reporters that his sons and at least one of his sons-in-law would go, and he hoped that even Nick Longworth would enlist. But Longworth remained in Congress. Eleanor recalled that "Uncle Ted was always urging Franklin to resign" from his post in the Navy Department so that he could go to war. TR also pressured Bamie and Fanny Parsons to allow their only sons to enlist. Nineteen-year-old Quentin enrolled in flight school in Mineola, while Ted and Archie prevailed on their father to help them get commissions with General John Pershing's army. TR wrote candidly to a friend "how glad I would be if I could see Ted, Kermit, Archie, Quentin and Dick all coming permanently home in a bunch, shy, say, three arms and two legs, evenly distributed among them!" He was deadly serious.[14]

Roosevelt had raised his sons to compete with one another for his favor. Kermit, the sensitive one, had not trained long enough at Plattsburg to be commissioned in the American army, so the best he could hope for was to have his father urge Lloyd George to get him a second lieutenant's commission in the British army in Mesopotamia. When it looked as if Ted and Archie would beat him into battle, Kermit admitted to his father that he was envious because he had never before been left behind in contests among the brothers.[15]

ETHEL'S SECOND CHILD, named Edith and born on June 17, brought the "first sunshine" into the family all year. Theodore spent more time than he could afford each day playing with good-natured three-year-old Richard and baby Edie, whom he loved to rock for a half hour on the piazza with his weathered hand engulfing her small one. When Richard told him that he would miss him when he went into the city, his grandfather recognized what solace Ethel's babies were to him and how much he needed them when his four sons faced danger. As each of his sons left for war, he feared that Wilson's bungled management of it would doom them. Sagamore Hill felt deserted, and Edith sent Kermit "ever so much love from the poor little remnant of a family" left behind.[16]

As the summer grew warmer, the American Defense Society, with Roosevelt's blessing, organized a New York Vigilance Committee to patrol for seditious street-corner speakers. They heckled an Irish Freedom meeting and antiwar speakers before turning them over to the police. They drove cars through a crowd of five thousand attending Irish independence meetings. Caught up in the intolerance of wartime, TR also urged the Boy Scouts to root out sissies and pacifists in their midst and to train boys for war.[17]

Wilson feared disloyalty so much that he did a great deal more than set up groups to harass street-corner speakers. He gained broad authority over the war culture with the passage of the Espionage Act, which could send saboteurs, spies, or even peaceful opponents of war to jail for twenty years. By executive order he revived the infamous Alien Enemies Act of 1798 and prohibited Americans born in enemy countries from criticizing the army or the government. Over two thousand enemy aliens were interned in camps. Wilson allowed members of his administration to punish dissent; ban antiwar magazines; censor news reports, telegrams, phone calls, letters, motion pictures, and overseas cables; infiltrate labor unions, and bribe labor leaders to support the war.[18]

The President gained expansive power over public consciousness using the Committee on Public Information, or C.P.I., run by George Creel. Although Creel started out by appealing to the press voluntarily to stop printing crucial military information about troop and train movements, he was soon pressuring newspapers and suppressing nonmilitary news that would make the administration look bad. He even browbeat some reporters into a "pact of silence" to bury the embarrassing news that members of the National Woman's Party had been jailed for lawful picketing outside the White House.[19]

TR heartily approved of a military curriculum in the colleges and many of Wilson's harshest attempts to inculcate loyalty, but he grew suspicious of domestic intelligence agencies and considered Creel a "scoundrel and liar" because of his use of the C.P.I. for partisan purposes. Creel was not alone in ignoring the First Amendment to garner support for the war and Wilson. Postmaster General Albert Burleson banned *The Nation,* not for sedition, but for criticizing Wilson's ally Samuel Gompers. TR granted the administration some wartime license to enforce uniformity of belief in extraordinary ways, but he hated its partisan methods.[20]

When the C.P.I. solicited TR's advice for techniques to arouse the public's war spirit, he recommended dramatizing the "hideous iniquities" committed by Germany, such as the burning of Louvain and the enslavement of Belgian men. Soon C.P.I. posters portrayed beastlike Huns dragging young girls away to be raped. But when Hermann Hagedorn offered the C.P.I. the services of the writers in the Vigilantes, Creel answered: "We don't want you! You're all Roosevelt men." Nevertheless, many Vigilantes did help out with the C.P.I., and Creel went far beyond TR's suggestions to create an extensive propaganda agency. Medill McCormick came up with the idea for the Four Minute Men who gave brief, but emotional patriotic speeches in movie theaters and often led audiences in singing "Pack Up Your Troubles" or "Keep the Home Fires Burning."[21]

Everywhere war acted to unleash social conflicts. Lynchings, riots, vigilantism, and mob violence increased across the land. TR tried much harder than Wilson to stop the racial violence that the war and migration set off. He spoke out more sharply than any other white national leader against the "appalling brutality" of the bloody East St. Louis riots of July where whites killed thirty-nine blacks. At a public gathering honoring Russia's new Kerensky government, Roosevelt took the opportunity to attack the "outbreak of savagery" in East St. Louis for which "there was no real provocation." At the same podium, Gompers defended the white workers for rioting because black strikebreakers posed an economic threat to them.[22]

When he heard Gompers' remarks, TR crossed the stage and shook his fist in a menacing way in the labor leader's face. The fury of his gestures left some observers with the impression that he had hit Gompers. TR declared, "Murder is murder, whether black or white," and he called for an investigation of the riot. He denounced Gompers for excusing the "the brutal infamies imposed on colored people." The audience of workers, socialists, and labor people responded with boos and cheers, and, in the pandemonium that followed, Roosevelt had to be escorted out of the hall by the police. The African-American press and the *Jewish Daily Forward* called the riot a "pogrom" and praised the ex-president's remarks.[23]

More riots broke out in Houston when black soldiers fought against insults perpetrated by local whites. Although white rioters went unpunished, Wilson allowed six black soldiers to be hanged for retaliating against those who had attacked them, leaving a blot on his record worse than Brownsville.[24]

FIGHTING AGAINST his own despair, Theodore joked in letters to his sons that he was useless baggage in wartime: "Every body works but Father!" But his work for the war effort had become speaking out for loyalty and reform. By August his frantic pace giving patriotic "bugle-call" speeches and defending Bull Moose ideas had left him exhausted.[25]

Edith had judged her husband "fine and hearty" after a "wonderful row, far, far out into the Sound" with "the most lovely calm water, and lights and shadows." He had moved her Philip Laszlo portrait so that he could see it from his desk in the library as he wrote, and she hoped he would content himself finally to home life with her. He regularly went to his office at the *Metropolitan*, where his visitors overflowed into Finley Peter Dunne's office. On August 17, TR returned from his writing and speechmaking in the city "light-headed" and then came down with "a bad go of fever." He felt so "wretched" he could not eat.[26]

Edith anxiously cared for him for several days while he was "sitting about with a bad head and back and poor leg done up in anti-photogrestine." That summer she helped to moderate TR's tendency toward furious activity followed by depths of weary depression. He described himself as "depressed" more often in the second half of 1917 than ever before. Edith, too, was dispirited, and she told Bamie, whose nineteen-year-old son, Sheffield, wanted to fight, what she could not say to Theodore. She confessed that her stoicism about her sons, especially Quentin, going to war was mingled with anguish and deep regret: "I cannot be reconciled to boys of his age taking irrevocable steps."[27]

On July 4, Archie had marched with the Sixteenth Infantry through Paris, where crowds cheered American soldiers as the "Les Teddies." The American forces parading with General Pershing struck Edith Wharton as a "really splendid" sight, and she did relief work and made the Roosevelt boys welcome in her home. TR hoped Kermit would reach the British army in time for the fall of Constantinople, but their eyes were on France, where Ted, Archie, and Quentin waited for battle. Edith and Theodore admitted they had some qualms about Quentin's precipitous engagement to Flora Whitney whose immature character and smart set, yachting, and rich family gave them pause, but Quentin lived with a grown man's dangers now and could make his own decisions. Edith recalled with sad nostalgia the days when Archie strummed his mandolin while Quentin played "The Bird in Nellie's Hat" on the piano in the North Room. During his illness, TR joked that Edith felt "very woebegone" because she "realized that she was mated to a dull-nerved, coarse-natured unappreciative and non-understanding boor," but he observed that when his wife's "life stretched before and behind in a straight, monotonous, dusty road of uncheered duty," all it took was a three-hour row with him on Long Island Sound to lift her spirits.[28]

Recovered enough to inspect an aviation training camp in Garden City in September, TR slipped away from the generals long enough to find a test pilot, to whom he said: "Take me up!" The exhilaration of flying five thousand feet above Long Island made him wish Edith could have tried it, too. With summer fading, Roosevelt had to make choices about how to expend what energy he had left. Pleading lack of expertise, he turned down a place on Herbert Hoover's Food Commission. He did not want to pass the war talking the consumer into wheatless Mondays and meatless Thursdays. He still wondered if the President would offer him a "disagreeable or useless" job before his searing anti-Wilson diatribe, *The Foes of Our Own Household*, came out. He finally decided the best role he could play on the home front was to stir up patriotism and claim the war for the forces of reform. He had always seen war as a reorganizing crucible which could nationalize and inspire truer citizenship, as he believed the Civil War had done. When Bull Moosers Harold Ickes, Hiram Johnson, and Gifford Pinchot called for the war to bring about social justice via a corporate profits tax, progressive income and estate tax policies, woman suffrage, and a "more equitable distribution of wealth," he spoke out in agreement with them.[29]

Roosevelt made a Labor Day speech at the Columbia County Fair in Chatham, New York, where he called for an excess war profits tax of 80 percent and renewed his plea for health, old-age, and unemployment insurance, a position to the left of even the most progressive senators. He urged government "to ensure a reasonably equitable division" of the profits earned during the war. TR also spoke out for "the democratization of industry" and heavily graduated inheritance and income taxes. He was eager to campaign further for wartime reform, but complained that it was hard to get anything but war articles published. When he made reform speeches newspapers ignored them and played up his "bugle-call" lectures instead.[30]

TR told Bridgeport, Connecticut, munitions workers that if employers would not guarantee health insurance, high wages, and pensions "as matters of right not as matters of favor," then government action and the "sanction of law" would be needed. When the high price of milk caused a serious health problem for poor children in New York City, he called for the "establishment of government markets" or legislation to make sure that poor children did not go without milk. He argued that the only sincere way to promote democracy abroad was "to make it just" at home. Many patriotic groups opposed the public expression of such reformist ideas because they saw it as "indirect treason" to call for so much government involvement in the economy, but Roosevelt was too great a national hero for easy attack.[31]

Though he described himself disparagingly as "an elderly male Cassandra has been," TR desperately wanted his national audience back so that he could promote reform. He and Edith hosted a mammoth reception at Sagamore Hill for five hundred guests of the New York State Woman Suffrage Campaign. He volunteered as a speaker in the campaign to win what veteran suffrage leader Carrie Chapman Catt called "the Gettysburg of the woman suffrage movement." When suffrage passed in New York in 1917, Roosevelt celebrated the victory with Anna Howard Shaw, who burst into tears at the enormity of their accomplishment, and he predicted to an enthusiastic audience that New York's example would lead the nation toward the passage of the Susan B. Anthony Amendment. To make sure his prediction came true, suffrage forces reaffirmed their national policy of reprisal, which Alice Paul had discussed with Roosevelt earlier, and they campaigned actively against anti-suffrage candidates, who were often Democrats.[32]

TR tried to make women's equality a patriotic issue. He denounced Germany as the country in which "women come nearest to being treated as a servile and inferior class, a class of drudges, born only for service to men," and he called for America to make its women full citizens in wartime and encourage them to serve in the workplace, in war industries, in hospitals, and even as nurses alongside men at the front. He gave money and praise to the National League for Women's Service, which had organized a women's rifle corps. He praised women's college volunteers in the Women's Land Army, which grew food to make up for wartime shortages. He told suffragists that he counted on them for support of the war as well as for the extension of social and economic justice. He believed in a woman's draft requiring universal service, "although the precise kind of service may be different" from men's service. During the New Deal his niece Eleanor took her uncle's idea and turned it into a proposal for a year of community service for women with the same wages as men who were drafted.[33]

On September 20 he began an ambitious pro-war speaking tour through Kansas, Illinois, Wisconsin, and Minnesota. Edith joined him for part of the trip to watch over his health as much as she could. He was waging a rhetorical war on "the Huns within our gates," attacking in particular the organizers of peace ships like Henry Ford, the foreign language press which he termed "our most dangerous foe," sissy pacifists, and dangerous "copperheads" like Senators William Stone and La Follette, and Congressman Jeff McLemore. He was not going to understate his case.[34]

At roughly the same time, La Follette argued in St. Paul that America had gone to war foolishly to defend "technical rights." Hurrying to press with an unedited report, the Associated Press quoted him saying "We had no grievances" against Germany. Believing the report, Roosevelt led the public outcry against La Follette and called for his ouster from the Senate. He stated in public that it was a shame not to send "an unhung traitor" like La Follette to his friend the kaiser. Newspapers broke the story that the German government had spent large amounts of money trying to influence Congress, which further intensified suspicion of the senator. A "pale and strained" La Follette defended himself and argued for freedom of speech in wartime. As sloppy journalism sparked wartime hysteria, TR grasped the chance to turn an old political foe into an enemy of the state. He called La Follette "the worst enemy that democracy has now alive" and the Senate opened expulsion hearings. TR's speaking tour was now big national news; he had used his influence with the public recklessly by preaching that a principled man should lose his Senate seat because of unpopular views.[35]

Competition with Wilson for leadership of the war also animated Roosevelt's desire to personify the home-front spirit. He devoted himself to the war effort by serving on the board of the local Red Cross, making speeches for Liberty Loans, and popularizing the slogan "Farm and Arm" as he and other wealthy Long Islanders turned portions of their estates into Victory Gardens. He did not tell Edith that his patriotism cost the family a large chunk of its life savings when he impulsively bought $60,000 in Liberty Bonds, but she found out later that he had, on the spur of the moment, given several pieces of family silver to the Camp Fire Girls to be melted down for the war. But, soon enough, weariness set in. Wilson was still president, and TR felt old, defunct, useless, and angry once more.[36]

The best he could do if he could not fight at the front would be to fight for America's soul, but his attacks on internal foes fueled the already spreading grass-roots drama of neighbor attacking neighbor for their failure to support the war. In Racine, Wisconsin, after repeatedly urging people to root out the "Huns within our gates," Roosevelt told his audience that "the hour for action in the name of loyalty to America has struck." A month later, four hundred miles away, Herbert Bigelow, a pacifist and socialist minister, was kidnapped by robed men and taken into the woods, where they horsewhipped him with a blacksnake whip "in the name of the poor women and children of Belgium."[37]

Roosevelt denied paternity of the monstrosity emerging from the war spirit: It did not strike him as the noble patriotic infant he had intended to raise. Although he approved of hating Germany, he insisted he did not preach domestic hate or violence: "I am utterly against any 'hymn of hate' in this country as against any nationality." He urged his countrymen not to discriminate against loyal German-Americans, but evidently he did not mind if opponents of war were attacked.[38]

The heat of Roosevelt's rhetoric against hyphenated Americans, the foreign language press, and his call for deporting immigrants who did not learn to speak English within five years struck a responsive chord with nativists, who viewed new immigrants as foreign intruders. He declared: "There is no room for the hyphen in our citizenship. . . . We have room in this country for but one flag. . . . We have room for but one language," and called for assimilation and Americanization programs. Yet he denied he was encouraging anti-immigrant prejudice, as he insisted that it was wrong to discriminate against any loyal American because of his ethnic or national origins. Unfortunately, that fine distinction was lost on audiences already inclined toward nativism.[39]

Nevertheless, many immigrants, blacks, and a wide variety of ethnic groups applauded Roosevelt's Americanism speeches. Immigrants often saw the Y.M.C.A. and other Americanization programs supported by industry as the price they paid for employment and greater social acceptance, but others regarded the patriotic teachings of Americanizers like Roosevelt as "humiliating tripe." Developing a stronger American civic folk culture had been a longstanding goal of progressive urban reformers who hoped to find common ground between old- and new-stock city people, but in wartime public pageantry was taken over by groups who sought to "nationalize" the masses for war, sometimes using coercion. Yet, Americanizers from within the working class taught new immigrants labor radicalism along with patriotism, so at the grass-roots level nationalist rhetoric often served the local agenda of increasing union membership and bargaining power. TR was invited to speak to many working-class audiences, and he applauded their use of blue-collar Americanism to gain an eight-hour day and better wages.[40]

Americanism, however, soon became a fire burning out of control, and Roosevelt's stark public pronouncements worked on it like kerosene. When patriots asked the conductor Karl Muck, a German citizen, to lead the Boston Symphony in the "Star-Spangled Banner" he replied it would be out of place in his classical program. Roosevelt charged that anyone who refused to play the national anthem "in this time of national crisis, should be forced to pack up and return to the country he came from." Muck finally played the anthem, but the Bureau of Investigation jailed him anyway.[41]

In the West job actions organized by the Industrial Workers of the World (I.W.W.) threatened the production of copper needed for armaments, and when a strike was rumored in Bisbee, Arizona, Phelps-Dodge mine manager and Rough Rider John Greenway, along with other vigilantes, deported at gunpoint 1,386 mine workers and local bystanders. They put the workers in boxcars, then left them in the New Mexico desert. The workers had not been charged with crimes but they were herded like cattle anyway. Roosevelt thought repression of the "criminal" I.W.W. "in times of danger" was justified, but he told Greenway that the government and not vigilantes should have "proceeded with the utmost rigor against the I.W.W.'s." His friend Judge Learned Hand commented: "As usual with Teddy, he speaks before he has any adequate knowledge of the facts and when he is wrong, he is all-fired wrong."[42]

On occasion, Roosevelt stood up against patriotic excess. Wilson's closest advisors assumed that disloyalty was rampant among newer immigrants and so ruled that foreign-born citizens and their children be banned from service in the Red Cross. Outraged, banker Jacob Schiff complained to Roosevelt that the administration assumed that immigrants could not be trusted to be loyal or to do war work. Roosevelt protested the order and declared in public addresses that he saw no reason to discriminate against immigrants or any ethnic or racial group as long as they supported America in the war.[43]

Insistent that loyalty superseded ethnicity or race, Roosevelt asked if he could speak before the 367th Negro Infantry at Camp Upton to pay his respects to black soldiers fighting for their country. TR donated part of his Nobel Peace Prize money to Negro war relief and told the 367th and other men in uniform: "It is only you and your kind who have the absolutely clear title to the management of this Republic." Edith wrote Kermit that she was proud of her husband on the occasion of his emotional address. After the speech the 367th sang "Old Black Joe," which, Edith said, "nearly reduced me to tears."[44]

But loyalty was not something TR could take for granted. He urged Schiff and others to reaffirm their allegiance by signing loyalty oaths. He also endorsed the loyalty oath campaign in the New York public schools and approved of firing teachers who had shown even "the slightest symptoms of disloyalty to this nation." Annoyed that Wilson had allowed draft exemptions for the son of newspaper magnate E. W. Scripps and the son of pacifist and Democratic Party benefactor Henry Ford, TR personally turned in names of men who had gained false exemptions from local draft boards. He even called for conscientious objectors, mostly Quakers or Mennonites, to lose their right to vote, or, better yet, for them to be put on minesweepers or forced to dig trenches at the front.[45]

As the Wilson administration and TR attacked disloyalty, the President's Bureau of Investigation enlisted volunteers from the American Protective League and other patriotic groups to spy on their neighbors. A.P.L. volunteers turned in three million people for alleged disloyalty, though a lack of credible evidence resulted in few convictions. Wilson's sloppily administered intelligence agencies imagined subversion in unlikely places and even used the Secret Service to spy on the collector of the Port of New York, Dudley Field Malone, who had criticized the President's attitude toward woman suffrage picketers. Roosevelt began to see the excesses in the hunt for internal subversion when it came too close to home. He wondered if, beyond censoring his overseas letters, the administration tapped his phone. He knew that the government eavesdropped on its critics, so he started communicating with Lodge by telegram because "I do not dare to use the telephone." He told Archie he could not write him freely for "I too fear the censor and dare not write you as fully as I would like."[46]

Roosevelt spotted big domestic foes Wilson had not criticized. In *The Foes of Our Own Household* he vented his anger at the enemies of true reform, the conservatives who resisted his Bull Moose ideas. They were those rich and selfish people who "oppose, or are inertly indifferent to, the effort to remove the causes of that preventable misery and wrong which drive honest poor men to follow the false prophets of evil."[47]

He also charged that Wilson was another "foe of our own household" because he had left the country so vulnerable that American troops arrived late to the war and had to be transported in British ships and defended by French guns. Roosevelt called the President a domestic foe because he failed to produce airplanes or field guns and had left American training camps short of rifles, tents, and clothing. Indeed, Wilson qualified further as a "foe of our own household" because he had "drugged" into stupor the nationalism and "moral sense of our people." He also directly attacked Wilson for his bloody occupation of Haiti and Santo Domingo, which he said proved that the President had no intention of making the "world safe for democracy."[48]

Wilson and his cabinet watched TR's criticisms of their inadequate "broomstick preparedness" in his *Kansas City Star* editorials, and they were ready to prosecute him if he crossed over into clearly seditious territory. They had sent many less famous men to jail for milder criticisms, but when Wilson received complaints about TR's "outbursts" he merely said: "I really think the best way to treat Mr. Roosevelt is to take no notice of him. That breaks his heart and is the best punishment that can be administered. After all, while what he says is outrageous in every particular, he does, I am afraid, keep within the limits of the law, for he is as careful as he is unscrupulous."[49]

WHEN, in December, Allied defeat loomed near, TR blamed it on Wilson's failure to prepare and considered the collapse of Russia and the defeat of the Italians at Caporetto "very grave." About 300,000 men had died at Passchendaele, leaving the British to wonder how much longer they could go on. Still eager to get American help to the Allies before it was too late, TR called for Wilson to declare war on Austria-Hungary. Wilson complied, though he persisted in referring to the United States as an associate rather than a full ally, which further annoyed Roosevelt.[50]

After the Bolsheviks gained power in Russia, they deserted the Allies and opened negotiations for a separate peace with Germany. Five million Russians had died fighting the czar's war, so war-weary peasants wanted peace and bread more than victory. Even TR admitted the Bolsheviks governed better at first than the Romanoffs. A Bolshevik separate peace, however, tainted all other negotiations. The French jailed former prime minister Joseph Caillaux, among other offenses, for advocating peace with Germany. Wilson had warned that those who "intrigue for peace" were pro-German and disloyal, and mobs had followed his lead by attacking peace advocates on the streets. His C.P.I. agent Edgar Sisson made inquiries in Petrograd to ascertain if Lenin might not be a paid agent of the German government.[51]

Bolshevik ascendancy in Russia reverberated fearfully around the world. If a small group of partisans could overturn a large government in disarray in Russia, revolution could happen anywhere, especially where war had allowed autocratic tendencies to grow in previous democracies. In fact, Leon Trotsky, in *The Bolsheviki and World Peace,* predicted that the Great War would usher in revolution around the world.

The Bolshevik threat hung over American politics by the end of 1917. Wilson feared domestic Bolsheviks and preached liberal internationalism and America's mission in order to stop revolutionary socialism from spreading outward from Russia. The success of a small Bolshevik cadre in Russia increased public suspicion against liberals and radicals in the United States. Because of Jane Addams' peace activism, her office doorway was vandalized and she was denounced as "a foolish virgin."[52]

Roosevelt worried that the triumph of Bolshevism in Russia had freed German troops to fight an all-out war to end the stalemate on the western front. Germany expected to win the war before Americans reached the front and dismissed the proposed million-man American army as a "bluff." German newspapers tried to belittle America's military prowess by spreading the word that the famous Rough Riders were mostly Negroes.[53]

Perhaps American "bluff" was right. War mobilization still floundered. Wilson had taken over the railroads, telegraphs, and telephones and had regulated wages and prices, but he had not come close to war readiness. Lodge alerted Roosevelt that after six months of fumbling the administration had failed to produce any American-made machine guns, and he warned that graft might be to blame. Stalled airplane production, unheated hospitals, lack of rifles and ammunition, and pneumonia in training camps worried Roosevelt, not only because his sons and the other soldiers were fighting in a badly run war effort, but also because leaders had "put us in such a humiliating and unworthy position." For Americans like TR who were privy to stories about British officers looking down on American troops as colonial inferiors who should fight only under Allied command, the President's failure to make a strong military showing was upsetting because it invited national humiliation.[54]

The Republican Party sent Senator Reed Smoot and Congressman Martin Madden to Sagamore Hill accompanied by the Republican Publicity Association's Jonathan Bourne to enlist TR's help in a "drive against the President" to oppose Wilson's sluggish failure to aid the Allies, his careless spending, his aggressive use of censorship, and, worst of all, his grab for more executive power. TR promised to lead the anti-Wilson forces. He was already planning to fire off attacks on Wilson's "fatuous and sinister censorship" and his sending American troops coffins instead of shoes and guns. They also talked about Congress limiting the President's powers before he took over any other major industries.[55]

He launched a full-scale onslaught against Wilson and came close to taunting the President to arrest him. The restraint of advisors, especially

Edith and Lodge, had moderated his impulsive actions in the White House, but by 1918, King Lear raged with little restraint. As he spoke around the country Roosevelt came perilously close to branding Wilson a traitor. His attacks on the President often violated the repressive spirit of the Espionage Act, which the attorney general applied loosely to forbid criticism of Wilson and to punish speech or print which tended to "impugn the motives of the government and thus encourage insubordination."[56]

In the depths of January 1918, Republicans and a few Democrats also launched a full-scale attack on Wilson's conduct of the war. Senator George Chamberlain, a Democrat, charged that young men had died in training camps because of government incompetence. Northeasterners were especially disgruntled because Wilson's fuel administrator closed factories and businesses for five days due to a coal shortage. TR and other administration critics came to Washington and told the press that Wilson's mismanagement of the war was claiming lives and that a coalition war cabinet was needed. Secretary of the Navy Josephus Daniels thought Roosevelt had come to Washington to set up a rump government. Wilson replied that a coalition war cabinet would pass only when "he was dead." As the emerging leader of the wartime opposition, TR faced a dilemma—how to attack the President's failures without giving "comfort to the opponents of the war."[57]

Because of Roosevelt's diatribes criticizing Wilson's inadequate planning for war, the mayor of Abilene, Kansas, called him "a seditious conspirator who ought to be shot dead." TR answered that it was a "foolish deceit" not to want to hear the truth that nine months after Germany's declaration of all-out submarine warfare, America was still not helping the Allies militarily in any significant numbers and Americans were "still wholly unable to defend ourselves."[58]

When German victory seemed near as the Allies braced themselves for a fierce German offensive, Roosevelt was called upon to stop "heckling the Commander-in-Chief when we [are] at war." He insisted that it was "unpatriotic not to criticize" the President, but his friends cautioned him that what he was doing would undermine his political future. When the Senate debated the sedition bill intended to silence Wilson's critics (especially TR) by banning "contemptuous or slurring language about the President," Roosevelt called it "sheer treason to the United States." Civil libertarian Roger Baldwin warned Wilson's advisor Colonel House that the sedition bill could be used to ban the Republican Party and prohibit all criticism of the government. On the floor of the Senate, Senator Hiram Johnson, TR's 1912 running mate, cautioned that the sedition bill would bring autocracy to America: "We are at war against a ruthless enemy. But good God, Mr. President, when did it become a war upon the American people?"[59]

If the sedition bill was passed, TR promised, "I shall certainly give the Government the opportunity to test its constitutionality." He did not, however, differ with the bill's basic assumption that speech encouraging draft resistance, defending Germany, or attacking the Allies was seditious. Indeed, he thought the bill was too extreme only when it prohibited loyal criticism of the government. He urged the government to "shoot the spy or the traitor," but to leave loyal dissenters alone. In the *Kansas City Star* he wrote that "the suppression of the truth by and about the Administration has been habitual," an assertion proven in part by the fact that Burleson's post office had recently destroyed anti-censorship pamphlets written by Norman Angell, and U.S. marshals had jailed citizens for mild public criticisms of President Wilson. The post office had already made it dangerous for newspapers to report the truth, Roosevelt contended, and it was downright reckless in a democracy to pass laws giving the President "absolute power."[60]

TR charged that the Wilson administration had "successfully endeavored to prevent expression of opinion hostile to it" by censoring the press. Burleson had already admitted that he would not allow anyone to print the opinion "that this Government got in the war wrong, that it is in it for the wrong purposes, or anything that will impugn the motives of the Government for going into the war." That spring the New York Post Office had tried to suppress the issue of *Metropolitan* which included Roosevelt's "Put the Blame Where It Belongs" and his "Lincoln and Free Speech." After that Roosevelt became a defender of wartime free speech because he believed the administration was wrong in using "the very real war powers of the government over the public press to stifle honest criticism of government inefficiency or misconduct."[61]

Burleson reacted angrily to TR's accusations of partisanship in censorship and dared him to produce evidence or to retract his statement. Roosevelt answered with a detailed list of cases when the administration had censored its political critics, including loyal black newspapers like the *New York News*, critical of Wilson's race policies, and the radical magazine *The Public*, opposed to Wilson's tax schemes. By all accounts, TR hit home with his scathing reply, and he helped inhibit autocratic leanings in Washington.[62]

The Nation asked "Why Is Roosevelt Unjailed?" in an editorial criticizing the administration's bad habit of jailing less famous adversaries. The editorial credited the ex-president with having saved the right of free speech in wartime. TR had argued clearly and effectively for a free press, using the same reasoning as Roger Baldwin and his National Civil Liberties Bureau, later the American Civil Liberties Union. In truth, however, TR was no Baldwin nor did he really defend complete free speech in wartime. He bemoaned

Wilson's failure to censor Hearst for defending Germany's right to sink the *Lusitania* and repeatedly criticizing the Allies.[63]

Though he lost his war against the Sedition Act when Congress passed it in 1918, Roosevelt had made some inroads in his battle to mobilize public opinion against political censorship. Villard's *New York Evening Post* conceded that TR's fight against Burleson had "great force." Vice President Thomas Marshall, in a speech advocating a third term for Wilson, ridiculed "Lady Theodora" for complaining too much and publishing in a seditious newspaper, the *Kansas City Star*, and afterward even the pro-administration *New York Times* denounced Marshall for his "bad taste."[64] Wilson's cabinet also considered censoring TR's anti-administration diatribes in the *Star*, but its censorship plans got lost in jurisdictional quarrels. TR wrote Archie that he wished Wilson dared jail him. It pleased him that "the Administration loathes me," and he said he wanted Wilson to arrest him because it "would make my voice carry farther."[65]

IN THE MIDDLE of his war of words against Wilson, Edith finally talked her husband into doing something about his health. His horse had gone lame from carrying him, so he enrolled at Jack Cooper's sanitarium and physical culture farm in Stamford, Connecticut, to lose weight, as Edith put it, "from that too substantial form." Cooper's later recollections inflated TR's salvation under his guidance. The ex-prizefighter recalled that the old Bull Moose came to him "on the verge of collapse" and told him, "I feel myself slipping a bit both mentally and physically." Cooper judged him to be overworked and thirty-five pounds overweight with high blood pressure. The trainer set him to early-morning walks, six half-mile runs, muscle-building exercises, and a half hour on the Reducycle each day. Boredom set in soon enough, though Theodore busied himself making friends with the kitchen staff and the sick patients at the sanitarium. When he came home he told Edith that he "had had enough of his trainers."[66]

Lodge and Connecticut political boss John T. King fueled TR's hopes for 1920. Roosevelt said he had decided to "strike hands with anyone who is sound on Americanism and on speeding up the war and putting it through to the finish," which left him with opportunistic bedfellows who did not agree with him that "we ought to take heed of our industrial and social matters." When Warren G. Harding cozied up to Alice in Washington to let her know his interest in her father's 1920 prospects, winning, not reform, was his agenda. TR rationalized his new associations with hidebound conservatives and superpatriots as expediency in wartime, but he also deluded himself that his charm would be overpowering enough to move the Republican Party toward a more progressive domestic agenda after the war.[67]

Roosevelt remained uneasy about his role: to be so revered, so famous, so able to inspire audiences made it more painful to feel so powerless. In early December 1917, Edith thought she had never seen her husband "looking better or more full of life," and she convinced him to leave politics and writing long enough to see a play with her in the city. When he walked into the theater, the audience went wild, even though Sarah Bernhardt was in attendance, too. As requests for public appearances multiplied, he found he disliked "serving as an end man in an amateur minstrel show." He nevertheless understood that he owed it to society to use the power of his celebrity to help good causes. He agreed to appear as part of the wartime fundraising "entertainment" along with Lillian Russell or pianist Josef Hoffman. Corinne talked him into appearing at Hero Land, the great Allied bazaar which activist women organized at Grand Central Plaza where she raised money for the Fatherless Children of France by charging each person fifty cents for a handshake with her brother. Desirous of pleasing his sister, he longed for more from his ex-presidency than to be an aging Buffalo Bill displayed before audiences as an artifact of the past.[68]

Roosevelt never relinquished the widespread progressive hope that a better world would emerge from the war. Many progressives saw in Wilson's centralization of power the promise of a stronger and more coordinated reform-minded postwar state. But progressive moral reform arose from the war first, with men in training camps and soldiers at the front made special objects of reform by the Anti-Swearing League, as well as anti-prostitution and prohibition forces. To prevent the "bestial demoralization" of the men by prostitutes and drink, Wilson put Raymond Fosdick in charge of the Commission on Training Camp Activities, which applied the well-worn muscular Christian recreational and moral tonic to uplift the soldiers' character and give them "invisible armour" against sin after the war.[69]

Roosevelt had been saying for a long time that proper military training could effect a cultural cure by taking "the moral stoop out of" each soldier's "shoulders as well as his physical stoop." His daughter-in-law Eleanor went to France to work for the Y.M.C.A., and he praised the Y's creation of clean recreation centers and their moral work among the troops. He agreed that prostitutes and drink should be kept away from the soldiers, and he wrote a social hygiene pamphlet warning men about the dangers of social disease. He urged them to "lead clean lives" "because its [*sic*] the straight, decent self-respecting thing to do; next because its the only way in which to give the square deal to women of the right type, who, Heaven knows, need the square deal; and finally because they owe it to the country not to ruin their efficiency as soldiers and citizens." However, contraceptives more than chastity were responsible for the fact that American soldiers had lower rates of venereal disease after enlistment than they had as civilians.[70]

While for many progressives improving the individual's character remained the ultimate goal of reform, for TR it had come to mean an overhaul of the social and economic system. He had begun his political career assuming that economic differences were natural and probably reflected just deserts, but he gradually had come to the belief that government should make sure everyone had a chance to make good in life. He viewed Wilson's wartime pressure on business to accept collective bargaining with labor and the eight-hour day, his tiny federal housing projects, and veterans benefits as only the first halting steps toward government reorganization of society to bring greater economic equality and to banish poverty and hunger. Roosevelt, Herbert Croly, John Dewey, Walter Lippmann, and Thorstein Veblen felt that wartime "national collectivism" was "full of benign possibilities for peace." The wartime centralization of the economy and the strengthening of the nation-state heartened nationalistic progressives because the federal government finally could pose a countervailing force to all-powerful corporations.[71]

Roosevelt's final vision of government-mediated social justice promised, not socialism or communism, but democratic legislation to achieve economic redistribution. In December 1917, as they sat before the fireplace in the North Room, Ethel stayed up late to talk over labor problems with her father, who told her:

> After declaring that all men are equal we cannot expect that permanently the 3% will own the property & have the power: the 97% will become restless, are restless. And perhaps the best way to meet it is that the 3% recognize the claim of all the others—& give them sickness insurance & old age pensions & a share in the stock & profits etc. Then of course comes the grave danger of too much paternalism. Father is going to bend his efforts to solving it—& thinks probably the people will turn to La Follette![72]

His solution for redistribution was, at one end of the spectrum, to use inheritance and progressive income taxes to diminish great fortunes, and at the other to exert government pressure for higher wages and government old-age, illness, and unemployment insurance to prevent a family from falling into poverty.[73]

Full employment and a rearrangement of worker-employer relationships would increase redistribution, too. TR spread the word of his plans for "cooperative ownership and management" of industry to employers and worker audiences alike, though he never made clear how these goals would be reconciled with the profit motive and capitalism, which he did not want to undermine. If he thought employers would willingly relinquish control or profit he was mistaken. What he meant by the "democratization of our industries" was workers' councils which would give employees profit sharing via stock options and more say in factory conditions. "Genuine social and industrial justice" would require government to insist that industry protect war workers from accidents and disease. Government should guarantee workers, he wrote, the "right to collective action and their safety from sweating and any other detrimental practice."[74]

As he looked forward to 1920, TR wanted wartime patriotism and Republican support for suffrage to win women voters. New York Woman Suffrage Party chairman Vira Whitehouse, treasurer Helen Reid, and Gifford Pinchot and his wife, Cornelia, came to Sagamore Hill to dine with the Roosevelts and John T. King. They talked over strategies for passing the Anthony Amendment and bringing the new voters into the Republican Party. Whitehouse intended to extend nationwide her successful New York suffrage strategy by having suffragists do useful war work, such as raising Red Cross and other relief funds and conducting the military census so that states would know which men were of draft age. "Woman power" in relief, war industries, and patriotic activities built a strong case for suffrage, but it was clear that many men, notably those on the Councils of National Defense and in control of both parties, were not prepared to accept women as anything but subordinates.[75]

Cornelia Pinchot urged Roosevelt to write to all the Republican chairmen in suffrage states to appoint women committee members and to integrate women into party councils, and he agreed to do so. She also wanted TR to remind the conservatives in the party that he alone could deliver progressive votes. Her husband was weighing his chances of unseating Boies Penrose in the Senate, but everything depended on how progressive the voters would be by November 1918. Nine million new female voters might put Roosevelt back into the White House in 1920, but the largest women's organization in the country, the Woman's Christian Temperance Union, was riding in the front of Bryan's prohibition wagon. While Roosevelt had favored a restricted wartime prohibition to save grain, he thought the war on the saloon misguided because ongoing changes in the workplace were already forcing sobriety on bosses and wage earners alike. He believed that national prohibition would bring free rum to every city in America, but he shrewdly left both sides on the liquor question convinced that he supported their viewpoint. TR was betting on social justice issues, not moral reform, for 1920.[76]

Roosevelt kept up his ties with the women's reform network. After touring schools and tenements with the Woman's Municipal League and social workers, he had launched an investigation of malnutrition among New York's children due to the milk shortage. He told the press that because one out of ten children in New York suffered from malnutrition, "he wanted to see the most radical action taken to secure an ample supply of milk to every child in the city." He favored government-funded free school lunches, but Hearst's "ponderous-minded" Mayor John Hylan did nothing.[77]

The year 1920 looked like a time for reform to TR, but for his new manager, John T. King, it seemed a chance to make deals. King visited Alice about her father's future presidential bid and told her of the funds and allies he had already solicited. Alice warily saw King as Penrose's henchman, so it did not surprise insiders when King scheduled a peace talk between TR and Penrose. But TR blindly told himself that King must be a true progressive who simply had a gift for making friends among the stand-patters and big donors.[78]

FROM THE trenches of France, Ted reported to his father that the "nervous and frayed out" Archie was showing "signs of strain." In "heartbroken letters" home, Archie said Sherman's claim, "War is hell," was a gross understatement. But neither son would accept a safe staff position because each understood it would be used against his father politically. Ted admitted to his superior officer that he feared disappointing his father, whose "dearest wish was that he should lead his battalion in action."[79]

Edith described her husband as incapable of happiness because he was anxious about his sons and "uneasy about public affairs." But Theodore's concern for his boys' well-being did not stop him from pressing them into battle. After describing his pride in Archie's, and Ted's wartime feats, TR wrote pointedly to Kermit: "I am looking forward eagerly to your letter which I suppose may at any time tell of your participation in the fighting."[80]

Early in 1918, Edith and Theodore discovered that Quentin was downhearted because Archie and Ted had been berating him for failing to get into the fighting as they had. Quentin was angry at his superiors and the dearth of airplanes for standing in the way of his chance to become a hero, flying over German lines. For Archie to belittle Quentin as the "weak link" in the family struck Ethel as "too absurd and horrid." Edith and Theodore were also "very angry" with Ted and Archie, and they immediately sent Quentin a cable of support. Yet, having raised his sons to become soldiers and having pushed them to compete with one another, TR would have to apply all his powers of denial to avoid feeling some responsibility for his sons demeaning each other about their war service.[81]

When he spoke before the National Security League in early 1918, he warned that America's mobilization for the Great War had been late and slapdash. He privately feared that Wilson's incompetence might cause "the little army we now have in France" to be "sacrificed," including his sons.[82]

At the exact moment the Allies braced for a German assault, Theodore was struck down by a nearly fatal illness. A cold went to his ears in the first days of February. Irritated by hemorrhoids, his unhealed Brazilian wound, an anal abscess with a fistula to the surface, became infected and hemorrhaged until his entire right buttock was swollen and red. Then fever knocked him out, though he still hoped to leave for a speaking engagement in Boston. On February 4, Dr. Walton Martin performed stopgap surgery with local anesthesia, which left the patient miserable but able to go to the Langdon Hotel, where he and Edith kept an apartment, to work from a couch where he dictated letters to Josephine Stricker.[83]

Edith, Alice, and Stricker stood by helplessly while Theodore was "suffering intensely." He refused to stop working or meeting his appointments at the *Metropolitan* offices and the Harvard Club. He had to see King, who was on his way to the St. Louis meeting of the Republican National Committee, where Roosevelt's plan to make King head of the committee met opposition and had to give way to his second choice, Will Hays of Indiana. When his secretary suggested that his mail could be postponed until he was not in so much pain, he replied sharply, "Miss Stricker, when I was President I instituted a rule to clear my desk each day of the day's work, and I shall stick to it." Shortly thereafter Stricker brought him a "stiff hooker of whiskey" for the pain, and he passed out.[84]

After another night of high fever, a "terribly white" TR was driven to Roosevelt Hospital where he agreed to have Dr. Martin put him under ether for his ears to be punctured and his abscesses excised in hopes that his health could be "fixed up once for all." Edith, Corinne, Alice, and Ethel waited out the operation together, and though he was "still hazy with ether" he woke up and recognized Edith right away.[85]

The next day his serious infection of the inner ear looked so bad that a specialist, Dr. Duel, told the family he thought TR's condition was "hopeless," because "a severe infection of the labyrinth" could spread to the meninges and dangerous brain surgery might be required.[86]

Edith had requested a room for the press in the hospital, and she saw that they were provided with food and coffee while they held a "death watch." She asked her husband's old friend John J. Leary to help Stricker with news releases that would prevent rumors from getting into print. Nevertheless, while he was in critical condition, some papers reported that TR had died.

In the first week after surgery, he went through "great suffering" from his ears. He was too ill to see many visitors for the next several days, but a few were allowed in: FDR, Ben Lindsey, Corinne, Bamie, Fanny Parsons, and Harriot Stanton Blatch of the League of Self-Supporting Women and the Women's Political Union.[87] Edith responded to the barrage of reporters, telegrams, and visitors with the composure learned from her long career as a political wife, yet in private she remained anxious about her husband's nearness to death.

Delirious when he dictated a letter to Archie on the eighth, he raged against a "very unjust world" in which the root evil was Wilson. All the Roosevelts had "to pay for the slothful and utterly selfish ambitions of a cold-blooded and unprincipled demagogue." He promised he would write a "full and truthful record" detailing Wilson's wrongdoing. Roosevelt's hatred of Wilson may have been the passion that kept him going.[88]

Edith found her husband "quite dauntless" as he fought for recovery in the hospital, and as she wrote Kermit, "He thinks of you boys the entire time—with such an aching longing to be in bodily danger with you." He wished he could "act as offering to the Gods" and somehow "save some of [his] boys from suffering or death by dying [him]self."[89]

After February 12, Edith began reporting more regularly in her diary her husband's gradual improvement and nights undisturbed by pain. He nevertheless remained a very sick man who suffered from vertigo. Even before he was able to walk again he turned to writing a major statement of how postwar American society could be reconstructed with progressive policies which he hoped would be the catalyst for transforming the Republican Party into "a constructive liberal party." The recent British Labour Party platform had been hailed by *The New Republic* and *The Outlook* as worth a serious look, and Roosevelt was determined in his keynote speech for the 1918 campaign to make the country reconsider the idea of a national minimum wage, a standard of living below which no American should fall. He called on Leary to set up a meeting about such ideas with friendly journalists at Sagamore Hill.[90]

After reading Labour Party plans to establish a minimum standard of living for all and some government ownership or supervision of natural resources, Roosevelt wrote: "I think that English labor party is about 90% right, although there may be 20% of it which would be damaging to try to hurry too fast." He had already praised its public housing plan.[91]

His main political concerns remained the problem of pushing the G.O.P. left. He had to find a tactful way to let George Perkins know that he had been supplanted by King as his manager. Meanwhile, Will Hays, the new "Billy Sunday of the Republican party," worked on Roosevelt's behalf in Washington giving a Republican Congressional Committee reception to Bull Moose and other Republican women which included even the courageous congresswoman Jeannette Rankin, who had voted against the war. Knowing that Wilson still reigned "supreme in the hearts of millions of his countrymen," TR asked King to counter the Democratic Party's publicity bureau by creating a Republican bureau that would speak up for progressive ideas.[92]

On March 7 Charles Lee drove TR back to Sagamore Hill where Richard waited on the piazza to greet his grandfather with hugs and kisses. Happy to be home in time to celebrate Richard's fourth birthday, TR was chastened momentarily by his close call, and he talked with Edith about what life would be like when the war was over and the boys were home again. They hoped to go to Fiji, Samoa, or Tahiti, to have a retirement of travel and reflection with their family nearby.[93]

IN FRANCE at the front, with his men under fire, Ted thought often how difficult it must be for his father "to be out of this veritable 'Armageddon.' " The American army raided the German lines near Toul after artillery barrages had softened up enemy defenses, but when Germans sent shells back, they exploded in the trenches that Major Theodore Roosevelt, Jr., commanded, knocking down two of TR's sons at once.[94]

On March 13 the United Press called TR with the news that Archie had been awarded the croix de guerre "under dramatic circumstances." As Theodore and Edith waited in "great suspense" contradictory news came in piece by piece—the War Department reported only slight wounds while Ted cabled that Archie's wounds were serious, but not life-threatening. On March 11 at 5 a.m. two German shells had knocked Ted down and blown Archie across the trench. As his brother's commanding officer, Ted picked himself up and sent stretcher-bearers to transport Archie to a first-aid station, but Archie did not get full medical attention until evening. Archie's arm was splintered in a compound fracture, his kneecap and leg wounded by shrapnel, and he was shell-shocked. Dick Derby went to see him and found him suffering.[95]

TR said his own "heart [was] torn with anxiety" as news of Archie's wounds poured in, so he appreciated that his wife, "the adamantine," reacted "as gallantly as any heroine of history." At lunch he looked at Edith, "her eyes shining, her cheeks flushed, as pretty as a picture," as she ordered Madeira, and the family drank a toast to Archie's bravery and then followed her lead by smashing their glasses on the floor.[96]

Before he knew the full extent of Archie's injuries, TR was so excited that he told the papers how proud he was of his son and that he was sure Archie would be back in action soon. Ted admitted he envied his brother's wound and medal, but their father's extravagant praise—"the scars will be badges of honor for all time"—and his solicitude for Archie galled Ted most. Ted wrote his father edgily that one of your sons "has an honourable wound, will have a scar & will be otherwise sound as a bell. 'There's glory for you.' "[97]

In response to prodding by Roosevelt and other Republicans, Wilson called up more men and hurried war production. The Committee on Public Information released pictures of hundreds of airplanes being sent to France and promised that thousands more would be ready soon. But the Senate Committee on Military Affairs exposed the administration's prevarications. Based on Naval Intelligence sources, Senator Lee Overman of North Carolina blamed spies in the Curtiss airplane plant for the fact that instead of 12,000, the American program had produced only 37 planes. Telling the public that "all great plants engaged in war work are more or less menaced by spies" was the way the administration excused its own failure to organize efficient war production. Privately Wilson admitted to the British spy William Wiseman that he was puzzled by Britain's desperate calls for manpower and their claims that Germany was close to winning the war.[98]

Near the end of March, Roosevelt's dizziness had abated just enough for him to put aside the cane he used to steady himself. Just a few weeks earlier the family had teased him when he had clumsily stepped on Edith's skirts as they went in to dinner, but now he found he had enough equilibrium to chop wood. Riding would have to wait. He began to laugh heartily again when friends told him humorous political stories, like the man who said to Secretary of Treasury William G. McAdoo: " 'Wilson always follows TR. Eventually I suppose soon we will hear he is deaf in one ear.' To which came the quick response 'Many think him already deaf in both!' "[99]

Roosevelt's doctors told him he was not strong enough to speak to the state Republican convention in Portland, Maine, but since he hoped to push the G.O.P. leftward through the speech he would deliver there, he went anyway, despite a bad cold. He focused what little energy he had left on the Maine talk because, as he told William Allen White, Bull Moosers did not need forgiveness for 1912, they needed the Old Guard to accept their "frank equality" and their new ideas on social and economic questions. He sent drafts to several politicians to test how well the progressive content of the speech would sit with them.[100]

Henry Cabot Lodge did not care for the more liberal views his friend outlined in his early drafts of the speech, especially his advocacy of heavy excess profits taxes which, the senator claimed, would hurt business. Any hint of government ownership and too many specific reforms would divide the party, Lodge warned. When TR's old conservative allies Root, Lodge, and Longworth urged him to take out of his Portland speech the section calling for an inheritance tax, he complied but allowed that in the future compromise would be a two-way street. But he kept in his call for heavy excess profits taxes. He and William Howard Taft had long since made up after all that had happened to their friendship in 1912, but TR did not consult Taft. Instead he gave drafts to Hiram Johnson and Congressman Joseph Nolan of San Francisco, as well as to labor and Grange representatives for a chance to recommend changes to his speech, but they liked it the way it was.[101]

As he delivered his impassioned three-hour speech to an enthusiastic crowd of four thousand, TR impressed observers that he was still "the livest man in the country." He called for the nation to support the President in wartime, but he hit hard at the administration's "grave incompetence" in waging war. The reform section of his speech was probably the most radical a Maine Republican convention had ever heard. He called on America to "use our collective power to prevent individual wrongdoing or individual suffering" "to achieve this economic power and dignity for the worker." As he spelled out his updated Bull Moose ideas his vision of a progressive reconstruction of society after the war had come through loud and clear.[102]

Following a warm response to his speech, delegates and cronies lined up to greet him and have their pictures taken with him. They played "Hail to the Chief" and brought Bill Sewall up to have a reunion with his old friend. But for all the hoopla and talk of victory in 1920, the convention still voted against one of TR's causes, woman suffrage. Perhaps it would be another year of "love him, but hate his views." The applause was balm for him, even if he had changed few minds.

Newspapers were impressed by Roosevelt's forceful speech, but most of them chose to bury its progressive content. The Republican *New York Tribune* highlighted his nationalism, but merely reported the reform details of the speech. The Delaware House of Representatives came within one vote of passing a resolution calling on the Department of Justice to act against him because of his criticism of Wilson. John T. King's reaction was perhaps the most important: he said his candidate was well launched for 1920.[103]

TR was dismayed that the war short-circuited any serious public response to the reform message of his Maine speech and that magazines were refusing his reform articles. Many of his conservative allies in the preparedness movement believed that any talk of social justice was "socialism pure and simple," a view TR considered Romanoff and reactionary. When he wrote that Herbert Spencer's opposition to public schools was "anti-social" and that it was the American people's duty to see that all its children, including the immigrant kids living in semi-starvation on the East Side, were well fed and well educated, only the *Metropolitan* would print it. But by mid-1918 the *Metropolitan* also would not publish articles he sent them extending the reform ideas of his Maine speech, and they lay dormant for the rest of TR's life. Frustrated that he could not find a wider magazine audience for his proposals, TR wondered whether "the prophet business can be combined with keeping up circulation."[104]

TR HAD arranged for Kermit to be transferred to the American Expeditionary Force in France, where Edith urged him to seek out Quentin right away because he was still "hurt terribly" by Ted's and Archie's taunts. She asked Kermit to "hearten him up" because the homesick Quentin "is only 20, & still really ought to be at college!" After she heard Quentin had been in a motorcycle accident, Flora Whitney was trying to get a passport to sail to France to marry him. Edith and Theodore missed their sons so much that they planned to accompany Flora, but they could not get permission to go over.[105]

Quentin cabled home saying he and his Groton friend Hamilton Coolidge had been sent to the front, and after days of moving medical stations close to the front lines to treat gas victims, Dick Derby was knocked down by a shell which killed the man next to him. Finally, TR was growing sated with his sons' heroics, and he wrote Kermit: "I should like to see all of you come home, and watch Mother's face as she greets you."[106]

Yet, as the German army neared Paris in the spring of 1918, TR was sickened by excesses on the home front. The anti-German hysteria which he had encouraged reached its height when vigilantes forced German-Americans to kiss the flag and tarred and feathered them. Then, on April 5, an Illinois mob lynched German-American Robert Prager, who had committed no crime. TR was among the first political leaders to condemn the killing and denounce mob violence. He had said years earlier: "Everything is un-American that tends either to government by a plutocracy, or government by a mob." The Wilson administration drew a different lesson from the lynching: Attorney General Thomas Gregory said the Prager incident proved the government needed stronger sedition laws.[107]

Roosevelt had become the embodiment of wartime patriotism, much admired even though his calls to reform and his denunciation of mob violence were largely ignored. Popular magazines again held him up as an ideal family man, pictured with his grandchildren in a widely circulated photo. As his sons became war heroes, the entire family came to embody national pride. Kermit was decorated for bravery with the British Military Cross, and in late June, Ted led his men in the Battle of Cantigny even after he had been nearly blinded by poison gas. Archie's courage at Toul and his serious injuries had made him a war hero, too. Their prominence in the famed First Division, the vanguard of America's military contribution to winning the war, enhanced Archie's and Ted's fame. The *Chicago Tribune* honored the Roosevelt boys as the "American Samurai" and the four "Roosevelt daredevils" were praised by newspapers around the country.[108]

In June 1918, German submarines were reported to have sunk American ships off the East Coast. FDR warned Eleanor, who was at Campobello with their children, to run into the woods and hide if Germans attacked. With dimmed lights and anti-aircraft guns ready to meet the enemy, New York and Boston prepared for German submarine or airplane assaults. The fear of imminent attack, TR hoped, might bring the war "home to our people" as never before.[109]

In late spring TR had to rest every afternoon to make it through the day, but when Richard asked him to read George Catlin's Indian or buffalo books and make the appropriate animal noises, the indulgent grandfather could not resist. Ethel reprimanded him because he spent so much time holding and entertaining little Edie that she was getting spoiled. The old Bull Moose sat on the piazza watching Richard ride Archie's old pony, Algonquin, up the road, and he basked in pleasant memories of the days when his children made Sagamore Hill their playground. At the *Metropolitan* offices TR looked to co-workers "unutterably weary, stricken in spirit and disconsolate." Edith saw that her husband was near the breaking point again, and she insisted that whenever he left Sagamore to make speeches, he take James Amos with him, for he is "not only intelligent but devoted and understands Father."[110]

The day that H. J. Whigham, editor of the *Metropolitan*, brought out Maria Bochkareva, the commander of the Russian Women's Battalion of Death, a peasant warrior wounded four times in the Great War, TR spoke approvingly of her plan to have 70,000 Allied troops and 30,000 Japanese join General Gregory Semenov to fight the Bolsheviks from Vladivostok.

Bochkareva dreamed out loud of taking a small force to assassinate the kaiser, but after she departed he wrote that he "hated my impotence to help her." Later the Roosevelts had a visit from Bull Mooser Raymond Robins, who was using his position as head of Red Cross operations in Russia to aid the anti-Bolshevik White Russians. TR wholeheartedly supported Wilson's intervention in the Russian civil war, especially his use of humanitarian aid and the Siberian expedition to help the White Russians defeat the Bolsheviks.[111]

TR felt great pride after word arrived that Ted had been shot in the leg and cited for gallantry in battle. He wrote Ted's wife that she and his sons "have justified my life as nothing that I have ever myself done has justified it."[112] Flight commander Quentin wrote proudly to his father on July 4 that in his first "dog fight" as he offered protection to infantry and artillery over Château-Thierry, he had shot down his first German plane. That day at Passaic High School in New Jersey twelve thousand people, many of them immigrants and children of immigrants, heard TR call for fair treatment of loyal immigrants and the establishment of a Jewish homeland in Palestine and an independent state for Armenia.[113]

Reports that the best German pilots, including the Richthofen Flying Circus, had been sent to counter the American fliers had reached the Roosevelts. One evening when TR was dining alone with Fanny Parsons at the Langdon Hotel, news was brought to him that Quentin had flown into the middle of a German air formation eight miles inside enemy lines and shot one plane down and then escaped unharmed. Then, on Tuesday, July 16, Colonel Roosevelt was in the middle of preparation for the state Republican convention in Saratoga, when sometime after 11 p.m. a United Press reporter showed him a censored telegram he had received urging him to "WATCH SAGAMORE HILL." Roosevelt took this to mean that something had happened to one of the boys. He said nothing to Edith until more definite news came the next day that Quentin was missing. They telegraphed Ethel, who was vacationing in Maine, and Alice, who rushed home immediately. Ted's wife, Eleanor, cabled from France saying the report was false. Dick, Archie, and Kermit waited anxiously for news with Eleanor and Edith Wharton in Paris, where they heard conflicting reports that Quentin was captured behind German lines or simply missing in action. By the eighteenth newspapers confirmed that Quentin had been shot down and killed by a German plane. At Sagamore Hill, Theodore gathered Edith, Ethel, and Alice on the piazza and read them the passage from Sir William Napier's history of the Peninsular War: "None fell with greater glory, though many fell, and there was much glory."[114]

Despite the shock, TR insisted on speaking at the convention on the nineteenth. At Saratoga he asked the new women delegates to work hard so that the surviving soldiers of the Great War could "come home to a nation which they can be proud to have fought for and could be proud to have died for." Though everyone in the hall could see that Roosevelt was more subdued than usual, the delegates cheered his speech enthusiastically and called for him to run for governor of New York.[115]

Meanwhile, reports that Quentin had landed safely or might be held as a prisoner kept cropping up, and TR told the press that the family still waited for encouraging news. At Saratoga, Fanny and Corinne lunched with him, and as he rode back on the train to New York with Corinne she saw that he was unable to concentrate on the book he was reading: "His sombre eyes were fixed on the swiftly passing woodlands and the river" for an "all-embracing grief" had "enveloped" him. When Corinne still pushed him to run for governor, TR replied: "Corinne, I have only one fight left in me, and I think I should reserve my strength in case I am needed in 1920."[116]

Official confirmation of Quentin's death reached Sagamore Hill on the twentieth. TR wrote bitterly to Archie that "gallant Quentin and many thousands like him, will have paid with their blood for the sins of the pacifists and sharp political demagogues and dull military pedants and tape-enmeshed bureaucrats." It was "terribly hard" for Edith, and Ethel read her mother to sleep while many friends gathered around Theodore in the afternoon. News reached them that day that Archie was being sent home to recover, and Eleanor cabled that Ted had been shot in the leg behind the left knee.[117]

Theodore and Edith could not bear to stay at Sagamore Hill where memories of Quentin were everywhere, so in a few days they joined Ethel, Richard, and Edie at Dark Harbor, Maine, where Ethel would feed her father lobsters and they could shield themselves from national attention as they mourned. The closest TR came to expressing regrets about raising his sons to seek an honorable death in war was to write: "It is rather awful to know that he paid with his life, and that my other sons may pay with their lives, to try to put in practice what I preached." But he hurriedly added, "Of course I would not have it otherwise."[118]

Quentin became an overnight hero, and TR hoped that his son would take the place that Robert Gould Shaw held in the Civil War. Underneath the glory, he felt responsible for Quentin's death when he wrote: "To feel that one has inspired a boy to conduct that has resulted in his death, has a pretty serious side for a father."[119]

At Dark Harbor, Edith found it a relief to escape the incessant din of the phone, the piles of mail, and the unwelcome questions from reporters. Richard made it his special task to soothe and cuddle his grandmother. TR loved "the underfoot world" of Edie and Richard and took Richard and "march[ed] down to the village store to get him a red railway train for which his soul yearns."[120]

When they finally returned home on August 10, Alice was waiting on the steps of Sagamore Hill, and Edith wrote: "I can't say what it meant to see her there." Also waiting for them were Quentin's last letters to them—bright, loving, and excruciating to read. Theodore and Edith sat in the North Room reading condolence letters together, and he wrote to a complete stranger that Edith suffered most from the loss: "Quentin was her baby, the last child left in the home nest; on the night before he sailed, a year ago, she did as she always had done and went upstairs to tuck him in bed—the huge, laughing, gentle-hearted boy." He told Edith Wharton that he could not write about Quentin because "I should break down if I tried."[121]

By summer's end, TR had returned to hard work, and was strong enough to ride, swim, walk, or row with Edith every afternoon. Their spirits were lifted by the expectation that Archie would be home soon, but, based on warnings from Ted and Kermit, they were prepared for him to be irascible. Archie wrote that Ted had surpassed him in the war and he felt like a "slacker and a loafer," despite his crutches and limp arm.[122]

The strain of war, illness, and loss was telling on Theodore. In hastily scrawled letters he was getting the names of his children and in-laws mixed up and the dates wrong. And he was losing his grasp on politics. Gifford Pinchot warned him that he was getting political advice about the Non-Partisan League from an "exceedingly dangerous adviser in farm matters" who worked for the Pennsylvania Chamber of Commerce, but TR did not listen. Instead, he heeded his old cowhand friends from the West who saw the Non-Partisan Leaguers as Bolsheviks in overalls.[123]

In the fall the congressional campaigns were a "gloves off" affair. The Democrats used Liberty Loan meetings to hand out cards urging voters to "stand up for Wilson over here. Don't let the elections go against the Government." Democrats around the country called the prospect of a Republican Congress "a source of comfort and elation to the Kaiser and his cohorts."[124]

Roosevelt's dilemma in the campaigns was a stark one. His militancy about the war brought him into alliance with conservative anti-Wilson forces, yet he was still deeply committed to domestic reform and progressive candidates who were left of center. Thus, he sometimes had to choose between war and reform. The decision was easy when pro-war progressive and friend Medill McCormick ran for the Senate in Illinois; TR supported him and McCormick went to the Senate to fight child labor. Often, he spoke enthusiastically for local progressive candidates, like Sadie Kost in the 22nd Congressional District in New York, who campaigned for suffrage and the improvement of working conditions for women. One Senate candidate who was lukewarm about the war even won TR's backing because of his strong support for farmers. In many cases, however, the urgency of the war prevailed over reform.[125]

Will Hays warned that the Democrats "will go to any lengths" to win in November, and many Republicans feared that Wilson sought a negotiated end to the war before the election for partisan reasons. Only a Republican Congress could block Wilson's postwar plans to bring the Fourteen Points into being, so Roosevelt endorsed Senator John Weeks of Massachusetts and a number of politicians whom he had called crooks and reactionaries in the past.[126]

That fall TR and Taft began acting in concert to "go in on a League of Nations," if universal military training and universal youth service as in Switzerland or Australia were a feature and no disarmament were part of the scheme. In private Roosevelt expressed concern that the wrong kind of league "would at the end of the war deliver us over, bound hand and foot" to our enemies. He had heard through a secret source in September that Wilson would try for a negotiated peace and then make himself the first president of the League of Nations. He also believed the rumor that Colonel House planned a postwar economic alliance with Germany against England, which hardened his contempt for "Peace-God" Wilson and his league.[127]

In public, Roosevelt said: "I shall be delighted to support the movement for a League to Enforce Peace, or for a League of Nations, if it is developed as a supplement to and not a substitute for the preparation of our own strength," yet newspapers reported that he opposed the league idea. But a league which included Germany, Austria, and Turkey was, in TR's eyes, like trying to fight crime in New York "by inviting all the burglars and gunmen to join the Police Force."[128]

TR did reflect fleetingly upon the possibility that his hatred of Wilson and his intense emotion about the war had skewed his better judgment. When he bragged in letters that with the Roosevelt Division, America could have made more of a difference in the war, he admitted he was making an "evil-natured boast." He would claim to friends that if he had been president the Great War and the conflict with Mexico could have been avoided, but then he confessed that perhaps avoiding the war might have been too much of a diplomatic challenge even for his skill.[129]

When author Owen Wister visited Sagamore Hill in October he saw TR fired up about Wilson's latest iniquities, and afterward he wrote Edith: "I wish

Theodore had a Colonel House. I'd like to be his Colonel House. You could be, I think." For many years she had been her husband's political alter ego. Since her near-fatal accident in 1911 Edith had had insufficient stamina to temper her husband's public tirades. Wister was right: TR badly needed to have his angry tongue moderated by a wise advisor. His emotions and moods governed his judgment more than ever before: he unwisely accepted hysterical rumors as "facts," like the purported presence within American borders of a quarter of a million German spies and agents. When TR worked late enough to spend the night at the Langdon Hotel, his neighbor was the war correspondent and mystery writer Mary Roberts Rinehart, who often brought to him men claiming to be Secret Service agents with proof of radical and pro-German plots. Then, TR spread the "facts" to his public.[130]

In the end the old Bull Moose talked repression and liberal reconstruction at the same time. In the fall congressional campaigns many Old Guard Republicans tried to get Roosevelt to temper his progressive views. But if they wanted him and his public following badly enough, TR believed that the party would have to accept his ideas. John T. King held meetings and set up informal groups of Roosevelt supporters who would exert pressure on mainstream Republicans to move toward TR's policies. In many places his ideas about reconstruction won votes away from the Democrats: in Wisconsin, Wilsonites talked loyalty, but Republicans beat them by talking tax justice and other kinds of reform. To win in the congressional races of 1918 across the nation the Republican National Committee used TR's patriotic but progressive Maine speech as a campaign document.[131]

At Sagamore Hill, Edith insisted that wallowing in the "death pangs" of grief was "selfish." But that fall she often sat impassive and wordless. Ethel thought she "might have been Buddha contemplating, so distant was she!" TR became "very quiet, very watchful of Mrs. Roosevelt." He saw her break down and cry for a few minutes at a time, then return to her "very, very brave" self-possession. Friends viewed TR sobbing quietly in the old barn one day as he draped his arm around his horse's neck.[132]

When Archie came home from the war he found his father grayer but still as "full of life and enthusiasm" as ever. The family thought Archie looked "very nervous and white," and he proved to be unreliable in his reporting of events. He also raved that all the Germans, enlisted or not, should be killed. Archie was stunned that people recognized him on the street because he was a war hero, and his celebrity enabled him to raise money speaking for the Liberty Loan.[133]

Theodore and Edith hurried to Corinne's country home, Henderson House, to comfort her when Douglas Robinson died on September 12.

Corinne's loss had a "particular poignancy" because the match had been so unhappy. When they played "Onward Christian Soldiers" at his funeral, Edith reminisced about the happier days of the Progressive convention when Oscar Straus sang along with his Christian friends. TR wrote that the death of his generation could not be as sad as the death of the young because "we have warmed both hands before the fire of life!"[134]

Three days after Roosevelt returned home, Wilson, without consulting the Allies, opened negotiations for peace with Germany. TR countered that it was "no time for notes" but for complete victory. After a nationwide "storm of angry protest" against the premature peace initiative, Wilson, in TR's words, "instantly turned his usual somersault" and came out for unconditional surrender, too. America's wartime hysteria now raged so irrationally against Germany that public health officials warned without evidence that German submarines had brought the Spanish influenza epidemic then spreading in New York and in training camps. Gregory's successor as attorney general, A. Mitchell Palmer, wanted to be president and declared the entire U.S. liquor industry pro-German, and then he launched an investigation of Hearst's crony Arthur Brisbane, suspected of having secret ties with German-American brewers.[135]

TR and the public protests over his unilateral peace negotiations so unnerved Wilson that on October 25 he made a partisan appeal to elect a Democratic Congress in order to allow him to "continue to be your unembarrassed spokesman in affairs at home and abroad." His opponents, he complained, "have sought to take the choice of policy and the conduct of the war out of my hands and put it under the control of instrumentalities of their own choosing." Wilson also insisted that "the return of a Republican majority to either house of Congress would, moreover, certainly be interpreted on the other side of the water as repudiation of my leadership." Colonel House recognized the speech was a colossal political error.[136]

Alice arrived at Sagamore Hill, and the family congregated, "foaming with rage" at Wilson's turning "his high office into an electioneering rostrum for one party." Favoring impeachment, Ethel predicted that her father would soon set the country straight about Wilson's call for a Democratic Congress, which he did by charging that Wilson had shown himself to be "a partisan leader first and President of all the people second."[137]

The next day TR met his public again at Carnegie Hall. Though in pain from rheumatism, he spoke for two hours, denouncing the administration for its "intolerable invasion of the rights of free speech and of a free press." But proving the axiom that politicians develop amnesia around election time, TR also made the incredible claim that he and like-minded Republicans had since April 1917 "cast all thoughts of politics aside and put ourselves unreservedly at the service of the President."[138]

In the end, Wilson could not produce peace by November 5, and Republicans swept Democrats out of office all over the country. Though Democrats attacked his loyalty, progressive Irvine Lenroot, TR's ally, was elected to the Senate from Wisconsin. With the Senate balanced precariously between 49 Republicans and 47 Democrats, Senator La Follette gained strategic importance. His expulsion was shelved by talk of a renewed progressive coalition of Arthur Capper, Cummins, Johnson, Norris, and Poindexter as his possible allies.[139]

TR'S HEALTH, weakened by the rigors of his speaking schedule, was collapsing once more. He had been in such pain with rheumatism on November 1 that he had been unable to sleep, and his exhaustion and gout finally convinced his doctors to confine him to bed. Throughout the first ten days of the month the family noted that he was "having a horrid suffering time." Yet when W.E.B. Du Bois invited Roosevelt to speak before the Circle for Negro War Relief, he accepted. The circle had been founded "for the purpose of making the conditions under which the colored soldier trains and fights the same as those which exist for the white soldier." Du Bois had once called himself a "strong Roosevelt partisan," but he had been alienated ever since TR rejected his racial equality platform at the Bull Moose convention in 1912.[140]

Their mutual friend Joel Spingarn thought Roosevelt and Du Bois had a lot in common: both were proud men who hated to admit they were wrong. Their meeting, however, told a great deal about how much TR had changed. The young racialist hothead of the nineties had died. He had missed his chance to remake race relations as president and again in 1912, but his views had finally changed and late in life he had served as a trustee of Tuskegee Institute and Howard University and on the Spingarn medal committee of the N.A.A.C.P. to recognize African-American achievement. President of Bethune-Cookman College Mary McLeod Bethune remembered him as one of black educators' "strongest friends and advocates." He met Du Bois with hope of future cooperation.[141]

For the rest of his life Du Bois remembered that night, November 2, when TR, in his last public appearance, praised him as a leader worthy to sit at any national council as an equal of any white man. As they stood together on the stage at Carnegie Hall, the two Harvard men—the white one whose words carried weight internationally and the black one whose calls for change had been ignored for years—praised each other warmly before a large, racially mixed audience. Du Bois said later that he knew that Roosevelt "had lived to regret" choosing in 1912 the "progressive South" over being on the right side of race.[142]

Knowing the war was nearly over and the shape of America's domestic future was up for grabs, TR moved slowly with his swollen gouty ankle onto the stage. He told the audience: "Terrible though this war has been, I think it has been also fraught with the greatest good for our national soul" because Americans, "our men on the other side, our sons and brothers on the other side, white men and black, white soldiers and colored soldiers," had prevented German victory, and "every American can now walk with his head up and look the citizen of any country in the world straight in the eyes." Black and white manliness united had won the Great War. The audience applauded when Roosevelt called for equal "civil and political rights" and the "right to work." In what proved to be his final public declaration of deeply felt political commitment, Roosevelt promised the audience to work "toward securing a juster and fairer treatment in this country of colored people." He was applauded warmly when he said, "I will do everything I can to aid, to bring about, to bring nearer, the day when justice, the square-deal, will be given as between black man and white."[143]

He was too ill to speak out of calculation: he spoke from his heart about what he wished he could do about race. He was no more likely to be free to gamble his 1920 presidential bid by tying it to an electorally suicidal platform for racial progress than he had been in 1912. Nevertheless, while other white leaders talked disenfranchisement and the repeal of the Fifteenth Amendment, he spoke of overdue racial justice. He had done more than talk: he had fought peonage as president and he had used some of his Nobel Prize funds to finance black women's war relief agencies. Yet he could bend open the iron cages of race prejudice only so far: not long before he had entertained doubts about southern blacks' fitness to vote, due to their high illiteracy rates.[144]

Edith said that her husband returned from his speech for Du Bois limping and in "great pain." He canceled all appointments. The only time he left the house was on election day to vote, memorable because Edith cast her first statewide vote ever. Within days, Theodore was "flat on his back with gout" and he dictated letters to Edith from his bed. They heard that Ted, Dick, and Kermit had gone to the front, and Sagamore Hill again feared telegrams carrying fatal news. TR was so ill he was "unable to stir from bed" on the tenth, so Edith called the doctor.[145]

At six in the morning in Oyster Bay on November 11, sirens and bells announced that the Great War was over. In Washington, Alice, after a late social evening, walked "alone in the November night" listening to the whistles across town making a "wailing melody." On Armistice Day a "very suffering" TR was taken by ambulance to Roosevelt Hospital with rheumatism and gout. For the next six weeks he lived in pain at the hospital, not in danger as he had been in February, but suffering local discomfort in his leg, arm, and hand. Doctors puzzled over the deeper trouble underlying his failed health, which could be his fever, newly discovered anemia, arteriosclerosis, or perhaps an embolism.[146]

Even while she stationed herself in an adjoining room to guard her husband's recovery, Edith lapsed into reveries of grief, speculating if Richard would someday have to die a death like Quentin. The German government had photographed Quentin's crushed body and circulated it to raise morale among its war-weary people. Edith wondered sadly to herself if, with the world in chaos, Quentin "may have given his life in vain."[147]

TR still planned for 1920 as he sat up in his hospital bed, discussing strategy for a progressive policy of postwar reconstruction with H. J. Whigham. When William Allen White arrived TR showed him "a rather radical article he had written" which White believed would have brought the New Deal in 1921.[148]

Just days before Wilson's party was to sail to the Paris Peace Conference to negotiate a treaty ending the war, TR spoke up as the leader of the opposition party. From his hospital bed he issued a press release to "our allies and our enemies" stating that "Mr. Wilson has no authority whatever to speak for the American people at this time. His leadership has just been emphatically repudiated by them."[149]

The tragedy of their wartime rivalry was that TR and Wilson had once shared many beliefs about domestic reform, and TR agreed with many of the Fourteen Points and even with a modified League of Nations. Yet conflict between parties and the egotism of their leaders made compromise and therefore true governance nearly impossible.[150]

Henry Cabot Lodge visited his old friend twice in the hospital. There TR approved a Republican plan to hold up appropriation bills, call an extra session of Congress, and then launch a congressional investigation of financial malfeasance in the conduct of the war.[151]

Later, Lodge invented a deathbed plot myth. He claimed that during his visits he and Roosevelt contrived a campaign against ratifying the Treaty of Versailles. No such plot existed. During the treaty fight, Lodge would ask Alice and Edith to write that one of TR's last wishes was the defeat of the league and the treaty, but the senator had forgotten that he visited TR in the hospital before a treaty existed and before Wilson had set foot in Paris. To the end of his life, TR believed that at Versailles Allied leaders might revise Wilson's proposals enough so "that the League of Nations [would] be modified into a pact more nearly resembling" his own views. TR's letters in his last several months show that he was unalterably opposed to a world federation headed by Wilson or to an open-ended collective security pact. Yet the league idea had appealed to him if national sovereignty and preparedness were guaranteed and no one promised the "millennium" could be achieved tomorrow.[152]

Around the time TR started taking serum treatments for his anemia, Richard was diagnosed with asthma. His grandfather mentioned the boy's asthma in his letters, but did not write about what it meant to him to see the grandson he adored struggling to breathe as he had as a child. Doctors decided Richard's asthma should be treated, as Ted's had been, with the removal of his tonsils and adenoids to reduce the likelihood of respiratory infections. After the operation Richard and his grandfather recovered together, and the two patients had a "great game" over TR's watch, which Richard called the "big brother" of his little one.[153]

Richard was expected to bounce back, but before TR left the hospital on Christmas morning doctors told him he might be a permanent invalid "tied to a chair." He reportedly replied: "All right! I can work and live that way, too." While he was in the hospital, he suffered "curious trouble with his chest," but no one knew its origin.[154]

TR spent a subdued Christmas at Sagamore Hill. Then doctors advised Ethel to take Richard to recuperate from bronchitis in a warmer climate, and she left on January 1 for Aiken, South Carolina. Because TR's fever and painful hand made him miserable, he stayed on the sofa in the Gate Room near its fireplace. One of his plans for 1919 was to write a book about Woodrow Wilson, an exposé of the true history of the President and the war. He had hired a researcher, George Garner, whom he asked to move to New York so that they could start on the book. Taft had found documents to prove that Wilson had not originally planned to send any troops abroad to aid the Allies, a fact which the two former presidents intended to publicize.[155]

On January 3, Edith wrote Ethel, "Father was so melancholy," but he found the energy to write senators to urge their support of the Anthony Amendment. When she checked on him at one in the morning she saw that he had been unable to sleep. Edith kept up her brisk morning walks with their new dog, yet she was exhausted, so she asked James Amos and a Scottish nurse to share her night vigils watching over TR, who had another "very suffering night and day."[156]

He never expected "to escape a certain grayness in the afternoon of life" because he knew that few lives "end in the splendor of a golden sunset." He felt grateful for Edith and the life they had led at Sagamore Hill to the end. He had worn himself out in fighting against his own dormancy, yet, as she watched him fading, Edith thought it was grief over Quentin that had taken "the fight" out of her husband. Theodore told her baldly that "it doesn't matter what happens to me now—The boys are coming home."[157]

On January 5, TR worked on page proofs for the *Metropolitan*, where several of his articles on postwar reform still awaited publication. Edith played solitaire near him as he read, and they talked about the children and Sagamore Hill. She could not resist kissing him each time she passed him that day. Then, about 10 p.m. he asked his wife "to help him to sit up as he felt oddly as if his heart was about to stop or his breathing." He said, "I know it is not going to happen, but it is such a strange feeling." She gave him sal volatile and called the nurse and doctor, who found his heart, lungs, and pulse fine. Unsettled, TR asked Edith to stay up with him for a while. Dr. Bigelow had urged her to provide Theodore with morphine if the pain interfered with sleep, so the nurse gave him a hypodermic.[158]

Then around midnight, after Theodore asked James Amos to turn off the light, Edith went to sleep in the master bedroom. She checked on her husband at 12:30 and 2 a.m. and found he was sleeping comfortably on his side, while Amos kept watch by the fire. At four in the morning the nurse woke Edith to tell her that her husband had stopped breathing. She tried to revive him with brandy and summoned the doctor, but TR was gone. Because none of the doctors had been apprehensive about any of his ailments being fatal, his death came as a shock. Dr. George Faller said "the embolism" had killed TR, and he sat with Edith by the fire in the library in stunned silence until dawn. A strenuous life was over.[159]

Epilogue

William Allen White grieved for TR as he had when his own father died and wrote later: "I have never known another person so vital nor another man so dear." Many of TR's friends reacted as John Quinn had: "I could not believe it this morning when I heard the news of his death. He seemed to be a great elemental force, like Niagara or the Hudson River." For Corinne, when "the desperate sorrow of losing Theodore" came, she fell into despair because "life would always have glamour, enchantment, inspiration and delight as long as he lived,—and now he is gone." Bamie, who was confined to a wheelchair with rheumatism, proved as stoic as her sister was emotive, but she shared William Sturgis Bigelow's sentiment that "it's not clear what we are any of us going to do without him."[1]

The family dealt with nationwide expressions of grief as graciously as they could. World War I–era mourners so often turned to spiritualism that Ethel was left to respond to over 150 people who claimed they had made contact with TR's spirit through mediums or séances. Fan clubs, memorial associations, monuments, national days of remembrance, stamps, centennials, and pilgrimages demanded the family's attention, but they did not always agree on how best to honor TR's memory. Corinne turned her loss into a career of speaking and writing about her brother and supporting the Roosevelt Memorial Association (R.M.A.) and the Woman's Roosevelt Memorial Association. Her book, *My Brother Theodore Roosevelt*, would keep his memory alive in the twenties, and she often addressed radio audiences with stories about his heroic days. Ted wrote in his diary that his Aunt Corinne "unquestionably is deranged on the subject of father. She has talked so much, with her rather emotional nature, about him that I really believe that she is more or less convinced that she is he now."[2]

War had tested young men's courage and endurance, as TR had hoped, but it did not turn out to be just a Galahad story for everyone. After a bout of Spanish influenza, Dick Derby would return to Ethel prematurely gray and aged, haunted by the ghastly memories of the surgeon's table on the front lines. Ted, who had learned to lead men bravely but without much humility, had been primed to build a career on familiar scaffolding—he came home to seek positions that reinforced the junior in his name, a New York State legislator, New York governor, and assistant secretary of the navy. Edith watched her remaining sons grow to manhood with mixed feelings about how they had been raised. Observing Ted's taut dissatisfaction with himself, despite his successful business career and happy marriage, Edith wrote him, "Honestly, as I look back, you fared worst because Father tried to 'toughen' you, but happily was too busy to exert the same pressure on the others!"[3]

Kermit, who had lost preeminence in the family's affections when his war service did not compare with his brothers', drank more after the war. Later, he was too sensitive to live the life he had chosen and too loyal to strike too far away from the family tree. When his thumb became chronically infected, he had it cut off. Though he remained a loving son to Edith as long as he could, and he had a respectable career as a steamship executive and explorer, ahead of Kermit was drink, decline, and, at last, suicide.

TR had described Archie as a "permanent cripple" who had told his father "he never expected again to be able to ride a spirited horse, or a pulling horse, or to jump fences, or to row." Theodore had planned to take his injured son devil fishing in early 1919 to rebuild his body and cheer him up. Yet in his last weeks of life, TR had had no idea how to respond emotionally to each "burst of woe" from Archie. Archie's later memoirs and letters overflowed with bitterness about his life with Father. In his last years he favored a brand of white supremacy that called for reinstituting a form of racial "servitude." He published quotations from his father to justify his racist and anti-communist John Birch Society views. He embarrassed and annoyed the rest of the family, despite their loyalty to him. No matter how far they deviated from his thinking politically, the Roosevelt boys never stopped being their father's sons. They remained brave to the end. They all came back for another world war, when Ted became the family's hero once again on D-Day.[4]

The white trillium that had been their wildflower still bloomed as an annual reminder to Edith of the years she had shared with her husband. When she visited places where they had been, the memories evoked "a curious sort of almost insupportable loneliness." She said she missed him as the biblical ewe lamb missed her lost wayward children. In a rare moment of complaint Edith wrote that when "so many women could so easily spare their husbands," it was cruel that she had lost a husband who had been indispensable to her happiness.[5]

Despite her grief Edith kept living a strenuous life for nearly thirty more years at Sagamore Hill, reading and traveling. She kept up with Louisa Lee Schuyler and Sara Delano Roosevelt, and sewed clothes for the Jacob Riis Settlement House. She even made a rare public speech to endorse her husband's supporter Herbert Hoover for president. She wrote books about her adventures and her own family history, and then settled back into the same quiet seasons of life she had shared with her husband and children. Theodore survived as a loving presence in her dreams: "I was bothered about something & was dozing & Father stood beside the bed & kissed me. I felt his little scrubby moustache—and waked. But it was so comfortable."[6]

Sharing her husband with the public remained the bane of her marriage. For many years she welcomed the Bull Moose faithful and incense swingers to annual graveside memorial services and reminiscences in the North Room. Though she admired the history education Hermann Hagedorn and his staff at the Roosevelt Memorial Association did with children, receptions at the Theodore Roosevelt birthplace year after year became a trial. She told Ethel: "I feel so deeply the responsibility of carrying on for Father," so she assisted Quentin's friend Earle Looker in putting together *The White House Gang*, an affectionate reminiscence of a boy's eye view of White House life, and she helped edit letters that Henry Cabot Lodge and her two eldest sons published.[7]

She proved to be the historian's nightmare, a protective wife who denied most scholars access to the papers that her husband had wanted open at the Library of Congress. She feared his candor would once more be misunderstood. When Hagedorn convinced her to cooperate with Henry Pringle and the resulting biography turned out to be nasty and dismissive of the man she loved, she was deeply hurt and not a little embittered. Behind his back she and Ethel called Hagedorn "Hermie Mermie" and resented his endless questions and requests for letters, appearances, and donations.[8]

When their father died Alice and Ethel promised to remain close forever, even as they headed in different directions. Alice haunted the Senate galleries during the League of Nations fight, and offended her companions at dinner parties when she said in 1919 after Wilson's stroke that the "illness of that swine in the White House" was probably mental. When she missed her father too much, she retreated to Auntie Bye's house or visited Ted or Ethel. Like her cousin Eleanor whose "My Day" column gave advice and sounded a note of Social Gospel cultural leadership much like TR, Alice became a newspaper columnist for a while. While Eleanor specialized in humanitarianism and human rights, Alice became an irreverent Washington savant and wit.[9]

Alice and Ethel agreed that the Kennedy family had copied the Theodore Roosevelts rather shamelessly—promoting vigor, jumping in swimming pools fully clothed as Alice had done, entertaining Pablo Casals and Robert Frost—every morsel of their élan had an imitative quality. Still, Alice enjoyed the Kennedys' parties and their friendship. The Kennedys, after all, understood something of the Galahad at Camelot spirit. Being an insider and a celebrity never lost its appeal for Alice, and she stood out as an irreverent Washington landmark until the end.[10]

The family stalwart, Ethel, looked after her mother until Edith's death in 1948, while Alice soured on her stepmother and recalled in her memoirs her adolescent difficulties with her rather than their closeness in her father's last years. During the New Deal, Alice liked to mimic the first lady and poke fun at all of Washington's alphabet agencies. At lunch one day at Sagamore Hill in 1933, when Alice complained that Franklin was "three parts Eleanor and one part slush," Ethel tried to quiet her down because New Dealers were present. Alice became a Robert Taft Republican who often sided with Archie, while Ethel remained a liberal Republican who delighted in hearing her cousin Eleanor denounce the pending anti-union "right to work" legislation as "reactionary." Ethel was filled with pride when she went to see Eleanor chairing the United Nations Human Rights Commission, and she liked to think that her father and Thee would have been, too. Eleanor's stewardship of the Universal Declaration of Human Rights was historic because it gained a worldwide agreement about the minimum rights that all people should have, a Bull Moose–like accomplishment that made Ethel proud to be a Roosevelt.[11]

Because she lived at home and worked so closely with her father during his leftward years, Ethel turned out to be his most Bull Moose child. She knew him in what were "his quieter, more peaceful moments when he stops being a regiment of cavalry for a little while and is the Audubon society." She supported the internationalist Cord Meyer in the United World Federalists as a successor to TR's internationalism and his league ideas. She had been raised to "brighten up the corner where we live," so she finally did make her Jane Addams mark on the world by starting social work services at St. Luke's Hospital. She exercised political skill blocking a bridge planned by Robert Moses that would have cut through Oyster Bay, and in the sixties she took a sympathetic view of movements to integrate housing on Long Island. Like her cousin Eleanor, she resigned from the Daughters of the American Revolution because she could not change its discriminatory racial policies.[12]

Ethel and Alice never stopped adoring their father, and they grieved together when young Richard Derby died suddenly in childhood. With Richard's death a link to their father's last days of kangaroo dances and petting "buppies" was gone forever. But they kept their father's spirit alive in different ways. Alice wrote crotchety memoirs about family life which still testified to her ambivalent but passionate devotion to her father. After Edith died Ethel worked to save Sagamore Hill as a historic site. She also helped Hermann Hagedorn collect the research for his best-selling *The Roosevelt Family of Sagamore Hill,* which romanticized her father and the childhood she remembered so fondly. She helped collect the letters that made possible the Theodore Roosevelt Collection at Harvard and the well-edited publication of eight volumes of his letters. Ethel was glad that so "many people had warmed their hands by the happy fire side of our family life."[13]

After Hagedorn died, Ethel stood by the refurbished and more scholarly Theodore Roosevelt Association and kept up the family's long-standing interest in the American Museum of Natural History. She was delighted when Felix Frankfurter remembered for television cameras a conversation when TR said: "This country will never really demonstrate that it is a democracy in the full reach and range of that conception until we will have had both a Negro and Jewish president of the United States." Ethel Roosevelt Derby did not live into the 1990s when congressional assaults on the budget of the National Park Service threatened to shut down Sagamore Hill. In her place, her daughters, other Roosevelt relatives, and John Gable, the director of the Theodore Roosevelt Association, defended its historic value once again.[14]

FOLLOWING Roosevelt's death the *Metropolitan* finally printed some of his controversial articles, an epitaph for his final critique of American life. Never willing to abandon capitalism altogether, TR viewed it in the end as a cruel system unless it was moderated by humane values and a government-promoted defense of the public good. In the end, he wrote, America was a "backward" country because:

> our system, or rather no-system, of attempting to combine political democracy with industrial autocracy, and tempering the evil of the boss and the machine politician by the evil of the doctrinaire and the demagogue, has now begun to creak and strain so as to threaten a breakdown.[15]

Capitalists who "with gross injustice" rake in huge profits which they should have shared with inventors, managers, and workers found themselves opposed by "labor union tyranny." Such polarization posed, in Roosevelt's mind, a "grave danger to the whole social fabric."[16]

The only way he saw out of the dilemma of greed, class conflict, and exploitation was for a democratic government to insist that workers get pensions, job security, and insurance against disease, accident, ill health, and old age. He called for labor to be represented on corporate boards, and for the government to regulate migrant labor under a federal bureau. He wanted to give uncultivated land, as Canada had, to reward veterans of the Great War. Otherwise, without drastic reform, the American system would fail.[17]

TR's last writings were the final chapter of his long education about America. From his days of boyhood in old New York greeting homeless newsboys at his father's side to his tenement tours with Gompers and Riis, Roosevelt had been an open-minded student who could learn from books and even more from meeting people. When the young duke died, a soldier, a cowboy, an adventurer, and a leader took his place, but always he was a man who hoped to show his faith by his works. He grew up willing to learn and change his views at the same time industrial America emerged and matured.

His final articles reaffirmed his belief in "collective action" and the expansion of public space for the public good. He told the story of an Oyster Bay controversy over who should have access to beachfronts. The question was put to a vote. Voters, many of them small taxpayers who did not want to pay taxes for the "collective ownership of a portion of the waterfront," defeated a proposal for a public beachfront. Thus, private ownership prevailed and most of the shoreline near Sagamore Hill was closed to public access, as it remains today. TR saw the beachfront controversy as a parable of shortsightedness. More than anything else, he regretted "backward" America's inability to see and promote the common good.[18]

In death he was remembered more for his colorful personality than for his radical ideas. He looked more like an amusing object of "genuine Americana" than a true prophet. Sir Arthur Conan Doyle hailed him as "a Superman if there ever was one," while others revered him for his "tender and sympathetic nature," his vast range of intellectual interests, and for being a moral voice and "an enemy of unclean men."[19]

Only a few of his contemporaries recalled his last years accurately. John Dewey remembered TR as "the prophet of a new social day," and William Allen White regarded him as a "great agitator" who issued radical attacks against "predatory wealth." After TR died, conservatives inflicted a reign of aggressive Americanism and nativism on the country through the Red Scare and into the twenties, and when Ted served in the New York State Assembly he voted against unseating five socialists for their political views. Edith was chagrined that they should be removed without being convicted of any crime, but she did not see it as her place to speak out against the ugly turn that patriotism took after her husband's death. White declared that if Theodore Roosevelt were to be brought to life again in the twenties, to speak out for progressive causes, "the various defense societies, security leagues, minute men of the republic, and 100 per cent Americans would start a whispering campaign that his real name was Feodor Roosevisky and that he was sent here as an agent of the Bolsheviki."[20]

Over time, America lost sight of the radical Theodore Roosevelt. The Bull Moose mantle was grasped by false claimants, including the reactionary Warren G. Harding, who had called TR a communist in 1912 but who exploited his memory to win the White House in 1920. Harding insisted that TR had been "really less the radical than he ofttimes appeared."[21]

Even though she had sat on the same podium with Roosevelt in the long years when he supported the federal suffrage amendment and Wilson did not, Anna Howard Shaw chose to give Wilson credit for his eleventh-hour help when women won the vote, and Roosevelt's post-presidential feminist legacy was erased from American memory. By the end of the twentieth century a new generation of feminists would remember him only as a mastermind of the "Teddy Bear patriarchy" because of his pronouncements on "race suicide," his defense of imperialism, and his muscular Christianity.[22]

In the long run, TR belonged to everyone and his legacy proved to be an elastic one. He touched the lives of later presidents as a role model and sometimes as a fond memory. He had proven to be a good mentor to a certain nephew by marriage. When that other master of patrician folksiness, FDR, became president, he and Eleanor invited Fanny Parsons to the White House. FDR told her: "You know how it was when Uncle Ted was there—how gay and homelike! Well, that's how we mean to have it!" In policy as well as style FDR invoked the progressive heritage of "uncle Theodore" often and had his staff find out what TR had done as president so that he could benefit from the judgment of his political hero.[23]

Ironically, Richard M. Nixon also felt a kinship for TR, especially his reversion to combat when faced with enemies. Nixon's hard early life made him spoil for a fight as readily as Roosevelt, and he used intelligence agencies with even more abandon to attack his enemies. Strange, too, that in Nixon's time, as in TR's with Ben Tillman, racial conservatives like Sam Ervin helped defend the Constitution and thwart the "imperial presidency." As he left office in disgrace over the Watergate scandal, Nixon quoted TR's memorial to Alice Lee because Roosevelt's words expressed grief with emotional candor. Yet TR and Nixon are ultimately not much alike. Roosevelt's spirit of intellectual curiosity and fun, his devotion to children and the strenuous life, his integrity and energy for facing the problems of his own time make him a presidential personality beyond compare.[24]

Theodore Roosevelt in death brooked as many resurrections as he did in life. His youthful struggles to overcome asthma have inspired generations of asthma sufferers who fight to live normal lives. Asthma had provided the central Horatio Alger story he told about himself, and it remained one of the most powerful inspirational stories repeated in self-help medical guides and children's literature.

But TR's other inspirational Alger story has not often been told to children. Certainly historians have neglected the tale, preferring the oft-repeated accounts of warmongering instead. Yet the other story is worth telling because it is true. He struggled throughout his life to open the prejudices that encased the Victorian world into which he had been born. We might wish he had fought harder, but in his last years he had looked at race, class, and gender with more compassionate and comprehending eyes. Women remained natural mothers of the race and inevitably in need of protection by men. Yet woman suffrage, women in the professions, and women in reform advanced further because Roosevelt defended female capacity for "statesmanship." As a political partner of formidable women, including Frances Kellor, Florence Kelley, and Jane Addams, he made progressivism a national force that reshaped American history.[25]

Class, too, had once been a cause for him to feel superior. The young man who had worried about the antecedents of his classmates at Harvard grew up to become a traitor to his class. While he continued to live the privileged life of landed gentry, he had reached out in a democratic spirit in politics to men in shirtsleeves and women who knew no pedigree. When crowds heckled him, he had listened. He spoke out for the government to equalize wealth, and he urged the middle classes to make more room for upwardly mobile newcomers. Despite a few imperial moments in the White House, Theodore Roosevelt stands historically as a defender of democracy, in political and economic terms, and for most of the last decade of his life he waged a sincere campaign for social democratic principles.[26]

Many of TR's youthful prejudices had faded with experience and maturity. As a young man he had seen a dead Spanish soldier as a jackrabbit and blacks as hopelessly inferior. He advocated certain immigration restriction schemes and failed to speak out against racial segregation. Yet the rising tide of scientific racism and anti-Semitism which spread across national borders at the end of the Great War finally made him sick.

Madison Grant, a defender of the scientifically sanctified racial superiority of Anglo-Saxons, wrote TR about a man who claimed he had evidence that old-stock American units from New England fought better than other races in the Great War. Roosevelt called that man "an addlepated ass." He insisted to Grant that race and ethnicity did not matter because men of foreign parentage across the nation fought well, including Jews. All American men who had a spark of Galahad, he believed, did their part in the Great War, regardless of race or ethnicity. He agreed with the verdict of *The Independent* and *The Crisis* that Americans were performing well in the war because they fought German "race prejudice" and its "unendurable" Teutonism, for "race prejudice is pro-Germanism."[27]

Theodore Roosevelt shared the late-nineteenth-century racialist past which infected most Western nations and spawned pan-Germanism, Teutonism, and eventually Nazi racism, as well as a resurgent American Ku Klux Klan in the teens and twenties. Of course, throughout this era, people in every country battled racialist thought and racist political movements. Impressed by the adaptation and accomplishment he had seen among blacks and their patriotic support for the Great War, Roosevelt took the final step toward believing in racial equality. At the end of his life TR repudiated the Madison Grants and other racists and promised W.E.B. Du Bois to work with more energy for racial justice. It took as much courage to break away from bankrupt prejudices of the past as it did to "make his own body."

The N.A.A.C.P. editorialized in *The Crisis* when TR died:

> A great man has died and the whole world stands shocked and mourning. Humanity has lost its greatest exemplar of noble aims and single-minded devotion to the development of national welfare and glory. The youth of America had no finer inspiration toward which to strive and with the passing of THEODORE ROOSEVELT passes the world's greatest protagonist of lofty ideals and principles. Take him all in all he was a man, generous, impulsive, fearless, loving the public eye, but intent on achieving the public good. . . . We mourn with the rest of the world as is fitting, but there is too in our sorrow a quality peculiar and apart. We have lost a friend. That he was our friend proves the justice of our cause, for Roosevelt never championed a cause which was not in essence right. He had his faults—of the head, not of the heart—and even when we suffered as the result of an impulse which we could not reconcile with what we expected at his hands, we were more grieved because he had hurt us than at the hurt itself. Even in our hot bitterness over the Brownsville affair we

> knew that he believed he was right, and he of all men had to act in accordance with his beliefs. It is good to remember that in 1917 he justified our trust when at the time of the East St. Louis riots he alone, of all Americans prating of liberty and democracy, uttered his courageous pronouncement at the meeting in Carnegie Hall.[28]

Of all the contradictory positions he had taken during his long political career, his denunciation of the East St. Louis race riots held the final, mature TR, according to *The Crisis:* "Justice with me," he had shouted, "is not a mere form of words!" Perhaps his long struggle to gain a stronger body had helped him in his longer and more heroic struggle to see beyond the bigotry of his own time.[29]

Theodore Roosevelt would endure through time as America's most fascinating president because he captured the American spirit of self-improvement, change, and growth. Not a picture-perfect hero, Roosevelt set a poor example for open-mindedness and tolerance for dissent during wartime. He loved democracy as expressed by cheering crowds but grew impatient with democracy in the form of constitutional checks on his power. He represents America's aggressiveness as well as its profound democratic spirit. Most of all, his life proved the malleability and importance of character and the need for the individual to feel an obligation to the community. Economic justice was his final ideal for America. In his maturity he thought the United States would be a less "backward" and more democratic country if it equalized wealth and tamed its corporations. People came first, property second. Theodore Roosevelt's life, then, stands as prophecy unheard, yet even prophets speaking in the wilderness can be resurrected.

Notes

Key to Names

TR	Theodore Roosevelt, president 1901–1909, 1858–1919
TRSR	Theodore Roosevelt Senior (Thee), the President's father, 1831–1878
MBR	Martha Bulloch Roosevelt (Mittie), the President's mother, 1834–1884
MSEB	Martha Stewart Elliott Bulloch, TR's grandmother, 1799–1864
SEW	Susan Elliott West, TR's aunt, 1820–1895
ABG	Anna Louisa Bulloch Gracie, TR's aunt, 1833–1893
RBR	Robert Barnwell Roosevelt, TR's uncle, 1829–1906
ARC	Anna Roosevelt Cowles (called Bamie or Bye), TR's sister, 1855–1931
WSC	William Sheffield Cowles, ARC's husband, 1846–1923
ER	Elliott Roosevelt, TR's brother, 1860–1894
AR	Anna Rebecca Hall Roosevelt, ER's wife, 1863–1892
CRR	Corinne Roosevelt Robinson, TR's sister, 1861–1933
DR	Douglas Robinson, CRR's husband, 1855–1918
AHLR	Alice Hathaway Lee, the first Mrs. Theodore Roosevelt, 1861–1884
EKR	Edith Kermit Carow Roosevelt, the second Mrs. Theodore Roosevelt, first lady 1901–1909, 1861–1948
ARL	Alice Lee Roosevelt Longworth, AHLR and TR's daughter, 1884–1980
NL	Nicholas Longworth, ARL's husband, 1869–1931
TRJR	Theodore Roosevelt, EKR and TR's son, 1887–1944
EBAR	Eleanor Butler Alexander Roosevelt, TRJR's wife, 1889–1960
KR	Kermit Roosevelt, EKR and TR's son, 1889–1943
BR	Belle Wyatt Willard Roosevelt, KR's wife, 1892–1968
ERD	Ethel Carow Roosevelt Derby, EKR and TR's daughter, 1891–1977
RD	Richard Derby, ERD's husband, 1881–1963
ABR	Archibald Bulloch Roosevelt, EKR and TR's son, 1894–1979
QR	Quentin Roosevelt, EKR and TR's son, 1897–1918
AER	Anna Eleanor Roosevelt, ER's daughter and TR's niece, first lady 1933–1945, 1884–1962
FDR	Franklin Delano Roosevelt, AER's husband, TR's fifth cousin and nephew by marriage, President 1933–1945, 1882–1945
HCL	Henry Cabot Lodge, Massachusetts congressman and senator, 1850–1924
ACMDL	Anna Cabot Mills Davis Lodge (Nannie), HCL's wife, 1850–1915

Key to Sources Frequently Cited

AUTO	Theodore Roosevelt, *An Autobiography* (1913; reprint, New York, 1985)
MEM	Theodore Roosevelt, *The Works of Theodore Roosevelt*, Memorial Edition (New York, 1919–26)
MOR	Elting E. Morison, John Morton Blum, and Alfred Chandler, eds., *The Letters of Theodore Roosevelt* (Cambridge, Mass., 1951–54)
TR/HCL	Henry Cabot Lodge, ed., *Selections from the Correspondence of Theodore Roosevelt and Henry Cabot Lodge, 1884–1918*, 2 vols. (New York, 1925)

Manuscripts

TRC-HU	Theodore Roosevelt Collection, Houghton Library, Harvard College Library
ARC-MS	Anna Roosevelt Cowles' memoirs of family life, "The Story of the Roosevelt Family"
EKR-Di	Edith Kermit (Carow) Roosevelt Diaries
ERD-Di	Ethel Carow (Roosevelt) Derby Diaries
MOR-REJ	Rejected letters collected from archives around the world by Elting Morison, John Blum, and Alfred Chandler, for their eight-volume *Letters of Theodore Roosevelt*; many are also available in TRP-LC
NSC	The Newspaper Scrapbook Collection, including the Mabel Styles Collection
PPA-TRC	Progressive Party Archives
TR-SP	TR's speeches, many taken down verbatim by stenographers, including his replies to challenges from the crowd
TRSR-LB	Theodore Roosevelt Senior Letterbooks, 1869–1878
SUBJ-TRC	Subject Files
MHS	Massachusetts Historical Society
HCL-MHS	Henry Cabot Lodge Papers and Roosevelt-Lodge Correspondence
LC	Library of Congress
ABR-LC	Archibald Bulloch Roosevelt Papers in Series 16 TR Papers
ARL-LC	Alice Roosevelt Longworth Papers, used with permission of Joanna Sturm
ARL-Di	Alice's Diaries, ARL-LC, used with permission of Joanna Sturm
GP-LC	Gifford Pinchot Papers
KBR-LC	Kermit and Belle Wyatt (Willard) Roosevelt Papers
KR-Di	Kermit Roosevelt's Diaries, KBR-LC
TRJR-LC	Theodore Roosevelt, Jr., Papers
TRP-LC	Theodore Roosevelt Papers
RFP-LC	Roosevelt Family Papers
FDR	Franklin Roosevelt Library
FDRN-FDR	Franklin Roosevelt Papers as Assistant Secretary of the Navy
RFP-FDR	Roosevelt Family Papers (includes family papers donated by the children)
JIG-ARIZ	John Greenway and Isabella Ferguson Greenway Papers, Arizona Historical Society
NR-SYR	Nicholas Roosevelt Papers at the George Arents Library, Syracuse University
TR-SYR	Theodore Roosevelt Papers at the George Arents Library, Syracuse University
NYHS	New-York Historical Society
ORHO-COL	Columbia Oral History Project, Columbia University
SHC	Bulloch Papers, Southern Historial Collection, University of North Carolina
TRP-BP	Theodore Roosevelt Collection at the TR Birthplace, National Park Service, New York

TRP-SAHI Theodore Roosevelt Family Papers, National Park Service Headquarters, Old Orchard House, at Sagamore Hill Historic Site, Oyster Bay, New York

INTRODUCTION

1. *American Heritage Dictionary of the English Language,* College Edition (Boston, 1976), 204.

2. Ferdinand C. Iglehart to TR (see Key to Sources Frequently Cited), July 11, 1912, TRP-LC; Nathan G. Hale, Jr., *Freud and the Americans: The Beginnings of Psychoanalysis in the United States, 1876–1917* (New York, 1971), 45; see also Kathleen Dalton, "Why America Loved Teddy Roosevelt: Or, Charisma Is in the Eyes of the Beholders," in Robert J. Brugger, ed., *OurSelves/Our Past: Psychological Approaches to American History* (Baltimore, 1981). TR wrote advice literature in "What We Can Expect of the American Boy," *St. Nicholas* 27, no. 7 (May 1900): 571–74; "Who Should Go West?" *Harper's Weekly,* Jan. 2, 1886, 7; "Manliness and Decency," *Men* 22, no. 39 (Feb. 6, 1897); "Americans Should Be Educated at Home," *Harvard Graduates' Magazine* 19, no. 73 (September 1910): 14–17; "Books That I Read and When and How I Do My Reading," *Ladies' Home Journal,* April 1915; "Civic Helpfulness," *Century Magazine,* October 1900, 939–44; "The College Graduate and Public Life," *Atlantic,* August 1894, 255–60; "The Emancipation of Education," *Good Housekeeping,* December 1908, 624–27; "Fellow-feeling as a Political Factor," *The Century,* January 1900, 466–71; "The President," series of articles in 1906–1907, *Ladies' Home Journal,* and "Men," series of anonymous articles, *Ladies' Home Journal,* October 1916–June 1917, August–October 1917; "A Message to All the Boys of America," *Boy Scouts' Year Book* (New York, 1915), 46–47; "Reform Through Social Work; Some Forces That Tell for Decency in New York City," *McClure's Magazine,* March 1901, 448–54, and *Fortnightly Review,* Nov. 1, 1901, 739–47; "Shall We Do Away with the Church? I Know All the Reasons for Not Going," *Ladies' Home Journal,* October 1917, 12, 119; "The Successful Mother," White House address, Mar. 10, 1908, to the delegates to the first International Congress in America on the Welfare of the Child, in *Ladies' Home Journal,* June 1908, 11.

3. *Newsweek,* Aug. 6, 1979.

4. Once rated by professional historians as deserving a place among the near-great presidents, he has recently moved up to be ranked as a great president alongside Lincoln, Washington, FDR, and Thomas Jefferson: David L. Porter, "American Historians Rate Our Presidents," in William D. Pederson and Ann M. McLaurin, eds., *The Rating Game in American Politics: An Interdisciplinary Approach* (New York, 1987), 15.

5. EKR to ARC, Mar. 11, n.y. (no year) [1889], TRC-HU.

6. ERD did not want Kermit's suicide to get out; EKR burned TR's letters to her on two different occasions; ARC edited out sections of TR's letters to her (*Letters from Theodore Roosevelt to Anna Roosevelt Cowles, 1870–1918* [New York, 1924]), and CRR told a highly selective story of TR's life in her book about him, *My Brother Theodore Roosevelt* (New York, 1929); HCL, with EKR's help, edited and even rewrote portions of TR's letters before he published them (*TR/HCL*); Will Irwin edited out references to ABR's mental slowness and other sore subjects in *Letters to Kermit from Theodore Roosevelt, 1902–1908* (New York, 1946); expurgated versions of TR's letters to his children have been published: Joseph Bucklin Bishop, ed., *Theodore Roosevelt's Letters to His Children* (New York, 1929) and Joan Paterson Kerr, ed., *A Bully Father: Theodore Roosevelt's Letters to His Children* (New York, 1995); the original letters are in TRC-HU, HCL-MHS, KBR-LC, TRP-LC, and TRJR-LC.

7. TR to ARC, May 15, 1886, *Letters from Theodore Roosevelt to Anna Roosevelt Cowles,* 81; see G. Edward White, *The Eastern Establishment and the Western Experience* (New York, 1968), 84.

8. Mark Twain [Samuel Clemens], *Life on the Mississippi*, in *Mississippi Writings* (1883; reprint, New York, 1982), 501.

9. MEM 18:52.

10. TR often called Wilson a "time-server" and "cold-blooded" for lacking the heroic spirit and physical courage: TR to KR and BR, Nov. 2, 1915, TRC-HU.

11. "Aggressive fighting" in TR, *The Free Citizen: A Summons to Service of the Democratic Ideal*, ed. Hermann Hagedorn (New York, 1958), 80; "corruption" in TR, "Administering the New York Police Force," *Atlantic Monthly*, September 1897, MEM 15:174.

12. See MEM 5:533; TR, "The Higher Life of American Cities," *Outlook* (Dec. 21, 1895), MEM 15:141.

13. Joseph Bucklin Bishop, *Theodore Roosevelt and His Time Shown in His Own Letters*, (New York, 1920), 1:2; Edward H. Cotton, *Theodore Roosevelt the American* (Boston, 1926); Jacob A. Riis, *Theodore Roosevelt the Citizen* (New York, 1904); Edward Marshall, *The Story of the Rough Riders* (New York, 1890); Hermann Hagedorn, *The Roosevelt Family of Sagamore Hill* (New York, 1954), 80; Hermann Hagedorn to ERD, Feb. 2, 1960, TRC-HU.

14. "almost single-handedly" in Edmund Morris, *The Rise of Theodore Roosevelt* (New York, 1979), book jacket, and on TR being "almost infallibly truthful" see 790 *n.* 65; "doubts" in Morris, "Theodore Roosevelt, President," *American Heritage* 32, no. 4 (June/July 1981): 8; John A. Gable, executive director of the Theodore Roosevelt Association, told the editor of the *Journal of American History* that TR never lied: 87, no. 3 (December 2000): 1171–72; "in a class" in Frederick W. Marks III, *Velvet on Iron: The Diplomacy of Theodore Roosevelt* (Lincoln, Nebr., 1979), 198–99.

15. Henry F. Pringle, *Theodore Roosevelt: A Biography* (1931; reprint, New York, 1956), 4; Pringle wrote: "It has been said that Theodore Roosevelt's life was the ultimate dream of every typical American boy: he fought in a war, killed lions, became President, and quarreled with the Pope. The years in the Bad Lands constituted an earlier role that nearly every boy plays in imagination. Roosevelt wore gaudy clothes. He was a deputy sheriff. He caught some thieves," 71; Teddy Brewster in *Arsenic and Old Lace* is a madder version of Pringle's boyish Roosevelt.

16. Richard Hofstadter, *The American Political Tradition and the Men Who Made It* (New York, 1948), 229, 231.

17. Bernard de Voto, ed., *Mark Twain in Eruption* (New York, 1940), 8; "Bryan on Roosevelt," newspaper clipping from 1904 campaign, TRP-LC; Henry Adams to Elizabeth Cameron, Feb. 25, 1912, in *Letters of Henry Adams*, ed. Worthington C. Ford (Boston, 1938), 2:587.

18. Thomas A. Bailey, *Presidential Greatness: The Image and the Man from George Washington to the Present* (New York, 1966), 307; Richard Saltus, "Manic-Depression Caused by Gene, Study Indicates," *Boston Globe*, Feb. 26, 1987.

19. TR, "The Presidency," *Youth's Companion*, Nov. 6, 1902, MEM 15:213.

20. Kathleen Dalton, "Between the Diplomacy of Imperialism and the Achievement of World Order by Supranational Mediation: Ethnocentrism and Theodore Roosevelt's Changing Views of World Order," in Pierre Melandri and Serge Ricard, eds., *Ethnocentrisme et diplomatie: L'Amérique et le monde au XXᵉ siècle* (Paris, 2001), 27–47.

21. "bad disposition" in Hutchins Hapgood, *A Victorian in the Modern World* (New York, 1939), 302. Because he talked so much about manhood and valued the friendship and companionship of other men on the hunt and in political battle, TR is often thought of as a "man's man," and never a "ladies' man," but his friend Arthur Lee got it right when he said TR was "essentially a boy's man" who understood the wonder and energy of boyhood: MEM 13:281; David Levering Lewis, *W.E.B. Du Bois: Biography of a Race, 1868–1919* (New York, 1993), 1:384; Lewis Einstein, *Roosevelt: His Mind in Action* (Boston, 1930), 97.

CHAPTER ONE: THE HANDICAP OF RICHES

1. MOR 1:67.

2. CRR, *My Brother*, 4.

3. TR and FDR were descendants of early Dutch settler Claes Martenzsen Van Rosenvelt. Roosevelts owned slaves and allowed one of them to be burned at the stake due to an alleged slave revolt in New Amsterdam: Daniel Horsmanden, *The New York Conspiracy*, intro. Thomas J. Davis (1744; reprint, Boston, 1971), 471, and "The Roosevelt Family in America: A Genealogy," *Theodore Roosevelt Association Journal* 16, nos. 1–3 (Winter/Spring/Summer 1990); I thank Jill Lepore for alerting me to their slave-owning; on the Tory farm, Eric Homberger, *The Historical Atlas of New York* (New York, 1994), 60–61; Kathleen Dalton, "The Early Life of Theodore Roosevelt" (Ph.D. diss., Johns Hopkins University, 1979); Edward Pessen, *Riches, Class and Power Before the Civil War* (Lexington, Mass., 1973), 136, 76, 10, 292; see also Edward K. Spann, *The New Metropolis: New York City, 1840–1857* (New York, 1981), 207–26; for C.V.S. Roosevelt's property, see NR-SYR, TRSR-LB, Roosevelt Family Deeds in De Witt, Lockman & Kip Lawyers, Miscellaneous Manuscripts, NYHS; Howard K. Beale, "Theodore Roosevelt's Ancestry: A Study in Heredity," N.Y. *Genealogical and Biographical Record*, October 1954, 200; ARC-MS; *History of the Chemical Bank, 1823–1913* (New York, 1913), 163, 165, 109; Roosevelt and Son, the Roosevelt piers, and Broadway Improvement Company paid off well into the twentieth century.

4. James C. Mohr, *The Radical Republicans and Reform in New York During Reconstruction* (Ithaca, N.Y., 1973); Robert Roosevelt owned, edited, and wrote articles for the organization's newspaper, *New York Citizen*, and served as an anti-Tammany Democratic congressman and member of the Committee of Seventy, which ousted Boss Tweed. Thee's brother James Alfred donated funds and his brother S. Weir Roosevelt was elected to the city's school board as a Citizens Association candidate. Thee signed petitions and endorsed Citizens Association candidates for office. Robert charged that Tammany was no more than "a howling mob of desperate wretches" who failed to represent real working people and stood for prizefighters and criminals. He blamed Tammany for the deaths of 7,000 New Yorkers "by the want of sanitary regulation": clipping, scrapbook #1, "Report of the Council of Hygiene and Public Health of the Citizens Association of New York upon the Sanitary Conditions of the City" (New York, 1865) and *New York Citizen*, Dec. 12, 1864, RBR Papers, NYHS; also RBR Papers, the Theodore Roosevelt Association offices; John Duffy, *A History of Public Health in New York City, 1866–1966* (New York, 1974); Seymour J. Mandelbaum, *Boss Tweed's New York* (New York, 1965); Alexander B. Callow, Jr., *The Tweed Ring* (New York, 1969); Leo Hershkowitz, *Tweed's New York: Another Look* (Garden City, N.Y., 1978); Timothy J. Gilfoyle, *City of Eros: New York City, Prostitution, and the Commercialization of Sex, 1790–1920* (New York, 1992); Edwin G. Burrows and Mike Wallace, *Gotham: A History of New York City to 1898* (New York, 1999).

5. TRSR-LB; "Roosevelt Family in America: Genealogy"; Charles Barney Whittelsey, *The Roosevelt Genealogy, 1649–1902* (Hartford, Conn., 1902); interview with P. James Roosevelt, Mar. 21, 1977; "The Roosevelt Copper Venture," *Copper*, June 1907, 20–22; Roosevelt and Son employed child labor and imported plate glass from London and Manchester Plate Glass Co., with factories in St. Helens, England, until January 1876, when they stopped importing due to competition from domestic manufacturers: LeGrand B. Randall to Hermann Hagedorn, Mar. 11, 1921, SUBJ-TRC and NR-SYR. As a banker Thee collected on mortgage interest and loans; see Roosevelt Family and Business Papers, NYHS and TRSR-LB; Elizabeth Christophers Hobson, *Recollections of a Happy Life* (New York, 1916), 79–90.

6. "mould" in TR, *New York* (New York, 1895), 188; Henry W. Bellows, *Historical Sketch of the Union League Club of New York: Its Origin, Organization, and Work, 1863–1879* (New York, 1879), 123–24.

7. Elizabeth Norris Emlen Roosevelt to ARC, Dec. 27, 1896, TRC-HU; ARC-MS; Constance (Mrs. Burton) Harrison, *Recollections Grave and Gay* (New York, 1911), 278; also Frederic Cople Jaher, "Style and Status: High Society in Late Nineteenth-Century New York," in Jaher, ed., *The Rich, the Well-Born, and the Powerful* (Urbana, Ill., 1973); Jaher, *The Urban Establishment* (Chicago, 1982); Kathleen M. Dalton, "Theodore Roosevelt, Knickerbocker Aristocrat," *New York History* 67, no. 1 (January 1986): 39–65; Roy Rosenzweig and Elizabeth Blackmar, *The Park and the People: A History of Central Park* (Ithaca, N.Y., 1991), 23; Edith Wharton, *The Age of Innocence* (New York, 1962).

8. "sacrifice" in J. A. Mangan, *Athleticism in the Victorian and Edwardian Public School: The Emergence and Consolidation of an Educational Ideology* (New York, 1981), 53; "physical courage" in Phillips Brooks, *Essays and Addresses Religious, Literary and Social* (New York, 1894), 323; on Hughes, ER to ARC, Nov. 21, n.y. [1880], RFP-FDR and Brian L. Stagg, "Tennessee's Rugby Colony," Robert M. McBride, ed., *More Landmarks of Tennessee History* (Nashville, 1969), 279; on muscular Christianity see Walter E. Houghton, *The Victorian Frame of Mind, 1830–1870* (New Haven, 1951); letter from President Roosevelt to John R. Mott in introduction, John R. Mott, ed., *The Claims and Opportunities of the Christian Ministry* (New York, 1913), 7–12; Thomas Hughes, *The Manliness of Christ* (London, 1879); C. Howard Hopkins, *History of the YMCA in North America* (New York, 1951); Lytton Strachey, *Eminent Victorians* (London, 1918); E. Anthony Rotundo, *American Manhood: Transformations in Masculinity from the Revolution to the Modern Era* (New York, 1994); Clifford Putney, *Muscular Christianity: Manhood and Sports in Protestant America, 1880–1920* (Cambridge, Mass., 2001); Laurence L. Doggett, *History of the Young Men's Christian Association* (New York, 1922); John Higham, "The Reorientation of American Culture in the 1890s," in Higham, ed., *Writing American History: Essays on Modern Scholarship* (Bloomington, Ind., 1970).

9. TRSR raised funds for the purchase of the Cesnola Collection, TRSR-LB; Nathaniel Burt, *Palaces for the People: A Social History of the American Art Museum* (Boston, 1977); Carol Duncan, "Art Museums and the Ritual of Citizenship," in Ivan Karp and Steven D. Lavine, eds., *Exhibiting Cultures: The Poetics and Politics of Museum Display* (Washington, D.C., 1991); "Higginson's revival" had sparked popular enthusiasm for sports, especially ice skating. Higginson wrote about "purity and vigor" as naturally interconnected virtues: *Out-door Papers* (Boston, 1863), 159, and *Atlantic Essays* (Boston, 1871); John A. Kouwenhoven, *Adventures in America, 1857–1900: A Pictorial Record from Harper's Weekly* (New York, 1938), picture 23; Sean Wilentz, *Chants Democratic: New York City and the Rise of the American Working Class, 1788–1850* (New York, 1986), 354; Mangan, *Athleticism in the Victorian and Edwardian Public School.*

10. Muscular Christians performed good works and fought pornography; see *Proceedings of the 18th Annual Convention of the Y.M.C.A. of North America*, 1873; Emma Brace, ed., *The Life of Charles Loring Brace: Chiefly Told in His Own Letters* (New York, 1894), 295; Charles Loring Brace, *The Dangerous Classes of New York, and Twenty Years' Work Among Them* (New York, 1880), 339. His system was controversial; many poor children left intact families only to be treated harshly as farmworkers: Miriam Z. Langsam, *Children West* (Madison, Wisc., 1964), viii; Robert Bremmer, *American Philanthropy* (Chicago, 1981), 64; see also Stephen O' Connor, *Orphan Trains: The Story of Charles Loring Brace and the Children He Saved and Failed* (Boston, 2001), and Marilyn Irvin Holt, *The Orphan Trains: Placing Out in America* (Lincoln, Nebr., 1992). Thee wanted the nature cure implicit in Brace's "placing out" system applied to other groups: sending the destitute inmates of New York's House of Refuge to teach them "manly vigor." Thee also took Theodore to rough it at Brace's camp in upstate New York.

11. E. Brace, ed., *Life of Charles Loring Brace*, 170; C. L. Brace, *Dangerous Classes*,

410, 177; State Charities Aid Association, *Theodore Roosevelt: Memorial Meeting* (New York, 1878); Union League Club of New York, *Theodore Roosevelt, Senior: A Tribute* (New York, 1878), TRSR-LB; SUBJ-TRC.

12. Nicholas Roosevelt, ms. draft of book on the Roosevelt family, NR-SYR, and Nicholas Roosevelt, *A Front Row Seat* (Norman, Okla., 1953); Franklin Delano Roosevelt, Notes on "Family," RFP-FDR; interview, WSC, Jr., Apr. 13, 1977.

13. AUTO, 12, 27; ARC-MS; Dr. J.G.B. Bulloch, *A History and Genealogy of the Families of Bulloch and Stobo and of Irvine of Cults* (privately printed, n.d.), 20; Clarece Martin, *A Glimpse of the Past: The History of Bulloch Hall and Roswell, Georgia* (Roswell, Ga., 1973), 6–8. MSEB refused to wed her sweetheart, James S. Bulloch, and married Senator John Elliott; Bulloch married Elliott's daughter Harriet. After Harriet and John died, MSEB and Bulloch were finally married. MSEB's children from her marriage to Elliott were Daniel, Georgia, and Susan. Susan married Silas Weir Roosevelt's brother-in-law Hilborne West. Hester and James' son was James Dunwody Bulloch. James Bulloch and MSEB's children were Anna Bulloch Gracie (1833–93), Martha Bulloch Roosevelt (1835–84), Charles Irvine Bulloch (1837–40), and Irvine Stephens Bulloch (1842–98); David McCullough, *Mornings on Horseback* (New York, 1981), 41–42.

14. Charles C. Jones, Jr., *The History of Georgia*, vol. 2, *Revolutionary Epoch* (Boston, 1883), 221, 229; ARC-MS; Martin, *Glimpse*, 6; Carleton Putnam, *Theodore Roosevelt: The Formative Years* (New York, 1958), 1.

15. AUTO, 29; Bishop, *Theodore Roosevelt*, 1:2; interview with Edith Derby Williams, June 15, 1994.

16. Abbie Graham, *Grace H. Dodge: Merchant of Dreams: A Biography* (New York, 1926), 49. In Thee's day evangelicals were activist Protestants who believed in "salvation by faith in the atoning death of Jesus Christ through personal conversion, the authority of Scripture, and the importance of preaching as contrasted with ritual,": *Webster's Seventh New Collegiate Dictionary* (Springfield, 1963), 287. Evangelicals could be liberal Protestants like Henry Ward Beecher who believed in a forgiving God and Christian evolutionism (and who rejected predestination and Hell) or fundamentalists who believed in the literal truth of the Bible and were hostile to evolutionary science and the secularization of public life. In the nineteenth century fundamentalism was not clearly associated with political conservatism. See George M. Marsden, *Fundamentalism and American Culture: The Shaping of Twentieth-Century Evangelicalism, 1870–1925* (New York, 1980). TR was a liberal Protestant, but Thee, if he had doctrinal concerns at all, probably held more sympathy with fundamentalism. Religious affiliation was a point of tension between Mittie and Thee: TR preferred his father's Dutch Reformed church to the Methodist church his mother attended; Mittie finally convinced Thee to join the Madison Square Presbyterian Church, then the Fifth Avenue Presbyterian Church, but he took Theodore on occasion to the Calvinist Collegiate Dutch Reformed Church, the church of C.V.S. Roosevelt, where the boy was confirmed: Collegiate Church, *Memorial Meeting to Honor Theodore Roosevelt* (New York, 1919). TR taught in an Episcopal Sunday school and considered joining the Congregational church when he was in college. He married Alice Hathaway Lee in a Unitarian church. He attended the Episcopal church in Oyster Bay with his second wife, Edith, but when he was president TR went to a local Dutch Reformed church.

17. TRSR to MBR, Jan. 12, 1862, and MBR to TRSR, May 16, [1855–58], TRC-HU; Ann Douglas Wood, " 'The Fashionable Diseases': Women's Complaints and Their Treatment in Nineteenth-Century America," in Mary S. Hartman and Lois Banner, eds., *Clio's Consciousness Raised: New Perspectives on the History of Women* (New York, 1974), 28; E. Anthony Rotundo, "American Fatherhood: A Historical Perspective," *American Behavioral Scientist* 29, no. 1 (September/October 1985): 7–25; Rotundo, *American Manhood.*

18. TRSR to MBR, Sept. 28, and MBR to TRSR, Oct. 12, 1853, TRC-HU.

19. MBR to TRSR, Sept. 14, 1853, TRC-HU; TRSR to Margaret Barnhill Roosevelt, July 1, 1851, and RBR to TRSR, July 17, 1853, RFP-LC; William Emlen Roosevelt interview, SUBJ-TRC.

20. TRSR to MBR, Dec. 19, 1861, and MBR to TRSR, May 19 and 21, 1855, TRC-HU.

21. Wharton, *Age of Innocence*, 45; TRSR to Elizabeth Emlen Roosevelt, Dec. 10, 1851, RFP, LC.

22. "*too hard*" in MBR to TRSR, Oct. 15, 1873, TRC-HU; on MBR's unhappiness, Lawrence F. Abbott, ed., *The Letters of Archie Butt, Personal Aide to President Roosevelt* (Garden City, N.Y., 1924), 279, and interview, WSC, Jr.

23. Interview, WSC, Jr.; MSEB to SEW, December 1858 and Oct. 28, 1858, TRC-HU.

24. By the mid-1850s, Mrs. Bulloch had sold Bulloch Hall in Roswell and moved in with her daughter Susan Elliott West and Hilborne West in Philadelphia: MSEB to SEW, [December 1858], TRC-HU; TRSR-LB.

25. MBR to TRSR, Oct. 5, 1853, and MSEB to SEW, Oct. 28, 1858, TRC-HU.

26. James D. Bulloch to Mrs. Stevens, July 11, 1849, James Dunwody Bulloch Letters #3318, SHC.

27. James D. Bulloch to Mrs. Stevens, July 11, 1849, James Dunwody Bulloch Letters #3318, SHC; MBR to ARC, July 28, 1868, TRSR to SEW, Mar. 3, 1877, and TRSR to TR, Oct. 27, 1876, TRC-HU. TR's daughter Alice Roosevelt Longworth was famous for similar quips, such as joking that President Calvin Coolidge looked like "he had been weaned on a pickle" and that presidential candidate Wendell Willkie sprang "from the grassroots of the country clubs of America": Michael Teague, *Mrs. L: Conversations with Alice Roosevelt Longworth* (Garden City, N.Y., 1981), xiv–xv.

28. ER to MBR, n.d. [1873], RFP-FDR.

29. Putnam, *Theodore Roosevelt*, 60: see John Fraser, *America and the Patterns of Chivalry* (New York, 1982), 78–83; duels were so common that Mittie's cousin joined an antidueling association: Thomas Gamble, *Savannah Duels and Duelists, 1733–1877* (Savannah, Ga., 1923).

30. "bloodthirstiness" in Bertram Wyatt-Brown, *Southern Honor: Ethics and Behavior in the Old South* (New York, 1982), 173; "manly qualities" in L. F. Abbott, ed., *Letters of Archie Butt*, 20, 67.

31. MBR to TRSR, [Oct. 5, 1853], TRC-HU. Her letters and family interviews show Mittie had a hypochondriac's self-centered preoccupation with symptoms: ARL, WSC, Jr., Corinne R. Alsop, ORHO-COL; interview, WSC, Jr.; EKR to Edith Derby Williams, Jan. 24, 1945, TRC-HU; Husbands sometimes shopped and made household orders for coal and other staple items, but wives managed servants and most details of housekeeping; TRSR-LB.

32. Harrison, *Recollections*, 278–79; ARC-MS.

33. "Bamie does not remember that the Deserter loves her and thinks often of her": MBR to ARC, Mar. 9, 1876, TRC-HU; "I think I was dastardly to leave home with my whole family under the weather": MBR to TRSR, n.d., TRC-HU. Birth control information and abortions were given discreetly to elite women by their doctors before state regulation: Carroll Smith-Rosenberg and Charles Rosenberg, "The Female Animal: Medical and Biological Views of Woman and Her Role in Nineteenth-Century America," in Judith Walzer Leavitt, ed., *Women and Health in America: Historical Readings* (Madison, Wisc., 1984), 17; William Marrs, M.D., *Confessions of a Neurasthenic*, quoted in John S. Haller, Jr., and Robin M. Haller, *The Physician and Sexuality in Victorian America* (New York, 1974), 8; Howard M. Feinstein, "The Use and Abuse of Illness in the James Family Circle: A View of Neurasthenia as a Social Phenomenon," in Robert J. Brugger, ed., *OurSelves/Our Past: Psychological*

Approaches to American History (Baltimore, 1981); Kathryn Kish Sklar, *Catharine Beecher: A Study in American Domesticity* (New York, 1973), 208; James C. Whorton, *Crusaders for Fitness: The History of American Health Reformers* (Princeton, 1982), 149. Today historians recognize that neurasthenia affects both sexes, but late-nineteenth-century America viewed it as a female phenomenon.

34. ARL said that Mittie "seems to have been moody, temperamental and, like most hypochondriacs, she enjoyed poor health": Teague, *Mrs. L*, 19; MBR, Commonplace Book, TRC-HU; CRR, *My Brother*, 18; Kathryn Kish Sklar, "All Hail to Pure Cold Water!" in Leavitt, ed., *Women and Health*, 250–51; Harry B. Weiss and Howard R. Kemble, *The Great American Water Cure: A History of Hydropathy in the United States* (Trenton, N.J., 1967); Jane B. Donegan, *"Hydropathic Highway to Health": Women and Water-cure in Antebellum America* (Westport, Conn., 1986); Susan E. Cayleff, *Wash and Be Healed: The Water-Cure Movement and Women's Health* (Philadelphia, 1987).

35. AUTO, 9, 8; TRSR to MBR, Apr. 9, 1860, TRC-HU.

36. MBR to TRSR, Dec. 9, 1861, MSEB to SEW, Nov. 7, 1861, and TRSR to MBR, Dec. 6, 1862, TRC-HU.

37. CRR, *My Brother*, 16.

38. ARC-MS; ABR to ERD, Apr. 26, 1975, TRC-HU; RBR to Elizabeth Ellis Roosevelt, June 4, 1862, RBR Papers, LC; *The Diary of Gideon Welles* (New York, 1911), 3:349; RBR to Elizabeth Ellis Roosevelt, May 31, 1862, copy formerly in possession of Mr. and Mrs. WSC, Jr.; interview with Jean Schermerhorn Roosevelt, Oyster Bay, N.Y., Mar. 20, 1977; ARL interview, ORHO-COL; Kathleen Dalton, "Theodore Roosevelt and the Idea of War," *Theodore Roosevelt Association Journal* 7, no. 4 (Fall 1981): 6–11.

39. Notice, May 17, 1861, meeting of Union Grays, Theodore Roosevelt, Secretary, in Notes on Building Expenses, 1861, TRC-HU; possibly part of Hiram Ketchum's Home Guards: *New York Times*, May 8, 1861; Tilton quoted in Basil Leo Lee, *Discontent in New York City, 1861–1865* (Washington, D.C., 1943), 110; Francis Parkman, "To the Lingerers," Aug. 12, 1862, in *The Letters of Francis Parkman*, ed. with an intro. by Wilbur R. Jacobs (Norman, Okla., 1960), 1:151–52; the Roosevelts were active in the Union Defense Committee, the Union League Club's Loyal Publication Society, and other groups; for TRSR and other Roosevelts' involvement in Loyal Publication Society see publications of L.P.S. in NR-SYR; James McCague, *The Second Rebellion: The Story of the New York City Draft Riots of 1863* (New York, 1968); George W. Smith and Charles B. Judah, eds., *Life in the North During the Civil War* (Albuquerque, N. Mex., 1966), 59; George M. Fredrickson, *The Inner Civil War: Northern Intellectuals and the Crisis of the Union* (New York, 1968), 151–76.

40. MSEB to SEW, July 14, 1863, TRC-HU; ARC-MS.

41. TRSR, Obituary, *New York Times*, Feb. 11, 1878; State Charities Aid Association, *Theodore Roosevelt: Memorial Meeting*; Union League Club, *Theodore Roosevelt, Senior: A Tribute*; Allotment Commission Books, NYHS; Theodore Roosevelt Senior Journal, TRC-HU; William Q. Maxwell, *Lincoln's Fifth Wheel: The Political History of the United States Sanitary Commission* (New York, 1956), 19; U.S. Allotment System, *Report to the President of the United States of the Commissioners for the State of New York* (New York, 1862).

42. TRSR to MBR, Jan. 1 and 23, 1862, TRC-HU; John Hay to TRSR, Feb. 4, 1862, TRP-LC; in 1863 he also raised money and volunteers on behalf of the Union League Club to replenish General Winfield Scott Hancock's troops. Three thousand men went to war because of Thee's efforts: Will Irwin, Earl Chapin May, and Joseph Hotchkiss, *A History of the Union League Club of New York City* (New York, 1952), 40; TRSR to MBR, Jan. 1, 1862, TRC-HU.

43. SUBJ-TRC; TRSR was an associate member of the Sanitary Commission and worked with the Women's Central Association of Relief to raise money to get supplies and

medical care to the front, and he was a leader in getting state and private groups to provide jobs and support to Union veterans; see U.S. Sanitary Commission #69, *Statement of the Objects and Methods of the Sanitary Commission,* Appointed by the Government of the U.S., June 13, 1861 (New York, 1863); Sanitary Commission Document #74, *Associate Members of the US Sanitary Commission,* Mar. 15, 1864; Charles J. Stillé, *History of the United States Sanitary Commission, Being the General Report of Its Work During the War of the Rebellion* (New York, 1868), 178–80; and Sanitary Commission pamphlets #68, #95; Union League Club, *Theodore Roosevelt, Senior: A Tribute;* State Charities Aid Association, *Theodore Roosevelt: Memorial Meeting;* Loyal Publication Society pamphlets; Frank Freidel, "The Loyal Publication Society: A Pro-Union Propaganda Agency," *Mississippi Valley Historical Review* 5, no. 26 (1939–40): 359–76; the L.P.S., the Protective War Claim Association, and the Soldiers Employment Bureau were funded by the Union League; TRSR was on its executive committee in 1864: Bellows, *Historical Sketch of the Union League;* Guy Gibson, "Lincoln's League: The Union League Movement During the Civil War" (Ph.D. diss., University of Illinois, 1957); on nationality see Fredrickson, *Inner Civil War.*

44. CRR, *My Brother,* 26; ARC-MS; TRSR to MBR, Feb. 7 and 14, 1862, TRC-HU; Francis B. C. Bradlee, *Blockade Running During the Civil War and the Effect of Land and Water Transportation on the Confederacy* (Salem, Mass., 1925), 54; James D. Bulloch, *The Secret Service of the Confederate States in Europe; or, How the Confederate Cruisers Were Equipped* (London 1883); U.S. Allotment System, *Report to the President,* 7.

45. ARC-MS; MBR to TRSR, Nov. 13 and Dec. 9, 1861, TRC-HU.

46. TRSR to MBR, Oct. 10, 1861, TRC-HU; Corinne Robinson Alsop interview, ORHO-COL; McCullough, *Mornings on Horseback,* 55, claims this event "never happened" but offers no evidence except that "a gesture so flamboyant would have been out of character" for Mittie, yet Confederate women were famous for flamboyant gestures; see Drew Gilpin Faust, *Mothers of Invention: Women of the Slaveholding South in the American Civil War* (Chapel Hill, N.C., 1996); Catherine Clinton, *Tara Revisited: Women, War & the Plantation Legend* (New York, 1995); B. Lee, *Discontent,* 26; Harold Melvin Hyman, *Era of the Oath: Northern Loyalty Tests During the Civil War and Reconstruction* (Philadelphia, 1954).

47. EBAR, *Day Before Yesterday: The Reminiscences of Mrs. Theodore Roosevelt, Jr.* (Garden City, N.Y., 1959), 38. The Roosevelts, like many "gentlemen of property and standing," disliked abolitionists before the war, but supported Lincoln during the war. The Roosevelts' close friends the Livingstons owned the cotton-trading boat captained by James D. Bulloch before the war, but no evidence of a Roosevelt connection with the cotton trade is available. After the war Irvine and James Bulloch became cotton brokers in Liverpool, however. The Roosevelts of TRSR's generation never became truly committed to racial equality and during Reconstruction Robert wrote that blacks were "inferior" and did not deserve voting rights: editorial, *The Citizen,* RBR Papers, NYHS; TRSR had been pro-slavery and anti-abolitionist in his youth: "Everyone in England broaches slavery as soon as they become sufficiently well acquainted, but I am really beginning to convince myself from arguing so much upon the subject that it is a blessing to all concerned, and that the fugitive slave law is correct in every particular": TRSR to James Alfred Roosevelt, July 10, 1851, RFP-LC; TRSR to MBR, Sept. 21, 1853, TRC-HU.

48. F. H. Morse to William Seward, July 19, 1861, in *War of the Rebellion: The Official Records of the War,* Series 3, 1:445; for more detail on the Roosevelts in the Civil War see Dalton, "Early Life"; Edward Boykin, *Ghost Ship of the Confederacy: The Story of the Alabama and Her Captain Raphael Semmes* (New York, 1957), vi, 69; Bulloch, *Secret Service;* Thomas S. Townsend, *The Honors of the Empire State in the War of the Rebellion* (New York, 1889), 79.

49. *Boston Herald,* Oct. 11, 1862, 4; Lee, *Discontent,* 190.

50. At first, Thee's branch of the Roosevelt family had opposed fighting a war over the South's secession. C.V.S.'s brother, "Uncle Judge," James I. Roosevelt, was a well-known Copperhead, a Democrat suspected of sympathizing with the South. But Thee, his father, and brothers were not "peace-at-any-price" men, as the popular Civil War phrase termed persistent opponents of war. After Fort Sumter, they became ardent supporters of the Union cause, and Thee became a Lincoln Republican. ARC-MS; MBR to TRSR, Dec. 15, 1861, TRC-HU.

51. *A Record of the Metropolitan Fair in Aid of the United States Sanitary Commission*, New York, April 1864 (New York, 1867); MSEB to SEW, Nov. 9, 1863, Nov. 20, n.y., and Oct. 20, 1863, TRC-HU.

52. ARC-MS; MSEB to SEW, Dec. 15, 1863, and TRSR to MBR, Feb. 14, 1862, TRC-HU.

53. CRR, *My Brother*, 33.

54. James Marten, *The Children's Civil War* (Chapel Hill, N.C., 1998); Emmy E. Werner, *Reluctant Witnesses: Children's Voices from the Civil War* (Boulder, Colo., 1998).

55. The Civil War was less "a rich man's war and a poor man's fight," especially measured by volunteer rates, than later American wars. Some historians see the riots as a continuation of ante-bellum class and racial violence: J. Mathew Gallman, *The North Fights the Civil War: The Home Front* (Chicago, 1994); Adrian Cook, *The Armies of the Streets: The New York City Draft Riots of 1863* (Lexington, Ky., 1974), 117; Iver Bernstein, *The New York City Draft Riots: Their Significance for American Society and Politics in the Age of the Civil War* (New York, 1990); A Volunteer Special, *The Volcano Under the City* (New York, 1876).

56. MSEB to SEW, July 14, 1863, TRC-HU; Cook, *Draft Riots*, 108, 118.

57. Bellows, *Historical Sketch of the Union League*, 54, 647, 83; Irwin et al., *Union League*, 30–36, 55; N.Y. Union League Club, *Report of the Committee on Volunteering*, Oct. 13, 1864 (New York), 24; Jacob A. Riis, "Theodore Roosevelt's Father," *Outlook* (Oct. 6, 1900): 306; Benjamin Quarles, *The Negro in the Civil War* (Boston, 1953), 190; Samuel Carter III, *Cyrus Field: Man of Two Worlds* (New York, 1968), 208–209; Cook, *Draft Riots*, 203; William Lawrence to ARC, n.d. [1878], TRC-HU; Burrows and Wallace, *Gotham*.

58. Like Brace, Lowell came around to the viewpoint that rather than sin, an unjust labor system, unemployment, and inhumanely low wages stood at the root of the problem of poverty. She and Thee co-authored a pamphlet on charity administration, after he helped secure her appointment as the first woman to serve as chair of the State Charities Aid Association board: William Rhinelander Stewart, *The Philanthropic Work of Josephine Shaw Lowell* (New York, 1911), 155; Joan Waugh, *Unsentimental Reformer: The Life of Josephine Shaw Lowell* (New York, 1997); Doris Groshen Daniels, *Always a Sister: The Feminism of Lillian D. Wald* (New York, 1989), 41–42; Louisa Lee Schuyler, "Forty-Three Years Ago; or, the Early Days of the State Charities Aid Association, 1872–1915," address, Feb. 25, 1915, TRC-HU.

59. Albert J. Beveridge, "The Autobiography of an American Boy," Beveridge Papers, LC; Marten, *Children's Civil War*.

60. At a time when thousands of returning soldiers were begging on the streets for food and money, Thee created an institution to get jobs for them, the Soldiers' Employment Bureau: LeGrand B. Randall to Hermann Hagedorn, Mar. 3, 1921, SUBJ-TRC; Patrick J. Kelly, *Creating a National Home: Building the Veterans' Welfare State, 1860–1900* (Cambridge, Mass., 1997); Marten, *Children's Civil War*, 167–86; James H. Moorhead, *American Apocalypse: Yankee Protestants and the Civil War, 1860–1869* (New Haven, 1978), 146; Fredrickson, *Inner Civil War*; Gerald F. Linderman, *Embattled Courage: The Experience of Combat in the American Civil War* (New York, 1987); Thomas J. Leonard, *Above the Battle: War-Making in America from Appomattox to Versailles* (New York, 1978).

61. Stefan Lorant, "The Boy in the Window," *American Heritage*, June 1955, 24–25; and EKR reminiscences in speech to the Woman's Roosevelt Memorial Association, Mar. 15, 1933, *Roosevelt House Bulletin*, Spring 1933; MSEB to SEW, Mar. 12, 1862, TRC-HU; *Theodore Roosevelt's Diaries of Boyhood and Youth* (New York, 1928), 162, 159, 155; the 30,000 Union soldiers who lost a limb in the war were more likely to be unemployed and homeless than their peers who had not met a surgeon's knife: Kelly, *National Home*, 10.

62. TRSR to MBR, Dec. 10, 1861, TRC-HU.

63. "They worshipped him": ARL, ORHO-COL; MOR 2:1443; Frances Theodora (Smith) Parsons, *Perchance Some Day* (privately printed, 1951), 261; TR, Private Diary, Dec. 11, 1878, TRP-LC.

64. ARC-MS; AUTO, 11. Mittie's stepbrother received no punishment for the crime but a Grand Tour of Europe; Mrs. Bulloch received affectionate letters from her former slaves after she sold Bulloch Hall and moved north. She had been responsible for gaining membership in the local church for local slaves, a practice which was discontinued after she left Roswell: Luke Mounar to MSEB, Nov. 8, 1858, TRC-HU.

65. AUTO, 11; CRR, *My Brother*, 17. Theodore's grandmother fasted and prayed through the grim battle news. Her depression and frequent outburst of tears after Confederate defeats put a damper on the household, especially on the small children who depended so much on her labors. She could not ignore the fact that Thee served on the 1864 Union League Club executive committee which judged secession "a crime," not a right. When he came home for good, Thee threw himself into monumental Union League projects: sending over 80,000 turkeys to the Union army and navy's 1863 Thanksgiving dinner. While Mittie and Thee enjoyed socializing at a brilliant reception they held downstairs on New Year's Day in 1864, Grandmother Bulloch, in a much more dour mood, sat upstairs sewing clothes to give to the poor children who came to Thee for help. Despondent when Confederate defeat seemed imminent, Grandmother Bulloch lapsed into a long illness which required Mittie or her sisters Susan West or Anna Bulloch to be in constant attendance. In July 1864, when front-page headlines announced that her stepson's ship, the *Alabama*, had been sunk off the coast of France, Grandmother Bulloch's grief and pain sundered her from the rejoicing that rang out across the North. Grandmother Bulloch finally died—within days of Theodore's sixth birthday in 1864. Anna Bulloch admitted that her mother's "heart was broken and I cannot wish her back now in all this trouble": ABG to Georgia King, Aug. 25, [1865], Thomas Butler King Papers, #1252, SHC; ABG to cousin, Jan. 23, 1866, Bulloch Family Papers #2750, SHC; Bellows, *Historical Sketch of the Union League*, 68–70, P. Kelly, *Creating a National Home*; MSEB to SEW, Jan. 1, 1864 and n.d. [December 1863], TRC-HU.

66. MBR to TRSR, Dec. 15, 1861, TRC-HU; MSEB to SEW, June 22 and Aug. 13, 1862, TRC-HU.

67. TR's speech at Bull Run in *New York World*, Nov. 16, 1902.

68. "Guidelines for the Diagnosis and Management of Asthma," *Pediatric Asthma Allergy and Immunology* 5, no. 2 (Summer 1991); P. M. Yellowlees and R. E. Ruffin, "Psychological Defenses and Coping Styles in Patients Following a Life-threatening Attack of Asthma," *Chest* 95 (1989): 1298–1303; Allan M. Weinstein, *Asthma: The Complete Guide to Self-Management of Asthma and Allergies for Parents and Their Families* (New York, 1987); TRSR-LB; albuterol, corticosteroids, cromolyn, and theophylline are commonly used today, but did not exist then. Coffee was the only stimulant available at the time that had an effect similar to theophylline, and TR became a lifelong heavy drinker of coffee, which probably served to reduce his asthma symptoms. Although there is no way to know for sure, TR probably had multiple allergies. McCullough traces one of the causes of TR's asthma to the boy's "peculiar and memorable fear of church," and dislike of the confining way his family

observed the Sabbath, 103; Paul Russell Cutright, *Theodore Roosevelt: The Making of a Conservationist* (Urbana, Ill., 1985), 22, refutes the Sabbath theory.

69. MBR to ARC, n.d. and July 31, 1870, TRC-HU; A. D. Rockwell, M.D., *Rambling Recollections: An Autobiography* (New York, 1920), 263; Dr. Metcalfe also diagnosed Theodore as having "strenmas opthalmia": MSEB to SEW, Apr. 8, 1863, TRC-HU; John S. Haller, Jr., *American Medicine in Transition, 1840–1910* (Chicago, 1981), 50; see also *n.* 40–41.

70. *Diaries of Boyhood and Youth,* 77.

71. Rockwell, *Recollections,* 261–63; TR's continuing acquaintance and correspondence with A. D. Rockwell runs until 1913, TR files, TRP-SAHI; George M. Beard, *American Nervousness: Its Causes and Consequences* (1881; reprint, New York, 1972), 287; George Stocking, Jr., *Victorian Anthropology* (New York, 1987), and *Race, Culture, and Evolution* (New York, 1968); Stephen Jay Gould, *The Mismeasure of Man* (New York, 1981).

72. Rockwell, *Recollections,* 261–63; Richard L. Bushman, *The Refinement of America: Persons, Houses, Cities* (New York, 1992), 443; Haller and Haller, *Physician and Sexuality in Victorian America,* 14; Beard, *American Nervousness,* 120–21; Whorton, *Crusaders,* 148–50.

73. Rockwell, *Recollections,* 261; G. M. Beard and A. D. Rockwell, *Practical Treatise on the Medical and Surgical Uses of Electricity* (New York: W. Wood & Co., 1881).

74. ERD, memorandum based on talk with EKR, Apr. 5, 1948, in possession of Edith Derby Williams; Hermann Hagedorn, "Talk with TR," SUBJ-TRC.

75. AUTO, 14.

76. MBR to ARC, Aug. 19 and 21, 1870, TRC-HU; TRSR to MBR, Sept. 2, 1870, TRSR-LB; MBR to ARC, July 25, 1870, TRC-HU; Sklar, "All Hail to Pure Cold Water!" 247; Haller and Haller, *Physician and Sexuality,* 26, 31; John Bell, M.D., *The Mineral and Thermal Springs of the United States and Canada* (Philadelphia, 1855), 51; some doctors believed that mineral waters were useful in the treatment of asthma: Cayleff, *Wash and Be Healed,* and Donegan, "*Hydropathic Highway.*"

77. TRSR to ARC, Aug. 14 and 23, 1870, TRC-HU. Mittie also followed dietary restrictions recommended by water-cure doctors, and even encouraged Elliott to improve his weak health by following the technique popularized by health reformer Sylvester Graham, chewing food very slowly to aid digestion.

78. *Diaries of Boyhood and Youth,* 237, 236, *Letters from Theodore Roosevelt to Anna Roosevelt Cowles,* 1. Other members were spending the summers in Oyster Bay by the late 1860s including C.V.S., Mary, and Silas Weir Roosevelt; see Silas Weir Roosevelt to ARC, Aug. 5, [n.y.], Oct. 29 and Aug. 20, 1869, and Mary West Roosevelt to ARC, n.d., TRC-HU.

79. Sklar, "All Hail to Pure Cold Water!" 253; Sklar, *Beecher,* 206. Resorts were filled with "multitudes of girls" but among men only "the solitary invalid, or clergyman, or artist": William Dean Howells, *The Rise of Silas Lapham* (New York, 1963), 27. Brace quoted in Hans Huth, *Nature and the American: Three Centuries of Changing Attitudes* (Berkeley, 1957), 108; RBR also ridiculed resorts in *Love and Luck: The Story of a Summer's Loitering on the Great South Bay* (New York, 1886).

80. George William Curtis, *Potiphar Papers* (New York, 1856), 133.

81. Ibid., 5, 29, 17; AUTO, 5.

82. Higginson, "Barbarism and Civilization," in *Out-door Papers,* 112. Many late-Victorian men believed that, because of these unsettling changes among women, men's power in society was at risk. Therefore men tried to etch out more carefully what they believed to be the essential and unchangeable—the so-called natural differences between the sexes. In science, medicine, the new social sciences, and politics, the late-Victorian age witnessed American men's quest for sexual essentials that would help them draw the line around

proper male rights and set the limits for the expansion in women's power that was well under way. Late-Victorian men "increasingly defined women as separate from and unlike men," at the same time they struggled to achieve redefinition and reassurance about what was truly masculine: Carroll Smith-Rosenberg, *Disorderly Conduct: Visions of Gender in Victorian America* (New York, 1985), 89. The men in the Roosevelt family watched even minor rearrangements in the sexual status quo with apprehension. When New York's women writers and professionals, led by Jane Cunningham Croly, founded the all-female Sorosis Club, Theodore's Uncle Rob wrote them a sarcastic letter asking to be admitted to their membership. Sorosis refused. TR wrote Higginson later attesting to the influence of his muscular Christian writings on his later views, TR to Thomas Wentworth Higginson, April 16, 1894, Theodore Roosevelt Papers, 1891–1935, in the Clifton Waller Barrett Library, Accession #5844, 5844-a, 5488-b, Albert H. and Shirley Small Special Collections Library, University of Virginia, Charlottesville, Va.

83. AUTO, 21; Parsons, *Perchance*, 28; Henry Fairfield Osborn, "Roosevelt, Student of Nature," *New York Sun*, Nov. 3, 1921.

84. Hermann Hagedorn, *The Boys' Life of Theodore Roosevelt* (New York, 1922), 22; AUTO, 29; MBR to ARC, July 28, 1868, TRC-HU.

85. Unidentified Bulloch relative note, n.d. [could be 1868 because of the reference to Mittie's trip south], enclosed in letter by Emma Izard, Bulloch Family Papers #2750, #19, SHC; MBR to ARC, n.d. [1868], TRC-HU.

86. MOR 1:3; ARC, *Women's Roosevelt Memorial Bulletin* 1, no. 3 (April 1920); MBR to ABG, July 28, 1872, TRC-HU; Putnam, *Theodore Roosevelt*, 79.

87. MBR to ABG, n.d., 1869, TRC-HU.

88. AUTO, 17; "An Autobiography of Albert S. Bickmore," with a historical sketch of the founding and early development of the American Museum of Natural History, typescript manuscript, 1908, Rare Book Room, American Museum of Natural History, New York; "First Annual Report of the American Museum of Natural History" (New York, 1870); Geoffrey T. Hellman, *Bankers, Bones and Beetles: The First Century of the American Museum of Natural History* (Garden City, N.Y., 1969), 23; John Richard Saunders, *The World of Natural History* (New York, 1952), 16–17; TR, "Record of the Roosevelt Museum," TRC-HU.

89. Martin Green, *The Mount Vernon Street Warrens: A Boston Story, 1860–1910* (New York, 1989); Aline B. Saarinen, *The Proud Possessors: The Lives, Times, and Tastes of Some Adventurous American Art Collectors* (New York, 1958); Williams Adams Brown, *Morris Ketchum Jesup* (New York, 1910), 138–41; Brian M. Fagan, *Rape of the Nile: Tomb Robbers, Tourists, and Archaeologists in Egypt* (New York, 1975); Douglass Shand-Tucci, *The Art of Scandal: The Life and Times of Isabella Stewart Gardner* (New York, 1997); Neil Harris, *Humbug: The Art of P. T. Barnum* (Boston, 1973), 173; Amy Henderson and Adrienne L. Kaeppler, eds., *Exhibiting Dilemmas: Issues of Representation at the Smithsonian* (Washington, D.C., 1997); Mittie collected ceramic art.

90. Higginson, *Out-door Papers*, 109–10. For a discussion of Primitive Masculinity see Dalton, "Early Life," 218–20, and Rotundo, *American Manhood*, 227–32, 287; also Marianna Torgovnick, *Gone Primitive: Savage Intellects, Modern Lives* (Chicago, 1990). Jesup promoted forest preservation as well as museums and urban reform: Ronald Rainger, *An Agenda for Antiquity: Henry Fairfield Osborn & Vertebrate Paleontology at the American Museum of Natural History, 1890–1935* (Tuscaloosa, Ala., 1991), 56–65, 110–22. Osborn praised the revival of Stone Age virtues by museums and contact with nature; he also encouraged research on the "missing link" and sent Roy Chapman Andrews to look for human origins in Central Asia. TR admired Osborn's work on Stone Age men; unlike TR, Osborn held on to notions of racial superiority and the idea of "a racial soul" past 1910 and eventually advocated eugenics and Nazi racial extermination: see Rainger, 147–51; Stanley Diamond, *In Search of the Primi-*

tive: A Critique of Civilization (New Brunswick, N.J., 1974); Gail Bederman, *Manliness and Civilization: A Cultural History of Gender and Race in the United States, 1880–1917* (Chicago, 1995); Donna Haraway, *Primate Visions: Gender, Race and Nature in Modern Science* (New York, 1989).

91. Paul R. Cutright, *Theodore Roosevelt the Naturalist* (New York, 1956); RBR, *Game Birds of the North Coasts and Lakes of the Northern States of America* (New York, 1866), 102–103; RBR, *The Game Fish of the Northern States and British Provinces* (New York, 1865); RBR, *Five Acres Too Much* (New York, 1885); William Irvine, *Apes, Angels, and Victorians: Darwin, Huxley, and Evolution* (New York, 1972); Sherrie L. Lyons, "Convincing Men They Are Monkeys," in Alan P. Barr, ed., *Thomas Henry Huxley's Place in Science and Letters* (Athens, Ga., 1997); Stephen Jay Gould, *Ever Since Darwin: Reflections in Natural History* (New York, 1977); Ernst Mayr, *The Growth of Biological Thought: Diversity, Evolution, and Inheritance* (Cambridge, Mass., 1982), 510.

92. Mayne Reid, *The Boy Hunters; or Adventures in Search of a White Buffalo* (Boston, 1858), 14, 57, and *Afloat in the Forest* (Boston, 1867), *The Boy Slaves* (Boston, 1865), *Bruin: The Great Bearhunt* (Boston, 1864); AUTO, 16–17; CRR clipping, Feb. 16, 1920, TRP-BP.

93. CRR, *My Brother*, 94.

94. Ibid., 34.

95. Based on conversations with ARC, "Each Room Has Many Memories," *Woman's Roosevelt Memorial Bulletin* 1, no. 3 (April 1920): 2–3; Alexander Lambert, "Roosevelt the Companion," MEM 3: xi.

96. Christian F. Reisner, *Roosevelt's Religion* (New York, 1922), 22.

97. CRR, *My Brother*, 36, 209; Parsons, *Perchance*, 28–29; MOR 1:10.

98. "Autograph Attempts at Writing Indian Sign Language," TRC-HU; *Diaries of Boyhood and Youth*, 5.

99. Putnam, *Theodore Roosevelt*, 100; Maud Elliott, "Copybook of the Dresden Literary American Club," TRC-HU; Parsons, *Perchance*, 20, 28.

100. Parsons, *Perchance*, 28; see also ER to MBR, July, n.y. [1873], RFP-FDR.

101. Parsons, *Perchance*, 27.

102. AUTO, 13; ARC-MS; Lincoln Steffens, *The Autobiography of Lincoln Steffens* (New York, 1958), 1:350.

103. MOR 8:829.

104. *Diaries of Boyhood and Youth*, 74; ARL, ORHO-COL.

105. Hagedorn, *Boys' Life*, 39–40; Robert Browning, "The Flight of the Duchess," in *Dramatic Lyrics: The Return of the Druses: A Blot in the 'Scutcheon: Colombe's Birthday Dramatic Romances: A Soul's Tragedy: Luria* (Boston, 1888), 289–309.

CHAPTER TWO: THE DEATH OF THE YOUNG DUKE

1. "sad" in MBR to ABG, June 6, 1869, TRC-HU. TR's diary documented the lingering effects of the war on the boy, for when he "met Jeff Davises [*sic*] son and some harsh words ensued." Thee, on the contrary, stood for reconciliation with the South on every level: *Diaries of Boyhood and Youth*, 16, 63, 103, and in slightly different form TR, Diaries, 1868–1877, TRC-HU; TRSR-LB; AUTO, 15. Compared to Henry James Senior, Mittie and Thee's ideas about educating their children were more limited, and they relied less on tutors and included the girls more than James did: Gay Wilson Allen, *William James, a Biography* (London, 1967); MBR to ABG, June 11, 1869 and n.d., 1869, TRC-HU; R.W.B. Lewis, *The Jameses, a Family Narrative* (New York, 1991), 80.

2. Sylvia Jukes Morris, *Edith Kermit Roosevelt: Portrait of a First Lady* (New York, 1980), 1–2.

3. AUTO, 16–17; EKR to CRR, Feb. 1, n.y. [1869], TRC-HU; MOR 1:4–5; ABG to CRR, Sept. 7, 1869, TRC-HU.

4. ARC-MS; interview, WSC, Jr.; ER to MBR, Oct. 18, 1874, RFP-FDR. Even Mittie confessed that as her invalidism increased she had become "the great laughing stock" of the family. Chronically late and unconscious of the needs of her family (and deaf in the last year or two of her life), she dithered over her inability to complete simple tasks and gave her husband the same pair of slippers for his birthday and Christmas. Yet Mrs. Roosevelt demanded efficient service from others: she hectored her butler to eliminate any household smell that irritated her: MBR to TR, Mar. 8, 1878, and TRSR to SEW, Jan. 6, 1877, TRC-HU; Roosevelt Women Interviews, ARC to CRR, May 25, 1926, TRC-HU; Mittie also admitted to ABG: "I am afraid of Thee," July 28, 1872, TRC-HU.

5. In July 1871, when the Tammany-run city government, fearing violence, banned an Irish Protestant parade to celebrate their victory over Catholics in the Battle of the Boyne, Thee and other city fathers cried foul and accused city hall of being dominated by Irish Catholic influence. At their urging, the governor ordered the parade to go on. Then, simmering old-country hatred between Protestant and Catholic Irish broke into the violent Orange Riot, which killed sixty-two people within a short walk of Twentieth Street; Thee indirectly helped start the riot, but its carnage only confirmed his belief that New York was in a state of crisis and to struggle against sinners "the best men" should reclaim urban politics: TRSR-LB; Thee's correspondence shows him to be anti-Catholic; see Michael A. Gordon, *The Orange Riots: Irish Political Violence in New York City, 1870 and 1871* (Ithaca, N.Y., 1993); Mandelbaum, *Boss Tweed's New York*; Callow, Jr., *Tweed Ring*; Hershkowitz, *Tweed's New York*; Mohr, *Radical Republicans*; Gilfoyle, *City of Eros*. Feminists and male Protestant reformers shared the assumption that abortions were used by immoral women and that reading lewd books would turn children toward the world of sin; Burrows and Wallace, *Gotham*. Tweed had used public funds to support Catholic Church schools and had encouraged the growth of unionism, which employers like Thee feared. The murder rate in New York City soared after the war, and prostitution and the many businesses that profited from it—brothels, concert saloons, theaters—defined more of the public life of the city than ever before. Visiting prostitutes had become a nearly universal recreation for men of Thee's class as well as others—Walt Whitman said nineteen out of twenty men frequented prostitutes. Brothel owners paid the police to look the other way.

6. Thee had been active in the Y.M.C.A. when it expanded in New York, but after it discontinued its early sponsorship of Comstock he also gave money directly to Comstock's Society for the Suppression of Vice, as did other members of the family; see *Annual Reports of the New York Society for the Suppression of Vice* (New York, 1875–90) and Records of the New York Society for the Suppression of Vice, LC; "A Memorandum Respecting New York as a Field for Moral and Christian Effort Among Young Men; Its Present Neglected Condition; and the Fitness of the New York Young Men's Christian Association as a Principal Agency for Its Due Cultivation," 1866, quoted in Heywood Broun and Margaret Leech, *Anthony Comstock: Roundsman for the Lord* (New York, 1927), 78; L. L. Doggett, *Life of Robert R. McBurney* (Cleveland, 1902), 65–80; Paul S. Boyer, *Purity in Print: The Vice-Society Movement and Book Censorship in America* (New York, 1968); D.R.M. Bennett, *Anthony Comstock: His Career of Cruelty and Crime* (New York, 1971); William A. Brown, *Morris K. Jesup: A Character Sketch* (New York, 1910); *Resolutions in Appreciation of Morris K. Jesup* (New York, 1908); Lowitt, *Dodge*, 321; Charles H. Hopkins, *John R. Mott: A Biography* (Grand Rapids, Mich., 1979); Comstock quoted in Timothy J. Gilfoyle, "City of Eros: New York City, Prostitution, and the Commercialization of Sex, 1790–1920" (Ph.D. diss., Columbia University, 1987), 313–14; Nicola Beisel, *Imperiled Innocents: Anthony Comstock and Family Reproduction in Victorian America* (Princeton, 1997); Anna Louise Bates, "Protective Custody: A

Feminist Interpretation of Anthony Comstock's Life and Laws" (Ph.D. diss., State University of New York, 1990); George Cooper, *Lost Love: A True Story of Passion, Murder, and Justice in Old New York* (New York, 1994); Eric Homberger, *Scenes from the Life of a City: Corruption and Conscience in Old New York* (New Haven, 1994).

7. Moody stayed with the Roosevelts' close friends during the revivals: Bernard A. Weisberger, *They Gathered at the River: The Story of the Great Revivalists and Their Impact upon Religion in America* (New York, 1979), 302, 205, 216; on Bellevue and charity networks, Hobson, *Recollections of a Happy Life* (New York, 1916), 186; Ira D. Sankey, *My Life and the Story of the Gospel Hymns* (Philadelphia, 1907), 84; William R. Moody, *D. L. Moody* (New York, 1930), 265.

8. Ethel heard Thee's saying about sickness from her father, ERD to KR, Jan. 28, 1918, KBR-LC; Henry Ward Beecher, *Twelve Lectures to Young Men, on Various Important Subjects*, rev. ed. (New York, 1879), 154–57, quoted in Ronald G. Walters, *Primers for Prudery: Sexual Advice to Victorian America* (Englewood Cliffs, N.J., 1974); Bruce Haley, *The Healthy Body and Victorian Culture* (Cambridge, Mass., 1978), 141; AUTO, 29–30. CRR told at least three contradictory versions of this conversation: "Impressions of TR," TRC-HU; *My Brother*, 50; "Piazza Saw Fun and Noisy Romps," *Woman's Roosevelt Memorial Bulletin*, April 1920, SUBJ-TRC.

9. TRSR to TR, Sept. 28, 1876, TRC-HU; CRR, *My Brother*, 50.

10. CRR, *My Brother*, 50; "owe" in TR, Private Diary, June 19, 1878, TRP-LC; "cousins" in ERD, memorandum based on talk with EKR, Apr. 5, 1948, in possession of Edith Derby Williams.

11. Rotundo, *American Manhood*, 51; Joseph Kett, *Rites of Passage: Adolescence in America, 1790 to the Present* (New York, 1977). Victorian society taught boys to negate the female influences of childhood and to separate emotionally from their mothers in order to build a male gender identity; see Rotundo, "Boy Culture," chapter 2 in *American Manhood*.

12. John Wood, "Helped Build Up Roosevelt's Muscle, Back in the 70's," *New York World Magazine*, Jan. 24, 1904, 5; CRR, *My Brother*, 50.

13. However, they might give him added strength to pull air in and out when he was in the middle of a serious attack.

14. AUTO, 30.

15. CRR to William Roscoe Thayer, Aug. 1, 1922, Thayer Papers, Houghton Library (hereafter Houghton).

16. For asthma episodes see EKR to ARC, 1890s letters in TRC; Richard Welling reported: "He entirely outgrew his asthma and the other weaknesses of boyhood days": "My Classmate Theodore Roosevelt," *American Legion Monthly*, January 1929, in Pringle Papers, Notes, TRC-HU.

17. MOR 1:61.

18. Copybook of the Dresden Literary American Club, TRC-HU.

19. Parsons, *Perchance*, 28.

20. AUTO, 20; Parsons, *Perchance*, 64; AUTO, 52.

21. RBR, *Superior Fishing, or, the Striped Bass, Trout, and Black Bass of the Northern States* (New York, 1865), vii; interview with Jean Schermerhorn Roosevelt; AUTO, 18–19; ER to TRSR, n.d., RFP-FDR.

22. AUTO, 43; interview, WSC, Jr.; MBR to ABG, Nov. 27, 1872, TRC-HU.

23. MBR to ABG, Jan. 12 and Feb. 3, 1873, TRC-HU; *Diaries of Boyhood and Youth*, 290; TR to ABG, Jan. 26, 1873, TRC-HU; CRR, *My Brother*, 56–57; TR to EKR, Apr. 13, and CRR to ABG, Dec. 27, 1873, TRC-HU.

24. CRR, *My Brother*, 57; AUTO, 18–19; ARC-MS; interview, WSC, Jr.

25. TR, "Remarks on Birds," 1874, TRC-HU; CRR, *My Brother*, 57; Ellen Emerson

letter quoted in Gay Wilson Allen, *Waldo Emerson: A Biography* (New York, 1981), 661; John McAleer, *Ralph Waldo Emerson: Days of Encounter* (Boston, 1984), 608.

26. CRR, *My Brother*, 80.

27. Elements of disagreement between Mittie and Thee over the proper treatment of TR's invalidism crop up in several letters, but most of the time Thee seems to have been in control of the more stoic approach they took after 1872: MBR to TRSR, August 1873, in Putnam, *Theodore Roosevelt*, 108–109. Mittie responded to her son's illness by writing him detailed accounts of her own symptoms: MBR to TR, July 17, and TR to TRSR, June 29, 8, and July 4, 1873, TRC-HU; ER to TRSR, June 15, 1873, RFP-FDR.

28. AUTO, 23.

29. Holmes, "The Soldier's Faith," May 30, 1895, in *Speeches by Oliver Wendell Holmes, Jr.* (Boston, 1934), 63.

30. Putnam, *Theodore Roosevelt*, 111; TR to TRSR, June 15 and 8, 1873, TRC-HU.

31. TR to ABG, June 15 and 8, and to TRSR, June 15, 1873, TRC-HU.

32. TR to TRSR, July 21, 1873, TRC-HU.

33. "A Woman's Story" and "Mrs. Field Mouse's Dinner Party," Notebook, Dresden Literary American Club, TRC-HU; CRR to TRSR, June 9, 1873. TR and ER had different feelings about Mittie. Mittie still held Elliott on her lap and babied him, but fifteen-year-old Theodore pulled away. In her eyes he would always be her baby, which often infuriated Theodore as he tried to achieve manhood. She aggravated him no end when she refused to stop calling him her "precious Teddy" long after he had sprouted whiskers: MOR 1:8, 13, 14; MBR to TR, Mar. 8, 1878, TRC-HU.

34. ER to Archibald Gracie, Nov. 9, 1873, RFP-FDR; ARC-MS; MOR 1:14; TRSR-LB; clipping, TR Scrapbook, TRC-HU; on the emergence of a national economic elite see Sven Beckert, *The Monied Metropolis: New York City and the Consolidation of the American Bourgeoisie, 1850–1896* (New York, 2001).

35. Ellen H. Fanshawe to EKR, Jan. 28, 1932, TRC-HU.

36. Constance (Mrs. Burton) Harrison, *Recollections Grave and Gay* (New York, 1911), 279; Putnam, *Theodore Roosevelt*, 119; RBR albums formerly in possession of Jean Roosevelt indicate RBR entertained Oscar Wilde in 1882; Lloyd Lewis and Henry Justin Smith, *Oscar Wilde Discovers America* (1882; reprint, New York, 1936), 45; TR to Ellen Gray, Mar. 31, 1897, TRJR-LC.

37. Tranquility was named after her ancestor Daniel Stewart's home Tranquil Hills: Mittie to Cousin Laura, Oct. 7, 1877, Bulloch Papers, SHC; MBR to TR, Mar. 8, 1878, and ARC to ERD, Nov. 24, 1923, TRC-HU.

38. CRR to MBR, Sept. 10, 1878, TRC-HU; after CRR had a serious breakdown TR recommended that she seek treatment from S. Weir Mitchell: WSC, Jr., and Mrs. Margaret Cowles, Corinne Robinson Alsop, Roosevelt Women Interviews, TRC-HU; ERD to Edith Derby Williams, Apr. 26, 1958, TRC-HU; ARL and ERD, ORHO-COL; see also Nicholas Roosevelt, *Theodore Roosevelt: The Man As I Knew Him* (New York, 1967), 29–37.

39. Helen Roosevelt Robinson, Roosevelt Women Interviews, TRC; TR to CRR, July 24, 1880, and "My Mother," Monroe D. Robinson, TRC-HU. Nicholas Roosevelt wrote: "Few people who did not know him well were aware of the intensity of his devotion to all those close to him. It was almost torrential, and constantly subject to spontaneous expression. Under the circumstances I can well understand that he had to take heroic steps to control himself," to Carleton Putnam, Apr. 5, 1958, NR-SYR; *Letters from Theodore Roosevelt to Anna Roosevelt Cowles*, 16.

40. Parsons, *Perchance*, 26; MBR to Laura, Oct. 7, [n.y.], Bulloch Papers, SHC; ARC to CRR, Nov. 24, 1923, and to ERD, Nov. 24, 1923, TRC-HU; *Letters from Theodore Roosevelt to Anna Roosevelt Cowles*, 16, 11.

41. EKR to TR, June 8, 1886, TRC-HU.

42. Ibid.

43. Cutler statement, SUBJ-TRC; Arthur Cutler to TRSR, Sept. 30, 1876, called TR "the brightest boy I ever expect to have," TRJR-LC; Putnam, *Theodore Roosevelt,* 127.

44. ER to TRSR, Oct. 1, 1874, RFP-FDR; McCullough, *Mornings on Horseback,* 145; Putnam, *Theodore Roosevelt,* 111. According to doctors consulted by Joseph Lash, Elliott's attacks were not due primarily to physical causes; TRSR to the Rev. Henry Coit, Oct. 7 and 11, 1875, TRSR-LB; see ER letters 1874–75 in RFP-FDR.

45. ER to Archibald Gracie, May 5, 1874, and ABG to ER, Jan. 8, 1882, RFP-FDR.

46. Elliott asked to go back to St. Paul's because it was hard for him to study at home when Theodore was so far ahead of him: ER to TRSR, Mar. 6, 1875, RFP-FDR.

47. EKR to TR, June 8, 1886, TRC-HU.

48. AUTO, 10.

49. TR to MBR, Mar. 4, 1876, MOR-REJ. Talk about uplifting the poor rang hollow because it was common knowledge that there would be a lot less vice in New York without so many rich brothel customers: Gilfoyle, *City of Eros,* 81–102; Christine Stansell, *City of Women: Sex and Class in New York, 1789–1860* (Urbana, Ill., 1986), 65, 79–139. Though they were fascinated by the recreation of the working class and their public expression of emotion, Protestant moral reformers contained their attraction to other ways by seeking to make other groups bend to their customs; *The Crusade for Children: A Review of Child Life in New York During 75 Years, 1853–1928* (New York, n.d.), 20; George Templeton Strong, *The Diary of George Templeton Strong* (New York, 1974), 4:382; Thomas Wentworth Higginson, *Cheerful Yesterdays: The American Negro; His History and Literature* (New York, 1968), 230; Wilentz, *Chants Democratic,* 263–70. All four Roosevelt children carried on their father's work in some form. Eventually, Theodore and Elliott's daughter Eleanor argued for government to care for society's neediest and aided in the building of a welfare state to guarantee minimum standards of living. She became the architect of the United Nations Declaration of Human Rights, which long after her death raised international expectations for how governments should treat their people. For the next century Thee's descendants credited his influence for their many good works: Joseph P. Lash, *Eleanor and Franklin: The Story of Their Relationship, Based on Eleanor Roosevelt's Private Papers* (New York, 1973), 29; interview, WSC, Jr., Edith Derby Williams.

50. MOR 1:14; William Emlen Roosevelt to ARC, July 13, 1876, TRC-HU; Arthur Cutler to TRSR, Sept. 30, 1876, TRJR-LC. His parents saw the Philadelphia Centennial Exposition with Mrs. Astor.

51. Seeing his father in idealized terms did not make it easier to separate from him. Theodore would sign himself Thee or TR Junior until he was in his twenties, though he didn't mind when Corinne, Mittie, or his college friends called him by the less august name Teddy. After the war Thee had come face-to-face with the kind of man he had paid to go to war with him: he and William Cullen Bryant had been judges when the "Left-Handed Corps" of right-hand amputees vied for penmanship prizes to prove how well they had adapted to their war wounds. Thee already suffered exhaustion and a mysteriously paralyzed hand, and he was being sued for running over someone with his carriage: TRSR-LB; P. Kelly, *National Home,* 58; ABR to ERD, Apr. 26, 1975, and TR to TRSR, Apr. 29, 1877, TRC-HU.

52. TRSR to TR, Oct. 27, 1876, TRC-HU; *Letters from Theodore Roosevelt to Anna Roosevelt Cowles,* 15–16. Thee probably knew Wyman from the Sanitary Commission: Morrill Wyman in Martin Kaufman, Stuart Galishoff, and Todd L. Savitt, eds., *Dictionary of American Medical Biography,* vol. 2 (Westport, Conn., 1984).

53. AUTO, 24; Hermann Hagedorn, interview of Richard Welling, 1880, Harvard, Welling Papers, Houghton.

54. For Harvard history see M. Green, *Mount Vernon Warrens*; Ronald Story, *The Forging of an Aristocracy: Harvard and the Boston Upper Class, 1800–1870* (Middletown, Conn., 1980); Samuel Eliot Morison, ed., *The Development of Harvard University Since the Inauguration of President Eliot, 1869–1929* (Cambridge., Mass, 1930); Morison, *Three Centuries of Harvard* (Cambridge., Mass., 1936); Helen Lefkowitz Horowitz, *Campus Life: Undergraduate Cultures from the End of the Eighteenth Century to the Present* (New York, 1987).

55. "emulation" in Putnam, *Theodore Roosevelt*, 131; Kim Townsend, *Manhood at Harvard: William James and Others* (Cambridge, Mass., 1996), 94–97; "astonishing" in *Letters from Theodore Roosevelt to Anna Roosevelt Cowles*, 16, 19.

56. Macaulay quoted in Mrinalini Sinha, *Colonial Masculinity: The "Manly Englishman" and the "Effeminate Bengali" in the Late Nineteenth Century* (Manchester, Eng., 1995), 15.

57. MOR 1:24; Nathaniel Southgate Shaler, *The Autobiography of Nathaniel Southgate Shaler with a Supplementary Memoir by His Wife* (Boston, 1909), 369; David N. Livingstone, *Nathaniel Southgate Shaler and the Culture of American Science* (London, 1987), 32, 186, 193.

58. On Harvard's muscular Christian atmosphere, Shaler, James, and Dudley Sargent see Townsend, *Manhood*, 31–79, 100–119 (113); Hagedorn interview of Welling, Harvard 1880; MOR 1:21; Morison, *Three Centuries*, 367–68; Phillips Brooks, *Essays and Addresses Religious, Literary and Social* (New York, 1894), 323.

59. Today Phillips Brooks House at Harvard continues the tradition of social service. Brooks, *Essays and Addresses*, 334.

60. Whorton, *Crusaders for Fitness*, 283; Washburn interview, SUBJ-TRC; Donald Wilhelm, *Theodore Roosevelt as an Undergraduate* (Boston, 1910), 9. Sewall later told an interviewer that TR had to bring a doctor with him on his first hunting trip in Maine: Alfred Gordon Munro, "Roosevelt: His Maine and Dakota Days," in SUBJ-TRC.

61. Putnam, *Theodore Roosevelt*, 219, 140; Wilhelm, *Undergraduate*, 32, 25.

62. Harry S. Rand and Charles William Eliot interviews, SUBJ-TRC. on resignation Palmer interview, SUBJ-TRC; Chauncey M. Depew, Speech before the Methodist Ministers' Association at the memorial service for Theodore Roosevelt at their chapel, New York, Jan. 13, 1919, privately printed, 18.

63. TR to MBR, Mar. 4, 1876, MOR-REJ; TRSR to TR, Dec. 16, 1877, TRC-HU; Mrs. Robert Bacon, William Hooper, William H. Thayer, and John Woodbury interviews, SUBJ-TRC. TR played minor roles as secretary of the Hasty Pudding Club, associate member of the Harvard Glee Club, steward on the Harvard Athletic Association board, and member of the board of editors of the Harvard *Advocate*: TR Scrapbook, TRC-HU.

64. *Boston Evening Gazette*, Nov. 9, 1879, 2–3, SUBJ-TRC; *Letters from Theodore Roosevelt to Anna Roosevelt Cowles*, 13.

65. MOR 2:1443; Henry E. Jackson interview, SUBJ-TRC; Dalton, "Early Life," 603.

66. Henry Davis Minot to Dr. Folsom, Apr. 18, 1878, Minot Family Papers, MHS.

67. Henry Davis Minot to TR, December 1879, and to Dr. Folsom, Apr. 18, 1878, Minot Family Papers, MHS; TR and H. D. Minot, *The Summer Birds of the Adirondacks in Franklin County, N.Y.*, pamphlet, TRC-HU.

68. TR to MBR, Mar. 4, 1876, MOR-REJ; TR, Private Diary, Apr. 30, 1878, TRP-LC.

69. Henry Davis Minot to Dr. Folsom, Apr. 18, 1878, and to TR, December 1879, Minot Family Papers, MHS; TR, Private Diary, Sept. 4, 1878, TRP-LC.

70. David M. Jordan, *Roscoe Conkling of New York: Voice in the Senate* (Ithaca, N.Y., 1971), 239–42; Claude Moore Fuess, *Carl Schurz, Reformer (1829–1906)* (New York, 1932), 226; Putnam, *Theodore Roosevelt*, 245; TRSR-LB.

71. For Conkling's attack on Hayes, Venila Lovina Shores, "The Hayes-Conkling Controversy 1877–1879," M.A. thesis, in *Smith College Studies in History* 4, no. 4, (July 1919):

225, 240, 245. TRSR financed and led the anti-Conkling movement. See also DeAlva Stanwood Alexander, *A Political History of the State of New York* (Port Washington, N.Y., 1969), 3:332.

72. Conkling may have had party-building rather than racial justice in mind in his support of a continued federal presence in the South, but when Frederick Douglass was kept off the dais at the opening ceremonies of the Philadelphia Centennial Exposition in 1876 it was Conkling who saw the affront and got Douglass admitted: Dee Alexander Brown, *The Year of the Century: 1876* (New York, 1966), 120.

73. Jordan, *Roscoe Conkling*, 245–46, 264, 271; see also Ari Arthur Hoogenboom, *Rutherford B. Hayes: Warrior and President* (Lawrence, Kans., 1995).

74. Paula Baker, "The Domestication of Politics: Women and American Political Society, 1780–1920," *American Historical Review* 89 (June 1984): 620–47, and Baker, *The Moral Frameworks of Public Life: Gender, Politics, and the State in Rural New York, 1870–1930* (New York, 1991), xiii. In 1894, TR argued in "The Merit System and Manliness in Politics" that a reformer needed to be manly to be credible in politics, and Richard Hofstadter credited him with overcoming the negative "stigma of effeminacy" with which Conkling and others had branded reformers: "Idealists and Professors and Sore-heads: The Genteel Reformers," *Columbia University Forum* 5, no. 2 (Spring 1962): 9; see also his *Anti-intellectualism in American Life* (New York, 1966).

75. MOR 1:30.

76. "fear" in TRSR to TR, Dec. 16, 1877, TRC-HU; "scientific man" in AUTO, 25.

77. MOR 1:30.

78. TR, Private Diary, Jan. 2 and Dec. 11, 1878, TRP-LC.

79. MOR 1:31; Elliott's Diary, Feb. 9, 1878, TRC-HU.

80. ARC-MS; TRSR to TR, Oct. 27, 1876, TRC-HU; TR, Private Diary, Mar. 7, 1878, TRP-LC.

81. TR, Private Diary, Mar. 3, 16, 6, 5, and 10, 1878, TRP-LC.

82. TR, Private Diary, July 11 and Apr. 18, 1878, TRP-LC; TR's Bible was in possession of WSC, Jr.

83. MBR to ARC, Sept. 9 and Jan. 18, 1880, TRC-HU; "proof of weakness" in E. Anthony Rotundo, "Manhood in America: The Northern Middle Class, 1770–1920" (Ph.D. diss., Brandeis University, 1982), 299; Dalton, "Early Life," 94; TR to CRR, Mar. 17, 1878, MOR-REJ; TR to Hal Minot, Jan. 11, 1879, MOR-REJ (also copy in Minot Family Papers, MHS).

84. MOR 1:28; he noted that his cousins had already gone into business, TR, Private Diary, June 13, 1878, TRP-LC.

85. N. Roosevelt, *Front Row Seat*, 25.

86. Mark Sullivan, "Visit Recalls Past of Mrs. Roosevelt," *Evening Star*, Aug. 11, 1932, in Roosevelt Women folder, SUBJ-TRC. S. Morris, *Edith Kermit Roosevelt*, offers the best description of EKR's relationship with the two Roosevelts in the 1870s; see 55–64.

87. TR, Private Diary, Aug. 21, 22, and 24, 1878, TRP-LC; Teague, *Mrs. L*, 30.

88. TR to ARC, Sept. 20, 1886, TRC-HU; S. Morris, *Edith Kermit Roosevelt*, 60–61; TR, Private Diary, Aug. 21, 22, and 24, 1878, TRP-LC.

89. TR, Private Diary, Nov. 2, 1878, TRP-LC.

90. See Geddes and the Rev. Prescott Evans interviews, SUBJ-TRC. There was some debate about whether the play was *Medea*, but two classmates seem to have agreed that this and similar events occurred late in TR's college career, Hagedorn interview of Richard Welling, Feb. 10, 1925, SUBJ-TRC. Years later when he sued an editor for calling him a drunk in the 1912 campaign, he was careful to testify under oath that never "in his maturity" had he been drunk, but he did not stop friends and family members from declaring that they

were sure he had never been drunk in his life; see *Roosevelt vs. Newett, A Transcript of the Testimony Taken and Depositions Read at Marquette, Michigan* (privately printed by W. Emlen Roosevelt, 1914).

91. Mrs. Robert Bacon interview, 1921, SUBJ-TRC.

92. George Santayana and Henry Adams quoted in Martin Green, *The Problem of Boston* (New York, 1966), 126, 215; Putnam, *Theodore Roosevelt*, 171; Thomas Lee interview, SUBJ-TRC. Brahmins were more likely to be abolitionists than Knickerbockers and more intellectually inclined: John T. Morse, Jr., *Memoir of Colonel Henry Lee with Selections from His Writings and Speeches* (Boston, 1905), 216; Edith Wharton, *The Age of Innocence* (New York, 1962), 119. George Cabot Lee opened the Union Safe Deposit vaults and invested heavily in real estate and railroads: History of Lee, Higginson & Co., Lee Papers, MHS; HCL to Thomas Wentworth Higginson, Oct. 10, 1907, Higginson Papers, Houghton.

93. TR to Hal Minot, July 5, 1880, Minot Family Papers, MHS; MOR 1:43.

94. George Cabot Lee, Jr., interviews, SUBJ-TRC; TR to MBR, Nov. 29, 1879, TRC-HU.

95. "flirt" in TR, Private Diary, Apr. 3, 1879, TRP-LC; "angel" in TR to ARC, Nov. 10, 1878, TRC-HU; MOR 1:35, 38.

96. TR to ARC, Aug. 25, and, n.d. [January], and to CRR, Oct. 13, 1879, MOR-REJ. Both Corinne and Fanny Smith Parsons later told Henry Pringle about the duel. CRR corrected the manuscript draft of Pringle's searing biography of TR; see CRR to Henry Pringle, Sept. 22, 1930, Pringle I, Biographers' Papers, TRC-HU. Otto H. Williams, Jr., to Charles F. Sprague (in TR's handwriting), Mar. 20, 1879, MOR-REJ and TR Scrapbook. Cleveland Amory, *Last Resorts* (New York, 1952), 317, claimed TR tried to kill himself over Alice but there is no corroborating evidence to prove it; in a similar circumstance TR's friend John Jay Chapman became so upset about a tumultuous courtship that he held his hand in a fire and burned it so badly it had to be amputated. Leverett Saltonstall Diary observes TR's behavior as relatively normal, Saltonstall Family Correspondence, Saltonstall Family Papers, MHS. Though a certain diagnosis is impossible, TR displayed a tendency toward cyclothymia, a common mood disorder which a small portion of high-functioning and extremely bright people suffer. His moods were a gift of creative energy and a rush of concentration when he needed it, though at times they took the form of sleeplessness and restlessness. It did not reach the disorder level because he kept it under control for most of his adult life, especially with the help of his second wife and their children, who learned that "taking care of Father" was necessary. Hypomanic symptoms include "inflated self-esteem or grandiosity," "decreased need for sleep, pressure of speech, flight of ideas, distractibility, increased involvement in goal-directed activities or psychomotor agitation," risk-taking, impulsiveness, and a "persistently elated, expansive, or irritable mood": *Diagnostic and Statistical Manual of Mental Disorders*, 4th ed., DSM-IV (Washington, D.C., 1994): 335–36; see Kay Redfield Jamison, *Touched by Fire: Manic-Depressive Illness and the Artistic Temperament* (New York, 1995) and *An Unquiet Mind: A Memoir of Moods and Madness* (New York, 1995).

97. TR, Private Diary, Oct. 10, 29, and 6, 1879; "drowning" in May 14, 1879, TRP-LC; TR to Henry Davis Minot, Jan. 11, 1879, Minot Family Papers, MHS.

98. TR to CRR, Oct. 13, 1879, and to ARC, n.d. [January 1880], MOR-REJ.

99. Henry Davis Minot to TR, December 1879, Minot Family Papers, MHS.

100. Ibid.

101. TR, Private Diary, Jan. 30, 1880, TRP-LC.

102. TR, Private Diary, Feb. 13, 1880, TRP-LC; TR to AHLR, Aug. 15, 1880, TRC-HU.

103. TR, "The Practicability of Equalizing Men and Women Before the Law," TRC-HU; TR, Private Diary, July 29, 1880, TRP-LC; Francis Parkman, "The Woman Question," *North American Review* 129 (October 1879): 303–21.

104. TR, Private Diary, Oct. 3, 1880, TRP-LC; TR to Henry Davis Minot, Feb. 13, 1880, Minot Family Papers, MHS; AHLR to MBR, Feb. 3, and to TR, Oct. 16, and TR to AHLR, Oct. 17, 1880, TRC-HU.

105. *Letters from Theodore Roosevelt to Anna Roosevelt Cowles*, 39; Sargent in Putnam, *Theodore Roosevelt*, 198.

106. TR, Private Diary, Oct. 3, 1880, TRP-LC; TR to MBR, Aug. 1 and Sept. 9, 1880, TRC-HU; Saltonstall Diary, MHS; "exercise" in AHLR to MBR, July 1, 1881, TRC-HU; "wild spirits" in Parsons, *Perchance*, 43.

CHAPTER THREE: "MY HEART WAS NEARLY BREAKING"

1. Putnam, *Theodore Roosevelt*, 198; Amos A. Lawrence Diaries and Account Books, Lawrence Papers, MHS.

2. Putnam, *Theodore Roosevelt*, 210 *n*. 31.

3. TR, Private Diary, Oct. 27, 1880, TRP-LC.

4. TR to John Burgess, Nov. 9, 1901, to MBR, Nov. 4, n.y. [1880], and to ARC, Nov. 10, n.y. [1880], MOR-REJ; SUBJ-TRC; Richard Hofstadter, *Social Darwinism in American Thought* (New York, 1955), 174–75.

5. ER to ARC, Aug. 29, 1880, RFP-FDR; ARC to AHLR, Feb. 1, 1880, TRC-HU; CRR to Henry Pringle, Sept. 22, 1930, Pringle Papers, TRC-HU; MBR to ER, Dec. 25, [1881], RFP-FDR; TR, Private Diary, June 11, 1878, TRP-LC.

6. TR to AHLR, Mar. 28, 1881, TRC-HU; TR, Private Diary, Dec. 20, 1880, TRP-LC; AHLR to TR, Apr. 5, 1881, TRC-HU; Michael Teague, "Theodore Roosevelt and Alice Hathaway Lee: A New Perspective," *Harvard Library Bulletin* 33, no. 3 (Summer 1985): 225–38.

7. AHLR to CRR, May 19, 1880, and TR to CRR, June 16, 1881, TRC-HU; TR to Bill Sewall, Sept. 5, 1887, TRP-LC.

8. TR to AHLR, Nov. 5 and Apr. 6, and AHLR to TR, Oct. 17, 1881, TRC-HU.

9. MBR to ER, n.d. [1880], and Dec. 7, 1880, RFP-FDR.

10. M. Hagedorn's Notes, Corinne Robinson Alsop, Roosevelt Women Interviews, TRC-HU; ER to ARC, May 8, 1881, RFP-FDR. TR to AHLR, Oct. 14, 1881, TRC-HU.

11. Garfield as a congressman had seriously considered restoring property qualifications for voting and he advocated Chinese exclusion: John G. Sproat, *"The Best Men": Liberal Reformers in the Gilded Age* (New York, 1971), 104; see also Ari Arthur Hoogenboom, *Outlawing the Spoils: A History of the Civil Service Reform Movement, 1865–1883* (Urbana, Ill., 1968); Andrew Gyory, *Closing the Gate: Race, Politics, and the Chinese Exclusion Act* (Chapel Hill, N.C., 1998), 191.

12. Allan Peskin, "Who Were the Stalwarts? Who Were Their Rivals?: Republican Factions in the Gilded Age," *Political Science Quarterly* 99, no. 4 (Winter 1984–Winter 1985): 703–16. The Edmunds anti-polygamy bill passed in 1882 and the Edmunds-Tucker Act took the vote away from Utah's women: see Joan Iversen, *The Antipolygamy Controversy in U.S. Women's Movements, 1880–1925: A Debate on the American Home* (New York, 1997); George F. Edmunds: Centenary Exercises, 1828–1928 (privately printed, 1928); Charles E. Rosenberg, *The Trial of Assassin Guiteau: Psychiatry and Law in the Gilded Age* (Chicago, 1968); Hoogenboom, *Hayes*, 471; Henry Adams believed Blaine had somehow put Guiteau up to the killing, Edward Chalfant, *Better in Darkness: A Biography of Henry Adams, His Second Life 1862–1891* (Hamden, Conn., 1994), 816.

13. Clipping, *New York Evening Post*, Nov. 7, 1881, and "hereditary claims" in Dr. A. S. Heath to TR, Oct. 27, 1881, TR Scrapbook, TRC-HU; *New York Times*, Nov. 10, 1881.

14. One of TR's western friends, Seth Bullock, hired repeaters from a fort in North Dakota: Howard R. Lamar, *Dakota Territory, 1861–1889* (New Haven, 1956), 165; on the Irish, TR, Private Diary, Jan. 2, 1883, TRP-LC.

15. Burrows and Wallace, *Gotham*, 862; MBR to ER, Dec. 4, 1881, RFP-FDR; Frederick S. Wood, ed., *Roosevelt as We Knew Him: The Personal Recollections of One Hundred and Fifty of His Friends and Associates* (Philadelphia, 1927), 9.

16. Memorandum of Hermann Hagedorn's conversation with I. Hunt and George Spinney, SUBJ-TRC; Kevin J. Mumford, " 'Lost Manhood' Found: Male Sexual Impotence and Victorian Culture in the United States," in John C. Fout and Maura Shaw Tantillo, eds., *American Sexual Politics: Sex, Gender, and Race Since the Civil War* (Chicago, 1993), 86–87.

17. AUTO, 64, 88.

18. Eileen Boris, *Home to Work: Motherhood and the Politics of Industrial Homework in the United States* (New York, 1995), 37.

19. Harbaugh, *Power and Responsibility*, 40–41; Thee worked to expand the reach of government responsibility on several fronts, successfully lobbying state and city officials to cover more of the costs of private charities, including his Orthopaedic Dispensary, and defending federal veterans' benefits and the federal soldiers' homes, which became the major federal welfare program of the nineteenth century. Thee had also moved beyond private philanthropy to chair the New York Bureau of Charities and serve on the State Board of Charities because he said they had "a power for good beyond anything unaided by the State." To raise money for his public causes he had sought to use visual images, much like the later efforts of Jacob Riis, Lewis Hine, and progressive reformers, to show prospective donors shocking photographs of children with diseases of the spine and hip joints. He and his partner in reform, Josephine Shaw Lowell, also used the state board as a public agency empowered to regulate and rid New York of corrupt and inefficient private philanthropies. He praised the international trend toward nation-building by organizing America's celebration of Italian unification. He raised funds for the Cesnola Collection and served on the committee that agreed to a separate Metropolitan Museum building in May 1871 and supported Hobson's Bellevue Training School for Nurses: TRSR-LB; D. Willis James in State Charities Aid Association, *Theodore Roosevelt: Memorial Meeting*, 34; TRSR to ARC, June 6, 1875, TRC-HU. Thee had been an advocate of hiring Civil War veterans with amputated hands and legs, and he had set up the Soldier's Employment Bureau and the Protective War Claims Association to help vets get back pay and jobs: Kelly, *National Home*. About a quarter of the federal budget went to veterans' benefits after the war; see Theda Skocpol, "America's First Social Security System: The Expansion of Benefits to Civil War Veterans," *Political Science Quarterly* 108, no. 1 (1993): 85–116.

20. AUTO, 86; TR to AHLR, Dec. 31, 1882, TRC-HU; Howard Lawrence Hurwitz, *Theodore Roosevelt and Labor in New York State, 1880–1900* (New York, 1943), 103; New York State Assembly, *Journal* (1884); TR to A. J. Heath, Mar. 12, 1883, the cartoon in *The Judge*, Mar. 3, 1883, in private collection of Lawrence and Doris Budner; Frederick Law Olmsted, *Forty Years of Landscape Architecture: Central Park* (Cambridge, Mass., c. 1928, 1973) 2:154.

21. TR to Olmsted, Mar. 19, 1882, in MOR 1:63; Mark Wahlgren Summers, *Rum, Romanism, and Rebellion: The Making of the President 1884* (Chapel Hill, N.C., 2000), 120; AUTO, 77–78.

22. MOR 1:50.

23. TR to AHLR, Oct. 14, 1881, TRC-HU. TR visited with James D. Bulloch several times: on both his Grand Tours, when Bulloch came to New York in 1877, and on his 1881 honeymoon with Alice; see Bulloch Papers, SHC. Richard W. Turk, *The Ambiguous Relationship: Theodore Roosevelt and Alfred Thayer Mahan* (New York, 1987). Contributions in *Military Studies* 63 (New York, 1987); Frank Conahan argues that TR's early advocacy of

naval preparedness stemmed from the lessons of the Confederate navy: "Theodore Roosevelt: Navalist Before Mahan," Harvard Extension School paper June 21, 1999. TR encouraged his uncle James D. Bulloch to write *The Secret Service of the Confederate States in Europe* (London, 1883); Peter Karsten, "The Nature of 'Influence': Roosevelt, Mahan and the Concept of Sea Power," *American Quarterly* 23, no. 4 (October 1971): 585–600; Mark Russell Shulman, "The Influence of History upon Sea Power: The Navalist Reinterpretation of the War of 1812," *Journal of Military History* 56, no. 2 (April 1982): 183–206.

24. MEM 7:xviii.

25. "abilities" in MOR 1:50; TRSR-LB shows Thee was not sympathetic to Grant's threatened intervention in Cuba; Robert Seager II, "Ten Years Before Mahan: The Unofficial Case for the New Navy, 1880–1890," *Mississippi Valley Historical Review* 40 (1953): 491–512.

26. TR to AHLR, Apr. 6, 1881, TRC-HU; see S. Morris, *Edith Kermit Roosevelt*, 69–75.

27. AUTO, 55; ARL interview, 1977; Election Expenses of TR in 1882, and George Haven Putnam, Partnership Agreement to Form the Firm of George Putnam's Sons, TRC-HU; MOR 1:56; see Cutwright, *Making of a Conservationist*, 132. Pringle, *Biography*, 39.

28. ER's Diary, TRC-HU; "ladies not" in EKR quoted in notes on January 1941 interview with Jean S. Schermerhorn Roosevelt, TRC-HU.

29. ER to ARC, May 8, 1881, RFP-FDR. MBR told Theodore how she preferred to sled with Elliott: MBR to ER, June 16, 1882, RFP-FDR. Mittie's preoccupations did not interest Theodore, but Elliott listened to her even when her mind wandered: ABG to ER, July 1, 1883, RFP-FDR.

30. TR to Mr. and Mrs. John Ellis Roosevelt, Sept. 4 and Aug. 28, 1881, and to John Ellis Roosevelt, Aug. 28, 1881, TRC-HU; see "The Roosevelt Family in America: A Genealogy," 46–47.

31. See Teague, "Theodore Roosevelt and Alice Hathaway Lee"; TR to AHLR, Apr. 6, 1882, TRC-HU.

32. "bored" in TR to CRR, July 1, 1883, TRC-HU; "excitement" in Henry Davis Minot to William Minot, Aug. 21, 1883, Minot Family Papers, MHS.

33. TR to MBR, Sept. 4, and to AHLR, Sept. 14, and 23, 1883, TRC-HU; ARC to Hermann Hagedorn, n.d., TRP-BP.

34. TR to AHLR, Sept. 23, 1883, TRC-HU.

35. TR to AHLR, Feb. 6, 1884, TRC-HU.

36. Memorandum of Hermann Hagedorn's conversation with I. Hunt and George Spinney, SUBJ-TRC; MOR 1:64–65; see TR to AHLR, November 1883–February 1884, TRC-HU.

37. AHLR to TR, Feb. 11, 1884, TRC-HU; ABG, "Account of Birth of Alice [Roosevelt] Longworth and Death of Alice Hathaway [Lee] Roosevelt," TRC-HU. The day Alice died TR wrote: "The light has gone out of my life": Private Diary, Feb. 14, 1884, TRP-LC.

38. TR did not rush home when news of illness or labor pains reached him; he grew uneasy when a loved one was ill and his usual warmth failed him. Edith wrote that when she was in pain their son Ted was "splendid in a sick room. I shall never forget how I clung to his hand & he recited King Olaf and Don Juan—Darling Father was not good for he always gave me the feeling that he was restless & he was too strenuous in his recitation!": EKR to ERD, July 5, 1927, TRC-HU; ABG, "Account of Birth of Alice [Roosevelt] Longworth and Death of Alice Hathaway [Lee] Roosevelt," TRC-HU.

39. Peabody wrote this Feb. 19, 1884: Frank D. Ashburn, *Peabody of Groton: A Portrait* (New York, 1944), 104; TR, "The Strenuous Life," MEM 15:281; MOR 1:67–68; TR mentions Alice in TR to Henry Davis Minot, Feb. 21 and Mar. 9, 1884, Minot Family Papers, MHS; TR also mentions Alice in TR to E. N. Buxton, June 8, 1899, MOR-REJ.

40. "not . . . so devoted" in Teague, *Mrs. L*, 20; TR, "In Memory of My Darling Wife Alice Hathaway Roosevelt and of My Beloved Mother, Martha Bulloch Roosevelt" (New York, 1884); Rosenberg, *Assassin Guiteau*, 246; TR feared there was a "veritable fatality in our family": TR to ARC, Feb. 3, 1895, MOR-REJ.

41. TR, Private Diary, Feb. 16, 1884, TRP-LC. In addition to the inheritance from his father he owned railroad stock, stock in the United Trust Company, shares of Roosevelt and Son, and a partnership in Putnam's. Russell Sturgis had been the architect of the West Fifty-seventh Street house, but TR hired Rich and Lamb to design and John A. Wood to build Sagamore Hill. Christopher Grant La Farge, the son of the painter and stained-glass artist of Boston's Trinity Church, John La Farge, designed the North Room addition in 1905 (it is finished in part in Philippine mahogany). The original 155 acres TR bought in 1883 cost $30,000, but when he needed money he sold 95 acres to Bamie, Uncle Jim (James A. Roosevelt), and other relatives. The name Leeholm is probably a play on Holm Lea, Charles Sprague Sargent's estate near Alice's home in Chestnut Hill; Sargent was a pioneer conservationist and co-designer (with Frederick Law Olmsted) of the Boston Park System and director of Arnold Arboretum and director of Harvard's Botanic Garden: Cynthia Zaitzevsky, *Frederick Law Olmsted and the Boston Park System* (Cambridge, Mass., 1982), 58–64.

42. MOR 1:66; TR to ARC, June 23, 1884, TRC-HU; Rosenberg, *Assassin Guiteau*; TR, Diary, Feb. 16, 1884, TRP-LC; ARC-MS; for real estate transactions see E. Morris, *Rise*, 248.

43. TR to Will Sewall, Mar. 9, 1884, TRP-LC, TR to ARC, Mar. 26, 1884, TRC-HU.

44. ER to AR, n.d. [June 1883], and ER to Mary Ludlow Hall, July 13, 1884, RFP-FDR. Bamie decided to overrule her brother's dictum about Baby Lee's name. His wife had wanted her child to be called Alice, and so she would be; *racialist* means accepting cultural evolutionary categories that define whites and/or Caucasians as superior to blacks and Asians, whereas here *racist* mean taking hostile action on the basis of presumed racial superiority. In terms of these definitions, TR was a racialist.

45. The Fisher letters showed that Blaine got a kickback in bonds of more than $150,000 for seeking a land grant renewal in his position as Speaker of the House: David Saville Muzzey, *James G. Blaine: A Political Idol of Other Days* (New York, 1935), 85–100; Summers, *Rum, Romanism, and Rebellion*, 62; Blaine was also a racist and an advocate of the Chinese Exclusion Act: Gyory, *Closing the Gate*; Bernhard Gillam, *Puck*, June 4, 1884.

46. John A. Garraty, *Henry Cabot Lodge: A Biography* (New York, 1953), 78; Sproat, *"The Best Men,"* 121.

47. Horace White's letter to the editor of the *New York Times*, Oct. 20, 1884, and TR from Boston, clipping, Oct. 21, [1884], SUBJ-TRC; MEM 16:76–78.

48. TR to HCL, June 18, 1884, HCL-MHS; Summers, *Rum, Romanism, and Rebellion*, 208.

49. TR to HCL, Aug. 12, 1884, HCL-MHS; SUBJ-TRC.

50. "effeminate" in Summers, *Rum, Romanism, and Rebellion*, 7, 17; HCL note on bottom of telegram notifying him of TR's death: CRR to HCL, Jan. 6, 1919, HCL-MHS. When HCL edited his correspondence with TR he corrected misspellings, deleted several negative remarks about McKinley and ethnic groups, and, worst of all, bowdlerized, invented, and rearranged portions of their letters; TR description of his friendship with Lodge comes in a memorandum, Feb. 10, 1908, HCL-MHS: "Altho I had met Cabot Lodge once or twice in the Porcellian Club, I never really knew him until the spring of 1884 when we came together in connection with the effort to prevent Blaine's nomination for President. We both took the same view, namely: that if possible Blaine should not be nominated, but that if nominated we would support him. From that time on he was my closest friend, personally, politically, and in

every other way, and occupied toward me a relation that no other man has ever occupied or ever will occupy. We have not always agreed, but our subjects of disagreement have been of but little weight compared to the matters upon which we did agree. For the past twenty-four years I have discust [*sic*] almost every move I have made in politics with him, provided he was at hand and it was possible for me to discuss it; and as regards many matters of policy and appointment, it would be quite impossible for me now to say whether it was he or I who first suggested the appointment I made or the course that I followed. Thus I have quite forgotten whether it was I who first suggested that Moody should come into the Cabinet or whether it was Lodge who made the suggestion."

51. TR to HCL, June 18, 1884 (incorrectly listed as part of Aug. 12, 1884, letter in published *TR/HCL* letters), HCL-MHS. Newspapers also found a personal scandal in Blaine's life: Blaine's first child was born three months after the Blaines were married and he was accused of being a "man-kisser": Summers, *Rum, Romanism, and Rebellion*, 188–90.

52. MEM 16:91.

53. William Rhinelander Stewart, *The Philanthropic Work of Josephine Shaw Lowell* (New York, 1911), 64; quotations from TR to HCL, April 16, 1886, August 20, 1887, March 8, 1885, and March 27, 1886, HCL-MHS; on the 1884 campaign see MEM 16:69–94.

54. AUTO, 151; TR to William Roscoe Thayer, July 12, 1884, TRC-HU.

55. HCL, *Early Memories* (New York, 1913), 44–50, 118, 129–130.

56. "Feline" in Teague, *Mrs. L*, 113–14; "dilettantism" in Garraty, *Lodge*, 226, and William C. Widenor, *Henry Cabot Lodge and the Search for an American Foreign Policy* (Berkeley, 1980), 24; HCL, *Early Memories*, 125.

57. TR to ARC, n.d. [1885], TRC-HU; TR to HCL, Jan. 7 and 11, 1886, HCL-MHS.

58. *TR/HCL*, 1:45.

59. TR to HCL, June 7, 1886, HCL-MHS. She was prominent in the Women's City Club and was considered "perhaps the most scholarly woman in society in the Capitol" because of her specialty in Greek studies and her wide reading. Edith gave him a clipping about Nannie which he enclosed in TR to ACMDL, Jan. 31 and Feb. 19, 1886, HCL-MHS. He gave part of his Nobel Peace Prize money to the Visiting Nurses Association because of Nannie: TR to Mrs. Frederick W. Vanderbilt, Feb. 4, 1907, MOR-REJ.

60. New York Supreme Court, New York County, Peter A. Juley, Plaintiff, against Town Topics Publishing Company, Defendant, deposition of Theodore Roosevelt taken March 20, 1919, TR File, TRP-SAHI. "Address of Colonel Theodore Roosevelt at Laying of Corner-Stone of Carnegie Library, Fargo College," Sept. 5, 1910, TR-SP.

61. TR to ARC, Mar. 19, 1885, and CRR to ARC, n.d. [1885], TRC-HU; *Letters from Theodore Roosevelt to Anna Roosevelt Cowles*, 86–87.

62. HCL, "Theodore Roosevelt," address before Congress, 1919, 6; Parsons, *Perchance*, 62–64; ER to ARC July 1, 1885, TRC-HU; CRR to Cousin Laura, Nov. 29, 1885, Bulloch Papers, SHC; Lilian Rixey, *Bamie: Theodore Roosevelt's Remarkable Sister* (New York, 1963), 53–62; ARC-MS.

63. Robert Crawford Munro Ferguson (hereafter Bob Ferguson) to ARC, Aug. 7, 1919, TRC-HU. She served as vice president of the Ladies Board of the Orthopaedic Hospital. For a while TR and ARC pooled their financial resources: *Letters from Theodore Roosevelt to Anna Roosevelt Cowles*, 82; she and Corinne asked Bill Sewall to keep them informed about TR's health. He still took heart medicine and had asthma attacks in the West. TR spent $85,000 of his inheritance on 300 head of cattle: Putnam, *Theodore Roosevelt*, 523; ARC to EKR, Oct. 23, 1886, TRC-HU.

64. TR to DR, June 28, 1886, TRC-HU; MOR 1:73; Henry E. Jackson interview, SUBJ-TRC.

65. MOR 1:82; TR, *Hunting Trips of a Ranchman: Sketches of Sport on the Northern Cattle Plains* (New York, 1885), 197; CRR to ARC, Apr. 4, 1886, TRC-HU; TR to Marquis de Mores, n.d. [Sept. 3, 1885], MOR-REJ.

66. AUTO, 43; Ned Buntline, *Buffalo Bill and His Adventures in the West* (New York, 1886), 90.

67. TR, *Wilderness Writings*, ed. Paul Schullery (Salt Lake City, 1986), 54.

68. TR, "My Life as a Naturalist," *American Museum Journal* 18, no. 5 (May 1918): 322; Will H. Hays, *Memoirs* (Garden City, N.Y., 1955), 245; TR, Private Diary, Aug. 25, 1880, TRP-LC; Owen Wister turned TR's character into *The Virginian*, which became a popular novel, play, and, eventually, television series.

69. "Hitched" in Cutwright, *Making of a Conservationist*, 111; "Life on the Cattle Plains," *Literary World*, Oct. 17, 1885; Hermann Hagedorn in *Roosevelt in the Bad Lands* (Boston, 1921) stated that TR spent "most of that summer" of 1887 at Elkhorn Ranch, but letters show he did not: Hagedorn, *Bad Lands*, 101, 253, 447, 39; MEM 2:413.

70. *Hunting Trips of a Ranchman*, 159.

71. "Mr. Roosevelt Among the Cowboys," *New York Tribune* clipping, July 30, 1884, SUBJ-TRC.

72. TR to HCL, Aug. 20, 1886, *TR/HCL*, 1:45.

73. Richard Henry Dana, *Two Years Before the Mast*, quoted in Richard White, *"It's Your Misfortune and None of My Own": A New History of the American West* (Norman, Okla., 1991), 49; TR, *Ranch Life and the Hunting Trail*, MEM, 4:367.

74. Putnam, *Theodore Roosevelt*, 460–61.

75. TR, *Ranch Life and the Hunting Trail*, MEM 4:367; William H. Goetzmann and William N. Goetzmann, *The West of the Imagination* (New York, 1986); Lee Clark Mitchell, *Westerns: Making the Man in Fiction and Film* (Chicago, 1996); Patricia Nelson Limerick, *The Legacy of Conquest: The Unbroken Past of the American West* (New York, 1987). In the West, Theodore tried to write himself into the dime novel. He was not alone; Harvard men of his generation regularly took a western post-graduate cure for their effeteness: Caspar Whitney punched cows in Rio Arriba, New Mexico, Endicott Peabody preached to desperadoes in Tombstone, Arizona: see also MEM 2:297.

76. TR to CRR, Aug. 7, 1886, TRC-HU; *Letters from Theodore Roosevelt to Anna Roosevelt Cowles*, 59; "spokesman" from R.W.G. Vail, quoted in Nora E. Cordingly, "Extreme Rarities in the Published Works of Theodore Roosevelt," *Papers of the Bibliographical Society of America*, vol. 39 (1945), 49.

77. TR, "Who Should Go West?" *Harper's Weekly*, Jan. 2, 1886.

78. And later Pawnee Bill's Historical Wild West, Indian Museum and Encampment and Zack Mulhall's show. He was delighted to have a chance to catch boat thieves and took time to photograph himself with two of his men for the magazine article he would write about the adventure: Goetzmann and Goetzmann, *West of the Imagination*, 243. TR wrote Stephen Crane, Aug. 18, 1896: "Some day I want you to write another story of the frontiersman & the Mexican Greaser in which the frontiersman shall come out on top; it is more normal that way!": Stephen Crane Papers, Columbia University, quoted in Christopher P. Wilson, "Stephen Crane and the Police," *American Quarterly* 48, no. 2 (June 1996): 273–315; on the frontier myth, wilderness, and TR see William Cronon, "The Trouble with Wilderness; or, Getting Back to the Wrong Nature," in Cronon, ed., *Uncommon Ground: Toward Reinventing Nature* (New York, 1995).

79. TR address, Carnegie Library, Fargo College, Sept. 5, 1910, TR-SP; TR also quoted in Lawrence Hyman Budner, "Hunting, Ranching, and Writing: The Influence of Theodore Roosevelt's Western Experiences in His Later Career and Political Thought" (M.A. thesis, Southern Methodist University, 1990), 1.

80. Lincoln A. Lang, *Ranching with Roosevelt* (Philadelphia, 1926), 114; Putnam, *Theodore Roosevelt*, 597–600.

81. AUTO, 103–104. He said: "I never would have been President if it had not been for my experiences in North Dakota": Elwyn B. Robinson, *History of North Dakota* (Lincoln, Nebr., 1966), 559, 241.

82. TR, "Books for Holidays in the Open," MEM 4:187–96; TR to CRR, July 5, 1886, TRC-HU; TR to Jonas Van Duzer, May 17, 1885, MOR-REJ; TR to CRR, May 12, 1886, TRC-HU.

83. TR to HCL, June 7, 1886, *TR/HCL* 1:41.

84. He conceded that western expansionists were personally immoral and had a "piratical way of looking at neighboring territory," TR, *Life of Thomas Hart Benton* (Boston, 1887), 15, 17.

85. TR also berated John Tyler as "a politician of monumental littleness," TR, *Benton*, 239.

86. CRR to Cousin Laura, Nov. 29, 1885, Bulloch Papers, SHC; MOR 1:34.

87. TR interview, *Pall Mall Gazette*, Dec. 9, 1886, in Christopher Silvester, ed., *The Penguin Book of Interviews: An Anthology from 1859 to the Present Day* (New York, 1993), 70 (I thank Gay Talese for sending me this interview); MEM 2:340; TR, "Cross-Country Riding in America, Riding to the Hounds on Long Island," *The Century* 32, no. 3 (July 1886): 337–42.

88. Putnam, *Theodore Roosevelt*, 561.

89. TR to EKR, Nov. 12, 1909, TRC-HU.

90. EKR to TR, June 8, 1886, TRC-HU. "Making love" in nineteenth-century parlance meant courting behavior, not intercourse, "Love-making" can mean courtship behavior: *The Compact Edition of the Oxford English Dictionary* (New York, 1986), 1:1670.

91. EKR to TR, June 8, 1886, TRC-HU.

92. If TR saw Edith again in November and proposed in December, as diaries and letters prove, then his mixed feelings about being untrue to Alice's memory, if confessed to Mrs. Selmes, were probably expressed during his engagement to Edith; Hermann Hagedorn interview of A. W. Merrifield, June 1919, and Hagedorn's Notes in Roosevelt Women Interviews, and Gaspar Griswold to ARC, July 15, 1885, TRC-HU. ARL said: "he never mentioned her name to *anyone*" in Teague, *Mrs. L*, 5.

93. TR to CRR, July 5, 1886, TRC-HU.

94. TR to ARC, Sept. 20, 1886, TRC-HU.

95. ARL, Roosevelt Women Interviews, TRC-HU; ARC to ACMDL, n.d. [1886], quoted in Rixey, *Bamie*, (New York, 1963), 62.

96. Silvester, *Penguin Book of Interviews*; "party standing," *TR/HCL*, 1:48–49; MOR 1:113; "implored" in Parsons, *Perchance*, 64.

97. *New York Times*, Oct. 24, 1886; Louis F. Post and Fred C. Leubuscher, *Henry George's 1886 Campaign* (Westport, Conn., 1976), 23; Henry George, *Progress and Poverty* (New York, 1926); Henry George, Jr., *The Life of Henry George* (New York, 1960); David Montgomery, "The Excommunication of Rev. Edward McGlynn: Alienation from the Land and the Reconfiguration of Working-Class Americanism," paper delivered at the Charles Warren Center, Harvard University, Cambridge, Mass., 1999; on 150 incidents see Sven Beckert, *The Monied Metropolis: New York and The Consolidation of the American Bourgeoisie*, 1850–1896 (New York, 2001).

98. Silvester, *Penguin Book of Interviews*, 71–72.

99. Hurwitz, *Theodore Roosevelt and Labor*, 109; MOR 1:114; he owned, in addition to Sagamore Hill and two ranches in the west, 28 East Twentieth Street, considerable property along Broadway and other streets in Manhattan, the piers, and other shares of land through Roosevelt and Son.

100. Hurwitz, *Theodore Roosevelt and Labor*, 137; TR to HCL, Oct. 28, 1886, HCL-MHS.

101. TR to ARC, Jan. 6, 1887, *Letters from Theodore Roosevelt to Anna Roosevelt Cowles*, 90–91.

102. "Old Bullion," *New York Herald*, Jan. 31, 1887; TR Scrapbook, TRC-HU.

103. "Summum Bonum," by Ethel Armes, TRB Anecdotes file, TRP-BP; Budner, "Hunting, Ranching, and Writing," 26; TR to CRR, Feb. 8, 1886, TRC-HU.

104. EKR to TR, Jan. 1, 1886, TRC-HU; Parsons, *Perchance*, 279.

CHAPTER FOUR: THE SENSITIVE PLANT

1. "White hour" in MOR 8:1347; EKR to ERD, May 11, 1913, TR to CRR, Nov. 22, 1886 and Feb. 8, 1886 [really 1887], and to ERD, May 1, 1913, TRC-HU.

2. TR to CRR, Jan. 22 and Feb. 8, 1887, and to ARC, Sept. 20, 1886, TRC-HU; Parsons, *Perchance*, 279.

3. ARL, Helen Roosevelt Robinson, ORHO-COL; Teague, *Mrs. L*, 37.

4. "Eagles" in EKR to ERD, Sept. 17, 1927, TRC-HU; "cloying adulation" in Parsons, *Perchance*, 242; TR to BR, Feb. 17, 1915, TRC-HU.

5. TR to KR, Jan. 10, 1909, TRC-HU.

6. TR to KR, Apr. 1, 1911, TRC-HU.

7. TR to ABR, Aug. 23, 1917, TRC-HU; Henry James Forman, "Roosevelt the Husbandman," *American Review of Reviews*, Aug. 1910, 175–9, in SUBJ-TRC.

8. Carlos Baker, ed., *The Selected Poetry and Prose of Percy Bysshe Shelley* (New York, 1951), 271; EKR to TR, June 8, 1886; "sensitive plant" in EKR to ERD, May 5, 1913, TRC-HU.

9. EKR to ERD, May 31 and July 23, 1913, and TR to ARC, Jan. 17, 1887, TRC-HU.

10. TR to CRR, Nov. 22, 1886, TRC-HU.

11. *Letters from Theodore Roosevelt to Anna Roosevelt Cowles*, 93; TR to ARC, Jan. 10, 1887, TRC-HU; Hagedorn, *Roosevelt Family*, 12.

12. TR to ARC, Sept. 20, 1886, TRC-HU.

13. TR to ARC, May 16, 1887, TRC-HU; ARC-MS.

14. TR to Bill Sewall, July 10, 1887, TRP-LC; EKR to ARC, n.d. [May 1887], and TR to ARC, May 21, 1887, TRC-HU; Bamie gave him a gun rack.

15. TR to John Jay, May 28 and June 10, 1887, John Jay and Jay Family Papers, Columbia University; TR, *Gouverneur Morris*, 20.

16. The movement influenced art, architecture, historic preservation, and literature, and sparked popular interest in early America: Karal Ann Marling, *George Washington Slept Here: Colonial Revivals and American Culture, 1876–1986* (Cambridge, Mass., 1988); Michael Kammen, *A Season of Youth: The American Revolution and the Historical Imagination* (New York, 1978); Laurel Thatcher Ulrich, *The Age of Homespun: Objects and Stories in the Creation of an American Myth* (New York, 2001); TR to E. B. Livingston, June 20, 1891, MOR-REJ; TR on tracing descent, from clipping, TR letter to the editor of *The Athenaeum*, Apr. 18, 1891, 507; TR told a genealogist who had found that Edith was descended from William the Conqueror he hoped "my own plebian origin must not be thrown up against me": TR to J. Bayard Backus, Mar. 16, 1900, TRC-HU.

17. Arthur John, *The Best Years of the Century: Richard Watson Gilder, Scribner's Monthly, and the Century Magazine, 1870–1909* (Chicago, 1981), 197, 138; Paul Nagel, *This Sacred Trust: American Nationality, 1798–1898* (New York, 1971), 241; TR, "A Teller of Tales of Strong Men," *Harper's Weekly*, Dec. 21, 1895, in TR Scrapbook, TRC-HU; MEM 4, 194; Kathleen D. McCarthy, *Women's Culture: American Philanthropy and Art, 1830–1930*

(Chicago, 1991), 106; see Lawrence J. Oliver, "Theodore Roosevelt, Brander Matthews, and the Campaign for Literary Americanism," *American Quarterly* 41, no. 1 (March 1989): 93–111.

18. Clipping, *New York Tribune*, Oct. 14, 1888, TR Scrapbook, TRC-HU; Thomas Wentworth Higginson, "Americanism in Literature," *Atlantic Monthly* 25 (January 1870): 56–63. TR thought William Morris' folk tales anemic and Henry James' "uninteresting stories about the upper social classes of England" proof that James was a lifeless "miserable little snob": MOR 1:390.

19. He did admit the Federalists were sore losers to Jefferson and Madison and that the northern secessionism which Morris advocated was ill advised: TR, *Gouverneur Morris*, 109, 84; TR wrote: "It is well indeed for our land that we of this generation have at last learned to think nationally": 220; Marling, *Colonial Revivals*; see also Kammen, *Season of Youth*. TR wrote: "Voters of the labouring class in the cities are very emotional: they value in a public man what we are accustomed to consider virtues only to be taken into account when estimating private character. Thus if a man is open-handed and warm-hearted, they consider it as being a fair offset to his being a little bit shaky when it comes to applying the eighth commandment to affairs of state." In an article in *The Century* in November 1886, TR complained that "a large vicious population" of poor voters had been dominated by bossism, in James Bryce, *The American Commonwealth* (New York, 1908), 2:183*n*.5.

20. Clipping, "The Dakota Cowboy," *Detroit Tribune*, Oct. 1, 1888, TR Scrapbook, TRC-HU.

21. ERD to Edith Derby Williams, Nov. 11, 1947, TRC-HU.

22. ERD to Edith Derby Williams, Aug. 6, 1950, TRC-HU; TR, "The Danger," in Charles F. Horne, ed., *The Meaning of Modern Life* (New York, 1907), 1–3; TR, "Civic Helpfulness," MEM 15:434; EKR to TR, Oct. 14, n.y. [1900], TRC-HU.

23. *Letters from Theodore Roosevelt to Anna Roosevelt Cowles*, 95; TR to CRR, Aug. 14, 1887, TRC-HU.

24. Helen Roosevelt Robinson, Roosevelt Women Interviews, TRC-HU. TR told CRR: "I think that what Edith says is true and that you do spoil me": Nov. 28, 1893, MOR-REJ.

25. Corinne Robinson Alsop, Roosevelt Women Interviews, TRC-HU.

26. Ibid.; Fanny Smith Parsons often joined them on the flower and bird walks; on "bumps": ARL, *Crowded Hours: Reminiscences of Alice Roosevelt Longworth* (New York, 1933), 30–31.

27. Though Bamie served as the family's stickler for etiquette, she also had a talent for flattery and patient listening and "making other people appear at their best": ARL, Helen Roosevelt Robinson, ORHO-COL.

28. ARL, ORHO-COL. She did not put it in words until later in their marriage: EKR to KR, June 19, [1915], KBR-LC; ARC to CRR, Mar. 26, 1926, TRC-HU.

29. TR to ARC, Sept. 11, 1887, TRC-HU.

30. EKR to Mrs. Ralph Cross Johnson, n.d. [1909], Martha Waller Johnson Papers, Virginia Historical Society, Richmond; TR to CRR, Sept. 20, 1887, and to EBAR, July 30, 1911, TRC-HU; EKR, "Baby's Journal," TRJR-LC.

31. ARL, ORHO-COL; interview, WSC, Jr.

32. TR to Bob Ferguson, Dec. 22, [1895], JIG-ARIZ.

33. ABG to CRR, May 14, n.y., TRC-HU; AER, *This Is My Story* (Garden City, N.Y., 1961), 15, 45–46.

34. ERD to EKR, May 5, 1913, TRC-HU.

35. EKR to TR, Nov. 14 and 20, 1887, TRC-HU.

36. TR to CRR, May 3, 1894, TRC-HU; TR to Jacob Riis, Jan. 6, 1912, Jacob Riis Papers, LC.

37. EKR to ARC, n.d. [Feb. 20, 1888], TRC-HU.

38. MOR, 1:215.

39. For the way public opinion was awakened to the need for park preservation see Richard A. Bartlett, *Yellowstone: A Wilderness Besieged* (Tucson, Ariz., 1985), 137–43, 309–21; George Bird Grinnell, ed., *Hunting at High Altitudes: The Fifth Book of the Boone and Crockett Club* (New York, 1913); John F. Reiger, *American Sportsmen and the Origins of Conservation* (New York, 1975), 140–41; Alfred Runte, *National Parks: The American Experience* (Lincoln, Nebr., 1987), 7–74.

40. On the roots of TR's conservation views see Dalton, "Early Life"; RBR-NYHS; RBR Scrapbooks, RBR, *Superior Fishing, or, the Striped Bass, Trout, and Black Bass of the Northern States* (New York, 1865); Richard P. Harmond, "Robert Barnwell Roosevelt and the Early Conservation Movement," *Theodore Roosevelt Association Journal* 14, no. 3 (Fall 1988): 2–11; on RBR's influence see also Tweed Roosevelt, "Theodore Roosevelt, The Mystery of the Unrecorded Environmentalist," speech, in author's possession; Grinnell, ed., *Hunting at High Altitudes;* Reiger, *Sportsmen,* 140–41; on the theory that some strains of conservation thinking originated in public commons see Richard W. Judd, *Common Lands, Common People: The Origins of Conservation in Northern New England* (Cambridge, Mass., 1997), 42–43; Cutright, *Naturalist,* 70–73.

41. MOR 1:136.

42. Rayford W. Logan, *The Betrayal of the Negro: From Rutherford B. Hayes to Woodrow Wilson* (New York, 1997), 68; Xi Wang, *The Trial of Democracy: Black Suffrage and Northern Republicans, 1860–1910* (Athens, Ga., 1997), 241. Opponents of the Lodge bill included the *Springfield Republican,* high-tariff men and other pro-business forces, and mugwumps like Carl Schurz: Leon F. Litwack, *Trouble in Mind: Black Southerners in the Age of Jim Crow* (New York, 1998), 220–21; Glenda Elizabeth Gilmore shows they were not completely successful in disenfranchising black voters in North Carolina, *Gender and Jim Crow: Women and the Politics of White Supremacy in North Carolina, 1896–1920* (Chapel Hill, 1996); Lee D. Baker, *From Savage to Negro: Anthropology and the Construction of Race, 1896–1954* (Berkeley, 1998).

43. Daniel G. Brinton quoted in L. Baker, *From Savage to Negro,* 27.

44. TR, "Social Evolution," his review of Benjamin Kidd's book in the *North American Review* (July 1895), MEM 14:107–28. Cultural evolutionary racial views were not challenged in professional anthropology until 1909, when Franz Boas published his findings about how changeable the cephalic index size could be when immigrants moved to a healthier environment; even Boas expressed cultural evolutionary views like TR's before 1909 but also moved toward a belief in African "equipotentiality" as TR did. It is not clear how much of what Boas wrote TR read; see Vernon J. Williams, Jr., *Rethinking Race: Franz Boas and His Contemporaries* (Louisville, 1996); TR, "True Americanism and Expansionism," speech before the New York Society, Brooklyn, Dec. 21, 1898, in Thomas B. Reed, ed., *Modern Eloquence* (New York, 1903), 3:1003; Lo Hui-min, ed., *The Correspondence of G. E. Morrison* (Cambridge, Eng., 1976–78), 1:285, quoted in Michael H. Hunt, *Ideology and U.S. Foreign Policy* (New Haven, 1987), 126; see also George Sinkler, *The Racial Attitudes of American Presidents from Abraham Lincoln to Theodore Roosevelt* (Garden City, N.Y., 1971), and Ronald Takaki, *Iron Cages: Race and Culture in Nineteenth-century America* (New York, 1990); TR, "True Americanism and Expansionism," speech, in *Modern Eloquence,* 3:1004.

45. The best exploration of the complexity of TR's racial views is Thomas G. Dyer, *Theodore Roosevelt and the Idea of Race* (Baton Rouge, 1980).

46. TR, "True Americanism," *The Forum* (Apr. 1894) in MEM, and TR "The Hollander as an American," speech at the Holland Society dinner, Jan. 15, 1896, in T. Reed, ed.,

Modern Eloquence, 1000; MEM 15:25 and 18:59; Howard K. Beale, *Theodore Roosevelt and the Rise of America to World Power* (Baltimore, 1956), 45.

47. L. Baker, *From Savage to Negro*, 86. Labor movements disagreed about immigration restriction: Dennis Kearney wanted to keep Asian workers out of California but before 1881 Greenbackers, Socialist Labor Party members, the Workingmen's Party, and Adolph Strasser of the Cigarmakers' Union did not support restriction; see Gyory, *Closing the Gate*.

48. MOR 1:144, 145.

49. TR speech in Minneapolis, Oct. 12, 1888, TR-SP; clipping from *St. Paul Pioneer Press*, Oct. 13, 1888, TR-SP.

50. Memorandum of L. T. Michener quoted in Harry J. Sievers, *Benjamin Harrison: Hoosier President, The White House and After* (New York, 1968), 75.

51. MOR 1:166; Mark Sullivan, *The Education of an American* (New York, 1938), 273.

52. TR, "Justice and Partisanship," speech in the New York Assembly, Mar. 9, 1883, TR-SP; MOR 1:169; TR to HCL, Sept. 10, 1889, HCL-MHS.

53. ARC to Mr. Riddle, July 23, 1889, JIG-ARIZ; TR to Charles Dudley Warner, July 26, 1889, TRP-LC; "make his way" in AER, *This Is My Story*, 21; liked work in HCL to TR, Aug. 15, 1888, HCL-MHS.

54. "The Civil Service Record," clipping, March 1889, TR-SP; MOR 1:175; TR to CRR, July 28, 1889, TRC-HU.

55. MOR 1:168; TR to Edmund Clarence Stedman, Jan. 13, 1890, TRC-HU.

56. TR, *The Winning of the West* (New York, 1889), 1:133, 175, 15, 14, 8, 106.

57. George B. Utley, "Roosevelt's *The Winning of the West*: Some Unpublished Letters," *Mississippi Valley Historical Review* 30, no. 4 (March 1944): 495–506.

58. TR Scrapbook, clippings from the *New York Sun*, Sept. 29 and Oct. 10, 1889, TRC-HU; Gilmore was also angered by TR's personal attacks on the reliability of his histories: 1:182: *n*.1; MEM 10:170, see also 179–81.

59. Sherrill example in TR, *The Winning of the West* 1:292; James R. Gilmore, *The Rear-Guard of the Revolution* (1886; reprint, New York, 1903), 117; both describe the Cherokee as "baffled" after the Watauga onslaught of 1776: Gilmore, 118, Roosevelt, 292. Plagiarism has been interpreted many ways over time and place, but today in the U.S. it usually means using a significant idea or at least several exact words from another text without putting quotation marks around that material and footnoting the source: John Higham, *History: Professional Scholarship in America* (New York, 1965); for the historical profession's role in defining plagiarism and standards of citation see Jacqueline Goggin and Morey Rothberg, eds., *John Franklin Jameson and the Development of Humanistic Scholarship in America* (Athens, Ga., 1993–2001) 1–3; Thomas Mallon, *Stolen Words: Forays into the Origins and Ravages of Plagiarism* (New York, 1989); Anthony Grafton, *The Footnote: A Curious History* (Cambridge, Mass., 1997); John D. Mittlestaedt and Robert A. Mittlestaedt, "The Protection of Intellectual Property: Issues of Origination and Ownership," *Journal of Public Policy and Marketing* 16, no. 1 (Spring 1997): 14–25.

60. TR to HCL, Oct. 30, 1889, HCL-MHS. In describing a May 1792 native attack on settlers at Buchanan's station James R. Gilmore wrote: "The first alarm was given by the frightened cattle . . . the garrison withheld their fire till the Indians were within ten paces of the buildings. Then a simultaneous discharge burst from the fort, and was replied to by a heavy and constant fire, which the savages kept up for an hour, never falling back to a greater distance, though one unbroken sheet of flame streamed from the port-holes and mowed them down by dozens," in *The Advance-Guard of Western Civilization* (New York, 1888), 221–22; TR in *The Winning of the West* (New York, 1896), 4:144, wrote: "The alarm was given by the running of the frightened cattle, and when the sentinel fired at the assailants they were not ten

yards from the gate of the blockhouse. The barred door withstood the shock and the flame-flashes lit up the night as the gun-men fired through the loop-holes"; TR had plagiarized less than Alexander Theroux (*New York Times*, Mar. 3, 1995) or Stephen Ambrose (*New York Times*, Jan. 11, 2002), and he did so before scholarly standards of citation had been established; my conversations with John Higham and Carl Guarneri clarified the historical context of TR's plagiarism, and Higham believes it would not have constituted a clear violation of professional standards until the 1920s.

61. TR to ARC, Nov. 20, 1888, TRC-HU. Though they still worried about money, they joined Bamie in helping Uncle Jimmie Bulloch out of financial difficulties in his old age; TR to Bill Sewall, Nov. 2, 1890, and Apr. 17, 1891, TRP-LC.

62. "be the father" in TR to Mrs. James (Sarah) Leavitt, Oct. 7, 1901, TRC-HU; "love a great many things" in AUTO, 319; on TR's friendship for his children see Teague, *Mrs. L*, 112; after Archie's birth he said: "I begin to think that this particular branch of the Roosevelt family is getting to be numerous enough": MOR 1:376.

63. EKR to Arthur Lee, Jan. 24, 1928, Lee Papers, Courtauld Institute, London; ABR, Memoirs, TRC-HU; MOR 3:74–75; an interpretation of Guiney's chivalric anti-modernism can be found in T. J. Jackson Lears, *No Place of Grace: Antimodernism and the Transformation of American Culture, 1880–1920* (New York, 1981), 124–29; ERD to RD, June 23, 1918, TRC-HU.

64. "Dive" and "endurance tests" in Teague, *Mrs. L*, 42; EKR to KR, Dec. 17, [1909], KBR-LC; "tribe" in EKR to ERD, Aug. 22, 1927, TRC-HU.

65. TR to ARC, Jan. 6, 1896, MOR-REJ; TR to Brander Matthews, Dec. 15, 1891, in Lawrence J. Oliver, ed., *The Letters of Theodore Roosevelt and Brander Matthews* (Knoxville, Tenn., 1995), 29; TRJR, *All in the Family* (New York, 1929), 165–66.

66. Maria Longworth Storer, *In Memoriam Bellamy Storer* (privately printed, 1923), 22; "Roosevelt's Home Life," *New York Post*, Jan. 25, 1903, quotes TR: "I want my boys trained to be hardy, self-reliant, positive men . . . rather than see them grow up namby-pamby weaklings I would prefer to see them put to death," SUBJ-TRC; TR discovered a tall hollow tree and lowered each child down for twenty feet on a rope from the opening—just for the fun of it. Doctors had fitted Kermit with a painful steel leg brace to straighten his bones, and he followed his mother about the house irritably whimpering and asking for comfort. When TR watched three-year-old Ethel steal five-year-old Kermit's go-cart and bite him, he was not displeased when Kermit did a headstand and smashed Ethel on the head with his steel leggings: TR to CRR, July 20, 1896, SUBJ-TRC; TR to ARC, Feb. 4, 1894, MOR-REJ; ARL, ORHO-COL; Edith dosed them with Jamaican ginger and when the children asked TR to stop her he replied: "I don't dare interfere. I shall be fortunate if she does not give me ginger too": TRJR, *All in the Family*, 98, see also 88–92.

67. Though he has the year wrong, see Hagedorn, *Roosevelt Family*, 37–38. Hagedorn, "Good Living at Teddy Roosevelt's," *McCall's*, June 1956, SUBJ-TRC; EKR-Di, July 31, 1892; TR to ARC, Aug. 11, 1892, TRC-HU.

68. See EKR to Gertrude Carow letters; on ERD's birth and Ferguson and EKR and TR's relationship with Carows see EKR to ERD, Aug. 14, 1928, TRC-HU.

69. "united family" in ABR to EKR, July 15, 1944, TRC-HU; EKR to TR, Jan. 15, 1901, TRC-HU; for example, TR to EKR, n.d. [May 25, 1894], TRC-HU.

70. TR to Emily Carow, Feb. 10, 1890, TRC-HU; MOR 1:304; EKR-Di, Jan. 1892–Jan. 1894, for frequency of visits with Tafts; William Manners, *TR and Will: A Friendship That Split the Republican Party* (New York, 1969), 33; John La Farge, *The Manner Is Ordinary* (New York, 1954), 34.

71. Patricia O'Toole, *The Five of Hearts: An Intimate Portrait of Henry Adams and His Friends, 1880–1918* (New York, 1990), 202.

72. MOR 1:253; EKR to ARC, n.d. [Apr. 1, 1890], TRC-HU; O'Toole, *Five of Hearts*, 203, 291.

73. TR to ARC, n.d. [1892], TRC-HU; Belle La Follette and Fola La Follette, *Robert M. La Follette* (New York, 1953), 2:86.

74. TR to ARC, n.d. [1892], TRC-HU.

75. TR to ARC, n.d. [1892], TRC-HU; O'Toole, *Five of Hearts*, 91; EKR to ARC, n.d., TRC-HU; "Lodge Flower": TR to William Hallett Phillips, n.d., TRP-LC; Nannie found Edith self-sacrificing and excessively dutiful, *MOR 1:641*; William Sturgis Bigelow thought Mrs. Cameron "a minion of fashion . . . hard, brilliant, and slightly metallic": Akiko Murakata, "Selected Letters of Dr. William Sturgis Bigelow" (Ph.D. diss., George Washington University, 1971), 487.

76. Sandra Haarsager, *Organized Womanhood: Cultural Politics in the Pacific Northwest, 1840–1920* (Norman, Okla., 1997), 114; Theodora Penny Martin, *The Sound of Our Own Voices: Women's Study Clubs, 1860–1910* (Boston, 1987); Karen Blair, *The Clubwoman as Feminist: True Womanhood Redefined, 1868–1914* (New York, 1980). The W.C.T.U. and the General Federation of Women's Clubs had large and influential memberships; club membership provided a substitute for higher education and voting for some women; for others volunteer associations gave them power to do "village improvement" and lobby for reform, including the eight-hour day, suffrage, widow's and mother's pensions, the abolition of child labor, prenatal care, and temperance. Later in life she met friends at the Colony Club, which for her was primarily a center for lively talk and friendship, and the St. Hilda's Club at her church. Daisy Harriman and other members of the Colony Club actively supported the shirtwaist strikers in 1909, but Edith did not take any public stands on political issues while her husband was alive except for playgrounds and preparedness: EKR to TR, July 8, n.y., EKR to ARC, n.d. [early 1893], TRC-HU; WSC and Corinne Robinson Alsop, ORHO-COL; Eleanor Robson Belmont, *The Fabric of Memory* (New York, 1957), 108–109.

77. Bamie's report showed the influence of her friends Grace Dodge and Josephine Shaw Lowell, who made a career of helping the 200,000 women who worked in New York City, and she praised their work and that of the New York Consumer's League and Florence Kelley, who was then studying the workingwomen of Chicago: Jeanne Madeline Weimann, *The Fair Women* (Chicago, 1981), 386–87; Sonya Michel, "The Limits of Maternalism: Policies Toward Wage-Earning Mothers During the Progressive Era," in Seth Koven and Sonya Michel, eds., *Mothers of a New World: Maternalist Politics and the Origins of Welfare States* (New York, 1993), 284; Florence Lockwood, "Working Girl's Clubs," *The Century* 41 (March 1891): 793–94; telephone conversation and correspondence, Mary La Farge to author, Nov. 20–27, 2001; TR encouraged Grant's brother John to become a Catholic priest even though most of the La Farges disapproved: J. La Farge, *The Manner Is Ordinary*; see the La Farge Family Papers, NYHS; MOR 7:375; ARC-MS; see TR to ARC letters, 1893–94, TRC-HU.

78. ARC-MS; WSC and Corinne Robinson Alsop, ORHO-COL; ARC also took an interest in Montessori and kindergarten movements, which were new ideas in American education then, and she may have been the person who encouraged Edith to send Kermit to a kindergarten, which upper-class families typically did not do at the time. She was also assisted by newspaper writer Mary Gay Humphrey and a factory inspector named Margaret Finn: Weimann, *The Fair Women*, 386–87; TR to ARC, July 20 and 23, 1892, TRC-HU; Kathryn Kish Sklar, *Florence Kelley and the Nation's Work: The Rise of Women's Political Culture, 1830–1900* (New Haven, 1995), 146–49, 225; S. Sara Monoson, "The Lady and the Tiger: Women's Electoral Activism in New York City Before Suffrage," *Journal of Women's History* 2, no. 2 (1990): 100–35; see *A City Government That Serves* (New York, 1917) and other Woman's Municipal League publications which show how many women TR knew would join—CRR,

Helen Roosevelt Robinson, Florence Lockwood La Farge, Belle Moskowitz, Maud Nathan, Cornelia Pinchot, Grace Potter, Mary Simkhovitch, Dorothy Straight; see also David S. Hammack, *Power and Society: Greater New York at the Turn of the Century* (New York, 1982); on the roots of one branch of progressivism in women's club activism see Blair, *Clubwoman as Feminist,* 102–19; on women urban reformers see Daphne Spain, *How Women Saved the City* (Minneapolis, 2001); see also Charles Garrett, *The LaGuardia Years, Machine and Reform Politics in New York City* (New Brunswick, N.J., 1961).

79. Carlos A. Schwantes, *Coxey's Army: An American Odyssey* (Lincoln, Nebr., 1985), 3.

80. Harold K. Steen, ed., *Origins of the National Forests: A Centennial Symposium* (Durham, N.C., 1992), 4; he refused to let women apply for laborers' jobs but generally upheld a strict merit system. Congress wouldn't provide enough staff to supervise exams. TR to Hon. Secretary of Agriculture, Aug. 21, 1893, MOR-REJ; MOR 1:322; EKR to ARC, June 10, 1894 TRC-HU.

81. CRR to Owen Wister, July 23, 1930, Wister Papers, LC; MOR 1:237, 410–12.

82. EKR to ARC, n.d. [1890], TRC-HU; MOR 1:343.

83. TR to ARC, Dec. 24, 1890, ARC to CRR, Mar. 13, 1891, and TR to ARC, n.d., TRC-HU.

84. EKR to ARC, Mar. 11, n.y., TRC-HU; Corinne Robinson Alsop's granddaughter Elizabeth Winthrop, *In Her Mother's House* (Garden City, N.Y., 1988), describes sexual abuse of a daughter by a man who is modeled after Elliott; Ward, in *Before the Trumpet,* records that Edith's suggestion about sending Eleanor to a "good school" may have been "to keep her out of her father's hands," 365; EKR to ARC, Mar. 11, n.y., and TR to ARC, June 17, 1891, TRC-HU.

85. TR to ARC, Jan. 25, [1892], and July 21, 1891, TRC-HU; he helped manage some of DR's property in Abingdon.

86. TR to ARC, June 17 and 20, Mar. 20, July 2, and Feb. 15, 1891, TRC-HU.

87. TR, *The Wilderness Hunter,* 183–85; ER to Mary Ludlow Hall, May 19 and Nov. 11, and ER to ARC, June 12, 1892, from Abingdon, RFP-FDR.

88. TR to ARC, EKR to ARC n.d. [1892], CRR to ARC, n.d., TRC-HU; EKR-Di, Sept. 18, 1892.

89. EKR to ARC, n.d. [1893], and CRR to ARC, n.d., TRC-HU; ARC to Mary Ludlow Hall, n.d. [Feb. 15, 1893], and Mary Ludlow Hall to ARC, Aug. 2, 1893, RFP-FDR; locks in Ward, *Before the Trumpet,* 304; the unreliable version which proposes Elliott had a brain tumor is by his grandson Elliott Roosevelt and James Brough, *An Untold Story: The Roosevelts of Hyde Park* (New York, 1973), 27; CRR to ARC, Aug. 15, 1894, TRC-HU; TR and Elliott had been on friendly terms in 1894, but when Elliott's neighbors in Virginia asked Theodore to come down to stop his brother from drinking he refused. He said no one could stop Elliott; Mary Ludlow Hall to CRR, Aug. 25, 1894, Joseph Lash Papers, FDR; AER, *This Is My Story,* 34–35.

90. MOR 1:509, 342–43; Corinne Robinson Alsop, Helen Roosevelt Robinson, Roosevelt Women Interviews, TRC-HU; see also Betty Boyd Caroli, *The Roosevelt Women* (New York, 1998), 101–102. One of TR's favorite dinner companions, Bayard's niece (and Bamie's World's Fair assistant) Florence Bayard Lockwood, married John La Farge's son Christopher Grant La Farge, the first architect of the Cathedral of St. John the Divine and the early New York subway stations, and Sagamore Hill's North Room. Later in life TR held secret meetings with party bosses at the La Farges' house.

91. TR to HCL, Aug. 22, 1895, HCL-MHS.

92. Helen Roosevelt Robinson, Roosevelt Women Interviews, TRC-HU.

93. Though he, too, balked at her marriage, Lodge continued to speak through Bamie to British policymakers about America's desire for peace in the Venezuelan conflict, and

when he took an extended tour of England and the Continent he enjoyed meeting Bamie's many friends at her salon on Eaton Place: CRR to TR, Nov. 25, 1895, and Helen Roosevelt Robinson, Roosevelt Women Interviews, TRC-HU.

94. Schwantes, *Coxey's Army*, 1–21, 176–83; EKR thanked Cecil Spring Rice for looking after her sickly husband while he was in Washington, *The Letters and Friendships of Sir Cecil Spring Rice: A Record*, ed. Stephen Gwynn (Boston, 1929), 1:161.

95. Olney worked as attorney general while taking a full-time salary as a lawyer for the Burlington Railroad; Secret Service agents had infiltrated Coxey's Army to see if they were violent or tied in any way with anarchists or socialists: Schwantes, *Coxey's Army*, 167–70; *New York Times* quoted in Almont Lindsey, *The Pullman Strike: The Story of a Unique Experiment and of a Great Labor Upheaval* (Chicago, 1971), 347.

96. MOR 1:391; MEM 15:10, 7–8; TR, "True American Ideals," *Forum* 18 (February 1895): 746; Karen Sawislak, "The 'Labor Problem' in America, 1880–1905," Charles Warren Center Paper, Harvard University, 1999; Carl S. Smith, *Urban Disorder and the Shape of Belief: The Great Chicago Fire, the Haymarket Bomb, and the Model Town of Pullman* (Chicago, 1995), 247–70. Years later TR's views evolved and he wrote: "Mr. Cleveland, whom I like, was more completely controlled by the corporations—largely through Messrs. Whitney and Olney—than any President we have had in our time": MOR 3:639; Cleveland was flawed, TR said, because "he has never been brought into contact from the philanthropic side with wageworkers, with poor people. He knows nothing of sweatshops or of the east side": MOR 3:648.

97. Railroad business in James A. Roosevelt to ARC, Jan. 12 and Apr. 4, 1894, TRC-HU.

98. TR to ARC, Mar. 19, 1894, TRC-HU; for repeated references to TR's illnesses, see EKR-Di, Feb. 16–May 10, 1894; EKR to ARC, Mar. 5, n.y. [1894], TRC-HU.

99. EKR to ARC, n.d. [prob. spring 1894], TRC-HU.

100. *TR/HCL*, 1:160, 171.

101. MOR 3:86.

102. William R. Thayer to EKR, Jan. 7, 1919, TRC-HU; Earle Looker, *The White House Gang* (New York, 1929), 21; EKR to TR, Mar. 8, 1900, and HCL to EKR, June 28, 1898, HCL-MHS.

CHAPTER FIVE: SOLDIER AT THE MORAL FRONTIER AND AT WAR

1. "lying" in Jay Stuart Berman, *Police Administration and Progressive Reform: Theodore Roosevelt as Police Commissioner of New York* (Westport, Conn., 1987), 19; in 1894 it was easy to pin the depression on the Democrats; Gilfoyle, *City of Eros*, 251; MOR 1:419*n*.

2. EKR to ARC, Jan. 1, 1894, and n.d. [Sept. 28, 1894], TRC-HU.

3. TR to Bob Ferguson, Oct. 16, 1894, JIG-ARIZ.

4. EKR to ARC, n.d. [fall 1894], and TR to ARC, Oct. 13, 1894, TRC-HU.

5. EKR to ARC, n.d. [October 1894], TRC-HU; TR to HCL, Oct. 24, 1894, HCL-MHS; TR to Endicott Peabody, Oct. 10, 1894, Peabody Papers, copies at Houghton, originals at Groton School Archives.

6. TR to ARC, Dec. 30, 1894, MOR-REJ; Burrows and Wallace, *Gotham*, 1194.

7. MOR 1:417; TR to Bob Ferguson, Mar. 11, 1895, JIG-ARIZ.

8. MOR 1:427, 428.

9. EKR to HCL, n.d. [February 1895], HCL-MHS. Edith wrote Lodge that she did not understand why "we should have had such a sturm and drang period about the S. cleaning and nothing at all about" the police offer. Edith's alliance with Cabot in guiding his career amused Theodore. After they discovered he had invented the word "mutterless" in *The*

Winning of the West, TR good-naturedly described to Cabot how Edith "joined with you in denunciation and loudly insisted that I had not read to her that part of the proof": TR to HCL, June 10, 1896, HCL-MHS.

10. Berman, *Police,* 52; Byrnes, not TR, had connected station houses to Mulberry Street headquarters: Burrows and Wallace, *Gotham,* 1062.

11. TR, "Administering the New York Police Force," *Atlantic Monthly,* September 1897, MEM 15; MOR 1:459; Gilfoyle, *City of Eros,* 253; the best work on the subject is Berman, *Police,* 51, 53; see also Avery Andrews, "Citizen in Action: The Story of T.R. as Police Commissioner," TRC-HU.

12. Jacob A. Riis, *A Ten Year's War: An Account of the Battle with the Slum in New York* (New York, 1900), 34; Jacob A. Riis, *How the Other Half Lives: Studies Among the Tenements of New York* (New York, 1971).

13. Riis, *Theodore Roosevelt the Citizen,* 144; see James B. Lane, *Jacob A. Riis and the American City* (Port Washington, N.Y., 1974).

14. Gilfoyle, *City of Eros,* 232; TR to Endicott Peabody, Sept. 13, 1895, Peabody Papers; J. Stuart Blackton, "My Neighbor T.R." from the Motion Picture Department Files, Houghton.

15. "An Honorable Member Among Us," Wald File, Anecdotes File, TRP-BP; Lillian D. Wald, *Windows on Henry Street* (Boston 1934), 58.

16. James Lardner and Thomas Reppetto, *NYPD: A City and Its Police* (New York, 2000), 113; Robert C. Allen, *Horrible Prettiness: Burlesque and American Culture* (Chapel Hill, N.C., 1991), 222–24.

17. This was controversial because it left part of the homeless population without a place to sleep; Jacob A. Riis, *The Making of an American* (New York, 1943), 257–59.

18. EKR to ARC, Sept. 7, [1895], TRC-HU. TR took Riis, Stephen Crane, Lincoln Steffens, Hamlin Garland, Alex Lambert, and Bob Ferguson with him on midnight patrols.

19. His childhood friend Cleveland Dodge sent him outstanding young men he knew in the Y.M.C.A., like Otto Raphael, to work in Jewish neighborhoods: AUTO, 192; Burrows and Wallace, *Gotham,* 1088. Of course, he did not always stand up against prejudice in his own elite world of clubs and society as vigorously as possible. When the Union League Club blackballed Theodore Seligman for membership and the Four Hundred closed ranks against Jews, he did not protest. However, when the same blackballing occurred at the Federal Club he spoke out against it. Anti-Semitism shows up in family letters more often in the next generation. The Union League's proposal to fire its African-American workers made TR angry and he wrote a letter of protest saying the club, because it was founded to support Lincoln, should be "about the last Club in the country that ought to occupy such ground": MOR 3:62.

20. MOR 1:545; AUTO, 200.

21. Norman H. Clark, *Deliver Us from Evil: An Interpretation of American Prohibition* (New York, 1976), 2–3; W. J. Rorabaugh, *The Alcoholic Republic: An American Tradition* (New York, 1979), says that American consumption of alcohol had dropped by the end of the century.

22. The W.C.T.U. had lobbied with success for temperance education and local option; John C. Burnham in his path-breaking book, *Bad Habits: Drinking, Smoking, Taking Drugs, Gambling, Sexual Misbehavior, and Swearing in American History* (New York, 1993), and Timothy Gilfoyle, in *City of Eros,* portray the campaigns against minor bad habits as a fight against the commercialization of vice; commercialized vice triumphed because it was profitable, not because it made for a better society. The assumptions that vice was only a personal choice with no social or moral ramifications and the post-Freudian belief that any repression of impulse could be bad made it difficult to see that a profitable hedonism/consumerism had redefined Americanness by the mid-twentieth century; Clark, *Deliver Us from Evil,* 13.

23. TR, "Closing the New York Saloons on Sunday," *McClure's Magazine,* October 1895; MEM 15:164; Gilfoyle, *City of Eros,* 243–45. The Raines Law of 1896 raised excise fees on saloons but let hotels serve alcohol on Sunday, which had the unintended effect of encouraging prostitution to move into hotels.

24. "uncontrolled" in Rebecca Edwards, *Angels in the Machinery: Gender in American Party Politics from the Civil War to the Progressive Era* (New York, 1997), 113; the riots, crime, and disorder of the Gilded Age in addition to class-conscious populism provoked anxieties about law and order among respectables, especially Republican Party leaders, 199*n*.7. "Uncontrolled manhood" also worried moral reformers; W.C.T.U. president Frances Willard and other social purity reformers who wanted to stop prostitution believed this "social evil" would continue until men were punished for going to prostitutes. In 1890, Willard had called for a single standard of purity for women and men, "A White Life for Two," and the White Cross Society and other purity groups promoted the same single standard theory which lay behind TR's policy of punishing male customers as well as the prostitutes: Ian Tyrrell, *Woman's World, Woman's Empire: The Woman's Christian Temperance Union in International Perspective, 1880–1930* (Chapel Hill, N.C., 1991), 41; Willard, "A White Life for Two," in Richard W. Leeman, *"Do Everything" Reform: The Oratory of Frances Willard* (Westport, Conn., 1992), 159, 171; see also Burrows and Wallace, *Gotham,* 1161–69.

25. AUTO, 204; MEM 15:158–59; MOR 1:473; Jacob A. Riis, "Theodore Roosevelt's Father," *Outlook* (Oct. 6, 1900): 307; TR to ARC, Oct. 26, 1896, TRC-HU; TR to Riis, Dec. 15, 1896, Riis Papers, LC; TR to ARC, June 7, 1896, TRC-HU.

26. TR to W. P. Young, City Vigilance League, Dec. 27, 1895, TRP-SYR. The City Vigilance League was an offshoot of Howard Crosby's Society for the Prevention of Crime: Gilfoyle, *City of Eros,* 186–92; "urban posse," 188. Charles Gallaudet Trumbull, *Anthony Comstock, Fighter: Some Impressions of a Lifetime of Adventure in Conflict with the Powers of Evil* (New York, 1913); records of the New York Society for the Suppression of Vice, LC; on funding see Berman, *Police,* 105; Christopher P. Wilson, "Stephen Crane and the Police," *American Quarterly* 48, no. 2 (June 1996): 273–315; though they were old Roosevelt family friends Edith found Jesup and Dodge smug: EKR to ARC, n.d. [Jan. 31, 1891], TRC-HU; MOR 1:514.

27. TR to HCL, Aug. 22, 1895, HCL-MHS; MOR 1:469; Lardner and Reppetto, *NYPD,* 117.

28. Journal, July 12, 1895, quoted in E. Morris, *Rise,* 499.

29. MOR 1:491, 455; *TR/HCL,* 1:163.

30. *TR/HCL,* 1:179, 175.

31. *TR/HCL,* 1:183; William Sturgis Bigelow to HCL, Nov. 23, 1895, in Akiko Murakata, "Selected Letters of Dr. William Sturgis Bigelow," 136.

32. *TR/HCL,* 1:190.

33. *TR/HCL,* 1:228.

34. "taxed" and "nervousness" in TR to Parsons, July 10, 1896, in Parsons, *Perchance,* 111–13; Charles Samuels and Louise Samuels, *Once upon a Stage: The Merry World of Vaudeville* (New York, 1974), 233.

35. EKR to ARC, Sept. 7, [1895], and July 9 and 29, [1896], TRC-HU.

36. Berman, *Police,* 71.

37. "Shaken" in Kate Shippen Roosevelt to ARC, n.d., and TR to ARC, Oct. 27, 1895, TRC-HU; HCL, TR Boston, 1915; MEM 15:170; he also increased the native-born policemen to reach 94 percent, which meant that Tammany Hall appointees lost places; he made the police force less Irish; credit to Riis, see J. Lane, *Riis,* 118–19; *TR/HCL,* 1:168, 170.

38. C. Smith, *Urban Disorder,* 260; *New York Times,* Oct. 27, 1886; TR was delighted when the workingmen's clubs began to organize to support Harrison.

39. James Edmund Roohan, *American Catholics and the Social Question, 1865–1900* (New York, 1976), 442. The political divisions within the church were deep; for example, Bishop Corrigan tried to silence the radical priest Father Edward McGlynn. TR had not known much about how hard James Cardinal Gibbons had politicked with Rome to win a policy of toleration for Catholic members of the Knights of Labor, which many lay Catholics interpreted as proof that their church approved of peaceful worker activism. In the years ahead TR would make friends with the Social Gospel priests and Catholic Americans who preached patriotism and social reform, including Gibbons and Archbishop John Ireland: TR to ARC, Sept. 15, 1895, TRC-HU, enclosure clipping *New York Herald*, Sept. 6, 1895; *TR/HCL*, 1:167; see TR, "The Police and the Saloons," *Independent*, July 25, 1895.

40. MOR 4:889. E. Morris, *Rise*, identifies him incorrectly as O'Sullivan. Sullivan is well known for his dramatic support of Frances Perkins' 54 Hour Bill in 1912; see George Martin, *Madam Secretary: Frances Perkins* (Boston, 1976), 92–99; Daniel Czitrom, "Underworlds and Underdogs: Big Tim Sullivan and Metropolitan Politics in New York, 1889–1913," *Journal of American History* 78, no. 2 (September 1991): 536–58.

41. TR, "The Higher Life of Cities," *Outlook* (Dec. 21, 1895), in MEM 15:143; TR, "The Ethnology of the Police," *Munsey's*, June 1897, 397; see also MEM 14:204–213; TR to Hon. Washington Hesing, June 6, 1894, MOR-REJ; see his review of Charles H. Pearson, *National Life and Character: A Forecast*. He still believed in ethnic traits on the police force—that the Irish were quick and political, the Germans hesitant in a crisis, native-born police smarter, MEM 14:230–57.

42. TR, " 'Professionalism' in Sports," *North American Review* 15 (August 1890): 187, 191; TR knew Pierre de Coubertin and other advocates of the international Olympic competitions but because of unsportsmanlike fights at early games in private he believed it might provoke international tensions to engage in Olympic competition: TR to Theodore A. Cook, Oct. 20, 1908, MOR-REJ. But he entertained Olympic athletes at the White House and told them to "keep their heads shut" about politics and be good sports: TR to Arthur Lee, Sept. 17, 1908, MOR-REJ.

43. *American Big-Game Hunting, Hunting in Many Lands, Trail and Camp Fire*; Cutright, *Naturalist*, 73–85.

44. TR to Ellen La Valley Gray, Mar. 31, 1897, TRJR-LC.

45. MOR 1:565; TR, speech at St. Nicholas Society Dinner, Delmonico's, Dec. 12, 1896, TR-SP; TR's friend Andrew D. White dismissed TR's Populist opponents in 1896 as "unbalanced men and hysterical women" because women were active in Populist Party politics: R. Edwards, *Angels in the Machinery*, 121.

46. MOR 1:592; TR to W. R. Kilpatrick, Oct. 17, 1894, MOR-REJ.

47. LeRoy Ashby, *William Jennings Bryan: Champion of Democracy* (Boston, 1987), 54; TR to ARC, July 19, 1896, MOR-REJ.

48. Lawrence W. Levine, *Defender of the Faith: William Jennings Bryan, the Last Decade* (New York, 1965), 246.

49. R. Edwards, *Angels in the Machinery*, 147; Herbert Croly attributed McKinley's victory to Hanna's gift for keeping his candidate's "ingratiating personality" before the public (*Marcus Alonzo Hanna: His Life and Work* [New York, 1912], 214), but it was money, mass mailing, and tight control of who said what that beat Bryan.

50. TR, "The City in Modern Life," *Atlantic Monthly* (April 1895), MEM 14:204–13.

51. EKR to KR, Jan. 19, n.y. [1930], KBR-LC; TR had also indicted a McKinley supporter, Samuel Thomas, for illegal fundraising.

52. EKR to CRR, Dec. 23, n.y. [1896], TRC-HU; TR to Martha Selmes, Mar. 15, 1896, JIG-ARIZ; TR to ARC, Nov. 29, 1896, TRC-HU.

53. TR to ARC, May 3, 1896, TRC-HU; TR speech at Union League Club against

Report of Committee on Political Reform, TRC-HU; McKinley later complained to William Howard Taft that "Roosevelt is always in such a state of mind": Archibald Butt, *Taft and Roosevelt: The Intimate Letters of Archie Butt, Military Aide* (Garden City, N.Y., 1930), 2:441; MOR 1:569; McKinley knew that Roosevelt had been an enthusiastic supporter of Speaker of the House Tom Reed's presidential hopes, and TR had no real support from the powerful Platt machine. TR disliked McKinley's close friend, campaign manager and head of the R.N.C., Mark Hanna, because he found him "coarse" and not capable of seeing the big picture: TR to HCL, July 30, 1896, HCL-MHS; HCL to TR, Dec. 2, 1896, TRP-LC.

54. Without consulting Edith, he had invited Bamie to spend the summer with them at Sagamore Hill at the same time he promised his new chief, Secretary of the Navy John D. Long, that he would pass almost all of the summer in Washington. But when Theodore disappeared Bamie did not exactly quite move in on her: TR to F. R. Lounsbury, Dec. 9, and to ARC, Dec. 20, 1896, MOR-REJ.

55. Helen Roosevelt Robinson (and ARL) to FDR, Sept. 10, 1897, RFP-FDR; EKR-Di, July 2 and 5, 1897. TR had invited him "for as long as you can stay": TR to FDR, June 11, 1897, RFP-FDR.

56. TR to WSC, Aug. 9, 1897, MOR-REJ; furniture and ranch, TR to Martha Selmes, Aug. 8, 1897, JIG-ARIZ; EKR-Di, Aug. 1–13, 1897.

57. MOR 1:567; TR to Reuben Durrett, Apr. 27, 1894 TRC-HU.

58. Beale, *Rise of America*, 89; when Roosevelt mused about how quickly the U.S. could annex by force underfortified Canada, he was indulging himself in a fantasy that Charles Sumner, Presidents U. S. Grant and Benjamin Harrison, American Fenians, bribed Manitoban rebels, and other advocates of a North American union dreamed before him: Charles Vevier, "American Continentalism: An Idea of Expansion, 1845–1910," in Joel H. Silbey, ed., *National Development and Sectional Crisis, 1815–1860* (New York, 1970), 11–24; Tilden G. Edelstein, *Strange Enthusiasm: A Life of Thomas Wentworth Higginson* (New Haven), 384; Walter LaFeber, *The Cambridge History of American Foreign Relations*, vol. 2, *The American Search for Opportunity, 1865–1913* (New York, 1995), 61–63, 78–79; MOR 1:500–501.

59. HCL to Thomas Wentworth Higginson, Mar. 25, 1896, Thomas Wentworth Higginson Papers, Houghton; MOR 1:573, 798. The Cuban war for independence suffered double blows when Spain killed its leaders José Martí in 1895 and Antonio Maceo in 1896; on the yellow press and the Cuban war see Arthur Lubow, *The Reporter Who Would Be King: A Biography of Richard Harding Davis* (New York, 1992), 143, and David Nasaw, *The Chief: The Life of William Randolph Hearst* (Boston, 2000), 128–29.

60. TR to HCL, Aug. 17, 1897, HCL-MHS; TR Scrapbook. TR was also busy trying to promote football between West Point and the Naval Academy at Annapolis. The Wright Brothers later studied Langley's design: Roger E. Bilstein, *Flight in America, 1900–1983: From the Wrights to the Astronauts* (Baltimore, 1984), 9.

61. TR to ARC, Jan. 17, 1896 [really 1897], TRC-HU.

62. MOR 1:803; O'Toole, *Five of Hearts*; MOR 1:644; Rotundo, *American Manhood*, 232–35; Kristin L. Hoganson, *Fighting for American Manhood: How Gender Politics Provoked the Spanish-American and Philippine-American Wars* (New Haven, 1998); David Blight, *Race and Reunion* (New York, 2001); Dalton, "Theodore Roosevelt and the Idea of War," *Theodore Roosevelt Association Journal* 7 no. 4, 6–11; Gerald F. Linderman, *The Mirror of War: American Society and the Spanish-American War* (Ann Arbor, 1974).

63. The postwar Civil War syndrome or glorification of Civil War sacrifice had roots in prevailing redemptive explanations of the war. Julia Ward Howe's inspirational and apocalyptic "Battle Hymn of the Republic," sung by hundreds of Union war prisoners at Libby Prison and at stirring rallies across the North, told of the war as part of God's plan for bringing about

his kingdom on earth. Morehead, *American Apocalypse*; David W. Blight, *Frederick Douglass' Civil War: Keeping Faith in Jubilee* (Baton Rouge, 1989), 118, and his *Race and Reunion*; see *The Letters of Francis Parkman* (Norman, Okla., 1960), 1:157; Oliver Wendell Holmes, Jr., in *Speeches by Oliver Wendell Holmes, Jr.* (Boston, 1934), 62–63, and his Memorial Day address, May 30, 1884, 11; "The Soldier's Faith," May 30, 1895. Lodge fought the tameness of his times by riding to the hounds at Myopia Hunt Club, bathing nude at Nahant, and reimagining America's role in world politics (see Robert Grant, *Fourscore: An Autobiography* [Boston, 1934], 241); like TR, many of his other friends dreamed of military glory which would put them on a par with Civil War heroes: James R. Garfield Diary, May 30, 1886, Garfield Papers-LC.

64. TR to Bob Ferguson, Apr. 20, 1894, JIG-ARIZ; "National Preparedness: Military-Industrial-Social," TR speech in Kansas City, Mo., Memorial Day, 1916; Blight, *Frederick Douglass*, 106, and *Race and Reunion.*

65. Long to Thomas Wentworth Higginson, Apr. 10, 1897, Higginson-Barney MSS, Houghton; Riis, *Theodore Roosevelt the Citizen*, 165.

66. TR to EKR, Sept. 9, 1897, TRJR-LC.

67. TR to C. H. Davis, Nov. 3, 1897, MOR-REJ; "Theodore Roosevelt's Views on the Use of Liquor in the Navy," *New England Home Magazine*, Nov. 7, 1897 (supplement to *Boston Sunday Journal*).

68. MOR 1:755; TR to Stanford Newel, Jan. 31, 1898, MOR-REJ.

69. Wood later wrote that excessive individualism required that "we must nationalize our people" and heighten their attachment to the nation: Wood, "Universal Military Training," addresses and proceedings of the Fifty-fourth Annual Meeting of the National Education Association, 1916, 161; TR to Bob Ferguson, Jan. 22, 1898, Nov. 1, 1897, JIG-ARIZ.

70. TR to F. C. Selous, Feb. 15, 1898, MOR-REJ.

71. TR to S. Whitney Tillinghast, Nov. 23, and to Francis Higginson, Nov. 19, 1897, and to William L. Clowes, Jan. 14, 1898, MOR-REJ.

72. Enrique de Lôme quoted in Hoganson, *Fighting*, 89; TR to DR, Mar. 6, [1898], TRC-HU; "butt-end" in MOR 1:717.

73. TR to Theodore Douglas Robinson, Feb. 16, 1898, and to Franklin Edmonds, Nov. 19, 1914, MOR-REJ.

74. TR to DR, Mar. 6, [1898], TRC-HU; Louis A. Pérez, Jr., *The War of 1898: The United States and Cuba in History and Historiography* (Chapel Hill, N.C., 1998), 16; TR to WSC, Mar. 29, 1898, SUBJ-TRC.

75. TR to Winthrop Chanler, Feb. 15, 1898, TRC-HU; MOR 1:784–85.

76. TR to CRR, Mar. 16, [1898], TRC-HU; he did get sympathy from the Lodges and the Chanlers; Wintie Chanler commented to Margaret Chanler that TR had hired for Edith's care "a lot of perfectly incompetent doctors, taxidermists and veterinaries, good sportsmen and athletes, but medically null": Margaret Chanler, ed., *Winthrop Chanler's Letters* (New York, 1951), 65; MOR 1:791; TR to ARC, Mar. 6 and 7, 1898, TRC-HU; MOR 1:790; see S. Morris, *Edith Kermit Roosevelt*, 168–73; Hyman George Rickover, *How the Battleship Maine Was Destroyed* (Annapolis, Md., 1995), 46–70, 91.

77. MOR 2:801; Emily Tuckerman, an old friend from New York, took in Kermit, Ethel, and Archie, and she recorded that TR visited them twice a day. Tuckerman wrote that his wild play with the children disturbed her household: Tuckerman diary, NYHS.

78. TR to Alexander Lambert, Mar. 29, 1898, TRC-HU.

79. weak policy: Hoganson, *Fighting for American Manhood*, 94, 102–104, 91, see 232*n.*; on demonstrations see Pérez, Jr., *War of 1898*, 67–80; TR, Journal, 1898, TRC-HU, and Wallace Finley Dailey, ed., *TR Pocket Diary 1898: Theodore Roosevelt's Private Account of the War with Spain* (Cambridge, Mass., 1998); TR wrote to E. N. Buxton on May 2, 1898: "I have been

doing all I could to bring about this war," but he did not single-handedly cause the war: SUBJ-TRC; John L. Offner, *An Unwanted War: The Diplomacy of the United States and Spain over Cuba, 1895–1898* (Chapel Hill, N.C., 1992), 168.

80. Pérez, Jr., *War of 1898*, 19, 29.

81. MOR 2:804. On April 29, 1898, Winthrop Chanler wrote about TR: "I really think he is going mad. The President has asked him twice as a personal favor to stay in the Navy Dept., but Theodore is wild to fight and hack and hew. It really is sad. Of course this ends his political career for good. Even Cabot says this": M. Chanler, ed., *Winthrop Chanler's Letters*, 68–69.

82. ARL and Corinne Robinson Alsop interview, ORHO-COL; Putnam, *Theodore Roosevelt*, 48–49.

83. "fortnight" in MOR 2:831; "apprehension" in ARL, *Crowded Hours*, 21; Arthur Frank Wertheim and Barbara Bair, *The Papers of Will Rogers* (Norman, Okla., 1996), 1:194.

84. EKR to ERD, June 3, 1898, TRC-HU; the hotel is now part of the University of Florida.

85. *TR/HCL*, 1:306.

86. EKR to HCL, June [25], 1898, HCL-MHS.

87. MEM 13:53; EKR to TRJR, Nov. 20, n.y. [1929], TRJR-LC; hounds, Bob Ferguson to DR, July 31, 1898, JIG-ARIZ; MEM 13:57; the segregated U.S. Army sent black troops to fight alongside Cuban insurgents: Pérez, Jr., *War of 1898*, 86–90, bases his evaluation of *insurrectos'* contribution to victory on Cuban and Spanish sources which have long been ignored in the U.S.

88. Bob Ferguson to DR, n.d. [June 1898], TRC-HU; MEM 13:62–82; Ivan Musicant, *Empire by Default: The Spanish-American War and the Dawn of the American Century* (New York, 1998), 377–89; a controversy arose about the Tenth Cavalry's role saving the Rough Riders from an ambush at Las Guásimas and TR criticized black infantrymen unfairly for cowardice and superstition; he said white officers needed to lead black troops: TR, "The Rough Riders," *Scribner's Magazine* 25 (April 1899), MOR 2:1305; see William Larry Ziglar, "Negro Opinion of Theodore Roosevelt" (Ph.D. diss., University of Maine, 1972), 82–85; Amy Kaplan, "Black and Blue on San Juan Hill," in *Cultures of United States Imperialism*, ed. Amy Kaplan and Donald E. Pease (Durham, N.C., 1993), 219–36.

89. In private TR viewed Davis as a superficial society "cad" but behaved as his good friend in Cuba for instrumental reasons; TR also invited the Vitagraph Film Company to join his troops: Lubow, *Reporter Who Would Be King*, 166–80; EKR to TR, May 28, 1898, TRJR-LC; EKR to TR, May 20, n.y. [1898], and July 1, 1898, TRC-HU; EKR to HCL, June [25], 1898, HCL-MHS; Charles Herner, *Arizona Rough Riders* (Tucson, 1970), 15–16; Edward Marshall, *The Story of the Rough Riders* (New York, 1899).

90. McClay Weller to his mother, n.d., in private collection of Lawrence and Doris Budner, Dallas.

91. MEM 13:62–82; Musicant, *Empire by Default*, 405–22; Willard B. Gatewood, Jr., *"Smoked Yankees" and the Struggle for Empire: Letters from Negro Soldiers, 1898–1902* (Fayetteville, Ark., 1987), 42–46, 73–97; William Sanders to Helen Sanders, July 19, 1898, Sanders Papers, Houghton; Lubow, *Reporter Who Would Be King*, 186–87; David F. Trask, *The War with Spain in 1898* (New York, 1981).

92. Musicant, *Empire by Default*, 427–31; Lodge included the part about the disaster: TR to HCL, July 3, 1898, HCL-MHS.

93. Nasaw, *The Chief*, 145, 136; MOR 3:96.

94. HCL to TR, July 7, 1898, HCL-MHS; George Dewey, *Autobiography of George Dewey: Admiral of the Navy* (New York, 1913), 180–85, 254–67.

95. TR to DR, July 22, 1898, MOR-REJ; Margaret Chanler Aldrich, Roosevelt Women

Interviews, TRC-HU; "Digest of the Complete Report of Auxiliary No. 3 of the Red Cross," TRC-HU; "the President": TR to HCL, July 22, 1898, HCL-MHS.

96. TR to HCL, July 14, 1898, HCL-MHS; see Sanders Papers, Houghton, for more on misconduct of the war; the Dodge Commission heard from the ambitious Nelson A. Miles about "embalmed" beef, MOR 2:903.

97. James Ford Rhodes, *The McKinley and Roosevelt Administrations, 1897–1909* (New York, 1965), 76–78; Bob Ferguson to CRR, June 12, 1898, TRC-HU; TR testified about the putrid "embalmed" beef he had thrown overboard his transport and the sickening canned roasted beef they ate and other problems: MOR 2:911–13, 952–54.

98. Michael Pearlman, *To Make Democracy Safe for America: Patricians and Preparedness in the Progressive Era* (Urbana, Ill., 1984), 22; see Scott letter in Hagedorn Papers, TRC-HU; F. Wood, ed., *Roosevelt As We Knew Him*, 58; L. F. Abbott, ed., *Letters of Archie Butt*, 112; John Greenway to TR, Sept. 13, 1913, JIG-ARIZ; TR said the War Department did not want him to have the Medal of Honor because "I was not acting in accordance with orders. I had been told to *support* the attack of the Regulars with my regiment," but not to charge through the regulars to take the hill, MOR 2:892, 894–95; McKinley and the Vice President supported the medal, but the army and some members of Congress disagreed; other reports said it was for buying them a lot of beer; TR to Martha Selmes, July 31, 1898, JIG-ARIZ; TR, *Rough Riders*, MEM: 38.

99. TR to reporter in Irving C. Norwood, "Exit-Roosevelt, the Dominant," *Outing Magazine* 53 (March 1909): 722; on pride about wounds see MOR 2:969; "content to go" in TR to HCL, July 19, 1898, HCL-MHS.

100. EKR to TR, July 18, 1898, TRC-HU.

101. EKR to TR, July 5 and 7, 1898, TRC-HU.

102. John L. Offner, "From Canned Goods to Gugus: American Perceptions of Filipinos in 1898," in Pierre Melandri and Serge Ricard, eds., *Ethnocentrisme et diplomatie: L'Amérique et le monde au XXe siècle* (Paris, 2001), 83–99; Stuart Creighton Miller, *"Benevolent Assimilation": The American Conquest of the Philippines, 1899–1903* (New Haven, 1982); Frank Ninkovich, *The United States and Imperialism* (Malden, Mass., 2001).

CHAPTER SIX: A "WILD GALLUP, AT BREAKNECK SPEED"

1. *New York Tribune*, Sept. 8 and Oct. 6, 1898, quoted in G. Wallace Chessman, *Governor Theodore Roosevelt: The Albany Apprenticeship, 1898–1900* (Cambridge, Mass., 1965), 54.

2. Henry Seidel Canby, *The Age of Confidence* (New York, 1934), 204–205; Lodge also wrote a history of the war; TR gloated to his new friend British military observer Arthur Lee: "The day of the Latin races is over," MOR 2:890.

3. Don Russell, *The Lives and Legends of Buffalo Bill* (Norman, Okla., 1960), 419; Glenn Shirley, *Pawnee Bill: A Biography of Major Gordon W. Lillie* (Albuquerque, N. Mex., 1958), 76; Arthur Frank Wertheim and Barbara Bair, eds., *The Papers of Will Rogers* (Norman, Okla., 1996), 1:224–26; Roosevelt's Rough Rider Association, Constitution and By-laws, JIG-ARIZ. When he saw Mulhall's Wild West show at his 1900 Rough Riders reunion TR made friends with him and his expert cowgirl daughter Lucille and later invited them to perform at his and McKinley's inauguration in March 1901.

4. "hybrid" in Thomas Collier Platt, *The Autobiography of Thomas Collier Platt* (New York, 1910), 358, 365. Fusion had fallen apart in New York politics, but TR tried to get the support of both regular Republicans and independents like Josephine Shaw Lowell, Seth Low, and John Jay Chapman; see Chapman Papers, Houghton, for details of TR's controversy with the independents about running on their ticket. Platt called the independents "thoughtless

aristocrats"; see also Chessman, *Governor,* and Harold F. Gosnell, *Boss Platt and His New York Machine* (Chicago, 1924).

5. MOR 1:753; Chessman, *Governor,* 63; "State and National Issues," MEM 16:441 and *New York Times,* Oct. 20, 1898, TR-SP; John Proctor Clarke's Recollections of Campaigning with TR, SUBJ-TRC.

6. Robert L. Beisner, *Twelve Against Empire: The Anti-Imperialists, 1898–1900* (New York, 1968), 126; Ziglar, "Negro Opinion of Theodore Roosevelt," 89, 90–105; Gatewood, "*Smoked Yankees*"; William O'Neill to J. S. Van Duzer, Nov. 1, 1898, Van Duzer Family Papers, Cornell University; Nasaw, *The Chief,* 148; Chessman, *Governor,* 59; AUTO, 282.

7. EKR to HCL, n.d. [1898], and scribbled on the bottom of TR to HCL, Oct. 14, 1898, HCL-MHS.

8. The Roosevelts threatened to send ARL to Miss Spence's School but due to her resistance they hired a governess: ARL, *Crowded Hours,* 26; Frances Parsons, *Roosevelt House Bulletin,* Fall 1948, Roosevelt Women folder, SUBJ-TRC. EKR wrote to his allies and kept up their social obligations when TR was governor; see EKR to Seth Low, Oct. 18, 1898, Low Papers, Columbia University Library.

9. EKR to ARL, Dec. 13, 1899, TRC-HU; Char Miller, *Gifford Pinchot and the Making of Modern Environmentalism* (Washington, D.C., 2001), 173.

10. Ethel Armes, based on interview with Edward Riis, "In the Hour of Peril," Anecdotes File, TRP-BP; ABR, Memoirs, TRC-HU; TRJR, *All in the Family,* 80; AER to ARC, Jan. 21, [1899], TRC-HU.

11. "cathedral town" in MOR 2:931; EKR to ARC, n.d. [1899], TRC-HU; EKR-Di Jan. 1–5, 1899; "breakdown" in TR to Woodbury Kane, Jan. 5, 1899, MOR-REJ; Governor and Mrs. Roosevelt decided that Alice must turn down a free railroad pass sent by the new Republican senator Chauncey Depew, formerly of the New York Central Railroad, because progressive governors like La Follette in Wisconsin and Altgeld in Illinois had made campaign issues out of railroads' attempts to bribe lawmakers with free passes. Theodore and Edith were not as careful about gifts to the children (like a Tiffany gold watch sent anonymously to Ted) because no strings were attached.

12. Chessman, *Governor,* 10.

13. For La Follette's 1901–1905 career as reform governor, see B. and F. La Follette, *Robert M. La Follette, June 14, 1855–June 18, 1925,* 1:136–98; Robert S. Maxwell, *La Follette and the Rise of the Progressives in Wisconsin* (New York, 1973); and Unger, *La Follette.*

14. Hammack, *Power and Society,* 56–57, 148.

15. Jacob A. Riis, "Theodore Roosevelt's Father," *Outlook* (Oct. 6, 1900): 306.

16. MOR 2:948. His father's friend Morris K. Jesup had advocated the protection of the Adirondacks since the early 1880s: Alfred L. Donaldson, *A History of the Adirondacks,* vol. 2 (New York, 1921).

17. "limitations" in L. Abbott, ed., *Letters of Archie Butt,* 68; James Weldon Johnson, *Black Manhattan* (New York, 1930), 26; Ziglar, "Negro Opinion of Theodore Roosevelt," 114; Richard B. Sherman, *The Republican Party and Black America from McKinley to Hoover, 1896–1933* (Charlottesville, Va., 1973), 24–25; for messages as governor see MEM 17:3–33.

18. TR to Florence Kelley, Jan. 23, to Jacob Riis, Jan. 23, and to John Williams, June 2, 1899, TRP-LC; Dorothy Rose Blumberg, *Florence Kelley: The Making of a Social Pioneer* (New York, 1966), 172–75; K. Sklar, *Kelley,* 292–94.

19. Although he gets mixed up about the Kelley appointment, a useful source on the governorship is Hurwitz, *Theodore Roosevelt and Labor,* 191–225, 232; Maud Nathan, *Once Upon a Time and Today* (New York, 1933), 132.

20. Hurwitz, *Theodore Roosevelt and Labor,* 234. TR favored a fairly relaxed system of

evaluating teachers via exams or advanced courses, but the bill he finally signed did not bring this into effect; AUTO, 314–17; Daniel Allen Hearn, *Legal Executions in New York State: A Comprehensive Reference, 1639–1963* (Jefferson, N.C., 1997).

21. Chessman, *Governor*, 146; Platt, *Autobiography*, 374.

22. TR to Seth Low, Apr. 16, 1900, Low Papers, Columbia University Library; MOR 2:1068, 905–907; 60 to 88 percent poor in 1900 Report of the U.S. Industrial Commission: see Morton Keller, *Affairs of State: Public Life in Late Nineteenth Century America* (Cambridge, Mass., 1977), 373; Hurwitz, *Theodore Roosevelt and Labor*, 191.

23. TR to John Coyle, May 15, 1899, MOR-REJ; MOR 2:1004; MEM 17:49.

24. MEM 15:267–81, xiv–xv.

25. TR to Platt, July 1, 1899, and to Alice M. Robertson, June 7, 1899, MOR-REJ; MOR 2:1023; John L. Offner, "From Canned Goods to Gugus: American Perceptions of Filipinos in 1898," in Pierre Melandri and Serge Ricard, eds., *Ethnocentrisme et diplomatie: L'Amérique et le monde au XXe siècle*, 83–99, and Offner, "Imperialism by International Consensus: The United States and the Philippine Islands," in Daniela Rossini, ed., *From Theodore Roosevelt to FDR: Internationalism and Isolationism in American Foreign Policy* (Staffordshire, Eng. 1995), 45–54.

26. MOR 2:1062; *TR/HCL*, 1:418; MEM 13:320.

27. MEM 13:324, 265, 322; TR to Charles Scribner, Aug. 10, 1899, SUBJ-TRC; one of TR's friends joked when he read the book that it was "a fine imaginative study of Cromwell's qualifications for the governorship of New York": MEM 13:266; MOR 2:1043.

28. TR to HCL, Aug. 10, 1899, HCL-MHS; EKR to ARC, n.d., TRC-HU.

29. George Dewey, *Autobiography of George Dewey: Admiral of the Navy* (New York, 1913), 289–90; TR to Capt. Daniel Delehanty, Jan. 4, 1899, MOR-REJ; TR to HCL, Aug. 20, 1901, HCL-MHS; TR to Avery Andrews, Aug. 8, 1899, SUBJ-TRC; MOR 2:1091.

30. TR to ARC, Nov. 14, 1899, TRC-HU; Maria Longworth Storer, *In Memoriam Bellamy Storer* (privately printed, 1923), 30.

31. EKR to ARC, n.d. [Dec. 31, 1899], TRC-HU; MOR 2:1127; MEM 13:274; TR was ambivalent about the Boer War because of his admiration for the Boers, but in the end he supported the British. TR blocked the New York legislature from passing a resolution of support for the Boers and Lodge fought against similar resolutions in the Senate; TR to Col. John Jacob Astor, Nov. 9, 1900, JIG-ARIZ.

32. TR to Jacob Riis, May 23, 1900, Riis Papers, LC; TR, "Fellow-Feeling as a Political Factor," *The Century*, January 1900; ERD to John Greenway, Mar. 1, 1900, EKR to John Greenway, Mar. 30, [1900], JIG-ARIZ; on the Burleigh visit, EKR-Di, Jan. 23, 1900; they also entertained overnight the former Dartmouth football player, attorney William H. Lewis and his wife, later an ally of Booker T. Washington: Louis R. Harlan, *Booker T. Washington: The Wizard of Tuskegee 1901–1905*, 16.

33. TR to WSC, Jan. 22, 1900, and EKR to ARC, n.d. [March 1900], TRC-HU.

34. *Letters from Theodore Roosevelt to Anna Roosevelt Cowles*, 223; TR to CRR, Apr. 13, 1900, TRC-HU; both sisters recalled being the governor's main hostess when he came to Manhattan; CRR claimed that all the breakfasts were at her house on 422 Madison Avenue: *My Brother*, 185; the diaries and letters support Bamie's memory up to October 1899; Corinne liked to recall how her brother said to her: "Pussie, haven't we had fun being governor of New York State?": *My Brother*, 194.

35. TR to Bartlett S. Johnston, Sept. 4, 1899, SUBJ-TRC; Goran Rystad, *Ambiguous Imperialism: American Foreign Policy and Domestic Politics at the Turn of the Century* (Stockholm, 1975), 225–26.

36. Beale, *Rise of America*, 102–103; Lodge battled Hay in Washington until the furious

secretary of state resigned, but McKinley insisted that he stay in office; TR to Frederick William Holls, Feb. 15 and 26, 1900, Holls Papers, Houghton.

37. Beale, *Rise of America:* Hay quote on 103, Lee on 106; MOR 2:1186, 1192.

38. AUTO, 323–24; TR to J. W. Pond, Dec. 5, 1899, MOR-REJ; MOR 2:1345.

39. TR to Capt. F. Norton Goddard, Apr. 16, 1900, MOR-REJ.

40. TR to HCL, Jan. 30, 1900, HCL-MHS; TR to Charles Mitchell Harvey, May 3, 1900, MOR-REJ.

41. "torn" in EKR-Di, June 18, 1900; ARC to TR, Apr. 26, 1900, TRP-LC.

42. "melancholy" in TR to James R. Parsons, June 25, 1900, TRC-HU, "stood Mr. Platt" in TR to John Proctor Clarke, Apr. 13, 1900, TR-SYR; see EKR-Di, June and July 1900; EKR wrote that the vice president's wife was the least important person of all in official Washington, but she dreaded the vice presidency not for herself but for her husband: EKR to Emily Carow, July 8, n.y. [1900], TRC-HU.

43. Rough Rider Clubs in NSC; Wertheim and Bair, eds., *Papers of Will Rogers,* 1:194–98; Ben Yagoda, *Will Rogers: A Biography* (New York, 1993), 43–46, 189.

44. TR to Frederick Holls, July 31, 1900, Holls Papers, Houghton: EKR to Emily Carow, Aug. 19, 1900, TRC-HU; Elihu Root to William Roscoe Thayer, Thayer Papers, Houghton.

45. "strain" in TR to TRJR, Sept. 24, 1900, TRJR-LC; "Teddy at Green River," *Cheyenne Leader,* Sept. 24, 1900, TR-SP; TR and EKR watched the news about the Boxer Rebellion that summer. The Dowager Empress of China had lost the Mandate of Heaven when her country was beaten by Japan in 1895, after which famine and foreign incursions into mines and ports tore China apart. When the anti-foreign secret society called the Boxers began killing "foreign devils," especially in the Japanese and European legations, the empress supported their murderous intentions in order to bolster the tottering Manchu dynasty. Desperate cries for help from the American embassy made President McKinley worry that the U.S. was too weak to rescue its people alone, and he rued the day he was forced to post two-thirds of the American army to subdue the Philippines.

46. Finley Peter Dunne, *Mr. Dooley's Philosophy* (New York, 1906), 233; Elmer Ellis, *Mr. Dooley's America: A Life of Finley Peter Dunne* (New York, 1969), 149; William M. Gibson, *Theodore Roosevelt Among the Humorists: W. D. Howells, Mark Twain, and Mr. Dooley* (Knoxville, Tenn., 1980), 49.

47. MOR 2:1406.

48. On TR's campaign style, Jerome A. Hart, *In Our Second Century: From an Editor's Notebook* (San Francisco, 1931), 323; "Roosevelt in Rochester," *New York Times* clipping, Oct. 27, 1898, TR-SP. On Foster, Melanie Gustafson, "Partisan and Nonpartisan: The Political Career of Judith Ellen Foster, 1881–1910," in Gustafson, Kristie Miller, and Elisabeth I. Perry, eds., *We Have Come to Stay: American Women and Political Parties, 1880–1960* (Albuquerque, N. Mex., 1999), 8–9. As president he appointed Foster to study women and child workers in the U.S.; see Gustafson, *Women and the Republican Party, 1854–1924* (Urbana, Ill., 2001), 76. The Republican Party benefited often when women voted in the West; woman suffrage would have made faster progress through the states and on the national level without the complication of prohibition because where women voted they tended to be dry voters and in favor of reform, which gave liquor interests and those opposed to reform two extra reasons to block suffrage: Jo Freeman, *A Room at a Time: How Women Entered Party Politics* (Lanham, Md., 2000), 51.

49. Ethel Armes, "You Couldn't Hit Hard Enough Sir!" Anecdotes File, TRP-BP; embrace story from F. Wood, ed., *Roosevelt As We Knew Him,* 79; MOR 2:1371; Ellis, *Mr. Dooley's America,* 149.

50. "Tried to Stop Roosevelt," *New York Times* clipping, Oct. 14, 1900, TR-SP.

51. TR to TRJR, Nov. 19, 1900, TRJR-LC; Mark Sullivan, *Our Times: The United States, 1900–1925* (New York, 1926), 1:346; MOR 2:1406, see *n.*2.

52. Ashby, *Bryan*, 87; MEM 16:571; Beisner, *Twelve Against Empire*, 125.

53. MEM 16:404, 513; MOR 2:1416; Ashby, *Bryan*, 91; Robert W. Cherny, *A Righteous Cause: The Life of William Jennings Bryan* (Boston, 1985).

54. November 1904, *Mark Twain's Letters* (New York, 1917), 2:762–63, quoted in Gibson, *Theodore Roosevelt Among the Humorists*, 34; Sullivan, *Our Times*, 1:346, *New York Times*, Nov. 3, 1900; Ashby, *Bryan*, 93; see also William Allen White, *Masks in a Pageant* (New York, 1928).

55. EKR to ARC, n.d., and to TR, n.d. [September or October 1900] and Sept. 29, n.y. [1900], TRC-HU; the Roosevelt boys' memoirs and letters are filled with resentment against the muscular Christian regimen of Rector Peabody at Groton; see also Putney, *Muscular Christianity*, 106–108.

56. EKR to Emily Carow, [Sept. 14, 1900], TRC-HU; TR to Edward Sandford Martin, Nov. 22, 1900, MOR-REJ; *New York Daily Tribune*, Dec. 31, 1900, TR-SP.

57. EKR to TR, Jan. 7, to ARC, [Jan.] 9, and to TR, Jan. 16, [1901], TRC-HU.

58. EKR to Emily Carow, Mar. 8, 1901, TRC-HU; EKR-Di, Mar. 4, 1901.

59. "existence" in MOR 3:12; TR to EKR, Mar. 6, 1901, TRC-HU; Robert Bridges memorandum of conversation with Mrs. DR, Aug. 21 and 22, 1920, in regard to the contents of her new book, TRC-HU; he also considered being admitted to the bar in New York and joining Evarts and Choate after the vice presidency: TR to John Proctor Clarke, Mar. 29, 1901, TRP-SYR; TR to TRJR, Nov. 19, 1900, TRJR-LC.

60. Nicholas Murray Butler to HCL, Apr. 24, 1900, HCL-MHS; "melancholic" in Teague, *Mrs. L*, 112; TR to Frances Parsons, June 26, 1900, in Parsons, *Perchance*, 133–34; Edith felt her privacy violated when her childhood nurse, Mame, who now lived at Sagamore Hill and looked after the next generation, gave photographs of Edith's childhood to the newspapers: EKR to ARC, n.d. [1900–1901], TRC-HU.

61. TR to TRJR, Apr. 9, 1901, TRJR-LC; MOR 3:97.

62. He also made plans to visit Hull House and Tuskegee Institute, and he thought a lot about his political future. He took Kermit, Ted, and some cousins on a cruise of the South Bay and a hunt; see EKR-Di, June 1901. For his summer business see MOR 3:97–127.

63. "sympathize" in MOR 3:57 (TR also found McKinley aloof and marred by "cold-bloodedness," 56); William Allen White, *The Autobiography of William Allen White* (New York, 1946), 333.

64. EKR to ARC, Apr. 24, [1901], TRC-HU; TR to TRJR, May 7, 1901, TRJR-LC; MOR 3:74.

65. Woodrow Wilson to TR, July 28, 1901, TRC-HU; TR to Endicott Peabody, May 7, and July 12 and 18, 1901, Peabody Papers, Houghton; Ashburn, *Peabody*, 220.

66. MOR 3:69, 80.

67. Hamlin Garland, *Companions on the Trail: A Literary Chronicle* (New York, 1931), 82; TR to ERD, Aug. 8, 1901, TRC-HU.

68. EKR-Di, Aug. 15–17, 1901.

69. EKR-Di, Aug. 22–31, 1901; EKR to ARC, n.d. [Aug. 30 and 31, Sept. 12, 1901], TRC-HU; TR to HCL, Sept. 9, 1901, HCL-MHS.

70. Robert Rydell, *All the World's a Fair: Visions of Empire at American International Expositions, 1876–1916* (Chicago, 1984). Efficiency expert Frederick Winslow Taylor had directed the concessions, and exhibition organizers, including Latin American sponsors, celebrated electricity, technology, and trade. Anthropological knowledge represented at the exposition was filled with racial hierarchy and stereotyping: Darkest Africa, Red Men's Day, and "our little brown brothers." Ansley Wilcox Scrapbook, T.R. Inaugural Site, Buffalo; *New*

York Evening Journal, Apr. 10, 1901, quoted in W. A. Swanberg, *Citizen Hearst: A Biography of William Randolph Hearst* (New York, 1961), 227.

71. EKR to ARC, Sept. 12, [1901], TRC-HU.

72. EKR-Di, Sept. 8, 11, 1901, Ansley Wilcox Scrapbook.

73. EKR-Di, Sept. 13, 1901, on the twelfth they camped at Colden Camp.

74. EKR-Di, Sept. 14, 1901; S. Morris, *Edith Kermit Roosevelt*, 211–15; William Chapman White, *Just About Everything in the Adirondacks* (Syracuse, N.Y., 1994), 80–81; Hazel was later famous for sentencing birth control advocate Margaret Sanger to jail; Bob Ferguson to Edith Munro Ferguson, Sept. 20, 1901, TRC-HU; Ansley Wilcox, "Theodore Roosevelt, President," statement included in David Wallace, *Ansley Wilcox House and Its Furnishings*, (Buffalo, N.Y., Theodore Roosevelt Inaugural National Historic Site, 1989).

75. Bob Ferguson to Edith Munro Ferguson, Sept. 20, 1901, TRC-HU; Wilcox, "Theodore Roosevelt, President"; see Exhibits and Ansley Wilcox Scrapbook 1901; see also E. Morris, *Rise*, 737–41.

76. EKR to TR, Sept. 21, [1901], TRC-HU; EKR-Di, Sept. 16, 1901.

CHAPTER SEVEN: THE STRONG MAN AND A WEAK STATE

1. Lyman Abbott, "Theodore Roosevelt As We See Him," *Outlook* (Oct. 12, 1912): 2; Elihu Root quoted in George E. Mowry, *The Era of Theodore Roosevelt and the Birth of Modern America, 1900–1912* (New York, 1962), 111. The best sources on Roosevelt's presidential years are Mowry, *Era*, William H. Harbaugh, *Power and Responsibility: The Life and Times of Theodore Roosevelt* (Newtown, Conn., 1997), and Lewis L. Gould, *The Presidency of Theodore Roosevelt* (Lawrence, Kans., 1991) and *Reform and Regulation: American Politics from Roosevelt to Wilson* (New York, 1986); for further reading see their bibliographies.

2. I described the scene of his walking to the White House, his dinner with his sisters, and his first days in more detail in Dalton, "Early Life"; see Rixey, *Bamie*, 172–82; *New York Times* and *New York World*, Sept. 23 and 24, 1901; Nicholas Murray Butler, *Across the Busy Years* (New York, 1939–40), 2:87; Rosamond Gilder, ed., *Letters of Richard Watson Gilder* (Boston, 1916), 210; White, *Autobiography*, 338–39; see also Political Scrapbook, TRP-LC.

3. TR to Brander Matthews, Mar. 21, 1901, MOR-REJ; Henry Adams, *Selected Letters* (New York, 1951), 2:364; Nathaniel Wright Stephenson, *Nelson W. Aldrich: A Leader in American Politics* (New York, 1930), 203; Parsons, *Perchance*, 234; Will Irwin, *Making of a Reporter* (New York, 1942), 157.

4. Matthew Josephson, *The President Makers* (New York, 1940), 108; Butler to HCL, May 28, 1901, HCL-MHS; *New York World*, Sept. 14, 1901; White, *Autobiography*, 339.

5. On Kentucky see Isaac Frederick Marcosson, *"Marse Henry": A Biography of Henry Watterson* (New York, 1951), 170; Twain quoted in W. Fitzhugh Brundage, ed., *Under Sentence of Death: Lynching in the South* (Chapel Hill, N.C., 1997), 1; white and black Republicans were also killed in order to maintain Democratic supremacy in the Solid South; Vardaman quoted in Stewart E. Tolnay and E. M. Beck, *A Festival of Violence: An Analysis of Southern Lynchings, 1882–1930* (Chicago, 1995), 25.

6. On anti-Semitism, Marcia Graham Synnott, "Anti-Semitism and American Universities: Did Quotas Follow the Jews?," in Jeffrey S. Gurock, ed., *American Jewish History* (New York, 1998), 6, 2:473–51; Pete Daniel, *The Shadow of Slavery: Peonage in the South, 1901–1969* (Chicago, 1990), 96–98, 67.

7. Louis Galambos, *The Public Image of Big Business, 1880–1940* (Baltimore, 1975), 86, 91.

8. Glenn Shirley, *Pawnee Bill: A Biography of Major Gordon W. Lillie* (Albuquerque,

N. Mex., 1958), 162. Charges of arson were evidently false, but spying, intimidation, and bullying tactics characterized the consolidation of oil refinery and marketing: Ron Chernow, *The House of Morgan: An American Banking Dynasty and the Rise of Modern Finance* (New York, 1990); see also Glenn Porter, *The Rise of Big Business, 1860–1910* (Arlington Heights, Ill., 1973).

9. Elliott J. Gorn, *Mother Jones: The Most Dangerous Woman in America* (New York, 2001), 138; Naomi R. Lamoreaux, *The Great Merger Movement in American Business, 1895–1904* (New York, 1988); on courts, Gerald Berk, *Alternative Tracks: The Constitution of American Industrial Order, 1865–1917* (Baltimore, 1994), 96, and Christopher L. Tomlins, *The State and the Unions: Labor Relations, Law, and the Organized Labor Movement in America, 1880–1960* (New York, 1985), 50; *In Re Debs* in Henry Steele Commager, *Documents of American History* (New York, 1947), 2:164; Beckert, *The Monied Metropolis*.

10. Forty percent of the national committee's campaign funds in 1888 came from Pennsylvania's manufacturers or financiers: Bradley A. Smith, "Faulty Assumptions and Undemocratic Consequences of Campaign Finance Reform," *Yale Law Journal* 105 (January 1996): 1049–68.

11. Gifford Pinchot, *Breaking New Ground* (New York, 1947), 112; Michael P. Cohen, *The Pathless Way: John Muir and American Wilderness* (Madison, Wisc., 1984), 277.

12. Owen M. Fiss, *Troubled Beginnings of the Modern State, 1888–1910* (New York, 1993); Tomlins, *State and the Unions*, 51; see Berk, *Alternative Tracks*, 107.

13. *New York Times*, Sept. 24, 1901; "dreadful" in *TR/HCL*, 1:506; "thought of Father" in TR to Mrs. James Leavitt, Oct. 7, 1901, TRC-HU; "confidence" in Butler, *Across the Busy Years*, 2:88.

14. CRR, *My Brother*, 206; Rixey, *Bamie*, 178; Dalton, "Early Life," 9.

15. While TR still held the floor, as he often did at presidential dinners, coffee was served along with the customary boutonniere, this night a yellow saffron rose. Corinne remembered that her brother was taken aback at the sight of the rose; his "face flushed." TR exclaimed: "Is it not strange! This is the rose we all connect with my father. . . . I think there is a blessing connected with this," CRR, *My Brother*, 206–207; Dalton, "Early Life."

16. TR belonged to William James' American Society for Psychical Research, which brought scientific research about the mind to the attention of a small circle of scholars, but there is not much evidence he was a believer in spiritualism; in TR's circle of friends Gifford Pinchot, Caroline Drayton Phillips, and many others took spiritualism very seriously: C. Miller, *Pinchot*, 192–93; CRR, *My Brother*, 206.

17. TR to TRJR, Nov. 20, 1908, TRJR-LC.

18. SUBJ-TRC; MOR 3:300; Lincoln Steffens later claimed that he invented the phrase "the square deal" but his accounts are often self-aggrandizing and unreliable: Peter Lyon, *Success Story: The Life and Times of S. S. McClure* (New York, 1963), 228; "treat each man" in MEM 18:69; for other references to the Square Deal see Albert Bushnell Hart and Herbert Ronald Ferleger, eds., *Theodore Roosevelt Cyclopedia* (New York, 1941), 582–83; the linguistic Americanism "square deal" predates TR; it appeared in *The Century*, June 1895, 279, *The Compact Edition of the Oxford English Dictionary* (New York, 1986), 2:4070.

19. "full President" in Bishop, *Theodore Roosevelt*, 2:174; Gould, *Reform and Regulation*, 27.

20. Mark Hanna to TR, Oct. 12, 1901, in Bishop, *Theodore Roosevelt*, 1:179; Edith Wharton, *The Fruit of the Tree* (New York, 1907), 624.

21. MEM 15:10, 529.

22. "A pink-tea man shall stay in or go out . . . we need real men, and these men shall be rewarded": MOR 4:1090; "reborn" in L. F. Abbott, ed., *Letters of Archie Butt*, 369; Jusserand confirmed this came up in TR's talk often: Jean-Jules Jusserand, *What Me Befell: The Reminiscences of J. J. Jusserand* (New York, 1933), 221. McKinley appointed Pinchot chief

forester: T. H. Watkins, "Father of the Forests," *American Heritage* 42, no. 1 (February/March 1991): 91; Stephen Ponder, "Federal News Management in the Progressive Era: Gifford Pinchot and the Conservation Crusade," *Journalism History* 13, no. 2 (Summer 1986): 42–47; TR to William B. Weeden, Oct. 12, 1906, MOR-REJ.

23. TR to CRR, July 20, 1896, SUBJ-TRC; TR, "At the Founders' Day Banquet of the Union League," *Presidential Addresses and State Papers of Theodore Roosevelt* (New York, 1905), 1:220.

24. AUTO, 400; TR to Cecil A. Lyon, Sept. 17, 1901, Small Collections—Cecil A. Lyon Papers, TR correspondence, FDR.

25. H. G. Wells, *The Future in America: A Search After Realities* (London, 1906), 350, 343.

26. L. F. Abbott, ed., *Letters of Archie Butt*, 12; Jusserand in NSC.

27. The Department of Commerce and Labor, National Bureau of Standards, Bureau of Mines, Census Bureau, and Forest Service were added to the federal government in the first years of the century: James Leiby, *Carroll Wright and Labor Reform: The Origin of Labor Statistics* (Cambridge, Mass., 1960), 111; Wright worried about underconsumption and its economic effects, 136; *Remarks of President Roosevelt to the Committee and Assistant Committees on Department Methods*, at the residence of Mr. Pinchot, Washington, D.C., March 20, 1906 TRC-HU; George M. Kober, *Report of Committee on Social Betterment: A Report by the President's Homes Commission* (Washington, D.C., 1908); Charles Frederick Weller, *Neglected Neighbors: Stories of Life in the Alleys, Tenements and Shanties of the National Capital* (Philadelphia, 1909); AUTO, 364.

28. William Bayard Hale, A *Week in the White House with Theodore Roosevelt* (New York, 1908), 47; the tennis court came with the McKim, Mead, and White renovations; Taft later added the Oval Office.

29. Mark Sullivan, *The Education of an American* (New York, 1938), 273.

30. Arthur Wallace Dunn, *Gridiron Nights: Humourous and Satirical Views of Politics and Statesmen as Presented by the Famous Dining Club* (New York, 1915); Frank M. Chapman, *Autobiography of a Bird-Lover* (New York, 1933), 184; Rixey, *Bamie*, 191.

31. James Pinchot to Gifford Pinchot, Apr. 9, 1907, Gifford Pinchot Papers, LC, quoted in Char Miller, "Keeper of His Conscience?: Pinchot, Roosevelt, and the Politics of Conservation," in Natalie A. Naylor, Douglas Brinkley, and John Allen Gable, eds., *Theodore Roosevelt: Many-Sided American* (Interlaken, N.Y., 1992), 242; Ellis, *Mr. Dooley's America*, 146, 122.

32. John T. McCutcheon, *Drawn from Memory* (New York, 1950), 243.

33. Sullivan, *Our Times*, 3:241; on the newspaper cabinet's later years, John J. Leary, Jr., *Talks with T.R.: From the Diaries of John J. Leary, Jr.* (Boston, 1920), 123–42; George Juergens, *News from the White House: The Presidential-Press Relationship in the Progressive Era* (Chicago, 1981), 65, 17.

34. TR to George Cortelyou, Aug. 11, 1903, George Cortelyou Papers, LC; TR to Joseph B. Bishop, Mar. 12, Aug. 3, 5, and Oct. 22, 1903, Bishop Papers, Houghton; Juergens, *News from the White House*, 69.

35. On hunts, Jim Higgers, *The Adventures of Theodore* (Chicago, 1901); "discovered" in Juergens, *News from the White House*, 29.

36. George Juergens, *Joseph Pulitzer and the New York World* (Princeton, 1966), 186, 322, 294, 282; Swanberg, *Citizen Hearst*, 223.

37. Political Scrapbook, TRP-LC; *New York World*, Sept. 7, 1901, 3; TR to Owen Wister, Sept. 25, 1901, Wister Papers, LC; TR defended his comments to Elbert Hubbard, famous for Roycroft arts and crafts and *Message to Garcia*, by saying that the "filthy" came from stories about Paine for "not even getting out" of bed "to perform the operations of

nature": Jan. 22, 1907, MOR-REJ; "not fully trusted" in *New York World*, Sept. 7, 1901, 3; "strangest" in May 29, 1902, NSC.

38. NSC; Finley Peter Dunne, "Youth and Age," in *Mr. Dooley's Opinions* (New York, 1901), 186.

39. MOR 3:313.

40. See Daniel, *Shadow*.

41. D. Lewis, *Biography*, 1:238, 246; the Pullman lawyer, Abraham Lincoln's son Robert Todd Lincoln, proved uncooperative.

42. Louis R. Harlan, *The Making of a Black Leader, 1865–1901* (New York, 1983), 311, 316; Washington spoke out against segregation and lynching on occasion: August Meier, *Negro Thought in America, 1880–1915* (Ann Arbor, 1988), 108–109; "mingle freely" in "Progressive Presidents and Black Americans" (Ph.D. diss., Columbia University, 1974), 42; "miscegenationist" in William F. Holmes, *"The White Chief": James Kimble Vardaman* (Baton Rouge, 1970), 105; Litwack, *Trouble in Mind*, 223; R. Edwards, *Angels in the Machinery*, 140; on why Stewart was discussing patronage in Colorado with TR see John Morton Blum, *The Republican Roosevelt* (New York, 1967), 40–41; Stephen Kantrowitz, *Ben Tillman and the Reconstruction of White Supremacy* (Chapel Hill, N.C., 2000), 259.

43. *The Correspondence of W.E.B. Du Bois*, vol. 1, *1877–1934*, ed. Herbert Aptheker (Amherst, Mass., 1973), 175; anti-Tuskegee blacks sought a meeting to talk with TR about using the Justice Department to enforce voting rights and to put an end to segregated interstate transportation, but the President's relationship with Washington got in the way, 92–93.

44. Kenneth O'Reilly, *Nixon's Piano: Presidents and Racial Politics from Washington to Clinton* (New York, 1995), 66; TR to TRJR, Oct. 31, 1903, TRJR-LC. Mary Church Terrell attended the First International Congress on the Welfare of the Child; see clipping, NSC, Mar. 12, 1905; in November 1906 she also visited: NSC. His additional black political visitors besides Washington were Bishop Walters and Grant, H. A. Rucker, Kelly Miller, and others who wanted TR to fight disenfranchisement in the South; he refused; see "Negro Guests at White House," Jan. 21, 1907, NSC; W. T. Vernon and other blacks attended a diplomatic reception. EKR went with the Cortelyous to hear the concert and her motives were probably more musical than racial: EKR-Di, Mar. 1, 1905; Constance McLaughlin Green, *Washington: Capital City, 1879–1950* (Princeton, 1963), 200; White House social events except for Mother's Clubs and other groups of its kind were usually segregated in this period; when the Playground Association scheduled a play on the White House grounds TR told the planners to make sure the black section had seats as good as the white one: Oct. 12, 1908, MOR-REJ.

45. TR to Joseph Bucklin Bishop, Oct. 5, 1904, Bishop Papers, Houghton; TR did not prosecute but he urged George Cortelyou to circulate the Heflin quotation to win votes in 1904: TR to Cortelyou, Oct. 5, 1904, Cortelyou Papers, LC; Kantrowitz, *Tillman*, 254.

46. "slight respect" in EKR to Emily Carow, n.d. [Feb. 14, 1903], TRC-HU; "never thought" in TR to Carl Schurz, Jan. 2, 1904, MOR-REJ; "melancholy," TR to Joseph B. Bishop, Oct. 21, 1901, Bishop Papers, Houghton; Social Gospel minister Charles Sheldon spoke for many northern liberal Protestants when he said: "Any man who is privileged to have Booker Washington to eat with him at his table should feel himself honored": Ralph E. Luker, *The Social Gospel in Black and White: American Racial Reform, 1885–1912* (Chapel Hill, N.C., 1991), 141.

47. "saddest things" in EKR, "How I Went to the White House," Administrative Records: Principal's Files, Hermann Hagedorn Files, Box 5, Folder 19, TRP-BP; see also *Roosevelt House Bulletin*, Fall 1933; EKR to ARL, Sept. 17, [1901], ARL-LC.

48. EKR to Christine G. Kean Roosevelt, n.d. but postmarked Nov. 4, 1901, TRC-HU; EKR to ARL, Sept. 17, n.y. [1901], ARL-LC.

49. Teague, *Mrs. L*, 77; EKR to ARL, n.d., ARL-LC; ARC to CRR, Mar. 6, 1904,

TRC-HU; letters to Alice from Grandmother Lee and ARC show that Alice did not save all of her tantrums and demands for more money or privileges for her stepmother.

50. White, *Autobiography*, 341; Irwin Hood "Ike" Hoover, *Forty-two Years in the White House* (Boston, 1934), 110, 289, 37; "magnificent" in EKR to ARL, n.d. [Oct. 2, 1901], ARL-LC; L. F. Abbott, ed., *Letters of Archie Butt*, 29–30, 271; clipping, Mark Sullivan, "Mrs. Theodore Roosevelt Dies in Her Sagamore Hill Home," *New York Herald Tribune*, Oct. 1, 1948, enclosed in ERD to Edith Derby Williams, May 5, 1968, TRC-HU; Stacy A. Cordery, "Edith Kermit (Carow) Roosevelt," in *American First Ladies: Their Lives and Legacies*, ed. Lewis L. Gould (New York, 1996), 307–12; Sylvia Jukes Morris, "Portrait of a First Lady," in Naylor, Brinkley, and Gable, eds., *Theodore Roosevelt: Many-Sided American*; Allida M. Black, "The Modern First Lady and Public Policy: From Edith Wilson Through Hillary Rodham Clinton," *Organization of American Historians Magazine of History* 15, no. 3 (Spring 2001): 15–20.

51. DR to Corinne Robinson Alsop, Feb. 13, 1900, TRC-HU.

52. On the presidential yacht *Sylph*, EKR, TR, and KR visited the Twin Island Fresh Air Home of Jacob A. Riis House; see Riis, *Theodore Roosevelt the Citizen*, 355; TR to ARL, Nov. 29, 1901, ARL-LC.

53. James E. Amos, *Theodore Roosevelt: Hero to His Valet* (New York, 1927), 8, 10, 129; Amos served as caretaker of the younger children, second butler, and finally as occasional valet and aide and "head man," at Sagamore Hill.

54. Hoover, *Forty-two Years*, 28; Edith's childhood nurse, Mame Ledwith, could not control Archie and Quentin either; TR to TRJR, Oct. 31, 1903, TRJR-LC; when Quentin and Charley Taft threw spitballs on paintings TR told them it was a "disgrace" to behave so badly in a gentleman's house "and especially the house of the nation": TR to ABR, Apr. 11, 1908, TRP-LC; on another occasion, when Quentin confided to his father that he hit his teacher in the face with a spitball, the President personally came to school with flowers the next day to say he was sorry for his son's misdeed: Looker, *White House Gang*, 208–16, 180–82, 149, 165.

55. Looker, *White House Gang*, 208–16, 180–82; Jean-Baptiste Duroselle, *France and the United States: From the Beginnings to the Present* (Chicago, 1978); "Knox" in White, *Autobiography*, 342; Amos, *Theodore Roosevelt*, 12, 149.

56. Harbaugh, *Power and Responsibility*, 344–45; Joan M. Jensen, *The Price of Vigilance* (Chicago, 1969), 12–13, 117, 150.

57. Text of TR speech not delivered in St. Louis, Feb. 9, 1918, not delivered because of his illness but released to the press, TR-SP, TRC-HU.

58. Frederick M. Davenport letter to Hermann Hagedorn, Dec. 31, 1948, SUBJ-TRC; G. Pinchot, *Breaking*, 314; Garfield served admirably as civil service commissioner, commissioner of corporations, and secretary of the interior under TR; see Jack M. Thompson, "James R. Garfield: The Career of a Rooseveltian Progressive, 1895–1916" (Ph.D. diss., University of South Carolina, 1958).

59. TR to HCL, Oct. 19, 1901, HCL-MHS. The anti-anarchist law passed in New York State to prohibit speech or writing advocating the violent overthrow of the government or assassination was later used to prosecute peaceful labor organizers and advocates of a general strike; Zechariah Chafee, Jr., *Freedom of Speech* (New York, 1920), 187–88; see TR's first Annual Message, MEM 17; and Roy L. Garis, *Immigration Restriction: A Study of the Opposition to and the Regulation of Immigration into the United States* (New York, 1927), 102–103; see Sidney Fine, "Anarchism and the Assassination of McKinley," *American Historical Review* 60 (July 1955): 777–99; TR, "National Life and Character," *Sewanee Review* 2 (August 1894), and "The Law of Civilization and Decay," *The Forum* 23 (January 1897): 578, 581; Hurwitz, *Theodore Roosevelt and Labor*, 282; after the 1878 decision *In re Ah Yup*, Chinese immigrants could not become citizens.

60. *Springfield Republican* clipping, Sept. 20, 1901, TRP-LC; TR to Stuart Bulloch, Nov. 1, 1901, MOR-REJ; EKR to Emily Carow, Sept. 15, 1901, TRC-HU; EKR to John Proctor Clarke, Sept. 22, [1901], TRP-SYR; on security see ARC to Bob Ferguson, Oct. 16, 1901, JIG-ARIZ; Edward J. Renehan, *John Burroughs* (Post Mills, Vt., 1992), 244.

61. Elizabeth Mills Reid to ARC, May 9, 1909, TRC-HU; TR to ARL, Nov. 29, 1901, ARL-LC.

62. ARC to CRR, Nov. 21, 1901, TRC-HU; *New York World*, Dec. 3, 1901, NSC; Ashburn, *Peabody*, 203; interview with WSC, Jr.

63. ARC to Bob Ferguson, Apr. 27, 1906, JIG-ARIZ; ARC to CRR, Apr. 13, 1902, and Apr. 30, 1903, TRC-HU.

64. "run Mrs. Theodore" from Margaret Chanler Aldrich, Roosevelt Women Interviews, TRC-HU; "counted" from Samuel Gompers, quoted in Julie Greene, "Dinner-Pail Politics: Employers, Workers, and Partisan Culture in the Progressive Era," in Eric Arnesen, Julie Greene, and Bruce Laurie, eds., *Labor Histories: Class, Politics, and the Working-Class Experience* (Chicago, 1998), 80; the Brahmin was Robert Winthrop, see his letter to ARC, March n.d., [1902]: TR to HCL, Mar. 14, 1902, and HCL to Robert Winthrop, Mar. 15, [1902], HCL-MHS; EKR to TR, Feb. 6, 1901, TRC-HU; ARC was often at the White House but she complained that she saw her brother too "seldom" to CRR, Nov. 21, 1901, TRC-HU.

65. "self-conscious" in TR to Owen Wister, Nov. 2, 1901, Wister Papers, LC; "washed face" and "idolize" from clipping enclosed in ARC to CRR, Nov. 3, 1901, TRC-HU; Edith complained about CRR's relationship with the press in 1898 and Bamie reprimanded her sister for talking too freely to the newspapers: ARC to CRR, Mar. 1, 1900, and Apr. 13, 1902, TRC-HU.

66. EKR to ARC, Feb. 18, 1902, TRC-HU.

67. TR to HCL, Feb. 10, 1902, HCL-MHS; Carroll Hodges' death was also attributed to meningitis in some papers: *New York Herald*, Feb. 9, 1902, NSC.

68. ABR, Memoirs, TRC-HU; *TR/HCL*, 1:509; TR to HCL, Oct. 19, 1901, HCL-MHS; TR to Endicott Peabody, Jan. 4 and 13, 1902, Peabody Papers, Houghton; EKR would not let ARL come with her at first but relented: ARL-Di, Feb. 8–21, 1902.

69. Elmer Ellis, ed., *Mr. Dooley at His Best* (New York, 1938), 104–105.

70. The anti-Semitic Morgan had contempt for Jewish bankers like Jacob Schiff associated with Harriman: Chernow, *House of Morgan*, 93.

71. Ibid., 105.

72. CRR, *My Brother*, 106; Thee had entertained Morgan when they founded the American Museum of Natural History but he was not a personal friend or business associate. Thee knew D. Willis James from the Y.M.C.A. and other civic activities. James gave a eulogy; see Union League Club, *Theodore Roosevelt, Senior: A Tribute*; ARC-MS; TRSR-LB; Balthasar Henry Meyer, A *History of the Northern Securities Case* (Madison, Wisc., 1906), 325.

73. MEM 18: 17–18. Just before he died McKinley wrote speeches advocating federal collection of data on the business activities of trusts, but he was not the trustbuster that even Cleveland attempted to be: Berk, *Alternative Tracks;* see also Tony Freyer, *Regulating Big Business: Antitrust in Great Britain and America, 1880–1990* (New York: 1992), and Leroy G. Dorsey, "Theodore Roosevelt and Corporate America, 1901–1909: A Reexamination," *Presidential Studies Quarterly* 25, no. 4 (Fall 1995): 725; George Bittlingmayer, "Antitrust and Business Activity: The First Quarter Century," *Business History Review* 70, no. 3 (August 1996): 363–401; *Addresses and Presidential Messages of Theodore Roosevelt* 1902–1904 (New York, 1971, c. 1904) 15; Dalton, "Why America Loved Teddy Roosevelt," in Brugger, ed., *Our-Selves/Our Past.* Historians who argue that Taft's more frequent anti-trust prosecutions out-

weigh TR's more dramatic ones miss the point: Taft, whose judicial career marked him as a defender of the status quo, would not have taken the initiative to use the law to challenge the merger movement if TR had not set the precedent.

74. NSC-AUTO, 575–589.

75. NSC; ARL interview, ORHO-COL; interview, WSC, Jr., April 13, 1977; Margaret Krech Cowles and WSC, Jr., and Mrs. Richard M. Bissell, Roosevelt Women Interviews, TRC-HU, and ARC-MS.

76. *New York Herald*, Jan. 26, 1902, and Clifford Howard, "The President's Daughter," *Ladies' Home Journal*, April 1902, NSC; Caroline Lee to ARL, July 16, 1903, ERD to ARL, n.d. [1902], and ARC to ARL, June 23, 1903, ARL-LC; February 1902, NSC.

77. TR to Oswald Garrison Villard, Mar. 22, 1902, Villard Papers, Houghton; *New York Times*, Apr. 4, 1902; Blum, *Republican Roosevelt*, 40–49.

78. Beveridge to David Graham Phillips, Aug. 27, 1901, quoted in Claude G. Bowers, *Beveridge and the Progressive Era* (New York, 1932), 156; Hoganson, *Fighting*, 134. Historians and demographers debate the casualty numbers because a cholera epidemic coincided with the war; see Glenn A. May, "150,000 Missing Filipinos: A Demographic Crisis in Batangas, 1887–1903," *Annales de démographie historique*, 1985, 215–43; John M. Gates, *Schoolbooks and Krags: The United States Army in the Philippines, 1898–1902* (Westport, Conn., 1973). Hoganson, *Fighting*, 146. Before he became president TR thought the army should "assume aggressive operations and . . . harass and smash the insurgents in every way until they are literally beaten into peace; entertaining no proposition from them save that of unconditional surrender": Brian McAllister Linn, *The Philippine War, 1899–1902* (Lawrence, Kans., 2000), 90; controversy erupted later over the land owned by the Catholic Church, but TR won over Catholic voters on the issue, see Frank T. Reuter, *Catholic Influence on American Colonial Policies 1898–1904* (Austin, Tex., 1967), 88–136.

79. Jim Zwick, ed., *Mark Twain's Weapons of Satire: Anti-Imperialist Writings on the Philippine-American War* (Syracuse, N.Y., 1992), 19, 33, 37.

80. The water cure was forcing water down a prisoner's throat until he agreed to talk: Richard E. Welch. Jr., *Response to Imperialism: The United States and the Philippine-American War, 1899–1902* (Chapel Hill, N.C., 1979), 141. For a view of army behavior as a response to guerrilla tactics see Brian McAllister Linn, *The U.S. Army and Counterinsurgency in the Philippine War, 1899–1902* (Chapel Hill, N.C., 1989) and *Guardians of Empire: The U.S. Army and the Pacific, 1902–1940* (Chapel Hill, N.C., 1997); Stuart Creighton Miller, "The American Soldier and the Conquest of the Philippines," in Peter W. Stanley, ed., A *Nation in the Making: The Philippines and the United States, 1899–1921* (Cambridge, Mass., 1974); James Claude Thomson, Stanley, and John Curtis Perry, *Sentimental Imperialists: The American Experience in East Asia* (New York, 1985).

81. MOR 3:240; Linn, *U.S. Army and Counterinsurgency*, 145–46; TR to Lyman Abbott, Dec. 24, 1901, MOR-REJ, TRC-HU.

82. TR to HCL, Feb. 10, 1902, HCL-MHS; Welch, *Response to Imperialism*, 136–49; Bigelow to HCL, May 26, 1902, Murakata, *Selected Letters*, 199; see also Walter LaFeber, *The Cambridge History of American Foreign Relations*, vol. II, *The American Search for Opportunity, 1865–1913* (New York, 1995), 165.

83. Linn, *Guardians*, 128.

84. Jim Tillman killed editor Narciso Gonzales but was acquitted; Kantrowitz, *Tillman*, 256; NSC; ARC to CRR, Apr. 13, 1902, and EKR to Emily Carow, n.d., TRC-HU.

85. NSC; seeWelch, *Responce to Imperialism*, 144–46.

86. "bandits" in MOR 3:279; NSC. TR ordered General Adna Chaffee to avoid force against the Moros if possible, but the Moro War resulted; John J. Pershing and Leonard Wood fought in the Moro War; its outcome was decided as much by military victories as by the

weakness of *insurrecto* leadership faced with a rich foe and the sanitation, schools, and roads brought by American rule; Stanley, ed., *Nation in the Making*.

87. Divorce only in civil marriages had been allowed earlier; Eileen J. Suarez Findlay, *Imposing Decency: The Politics of Sexuality and Race in Puerto Rico, 1870–1920* (Durham, N.C., 1999), 111; Rebecca J. Scott, "Defining the Boundaries of Freedom in the World of Cane: Cuba, Brazil, and Louisiana after Emancipation," *American Historical Review* 99, no. 1 (February 1994): 70–102. Within Cuba, "Cuba Libre" had been a cry for racial equality as well as independence, but slave emancipation was followed by the proletarianization of Afro-Cubans: Scott, *Slave Emancipation in Cuba: The Transition to Free Labor, 1860–1899* (Princeton, 1985), 287–93. National City Bank, Henry O. Havemeyer, and Rockefeller interests benefited from the newly favorable climate for foreign investors: César J. Ayala, *American Sugar Kingdom: The Plantation Economy of the Spanish Caribbean, 1898–1934* (Chapel Hill, N.C., 1999), 74–85; Louis A. Pérez, *Cuba Between Empires, 1878–1902* (Pittsburgh, 1983), chap. 2; José M. Hernández, *Cuba and the United States: Intervention and Militarism, 1868–1933* (Austin, Tex., 1993).

88. Walter Lippmann, *Drift and Mastery: An Attempt to Diagnose the Current Unrest* (1914; reprint, Englewood Cliffs, N.J., 1961); George Rothwell Brown, *The Leadership of Congress* (Indianapolis, 1922), 112; however, in the end tariff relief in Cuba gave the Sugar Trust even more reason to take over plantations and dispossess Cubans of their land. The proletarianization of labor was one of the many unintended consequences of American dominion over Cuba; see Ayala, *American Sugar Kingdom*; MOR 3:392.

89. TR, "Camera Shots at Wild Animals," *World's Work*, December 1901; MOR 1:799.

90. TR, "The Presidency," *Youth's Companion*, Nov. 6, 1902, MEM 15:213–23; Bigelow to TR, Mar. 1, 1902, in Murakata, *Selected Letters*, 192–93; paleontology in Alexander Lambert, "Roosevelt the Companion," in MEM 3:xviii.

91. He recalled that during the Spanish-American War "the night before each fight, I never dared to think of either my wife or children because it really tended to unman me": TR to Mrs. John C. Graham, Mar. 5, 1915, TRC-HU; TR to William Sturgis Bigelow, Apr. 1, 1902, MOR-REJ; EKR to Christine Kean Roosevelt, n.d. [postmarked May 6, 1902], TRC-HU.

92. EKR-Di, June–September 1902; ARL-Di, May 8, 1902; NSC; S. Morris, *Edith Kermit Roosevelt*, 237.

93. TR to ERD, June 19, 1902, TRC-HU; TR to Winthrop Chanler, June 10, 1902, MOR-REJ.

94. Several assassination attempts occurred during TR's presidency, see Riis, *Theodore Roosevelt the Citizen*, 283; "Notes on a Summer at Oyster Bay in 1902," by Walter S. Hinchman, Kermit's tutor for Groton, told of William Craig's rescue of TR, SUBJ-TRC; in September 1903 another armed man approached him on the piazza: *New York Herald*, Sept. 2, 1903; a crank broke through security at Uncle Jimmie Gracie's funeral in New York in November 1903, TR to DR, Dec. 1, 1903, MOR-REJ.

95. "Christian men" in Tomlins, *State and the Unions*, 73. Mark Hanna owned coal mines and had tried locking strikers out and hiring scabs, but he came to favor negotiation as an easier way to get miners back to work; see the pro-Hanna Rhodes, *McKinley and Roosevelt Administrations*, 237; Donald L. Miller and Richard E. Sharpless, *The Kingdom of Coal: Work, Enterprise, and Ethnic Communities in the Mine Fields* (Philadelphia, 1985), 276.

96. NSC, 1902; EKR to Emily Carow, Sept. 5, 1902, TRC-HU; some accounts of the accident describe TR swearing at the motorman: "Roosevelt's Narrow Escape from Death in Smash-Up," Capt. George A. Lung account of September 1902 crash in *Brooklyn Eagle*, Jan. 8, 1919, SUBJ-TRC.

97. "virility" in Eugene Thwing, *The Life and Meaning of Theodore Roosevelt* (New York, 1919), 261; Ellis, ed., *Mr. Dooley at His Best*, 104, 106.

98. EKR-Di, Sept. 24, 1902; Stephenson, *Aldrich,* 194–99; doctors in Indiana had aspirated it; ARL-Di, Sept. 4 and 16, 1902; EKR to ARC, n.d. [September 1902], TRC-HU.

99. EKR to CRR, Oct. 1, 1902, TRC-HU; MOR 3:327, 338; Robert H. Wiebe, "The Anthracite Coal Strike of 1902: A Record of Confusion," *Mississippi Valley Historical Review* 48 (1961); Miller and Sharpless, *Kingdom of Coal,* 278; TR to Jacob Riis, Oct. 8, 1902, Riis Papers, LC.

100. EKR to Emily Carow, Sept. 24, 1902, TRC-HU; TR to Albert Shaw, Oct. 1, 1902, MOR-REJ; TR to Jacob Riis, Oct. 8, 1902, Riis Papers, LC.

101. EKR to Emily Carow, Oct. 5, 1902, TRC-HU; Bamie passed her brother some privileged information from her Harriman contacts, but it was not clear what the information was: TR to ARC, Sept. 15, 1902, TRC-HU.

102. G. Pinchot, *Breaking,* 194; Gould, *Reform and Regulation,* 32; John Milton Hay, *Letters of John Hay and Extracts from Diary* (New York, 1969), 258.

103. John Burroughs, *Camping and Tramping with Roosevelt* (Boston, 1907), 22; Shelby Foote's grandfather was one of the guides on the trip.

104. TR to Kermit, Dec. 4, 1902, MOR-REJ; EKR to Emily Carow, n.d. [Jan. 4, 1903], TRC-HU.

105. Willard B. Gatewood, Jr., *Theodore Roosevelt and the Art of Controversy: Episodes of the White House Years* (Baton Rouge, 1970), 76.

106. When Vardaman ran for governor he called for the curtailment of public education for black children because he said book learning ruined good field hands; see W. Holmes, "*The White Chief*"; Gatewood, *Art of Controversy,* 84.

107. W. Holmes, "*The White Chief*"; George Coleman Osborn, *John Sharp Williams: Planter-Statesman of the Deep South* (Baton Rouge, 1943), 150.

108. Paul Morton gave illegal rebates but still became TR's secretary of the navy, 1904–1905. When Vardaman was governor he personally stopped several lynchings but otherwise aggravated race relations horribly; see W. Holmes, "*The White Chief.*" TR fought for increased power for the Interstate Commerce Commission in the Hepburn-Dolliver Act but he did not endorse rate-fixing by the government: Berk, *Alternative Tracks,* 158.

109. *New York Times,* Oct. 28, 1902; see *New York Evening Journal,* Oct. 28, 1902; the fireworks celebration Hearst had planned for 40,000 spectators in Madison Square Garden exploded and killed 18 people: Swanberg, *Citizen Hearst,* 239–44; Nasaw, *The Chief,* 162–64.

110. MOR 3:357; *TR/HCL,* 2:65; Eric F. Goldman, *Charles J. Bonaparte: Patrician Reformer, His Earlier Career* (Baltimore, 1943), 60.

111. MOR 3:386 *n.* 1, 396–400.

112. MOR 3: 389–400; EKR to Emily Carow, Dec. 14, 1902, TRC-HU.

113. "out of the woods" in MOR 3:396; Serge Ricard, "The Anglo-German Intervention in Venezuela and Theodore Roosevelt's Ultimatum to the Kaiser: Taking a Fresh Look at an Old Enigma," in Ricard and Hélène Christol, eds., *Anglo-Saxonism in U.S. Foreign Policy: The Diplomacy of Imperialism, 1899–1919* (Aix-en-Provence, France, 1991), 65–77; international lawyer Frederick Holls called TR on Dec. 24, 1902, to urge him not to arbitrate personally but to use The Hague in order to establish its credibility and help the arbitration movement: Holls Papers, Houghton; AUTO, 526; I thank William Tilchin for calling my attention to the importance of the Ricard discoveries.

114. AUTO, 526; TR confided in Jusserand that toward the kaiser he "had an inclination for a year or two" before he recognized his aggressive intentions: Jusserand, *What Me Befell,* 127, 107, 267; Bishop, *Theodore Roosevelt,* 1:377; Gordon Craig, *Germany, 1866–1945* (New York, 1978), 240.

115. MOR 3:406, 423; EKR-Di, Feb. 13, 1903.

116. "I feel," Hermann Speck von Sternberg, Feb. 19, 1903, quoted in Ricard, "Anglo-

German Intervention," 74; Edmond Taylor, *The Fall of the Dynasties: The Collapse of the Old Order, 1905–1922* (New York, 1963), 156. Naval College war games showed that German ships would likely defeat American ships; one historian believes that TR knew the U.S. might lose a Caribbean fight against the Germans: Ronald Spector, "Roosevelt, the Navy, and the Venezuela Controversy: 1902–1903," *American Neptune* 32, no. 4 (1972): 257–63; diplomat Lewis Einstein in *Roosevelt: His Mind in Action*, 129, recalled that the U.S. Navy was strong enough to have beaten Germany in the Caribbean.

117. "driven" in TR to James Russell Parsons, Feb. 12, and "beings" in ARC to CRR, Mar. 2, 1903, TRC-HU; "conspicuous" in ARL-Di, Mar. 8, 1903; ARL overspent roughly $19,000 in current value: EKR-Di, Mar. 23 and 30, 1903.

118. TR, "My Life as a Naturalist," *American Museum Journal* 18, no. 5 (May 1918): 321–31 (329); Alton A. Lindsey, "Was Theodore Roosevelt the Last to See Wild Passenger Pigeons?" *Proceedings of the Indiana Academy of Science* 86 (1977): 349–56; C. Hart Merriam, "Roosevelt, the Naturalist," *Science* 75, no. 1937 (Feb. 12, 1932): 181–83.

119. TR, *Address of President Roosevelt Before the National Editorial Association at Jamestown, Virginia, June 10, 1907* (Washington, D.C., 1907), 10, quoted in Lawrence Hyman Budner, "Hunting, Ranching, and Writing: The Influence of Theodore Roosevelt's Western Experiences in His Later Career and Political Thought" (M.A. thesis, Southern Methodist University, 1990), 79.

120. Irwin, *Making of a Reporter*, 171.

121. TR to Frank Chapman quoted in Chapman, *Autobiography*, 181; "intellect" in TR to John Burroughs, Sept. 27, 1905; to William Dutcher, July 18, 1906; to John Burroughs, Sept. 27, 1905, MOR-REJ; see also TR to J. H. Bowles, Mar. 7, 1908, and to Philip B. Stewart, Feb. 19, 1907, MOR-REJ; he tried to order banning the killing of all manatee off Florida's coasts: TR to Charles E. Magoon, Jan. 9, 1909, MOR-REJ; MOR 3:442. Environmental historians used to find the dichotomy of the utilitarian or "conservation for use" policy opposed to preservationism as the key to this period; TR does not fit into either side neatly; see also C. Miller, *Pinchot*, which suggests that the dichotomy is false and that Pinchot was also a more complex figure.

122. Burroughs, *Camping and Tramping*, xiv.

123. Cohen, *Pathless Way*, 14, 177, "geography" on 240.

124. "Mr. Roosevelt Sees a Cowboy Festival," clipping, Apr. 26, 1903, TR-SP; TR to John Hay, Aug. 9, 1903, TRC-HU.

125. Emerson in Renehan, *Burroughs*, 106; Burroughs, *Camping and Tramping*, 39; TR to W. Broadfoot, May 27, 1903, MOR-REJ.

126. Paul Schullery, "A Partnership in Conservation: Roosevelt and Yellowstone," *Montana: The Magazine of Western History*, Summer 1978, 6.

127. "temple" in Cutright, *Making of a Conservationist*, 247; "Bully!" in Thurman Wilkins, *John Muir: Apostle of Nature* (Norman, Okla., 1995), 217.

128. "love" in Stephen R. Fox, *John Muir and His Legacy: The American Conservation Movement* (Boston, 1981), 126; Frank McCoy, SUBJ-TRC; TR to William H. Moody, May 18, 1904, MOR-REJ; on their trip see Cohen, *Pathless Way*, and Linnie Marsh Wolfe, *Son of the Wilderness: The Life of John Muir* (New York, 1945).

129. George L. Knapp, "The Other Side of Conservation," *North American Review* 191 (April 1910): 481; George Bird Grinnell, ed., *Brief History of the Boone and Crockett Club* (New York, 1910), 45.

130. He created the National Bison Range to prevent extinction of an endangered species, "Refuge System Spans 75 Years of Varied and Colorful History," *Fish and Wildlife News*, Fish and Wildlife Service, U.S. Department of Interior, December 1978–January 1979, 4–8; he also wrote that the camera should replace the rifle if "so-called" civilized countries

wanted to stop the extermination of animals: TR to Warburton Pike, Jan. 18, 1905, MOR-REJ.

131. G. Pinchot, *Breaking*, 204–205, 240.

132. MEM 5:104; his uncle Robert B. Roosevelt had advocated fish preservation via culture since TR's childhood; for a listing of the preserves see MEM 4:609–12; Blair, *Clubwoman as Feminist*, 106; see "Conservation of Natural Resources," *Federation Bulletin* 5 (May 1908): 248–49; MEM 17: 607–18.

133. Gould, *Presidency*, 40; Thomas R. Dunlap, *Saving America's Wildlife: Ecology and the American Mind, 1850–1990* (Princeton, 1988), 7; TR, "Big Game Disappearing in the West," *Forum* 15 (August 1893): 767–74; TR, "Forests Vital to Our Welfare," *National Geographic Magazine* 16 (November 1905): 515–16; TR, "Two Great Undertakings Letter to the Congress of Irrigation Engineers," *National Geographic Magazine* 17 (November 1906): 645–47; TR, "Conservation of Natural Resources," *Chautauqua* 55 (June 1909): 33–43; Shirley, *Pawnee Bill*, 155.

134. Cutright, *Making of a Conservationist*, 211; TR was also a strong advocate of planting new trees on Arbor Day.

135. The Fulton amendment to the agricultural bill of 1907 blocked further reserves in Colorado, Montana, Oregon, Washington, and Wyoming; see the more detailed treatment in C. Miller, *Pinchot*, 163–64.

136. Gregory Randall Graves says TR added 150 million acres to forest reserves: Graves, "Anti-Conservation and Federal Forestry in the Progressive Era" (Ph.D. diss., University of California at Santa Barbara, 1987), 190, 165; "peons" in Michael McCarthy, "The First Sagebrush Rebellion: Forest Reserves and States Rights in Colorado and the West, 1891–1907," in Harold K. Steen, ed., *Origins of the National Forests: A Centennial Symposium* (Durham, N.C., 1992), 190–92; Robert E. Wolf, "National Forest Timber Sales and the Legacy of Gifford Pinchot: Managing a Forest and Making It Pay," in Char Miller., ed., *American Forests: Nature, Culture, and Politics* (Lawrence, Kans., 1997), 87–105; Doug Stewart, Lisa Drew, and Mark Wexler, "Diary of a Century: How Conservation Grew from a Whisper to a Roar," *National Wildlife*, December 1999/January 2000; about 1,755,400 acres of forestland belonging to native people were taken away to become national forests under TR; timber cutting was often allowed in forest reserves; see also Samuel P. Hays, *Conservation and the Gospel of Efficiency: The Progressive Conservation Movement, 1890–1920* (Cambridge, Mass., 1959).

137. TR to TRJR, May 12, 1908, TRJR-LC; G. Pinchot, *Breaking*, 190–91; Marc Reisner, excerpt from *Cadillac Desert*, in Merchant, *Major Problems*, 372. Too many dams in the long run lowered the water table, disrupted rivers, streams, and animal habitats, and encouraged oversettlement of arid environments.

138. Newlands was irritated about TR's taking credit. *The Public Papers of Francis G. Newlands*, ed. Arthur B. Darling (Boston, 1932), 1:81; TR believed Newlands should not be given credit for the Reclamation Act: MOR 3:317; AUTO, 408–36.

139. C. Miller, *Pinchot*, 159; the Supreme Court in *U.S.* v. *Grimaud* and *U.S.* v. *Light* approved Pinchot's use of federal authority to stop illegal grazing and other abuses of the forest reserves, 161; MOR 6:1065–66.

140. E. C. Blackorby, "Theodore Roosevelt's Conservation Policies and Their Impact upon America and the American West," *North Dakota History* 25, no. 4 (October 1958): 106–17; Stephen Edward Ponder, "News Management in the Progressive Era, 1898–1909: Gifford Pinchot, Theodore Roosevelt and the Conservation Crusade" (Ph.D. diss., University of Washington, 1985), 194–201.

141. Ecology as a field did not emerge until later, but scientists talked about interdependence and "life zones": Dunlap, *Saving America's Wildlife*, 41–46; Mrs. William Starr Dana (Frances Theodora Parsons), *How to Know the Wild Flowers: A Guide to the Names, Haunts,*

and Habits of Our Common Wild Flowers (1893; reprint, Boston, 1989). Though he liked to take his children to pick wildflowers when they were young, as he aged TR increasingly viewed wildflower picking as wrong: EKR to ERD, May 14, 1927, TRC-HU.

142. C. Miller, *Pinchot*, 172; first called the Alexander Archipelago National Forest: David E. Conrad, "Creating the Nation's Largest Forest Reserve: Roosevelt, Emmons, and the Tongass National Forest," *Pacific Historical Review* 46, no. 1 (February 1977): 65–83; TR, "Message to Congress," Dec. 5, 1905, *Presidential Addresses and State Papers of Theodore Roosevelt*, 4:638.

143. Runte, *National Parks*, 71–73.

144. "without" in MOR 6:1446; Fox, *Muir*, 124. TR did give credit to Garfield and Pinchot; see AUTO and MOR 6:1522*n*.1. For a detailed listing of TR-created national forests, national monuments, federal bird reservations, national parks, and national game preserves see *Theodore Roosevelt Association Journal* 10 (1984): 8–9.

CHAPTER EIGHT: A BETTER DEMOCRAT

1. He was writing sympathetically about how difficult it would be for President Wilson to lead a Democratic Party filled with politicians more conservative than he: TR to Joseph Bucklin Bishop, Feb. 10, 1913, Bishop Papers, Houghton.

2. TR, "True Americanism and Expansionism," speech 1003; MOR 3:520.

3. TR to John Burroughs, May 19, 1903, MOR-REJ; Burroughs, *Camping and Tramping; TR/HCL*, 2:10–26; TR made the anti-Hearst order in July, MOR 3:518; see also Nasaw, *The Chief*, 170.

4. EKR to ARC, n.d. [April 1903], TRC-HU; *TR/HCL*, 2:8; EKR to Emily Carow, Apr. 12, 1903 and June 8, n.y. [1903], and ARC to CRR, Apr. 27, 1903, TRC-HU; *Letters to Kermit from Theodore Roosevelt, 1902–1908*, ed. Will Irwin (New York, 1946), 38.

5. "really count" in ARL-Di, May 5, 1903; Cassandra Tate, *Cigarette Wars: The Triumph of "The Little White Slaver"* (New York, 1999), 99–100.

6. "stale" in MOR 3:535; "poor dears" in ARL-Di, June 11, 1903; Grandfather Lee covered her overdraft and gave her extra money: George Cabot Lee to ARL, Nov. 5, 1903, ARL-LC; she wrote in her diary, June 11, 1903: "If Fa & Mo knew of some of the things I calmly talk about I think they would curl up and pass away with horror; friends warned Alice that because so many people viewed her as a "disgrace" to the President some crank might shoot her, ARL-Di, Feb. 13, 1904; Isabella Stewart Gardner refused to invite her to a party and ARL promised to seek revenge on "the old bitch," ARL-Di, Dec. 15, 1904."

7. ARL-Di, Aug. 28, 1903.

8. ARC to CRR, Aug. 21, 1903, TRC-HU.

9. ARL-Di, July 15, 1903; Ethel Barrymore, *Memories: An Autobiography* (New York, 1955), 131.

10. MOR 3:655.

11. EKR to Emily Carow, "like the cook" July 16, 1902, "prefers me thin" Sept. 7, n.y., [1900] TRC-HU.

12. When people complained that he had not singled out Nelson Miles for special honors on retirement, TR told Lodge: "We are a queer, emotional, hysterical people on occasions": *TR/HCL*, 2:52, 63; Rhodes, *McKinley and Roosevelt Administrations*, 286.

13. TR to HCL, Aug. 6, 1903, HCL-MHS; TR to Brooks Adams, July 18, 1903, TRC-HU; Lyon, *Success Story*, 222.

14. EKR to KR, n.d. [Oct. 21, 1903], KBR-LC; TR to Bob Ferguson, Oct. 24, 1903, JIG-ARIZ; HCL wrote TR that "the Canadians impress me as stupid and provincial in the highest degree": Sept. 5, 1904, HCL-MHS; see Gould, *Presidency*, 81–83, which explains British

favoritism toward the U.S. during the boundary dispute; on cavalry see Marks, *Velvet on Iron*, 62–63; Albert Shaw claimed to have talked TR into arbitration: Memorandum for Myself, Referring to a Letter of June 18, 1943, to Professor Nelson M. Blake, SUBJ-TRC; TR had earlier expressed an interest in Canadian territory: TR to General J. H. Wilson, Nov. 5, 1895, copy enclosed in ERD to Edith Derby Williams, Apr. 17, 1966, TRC-HU, says: "I want to take the entire valley of the St. Lawrence, the Saskatchewan and the Columbia. If we cannot wake up our people to this, then at least I wish us to be resolute about the Alaska boundary."

15. Helen Nicolay, *Our Capital on the Potomac* (New York, 1924), 475; Hay represented a link to Thee and to presidential history, some of it tragic. Hay had been close to three assassinated presidents—Lincoln, Garfield, and McKinley; TR had also summoned the Senate Big Four to spend the night at Sagamore Hill earlier in the month; *Letters of John Hay*, 275.

16. Philippe Bunau-Varilla, *From Panama to Verdun: My Fight for France* (Philadelphia, 1940), 113–116; Peter Larsen, "Theodore Roosevelt and the Moroccan Crisis, 1904–1906" (Ph.D. diss., Princeton University, 1984), 222; see Gould, *Presidency*; on Panama see Marks, *Velvet on Iron*, 96–105.

17. In February 1902 he told Lodge that the treaty to acquire the Danish Virgin Islands was "simply a method of safe-guarding the Isthmian Canal": TR to HCL, Feb. 10, 1902, HCL-MHS.

18. A. M. Beaupre to John Hay, Sept. 5, 1903, MOR-REJ; MOR 3:567; Richard L. Lael, *Arrogant Diplomacy: U.S. Policy Toward Colombia, 1903–1922* (Wilmington, Del., 1987), 4–5.

19. TR to Mark Hanna, Aug. 22, 1903, TRJR-LC; MOR 3:628; "alliance" in Bunau-Varilla, *From Panama*, 132–33; "taint of legality" in Rhodes, *McKinley and Roosevelt Administrations*, 271; "force of arms" in TR to William Roscoe Thayer, July 2, 1918, TRC-HU; on his relationship with Bunau-Varilla, TR to Silas McBee, Jan. 6, 1904, MOR-REJ; Walter LaFeber pointed out that Bunau-Varilla insisted that the U.S. give no sovereignty to Panama—Hay and TR had wanted it to be an independent country: *The Panama Canal: The Crisis in Historical Perspective* (New York, 1989), 23–36; many books call the revolution bloodless but at least one Chinese man was killed; Rhodes, 268*n*.3; see U.S. Department of State, *Papers Relating to the Foreign Relations of the United States* (Washington, D.C., 1903), 232; John Nikol and Francis X. Holbrook, "Naval Operations in the Panama Revolution 1903," *American Neptune* 37, no. 4 (1977): 253–61; TR said Nelson Cromwell was fomenting a revolution (as were others) which did not go off, but Bunau-Varilla's revolution succeeded first: TR to Julius Chambers, July 9, 1914, MOR-REJ.

20. Bunau-Varilla, *From Panama*, 176; Teller in Lael, *Arrogant Diplomacy*, 33; LaFeber pointed out that though Hay and TR had wanted Panama to be an independent country Bunau-Varilla insisted that the U.S. give it no real sovereignty: *Panama Canal*, 31.

21. John Major, *Prize Possession: The United States and the Panama Canal, 1903–1979* (New York, 1993), 62; *Letters of Henry Adams*, 2:419; TR to Richard Harding Davis, Dec. 12 and 22, 1903, MOR-REJ; TR to TRJR, Nov. 15, 1903, TRJR-LC; "eunuchs" in MOR 3:663.

22. TR to TRJR, Feb. 10, 1904, TRJR-LC.

23. TR to TRJR, Jan. 29, 1904, MOR 4:712–13; TR to Philander C. Knox, Dec. 30, 1903, MOR-REJ.

24. TR to Florence La Farge, Nov. 5, 1903, MOR-REJ.

25. MOR 4:772.

26. TR to TRJR, Feb. 6, 1904, TRJR-LC; TR to Dr. McKelway, Mar. 17, 1904, MOR-REJ; MOR 4:753.

27. MOR 4:795, 809.

28. *Letters to Kermit*, 555; TR to TRJR, Jan. 18, 1904, TRJR-LC.

29. On Hanna and N.A.W.S.A., EKR-Di, Feb. 15, 1904; on Edith's views, TR to Eli-

nor Vernon De Fresney, Aug. 15, 1911, MOR-REJ; clippings from *Leslie's Weekly*, Oct. 13, 1904, TRP-LC; Carolyn Merchant, "The Women of the Progressive Conservation Crusade, 1900–1915," in Merchant, *Major Problems in American Environmental History*, 373–82; women could vote for school board in several states.

30. Nasaw, *The Chief*, 174–75.

31. MOR 4:823, 839, 912.

32. EKR to ARL, Aug. 10, 1904, TRC-HU; on TR's defense of Alice see Ellen Maury Slayden, *Washington Wife: Journal of Ellen Maury Slayden from 1897–1919* (New York, 1963), 54–55; Mark Sullivan, *The Education of an American* (New York, 1938), 211–12; *Town Topics* was considered the *Police Gazette* for the Four Hundred and its reporting was often untrue: Andy Logan, *The Man Who Robbed the Robber Barons* (New York, 1965), 179, 48.

33. "awful trial" in MOR 4:853; ARL-Di, January 1904–December 1905; Nicholas Longworth to ARL, n.d., ARL-LC.

34. TR tried to convince Williams that his Panama policy was pro-southern, an extension of Jackson, Benton, and Houston expansionism, and the South generally supported TR's actions in Panama more heartily than the North or West: TR to John Sharp Williams (draft, unsigned), Dec. 5, 1904, MOR-REJ; Willard B. Gatewood, Jr., "Theodore Roosevelt and the 'Kinetoscope Fakes': An Incident in the Campaign of 1904," *Mid-America* 49, no. 3 (1967): 194.

35. Gatewood, "Theodore Roosevelt and the 'Kinetoscope Fakes,' " 199; on TR's views on the South, TR to Edward S. Martin, Nov. 16, 1904, manuscripts presented by Mrs. Edward S. Blagden, Houghton.

36. Hay Diary quoted in P. Larsen, "Moroccan Crisis," 20; TR to John Hay, June 15, 1904, MOR-REJ; Hay deserves credit for open door diplomacy and the peaceful Perdicaris resolution, but decision-making in the Boxer Reprisal, the Algeciras Conference, and the Alaskan Boundary Dispute were out of his hands: HCL to TR, Feb. 14, 1909, HCL-MHS.

37. Larsen, "Theodore Roosevelt and the Moroccan Crisis," 25, 72–73; Perdicaris later recommended that Raisuli be put in charge of Tangier, which prompted the *Washington Post* to suggest the kidnapping had been a hoax invented by two friends; Lewis Einstein, in *Roosevelt: His Mind in Action*, wrote that it was lucky that TR did not have to make good on his threat to capture Raisuli because U.S. Marines would have been unprepared to occupy and track him down in the Moroccan mountains, 133; Barbara Tuchman, "Perdicaris Alive or Raisuli Dead," *American Heritage* 10 (August 1959): 18–21, 98–101; HCL to TR, June 25, 1904, HCL-MHS.

38. HCL to TR, June 25, 1904, HCL-MHS; TR to TRJR, May 14, 1904, TRJR-LC.

39. HCL to TR, June 25, 1904, HCL-MHS; Harlan, *Wizard of Tuskegee*, 26–27.

40. HCL to TR, June 25, 1904, HCL-MHS.

41. "unhung" in MOR 4:947; EKR to KR, n.d. [June 1904], KBR-LC; though he was unlikely to win votes he visited South Carolina in April 1902, Tennessee and North Carolina in September 1902, Tennessee and Mississippi in November 1902, Missouri in April 1903 and November 1904, Texas in April 1905, North Carolina, Georgia, Florida, Alabama, Arkansas, and Louisiana in October 1905, Missouri, Tennessee, and Mississippi in October 1907; on his chances of election in the South, *Letters to Kermit*, 79–80; he also put a relative of Robert E. Lee on his staff and in the fall of 1905 he toured the South with a southern cousin and two southern Rough Riders, John Greenway and John McIlhenny.

42. EKR to ARC, n.d. [August 1904], TRC-HU.

43. *TR/HCL*, 2:15, 17; see also Edward G. Riggs to Roy E.T. Riggs, Feb. 7, 1921, in SUBJ-TRC; Lash, *Eleanor and Franklin*, 202.

44. HCL to TR, Oct. 18, 1904, HCL-MHS; Hoover, *Forty-two Years*, 248; HCL to TR, Sept. 5, 1904, HCL-MHS; "good angel": Eleanor quoted in Linda Donn, *The Roosevelt Cousins* (New York, 2001), 80; EKR to Emily Carow, Nov. 18, 1904, TRC-HU.

45. AUTO, 367; HCL to TR, June 1, 13, 25, July 20, 23, 25, Aug. 2, 8, Sept. 5, 9, Oct. 12, 15, 18, Nov. 3, 1904, Aug. 12, 1907, HCL-MHS.

46. Clippings from *New York World*, Oct. 9, 1904, TRP-LC; MOR 4:996; Bradley A. Smith, "Faulty Assumptions and Undemocratic Consequences of Campaign Finance Reform," *Yale Law Journal* 105 (January 1996). As president TR never fully supported campaign finance reform; see Robert Mutch, *Campaigns, Congress and Courts: The Making of Federal Finance Laws* (New York, 1988). During the Bull Moose campaign he favored but did not make a major issue of it.

47. Clippings from *New York World*, Oct. 9, 1904, TRP-LC.

48. "All Jews" in Gould, *Presidency*, 140; see also Gary Dean Best, *To Free a People: American Jewish Leaders and the Jewish Problem in Eastern Europe, 1890–1914* (Westport, Conn., 1982), 64–111; Ellis, *Mr. Dooley's America*, 154; NSC for TR's visit to the Lower East Side; on Ellis Island, Alan M. Kraut, *The Huddled Masses: The Immigrant in American Society, 1880–1921* (Wheeling, Ill., 1982), 70–71; on New York immigrant life, Richard Polenberg, *Fighting Faiths: The Abrams Case, the Supreme Court, and Free Speech* (New York, 1987), 4–11; *Puck*, July 10, 1889, TR Scrapbook, TRC-HU; Gould, *Presidency*, 140.

49. Clippings from *New York World, New York Press, New York Tribune, Worcester Telegram, American Herald*, TRP-LC; "sure things" in TR to Taft, Sept. 16, 1908, MOR-REJ.

50. " 'Monstrous,' Says Mr. Roosevelt," *Washington Post*, Nov. 5, 1904, TRP-LC; Sullivan in MOR 4:889; Sullivan also helped Frances Perkins get factory inspection legislation passed; ARL-Di, Nov. 3–7, 1904; EKR-Di, Nov. 4, 1904.

51. "fortnight" in TR to ACMDL, Nov. 10, 1904, HCL-MHS; HCL to TR, Nov. 3, 1904, HCL-MHS; EKR to KR, n.d. [Oct. 30, 1904], KBR-LC.

52. D. Lewis, *Biography*, vol. 1, 523; TR to John Byrnne, Sept. 14, 1903, and to Cornelius Bliss, Feb. 2, 1905, MOR-REJ; Harlan, *Making of a Black Leader*, 25–31; Linda O. McMurray, *To Keep the Waters Troubled: The Life of Ida B. Wells* (New York, 1998), 261–64, 277–78; James Weldon Johnson, *Along This Way* (New York, 1990); Adriane D. Smith, "The Autobiography of a Colored Man: James Weldon Johnson and Progressive Politics," paper given at the Organization of American Historians convention, Los Angeles, Apr. 28, 2001; Kevin K. Gaines, *Uplifting the Race: Black Leadership, Politics, and Culture in the Twentieth Century* (Chapel Hill, N.C., 1996); Matthew Frye Jacobson, *Barbarian Virtues: The United States Encounters Foreign Peoples at Home and Abroad, 1876–1917* (New York, 2000); TR looked for black talent in the federal government and elevated men like George Washington Ellis in the Census Office of the Interior Department, whom he appointed to a post in the U.S. embassy in Liberia; see Williams, *Rethinking Race*, 45.

53. ARL-Di, Nov. 7, 1904; EKR-Di, Nov. 8, 1904; *Letters to Kermit*, 85.

54. HCL to TR, Nov. 15, 1904, HCL-MHS; EKR to ARC n.d. [Nov. 10–17, 1904], and TR to Edward Sandford Martin, Nov. 16, 1904, TRC-HU; Lewis L. Gould argues that it was premeditated: *Reform and Regulation*, 72.

55. "exploiting savagery" in Rydell, *All the World's a Fair*, 276n.40, 168–76, 163–64; L. Baker, *From Savage*, 70–71.

56. David Glassberg, *American Historical Pageantry: The Uses of Tradition in the Early Twentieth Century* (Chapel Hill, N.C., 1990), 31; Moxie in Oliver, ed., *The Letters of Theodore Roosevelt and Brander Matthews*, 133; see President Roosevelt in Butler in Mark Bennitt, et al., eds., *History of the Louisiana Purchase Exposition . . . St. Louis World's Fair of 1904* (St. Louis, 1905).

57. *Letters to Kermit*, 87; he read James Ford Rhodes' fifth volume of his history of the U.S. on the train to St. Louis in order to be able to dictate a book review on the way back to Washington, and talked Corinne into staying up late to keep him company while he dic-

tated it: CRR, *My Brother,* 220; ARL-Di, Nov. 26, 1904; TR to James A. Hemenway, Dec. 1, 1904, MOR-REJ; MOR 4:1055; Bennitt, ed., *History of the Louisiana Purchase Exposition,* 379.

58. TR to Nannie Lodge, Nov. 10, 1904, HCL-MHS; Jusserand, *What Me Befell,* 346.

59. "make trouble" in HCL to TR, Aug. 6, 1906, HCL-MHS; TR's message to Congress, Dec. 6, 1904, in *Presidential Addresses and State Papers of Theodore Roosevelt,* 3:119–89; Charles Larsen, *The Good Fight: The Life and Times of Ben B. Lindsey* (Chicago, 1972), 91; Professor Lawrence Laughlin to Mary Hagedorn, SUBJ-TRC.

CHAPTER NINE: "I SO THOROUGHLY BELIEVE IN REFORM"

1. Harbaugh, *Power and Responsibility,* 208.

2. LeRoy Ashby, *Saving the Waifs: Reformers and Dependent Children, 1890–1917* (Philadelphia, 1984), 121; EKR-Di, Mar. 4, 1905; Uncle Robert announced to the press that TR might run in 1908, NSC; "elated" in TR to Mary Cadwalader Jones, Jan. 23, 1905, MOR-REJ.

3. Harbaugh, *Power and Responsibility,* 217, 219; AUTO, 384.

4. Gould, *Reform and Regulation,* 76–77.

5. "wild" and "mad" in *Letters to Kermit,* 93, 95; on Heyburn and the Senate see Mar. 1, 1905, NSC; Stephenson, *Aldrich,* 260–61.

6. Hoover, *Forty-two Years,* 234; Fortescue was Robert Roosevelt's illegitimate son.

7. TR to Jane Addams, Jan. 24, 1906, MOR 5:140, and Charles P. O'Neill to Jane Addams, Jan. 29, 1906, in Jane Addams Papers, Swarthmore College; TR, "Where I Stand on Child Labor," *Woman's Home Companion,* January 1907. Progressive reformers supported a wide variety of causes, some of them conflicting; for ways to understand progressivism see the bibliographical essays in Steven J. Diner, *A Very Different Age: Americans of the Progressive Era* (New York, 1998), and Arthur S. Link and Richard L. McCormick, *Progressivism* (Arlington Heights, Ill., 1983). Also see Richard Hofstadter, *The Age of Reform: From Bryan to F.D.R.* (New York, 1955); Robert H. Wiebe, *The Search for Order, 1877–1920* (New York, 1967); Nell Irvin Painter, *Standing at Armageddon: The United States, 1877–1919* (New York, 1987); John D. Buenker, John C. Burnham, and Robert M. Crunden, *Progressivism* (Cambridge, Mass., 1977); Anne Firor Scott, *Natural Allies: Women's Associations in American History* (Urbana, Ill., 1991); Blair, *Clubwoman as Feminist;* Robyn Muncy, *Creating a Female Dominion in American Reform, 1890–1935* (New York, 1991); Anne F. Scott and Andrew M. Scott, *One Half the People: The Fight for Woman Suffrage* (Philadelphia, 1975); John D. Buenker, *Urban Liberalism and Progressive Reform* (New York, 1973); Dorothy Salem, *To Better Our World: Black Women and Organized Reform, 1890–1920* (Brooklyn, 1990); Sidney M. Milkis and Jerome M. Mileur, eds., *Progressivism and the New Democracy* (Amherst, Mass., 1999); Clyde Griffen, "The Progressive Ethos," in Stanley Coben and Lorman Ratner, eds., *The Development of an American Culture* (Englewood Cliffs, N.J., 1970), 120–49; John Milton Cooper, Jr., *Pivotal Decades: The United States, 1900–1920* (New York, 1990); Kevin Mattson, *Creating a Democratic Public: The Struggle for Urban Participatory Democracy During the Progressive Era* (University Park, Pa., 1998); Seymour Martin Lipset and Gary Marks, *It Didn't Happen Here: Why Socialism Failed in the United States* (New York, 2000); Robert M. Crunden, *Ministers of Reform: The Progressives' Achievement in American Civilization 1889–1920* (New York, 1982); Martin J. Sklar, *The Corporate Reconstruction of American Capitalism, 1890–1916: The Market, Law, and Politics* (Cambridge, Mass., 1988).

8. TR to Edgar Gardner Murphy, Nov. 15, 1907, MOR-REJ; Jack Temple Kirby, *Darkness at the Dawning: Race and Reform in the Progressive South* (New York, 1972), 70.

9. TR to James A. Tawney, Jan. 29, 1907, MOR-REJ; Lodge supported TR's child

labor proposals for the district; it annoyed TR that Beveridge's national bill delayed the passage of the district bill by two years.

10. C. Green, *Washington*, 155; TR wrote the introduction to Charles Frederick Weller, *Neglected Neighbors: Stories of Life in the Alleys, Tenements and Shanties of the Nation's Capital* (Philadelphia, 1909), which attacked segregation; Robert Harrison, "The Ideal of a 'Model City': Federal Social Policy for the District of Columbia, 1905–1909," *Journal of Urban History* 15, no. 4 (August 1989): 444.

11. TR to James Bronson Reynolds, Feb. 24, 1906, and TR to John St. Loe Strachey, Jan. 9, 1905, MOR-REJ; Harrison, "Ideal of a 'Model City,' " 435–63; C. Green, *Washington*, 156.

12. Slayden, *Washington Wife*, 81.

13. "shambling" in TR to Henry S. Pritchett, Dec. 26, 1904, MOR-REJ; TR to Benjamin Ide Wheeler, Jan. 6, 1906, and "real party" in TR to ABR, Mar. 26, 1912, MOR-REJ; see also TR to TRJR, Oct. 4, 1903, and Nov. 20, 1908, TRJR-LC.

14. TR to Lyman Abbott, Aug. 8, 1904, TRP-LC.

15. Luker, *Social Gospel*, 222; see also Daniel, *Shadow*.

16. Mary White Ovington, *The Walls Came Tumbling Down* (New York, 1969), 154–64.

17. Daniel, *Shadow*, 71–88; the ruling in the *Bailey* case did not end peonage altogether; Daniel A. Novak, *The Wheel of Servitude: Black Forced Labor After Slavery* (Lexington, Ky., 1978), 46–64.

18. TR tried to get journalist George Kennan to publicize Judge Jones' efforts: MOR 3:514; TR may have encouraged Richard Barry to write about peonage (Barry later became a publicity man for the Republican National Committee): Barry, "Slavery in the South To-Day," *Cosmopolitan* 42 (March 1907): 481–91; TR praised Ray Stannard Baker, *Following the Color Line; American Negro Citizenship in the Progressive Era* (New York, 1964); Ellen Fitzpatrick, *Endless Crusade: Women Social Scientists and Progressive Reform* (New York, 1990), 140; Cecilia Kayes, "Roosevelt as a Phrasemaker," *Outlook* 124 (Jan. 7, 1920): 40.

19. Remarks of President Roosevelt to members of the Welfare Department of the Civic League at the White House, May 11, 1908, TR-SP.

20. TR to Albert Shaw, Feb. 3, 1903, MOR-REJ.

21. Daniel, *Shadow*, 83–84; when reviewing the Oklahoma state constitution and its application for statehood Bonaparte took a dim view of its grandfather clause: Clement E. Vose, *Constitutional Change: Amendment Politics and Supreme Court Litigation Since 1900* (Lexington, Mass., 1972), 32; MOR 4:1047; TR to John Sharp Williams, unsigned and unsent, Dec. 5, 1904, MOR-REJ; Booker T. Washington objected when TR used the word "black" rather than "colored" in his speeches: TR to Washington, Oct. 16, 1905, MOR-REJ.

22. TR to Henry S. Pritchett, Dec. 26, 1904, MOR-REJ; see EKR-Di, April–June 1905; ERD to Bob Ferguson, May 1, 1905, JIG-ARIZ.

23. TR to Margaret Chanler, Jan. 27, 1905, EKR-Di, January–March 1905. A descendant of Alexander Hamilton, Schuyler was "deeply attached" to Thee and TR, and had worked on a tenement reform bill with Thee before he died. She was one of TR's last visitors in the hospital in December 1918 and she remained close to EKR and CRR for the rest of her life: Louisa Lee Schuyler to CRR, June 16, 1923, TRC-HU; Edward T. James, ed., *Notable American Women, 1607–1950; a Biographical Dictionary*, 3 vols. (Cambridge, Mass., 1975), 244–246.

24. EKR to KR, n.d. [early 1905], KBR-LC; ARL-Di, Feb. 17, 1905.

25. Lash, *Eleanor and Franklin*, 201; FDR to Horace G. Knowles, Jan. 27, 1936, Papers as President, President's Personal File, Alphabetical Listings, FDR.

26. EKR to ERD, n.d. [December 1905], TRC-HU; ARC to Bob Ferguson, Aug. 20, 1903 and May 4, 1905, and Peachy to Isabella Selmes Ferguson Greenway, Sept. 14, [1905],

and "Home-Coming of Robt. Munro Ferguson," reprinted from the *Northern Weekly*, Aug. 17, 1905, and JIG-ARIZ; see EKR to KR and ERD to KR letters in 1905–1906, KBR-LC; TR to KR, Mar. 4, 1906, TRC-HU, deleted from *Letters to Kermit*; TR to KR, Feb. 20, 1906, TRC-HU.

27. TR to ARC, Apr. 9, 1905, TRC-HU; KR to TR, Apr. 30, 1905, and EKR to KR, n.d. [May 8, and April 15 and 30, 1905], KBR-LC; TR to ARL, May 6, 1905, TRC-HU.

28. "scooped" in Goldman, *Bonaparte*, 86; the Maryland state legislature passed a grandfather clause in 1908 and Bonaparte helped black voters sue the state after he left federal office: Vose, *Constitutional Change*, 26–28.

29. P. Larsen, "Moroccan Crisis," 115.

30. TR told Jusserand that the Russian ambassador lied to him and confessed his dislike for the effete new British ambassador Sir Mortimer Durand, who was not good at scrambles in Rock Creek Park.

31. *TR/HCL*, 2:128; TR to Curtis Guild, Jr., Apr. 2, 1906, MOR-REJ; EKR to KR, n.d. [June 18, 1905], KBR-LC.

32. Widenor, *Lodge*, 123.

33. *New York Times*, Jan. 24, 1906; TR to Joseph Bishop, Mar. 23, 1905, MOR-REJ.

34. Rhodes, *McKinley and Roosevelt Administrations*, 262; the Senate finally approved the protocol in 1907.

35. *TR/HCL*, 2:125; see TR to W. Cameron Forbes, Apr. 6, 1915, TRC-HU; William N. Tilchin, *Theodore Roosevelt and the British Empire* (New York, 1997), 216–17.

36. *TR/HCL*, 2:140.

37. Count Sergius Witte, "Count Witte's Memoirs," *The World's Work*, March 1921, 487; Tyler Dennett cites the indemnity at $7 billion; *Roosevelt and the Russo-Japanese War* (Garden City, N.Y., 1925), 255; TR judged Witte "utterly cynical, untruthful and unscrupulous": Sir Cecil Spring Rice, *The Letters and Friendships of Sir Cecil Spring Rice* ed. Stephen Gwynn, 2:9; (Boston, 1929), TR and EKR got information on Russia from Ambassador Meyer and Spring Rice, and TR often warned them about the menace posed by the kaiser: 2:1–17.

38. Witte, "Memoirs," 487, 494; Lloyd C. Griscom, *Diplomatically Speaking* (Boston, 1940), 261; *TR/HCL*, 2:121; Elizabeth Mills Reid, Ted, Quentin, and some of Bamie's other friends shared Witte's anti-Semitism; Dennett, *Roosevelt and the Russo-Japanese War*, 283; Akira Iriye, "Japan as a Competitor, 1895–1917," in Iriye, ed., *Mutual Images: Essays in American-Japanese Relations* (Cambridge, Mass., 1975), 73–99.

39. EKR to KR, n.d. [Aug. 15, 1905], KBR-LC; TR was not that well informed about Russia's reforms; Dennett, *Roosevelt and the Russo-Japanese War*, 292.

40. TR to Knute Nelson, June 23, 1905, MOR-REJ; MEM 13:270–71.

41. On the boycott see Harbaugh, *Power and Responsibility*, 282–85; see also Griscom, *Diplomatically Speaking*.

42. Stacey Cordery Rozek, "Alice Roosevelt and the 1905 Far Eastern Junket," in Naylor, Brinkley, and Gable, eds., *Theodore Roosevelt: Many-Sided American*, 361.

43. Raymond A. Esthus, *Double Eagle and Rising Sun: The Russians and Japanese at Portsmouth in 1905* (Durham, N.C., 1988), 156–57, 170; Princess Catherine Radziwill, "A Russian Appreciation of Theodore Roosevelt," *Outlook* 124 (Jan. 7, 1920): 18–19; Wilhelm II, *The Kaiser's Memoirs* (New York, 1922), 200; Akira Iriye, *Across the Pacific: An Inner History of American–East Asian Relations* (New York, 1967), 100–107.

44. Japan held for him, as it did for America's early Japan experts, William Sturgis Bigelow, Ernest Fenollosa, Lafcadio Hearn, and Edward S. Morse, a reminder of cultural possibilities that America lacked; he most likely read Shunsui Tamenaga's edition of *The Loyal Ronins: An Historical Romance* (New York, 1884): TR to Florence La Farge June 6, 1904, and Feb. 11, 1905, MOR-REJ; he read to his sons Tadayoshi Sakurai, *Human Bullets: A Soldier's*

Story of Port Arthur (Boston, 1907); see TR to Lieutenant Sakurai, Apr. 22, 1908, MOR-REJ; Roosevelt also read and admired the *Tales of the Genji* and Lafcadio Hearn, *Japan: An Attempt at Interpretation* (New York, 1904), and EKR brought Fenollosa to lecture at the White House; the emperor sent him the samurai swords made by the famed sword-maker Munemitsu of Jakushu. Admiral Togo, known then as the hero of the Russo-Japanese War, came to Sagamore Hill and gave TR a suit of Tokugawa armor and a Tokugama chest, which are still on display in the North Room: EKR to KR, Sept. 9, 1935, KBR-LC; TR was eager for his countrymen to learn more about Japan, so he wrote a pamphlet which the Japan Society distributed praising Japan's contribution to the Allied cause in World War I. Talk about keeping an open door in China or preserving its territorial integrity had always been a smoke screen for America's eagerness to join European powers in their ongoing competition over ports and trade concessions. The czar had stopped Standard Oil from gaining a foothold in Manchuria. Western powers including the U.S. still believed that they could extract great profits from "China's Illimitable Markets"; see Edward B. Parsons, "Roosevelt's Containment of the Russo-Japanese War," *Pacific Historical Review* 38, no. 1 (1969): 23. Root had organized the aggressive Boxer Reprisal, which killed countless Chinese and brought foreign armies deep into China. TR returned part of the Boxer Indemnity money China owed the U.S. to calm tension after the boycott. The Roosevelt administration finally signed the Root-Takahira agreement because it recognized that Japan was an Asian power with a protectorate over Korea and a special interest in Manchuria, and that the U.S. had limited military power in that region and no public support for a war over Korea to stop Japan's expansion; Peter Duus, *The Abacus and the Sword: The Japanese Penetration of Korea, 1895–1910* (Berkeley, 1995). TR believed that European powers and Japan would probably have to do the work of "civilization" in the weaker nations of Asia, and he wanted to maintain American access to Asian markets. He found the shock troops of U.S. investment in Manchuria, the Morgan-Hill banking and railroad interests, showed "literally astounding lack of insight and forethought," and their arrogance made it hard for him to protect their interests abroad: TR to Brooks Adams, July 18, 1903, TRC-HU. Even when he engaged in the basest promotion of American business interests overseas he viewed his efforts as an internationalist building a more stable world order; see Frank Ninkovich, *Modernity and Power* (Chicago, 1994).

45. Esthus, *Double Eagle*, 186.

46. Griscom, *Diplomatically Speaking*, 261–62; Jusserand, *What Me Befell*, 217; Esthus, *Double Eagle*, 186; Russia, looking for scapegoats to blame for its defeat by Japan, turned to a new round of pogroms against the Jews; Ute Mehnert, "German Weltpolitik and the American Two-Front Dilemma: The 'Japanese Peril' in German-American Relations, 1904–1917," *Journal of American History* (March 1996): 1452–77; D. Lewis, *Biography*, 1:370; Akira Iriye, *Cultural Internationalism and World Order* (Baltimore, 1997), 48.

47. TR to ARC, Sept. 1, 1905, TRC-HU; EKR-Di, Sept. 30, 1905; Esthus, *Double Eagle*, 174.

48. Ronald Takaki, *Strangers from a Different Shore: A History of Asian Americans* (New York, 1989), 201–203; Ian Mugridge, *The View from Xanadu: William Randolph Hearst and United States Foreign Policy* (Montreal, 1995), 50.

49. Kenneth Wimmel, *Theodore Roosevelt and the Great White Fleet: American Sea Power Comes of Age* (Washington, D.C., 1998), 216; *New York Times*, June 10, 1907; other West Coast states and British Columbia and Alberta had anti-Japanese outbreaks which required TR to work with William Mackenzie King, Canada's first deputy minister of labour (later advocate of old age pensions and prime minister) and the British government to ease tensions with Japan: Gould, *Presidency*, 262–63.

50. Hearst's claim about Japan's intent was false: Mugridge, *View from Xanadu*, 52.

51. TR to Charles Bonaparte, July 13, 1907, TRP-LC; Rixey, *Bamie*, 250.

52. MOR 4:1271; Mugridge, *View from Xanadu*, 24.

53. Richard W. Leopold, *Elihu Root and the Conservative Tradition* (Boston, 1954), 47–69.

54. See Ninkovich, *Modernity and Power*, and the reassessment of TR's foreign policy in Marks, *Velvet on Iron*; Gould, *Presidency*, 254.

55. See Frederick C. Leiner, "The Unknown Effort: Theodore Roosevelt's Battleship Plan and International Arms Limitation Talks, 1906–1907," *Military Affairs* 4 (1984): 174–79.

56. Walter Rauschenbusch, *Christianity and the Social Crisis* (New York, 1910), 378; Iriye, *Cultural Internationalism*; Barbara W. Tuchman, *The Proud Tower: A Portrait of the World Before the War, 1890–1914* (New York, 1966); Harbaugh, *Power and Responsibility*, 280–81; Griscom, *Diplomatically Speaking*, 275.

57. Hoganson, *Fighting*; Dalton, "Theodore Roosevelt and the Idea of War," 6–11.

58. Norman A. Graebner, ed., *Uncertain Tradition: American Secretaries of State in the Twentieth Century* (New York, 1961), 46; Judson C. Welliver, "The Epoch of Roosevelt," *American Review of Reviews*, February 1909, 339–46.

59. Dalton, "Between the Diplomacy of Imperialism," 27–47.

60. TR to TRJR, Oct. 10 and Nov. 5, 1905, TRJR-LC; "sin" in EKR to KR, n.d. [Sept. 26, 1908], KBR-LC; EKR to KR [Oct. 25, 1905], KBR-LC; ARC described Kermit as having "the look of a medieval saint & the wickedness of the 19th Century in his heart": EKR to Emily Carow, Oct. 8, n.y. [1904], TRC-HU; KR-Di, January–May 1905.

61. John Sayle Watterson, *College Football: History, Spectacle, Controversy* (Baltimore, 2000), 65; TR to F. J. Stimson, Nov. 25, 1905, MOR-REJ.

62. The western colleges substituted rugby: Watterson, *College Football*, 72, 95. Today the N.C.A.A. gives TR credit for the reform of football. Watterson states that others enacted the reforms, after TR started the conversation. Rector Endicott Peabody aided the President in his reform scheme by offering a set of rules put together by boarding schools but always saw himself as "the originator of a great scheme": Ashburn, *Peabody*, 208; Jeffrey C. Stewart, ed., *Paul Robeson: Artist and Citizen* (New Brunswick, N.J., 1999), 13.

63. Harbaugh, *Power and Responsibility*, 161; many years later Edith enjoyed reading Holmes' published letters but recalled, "Justice Holmes and my husband could not possibly understand each other!": EKR to Marion King, June 19, 1945, TRC-HU; Garraty, *Lodge*, 221.

64. Ethan Hitchcock called Bonaparte a "casuistical old woman": Goldman, *Bonaparte*, 40; Charles Bonaparte quoted in Goldman, Bonaparte, 129, see 53, and Robert Grant in *Fourscore* recalled Bonaparte's high-pitched voice and "rather florid manner," 254; HCL to TR, Oct. 13, 1906, HCL-MHS.

65. HCL to TR, June 27, 1903, and Sept. 1, 1906, HCL-MHS; Vose, *Constitutional Change*, 44.

66. HCL to TR, Aug. 6, 1906, HCL-MHS; Wang, *Trial of Democracy*, 263; TR to Secretary of the Treasury, Jan. 9, 1903, MOR-REJ.

67. Garraty, *Lodge*, 228.

68. Louis Filler, *The Muckrakers: Crusaders for American Liberalism* (Chicago, 1968), 214–16; Blum, *Republican Roosevelt*, 87–105; Gould, *Presidency*, 156–64; Harbaugh, *Power and Responsibility*, 234–44.

69. Richard Hofstadter, ed., *The Progressive Movement, 1900–1915* (Englewood Cliffs, N.J., 1963), 18–19; MOR 4:965; Orville Platt died under attack, too. TR considered Thomas W. Lawson's book *Frenzied Finance* (New York, 1906) unreliable and dangerous because so many people believed it to be proof that government was a willing co-conspirator with an insidious "System" which gave "colossal corporations" "an insolent disregard of law." Charles Edward Russell's exposé of the Beef Trust, *The Greatest Trust in the World* (New York, 1905), and his attack on James Garfield's investigation of it as a whitewash job, infuriated TR. TR

complained to magazine owner Robert J. Collier that Lincoln Steffens used gossip as his main source and wrote "impressionist paintings" instead of facts in his articles: TR to Collier, Nov. 4, 1907, MOR-REJ.

70. TR to Ray Stannard Baker, Apr. 9, 1906, MOR-REJ.

71. TR to KR, Nov. 7, 1906, TRC-HU; portions deleted from *Letters to Kermit*, 164; Ernest Crosby, "The Final Word on the 'Literature of Exposure,' " *Cosmopolitan* 42, no. 1 (November 1906), frontispiece.

72. "We'll get you" in Stephenson, *Aldrich*, 266; on the tariff ploy see Blum, *Republican Roosevelt*.

73. Sullivan, *Our Times*, 3:266; TR had already termed Spooner, Hale, and Foraker "a curse": Mowry, *Era*, 200. He wrote critically of Knox to Lodge, June 1, 1908, MOR-REJ; of Spooner to Joseph B. Bishop, Mar. 23, 1905, Bishop Papers, Houghton; Edward S. Corwin, *The President: Office and Powers 1787–1948: History and Analysis of Practice and Opinion* (New York, 1948), 498*n*.7.

74. "roused the people": president of the Rock Island Line to William Howard Taft; see Sidney M. Milkis and Michael Nelson, *The American Presidency: Origins and Development, 1776–1998* (Washington, D.C., 1999), 200; Gould, *Presidency*, 63.

75. Berk, *Alternative Tracks*, 160; Lamoreaux, *Great Merger Movement*, 170; Melvin I. Urofsky, "Proposed Federal Incorporation in the Progressive Era," *American Journal of Legal History* 26 (April 1982): 160–83; TR had promised Root he would "go slow" on corporate control: Dec. 26, 1904, MOR-REJ.

76. *New York Herald*, Feb. 1, 1905; Paolo E. Coletta, *William Jennings Bryan: Political Evangelist, 1860–1908* (Lincoln, Nebr. 1964), 354.

77. HCL to TR, Aug. 6, 1906, HCL-MHS.

78. On cataract see William H. Harbaugh, "The Theodore Roosevelts' Retreat in Southern Albemarle: Pine Knot, 1905–1908," reprinted from *Albemarle County History* 51 (1993); 30*n*.70; see William H. Wilmer to Henry Pringle, Oct. 31, 1930, TRC-HU. On his bone see TR to KR, Sept. 27, 1908, MOR-REJ; Edith wrote Kermit that Father had erythema, n.d. [Sept. 26, 1908], KBR-LC; "havoc" in TR to Edward North Buxton, Oct. 23, 1908, MOR-REJ.

79. TR to Stephen O'Meara, Oct. 2, 1906, and TRJR to TR, n.d., enclosed in HCL to TR, Oct. 4, 1906, HCL-MHS.

80. TR to ACMDL, Mar. 11, 1906, HCL-MHS. Despite Lodge's condescension toward organized labor and doubts about reform, TR took his advice on world affairs seriously throughout his presidency. Lodge proposed the corollary to the Monroe Doctrine and suggested the compromise that became the gentleman's agreement with Japan. Moody served as secretary of the navy (1902–1904), attorney general (1904–1906), and associate justice on the Supreme Court (1906–10). Pinchot and Garfield were closer to TR than Moody, and the pair were sometimes called "Mr. Pinchfield and Mr. Garchot": ERD to Edith Derby Williams, June 11, 1962, TRC-HU.

81. TR to E. H. Butler, May 7, 1906, MOR-REJ; Willard Gatewood, Jr., "Theodore Roosevelt and the Case of Mrs. Minor Morris," *Mid-America* 48, no. 1 (January 1966): 17.

82. TR kept track of the vote to table the investigation of the Morris incident: Gatewood, "Theodore Roosevelt and the Case of Mrs. Minor Morris," 11.

83. Locoweed is a legume that causes locoism in cattle. On pure food and drug reformers see Lorine Swainston Goodwin, *The Pure Food, Drink, and Drug Crusaders, 1879–1914* (Jefferson, N.C., 1999); George M. Kober, *Report of Committee on Social Betterment: A Report by the President's Homes Commission* (Washington, D.C., 1908), 268–70.

84. Goodwin, *Pure Food, Drink, and Drug Crusaders*, 162–70. After reading *The Jungle*, TR sent investigators to follow up on Upton Sinclair's exposé of unsanitary and inhumane

conditions in the meatpacking industry in Chicago; see also Peter Temin, *Taking Your Medicine: Drug Regulation in the United States* (New York, 1980).

85. Goodwin, *Pure Food, Drink, and Drug Crusaders*, 245.

86. "humbug" in Sullivan, *Our Times*, 3:283; Goodwin, *Pure Food, Drink, and Drug Crusaders*; Oscar E. Anderson, Jr., *The Health of a Nation: Harvey W. Wiley and the Fight for Pure Food* (Chicago, 1958), 172–96; TR suspected Wiley of being connected with a salicylic acid factory in New Jersey which he would be charged with regulating if the law passed: TR to James Wilson, May 28, 1906, MOR-REJ.

87. "damage" in MOR 5:219; "diffusion" in TR to Jacob Riis, June 26, 1906, MOR-REJ; "anarchist" in TR to Kermit, June 13, 1906, TRC-HU.

88. TR to Bishop William C. Doane, Jan. 26, 1905, NSC.

CHAPTER TEN: SAVING "OUR OWN NATIONAL SOUL"

1. The eyewitness report comes from William Phillips, *Ventures in Diplomacy* (Boston, 1953), 37–38; moral reformers in the Y.M.C.A. and many other groups' leaders believed he was their friend: the Anti-Cigarette League offices kept his picture on the wall: Tate, *Cigarette Wars*, 40; at a convention of the Anti-Saloon League TR was credited with encouraging a "great onward and upward movement" for purity: James H. Timberlake, *Prohibition and the Progressive Movement, 1900–1920* (New York, 1970), 33; Cecil Spring Rice wrote TR that if imperialist reformer Joseph Chamberlain "had really been a great man, he would have headed a movement for the regeneration of the national character—self-sacrifice, national defence and devotion of all departments to the good of the nation—a sort of general moral reform," which was what TR attempted as president: *Letters and Friendships of Sir Cecil Spring Rice*, 2:111.

2. Burnham, *Bad Habits*; Wiebe, *Search for Order*; Alison M. Parker, *Purifying America: Women, Cultural Reform, and Pro-Censorship Activism, 1873–1933* (Chicago, 1997); Mark Thomas Connelly, *The Response to Prostitution in the Progressive Era* (Chapel Hill, N.C., 1980); K. Austin Kerr, *Organized for Prohibition: A New History of the Anti-Saloon League* (New Haven, 1985); John D'Emilio and Estelle B. Freedman, *Intimate Matters: A History of Sexuality in America* (New York, 1988); David Musto, "Opium, Cocaine and Marijuana in American History," *Scientific American*, July 1991, 40–47; Joseph R. Gusfield, *Symbolic Crusade: Status Politics and the American Temperance Movement* (Chicago, 1972); Stephen Vaughn, "Morality and Entertainment: The Origins of the Motion Picture Production Code," *Journal of American History* 77 (1990): 39–65; Michael Schudson, *Discovering the News: A Social History of American Newspapers* (New York, 1978); Richard Christian Johnson, "Anthony Comstock: Reform, Vice, and the American Way" (Ph.D. diss., University of Wisconsin, 1973); Charles Matthew Feldman, *The National Board of Censorship (Review) of Motion Pictures, 1909–1922* (New York, 1977); Lillian Faderman, *Odd Girls and Twilight Lovers: A History of Lesbian Life in Twentieth Century America* (New York, 1991).

3. "national afternoon" in Stocking, *Race, Culture, and Evolution*, 67. TR did not agree with the oft-heard argument that Rome fell because of moral decline or the influx of foreigners; he was not sure its fall could be explained by decadence: "there is something of mystery that baffles comprehension when the spirit, determination, and capacity for achievement that have characterized a great people vanish from their lives"; see "Theodore Roosevelt on the Decadence of Various Peoples, Including the Romans," *Classical Weekly* 18, no. 15 (Feb. 16, 1925): 113. Elizabeth B. Grannis of the National Christian League for the Promotion of Social Purity to William Astor Chanler, Jan. 21, 1898, Chanler Family Papers, NYHS; Egal Feldman, "Prostitution, the Alien Woman and the Progressive Imagination, 1910–1915," *American Quarterly* 19 (1967): 193.

4. George Frisbie Hoar, "Public and Private Morals," *Collier's*, June 4, 1904, 9; David J. Langum, *Crossing Over the Line: Legislating Morality and the Mann Act* (Chicago, 1994), 20–22; "National Deterioration," *The Nation* 83 (Aug. 16, 1906): 134–35.

5. "decency" in TR to William Allen White, Oct. 7, 1908, White Papers, LC; TR to Baron de Coubertin, July 21, 1905, MOR-REJ; "gambling" in "Sayings of Theodore Roosevelt," *New York Times*, Feb. 9, 1919, in TRC-HU.

6. "thirst" in TR, "Women's Right . . . ," *Outlook* (Feb. 3, 1912): 266; "gilded youth," etc., in address of President Roosevelt to the Department of Superintendence of the National Educational Association at the White House, Feb. 26, 1905, TR-SP.

7. Remarks of President Roosevelt to the Central Juvenile Reformatory Committee at the White House, Dec. 15, 1905, TR-SP.

8. TR, speech to the National Congress of Mothers, Mar. 2, 1905, early drafts, TRC-HU.

9. TR to Bishop William C. Doane, Jan. 26, 1905, NSC; Nelson Manfred Blake, *The Road to Reno: A History of Divorce in the United States* (New York, 1962), 153, 125, 140; see George A. Bartlett, *Men, Women and Conflict* (New York, 1931), 11; MOR 7:363.

10. "The President's Views on a Uniform Divorce Law," 1906; TR, "The President," series of articles in the *Ladies' Home Journal*, 1906–1907, TRC-HU.

11. TR did not object to Grant's negative portrayal of clubwomen: Robert Grant, *Unleavened Bread* (New York, 1900); Newport morals were lax: "What with rich food, splendid apparel, perpetual self-indulgence, and the power which money gives them to gratify every whim, is it any wonder that they won't let a little thing like the marriage vow stand in the way of their individual preferences?": Grant, *The Undercurrent* (New York, 1904), 244.

12. TR, speech to the National Congress of Mothers, Mar. 2, 1905, third and fourth drafts; in earlier drafts he denounced apartment house living, TRC-HU.

13. TR was a positive eugenicist because he campaigned to encourage groups he consider racially fit to reproduce; see Molly Ladd-Taylor, "Eugenics, Sterilisation and Modern Marriage in the USA: The Strange Career of Paul Popenoe," *Gender and History* 13, no. 2 (August 2001).

14. Elizabeth Pleck, "The Whipping Post for Wife Beaters, 1876–1906," in David Levine et al., *Essays on the Family and Historical Change* (College Station, Tex., 1983), 127–49.

15. TR, speech to the National Congress of Mothers, early drafts, TRC-HU; TR also praised mothers in remarks to the delegates to the first International Congress in America on the Welfare of the Child at the White House, Mar. 10, 1908, TR-SP; he also took the categorical moral position that good mothers breastfed their babies: "By Godfrey, the woman who won't nurse her own babies, if she can, isn't fit to have a baby anyhow—I always say so": J. Lane, *Riis*, 111.

16. On circulation see John, *Best Years*, 235; "Mr. Roosevelt's Views on the Strenuous Life," *Ladies' Home Journal* 23 (May 17, 1906), TRC-HU.

17. Daniel Scott Smith, "Family Limitation, Sexual Control, and Domestic Feminism in Victorian America," in Nancy F. Cott and Elizabeth H. Pleck, eds., *A Heritage of Her Own: Toward a New Social History of American Women* (New York, 1979), 226.

18. TR quoted in Linda Gordon, *Woman's Body, Woman's Right: A Social History of Birth Control in America* (New York, 1976), 140; TR to Bessie Van Vorst, Oct. 18, 1902, MOR 3:355–56; NSC; TR, sixth annual message to Congress, Dec. 3, 1903.

19. Elaine Tyler May, *Barren in the Promised Land: Childless Americans and the Pursuit of Happiness* (Cambridge, Mass., 1997), 73; Connelly, *Response to Prostitution*, 75.

20. Howe quoted in Gordon, *Woman's Body*, 143, 150; Howe would not allow anyone to utter a negative word about TR in her presence; Rauschenbusch, *Christianity and the Social Crisis*, 274–79; Teague, *Mrs. L*, 82.

21. TR also opposed birth control and abortion: TR to Franklin C. Smith, Jan. 24, 1906, MOR-REJ; Linda Gordon, "Putting Children First: Women, Maternalism, and Welfare in the Early Twentieth Century," in Linda K. Kerber, Alice Kessler-Harris, and Kathryn Kish Sklar, eds., *U.S. History as Women's History: New Feminist Essays* (Chapel Hill, N.C., 1995), 75; Francis Amasa Walker used statistics to argue that foreign-born families had a higher birthrate than native-born Americans: Gordon, *Woman's Body*, 138.

22. Parker, *Purifying America*; David Pivar, *Purity Crusade: Sexual Morality and Social Control, 1868–1900* (Westport, Conn., 1973); Boyer, *Purity in Print.* TR also believed that authors should exercise more self-censorship and choose not to expose the reading public to corrupting or sensational images. He feared that if children read about violent behavior they might try it. He attempted to get Owen Wister to delete from his story a vivid description of gouging out a horse's eye: Fanny Kemble Wister, ed., *Owen Wister Out West: His Journals and Letters* (Chicago, 1968), 96. He also wrote S. S. McClure that he had destroyed a piece written by Ida Tarbell which *McClure's Magazine* had considered publishing; this suggests that his friendly relationship with the owner allowed him an informal prior restraint power over muckrakers: TR to S. S. McClure, July 20, 1905, MOR-REJ; Richard Butsch, *The Making of American Audiences: From Stage to Television, 1750–1990* (New York, 2000), 152.

23. The attorney called Thaw's moral outrage "dementia Americana": Paul R. Baker, *Stanny: The Gilded Life of Stanford White* (New York, 1989), 390; Michael Macdonald Mooney, *Evelyn Nesbit and Stanford White: Love and Death in the Gilded Age* (New York, 1976).

24. "The Exposure of Vice," *The Nation*, Feb. 21, 1907, 169; on their professional acquaintance see Paul Baker, *Stanny*, 338; TR and White also mixed in the same social circle, and their mutual friends were sculptor Augustus Saint-Gaudens, sportsman Winthrop Chanler, stained-glass artist John La Farge, and editor of *The Century* Richard Watson Gilder; re favoritism toward McKim, Mead, and White see TR to C. Grant La Farge, Mar. 21, 1903, MOR-REJ; TR entertained White's son, Lawrence Grant White, at Sagamore Hill later: Sagamore Hill Guest Book, SAHI.

25. Progressives tried to regulate sexuality in many ways, including raising the age of consent, advocating sex education in the schools, and censoring books and movies: D'Emilio and Freedman, *Intimate Matters*, 202–15; Paul Baker, *Stanny*, 387–88; Parker, *Purifying America*, 124; because of the Thaw trial movie, the movie industry established the National Board of Censorship: Leonard Courtney Archer, "The National Association for the Advancement of Colored People and the American Theatre: A Study of Relationships and Influences" (Ph.D. diss., Ohio State University, 1974), 353.

26. TR to Endicott Peabody, July 6, 1905, MOR-REJ; Ashby, *Saving the Waifs*, 25; see Mrs. David O. Mears, "The Home," first International Congress in America on the Welfare of the Child held under the auspices of the National Congress of Mothers in Washington, D.C., March 10–17, 1908 (National Congress of Mothers, 1908), 147–50; Peter G. Filene, *Him/Her/Self: Sex Roles in Modern America* (New York, 1975), 41–42.

27. *New York Times*, July 14, 1910; Parker, *Purifying America*, 140.

28. Mowry, *Era*, 111; MOR 7:249.

29. AUTO, 198; L. Baker, *From Savage to Negro*, 106–107.

30. Ashby, *Saving the Waifs*, 183.

31. F. L. Luther to TR, Aug. 8, 1912, TRP-LC.

32. America's conversations about race suicide and overcivilization begin with Thomas Wentworth Higginson, George William Curtis, Francis Amasa Walker, E. A. Ross; see chaps. 1 and 2, and Rotundo, *American Manhood*, chapters 10 and 11, especially pp. 251–55.

33. TR saw a connection in France between cultural decadence and family limitation: TR to William I. Nichols, Sept. 21, 1908, MOR-REJ.

34. Gould, *Presidency*, 54; see also G. Stanley Hall, "Feminization in School and Home," *World's Work* 16 (1908): 10237–44. However, mother's pensions also kept women home and prevented them from competing with men for jobs. TR's friends juvenile court justice Ben Lindsey and journalist William Hard, the Consumers' League, and the W.C.T.U. also assisted the mother's pensions movement; TR praised their efforts in letters to William Hard, Jan. 9, 1912, and to Mrs. Robert Park (suffrage leader Maud Wood Park, at the time Mrs. Robert Hunter), Dec. 5, 1911, MOR-REJ; Sonya Michel, "The Limits of Maternalism: Policies Toward American Wage-Earning Mothers During the Progressive Era," in Koven and Michel, eds., *Mothers of a New World*, 279.

35. Although Roosevelt was a gender reactionary who disliked the "new woman" career seekers of his day and found some women club activists annoying, he certainly did not complain if a million conservation-minded clubwomen wrote to their congressmen in support of his bills. He saw women's prominence in pure milk, clean water, and pure food and drug campaigns as a natural outgrowth of their roles as mothers. And he regarded women educating themselves and tackling political problems as a constructive, though sometimes amusing, development in American life. One day when the painter John Singer Sargent stayed for lunch at the White House after spending the morning trying to get TR to hold still long enough to paint his picture, the President learned that Sargent thought of the Midwest as a primitive cultural wasteland. TR urged William Allen White to tell Sargent the truth about the Midwest. "Chuckling and prodding" White, TR got him to inform Sargent how clubwomen in the heartland read learned papers about the true meaning of Sargent's art: White, *Autobiography*, 341; TR liked Edith Wharton's story "Xingu," which satirized the General Federation of Women's Clubs type as he saw her: TR to Edith Wharton, Jan. 5, 1912, MOR-REJ; TR, "The Cause of Decency," *Outlook* (1911); Edward Wagenknecht, *The Seven Worlds of Theodore Roosevelt* (New York, 1958), 90.

36. Vose, *Constitutional Change*, 182; TR, "Women's Right . . . ," *Outlook* (Feb. 3, 1912): 266.

37. Doris Groshen Daniels, "Theodore Roosevelt and Gender Roles," *Presidential Studies Quarterly* 26, no. 3 (1996): 648–65; Molly Ladd-Taylor, *Mother-Work: Women, Child Welfare, and the State*, 1890–1930 (Chicago, 1994), 48–49.

38. TR to Joseph Bucklin Bishop, June 3, 1902, Bishop Papers, Houghton; the phrase "me and my people" got TR into trouble: *Letters to Kermit*, 234; Connelly, *Response to Prostitution*, 25; Slayden, *Washington Wife*, 71.

39. MOR 7:266. On occasion doctors and states stepped into the breach and sterilized "feebleminded" people in institutions and the poor whom they considered unfit to "better" the race, and the General Federation of Women's Clubs, the National Congress of Mothers, and many other progressive reform groups on occasion supported them: Elaine May, *Barren in the Promised Land*; TR expressed interest in plans to limit the reproduction of the unfit, including sterilization: TR to Arthur Lee, July 7, 1913, Lee Papers, Courtauld Institute, London, and TR, "Birth Control from the Positive Side," *Outlook* (October 1917); Daniel J. Kevles, *In the Name of Eugenics: Genetics and the Uses of Human Heredity* (Cambridge, Mass., 1995); Alisa Klaus, "Depopulation and Race Suicide: Maternalism and Pronatalist Ideologies in France and the United States," in Koven and Michel, eds., *Mothers of a New World*, 203; African-Americans suffered from higher infant mortality rates than other groups in this "nadir" period of black history, but public health officials and politicians often attributed these rates to what they insisted was the physical inferiority of blacks; today poor nutrition, low birthweights, and lack of access to medical care are the prevailing medical explanations.

40. TR also warned white southerners that Anglo-Saxons would be outnumbered if blacks repoduced at a higher rate than they did: TR, "Mr. Roosevelt's Views on Race Suicide," *Ladies' Home Journal* 23 (February 21, 1906), TRC-HU.

41. Abortion and birth control when Comstock began his crusade in the 1870s were presumed to be tools of "bad women" or prostitutes; see Linda Gordon, *Woman's Body.* States sometimes forced the sterilization of poor and other women in this period, but not because of TR's views; see Elaine May, *Barren in the Promised Land.* On TR's backtracking see "the popular belief that I have advocated enormous families without regard to economic conditions has just about the same foundation as the Wall Street belief to the effect that I pass my time in reveling in drink, and tortured by a wild desire for blood": TR to E. A. Ross, July 11, 1911, MOR-REJ; TR complained that immigrants were not reproducing enough in "Race Decadence," *Outlook* (Apr. 8, 1911): 763–68.

42. Though he did not write the essay until later, his views had not changed on cultural nationalism since the 1890s: TR admitted that a fine sense of aesthetics was not one of the strong suits in American culture in "Nationalism in Literature and Art," "Art and the Republic," *Proceedings of the Thirty-Eighth Annual Convention,* American Institute of Architects, 1904 (Washington, D.C., 1905), 15–18; see Oliver, "Theodore Roosevelt, Brander Matthews."

43. "spiritually" in Walter Lippmann, "A Tribute to Theodore Roosevelt," *Roosevelt House Review* 7 (Spring 1949): 2; savoir-vivre in TR to ARC, Aug. 8, 1911, TRC-HU; salon idea from Owen Wister, *Roosevelt: The Story of a Friendship, 1880–1919* (New York, 1930), 124; "genuine Americana" in TR to William Welch, Jan. 22, 1909, MOR-REJ; poets in TR to CRR, June 16, 1915, TRC-HU.

44. TR to the Committee on Department Methods, Feb. 11, 1908, MOR-REJ; Willard B. Gatewood, Jr., "Theodore Roosevelt: Champion of 'Governmental Aesthetics,' " *Georgia Review* 21, no. 1 (1967): 172–83; TR later expressed sympathy with his friend Joel Spingarn's New Criticism: TR to Spingarn, Dec. 18, 1912, MOR-REJ; Burton R. Pollin, "Theodore Roosevelt to the Rescue of the Poe Cottage," *Mississippi Quarterly* 34, no. 1 (1980–81): 51–60; on his books see David H. Wallace, *Sagamore Hill: Sagamore Hill National Historic Site, Oyster Bay, New York* (Harpers Ferry, W. Va., 1991), 104, and see Roosevelt Book List, SAHI.

45. TR saw Jesse James taking the place of Robin Hood: Introduction, John A. Lomax, ed., *Cowboy Songs and Other Frontier Ballads* (New York, 1910), and see Robert Cantwell, *When We Were Good: The Folk Revival* (Cambridge, Mass., 1996), 7, and especially good on the Lomaxes and the cult of authenticity is Benjamin Filene, *Romancing the Folk: Public Memory and American Roots Music* (Chapel Hill, N.C., 2000), 32–73, 133–78.

46. Natalie Curtis, "Mr. Roosevelt and Indian Music: A Personal Reminiscence," *Outlook* 121 (Mar. 5, 1919): 399–400; J. P. Morgan had funded E. S. Curtis' ambitious attempt to use fieldwork and photography together to catalogue native life in the twenty-volume *The North American Indian,* for which TR wrote an enthusiastic introduction; on Lomax, Cantwell, *When We Were Good,* 7; on musical choices, David Bispham, *A Quaker Singer's Recollections* (New York, 1920), 317.

47. Remarks of President Roosevelt after listening to songs by the students of the Manassas Industrial School at the White House, Feb. 14, 1906, TR-SP; the Roosevelts owned Arthur A. Schomburg, *Bibliographica Americana: A Bibliographical Checklist of American Negro Poetry,* vol. 2 (New York, 1916) and the poetry of Phillis Wheatley; see Roosevelt Book List, SAHI; EKR-Di, Mar. 20, 1903; Record of White House Musicales, TRC-HU; TR encouraged the *Atlantic Monthly* to publish reviews of Indian and African-American folk tales, TR to *Atlantic Monthly,* Jan. 8, 1895, the Houghton Mifflin Co. Papers, Houghton.

48. TR's cronyism included hiring a few friends; his old friend Bill Sewall got to be postmaster of Island Falls, Maine, and Bat Masterson became a deputy U.S. marshal for the Southern District of New York. Roosevelt knew Masterson in the Dakotas, and he was convinced that he never did anything illegal: Robert K. De Arment, *Bat Masterson: The Man and the Legend* (Norman, Okla., 1979), 375; Russell, *Lives and Legends of Buffalo Bill,* 427; TR served as honorary vice president of the Buffalo Bill Memorial Association, 469.

49. TR had urged Lummis when they were at Harvard not to let boys haze him for his long hair: Dudley Gordon, *Charles F. Lummis: Crusader in Corduroy* (Los Angeles, 1972), 11. The Lummis' Sequoya League advocated improved treatment of native people and the Landmarks Club helped preserve the Spanish missions including San Juan Capistrano; Lummis campaigned in his magazines, *Land of Sunshine,* and *Out West* for that and other causes: Mark Thompson, *American Character: The Curious Life of Charles Fletcher Lummis and the Rediscovery of the Southwest* (New York, 2001), 185, 210–11; for a less romanticized view of missions see Limerick, *The Legacy of Conquest,* 256–58; TR was a big fan of western novels and bought himself a bronze of Kit Carson at Tiffany's in 1915: D. Wallace, *Sagamore Hill,* 106, 116. Lummis is also credited as the popularizer of mission-style architecture and furniture, though Gustav Stickley's designs popularized this style earlier; see Elizabeth Cumming and Wendy Kaplan, *The Arts and Crafts Movement* (New York, 1991), 125–26, 146; see also Juliet Kinchin, "Interiors: Nineteenth-century Essays on the 'Masculine' and the 'Feminine' Room," in Pat Kirkham, ed., *The Gendered Object* (Manchester, U.K., 1996).

50. Garland, *Companions Along the Way,* 247–48; TR to Augustus Saint-Gaudens, July 8, 1905, MOR-REJ; Roosevelt was especially pleased when wonderful exhibitions of leading American artists came to Washington, and he thought the best painting was Sargent's picture of the four doctors: TR to Whitelaw Reid, Feb. 17, 1907, MOR-REJ; see also the Smithsonian Institution Archives and Manuscript Catalog; James Conaway, *The Smithsonian: 150 Years of Adventure, Discovery, and Wonder* (New York, 1995); *The Smithsonian Experience: Science-History-The Arts . . . The Treasures of the Nation* (Washington, D.C., 1977).

51. Kathryn Dethier, "The Spirit of Progressive Reform: *The Ladies' Home Journal* House Plans, 1900–1902," *Journal of Design History,* June 1993, 241–61; Eileen Boris, *Art and Labor: Ruskin, Morris, and the Craftsman Ideal in America* (Philadelphia, 1986), 46, 162; David E. Shi, *The Simple Life: Plain Living and High Thinking in American Culture* (New York, 1985).

52. In his "Address of President Roosevelt before the Grand Lodge of the State of Pennsylvania upon the occasion of the Sesquicentennial Celebration of the Initiation of Brother George Washington," Nov. 5, 1902, TRC-HU (Wagner was a friend of Mlle. Souvestre, AER and ARC's teacher); Gwendolyn Wright, *Moralism and the Model Home: Domestic Architecture and Cultural Conflict in Chicago, 1873–1913* (Chicago, 1980). TR and Edith were friends of Maria Longworth Nichols Storer, the leading woman of the Arts and Crafts Movement, founder of Rookwood Pottery, and they kept one of her vases in Edith's drawing room: D. Wallace, *Sagamore Hill,* 109; Stickley's mission-style furniture was built by workers who enjoyed profit sharing, and at Hull House the Arts and Crafts Movement became an avenue for immigrants to become productive Americans: Boris, *Art and Labor,* 46, 162.

53. "minister" in L. F. Abbott, ed., *Letters of Archie Butt,* 356*n*.1; TR quoted in the *New York Sun* in Stephen J. Pyne, *How the Canyon Became Grand: A Short History* (New York, 1999), 38, 113.

54. Gatewood, "Theodore Roosevelt: Champion of 'Governmental Aesthetics,' " 177.

55. TR wrote that the changes made during the McKinley administration had "involved practically the extinction of the historic White House." He strongly opposed McKinley's idea that the President should live away from the White House altogether: TR, "Notes on the Improvement of the White House," TRC-HU; TR thought that Glenn Brown's idea of putting a second story over the East Terrace would be like cutting down one of the Calaveras trees: TR to Abby G. Baker, Dec. 5, 1908, MOR-REJ; C. Green, *Washington,* 132–46, at one point TR suggested that winding roads between the Capitol and the White House be substituted for the grand avenues Pierre L'Enfant had envisioned, but he listened

finally to the architects; Johnston was the niece and hostess of President James Buchanan and her collection of British paintings waited at the Corcoran Art Gallery until a national gallery was built; what was called the National Gallery in TR's day later became the National Collection of Fine Arts, which became the National Museum of American Art and more recently the Smithsonian American Art Museum; EKR-Di, Oct. 19, 1906; Edith also made a point of buying work by women artists: EKR to Emily Carow, Nov. 25, 1904, TRC-HU.

56. Oliver, *Letters of Theodore Roosevelt and Brander Matthews,* 39*n*.6; Brander Matthews, *Americanisms and Briticisms: With Other Essays on Other Isms* (New York, 1892); for the full simplified spelling story and a longer list of founders see Sullivan, *Our Times,* 3:162–90; Rauschenbusch, *Christianity and the Social Crisis,* 412; TR, *Cosmopolitan,* December 1892, in MEM 14:371, 368; Thomas R. Lounsbury, *English Spelling and Spelling Reform* (New York, 1909); MOR 5:378.

57. Oliver, *Letters of Theodore Roosevelt and Brander Matthews,* 184*n*.2; Sullivan, *Our Times,* 3:177, 181, 187.

58. TR to Fonetta Flansburg, Mar. 5, 1913, MOR-REJ; Sullivan, *Our Times,* 3:162; TR to Jacob Riis, Sept. 26, 1906, Riis-LC.

59. TR, "Men Who Misinterpret Nature," *Everybody's Magazine,* June 1907, 770–74 in MEM 6:369; Ralph H. Lutts, *The Nature Fakers: Wildlife, Science, and Sentiment* (Golden, Colo., 1990), 102, 108; "endow" through "liar" in TR to John Burroughs, May 23 and 27, 1907, MOR-REJ; Edward B. Clark, "Real Naturalists on Nature Faking," *Everybody's Magazine,* September 1907, 17:423–27.

60. "yellow journalists" in Lutts, *Nature Fakers,* 130, 136.

61. "calm" in EKR to KR, n.d. [May 23, 1906], KBR-LC; EKR-Di, February–July 1906; "prison" in Finley Peter Dunne, *Mr. Dooley in the Hearts of His Countrymen* (Boston, 1914), 123; "condition" in EKR to KR, Apr. 27, 1906, KBR-LC.

62. "discipline" in TR to ACMDL, June 9, 1906, HCL-MHS; "decrepit" in TR to ERD, June 17, 1906, MOR-REJ; "cheer me" in TR to ABR, June 13, 1906, MOR-REJ.

63. TR to George R. Carter, May 22, 1906, MOR-REJ.

64. TR to ABR, Nov. 9, 1907, TRP-LC; *Letters to Kermit,* 17; EKR-Di, March–June 1906. The eye problem was in March, the ankle in June.

65. David H. Burton, *Theodore Roosevelt: Confident Imperialist* (Philadelphia, 1968), 105–108; Ayala, *American Sugar Kingdom,* 74–85; Hernández, *Cuba and the United States,* 142–50; Charles Magoon ruled absolutely and brought in sanitation reforms and public works; Christopher A. Abe, "Controlling the Big Stick: Theodore Roosevelt and the Cuban Crisis of 1906," *Naval War College Review* 40, no. 3 (Summer 1987): 88–98.

66. "wipe" in Allan Nevins, *Henry White: Thirty Years of American Diplomacy* (New York, 1930), 255; *Letters to Kermit,* 157; Pérez, *War of 1898,* 33.

67. Ann J. Lane, *The Brownsville Affair: National Crisis and Black Reaction* (Port Washington, N.Y., 1971), and John D. Weaver, *The Brownsville Raid* (New York, 1973).

68. Stephenson, *Aldrich,* 327; James A. Tinsley, "Roosevelt, Foraker, and the Brownsville Affray," *Journal of Negro History* 41, no. 1 (1956): 53; Julian Hawthorne, "Tillman Lays All Blame for Race Trouble on Roosevelt," Jan. 12, 1907, NSC.

69. Slayden, *Washington Wife,* 97; Mary Church Terrell, *A Colored Woman in a White World* (New York, 1980), 274–78.

70. A. Lane, *Brownsville Affair,* 147–48; EKR to KR, n.d. [Jan. 3, 1907], KBR-LC; HCL to TR, June 20, 1907, HCL-MHS; Julia B. Foraker, *I Would Live It Again: Memories of a Vivid Life* (New York, 1932), 286–87, 295–97; Joseph Benson Foraker, *Notes of a Busy Life* (Cincinnati, 1916), 2:231–27; even the pro-Foraker biographer Everett Walters, *Joseph Benson Foraker: An Uncompromising Republican* (Columbus, Ohio, 1948), offers evidence that Foraker was a creature of the railroads.

71. Dyer, *Theodore Roosevelt and the Idea of Race*, 17, 22–44; MOR 3:76, 5:723, 4:795; L. Baker, *From Savage to Negro*, 84–87, 104–21.

72. Harlan, *Wizard of Tuskegee, 1901–1915* (New York, 1983), 303.

73. Zwick, ed., *Mark Twain's Weapons of Satire*, 155.

74. Jack C. Lane, *Armed Progressive: General Leonard Wood* (San Rafael, Calif., 1978), 126.

75. Ibid., 126–29; the massacre happened in 1906: Linn, *Guardians*, 38–39; Zwick, ed., *Mark Twain's Weapons of Satire*, 180; Frank Hindman Golay, *Face of Empire: United States–Philippine Relations, 1898–1946* (Madison, Wisc., 1998), 111–12; Offner, "From Canned Goods to Gugus," 83–99; clipping editorial, Nov. 8, 1906, enclosed in EKR to KR, Dec. 2, [1906], KBR-LC.

76. TR to KR, Nov. 23, 1906, JIG-ARIZ.

77. TR to KR, Nov. 20, 1906, JIG-ARIZ.

78. TR, "The Ancient Irish Sagas," *The Century* 73, no. 3 (January 1907) in MEM 14:384–401; TR to Fred Norris Robinson, Jan. 29, 1907, Robinson Papers, Houghton; years earlier, John Hay, knowing TR's fondness for the Celtic and Nordic stories, the Song of Roland, and the Arthurian cycle, had given him an original manuscript of William Morris' version of the Norse sagas. The President graciously thanked Hay but the Morris version proved rather too bloodless for his taste: AUTO, 400.

79. Daniel T. Rodgers, *Atlantic Crossings: Social Politics in a Progressive Age* (Cambridge, Mass., 1998), 65.

80. Rodgers sees TR as an advocate of "Tory social reform": ibid., 247.

81. Peter J. Coleman, *Progressivism and the World of Reform: New Zealand and the Origins of the American Welfare State* (Lawrence, Kans., 1987), 230*n*.10; TR, speech in Chautauqua, N.Y., Aug. 11, 1905, in *Presidential Addresses and State Papers of Theodore Roosevelt*, (New York, 1905), 4:453.

82. James T. Kloppenberg, *Uncertain Victory: Social Democracy and Progressivism in European and American Thought, 1870–1920* (New York, 1986), 210; Rodgers, *Atlantic Crossings*, 54, 57; TR praised Georges Clemenceau's 1906 speech attacking the socialism of Jean Jaurès and said Clemenceau's "program of legislation and of government acts is so much like my own": TR to Jules Jusserand, Aug. 15, 1906, MOR-REJ, but William Allen White believed that progressives were "fighting a common cause" with Jaurès; Clemenceau favored unemployment and old-age insurance, collective bargaining, and the nationalization of railroads and utilities, the last of which TR did not support.

83. Laurence M. Hauptman, "Governor Theodore Roosevelt and the Indians of New York State," *Proceedings of the American Philosophical Society* 119, no.1 (Feb. 21, 1975): 1–7, and William T. Hagan, *Theodore Roosevelt and Six Friends of the Indian* (Norman, Okla., 1997); I thank Lawrence Hauptman for his advice about TR and native peoples.

84. Hagan, *Six Friends*, 133, 153, 226.

85. "heart failure" in *Letters to Kermit*, 184; "strain" in EKR to Emily Carow, n.d. [Mar. 10, 1907], TRC-HU; EKR-Di, Mar. 1–19, 1907.

86. KR-Di, Mar. 26, June 20, Sept. 17, Nov. 28, 1907; EKR to ARC, n.d. [May 1, 1907], TRC-HU.

87. TR to DR, Feb. 9, 1906, MOR-REJ; in January, Edith took to her bed with a headache one week and backache the next.

88. KR-Di, Feb. 17, 1906; TR to Winthrop Chanler, Apr. 4, 1906, MOR-REJ; "anything but trouble" in Teague, *Mrs. L*, 128.

89. EKR-Di, June 8–9, 1905, Oct. 31–Nov. 4, 1906, May 17–22, 1907, May 7–10, 1908; EKR to John Greenway, Dec. 12, [1905], JIG-ARIZ; ERD to EKR n.d. [November 1905], TRC-HU; Harbaugh, "Theodore Roosevelts' Retreat."

90. MOR 5:198–99; the reports Wilkie sent back showed that most members of the W.F.M. were practical men, not wild-eyed assassins: TR to Edwin C. Stokes, Sept. 9, 1906, MOR-REJ; J. Anthony Lukas, *Big Trouble: A Murder in a Small Western Town Sets Off a Struggle for the Soul of America* (New York, 1997), 549; TR's Department of Commerce and Labor found there was no longer a threat of anarchism in the U.S.: William Preston, Jr., *Aliens and Dissenters: Federal Suppression of Radicals, 1903–1933* (New York, 1963), 33.

91. "pressure" and "mistake" in TR to Calvin Cobb, June 20, 1906, and "stupid men" in TR to Lyman Abbott, July 10, 1906, MOR-REJ.

92. "untruth" in Lukas, *Big Trouble*, 459; TR to William Emlen Roosevelt, Apr. 5, 1907, MOR-REJ.

93. Lukas, *Big Trouble*, 470–73; EKR to Emily Carow, May 4, 1907, TRC-HU; see *Letters to Kermit*, 193, for a more positive mood on the same day.

94. EKR-Di, May 17–22, 1907; *Letters to Kermit*, 199–200.

95. TR to Edwin C. Stokes, Sept. 9, 1906, MOR-REJ; EKR-Di, May 17–22, 1907; "terror" in EKR to KR, n.d. [May 22, 1907], KBR-LC.

96. EKR said her husband was like Thee, Ted, and Quentin in having a flare-up of temper, followed by quiet embers: EKR to ARC, May 5, 1912, TRC-HU; Hermann Hagedorn quoted Edith as he interviewed WSC, Jr., and Mrs. Margaret Cowles, and Corinne Robinson Alsop, Roosevelt Women Interviews, TRC-HU; EKR to KR, n.d. [July 30, 1907], KBR-LC.

97. TR to ABR, Dec. 13, 1908, TRP-LC; TR to Endicott Peabody, Feb. 12, 1907, MOR-REJ; ABR, Memoirs, TRC-HU; EKR-Di, Sept. 15–17, 1907.

98. TR to ACMDL, Sept. 20, 1907, HCL-MHS; TR to Edward A. Ross, Apr. 8, 1907, MOR-REJ.

99. Teresa Richardson to EKR, Oct. 24, 1907, TRC-HU; Chernow, *House of Morgan*, 13–128, does not depict a substantially different situation from Jean Strouse, *Morgan: American Financier* (New York, 1999).

100. HCL to TR, Aug. 12, 1907, HCL-MHS.

101. George Bittlingmayer, "Antitrust and Business Activity: The First Quarter Century," *Business History Review* 70 (Autumn 1996): 363–401.

102. *Letters to Kermit*, 224.

103. "savagery" in MOR 5:746*n*.1; TR later put pressure on Judge Landis to ease up on his prosecutions because restoring business confidence was the highest priority: MOR 5:779*n*.1, 784–85, 803; EKR to KR, n.d. [Nov. 18, 1907], KBR-LC.

104. "fanatic" in TR to ERD, Oct. 6, 1907, TRC-HU; on TR's health see Harbaugh, "Theodore Roosevelts' Retreat"; TR signed the letter to her, as he usually did, "Your Own lover": TR to EKR, Oct. 10, 1907, TRC-HU and TRP-SAHI; Dr. Rixey to EKR, Oct. 19, 1907, KBR-LC. Edith was not that pleased her husband went hunting in an "unattractive" canebrake; "constant companionship with the men who are with him would not amuse me at all!": EKR to Emily Carow, Oct. 12, [1907], and n.d., TRC-HU; EKR to KR, n.d. [Oct. 24, 1907], KBR-LC.

105. TR to T. R. Lounsbury, June 26, 1908, MOR-REJ; Gatewood, *Art of Controversy*, 229, 230, 233.

106. TR to HCL, Aug. 19, 1907, HCL-MHS.

107. "blows" in TR to TRJR, May 12, 1908, TRJR-LC; NSC; TR to Baron Kanekō, n.d., Nevins Collection, Columbia University; Kimitada Miwa, "Japanese Images of War with the United States," in Iriye, ed., *Mutual Images*, 115–37; mob violence against the Japanese was a factor in sending the fleet to the Pacific, 176–77: Canada had its own anti-Japanese riots in Vancouver in 1907 and a diplomatic gentleman's agreement to restrict immigration; see Neville Bennett, "The 'White Canada' Policy: British Columbia and Oriental Exclusion, 1897–1911—The Diplomatic Repercussions of Regionalism," in *Regionalism and National*

Identity: Multi-disciplinary Essays on Canada, Australia, and New Zealand, ed. Reginald Berry and James Acheson (Christ Church, N.Z., 1985), 475–83; Raymond A. Esthus, *Theodore Roosevelt and Japan* (Seattle, 1967).

108. James R. Reckner, *Teddy Roosevelt's Great White Fleet* (Annapolis, Md., 1988), 22–23; Iriye, "Japan as a Competitor," in Iriye, ed., *Mutual Images,* 85.

109. Akira Iriye, *Pacific Estrangement: Japanese and American Expansion, 1897–1911* (Cambridge, Mass., 1972), 117; Wimmel, *Theodore Roosevelt and the Great White Fleet;* TR to Albert Shaw, Sept. 3, 1907, MOR-REJ.

110. Reckner, *Great White Fleet,* 49, 78–79; Charles E. Neu, *An Uncertain Friendship: Theodore Roosevelt and Japan, 1906–1909* (Cambridge, Mass., 1967), 212; Thomas A. Bailey, *Theodore Roosevelt and the Japanese-American Crises* (Stanford, Calif., 1934), 211–15.

111. Robert A. Hart, *The Great White Fleet: Its Voyage Around the World, 1907–1909* (Boston, 1965), viii, 13.

112. Reckner, *Great White Fleet,* 49, 59.

113. Ibid., 49, 78–79.

114. Linn, *Guardians,* 86–87, 90.

115. MOR 7:396; "Dear Uncle Ted," FDR to TR, June 7, 1916, FDRN-FDR; TR to Albert Shaw, Sept. 3, 1907, MOR-REJ.

116. Hart, *Great White Fleet,* 299.

117. Beale, *Rise of America,* 388.

118. MOR 6:955, 889; TR to TRJR, Feb. 11, 1908, MOR-REJ; *Letters to Kermit,* 230.

119. HCL to TR, Jan. 2, and Elihu Root to HCL, Jan. 3, 1908, HCL-MHS.

120. MOR 6:925; TR to Arthur Lee, Sept. 16, 1910, MOR-REJ; Ashburn, *Peabody,* 210; MEM 18:95.

121. "nobody likes" in L. F. Abbott, ed., *Letters of Archie Butt,* 337; reported in *World,* Aug. 10, 1905, in NSC; Hutchins Hapgood, *A Victorian in the Modern World* (New York, 1939), 302; chrysanthemum in *New York Times,* letter to the editor Jan. 30, 1908, enclosed in EKR to KR, n.d. [Feb. 2, 1908], KBR-LC.

122. MOR 6:947–48, 925.

123. Stephen Ponder, "Federal News Management in the Progressive Era: Gifford Pinchot and the Conservation Crusade," *Journalism History* 13, no. 2 (Summer 1986): 42–48.

124. TR, Governors' Conference remarks, May 15, 1908, TR-SP; Pinchot, *Breaking,* 347; address at the opening of the conference on the Conservation of Natural Resources at the White House, May 13, 1908, MEM 18:165; Henry Clepper, "A Commemoration: The Historic White House Conference on Conservation," *American Forests* 89 (May 1983): 26–28.

125. Lawrence F. Abbott, *Impressions of Theodore Roosevelt* (Garden City, N.Y., 1919), 22; Abbott, ed., *Letters of Archie Butt,* 144.

126. Apr. 6, 1907, and Nov. 21, 1906, NSC; TR to William Howard Taft, Apr. 2, 1908, MOR-REJ.

127. TR to KR, June 17, 1908, with United Press account of the convention, TRC-HU; TR to HCL, June 15, 16, and 18 and HCL to TR, June 22, 1908, HCL-MHS.

128. TR to TRJR, Feb. 11, 1908, and to Frank C. Smith, Jan. 9, 1907, MOR-REJ; Swanberg, *Citizen Hearst,* 316; EKR to KR, n.d. [June 15, 1907], KBR-LC; he was a shareholder in the Chemical Bank, Feb. 28, 1907: TR to W. B. Ridgely, MOR-REJ.

129. Quentin would be a boarder at Episcopal High School, where he was regularly hazed, and when he came home he attached himself to Oscar Straus, who helped him with his coin collecting. Quentin had become the family's only baseball fan and Edith had him tutor her in its rules: Oscar S. Straus, *Under Four Administrations: From Cleveland to Taft* (Boston, 1922), 244–45. Archie was being held back a grade at Groton but Ted had finished Harvard in three years and newspapers chronicled his first day on the job in a Connecticut

carpet factory, where he planned to work his way up to a management job. Ethel was preparing for a much quieter White House debut than Alice's, followed by a debutante's season. TR found her minor rebellions—high jumping against his wishes on spirited horses—much more tolerable than Alice's, and when he saw women riding astride in California, rather than sidesaddle as they did in the East, he wrote Ethel that perhaps in her lifetime riding habits would change enough to give her and other women more freedom. Besides, it would be better for the horse: TR to ERD, May 10, 1903, TRC-HU.

130. TR to ABR, Jan. 2, 1908, ABR Papers, in TRP-LC; Edith liked to tease him about his loyal friends; she knew that Elihu Root as a corporation lawyer had practically invented the holding company, thereby enabling the Sugar Trust to gain a monopoly over sugar refining in America. When her husband fulminated in praise of Root, most likely over some piece of anti-trust advice, Edith interjected wryly: "Set a thief to catch a thief": ERD to Edith Derby Williams, Aug. 14, 1960, TRC-HU.

131. EKR-Di, Dec. 8, 1908; EKR to KR, n.d. [Dec. 9] and [16, 1908], KBR-LC; on historical work see TR to TRJR, Dec. 3, 1908, MOR-REJ.

132. TR to TRJR, Jan. 4, 1909, MOR-REJ.

133. TR to Bob Ferguson, Jan. 17, 1909, MOR-REJ.

134. Harbaugh, *Power and Responsibility*, 344–45; Joan M. Jensen, *The Price of Vigilance* (Chicago, 1968), 12–13, 117, 150; Christopher M. Andrew, *For the President's Eyes Only: Secret Intelligence and the American Presidency from Washington to Bush* (New York, 1996), 26–29; Rhodin Jeffrys-Jones, *American Espionage: From Secret Service to CIA* (New York, 1977), 17–48; Andrew, *Intelligence and International Relations, 1900–1945* (Exeter, Eng., 1987); Andrew and David Dilks, eds., *The Missing Dimension* (London, 1984); "usurp" in AUTO, 346; army in Gatewood, *Art of Controversy*, 238.

135. NSC; Gatewood, *Art of Controversy*, 236–87.

136. Slayden, *Washington Wife*, 116; Feb. 8, 1909, NSC.

137. "sixteen lions" in L. F. Abbott, ed., *Letters of Archie Butt*, 104; Vose, *Constitutional Change*, 25; TR also felt that way about the *World* and other newspapers, see Gould, *Presidency*, for a clear explanation of TR's attempt to jail Pulitzer for libel.

138. Stanley Karnow, *In Our Image: America's Empire in the Philippines* (New York, 1989); Welch, *Response to Imperialism*, 136–49; Gould, *Presidency*, 253.

139. For TR as a transitional figure see Dalton, "Between the Diplomacy of Imperialism," and Frank Ninkovich, "Theodore Roosevelt: Civilization as Ideology," *Diplomatic History* 10, no. 3 (1986): 221–45. The ultimate effects of his naval buildup and the Great White Fleet's voyage are debated by historians; many Japanese observers viewed the voyage as having peaceful and stabilizing intent: Iriye, *Pacific Estrangement;* Wimmel, *Theodore Roosevelt and the Great White Fleet;* Reckner, *Great White Fleet;* Richard D. Challener, *Admirals, Generals and American Foreign Policy, 1898–1914* (Princeton, 1973); Bailey, *Theodore Roosevelt and the Japanese-American Crises;* Esthus, *Theodore Roosevelt and Japan*; Iriye, ed., *Mutual Images;* May 6, 1910, NSC; MOR 7:83; TR, "International Peace," address before the Nobel Prize Committee, Christiania, Norway, May 5, 1910; see Serge Ricard, "Anti-Wilsonian Internationalism: Theodore Roosevelt in the *Kansas City Star,*" in Daniela Rossini, ed., *From Theodore Roosevelt to FDR: Internationalism and Isolationism in American Foreign Policy* (Bodmin, Eng., 1995).

140. AER to William Harbaugh, which he repeated during "Writing Theodore Roosevelt Across the Generations," Organization of American Historians panel, Apr. 27, 2001, Los Angeles. After F.D.R. spoke in praise of TR he wrote: "It is because I really admired and respected and loved T.R. that I felt every word of what I said": FDR to Horace G. Knowles, Jan. 27, 1936, FDR Papers, Papers as President, President's Personal Files, TR 787, FDR. Par-

sons, *Perchance*, 340; Harold T. Pinkett, "The Keep Commission, 1905–1909: A Rooseveltian Effort for Administrative Reform," *Journal of American History* 52, no. 2 (1965): 299.

141. Ray Eldon Hiebert, *Courtier to the Crowd: The Story of Ivy Lee and the Development of Public Relations* (Ames, Iowa, 1966).

142. Harbaugh, *Power and Responsibility*, 318.

143. HCL to CRR, Sept. 18, 1921, TRC-HU; EKR to HCL, n.d. [Nov. 11, 1908], HCL-MHS.

144. Archie Butt to his mother, May 15, [1908], in L. F. Abbott, ed., *Letters of Archie Butt*, 7.

145. TR to ACMDL, June 19, 1908, HCL-MHS; Abbott, ed., *Letters of Archie Butt*, 323.

CHAPTER ELEVEN: THE WORLD CITIZEN

1. Mar. 23, 1909, NSC.

2. EKR to KR, Nov. 28 and Dec. 17, [1909], KBR-LC; KR-Di, Mar. 23, 1909; Lodge told TR, "I was not prepared for the intensity of the popular interest in you after you left office": HCL to TR, n.d. [end of March 1909] and Apr. 29, 1909, HCL-MHS; see also *TR/HCL*, 2:330 and 335; Mar. 23, 1909, NSC.

3. "dull thud" in L. F. Abbott, ed., *Letters of Archie Butt*, 42; Henry L. Stoddard, *It Costs to Be President* (New York, 1938), 175.

4. *Boston Transcript*, June 18, 1910, NSC. His inheritance income came from the remaining capital from his bequests by Thee, Mittie, Uncle James K. Gracie, the Roosevelt pier, and the Broadway Improvement Company; Edith's annual income from her uncle John's bequest was $6,101.55 in 1909 and $6,214.12 in 1910: see back of EKR-Di, 1894–1919; TR to TRJR, Nov. 11, 1910, and Aug. 22, 1911, TRJR-LC; DR to ARC, Nov. 7, 1912, TRC-HU; William Leuchtenburg, ed., *Theodore Roosevelt: The New Nationalism* (Englewood Cliffs, N.J., 1961), 104.

5. TR to C. H. Sherrill, Mar. 3, 1913, MOR-REJ; Joseph Bucklin Bishop, *A Chronicle of One Hundred and Fifty Years: The Chamber of Commerce of the State of New York, 1768–1918* (New York, 1918), 199; among the many post-presidential positions suggested to TR were the presidency of Harvard and heading the Boy Scouts.

6. EKR to KR, June 6, 1909, KBR-LC; Mar. 24, 1909, NSC.

7. KR-Di, June 1909; TR had asked to see Florence La Farge at the farewell luncheon: TR to CRR, n.d. [Mar. 13, 1909], TRC-HU.

8. "Close Range Impressions of Theodore Roosevelt," 1909, SUBJ-TRC.

9. KR-Di describes the trip, Mar.–June, 1909; R.W.B. Lewis, *Edith Wharton*, 261; March 1909, NSC; Thomas M. Pitkin, *The Black Hand: A Chapter in Ethnic Crime* (Totowa, N.J., 1977).

10. John T. McCutcheon, *In Africa: Hunting Adventures in the Big Game Country* (Indianapolis, 1910), 187; the Roosevelt party made their way through the Suez Canal to Mombasa accompanied by a young United Press reporter, Warrington Dawson, who had been recommended by Henry White and Bamie. Roosevelt occasionally invited Dawson into his camp to gather small snippets of accurate hunting news which could be given to reporters who followed the party at a distance or who waited in Nairobi. Even so, newspapers spread the amusing falsehood that TR did a war dance when he shot his first lion. TR joked about offering rewards if cannibals rid him of reporters on his trip: L. F. Abbott, ed., *Letters of Archie Butt*, 203; Warrington Dawson, *Opportunity and Theodore Roosevelt* (Chicago, 1923), 73–74; see also Gary Rice, "Trailing a Celebrity: Press Coverage of Theodore Roosevelt's African Safari, 1909–1910," *Theodore Roosevelt Association Journal* 21, no. 3 (Fall 1996): 4–16.

11. Mar. 8, 1909, NSC; when TR finished his hunt he joked to reporters in Khartoum that Professor Starr would have to "guess again."

12. Apr. 1, 1909, NSC; Rice, "Trailing a Celebrity."

13. *TR/HCL,* 2:358–59; Dec. 3, 1909, NSC; HCL to TR, June 21, 1909, and TR to HCL, July 26, 1909, HCL-MHS.

14. KR-Di, Mar. 5 and 6, 1909; MOR 7:46–47; see *African Game Trails* MEM 5, where TR offers different death tolls.

15. MOR 7:17, 26; MEM 2:85, 345; TR, 1909 Diary, Nov. 19–20, TRC-HU.

16. MEM 2:209, 216–17; MOR 7:24.

17. MEM 2:300.

18. TR to KR, Aug. 21, 1909, TRC-HU; MEM 2:244–45; he told his editor: "The elephant that charged me was within a few feet," probably referring to the second elephant, MOR 7:34.

19. MEM 2:246–47.

20. MEM 2:276–77; TR to TRJR, May 5, 1909, TRJR-LC; TR to Will Sewall, July 16, 1909, TRP-LC.

21. TR to TRJR, May 5, 1909, TRJR-LC; to ARC, Oct. 17, 1909, TRC-HU; to Will Sewall, July 16, 1909, TRP-LC; to WSC, Jr., Mar. 19, 1910, and to William Loeb, Nov. 2, 1909, TRC-HU; TR letter quoted in KR, Jr., *A Sentimental Safari* (New York, 1963), 117.

22. MEM 2:100; TR also worried aloud to his friend Carl Akeley the problem his fame and accomplishments would create for his sons as they tried to find their niche in the world; see Akeley letters to Hagedorn, SUBJ-TRC.

23. MOR 7:38.

24. MEM 2:xxvii.

25. TR, "Wild Hunting Companions," MEM 4:125.

26. MEM 2:xxxi; TR to Kaiser Wilhelm, Jan. 2, 1909, MOR-REJ.

27. MEM 2:363.

28. *Outlook* 94 (January–June 1910): 7; he described himself as "a pretty good Imperialist" and gave the British and other imperial powers free advice about what they were doing wrong in Africa: MOR 7:32.

29. Kenneth M. Cameron, *Into Africa: The Story of the East African Safari* (London, 1990), 54.

30. MEM 2:xxii; KR-Di, May 6, 1909; in his diary TR excoriated himself for missed shots, but Kermit in his diary recorded more interest in the bisexuality of hyenas: TR, 1909 Diary, Aug. 7, 31, and Sept. 23, TRC-HU.

31. MEM 2:xv.

32. KR, Jr., *Sentimental Safari,* 101–103; Dawson, *Opportunity,* 73; TR, "Wild Hunting Companions," MEM 4:122–24.

33. HCL to TR, June 21, 1909, HCL-MHS; MOR 7:22.

34. He probably backed out because he did not trust Selig: *The Theodore Roosevelt Association Film Collection: A Catalog,* ed. Wendy White-Hensen and Veronica M. Gillespie (Washington, D.C., 1986), xiii, 12, 152, 6; Budd Schulberg, *Moving Pictures: Memories of a Hollywood Prince* (New York, 1982), 117–18; TR qualifies as the first motion picture and animated cartoon president.

35. Kermit went back to Africa, too, and made friends with Denys Finch-Hatton, Isak Dinesen's lover; see Ernest Hemingway, "The Short Happy Life of Francis Macomber," in *The Fifth Column, and the First Forty-Nine Stories* (New York, 1938), 105; *African Game Trails* and TR's adventures are the backdrop for the Macomber story with its crucible of "buck fever"; Cameron, *Into Africa,* 51, 97–104; see Kenneth S. Lynn, *Hemingway* (New York, 1987).

36. TR to CRR, May 19, 1909, TRC-HU.

37. ARL to EKR, Apr. 19, 1909, and EKR to KR, June 16, [1909], KBR-LC.

38. EKR to KR, Apr. 7, [1909], KBR-LC.

39. Ibid.

40. Symptoms of stroke or hysterical paralysis: EKR to KR, May 19, n.y., and June 16, [1909], KBR-LC. Gossips deplored the Tafts' lack of savoir-faire: EKR to KR, n.d. [June 2, 1909], KBR-LC.

41. EKR to KR, May 26, [1909], KBR-LC.

42. TR to KR, Sept. 27, 1908, MOR-REJ; KR, Jr., *Sentimental Safari*, 16–17.

43. TRJR to Endicott Peabody, Apr. 16, 1909, Peabody Papers, Houghton.

44. TR to ERD, Sept. 3, 1909, TRC-HU.

45. The Fairy Orchard was a meadow with apple trees not far from the house, now a parking lot: EKR to TR, n.d. [Nov. 1, 1891], and to ERD, May 14, 1928, TRC-HU.

46. TR to EKR, Nov. 12, 1909, TRC-HU.

47. EKR to KR, n.d. [June 2, 1909], KBR-LC; MOR 7:83.

48. ARL to EKR, Apr. 7, 1909, KBR-LC; see Butt on Taft learning the job in *Taft and Roosevelt*, 1:24–75.

49. Clipping enclosed in EKR to KR, June 2, 1909, KBR-LC; March 1909, NSC.

50. Bowers, *Beveridge and the Progressive Era*, 300; L. F. Abbott, ed., *Letters of Archie Butt*, 271–73; H. H. Kohlsaat, *From McKinley to Harding* (New York, 1923), 185.

51. TR's 1908 message to Congress in MEM 17:575–641; TR found it irritating that Taft had removed Henry White from the diplomatic service, but would make no public statement against the President. Roosevelt had sent advice to Taft through Lodge that the tariff bill should be "managed as to give Taft the chance to appear" as an effective champion of reduction even if his efforts to get it through Congress failed, but such advice went unheeded: TR to HCL, Sept. 10, 1909, HCL-MHS.

52. HCL to TR, Nov. 30, 1909, HCL-MHS; *New York Times*, Mar. 24, 1910.

53. Teague, *Mrs. L*, 140. Lodge advised Roosevelt that Taft was hurting himself by speaking around the country about the tariff and the courts. Lodge reported that he had visited J. P. Morgan in New York and found him immensely disappointed in Taft's leadership. Lodge added, alluding most likely to Morgan's large secret campaign donation: "I do not think there is anybody in the country who is more anxious for Taft's success than Morgan—for reasons which delicacy forbids me to enter into": HCL to TR, Nov. 30, 1909, HCL-MHS. Rumors reached Edith that Bamie criticized her brother for trying to foist Loeb on Taft for a cabinet post, and Edith reminded her that TR had not interfered in cabinet choices: EKR to ARC, n.d. [1910], TRC-HU.

54. EKR to KR, Jan. 7, [1910], KBR-LC; ARL-Di, Jan. 8, 1910. Alice went to Mabel Boardman's salon and talked with several congressmen to gather information for her father: ARL-Di, Jan. 31, 1910.

55. Several Roosevelt family members and friends belonged to the Colony Club: *New York Times*, Dec. 22, 1909, 8:1; Dec. 15, 1909, 8:1. The Colony Club had been founded by Daisy Harriman and other wealthy society women to provide a social and intellectual center and athletic club for women. Its members divested themselves of stock in companies known to treat workers harshly; Edith entertained out of the club and her picture appears in its history: Anne F. Cox, *The History of the Colony Club, 1903–1984* (New York, 1984), 11–39; Lamoreaux, *Great Merger Movement*, 172–73.

56. Lawrence Abbott traveled with them: EKR-Di, Feb. 16, 1910; EKR to KR, Feb. 10 and 20, [1910], KBR-LC. Alice was so jealous of the gifts and press attention her stepmother and stepsister received at the time of their departure she began a new flirtation with one of the many young men who pursued her: ARL-Di, Mar. 2, 1910.

57. EKR-Di, Mar. 14, 1910; TR to TRJR, Mar. 21, 1910, TRJR-LC; EKR approved of

EBAR because she was a book lover and very unselfish, and she had "been brought up very carefully in the old-fashioned way, always with her mother": EKR to Mrs. Ralph Cross Johnson, n.d. [1910], Martha Waller Johnson Papers, Virginia Historical Society, Richmond.

58. TR to Secretary of the Smithsonian Institution, Dec. 12, 1909, MOR-REJ; *New York Times,* Dec. 15, 1909; TR to Charles Walcott, Feb. 2, 1915, HCL-MHS; clipping enclosed in EKR to KR, Feb. 20, 1910, KBR-LC.

59. EKR to TRJR, Mar. 12, [1910], SUBJ-TRC; Mar. 23, 1910, NSC.

60. EKR to KR, July 28, 1909, May 12 and June 2, [1909], KBR-LC; MOR 7:64; TR, 1910 Diary, Apr. 23, TRC-HU.

61. EKR to TRJR, Apr. 11, 1910, SUBJ-TRC; MOR 7:50; KR, Jr. *Sentimental Safari,* 40; NSC; Edith and Theodore began April 1910 in Naples and after Rome returned to Spezzia, where a carriage took them to visit the scenes of their honeymoon: MOR 7:364.

62. MOR 7:385.

63. Lois Scharf and Joan M. Jensen, eds., *Decades of Discontent: The Women's Movement, 1920–1940* (Boston, 1983), 15; quoting Edith Wharton, A *Backward Glance,* in R.W.B. Lewis, *Wharton,* 281; William Morton Fullerton, "Mr. Roosevelt and France," *Scribner's Magazine* 48 (July–December 1910): 370; the institute includes the Académie des sciences morales et politiques and four other academies; I thank Serge Ricard for clarifying the divisions. William James, then visiting his brother Henry in Britain, wrote his comment to Wharton: Lewis, *Wharton,* 290.

64. EKR to TRJR, May 1, 1910, SUBJ-TRC.

65. EKR to TRJR, May 8, 1910, SUBJ-TRC; May 6, 1910, NSC; MOR 7:387; TR, "International Peace," address before the Nobel Prize Committee, Christiania, Norway, May 5, 1910, MEM 3:xv, 410–15. TR wrote: "Throughout the effort to obtain for our country a vertebrate military policy there can be likewise obtained for our people a social efficiency, a discipline, a sense of international responsibility that . . . will do much to hasten the day of 'the parliament of man and the federation of the world' ": TR, "Democracy and Military Preparation," *Outlook* (Nov. 25, 1914): 665; Jane Addams praised his speech.

66. Fullerton, "Mr. Roosevelt and France," 370; MOR 7:292, 343, 377–79. TR judged the kaiser "vain as a peacock": Butt, *Taft and Roosevelt,* 1:421.

67. MOR 7:396; the peace conference that Carnegie had planned for TR's visit in Britain was not held because of King Edward's death.

68. MOR 7:402–404; Sir Arthur Conan Doyle, *Memories and Adventures* (Boston, 1924), 236–37. Doyle recalled a TR story: On a long whistle-stop train trip the President had been awakened and his secretary urged him to dress to greet the waiting rural crowds: "They have come sixty miles to see you," he said. The President replied: "They would have come a hundred to see a cat with two heads."

69. *Felix Frankfurter Reminisces: Recorded in Talks with Dr. Harlan B. Phillips* (New York, 1960), 51–52; ERD to KR, Aug. 4, 1913, KBR-LC; Arthur Lee, *Good Innings: The Private Papers of Viscount Lee of Fareham,* ed. Alan Clark (London, 1974), 1:421.

70. TR, 1910 Diary, memoranda pages at end, TRC-HU; MOR 7:64.

71. *New York Times,* Apr. 24, 1910; TR to HCL, Apr. 6 and 11, 1910, HCL-MHS; see Rodgers, *Atlantic Crossings;* Daniel Levine, *Poverty and Society: The Growth of the American Welfare State in International Comparison* (New Brunswick, N.J., 1988); Coleman, *Progressivism and the World of Reform;* Kloppenberg, *Uncertain Victory;* MOR 7:366, 368, 380, 385; John Callan O'Laughlin, *From the Jungle Through Europe with Roosevelt* (Boston, 1910), 135; MOR 7:406.

72. About conditions in Italy TR admitted "a very strong sympathy with some of the Socialistic aims, and a very profound distrust of most of the Socialistic methods": MOR 7:359;

he praised Germany's timber management: TR's speech in Spencer, N.Y., Oct. 24, 1910, TR-SP.

73. *New York Times,* June 12, 1910, SUBJ-TRC.

74. *New York Times,* June 19, 1910; see *Film Collection Guide* and the films within the TRA Film Collection, Motion Picture Division, LC, especially FEA 9040 and FAB 1791.

75. Josephine Goldmark, *Impatient Crusader: Florence Kelley's Life Story* (Urbana, Ill., 1953), 68–69; Ira V. Brown, *Lyman Abbott, Christian Evolutionist: A Study in Religious Liberalism* (Cambridge, Mass., 1953), 192.

76. TR to EBAR, July 13, 1911, TRJR-LC; MOR 7:413; KR, Jr., *Sentimental Safari,* 47, 234; TR to KR, July 19, 1910, TRC-HU.

77. MOR 7:45, 73, 80; TR conceded that Taft was a better president than McKinley and probably even better than Harrison, but he disliked his domestic and foreign policies: TR to Arthur Lee, Sept. 9, 1910, MOR-REJ. Taft may have been a mild progressive in pursuing anti-trust prosecutions, but he appointed anti-labor Supreme Court justices who deified liberty of contract. His Department of State turned foreign affairs into an extension of Wall Street. Lodge and TR agreed that the divided and discredited Republican Party was doomed temporarily in the 1910 congressional elections and probably in the 1912 presidential vote. TR did not want to support the tariff bill, and he wondered to Lodge how he could endorse party regulars who had torn down his policies: TR to HCL, Apr. 11, 1910, HCL-MHS; Frankfurter observed after working with both men that TR, unlike Taft, "thought profoundly or at least got all the available thinking of others" but did not get credit for being deliberative because "he acted expeditiously and pyrotechnically": *From the Diaries of Felix Frankfurter,* ed. Joseph P. Lash (New York, 1975), 107.

78. *New York Times,* June 28, 1910; Robert M. La Follette, *La Follette's Autobiography: A Personal Narrative of Political Experiences by Robert M. La Follette* (Madison, Wisc., 1968), 209.

79. TRJR to TR, undated fragment [1910], TRJR-LC; Ted, who hoped for a place in California politics, supported Hiram Johnson for governor, and Johnson campaigned by calling out "Bully!" to link himself with TR. La Follette had taken a clearer stand for suffrage than other major political leaders, while TR admitted privately a "contemptuous dislike" of many suffrage leaders and a belief that it was not an important reform: TR to Miss Stevenson, May 22, 1911, MOR-REJ.

80. TR to Ray Stannard Baker, Nov. 23, 1911, MOR-REJ; TR to TRJR, Nov. 21, 1910, TRJR-LC; TR to Florence Cole, Sept. 22, 1910, MOR-REJ; David P. Thelen, *Robert M. La Follette and the Insurgent Spirit* (Boston, 1976), 76.

81. EKR to Mary Cadwalader Jones, Mar. 6, 1910, TRC-HU; HCL to TR, Apr. 19 and 25, 1910, and TR to HCL, Apr. 6 and 11, 1910, HCL-MHS.

82. NSC; TR to Endicott Peabody, Aug. 10, 1910, Peabody Papers, Houghton; EKR to ARC, July 15, [1910], TRC-HU.

83. TR to TRJR, Aug. 10, 1910, TRJR-LC; TR urged his son to show his letter of support for insurgency to Fremont Older and other California progressives.

84. TR to KR, July 19, 1910, TRC-HU. M. Nelson McGeary, *Gifford Pinchot: Forester-Politician* (Princeton, 1960), 193, claims Pinchot wrote the New Nationalism speech, but it is only certain that he worked on one draft of it, not necessarily the final one; C. Miller, *Pinchot,* says that Herbert Croly and then Pinchot drafted the New Nationalism speech, 234–35; EKR to KR, Aug. 7, [1910], and n.d., KBR-LC.

85. Leuchtenburg, ed., *New Nationalism,* 22, 27, 30; MOR 8:1043; George Martin, *Madam Secretary: Frances Perkins* (Boston, 1976), 71, says the Pittsburgh survey influenced his New Nationalism speech; Lodge had urged TR to read Croly's nationalist *The Promise of*

American Life, but Croly's idea that true democracy and social justice would be served better by a strong central government than by parochial states' rights was not news to the ex-president: Charles Forcey, *The Crossroads of Liberalism: Croly, Weyl, Lippmann, and the Progressive Era, 1900–1925* (New York, 1967), 128–29; Robert S. LaForte, "Theodore Roosevelt's Osawatomie Speech," *Kansas Historical Quarterly* 32 (1966): 199; the 1905 *Lochner,* or *Bakeshop,* decision infuriated TR because the Court stated that liberty of contract was more important than labor's need for decent working conditions. The 1909 strike of 30,000 shirtwaist makers in New York City showed him that labor, including women, was ready to organize to demand better conditions and higher wages. Boss William Lorimer had a slush fund of corporate donations from corrupt Illinois legislators to buy his election to the U.S. Senate in 1909, which the *Chicago Tribune* had exposed. By 1912 the Senate had forced him to resign, but Lorimerism still corrupted the political process. Bossism and its ties to corporate power would not unravel without concerted political pressure; TR was sympathetic to the reasoning in the Brandeis brief in the *Muller* v. *Oregon* case, which he believed provided a good justification for protective legislation for women because of their role as mothers. Reformers like Florence Kelley argued that labor laws for women would provide an "entering wedge" of precedent to gain later labor laws protecting all workers, and their reasoning swayed TR. On women reformers and protective legislation see Nancy Woloch, *Muller v. Oregon: A Brief History with Documents* (Boston, 1996); Nancy Schrom Dye, *As Equals and as Sisters: Feminism, the Labor Movement, and the Women's Trade Union League of New York* (Columbia, Mo., 1980); Susan Lehrer, *Origins of Protective Labor Legislation for Women, 1905–1925* (Albany, N.Y., 1987); Judith A. Baer, *The Chains of Protection: The Judicial Response to Women's Labor Legislation* (Westport, Conn., 1978); Goldmark, *Impatient Crusader.*

86. TR to Jack Greenway, Dec. 19, 1910, JIG-ARIZ; Leuchtenburg, ed., *New Nationalism,* 28–29; TR's quote from Lincoln echoed almost word for word Gompers' plea on behalf of labor to the Republican platform committee in 1908, TR to KR, June 18, 1908, U.P. enclosure, TRC-HU. Workmen's compensation laws were supported by many businesses because they limited the company's liability; TR also said: "The man who wrongly holds that every human right is secondary to his profit must now give way to the advocate of human welfare, who rightly maintains that every man holds his property subject to the general right of the community to regulate its use to whatever degree the public welfare may require it."

87. Leuchtenburg, ed., *New Nationalism,* 33–34; Ben B. Lindsey, "The Beast and the Jungle," *Everybody's Magazine,* 1910; C. Larsen, *Ben Lindsey,* 116–20; F. Wood, *Roosevelt As We Knew Him,* 238; *New York Times,* July 21, 1910; "caged" in EKR to KR, Oct. 31, [1910], KBR-LC; "alive" in TR to KR, July 19, 1910, TRC-HU.

88. Villard in LaForte, "Osawatomie Speech," 197; Paris Commune in TR to James Bryce, Sept. 13, 1910, MOR-REJ. In private letters TR sized up the political situation and decided not to run in 1912; he predicted that Taft could manipulate the fake delegates of the South and get the support of the moneyed interests of the East to win the nomination, but he also noted that from the Alleghenies west the "general sentiment is overwhelmingly for me": TR to Arthur Lee, Sept. 16, 1910, MOR-REJ; and Wall Street in TR to TRJR, Sept. 21, 1910, TRJR-LC.

89. TR to TRJR, Oct. 16, 1910, TRJR-LC.

90. MOR 7:135; TR to TRJR, Sept. 21, 1910, TRJR-LC.

91. Joel Spingarn, the literature professor famous for his advocacy of the New Criticism and his leadership roles in the N.A.A.C.P., was one of many young men inspired to public service by Roosevelt: Amos Pinchot, *History of the Progressive Party, 1912–1916* (New York, 1958), 236; Stimson favored federal incorporation of interstate corporations, and after refusing to act as Gifford Pinchot's counsel in the Ballinger-Pinchot controversy, he had helped his close friend Gifford Pinchot hire the well-known labor lawyer Louis Brandeis. Like Roo-

sevelt, Stimson often tried to get Pinchot to tone down his crusading zeal to win his case. But Pinchot had been determined to prove that Ballinger sought to give away Alaskan lands to Guggenheim mining interests, so the fact that his evidence was flimsy was less important to Pinchot than gaining publicity for his larger war against "the special interests": Elting E. Morison, *Turmoil and Tradition: A Study of the Life and Times of Henry L. Stimson* (Boston, 1960), 139; see Miller, *Pinchot*, on Ballinger-Pinchot and on the N.C.A.

92. Morison, *Turmoil*, 139; F. Wood, *Roosevelt As We Knew Him*, 244–47; TR speech at the American Locomotive Works, Schenectady, N.Y., Oct. 17, 1910, TR-SP.

93. Griscom, *Diplomatically Speaking*, 351; TR to TRJR, Nov. 11, 1910, TRJR-LC; TR speech in Oswego, N.Y., Oct. 24, 1910, TR-SP.

94. TR, Kismet Hall speech, Oct. 29, 1910; TR, speeches in Kingston, Oct. 29, and in Utica, N.Y., Oct. 27, 1910, TR-SP.

95. Rita Halle Kleeman, *Gracious Lady, the Life of Sara Delano Roosevelt* (New York, 1935), 204; Geoffrey C. Ward, *A First-Class Temperament: The Emergence of Franklin Roosevelt* (New York, 1989), 106.

96. "never be President" in Morison, *Turmoil*, 179 (Senator Dolliver described President Taft by 1911 as "a large amiable island surrounded entirely by persons who knew exactly what they wanted"); on TR's political musings see TR to TRJR, Oct. 16, 1910, TRJR-LC, and *From the Diaries of Felix Frankfurter.*

CHAPTER TWELVE: A PROGRESSIVE WORLD MOVEMENT

1. Rumors of his drunkenness were not based on fact. On election night 1910, for example, he took a glass of Madeira at his house and then had two glasses of cider at Stimson's nearby home: *Felix Frankfurter Reminisces*, 51–52; TR to Charles C. Bull, Nov. 24, 1911, MOR-REJ; EKR to KR, Oct. 31, [1910], KBR-LC, EKR-Di, Nov. 6, 1910; TR to TRJR, Oct. 19 and Nov. 21, 1910, TRJR-LC.

2. Butt, *Taft and Roosevelt*, 2:579; TR to Benjamin Ide Wheeler, Nov. 21, 1910, TRJR-LC.

3. TR to EBAR, Nov. 27, 1910, TRJR-LC.

4. Lincoln Steffens, "The Boss of All the Bosses," *Everybody's* 23 (September 1910): 291–98; *Letters of Louis D. Brandeis*, ed. Melvin I. Urofsky and David W. Levy (Albany, N.Y., 1972), quoted in 2:36*n*.3; Herbert F. Margulies, "La Follette, Roosevelt and the Republican Presidential Nomination of 1912," *Mid-America* 58, no. 1 (January 1976): 54–76.

5. TR to TRJR, Jan. 2, 1911, TRJR-LC; TR to Robert Perkins Bass, Dec. 23, 1910, MOR-REJ; TR to ABR, Dec. 12, 1910, MOR-REJ. Louis Brandeis had helped negotiate a "protocol of peace" in the cloakmakers' strike and social worker Henry Moskowitz became secretary of the Board of Arbitration set up to resolve future disputes; see *Letters of Louis D. Brandeis*, 2:568–69.

6. *Letters of Louis D. Brandeis*, 2:568–69; on the lunch, Gifford Pinchot Diary, Feb. 20, 1911, GP-LC.

7. MOR 7:216; Leon Stein, *The Triangle Fire* (New York, 1962), 207.

8. Daniel Czitrom, "Underworlds and Underdogs: Big Tim Sullivan and Metropolitan Politics in New York, 1889–1913," *Journal of American History* 78, no. 2 (September 1991): 536–58. The membership of the Committee of 25 included future Bull Moosers Mary Dreier, John A. Kingsbury, Anne Morgan, Frances Perkins, George W. Perkins, and Amos Pinchot; the owners of the Asch building settled for $75 per death compensation: see Stein, *Triangle Fire*, 207–12; TR, "The Coal Miner at Home," *Outlook* (Dec. 24, 1910): 899–908; on ties between New York City reformers and TR see Elizabeth Israels Perry, *Belle Moskowitz: Feminine Politics and the Exercise of Power in the Age of Alfred E. Smith* (New York, 1992), 68–114.

9. TR, speech on Workmen's Compensation to National Civic Federation, Jan. 13, 1911, TR-SP; TR, "The Conservation of Womanhood and Childhood," typescripts with handwritten corrections, speech in Milwaukee, Oct. 10, 1911, TRC-HU; MEM 18:244–75. Addresses by Colonel Roosevelt in Birmingham, Alabama, Mar. 10, 1911, TR-SP; he went there to give a speech urging the South to adopt child labor laws: "The Conservation of Childhood," address at the National Child Labor Conference, Mar. 10–11, 1911, TR-SP.

10. Lela B. Costin, *Two Sisters for Social Justice: A Biography of Grace and Edith Abbott* (Chicago, 1983), 47; some date this conversion to March 1911: John C. Farrell, *Beloved Lady: A History of Jane Addams' Ideas on Reform and Peace* (Baltimore, 1967), 125–26; TR to Bob Ferguson, Feb. 2, 1911, MOR-REJ; see Levine, *Poverty and Society;* reformers convinced TR that woman suffrage would improve the chance of passing labor legislation he favored and curbing the white slave trade. TR to Elinor Vernon DeFresney before his change of heart, Aug. 15, 1911, MOR-REJ; TR to Florence Kelley, Dec. 26, 1911, and Jan. 9, 1912, MOR-REJ; MOR 7:475; TR to Maud Nathan, Oct. 26, 1911, MOR-REJ; Joseph Bucklin Bishop, who wrote TR's authorized biography, said TR supported the Anthony Amendment in 1911: MEM 23, Bishop, *Theodore Roosevelt,* 1:132; see Nathan, *Once Upon a Time and Today,* 144; TR to Mrs. Roger Wolcott, Dec. 19, 1911, MOR-REJ. TR wanted to discuss suffrage with women who understood workingwomen's problems and he wanted suffragists to help him lobby Lawrence Abbott to change *The Outlook*'s editorial policy on suffrage; less reliable versions of TR's change of mind on suffrage are abundant; see a George Junior Republic visit "Between You and Me!" Anecdotes File, TRP-BP. TR had already come to positions like the woman suffrage and labor movements on women's property, inheritance, and custody rights: TR to William Hard, Jan. 8, 1912, MOR-REJ; D. Daniels, "Theodore Roosevelt and Gender."

11. ABR, Memoirs, TRC-HU; TR to ABR, Jan. 5, 1911, MOR-REJ; Archie wanted to go straight to Harvard and not return to Groton, but his father said he was not ready for Harvard: TR to ABR, Feb. 2, 1912, MOR-REJ.

12. TR, "Charter Day Address," Berkeley, Calif., Mar. 23, 1911; Apr. 6, 1911, NSC; TR was offended by a commercial club skit in Portland featuring "Queen Mombassa" lecturing him on race suicide in a Negro dialect. He didn't think it was funny and said so. Apr. 5, 1911, NSC; Nathan, *Once Upon a Time and Today,* 137; MOR 7:269; Gifford Pinchot Diary, May 16, 1911, GP-LC.

13. TR to Edward North Buxton, July 24, and to Lady Delamere, Mar. 3, 1911, MOR-REJ; he was called before a congressional committee to defend his approval of the merger in the Tennessee Coal and Iron case, and after he testified he wrote TRJR that he did not think it right for ex-presidents to be subpoenaed: Aug. 9, 1911, TRJR-LC; EKR had clematis and other vines transplanted from the White House, EKR to Emily Carow, Oct. 19, 1902, TRC-HU.

14. TR still pondered what he should do about 1912, but he did little more than issue criticism of Taft's arbitration treaties for taking constitutional power out of the hands of the Senate and the President and giving them to an independent commission: EKR to ARC, Aug. 19, 1914, TRC-HU; TR to TRJR, Sept. 22, 1911, TRJR-LC; *New York Times,* May 27, 1911; TR spoke out against the McNamara brothers, union leaders accused of bombing the Los Angeles Times Building even before they confessed; Archie failed the Harvard entrance exams in geometry and civics, but got a C in history and a D in French, so his father felt that tutoring had done some good: TR to David Evans, Oct. 2, 1911, MOR-REJ; MOR 7:281, 199; Ethel had reached a marriageable age and had several young men interested in her, including Dick Derby, Clarence Hay, Rough Rider John Greenway, and Fairman Dick. She did charity work with the Manhattan Junior League and raised money for West Side children: ERD to Josephine Osborn, Apr. 9 and 12, 1911, Ethel Carow Roosevelt Derby Papers inven-

tory, Baker University Archives, Baldwin City, Kans.; ERD-Di, April–November 1911. TR doubted he was patient enough when he tried to teach Quentin tennis, but he played more congenially with Archie, cousin Philip, and Ethel. The "very chubby and affectionate" Quentin cared little for sports but preferred taking apart machines like his wireless radio. He attempted baseball with James Amos, the butler, and tried to start his own beehive dressed in makeshift armor; Theodore remembered Edith's birthday for a change because it was her fiftieth, and he wrote Bamie that we all gave her presents "with all of which she was delighted; which does not always happen with Edith, as occasionally she shares our own mother's way of looking at a present of which she does not approve": TR to ARC, Aug. 8, 1911, TRC-HU.

15. TR to CRR, Oct. 5, 1911, TRC-HU; also TR to ARC, Oct. 2, 1911, MOR-REJ.

16. TR to Endicott Peabody, Oct. 10, 1911, MOR-REJ.

17. TR to TRJR, Oct. 13, 1911, TRJR-LC, and Oct. 5, 1911, MOR-REJ; TR dictated one of his most candid and lengthy letters ever on Oct. 1, the day after the accident, to the historian George Trevelyan.

18. TR to TRJR, Oct. 30, 1911, TRJR-LC; ERD-Di, Oct. 16, 1911; TR to TRJR, Nov. 9, 1911, TRJR-LC.

19. Pauline Goldmark and Owen Lovejoy prepared a memo for TR on industrial problems (which TR wrote upon) and used for his speech; see TR, "The Conservation of Womanhood and Childhood," speech draft includes the memo, TRC-HU; TR did not use all the National Child Labor Committee's arguments about the spread of disease from home work, nor did he borrow Goldmark's phrase "the conservation of Fatherhood" in this talk.

20. *New York Times*, Oct. 21, 1911.

21. Lash, *From the Diaries of Felix Frankfurter*, 112*n*.1; MOR 7:429–30; TR had already called Taft "a flubdub with a streak of the second-rate and the common in him," and complained that he had no idea what America needed to address the problems of the new industrial age: TR to TRJR, Aug. 22, 1911, TRJR-LC; James C. German, Jr., "Taft, Roosevelt, and United States Steel," *Historian* 34 (1972): 610; TR, "The Trusts, the People, and the Square Deal," *Outlook* 99 (Nov. 18, 1911): 655; MOR 7:278, 429, 454; "Taft to Urge Trust Law Change," *New York Tribune*, Jan. 21, 1912.

22. On Taft's ignorance of the suit see Donald F. Anderson, *William Howard Taft: A Conservative's Conception of the Presidency* (Ithaca, N.Y., 1968), 79–82; "Roosevelt May Repudiate Perkins," NSC; TR's letters indicate growing sympathy with progressives in the fall of 1911; TR told one friend it would be "cowardice" not to run in 1912: Grant, *Fourscore*, 320.

23. MOR 7:423, 421, 466; TR to James R. Garfield, Dec. 2, 1911, Garfield Papers, LC.

24. TR to Bob and Isabella Ferguson, Dec. 5, 1911, JIG-ARIZ; ERD-Di, Dec. 25, 1911; TR to Florence La Farge, Dec. 15, 1911, MOR-REJ; TR to KR, Jan. 7, 1912, TRC-HU; TR saw Fanny Parsons alone and she evidently encouraged him to run: TR to Frances Parsons, Dec. 27, 1911, Jan. 15, Feb. 5, 1912, Parsons Papers, Houghton Library.

25. *Congressional Record*, 62nd Cong., 2nd Sess., 2,245, 2,499–502; Ardis Cameron, *Radicals of the Worst Sort: Laboring Women in Lawrence, Massachusetts, 1860–1912* (Urbana, Ill., 1993).

26. TR to Julian Harris, Dec. 5, 1911, MOR-REJ; TR, "Lynching and the Miscarriage of Justice," *Outlook* (Nov. 25, 1911): 706–707; Charles Flint Kellogg, *NAACP: A History of the National Association for the Advancement of Colored People*, vol. 1, *1909–1920* (Baltimore, 1967), 211–13; compare "Women's Rights and the Duties of Both Men and Women," handwritten and corrected draft, TRC-HU; TR to Florence Kelley, Dec. 26, 1912, MOR-REJ.

27. TR to Joseph Bucklin Bishop, Dec. 13, 1911, Bishop Papers, Houghton; MOR 7:445.

28. Thelen, *La Follette*, 88–90; for the many overtures TR made to La Follette and the reasons the senator avoided him in 1911 and early 1912 see Nancy C. Unger, *Fighting Bob La*

Follette: The Righteous Reformer (Chapel Hill, N.C., 2000), 194–213; the best sources on TR and the 1912 election are John Gable, *The Bull Moose Years: Theodore Roosevelt and the Progressive Party* (Port Washington, N.Y., 1978), hereafter Gable book, and Gable, "The Bull Moose Years: Theodore Roosevelt and the Progressive Party, 1912–1916" (Ph.D. diss., Brown University 1972), hereafter Gable diss.; Pinchot, *History of the Progressive Party*, 134–35.

29. "Mr. La Follette, as Seen by his Party Press," *Literary Digest* 40 (Feb. 17, 1912): 319.

30. Minutes of a meeting at the Congress Hotel, Chicago, Feb. 10, 1912, TRP-LC.

31. Harbaugh, *Power and Responsibility*, 395–99; MOR 7:484–85; Gifford Pinchot Diary, Feb. 5, 1912, GP-LC; he originally opposed some forms of recall: MOR 7:232, 260; he was in favor of the Massachusetts system of recall which provided for the removal of a judge by both houses of the legislature.

32. They also had tea with E. A. Robinson: EKR to KR, [Feb. 12, 1912], KBR-LC; TR to Mrs. Augustus Tyler, Jan. 12, 1912, MOR-REJ.

33. Gifford Pinchot Diary, Feb. 16, 1912, GP-LC; see ARL-Di, February 1912; Alice was in close touch with Medill McCormick so she knew TR had decided to run: ARC to WSC, Feb. 24, 1912, TRC-HU; he repeatedly told friends he knew he could not win, but he was more likely to speak his deepest feelings to his immediate family.

34. *New York Times*, Feb. 23, 1912; MOR 7:508; ARL-Di, Feb. 21 and 26, 1912; *TR/HCL*, 2:423–24.

35. Ward, *First-Class Temperament*, 187.

36. Manners, *TR and Will*, 230. The Pinchots had been major financial backers of La Follette and had seriously supported him until December 1911; see Margulies, "La Follette, Roosevelt and the Republican Presidential Nomination of 1912," 54–76.

37. TR to ARC, Mar. 3, 1912, TRC-HU; J. Anderson, *Taft*, 233.

38. ARL-Di, Mar. 3, 1912; Gilson Gardner, *Lusty Scripps: The Life of E. W. Scripps* (New York, 1932), 188–89.

39. ARL-Di, Mar. 8 and 15, 1912.

40. TR to KR, Mar. 9, 1912, TRC-HU.

41. TR to ARC, Mar. 3, 1912, TRC-HU; Swanberg, *Citizen Hearst*, 333; ARL-Di, Mar. 14 and 16, May 5, 1912.

42. EKR to KR, Dec. 15, n.y. [1917], KBR-LC.

43. C. Larsen, *Ben Lindsey*, 115.

44. Other major donors were Roosevelt and Son, Bob Bacon, Alexander Smith Cochrane, August Heckscher, Elon Hooker, Frank Munsey, George Perkins, and Emlen Roosevelt: 1912 Bound Ledger, PPA-TRC; ERD raised money via the Women's National Committee.

45. TR, speech at Niblo's Garden, New York, Mar. 25, 1912, TRC-HU.

46. Mar. 8, 1912, NSC.

47. TR, speech at Star Casino, New York, Mar. 25, 1912, TR-SP.

48. "fussed" in EKR to KR, [Apr. 2, 1912], KBR-LC; Gifford Pinchot-Di, Apr. 9, 1912 GP-LC; speech in Pittsburgh, Apr. 10, 1912, TR-SP.

49. Apr. 13, 1912, NSC; TR, speech in Omaha, Nebr., Apr. 17, 1912, TR-SP.

50. Taft quoted in George E. Mowry, *Theodore Roosevelt and the Progressive Movement* (New York, 1960), 216.

51. *New York Times*, Feb. 12, 1912; TR, speech in Worcester, Mass., Apr. 27, 1912, TR-SP.

52. Henry L. Stoddard, *It Costs to Be President* (New York, 1938), 161; "crazy" in Alice Forbes Perkins Hooper to Frederick Jackson Turner, Mar. 7, 1912, in Ray Allen Billington, ed., *"Dear Lady": The Letters of Frederick Jackson Turner and Alice Forbes Perkins Hooper* (San Marino, Calif., 1970), 117; Frank Harper to Charles Dwight Willard, May 13, 1912, MOR-

REJ; Gould, *Presidency*, 114; Marjorie Phillips, *Duncan Phillips and His Collection* (Boston, 1971), 45; J. Anderson, *Taft*, 232; May 30, 1912, NSC; John L. Heaton, *Cobb of "The World": A Leader in Liberalism; Compiled from His Editorial Articles and Public Addresses* (New York, 1924), 180.

53. TR, "Fundamental Principles," speech in Springfield, Ohio, May, 15 [1912], TR-SP; TR, speech in Lima, Ohio, May 16, 1912, TR-SP.

54. EKR to Arthur Lee, May 20, n.y. [1912], Lee Papers, Courtauld Institute; TR to R.H. Waterford, May 29, 1912, MOR-REJ; crowds responded favorably when TR announced in Canton: "I place the human right of a crippled brakeman above the property rights of a railroad corporation": "Throng Battles for Places to Hear Colonel," May 1912, Misc. Clippings, TR-SP; TR, speech in Marion, Ohio, May 18, 1912, TR-SP.

55. "blackguard" in TR to Arthur Lee, May 10, 1912, Lee Papers, Courtauld Institute; Taft to Horace D. Taft, Apr. 14, 1912, Taft Papers, LC, quoted in Henry F. Pringle, *The Life and Times of William Howard Taft* (New York, 1939), 1:772; Pringle, *Theodore Roosevelt*, 778; Gable diss., 37; on the mutual friend see Harbaugh, *Power and Responsibility*, 392; TR, speech in Cleveland, May 19, 1912, TR-SP.

56. TR to Cecil A. Lyon, May 27, 1912, Cecil A. Lyon Papers, TR Correspondence—FDR; Gable diss., 37–38.

57. KR-Di, Apr. 30, 1912; "campaign is all" in ERD-Di, May 23, 1912; "dear & kind" in ARL-Di, May 19, 1912.

58. ARL-Di, Apr. 12, 15, and 17, 1912.

59. TR to Endicott Peabody, Apr. 23, 1912, MOR-REJ; Kermit also got in trouble at Harvard: TR to KR, May 27, 1912, TRC-HU.

60. "uphill fight," etc., in EKR to Arthur Lee, Apr. 19, [1912], Lee Papers, Courtauld Institute; "big tender heart" in EKR to ARC, May 5, 1912, TRC-HU; EKR to ARC, Apr. 27, 1912, TRC-HU; Dr. Bigelow pointedly reported to Lodge that TR was "surprised and hurt" by Gardner's attack; he mentioned it repeatedly when he stayed with Dr. Bigelow in Boston: Akiko Murakata, *Selected Letters of Dr. William Sturgis Bigelow*, 343.

61. Gould, *Presidency*, 114–15. These are AP numbers; see Victor Rosewater, *Back Stage in 1912: The Inside Story of the Split Republican Convention* (Philadelphia, 1932), 118.

62. On Tafts, ARL-Di, Apr. 4, 1912; TR to Civic Forum, *Boston Journal*, Apr. 27, 1912, TR-SP; "Machiavellian" in June 10, 1912, NSC.

63. William Roscoe Thayer, *Theodore Roosevelt: An Intimate Portrait* (New York, 1919), 359; Nicholas Roosevelt to Dear Family, [June 1912], NR-SYR; F. Wood, *Roosevelt As We Knew Him*, 273; William Jennings Bryan, *A Tale of Two Conventions* (New York, 1912), 7.

64. TR, "The Case Against the Reactionaries," speech at the Chicago Auditorium, June 17, 1912, in TR, *Social Justice and Popular Rule Works*, national edition (New York, 1926), 17:204–31.

65. Bryan, *Tale of Two Conventions*, 27; ARL-Di, June 17, 1912.

66. Edna Ferber, *A Peculiar Treasure* (New York, 1939), 196; ERD-Di, June 16, 1912; ARL-Di, June 16, 1912; Nicholas Roosevelt to Dear Family, n.d. [June 1912], NR-SYR.

67. ERD-Di, June 16, 1912; Pinchot, White, and Hiram Johnson were present during the third-party debate according to A. T. Packard 1920 Statement, SUBJ-TRC, June 1912; MOR 7:561.

68. Extract from George Rublee's Reminiscences, SUBJ-TRC; MOR 7:561; Rublee later promoted reform under Wilson and F.D.R. and pressed the need to admit Jewish refugees to the United States in the 1930s.

69. Goldmark, *Impatient Crusader*, 140–41; Allen F. Davis, "The Social Workers and the Progressive Party, 1912–1916," *American Historical Review* 69 (April 1964): 671–88; June 7, 1912, NSC; Jane Addams, *The Second Twenty Years at Hull-House* (New York, 1930), 27–30;

and *One Hundred Years at Hull-House*, ed. Mary Lynn McCree Bryan and Allen F. Davis (Bloomington, Ind., 1990).

70. Amos, *Hero to His Valet*, 142–44. Kermit, who served as a sergeant at arms in the Maine delegation, watched Taft men gather anti-Roosevelt votes all around him.

71. Nicholas Roosevelt to Dear Family, n.d. [June 1912], NR-SYR; Walter Davenport, *Power and Glory: The Life of Boies Penrose* (New York, 1931), 184, 210.

72. There is no consensus about what her advice was; some participants recall that she thought he should run no matter what, but EBAR recalled Edith said: "Theodore, remember that often one wants to do the hardest and the noblest thing, but sometimes it does not follow that it is the right thing": EBAR to Mary Hagedorn, Nov. 10, 1948, SUBJ-TRC. This sounds like advice not to persist with his candidacy, which is probably what she thought in June 1912. Hadley was conferring with Boies Penrose, a reason to ERD not to step aside: ERD-Di, June 21, 1912; Lawrence F. Abbott recalled that TR refused to cut deals to win the nomination: *Impressions of Theodore Roosevelt*, 84–85; Henry Stimson believed Root had done the right thing: "Relations of Col. Henry L. Stimson with Theodore Roosevelt," SUBJ-TRC.

73. "best to keep silent" in KR-Di, June 20, 1912; ERD-Di, June 19, 1912; ARL-Di, June 19, 1912. Whether this was a spontaneous or planned demonstration to head off a compromise Hadley nomination is unknown; see Rosewater, *Back Stage in 1912*, 179–80; Gable diss., 75 n. 71; MOR 7:559.

74. TR to Republican convention, June 20, 1912, TRC-HU; Pringle, *Taft*, 2: 798; "The Stolen Nomination for the Presidency," the facts of the Chicago convention of 1912, PPA-TRC; TR, "A Naked Issue of Right and Wrong," *Outlook* 101 (June 15, 1912).

75. ARL-Di, June 22, 1912.

76. John Kingsbury was the social worker; ARL-Di, June 22, 1912; Ethel Armes, "When It Was Up to John," Anecdotes File, TRP-BP; ERD-Di, June 22, 1912.

77. Bryan, *Tale of Two Conventions*, 99.

78. Ernest A. Bigelow to TR, July 22, 1912, TRP-LC; "crisis" and "incarnate[d]" in Dalton, "Why America Loved Teddy Roosevelt"; George Sylvester Viereck, "Political Notes," *The International* 6, no. 2 (July 1912).

79. Pringle, *Taft*, 815–16, 841; when his vice-presidential running mate, James S. Sherman, died, Taft replaced him with the president of Columbia University, Nicholas Murray Butler, whom TR called "more royalist than the King himself": TR to Arthur Lee, Sept. 16, 1910, MOR-REJ.

80. Chester Rowell statement to Hermann Hagedorn, Nov. 27, 1940, SUBJ-TRC; platform drafts in PPA-TRC; for Perkins' views on business regulation and the need to redistribute profits see George W. Perkins, "A Constructive Suggestion," speech to Chamber of Commerce, Youngstown, Ohio, Dec. 4, 1911, Political Publications, PPA-TRC; Goldmark, *Impatient Crusader*, 140–41; Allen F. Davis, *Spearheads for Reform: The Social Settlements and the Progressive Movement, 1890–1914* (New York, 1967), 197; the mother of social security, Frances Perkins, though she could not vote, supported TR: George Martin, *Madam Secretary: Frances Perkins* (Boston, 1976), 71.

81. Ben Lindsey, Jane Addams, Frances Kellor, and Florence Kelley probably had the most influence in changing his mind: AUTO, 163; Irwin, *Making of a Reporter*, 199, 339.

82. William P. Helm to Mary Hagedorn, n.d. 1948, and to Leona Bloch, July 12, 1924, SUBJ-TRC.

83. Gable diss., 197; W.E.B. Du Bois, "From McKinley to Wallace: My Fifty Years as an Independent," in David Levering Lewis, *W.E.B. Du Bois: A Reader* (New York, 1995), 485; W.E.B. Du Bois, *The Autobiography of W.E.B. Du Bois: A Soliloquy on Viewing My Life from the Last Decade of Its First Century* (New York, 1968), 263; a different version appears in Lewis, *Biography*, 1:422; W.E.B. Du Bois, *Dusk of Dawn: An Essay Toward an*

Autobiography of a Race Concept (New York, 1940), 233–34; according to some sources, Lillian Wald's personal friendship with TR won her support in 1912: Sept. 3, 1940, clipping from the *New York Herald* in President's Personal File, FDR; B. Joyce Ross, *J. E. Spingarn and the Rise of the NAACP, 1911–1939* (New York, 1972), 26.

84. Glenda Gilmore, *Gender and Jim Crow*, 65–89, 115, 135–38; Gable diss., 177; earlier TR had admitted the violation of black voting rights was an "iniquity," but he said he had nothing to gain politically from fighting it: TR to Charles A. Gardiner, Nov. 18, 1903, MOR-REJ.

85. TR, "Lynching and the Miscarriage of Justice," *Outlook* (Nov. 25, 1911): 706–707; though he had done so by saying "in the many cases in which the lynching is not for rape there is literally not the slightest excuse of any kind or sort that can be advanced for it," which suggested that lynching could sometimes be justified by rape; see Gilmore, *Gender and Jim Crow*, 99; Colonel Roosevelt's statement at the National Progressive Convention, Coliseum, Chicago, Aug. 6, 1912, TR-SP; TR to Will N. Haban, Sept. 16, 1907, MOR-REJ; Gable diss., 196–97.

86. Gable diss., 179.

87. Roosevelt's statement at the National Progressive Convention.

88. Sept. 3 and 30, 1912, NSC; black delegates released a statement: "The charge of lily-whitism against the Progressive Convention is false" because, in addition to northern delegates, Arkansas, Tennessee, Kentucky, Maryland, and West Virginia were represented by black delegates: "Official Statement of the Negro Delegates in the National Progressive Convention," in Roosevelt's statement at the National Progressive Convention; minutes of Platform Committee, PPA-TRC; Kellogg, *NAACP*, 1:179; "Know the Truth!" statement of the Entire Colored Delegation of the National Progressive Convention, Aug. 7, 1912, 1912 pamphlets, Campaign Literature Scrapbook, TRC-HU; Ziglar, "Negro Opinion of Theodore Roosevelt," 359.

89. Hays, *Memoirs*, 144; Harlan, *Wizard of Tuskegee*, 353–54; Washington chose 1912 to speak out against lynching and the unfair treatment of blacks: "Is the Negro Having a Fair Chance?" *The Century* 85 (November 1912): 46–55.

90. Lewis, *Biography*, 1:421; Calvin S. Morris, *Reverdy C. Ransom: Black Advocate of the Social Gospel* (New York, 1990), 150–51. Among those James Weldon Johnson includes as original participants in the meetings that led up to the founding of the N.A.A.C.P. were future supporters of the Progressive Party: Jane Addams, John Dewey, Mary E. McDowell, John E. Milholland, Henry Moskowitz, Joel Spingarn, and Lillian Wald; see also Kellogg, *NAACP*. On Layton see Gustafson, *Women and the Republican Party*, 161, and on the lily whitism in the party, 126–32. Black leaders John R. Gleed, Kelly Miller, Rev. William H. Mixon, Beauregard F. Moseley, May Childs Nervey, and Reverdy C. Ransom supported TR in 1912; see Douglas C. Strange, "The Making of a President—1912: The Northern Negroes' View," *Negro History Bulletin* 31, no. 7 (1968): 14–23. The Democratic convention had no black delegates, the Socialist convention only one, and the Republican convention many; "devilish" quote from *Richmond Planet*, Mar. 14, 1908, in Ziglar, "Negro Opinion," 335; TR to Bradley Gilman, July 14, 1912, TRJR-LC.

91. English reformers learned about one way to create old-age pensions and health and unemployment insurance from Germany; "programme" quote in Kenneth O. Morgan, ed., *Lloyd George: Family Letters, 1885–1936* (London, 1973), 164; for the influence of British reforms on American labor policies see Lyman Abbott, *Reminiscences* (Boston, 1915), 16; *From the Diaries of Felix Frankfurter*, 117; William Allen White said the Progressive Party would be like Lloyd George, the German Liberals, Briand, Clemenceau, and the Radicals in Italy: "Following the Campaign," *Outlook* 101 (Aug. 24, 1912): 915; George L. Record believed that America would have to make more "concessions to state socialism" in the form of public

ownership of utilities if it wanted to avoid socialism altogether, but in 1912, TR was willing to go beyond social democracy only in the form of municipal ownership of gas, water, and electric systems: Record, *How to Abolish Poverty* (Jersey City, N.J., 1936), 14; Progressives advocated a national quarantine power and a coordinated public health service: "The Health Plank of the Progressive Party Platform," in PPA-TRC.

92. "Pass Prosperity Around," Speech of Albert J. Beveridge, Temporary Chairman of the Progressive National Convention (New York, 1912); Mary Elizabeth Lease had seconded the nomination of James B. Weaver at the People's Party convention in 1892; Rebecca Edwards, who is working on a book about Lease, says it is Mary Elizabeth, not Mary Ellen as Hofstadter and others claimed; *New York Tribune*, Aug. 8, 1912; *New York Herald*, Aug. 8, 1912.

93. "A Contract with the People," platform of the Progressive Party adopted at its First National Convention, Chicago, Aug. 7, 1912 (New York, 1912).

94. Addams, *Second Twenty Years at Hull-House*, 32–33; TR, "The Progressives and the Colored Man," *Outlook* 101 (Aug. 24, 1912): 909–12; Gustafson, *Women and the Republican Party*, 11.

95. Dalton, "Why America Loved Teddy Roosevelt"; Gerald F. Roberts, "The Strenuous Life: The Cult of Manliness in the Era of Theodore Roosevelt" (Ph.D. diss., Michigan State University, 1970); Melanie Gustafson, "Partisan Women: Gender, Politics, and the Progressive Party of 1912" (Ph.D. diss., New York University, 1993), 190.

96. After Rabbi B. Levi offered a prayer, Roosevelt called for equality, conservation, a national department of public health, and government regulation of business when he addressed his convention, and his speech was interrupted 145 times by cheers and applause: *New York Times*, Aug. 4, 1912. The best estimate of the number of women who served as official delegates and alternates at the convention is 21 to 60, but that does not include advisors, women reporters, family members, and activists like Ruth McCormick: Melanie Gustafson, "Partisan Women in the Progressive Era: The Struggle for Inclusion in American Political Parties," *Journal of Women's History* 9, no. 2 (Summer 1997): 8–30; William Draper Lewis, *The Life of Theodore Roosevelt* (New York, 1919), 372; 1912 pamphlets, Campaign Literature Scrapbook, PPA-TRC; the membership of the convention reflected Roosevelt's move leftward. Major figures in the settlement house movement, social work, and the National Conference of Charities and Correction were eager to support him. La Follette men like Charles McCarthy of the Wisconsin Legislative Reference Bureau and many former Bryanites cheered themselves hoarse over Roosevelt. Hull House, the National Women's Trade Union League, Jacob Riis, the University Settlement's John Kingsbury, Madison House's Henry Moskowitz, Greenwich House's Mary Simkhovitch, the editor of *Survey* magazine Paul Kellogg, and major child labor reformers like Homer Folks and Owen Lovejoy became partisans for Roosevelt.

97. Fred D. Warren to Eugene V. Debs, Aug. 8, 1912, in *Letters of Eugene V. Debs*, vol. 1, 1874–1912, ed. J. Robert Constantine (Urbana, Ill., 1990), 535.

98. Gable diss., 231, 142, 89; Gable book, 76; Michael Harrington, *Socialism* (New York, 1972), 119–30. TR later disagreed with Watson's virulent anti-Catholicism; see Thomas G. Dyer, "Aaron's Rod: Theodore Roosevelt, Tom Watson, and Anti-Catholicism," *Research Studies* 44, no. 1 (March 1976): 60–68.

99. EKR to KR, Aug. 8, [1912], KBR-LC.

100. MOR 7:634; George Harvey, "Roosevelt's Personal Characteristics," *Houston Daily Post*, Oct. 7, 1912.

101. "Broadside Fired by Harvey Wiley," *Houston Post*, Oct. 3, 1912; dinner in Gable diss., 200; Eliot also let the Democrats issue a pamphlet in his name denouncing TR as impulsive and unreliable: "Why Dr. Eliot Will Vote for Wilson and Marshall," pamphlet,

1912 pamphlets, Campaign Literature Scrapbook, TRC-HU; TR's reply in *New York Times*, Oct. 16, 1912.

102. EKR to CRR, Aug. 22, [1912], SUBJ-TRC; Oct. 9, 1912, NSC.

103. Ethel asked Dorothy Whitney Straight for the money: ERD to KR, n.d. [Sept. 20, 1912], KBR-LC; small donors included most of Hull House and social work leaders; see Progressive Party Contributions-PPA-TRC; William Allen White said that Herbert Hoover gave $1,000: White, *Autobiography*, 486; donors included the well-known musical comedy star Lillian Russell, sanitarium doctor and cereal advocate John Harvey Kellogg of Battle Creek, Michigan, and William Wrigley of Wrigley chewing gum fame; ERD to KR, Oct. 4, 1912, KBR-LC; Richard Derby to KR, n.d. [Sept. 20, 1912], SUBJ-TRC; ERD to Josephine Osborn, [1912], Ethel Carow Roosevelt Derby Papers inventory, Baker University Archives, Baldwin City, Kans.; C. Miller, *Pinchot*, 178–79.

104. "Why Edison Is a Progressive," 1912 pamphlets, Campaign Literature Scrapbook, TRC-HU; Mary Kingsbury Simkhovitch, *Neighborhood: My Story of Greenwich House* (New York, 1938), 175.

105. ERD to KR, Oct. 4, 1912, KBR-LC; October 1912, NSC; Mrs. Willard Carpenter invented electric devices that flashed inside bandanna hats and Ruth McCormick created the Founder's Day promotions; Margaret Chanler and EKR were on the Founder's Day committee: *New York Press*, Oct. 20, 1912, NSC; Vassar and Wellesley had active Women's Progressive Clubs which Julia K. Knapp coordinated; at a national conference of Women Progressives, Jane Addams and Frances Kellor spoke, and many suffrage leaders, political organizers, and clubwomen gained useful political experience: *New York Times*, Oct. 2, 1912; the Roosevelts' friend Daisy Harriman did some of the same things for Wilson's campaign: Kristie Miller, " 'Eager and Anxious to Work': Daisy Harriman and the Presidential Election of 1912," in Gustafson, Miller, and Perry, eds., *We Have Come to Stay*; Margaret Dreier Robins was elected to the executive committee of the State Progressive Party: Mary E. Dreier, *Margaret Dreier Robins: Her Life, Letters, and Work* (New York, 1950), 89.

106. Alice H. Cook, *A Lifetime of Labor: The Autobiography of Alice H. Cook* (New York, 1998), 5; ERD to KR, Oct. 30, 1912, clipping enclosed, KBR-LC; on techniques, Nathan, *Once Upon a Time and Today*, 143. Margaret Dreier Robins wanted to use Lewis Hine photos of child labor in pamphlets with the Progressive Party platform in order to show why the minimum wage and the abolition of child labor were important: Robins to Mary Dreier, Sept. 17, 1912, Dreier Papers, Schlesinger Library (I found no evidence in PPA-TRC that they finally used Hine photos); La Follette joined hands with Boss Penrose to investigate where the Bull Moose Party got its funds, which Taft thought was good because it could stop wealthy people from making donations for fear of being publicly investigated: MOR 7:594–95; Progressive Party contribution ledgers in PPA-TRC show no corporate contributions except Roosevelt and Son; Armond Fields, *Lillian Russell: A Biography of "America's Beauty"* (Jefferson, N.C., 1999), 177–78; "moosus" in Fitzpatrick, *Endless Crusade*, 146.

107. Rather than live any longer in the flowery and overstuffed Victorian parlors decorated by their wives, many men by the 1890s preferred the new Craftsman furniture and the Arts and Crafts Movement's rustic and austere aesthetic: Miles Orvell, *The Real Thing: Imitation and Authenticity in American Culture, 1880–1940* (Chapel Hill, N.C., 1989), 159; Wagenknecht, *Seven Worlds*, 78; Boris, *Art and Labor*, 46, 76; Margaret Dreier Robins to Mary Dreier, Sept. 17, 1912, Mary Dreier Papers, Schlesinger Library; for Gustav Stickley's support of TR see his editorial in the August 1912 *Craftsman*; though my evidence contradicts it, for a view of Stickley and the American Arts and Crafts movement as conservative see Harvey Grech, *Fit for America: Health Fitness, Sport, and American Society* (Baltimore, 1986), 270–82.

108. EKR to ARC, Sept. 12, [1912], TRC-HU; ERD-Di, Aug. 14 and Sept. 2, 1912; ERD to KR, Dec. 27, [1912], KBR-LC. While her husband was away Edith found consolation in being a grandmother. Ted had taken a job on Wall Street as a bond salesman, and one-year-old Gracie was a frequent visitor to the Fairy Orchard; "making love" in TR to ERD, Aug. 21, 1912, TRC-HU; George Roosevelt, "1912 Diary," Xerox in possession of Sheldon Stern, John F. Kennedy Library, Boston, Mass.

109. TR, speech in Point of Pines, Mass., Aug. 17, 1912, TR-SP; "good place" in "Theodore Roosevelt, Fighter for Social Justice," Theodore Roosevelt Association film collection, Motion Picture Reading Room, LC; see also NSC, September and October 1912.

110. TR to ERD, Aug. 21, 1912, TRC-HU; James W. Beckman, "Impressions of Famous People I Have Seen or Known," SUBJ-TRC; Philip J. Roosevelt, "Politics of the Year 1912: An Intimate Progressive View," TRC-HU.

111. On Root, EKR to ERD, Oct. 22, 1927, TRC-HU; EKR to ARC, Oct. 29, [1912], TRC-HU; ERD to KR, [Oct. 27, 1912], KBR-LC; "shame" in TR, speech in Point of Pines, Mass., Aug. 17, 1912, TR-SP; *TR/HCL*, 2:424.

112. Philip J. Roosevelt to Christine G.K. Roosevelt, Oct. 12, 1912, TRC-HU; TR, speech to be delivered at Oshkosh, Wisc., Oct. 11, 1912, TRC-HU; Gable diss., 302. The candidates had real differences on race. Wilson had been the only Ivy League president to endorse the exclusion of black students, and he picked race baiter Josephus Daniels as his campaign manager. But he courted and won northern black support because of the Bull Moose Party's southern lily-white policy. As hostility between the Roosevelt and Wilson camps grew, the Roosevelt campaign heard from Princeton's new president that TR would not be allowed to speak on his campus: Arthur S. Link, "The Negro as a Factor in the Campaign of 1912," *Journal of Negro History* 32 (1947): 81–99; "Bull Moose at the Nass," *Princeton Alumni Weekly*, Mar. 28, 1980, 34; Sept. 3, 1912, NSC.

113. Edwin A. Weinstein, *Woodrow Wilson: A Medical and Psychological Biography* (Princeton, 1981), 240, 183–194, 289–91.

114. NSC and SUBJ-TRC.

115. Raymond Robins to Mary Dreier, Oct. 9 and Nov. 10, 1912, Mary Dreier Papers, Schlesinger Library; Gable diss., 374.

116. TR, speech on suffrage, St. Johnsbury, Vt., Aug. 30, 1912, TRC-HU; *New York Times*, Aug. 20, 1912.

117. Raymond Robins to Mary Dreier, Oct. 14, 1912, Mary Dreier Papers, Schlesinger Library.

118. Oct. 7, 1912, NSC; Philip J. Roosevelt to Christine G.K. Roosevelt, Oct. 12, 1912, TRC-HU.

119. Raymond Robins to Mary Dreier, Oct. 9, 1912, Mary Dreier Papers, Schlesinger Library.

120. Philip J. Roosevelt, "Politics of the Year 1912: An Intimate Progressive View," TRC-HU; O. K. Davis, "Eyewitness Account to George Perkins," Oct. 15, 1912, TRP-LC; *New York Evening Mail* Oct. 15, 1912; H. P. Weissenborn to Hermann Hagedorn, July 12, 1949, SUBJ-TRC; *New York Times*, Oct. 2, 15, and 31, 1912; TR's version is MOR 7:705; TR swore while in the hospital, 62; on Schrank's motives see Oliver E. Remey, et al., eds., *The Attempted Assassination of Ex-President Theodore Roosevelt* (Milwaukee, 1912), 196–97.

121. TR to EKR, Oct. 14, 1912, KBR-LC.

122. *New York Times*, Oct. 16, 1912; Joseph Colt Bloodgood to Dr. Loyal Davis, July 12, 1932, TRC-HU.

123. Addams in Oct. 18, 1912, NSC; patient in EKR to KR, Oct. 21 and 22, n.y. [1912], KBR-LC; EKR to ARC, Oct. 29, n.y. [1912], TRC-HU; Ferber, *Peculiar Treasure*, 228; ERD to KR, Nov. 4, n.y. [1912], KBR-LC.

124. Clipping "Good Out of Evil," ERD to KR, n.d. [Oct. 21–29, 1912], KBR-LC; Mark Sullivan, *The Education of an American* (New York, 1938), 304; ERD to KR, Oct. 22, 1912, and [Nov. 11, 1912] and clippings enclosed, KBR-LC; TR was supported by writers including Mary Antin, Herbert Croly, Richard Harding Davis, Edna Ferber, Hamlin Garland, Inez Haynes Gillmore, Hermann Hagedorn, Emerson Hough, Marion Couthouy Smith, William Allen White, and Owen Wister.

125. Oscar Straus in Cincinnati, Oct. 24, 1912, NSC; see also Stan Gores, "The Attempted Assassination of Teddy Roosevelt," *Wisconsin Magazine of History* 53 (Summer 1970): 269–77.

126. ERD-Di, Oct. 30, 1912; TR to Louisa Lee Schuyler, Dec. 31, 1912, MOR-REJ.

127. Oct. 28, 1912, NSC; ERD to KR, n.d. [Oct. 21–29, 1912], KBR-LC; *New York Times*, Nov. 3, 1912; EKR to KR, Nov. 6, n.y. [1912], KBR-LC; MOR 7:650–51.

128. ERD-Di, Nov. 5, 1912; *New York Times*, Nov. 12, 1912; Harlan, *Wizard of Tuskegee*, 357.

129. See Gable book and diss.; Allan J. Lichtman and Jack B. Lord, "Party Loyalty and Progressive Politics: Quantitative Analysis of the Vote for President in 1912," manuscript draft.

130. TR, "On the Need for Social Justice in the U.S.," typescript draft of Madison Square Garden speech, Oct. 26, 1912, TRP-LC; Mary Kingsbury Simkhovitch statement, Aug. 15, 1912, TRP-LC.

131. ERD-Di, Nov. 6, 1912; TR to Mary Dreier and Frances A. Kellor, Nov. 6, 1912, Mary Dreier Papers, Schlesinger Library; R.W.B. Lewis, *Edith Wharton* (New York, 1975), 330.

132. DR to ARC, Nov. 7, 1912, TRC-HU; bullet in EKR to KR, Apr. 26, n.y. [1913], KBR-LC; "babies" in DR to ARC, Nov. 7, 1912, TRC-HU; Dean of Howard University Kelly Miller made the 60 percent estimate: Gustafson, *Women and the Republican Party*, 132.

133. "slugger" in *From the Diaries of Felix Frankfurter*, 117; "dull thud" in J. J. Leary, SUBJ-TRC.

134. Clipping which quotes Watterson, Sept. 27, 1914, in James Callaway editorial, NSC; *Letters of Henry Adams*, 606.

135. EKR to KR, Dec. 15, n.y. [1912], and ERD to KR, Dec. 7, n.y. [1912], KBR-LC; Ira V. Brown, *Lyman Abbott, Christian Evolutionist: A Study in Religious Liberalism* (Cambridge, Mass., 1953), 211.

136. Hermann Hagedorn to Richard Derby, May 30, 1957, and Hagedorn to ERD, May 30, 1957, TRC-HU; Alexander Lambert to Hagedorn, memo, SUBJ-TRC. When Hagedorn was writing *The Roosevelt Family of Sagamore Hill* the Derbys asked him to delete the accurate account of TR's depression and write that Lambert came to Sagamore Hill of his own volition. They did not like the word "desolation," but accepted the phrase "bruised spirit," 328.

137. Hermann Hagedorn to Richard Derby, May 30, 1957, TRC-HU; *Current Opinion* 54, no. 3 (March 1913); TR, "Is Polar Exploration Worth While?" *Outlook* 103 (Mar. 1, 1913): 486.

138. MOR 7:648–49.

139. MEM 4:188.

140. TR to Joseph Bucklin Bishop, Feb. 10, 1913, Bishop Papers, Houghton; MOR 7:704.

141. TR to Joseph Bucklin Bishop, Feb. 10, 1913, Bishop Papers, Houghton; TR to Charles K. Warren, Jan. 7, 1913, MOR-REJ.

142. MOR 7:650.

143. MOR 7:679–80; *Roosevelt vs. Newett.*

144. TR to James H. Pound, Dec. 4, 1912, MOR-REJ; TR to John Callan O'Laughlin, Feb. 8, 1913, TRC-HU; MOR 7:653; the *New York World* attacked TR for being under the influence of trusts, Apr. 18, 1912; psychologist Morton Prince also subjected TR to long-distance psychoanalysis: "Roosevelt Analyzed by New Psychology," *Boston Herald*, Mar. 24, 1912, NSC.

145. MOR 7:655–56; TR to John Burroughs, Aug. 15, 1911, Barrett Collection, Alderman Library, University of Virginia; Stephen Jay Gould judged TR to be a better scientist than Thayer in "Red Wings in the Sunset," *Natural History* 94 (May 1985): 11–12, 18–24.

146. QR to ARC, n.d. [Dec. 5, 1912], TRC-HU.

147. ERD to RD, May 6, 1926, TRC-HU.

148. ERD to KR, June 12, n.y. [1913], KBR-LC; ARL to ARC, Jan. 31, 1914, TRC-HU. EKR to KR, Feb. 24, n.y. [1913], KBR-LC. Ethel saw the tragedy of Alice being exiled to live with Nick and his overbearing mother when "she really has wonderful capacities and is only letting them react on herself": ERD-Di, June 21 and July 29, 1912; Alice lived to regret her choice. Ethel reported years later that Alice kept "thinking 'Oh could I escape could I escape. Why did I not leave in 1912?' ": ERD to RD, May 6, 1926, TRC-HU.

149. Letter, Edith Derby Williams to author, Sept. 29, 1996; ERD to KR, June 23 and 29, 1913, KBR-LC. Derbys and Roosevelts had known each other in the old genteel world of Gramercy Park since before the Civil War. TR saw in Dick echoes of his own oblivious scholarly side; he said Dick at times resembled a "gentleman frog": MOR 7:742.

150. Ferdinand C. Iglehart, *Theodore Roosevelt: The Man As I Knew Him* (New York, 1919), 281; TR to KR, Nov. 11, 1912, TRC-HU.

151. TR to Frances Parsons, Nov. 14, 1912, Parsons Papers, Houghton; EKR to ERD, Dec. 1, 1927, TRC-HU.

152. MOR 7:660; EKR wrote to ARC: "I think many things that he had no time to think of during the campaign come to him now": Dec. 15, n.y. [1912], TRC-HU.

153. MOR 7:688; ERD to KR, Nov. 23, n.y. [1916], KBR-LC; HCL to TR, Oct. 20, 1909, HCL-MHS; he also gave a speech to military historians arguing for a dialogue between general historians and military specialists: TR, speech in Boston, Dec. 8, 1912, TR-SP; MEM 14 and 18; TR, *History as Literature*, 27, 28; Ray Allen Billington, *Frederick Jackson Turner: Historian, Scholar, Teacher* (New York, 1973), 288–89. Professional historians did not know that in private TR dismissed them as "academic pedants" and had called the professional historians' association "a preposterous little historical organization which, when I was just out of Harvard and very ignorant, I joined." He judged them "both absurd and mischievous" because of their collection of small facts and refusal to tell larger, heroic stories about the past: Bishop, *Theodore Roosevelt*, 2:139–40.

154. TR to William Sturgis Bigelow, Dec. 4, 1912, MOR-REJ; TR to ARC, Dec. 6 and 16, 1912, MOR-REJ; later Joseph Hodges Choate and others talked him out of resigning from all of his New York clubs. That Christmas Edith stopped Ethel from going to visit Kermit: "I would not be selfish and forbid her going but that I was not strong, that she was the only person I could turn to for help in the really heavy work of keeping accounts etc. straight, that besides Father had always been accustomed to having his friends here whenever he wished, and I might not have the strength to see that all went smoothly for them": EKR to KR, Mar. 2, n.y. [1913], KBR-LC; Stoddard, *It Costs to Be President*, 176.

CHAPTER THIRTEEN: THE BULL MOOSE UNHEARD

1. TR to QR, Feb. 14, and ERD to EKR, July 17, 1913, TRC-HU.

2. EKR-Di, Jan. 1, 1913.

3. MOR 7:646.

4. "never conquered asthma" in CRR to William R. Thayer, Aug. 8, 1922, Thayer Papers, Houghton. TR also wrote "I never found a permanent cure for asthma, but the spasms would be relieved by breathing Kidder's Asthmatic Pastiles [*sic*]. . . . I did not outgrow the asthma until I was about thirty-five years old," to Warren Francis Griffin, Apr. 21, 1913, MOR-REJ.

5. ERD to RD, n.d., TRC-HU.

6. TR to Mrs. Pinchot, June 20, 1913, MOR-REJ.

7. MOR 7:652, 677.

8. MOR 7:711, 646; Gerald Gunther, *Learned Hand: The Man and the Judge* (New York, 1994), 239.

9. TR opposed limiting presidential terms: TR to Joseph Bucklin Bishop, Feb. 10, 1913, Bishop Papers, Houghton; newspapers reported that TR was in favor of direct election of presidents and abolition of the electoral college: Feb. 11, 1911, NSC.

10. MOR 7:682.

11. Clippings, May 27, 1913, NSC; TR feared the loss of immigrant and labor votes if his party advocated prohibition. Many New York Progressives supported the municipal ownership of all public utilities, another issue that forever divided the party: TR Lincoln dinner speech, Feb. 13, 1913, NSC; *New York Evening Mail*, Feb. 13, 1913, NSC.

12. Wald, *Windows on Henry Street*, 299–300.

13. MOR 7:699.

14. MOR 7:700–701; later veterans of the Progressive Party would work with Florence Kelley, Frances Perkins, F.D.R., Al Smith, and Robert Wagner to pass labor legislation: Elizabeth Payne, *Reform, Labor, and Feminism: Margaret Dreier Robins and the Women's Trade Union League* (Chicago, 1988), 50; Dye, *As Equals and as Sisters;* and Meredith Tax, *The Rising of the Women: Feminist Solidarity and Class Conflict, 1880–1917* (New York, 1980); also see *Progressive Bulletin* for TR's cooperation with the early New York labor reformers.

15. Irving Greenberg, *Theodore Roosevelt and Labor; 1900–1918* (New York, 1988), 422; TR, speech at the National Conference of Progressive Service Workers, July 2, 1913, MEM 19:518.

16. "Woman Suffrage Demanded in the Interests of Good Government," speech at Metropolitan Opera House, New York City, May 2, 1913, TR-SP; *New York Tribune*, May 3, 1913; TR wrote many letters urging politicians to support state and national suffrage legislation; TR to Francis T. McGovern, n.d. [March 1913], MOR-REJ.

17. "Woman Suffrage Demanded in the Interests of Good Government"; suffragists Inez Mulholland and Pauline Frederick were in the pageant; Anna Howard Shaw shared the suffrage podium with TR, but she later refused to credit him with helping the cause and gave all the credit to President Wilson. Unlike Nathan and Addams, Shaw never forgave TR for failing to support the Anthony Amendment when he was president.

18. Newspaper clipping in file, TR, "The Progressive Party," speech in Rochester, N.Y., June 11, 1913, TR-SP; *Current Opinion* 54, no. 6 (June 1913): 455. M.I.T. biologist William T. Sedgwick warned that if women kept pressing for the vote and equal treatment, "rough male power" would reassert itself and man "will firmly shut down on the Feminist activities" and put women back in the home "where you belong. Now Stay there": George MacAdam, "Feminist Revolutionary Principle Is Biological Bosh," *New York Times*, Jan. 18, 1914; TR disagreed with Sedgwick.

19. TR, "Race Decadence," MEM 14:162, 166; Alice, Bamie, Corinne, Ethel, Isabella Ferguson, Fanny Parsons, Caroline Drayton Phillips, Lillian Wald, and others commented on his ability to take women seriously; Roosevelt Women Interviews; interview with Edith Derby Williams.

20. Parsons, *Perchance*, 260.

21. *New York Tribune*, May 3, 1913; Gable book, 170; Frances A. Kellor, "A New Spirit in Party Organization," *North American Review*, June 1914.

22. Gable book, 167; Fitzpatrick, *Endless Crusade*, 152–57; Payne, *Reform, Labor, and Feminism*, 162–65; on protective labor legislation for women being used as an "entering wedge" to win better laws for all, see Woloch, *Muller v. Oregon*.

23. MOR 7:672–76; see also *Progressive Bulletin.*

24. A. Davis, *Spearheads for Reform,* 206–17; Fitzpatrick, *Endless Crusade,* 149–57.

25. *Collier's,* January 1913; "whatever" in TR to Mary Dreier, Feb. 4, 1913, Mary Dreier Papers, Schlesinger Library.

26. "aggressive" in MOR 7:660, "too radical" in 665; ERD hoped prison reform would become a larger goal of the Progressive Party: ERD to KR, June 12, n.y. [1913], KBR-LC; TR's donations in TR to Theodore Douglas Robinson, Feb. 27, 1913, MOR-REJ; see John Milton Cooper, Jr., *The Warrior and the Priest* (Cambridge, Mass., 1983).

27. White, *Autobiography,* 510.

28. Dalton, "Why America Loved Teddy Roosevelt," 270; Hagedorn, *Roosevelt Family,* 333.

29. Clippings, May 14, 1913, NSC; EKR to ARC, n.d. [Feb. 26, 1913], and Mar. 5, n.y. [1913], TRC-HU.

30. *The Week, The Nation* 96, no. 2491 (Apr. 3, 1913): 321.

31. ERD to KR, n.d. [March 1913], KBR-LC; ERD to KR, June 12, 1913, KBR-LC; by the time they got around to hiring servants Edith encouraged them to hire more conventional ones; TR favored rehabilitation and giving prisoners the right to earn money in jail, MOR 7:696.

32. George Garner, Hagedorn interview, Feb. 22, 1932, Notes, SUBJ-TRC; African-American servants James Amos and Charles and Clara Lee helped EKR and ERD manage the flow of visitors at Sagamore Hill. After riding with Charles Lee, Ethel wrote in her diary that Mr. Lee's father had been Robert E. Lee's body servant when he surrendered at Appomattox and that the general had given him a sword, a house, 100 acres, and two mules in Lynchburg. ERD recorded: "Lee adores us all": ERD-Di, Aug. 13, 1912 (TR had made a point of putting Fitzhugh Lee, General Lee's grand-nephew, on his staff when he was president); during World War I the Lees sometimes cared for Richard Derby, Jr., and Edith Derby Williams, who were attached to them: ERD to RD, Feb. 2, 1918, TRC-HU; when TR was president, Charles Lee was refused the right to ride in a freight car to look after the President's horse, and TR complained to the Pennsylvania Railroad about its unwillingness to compromise its Jim Crow practices: TR to W. A. Patton, Mar. 6, 1908, MOR-REJ; Hermann Hagedorn also interviewed Lee, TRP-BP.

33. Belle Willard to KR, n.d., enclosed clipping from *New York Herald,* Apr. 5, 1913, KBR-LC; Apr. 4, 1913, NSC; Scott Joplin's "The Strenuous Life" ragtime was not written about TR, but several other ragtime pieces are connected with his presidency; ERD to KR, n.d. [April 1913], KBR-LC; EKR to ARC, Apr. 23, 1913, TRC-HU; EKR to KR, May 29, [1913], KBR-LC; after the wedding Theodore and Edith spent a quiet and happy hour with Gracie, and then Quentin read Edith to sleep with his favorite fairy tales and TR took Archie to chop logs: EKR to ARC, Apr. 23, 1913, TRC-HU; EKR to KR, May 29, n.y. [1913], KBR-LC. That spring TR brought Edith to dine with him and Lillian Wald and Jacob Riis at Henry Street Settlement.

34. EKR to ARC, Apr. 28, 1913, TRC-HU; Edith begged TR not to overwork and not to invite more guests to Sagamore Hill, but he promised only to try harder to be "very good and considerate" by keeping the flow of visitors to Sagamore Hill down: EKR to KR, Apr. 26, n.y. [1913], KBR-LC.

35. EKR to KR, May 24, n.y. [1913], KBR-LC; TR to Herbert S. Hadley, May 17, 1913, MOR-REJ; *New York Times,* May 26, 1913; TR to James Pound, Feb. 4, 1913, MOR-REJ; Marshall Van Winkle, *Sixty Famous Cases* (New York, 1956), 6:394.

36. Newspapers claimed he hired his own public relations advisor: NSC; Melvin G. Holli and C. David Tompkins, "Roosevelt vs. Newett: The Politics of Libel," *Michigan History* 47, no. 4 (December 1963): 338–56; *New York Times,* May 28, 1913; *Roosevelt vs. Newett,* 16.

37. Holli and Tompkins, "Roosevelt vs. Newett," 353.

38. Van Winkle, *Sixty Famous Cases,* 400.

39. Ibid., 423, 425.

40. EKR to ERD, June 3, 1913, TRC-HU.

41. There is no evidence TR was ever drunk at any time other than his college years: EKR to ERD, n.d. [May 1, 1913], TRC-HU; Archie Butt recalled that TR asked for a scotch and soda because he "needed" it when he visited President Taft: Butt, *Taft and Roosevelt,* 1:419.

42. W.E.D. Stokes to HCL, Feb. 11, 1919, HCL-MHS.

43. ERD to EKR, Mar. 16, 1928, TRC-HU. Emily refused the appendectomy unless her sister came over right away. Edith did not want to go, fearing that left unsupervised, her husband would go off to speaking engagements wearing "disreputable shirts" and what the family called his Eddie Foy hat: EKR to KR, June 8, n.y. [1913], KBR-LC; "hate" in TR to ERD, June 10 and 19, 1913, TRC-HU; TR sent his wife humorous news of home: their ailing dog, Ace, was convalescing in the barn where Bongo, the family cat, would bring him get-well gifts—dead rats. While Edith was gone, TR let his sociability run rampant and the daily guest list grew. Edith was irritated to hear that "just when everything should be managed to shield father," Ted and Alice "settled upon him like vampires—filling the house with the people they want to know using Father as a bait!": EKR to KR, July 6, n.y. [1913], KBR-LC.

44. Sung to the tune of "Maryland, My Maryland," a favorite of the Jane Addams Chorus of 1912: clipping in file, TR, "The Progressive Party," speech in Rochester, N.Y., June 11, 1913, TR-SP; SUBJ-TRC.

45. TR, "The Progressive Party," corrected typed draft, TR-SP.

46. TR, "The Progressive Party," and "The Progressive Party," *The Century* 86 (Oct. 1913): 826–36; for the influence of "the age of socialist inquiry" on Wilson see Thomas J. Knock, *To End All Wars: Woodrow Wilson and the Quest for a New World Order* (Princeton, 1992).

47. Vladimir G. Simkhovitch, *Marxism Versus Socialism* (New York, 1923); MOR 8:740. Instead of lecturing laborers about their duties as he had done earlier in his career, TR wrote a letter chastising the novelist Winston Churchill for declaring in *The Inside of the Cup* that the abolition of private property would bring the end of Christian civilization: TR to Winston Churchill, June 17, 1913, MOR-REJ. TR liked the book however: TR to H. J. Whigham, June 23, 1913, MOR-REJ. He praised (AER's brother) Hall Roosevelt for his work with George Lunn, the socialist mayor of Schenectady who built good parks and schools: TR to KR, Nov. 26, 1915, TRC-HU.

48. TR to Charles F. Clarke, Apr. 4, 1913, MOR-REJ; on anxiety about women gaining too much influence in education and men's hope that athleticism would rebuild their courage and manliness, see Putney, *Muscular Christianity,* David Tyack and Elisabeth Hansot, *Learning Together: A History of Coeducation in American Schools* (New Haven, 1990), and Lynn D. Gordon, *Gender and Higher Education in the Progressive Era* (New Haven, 1990); clipping, June 7 and May 9, 1913, NSC.

49. TR to His Excellency the Minister of Paraguay, June 24, 1913, and TR to Father Zahm, June 30, 1913, MOR-REJ; for a more detailed treatment of TR's South American trip see Joseph R. Ornig, *My Last Chance to Be a Boy: Theodore Roosevelt's South American Expedition of 1913–1914* (Mechanicsburg, Pa., 1994), 6.

50. EKR to KR, June 8 and 13, n.y. [1913], and July 6, n.y. [1913], KBR-LC; EKR to ERD, n.d. [August 1913], TRC-HU.

51. Ornig, *My Last Chance,* 27. Argentina, Chile, and Brazil paid TR at least $10,000 for his speaking engagements in their countries; TR had his $12,000 a year salary from *The Outlook* (and he would write political and social articles for them), and *Scribner's* was paying him

$15,000 for six to eight articles about his travels and the natural history of the interior which would later be published as a book. After paying for a large share of the cost of the expedition, TR still hoped to bring home a profit of $20,000. Zahm's benefactor, the Catholic industrialist Charles Schwab, paid for some of the expedition.

52. EKR to KR, July 15, [1913], KBR-LC.

53. EKR to ERD, Oct. 19, 1913, TRC-HU; TR said he "did not like Kermit to come on this trip with me": TR to EBAR, Dec. 10, 1913, TRJR-LC; TR wrote to Ethel that "I wish he would have gone straight to Belle. . . . I found that his feelings would really have been hurt if I had not let him come on this trip": TR to ERD, Dec. 10, 1913, TRC-HU.

54. Ornig, *My Last Chance*, 38; see also TR Farewell Dinner program, Progressive National Service and Progressive Service of the State of New York, New York, TRC-HU; TR wrote AER the morning he sailed: "Just a line to say how deeply touched and pleased I was to see you at the dinner. Give my love to Franklin. I hear from all sides how well he is doing. Your affectionate Uncle": TR to AER, Oct. 4, 1913, AER Papers, FDR; TR, speech, Oct. 3, 1913, New York, TRC-SP; his original speech had criticized Wilson's Mexican policy and defended his Panama Canal, but it was shortened at the request of Frances Kellor: clipping, Oct. 5, 1913, NSC; "intolerable burden" in TR to QR, Oct. 8, 1913, TRC-HU.

55. Parsons, *Perchance*, 249; clipping, Oct. 5, 1913, NSC; Ornig, *My Last Chance*, 41.

56. EKR to ARC, Oct. 15, 1913, TRC-HU.

57. MOR 7:746; HCL to TR, Nov. 7, and TR to HCL, Oct. 8, 1913, HCL-MHS; when HCL and EKR edited these letters for publication they left out Lodge bragging about his ulcer and Edith sleeping until lunch: *TR/HCL*, 2:444; for reports on dangers of the region, Neville B. Craig, *Recollections of an Ill-fated Expedition to the Headwaters of the Madeira River in Brazil* (Philadelphia, 1907), and Arnold Henry Savage Landor, *Across Unknown South America* (Boston, 1913).

58. EKR to ARC, Oct. 15, 1913, TRC-HU. TR's past friendship toward Brazil had grown by leaps and bounds after it quickly recognized Panama's independence; as president he elevated the Brazilian legation to an embassy and had sent his secretary of state, Elihu Root, there on a goodwill visit in 1906. The U.S. was Brazil's most important trading partner, and Brazil gave the U.S. trade preferences to encourage it to find more Brazilian markets for manufactured goods. In turn, Americans drank most of the coffee exported by Brazil; see E. Bradford Burns, *The Unwritten Alliance: Rio-Branco and Brazilian-American Relations* (New York, 1966).

59. Burns, *Unwritten Alliance*; Ornig, *My Last Chance*, 49–51; TR, *Through the Brazilian Wilderness*, 8–9.

60. Father John Augustine Zahm, "Roosevelt's Visit to South America," *Review of Reviews* 50 (July 1914): 85.

61. Henry Fairfield Osborn, "T.R., Naturalist," *Natural History Magazine*; Osborn, *Impressions of Great Naturalists, Reminiscences of Darwin, Huxley, Balfour, Cope and Others* (New York, 1924).

62. EKR to ERD, Nov. 13, 1913, TRC-HU. TR was especially eager to see where Kermit had lived and worked in São Paulo in his bridge-building days. When he saw the rough life his son had led, he grew nostalgic for his own youthful days on the Dakota frontier.

63. Burns, *Unwritten Alliance*, 163. The fear of strong government in America, TR said, had stopped states from protecting men, women, and children from working in unhealthy conditions in tenement houses. He denounced the U.S. Supreme Court's "inexcusable and reckless wantonness" in ruling consistently "on behalf of privilege, and against the interests of the very people for whom it is most needful that the power of the government should be invoked": TR, "Democratic Ideals," speech in Buenos Aires, TRP-LC; Rio speech, *New York Times*, Oct. 25, 1913.

64. He told Chileans that in preparing strategy for the Spanish-American War he had studied their military past and conceded that Latin Americans had handled the problem of slavery better than North Americans: TR, speech at the Municipal Theatre, Santiago de Chile, Nov. 24, 1913, TR-SP; Ornig, *My Last Chance*, 62–63.

65. TR described himself as a "beaten man": TR to William Allen White, Nov. 30, 1914, MOR-REJ. La Follette described him as politically dead in *Review of Reviews*, December 1913, 675; TR, *Through the Brazilian Wilderness* (New York, 1926), 27; see TR, "Montevideo," *Outlook* 106 (Feb. 28, 1914); "José Batlle," *Historic World Leaders*, vol. 4, *North and South America*, vol. AA-L, Anne Commire, ed. (Washington, D.C., 1994).

66. EKR to ERD, Nov. 7 and 14, n.y. [1913], TRC-HU; KR to Belle Willard, Nov. 14, 1913, KBR-LC.

67. KR to Belle Willard, Nov. 26, 1913, KBR-LC.

68. TR, *Through the Brazilian Wilderness*, 140; John Augustine Zahm, *Through South America's Southland, with an Account of the Roosevelt Scientific Expedition to South America* (New York, 1916), 378; Ornig, *My Last Chance*, 71.

69. KR to Belle Willard, Dec. 24, 1913, KBR-LC.

70. TR to EKR, Dec. 24, 1913, KBR-LC.

71. TR, *Through the Brazilian Wilderness*, 106–109.

72. KR, *The Happy Hunting-grounds* (London, 1920), 32; TR, *Through the Brazilian Wilderness*, 186.

73. TR, *Through the Brazilian Wilderness*, 174.

74. Ibid., 52; TR to EBAR, Oct. 8, 1913, TRJR-LC; TR liked Cherrie even more because he had named a new species of ant thrush after his favorite revolutionary, which struck Roosevelt as "delightful because of its practical combination of those not normally kindred pursuits, ornithology and gun-running": TR, "Up the Paraguay," *Scribner's* 55, no. 4 (April 1914): 408; piranha were already known as a danger in the Amazon, but TR's tales drew greater publicity to them in North America.

75. TR, "Up the Paraguay," 419.

76. TR, *Through the Brazilian Wilderness*, 175. John T. McCutcheon of the *Chicago Tribune* drew cartoons of TR on his South American adventure first with a Bull Moose reminding him, "Be sure to write," and second hunched over his pen while scribbling furiously in the jungle, the volumes mounting as he wrote his way through the jungle—"The Life History of the Armadillo," "Suffrage Movement on the Amazon," and "Pompous Days in Pampas Land"; "Colonel Roosevelt on the Progressive Party," *American Review of Reviews*, November 1913, TRC-HU.

77. TR, *Through the Brazilian Wilderness*, 126.

78. Zahm, *Through South America's Southland*, 479.

79. Cherrie Diary, Feb. 1, 1914, quoted in Ornig, *My Last Chance*, 117; TR's statement, Feb. 1, 1914, KBR-LC.

80. KR-Di, Feb. 3–26, 1914.

81. KR to EKR, Feb. 24, n.y. [1914], KBR-LC.

82. EKR to KR, Mar. 11, n.y. [1914], KBR-LC; she lunched with her old friend Sara Delano Roosevelt, but her main source of support remained her loyal and pregnant daughter Ethel. Ethel, fearful that it would displease her father to have a weakling grandchild, told her mother that she couldn't "bear" to give birth to a child who was "delicate." Richard Derby, Jr., was born March 6: ERD to EKR, Oct. 29, 1913, TRC-HU.

83. Ornig, *My Last Chance*, 145.

84. Candido Mariano da Silva Rondon, *Lectures Delivered on the 5th, 7th, and 9th of October, 1915*, trans. R. G. Reidy and E. Murray (Rio de Janeiro, 1916), 80–82.

85. TR, *Through the Brazilian Wilderness*, 275–77.

86. Ornig, *My Last Chance*, 150.

87. George Cherrie, *Roosevelt Memorial Meeting, the Explorer's Club, Mar. 1, 1919* (New York, 1919).

88. Ibid.

89. KR-Di, Apr. 2–5, 1914; Cherrie, *Roosevelt Memorial Meeting*.

90. KR, *The Long Trail* (New York, 1921), 75, and Ernest Bernbaum, ed., *Anthology of Romanticism* (New York, 1948), 177; TR, *Through the Brazilian Wilderness*, 42.

91. Cherrie, *Roosevelt Memorial Meeting;* TR later told a college classmate that he had also contemplated shooting himself to save his companions: Charles G. Washburn statement, SUBJ-TRC; see also Oscar King Davis, *Released for Publication: Some Inside Political History of Theodore Roosevelt and His Times, 1898–1918* (Boston, 1925), 431.

92. Rondon, *Lectures*, 109; KR-Di, Apr. 3, 1914, KBR-LC.

93. KR-Di, Apr. 5, 1914; Rondon, *Lectures*.

94. EKR to ARC, n.d. [Dec. 19, 1913], TRC-HU; EKR-Di, Mar. 31, 1914; EKR to ARC, Apr. 7, 1914, TRC-HU.

95. Rondon, *Lectures*, 116.

96. KR-Di, Apr. 8–12, 1914; Rondon, *Lectures*, 117.

97. Rondon, *Lectures*, 124.

98. KR-Di, Apr. 20, 1914.

99. TR, *Through the Brazilian Wilderness*, 78.

100. Ibid., 310; TR to Arthur Lee, May 4, and to Ruth and Arthur Lee, May 20, 1914, Lee Papers, Courtauld Institute.

101. TR, *Through the Brazilian Wilderness*, 317–18.

102. Ibid., 328.

103. Ibid., 328–29.

104. Clipping, May 19, 1914, NSC; clipping, *New York Times*, May 31, 1914.

105. EKR to ARC, n.d. [May 18, 1914], and to KR, May 24, n.y. [1914], KBR-LC; Parsons, *Perchance*, 251.

106. Joseph A. McCartin, *Labor's Great War: The Struggle for Industrial Democracy and the Origins of Modern American Labor Relations, 1912–1921* (Chapel Hill, N.C., 1997), 15–18; for Wilson's important domestic achievements up to 1915 see Arthur S. Link, *Woodrow Wilson and the Progressive Era, 1910–1917* (New York, 1963), Knock, *To End All Wars;* John Morton Blum, *Woodrow Wilson and the Politics of Morality* (Boston, 1956), and Cooper, *Pivotal Decades;* Henry Markham, Hamilton Rice, and Henry Savage Landor challenged TR's claim: TR to Arthur Lee, May 23, and to Ruth and Arthur Lee, May 20, 1914, Lee Papers, Courtauld Institute.

107. Gable book, 208–209, and George S. McGovern, *The Great Coalfield War* (Boston, 1972).

108. Kathleen L. Wolgemuth, "Woodrow Wilson and Federal Segregation," *Journal of Negro History*, April 1959, 158–73; Jane Lang Scheiber and Harry N. Scheiber, "The Wilson Administration and the Wartime Mobilization of Black Americans, 1917–18," *Labor History* 10 no. 3 (1969): 433–58.

109. "starving" in EKR to KBR, May 24, n.y. [1914], KBR-LC; "movie" in ARL, *Crowded Hours*, 231; ERD-Di. In the last days of May 1914 the Roosevelts held a Progressive conference and entertained Joe Alsop, Governor Robert Bass, Frank Chapman, George Cherrie, Corinne, Richard Harding Davis, Edmund Heller, Frank Knox, Mr. and Mrs. Ben B. Lindsey, Medill McCormick, Gifford Pinchot, Douglas Robinson, and Dr. Albert Shaw; see S. Morris, *Edith Kermit Roosevelt*, 403, on why Edith did not attend Kermit's wedding.

110. TR to EKR, June 11, 1914, KBR-LC; EKR-Di, June 23, 30, 1914.

111. TR, "Our Vanishing Wild Life," *Outlook* (Jan. 25, 1913), MEM 14:562; TR to J. Grinnell, July 10, 1914, MOR-REJ; TR, "The Conservation of Wild Life," *Outlook* (Jan. 20, 1915). Spreading knowledge about animal behavior increased public sympathy for game protection laws, so TR urged the study of the habits of killer whales on his friend Roy Chapman Andrews, a natural history writer and explorer who some said was later the model for the fictional Indiana Jones: TR to Andrews, July 14, 1914, MOR-REJ.

112. TR to John A. Hennessey, July 25, 1914, MOR-REJ.

113. TR to Charles Bonaparte, July 22, to Henry L. Stoddard, July 8, and to Everett Colby, July 6, 1914, MOR-REJ; clippings, July 3, 1914, FDRN-FDR and FDR Scrapbooks, FDR; CRR, *My Brother*, 279; TR to John M. Parker, July 6, 1914, MOR-REJ.

114. TR to General Theodore A. Biggham, July 9, 1914, MOR-REJ; EKR to KR, n.d. [July 28, 1914], and n.d. [June 28, 1914], KBR-LC; Alexander Lambert to unknown addressee [probably ARC or EKR, n.d. [summer 1914]: copy, TRC-HU and KBR-LC.

115. TR to John C. Shaffer, July 2, 1914, MOR-REJ; the Roosevelts attended Gifford Pinchot's wedding to Cornelia Bryce, EKR-Di, Aug. 15, 1914; a three-year contract with the *Metropolitan;* there was debate about the political reasons for his resignation from *The Outlook.* Abbott opposed woman suffrage and supported Wilson on the Panama Canal tolls controversy: clippings, July 4–10, 1914, NSC.

116. TRJR to KR, Oct. 22, 1914, KBR-LC; TR to ERD, Oct. 5, 1914, EKR to ARC, n.d. [late 1914], TRC-HU; Payne, *Reform, Labor, and Feminism,* 31; Gable book, 220.

117. TR to E. C. Stokes, and to Medill McCormick, Aug. 5, 1914, MOR-REJ; MOR 8:847–49; TR called the Clayton Anti-Trust Act an "economic absurdity" designed to thwart economic progress: speech in Pittsburgh, June 30, 1914, TR-SP.

118. TR to Henry F. Cochems, Nov. 7, 1914, MOR-REJ; "no longer fit" TR to BR, Nov. 7, 1914, TRC-HU. Long political experience taught the Roosevelts to be philosophical about the outcome. At least Alice, due to Nick's election, could escape Ohio and close contact with her mother-in-law to return to her beloved capital, and California had sent Hiram Johnson to the Senate: EKR to ERD, Nov. 3, n.y. [1914], TRC-HU; Ben Lindsey quoted in Gable book, 222. But T.R. still wanted to seek solutions to home-front problems with Thomas Edison, who had interested him in Henry Ford's advanced labor policies, and TR asked his *New Republic* friends to explore labor issues for him. TR had promised Lillian Wald that the Progressive Party would fight for the representation of women at the upcoming New York Constitutional Convention.

119. TR did not know that the German "submarine menace" stopped Ethel and Dick from landing in Southampton, but he and Edith could read that German zeppelins had dropped bombs on Paris not far from the hospital where they worked: ERD to Hermann Hagedorn, May 23, 1951, Correspondence Files, TRP-BP; ERD Travel Diary, n.d., TRC-HU; TR to ERD, October–November 1914, TRC.

120. TR to Arthur Lee, Aug. 1, 1914, Lee Papers, Courtauld Institute.

121. MOR 8:825–26; TR to Arthur Lee, Aug. 1, 1914, Lee Papers, Courtauld Institute.

122. MOR 8:857–60; TR's youthful admiration for German culture had grown into a full-blown wish that the U.S. emulate Germany in addressing social problems, for America provided fewer benefits to its orphans, widows, and destitute children than there, France, or England. Like so many turn-of-the-century American intellectuals, he viewed Germany as the seedbed of modern science and learning, and had been honored when a Roosevelt Professorship was created at the University of Berlin to exchange ideas. Roosevelt had often called for America to copy, under democratic conditions, the way "Germany has taken care of her working classes" by adopting "justice in wages, justice in housing, justice in sanitary conditions." But his lifelong admiration for German learning and culture did not make him

an admirer of German "racial ideas": *New York Times Magazine*, Sept. 19, 1915; Phyllis Keller, *States of Belonging: German-American Intellectuals and the First World War* (Cambridge, Mass., 1979), 95–97.

123. Selous to TR, Nov. 18, 1914, enclosed in TR to KR, Dec. 5, 1914, TRC-HU. Some eyewitnesses said that only 10 percent of the atrocities told about Belgium were true: James Morgan Read, *Atrocity Propaganda, 1914–1919* (New Haven, 1941), 29, refuted by Nicoletta F. Gullace, "Sexual Violence and Family Honor: British Propaganda and International Law During the First World War," *American Historical Review* 102, no. 3 (June 1997): 714–47. See also Great Britain, Treasury, *Report of the Committee on Alleged German Outrages* (London, 1915); *Reports on the Violations of the Rights of Nations and of the Laws and Customs of War in Belgium* (London 1915–16); Michael L. Sanders and Philip M. Taylor, *British Propaganda During the First World War* (London, 1982); Arthur Marwick, *The Deluge: British Society and the First World War* (London, 1970).

124. ERD to EKR, Oct. 6, 1914, TRC-HU; TR to Kenneth Hutchins, Apr. 23, 1918, MOR-REJ; KR to TR, June 28, n.y. [1915], KBR-LC; though for many years scholars believed German atrocities were exaggerated by British propagandists (they were), today historians recognize the valid evidence of real atrocities: see Gullace, "Sexual Violence," and John Horne and Alan Kramer, "German 'Atrocities' and Franco-German Opinion, 1914: The Evidence of German Soldiers' Diaries," *Journal of Modern History* 66 (March 1994): 1–33; while the need for U.S. intervention in World War I remains a debatable question, TR's genuine concerns about human rights violations and his eagerness for preparedness can no longer be dismissed as militarism or signs of his eagerness to fight any way, anytime.

125. TR, "An International Posse Comitatus," MEM 20:82–100; *New York Times*, Nov. 8, 1914; see *Philadelphia North American*, Nov. 8 and 15, 1914.

126. Clippings, Oct. 22, 1914, FDRN-FDR and FDR Scrapbooks, FDR; Jonathan Daniels, *The End of Innocence* (New York, 1954), 146, 150–52; Lodge's son-in-law, Augustus P. Gardner, led the attacks on the administration's failure to prepare, and TR and FDR were in fairly frequent contact about preparedness from 1914 to 1918.

127. ERD, Travel Diaries, and ERD, EKR, RD letters, November and December 1914, TRC-HU.

128. After the dictator Porfirio Díaz left office in 1911, moderate Francisco Madero emphasized constitutionalism, not economic reform. Taft's ambassador to Mexico, Henry Lane Wilson, aided the deposing of Madero by dictator Victoriano Huerta. At first, President Wilson banned arms sales to Huerta and refused to recognize his government, then as Pancho Villa, Venustiano Carranza, and Emiliano Zapata struggled to launch a revolution, Wilson recognized Huerta. Germany funded Huerta and hoped to start a war between the U.S. and Mexico; Germany aimed to sabotage American and Canadian munitions plants and the Canadian Pacific Railway to prevent the transportation of arms and Japanese and other troops headed to help Britain in the Great War: Reinhard R. Doerries, *Imperial Challenge: Ambassador Count Bernstorff and German-American Relations, 1908–1917* (Chapel Hill, N.C., 1989), 165–74.

129. John Womack, Jr., *Zapata and the Mexican Revolution* (New York, 1969), 65–82, 96–112, 394–400; unsympathetic to the social goals of the revolution, especially Zapata, is Robert E. Quirk, *The Mexican Revolution, 1914–1915: The Convention of Aguascalientes* (New York, 1963), 108; Wilson was more sympathetic with the revolutionaries' professed goal of bringing a better life to the peasants, but his bungled Mexican policy aided Carranza, who was the least likely to realize those goals. TR and Wilson had patronizing attitudes toward Mexicans, but TR was more concerned about law-and-order issues on the border.

130. TR, "An International Posse Comitatus," MEM 20:82–100; *New York Times*, Nov. 8, 1914; see *Philadelphia North American*, Nov. 8 and 15, 1914; George E. Mowry, *Theodore Roo-*

sevelt and the Progressive Movement (New York, 1960), 330; "Colonel Roosevelt on Our Responsibility in Mexico," *American Review of Reviews*, February 1915; *New York Times*, Dec. 6, 1914; Mexican oil fields supplied the British navy: Lloyd C. Gardner, "Woodrow Wilson and the Mexican Revolution," in *Woodrow Wilson and a Revolutionary World, 1913–1921*, ed. Arthur S. Link (Chapel Hill, N.C., 1982); MOR 7:245.

131. TR to KR, Feb. 22, 1915, TRC-HU; Leonard, *Above the Battle*, 88, 110; Tom Leonard also supplied the author with useful references about TR's attitude toward war; Barbara S. Kraft and Donald Smythe, "How T.R. Tried in Vain to Fight in World War I," *Smithsonian* 4, no. 7 (1973): 54–61 (56).

132. EKR-Di, Jan. 31–Feb. 3, 1915.

133. TR fashioned himself as the John Bright of the Great War. At the time of the U.S. Civil War, within the British government, Bright had communicated with Charles Sumner to work as the loyal opposition to prevent Britain from aiding the Confederacy. TR was desperate to stop the U.S. from aiding Germany, and he wanted to bring Britain and America closer together: see TR's letters in MOR and MOR-REJ; Robert A. Rosenstone, *Romantic Revolutionary: A Biography of John Reed* (New York, 1975), 211; Justin Kaplan, *Lincoln Steffens: A Biography* (New York, 1974), 230.

134. TR "Utopia or Hell: Theodore Roosevelt's Plan for the League of Nations," *The Independent* 81, no. 3448 (Jan. 4, 1915): 15–17; Hermann Hagedorn, Notes on a Conversation with Theodore Roosevelt, Sept. 27, 1914, SUBJ-TRC; talk of a league had circulated in European and American circles long before TR proposed it in his 1910 Nobel Prize speech: see Dalton, "Between the Diplomacy of Imperialism," 27–47, and Iriye, *Cultural Internationalism*.

135. TR, "Utopia or Hell."

136. Jonathan Daniels, *End of Innocence*, 63, 166–68, 176, 188–96, 210–13; see Caroline Drayton Phillips Papers, Schlesinger Library. Josephus Daniels proved to be a controversial leader of the navy. The *New York World* portrayed him as a yokel who did not understand sailors and would stop all drinking, tattoos, and singing of "It's a Long Way to Tipperary" in the navy: Daniels, *End*, 128–29, 157. The preparedness forces thought him incompetent.

137. TR, speech at the Ohio Society Dinner, Hotel Waldorf, New York City, Jan. 12, 1918, TR-SP.

138. TR, speech at the National Security League luncheon, Hotel Astor, New York City, Jan. 19, 1918, TR-SP; TR, speech at the Ohio Society Dinner, Jan. 12, 1918, TR-SP.

139. Pearlman, *To Make Democracy Safe for America*, 38; Walter Lippmann saw Leonard Wood as a "pseudo-Roosevelt" and a man who represented the spirit of the "coup d'etat": Walter Lippmann, "Leonard Wood," in *Early Writings* (New York, 1970), 158, 165.

140. TR, "Peace Purchased by Cowardice Invites War," *Metropolitan*, July 1916, *Metropolitan* Scrapbook, TRC-HU; *Congressional Record*, Appendix, vol. 55, part 8, 65th Cong., 1st Sess., 62, FDR; *Scribner's*, George Perkins and Frances Kellor had a falling-out over how to run and finance the Progressive National Service, and after Perkins told his version to the Roosevelts, TR took Perkins' side and Ethel wrote of Kellor, "That is an idol shattered alright": ERD-Di, Feb. 24, 1915; Fitzpatrick, *Endless Crusade*, 55–57.

141. "gallant" in TRJR to KR, July 21, 1915, KBR-LC; Harvard may have been sending a lot of volunteers to Plattsburg, but President Lowell almost dismissed Archie for organizing military training on campus, ABR, Memoirs, TRC-HU. On preparedness see Pearlman, *To Make America Safe for Democracy*; Robert W. Tucker, *The Just War: A Study in Contemporary American Doctrine* (Baltimore, 1960); John Garry Clifford, *The Citizen Soldiers: The Plattsburg Training Camp Movement, 1913–1920* (Lexington, Ky., 1972); John P. Finnegan, *Against the Specter of a Dragon: The Campaign for American Military Preparedness, 1914–1917* (Westport, Conn., 1974), Ralph Barton Perry, *The Plattsburg Movement: A Chapter of America's Par-*

ticipation in the World War (New York, 1921). Some class snobbery existed within the Roosevelt family: Archie disliked having so few gentlemen in his classes at Andover; TR instructed Ted that workplace equality did not mean a gentleman had to mingle socially with people with lower class standings: TR to TRJR, Nov. 20, 1908, TRJR-LC; and Edith wrote, "If one is not born a lady one can't grow to be one": EKR to ERD, Dec. 1, 1927, TRC-HU.

142. "remasculinize" in John Carver Edwards, *Patriots in Pinstripes: Men of the National Security League* (Washington, D.C., 1982), 33–36, 5; CRR, *My Brother*, 288–89. The Woman's Peace Party (including Leonora O'Reilly and Frances Perkins, who had worked with TR) accused the N.S.L. of being funded by munitions makers; a few preparedness leaders, such as Du Pont employee and inventor of one type of smokeless powder, Hudson Maxim, and T. Coleman du Pont, were in the munitions business. Bernard Baruch, Cleveland Dodge, T. Coleman du Pont, Henry Clay Frick, Simon Guggenheim, Hearst, Hudson Maxim, J. P. Morgan, George Perkins, Mortimer Schiff, and others funded the N.S.L., and Bull Mooser Elon Hooker of Hooker Electro-Chemical chaired the American Defense Society.

143. Gable book, 216–32; Victor Murdock, "A National Bureau of Employment," speech in the House of Representatives, May 1, 1914 (Washington, 1914).

144. TR to KR, Feb. 8, 1915, TRC-HU; MOR 8:1486–87; Mary Heaton Vorse, *A Footnote to Folly: Reminiscences of Mary Heaton Vorse* (New York, 1935), 56–74.

145. TR to KR, Jan. 10, 1915, TRC-HU.

146. TR to KR, Feb. 8, 1915, TRC-HU; "dining in town" in TRJR to KR, Mar. 24, 1915, KBR-LC.

147. "Hospitable inclinations" in TR to BR, Feb. 17, 1915, TRC-HU; ABR memoirs, TRC-HU; children said TR told them that Edith developed a "martyr complex" because of the demands life at Sagamore Hill made on her: ERD to Edith Derby Williams, Feb. 7, 1948, TRC-HU; EKR wrote that Uncle Jim and Aunt Lizzie (Elizabeth Emlen) Roosevelt sent her friend Teresa Richardson to tell TR that running Sagamore Hill with so many guests was "killing" his wife: Alice King memo about EKR correspondence with Marion King, TRC-HU; "clever people" and "deeply possessive" in ERD to Edith Derby Williams, Nov. 9, 1947, TRC-HU; "privilege of growing old" and TR's description of his life with EKR as a life of "old people": TR to BR, Jan. 16, 1915, TRC-HU.

148. EKR to ERD, Dec. 1, 1927, and ERD to Edith Derby Williams, Nov. 7, 1948, TRC-HU; Nicholas Roosevelt wrote to Carleton Putnam, Apr. 5, 1958, NR-SYR, that TR was "devoted to her, and greatly enjoyed the fun which they had together in talking about people and events—fun of a kind which he could never have with Edith, who, incidentally, I suspect of having always been jealous of Mrs. Parsons, and rather resented his fun with her."

149. Parsons, *Perchance*, 234; the best source on Parsons is her memoirs, *Perchance*; see Mrs. William Starr Dana (Frances Theodora Parsons), *How to Know the Wild Flowers* (1893; reprint, Boston, 1989) and her several other books; statement by Mrs. Parsons, Feb. 18, 1949, Correspondence File, TRP-BP; thanks to Frances Tennenbaum for information about her.

150. Lippmann, *Drift and Mastery*, 50.

151. Forcey, *Crossroads of Liberalism*, 192–212; David W. Levy, *Herbert Croly of the New Republic: The Life and Thought of an American Progressive* (Princeton, 1985), 194–202, 216–17, 240–43; Gunther, *Learned Hand*, 241–44.

152. "The Irish Players," *Outlook* (Dec. 6, 1911), MEM 14:402–404. On the American Renaissance of the Greenwich Village era, Van Wyck Brooks, *America's Coming-of-Age* (New York, 1915); Walter Lippmann, *A Preface to Politics* (Ann Arbor, 1962); Henry May, *The End of American Innocence* (Chicago, 1964); James Hoopes, *Van Wyck Brooks: In Search of American Culture* (Amherst, Mass., 1977); Freda Kirchwey, "Socialism's Edge Dulled on Dinner," *New York Tribune*, Dec. 31, 1913; Kenneth Lynn, "The Rebels of Greenwich Village," *Perspectives*

in American History 8 (1974): 335–77; Daniel Joseph Singal, "Towards a Definition of American Modernism," *American Quarterly* 39 (Spring 1987): 7–26; Albert Parry, *Garrets and Pretenders: A History of Bohemianism in America* (1933; reprint, New York, 1960); Christine Stansell, *American Moderns: Bohemian New York and the Creation of a New Century* (New York, 2000); K. McCarthy, *Women's Culture.*

153. B. L. Reid, *The Man from New York: John Quinn and His Friends* (New York, 1968), 116–18; *New York Times,* Nov. 29, 1911.

154. Reid, *Man from New York,* 148; TR, "A Layman's Views of an Art Exhibition," *Outlook* (March 29, 1913), MEM 14:405-10.

155. Reid, *Man from New York,* 201–202; Wagenknecht, *Seven Worlds,* 82–84; TR also attended the 1918 show "The Immigrant in America" at Gertrude Vanderbilt Whitney's studio.

156. TR, "Dante and the Bowery," *Outlook* (Aug. 26, 1911), in MEM 14:446.

157. TR, "Dante and the Bowery"; TR, "Nationalism in Literature and Art," MEM 14:456.

158. CRR, *My Brother,* 323–24; Forcey, *Crossroads of Liberalism,* 198; Roosevelt thought an American theater should be endowed, so that it would be a source of national pride and cultural advancement; B. Reid, *Quinn,* 273, 249.

159. Harbaugh, *Power and Responsibility,* 435; Hamilton Wright Mabie and others recalled how good TR was at teamwork and collegiality in his magazine writer years: Lyman Abbott, *Reminiscences,* 443.

160. John Muir and conservation pieces in *Outlook,* MEM 12:566–69, see also MEM 14:561–81; "Books for Holidays in the Open," *Ladies' Home Journal,* April 1915, MEM 4:187–96; *Collier's* 54 (Oct. 3, 1914): 10; Wagenknecht, *Seven Worlds,* 65; Edward Bok, *The Americanization of Edward Bok: An Autobiography* (New York, 1965), 197–203.

161. Granville Hicks, *John Reed: The Making of a Revolutionary* (New York, 1968), 178–79; Rosenstone, *Romantic Revolutionary,* 210.

162. On Vigilantes see P. Keller, *States of Belonging;* Douglas Fairbanks and Charles Dana Gibson were also Vigilantes; Hermann Hagedorn to CRR, Apr. 14, 1917, and ERD to RD, Apr. 3, 1918, TRC-HU; Hermann Hagedorn, *The Hyphenated Family: An American Saga* (New York, 1960), 233.

163. On EKR naming his books, TR to BR and KR, Dec. 10, 1915, TRC-HU; Ned Buxton to Nicholas Roosevelt, Dec. 30, 1947, NR-SYR.

164. TR's descriptions of EKR in TR to Endicott Peabody, Apr. 8, 1915, Peabody Papers, Houghton; "silver lining" in TR to KR, May 2, 1915, TRC-HU; EKR-Di, April and May 1915.

165. ERD to RD, n.d. [May 1915], and TR to KR, May 2, 1915, TRC-HU.

166. B. La Follette and F. La Follette, *Robert M. La Follette,* 2:879; Arthur S. Link, *Wilson: The Struggle for Neutrality, 1914–1915* (Princeton, 1960), 368–73; the shrapnel cases were not loaded.

167. Clippings, Apr. 22, 1915, NSC; TR, "Murder on the High Seas," MEM 20; Henry James Whigham, Statement in Re The Writing of "Murder on the High Seas," and TR to Whigham, May 11, 1915, TRC-HU; Link, *Struggle for Neutrality,* 382.

168. TR to ERD, May 12, 1915, TRC-HU. TR's position in the Barnes trial was more than awkward. He testified to having intimate knowledge of corrupt dealings perpetrated by bosses, yet not to be in any way morally compromised by them himself. When the prosecutor questioned him about why he as governor had not attacked Boss Platt, TR replied with great emotion: "I believe emphatically that you must have a due regard for opportunism in the choice of the time and methods of making the attack." He fought bosses when doing so no longer ruined a man's career. Supreme Court Appellate Division—Fourth Department,

William Barnes, Plaintiff-Appellant, against Theodore Roosevelt, Defendant-Respondent Case on Appeal, v.1 #12, 318–20.

169. EKR burned most of TR's letters, but she saved this fragment and sent it to AER in a letter, Oct. 31, 1921: FDRN-FDR.

170. "Roosevelt and Barnes," *Philadelphia North American*, May 26, 1915; TR to KR and BR, June 16, 1915, TRC-HU; TR to Endicott Peabody, June 29, 1915, Peabody Papers, Houghton.

171. For diplomatic and political background see Link, *Struggle for Neutrality*, and Ernest R. May, *The World War and American Isolation, 1914–1917* (Cambridge, Mass., 1959).

172. Arthur S. Link, *Wilson: Confusions and Crises, 1915–1916* (Princeton, 1964), 55–61; Jules Witcover, *Sabotage at Black Tom: Imperial Germany's Secret War in America, 1914–1917* (Chapel Hill, N.C., 1989); Reinhard R. Doerries, "Promoting Kaiser and Reich: Imperial German Propaganda in the United States During World War I," in Hans Jürgen-Schröeder, ed., *Confrontation and Cooperation: Germany and the United States in the Era of World War I, 1900–1924* (Oxford, Eng., 1993), 135–65; Frederic William Wile, *The German-American Plot: The Record of a Great Failure, The Campaign to Capture the Sympathy and Support of the United States* (London, 1915), 23; see also the contemporary tract which influenced public opinion, William H. Skaggs, *German Conspiracies in America* (London, 1917), 120. U.S. Ambassador to Germany James Gerard had heard from Under Secretary Zimmerman that Germany already had a half million reservists in the U.S.; Germany used the U.S. as the base for its anti-British subversion in India and Ireland: Doerries, *Imperial Challenge*, 141–90.

173. Doerries, *Imperial Challenge*, 189.

174. Doerries, "Promoting Kaiser," 135–65; Harry N. Scheiber, *The Wilson Administration and Civil Liberties, 1917–1921* (Ithaca, N.Y., 1960), 7.

175. TRJR to KR, Mar. 24, 1915, KBR-LC; Ted had set up a board of directors by March 1915: MOR 8:909; Thomas A. Rumer, *The American Legion: An Official History, 1919–1989* (New York, 1990), is not accurate on the founding of the organization. Ted and Dick contemplated political careers after the war; see RD Diary, and RD to ERD, Apr. 6, 9, 19, May 7, Oct. 30, and Nov. 1, 1919, TRC-HU.

176. *New York Times*, Dec. 14, 1918; Swanberg, *Citizen Hearst*, 352–53.

177. Marian Blackton Trimble, *J. Stuart Blackton: A Personal Biography by His Daughter* (Metuchen, N.J., 1985), 75. Local theaters and the distributor, Vitagraph, sued Henry Ford and other peace activists when they picketed the movie. Paramount made a newsreel of TR speaking about preparedness, "Shall We Prepare?" Feb. 1916, see *The Moving Picture World* 27, no. 8 (1916); *Theodore Roosevelt Association Film Collection*, ed. White-Hensen and Gillespie, 95–96; *Metropolitan* 43, no. 5 (1916): 72–73.

178. TR, *America and the World War*, MEM 20:178; Parsons, *Perchance*, 242; White in MOR 8:871*n*.; TR to Kermit, Dec. 2, 1914, TRC-HU; "cannon loose" in Jonathan Daniels, *End of Innocence*, 63.

179. "lick his wounds" in Parsons, *Perchance*, 242; MOR 8:910–11.

180. See Notes by Oswald Garrison Villard, [May 15, 1915], Villard Papers, Houghton, discussed in Doerries, "Promoting Kaiser," 135–65.

181. TR to KR, May 27, 1915, TRC-HU.

182. EKR to KR, Aug. 21, [1915], KBR-LC; TR to KR, May 27, 1915, TRC-HU.

183. TR to KR, May 31 and May 27, 1915, TRC-HU.

184. R. L. Duffus, *Lillian Wald: Neighbor and Crusader* (New York, 1938), 151–54; Charlotte Perkins Gilman, *The Man-Made World* (1911), 211, quoted in Degen, *History of the Woman's Peace Party*, 26, 31, Addams quoted, 11.

185. Allen F. Davis, *American Heroine: The Life and Legend of Jane Addams* (New York,

1973), 223; *New York Times*, Apr. 19, 20, and 23, 1915. TR's 1912 allies—Addams, Mary Dreier, Paul Kellogg, Amos Pinchot, and others—were active in the American Union Against Militarism, and pressed for graduated income and inheritance taxes to pay the cost of preparing for war; see Erika A. Kuhlman, *Petticoats and White Feathers: Gender Conformity, Race, the Progressive Peace Movement, and the Debate over War, 1895–1919* (Westport, Conn., 1997), 66; most of them finally supported American involvement in World War I. His frienship with Addams remained close.

186. Harriet Hyman Alonso, *Peace as a Women's Issue: A History of the U.S. Movement for World Peace and Women's Rights* (Syracuse, N.Y., 1993), 70.

187. TRJR to KR, Sept. 23, 1915, KBR-LC; *Letters from Theodore Roosevelt to Anna Roosevelt Cowles*, 310; TRJR to KR, July 14, 1915, KBR-LC.

188. "Bird Reserves," MEM 4:215, 198; EKR-Di, June 6–14, 1915.

189. TR to KR and BR, June 16, 1915, TRC-HU; EKR-Di, June 14 and Aug. 25, 1915; TR, "Standing by the President," *Current History*, October 1915, 19–20, 21.

190. TR, "Armenian Outrages," MEM 20; TR to KR, Oct. 15, 1915, TRC-HU; Theodore was happy to have the whole Derby family and Quentin and Archie and their friends at Sagamore Hill that summer. In July, TR and Edith traveled to Canada and saw Banff and Lake Louise. They attended Roosevelt Day at the Panama-Pacific Exposition and TR spoke at the American Historical Congress in San Francisco and then to more than 20,000 people in San Diego. After the *Lusitania*, he found much more popular enthusiasm for preparedness and a renewed national following.

191. Lambert worked on the Judicial Council of the A.M.A. and on the American Association for Labor Legislation's Social Insurance Committee, but the post–World War I Red Scare and the rise of coercive Americanism defeated his campaign: Beatrix Hoffman, *The Wages of Sickness: The Politics of Health Insurance in Progressive America* (Chapel Hill, N.C., 2001), 70–71.

192. TR, "A Curious Experience," MEM 4:232–33.

193. When he called it racial he often meant national competition. "A Curious Experience," 249–53, Appendix C, "My Life as a Naturalist," 605; TR to KR, Oct. 1, 1915, TRC-HU.

194. E. R. May, *World War and American Isolation;* "out-Teddy": Herbert Croly quoted in Forcey, *Crossroads of Liberalism*, 154.

195. Link, *Struggle for Neutrality*, 645–51; *New York Times*, Oct. 13 and Dec. 8, 1915; Link, *Confusions and Crises*, 36–37; Frederick C. Luebke, *Bonds of Loyalty: German-Americans and World War I* (De Kalb, Ill., 1974), 145–47; "A 'Swat the Hyphen' Movement," *Literary Digest* 51 (Oct. 30, 1915): 943–44.

196. TR to KR, Aug. 6, 1915, TRC-HU.

197. TR to KR, Oct. 24 and 26, and to BR and KR, Dec. 10, Nov. 11, and Oct. 24, 1915, TRC-HU.

198. "Buppies" and "rapture" in TR to BR and KR, Dec. 27, 1915, TRC-HU; on ARL's "help" see TR to KR, Nov. 26, 1915, TRC-HU; David H. Wallace, *Sagamore Hill: Historic Furnishings Report*, vol. 1, Historical Data (Harpers Ferry, W.Va., 1989), 101; TRJR to KR, Dec. 28, 1915, KBR-LC; TR was already discussing with HCL which progressive candidate would be acceptable to both sides, Dec. 4, 1915, HCL-MHS.

199. TR to KR, Aug. 6, 1915, TRC-HU; MOR 8:881; TR to Frank Knox, Dec. 21, 1915, and to KR, Jan. 19, 1916, TRC-HU.

200. *New York Times*, May 11, 1916; when in May 1916, Woodrow Wilson and Samuel Gompers lined up approvingly with the organizers of the League to Enforce the Peace, including Taft and president A. Lawrence Lowell of Harvard, defenders of the idea of a world organization to encourage peace resembled a reunion of TR's worst enemies: Degen, *History of the Woman's Peace Party*, 167; "New York's Parade of Preparedness," *Survey* 36 (1916): 197–98.

201. Joseph Tumulty, *Woodrow Wilson As I Know Him* (Garden City, N.Y., 1921), 246–47; TR to Ruth and Arthur Lee, Nov. 1, 1915, Lee Papers, Courtauld Institute.

202. Ward, *First-Class Temperament*, 323.

203. EKR-Di, Feb. 12–Mar. 24, 1916; "social reform" in ERD-Di, Apr. 2, 1916; on his recurring fevers, TRJR to KR, Mar. 8, 1916, KBR-LC; "heroic" in TR, speech in Port-of-Spain, Trinidad, British West Indies, Mar. 9, 1916, TR-SP.

204. Gable book, 229–49; Mowry, *Theodore Roosevelt and the Progressive Movement*, 342–43; Roosevelt Non-Partisan Leaguers converged on Sagamore Hill to show their support for TR's candidacy: P. C. Desmond to William Roscoe Thayer, May 24, n.y. [1916], Thayer Papers, Houghton.

205. TR to Ida Husted Harper, Sept. 16, 1918, MOR-REJ.

206. ERD-Di, June 5 and 14, 1916; "majorities" in ARL, *Crowded Hours*, 218.

207. Harold L. Ickes, "Who Killed the Progressive Party?" *American Historical Review* 46 (January 1941), 306–37; Lippmann, "At the Chicago Convention," in *Early Writings*, 122; ERD-Di, June 6–10, 1916.

208. Swanberg, *Citizen Hearst*, 359.

209. MOR 8:1066; see J. Joseph Huthmacher, "Charles Evans Hughes and Charles Francis Murphy: The Metamorphosis of Progressivism," *New York History*, January 1965, 25–40; after TR's bout with croup his cough persisted and caused him to pull a ligament: EKR-Di, June, 13, 1916; TR to CRR, June 23, 1916, TRC-HU.

210. Lippmann, "At the Chicago Convention," 126–27; followers who had "found their political souls" through TR never forgave him for giving up the Bull Moose banner in 1916; Thomas Robins mss. quoted in MOR 8:1074; tearful delegates ripped their Roosevelt badges off and left the hall in disgust: T. H. Watkins, *Righteous Pilgrim: The Life and Times of Harold L. Ickes, 1874–1952* (New York, 1990), 146. A few die-hards hung on to the Bull Moose Party but later they drifted to the Prohibition Party in 1917 or joined the National Woman's Party. Others met again after the Great War in the Committee of 48, modeled after the British Labour Party with its program of public ownership of utilities and a nationally guaranteed minimum standard of living: Nancy F. Cott, *The Groundings of Modern Feminism* (New Haven, 1987), 64–65, Mowry, *TR and the Progressive Party*, 367, Gable book, 250–52; see Eugene M. Tobin, *Organize or Perish: America's Independent Progressives, 1913–1933* (Westport, Conn., 1986). The anger of true believers bothered TR less than being rejected by the GOP. Because party regulars had been "intent upon disciplining me and teaching a lesson in party regularity," he insisted, as he had so many other times, he had reached the end of his political career: TR to Isaac Russell, June 16, 1916, MOR 8:1063; TR to CRR, June 23, 1916, TRC-HU.

211. Republican National Committee, *Republican Campaign Text-Book 1916* inside cover, 226, 240, 376; Gustafson, *Women and the Republican Party*, 170; "Men and Commodities," *Metropolitan*, September 1916, *Metropolitan* Scrapbook, TRC-HU; "be human" in ERD-Di, June 29, 1916; TR was preoccupied by the end of June organizing a cavalry division to go to Mexico, where the President had just sent troops, and he volunteered to work with the Board of Health to enforce a quarantine because of a polio epidemic in Oyster Bay: EKR to Emily Carow, July 30, and ERD to DR, June 29, 1916, TRC-HU; TR to Frank McCoy, July 9, 1916, TRP-LC; ERD-Di June 23–29, 1916.

212. Doerries, *Imperial Challenge*, 188–89; Witcover, *Sabotage at Black Tom;* Doerries, "Promoting Kaiser," 135–65.

213. ERD, Recollections of Richard Derby, Jr., TRC-HU; MOR 8:1105.

214. "rescue act" in press release, Aug. 27, 1916, FDRN-FDR; on the challenge for TR of campaigning for the Republican National Committee: ERD to RD, Aug. 26, 1916, TRC-HU.

215. Hermann Hagedorn, *The Bugle That Woke America: The Saga of Theodore Roosevelt's Last Battle for His Country* (New York, 1940), 113; MOR 8:1078; TR to W. A. Wadsworth, June 23, 1916, TRP-LC.

216. "invited" in "He Kept Us Out of War," *Literary Digest*, Oct. 14, 1916, 934; the Mexican press criticized America's failure to stand up to German insult and said it would cause "through all centuries of time to come . . . the brand of disgrace [to] cling to their countenance": *El Radical* quoted by TR in "Peace Purchased by Cowardice Invites War," *Metropolitan*, July 1916, *Metropolitan* Scrapbook, TRC-HU; MOR 8:1092.

217. TR approved of the Congressional Union and then the Woman's Party policy of campaigning against Democrats for their failure to support universal suffrage. His friend Alice Carpenter brought Paul to see him; conversations with Alice Paul: Woman Suffrage and the Equal Rights Amendment, Bancroft Library, University of California, Berkeley; Inez Haynes Gillmore, *The Story of the Woman's Party* (New York, 1921), 161; both parties were on record favoring suffrage if states voted for it one by one, but the movement wanted a national amendment; "Why Hughes Finds Wilson Wanting," *Literary Digest* 53 (Aug. 12, 1916): 335–36, and "Mr. Hughes' New Suffrage Plank," 337; MOR 8:1081–82.

218. C. K. MacFarland and Nevin E. Neal, "The Reluctant Reformer: Woodrow Wilson and Woman Suffrage, 1913–1920," *Rocky Mountain Social Science Journal* 11 (1974): 33–43 (37); on domestic issues Wilson's strategists aimed to win over Bull Moose followers. It was painful for TR to see his old friends Jane Addams, Bainbridge Colby, Mathew Hale, Francis J. Heney, Ben Lindsey, and Lillian Wald support Wilson. TR nevertheless welcomed Lindsey to Sagamore Hill and publicly endorsed his reelection bid to the Denver Juvenile Court.

219. Link, *Wilson and the Progressive Era*, 192–96; Richard Lowitt, *George W. Norris: The Persistence of a Progressive, 1913–1933* (Urbana, Ill., 1971), 86; see TR's 1916 speeches and TR, "Good Americans Should Support Mr. Hughes," *Metropolitan*, December 1916, *Metropolitan* Scrapbook, TRC-HU.

220. Josephus Daniels, *The Cabinet Diaries of Josephus Daniels, 1913–1921*, ed. E. David Cronon (Lincoln, Nebr., 1963), 180–87.

221. Hughes ignored racial issues in 1916: Nancy J. Weiss, "The New Negro and the New Freedom: Fighting Wilsonian Segregation," *Political Science Quarterly* 84, no. 1 (March 1969): 61–79; see also Wolgemuth, "Woodrow Wilson and Federal Segregation"; Scheiber and Scheiber, "Wilson Administration and the Wartime Mobilization of Black Americans."

222. Walton E. Bean, "George Creel and His Critics: A Study of the Attacks on the Committee on Public Information, 1917–1919" (Ph.D. diss., University of California at Berkeley, 1941), 19; Mark Sullivan, "George Creel—Censor," *Collier's* 60, no. 10 (November 1917): 12–13, 36; Creel had been a child labor reformer and a friend of Ben Lindsey in Denver, where he had become a local laughingstock trying to promote temperance among the police: George Creel, *A Rebel at Large* (New York, 1947), 148–56; S. D. Lovell, *The Presidential Election of 1916* (Carbondale, Ill., 1980), 179.

223. Arthur S. Link, ed., *The Papers of Woodrow Wilson* (Princeton, 1966–94) 5:111, 97–108; *New York Times*, Oct. 25, Nov. 2 and 5, 1916; Luebke, *Bonds of Loyalty*, 176–77.

224. Keller, *States of Belonging*, 110–12, 199; Doerries, *Imperial Challenge*, 199.

225. *New York World*, Oct. 10, 1916; House Diary, Oct. 20, 1916, in Link, ed., *Papers of Woodrow Wilson*, 5:174.

226. *New York Times*, Sept. 29, 1916; Link, ed., *Papers of Woodrow Wilson*, 5:176; David R. Woodward, "Great Britain and President Wilson's Efforts to End World War I in 1916," *Maryland Historian* 1, no. 1 (1970): 45–58; "lily-livered" in TR to KR, Mar. 1, 1917, MOR-REJ.

227. TR's train trip: Ned Lewis to Ma, Oct. 17, 18, 1916, Anecdotes File, TRP-BP.

228. Ned Lewis to Pa, Oct. 17, 18, and 21, 1916, Anecdotes File, TRP-BP; Link, ed.,

Papers of Woodrow Wilson, 5:108; TR, speech in Albuquerque, N. Mex., Oct. 24, 1916, TR Essays and Addresses, TRC-HU.

229. Ned Lewis to Ma, Oct. 25, 1916, Anecdotes File, TRP-BP. CRR, *My Brother*, used the same series of Lewis letters, but tells a different story of TR's tour; see 309–19.

230. Ned Lewis to Ma, Oct. 27, 1916, Anecdotes File, TRP-BP; TR to James Garfield, Sept. 28, and to George W. Perkins, Oct. 25, 1916, TRP-LC; Carl Wittke, *German-Americans and the World War* (Columbus, Ohio, 1936), 89; Lovell, *Presidential Election of 1916*, 147–53.

231. Ned Lewis to Ma, Oct. 25, 1916, Anecdotes File, TRP-BP; *New York Tribune*, Oct. 24–27, 1916; Frances Kellor organized the Hughes Women's Train; Molly M. Wood, "Mapping a National Campaign Strategy: Partisan Women in the Presidential Election of 1916," in Gustafson, Miller, and Perry, eds., *We Have Come to Stay*, 1999.

232. TR to Robert P. Bass, July 28, 1916, TRP-LC; Ned Lewis to Ma, Oct. 27, 1916, Anecdotes File, TRP-BP.

233. TR to William Russell Willcox, Aug. 21, 1916, MOR 8:1101; TR to Charles Evans Hughes, Oct. 26, 1908, MOR-REJ.

234. Christine A. Lunardini and Thomas J. Knock, "Woodrow Wilson and Woman Suffrage: A New Look," *Political Science Quarterly* 95 (Winter 1980–81): 655–57; MOR 8:1135, 1131, 1137–39; Ward, *First-Class Temperament*, 325*n*.26.

235. Sally Hunter Graham, "Woodrow Wilson, Alice Paul, and the Woman Suffrage Movement," *Political Science Quarterly* 98, no. 4 (Winter 1983–84); 665–79; Lunardini and Knock, "Wilson and Woman Suffrage," 655–57.

236. MacFarland and Neal, "Reluctant Reformer," 33–43; MOR 8:885; Link, *Wilson and the Progressive Era*, 229.

CHAPTER FOURTEEN: WHY IS ROOSEVELT UNJAILED?

1. *Literary Digest* 53 (Nov. 25, 1916): 1393; EKR-Di, Jan. 12, 1917, TRC-HU; MOR 8:1113–14.

2. MOR 8:1114.

3. William E. Leuchtenburg, *The Perils of Prosperity, 1914–32* (Chicago, 1958), 26.

4. TR to William Allen White, Feb. 17, 1917, TRC-HU; Edmund S. Burke to TR, Patriot's Day, 1917 in TR-World War I File—Potential Recruits for TR Proposed Division, SAHI; Major General J. A. Harbord, "The Story of the Roosevelt Division," *American Legion Monthly* 16, no. 4 (April 1934); remarks of Theodore Roosevelt at Circle for Negro War Relief meeting, Carnegie Hall, Nov. 2, 1918, TR-SP; Elliott M. Rudwick, *Race Riot at East St. Louis, July 2, 1917* (New York, 1966); Hamilton Fish, Sr., "Theodore Roosevelt and the Race Riots of 1917," *Theodore Roosevelt Association Journal* 1, no. 1 (Winter/Spring 1975).

5. Address to the country, Mar. 4, 1917, in Ray Stannard Baker and William E. Dodd, eds., *Public Papers of Woodrow Wilson* (New York, 1925), 4:433–35; Arthur S. Link, *Wilson: Campaigns for Progressivism and Peace, 1916–1917* (Princeton, 1965), 419–21, 342–62; Hoover in Edwin A. Weinstein, *Woodrow Wilson: A Medical and Psychological Biography* (Princeton, 1981), 312; TR judged the "willful men" to be traitors, but blamed the "helpless and contemptible" state of America on Wilson for failing to accept the inevitability of war with Germany: TR to John Callan O'Laughlin, Mar. 8, 1917, MOR 8:1161; *Letters of Louis D. Brandeis*, 4:274.

6. N. Gordon Levin, Jr., *Woodrow Wilson and World Politics: America's Response to War and Revolution* (New York, 1968), 43.

7. ARL, *Crowded Hours*, 246; *New York Times*, Apr. 11, 1917, clippings, Apr. 11, 1917, NSC; Creel, *Rebel at Large*, 188.

8. *New York Times*, Apr. 11, 1917; Tumulty, *Wilson As I Know Him*, 288; TR to Joseph Tumulty, Apr. 12, 1917, MOR-REJ; Seward W. Livermore, *Politics Is Adjourned: Woodrow Wilson and the War Congress, 1916–1918* (Middletown, Conn., 1966), 19; TR to Lydiard Horton, Apr. 25, 1917, Horton Papers, Columbia University.

9. TR also wanted many men of German descent: TR to E. A. Koehr, Apr. 10, 1917, MOR-REJ; Apr. 14, 1917, NSC.

10. TR to Arthur D. Hill, May 28, 1917, MOR-REJ.

11. Wynn, *Progressivism to Prosperity*, 177; Scheiber and Scheiber, "Wilson Administration and the Wartime Mobilization of Black Americans," 441; Fish, "Roosevelt and the Race Riots of 1917"; Hasia R. Diner, *In the Almost Promised Land: American Jews and Blacks, 1915–1935* (Westport, Conn, 1977), 134; on the division and draft politics see Livermore, *Politics Is Adjourned;* Major General Tasker H. Bliss memorandum for Adjutant General, Apr. 14, 1917, in Morris J. MacGregor and Bernard C. Nalty, *Blacks in the United States Armed Forces: Basic Documents* (Wilmington, Del., 1977), 4:6–7; TR to Hiram Johnson, May 24, 1917, MOR-REJ; Newton D. Baker to TR, Apr. 13, 1917, TRC-HU.

12. TR to Henry K. Warren, June 20, 1917, MOR-REJ; in 1918, Prime Minister David Lloyd George opened a secret communication with TR to encourage him to make a trip to inspire the war-weary British armies, but TR feared that he would be seen as a meddler: TR to Arthur Lee, Feb. 21, 1918, MOR-REJ; to TRJR, May 23, 1917, TRJR-LC; to BR, May 23, 1917, TRC-HU.

13. *New York Times*, June 8, 1917; TR speech to the American Medical Association, June 7, 1917, TR-SP.

14. TR to KR, June 8, 1917, KBR-LC; Ward, *First-Class Temperament*, 346; interviews with Louis Eisner, Frank Freidel, FDR; TR to Arthur Lee, Apr. 12, 1918, MOR-REJ.

15. TR to David Lloyd George, June 20, 1917, and KR to TR, June 11 and 19, 1917, TRC-HU.

16. ERD-Di, June 20, 1917, and EKR to KR, n.d. [June 18, 1917], and July 22, n.y. [1917], KBR-LC; TR to TRJR, Jan. 6, 1918, TRJR-LC; TR to KR, Jan. 7 and 14, 1918, KBR-LC.

17. *New York Times*, Aug. 19, 1917; John Carver Edwards, "Playing the Patriot Game: The Story of the American Defense Society, 1915–1932," *Studies in History and Society* 1, no. 1 (1976): 54–72; Shi, *Simple Life*, 212; TR, "A Message to All the Boy Scouts of America," *Boy Scout Yearbook*, 1915, 47.

18. The War Department censored telegrams and telephone calls; the Navy Department censored overseas cables; the post office censored letters; news from the front seems to have been censored by a combination of the Committee on Public Information, the War Department, and the Censorship Board; Creel censored movies: Vaughn, "First Amendment Liberties and the Committee on Public Information" 95–119, Scheiber, *Wilson Administration and Civil Liberties*, 7; Learned Hand of the Southern District of New York in the *Masses* case later restricted the scope of the Espionage Act.

19. Ray Stannard Baker, *Woodrow Wilson: Life and Letters, War Leader, April 6, 1917–February 28, 1918* (New York, 1939), 7:111; Sally Hunter Graham, "Wilson, Alice Paul, and the Woman Suffrage Movement," *Political Science Quarterly* 98, no. 4 (Winter 1983–84): 665–79; Mark Sullivan, "George Creel—Censor," *Collier's* 60, no. 10 (November 1917): 12–13, 36; N.A.W.S.A. had put Creel up to it according to Sara Hunter Graham, *Woman Suffrage and the New Democracy* (New Haven, 1996), 108–109.

20. TR to Marie Meloney, Jan. 15, 1917, Meloney Papers, Columbia University; Donald Johnson, "Wilson, Burleson, and Censorship in the First World War," *Journal of Southern History* 28 (1962): 46–58; Stanley Shapiro, "The Great War and Reform: Liberals and Labor, 1917–1919," *Labor History* 12 (1971): 323–44 (333).

21. TR to William M. Blair, Aug. 14, 1917, MOR-REJ; P. Keller, *States of Belonging,* 236; James Robert Mock, *Words That Won the War: The Story of the Committee on Public Information, 1917–1919* (Princeton, 1939), 115, 124.

22. *New York Times,* July 7, 1917.

23. Ibid.; Fish, "Roosevelt and the Race Riots of 1917"; Rudwick, *Race Riot,* 134–35; Diner, *In the Almost Promised Land,* 43, 48; Kellogg, *NAACP,* 227. At the same time, Wilson refused to meet with black representatives who called for anti-lynching legislation and declined to order a formal investigation of the riots. It took the President until July 1918 to speak out against mob violence.

24. Wilson's secretary of the navy, Josephus Daniels, summarized the cabinet's discussion of the Houston riots: "Race prejudice. Fight in Houston, Texas. Negro in uniform wants the whole sidewalk": Daniels, *Cabinet Diaries,* 195; Kellogg, *NAACP,* 262.

25. TR to EBAR, Aug. 23, 1917, TRJR-LC.

26. "bad go of fever" in ERD-Di, Aug. 17, 1917; on his health, EKR-Di, Aug. 17–23, 1917; EKR to KR, Aug. 12, n.y. [1917], KBR-LC; Sonya Levien, "The Great Friend," *Woman's Home Companion* 46, no. 10 (October 1919).

27. EKR-Di, August 1917; "irrevocable steps" in EKR to ARC, Jan. 29, 1918, TRC-HU; TR wrote: "I am depressed & concerned at all that has occurred" and he said that if "disaster comes" and Germany wins it will be America's fault: TR to BR, Dec. 10, 1917, TRC-HU; Ethel described TR as "terribly depressed": ERD-Di, Nov. 3, 1917; EKR to ARC, Jan. 29, 1918, TRC-HU.

28. RD to ERD, Dec. 18 and Sept. 2, 1917, TRC-HU; R.W.B. Lewis, *Edith Wharton,* 405; Wallace, *Sagamore Hill,* 114; "woebegone . . . boor" in TR to EBAR, Aug. 23, 1917, TRJR-LC.

29. This was his second flight; the first was with Arch Hoxsey in 1910: TR to TRJR, Sept. 13, 1917, TRJR-LC; clipping, Sept. 14, 1917, NSC; TR to EBAR, Sept. 17, 1917, TRJR-LC; TR, "Statement Declining Post on the Food Commission," Aug. 3, 1917, John J. Leary Papers, Houghton; *New York Times,* Apr. 23, 1917; Otis Graham, *Reform and War in America, 1900–1928* (Englewood Cliffs, N.J., 1971); Wynn, *Progressivism to Prosperity,* 36; clipping, May 9, 1917, NSC.

30. *New York Times,* Sept. 6, 1917; TR, speech, Sept. 5, 1917, Columbia County Fair, and speech, May 9, 1917, and speech to Railroad Brotherhoods, TR-SP; MOR 8:1237; TR to Dr. Edward Rumely, May 19, 1917, MOR-REJ.

31. TR, speech in Bridgeport, Nov. 3, 1917, TR-SP; TR, speech to the women, Nov. 20, 1917, TR-SP; Lewis Paul Todd, *Wartime Relations of the Federal Government and the Public Schools, 1917–1918* (New York, 1945), 68; see David M. Kennedy, *Over Here: The First World War and American Society* (New York, 1980), 58.

32. TR to QR, Sept. 1, 1917, MOR 8:1234; in 1915, New York's suffrage campaign was guilty of nativism, but by the 1917 campaign the organizers had changed their approach and Lillian Wald's well-canvassed immigrant precincts voted much more heavily for suffrage than they had in 1915: Doris Daniels, "Building a Winning Coalition: The Suffrage Fight in New York State," *New York History* 60, no. 1 (January 1979): 59–80; Mary Garrett Hay put the wives of local Tammany bosses on the local suffrage boards, and the Woman's Suffrage Party's winning coalition included Socialist Party members and the Women's Trade Union League: Sara H. Graham, *Woman Suffrage,* 112–13; *New York Times,* Nov. 21, 1917; John D. Buenker, "The Urban Political Machine and Woman Suffrage: A Study in Political Adaptability," *Historian* 33 (1971): 264–79.

33. TR, speech to the women, Nov. 20, 1917, TR-SP; he had initially opposed his daughter-in-law Eleanor's service in France with the Y.M.C.A. but he changed his mind when she set up rest areas for soldiers. She also provided his sons with medical care and a

home away from home in Paris; *New York Times*, Apr. 28, 1917; June Sochen, *Movers and Shakers: American Women Thinkers and Activists, 1900–1970* (New York, 1973), 160.

34. TR, "Why We Are at War," Sept. 24, 1917, TR-SP; TR to TRJR, Sept. 1, 1917, TRJR-LC.

35. *New York Times*, May 24, 1918; *Letters of Louis D. Brandeis*, 4: 314; *New York Times*, Sept. 21, 22, and 25, 1917.

36. *New York Times*, Apr. 25, 1918; reminiscence of Guernsey Curran, "A Subscription for the Oyster Bay Quota for the Red Cross Drive," TRC-HU.

37. TR, "The Huns Within Our Gates," speech in Racine, Wisc., Sept. 27, 1917, TR-SP; *New York Times*, Oct. 30, 1917.

38. Apr. 21, 1917, clippings, NSC; *New York Times*, Apr. 22, 1917; TR to Charles G. Washburn, July 2, 1917, MOR-REJ.

39. David C. Stephenson, "Roosevelt's Unfinished Program," *McClure's* 57, no. 2 (June 1924).

40. "tripe" in Norbert Wiener, *Ex Prodigy: My Childhood and Youth* (New York, 1953), 266–67. Leonard Wood called for turning up the heat on the assimilation melting pot during the war: David Glassberg, *American Historical Pageantry: The Uses of Tradition in the Early Twentieth Century* (Chapel Hill, N.C., 1990), 222. For immigrant support for Americanization see Hagedorn, *Hyphenated Family;* P. Keller, *States of Belonging;* TR, speech in Bridgeport, Nov. 3, 1917, TR-SP; Paul McBride, "Peter Roberts and the YMCA Americanization Program, 1907–World War I," *Pennsylvania History* 44 (1977): 145–62; James R. Barrett, "Americanization from the Bottom Up: Immigration and the Remaking of the Working Class in the United States, 1880–1930," *Journal of American History* 79, no. 3 (December 1992): 996–1020; David Montgomery, "Nationalism, American Patriotism, and Class Consciousness Among Immigrant Workers in the United States in the Epoch of World War I," in Dirk Hoerder, ed., *"Struggle a Hard Battle": Essays on Working-Class Immigrants* (De Kalb, Ill., 1986), 327–51; Sean Wilentz, "Against Exceptionalism: Class Consciousness and the American Labor Movement, 1790–1920," *International Labor and Working-Class History* 26 (Fall 1984): 1–24; David Montgomery, "Labor and the Republic in Industrial America: 1860–1920," *Le Mouvement sociale* 110 (1980): 211–15; Eric Hobsbawm and Terence Ranger, eds., *The Invention of Tradition* (New York, 1983).

41. *New York Times*, Nov. 3, 1917; clippings in ERD to RD, Mar. 27, 1918, TRC-HU.

42. John H. Lindquist and James Fraser, "A Sociological Interpretation of the Bisbee Deportation," *Pacific Historical Review* 37 (1968): 401–22; James W. Byrkit, *Forging the Copper Collar: Arizona's Labor Management War of 1901–1921* (Tucson, 1982); Robert L. Tyler, *Rebels of the Woods: The I.W.W. in the Pacific Northwest* (Eugene, Oreg., 1967); the Phelps-Dodge Company was eventually charged with kidnapping but found not guilty; Greenway went to war, became a millionaire, and married Bob Ferguson's widow; TR to Felix Frankfurter, Dec. 19, 1917, MOR 8:1262, 1265; Michael R. Johnson, "The IWW and Wilsonian Democracy," *Science and Society* 28, no. 3 (1964): 258–74; Philip Taft, "The Federal Trials of the IWW," *Labor History* 3 (1962): 57–91; Philip Taft, "The Bisbee Deportation," *Labor History* 13 (1972): 3–40; TR to John Greenway, July 23 and 11, 1917, JIG-ARIZ; Gunther, *Learned Hand*, 355; more patriotic repression followed. Despite credible evidence they had committed no crime, Wilson ordered the arrest of 184 I.W.W. members for conspiracy to commit sabotage against the war and to obstruct the draft.

43. TR's speech in Forest Hills, N.Y., TR-SP; *New York Times*, July 7, 1917.

44. Scheiber and Scheiber, "Wilson Administration and the Wartime Mobilization of Black Americans," 445–50; *New York Times*, Nov. 19, 1917; EKR to KR, Nov. 20, n.y. [1917], KBR-LC.

45. TR to William Temple Hornaday, Nov. 25, 1917, TRC-HU; TR to Captain Hans,

Freeport Police Force, May 15, 1915, MOR-REJ; *New York Times*, May 29 and Aug. 31, 1917. Newton D. Baker ignored TR and consulted civil libertarian Roger Baldwin, who suggested nonpunitive treatment, conscientious objector cantonments, and employment on the home front. The Wilson administration finally permitted the hazing and jailing of a great many C.O.s and had Baldwin's National Civil Liberties Bureau investigated by Military Intelligence; the starving and beating of C.O.s resulted from local camp commanders ignoring Baker's orders. At Camp Grant, C.O.s were given a bread-and-water diet and treated like prisoners of war. Wilson finally granted C.O.s the right to choose noncombatant service but the army court-martialed many of them anyway; see Donald D. Johnson, *The Challenge to American Freedoms: World War I and the Rise of the American Civil Liberties Union* (Lexington, Ky., 1963), 26–47.

46. *TR/HCL*, 2:544; TR to HCL, Nov. 22, 1918, HCL-MHS; TR expected his letters not only to be censored for sensitive war information, but to be confiscated for political reasons, too: TR to ABR, Jan. 20, 1918, TRC-HU. The Roosevelts sometimes wrote about politics to loved ones at the front in a kind of code. Ethel, when she wanted to tell Dick about what Lord Lee had told her father about British strategy, referred to Lee as Richard's godmother's husband. When Wilson allowed local officials to arrest and imprison suffragists picketing peacefully outside the White House, TR wrote to suffrage leader Abby Scott Baker that he was astounded by "the absurdity of arresting you for carrying banners containing only statements which are quoted from Pres. Wilson's own speeches": July 31, 1917, MOR-REJ; H. C. Peterson and Gilbert C. Fite, *Opponents of War, 1917–1918* (Madison, Wisc., 1957), 19; Andrew, *For the President's Eyes Only*, 54–55; *New York Times*, Nov. 21, 1917; on Malone see Sally H. Graham, "Wilson, Alice Paul, and the Woman Suffrage Movement," 665–79. The National Security League was given franking privileges by the C.P.I. and invited by the New York City Board of Education to run weekly meetings to instruct public school teachers in loyalty. Teachers were fired for opposing the war. John Carver Edwards, "Princeton's Passionate Patriot: McElroy's Committee on Patriotism Through Education," *New Jersey History* 95 (1977): 207–26 (213).

47. TR, "Foes of Our Own Household," MEM 21:7.

48. Ibid., 12, 3, 7, 11. TR encouraged the N.A.A.C.P.'s James Weldon Johnson to go on a fact-finding trip to Haiti, where 3,000 had died under Wilsonian rule: Johnson, *Along This Way*, 357–60.

49. Josephus Daniels, *Cabinet Diaries*, 216; Baker, *Wilson: Life and Letters*, 7:423–24.

50. TR to KR, Nov. 9, 1917, KBR-LC.

51. TR to KR, Feb. 28, 1918, MOR-REJ; Wilson, address of June 14, 1917, *Congressional Record* (65th Cong., 1st Sess.), 55: Appendix, 334; the documents were fakes: George F. Kennan, "The Sisson Documents," *Journal of Modern History* 28 (June 1956): 130–54.

52. Degen, *History of the Woman's Peace Party*, 198–200, 215, 201; Jane Addams, *Peace and Bread in Time of War* (New York, 1972), 128.

53. *New York Times*, Sept. 6, 1917.

54. HCL to TR, Dec. 18, 1917, HCL-MHS; TR, "Broomstick Preparedness—A Study in Cause and Effect," Dec. 27, 1917, in *Roosevelt in the Kansas City Star*, ed. Ralph Stout (Boston, 1921), 76–77; see Ricard, "Anti-Wilsonian Internationalism," in Rossini, ed., *From Theodore Roosevelt to FDR*, 25–44.

55. Bourne, a Bull Mooser, had been an insurgent senator opposed to Taft. The Republican Publicity Association advanced TR's wing of the party; see Arthur H. Bone, ed., *Oregon Cattleman, Governor, Congressman: Memoirs and Times of Walter M. Pierce* (Portland, Oreg., 1981), 296; Leonard Schlup, "Republican Insurgent: Jonathan Bourne and the Politics of Progressivism, 1908–1912," *Oregon Historical Quarterly* 87, no. 3 (1986): 229–44; TR, *Roosevelt in the Kansas City Star*, 92; TR had based his claim about coffins on Archie's letters, which

proved to be inaccurate: TR to ABR, Feb. 2, and ERD to RD, Mar. 6 and Dec. 6, 1918, TRC-HU; *New York Times,* Jan. 20, 1918.

56. TR, "The Huns Within Our Gates," speech in Racine, Sept. 27, 1917, TR-SP; O. A. Hilton, "Freedom of the Press in Wartime, 1917–19," *Southwestern Social Science Quarterly* 28 (1948): 348–49.

57. Daniels, *Cabinet Diaries,* 272; August Heckscher, *Woodrow Wilson* (New York, 1991), 456; TR to KR, Sept. 28, 1917, MOR-REJ.

58. Clipping in EKR to KR, Nov. 10, 1917, KBR-LC; Gifford Pinchot tried to talk TR out of his vitriolic attacks against the Non-Partisan League, a farmers' group with many reform views Pinchot and Roosevelt shared, but Roosevelt took newspaper attacks on the N.P.L.'s disloyalty seriously and lumped the group with his old rival La Follette—traitors who played the German game: Pinchot to TR, Oct. 16, 1918, MOR-REJ. Swept along with legions of ordinarily moderate people in the wave of war enthusiasm (William Howard Taft told preparedness rallies that traitors should be "given the short shrift of a firing squad"), TR was hardly alone in his blindness to the excesses of this historic moment. Assistant Attorney General Charles Warren proposed a "court martial bill" which would have made any person obstructing the war effort subject to military justice and the death penalty: Harry Scheiber, *The Wilson Administration and Civil Liberties: 1917–1921* (Ithaca, N.Y., 1960), 49–50.

59. TR to George E. Miller, Dec. 23, 1918, MOR-REJ; *Pearson's* 39, no. 6 (October 1918); TR to Dr. Manning, July 3, 1918, and TR to Alfred Holman, Apr. [23?], 1918, MOR-REJ; Senator Overman said that the amendments had prohibited criticism of the President, but the final bill did not: *New York Times,* Apr. 8, 1918; TR believed the bill was unconstitutional: "Citizens or Subjects," Apr. 6, 1918, in *Roosevelt in the Kansas City Star,* 129–32. The Sedition Act banned "uttering, printing, writing, or publishing any disloyal, profane, scurrilous, or abusive language intended to cause contempt, scorn, contumely or disrepute" for the government and the military or opposing the U.S. in the war: H. Scheiber, *Wilson Administration and Civil Liberties,* 24. The Justice Department Volunteer Union League Club patriots raided the offices of the National Civil Liberties Bureau on Aug. 31, 1918: D. Johnson, *Challenge to American Freedoms,* 75, 70. Hiram Johnson and TR were acting in concert against the sedition bill: *New York Times,* Apr. 25, 1918; A. Lincoln, "My Dear Friend and Champion: Letters Between Theodore Roosevelt and Hiram Johnson in 1918," *California Historical Society Quarterly* 48, no. 1 (1969): 19–36 (27).

60. TR, "Citizens or Subjects," Apr. 6, 1918, in *Roosevelt in the Kansas City Star,* 129–32, 137; see Ricard, "Anti-Wilsonian Internationalism," 25–44; Peterson and Fite, *Opponents of War,* 100; MOR 8:1323; TR to Hiram Johnson, Apr. 23, 1918, MOR-REJ.

61. "Mr. Burleson to Rule the Press," *Literary Digest* 55 (Oct. 6, 1917): 12; MOR 8:1320–35; see also TR, "Lincoln and Free Speech," originally titled "Patriotism, Sedition, and Servility," galley proofs, TRC-HU.

62. TR fought back by citing cases where the administration had censored and bullied its critics to silence: the March issue of the anti-administration but pro-war *Metropolitan* had been declared unmailable; the Justice Department had tracked down one of the magazine's advertisers and grilled him about his loyalty.

63. TR to Miles Poindexter, May 12, 1918, MOR 8:1320–35; *New York Times,* May 11, 1918; "Why Is Roosevelt Unjailed?" *The Nation* 107, no. 2784 (November 1918); D. Johnson, *Challenge to American Freedoms,* 200–201. TR was no civil libertarian: he turned over to the Department of Justice for prosecution sedition letters written to him by critics of the U.S. government and the Allies: TR to Department of Justice, Aug. 21, 1918, MOR-REJ; "Mr. Hearst's Loyalty," *Literary Digest,* May 25, 1918, 12–13.

64. TR to Poindexter, May 12, 1918, MOR 8:1320–35; Hays, *Memoirs,* 161–62.

65. TR to TRJR, June 1, 1918, TRJR-LC; TR to ABR, Jan. 20, 1918, TRC-HU.

66. EKR to KR, Oct. 10, n.y. [1917], KBR-LC. TR told John J. Leary he had had arteriosclerosis since he was forty: Leary, *Talks with T.R.*, 20; Ethel Armes, "Fine Day! How are you?" Anecdotes File, and Armes, "TR at Jack Cooper's," TRP-BP; EKR to ERD, Oct. 12, and to QR, Oct. 14, 1917, TRC-HU; EKR to KR, Oct. 27, n.y. [1917], KBR-LC.

67. TR to TRJR, Nov. 29, 1917, TRJR-LC; ARL, *Crowded Hours*, 261; Matthew J. Glover, "What Might Have Been: Theodore Roosevelt's Platform for 1920," in Naylor, Brinkley, and Gable, eds., *Theodore Roosevelt: Many-Sided American.*

68. EKR to KR, Dec. 15, n.y. [1917], KBR-LC; TR to QR, Nov. 28, 1917, MOR-REJ; *New York Times*, Feb. 4, 1918; CRR, *My Brother*, 332.

69. Ray H. Abrams, *Preachers Present Arms* (New York, 1933), 169; Penn Borden, *Civilian Indoctrination of the Military: World War I and Future Implications for the Military-Industrial Complex* (New York, 1989), 66; Newton D. Baker, "Invisible Armor," *Playground* 11 (1918): 473–81.

70. TR, speech at the National Security League luncheon, Hotel Astor, New York City, Jan. 19, 1918, TR-SP, TRC-HU; American Defense Society pamphlet, *Don't Take a Chance*, MOR-REJ; Nancy K. Bristow, *Making Men Moral: Social Engineering During the Great War* (New York, 1996), 206; Allen F. Davis, "Welfare, Reform and World War I," *American Quarterly* 19 (1967): 516–33; TR to Bishop Sumner, May 5, 1917, MOR-REJ; TR did say, however, that in wartime "patriotism is an even higher obligation than progressivism": TR to Earnest E. Smith, Aug. 31, 1917, MOR-REJ.

71. Even Democrats like Wilson and Joseph Tumulty, who took an interest in the British Labour Party platform, stood to the right of TR on domestic reform in 1918; see John Morton Blum, *Joe Tumulty and the Wilson Era* (New York, 1969), 146–51; Charles Hirschfeld, "Nationalist Progressivism and World War I," *Mid-America* 45, no. 3 (July 1963): 139–56. Thorstein Veblen, like TR a critic of the Gilded Age nouveaux riches, likewise imagined that "invidious distinctions of class, sex, wealth and privilege" might disappear when the country pulled together against a common enemy: David B. Danbom, " 'For the Record of the War': Thorstein Veblen, Wartime Exigency, and Social Change," *Mid-America* 62 (1980): 91–95; TR also reiterated his commitment to the Social Gospel and to "the great law of service" during the war. In a plea for people to come back to the churches, "Shall We Do Away with the Church?" *Ladies' Home Journal*, October 1917, 12, 119, TR wrote: "Unless it is the poor man's church it is not a Christian church at all in any real sense."

72. ERD to RD, Dec. 14, 1917, TRC-HU.

73. Melvyn Dubofsky, "Organized Labor in New York City and the First World War, 1914–1918," *New York History* 42 (1961): 388.

74. MOR 8:1000, 1143, 1144, 1147; TR, text of speech in Des Moines, Iowa, Feb. 11, 1918, not given on account of sickness, TR-SP; Roosevelt spoke out for the appointment of women to the National War Labor Board to improve its awareness of problems women workers faced. Taft told TR that no legal power existed to change the membership: Valerie J. Conner, "The Mothers of the Race in World War I: The National War Labor Board and Women in Industry," *Labor History* 21 (1980): 31–54 (41); *New York Times*, Apr. 22, 1917.

75. Whitehouse was an advocate of white suffragists working for the vote for black women: Sara H. Graham, *Woman Suffrage*, 102; Cott, *Groundings of Modern Feminism*, 295; Barbara J. Steinson, *American Women's Activism in World War I* (New York, 1982), 301.

76. See, for example, TR to Frank B. Kellogg, Apr. 26, 1918, MOR-REJ; Wilson vetoed the Eighteenth Amendment; Leary, *Talks with T.R.*, 291–95. TR's Sunday closing campaign and his moral rhetoric won him support among many New York Prohibitionists; in at least one 1912 speech he declared support for local prohibition. TR shared the common Prohibitionist belief that the saloon power was aligned with corrupt Democratic bosses, but he dis-

liked the Prohibition movement even though many Prohibitionists believed him to be an ally: Ferdinand C. Iglehart, *King Alcohol Dethroned* (New York, 1917); TR to Joel Borton, July 25, 1914, MOR-REJ.

77. *New York Times*, Jan. 17 and 18, 1918, and Aug. 15, 1951.

78. ARL, *Crowded Hours*, 269, 264; MOR 8:1131.

79. TRJR to TR, Dec. 24, 1917, and n.d. [December 1917], TRJR-LC; TR to George Roosevelt, Jan. 7, 1918, MOR-REJ; TR to KR, Dec. 2, 1917, KBR-LC; B. B. Buck to TR, Dec. 25, 1917, TRJR-LC; TR asked his sons not to refuse staff positions if military necessity required it: TR to ABR, Jan. 20, 1918, TRC-HU.

80. EKR to KR, Jan. 6, n.y. [1918], KR-LC; Archie remembered that they all enlisted to please their father: Henry Berry, *Make the Kaiser Dance* (Garden City, N.Y., 1978), 135; TR to KR, Jan. 1, 1918, KBR-LC; Edith tried to look the other way as her husband pushed his sons toward danger. She believed fighting for their country was the right thing to do, but rather than think too long about what they faced in the trenches, she preferred to be "dazed with emotion" when she heard eighteen-year-old Jascha Heifetz play the violin and Enrico Caruso sing: EKR to KR, Jan. 13, n.y. [1918], KR-LC.

81. TR to KR, Jan. 27, 1918, KBR-LC; "weak link" and "too absurd" in ERD to RD, Jan. 19, 1918, TRC-HU; ERD to RD, Feb. 2, 1918, TRC-HU.

82. TR to KR, Jan. 20, 1918, KBR-LC.

83. On TR's medical condition see EKR-Di, Feb. 2–12, 1918, EKR to ARC, n.d. [winter 1918], and Walton Martin to RD, Feb. 16, 1918; TRC-HU; John J. Leary, "The Colonel's Close Call," February 1918, SUBJ-TRC.

84. Josephine Stricker, "Roosevelt at Close Range," *The Delineator*, September 1919, 31; Leary, "The Colonel's Close Call"; RD to RDJR, Feb. 6, 1918, TRC-HU; *New York Times*, Feb. 7, 1918.

85. "terribly white" and "hazy" in ERD to RD, Feb. 6, 1918, TRC-HU.

86. Leary, "The Colonel's Close Call"; EKR-Di, February–March 1918; ERD to RD, Feb. 7, and Walton Martin to RD, Feb. 16, 1918, TRC-HU; *New York Times*, Feb. 9–11, 1918.

87. EKR-Di, Feb. 8, 1918, Leary, "The Colonel's Close Call."

88. TR to ABR, Feb. 8, 1918, TRC-HU.

89. EKR to KR, Feb. 5, 1918, KBR-LC; TR to Bob Perkins, July 22, 1918, TRJR-LC.

90. TR to Will H. Hays, May 15, 1918, MOR-REJ; " 'After the War' Reconstruction in Great Britain—Some Radical Proposals," *Outlook* (Feb. 27, 1918). Though *The Outlook* took a Y.M.C.A. view of many social issues it favored an expansion of the federal government's role in guaranteeing the public's well-being. TR believed in public control (though not necessarily ownership) of mines, forests, and rivers: Saght of the *World*, Jennings of the *Herald*, Leonard Smith of the *Times*, and Cronyn of the *Sun*, in Leary, "The Colonel's Close Call." He already had the ear of Ogden and Helen Reid, who owned the *New York Tribune*; *New York Times*, Feb. 17, 1918.

91. TR to Meyer Lissner, Mar. 26, 1918, MOR-REJ; he was most critical of the sections that called for immediate nationalization of railways, mines, and the production of electricity: TR to Lissner, Apr. 19, 1918, MOR-REJ; Paul U. Kellogg and Arthur Gleason, *British Labor and the War* (New York, 1919). The new National Party and Socialists expressed their enthusiasm about the British Labour Party platform, and even Woodrow Wilson was reading it.

92. Hays, *Memoirs*, 154–55; *New York Times*, Feb. 27, 1918; TR to John T. King, Feb. 28, 1918, MOR-REJ.

93. *New York Times*, Mar. 8, 1918; EKR to KR, Mar. 10, n.y. [1918], KR-LC; TR also talked with Mary Roberts Rinehart of going on a trip to Mexico: Rinehart, *My Story* (New York, 1931), 242–43.

94. TRJR to TR, Apr. 23, 1918, TRJR-LC; Ted and Archie had been living in trenches full of snow when news came that their Long Island neighbor aviator Tommy Hitchcock had been captured by the Germans; TR and Edith knew that fate could strike even closer to home at any moment. General Peyton March came back from the front denouncing the administration's refusal to let reporters send home detailed war news. Ethel thought Wilson's censorship of war news was "too terribly cruel" because no one at Sagamore Hill could find out whether members of their family were involved in the heavy fighting reported: ERD to RD, Feb. 2, 1918, TRC-HU.

95. EKR to Mrs. Willard, Apr. 9, n.y. [1918], KBR-LC; EKR to KR, Mar. 17, 24, and 31, n.y. [1918], KBR-LC; TRJR to TR, n.d. [March 1918], TRJR-LC; *New York Times*, Mar. 14 and 16, 1918; RD to ERD, Mar. 12, 1918; RD Diary, Mar. 12, 1918, TRC-HU.

96. TR to QR, Dec. 24, 1917, MOR 8:1266; TR to Ted, Mar. 14, 1918, TRJR-LC; TR to ABR, Mar. 3, 1918, and ERD to RD, Mar. 13, 1918, TRC-HU.

97. *New York Times*, Mar. 16, 1918; TR to TRJR, Mar. 18, 1918, TRJR-LC; TRJR to TR, n.d. [March 1918], TRJR-LC.

98. *New York Times*, Mar. 29, 1918; W. B. Fowler, *British-American Relations 1917–1918: The Role of Sir William Wiseman* (Princeton, 1969), 142.

99. The story came from Guy Emerson: ERD to RD, Mar. 27, 1918, TRC-HU; Wallace, *Sagamore Hill*, 1:101.

100. TR to ABR, Mar. 31, 1918, and EKR to ARC, Mar. 18, 1918, TRC-HU; *New York Times*, Mar. 27, 1918; TR to William Allen White, Apr. 2, 1918, MOR-REJ.

101. HCL to TR, Mar. 5, 1918, HCL-MHS; TR replied that the inheritance tax proposal might be complicated enough to be better discussed elsewhere: TR to HCL, Mar. 8, 1918, HCL-MHS; MOR 8:1294*n*.2; TR to TRJR, Mar. 31, 1918, TRJR-LC; TR to Meyer Lissner, Mar. 26, 1918, MOR-REJ.

102. "Start of the Political Drive," *Literary Digest* 57 (Apr. 13, 1918): 14–15. The Senate was already holding hearings to consider outlawing the German-American Alliance; see U.S. Senate, Subcommittee of the Committee on the Judiciary, "National German-American Alliance," Hearings on Senate Bill 3529, 65th Cong., 2nd Sess., Feb. 23–Apr. 13, 1918. The charter was repealed in July 1918; see Austin J. App, "The Germans," in Joseph P. O'Grady, *The Immigrants' Influence on Wilson's Peace Policies* (Lexington, Ky., 1967), 34; the National Education Association got Congress to pass the Smith-Towner Act, which cut off federal funds to states unless they required that private and public schools teach in English: Luebke, *Bonds of Loyalty*, 312.

103. TR to TRJR, Mar. 24, 1918, TRJR-LC; *Roosevelt in the Kansas City Star*, 131; EKR-Di, Apr. 8, 1918; *New York Times*, Mar. 30, 1918; *The Stars and Stripes*, Apr. 5, 1918.

104. EKR-Di, Mar. 19, 1918; EKR to QR, Mar. 22, 23, and 31, 1918, TR to ABR, Mar. 31, 1918, and ERD to RD, Mar. 27, 1918, TRC-HU; Editor, "Social Justice and Social-ism," *North American Review* 196 (July 1917): 1–8; TR, "A Visit to the East Side," *Metropolitan*, April 1918, *Metropolitan* Scrapbook, TRC-HU; H. J. Whigham decided to publish TR's more radical views after he died; TR to Henry A. Wise Wood, July 3, 1918, MOR-REJ; MOR 8:1312; on the *Kansas City Star*'s refusal to print some of his harsher attacks on Wilson see ERD to RD, Apr. 22, 1918, TRC-HU.

105. EKR to KR, Apr. 21, n.y. [1918], KBR-LC; EKR to QR, Apr. 28, 1918, TRC-HU.

106. TR to KR, Apr. 21, 1918, KBR-LC.

107. TR to Stanwood Menken, Jan. 10, 1916, MOR 8:1143. TR still favored the expulsion of Robert M. La Follette from the Senate; see MOR 8:1307. Peterson and Fite, *Opponents of War*, 212; Meirion Harries and Susie Harries, *The Last Days of Innocence: America at War, 1917–1918* (New York, 1997), 296.

108. TR to Viscount K. Kanekō, Aug. 21, 1918, MOR-REJ; TR to TRJR and EBAR,

Sept. 9, 1918, TRJR-LC; in 1918 alone TR received an average of 4,000 to 5,000 letters a week, most of them from admirers: Lewis L. Gould, "The Price of Fame: Theodore Roosevelt as a Celebrity, 1909–1919," *Lamar Journal of the Humanities* 10 (Fall 1984):11.

109. *New York Times*, June 12, 1918; the *Times* reported U-boats sank barges off Orleans on Cape Cod and Gloucester fishing boats: July 22 and 24, 1918; more enemy aliens were interned as a result of the U-boat attacks; " 'U'-Boats Reduced to War on Our Coasting Smacks," *Literary Digest* 57 (June 15, 1918): 7–8; TR to Bishop Sumner, June 1, 1918, MOR-REJ.

110. TR to ABR, Apr. 14 and 28, 1918, TRC-HU; EKR-Di, April–June 1918; when Margaret Robins lunched with the Roosevelts she said she believed Russia was not out of the war for good: ERD-Di, Apr. 15, 1918; "weary" in Sonya Levien statement, SUBJ-TRC; Amos in EKR to KR, June 2, n.y. [1918], KBR-LC.

111. For a long but incomplete list of guests see Sagamore Hill Guest Book, SAHI, and my talk "Famous Visitors to Sagamore Hill," SAHI, May 27, 2001: guests included Eleanor and Franklin Roosevelt, Edna Ferber, Mark Twain, John L. Sullivan, Alice Paul, Taft, Wilson, La Follette, Admiral Togo, Maria Bochkareva, Riis, Stimson, Charles McKim, Cecilia Beaux, Edith Wharton, Will Hays, James M. Barrie, John Burroughs, Frederic Remington, Owen Wister, Thomas Edison, Harvey Firestone, John Muir, and John Burroughs. TR left for a midwestern speaking tour for the Committee on Patriotism Through Education of the National Security League: ERD to RD, May 17, 1918, TRC-HU; TR to CRR, July 3, 1918, MOR-REJ; TR to Grace Lockwood Roosevelt, June 19, 1918, TRC-HU; Christopher Lasch, *The American Liberals and the Russian Revolution* (New York, 1972), 97–126; TR evidently told Oscar Straus later that year that the Russian civil war was "not our business": Straus, *Under Four Administrations*, 392; Emily S. Rosenberg, *Spreading the American Dream: American Economic and Cultural Expansion, 1890–1945* (New York, 1989), 78.

112. TR to EBAR, June 20 and 28, n.y. [1918], TRJR-LC.

113. *New York Times*, July 4 and 5, 1918; QR to TR, July 4, 1918, TRP-SAHI; TR believed that an American Jew who became a citizen of Palestine could no longer be an American citizen as well: MOR 8:1372; Wilson supported the Balfour Declaration in public in September 1918, and earlier through diplomatic channels, Fowler, *Sir William Wiseman*, 94.

114. *New York Times*, July 7, 11, and 18, 1918; Sir William Napier, *English Battles and Sieges in the Peninsula* (London, 1990); TR reprimanded Ted for writing only to him during the war and asked that he write only to his mother from then on: July 12, 1918, TRJR-LC; Parsons, *Perchance*, 174; EKR-Di, July 1918; Philip Thompson, "Roosevelt and His Boys," *McClure's* 50 (November 1918): 10–12; ERD to RD, and RD to ERD, July 17, 1918, TRC-HU; Frank Freidel, *Over There: The Story of America's First Great Overseas Crusade* (Philadelphia, 1990), 139–40; ERD-Di inside panel of diary 1921–26; President Wilson cabled condolences.

115. *New York Times*, July 19, 1918; the Saratoga convention endorsed the federal suffrage amendment.

116. Quotations from CRR, *My Brother*, 344–46; political speculation about a "Roosevelt vs. Roosevelt" governor's race in November recalled talk of TR and FDR running against each other for the Senate in 1914, but the press admitted that after his recent fight against Tammany FDR was unlikely to be nominated: *New York Times*, July 21, 1918; TR to TRJR and EBAR, July 29, 1918, TRJR-LC; Hermann Hagedorn said at Saratoga that TR had agreed to run for governor, but that Edith talked him out of it when he got home: Notes on RMA Meeting, SUBJ-TRC.

117. TR to ABR, July 21, 1918, ABR, Memoirs, TRC-HU; EKR-Di; TR wrote Lady Gregory that their sons had died because of the President's slowness in war preparation: Sept. 11, 1918, MOR-REJ; Flora Whitney, the Cortelyous, Bob Perkins, WSC, Jr., and George

Perkins were there; "terribly hard" in ERD to RD, July 21, 1918, TRC-HU; RD to ERD, July 21, 1918, TRC-HU, ERD-Di, July 18, 1918.

118. ERD to RD, July 22, 1918, TRC-HU; TR to President of Allegheny College, William B. Crawford, July 24, 1918, MOR-REJ.

119. MOR 8:1355.

120. MOR 8:1357; TR to ERD, Aug. 13, 1918, TRC-HU; TR to KR, July 28, 1918, KBR-LC; TR to TRJR and EBAR, Aug. 4, 1918, TRJR-LC.

121. EKR to KR, Aug. 11, n.y. [1918], KBR-LC; TR to TRJR and EBAR, Aug. 15, 1918, TRJR-LC; TR letter quoted in Andrew Carroll, *War Letters: Extraordinary Correspondence from American Wars* (New York, 2001), 146; TR to Edith Wharton, Aug. 15, 1918, MOR-REJ.

122. EKR to KR, Aug. 18, n.y. [1918], KBR-LC; TR to KR, Aug. 22, 1918, MOR-REJ; TR to TRJR and EBAR, Aug. 15 and 21, 1918, TRJR-LC.

123. TR to TRJR and EBAR, Aug. 29 and Sept. 13, 1918, TRJR-LC. He would also get names of people he knew well mixed up; see, e.g., MOR 8:1407.

124. MOR 8:1378; Hays, *Memoirs*, 172; Tammany's Al Smith attacked TR for saying at Saratoga that the War Department was inefficient and recalled that TR had said in 1898 it was dangerous to turn out of office the incumbent party in wartime.

125. TR to Mrs. Sadie Kost, Oct. 30, 1918, MOR-REJ; *New York Times*, Nov. 3, 1918; Mor 8:1366; TR supported pro-war conservative Albert Fall for senator in New Mexico and anti–Non-Partisan League Republicans in South Dakota.

126. Hays, *Memoirs*, 170; *New York Times*, Oct. 29, 1918; Roosevelt considered Senator Weeks so reactionary that when postwar reconstruction came "he will be a good deal like an Egyptian mummy." New alliances were forming out of the war, and Weeks, who had opposed suffrage, Louis Brandeis' nomination to the Supreme Court, and taxing excess profits, had been targeted for defeat by Bay State suffrage forces allied with Jews, labor, and progressive reformers who shared many of TR's domestic views. But again TR held his nose and endorsed Weeks for being a critic of Wilson's conduct of the war. Weeks lost anyway.

127. TR to Taft, Aug. 26, and to KR, Sept. 26, 1918, MOR-REJ, but he also counseled Albert J. Beveridge, "We are willing to experiment with it": Oct. 16, 1918, MOR-REJ; TR to George Haven Putnam, Nov. 15, 1918, SUBJ-TRC; TR described his source as "a prominent German-Jew banker": TR to BR and KR, Oct. 20, 1918, KBR-LC.

128. TR, "Colonel Roosevelt's Address at Lafayette Day Exercises Aldermanic Chambers, New York, Sept. 6, 1918," TR-SP; *New York Times*, Sept. 7 and Oct. 13, 1918.

129. "evil-natured" in TR to George Roosevelt, Jan. 7, 1918, MOR-REJ; avoiding the war in Caroline Drayton Phillips, Journal, July 12, 1916, Caroline Drayton Phillips Papers, Schlesinger Library; TR had predicted World War I in 1911 according to Tyler Dennett, "Could T.R. Have Stopped the War?" *The World's Work*, February 1925, 392–99.

130. Owen Wister to EKR, Oct. 25, 1918, TRC-HU; Rinehart, *My Story*, 242–43; *Roosevelt in the Kansas City Star*, 223.

131. Lorin Lee Cary, "The Wisconsin Loyalty Legion, 1917–1918," *Wisconsin Magazine of History* 53 (1969): 33–50; King, who had lined up Colonel William Boyce Thompson, Otto Kahn, Julius Kahn, and other major donors to finance TR's 1920 run, got Thompson to lay out $300,000 to fund the Republican congressional races in 1918. Thompson had spent large sums of his own money to stabilize the Russian Kerensky government. Hays recorded in his diary one day in his eager search to put together a coalition to beat the Democrats in November; it included whirlwind meetings with TR, George Perkins, Billy Barnes, Charles Evans Hughes, Henry Clay Frick, Governor Carl E. Millikin of Maine, Senator James A. Hemenway, Judge Elbert Gary, the presidents of several steel companies, Governor Charles S. Whitman of New York, the editor of the *Evening Mail*, and several others interested in affecting the election: Hays *Memoirs*, 157–59; Fowler, *Sir William Wiseman*, 108; TR to HCL, Sept. 8,

1917, MOR-REJ; *New York Tribune*, July 19, 1918. In many races TR and the National Security League worked against each other; see Robert D. Ward, "The Origin and Activities of the National Security League, 1914–1919," *Mississippi Valley Historical Review* 47 (1960): 51–65. TR was irritated by the scandals and mismanagement of the overzealous leaders of the American Defense Society and threatened to resign: Edwards, "Playing the Patriot Game," 54–72.

132. EKR to KR, Sept. 29, n.y. [1918], KBR-LC; ERD to RD, Oct. 3, 1918, TRC-HU; Rinehart, *My Story*, 260; TR to Robert P. Perkins, July 22, 1918, TRJR-LC. Grief also sent TR into manic eating; at one meal two plates of applesauce, two plates of tomatoes, one plate of potatoes, and eighteen spare ribs before he made Ethel stop counting: ERD to RD, Oct. 15, 1918, TRC-HU.

133. ABR to KR, Oct. 23, 1918, KBR-LC; ABR to CRR, Sept. 10, 1918, TRC-HU; TR to TRJR and EBAR, Oct. 20, 1918, TRJR-LC; ERD to RD, Oct. 3 and 4, 1918, TRC-HU.

134. TR to TRJR and EBAR, Sept. 13, 1918, TRJR-LC; ERD to KR, Sept. 15, n.y. [1918], KBR-LC; TR wrote that DR, WSC, and Emlen Roosevelt were his three closest friends: Sept. 15, 1918, MOR-REJ, a list of loyal family members who helped him in 1912, also a list which leaves out HCL; EKR to KR, Sept. 13, [1918], KBR-LC; Archie stayed with his parents when he first came home and went into the city for medical treatments. As she faced life alone, Corinne could not lean on her sons, who were "frail reeds," but her capable daughter Corinny and son-in-law Joseph Alsop found the Robinson family property had been mismanaged and set out to help her set things aright: ERD to RD, Oct. 29, 1918, TRC-HU; Fanny sat across from the Roosevelts in the Pullman car while Theodore showed he was not too overcome by grief to lecture his niece Eleanor on the urgent need for Franklin to enlist immediately: Jonathan Daniels, *End of Innocence*, 270–71; Parsons, *Perchance*, 280.

135. ERD to RD, Oct. 13, 1918, and n.d., frag. clippings, TRC-HU; TR to TRJR and EBAR, Oct. 13 and 20, 1918, TRJR-LC; *New York Times*, Sept. 19 and Oct. 14, 1918; that fall TR also made a Liberty Loan speaking tour.

136. Baker and Dodd, eds., *Public Papers of Woodrow Wilson*, 6:286–88. Wilson's key advisor allowed the President to blunder because he was preoccupied with peace negotiations; on the blunder see House Diary, October 1918, and on Wilson's irritation with TR's criticisms see Phyllis Lee Levin, *Edith and Woodrow: The Wilson White House* (New York, 2001), 217–19. Levin offers plentiful evidence of Wilson's breaches of security in sharing information with Mrs. Wilson during the war, but most presidents have relied on their family's discretion in the same way. Edith Roosevelt had almost as much access to privileged information as Edith Wilson.

137. MOR 8:1388; ERD to RD, Oct. 29, 1918, TRC-HU; *New York Times*, Oct. 26, 1918.

138. TR speech at Carnegie Hall: *New York Evening Sun*, Oct. 28, 1918; *New York Times*, Oct. 29, 30, 1918; TR would not let Archie attend because such a "fighting political speech" might upset him: TR to TRJR, Nov. 3, 1918, TRJR-LC.

139. Though his domestic views had not changed, Lenroot spoke "the words that patriotism demand" and won the primary by attacking the loyalty of his former ally La Follette. The Democrats emphasized loyalty even more than the Republicans in the general election in Wisconsin; see B. La Follette and F. La Follette, *Robert M. La Follette*, 2:866–73, 902.

140. "suffering time" in scribbled note about TR's gout: EKR to TRJR, Nov. 10, 1918, TRJR-LC; EKR-Di, November 1918; ERD-Di, Nov. 11, 1918. W.E.B. Du Bois, in an editorial in *The Crisis*, had denounced "the unspeakable Theodore Roosevelt" for rejecting his civil rights Bull Moose plank: Du Bois, "The Last Word in Politics," *The Crisis*, 1912; "The Circle for Negro War Relief, Inc.," *The Crisis*, November 1918; Du Bois, "From McKinley to Wallace," in D. Lewis, *Reader*, 484–85.

141. Langston Hughes, *Fight for Freedom: The Story of the* NAACP (New York, 1962), 67; Mary McLeod Bethune to CRR, Feb. 27, 1931, TRC-HU; Julius Rosenwald recollections

of TR in F. Wood, *Roosevelt As We Knew Him*, 345–54; Ziglar, "Negro Opinion of Theodore Roosevelt," 359.

142. W.E.B. Du Bois, "My Campaign for Senator," in Du Bois, "An Essay Toward a History of the Black Man in the Great War," *The Crisis*, June 1919, in D. Lewis, *Reader*, 787. By 1918, TR and Du Bois were more like-minded than in 1912. They both strongly supported the war, wanted the outstanding black military man of his generation, Colonel Charles Young, to lead troops in France (the Wilson administration declared him physically unfit), advocated training camps for black officers, and urged black men to enlist because war service could improve the status of their race. They were united in raising funds to relieve the hardships of black veterans and their families.

143. Remarks of Theodore Roosevelt at the Circle for Negro War Relief meeting, Carnegie Hall, Nov. 2, 1918, TR-SP; *New York Times*, Nov. 3, 1918; "Roosevelt's Last Public Speech—A Tribute to the Colored Soldiers," Anecdotes File, TRP-BP.

144. MOR 8:1132, 1364. There was a movement to repeal the Fifteenth Amendment during the war; Senator William Borah said it had been a mistake to let blacks vote after the Civil War; in 1918 no amount of courageous service in the war could buy African-Americans respect. White American officers had proven "more anxious to insult Negroes than to fight Germans," because the Wilson administration had allowed "the customs of the Solid South" to prevail throughout the American army: *Correspondence of W.E.B. Du Bois*, 1:340; see Du Bois, "Essay Toward a History of the Black Man in the Great War," *The Crisis*, June 1919, in D. Lewis, *Reader.*

145. EKR to KR, Nov. 3, n.y. [1918], KBR-LC; TR to TRJR (in Edith's handwriting), Nov. 10, 1918, TRJR-LC.

146. "alone" and "wailing" in ARL, *Crowded Hours*, 275. The news of peace didn't reach Dick until nighttime because the Second Division was still fighting its way across the Meuse River. Immensely relieved, he wrote home to Ethel that he hoped their children "will be spared this dreadful experience": RD to ERD, Nov. 15, 1918, TRC-HU; EKR-Di, Nov. 11–25, 1918; ERD-Di, Dec. 1–31, 1918; news reports variably described the ailment as gout, lumbago, sciatica, and inflammatory rheumatism.

147. EKR to KR, Oct. 13, n.y. [1918], and to BR, Oct. 25, n.y. [1918], KBR-LC.

148. H. J. Whigham, "The Colonel As We Saw Him," *Metropolitan* Scrapbook, TRC-HU; White, *Autobiography*, 549.

149. This statement was an answer to Wilson's call for a Democratic Congress. Both used the word "repudiate": *Roosevelt in the Kansas City Star*, 272–77; Tumulty, *Woodrow Wilson As I Know Him*, 340; many people had urged Wilson to take Roosevelt, as the leader of the opposition party, with him to Paris, but the President, equally bitter, refused, saying it "has been my unfortunate experience that the man you mention seeks to take charge of anything he has a part in, and to take charge in a way thoroughly disloyal to his associates": Arthur S. Link, ed., *The Papers of Woodrow Wilson*, vol. 53 (Princeton, N.J., 1986), 117 (Nov. 18, 1918).

150. Livermore, *Politics Is Adjourned*, is the best study of this conflict; see TR to Philip J. Roosevelt, Dec. 19, 1918, TRC-HU; *Roosevelt in the Kansas City Star*, 243–50, 261–65, 277–81, 292–95.

151. HCL to TR, Dec. 2, 1918, HCL-MHS.

152. CRR, *My Brother*, 361–62, says TR and Lodge talked over the "contingencies" rather than the specifics of the league when TR was in the hospital; HCL later wrote to CRR that he hoped she wasn't saying that the specific reservations were prepared in TR's hospital room because, at most, "the essence of the reservations, the principles which they embodied, were considered by Theodore and by me in the conversation which you heard": HCL to CRR, Nov. 5, 1920, TRC-HU.

153. On the day that Richard had a bad attack of asthma, TR was taken with a "severe

chill and cough" followed by a high fever which left him "feeling very depressed": ERD to RD, Dec. 8 and 19, 1918; for a few nights TR could sleep without opiates, but his pain persisted: watches in ERD-Di, Dec. 19, 1918; ERD to RD, Dec. 19, 1918, TRC-HU; TR to KR, Dec. 27, 1918, KBR-LC; EKR-Di, December 1918.

154. Dr. John T. Faris, interview notes, SUBJ-TRC; Hagedorn, *Bugle That Woke America,* 181–91; Cleveland Dodge talked with TR in late 1918: F. Wood, *Roosevelt As We Knew Him,* 314; ERD-RD, Jan. 8, 1919, TRC-HU.

155. Richard and little Edie had enjoyed their stockings and the Christmas tree in the parlor at Sagamore Hill before TR, Edith, Alice, Archie, and Gracie arrived. On Christmas Day Ethel wrote Dick: "Father looks very white—& as if he had been through a good deal as indeed he has. So thankful to be back to his own things—among his own people": ERD to RD, Dec. 25, 1918; but within days, Richard came down with bronchitis and TR developed a fever of 103 degrees: EKR-Di, Dec. 25, 1918–Jan. 6, 1919; ERD-Di, Dec. 25–Jan. 1, 1918; ERD to RD, Dec. 30, 1918; Pringle, *Taft,* 2:907–909; MOR 8:1337*n.*; George Garner interview, Feb. 22, 1932, SUBJ.

156. EKR to ERD, Jan. 4, 5, and 6, 1919: Dr. Faller gave him hypodermics filled with arsenic two days before he died; Carrie Chapman Catt and Nettie Rogers Shuler, *Woman Suffrage and Politics: The Inner Story of the Suffrage Movement* (New York, 1923), 333.

157. MOR 8:892; ERD to RD, Jan. 6, 1919.

158. HCL to William Sturgis Bigelow, Jan. 10, 1919, HCL-MHS.

159. EKR to KR, Jan. 12, n.y. [1919], KBR-LC; ERD to RD, Jan. 8, 1919, TRC-HU; Dr. Faller might have known about "the embolism."

EPILOGUE

1. White, *Autobiography,* 552; B. Reid, *Quinn,* 389–90; CRR to Arthur Lee, Mar. 19, 1919, Lee Papers, Courtauld Institute; TRJR Diary, Feb. 19, 1922, TRJR-LC; William Sturgis Bigelow to HCL, Jan. 6, 1919, enclosed in HCL to CRR, Jan. 11, 1919, TRC-HU.

2. Josephus Daniels, *Cabinet Diaries,* 462; see Kathleen M. Dalton, "The Bully Prophet: Theodore Roosevelt and American Memory," in Naylor, Brinkley, and Gable, eds., *Theodore Roosevelt: Many-Sided American,* 559–76; Dalton, "Famous Visitors to Sagamore Hill."

3. EKR to TRJR, July 25, 1939, SUBJ-TRC.

4. TR to KR, Dec. 29, and to BR, Dec. 7, 1918, MOR-REJ; ABR, ed., *Theodore Roosevelt on Race, Riots, Reds, Crime* (Metairie, La., 1968). Roosevelt's hope that war would alter a generation of young men and unify a nation to achieve reform at home would be proven wrong by the Great War, though he never admitted it. America after the war remained divided and even less so inclined. Red Cross officials estimated that 25 percent of the American soldiers returning from France suffered from "shell-shock" or other types of mental illness. Ironically, Plattsburg, where TR had pinned his hopes on remaking American manhood, became a shell-shock treatment center. To reevaluate the "bully father" myth compare Archie's memoirs with Joan Kerr, *The Bully Father,* and Hermann Hagedorn, *The Roosevelt Family of Sagamore Hill;* TR urged the boys to compete ruthlessly with each other, and could not tolerate weakness or illness in them. He was a better father to his daughters. In Alice's youth he overindulged her, though he did work out a more appreciative and warm relationship with her after she took an interest in politics. Ethel might have wanted to perpetuate the perfect father myth because she had the closest and best relationship with him in his last years, even though he discouraged her career aspirations. He had more time to be a nurturant and expressive father and grandfather in his last years.

5. EKR to Arthur Lee, Dec. 17, 1924, Lee Papers, Courtauld Institute.

6. EKR to ERD, May 14, 1928, TRC-HU.

7. EKR to ERD, Dec. 15, 1932, TRC-HU.

8. Interview, Edith Derby Williams, June 15, 1994; EKR's temperament changed as she aged and she became somewhat more waspish and did not get along as well with ARL and other family members: S. Morris, *Edith Kermit Roosevelt*; she refused historians' access to some of her husband's papers and then asked J. Franklin Jameson to restrict the papers on her behalf: Jacqueline Goggin and Morey Rothberg, eds., *John Franklin Jameson and the Development of Humanistic Scholarship in America*, 3:296–97; in politics she became more conservative and endorsed Hoover and privately criticized FDR as "Franklin Mussolini": EKR to TRJR, n.d. [1933], TRJR-LC.

9. ARL to ARC, Oct. 27, [1919], TRC-HU.

10. ERD to Edith Derby Williams, Nov. 10, 1963, and clipping about ARL jumping in a pool with her clothes on on her trip to Asia in 1905 and its similarity to Kennedy family antics, TRC-HU.

11. Caroline Drayton Phillips Journal, Sept. 12, 1933, Caroline Drayton Phillips Papers, Schlesinger Library; ERD to Edith Derby Williams, Sept. 21, 1958, TRC-HU; Mrs. Derby held views that would have qualified her as a Rockefeller Republican, but she believed Rockefeller failed to live up to TR's moral standards.

12. Clipping enclosed in EKR to KR, June 13, n.y. [1915], KBR-LC; ERD to Edith Derby Williams, July 14, 1957, TRC-HU; Bamie disliked Eleanor's choice of female friends (Alice called them "female impersonators": Teague, *Mrs. L*, 160) and her lack of interest in her appearance: ARC to CRR, Dec. 11, 1923, TRC-HU; Alice "derided" noble, high-minded people like the Derbys for dreaming of one world; Corinny Alsop got mad and told Alice that anyone who lacked a vision of a better world was a "damned fool." Ethel thought Archie's "communist under every bed" views were dangerous and she told him so: ERD to Edith Derby Williams, Oct. 11, 1953, TRC-HU; see also ERD to Edith Derby Williams, Nov. 1, 1953, TRC-HU; TR's secretary William Loeb had a difficult and unreliable son who years later made a name for himself attacking liberals in the *Manchester Union Leader.* His column attacking "those dull friends of Ethel's" hit at Learned Hand among others. Loeb called one of Ethel's friends a communist because she was in the League of Women Voters: ERD to Edith Derby Williams, Jan. 31, 1954, and May 26, 1957, TRC-HU; EBAR was more enthusiastic about Joe McCarthy than ERD and RD; when Archie was outraged on racial grounds that the Theodore Roosevelt Association gave Nobel Peace Prize winner and undersecretary-general for special political affairs of the United Nations Ralph Bunche its medal, EBAR stood by ERD and ARL in supporting Bunche. At the award dinner Bunche told ERD he had been raised to believe that there had been two great Americans, Booker T. Washington and TR; ERD to Edith Derby Williams, Oct. 24 and 31, 1954, TRC-HU; ERD liked Carleton Putnam's book about her father but found his white supremacist views abhorrent and sympathized instead with James Meredith: ERD to Edith Derby Williams, Sept. 6, 1959, and Oct. 7, 1962, TRC-HU. The resurgence of the Klan, the nomination of Goldwater, and the flying of the Confederate flag over Montgomery upset her. She joined the Ripon Society, and disliked the drift of the party and that "dreadful Phyllis Schaffley [*sic*]": ERD to Edith Derby Williams, Apr. 9, 1965, and July 10, 1967, TRC-HU; race caused tensions between ABR and ERD near the end of their lives, especially when she had her book class read *The Autobiography of Malcolm X* and she became an admirer of Martin Luther King, Jr., and Coretta Scott King: ERD to Edith Derby Williams, Dec. 5, 1965 and Mar. 2, 1969, TRC-HU.

13. ERD, Recollections of RD, Jr., TRC-HU; ERD was involved in the Visiting Nurses Association, Progressive Mother's Club, Edith Kermit Roosevelt Women's Republican Club, and other local activities.

14. ERD to Edith Derby Williams, Jan. 4, 1970, TRC-HU.

15. TR, "The Industrial Problems of Peace," January 1920, *Metropolitan* Scrapbook, TRC-HU.

16. Ibid.

17. TR, "The Problems of Peace," Part 2, February 1920, and "Eyes to the Front," February 1919, *Metropolitan* Scrapbook, TRC-HU; he also called for a unified national system of transportation "under about as close government supervision as that exercised over the Federal National Bank."

18. TR, "A Big Success and a Small Failure in Applied Democracy," July 1919, *Metropolitan* Scrapbook, TRC-HU.

19. *Boston Herald*, Jan. 12, 1919.

20. EKR to KR, Jan. 25, n.y. [1920], KBR-LC; John Dewey, "Theodore Roosevelt," *The Dial*, Feb. 8, 1919, 115–17; "Honor Memory of Roosevelt on Navy Day"; William Allen White, speech at the College of Emporia, Emporia, Kans., Oct. 27, 1926, Roosevelt clippings, TRC-HU.

21. Warren G. Harding, *Tribute to Theodore Roosevelt*, pamphlet, TR-SYR.

22. Anna Howard Shaw to Medill McCormick, n.d., Anna Howard Shaw Papers, Part A, Reel 18, frame 564, Women's Studies Manuscripts, Women's Suffrage, Series I-SL, Schlesinger Library; Vice President Thomas Marshall testified to Wilson's personal opposition to suffrage until the end of his life: Caroline Drayton Phillips, Journal, Jan. 27, 1919, Caroline Drayton Phillips Papers, Schlesinger Library; Donna Jeanne Haraway, *Primate Visions: Gender, Race, and Nature in the World of Modern Science* (New York, 1989); Gail Bederman, *Manliness & Civilization: A Cultural History of Gender and Race in the United States, 1880–1917* (Chicago, 1995).

23. Parsons, *Perchance*, 340; Alan R. Havig, "Theodore and Franklin: F.D.R.'s Use of the Theodore Roosevelt Image, 1920–1936," *Theodore Roosevelt Association Journal* 5, no. 2 (Spring 1979): 6–10; Havig, "Presidential Images, History and Homage: Memorializing Theodore Roosevelt, 1919–1967," *American Quarterly* 30 (Fall 1978): 514–32; James L. Golden, "FDR's Use of the Symbol of TR in the Formation of His Political Persona and Philosophy," and John Robert Greene, "The Men in the Arena: Presidential Co-option of the Image of Theodore Roosevelt, 1916–1989," in Naylor, Brinkley, and Gable, eds., *Theodore Roosevelt: Many-Sided American*.

24. Republican presidential candidate Barry Goldwater described himself as a TR type: clipping enclosed in ERD to Edith Derby Williams, Mar. 14, 1964, TRC-HU.

25. TR to William Ridgway, Nov. 9, 1908, MOR-REJ; "Biological Analogies," MEM 14:65–106.

26. TR, "The Problems of Peace," Part 2, February 1920, and "Eyes to the Front," February 1919, *Metropolitan* Scrapbook, TRC-HU.

27. MOR 8:1419; "Race Superiority," *The Crisis* (November 1918): 24; W.E.B. Du Bois, "World War and the Color Line," *The Crisis* (November 1914): 28–30.

28. "Editorial: Theodore Roosevelt," *The Crisis* 17, no. 4 (February 1919): 163.

29. Ibid.

Bibliography

Manuscript Sources

Harvard University, Cambridge, Massachusetts

Theodore Roosevelt Collection, Houghton Library, Harvard College Library, includes papers of TR, ARC, CRR, ABR, KR, EKR, ERD, and other family members, Hermann Hagedorn Papers, Avery D. Andrews Papers, Alsop Papers, Alice Gore King Papers, Edward Van Valkenberg Papers, Frances Theodora Smith Dana Parsons Papers, Joseph Bucklin Bishop Papers, John J. Leary Papers, John Callan O'Laughlin Papers, Josephine Preston Peabody Papers, Houghton Mifflin Co. Papers, William H. Sanders Papers, manuscripts deposited by Mrs. Harold Peabody, manuscripts bequeathed by Mrs. Southworth Lancaster, Richard Welling Papers, Edith Kermit Roosevelt Diaries, Ethel Carow Roosevelt Derby Diaries, photostats of rejected letters collected from archives around the world when Elting Morison and John Blum collected their eight volumes of Theodore Roosevelt letters, the Newspaper Scrapbook Collection, including the Mabel Styles Collection, Progressive Party Archives, Theodore Roosevelt diaries, Theodore Roosevelt Senior Letterbooks, Subject Files, Biographers Papers, Original Cartoon Collection, and many other related papers, as well as published sources in Widener Library

Additional Collections at the Houghton Library

Mrs. Edward S. Blagden Papers, Endicott Peabody Papers (originals now returned to Groton School Archives), William Roscoe Thayer Papers, Thomas Wentworth Higginson Papers, James Freeman Clarke Papers, William Dean Howells Papers, Alan Seeger Papers, Oswald Garrison Villard Papers, Robert Grant Papers, Frederick W. Holls Papers, Norton Family Papers, Walter Hines Page Papers, E. L. Godkin Papers, Charles Follen Adams Papers, the Rockhill Papers, George Edward Woodberry Papers, Charles Sanders Pierce Papers

Schlesinger Library, Radcliffe Institute for Advanced Study, Harvard University

Caroline Drayton Phillips Journal, Caroline Drayton Phillips Papers, Harriet Laidlaw Papers, Mary Dreier Papers, Anna Howard Shaw Papers in Women's Studies Manuscripts, Maud Nathan Papers, Jane Addams Papers from Swarthmore College Library (microfilm edition)

Massachusetts Historical Society, Boston

Lodge-Roosevelt Correspondence P-490, Henry Cabot Lodge Papers (1850–1924) P-525, Minot Family Papers, Amos A. Lawrence Papers, Leverett Saltonstall Papers, Lee Family Papers

Library of Congress, Washington, D.C.

Archibald Bulloch Roosevelt Papers in Series 16 TR Papers, Alice Roosevelt Longworth Papers (used with permission of Joanna Sturm), Gifford Pinchot Diary and Gifford Pinchot Papers, Hermann Hagedorn Papers, James Garfield Papers, Kermit and Belle Wyatt (Willard) Roosevelt Papers, Owen Wister Papers, Theodore Roosevelt Association Film Collection, Theodore Roosevelt Jr. Papers, Theodore Roosevelt Papers (microfilmed and Series 13-J clippings not filmed), William Allen White Papers, George Cortelyou Papers, Robert Barnwell Roosevelt Papers, Records of the New York Society for the Suppression of Vice, William McKinley Papers, Albert Beveridge Papers, Robert M. La Follette Papers, William Howard Taft Papers, Joseph Hodges Choate Papers

Franklin Delano Roosevelt Library, Hyde Park, New York

Franklin Roosevelt Papers as assistant secretary of the navy, Roosevelt Family Papers (includes Family Papers Donated by the Children), Joseph Lash Papers, Eleanor Roosevelt Papers *Small Collections*—TR and Other Papers, F.D.R. Papers: Papers as President, President's Personal File, F.D.R. Scrapbooks

Smaller Roosevelt Manuscript Sources

Courtauld Institute, London: Arthur Lee Papers

University of North Carolina, Chapel Hill, Southern Historical Collection, Wilson Library: Bulloch Family Papers #2750, James Dunwody Bulloch Letters #3318, and Thomas Butler King Papers #1252

Arizona Historical Society, Tucson: John Greenway and Isabella Ferguson Greenway Papers, Robert Munro Ferguson Papers

Syracuse University Library, Syracuse, New York, Department of Special Collections: Nicholas Roosevelt and Theodore Roosevelt Papers

Theodore Roosevelt Birthplace, New York, National Park Service: Theodore Roosevelt Collection, Anecdotes File

New York Public Library: Theodore Roosevelt Letters, Dodge Papers, Samuel Ward Papers

Columbia University, New York, Special Collection Division, Butler Library: Theodore Roosevelt Association Papers, Lincoln Steffens Collection, Cornelius Rea Agnew Collection, Frederick Davenport Papers, Frederick W. Holls Papers, Nicholas Murray Butler Papers, Marie Meloney Collection, Belmont Papers, Seth Low Papers, Dix Papers, Marriner Collection, Jay Family Papers, Nevins Collection, Columbia Oral History Project

New York Historical Society: Robert Barnwell Roosevelt Papers, Roosevelt Family Papers, Henry Fairfield Osborn Papers, Chanler Family Papers, Emily Tuckerman Diary, Stanford White Papers, Allotment Commission Books

American Museum of Natural History, New York, Rare Book Room: "An Autobiography of Albert S. Bickmore," with a historical sketch of the Founding and Early Development of the American Museum of Natural History, typescript manuscript, 1908

Cornell University, Ithaca, New York, Department of Manuscripts and University Archives, John M. Olin Library: Van Duzer Family Papers, Andrew Dickson White Papers,

Jacob Gould Schurman Papers, Goldwin Smith Papers, Oral History Interview with A. B. Recknagel

Stanford University Libraries, Stanford, California, Department of Special Collections: Stephen Mallory White Papers, Meyer Lissner Papers

Hoover Institution on War, Revolution and Peace, Stanford University: John Callan O'Laughlin Papers

University of California, Berkeley, Bancroft Library: Woman Suffrage and the Equal Rights Amendment Papers (available on-line)

Theodore Roosevelt Association, Oyster Bay, New York: Theodore Roosevelt Association and Roosevelt Memorial Association Papers, held in the offices of the T.R.A.

Sagamore Hill Historic Site, National Park Service Headquarters, Old Orchard House: Theodore Roosevelt Family Papers, Roosevelt Division Archives, Sagamore Hill Accounts Book, Book List, Visitors' Log Book

Baker University Library, Baldwin City, Kansas: Ethel Roosevelt Derby Papers

Virginia Historical Society Collections, Richmond: Martha Waller Johnson Papers

University of Virginia, Charlottesville, Manuscript Department, Alderman Library: Barrett Papers

Privately Held Manuscripts

Robert Barnwell Roosevelt Papers, scrapbook and letters, formerly in possession of Jean Schermerhorn Roosevelt, now at the Theodore Roosevelt Association offices, Oyster Bay, New York

Roosevelt Family Papers, formerly in possession of William Sheffield Cowles, Jr., Old Gate, Farmington, Connecticut, currently in possession of his son Evan S. Cowles

Collection of Lawrence H. and Doris A. Budner, Dallas

Published Primary Sources

For a collection of primary and secondary sources see Harvard University Library. *Theodore Roosevelt Collection: Dictionary Catalogue and Shelflist.* 6 vols. Cambridge, Mass., 1986, soon to be posted on-line.

Abbott, Lawrence F. *Impressions of Theodore Roosevelt.* Garden City, N.Y.: Doubleday, Page, 1919.

——, ed. *The Letters of Archie Butt, Personal Aide to President Roosevelt.* Garden City, N.Y.: Doubleday, Page, 1924.

Abbott, Lyman. *Reminiscences.* Boston: Houghton Mifflin, 1915.

Adams, Henry. *Letters of Henry Adams,* ed. Worthington C. Ford. 2 vols. Boston: Houghton Mifflin, 1930 and 1938.

——. *Selected Letters.* New York: Farrar, Straus, and Young, 1951.

Addams, Jane. *One Hundred Years at Hull-House,* ed. Mary Lynn McCree Bryan and Allen F. Davis. Bloomington: University of Indiana Press, 1990.

——. *Peace and Bread in Time of War.* New York: Garland, 1972.

——. *The Second Twenty Years at Hull-House.* New York: Macmillan, 1930.

——. *Twenty Years at Hull-House.* New York: New American Library, 1961.

Amos, James E. *Theodore Roosevelt: Hero to His Valet.* New York: John Day, 1927.

Baker, Ray Stannard. *Woodrow Wilson: Life and Letters.* 8 vols. Garden City, N.Y.: Doubleday, Page, and Doubleday, Doran, 1927–39.

——, and William E. Dodd, eds. *Public Papers of Woodrow Wilson.* 6 vols. New York: Harper & Bros., 1925.

Belmont, Eleanor Robson. *The Fabric of Memory*. New York: Farrar, Straus, and Cudahy, 1957.

Bispham, David S. A *Quaker Singer's Recollections*. New York: Macmillan, 1920.

Blatch, Harriot Stanton, and Alma Lutz. *Challenging Years: The Memoirs of Harriot Stanton Blatch*. New York: Putnam's, 1940.

Bok, Edward W. *The Americanization of Edward Bok: An Autobiography*. New York: Pocket Books, 1965.

Brace, Charles Loring. *The Dangerous Classes of New York, and Twenty Years' Work Among Them*. New York: Wynkoop & Hallenbeck, 1880.

Brace, Emma, ed. *The Life of Charles Loring Brace: Chiefly Told in His Own Letters*. New York: Sampson, Low, Marston, 1894.

Brandeis, Louis D. *Letters of Louis D. Brandeis*, ed. Melvin I. Urofsky and David W. Levy. 5 vols. Albany, N.Y.: State University of New York Press, 1971–75.

Bryan, William Jennings. A *Tale of Two Conventions*. New York: Funk & Wagnalls, 1912.

Bryan, William Jennings, with Mary Baird Bryan. *The Memoirs of William Jennings Bryan*. New York: Haskell House, 1971.

Burroughs, John. *Camping and Tramping with Roosevelt*. Boston: Houghton Mifflin, 1907.

Butler, Nicholas Murray. *Across the Busy Years: Recollections & Reflections*. New York: Scribner's, 1939–40.

Butt, Archibald. *Taft and Roosevelt: The Intimate Letters of Archie Butt, Military Aide*. 2 vols. Garden City, N.Y.: Doubleday, Doran, 1930.

Chanler, Winthrop. *Winthrop Chanler's Letters*, ed. Margaret Chanler. New York: privately printed, 1951.

Chapman, John Jay. *John Jay Chapman and His Letters*, ed. M. A. DeWolfe Howe. Boston: Houghton Mifflin, 1937.

Creel, George. A *Rebel at Large: Recollections of Fifty Crowded Years*. New York: Putnam's, 1947.

Daniels, Josephus. *The Cabinet Diaries of Josephus Daniels, 1913–1921*, ed. E. David Cronon. Lincoln: University of Nebraska Press, 1963.

Davis, Oscar King. *Released for Publication: Some Inside Political History of Theodore Roosevelt and His Times, 1898–1918*. Boston: Houghton Mifflin, 1925.

Doyle, Sir Arthur Conan. *Memories and Adventures*. Boston: Little, Brown, 1924.

Du Bois, W.E.B. *The Autobiography of W.E.B. Du Bois: A Soliloquy on Viewing My Life from the Last Decade of Its First Century*. New York: International Publishers, 1968.

———. *The Correspondence of W.E.B. Du Bois*, vol. 1, *Selections, 1877–1934*, ed. Herbert Aptheker. Amherst: University of Massachusetts Press, 1973.

———. *Dusk of Dawn: An Essay Toward an Autobiography of a Race Concept*. New York: Schocken, 1968.

Dunn, Arthur Wallace. *From Harrison to Harding: A Personal Narrative, Covering a Third of a Century, 1888–1921*. New York: Putnam's, 1922.

Dunne, Finley Peter. *Gridiron Nights: Humourous and Satirical Views of Politics and Statesmen as Presented by the Famous Dining Club*. New York: Stokes, 1915.

———. *Mr. Dooley at His Best*, ed. Elmer Ellis. New York: Scribner's, 1938.

———. *Mr. Dooley's Philosophy*. New York: Scribner's, 1906.

Ferber, Edna. A *Peculiar Treasure*. New York: Doubleday, Doran, 1939.

Foraker, Joseph Benson. *Notes of a Busy Life*. 2 vols. Cincinnati: Stewart & Kidd, 1916.

Foraker, Julia B. *I Would Live It Again: Memories of a Vivid Life*. New York: Harper & Bros., 1932.

Foster, Judith Ellen. *The Saloon Must Go*. New York: National Temperance Society and Publication House, 1889.

Frankfurter, Felix. *Felix Frankfurter Reminisces: Recorded in Talks with Dr. Harlan B. Phillips*. New York: Reynal, 1960.

——. *From the Diaries of Felix Frankfurter*, ed. Joseph P. Lash. New York: Norton, 1975.

Garland, Hamlin. *Companions on the Trail: A Literary Chronicle*. New York: Macmillan, 1931.

Gatewood, Willard B., Jr. *"Smoked Yankees" and the Struggle for Empire: Letters from Negro Soldiers, 1898–1902*. Fayetteville: University of Arkansas Press, 1987.

Gilder, Richard Watson. *Letters of Richard Watson Gilder*, ed. Rosamond Gilder. Boston: Houghton Mifflin, 1916.

Grant, Robert. *Fourscore: An Autobiography*. Boston: Houghton Mifflin, 1934.

Hale, William Bayard. *A Week in the White House with Theodore Roosevelt*. New York: Putnam's, 1908.

Harriman, Florence Jaffray. *From Pinafores to Politics*. New York: Holt, 1923.

Hart, Albert Bushnell, and Herbert Ronald Ferleger, eds. *Theodore Roosevelt Cyclopedia*. New York: Roosevelt Memorial Association, 1941.

Hart, Jerome A. *In Our Second Century: From an Editor's Notebook*. San Francisco: Pioneer Press, 1931.

Hays, Will H. *Memoirs*. Garden City, N.Y.: Doubleday, 1955.

Higginson, Thomas Wentworth. *Cheerful Yesterdays: The American Negro, His History and Literature*. New York: Arno Press, 1968.

Hoover, Irwin Hood "Ike." *Forty-two Years in the White House*. Boston: Houghton Mifflin, 1934.

Irwin, Will. *Making of a Reporter*. New York: Putnam's, 1942.

Johnson, James Weldon. *Along This Way: The Autobiography of James Weldon Johnson*. New York: Penguin Books, 1990.

Jusserand, Jean-Jules. *What Me Befell: The Reminiscences of J. J. Jusserand*. Boston: Houghton Mifflin, 1933.

Kelley, Florence. "Twenty-five Years of the Consumers' League Movement," *Survey*, Nov. 27, 1915.

Kellor, Frances. "A New Spirit in Party Organization," *North American Review*, June 1914.

——. "The Protection of Immigrant Women," *Atlantic*, February 1908.

La Farge, John. *The Manner Is Ordinary*. New York: Harcourt Brace, 1954.

La Follette, Robert M. *La Follette's Autobiography: A Personal Narrative of Political Experiences*. Madison, Wisc.: R. M. La Follette Co., 1968.

Leary, John J., Jr. *Talks with T.R.: From the Diaries of John J. Leary, Jr.* Boston: Houghton Mifflin, 1920.

Lee, Arthur Hamilton, Viscount. *Good Innings: The Private Papers of Viscount Lee of Fareham*, ed. Alan Clark. London: J. Murray, 1974.

Lodge, Henry Cabot, ed. *Selections from the Correspondence of Theodore Roosevelt and Henry Cabot Lodge, 1884–1918*. 2 vols. New York: Da Capo, 1925.

Longworth, Alice Roosevelt. *Crowded Hours: Reminiscences of Alice Roosevelt Longworth*. New York: Scribner's, 1933.

Looker, Earle. *The White House Gang*. New York: Revell, 1929.

McCutcheon, John T. *Drawn from Memory*. New York: Bobbs-Merrill, 1950.

Nathan, Maud. *Once Upon a Time and Today*. New York: Putnam's, 1933.

——. *Story of an Epoch-Making Movement*. Garden City, N.Y.: Doubleday, Page, 1926.

Newlands, Francis G. *The Public Papers of Francis G. Newlands*, ed. Arthur B. Darling. 2 vols. Boston: Houghton Mifflin, 1932.

O'Laughlin, John Callan. *From the Jungle Through Europe with Roosevelt.* Boston: Chapple, 1910.

Oliver, Lawrence J., ed. *The Letters of Theodore Roosevelt and Brander Matthews.* Knoxville: University of Tennessee Press, 1995.

Park, Maud Wood. *Front Door Lobby.* Boston: Beacon, 1960.

Parsons, Frances Theodora (Smith). *Perchance Some Day.* New York: privately printed, 1951.

Phillips, William. *Ventures in Diplomacy.* Boston: Beacon, 1953.

Pinchot, Amos. *History of the Progressive Party, 1912–1916.* New York: New York University Press, 1958.

Pinchot, Gifford. *Breaking New Ground.* New York: Harcourt Brace, 1947.

Platt, Thomas Collier. *The Autobiography of Thomas Collier Platt,* ed. Louis J. Lang. New York: Dodge, 1910.

Rauschenbusch, Walter. *Christianity and the Social Crisis.* New York: Macmillan, 1910.

Riis, Jacob A. *How the Other Half Lives: Studies Among the Tenements of New York.* 1890; reprint, New York: Macmillan, 1971.

——. *The Making of an American.* New York: Macmillan, 1943.

——. *A Ten Year's War: An Account of the Battle with the Slum in New York.* Boston: Houghton Mifflin, 1900.

——. *Theodore Roosevelt the Citizen.* New York: The Outlook Co., 1904.

Rinehart, Mary Roberts. *My Story.* New York: Farrar & Rinehart, 1931.

Robinson, Corinne Roosevelt. *My Brother Theodore Roosevelt.* New York: Scribner's, 1929.

Rockwell, A. D., M.D. *Rambling Recollections: An Autobiography.* New York: Hoeber, 1920.

Roosevelt, Anna Eleanor. *This Is My Story.* Garden City, N.Y.: Doubleday, 1961.

Roosevelt, Edith Kermit Carow, Belle Willard Roosevelt, Kermit Roosevelt, Richard Derby, and Kermit Roosevelt. *Cleared for Strange Ports.* New York: Scribner's, 1927.

Roosevelt, Edith Kermit Carow, and Kermit Roosevelt, eds. *American Backlogs: The Story of Gertrude Tyler and Her Family.* New York: Scribner's, 1928.

Roosevelt, Eleanor Butler Alexander. *Day Before Yesterday: The Reminiscences of Mrs. Theodore Roosevelt, Jr.* Garden City, N.Y.: Doubleday, 1959.

Roosevelt, Elliott. *Hunting Big Game in the Eighties: The Letters of Elliott Roosevelt, Sportsman,* ed. Anna Eleanor Roosevelt. New York: Scribner's, 1932.

Roosevelt, Elliott, and James Brough. *An Untold Story: The Roosevelts of Hyde Park.* New York: Dell, 1973.

Roosevelt, Kermit. *The Happy Hunting-grounds.* London: Hodder & Stroughton, 1920.

——. *War in the Garden of Eden.* New York: Scribner's, 1919.

Roosevelt, Nicholas. *A Front Row Seat.* Norman: University of Oklahoma Press, 1953.

——. *Theodore Roosevelt: The Man As I Knew Him.* New York: Dodd, Mead, 1967.

Roosevelt, Theodore. *An Autobiography.* 1913; reprint, New York: Da Capo, 1985.

——. *A Bully Father: Theodore Roosevelt's Letters to His Children,* ed. Joan Paterson Kerr. New York: Random House, 1995.

——. *Letters from Theodore Roosevelt to Anna Roosevelt Cowles, 1870–1918,* ed. Anna Roosevelt Cowles. New York: Scribner's, 1924.

——. *The Letters of Theodore Roosevelt,* ed. Elting E. Morison, John Morton Blum, and Alfred Chandler. 8 vols. Cambridge, Mass.: Harvard University Press, 1951–54.

——. *Pocket Diary 1898: Theodore Roosevelt's Private Account of the War with Spain,* ed.

Wallace Finley Dailey. Cambridge, Mass.: Theodore Roosevelt Collection, Harvard College Library, Houghton Library, Harvard University, 1998.

——. *Roosevelt in the Kansas City Star: War-time Editorials by Theodore Roosevelt*, ed. Ralph Stout. Boston: Houghton Mifflin, 1921.

——. *Theodore Roosevelt's Diaries of Boyhood and Youth*. New York, Scribner's, 1928.

——. *The Works of Theodore Roosevelt*, Memorial Edition. New York: Scribner's, 1919–26.

MEM 1 *Hunting Trips of a Ranchman*. 1885.

"Game Shooting in the West," *Outing*, 1886.

Good Hunting. 1907.

MEM 2 *The Wilderness Hunter*. 1893.

MEM 3 *Outdoor Pastimes of an American Hunter*. 1905.

MEM 4 *A Book-Lover's Holidays in the Open*. 1916.

MEM 5 *African Game Trails*. 1910.

MEM 6 *Through the Brazilian Wilderness*. 1914.

MEM 7 *The Naval War of 1812*. 1882.

MEM 8 *Thomas Hart Benton*. 1887.

Gouverneur Morris. 1888.

MEM 9 *Hero Tales from American History* (with Henry Cabot Lodge). 1895.

MEM 10 *The Winning of the West*. 1889–96.

MEM 11 *The Winning of the West*.

MEM 12 *The Winning of the West*.

MEM 13 *The Rough Riders*. 1899.

Oliver Cromwell. 1900.

MEM 14 *Literary Essays*.

MEM 15 *American Ideals*. 1897.

The Strenuous Life. 1900.

Realizable Ideals. 1912.

MEM 16 Campaigns and Controversies. Pre-presidential speeches and articles.

MEM 17 State Papers as Governor and President.

MEM 18 American Problems.

MEM 19 Social Justice and Popular Rule. Speeches and articles related to his leftward shift from 1910 to 1919.

MEM 20 *America and the World War*. 1915.

MEM 21 *The Foes of Our Own Household*. 1917.

The Great Adventure. 1918.

Letters to His Children.

MEM 22 *Autobiography*. 1913.

MEM 23 and 24 Joseph B. Bishop, *Theodore Roosevelt and His Time*.

——. "Better Life on the Farm," *Journal of Education*, Aug. 27, 1908, 189–90.

——. "Social Values and National Existence," address to the American Sociological Society, printed in *Current History*, February 1916.

Roosevelt, Theodore, Jr. *All in the Family*. New York: Putnam's, 1929.

Roosevelt vs. Newett, A Transcript of the Testimony Taken and Depositions Read at Marquette, Michigan. Privately printed by W. Emlen Roosevelt, 1914.

Simkhovitch, Mary Kingsbury. *Neighborhood: My Story of Greenwich House*. New York: Norton, 1938.

Slayden, Ellen Maury. *Washington Wife: Journal of Ellen Maury Slayden from 1897–1919*. New York: Harper & Row, 1963.

Spring Rice, Cecil. *The Letters and Friendships of Sir Cecil Spring Rice: A Record*, ed. Stephen Gwynn. 2 vols. Boston: Houghton Mifflin, 1929.

State Charities Aid Association, *Theodore Roosevelt: Memorial Meeting*. New York: privately printed, 1878.

Steffens, Lincoln. *The Autobiography of Lincoln Steffens*. 2 vols. New York: Harcourt Brace, 1958.

Straus, Oscar S. *Under Four Administrations, from Cleveland to Taft: Recollections of Oscar S. Straus*. Boston: Houghton Mifflin, 1922.

Strong, George Templeton. *The Diary of George Templeton Strong*, ed. Allan Nevins and Milton Halsey Thomas. New York, Octagon, 1974.

Teague, Michael. *Mrs. L: Conversations with Alice Roosevelt Longworth*. Garden City, N.Y.: Doubleday, 1981.

Terrell, Mary Church. *A Colored Woman in a White World*. Washington, D.C.: Ransdell, 1940.

Thayer, William R. *The Life and Letters of John Hay*. 2 vols. Boston: Houghton Mifflin, 1915.

Tumulty, Joseph P. *Woodrow Wilson As I Know Him*. Garden City, N.Y.: Doubleday Page, 1921.

Union League Club of New York. *Theodore Roosevelt, Senior: A Tribute, the Proceedings at a Meeting, Feb. 14, 1878*. New York: Irving Press, 1902.

Villard, Oswald Garrison. *Women in the New York Municipal Campaign of 1901*. Boston: Youngjohn, 1902.

Vorse, Mary Heaton. *A Footnote to Folly: Reminiscences of Mary Heaton Vorse*. New York: Farrar and Rinehart, 1935.

Wald, Lillian D. *Windows on Henry Street*. Boston: Little, Brown, 1934.

White, William Allen. *The Autobiography of William Allen White*. New York: Macmillan, 1946.

——. *Masks in a Pageant*. New York: Macmillan, 1928.

William II, Emperor. *The Kaiser's Memoirs*. New York: Harper, 1922.

Wister, Owen. *Roosevelt: The Story of a Friendship, 1880–1919*. New York: Macmillan, 1930.

Wood, Frederick S., ed. *Roosevelt As We Knew Him: The Personal Recollections of One Hundred and Fifty of His Friends and Associates*. Philadelphia: Winston, 1927.

Zahm, John Augustine. *Through South America's Southland, with an Account of the Roosevelt Scientific Expedition to South America*. New York: Appleton, 1916.

Zwick, Jim, ed. *Mark Twain's Weapons of Satire: Anti-Imperialist Writings on the Philippine-American War*. Syracuse, N.Y.: Syracuse University Press, 1992.

Selected Published Secondary Sources

Adams, Graham, Jr. *Age of Industrial Violence, 1910–1915: The Activities and Findings of the United States Commission on Industrial Relations*. New York: Columbia University Press, 1966.

Adler, Cyrus. *Jacob H. Schiff: His Life and Letters*. 2 vols. Garden City, N.Y.: Doubleday, Doran, 1928.

Alexander, DeAlva Stanwood. *A Political History of the State of New York*. Empire State historical publication series, no. 69. Port Washington, N.Y.: Friedman, 1969.

Alonso, Harriet Hyman. *Peace as a Women's Issue: A History of the U.S. Movement for World Peace and Women's Rights*. Syracuse, N.Y.: Syracuse University Press, 1993.

Ambrosius, Lloyd E. *Wilsonian Statecraft: Theory and Practice of Liberal Internationalism During World War I*. Wilmington, Del.: SR Books, 1991.

Anderson, Judith Icke. *William Howard Taft: An Intimate History*. New York: Norton, 1981.

Anderson, Oscar E., Jr. *The Health of a Nation: Harvey W. Wiley and the Fight for Pure Food*. Chicago: University of Chicago Press, 1958.

Andrew, Christopher M. *For the President's Eyes Only: Secret Intelligence and the American Presidency from Washington to Bush*. New York: Harper Perennial, 1996.

Ashburn, Frank D. *Peabody of Groton: A Portrait*. New York: Coward McCann, 1944.

Ashby, LeRoy. *Saving the Waifs: Reformers and Dependent Children, 1890–1917*. Philadelphia: Temple University Press, 1984.

——. *William Jennings Bryan: Champion of Democracy*. Boston: Twayne, 1987.

Ayala, César J. *American Sugar Kingdom: The Plantation Economy of the Spanish Caribbean, 1898–1934*. Chapel Hill, N.C.: University of North Carolina Press, 1999.

Baer, Judith A. *The Chains of Protection: The Judicial Response to Women's Labor Legislation*. Westport, Conn.: Greenwood Press, 1978.

Bailey, Thomas A. *Theodore Roosevelt and the Japanese-American Crises*. Stanford, Calif.: Stanford University Press, 1934.

Baker, Lee D. *From Savage to Negro: Anthropology and the Construction of Race, 1896–1954*. Berkeley: University of California Press, 1998.

Baker, Paul R. *Stanny: The Gilded Life of Stanford White*. New York: Free Press, 1989.

Baker, Paula. "The Domestication of Politics: Women and American Political Society, 1780–1920," *American Historical Review* 89 (June 1984): 620–47.

Barrett, James R. "Americanization from the Bottom Up: Immigration and the Remaking of the Working Class in the United States, 1880–1930," *Journal of American History* 79, no. 3 (December 1992): 996–1020.

Bartlett, Richard A. *Yellowstone: A Wilderness Besieged*. Tucson: University of Arizona Press, 1985.

Beale, Howard K. *Theodore Roosevelt and the Rise of America to World Power*. Baltimore: Johns Hopkins Press, 1956.

Bean, Walton E. "George Creel and His Critics: A Study of the Attacks on the Committee on Public Information, 1917–1919," Ph.D. diss., University of California at Berkeley, 1941.

Beckert, Sven. *The Monied Metropolis: New York City and the Consolidation of the American Bourgeoisie, 1850–1896*. New York: Cambridge University Press, 2001.

Beisner, Robert L. *Twelve Against Empire: The Anti-Imperialists, 1898–1900*. New York: McGraw-Hill, 1968.

Beringause, Arthur F. *Brooks Adams: A Biography*. New York: Knopf, 1955.

Berk, Gerald. *Alternative Tracks: The Constitution of American Industrial Order, 1865–1917*. Baltimore: Johns Hopkins University Press, 1994.

Berman, Jay Stuart. *Police Administration and Progressive Reform: Theodore Roosevelt as Police Commissioner of New York*. Westport, Conn.: Greenwood, 1987.

Bernstein, Iver. *The New York City Draft Riots: Their Significance for American Society and Politics in the Age of the Civil War*. New York: Oxford University Press, 1990.

Best, Gary Dean. *To Free a People: American Jewish Leaders and the Jewish Problem in Eastern Europe, 1890–1914*. Westport, Conn.: Greenwood Press, 1982.

Bishop, Joseph Bucklin. *Theodore Roosevelt and His Time Shown in His Own Letters*. New York: Scribner's, 1920.

Bittlingmayer, George. "Antitrust and Business Activity: The First Quarter Century," *Business History Review* 70 (Autumn 1996) 7:363–401.

Blair, Karen. *The Clubwoman as Feminist: True Womanhood Redefined, 1868–1914*. New York: Holmes & Meier, 1980.

Blake, Nelson Manfred. *The Road to Reno: A History of Divorce in the United States*. New York: Macmillan, 1962.

Blight, David W. "For Something Beyond the Battlefield: Frederick Douglass and the Struggle for the Memory of the Civil War," *Journal of American History* 75 (March 1989): 1156–78.

——. *Frederick Douglass' Civil War: Keeping Faith in Jubilee*. Baton Rouge: Louisiana State University Press, 1989.

——. *Race and Reunion: The Civil War in American Memory*. Cambridge, Mass.: Harvard University Press, 2001.

Blum, John Morton. *Joe Tumulty and the Wilson Era*. Hamden, Conn.: Archon, 1969.

——. *The Republican Roosevelt*. New York: Atheneum, 1967.

Borden, Penn. *Civilian Indoctrination of the Military: World War I and Future Implications for the Military-Industrial Complex*. Westport, Conn.: Greenwood Press, 1989.

Bordin, Ruth B. *Woman and Temperance: The Quest for Power and Liberty, 1873–1900*. Philadelphia: Temple University Press, 1981.

Boris, Eileen. *Art and Labor: Ruskin, Morris, and the Craftsman Ideal in America*. Philadelphia: Temple University Press, 1986.

——. *Home to Work: Motherhood and the Politics of Industrial Homework in the United States*. New York: Cambridge University Press, 1995.

Bowers, Claude G. *Beveridge and the Progressive Era*. New York: Literary Guild, 1932.

Boyer, Paul S. *Purity in Print: The Vice-Society Movement and Book Censorship in America*. New York: Scribner, 1968.

——. *Urban Masses and Moral Order in America, 1820–1920*. Cambridge, Mass.: Harvard University Press, 1978.

Braeman, John. *Albert J. Beveridge: American Nationalist*. Chicago: University of Chicago Press, 1971.

Bristow, Nancy K. *Making Men Moral: Social Engineering During the Great War*. New York: New York University Press, 1996.

Brown, Dee Alexander. *The Year of the Century: 1876*. New York: Scribner, 1966.

Buenker, John D. "The Urban Political Machine and Woman Suffrage: A Study in Political Adaptability," *Historian* 33 (1971): 264–79.

——. *Urban Liberalism and Progressive Reform*. New York: Scribner, 1973.

Buenker, John D., John C. Burnham, and Robert M. Crunden. *Progressivism*. Cambridge, Mass.: Shenkman, 1977.

Burnham, John C. *Bad Habits: Drinking, Smoking, Taking Drugs, Gambling, Sexual Misbehavior, and Swearing in American History*. New York: New York University Press, 1993.

Burrows, Edwin G., and Mike Wallace. *Gotham: A History of New York City to 1898*. New York: Oxford University Press, 1999.

Burton, David H. *Theodore Roosevelt: Confident Imperialist*. Philadelphia: University of Pennsylvania Press, 1968.

Butsch, Richard. *The Making of American Audiences: From Stage to Television, 1750–1990*. New York: Cambridge University Press, 2000.

Byrkit, James W. *Forging the Copper Collar: Arizona's Labor Management War of 1901–1921*. Tucson: University of Arizona Press, 1982.

Callow, Alexander B., Jr. *The Tweed Ring*. New York: Oxford University Press, 1969.

Caroli, Betty Boyd. *The Roosevelt Women*. New York: Basic Books, 1998.

Cavallo, Dominick. *Muscles and Morals: Organized Playgrounds and Urban Reform, 1880–1920*. Philadelphia: University of Pennsylvania Press, 1981.

Chalfant, Edward. *Better in Darkness: A Biography of Henry Adams, His Second Life 1862–1891*. Hamden, Conn.: Archon Books, 1994.

Challener, Richard D. *Admirals, Generals and American Foreign Policy, 1898–1914*. Princeton: Princeton University Press, 1973.

Chernow, Ron. *The House of Morgan: An American Banking Dynasty and the Rise of Modern Finance*. New York: Atlantic Monthly Press, 1990.

Cherny, Robert W. *American Politics in the Gilded Age, 1868–1900*. Wheeling, Ill.: Davidson, 1997.

———. *A Righteous Cause: The Life of William Jennings Bryan*. Boston: Little, Brown, 1985.

Chessman, G. Wallace. *Governor Theodore Roosevelt: The Albany Apprenticeship, 1898–1900*. Cambridge, Mass.: Harvard University Press, 1965.

Clifford, John Garry. *The Citizen Soldiers: The Plattsburg Training Camp Movement, 1913–1920*. Lexington: University Press of Kentucky, 1972.

Cohen, Michael P. *The Pathless Way: John Muir and American Wilderness*. Madison: University of Wisconsin Press, 1984.

Coleman, Peter J. *Progressivism and the World of Reform: New Zealand and the Origins of the American Welfare State*. Lawrence: University Press of Kansas, 1987.

Coletta, Paolo E. *The Presidency of William Howard Taft*. Lawrence: University Press of Kansas, 1973.

———. *William Jennings Bryan: Political Evangelist, 1860–1908*. 3 vols. Lincoln: University of Nebraska Press, 1964–69.

Connelly, Mark Thomas. *The Response to Prostitution in the Progressive Era*. Chapel Hill: University of North Carolina Press, 1980.

Conner, Valerie J. "The Mothers of the Race in World War I: The National War Labor Board and Women in Industry," *Labor History* 21 (1980): 31–54.

Cook, Adrian. *The Armies of the Streets: The New York City Draft Riots of 1863*. Lexington: University of Kentucky Press, 1974.

Cooper, John Milton, Jr. *Pivotal Decades: The United States, 1900–1920*. New York: Norton, 1990.

———. *The Warrior and the Priest*. Cambridge, Mass.: Belknap, 1983.

Cortissoz, Royal. *The Life of Whitelaw Reid*. 2 vols. New York: Scribner's, 1921.

Cott, Nancy F. *The Groundings of Modern Feminism*. New Haven: Yale University Press, 1987.

Cott, Nancy F., and Elizabeth H. Pleck, eds. *A Heritage of Her Own: Toward a New Social History of American Women*. New York: Simon & Schuster, 1979.

Cutright, Paul Russell. *Theodore Roosevelt: The Making of a Conservationist*. Urbana: University of Illinois Press, 1985.

———. *Theodore Roosevelt the Naturalist*. New York: Scribner's, 1956.

Dalton, Kathleen. "Between the Diplomacy of Imperialism and the Achievement of World Order by Supranational Mediation: Ethnocentrism and Theodore Roosevelt's Changing Views of World Order," in Pierre Melandri and Serge Ricard, eds., *Ethnocentrisme et diplomatie: L'Amérique et le monde au XXe siècle*. Paris: Editions l'Harmattan, 2001.

———. "The Bully Prophet: Theodore Roosevelt and American Memory," in Natalie A. Naylor, Douglas Brinkley, and John Allen Gable, eds., *Theodore Roosevelt: Many-Sided American*. Interlaken, N.Y.: Heart of the Lakes Publishing/Hofstra University, 1992.

———. "The Early Life of Theodore Roosevelt," Ph.D. diss., Johns Hopkins University, 1979.

———. "President Clinton, You're No Teddy Roosevelt," *Los Angeles Times*, Jan. 26, 1997.

———. "Teaching New Perspectives on Theodore Roosevelt and His Era: Was Theodore

Roosevelt a Warmonger?" for a special edition on the Progressive Era in the Organization of American Historians' *Magazine of History* 13, no. 3 (Spring 1999): 31–36.

——. "Theodore Roosevelt and the Idea of War," *Theodore Roosevelt Association Journal* 7, no. 4 (Fall 1981): 6–11.

——. "Theodore Roosevelt, Knickerbocker Aristocrat," *New York History* 67, no. 1 (January 1986): 39–65.

——. "Why America Loved Teddy Roosevelt: Or, Charisma Is in the Eyes of the Beholders," in Robert J. Brugger, ed., *OurSelves/Our Past: Psychological Approaches to American History*. Baltimore: Johns Hopkins University Press, 1981.

Danbom, David B. " 'For the Record of the War': Thorstein Veblen, Wartime Exigency, and Social Change," *Mid-America* 62 (1980): 91–95.

Daniel, Pete. *The Shadow of Slavery: Peonage in the South, 1901–1969*. Chicago: University of Illinois Press, 1990.

Daniels, Doris. "Building a Winning Coalition: The Suffrage Fight in New York State," *New York History* 60, no. 1 (January 1979): 59–80.

——. "Theodore Roosevelt and Gender Roles," *Presidential Studies Quarterly*, 1996 26(3): 648–65.

Daniels, Jonathan. *The End of Innocence*. Philadelphia: Lippincott, 1954.

Daniels, Josephus. *The Wilson Era: Years of Peace, 1910–1917*. Chapel Hill: University of North Carolina Press, 1944.

Davies, Wallace Evan. *Patriotism on Parade: The Story of Veterans' and Hereditary Organizations in America, 1783–1900*. Cambridge, Mass.: Harvard University Press, 1955.

Davis, Allen F. *American Heroine: The Life and Legend of Jane Addams*. New York: Oxford University Press, 1973.

——. "The Social Workers and the Progressive Party, 1912–1916," *American Historical Review* 69 (April 1964): 671–88.

——. *Spearheads for Reform: The Social Settlements and the Progressive Movement, 1890–1914*. New York: Oxford University Press, 1967.

——. "Welfare, Reform and World War I," *American Quarterly* 19 (1967): 516–33.

Davis, Calvin DeArmond. *The United States and the Second Hague Peace Conference: American Diplomacy and International Organization, 1899–1914*. Durham, N.C.: Duke University Press, 1975.

Degen, Marie Louise. "The History of the Woman's Peace Party," *The Johns Hopkins University Studies in Historical and Political Science*, series 57, no. 3. Baltimore: Johns Hopkins University Press, 1939.

D'Emilio, John, and Estelle B. Freedman. *Intimate Matters: A History of Sexuality in America*. New York: Harper & Row, 1988.

Dennett, Tyler. *John Hay: From Poetry to Politics*. New York: Dodd, Mead, 1933.

——. *Roosevelt and the Russo-Japanese War*. Garden City, N.Y.: Doubleday, Page, 1925.

Diner, Hasia R. *In the Almost Promised Land: American Jews and Blacks, 1915–1935*. Westport, Conn.: Greenwood Press, 1977.

Diner, Steven J. *A Very Different Age: Americans of the Progressive Era*. New York: Hill & Wang, 1998.

Doerries, Reinhard R. *Imperial Challenge: Ambassador Count Bernstorff and German-American Relations, 1908–1917*. Chapel Hill: University of North Carolina Press, 1989.

——. "Promoting Kaiser and Reich: Imperial German Propaganda in the United States During World War I," in Hans Jürgen-Schröder, ed., *Confrontation and Cooperation: Germany and the United States in the Era of World War I, 1900–1924*, Oxford, Eng.: Berg, 1993.

Doughty, Robin W. *Feather Fashions and Bird Preservation: A Study in Nature Protection*. Berkeley: University of California Press, 1975.

Dreier, Mary E. *Margaret Dreier Robins: Her Life, Letters, and Work.* New York: Island Press Cooperative, 1950.

Dubofsky, Melvyn. "Organized Labor in New York City and the First World War, 1914–1918," *New York History* 42 (1961).

Duffus, R. L. *Lillian Wald, Neighbor and Crusader.* New York: Macmillan, 1938.

Dunlap, Thomas R. *Saving America's Wildlife: Ecology and the American Mind, 1850–1990.* Princeton: Princeton University Press, 1988.

Duus, Peter. *The Abacus and the Sword: The Japanese Penetration of Korea, 1895–1910.* Berkeley: University of California Press, 1995.

Dye, Nancy Schrom. *As Equals and as Sisters: Feminism, the Labor Movement, and the Women's Trade Union League of New York.* Columbia: University of Missouri Press, 1980.

Dyer, Thomas G. *Theodore Roosevelt and the Idea of Race.* Baton Rouge: Louisiana State University Press, 1980.

Edwards, John Carver. *Patriots in Pinstripes: Men of the National Security League.* Washington, D.C.: University Press of America, 1982.

Edwards, Rebecca. *Angels in the Machinery: Gender in American Party Politics from the Civil War to the Progressive Era.* New York: Oxford University Press, 1997.

Einstein, Lewis. *Roosevelt: His Mind in Action.* Boston: Houghton Mifflin, 1930.

Ellis, Edward Robb. *Echoes of Distant Thunder: Life in the United States, 1914–1918.* New York: Coward, McCann and Geoghegan, 1975.

Ellis, Elmer. *Mr. Dooley's America: A Life of Finley Peter Dunne.* Hamden, Conn.: Archon, 1969.

Esthus, Raymond A. *Double Eagle and Rising Sun: The Russians and Japanese at Portsmouth in 1905.* Durham, N.C.: Duke University Press, 1988.

——. *Theodore Roosevelt and the International Rivalries.* Waltham, Mass.: Ginn-Blaisdell, 1970.

——. *Theodore Roosevelt and Japan.* Seattle: University of Washington Press, 1967.

Faderman, Lillian. *Surpassing the Love of Men: Romantic Friendships and Love Between Women from the Renaissance to the Present.* New York: Morrow, 1981.

Farrell, John C. *Beloved Lady: A History of Jane Addams' Ideas on Reform and Peace.* Baltimore: Johns Hopkins University Press, 1967.

Feinstein, Howard M. *Becoming William James.* Ithaca, N.Y.: Cornell University Press, 1984.

Filene, Peter G. "An Obituary for 'The Progressive Movement,' " *American Quarterly* 22 (Spring 1970): 30.

Filler, Louis. *The Muckrakers: Crusaders for American Liberalism.* Chicago: University of Chicago Press, 1968.

Findlay, Eileen J. Suarez. *Imposing Decency: The Politics of Sexuality and Race in Puerto Rico, 1870–1920.* Durham, N.C.: Duke University Press, 1999.

Fink, Leon, ed. *Major Problems in the Gilded Age and the Progressive Era.* Lexington, Mass.: Heath, 1993.

Finnegan, John P. *Against the Specter of a Dragon: The Campaign for American Military Preparedness, 1914–1917.* Westport, Conn.: Greenwood, 1974.

Fiss, Owen M. *Troubled Beginnings of the Modern State, 1888–1910.* New York: Macmillan, 1993.

Fitzpatrick, Ellen. *Endless Crusade: Women Social Scientists and Progressive Reform.* New York: Oxford University Press, 1990.

Forcey, Charles. *The Crossroads of Liberalism: Croly, Weyl, Lippmann, and the Progressive Era, 1900–1925.* New York: Oxford University Press, 1967.

Fox, Stephen R. *The Guardian of Boston, William Monroe Trotter.* New York: Atheneum, 1970.

———. *John Muir and His Legacy: The American Conservation Movement.* Boston: Little, Brown, 1981.

Fraser, John. *America and the Patterns of Chivalry.* New York: Cambridge University Press, 1982.

Fredrickson, George M. *The Black Image in the White Mind: The Debate on Afro-American Character and Destiny, 1817–1914.* New York: Harper & Row, 1971.

———. *The Inner Civil War: Northern Intellectuals and the Crisis of the Union.* New York: Harper & Row, 1968.

Freeman, Jo. *A Room at a Time: How Women Entered Party Politics.* Lanham, Md.: Rowman & Littlefield, 2000.

Freidel, Frank. *Over There: The Story of America's First Great Overseas Crusade.* Philadelphia: Temple University Press, 1990.

Freyer, Tony. *Regulating Big Business: Antitrust in Great Britain and America, 1880–1990.* New York: Cambridge University Press, 1992.

Fuess, Claude Moore. *Carl Schurz, Reformer (1829–1906).* American Political Leaders series. New York: Dodd, Mead, 1932.

Gable, John. *The Bull Moose Years: Theodore Roosevelt and the Progressive Party.* Port Washington, N.Y.: Kennikat, 1978.

———. "The Bull Moose Years: Theodore Roosevelt and the Progressive Party, 1912–1916," Ph.D. diss., 1972.

Gallman, J. Matthew. *The North Fights the Civil War: The Home Front.* Chicago: University of Chicago Press, 1994.

Gardner, Gilson. *Lusty Scripps: The Life of E. W. Scripps.* New York: Vanguard, 1932.

Garraty, John A. *Henry Cabot Lodge: A Biography.* New York: Knopf, 1953.

Gatewood, Willard B., Jr. *Theodore Roosevelt and the Art of Controversy: Episodes of the White House Years.* Baton Rouge: Louisiana State University Press, 1970.

———. "Theodore Roosevelt: Champion of 'Governmental Aesthetics,' " *Georgia Review* 21, no. 1 (1967): 172–83.

George, Henry, Jr. *The Life of Henry George, by His Son.* 1900; reprint, New York: Robert Schalkenbach Foundation, 1960.

Gibson, William M. *Theodore Roosevelt Among the Humorists: W. D. Howells, Mark Twain, and Mr. Dooley.* Knoxville: University of Tennessee Press, 1980.

Gilfoyle, Timothy J. *City of Eros: New York City, Prostitution, and the Commercialization of Sex, 1790–1920.* New York: Norton, 1992.

Gilmore, Glenda Elizabeth. *Gender and Jim Crow: Women and the Politics of White Supremacy in North Carolina, 1896–1920,* Chapel Hill: University of North Carolina Press, 1996.

Golay, Frank Hindman. *Face of Empire: United States–Philippine Relations, 1898–1946.* Madison: University of Wisconsin Press, 1998.

Goldman, Eric F. *Charles J. Bonaparte, Patrician Reformer: His Earlier Career.* Baltimore: Johns Hopkins Press, 1954.

———. *Rendezvous with Destiny: A History of Modern American Reform.* New York: Knopf, 1966.

Goldmark, Josephine. *Impatient Crusader: Florence Kelley's Life Story.* Urbana: University of Illinois Press, 1953.

Goodwin, Lorine Swainston. *The Pure Food, Drink, and Drug Crusaders, 1879–1914.* Jefferson, N.C.: McFarland, 1999.

Goodwyn, Lawrence. *The Populist Moment.* New York: Oxford University Press, 1978.

Gordon, Dudley. *Charles F. Lummis: Crusader in Corduroy*. Los Angeles: Cultural Assets Press, 1972.

Gordon, Lynn D. *Gender and Higher Education in the Progressive Era*. New Haven: Yale University Press, 1990.

Gosnell, Harold F. *Boss Platt and His New York Machine*. Chicago: University of Chicago Press, 1924.

Gossett, Thomas F. *Race: The History of an Idea in America*. New York: Schocken, 1965.

Gould, Lewis L. *The Presidency of Theodore Roosevelt*. Lawrence: University Press of Kansas, 1991.

——. "The Price of Fame: Theodore Roosevelt as a Celebrity, 1909–1919," *Lamar Journal of the Humanities* 10 (Fall 1984): 7–18.

——. *Reform and Regulation: American Politics from Roosevelt to Wilson*. New York: Knopf, 1986.

Gould, Stephen Jay. *Ever Since Darwin: Reflections in Natural History*. New York: Norton, 1977.

Graebner, Norman A., ed. *Uncertain Tradition: American Secretaries of State in the Twentieth Century*. New York: McGraw-Hill, 1961.

Graham, Abbie. *Grace H. Dodge: Merchant of Dreams, a Biography*. New York: Woman's Press, 1926.

Graham, Otis. *An Encore for Reform: The Old Progressives and the New Deal*. London: Oxford University Press, 1967.

Graham, Sally Hunter. "Woodrow Wilson, Alice Paul, and the Woman Suffrage Movement," *Political Science Quarterly* 98, no. 4 (Winter 1983–84): 665–79.

Graham, Sara Hunter. *Woman Suffrage and the New Democracy*. New Haven: Yale University Press, 1996.

Green, Constance McLaughlin. *Washington: Capital City, 1879–1950*. Princeton: Princeton University Press, 1963.

Green, Martin. *The Mount Vernon Street Warrens: A Boston Story, 1860–1910*. New York: Scribner's, 1989.

——. *The Problem of Boston*. New York: Norton, 1966.

Greenberg, Irving. *Theodore Roosevelt and Labor, 1900–1918*. New York: Garland, 1988.

Griscom, Lloyd C. *Diplomatically Speaking*. Boston: Little, Brown, 1940.

Gunther, Gerald. *Learned Hand: The Man and the Judge*. New York: Knopf, 1994.

Gusfield, Joseph R. *Symbolic Crusade: Status Politics and the American Temperance Movement*. Chicago: University of Chicago Press, 1972.

Gustafson, Melanie. "Partisan Women in the Progressive Era: The Struggle for Inclusion in American Political Parties," *Journal of Women's History* 9, no. 2, (Summer 1997): 8–30.

——. *Women and the Republican Party, 1854–1924*. Urbana: University of Illinois Press, 2001.

Gustafson, Melanie, Kristie Miller, and Elisabeth I. Perry, eds. *We Have Come to Stay: American Women and Political Parties, 1880–1960*. Albuquerque: University of New Mexico Press, 1999.

Hagan, William T. *Theodore Roosevelt and Six Friends of the Indian*. Norman: University of Oklahoma Press, 1997.

Hagedorn, Hermann. *The Boys' Life of Theodore Roosevelt*. New York: Harper & Bros., 1922.

——. *The Bugle That Woke America: The Saga of Theodore Roosevelt's Last Battle for His Country*. New York: Day, 1940.

——. *The Hyphenated Family: An American Saga*. New York: Macmillan, 1960.

——. *The Roosevelt Family of Sagamore Hill*. New York: Macmillan, 1954.

———. *Roosevelt in the Bad Lands*. Boston: Houghton Mifflin, 1921.

———. *The Rough Riders: A Romance*. New York; London: Harper & Bros., 1927.

Haley, Bruce. *The Healthy Body and Victorian Culture*. Cambridge, Mass.: Harvard University Press, 1978.

Haller, Mark H. *Eugenics: Hereditarian Attitudes in American Thought*. New Brunswick, N.J.: Rutgers University Press, 1963.

Hammack, David S. *Power and Society: Greater New York at the Turn of the Century*. New York: Russell Sage Foundation, 1982.

Harbaugh, William H. *Power and Responsibility: The Life and Times of Theodore Roosevelt*. New York: Farrar, Straus & Cudahy, 1961.

———. "The Theodore Roosevelts' Retreat in Southern Albemarle: Pine Knot, 1905–1908," reprinted from *Albemarle County History* 51 (1993).

Harlan, Louis R. *Booker T. Washington: The Making of a Black Leader, 1865–1901*. New York: Oxford University Press, 1972.

———. *Booker T. Washington: The Wizard of Tuskegee, 1901–1915*. New York: Oxford University Press, 1983.

Harries, Meirion, and Susie Harries. *The Last Days of Innocence: America at War, 1917–1918*. New York: Random House, 1997.

Harrison, Robert. "The Ideal of a 'Model City': Federal Social Policy for the District of Columbia, 1905–1909," *Journal of Urban History* 15, no. 4 (August 1989).

Hart, Robert A. *The Great White Fleet: Its Voyage Around the World, 1907–1909*. Boston: Little, Brown, 1965.

Havig, Alan R. "Presidential Images, History and Homage: Memorializing Theodore Roosevelt, 1919–1967," *American Quarterly* 30 (Fall 1978).

———. "Theodore and Franklin: F.D.R.'s Use of the Theodore Roosevelt Image, 1920–1936," *Theodore Roosevelt Association Journal* 5, no. 2 (Spring 1979): 6–10.

Hays, Samuel P. *Conservation and the Gospel of Efficiency: The Progressive Conservation Movement, 1890–1920*. Cambridge, Mass.: Harvard University Press, 1959.

Heckscher, August. *Woodrow Wilson*. New York: Scribner's, 1991.

Hernández, José M. *Cuba and the United States: Intervention and Militarism, 1868–1933*. Austin, Tex.: University of Austin Press, 1993.

Hershkowitz, Leo. *Tweed's New York: Another Look*. Garden City, N.Y.: Doubleday, Doran, 1978.

Hiebert, Ray Eldon. *Courtier to the Crowd: The Story of Ivy Lee and the Development of Public Relations*. Ames: Iowa State University Press, 1966.

Hirschfeld, Charles. "Nationalist Progressivism and World War I," *Mid-America* 45, no. 3 (July 1963): 139–56.

Hoffman, Beatrix. *The Wages of Sickness: The Politics of Health Insurance in Progressive America*. Chapel Hill: University of North Carolina Press, 2001.

Hofstadter, Richard. *The Age of Reform: From Bryan to F.D.R.* New York: Vintage, 1955.

———. *The American Political Tradition and the Men Who Made It*. New York: Knopf, 1948.

———. *Anti-Intellectualism in American Life*. New York: Knopf, 1966.

Hoganson, Kristin L. *Fighting for American Manhood: How Gender Politics Provoked the Spanish-American and Philippine-American Wars*. New Haven: Yale University Press, 1998.

Holmes, William F. *"The White Chief": James Kimble Vardaman*. Baton Rouge: Louisiana State University Press, 1970.

Hoogenboom, Ari Arthur. *Outlawing the Spoils: A History of the Civil Service Reform Movement, 1865–1883*. Urbana: University of Illinois Press, 1968.

——. *Rutherford B. Hayes: Warrior and President.* Lawrence: University Press of Kansas, 1995.

Hoopes, James. *Van Wyck Brooks: In Search of American Culture.* Amherst: University of Massachusetts Press, 1977.

Hopkins, C. Howard. *History of the YMCA in North America.* New York: Association Press, 1951.

Horne, John, and Alan Kramer. "German 'Atrocities' and Franco-German Opinion, 1914: The Evidence of German Soldiers' Diaries," *Journal of Modern History* 66 (March 1994): 1–33.

Horowitz, Helen Lefkowitz. *Campus Life: Undergraduate Cultures from the End of the Eighteenth Century to the Present.* New York: Knopf, 1987.

——. *Culture and the City: Cultural Philanthropy in Chicago from the 1880s to 1917.* Lexington: University Press of Kentucky, 1976.

Hughes, Langston. *Fight for Freedom: The Story of the NAACP.* New York: Berkley, 1962.

Hunt, Michael H. *Ideology and U.S. Foreign Policy.* New Haven: Yale University Press, 1987.

Hurwitz, Howard Lawrence. *Theodore Roosevelt and Labor in New York State, 1880–1900.* New York: Columbia University Press, 1943.

Huth, Hans. *Nature and the American: Three Centuries of Changing Attitudes.* Berkeley: University of California Press, 1957.

Iriye, Akira. *Across the Pacific: An Inner History of American–East Asian Relations.* New York: Harcourt Brace & World, 1967.

——. *Cultural Internationalism and World Order.* Baltimore: Johns Hopkins University Press, 1997.

——. *Pacific Estrangement: Japanese and American Expansion, 1897–1911.* Cambridge, Mass.: Harvard University Press, 1972.

——, ed. *Mutual Images: Essays in American-Japanese Relations.* Cambridge, Mass.: Harvard University Press, 1975.

Israel, Jerry. *Progressivism and the Open Door: America and China, 1905–1921.* Pittsburgh: University of Pittsburgh Press, 1971.

Iversen, Joan. *The Antipolygamy Controversy in U.S. Women's Movements, 1880–1925: A Debate on the American Home.* New York: Garland, 1997.

Jacoby, Robin Miller. *The British and American Women's Trade Union Leagues, 1890–1925.* Brooklyn, N.Y.: Carlson, 1994.

Jaher, Frederic Cople. *The Urban Establishment.* Chicago: University of Illinois Press, 1982.

——, ed. *The Rich, the Well-Born, and the Powerful.* Urbana: University of Illinois Press, 1973.

Jameson, J. Franklin (John Franklin). *John Franklin Jameson and the Development of Humanistic Scholarship in America*, ed. Jacqueline Goggin and Morey Rothberg. Athens: University of Georgia Press, 1993–2001.

Jensen, Joan M. *The Price of Vigilance.* Chicago: Rand McNally, 1969.

Jessup, Philip C. *Elihu Root.* 2 vols. New York: Dodd, Mead, 1938.

John, Arthur. *The Best Years of the Century: Richard Watson Gilder, Scribner's Monthly, and the Century Magazine, 1870–1909.* Chicago: University of Chicago Press, 1981.

Johnson, Donald D. *The Challenge to American Freedoms: World War I and the Rise of the American Civil Liberties Union.* Lexington: University Press of Kentucky, 1963.

——. "Wilson, Burleson, and Censorship in the First World War," *Journal of Southern History* 28 (1962): 46–58.

Johnson, Michael R. "The IWW and Wilsonian Democracy," *Science and Society* 28, no. 3 (1964): 258–74.

Johnson, Richard Christian. "Anthony Comstock: Reform, Vice, and the American Way," Ph.D. diss., University of Wisconsin, 1973.

Johnson, Robert. *The Peace Progressives and American Foreign Policy*. Cambridge, Mass.: Harvard University Press, 1995.

Jordan, David M. *Roscoe Conkling of New York: Voice in the Senate*. Ithaca, N.Y.: Cornell University Press, 1971.

Jordan, Winthrop D. *White over Black: American Attitudes Toward the Negro, 1550–1812*. Chapel Hill: University of North Carolina Press, 1968.

Juergens, George. *Joseph Pulitzer and the New York World*. Princeton: Princeton University Press, 1966.

——. *News from the White House: The Presidential-Press Relationship in the Progressive Era*. Chicago: University of Chicago Press, 1981.

Kantrowitz, Stephen. *Ben Tillman and the Reconstruction of White Supremacy*. Chapel Hill: University of North Carolina Press, 2000.

Kaplan, Justin. *Lincoln Steffens: A Biography*. New York: Simon & Schuster, 1974.

Kaplan, Wendy, et al. *"The Art That Is Life": The Arts and Crafts Movement in America, 1875–1920*. Boston: Museum of Fine Arts, 1987.

Karnow, Stanley. *In Our Image: America's Empire in the Philippines*. New York: Ballantine, 1989.

Kazin, Michael. *The Populist Persuasion: An American History*. Ithaca, N.Y.: Cornell University Press, 1998.

Keller, Morton. *Affairs of State: Public Life in Late Nineteenth Century America*. Cambridge, Mass.: Belknap, 1977.

Keller, Phyllis. *States of Belonging: German-American Intellectuals and the First World War*. Cambridge, Mass.: Harvard University Press, 1979.

Kellogg, Charles Flint. *NAACP: A History of the National Association for the Advancement of Colored People*, vol. 1, *1909–1920*. Baltimore: Johns Hopkins University Press, 1967.

Kelly, Patrick J. *Creating a National Home: Building the Veterans' Welfare State, 1860–1900*. Cambridge, Mass.: Harvard University Press, 1997.

Kennedy, David M. *Over Here: The First World War and American Society*. New York: Oxford University Press, 1968.

Kerber, Linda K., Alice Kessler-Harris, and Kathryn Kish Sklar, eds. *U.S. History as Women's History: New Feminist Essays*. Chapel Hill: University of North Carolina Press, 1995.

Kerr, K. Austin. *Organized for Prohibition: A New History of the Anti-Saloon League*. New Haven: Yale University Press, 1985.

Kevles, Daniel J. *In the Name of Eugenics: Genetics and the Uses of Human Heredity*. Cambridge, Mass.: Harvard University Press, 1995.

Kloppenberg, James T. *Uncertain Victory: Social Democracy and Progressivism in European and American Thought, 1870–1920*. New York: Oxford University Press, 1986.

Knock, Thomas J. *To End All Wars: Woodrow Wilson and the Quest for a New World Order*. Princeton: Princeton University Press, 1992.

Koven, Seth, and Sonya Michel, eds. *Mothers of a New World: Maternalist Politics and the Origins of Welfare States*. New York: Routledge, 1993.

Ladd-Taylor, Molly. "Eugenics, Sterilisation and Modern Marriage in the USA: The Strange Career of Paul Popenoe," *Gender & History* 13, no. 2 (August 2001): 301.

——. *Mother-Work: Women, Child Welfare, and the State, 1890–1930*. Chicago: University of Illinois Press, 1994.

Lael, Richard L. *Arrogant Diplomacy: U.S. Policy Toward Colombia, 1903–1922.* Wilmington, Del.: Scholarly Resources, 1987.

La Follette, Belle Case, and Fola La Follette. *Robert M. La Follette.* 2 vols. New York: Macmillan, 1953.

Lamoreaux, Naomi R. *The Great Merger Movement in American Business, 1895–1904.* New York: Cambridge University Press, 1988.

Lane, Ann J. *The Brownsville Affair: National Crisis and Black Reaction.* Port Washington, N.Y.: Kennikat, 1971.

Lane, James B. *Jacob A. Riis and the American City.* Port Washington, N.Y.: Kennikat, 1974.

Langum, David J. *Crossing Over the Line: Legislating Morality and the Mann Act.* Chicago: University of Chicago Press, 1994.

Lardner, James, and Thomas Reppetto. *NYPD: A City and Its Police.* New York: Holt, 2000.

Larsen, Charles. *The Good Fight: The Life and Times of Ben B. Lindsey.* Chicago: Quadrangle, 1972.

Larsen, Peter. "Theodore Roosevelt and the Moroccan Crisis, 1904–1906," Ph.D. diss., Princeton University, 1984.

Lasch, Christopher. *The New Radicalism in America, 1889–1963.* New York: Knopf, 1965.

Lasch-Quinn, Elizabeth. *Black Neighbors: Race and the Limits of Reform in the American Settlement House Movement, 1890–1945.* Chapel Hill: University of North Carolina Press, 1993.

Lash, Joseph P. *Eleanor and Franklin: The Story of Their Relationship, Based on Eleanor Roosevelt's Private Papers.* New York: New American Library, 1973.

Lears, T. J. Jackson. *No Place of Grace: Antimodernism and the Transformation of American Culture, 1880–1920.* New York: Pantheon, 1981.

Lee, Basil Leo. *Discontent in New York City, 1861–1865.* Washington, D.C.: Catholic University of America Press, 1943.

Leech, Margaret. *In the Days of McKinley.* New York: Harper, 1959.

Lehrer, Susan. *Origins of Protective Labor Legislation for Women, 1905–1925.* Albany, N.Y.: State University of New York Press, 1987.

Leiby, James. *Carroll Wright and Labor Reform: The Origin of Labor Statistics.* Cambridge, Mass.: Harvard University Press, 1960.

Leonard, Thomas J. *Above the Battle: War-Making in America from Appomattox to Versailles.* New York: Oxford University Press, 1978.

Leopold, Richard W. *Elihu Root and the Conservative Tradition.* Boston: Little, Brown, 1954.

Leuchtenburg, William E. *The Perils of Prosperity, 1914–32.* Chicago: University of Chicago Press, 1958.

Levin, N. Gordon, Jr. *Woodrow Wilson and World Politics: America's Response to War and Revolution.* New York: Oxford University Press, 1968.

Levin, Phyllis Lee. *Edith and Woodrow: The Wilson White House.* New York: Scribner, 2001.

Levine, Daniel. *Jane Addams and the Liberal Tradition.* Madison: State Historical Society of Wisconsin, 1971.

——. *Poverty and Society: The Growth of the American Welfare State in International Comparison.* New Brunswick, N.J.: Rutgers University Press, 1988.

Levy, David W. *Herbert Croly of The New Republic: The Life and Thought of an American Progressive.* Princeton: Princeton University Press, 1985.

Lewis, David Levering. *W.E.B. Du Bois: Biography of a Race, 1868–1919*, 2 vols. New York: Holt, 1993.

——. *W.E.B. Du Bois: A Reader.* New York: Holt, 1995.

Linderman, Gerald F. *The Mirror of War: American Society and the Spanish-American War.* Ann Arbor: University of Michigan Press, 1974.

Lindquist, John H., and James Fraser. "A Sociological Interpretation of the Bisbee Deportation," *Pacific Historical Review* 37 (1968): 401–22.

Link, Arthur S. *Wilson: Campaigns for Progressivism and Peace, 1916–1917.* Princeton: Princeton University Press, 1965.

——. *Wilson: Confusions and Crises, 1915–1916.* Princeton: Princeton University Press, 1964.

——. *Wilson: The New Freedom.* Princeton: Princeton University Press, 1956.

——. *Wilson: The Road to the White House.* Princeton: Princeton University Press, 1968.

——. *Wilson: The Struggle for Neutrality, 1914–1915.* Princeton: Princeton University Press, 1960.

——. *Wilson the Diplomatist: A Look at His Major Foreign Policies.* New York: New Viewpoints, 1974.

——. *Woodrow Wilson: A Brief Biography.* Cleveland: World, 1963.

——. *Woodrow Wilson: Revolution, War and Peace.* Arlington Heights, Ill.: Davidson, 1979.

——. *Woodrow Wilson and the Progressive Era, 1910–1917.* New York: Harper Torchbooks, 1963.

——. *Woodrow Wilson and a Revolutionary World, 1913–1921.* Supplementary volumes to *The Papers of Woodrow Wilson.* Chapel Hill: University of North Carolina Press, 1982.

——, ed. *The Papers of Woodrow Wilson.* 69 vols. Princeton: Princeton University Press, 1966–94.

Link, Arthur S., and Richard L. McCormick. *Progressivism.* Arlington Heights, Ill.: Davidson, 1983.

Linn, Brian McAllister. *Guardians of Empire: The U.S. Army and the Pacific, 1902–1940.* Chapel Hill: University of North Carolina Press, 1997.

——. *The Philippine War, 1899–1902.* Lawrence: University Press of Kansas, 2000.

——. *The U.S. Army and Counterinsurgency in the Philippine War, 1899–1902.* Chapel Hill: University of North Carolina Press, 1989.

Lippmann, Walter. *Drift and Mastery: An Attempt to Diagnose the Current Unrest.* 1914; reprint, Englewood Cliffs, N.J.: Prentice-Hall, 1961.

Litwack, Leon F. *Trouble in Mind: Black Southerners in the Age of Jim Crow.* New York: Knopf, 1998.

Livermore, Seward W. *Politics Is Adjourned: Woodrow Wilson and the War Congress, 1916–1918.* Middletown, Conn.: Wesleyan University Press, 1966.

Lockmiller, David A. *Magoon in Cuba: A History of the Second Intervention, 1906–1909.* Chapel Hill: University of North Carolina Press, 1938.

Logan, Rayford W. *The Betrayal of the Negro: From Rutherford B. Hayes to Woodrow Wilson.* New York: Da Capo, 1997.

Lovell, S. D. *The Presidential Election of 1916.* Carbondale: Southern Illinois University Press, 1980.

Lowitt, Richard. *George W. Norris: The Persistence of a Progressive, 1913–1933.* Urbana: University of Illinois Press, 1971.

——. *A Merchant Prince of the Nineteenth Century: William E. Dodge.* New York: Columbia University Press, 1954.

Lubow, Arthur. *The Reporter Who Would Be King: A Biography of Richard Harding Davis*. New York: Scribner, 1992.

Luebke, Frederick C. *Bonds of Loyalty: German-Americans and World War I*. De Kalb: Northern Illinois University Press, 1974.

Lukas, J. Anthony. *Big Trouble: A Murder in a Small Western Town Sets Off a Struggle for the Soul of America*. New York: Simon & Schuster, 1997.

Luker, Ralph E. *The Social Gospel in Black and White: American Racial Reform, 1885–1912*. Chapel Hill: University of North Carolina Press, 1991.

Lunardini, Christine A., and Thomas J. Knock. "Woodrow Wilson and Woman Suffrage: A New Look," *Political Science Quarterly* 95 (Winter 1980–81): 655–57.

Lutts, Ralph H. *The Nature Fakers: Wildlife, Science, and Sentiment*. Golden, Colo.: Fulcrum, 1990.

Lynn, Kenneth S. *William Dean Howells: An American Life*. New York: Harcourt Brace, 1970.

Lyon, Peter. *Success Story: The Life and Times of S. S. McClure*. New York: Scribner's, 1963.

MacFarland, C. K., and Nevin E. Neal. "The Reluctant Reformer: Woodrow Wilson and Woman Suffrage, 1913–1920," *Rocky Mountain Social Science Journal* 11 (1974): 33–43.

McCarthy, Kathleen D. *Women's Culture: American Philanthropy and Art, 1830–1930*. Chicago: University of Chicago Press, 1991.

McCartin, Joseph A. *Labor's Great War: The Struggle for Industrial Democracy and the Origins of Modern American Labor Relations, 1912–1921*. Chapel Hill: University of North Carolina Press, 1997.

McClymer, John F. *War and Welfare: Social Engineering in America, 1890–1925*. Westport, Conn.: Greenwood, 1980.

McCullough, David. *Mornings on Horseback*. New York: Simon & Schuster, 1981.

McDonough, Peter. *Men Astutely Trained: A History of the Jesuits in the American Century*. New York: Free Press, 1992.

McGeary, M. Nelson. *Gifford Pinchot: Forester-Politician*. Princeton: Princeton University Press, 1960.

McGovern, George S. *The Great Coalfield War*. Boston: Houghton Mifflin, 1972.

McLoughlin, William G. *Revivals, Awakenings, and Reform: An Essay on Religion and Social Change in America, 1607–1977*. Chicago: University of Chicago Press, 1978.

Mandelbaum, Seymour J. *Boss Tweed's New York*. New York: Wiley, 1965.

Mangan, J. A. *Athleticism in the Victorian and Edwardian Public School: The Emergence and Consolidation of an Educational Ideology*. New York: Cambridge University Press, 1981.

Manners, William. *T.R. and Will: A Friendship That Split the Republican Party*. New York: Harcourt Brace & World, 1969.

Marchand, C. Roland. *The American Peace Movement and Social Reform, 1898–1918*. Princeton: Princeton University Press, 1972.

Marcosson, Isaac Frederick. *"Marse Henry": A Biography of Henry Watterson*. New York: Dodd, Mead, 1951.

Marks, Frederick W., III. *Velvet on Iron: The Diplomacy of Theodore Roosevelt*. Lincoln: University of Nebraska Press, 1979.

Marling, Karal Ann. *George Washington Slept Here: Colonial Revivals and American Culture, 1876–1986*. Cambridge, Mass.: Harvard University Press, 1988.

Marsden, George M. *Fundamentalism and American Culture: The Shaping of Twentieth-Century Evangelicalism, 1870–1925*. New York: Oxford University Press, 1980.

Marten, James. *The Children's Civil War*. Chapel Hill: University of North Carolina Press, 1998.

Martin, Clarece. *A Glimpse of the Past: The History of Bulloch Hall and Roswell, Georgia.* Roswell, Ga.: Lake, 1987.

Maxwell, Robert S. *La Follette and the Rise of the Progressives in Wisconsin.* New York: Russell & Russell, 1973.

May, Elaine Tyler. *Barren in the Promised Land: Childless Americans and the Pursuit of Happiness.* Cambridge, Mass.: Harvard University Press, 1997.

May, Ernest R. *Imperial Democracy: The Emergence of America as a Great Power.* New York: Harcourt Brace & World, 1961.

——. *The World War and American Isolation, 1914–1917.* Cambridge, Mass.: Harvard University Press, 1959.

May, Henry. *The End of American Innocence.* Chicago: Quadrangle, 1964.

Mayr, Ernst. *The Growth of Biological Thought: Diversity, Evolution, and Inheritance.* Cambridge, Mass.: Belknap, 1982.

Meier, August. *Negro Thought in America, 1880–1915.* Ann Arbor: University of Michigan Press, 1988.

Merchant, Carolyn. *Major Problems in American Environmental History: Documents and Essays.* Lexington, Mass.: Heath, 1993.

Miller, Char. *Gifford Pinchot and the Making of Modern Environmentalism.* Washington, D.C.: Island Press, 2001.

——, ed. *American Forests: Nature, Culture, and Politics.* Lawrence: University Press of Kansas, 1997.

Miller, Donald L., and Richard E. Sharpless. *The Kingdom of Coal: Work, Enterprise, and Ethnic Communities in the Mine Fields.* Philadelphia: University of Pennsylvania Press, 1985.

Miller, Stuart Creighton. *"Benevolent Assimilation": The American Conquest of the Philippines, 1899–1903.* New Haven: Yale University Press, 1982.

Millis, Walter. *The Martial Spirit: A Study of Our War with Spain.* Boston: Houghton Mifflin, 1931.

——. *Road to War: America 1914–1917.* Boston: Houghton Mifflin, 1935.

Mock, James Robert. *Words That Won the War: The Story of the Committee on Public Information, 1917–1919.* Princeton: Princeton University Press, 1939.

Mohr, James C. *The Radical Republicans and Reform in New York During Reconstruction.* Ithaca, N.Y.: Cornell University Press, 1973.

Moorhead, James H. *American Apocalypse: Yankee Protestants and the Civil War, 1860–1869.* New Haven: Yale University Press, 1978.

Morgan, H. Wayne. *From Hayes to McKinley: National Party Politics, 1877–1896.* Syracuse, N.Y.: Syracuse University Press, 1969.

——. *William McKinley and His America.* Syracuse, N.Y.: Syracuse University Press, 1963.

Morison, Elting E. *Turmoil and Tradition: A Study of the Life and Times of Henry L. Stimson.* Boston: Houghton Mifflin, 1960.

Morris, Calvin S. *Reverdy C. Ransom: Black Advocate of the Social Gospel.* Lanham, Md.: University Press of America, 1990.

Morris, Edmund. *The Rise of Theodore Roosevelt.* New York: Coward, McCann and Geoghegan, 1979.

Morris, Sylvia Jukes. *Edith Kermit Roosevelt: Portrait of a First Lady.* New York: Coward, McCann and Geoghegan, 1980.

Mowry, George E. *The Era of Theodore Roosevelt and the Birth of Modern America, 1900–1912.* New York: Harper Torchbooks, 1962.

——. *Theodore Roosevelt and the Progressive Movement.* New York: Hill & Wang, c. 1946, 1960.

Muncy, Robyn. *Creating a Female Dominion in American Reform, 1890–1935*. New York: Oxford University Press, 1991.

Musicant, Ivan. *Empire by Default: The Spanish-American War and the Dawn of the American Century*. New York: Holt, 1998.

Musto, David. "Opium, Cocaine and Marijuana in American History," *Scientific American*, July 1991, 40–47.

Nasaw, David. *The Chief: The Life of William Randolph Hearst*. Boston: Houghton Mifflin, 2000.

Nash, Roderick. *Wilderness and the American Mind*. New Haven: Yale University Press, 1976.

Naylor, Natalie A., Douglas Brinkley, and John Allen Gable, eds. *Theodore Roosevelt: Many-Sided American*. Interlaken, N.Y.: Heart of the Lakes Publishing, 1992.

Neu, Charles E. *An Uncertain Friendship: Theodore Roosevelt and Japan, 1906–1909*. Cambridge, Mass.: Harvard University Press, 1967.

Nevins, Allan. *Henry White: Thirty Years of American Diplomacy*. New York: Harper & Bros., 1930.

Ninkovich, Frank. *Modernity and Power*. Chicago: University of Chicago Press, 1994.

——. "Theodore Roosevelt: Civilization as Ideology," *Diplomatic History* 10, no. 3 (1986): 221–45.

——. *The United States and Imperialism*. Malden, Mass.: Blackwell, 2001.

Nish, Ian Hill. *The Origins of the Russo-Japanese War*. New York: Longman, 1985.

Novak, Daniel A. *The Wheel of Servitude: Black Forced Labor After Slavery*. Lexington: University of Kentucky Press, 1978.

Odem, Mary E. *Delinquent Daughters: Protecting and Policing Adolescent Sexuality in the United States, 1885–1920*. Chapel Hill: University of North Carolina Press, 1995.

Offner, John L. *An Unwanted War: The Diplomacy of the United States and Spain over Cuba, 1895–1898*. Chapel Hill: University of North Carolina Press, 1992.

Oliver, Lawrence J. "Theodore Roosevelt, Brander Matthews, and the Campaign for Literary Americanism," *American Quarterly* 41, no. 1 (March 1989): 93–111.

Olson, Keith W. *Biography of a Progressive: Franklin K. Lane*. Westport, Conn.: Greenwood, 1979.

O'Reilly, Kenneth. *Nixon's Piano: Presidents and Racial Politics from Washington to Clinton*. New York: Free Press, 1995.

Ornig, Joseph R. *My Last Chance to Be a Boy: Theodore Roosevelt's South American Expedition of 1913–1914*. Mechanicsburg, Pa.: Stackpole, 1994.

Orvell, Miles. *The Real Thing: Imitation and Authenticity in American Culture, 1880–1940*. Chapel Hill: University of North Carolina Press, 1989.

Osborn, George Coleman. *John Sharp Williams: Planter-Statesman of the Deep South*. Baton Rouge: Louisiana State University Press, 1943.

O'Toole, Patricia. *The Five of Hearts: An Intimate Portrait of Henry Adams and His Friends, 1880–1918*. New York: Ballantine, 1990.

Ovington, Mary White. *The Walls Came Tumbling Down*. New York: Arno, 1969.

Painter, Nell Irvin. *Standing at Armageddon: The United States, 1877–1919*. New York: Norton, 1987.

Parker, Alison M. *Purifying America: Women, Cultural Reform, and Pro-Censorship Activism, 1873–1933*. Chicago: University of Chicago Press, 1997.

Payne, Elizabeth. *Reform, Labor, and Feminism: Margaret Dreier Robins and the Women's Trade Union League*. Chicago: University of Illinois Press, 1988.

Pearlman, Michael. *To Make Democracy Safe for America: Patricians and Preparedness in the Progressive Era*. Urbana: University of Illinois Press, 1984.

Pérez, Louis A. Jr., *Cuba: Between Reform and Revolution.* New York: Oxford University Press, 1988.

——. *Cuba: Between Empires, 1878–1902.* Pittsburgh: University of Pittsburgh Press, 1983.

——. *Cuba Under the Platt Amendment, 1902–1934.* Pittsburgh: University of Pittsburgh Press, 1986.

——. *The War of 1898: The United States and Cuba in History and Historiography.* Chapel Hill: University of North Carolina Press, 1998.

Perry, Ralph Barton. *The Plattsburg Movement: A Chapter of America's Participation in the World War.* New York: Dutton, 1921.

Peterson, H. C. *Propaganda for War: The Campaign Against American Neutrality, 1914–1917.* Norman: University of Oklahoma Press, 1939.

Peterson, H. C., and Gilbert C. Fite. *Opponents of War, 1917–1918.* Seattle: University of Washington Press, 1957.

Pivar, David. *Purity Crusade: Sexual Morality and Social Control, 1868–1900.* Westport, Conn.: Greenwood, 1973.

Pleck, Elizabeth H. "The Whipping Post for Wife Beaters, 1876–1906," in David Levine et al., *Essays on the Family and Historical Change.* College Station: Texas A & M University Press, 1983.

Porter, Glenn. *The Rise of Big Business, 1860–1910.* Arlington Heights, Ill.: AHM, 1973.

Preston, William Jr. *Aliens and Dissenters: Federal Suppression of Radicals, 1903–1933.* New York: Harper & Row, 1963.

Pringle, Henry F. *The Life and Times of William Howard Taft.* 2 vols. New York: Farrar & Rinehart, 1939.

——. *Theodore Roosevelt: A Biography.* New York: Harcourt Brace, 1931.

Putnam, Carleton. *Theodore Roosevelt: The Formative Years, 1858–1886.* New York: Scribner's, 1958.

Putney, Clifford. *Muscular Christianity: Manhood and Sports in Protestant America, 1880–1920.* Cambridge, Mass.: Harvard University Press, 2001.

Pyne, Stephen J. *How the Canyon Became Grand: A Short History.* New York: Viking, 1999.

Rainger, Ronald. *An Agenda for Antiquity: Henry Fairfield Osborn & Vertebrate Paleontology at the American Museum of Natural History, 1890–1935.* Tuscaloosa: University of Alabama Press, 1991.

Reckner, James R. *Teddy Roosevelt's Great White Fleet.* Annapolis, Md.: Naval Institute Press, 1988.

Reid, B. L. *The Man from New York: John Quinn and His Friends.* New York: Oxford University Press, 1968.

Reiger, John F. *American Sportsmen and the Origins of Conservation.* New York: Winchester, 1975.

Reisner, Christian F. *Roosevelt's Religion.* New York: Abingdon, 1922.

Rhodes, James Ford. *The McKinley and Roosevelt Administrations, 1897–1909.* 1922; reprint, Port Washington, N.Y.: Kennikat, 1965.

Ricard, Serge. "The Anglo-German Intervention in Venezuela and Theodore Roosevelt's Ultimatum to the Kaiser: Taking a Fresh Look at an Old Enigma," in Ricard and Hélène Christol, eds., *Anglo-Saxonism in U.S. Foreign Policy: The Diplomacy of Imperialism, 1899–1919.* Aix-en-Provence, France: Université de Provence, 1991.

——. "Anti-Wilsonian Internationalism: Theodore Roosevelt in the *Kansas City Star,*" in Daniela Rossini, ed., *From Theodore Roosevelt to FDR: Internationalism and Isolationism in American Foreign Policy.* Bodmin, Eng.: Keele University Press, 1995.

Rixey, Lilian. *Bamie: Theodore Roosevelt's Remarkable Sister.* New York: McKay, 1963.

Rosenstone, Robert A. *Romantic Revolutionary: A Biography of John Reed.* New York: Knopf, 1975.

Ross, B. Joyce. *J. E. Spingarn and the Rise of the NAACP, 1911–1939.* New York: Atheneum, 1972.

Rothman, Ellen. *Hands and Hearts: A History of Courtship in America.* New York: Basic Books, 1984.

Rotundo, E. Anthony. "After the Revolution: Changes in Mother-Son Relationships in Nineteenth-Century Middle Class Families," *Psychoanalysis and Psychotherapy* 12, no. 1 (1995).

——. "American Fatherhood: A Historical Perspective," *American Behavioral Scientist* 29, no. 1 (September/October 1985): 7–25.

——. *American Manhood: Transformations in Masculinity from the Revolution to the Modern Era.* New York: Basic Books, 1994.

——. "Body and Soul: Changing Ideals of Middle-Class Manhood, 1770–1920," *Journal of Social History*, June 1983.

——. "Learning About Manhood: Gender Ideals in Nineteenth-Century America," in J. A. Mangan and James Walvin, eds., *Morality and Manliness: Nineteenth-Century Images in the Old and New World.* New York: St. Martin's, 1987.

Rudwick, Elliott M. *Race Riot at East St. Louis, July 2, 1917.* Cleveland: World, 1966.

Runte, Alfred. *National Parks: The American Experience.* Lincoln: University of Nebraska Press, 1987.

Russell, Don. *The Lives and Legends of Buffalo Bill.* Norman: University of Oklahoma Press, 1960.

Rydell, Robert W. *All the World's a Fair: Visions of Empire at American International Expositions, 1876–1916.* Chicago: University of Chicago Press, 1984.

Saarinen, Aline B. *The Proud Possessors: The Lives, Times, and Tastes of Some Adventurous American Art Collectors.* New York: Random House, 1958.

Salem, Dorothy. *To Better Our World: Black Women in Organized Reform, 1890–1920.* Brooklyn, N.Y.: Carlson, 1990.

Scheiber, Harry N. *The Wilson Administration and Civil Liberties, 1917–1921.* Ithaca, N.Y.: Cornell University Press, 1960.

Scheiber, Jane Lang, and Harry N. Scheiber, "The Wilson Administration and the Wartime Mobilization of Black Americans, 1917–18," *Labor History* 10, no. 3 (1969): 433–58.

Schudson, Michael. *Discovering the News: A Social History of American Newspapers.* New York: Basic Books, 1978.

Schwantes, Carlos A. *Coxey's Army: An American Odyssey.* Lincoln: University of Nebraska Press, 1985.

Scott, Anne Firor. *Natural Allies: Women's Associations in American History.* Urbana: University of Illinois Press, 1991.

Scott, Anne Firor, and Andrew M. Scott. *One Half the People: The Fight for Woman Suffrage.* Philadelphia: Lippincott, 1975.

Shapiro, Stanley. "The Great War and Reform: Liberals and Labor, 1917–1919," *Labor History* 12 (1971): 323–44.

Sherman, Richard B. *The Republican Party and Black America from McKinley to Hoover, 1896–1933.* Charlottesville: University Press of Virginia, 1973.

Shi, David E. *The Simple Life: Plain Living and High Thinking in American Culture.* New York: Oxford University Press, 1985.

Sievers, Harry J. *Benjamin Harrison.* 3 vols. New York: University Publishers, 1959–68.

Simkhovitch, Vladimir G. *Marxism Versus Socialism.* New York: Columbia University Press, 1923.

Sinkler, George. *The Racial Attitudes of American Presidents from Abraham Lincoln to Theodore Roosevelt.* Garden City, N.Y.: Doubleday, 1971.

Sklar, Kathryn Kish. *Florence Kelley and the Nation's Work: The Rise of Women's Political Culture, 1830–1900.* New Haven: Yale University Press, 1995.

——. "Women and the Creation of the American Welfare State," in Carl J. Guarneri, ed., *America Compared: American History in International Perspective,* vol. 2. Boston: Houghton Mifflin, 1997.

Sklar, Martin. *The Corporate Reconstruction of American Capitalism, 1890–1916: The Market, Law, and Politics.* Cambridge, Mass.: Harvard University Press, 1988.

Smith, Carl S. *Urban Disorder and the Shape of Belief: The Great Chicago Fire, the Haymarket Bomb, and the Model Town of Pullman.* Chicago: University of Chicago Press, 1995.

Smith, Mary Ann. *Gustav Stickley: The Craftsman.* Syracuse, N.Y.: Syracuse University Press, 1983.

Smith-Rosenberg, Carroll. *Disorderly Conduct: Visions of Gender in Victorian America.* New York: Knopf, 1985.

Solomon, Barbara Miller. *Ancestors and Immigrants: A Changing New England Tradition.* Cambridge, Mass.: Northeastern University Press, 1956.

Southern, David W. *The Malignant Heritage: Yankee Progressives and the Negro Question, 1901–1914.* Chicago: University of Chicago Press, 1968.

Sproat, John G. *"The Best Men": Liberal Reformers in the Gilded Age.* New York: Oxford University Press, 1971.

Sprout, Harold, and Margaret Sprout. *The Rise of American Naval Power, 1776–1918.* Princeton: Princeton University Press, 1946.

Stanley, Peter W. *A Nation in the Making: The Philippines and the United States, 1899–1921.* Cambridge, Mass.: Harvard University Press, 1974.

——, ed. *Reappraising an Empire: New Perspectives on Philippine-American History.* Cambridge, Mass.: Harvard University Press, 1984.

Stansell, Christine. *City of Women: Sex and Class in New York, 1789–1860.* Urbana: University of Illinois Press, 1986.

Stanton, Elizabeth Cady, Susan B. Anthony, and Matilda Joslyn Gage, eds. *History of Woman Suffrage.* New York: Arno, 1969.

Stasz, Clarice. *The Vanderbilt Women: Dynasty of Wealth, Glamour, and Tragedy.* New York: St. Martin's, 1991.

Steinson, Barbara J. *American Women's Activism in World War I.* New York: Garland, 1982.

Stephenson, Nathaniel Wright. *Nelson W. Aldrich: A Leader in American Politics.* New York: Scribner's, 1930.

Stocking, George W., Jr. *Race, Culture, and Evolution, or Essays in the History of Anthropology.* Chicago: University of Chicago Press, 1968.

Sullivan, Mark. *Our Times: The United States, 1900–1925.* 6 vols. New York: Scribner's, 1926–35.

Summers, Mark Wahlgren. *Rum, Romanism, and Rebellion: The Making of the President 1884.* Chapel Hill: University of North Carolina Press, 2000.

Swanberg, W. A. *Citizen Hearst: A Biography of William Randolph Hearst.* New York: Scribner's, 1961.

Taft, Philip. "The Bisbee Deportation," *Labor History* 13 (1972): 3–40.

Takaki, Ronald. *Iron Cages: Race and Culture in Nineteenth-Century America.* New York: Oxford University Press, 1990.

——. *Strangers from a Different Shore: A History of Asian Americans.* Boston: Little, Brown, 1989.

Tate, Cassandra. *Cigarette Wars: The Triumph of "The Little White Slaver."* New York: Oxford University Press, 1999.

Tax, Meredith. *The Rising of the Women: Feminist Solidarity and Class Conflict, 1880–1917.* New York: Monthly Review Press, 1980.

Teague, Michael. "Theodore Roosevelt and Alice Hathaway Lee: A New Perspective," *Harvard Library Bulletin* 33, no. 3 (Summer 1985): 225–38.

Thelen, David P. *Robert M. La Follette and the Insurgent Spirit.* Boston: Little, Brown, 1976.

Thompson, Mark. *American Character: The Curious Life of Charles Fletcher Lummis and the Rediscovery of the Southwest.* New York: Arcade, 2001.

Thomson, James Claude, Peter W. Stanley, and John Curtis Perry. *Sentimental Imperialists: The American Experience in East Asia.* New York: Harper & Row, 1985.

Thwing, Eugene. *The Life and Meaning of Theodore Roosevelt.* New York: Current Literature Publishing Co., 1919.

Tilchin, William N. *Theodore Roosevelt and the British Empire: A Study in Presidential Statecraft.* New York: St. Martin's, 1997.

Timberlake, James H. *Prohibition and the Progressive Movement, 1900–1920.* Cambridge, Mass.: Harvard University Press, 1966.

Tobin, Eugene M. *Organize or Perish: America's Independent Progressives, 1913–1933.* Westport, Conn.: Greenwood, 1986.

Tomlins, Christopher L. *The State and the Unions: Labor Relations, Law, and the Organized Labor Movement in America, 1880–1960.* New York: Cambridge University Press, 1985.

Trani, Eugene P. *The Treaty of Portsmouth: An Adventure in American Diplomacy.* Lexington: University Press of Kentucky, 1969.

Trask, David F. *The War with Spain in 1898.* New York: Macmillan, 1981.

Turk, Richard W. *The Ambiguous Relationship: Theodore Roosevelt and Alfred Thayer Mahan.* Westport, Conn.: Greenwood, 1987.

Tyack, David, and Elisabeth Hansot. *Learning Together: A History of Coeducation in American Schools.* New Haven: Yale University Press, 1990.

Urofsky, Melvin I. "Proposed Federal Incorporation in the Progressive Era," *American Journal of Legal History* 26 (April 1982): 160–83.

U.S. Department of State. *Papers Relating to the Foreign Relations of the United States, 1903.* Washington, D.C.: Government Printing Office, 1904.

Vaughn, Stephen. "First Amendment Liberties and the Committee on Public Information," *American Journal of Legal History* 23 (1979): 95–119.

——. "Morality and Entertainment: The Origins of the Motion Picture Production Code," *Journal of American History* 77 (1990): 39–65.

Vose, Clement E. *Constitutional Change: Amendment Politics and Supreme Court Litigation Since 1900.* Lexington, Mass.: Lexington Books, 1972.

Wagenknecht, Edward. *The Seven Worlds of Theodore Roosevelt.* New York: Longmans, Green, 1958.

Wallace, David H. *Sagamore Hill: Sagamore Hill National Historic Site, Oyster Bay, New York.* Harpers Ferry, W. Va.: National Park Service, 1991.

Walters, Ronald G. *American Reformers, 1815–1860.* New York: Hill & Wang, 1978.

Wang, Xi. *The Trial of Democracy: Black Suffrage and Northern Republicans, 1860–1910.* Athens, Ga.: University of Georgia Press, 1997.

Ward, Geoffrey C. *Before the Trumpet: Young Franklin Roosevelt, 1882–1905.* New York: Harper & Row, 1985.

——. *A First-Class Temperament: The Emergence of Franklin Roosevelt.* New York: Harper & Row, 1989.

Watts, Sarah Lyons. *Order Against Chaos: Business Culture and Labor Ideology in America, 1880–1915.* Westport, Conn.: Greenwood, 1991.

Waugh, Joan. *Unsentimental Reformer: The Life of Josephine Shaw.* Cambridge, Mass.: Harvard University Press, 1997.

Weaver, John D. *The Brownsville Raid.* New York: Norton, 1973.

Weinstein, James. *The Corporate Ideal in the Liberal State, 1900–1918.* Westport, Conn.: Greenwood, 1968.

Weiss, Nancy J. "The New Negro and the New Freedom: Fighting Wilsonian Segregation," *Political Science Quarterly* 84, no. 1 (March 1969): 61–79.

Welch, Richard E., Jr., *Response to Imperialism: The United States and the Philippine-American War, 1899–1902.* Chapel Hill: University of North Carolina Press, 1979.

White, G. Edward. *The Eastern Establishment and the Western Experience.* New Haven: Yale University Press, 1968.

White-Hensen, Wendy, and Veronica M. Gillespie, eds., *The Theodore Roosevelt Association Film Collection.* Washington, D.C.: Library of Congress, 1986.

Whorton, James C. *Crusaders for Fitness: The History of American Health Reformers.* Princeton: Princeton University Press, 1982.

Widenor, William C. *Henry Cabot Lodge and the Search for an American Foreign Policy.* Berkeley: University of California Press, 1980.

Wiebe, Robert H. *The Search for Order, 1877–1920.* New York: Hill & Wang, 1967.

Wilentz, Sean. *Chants Democratic: New York City and the Rise of the American Working Class, 1788–1850.* New York: Oxford University Press, 1986.

Wilhelm, Donald. *Theodore Roosevelt as an Undergraduate.* Boston: Luce, 1910.

Williams, Vernon J., Jr. *Rethinking Race: Franz Boas and His Contemporaries.* Louisville: University Press of Kentucky, 1996.

Wilson, Derek. *The Astors, 1763–1992: Landscape with Millionaires.* London: Weidenfeld & Nicolson, 1993.

Wimmel, Kenneth. *Theodore Roosevelt and the Great White Fleet: American Sea Power Comes of Age.* Washington, D.C.: Brassey's, 1998.

Witcover, Jules. *Sabotage at Black Tom: Imperial Germany's Secret War in America, 1914–1917.* Chapel Hill, N.C.: Algonquin, 1989.

Wittke, Carl. *German-Americans and the World War.* Columbus: Ohio State Archaeological and Historical Society, 1936.

Wolgemuth, Kathleen L. "Woodrow Wilson and Federal Segregation," *Journal of Negro History,* April 1959, 158–73.

Woloch, Nancy. *Muller v. Oregon: A Brief History with Documents.* Boston: Bedford, 1996.

Womack, John. *Zapata and the Mexican Revolution.* New York: Vintage, 1970.

Wyatt-Brown, Bertram. *Southern Honor: Ethics and Behavior in the Old South.* New York: Oxford University Press, 1982.

Wynn, Neil A. *From Progressivism to Prosperity: World War I and American Society.* New York: Holmes & Meier, 1986.

Ziglar, William Larry. "Negro Opinion of Theodore Roosevelt." Ph.D. diss., University of Maine, 1972.

Acknowledgments

When a scholar works on a topic for over twenty-five years, the list of debts to colleagues grows long. At Mills College Charles Larsen, biographer of "bull mouse" Ben Lindsey, and Reynold M. Wik, chronicler of Henry Ford's rapport with plain folks, launched me as a student of history. My loyalty to Mills owes much to their wise guidance, the kindness of their wives, Grace Larsen and Helen Wik, and to my beloved friends Elizabeth Wray, Alice Pulliam, and Roberta Copernoll Johnson, who still drag me away from the library.

It was fortunate that in my Johns Hopkins University graduate school years Kenneth S. Lynn and David Donald spoke up for biography despite the fact that scholarly fashions ran the other way. After teaching me recent political history through the prism of the Chandler-Galambos organizational synthesis, Louis P. Galambos poured the celebratory Teacher's Scotch the day I passed my doctoral exams. Jack Greene kindly helped me find an agent. Ronald G. Walters shaped my social history vision and my writing, and most important he was the benign role model I needed to see myself as a professional historian. Linda Ramsey, Elisabeth Griffith, and Daniel Wilson shared the joys and misery of graduate school with me.

I came to my understanding of TR and his times in conversation with other seekers on the same journey. William Harbaugh, author of a superb one-volume biography of TR, has read many drafts of my chapters. I thank Bill for a rare friendship across generations. Lewis Gould offered encouragement and advice along the way, and the Executive Director of the Theodore Roosevelt Association, John Gable, despite our many differences of opinion, has been endlessly generous in providing information and analyzing my chapters. In addition to the domestic history reading Charles Larsen did, three experts on foreign policy read and commented perceptively on portions of my book: Akira Iriye, Serge Ricard, and Frank Ninkovich. Lawrence Budner read some of my chapters, showed me the wonderful TR collection he and his wife, Doris, have gathered, and made copies of rare photos for me. Amy Verone, Kathleen Sheedy-Young, Charles Markis, and other National Park Service experts have helped me when I have been in Oyster Bay, and they also sent me useful information from Sagamore Hill and the TR Birthplace.

I appreciate the help I got—often in the form of Xeroxed articles or proofreading—from Sarah Phillips, Amy Johnson, Dan Schneider, Jeanne LaSaffre, Morey Rothberg, Connor Cooper, Daniel Joseph Ankeles, and Jessica Spradling, and the eager support from my students at Phillips Academy and Harvard Extension School, especially Adam Berg, Jeff Kehoe, Susanah Rubin, Barbara Cutter, and Melissa Burrage. An endowed chair, a Charles Warren fellowship, and William R. Kenan grants funded this book. Vic Henningsen, Kelly Wise, Tom Lyons, and Phil Zaeder deserve gratitude for accommodating my scholarly endeavors at

Phillips Academy. Director of the Peabody Museum Jim Bradley helped me understand the history of anthropology and Associate Curator of the Addison Gallery of Art Susan Faxon improved my understanding of "genuine Americana." Many librarians and archivists put in extra effort to make my work easier, especially Edward Lyon, Cheryl Laguardia, Mary Wolfskill, Mark Renovitch, Elizabeh Lawson, Gregory Schwarz, Susan Halpert, Denison Beach, Marie-Hélène Gold, Fran Gallagher, Ruth Quattlebaum, Bobbie McDonnell, Rachel Penner, Tim Sprattler, and Peter Drummey. The chivalrous guard Bob Abrams insisted upon carrying my bulky computer into the Houghton manuscript room every day for almost two years, and his colleague Phil Capernaros advised me on military history and became my friend.

The Houghton Library with its rich research trove has become my second home. All serious Theodore Roosevelt scholars respect the archival genius and professionalism of Wallace F. Dailey, the curator of the Theodore Roosevelt Collection. He runs a much-in-demand manuscript and photo archive as important as any presidential library, and he does it as a second job. None of us could conduct our research without him, and his extensive knowledge and selfless devotion to promoting scholarship is heroic. My debt to him is great.

The families of famous people often make life difficult for researchers. Fortunately, the Roosevelts are history-minded. P. James Roosevelt, Jean Schermerhorn Roosevelt, Mr. and Mrs. William Sheffield Cowles, Jr., and the granddaughter TR hugged so fondly, Edith Derby Williams, gave me full and useful interviews and loaned me family treasures to study. Tweed Roosevelt commented on my Brazil section and shared the fun of discovery as I dug through the archives in search of his great-grandfather. Many years ago Alice Roosevelt Longworth answered my questions over the phone, and Ethel Roosevelt Derby talked with me about her father at a Theodore Roosevelt Association dinner in 1976. Descendants of other figures in Progressive Era history also aided my research, especially Nick Baker of the American Newspaper Depository, Mary La Farge, and William and Caroline Drayton Phillips' daughter Ann Bryant.

During the long years of research on TR and his times, I have sought out other scholars to help me figure out the past, notably James B. Gilbert, Sven Beckert, Sarah Watts, Leon Fink, Susan Levine, Karen Sawislak, Elisabeth Perry, Carl Guarneri, Susan M. Lloyd, John Higham, Dom Cavallo, Thomas J. Knock, Elizabeth Pleck, Kathryn Kish Sklar, Hélène Lipstadt, Dr. Miles Shore, David Mayberry Lewis, Gerry Sweeney, Elaine Tyler May, Vincente Rafael, Robyn Muncy, and Melanie Gustafson. I especially thank Char Miller, Nancy Unger, Joan Waugh, and David Nasaw for sharing their bound galleys and extensive knowledge. The late Stephen Jay Gould talked over evolution, Lamarck, and his views on TR with me and shared his Red Sox tickets with my family.

My five years at the Warren Center at Harvard, first as a fellow, then as an associate, enriched my professional development. I thank Laurel Ulrich, Akira Iriye, William Gienapp, Ernest May, Bernard Bailyn, Susan Hunt, and Pat Denault for their hospitality. Jill Lepore, Bruce Schulman, Nina Silber, Kristin Hoganson, and David Blight were Warren Fellows with me and have been inspirations as I have worked on my book. Jill Lepore and her husband, Tim Leak, deserve special thanks for friend-service beyond the usual, taking care of my son when my daughter was having surgery. And Bruce and Jill offered me immense moral support and renewed my faith in the profession.

Brett Williams' friendship and hospitality made it enjoyable for me to do research at the Library of Congress one summer, and she has helped me keep academic life in perspective ever since our early teaching days together at American University. My husband's Brandeis graduate school peers and teachers have remained our dear friends over the years. John and Virginia Demos, Ellen Rothman, Ted Byers, Judy Taylor, Mike Grossberg, Tina Manuel, and Ellen Fitzpatrick egged me on with good cheer as I persisted with an almost interminable project, and both Ellens read the manuscript, which is a lot to ask of friends. John Demos at a crucial moment recommended my work to Gerry McCauley, which opened a door of immense importance to me.

Several supportive friends helped me keep writing over the years: Bob Krauss and Lois Putnam, Regina Morantz-Sanchez, Harriet Alonso, Andrea Sedlak, Bruce Mazlish, Helen and Dan Horowitz, Jan Lewis, Barry Bienstock, Jay Rogers, Peter Filene, Ted and Nancy Sizer, Carole Gras, Kathy Grammar, Carl and Elizabeth Krumpe, and Gerald, Lucas, and Jenny Platt. Whether it was teaching me to love New York or fixing the car that died between archives or giving me Tillie Olson's *Silences* when my children's needs came before my research agenda or that big hug on Monday morning before classes started, they got me through the rough spots.

In addition to raising our daughters in tandem and helping us during asthma crises, Terry and Doug Kuhlmann have edited, printed out, and listened to me think about writing this book for years; their daughter Georgiana also checked some of the endnotes. Peter and Lisa Smith have administered laugh-therapy when needed. I am also grateful that my friend Barbara Dailey volunteered to turn awkward sentences into smooth ones at the very last minute. Jonathan Fasman and Luba Ostashevsky provided crucial aid in the last stages of bringing the book to light. Fred Scott kindly gave me a general history audience reading. Doctors Curtis Moody and Richard Horan educated me about asthma, and my own doctor Christina Iacobo read the medical sections for me.

Extended families, East and West, kept me rooted while I researched and wrote. My late mother, Kathleen Mildred Nelson Dalton, and my father, William Connolly Dalton, encouraged me to aim high, even to be the first woman to graduate from college in our family. My extended family in California—my stepmother, Faye Dalton, my stepsiblings, Rick Moen and Michele Strickland, my cousin Lynne Dalton Neumayer, my uncle Mont Nelson, and my cousin Kathleen Nelson Hurley—have made so many contributions to my life and work I cannot list them all. Faye has been exceptionally kind to my father in his eighties, and my substitute sister, Alison Di Pace, brings good cheer to my father—in part on my behalf—every Friday at his nursing home. Since 1961, Candy Buchanan has been my feisty and stalwart friend and should take credit for helping me reach maturity with horizons broader than the Suisun Bay.

On the East Coast, my sister-in-law Ruth Ann Whitney talked over TR's developmental issues with me and edited my manuscript as did our friends and adopted family members Robert and Jorinda Gershon, whose fine literary sensibilities helped me think about how to tell a story. My sister-in-law Peggy Rotundo and her husband, Danny Danforth, their children, Ann and Nick (who searched the Yale stacks for a rare TR cartoon), Newell and Dalli Bacon, Barry and Donna Griffiths, and Aunt Rose Rotundo offered me intangible gifts of love and patience. Danny also remains my best native informant on anthropology, ornithology, and nationalism. Cousin Richard Laub took us to see Mittie's house in Roswell, and Uncle Ralph Bristol performed the extraordinarily generous act of going through and photocopying the Arizona State Historical Society's Greenway and Ferguson Papers for me while he was on vacation.

I wrote much of this book on my mother-in-law's dining room table on weekends when I could escape dormitory parenthood. Barbara Bristol Rotundo has been a fierce advocate of my writing career. She looked for photos, too, and shared her vast knowledge of the nineteenth century and Brahmin personalities with me. I am lucky to be related to her.

Gerry McCauley has given me excellent professional advice over the years, and my editor at Knopf, Ashbel Green, understood my insights and then sharpened my ideas and language to make this a better book. I thank both of them for giving me the opportunity to write for a larger audience.

It is impossible to raise children, teach in a boarding school, do research as a fellow at a major research university, and write a book like this. My partner in the impossible deserves more than the dedication and more than thanks. I met E. Anthony Rotundo because we were writing about TR and nineteenth-century manliness, and I thank TR for being a good posthumous matchmaker. Tony and I have managed to live an active dual life of the mind, even through hectic dorm counseling and job-sharing years when our children Barbara Dalton Rotundo and Peter William Dalton Rotundo were little. After Tony wrote *American Manhood*, we shifted family gears so my work could get done, too. My book benefited from my marriage to a pioneering historian who is also a discerning and tough-minded editor. I thank Tony above all others for the work he did to support me so I could finish this book. Barbara and Peter have variously worked as typists, photocopiers, photographers, proofreaders, and computer repair specialists. Both of them have been affectionate toward and bemused by their author-mother. My family's love has made all the difference, and next time I promise I'll write faster.

Index

PERMISSIONS ACKNOWLEDGMENTS

Grateful acknowledgment is made to the following for permission to reprint previously unpublished material:

Massachusetts Historical Society: Excerpted material from Lodge-Roosevelt Correspondence; the Henry Cabot Lodge Papers, 1745–1966; Minot Family Papers, 1658–1939; and the Amos A. Lawrence diaries and account books. Reprinted by permission of the Massachusetts Historical Society.

Mary Minot Mulligan: Excerpts from the Henry Davis Minot correspondence in the Minot Family Papers. Reprinted by permission of Mary Minot Mulligan.

Syracuse University Library: Excerpts from the Theodore Roosevelt and Nicholas Roosevelt Papers. Syracuse University Library, Department of Special Collections. Reprinted by permission of the Syracuse University Library.

Theodore Roosevelt Association: Excerpted material from Theodore Roosevelt and Eleanor Roosevelt's letters and diaries; letters from various family members' papers; Alice Longworth papers; and the RMA Minutes. Reprinted by permission of the Theodore Roosevelt Association, Oyster Bay, NY.

Houghton Library, Harvard University: Excerpted material from letters, diaries, and other unpublished sources written by Theodore Roosevelt and other Roosevelt family members. Theodore Roosevelt Collection, Harvard College Library, Houghton Library, Harvard University. Reprinted by permission of the Houghton Library, Harvard University.

The University of North Carolina at Chapel Hill: Excerpts from the Bulloch Family Papers, #2750; the James Dunwody Bulloch Letters, #3318; and the Thomas Butler King Papers, #1252. Southern Historical Collection, Wilson Library, the University of North Carolina at Chapel Hill. Reprinted by permission of the University of North Carolina at Chapel Hill.

A NOTE ABOUT THE AUTHOR

Kathleen Dalton is Associate Fellow at the Charles Warren Center for Studies in American History at Harvard University and a Research Fellow at the Gilder Lehrman Institute of American History. She is on leave as Cecil F. P. Bancroft Instructor of History and Social Science at Phillips Academy, Andover. Educated at Mills College and Johns Hopkins University, she has been studying Theodore Roosevelt since 1975. She lives in Andover, Massachusetts, with her husband, the historian E. Anthony Rotundo, and their two children.

A NOTE ON THE TYPE

The text of this book was set in Electra, a typeface designed by W. A. Dwiggins (1880–1956). This face cannot be classified as either modern or old style. It is not based on any historical model, nor does it echo any particular period or style. It avoids the extreme contrasts between thick and thin elements that mark most modern faces, and it attempts to give a feeling of fluidity, power, and speed.

Composed by North Market Street Graphics, Lancaster, Pennsylvania
Printed and bound by R. R. Donnelley & Sons, Harrisonburg, Virginia
Designed by Robert C. Olsson